THE ESSENTIALS OF

Computer Organization and Architecture

FOURTH EDITION

Linda Null
The Pennsylvania State University

Julia Lobur
The Pennsylvania State University

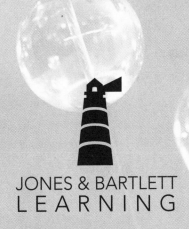

JONES & BARTLETT
LEARNING

World Headquarters
Jones & Bartlett Learning
5 Wall Street
Burlington, MA 01803
978-443-5000
info@jblearning.com
www.jblearning.com

Jones & Bartlett Learning books and products are available through most bookstores and online booksellers. To contact Jones & Bartlett Learning directly, call 800-832-0034, fax 978-443-8000, or visit our website, www.jblearning.com.

Substantial discounts on bulk quantities of Jones & Bartlett Learning publications are available to corporations, professional associations, and other qualified organizations. For details and specific discount information, contact the special sales department at Jones & Bartlett Learning via the above contact information or send an email to specialsales@jblearning.com.

03314-4

Production Credits
Executive Publisher: William Brottmiller
Publisher: Cathy L. Esperti
Acquisitions Editor: Laura Pagluica
Editorial Assistant: Brooke Yee
Director of Production: Amy Rose
Senior Production Editor: Tiffany Sliter
Associate Production Editor: Sara Fowles
Associate Marketing Manager: Cassandra Peterson
VP, Manufacturing and Inventory Control: Therese Connell
Composition: Laserwords Private Limited, Chennai, India
Cover and Title Page Design: Kristin E. Parker
Director of Photo Research and Permissions: Amy Wrynn
Cover and Title Page Image: © Eugene Sergeev/ShutterStock, Inc.
Printing and Binding: Edwards Brothers Malloy
Cover Printing: Edwards Brothers Malloy

To order this product, use ISBN: 978-1-284-07448-2

The Library of Congress has cataloged the first printing as follows:
Null, Linda.
  The essentials of computer organization and architecture / Linda Null and Julia Lobur. -- Fourth edition.
    pages ; cm
  Includes index.
  ISBN 978-1-284-03314-4 (pbk.) -- ISBN 1-284-03314-7 (pbk.) 1. Computer organization. 2. Computer architecture. I. Lobur, Julia. II. Title.
  QA76.9.C643N85 2015
  004.2'2--dc23
                                        2013034383

6048

Printed in the United States of America
18 17 16 15   10 9 8 7 6 5 4

In memory of my father, Merrill Cornell, a pilot and man of endless talent and courage, who taught me that when we step into the unknown, we either find solid ground, or we learn to fly.

—L. M. N.

To the loving memory of my mother, Anna J. Surowski, who made all things possible for her girls.

—J. M. L.

Contents

CHAPTER 3

Boolean Algebra and Digital Logic   137

CHAPTER
4

MARIE: An Introduction to a Simple Computer   215

CHAPTER
5

A Closer Look at Instruction Set Architectures

CHAPTER
6

Memory   341

CHAPTER

8

System Software   495

CHAPTER 13

Selected Storage Systems and Interfaces   743

Preface

TO THE STUDENT

This is a book about computer organization and architecture. It focuses on the function and design of the various components necessary to process information digitally. We present computing systems as a series of layers, starting with low-level hardware and progressing to higher-level software, including assemblers and operating systems. These levels constitute a hierarchy of virtual machines. The study of computer organization focuses on this hierarchy and the issues involved with how we partition the levels and how each level is implemented. The study of computer architecture focuses on the interface between hardware and software, and emphasizes the structure and behavior of the system. The majority of information contained in this textbook is devoted to computer hardware, computer organization and architecture, and their relationship to software performance.

Students invariably ask, "Why, if I am a computer science major, must I learn about computer hardware? Isn't that for computer engineers? Why do I care what the inside of a computer looks like?" As computer users, we probably do not have to worry about this any more than we need to know what our cars look like under the hood in order to drive them. We can certainly write high-level language programs without understanding how these programs execute; we can use various application packages without understanding how they really work. But what happens when the program we have written needs to be faster and more efficient, or the application we are using doesn't do precisely what we want? As computer scientists, we need a basic understanding of the computer system itself in order to rectify these problems.

There is a fundamental relationship between the computer hardware and the many aspects of programming and software components in computer systems. In order to write good software, it is very important to understand the computer system as a whole. Understanding hardware can help you explain the mysterious errors that sometimes creep into your programs, such as the infamous segmentation fault or bus error. The level of knowledge about computer organization and computer architecture that a high-level programmer must have depends on the task the high-level programmer is attempting to complete.

For example, to write compilers, you must understand the particular hardware to which you are compiling. Some of the ideas used in hardware (such as pipelining) can be adapted to compilation techniques, thus making the compiler faster and more efficient. To model large, complex, real-world systems, you must understand how floating-point arithmetic should, and does, work (which are not necessarily the same thing). To write device drivers for video, disks, or other I/O devices, you need a good understanding of I/O interfacing and computer architecture in general. If you want to work on embedded systems, which are usually very resource constrained, you must understand all of the time, space, and price trade-offs. To do research on, and make recommendations for, hardware systems, networks, or specific algorithms, you must acquire an understanding of benchmarking and then learn how to present performance results adequately. Before buying hardware, you need to understand benchmarking and all the ways that others can *manipulate* the performance results to "prove" that one system is better than another. Regardless of our particular area of expertise, as computer scientists, it is imperative that we understand how hardware interacts with software.

You may also be wondering why a book with the word *essentials* in its title is so large. The reason is twofold. First, the subject of computer organization is expansive and it grows by the day. Second, there is little agreement as to which topics from within this burgeoning sea of information are truly essential and which are just helpful to know. In writing this book, one goal was to provide a concise text compliant with the computer architecture curriculum guidelines jointly published by the Association for Computing Machinery (ACM) and the Institute of Electrical and Electronic Engineers (IEEE). These guidelines encompass the subject matter that experts agree constitutes the "essential" core body of knowledge relevant to the subject of computer organization and architecture.

We have augmented the ACM/IEEE recommendations with subject matter that we feel is useful—if not essential—to your continuing computer science studies and to your professional advancement. The topics that we feel will help you in your continuing computer science studies include operating systems, compilers, database management, and data communications. Other subjects are included because they will help you understand how actual systems work in real life.

We hope that you find reading this book an enjoyable experience, and that you take time to delve deeper into some of the material that we have presented. It is our intention that this book will serve as a useful reference long after your formal course is complete. Although we give you a substantial amount of information, it is only a foundation upon which you can build throughout the remainder of your studies and your career. Successful computer professionals continually add to their knowledge about how computers work. Welcome to the start of your journey.

TO THE INSTRUCTOR

This book is the outgrowth of two computer science organization and architecture classes taught at Penn State Harrisburg. As the computer science curriculum evolved, we found it necessary not only to modify the material taught in the courses, but also to condense the courses from a two-semester sequence into a three-credit, one-semester course. Many other schools have also recognized the need to compress material in order to make room for emerging topics. This new course, as well as this textbook, is primarily for computer science majors and is intended to address the topics in computer organization and architecture with which computer science majors must be familiar. This book not only integrates the underlying principles in these areas, but it also introduces and motivates the topics, providing the breadth necessary for majors while providing the depth necessary for continuing studies in computer science.

Our primary objective in writing this book was to change the way computer organization and architecture are typically taught. A computer science major should leave a computer organization and architecture class with not only an understanding of the important general concepts on which the digital computer is founded, but also with a comprehension of how those concepts apply to the real world. These concepts should transcend vendor-specific terminology and design; in fact, students should be able to take concepts given in the specific and translate to the generic and vice versa. In addition, students must develop a firm foundation for further study in the major.

The title of our book, *The Essentials of Computer Organization and Architecture*, is intended to convey that the topics presented in the text are those for which every computer science major should have exposure, familiarity, or mastery. We do not expect students using our textbook to have complete mastery of all topics presented. It is our firm belief, however, that there are certain topics that must be mastered; there are those topics about which students must have a definite familiarity; and there are certain topics for which a brief introduction and exposure are adequate.

We do not feel that concepts presented in sufficient depth can be learned by studying general principles in isolation. We therefore present the topics as an integrated set of solutions, not simply a collection of individual pieces of information. We feel our explanations, examples, exercises, tutorials, and simulators all combine to provide the student with a total learning experience that exposes the inner workings of a modern digital computer at the appropriate level.

We have written this textbook in an informal style, omitting unnecessary jargon, writing clearly and concisely, and avoiding unnecessary abstraction, in hopes of increasing student enthusiasm. We have also broadened the range of topics typically found in a first-level architecture book to include system software, a brief tour of operating systems, performance issues, alternative architectures, and a concise introduction to networking, as these topics are intimately related to computer hardware. Like most books, we have chosen an architectural model, but it is one that we have designed with simplicity in mind.

Relationship to CS2013

In October 2013, the ACM/IEEE Joint Task Force unveiled Computer Science Curricula 2013 (CS2013). Although we are primarily concerned with the Computer Architecture knowledge area, these new guidelines suggest integrating the core knowledge throughout the curriculum. Therefore, we also call attention to additional knowledge areas beyond architecture that are addressed in this book.

CS2013 is a comprehensive revision of CS2008, mostly the result of focusing on the *essential concepts* in the Computer Science curriculum while still being flexible enough to meet individual institutional needs. These guidelines introduce the notion of Core Tier-1 and Core Tier-2 topics, in addition to elective topics. Core Tier-1 topics are those that should be part of every Computer Science curriculum. Core Tier-2 topics are those that are considered essential enough that a Computer Science curriculum should contain 90–100% of these topics. Elective topics are those that allow curricula to provide breadth and depth. The suggested coverage for each topic is listed in lecture hours.

The main change in the Architecture and Organization (AR) knowledge area from CS2008 to CS2013 is a reduction of lecture hours from 36 to 16; however, a new area, System Fundamentals (SF), has been introduced and includes some concepts previously found in the AR module (including hardware building blocks and architectural organization). The interested reader is referred to the CS2013 guidelines (http://www.acm.org/education/curricula-recommendations) for more information on what the individual knowledge areas include.

We are pleased that the fourth edition of *The Essentials of Computer Organization and Architecture* is in direct correlation with the ACM/IEEE CS2013 guidelines for computer organization and architecture, in addition to integrating material from additional knowledge units. Table P.1 indicates which chapters of this textbook satisfy the eight topics listed in the AR knowledge area. For the other knowledge areas, only the topics that are covered in this textbook are listed.

AR – Architecture	Core Tier 1 Hours	Core Tier 2 Hours	Includes Electives	Chapters
Digital Logic and Digital Systems		3	N	1, 3, 4
Machine-Level Representation of Data		3	N	1, 2
Assembly-Level Machine Organization		6	N	1, 4, 5, 7, 8, 9
Memory System Organization and Arch		3	N	2, 6, 7, 13
Interfacing and Communication		1	N	4, 7, 12
Functional Organization			Y	4, 5
Multiprocessing and Alternative Archs			Y	9
Performance Enhancements			Y	9, 11
NC – Networking and Communication	**Core Tier 1 Hours**	**Core Tier 2 Hours**	**Includes Electives**	**Chapters**
Introduction	1.5		N	12
Networked Applications	1.5		N	12
Reliable Data Delivery		2	N	12
Routing and Forwarding		1.5	N	12
OS – Operating Systems	**Core Tier 1 Hours**	**Core Tier 2 Hours**	**Includes Electives**	**Chapters**
Overview of Operating Systems	2		N	8
Memory Management		3	N	6
Virtual Machines			Y	8
File Systems			Y	7
Real-Time and Embedded Systems			Y	10
System Performance Evaluations			Y	6, 11
PD – Parallel and Distributed Computing	**Core Tier 1 Hours**	**Core Tier 2 Hours**	**Includes Electives**	**Chapters**
Parallel Architecture	1	1	N	9
Distributed Systems			Y	9
Cloud Computing			Y	1, 9, 13
SF – Systems Fundamentals	**Core Tier 1 Hours**	**Core Tier 2 Hours**	**Includes Electives**	**Chapters**
Computational Paradigms	3		N	3, 4, 9
State and State Machines	6		N	3
Parallelism	3		N	9
Evaluation	3		N	11
Proximity		3	N	6
SP – Social Issues and Professional Practice	**Core Tier 1 Hours**	**Core Tier 2 Hours**	**Includes Electives**	**Chapters**
History			Y	1

TABLE P.1 ACM/IEEE CS2013 Topics Covered in This Book

Why Another Text?

No one can deny there is a plethora of textbooks for teaching computer organization and architecture already on the market. In our 35-plus years of teaching these courses, we have used many very good textbooks. However, each time we have taught the course, the content has evolved, and eventually, we discovered we were writing significantly more course notes to bridge the gap between the material in the textbook and the material we deemed necessary to present in our classes. We found that our course material was migrating from a computer engineering approach to organization and architecture toward a computer science approach to these topics. When the decision was made to fold the organization class and the architecture class into one course, we simply could not find a textbook that covered the material we felt was necessary for our majors, written from a computer science point of view, written without machine-specific terminology, and designed to motivate the topics before covering them.

In this textbook, we hope to convey the spirit of design used in the development of modern computing systems and what effect this has on computer science students. Students, however, must have a strong understanding of the basic concepts before they can understand and appreciate the intangible aspects of design. Most organization and architecture textbooks present a similar subset of technical information regarding these basics. We, however, pay particular attention to the level at which the information should be covered, and to presenting that information in the context that has relevance for computer science students. For example, throughout this book, when concrete examples are necessary, we offer examples for personal computers, enterprise systems, and mainframes, as these are the types of systems most likely to be encountered. We avoid the "PC bias" prevalent in similar books in the hope that students will gain an appreciation for the differences, the similarities, and the roles various platforms play in today's automated infrastructures. Too often, textbooks forget that motivation is, perhaps, the single most important key in learning. To that end, we include many real-world examples, while attempting to maintain a balance between theory and application.

Features

We have included many features in this textbook to emphasize the various concepts in computer organization and architecture, and to make the material more accessible to students. Some of the features are:

- *Sidebars.* These sidebars include interesting tidbits of information that go a step beyond the main focus of the chapter, thus allowing readers to delve further into the material.

- *Real-World Examples.* We have integrated the textbook with examples from real life to give students a better understanding of how technology and techniques are combined for practical purposes.

- *Chapter Summaries.* These sections provide brief yet concise summaries of the main points in each chapter.

- *Further Reading.* These sections list additional sources for those readers who wish to investigate any of the topics in more detail, and contain references to definitive papers and books related to the chapter topics.
- *Review Questions.* Each chapter contains a set of review questions designed to ensure that the reader has a firm grasp of the material.
- *Chapter Exercises.* Each chapter has a broad selection of exercises to reinforce the ideas presented. More challenging exercises are marked with an asterisk.
- *Answers to Selected Exercises.* To ensure that students are on the right track, we provide answers to representative questions from each chapter. Questions with answers in the back of the text are marked with a blue diamond.
- *Special "Focus On" Sections.* These sections provide additional information for instructors who may wish to cover certain concepts, such as Kmaps and data compression, in more detail. Additional exercises are provided for these sections as well.
- *Appendix.* The appendix provides a brief introduction or review of data structures, including topics such as stacks, linked lists, and trees.
- *Glossary.* An extensive glossary includes brief definitions of all key terms from the chapters.
- *Index.* An exhaustive index is provided with this book, with multiple cross-references, to make finding terms and concepts easier for the reader.

About the Authors

We bring to this textbook not only 35-plus years of combined teaching experience, but also 30-plus years of industry experience. Our combined efforts therefore stress the underlying principles of computer organization and architecture and how these topics relate in practice. We include real-life examples to help students appreciate how these fundamental concepts are applied in the world of computing.

Linda Null holds a PhD in computer science from Iowa State University, an MS in computer science from Iowa State University, an MS in computer science education from Northwest Missouri State University, an MS in mathematics education from Northwest Missouri State University, and a BS in mathematics and English from Northwest Missouri State University. She has been teaching mathematics and computer science for more than 35 years and is currently the computer science graduate program coordinator and associate program chair at the Pennsylvania State University Harrisburg campus, where she has been a member of the faculty since 1995. She has received numerous teaching awards including the Penn State Teaching Fellow Award and the Teaching Excellence Award. Her areas of interest include computer organization and architecture, operating systems, computer science education, and computer security.

Julia Lobur has been a practitioner in the computer industry for more than 30 years. She has held positions as systems consultant, staff programmer/analyst, systems and network designer, software development manager, and project manager, in addition to part-time teaching duties. Julia holds an MS in computer science and is an IEEE Certified Software Development Professional.

Prerequisites

The typical background necessary for a student using this textbook includes a year of programming experience using a high-level procedural language. Students are also expected to have taken a year of college-level mathematics (calculus or discrete mathematics), as this textbook assumes and incorporates these mathematical concepts. This book assumes no prior knowledge of computer hardware.

A computer organization and architecture class is customarily a prerequisite for an undergraduate operating systems class (students must know about the memory hierarchy, concurrency, exceptions, and interrupts), compilers (students must know about instruction sets, memory addressing, and linking), networking (students must understand the hardware of a system before attempting to understand the network that ties these components together), and of course, any advanced architecture class. This text covers the topics necessary for these courses.

General Organization and Coverage

Our presentation of concepts in this textbook is an attempt at a concise yet thorough coverage of the topics we feel are essential for the computer science major. We do not feel the best way to do this is by "compartmentalizing" the various topics; therefore, we have chosen a structured yet integrated approach where each topic is covered in the context of the entire computer system.

As with many popular texts, we have taken a bottom-up approach, starting with the digital logic level and building to the application level that students should be familiar with before starting the class. The text is carefully structured so that the reader understands one level before moving on to the next. By the time the reader reaches the application level, all the necessary concepts in computer organization and architecture have been presented. Our goal is to allow the students to tie the hardware knowledge covered in this book to the concepts learned in their introductory programming classes, resulting in a complete and thorough picture of how hardware and software fit together. Ultimately, the extent of hardware understanding has a significant influence on software design and performance. If students can build a firm foundation in hardware fundamentals, this will go a long way toward helping them to become better computer scientists.

The concepts in computer organization and architecture are integral to many of the everyday tasks that computer professionals perform. To address the numerous areas in which a computer professional should be educated, we have taken a high-level look at computer architecture, providing low-level coverage only when deemed necessary for an understanding of a specific concept. For example, when discussing ISAs, many hardware-dependent issues are introduced in the context of different case studies to both differentiate and reinforce the issues associated with ISA design.

The text is divided into 13 chapters and an appendix, as follows:

- **Chapter 1** provides a historical overview of computing in general, pointing out the many milestones in the development of computing systems and allowing the reader to visualize how we arrived at the current state of computing. This chapter introduces the necessary terminology, the basic components in a computer system, the various logical levels of a computer system, and the von Neumann computer model. It provides a high-level view of the computer system, as well as the motivation and necessary concepts for further study.

- **Chapter 2** provides thorough coverage of the various means computers use to represent both numerical and character information. Addition, subtraction, multiplication, and division are covered once the reader has been exposed to number bases and the typical numeric representation techniques, including one's complement, two's complement, and BCD. In addition, EBCDIC, ASCII, and Unicode character representations are addressed. Fixed- and floating-point representation are also introduced. Codes for data recording and error detection and correction are covered briefly. Codes for data transmission and recording are described in a special "Focus On" section.

- **Chapter 3** is a classic presentation of digital logic and how it relates to Boolean algebra. This chapter covers both combinational and sequential logic in sufficient detail to allow the reader to understand the logical makeup of more complicated MSI (medium-scale integration) circuits (such as decoders). More complex circuits, such as buses and memory, are also included. We have included optimization and Kmaps in a special "Focus On" section.

- **Chapter 4** illustrates basic computer organization and introduces many fundamental concepts, including the fetch–decode–execute cycle, the data path, clocks and buses, register transfer notation, and, of course, the CPU. A very simple architecture, MARIE, and its ISA are presented to allow the reader to gain a full understanding of the basic architectural organization involved in program execution. MARIE exhibits the classic von Neumann design and includes a program counter, an accumulator, an instruction register, 4096 bytes of memory, and two addressing modes. Assembly language programming is introduced to reinforce the concepts of instruction format, instruction mode, data format, and control that are presented earlier. This is not an assembly language textbook and was not designed to provide a practical course in assembly language programming. The primary objective in introducing assembly is to further the understanding of computer architecture in general. However, a simulator for MARIE is provided so assembly language programs can be written, assembled, and run on the MARIE architecture. The two methods of control, hardwiring and microprogramming, are introduced and compared in this chapter. Finally, Intel and MIPS architectures are compared to reinforce the concepts in the chapter.

- **Chapter 5** provides a closer look at instruction set architectures, including instruction formats, instruction types, and addressing modes. Instruction-level pipelining is introduced as well. Real-world ISAs (including Intel®, MIPS® Technologies, ARM, and Java™) are presented to reinforce the concepts presented in the chapter.

- **Chapter 6** covers basic memory concepts, such as RAM and the various memory devices, and also addresses the more advanced concepts of the memory hierarchy, including cache memory and virtual memory. This chapter gives a thorough presentation of direct mapping, associative mapping, and set-associative mapping techniques for cache. It also provides a detailed look at paging and segmentation, TLBs, and the various algorithms and devices associated with each. A tutorial and simulator for this chapter is available on the book's website.

- **Chapter 7** provides a detailed overview of I/O fundamentals, bus communication and protocols, and typical external storage devices, such as magnetic and optical disks, as well as the various formats available for each. DMA, programmed I/O, and interrupts are covered as well. In addition, various techniques for exchanging information between devices are introduced. RAID architectures are covered in detail. Various data compression formats are introduced in a special "Focus On" section.

- **Chapter 8** discusses the various programming tools available (such as compilers and assemblers) and their relationship to the architecture of the machine on which they are run. The goal of this chapter is to tie the programmer's view of a computer system with the actual hardware and architecture of the underlying machine. In addition, operating systems are introduced, but only covered in as much detail as applies to the architecture and organization of a system (such as resource use and protection, traps and interrupts, and various other services).

- **Chapter 9** provides an overview of alternative architectures that have emerged in recent years. RISC, Flynn's Taxonomy, parallel processors, instruction-level parallelism, multiprocessors, interconnection networks, shared memory systems, cache coherence, memory models, superscalar machines, neural networks, systolic architectures, dataflow computers, quantum computing, and distributed architectures are covered. Our main objective in this chapter is to help the reader realize we are not limited to the von Neumann architecture, and to force the reader to consider performance issues, setting the stage for the next chapter.

- **Chapter 10** covers concepts and topics of interest in embedded systems that have not been covered in previous chapters. Specifically, this chapter focuses on embedded hardware and components, embedded system design topics, the basics of embedded software construction, and embedded operating systems features.

- **Chapter 11** addresses various performance analysis and management issues. The necessary mathematical preliminaries are introduced, followed by a discussion of MIPS, FLOPS, benchmarking, and various optimization issues with which a computer scientist should be familiar, including branch prediction, speculative execution, and loop optimization.

- **Chapter 12** focuses on network organization and architecture, including network components and protocols. The OSI model and TCP/IP suite are introduced in the context of the Internet. This chapter is by no means intended to be comprehensive. The main objective is to put computer architecture in the correct context relative to network architecture.

- **Chapter 13** introduces some popular I/O architectures suitable for large and small systems, including SCSI, ATA, IDE, SATA, PCI, USB, and IEEE 1394. This chapter also provides a brief overview of storage area networks and cloud computing.

- **Appendix A** is a short appendix on data structures that is provided for those situations in which students may need a brief introduction or review of such topics as stacks, queues, and linked lists.

The sequencing of the chapters is such that they can be taught in the given numerical order. However, an instructor can modify the order to better fit a given curriculum if necessary. Figure P.1 shows the prerequisite relationships that exist between various chapters.

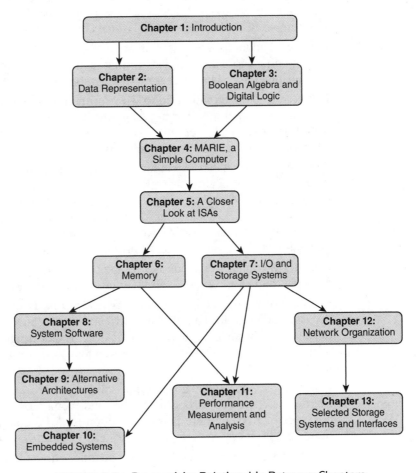

FIGURE P.1   Prerequisite Relationship Between Chapters

What's New in the Fourth Edition

In the years since the third edition of this book was created, the field of computer architecture has continued to grow. In this fourth edition, we have incorporated many of these new changes in addition to expanding topics already introduced in the first three editions. Our goal in the fourth edition was to update content and references, add new material, expand current discussions based on reader comments, and expand the number of exercises in all of the core chapters. Although we cannot itemize all the changes in this edition, the list that follows highlights those major changes that may be of interest to the reader:

- **Chapter 1** has been updated to include new examples and illustrations, tablet computers, computing as a service (Cloud computing), and cognitive computing. The hardware overview has been expanded and updated (notably, the discussion on CRTs has been removed and a discussion of graphics cards has been added), and additional motivational sidebars have been added. The non-von Neumann section has been updated, and a new section on parallelism has been included. The number of exercises at the end of the chapter has been increased by 26%.

- **Chapter 2** contains a new section on excess-M notation. The simple model has been modified to use a standard format, and more examples have been added. This chapter has a 44% increase in the number of exercises.

- **Chapter 3** has been modified to use a prime ($'$) instead of an overbar to indicate the NOT operator. Timing diagrams have been added to help explain the operation of sequential circuits. The section on FSMs has been expanded, and additional exercises have been included.

- **Chapter 4** contains an expanded discussion of memory organization (including memory interleaving) as well as additional examples and exercises. We are now using the "0x" notation to indicate hexadecimal numbers. More detail has been added to the discussions on hardwired and microprogrammed control, and the logic diagrams for MARIE's hardwired control unit and the timing diagrams for MARIE's microoperations have all been updated.

- **Chapter 5** contains expanded coverage of big and little endian and additional examples and exercises, as well as a new section on ARM processors.

- **Chapter 6** has updated figures, an expanded discussion of associative memory, and additional examples and discussion to clarify cache memory. The examples have all been updated to reflect hexadecimal addresses instead of decimal addresses. This chapter now contains 20% more exercises than the third edition.

- **Chapter 7** has expanded coverage of solid state drives and emerging data storage devices (such as carbon nanotubes and memristors), as well as additional coverage of RAID. There is a new section on MP3 compression and in addition to a 20% increase in the number of exercises at the end of this chapter.

- **Chapter 8** has been updated to reflect advances in the field of system software.

- **Chapter 9** has an expanded discussion of both RISC vs. CISC (integrating this debate into the mobile arena) and quantum computing, including a discussion of the technological singularity.
- **Chapter 10** contains updated material for embedded operating systems.
- **Chapter 12** has been updated to remove obsolete material and integrate new material.
- **Chapter 13** has expanded and updated coverage of USB, expanded coverage of Cloud storage, and removal of obsolete material.

Intended Audience

This book was originally written for an undergraduate class in computer organization and architecture for computer science majors. Although specifically directed toward computer science majors, the book does not preclude its use by IS and IT majors.

This book contains more than sufficient material for a typical one-semester (14 weeks, 42 lecture hours) course; however, all the material in the book cannot be mastered by the average student in a one-semester class. If the instructor plans to cover all topics in detail, a two-semester sequence would be optimal. The organization is such that an instructor can cover the major topic areas at different levels of depth, depending on the experience and needs of the students. Table P.2 gives the instructor an idea of the amount of time required to cover the topics, and also lists the corresponding levels of accomplishment for each chapter.

It is our intention that this book serve as a useful reference long after the formal course is complete.

Chapter	One Semester (42 Hours)		Two Semesters (84 Hours)	
	Lecture Hours	Expected Level	Lecture Hours	Expected Level
1	3	Mastery	3	Mastery
2	6	Mastery	6	Mastery
3	6	Mastery	6	Mastery
4	8	Mastery	8	Mastery
5	4	Familiarity	6	Mastery
6	3	Familiarity	8	Mastery
7	2	Familiarity	6	Mastery
8	2	Exposure	7	Mastery
9	2	Familiarity	7	Mastery
10	1	Exposure	5	Familiarity
11	2	Exposure	9	Mastery
12	2	Exposure	7	Mastery
13	1	Exposure	6	Mastery

TABLE P.2 Suggested Lecture Hours

Support Materials

A textbook is a fundamental tool in learning, but its effectiveness is greatly enhanced by supplemental materials and exercises, which emphasize the major concepts, provide immediate feedback to the reader, and motivate understanding through repetition. We have, therefore, created the following ancillary materials for the fourth edition of *The Essentials of Computer Organization and Architecture*:

- *Test bank.*
- *Instructor's Manual.* This manual contains answers to exercises. In addition, it provides hints on teaching various concepts and trouble areas often encountered by students.
- *PowerPoint Presentations.* These slides contain lecture material appropriate for a one-semester course in computer organization and architecture.
- *Figures and Tables.* For those who wish to prepare their own lecture materials, we provide the figures and tables in downloadable form.
- *Memory Tutorial and Simulator.* This package allows students to apply the concepts on cache and virtual memory.
- *MARIE Simulator.* This package allows students to assemble and run MARIE programs.
- *Datapath Simulator.* This package allows students to trace the MARIE datapath.
- *Tutorial Software.* Other tutorial software is provided for various concepts in the book.

The exercises, sample exam problems, and solutions have been tested in numerous classes. The *Instructor's Manual*, which includes suggestions for teaching the various chapters in addition to answers for the book's exercises, suggested programming assignments, and sample example questions, is available to instructors who adopt the book. (Please contact your Jones & Bartlett Learning representative at 1-800-832-0034 for access to this area of the website.)

The Instructional Model: MARIE

In a computer organization and architecture book, the choice of architectural model affects the instructor as well as the students. If the model is too complicated, both the instructor and the students tend to get bogged down in details that really have no bearing on the concepts being presented in class. Real architectures, although interesting, often have far too many peculiarities to make them usable in an introductory class. To make things even more complicated, real architectures change from day to day. In addition, it is difficult to find a book incorporating a model that matches the local computing platform in a given department, noting that the platform, too, may change from year to year.

To alleviate these problems, we have designed our own simple architecture, MARIE, specifically for pedagogical use. MARIE (Machine Architecture that is Really Intuitive and Easy) allows students to learn the essential concepts of computer organization and architecture, including assembly language, without getting caught up in the unnecessary and confusing details that exist in real architectures. Despite its simplicity, it simulates a functional system. The MARIE machine simulator, MarieSim, has a user-friendly GUI that allows students to (1) create and edit source code, (2) assemble source code into machine object code, (3) run machine code, and (4) debug programs.

Specifically, MarieSim has the following features:

- Support for the MARIE assembly language introduced in Chapter 4
- An integrated text editor for program creation and modification
- Hexadecimal machine language object code
- An integrated debugger with single step mode, break points, pause, resume, and register and memory tracing
- A graphical memory monitor displaying the 4096 addresses in MARIE's memory
- A graphical display of MARIE's registers
- Highlighted instructions during program execution
- User-controlled execution speed
- Status messages
- User-viewable symbol tables
- An interactive assembler that lets the user correct any errors and reassemble automatically, without changing environments
- Online help
- Optional core dumps, allowing the user to specify the memory range
- Frames with sizes that can be modified by the user
- A small learning curve, allowing students to learn the system quickly

MarieSim was written in the Java language so that the system would be portable to any platform for which a Java Virtual Machine (JVM) is available. Students of Java may wish to look at the simulator's source code, and perhaps even offer improvements or enhancements to its simple functions.

Figure P.2, the MarieSim Graphical Environment, shows the graphical environment of the MARIE machine simulator. The screen consists of four parts: the menu bar, the central monitor area, the memory monitor, and the message area.

Menu options allow the user to control the actions and behavior of the MARIE simulator system. These options include loading, starting, stopping, setting breakpoints, and pausing programs that have been written in MARIE assembly language.

The MARIE simulator illustrates the process of assembly, loading, and execution, all in one simple environment. Users can see assembly language statements

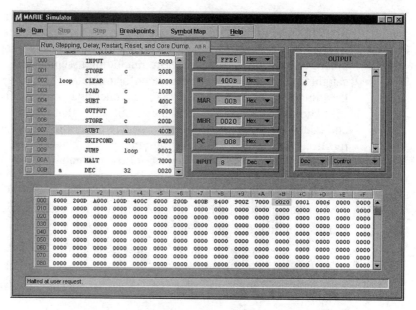

FIGURE P.2 The MarieSim Graphical Environment

directly from their programs, along with the corresponding machine code (hexadecimal) equivalents. The addresses of these instructions are indicated as well, and users can view any portion of memory at any time. Highlighting is used to indicate the initial loading address of a program in addition to the currently executing instruction while a program runs. The graphical display of the registers and memory allows the student to see how the instructions cause the values in the registers and memory to change.

If You Find an Error

We have attempted to make this book as technically accurate as possible, but even though the manuscript has been through numerous proofreadings, errors have a way of escaping detection. We would greatly appreciate hearing from readers who find any errors that need correcting. Your comments and suggestions are always welcome; please send on email to ECOA@jblearning.com.

Credits and Acknowledgments

Few books are entirely the result of one or two people's unaided efforts, and this one is no exception. We realize that writing a textbook is a formidable task and only possible with a combined effort, and we find it impossible to adequately thank those who have made this book possible. If, in the following acknowledgments, we inadvertently omit anyone, we humbly apologize.

A number of people have contributed to the fourth edition of this book. We would first like to thank all of the reviewers for their careful evaluations of previous editions and their thoughtful written comments. In addition, we are grateful for the many readers who have emailed useful ideas and helpful suggestions. Although we cannot mention all of these people here, we especially thank John MacCormick (Dickinson College) and Jacqueline Jones (Brooklyn College) for their meticulous reviews and their numerous comments and suggestions. We extend a special thanks to Karishma Rao and Sean Willeford for their time and effort in producing a quality memory software module.

We would also like to thank the individuals at Jones & Bartlett Learning who worked closely with us to make this fourth edition possible. We are very grateful to Tiffany Silter, Laura Pagluica, and Amy Rose for their professionalism, commitment, and hard work on the fourth edition.

I, Linda Null, would personally like to thank my husband, Tim Wahls, for his continued patience while living life as a "book widower" for a fourth time, for listening and commenting with frankness about the book's contents and modifications, for doing such an extraordinary job with all of the cooking, and for putting up with the almost daily compromises necessitated by my writing this book—including missing our annual fly-fishing vacation and forcing our horses into prolonged pasture ornament status. I consider myself amazingly lucky to be married to such a wonderful man. I extend my heartfelt thanks to my mentor, Merry McDonald, who taught me the value and joys of learning and teaching, and doing both with integrity. Lastly, I would like to express my deepest gratitude to Julia Lobur, as without her, this book and its accompanying software would not be a reality. It has been both a joy and an honor working with her.

I, Julia Lobur, am deeply indebted to my lawful spouse, Marla Cattermole, who married me despite the demands that this book has placed on both of us. She has made this work possible through her forbearance and fidelity. She has nurtured my body through her culinary delights and my spirit through her wisdom. She has taken up my slack in many ways while working hard at her own career. I would also like to convey my profound gratitude to Linda Null: first, for her unsurpassed devotion to the field of computer science education and dedication to her students and, second, for giving me the opportunity to share with her the ineffable experience of textbook authorship.

CHAPTER 1
Introduction

1.1 OVERVIEW

D r. Negroponte is among many who see the computer revolution as if it were a force of nature. This force has the potential to carry humanity to its digital destiny, allowing us to conquer problems that have eluded us for centuries, as well as all of the problems that emerge as we solve the original problems. Computers have freed us from the tedium of routine tasks, liberating our collective creative potential so that we can, of course, build bigger and better computers.

As we observe the profound scientific and social changes that computers have brought us, it is easy to start feeling overwhelmed by the complexity of it all. This complexity, however, emanates from concepts that are fundamentally very simple. These simple ideas are the ones that have brought us to where we are today and are the foundation for the computers of the future. To what extent they will survive in the future is anybody's guess. But today, they are the foundation for all of computer science as we know it.

Computer scientists are usually more concerned with writing complex program algorithms than with designing computer hardware. Of course, if we want our algorithms to be useful, a computer eventually has to run them. Some algorithms are so complicated that they would take too long to run on today's systems. These kinds of algorithms are considered **computationally infeasible**. Certainly, at the current rate of innovation, some things that are infeasible today could be feasible tomorrow, but it seems that no matter how big or fast computers become, someone will think up a problem that will exceed the reasonable limits of the machine.

To understand why an algorithm is infeasible, or to understand why the implementation of a feasible algorithm is running too slowly, you must be able to see the program from the computer's point of view. You must understand what makes a computer system tick before you can attempt to optimize the programs that it runs. Attempting to optimize a computer system without first understanding it is like attempting to tune your car by pouring an elixir into the gas tank: You'll be lucky if it runs at all when you're finished.

Program optimization and system tuning are perhaps the most important motivations for learning how computers work. There are, however, many other reasons. For example, if you want to write compilers, you must understand the hardware environment within which the compiler will function. The best compilers leverage particular hardware features (such as pipelining) for greater speed and efficiency.

If you ever need to model large, complex, real-world systems, you will need to know how floating-point arithmetic should work as well as how it really works in practice. If you wish to design peripheral equipment or the software that drives peripheral equipment, you must know every detail of how a particular computer deals with its input/output (I/O). If your work involves embedded systems, you need to know that these systems are usually resource-constrained. Your understanding of time, space, and price trade-offs, as well as I/O architectures, will be essential to your career.

All computer professionals should be familiar with the concepts of benchmarking and be able to interpret and present the results of benchmarking systems. People who perform research involving hardware systems, networks, or algorithms find benchmarking techniques crucial to their day-to-day work. Technical managers in charge of buying hardware also use benchmarks to help them buy the best system for a given amount of money, keeping in mind the ways in which performance benchmarks can be manipulated to imply results favorable to particular systems.

The preceding examples illustrate the idea that a fundamental relationship exists between computer hardware and many aspects of programming and software components in computer systems. Therefore, regardless of our areas of expertise, as computer scientists, it is imperative that we understand how hardware interacts with software. We must become familiar with how various circuits and components fit together to create working computer systems. We do this through the study of **computer organization**. Computer organization addresses issues such as control signals (how the computer is controlled), signaling methods, and memory types. It encompasses all physical aspects of computer systems. It helps us to answer the question: How does a computer work?

The study of **computer architecture**, on the other hand, focuses on the structure and behavior of the computer system and refers to the logical and abstract aspects of system implementation as seen by the programmer. Computer architecture includes many elements such as instruction sets and formats, operation codes, data types, the number and types of registers, addressing modes, main memory access methods, and various I/O mechanisms. The architecture of a system directly affects the logical execution of programs. Studying computer architecture helps us to answer the question: How do I design a computer?

The computer architecture for a given machine is the combination of its hardware components plus its **instruction set architecture (ISA)**. The ISA is the agreed-upon interface between all the software that runs on the machine and the hardware that executes it. The ISA allows you to talk to the machine.

The distinction between computer organization and computer architecture is not clear-cut. People in the fields of computer science and computer engineering hold differing opinions as to exactly which concepts pertain to computer organization and which pertain to computer architecture. In fact, neither computer organization nor computer architecture can stand alone. They are interrelated and interdependent. We can truly understand each of them only after we comprehend both of them. Our comprehension of computer organization and architecture ultimately leads to a deeper understanding of computers and computation—the heart and soul of computer science.

1.2 THE MAIN COMPONENTS OF A COMPUTER

Although it is difficult to distinguish between the ideas belonging to computer organization and those ideas belonging to computer architecture, it is impossible to say where hardware issues end and software issues begin. Computer scientists design algorithms that usually are implemented as programs written in some computer language, such as Java or C++. But what makes the algorithm run? Another algorithm, of course! And another algorithm runs that algorithm, and so on until you get down to the machine level, which can be thought of as an algorithm implemented as an electronic device. Thus, modern computers are actually implementations of algorithms that execute other algorithms. This chain of nested algorithms leads us to the following principle:

> **Principle of Equivalence of Hardware and Software:** *Any task done by software can also be done using hardware, and any operation performed directly by hardware can be done using software.*[1]

A special-purpose computer can be designed to perform any task, such as word processing, budget analysis, or playing a friendly game of Tetris. Accordingly, programs can be written to carry out the functions of special-purpose computers, such as the embedded systems situated in your car or microwave. There are times when a simple embedded system gives us much better performance than a complicated computer program, and there are times when a program is the preferred approach. The Principle of Equivalence of Hardware and Software tells us that we have a choice. Our knowledge of computer organization and architecture will help us to make the best choice.

We begin our discussion of computer hardware by looking at the components necessary to build a computing system. At the most basic level, a computer is a device consisting of three pieces:

1. A processor to interpret and execute programs

2. A memory to store both data and programs

3. A mechanism for transferring data to and from the outside world

---

[1]What this principle does not address is the speed with which the equivalent tasks are carried out. Hardware implementations are almost always faster.

We discuss these three components in detail as they relate to computer hardware in the following chapters.

Once you understand computers in terms of their component parts, you should be able to understand what a system is doing at all times and how you could change its behavior if so desired. You might even feel like you have a few things in common with it. This idea is not as far-fetched as it appears. Consider how a student sitting in class exhibits the three components of a computer: The student's brain is the processor, the notes being taken represent the memory, and the pencil or pen used to take notes is the I/O mechanism. But keep in mind that your abilities far surpass those of any computer in the world today, or any that can be built in the foreseeable future.

1.3   AN EXAMPLE SYSTEM: WADING THROUGH THE JARGON

This text will introduce you to some of the vocabulary that is specific to computers. This jargon can be confusing, imprecise, and intimidating. We believe that with a little explanation, we can clear the fog.

For the sake of discussion, we have provided a facsimile computer advertisement (see Figure 1.1). The ad is typical of many in that it bombards the reader with phrases such as "32GB DDR3 SDRAM," "PCIe sound card," and "128KB L1 cache." Without having a handle on such terminology, you would be hard-pressed to know whether the stated system is a wise buy, or even whether the

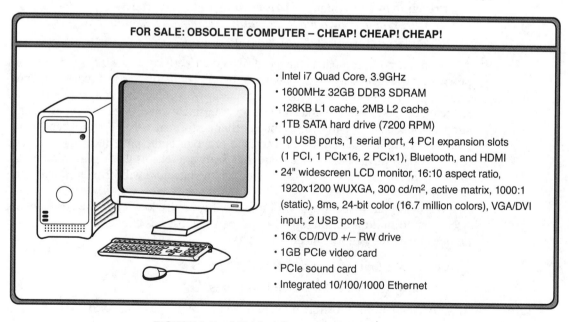

FIGURE 1.1   A Typical Computer Advertisement

system is able to serve your needs. As we progress through this text, you will learn the concepts behind these terms.

Before we explain the ad, however, we need to discuss something even more basic: the measurement terminology you will encounter throughout your study of computers.

It seems that every field has its own way of measuring things. The computer field is no exception. For computer people to tell each other how big something is, or how fast something is, they must use the same units of measure. The common prefixes used with computers are given in Table 1.1. Back in the 1960s, someone decided that because the powers of 2 were close to the powers of 10, the same prefix names could be used for both. For example, 2^{10} is close to 10^3, so "kilo" is used to refer to them both. The result has been mass confusion: Does a given prefix refer to a power of 10 or a power of 2? Does a kilo mean 10^3 of something or 2^{10} of something? Although there is no definitive answer to this question, there are accepted "standards of usage." Power-of-10 prefixes are ordinarily used for power, electrical voltage, frequency (such as computer clock speeds), and multiples of bits (such as data speeds in number of bits per second). If your antiquated modem transmits at 28.8kb/s, then it transmits 28,800 bits per second (or 28.8×10^3). Note the use of the lowercase "k" to mean 10^3 and the lowercase "b" to refer to bits. An uppercase "K" is used to refer to the power-of-2 prefix, or 1024. If a file is 2KB in size, then it is 2×2^{10} or 2048 bytes. Note the uppercase "B" to refer to byte. If a disk holds 1MB, then it holds 2^{20} bytes (or one megabyte) of information.

Not knowing whether specific prefixes refer to powers of 2 or powers of 10 can be very confusing. For this reason, the International Electrotechnical Commission, with help from the National Institute of Standards and Technology, has approved standard names and symbols for binary prefixes to differentiate them from decimal prefixes. Each prefix is derived from the symbols given in Table 1.1 by adding an "i." For example, 2^{10} has been renamed "kibi" (for kilobinary) and

Prefix	Symbol	Power of 10	Power of 2	Prefix	Symbol	Power of 10	Power of 2
Kilo	K	1 thousand = 10^3	2^{10} = 1024	Milli	m	1 thousandth = 10^{-3}	2^{-10}
Mega	M	1 million = 10^6	2^{20}	Micro	μ	1 millionth = 10^{-6}	2^{-20}
Giga	G	1 billion = 10^9	2^{30}	Nano	n	1 billionth = 10^{-9}	2^{-30}
Tera	T	1 trillion = 10^{12}	2^{40}	Pico	p	1 trillionth = 10^{-12}	2^{-40}
Peta	P	1 quadrillion = 10^{15}	2^{50}	Femto	f	1 quadrillionth = 10^{-15}	2^{-50}
Exa	E	1 quintillion = 10^{18}	2^{60}	Atto	a	1 quintillionth = 10^{-18}	2^{-60}
Zetta	Z	1 sextillion = 10^{21}	2^{70}	Zepto	z	1 sextillionth = 10^{-21}	2^{-70}
Yotta	Y	1 septillion = 10^{24}	2^{80}	Yocto	y	1 septillionth = 10^{-24}	2^{-80}

TABLE 1.1 Common Prefixes Associated with Computer Organization and Architecture

is represented by the symbol Ki. Similarly, 2^{20} is mebi, or Mi, followed by gibi (Gi), tebi (Ti), pebi (Pi), exbi (Ei), and so on. Thus, the term *mebibyte*, which means 2^{20} bytes, replaces what we traditionally call a megabyte.

There has been limited adoption of these new prefixes. This is unfortunate because, as a computer user, it is important to understand the true meaning of these prefixes. A kilobyte (1KB) of memory is *typically* 1024 bytes of memory rather than 1000 bytes of memory. However, a 1GB disk drive might actually be 1 billion bytes instead of 2^{30} (which means you are getting less storage than you think). All 3.5" floppy disks are described as storing 1.44MB of data when in fact they store 1440KB (or $1440 \times 2^{10} = 1474560$ bytes). You should always read the manufacturer's fine print just to make sure you know exactly what 1K, 1KB, or 1G represents. See the sidebar "When a Gigabyte Isn't Quite . . ." for a good example of why this is so important.

Who Uses Zettabytes and Yottabytes Anyway?

The National Security Agency (NSA), an intelligence-gathering organization in the United States, announced that its new Intelligence Community Comprehensive National Cybersecurity Initiative Data Center, in Bluffdale, Utah, was set to open in October 2013. Approximately 100,000 square feet of the structure is utilized for the data center, Whereas the remaining 900,000+ square feet houses technical support and administration. The new data center will help the NSA monitor the vast volume of data traffic on the Internet.

It is estimated that the NSA collects roughly 2 million gigabytes of data every hour, 24 hours a day, seven days a week. This data includes foreign and domestic emails, cell phone calls, Internet searches, various purchases, and other forms of digital data. The computer responsible for analyzing this data for the new data center is the Titan supercomputer, a water-cooled machine capable of operating at 100 petaflops (or 100,000 trillion calculations each second). The PRISM (Planning Tool for Resource Integration, Synchronization, and Management) surveillance program will gather, process, and track all collected data.

Although we tend to think in terms of gigabytes and terabytes when buying storage for our personal computers and other devices, the NSA's data center storage capacity will be measured in zettabytes (with many hypothesizing that storage will be in thousands of zettabytes, or yottabytes). To put this in perspective, in a 2003 study done at the University of California (UC) Berkeley, it was estimated that the amount of new data created in 2002 was roughly 5EB. An earlier study by UC Berkeley estimated that by the end of 1999, the sum of all information, including audio, video, and text, created by humankind was approximately 12EB of data. In 2006, the combined storage space of every computer hard drive in the world was estimated at 160EB; in 2009, the Internet as a whole was estimated to contain roughly 500 total exabytes, or a half zettabyte, of data. Cisco, a U.S. computer network hardware manufacturer, has estimated that by 2016, the total volume of data on the global internet will be 1.3ZB, and Seagate Technology, an American manufacturer of hard drives, has estimated that the total storage capacity demand will reach 7ZB in 2020.

The NSA is not the only organization dealing with information that must be measured in numbers of bytes beyond the typical "giga" and "tera." It is estimated that Facebook collects 500TB of new material per day; YouTube observes roughly 1TB of new video information every four minutes; the CERN Large Hadron Collider generates 1PB of data per second; and the sensors on a single, new Boeing jet engine produce 20TB of data every hour. Although not all of the aforementioned examples require permanent storage of the data they create/handle, these examples nonetheless provide evidence of the remarkable quantity of data we deal with every day. This tremendous volume of information is what prompted the IBM Corporation, in 2011, to develop and announce its new 120-PB hard drive, a storage cluster consisting of 200,000 conventional hard drives harnessed to work together as a single unit. If you plugged your MP3 player into this drive, you would have roughly two billion hours of music!

In this era of smartphones, tablets, Cloud computing, and other electronic devices, we will continue to hear people talking about petabytes, exabytes, and zettabytes (and, in the case of the NSA, even yottabytes). However, if we outgrow yottabytes, what then? In an effort to keep up with the astronomical growth of information and to refer to even bigger volumes of data, the next generation of prefixes will most likely include the terms *brontobyte* for 10^{27} and *gegobyte* for 10^{30} (although some argue for *geobyte* and *geopbyte* as the prefixes for the latter). Although these are not yet universally accepted international prefix units, if history is any indication, we will need them sooner rather than later.

When a Gigabyte Isn't Quite . . .

Purchasing a new array of disk drives should be a relatively straightforward process once you determine your technical requirements (e.g., disk transfer rate, interface type, etc.). From here, you should be able to make your decision based on a simple price/capacity ratio, such as dollars per gigabyte, and then you'll be done. Well, not so fast.

The first boulder in the path of a straightforward analysis is that you must make sure that the drives you are comparing all express their capacities either in formatted or unformatted bytes. As much as 16% of drive space is consumed during the formatting process. (Some vendors give this number as "usable capacity.") Naturally, the price–capacity ratio looks much better when unformatted bytes are used, although you are most interested in knowing the amount of *usable* space a disk provides.

Your next obstacle is to make sure that the same radix is used when comparing disk sizes. It is increasingly common for disk capacities to be given in base 10 rather than base 2. Thus, a "1GB" disk drive has a capacity of $10^9 = 1,000,000,000$ bytes, rather than $2^{30} = 1,073,741,824$ bytes—a reduction of about 7%. This can make a huge difference when purchasing multigigabyte enterprise-class storage systems.

As a concrete example, suppose you are considering purchasing a disk array from one of two leading manufacturers. Manufacturer *x* advertises an array of 12 250GB disks for $20,000. Manufacturer *y* is offering an array of 12 212.5GB disks for $21,000. All other things being equal, the cost ratio overwhelmingly favors Manufacturer *x*:

Manufacturer *x*: $20,000 ÷ (12 × 250GB) ≅ $6.67 per GB
Manufacturer *y*: $21,000 ÷ (12 × 212.5GB) ≅ $8.24 per GB

Being a little suspicious, you make a few telephone calls and learn that Manufacturer *x* is citing capacities using unformatted base 10 gigabytes and Manufacturer *y* is using formatted base 2 gigabytes. These facts cast the problem in an entirely different light: To start with, Manufacturer *x*'s disks aren't really 250GB in the way that we usually think of gigabytes. Instead, they are about 232.8 base 2 gigabytes. After formatting, the number reduces even more to about 197.9GB. So the real cost ratios are, in fact:

Manufacturer *x*: $20,000 ÷ (12 × 197.9GB) ≅ $8.42 per GB
Manufacturer *y*: $21,000 ÷ (12 × 212.5GB) ≅ $8.24 per GB

Indeed, some vendors are scrupulously honest in disclosing the capabilities of their equipment. Unfortunately, others reveal the facts only under direct questioning. Your job as an educated professional is to ask the right questions.

When we want to talk about how fast something is, we speak in terms of fractions of a second—usually thousandths, millionths, billionths, or trillionths. Prefixes for these metrics are given in the right-hand side of Table 1.1. Generally, negative powers refer to powers of 10, not powers of 2. For this reason, the new binary prefix standards do not include any new names for the negative powers. Notice that the fractional prefixes have exponents that are the reciprocal of the prefixes on the left side of the table. Therefore, if someone says to you that an operation requires a microsecond to complete, you should also understand that a million of those operations could take place in one second. When you need to talk about how many of these things happen in a second, you would use the prefix *mega-*. When you need to talk about how fast the operations are performed, you would use the prefix *micro-*.

Now to explain the ad. The microprocessor in the ad is an Intel i7 Quad Core processor (which means it is essentially four processors) and belongs to a category of processors known as multicore processors (Section 1.10 contains more information on multicore processors). This particular processor runs at 3.9GHz. Every computer system contains a clock that keeps the system synchronized. The clock sends electrical pulses simultaneously to all main components, ensuring that data and instructions will be where they're supposed to be, when they're supposed to be there. The number of pulsations emitted each second by the clock is its frequency. Clock frequencies are measured in cycles per second, or **hertz**. If computer system clocks generate millions of pulses per second, we say that they operate in the **megahertz (MHz)** range. Most computers today operate in the **gigahertz (GHz)** range, generating billions of pulses per second. And because nothing much gets done in a computer system without microprocessor involvement, the frequency rating of the microprocessor is crucial to overall system speed. The microprocessor of the system in our advertisement operates at 3.9 billion cycles per second, so the seller says that it runs at 3.9GHz.

The fact that this microprocessor runs at 3.9GHz, however, doesn't necessarily mean that it can execute 3.9 billion instructions every second or, equivalently, that every instruction requires 0.039 nanoseconds to execute. Later in this text, you will see that each computer instruction requires a fixed number of cycles to execute. Some instructions require one clock cycle; however, most instructions require more than one. The number of instructions per second that a microprocessor can actually execute is *proportionate* to its clock speed. The number of clock cycles required to carry out a particular machine instruction is a function of both the machine's organization and its architecture.

The next thing we see in the ad is "1600MHz 32GB DDR3 SDRAM." The 1600MHz refers to the speed of the system **bus**, which is a group of wires that moves data and instructions to various places within the computer. Like the microprocessor, the speed of the bus is also measured in MHz or GHz. Many computers have a special local bus for data that supports very fast transfer speeds (such as those required by video). This local bus is a high-speed pathway that connects memory directly to the processor. Bus speed ultimately sets the upper limit on the system's information-carrying capability.

The system in our advertisement also boasts a memory capacity of 32 gigabytes (GB), or about 32 billion characters. Memory capacity not only determines the size of the programs you can run, but also how many programs you can run at the same time without bogging down the system. Your application or operating system manufacturer will usually recommend how much memory you'll need to run its products. (Sometimes these recommendations can be hilariously conservative, so be careful whom you believe!)

In addition to memory size, our advertised system provides us with a memory type, **SDRAM**, short for **synchronous dynamic random access memory**. SDRAM is much faster than conventional (nonsynchronous) memory because it can synchronize itself with a microprocessor's bus. The system in our ad has **DDR3 SDRAM**, or **double data rate** type three SDRAM (for more information on the different types of memory, see Chapter 6).

A Look Inside a Computer

Have you ever wondered what the inside of a computer really looks like? The example computer described in this section gives a good overview of the components of a modern PC. However, opening a computer and attempting to find and identify the various pieces can be frustrating, even if you are familiar with the components and their functions.

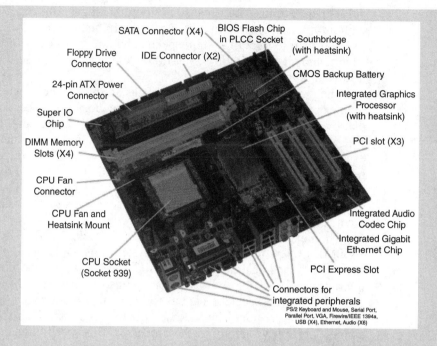

Photo courtesy of Moxfyre at en.wikipedia (from http://commons.wikimedia.org/wiki/File:Acer_E360_Socket_939_motherboard_by_Foxconn.svg).

If you remove the cover on your computer, you will no doubt first notice a big metal box with a fan attached. This is the power supply. You will also see various drives, including a hard drive and a DVD drive (or perhaps an older floppy or CD drive). There are many integrated circuits—small, black rectangular boxes with legs attached. You will also notice electrical pathways, or buses, in the system. There are printed circuit boards (expansion cards) that plug into sockets on the motherboard, the large board at the bottom of a standard desktop PC or on the side of a PC configured as a tower or mini-tower. The motherboard is the printed circuit board that connects all the components in the computer, including the CPU, and RAM and ROM, as well as an assortment of other essential components. The components on the motherboard tend to be the most difficult to identify. Above you see an Acer E360 motherboard with the more important components labeled.

The Southbridge, an integrated circuit that controls the hard disk and I/O (including sound and video cards), is a hub that connects slower I/O devices to the system bus. These devices connect via the I/O ports at the bottom of the board. The PCI slots allow for expansion boards belonging to various PCI devices. This motherboard also has PS/2 and Firewire connectors. It has serial and parallel ports, in addition to four USB ports. This motherboard has two IDE connector slots, four SATA connector slots, and one floppy disk controller. The super I/O chip is a type of I/O controller that controls the floppy disk, both the parallel and serial ports, and the keyboard and mouse. The motherboard also has an integrated audio chip, as well as an integrated Ethernet chip and an integrated graphics processor. There are four RAM memory banks. There is no processor currently plugged into this motherboard, but we see the socket where the CPU is to be placed. All computers have an internal battery, as seen in the top middle of the picture. The power supply plugs into the power connector. The BIOS flash chip contains the instructions in ROM that your computer uses when it is first powered up.

A note of caution regarding looking inside the box: There are many safety issues, for both you and your computer, involved with removing the cover. There are many things you can do to minimize the risks. First and foremost, make sure the computer is turned off. Leaving it plugged in is often preferred, as this offers a path for static electricity. Before opening your computer and touching anything inside, you should make sure you are properly grounded so static electricity will not damage any components. Many of the edges, both on the cover and on the circuit boards, can be sharp, so take care when handling the various pieces. Trying to jam misaligned cards into sockets can damage both the card and the motherboard, so be careful if you decide to add a new card or remove and reinstall an existing one.

The next line in the ad, "128KB L1 cache, 2MB L2 cache" also describes a type of memory. In Chapter 6, you will learn that no matter how fast a bus is, it still takes "a while" to get data from memory to the processor. To provide even faster access to data, many systems contain a special memory called **cache**. The system in our advertisement has two kinds of cache. Level 1 cache (L1) is a small, fast memory cache that is built into the microprocessor chip and helps speed up access to frequently used data. Level 2 cache (L2) is a collection of fast, built-in memory chips situated between the microprocessor and main memory. Notice that the cache in our system has a capacity of kilobytes (KB), which is much smaller than main memory. In Chapter 6, you will learn how cache works, and that a bigger cache isn't always better.

On the other hand, everyone agrees that the more fixed disk capacity you have, the better off you are. The advertised system has a 1TB hard drive, an average size by today's standards. The storage capacity of a fixed (or hard) disk is not the only thing to consider, however. A large disk isn't very helpful if it is too slow for its host system. The computer in our ad has a hard drive that rotates at 7200 revolutions per minute (RPM). To the knowledgeable reader, this indicates (but does not state outright) that this is a fairly fast drive. Usually, disk speeds are stated in terms of the number of milliseconds required (on average) to access data on the disk, in addition to how fast the disk rotates.

Rotational speed is only one of the determining factors in the overall performance of a disk. The manner in which it connects to—or **interfaces** with—the rest of the system is also important. The advertised system uses a **SATA (serial advanced technology attachment** or **serial ATA)** disk interface. This is an evolutionary storage interface that has replaced **IDE**, or **integrated drive electronics.** Another common interface is **EIDE, enhanced integrated drive electronics**, a cost-effective hardware interface alternative for mass storage devices. EIDE contains special circuits that allow it to enhance a computer's connectivity, speed, and memory capability. Most ATA, IDE, and EIDE systems share the main system bus with the processor and memory, so the movement of data to and from the disk is also dependent on the speed of the system bus.

Whereas the system bus is responsible for all data movement internal to the computer, **ports** allow movement of data to and from devices external to the computer. Our ad speaks of two different ports with the line, "10 USB ports, 1 serial port." Serial ports transfer data by sending a series of electrical pulses across one or two data lines. Another type of port some computers have is a parallel port. Parallel ports use at least eight data lines, which are energized simultaneously to transmit data. Many new computers no longer come with serial or parallel ports, but instead have only USB ports. USB (**universal serial bus**) is a popular external bus that supports **Plug-and-Play** installation (the ability to configure devices automatically) as well as **hot plugging** (the ability to add and remove devices while the computer is running).

Expansion slots are openings on the motherboard where various boards can be plugged in to add new capabilities to a computer. These slots can be used for such things as additional memory, video cards, sound cards, network cards, and modems. Some systems augment their main bus with dedicated I/O buses using these expansion slots. **Peripheral Component Interconnect** (**PCI**) is one such I/O bus standard that supports the connection of multiple peripheral devices. PCI, developed by the Intel Corporation, operates at high speeds and also supports Plug-and-Play.

PCI is an older standard (it has been around since 1993) and was superseded by PCI-x in 2004. PCI-x basically doubled the bandwidth of regular PCI. Both PCI and PCI-x are parallel in operation. In 2004, PCI express (PCIe) replaced PCI-x. PCIe operates in serial and is currently the standard in today's computers. In the ad, we see the computer has 1 PCI slot, 1 PCI x 16 slot, and 2 PCI x 1 slots. This computer also has Bluetooth (a wireless technology allowing the transfer of information over short distances) and an HDMI port (High-Definition Multimedia Interface, used to transmit audio and video).

PCIe has not only superseded PCI and PCI-x, but in the graphics world, it has also progressively replaced the **AGP** (**accelerated graphics port**) graphics interface designed by Intel specifically for 3D graphics. The computer in our ad has a PCIe video card with 1GB of memory. The memory is used by a special **graphics processing unit** on the card. This processor is responsible for performing the necessary calculations to render the graphics so the main processor of the computer is not required to do so. This computer also has a PCIe sound card; a sound card contains components needed by the system's stereo speakers and microphone.

In addition to telling us about the ports and expansion slots in the advertised system, the ad supplies us with information on an **LCD** (**liquid crystal display**) monitor, or "flat panel" display. Monitors have little to do with the speed or efficiency of a computer system, but they have great bearing on the comfort of the user. This LCD monitor has the following specifications: 24", 1920 × 1200 WUXGA, 300 cd/m^2, active matrix, 1000:1 (static), 8ms, 24-bit color (16.7 million colors), VGA/DVI input, and 2USB ports. LCDs use a liquid crystal material sandwiched between two pieces of polarized glass. Electric currents cause the crystals to move around, allowing differing levels of backlighting to pass through, creating the text, colors, and pictures that appear on the screen. This is done by turning on/off different **pixels**, small "picture elements" or dots on the screen. Monitors typically have millions of pixels, arranged in rows and columns. This monitor has 1920×1200 (more than a million) pixels.

Most LCDs manufactured today utilize active matrix technology, Whereas passive technology is reserved for smaller devices such as calculators and clocks. **Active matrix** technology uses one transistor per pixel; **passive matrix** technology uses transistors that activate entire rows and columns. Although passive technology is less costly, active technology renders a better image because it drives each pixel independently.

The LCD monitor in the ad is 24", measured diagonally. This measurement affects the **aspect ratio** of the monitor—the ratio of horizontal pixels to vertical pixels that the monitor can display. Traditionally, this ratio was 4:3, but newer widescreen monitors use ratios of 16:10 or 16:9. Ultra-wide monitors use a higher ratio, around 3:1 or 2:1.

When discussing resolution and LCDs, it is important to note that LCDs have a **native resolution**; this means LCDs are designed for a specific resolution (generally given in horizontal pixels by vertical pixels). Although you can change the resolution, the image quality typically suffers. Resolutions and aspect ratios are often paired. When listing resolutions for LCDs, manufacturers often use the following abbreviations: XGA (extended graphics array); XGA+ (extended graphics array plus); SXGA (super XGA); UXGA (ultra XGA); W prefix (wide); and WVA (wide viewing angle). The viewing angle specifies an angle, in degrees, that indicates at which angle a user can still see the image on the screen; common angles range from 120 to 170 degrees. Some examples of standard 4:3 native resolutions include XGA (1024×768), SXGA (1280×1024), SXGA+ (1400×1050), and UXGA (1600×1200). Common 16:9 and 16:10 resolutions include WXGA (1280×800), WXGA+ (1440×900), WSXGA+ (1680×1050), and WUXGA (1920×1200).

LCD monitor specifications often list a **response time**, which indicates the rate at which the pixels can change colors. If this rate is too slow, ghosting and blurring can occur. The LCD monitor in the ad has a response time of 8ms. Originally, response rates measured the time to go from black to white and back to black. Many manufacturers now list the response time for gray-to-gray transitions (which is generally faster). Because they typically do not specify which transition has been measured, it is very difficult to compare monitors. One manufacturer may specify a response time of 2ms for a monitor (and it measures gray-to-gray), while another manufacturer may specify a response rate of 5ms for its monitor (and it measures black-to-white-to-black). In reality, the monitor with the response rate of 5ms may actually be faster overall.

Continuing with the ad, we see that the LCD monitor has a specification of 300 cd/m^2, which is the monitor's luminance. **Luminance** (or image brightness) is a measure of the amount of light an LCD monitor emits. This measure is typically given in candelas per square meter (cd/m^2). When purchasing a monitor, the brightness level should be at least 250 (the higher the better); the average for computer monitors is from 200 to 300 cd/m^2. Luminance affects how easy a monitor is to read, particularly in low light situations.

Whereas luminance measures the brightness, the **contrast ratio** measures the difference in intensity between bright whites and dark blacks. Contrast ratios can be **static** (the ratio of the brightest point on the monitor to the darkest point on the monitor that can be produced at a given instant in time) or **dynamic** (the ratio of the darkest point in one image to the lightest point in another image produced at a separate point in time). Static specifications are typically preferred. A low static ratio (such as 300:1) makes it more difficult to discern shades; a good static ratio is 500:1 (with ranges from 400:1 to 3000:1). The monitor in the ad has a static contrast ratio of 1000:1. LCD monitors can have dynamic ratios of 12,000,000:1 and higher, but a higher dynamic number does not necessarily mean the monitor is better than a monitor with a much lower static ratio.

The next specification given for the LCD monitor in the ad is its **color depth**. This number reflects the number of colors that can be displayed on the screen at one time. Common depths are 8-bit, 16-bit, 24-bit, and 32-bit. The LCD monitor in our ad can display 2^{24}, or roughly 16.7 million colors.

LCD monitors also have many optional features. Some have integrated USB ports (as in this ad) and/or speakers. Many are HDCP (high bandwidth digital content protection) compliant (which means you can watch HDCP-encrypted materials, such as Blu-ray discs). LCD monitors may also come with both VGA (video graphics array) and DVI (digital video interface) connections (as seen in the ad). VGA sends analog signals to the monitor from the computer, which requires digital-to-analog conversion; DVI is already digital in format and requires no conversion, resulting in a cleaner signal and crisper image. Although an LCD monitor typically provides better images using a DVI connection, having both connectors allows one to use an LCD with existing system components.

Now that we have discussed how an LCD monitor works and we understand the concept of a pixel, let's go back and discuss graphics cards (also called video cards) in more detail. With millions of pixels on the screen, it is quite challenging to determine which ones should be off and which ones should be on (and in what color). The job of the graphics card is to input the binary data from your computer and "translate" it into signals to control all pixels on the monitor; the graphics card therefore acts as a "middleman" between the computer's processor and monitor. As mentioned previously, some computers have integrated graphics, which means the computer's processor is responsible for doing this translation, causing a large workload on this processor; therefore, many computers have slots for graphics cards, allowing the processor on the graphics card (called a **graphics processing unit**, or **GPU**) to perform this translation instead.

The GPU is no ordinary processor; it is designed to most efficiently perform the complex calculations required for image rendering and contains special programs allowing it to perform this task more effectively. Graphics cards typically contain their own dedicated RAM used to hold temporary results and information, including the location and color for each pixel on the screen. A **frame buffer** (part of this RAM) is used to store rendered images until these images are intended to be displayed. The memory on a graphics card connects to a **digital-to-analog converter** (DAC), a device that converts a binary image to analog signals that a monitor can understand and sends them via a cable to the monitor. Most graphics cards today have two types of monitor connections: DVI for LCD screens and VGA for the older CRT (cathode ray tube) screens.

Most graphics cards are plugged into slots in computer motherboards, so are thus powered by the computers themselves. However, some are very powerful and actually require a connection directly to a computer's power supply. These high-end graphics cards are typically found in computers that deal with image-intensive applications, such as video editing and high-end gaming.

Continuing with the ad, we see that the advertised system has a 16x DVD +/− RW drive. This means we can read and write to DVDs and CDs. "16x" is a measure of the drive speed and measures how quickly the drive can read and write. DVDs and CDs are discussed in more detail in Chapter 7.

Computers are more useful if they can communicate with the outside world. One way to communicate is to employ an Internet service provider and a modem. There is no mention of a modem for the computer in our ad, as many desktop owners use external modems provided by their Internet service provider (phone modem, cable modem, satellite modem, etc). However, both USB and PCI modems are available that allow you to connect your computer to the Internet using the phone line; many of these also allow you to use your computer as a fax machine. I/O and I/O buses in general are discussed in Chapter 7.

A computer can also connect directly to a network. Networking allows computers to share files and peripheral devices. Computers can connect to a network via either a wired or a wireless technology. Wired computers use **Ethernet** technology, an international standard networking technology for wired networks, and there are two options for the connection. The first is to use a **network interface card (NIC)**, which connects to the motherboard via a PCI slot. NICs typically support 10/100 Ethernet (both Ethernet at a speed of 10Mbps and fast Ethernet at a speed of 100Mbps) or 10/100/1000 (which adds Ethernet at 1,000Mbps). Another option for wired network capability is integrated Ethernet, which means that the motherboard itself contains all necessary components to support 10/100 Ethernet; thus no PCI slot is required. Wireless networking has the same two options. Wireless NICs are available from a multitude of vendors and are available for both desktops and laptops. For installation in desktop machines, you need an internal card that will most likely have a small antenna. Laptops usually use an expansion (PCMCIA) slot for the wireless network card, and vendors have started to integrate the antenna into the back of the case behind the screen. Integrated wireless (such as that found in the Intel Centrino mobile technology) eliminates the hassle of cables and cards. The system in our ad employs integrated Ethernet. Note that many new computers may have integrated graphics and/or integrated sound in addition to integrated Ethernet.

Although we cannot delve into all of the brand-specific components available, after completing this text, you should understand the concept of how most computer systems operate. This understanding is important for casual users as well as experienced programmers. As a user, you need to be aware of the strengths and limitations of your computer system so you can make informed decisions about applications and thus use your system more effectively. As a programmer, you need to understand exactly how your system hardware functions so you can write effective and efficient programs. For example, something as simple as the algorithm your hardware uses to map main memory to cache and the method used for memory interleaving can have a tremendous effect on your decision to access array elements in row versus column-major order.

Throughout this text, we investigate both large and small computers. Large computers include mainframes, enterprise-class servers, and supercomputers. Small computers include personal systems, workstations, and handheld devices. We will show that regardless of whether they carry out routine chores or perform sophisticated scientific tasks, the components of these systems are very similar. We also visit some architectures that lie outside what is now the mainstream of computing. We hope that the knowledge you gain from this text will ultimately serve as a springboard for your continuing studies the vast and exciting fields of computer organization and architecture.

Tablet Computers

Ken Olsen, the founder of Digital Equipment Corporation, has been unfairly ridiculed for saying "There is no reason for any individual to have a computer in his home." He made this statement in 1977 when the word, *computer*, evoked a vision of the type of machine made by his company: refrigerator-sized behemoths that cost a fortune and required highly skilled personnel to operate. One might safely say that no one—except perhaps a computer engineer—ever had such a machine in his or her home.

As already discussed, the "personal computing" wave that began in the 1980s erupted in the 1990s with the establishment of the World Wide Web. By 2010, decennial census data reported that 68% of U.S. households claimed to have a personal computer. There is, however, some evidence that this trend has peaked and is now in decline, owing principally to the widespread use of smartphones and tablet computers. According to some estimates, as many as 65% of Internet users in the United States connect exclusively via mobile platforms. The key to this trend is certainly the enchanting usability of these devices.

We hardly need the power of a desktop computer to surf the Web, read email, or listen to music. Much more economical and lightweight, tablet computers give us exactly what we need in an easy-to-use package. With its booklike form, one is tempted to claim that a tablet constitutes the perfect "portable computer."

The figure on the next page shows a disassembled Pandigital Novel tablet computer. We have labeled several items common to all tablets. The mini USB port provides access to internal storage and the removable SD card. Nearly all tablets provide Wi-Fi connection to the Internet, with some also supporting 2G, 3G, and 4G cellular protocols. Battery life can be as much as 14 hours for the most efficient high-end tablet computers. Unlike the Pandigital, most tablets include at least one camera for still photography and live video.

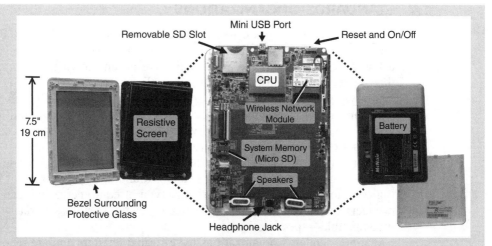

A Disassembled Tablet Computer
Courtesy of Julia Lobur.

A touchscreen dominates the real estate of all portable devices. For consumer tablets and phones, touchscreens come in two general types: resistive and capacitive. **Resistive** touchscreens respond to the pressure of a finger or a stylus. **Capacitive** touchscreens react to the electrical properties of the human skin. Resistive screens are less sensitive than capacitive screens, but they provide higher resolution. Unlike resistive screens, capacitive screens support multitouch, which is the ability to detect the simultaneous press of two or more fingers.

Military and medical computer touchscreens are necessarily more durable than those intended for the consumer market. Two different technologies, **surface acoustic wave touch sense** and **infrared touch sense**, respectively, send ultrasonic and infrared waves across the surface of a ruggedized touchscreen. The matrix of waves is broken when a finger comes in contact with the surface of the screen.

Because of its high efficiency, cell phone CPU technology has been adapted for use in the tablet platform. The mobile computing space has been dominated by ARM chips, although Intel and AMD have been gaining market share. Operating systems for these devices include variants of Android by Google and iOS by Apple. Microsoft's Surface tablets running Windows 8 provide access to the Microsoft Office suite of products.

As tablet computers continue to replace desktop systems, they will also find uses in places where traditional computers—even laptops—are impractical. Thousands of free and inexpensive applications are available for all platforms, thereby increasing demand even further. Educational applications abound. With a size, shape, and weight similar to a paperback book, tablet computers are replacing paper textbooks in some U.S. school districts. Thus, the elusive dream of "a computer for every student" is finally coming true—thanks to the tablet. By 1985, people were already laughing at Olsen's "home computer" assertion. Would perhaps these same people have scoffed if instead he would have predicted a computer in every backpack?

1.4 STANDARDS ORGANIZATIONS

Suppose you decide you'd like to have one of those nifty new LCD widescreen monitors. You figure you can shop around a bit to find the best price. You make a few phone calls, surf the Web, and drive around town until you find the one that gives you the most for your money. From your experience, you know you can buy your monitor anywhere and it will probably work fine on your system. You can make this assumption because computer equipment manufacturers have agreed to comply with connectivity and operational specifications established by a number of government and industry organizations.

Some of these standards-setting organizations are ad hoc trade associations or consortia made up of industry leaders. Manufacturers know that by establishing common guidelines for a particular type of equipment, they can market their products to a wider audience than if they came up with separate—and perhaps incompatible—specifications.

Some standards organizations have formal charters and are recognized internationally as the definitive authority in certain areas of electronics and computers. As you continue your studies in computer organization and architecture, you will encounter specifications formulated by these groups, so you should know something about them.

The **Institute of Electrical and Electronics Engineers (IEEE)** is an organization dedicated to the advancement of the professions of electronic and computer engineering. The IEEE actively promotes the interests of the worldwide engineering community by publishing an array of technical literature. The IEEE also sets standards for various computer components, signaling protocols, and data representation, to name only a few areas of its involvement. The IEEE has a democratic, albeit convoluted, procedure established for the creation of new standards. Its final documents are well respected and usually endure for several years before requiring revision.

The **International Telecommunications Union (ITU)** is based in Geneva, Switzerland. The ITU was formerly known as the *Comité Consultatif International Télégraphique et Téléphonique*, or the International Consultative Committee on Telephony and Telegraphy. As its name implies, the ITU concerns itself with the interoperability of telecommunications systems, including telephone, telegraph, and data communication systems. The telecommunications arm of the ITU, the ITU-T, has established a number of standards that you will encounter in the literature. You will see these standards prefixed by ITU-T or the group's former initials, **CCITT**.

Many countries, including the European Community, have commissioned umbrella organizations to represent their interests in various international groups. The group representing the United States is the **American National Standards Institute (ANSI)**. Great Britain has its **British Standards Institution (BSI)** in addition to having a voice on the **CEN (Comité Européen de Normalisation)**, the European committee for standardization.

The **International Organization for Standardization (ISO)** is the entity that coordinates worldwide standards development, including the activities of ANSI with BSI, among others. ISO is not an acronym, but derives from the Greek word, *isos*, meaning "equal." The ISO consists of more than 2800 technical committees, each of which is charged with some global standardization issue. Its interests range from the behavior of photographic film to the pitch of screw threads to the complex world of computer engineering. The proliferation of global trade has been facilitated by the ISO. Today, the ISO touches virtually every aspect of our lives.

Throughout this text, we mention official standards designations where appropriate. Definitive information concerning many of these standards can be found in excruciating detail on the website of the organization responsible for establishing the standard cited. As an added bonus, many standards contain "normative" and informative references, which provide background information in areas related to the standard.

1.5 HISTORICAL DEVELOPMENT

During their 60-year life span, computers have become the perfect example of modern convenience. Living memory is strained to recall the days of steno pools, carbon paper, and mimeograph machines. It sometimes seems that these magical computing machines were developed instantaneously in the form that we now know them. But the developmental path of computers is paved with accidental discovery, commercial coercion, and whimsical fancy. And occasionally computers have even improved through the application of solid engineering practices! Despite all the twists, turns, and technological dead ends, computers have evolved at a pace that defies comprehension. We can fully appreciate where we are today only when we have seen where we've come from.

In the sections that follow, we divide the evolution of computers into generations, each generation being defined by the technology used to build the machine. We have provided approximate dates for each generation for reference purposes only. You will find little agreement among experts as to the exact starting and ending times of each technological epoch.

Every invention reflects the time in which it was made, so one might wonder whether it would have been called a computer if it had been invented in the late 1990s. How much computation do we actually see pouring from the mysterious boxes perched on or beside our desks? Until recently, computers served us only by performing mind-bending mathematical manipulations. No longer limited to white-jacketed scientists, today's computers help us to write documents, keep in touch with loved ones across the globe, and do our shopping chores. Modern business computers spend only a minuscule part of their time performing accounting calculations. Their main purpose is to provide users with a bounty of strategic information for competitive advantage. Has the word *computer* now become a misnomer? An anachronism? What, then, should we call them, if not computers?

We cannot present the complete history of computing in a few pages. Entire texts have been written on this subject and even they leave their readers wanting more detail. If we have piqued your interest, we refer you to some of the books cited in the list of references at the end of this chapter.

1.5.1   Generation Zero: Mechanical Calculating Machines (1642–1945)

Prior to the 1500s, a typical European businessperson used an abacus for calculations and recorded the result of his ciphering in Roman numerals. After the decimal numbering system finally replaced Roman numerals, a number of people invented devices to make decimal calculations even faster and more accurate. Wilhelm Schickard (1592–1635) has been credited with the invention of the first mechanical calculator, the Calculating Clock (exact date unknown). This device was able to add and subtract numbers containing as many as six digits. In 1642, Blaise Pascal (1623–1662) developed a mechanical calculator called the Pascaline to help his father with his tax work. The Pascaline could do addition with carry and subtraction. It was probably the first mechanical adding device actually used for a practical purpose. In fact, the Pascaline was so well conceived that its basic design was still being used at the beginning of the twentieth century, as evidenced by the Lightning Portable Adder in 1908 and the Addometer in 1920. Gottfried Wilhelm von Leibniz (1646–1716), a noted mathematician, invented a calculator known as the Stepped Reckoner that could add, subtract, multiply, and divide. None of these devices could be programmed or had memory. They required manual intervention throughout each step of their calculations.

Although machines like the Pascaline were used into the twentieth century, new calculator designs began to emerge in the nineteenth century. One of the most ambitious of these new designs was the Difference Engine by Charles Babbage (1791–1871). Some people refer to Babbage as "the father of computing." By all accounts, he was an eccentric genius who brought us, among other things, the skeleton key and the "cow catcher," a device intended to push cows and other movable obstructions out of the way of locomotives.

Babbage built his Difference Engine in 1822. The Difference Engine got its name because it used a calculating technique called the **method of differences**. The machine was designed to mechanize the solution of polynomial functions and was actually a calculator, not a computer. Babbage also designed a general-purpose machine in 1833 called the Analytical Engine. Although Babbage died before he could build it, the Analytical Engine was designed to be more versatile than his earlier Difference Engine. The Analytical Engine would have been capable of performing any mathematical operation. The Analytical Engine included many of the components associated with modern computers: an arithmetic processing unit to perform calculations (Babbage referred to this as the **mill**), a memory (the **store**), and input and output devices. Babbage also included a conditional branching operation where the next instruction to be performed was determined by the result of the previous operation. Ada, Countess of Lovelace and daughter of poet Lord Byron, suggested that Babbage write a plan for how the machine would calculate numbers. This is regarded as the first computer program, and Ada is considered to be the first computer programmer. It is also rumored that she suggested the use of the binary number system rather than the decimal number system to store data.

A perennial problem facing machine designers has been how to get data into the machine. Babbage designed the Analytical Engine to use a type of punched card for input and programming. Using cards to control the behavior of a machine did not originate with Babbage, but with one of his friends, Joseph-Marie Jacquard (1752–1834). In 1801, Jacquard invented a programmable weaving loom that could produce intricate patterns in cloth. Jacquard gave Babbage a tapestry that had been woven on this loom using more than 10,000 punched cards. To Babbage, it seemed only natural that if a loom could be controlled by cards, then his Analytical Engine could be as well. Ada expressed her delight with this idea, writing, "[T]he Analytical Engine weaves algebraical patterns just as the Jacquard loom weaves flowers and leaves."

The punched card proved to be the most enduring means of providing input to a computer system. Keyed data input had to wait until fundamental changes were made in how calculating machines were constructed. In the latter half of the nineteenth century, most machines used wheeled mechanisms, which were difficult to integrate with early keyboards because they were levered devices. But levered devices could easily punch cards and wheeled devices could easily read them. So a number of devices were invented to encode and then "tabulate" card-punched data. The most important of the late-nineteenth-century tabulating machines was the one invented by Herman Hollerith (1860–1929). Hollerith's machine was used for encoding and compiling 1890 census data. This census was completed in record time, thus boosting Hollerith's finances and the reputation of his invention. Hollerith later founded the company that would become IBM. His 80-column punched card, the **Hollerith card**, was a staple of automated data processing for more than 50 years.

A Pre-Modern "Computer" Hoax

The latter half of the sixteenth century saw the beginnings of the first Industrial Revolution. The spinning jenny allowed one textile worker to do the work of twenty, and steam engines had power equivalent to hundreds of horses. Thus began our enduring fascination with all things mechanical. With the right skills applied to the problems at hand, there seemed no limits to what humankind could do with its machines!

Elaborate clocks began appearing at the beginning of the 1700s. Complex and ornate models graced cathedrals and town halls. These clockworks eventually morphed into mechanical robots called **automata**. Typical models played musical instruments such as flutes and keyboard instruments. In the mid-1700s, the most sublime of these devices entertained royal families across Europe. Some relied on trickery to entertain their audiences. It soon became something of a sport to unravel the chicanery. Empress Marie-Therese of the Austria-Hungarian Empire relied on a wealthy courtier and tinkerer, Wolfgang von Kempelen, to debunk the spectacles on her behalf. One day, following a particularly impressive display, Marie-Therese challenged von Kempelen to build an automaton to surpass all that had ever been brought to her court.

von Kempelen took the challenge, and after several months' work, he delivered a turban-wearing, pipe-smoking, chess-playing automaton. For all appearances, "The Turk" was a formidable opponent for even the best players of the day. As an added touch, the machine contained a set of baffles enabling it to rasp "Échec!" as needed. So impressive was this machine that for 84 years it drew crowds across Europe and the United States.

Of course, as with all similar automata, von Kempelen's Turk relied on trickery to perform its prodigious feat. Despite some astute debunkers correctly deducing how it was done, the secret of the Turk was never divulged: A human chess player was cleverly concealed inside its cabinet. The Turk thus pulled off one of the first and most impressive "computer" hoaxes in the history of technology. It would take another 200 years before a real machine could match the Turk—without the trickery.

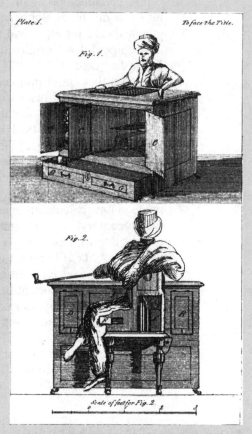

The mechanical Turk
Reprinted from Robert Willis, *An attempt to Analyse the Automaton Chess Player of Mr. de Kempelen.* JK Booth, London. 1824.

1.5.2   The First Generation: Vacuum Tube Computers (1945–1953)

Although Babbage is often called the "father of computing," his machines were mechanical, not electrical or electronic. In the 1930s, Konrad Zuse (1910–1995) picked up where Babbage left off, adding electrical technology and other improvements to Babbage's design. Zuse's computer, the Z1, used electromechanical relays instead of Babbage's hand-cranked gears. The Z1 was programmable and had a memory, an arithmetic unit, and a control unit. Because money and resources were scarce in wartime Germany, Zuse used discarded movie film instead of punched cards for input. Although his machine was designed to use vacuum tubes, Zuse, who was building his machine on his own, could not afford the tubes. Thus, the Z1 correctly belongs in the first generation, although it had no tubes.

Zuse built the Z1 in his parents' Berlin living room while Germany was at war with most of Europe. Fortunately, he couldn't convince the Nazis to buy his machine. They did not realize the tactical advantage such a device would give them. Allied bombs destroyed all three of Zuse's first systems, the Z1, Z2, and Z3. Zuse's impressive machines could not be refined until after the war and ended up being another "evolutionary dead end" in the history of computers.

Digital computers, as we know them today, are the outcome of work done by a number of people in the 1930s and 1940s. Pascal's basic mechanical calculator was designed and modified simultaneously by many people; the same can be said of the modern electronic computer. Notwithstanding the continual arguments about who was first with what, three people clearly stand out as the inventors of modern computers: John Atanasoff, John Mauchly, and J. Presper Eckert.

John Atanasoff (1904–1995) has been credited with the construction of the first completely electronic computer. The Atanasoff Berry Computer (ABC) was a binary machine built from vacuum tubes. Because this system was built specifically to solve systems of linear equations, we cannot call it a general-purpose computer. There were, however, some features that the ABC had in common with the general-purpose ENIAC (Electronic Numerical Integrator and Computer), which was invented a few years later. These common features caused considerable controversy as to who should be given the credit (and patent rights) for the invention of the electronic digital computer. (The interested reader can find more details on a rather lengthy lawsuit involving Atanasoff and the ABC in Mollenhoff [1988].)

John Mauchly (1907–1980) and J. Presper Eckert (1929–1995) were the two principal inventors of the ENIAC, introduced to the public in 1946. The ENIAC is recognized as the first all-electronic, general-purpose digital computer. This machine used 17,468 vacuum tubes, occupied 1800 square feet of floor space, weighed 30 tons, and consumed 174 kilowatts of power. The ENIAC had a memory capacity of about 1000 information bits (about 20 10-digit decimal numbers) and used punched cards to store data.

John Mauchly's vision for an electronic calculating machine was born from his lifelong interest in predicting the weather mathematically. While a professor of physics at Ursinus College near Philadelphia, Mauchly engaged dozens of adding machines and student operators to crunch mounds of data that he believed would reveal mathematical relationships behind weather patterns. He felt that if he could have only a little more computational power, he could reach the goal that seemed just beyond his grasp. Pursuant to the Allied war effort, and with ulterior motives to learn about electronic computation, Mauchly volunteered for a crash course in electrical engineering at the University of Pennsylvania's Moore School of Engineering. Upon completion of this program, Mauchly accepted a teaching position at the Moore School, where he taught a brilliant young student, J. Presper Eckert. Mauchly and Eckert found a mutual interest in building an electronic calculating device. In order to secure the funding they needed to build their machine, they wrote a formal proposal for review by the school. They portrayed their machine as conservatively as they could, billing it as an "automatic calculator." Although they probably knew that computers would be able to function most efficiently using the binary numbering system, Mauchly and Eckert

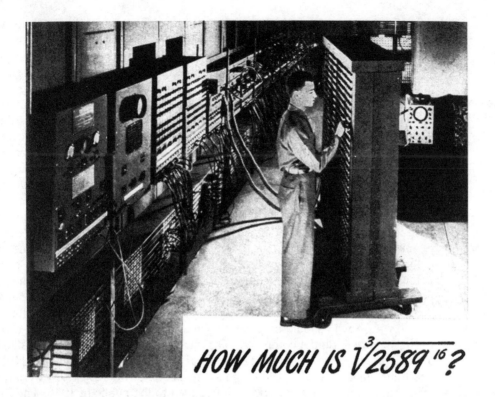

HOW MUCH IS $\sqrt[3]{2589}\,^{16}$?

The Army's ENIAC can give you the answer in a fraction of a second!

Think that's a stumper? You should see *some* of the ENIAC's problems! Brain twisters that if put to paper would run off this page and feet beyond . . . addition, subtraction, multiplication, division — square root, cube root, any root. Solved by an incredibly complex system of circuits operating 18,000 electronic tubes and tipping the scales at 30 tons!

The ENIAC is symbolic of many amazing Army devices with a brilliant future for you! The new Regular Army needs men with aptitude for scientific work, and as one of the first trained in the post-war era, you stand to get in on the ground floor of important jobs which have never before existed. You'll find that an Army career pays off.

The most attractive fields are filling quickly. Get into the swim while the getting's good! 1½, 2 and 3 year enlistments are open in the Regular Army to ambitious young men 18 to 34 (17 with parents' consent) who are otherwise qualified. If you enlist for 3 years, you may choose your own branch of the service, of those still open. Get full details at your nearest Army Recruiting Station.

YOUR REGULAR ARMY SERVES THE NATION AND MANKIND IN WAR AND PEACE

A GOOD JOB FOR YOU
U. S. Army
CHOOSE THIS
FINE PROFESSION NOW!

U.S. Army, 1946.

designed their system to use base 10 numbers, in keeping with the appearance of building a huge electronic adding machine. The university rejected Mauchly and Eckert's proposal. Fortunately, the U.S. Army was more interested.

During World War II, the army had an insatiable need for calculating the trajectories of its new ballistic armaments. Thousands of human "computers" were engaged around the clock cranking through the arithmetic required for these firing tables. Realizing that an electronic device could shorten ballistic table calculation from days to minutes, the army funded the ENIAC. And the ENIAC did indeed shorten the time to calculate a table from 20 hours to 30 seconds. Unfortunately, the machine wasn't ready before the end of the war. But the ENIAC had shown that vacuum tube computers were fast and feasible. During the next decade, vacuum tube systems continued to improve and were commercially successful.

What Is a Vacuum Tube?

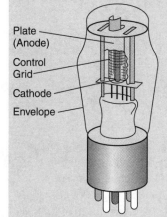

Plate
(Anode)

Control
Grid

Cathode

Envelope

The wired world that we know today was born from the invention of a single electronic device called a **vacuum tube** by Americans and—more accurately—a **valve** by the British. Vacuum tubes should be called valves because they control the flow of electrons in electrical systems in much the same way as valves control the flow of water in a plumbing system. In fact, some mid-twentieth-century breeds of these electron tubes contain no vacuum at all, but are filled with conductive gases, such as mercury vapor, which can provide desirable electrical behavior.

The electrical phenomenon that makes tubes work was discovered by Thomas A. Edison in 1883 while he was trying to find ways to keep the filaments of his light bulbs from burning away (or oxidizing) a few minutes after electrical current was applied. Edison reasoned correctly that one way to prevent filament oxidation would be to place the filament in a vacuum. Edison didn't immediately understand that air not only supports combustion, but also is a good insulator. When he energized the electrodes holding a new tungsten filament, the filament soon became hot and burned out as the others had before it. This time, however, Edison noticed that electricity continued to flow from the warmed negative terminal to the cool positive terminal within the light bulb. In 1911, Owen Willans Richardson analyzed this behavior. He concluded that when a negatively charged filament was heated, electrons "boiled off" as water molecules can be boiled to create steam. He aptly named this phenomenon **thermionic emission**.

Thermionic emission, as Edison had documented it, was thought by many to be only an electrical curiosity. But in 1905, a British former assistant to Edison, John A. Fleming, saw Edison's discovery as much more than a novelty. He knew that thermionic emission supported the flow of electrons in only one direction: from the negatively charged **cathode** to the positively charged **anode**, also called a **plate**. He realized that this behavior could *rectify* alternating current. That is, it could change alternating current into the direct current that was essential for the proper operation of telegraph equipment. Fleming used his ideas to invent an electronic valve later called a **diode tube** or **rectifier**.

The diode was well suited for changing alternating current into direct current, but the greatest power of the electron tube was yet to be discovered. In 1907, an American named Lee DeForest added a third element, called a **control grid**. The control grid, when carrying a negative charge, can reduce or prevent electron flow from the cathode to the anode of a diode.

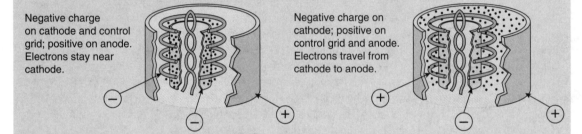

Negative charge on cathode and control grid; positive on anode. Electrons stay near cathode.

Negative charge on cathode; positive on control grid and anode. Electrons travel from cathode to anode.

When DeForest patented his device, he called it an **audion tube**. It was later known as a **triode**. The schematic symbol for the triode is shown at the left.

A triode can act as either a switch or an amplifier. Small changes in the charge of the control grid can cause much larger changes in the flow of electrons between the cathode and the anode. Therefore, a weak signal applied to the grid results in a much stronger signal at the plate output. A sufficiently large negative charge applied to the grid stops all electrons from leaving the cathode.

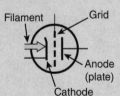

Filament   Grid

Anode (plate)

Cathode

Additional control grids were eventually added to the triode to allow more exact control of the electron flow. Tubes with two grids (four elements) are called **tetrodes**; tubes with three grids are called **pentodes**. Triodes and pentodes were the tubes most commonly used in communications and computer applications. Often, two or three triodes or pentodes would be combined within one envelope so they could share a single heater, thereby reducing the power consumption of a particular device. These latter-day devices were called "miniature" tubes because many were about 2 inches (5cm) high and 0.5 inch (1.5cm) in diameter. Equivalent full-sized diodes, triodes, and pentodes were a little smaller than a household light bulb.

Vacuum tubes were not well suited for building computers. Even the simplest vacuum tube computer system required thousands of tubes. Enormous amounts

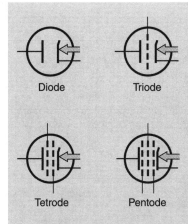

Diode Triode

Tetrode Pentode

of electrical power were required to heat the cathodes of these devices. To prevent a meltdown, this heat had to be removed from the system as quickly as possible. Power consumption and heat dissipation could be reduced by running the cathode heaters at lower voltages, but this reduced the already slow switching speed of the tube. Despite their limitations and power consumption, vacuum tube computer systems, both analog and digital, served their purpose for many years and are the architectural foundation for all modern computer systems.

Although decades have passed since the last vacuum tube computer was manufactured, vacuum tubes are still used in audio amplifiers. These "high-end" amplifiers are favored by musicians who believe that tubes provide a resonant and pleasing sound unattainable by solid-state devices.

1.5.3 The Second Generation: Transistorized Computers (1954–1965)

The vacuum tube technology of the first generation was not very dependable. In fact, some ENIAC detractors believed that the system would never run because the tubes would burn out faster than they could be replaced. Although system reliability wasn't as bad as the doomsayers predicted, vacuum tube systems often experienced more downtime than uptime.

In 1948, three researchers with Bell Laboratories—John Bardeen, Walter Brattain, and William Shockley—invented the transistor. This new technology not only revolutionized devices such as televisions and radios, but also pushed the computer industry into a new generation. Because transistors consume less power than vacuum tubes, are smaller, and work more reliably, the circuitry in computers consequently became smaller and more reliable. Despite using transistors, computers of this generation were still bulky and quite costly. Typically only universities, governments, and large businesses could justify the expense. Nevertheless, a plethora of computer makers emerged in this generation; IBM, Digital Equipment Corporation (DEC), and Univac (now Unisys) dominated the industry. IBM marketed the 7094 for scientific applications and the 1401 for business applications. DEC was busy manufacturing the PDP-1. A company founded (but soon sold) by Mauchly and Eckert built the Univac systems. The most successful Unisys systems of this generation belonged to its 1100 series. Another company, Control Data Corporation (CDC), under the supervision of Seymour Cray, built the CDC 6600, the world's first supercomputer. The $10 million CDC 6600 could perform 10 million instructions per second, used 60-bit words, and had an astounding 128 kilowords of main memory.

What Is a Transistor?

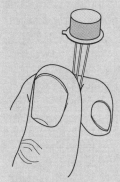

The transistor, short for **transfer resistor**, is the solid-state version of the triode. There is no such thing as a solid-state version of the tetrode or pentode. Electrons are better behaved in a solid medium than in the open void of a vacuum tube, so there is no need for the extra controlling grids. Either germanium or silicon can be the basic "solid" used in these solid-state devices. In their pure form, neither of these elements is a good conductor of electricity. But when they are combined with trace amounts of elements that are their neighbors in the Periodic Chart of the Elements, they conduct electricity in an effective and easily controlled manner.

Boron, aluminum, and gallium can be found to the left of silicon and germanium on the Periodic Chart. Because they lie to the left of silicon and germanium, they have one less electron in their outer electron shell, or **valence**. So if you add a small amount of aluminum to silicon, the silicon ends up with a slight imbalance in its outer electron shell, and therefore attracts electrons from any pole that has a negative potential (an excess of electrons). When modified (or **doped**) in this way, silicon or germanium becomes a **P-type** material.

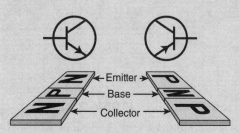

Emitter
Base
Collector

Similarly, if we add a little boron, arsenic, or gallium to silicon, we'll have extra electrons in valences of the silicon crystals. This gives us an **N-type** material. A small amount of current will flow through the N-type material if we provide the loosely bound electrons in the N-type material with a place to go. In other words, if we apply a positive potential to N-type material, electrons will flow from the negative pole to the positive pole. If the poles are reversed, that is, if we apply a negative potential to the N-type material and a positive potential to the P-type material, no current will flow. This means we can make a solid-state diode from a simple junction of N- and P-type materials.

The solid-state triode, the transistor, consists of three layers of semiconductor material. Either a slice of P-type material is sandwiched between two N-type materials, or a slice of N-type material is sandwiched between two P-type materials. The former is called an NPN transistor, the latter a PNP transistor. The inner layer of the transistor is called the base; the other two layers are called the collector and the emitter.

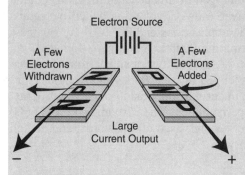

Electron Source
A Few Electrons Withdrawn
A Few Electrons Added
Large Current Output
−
+

The figure at the left shows how current flows through NPN and PNP transistors. The base in a transistor works just like the control grid in a triode tube: Small changes in the current at the base of a transistor result in a large electron flow from the emitter to the collector.

A **discrete-component** transistor is shown in "TO-50" packaging in the figure at the top of this sidebar. There are only three wires (leads) that connect the base, emitter, and collector of the transistor to the rest of the circuit. Transistors are not only smaller than vacuum tubes, but they also run cooler and are much more reliable. Vacuum tube filaments, like light bulb filaments, run hot and eventually burn out. Computers using transistorized components will naturally be smaller and run cooler than their vacuum tube predecessors. The ultimate miniaturization, however, is not realized by replacing individual triodes with discrete transistors, but in shrinking entire circuits onto one piece of silicon.

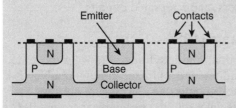

Integrated circuits, or **chips**, contain hundreds to billions of microscopic transistors. Several different techniques are used to manufacture integrated circuits. One of the simplest methods involves creating a circuit using computer-aided design software that can print large maps of each of the several silicon layers forming the chip. Each map is used like a photographic negative where light-induced changes in a photoresistive substance on the chip's surface produce the delicate patterns of the circuit when the silicon chip is immersed in a chemical that washes away the exposed areas of the silicon. This technique is called **photomicrolithography**. After the etching is completed, a layer of N-type or P-type material is deposited on the bumpy surface of the chip. This layer is then treated with a photoresistive substance, exposed to light, and etched as was the layer before it. This process continues until all the layers have been etched. The resulting peaks and valleys of P- and N-type material form microscopic electronic components, including transistors, that behave just like larger versions fashioned from discrete components, except that they run a lot faster and consume a small fraction of the power.

1.5.4 The Third Generation: Integrated Circuit Computers (1965–1980)

The real explosion in computer use came with the integrated circuit generation. Jack Kilby invented the integrated circuit (IC), or **microchip**, made of germanium. Six months later, Robert Noyce (who had also been working on integrated circuit design) created a similar device using silicon instead of germanium. This is the silicon chip upon which the computer industry was built. Early ICs allowed dozens of transistors to exist on a single silicon chip that was smaller than a single "discrete component" transistor. Computers became faster, smaller, and cheaper, bringing huge gains in processing power. The IBM System/360 family of computers was among the first commercially available systems to be built entirely of solid-state components. The 360 product line was also IBM's first offering in which all the machines in the family were compatible, meaning they all used the same assembly language. Users of smaller machines could upgrade to larger systems without rewriting all their software. This was a revolutionary new concept at the time.

The IC generation also saw the introduction of time-sharing and multiprogramming (the ability for more than one person to use the computer at a time). Multiprogramming, in turn, necessitated the introduction of new operating systems for these computers. Time-sharing minicomputers such as DEC's PDP-8 and PDP-11 made computing affordable to smaller businesses and more universities.

IC technology also allowed for the development of more powerful supercomputers. Seymour Cray took what he had learned while building the CDC 6600 and started his own company, the Cray Research Corporation. This company produced a number of supercomputers, starting with the $8.8 million Cray-1, in 1976. The Cray-1, in stark contrast to the CDC 6600, could execute more than 160 million instructions per second and could support 8MB of memory. See Figure 1.2 for a size comparison of vacuum tubes, transistors, and integrated circuits.

1.5.5 The Fourth Generation: VLSI Computers (1980–????)

In the third generation of electronic evolution, multiple transistors were integrated onto one chip. As manufacturing techniques and chip technologies advanced, increasing numbers of transistors were packed onto one chip. There are now various levels of integration: SSI (small-scale integration), in which there are 10 to 100 components per chip; MSI (medium-scale integration), in which there are 100 to 1000 components per chip; LSI (large-scale integration), in which there are

FIGURE 1.2 Comparison of Computer Components
Clockwise, starting from the top:
1) Vacuum tube
2) Transistor
3) Chip containing 3200 2-input NAND gates
4) Integrated circuit package (the small silver square in the lower left-hand corner is an integrated circuit)
Courtesy of Linda Null.

1000 to 10,000 components per chip; and finally, VLSI (very-large-scale integration), in which there are more than 10,000 components per chip. This last level, VLSI, marks the beginning of the fourth generation of computers. The complexity of integraged circuits continues to grow, with more transistors being added all the time. The term *ULSI* (ultra-large-scale integration) has been suggested for integrated circuits containing more than 1 million transistors. In 2005, billions of transistors were put on a single chip. Other useful terminology includes: (1) WSI (wafer-scale integration, building superchip ICs from an entire silicon wafer; (2) 3D-IC (three-dimensional integrated circuit); and (3) SOC (system-on-a-chip), an IC that includes all the necessary components for the entire computer.

To give some perspective to these numbers, consider the ENIAC-on-a-chip project. In 1997, to commemorate the fiftieth anniversary of its first public demonstration, a group of students at the University of Pennsylvania constructed a single-chip equivalent of the ENIAC. The 1800-square-foot, 30-ton beast that devoured 174 kilowatts of power the minute it was turned on had been reproduced on a chip the size of a thumbnail. This chip contained approximately 174,569 transistors—an order of magnitude fewer than the number of components typically placed on the same amount of silicon in the late 1990s.

VLSI allowed Intel, in 1971, to create the world's first microprocessor, the 4004, which was a fully functional, 4-bit system that ran at 108KHz. Intel also introduced the random access memory (RAM) chip, accommodating four kilobits of memory on a single chip. This allowed computers of the fourth generation to become smaller and faster than their solid-state predecessors.

VLSI technology, and its incredible shrinking circuits, spawned the development of microcomputers. These systems were small enough and inexpensive enough to make computers available and affordable to the general public. The premiere microcomputer was the Altair 8800, released in 1975 by the Micro Instrumentation and Telemetry (MITS) corporation. The Altair 8800 was soon followed by the Apple I and Apple II, and Commodore's PET and Vic 20. Finally, in 1981, IBM introduced its PC (Personal Computer).

The Personal Computer was IBM's third attempt at producing an "entry-level" computer system. Its Datamaster and its 5100 Series desktop computers flopped miserably in the marketplace. Despite these early failures, IBM's John Opel convinced his management to try again. He suggested forming a fairly autonomous "independent business unit" in Boca Raton, Florida, far from IBM's headquarters in Armonk, New York. Opel picked Don Estridge, an energetic and capable engineer, to champion the development of the new system, code-named the Acorn. In light of IBM's past failures in the small-systems area, corporate management held tight rein on the Acorn's timeline and finances. Opel could get his project off the ground only after promising to deliver it within a year, a seemingly impossible feat.

Estridge knew that the only way he could deliver the PC within the wildly optimistic 12-month schedule would be to break with IBM convention and use as many "off-the-shelf" parts as possible. Thus, from the outset, the IBM PC was conceived with an "open" architecture. Although some people at IBM may have later regretted the decision to keep the architecture of the PC as nonproprietary as possible, it was this very openness that allowed IBM to set the standard for the industry. While IBM's competitors were busy suing companies for copying their system designs, PC clones proliferated. Before long, the price of "IBM-compatible" microcomputers came within reach for just about every small business. Also, thanks to the clone makers, large numbers of these systems soon began finding true "personal use" in people's homes.

IBM eventually lost its microcomputer market dominance, but the genie was out of the bottle. For better or worse, the IBM architecture continues to be the de facto standard for microcomputing, with each year heralding bigger and faster systems. Today, the average desktop computer has many times the computational power of the mainframes of the 1960s.

Since the 1960s, mainframe computers have seen stunning improvements in price–performance ratios owing to VLSI technology. Although the IBM System/360 was an entirely solid-state system, it was still a water-cooled, power-gobbling behemoth. It could perform only about 50,000 instructions per second and supported only 16MB of memory (while usually having *kilobytes* of physical memory installed). These systems were so costly that only the largest businesses and universities could afford to own or lease one. Today's mainframes—now called "enterprise servers"—are still priced in the millions of dollars, but their processing capabilities have grown several thousand times over, passing the billion-instructions-per-second mark in the late 1990s. These systems, often used as Web servers, routinely support hundreds of thousands of transactions *per minute!*

The processing power brought by VLSI to supercomputers defies comprehension. The first supercomputer, the CDC 6600, could perform 10 million instructions per second, and had 128KB of main memory. By contrast, supercomputers of today contain thousands of processors, can address terabytes of memory, and will soon be able to perform a *quadrillion* instructions per second.

What technology will mark the beginning of the fifth generation? Some say the fifth generation will mark the acceptance of parallel processing and the use of networks and single-user workstations. Many people believe we have already crossed into this generation. Some believe it will be quantum computing. Some people characterize the fifth generation as being the generation of neural network, DNA, or optical computing systems. It's possible that we won't be able to define the fifth generation until we have advanced into the sixth or seventh generations, and whatever those eras will bring.

The Integrated Circuit and Its Production

Integrated circuits are found all around us, from computers to cars to refrigerators to cell phones. The most advanced circuits contain hundreds of millions (and even billions) of components in an area about the size of your thumbnail. The transistors in these advanced circuits can be as small as 45nm, or 0.000045 millimeters, in size. Thousands of these transistors would fit in a circle the diameter of a human hair.

How are these circuits made? They are manufactured in semiconductor fabrication facilities. Because the components are so small, all precautions must be taken to ensure a sterile, particle-free environment, so manufacturing is done in a "clean room." There can be no dust, no skin cells, no smoke—not even bacteria. Workers must wear clean room suits, often called "bunny suits," to ensure that even the tiniest particle does not escape into the air.

The process begins with the chip design, which eventually results in a mask, the template or blueprint that contains the circuit patterns. A silicon wafer is then covered by an insulating layer of oxide, followed by a layer of photosensitive film called photo-resist. This photo-resist has regions that break down under UV light and other regions that do not. A UV light is then shone through the mask (a process called photolithography). Bare oxide is left on portions where the photo-resist breaks down under the UV light. Chemical "etching" is then used to dissolve the revealed oxide layer and also to remove the remaining photo-resist not affected by the UV light. The "doping" process embeds certain impurities into the silicon that alters the electrical properties of the unprotected areas, basically creating the transistors. The chip is then covered with another layer of both the insulating oxide material and the photo-resist, and the entire process is repeated hundreds of times, each iteration creating a new layer of the chip. Different masks are used with a similar process to create the wires that connect the components on the chip. The circuit is finally encased in a protective plastic cover, tested, and shipped out.

As components become smaller and smaller, the equipment used to make them must be of continually higher quality. This has resulted in a dramatic increase in the cost of manufacturing ICs over the years. In the early 1980s, the cost to build a semiconductor factory was roughly $10 million. By the late 1980s, that cost had risen to approximately $200 million, and by the late 1990s, an IC fabrication factory cost more or less around $1 billion. In 2005, Intel spent approximately $2 billion for a single fabrication facility and, in 2007, invested roughly $7 billion to retool three plants in order to allow them to produce a smaller processor. In 2009, AMD begin building a $4.2 billion chip manufacturing facility in upstate New York.

The manufacturing facility is not the only high-dollar item when it comes to making ICs. The cost to design a chip and create the mask can run anywhere from $1 million to $3 million—more for smaller chips and less for larger ones. Considering the costs of both the chip design and the fabrication facility, it truly is amazing that we can walk into our local computer store and buy a new Intel i3 microprocessor chip for around $100.

1.5.6 Moore's Law

So where does it end? How small can we make transistors? How densely can we pack chips? No one can say for sure. Every year, scientists continue to thwart prognosticators' attempts to define the limits of integration. In fact, more than one skeptic raised an eyebrow when, in 1965, Intel founder Gordon Moore stated, "The density of transistors in an integrated circuit will double every year." The current version of this prediction is usually conveyed as "the density of silicon chips doubles every 18 months." This assertion has become known as **Moore's Law**. Moore intended this postulate to hold for only 10 years. However, advances in chip manufacturing processes have allowed this assertion to hold for almost 40 years (and many believe it will continue to hold well into the 2010s).

Yet, using current technology, Moore's Law cannot hold forever. There are physical and financial limitations that must ultimately come into play. At the current rate of miniaturization, it would take about 500 years to put the entire solar system on a chip! Clearly, the limit lies somewhere between here and there. Cost may be the ultimate constraint. **Rock's Law**, proposed by early Intel capitalist Arthur Rock, is a corollary to Moore's Law: "The cost of capital equipment to build semiconductors will double every four years." Rock's Law arises from the observations of a financier who saw the price tag of new chip facilities escalate from about $12,000 in 1968 to $12 million in the mid-1990s. In 2005, the cost of building a new chip plant was nearing $3 billion. At this rate, by the year 2035, not only will the size of a memory element be smaller than an atom, but it would also require the entire wealth of the world to build a single chip! So even if we continue to make chips smaller and faster, the ultimate question may be whether we can afford to build them.

Certainly, if Moore's Law is to hold, Rock's Law must fall. It is evident that for these two things to happen, computers must shift to a radically different technology. Research into new computing paradigms has been proceeding in earnest during the last half decade. Laboratory prototypes fashioned around organic computing, superconducting, molecular physics, and quantum computing have been demonstrated. Quantum computers, which leverage the vagaries of quantum mechanics to solve computational problems, are particularly exciting. Not only would quantum systems compute exponentially faster than any previously used method, but they would also revolutionize the way in which we define computational problems. Problems that today are considered ludicrously infeasible could be well within the grasp of the next generation's schoolchildren. These schoolchildren may, in fact, chuckle at our "primitive" systems in the same way that we are tempted to chuckle at the ENIAC.

1.6   THE COMPUTER LEVEL HIERARCHY

If a machine is to be capable of solving a wide range of problems, it must be able to execute programs written in different languages, from Fortran and C to Lisp and Prolog. As we shall see in Chapter 3, the only physical components we have to work with are wires and gates. A formidable open space—a **semantic gap**—exists between these physical components and a high-level language such as C++. For a system to be practical, the semantic gap must be invisible to most of the users of the system.

Programming experience teaches us that when a problem is large, we should break it down and use a "divide and conquer" approach. In programming, we divide a problem into modules and then design each module separately. Each module performs a specific task, and modules need only know how to interface with other modules to make use of them.

Computer system organization can be approached in a similar manner. Through the principle of abstraction, we can imagine the machine to be built from a hierarchy of levels, in which each level has a specific function and exists as a distinct hypothetical machine. We call the hypothetical computer at each level a **virtual machine**. Each level's virtual machine executes its own particular set of instructions, calling upon machines at lower levels to carry out the tasks when necessary. By studying computer organization, you will see the rationale behind the hierarchy's partitioning, as well as how these layers are implemented and interface with each other. Figure 1.3 shows the commonly accepted layers representing the abstract virtual machines.

Level 6, the User Level, is composed of applications and is the level with which everyone is most familiar. At this level, we run programs such as word processors, graphics packages, or games. The lower levels are nearly invisible from the User Level.

Level 5, the High-Level Language Level, consists of languages such as C, C++, Fortran, Lisp, Pascal, and Prolog. These languages must be translated

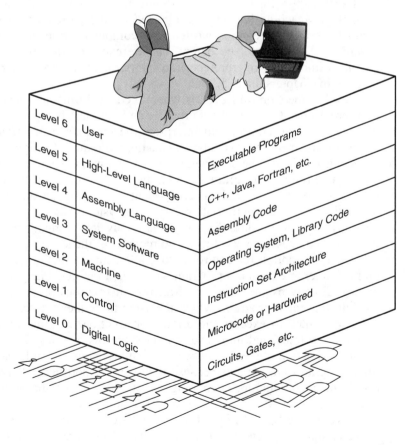

FIGURE 1.3   The Abstract Levels of Modern Computing Systems

(using either a compiler or an interpreter) to a language the machine can understand. Compiled languages are translated into assembly language and then assembled into machine code. (They are translated to the next lower level.) The user at this level sees very little of the lower levels. Even though a programmer must know about data types and the instructions available for those types, he or she need not know about how those types are actually implemented.

Level 4, the Assembly Language Level, encompasses some type of assembly language. As previously mentioned, compiled higher-level languages are first translated to assembly, which is then directly translated to machine language. This is a one-to-one translation, meaning that one assembly language instruction is translated to exactly one machine language instruction. By having separate levels, we reduce the semantic gap between a high-level language, such as C++, and the actual machine language (which consists of 0s and 1s).

Level 3, the System Software Level, deals with operating system instructions. This level is responsible for multiprogramming, protecting memory, synchronizing processes, and various other important functions. Often, instructions translated from assembly language to machine language are passed through this level unmodified.

Level 2, the Instruction Set Architecture (ISA), or Machine Level, consists of the machine language recognized by the particular architecture of the computer system. Programs written in a computer's true machine language on a hardwired computer (see below) can be executed directly by the electronic circuits without any interpreters, translators, or compilers. We will study ISAs in depth in Chapters 4 and 5.

Level 1, the Control Level, is where a **control unit** makes sure that instructions are decoded and executed properly and that data is moved where and when it should be. The control unit interprets the machine instructions passed to it, one at a time, from the level above, causing the required actions to take place.

Control units can be designed in one of two ways: They can be **hardwired** or they can be **microprogrammed**. In hardwired control units, control signals emanate from blocks of digital logic components. These signals direct all the data and instruction traffic to appropriate parts of the system. Hardwired control units are typically very fast because they are actually physical components. However, once implemented, they are very difficult to modify for the same reason.

The other option for control is to implement instructions using a microprogram. A microprogram is a program written in a low-level language that is implemented directly by the hardware. Machine instructions produced in Level 2 are fed into this microprogram, which then interprets the instructions by activating hardware suited to execute the original instruction. One machine-level instruction is often translated into several microcode instructions. This is not the one-to-one correlation that exists between assembly language and machine language. Microprograms are popular because they can be modified relatively easily. The disadvantage of microprogramming is, of course, that the additional layer of translation typically results in slower instruction execution.

Level 0, the Digital Logic Level, is where we find the physical components of the computer system: the gates and wires. These are the fundamental building blocks, the implementations of the mathematical logic, that are common to all computer systems. Chapter 3 presents the Digital Logic Level in detail.

1.7   CLOUD COMPUTING: COMPUTING AS A SERVICE

We must never forget that the ultimate aim of every computer system is to deliver functionality to its users. Computer users typically do not care about terabytes of storage and gigahertz of processor speed. In fact, many companies and government agencies have "gotten out of the technology business" entirely by outsourcing their data centers to third-party specialists. These outsourcing agreements tend to be highly complex and prescribe every aspect of the hardware configuration. Along with the detailed hardware specifications, **service-level agreements (SLAs)** provide penalties if certain parameters of system performance and availability are not met. Both contracting parties employ individuals whose main job is to monitor the contract, calculate bills, and determine SLA penalties when needed. Thus, with the additional administrative overhead, data center outsourcing is neither a cheap nor an easy solution for companies that want to avoid the problems of technology management.

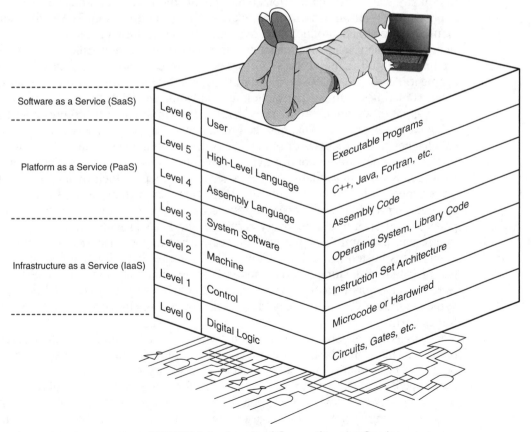

FIGURE 1.4   Levels of Computing as a Service

A somewhat easier approach may be found in the emerging field of Cloud computing. **Cloud computing** is the general term for any type of virtual computing platform provided over the Internet. A Cloud computing platform is defined in terms of the services that it provides rather than its physical configuration. Its name derives from the cloud icon that symbolizes the Internet on schematic diagrams. But the metaphor carries well into the actual Cloud infrastructure, because the computer is more abstract than real. The "computer" and "storage" appear to the user as a single entity in the Cloud but usually span several physical servers. The storage is usually located on an array of disks that are not directly connected to any particular server. System software is designed to give this configuration the illusion of being a single system; thus, we say that it presents a **virtual machine** to the user.

Cloud computing services can be defined and delivered in a number of ways based on levels of the computer hierarchy shown again in Figure 1.4. At the top of the hierarchy, where we have executable programs, a Cloud provider might offer an entire application over the Internet, with no components installed locally. This is called **Software as a Service**, or **SaaS**. The consumer of this service does not maintain the application or need to be at all concerned with the infrastructure in any way. SaaS applications tend to focus on narrow, non-business-critical applications. Well-known examples include Gmail, Dropbox, GoToMeeting, and Netflix. Specialized products are available for tax return preparation, payroll, fleet management, and case management, to name only a few. Salesforce.com is a pioneering, full-featured SaaS offering designed for customer relationship management. Fee-based SaaS is typically billed monthly according to the number of users, sometimes with per-transaction fees added on as well.

A great disadvantage of SaaS is that the consumer has little control over the behavior of the product. This may be problematic if a company has to make radical changes to its processes or policies in order to use a SaaS product. Companies that desire to have more control over their applications, or that need applications for which SaaS is unavailable, might instead opt to deploy their own applications on a Cloud-hosted environment called **Platform as a Service**, or **PaaS**. PaaS provides server hardware, operating systems, database services, security components, and backup and recovery services. The PaaS provider manages performance and availability of the environment, whereas the customer manages the applications hosted in the PaaS Cloud. The customer is typically billed monthly per megabytes of storage, processor utilization, and megabytes of data transferred. Well-known PaaS providers include Google App Engine and Microsoft Windows Azure Cloud Services [as well as Force.com (PaaS provided by Salesforce.com)].

PaaS is not a good fit in situations where rapid configuration changes are required. This would be the case if a company's main business is software development. The formality of change processes necessary to a well-run PaaS operation impedes rapid software deployment [by forcing a company to play by the service provider's rules]. Indeed, in any company where staff is capable of managing operating system and database software, the **Infrastructure as a Service (IaaS)** Cloud model might be the best option. IaaS, [the most basic of the models,] provides only server hardware, secure network access to the servers, and backup and recovery services. The customer is responsible for all system software including the operating system and databases. IaaS is typically billed by the number of virtual machines used, megabytes of storage, and megabytes of data transferred, but at a lower rate than PaaS. The biggest names in IaaS include Amazon EC2, Google Compute Engine, Microsoft Azure Services Platform, Rackspace, and HP Cloud.

Not only do PaaS and IaaS liberate the customer from the difficulties of data center management, they also provide **elasticity**: the ability to add and remove resources based on demand. A customer pays for only as much infrastructure as is needed. So if a business has a peak season, extra capacity needs to be allocated only for the duration of the peak period. This flexibility can save a company a great deal of money when it has large variations in computing demands.

Cloud storage is a limited type of IaaS. The general public can obtain small amounts of Cloud storage inexpensively through services such as Dropbox, Google Drive, and Amazon.com's Cloud Drive—to name only a few among a crowded field. Google, Amazon, HP, IBM, and Microsoft are among several vendors that provide Cloud storage for the enterprise. As with Cloud computing in general, enterprise-grade Cloud storage also requires careful management of performance and availability.

The question that all potential Cloud computing customers must ask themselves is whether it is less expensive to maintain their own data center or to buy Cloud services—including the allowances for peak periods. Moreover, as with traditional outsourcing, vendor-provided Cloud computing still involves considerable contract negotiation and management on the part of both parties. SLA management remains an important activity in the relationship between the service provider and the service consumer. Moreover, once an enterprise moves its assets to the Cloud, it might be difficult to transition back to a company-owned data center, should the need arise. Thus, any notion of moving assets to the Cloud must be carefully considered, and the risks clearly understood.

The Cloud also presents a number of challenges to computer scientists. First and foremost is the technical configuration of the data center. The infrastructure must provide for uninterrupted service, even during maintenance activities. It must permit expedient allocation of capacity to where it is needed without degrading or interrupting services. Performance of the infrastructure must be carefully monitored and interventions taken whenever performance falls below certain defined thresholds; otherwise, monetary SLA penalties may be incurred.

On the consumer side of the Cloud, software architects and programmers must be mindful of resource consumption, because the Cloud model charges fees in proportion to the resources consumed. These resources include communications bandwidth, processor cycles, and storage. Thus, to save money, application programs should be designed to reduce trips over the network, economize machine cycles, and minimize bytes of storage. Meticulous testing is crucial prior to deploying a program in the Cloud: An errant module that consumes resources, say, in an infinite loop, could result in a "surprising" Cloud bill at the end of the month.

With the cost and complexity of data centers continuing to rise—with no end in sight—Cloud computing is almost certain to become the platform of choice for medium- to small-sized businesses. But the Cloud is not worry-free. A company might end up trading its technical challenges for even more vexing supplier management challenges.

1.8   THE VON NEUMANN MODEL

In the earliest electronic computing machines, programming was synonymous with connecting wires to plugs. No layered architecture existed, so programming a computer was as much of a feat of electrical engineering as it was an exercise in algorithm design. Before their work on the ENIAC was complete, John W. Mauchly and J. Presper Eckert conceived of an easier way to change the behavior of their calculating machine. They reckoned that memory devices, in the form of mercury delay lines, could provide a way to store program instructions. This would forever end the tedium of rewiring the system each time it had a new problem to solve, or an old one to debug. Mauchly and Eckert documented their idea, proposing it as the foundation for their next computer, the EDVAC. Unfortunately, while they were involved in the top secret ENIAC project during World War II, Mauchly and Eckert could not immediately publish their insight.

No such proscriptions, however, applied to a number of people working at the periphery of the ENIAC project. One of these people was a famous Hungarian mathematician named John von Neumann (pronounced *von noy-man*). After reading Mauchly and Eckert's proposal for the EDVAC, von Neumann published and publicized the idea. So effective was he in the delivery of this concept that history has credited him with its invention. All stored-program computers have come to be known as **von Neumann systems** using the **von Neumann architecture**. Although we are compelled by tradition to say that stored-program computers use the von Neumann architecture, we shall not do so without paying proper tribute to its true inventors: John W. Mauchly and J. Presper Eckert.

Today's version of the stored-program machine architecture satisfies at least the following characteristics:

- Consists of three hardware systems: A **central processing unit (CPU)** with a control unit, an **arithmetic logic unit (ALU)**, **registers** (small storage areas), and a program counter; a **main memory system**, which holds programs that control the computer's operation; and an **I/O system**.
- Capacity to carry out sequential instruction processing.
- Contains a single path, either physically or logically, between the main memory system and the control unit of the CPU, forcing alternation of instruction and execution cycles. This single path is often referred to as the **von Neumann bottleneck**.

Figure 1.5 shows how these features work together in modern computer systems. Notice that the system shown in the figure passes all of its I/O through the arithmetic logic unit (actually, it passes through the accumulator, which is part of the ALU). This architecture runs programs in what is known as the **von Neumann execution cycle** (also called the **fetch-decode-execute cycle**), which describes how the machine works. One iteration of the cycle is as follows:

1. The control unit fetches the next program instruction from the memory, using the program counter to determine where the instruction is located.

2. The instruction is decoded into a language the ALU can understand.

3. Any data operands required to execute the instruction are fetched from memory and placed in registers in the CPU.

4. The ALU executes the instruction and places the results in registers or memory.

The ideas present in the von Neumann architecture have been extended so that programs and data stored in a slow-to-access storage medium, such as a hard disk, can be copied to a fast-access, volatile storage medium such as RAM prior to execution. This architecture has also been streamlined into what is currently called the **system bus model**, which is shown in Figure 1.6. The data bus moves data from main memory to the CPU registers (and vice versa). The address bus holds the

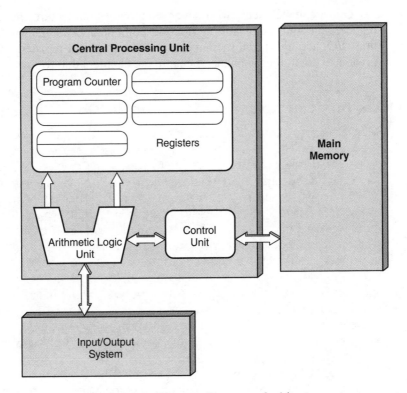

FIGURE 1.5 The von Neumann Architecture

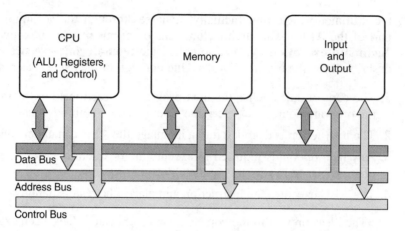

FIGURE 1.6 The Modified von Neumann Architecture, Adding a System Bus

address of the data that the data bus is currently accessing. The control bus carries the necessary control signals that specify how the information transfer is to take place.

Other enhancements to the von Neumann architecture include using index registers for addressing, adding floating-point data, using interrupts and asynchronous I/O, adding virtual memory, and adding general registers. You will learn a great deal about these enhancements in the chapters that follow.

Quantum Leap for Computers: How Small Can We Go?

VLSI technology has allowed us to put billions of transistors on a single chip, but there is a limit to how small we can go with current transistor technology. Researchers at the University of New South Wales' Centre for Quantum Computer Technology and the University of Wisconsin–Madison have taken "small" to an entirely new level. In May 2010, they announced the 7-atom transistor, a working transistor embedded in silicon that is only 7 atoms in size. Transistors 1 atom in size that allowed the flows of electrons were reported as early as 2002, but this transistor is different in that it provides all the functionality of a transistor as we know it today.

The 7-atom transistor was created by hand, using a scanning tunneling microscope. It's a long way from being mass produced, but the researchers hope to make it commercially available by 2015. The transistor's tiny size means smaller but more powerful computers. Experts estimate it may shrink microchips by a factor of 100, while enabling an exponential speedup in processing. This means our computers could become one hundred times smaller, but at the same time, also one hundred times faster.

In addition to replacing traditional transistors, this discovery may be fundamental in the efforts to build a quantum computer in silicon. Quantum computing is expected to be the next significant leap in computer technology. Small quantum computers now exist that perform calculations millions of times faster than conventional computers, but these computers are too small to be of much use. A large-scale, working quantum computer would enable us to perform calculations and solve problems that would take a conventional computer more than 13 billion years. That could change the way we view the world. For one thing, every encryption algorithm employed today would be useless against that kind of computing power. On the other hand, ultra-secure communications would be possible using new quantum technologies.

Quantum computers have significant potential. Current applications, including special effects for movies, cryptography, searching large data files, factoring large numbers, simulating various systems (such as nuclear explosions and weather patterns), military and intelligence gathering, and intensive, time-consuming computations (such as those found in astronomy, physics, and chemistry), would all see tremendous performance increases if quantum computing were used. New applications we have not yet discovered are likely to evolve as well.

In addition to its potential to change computing as we know it today, this new 7-atom transistor is significant for another reason. Recall Moore's Law; this law is not so much a law of nature, but rather an expectation of innovation and a significant driving force in chip design. Moore's Law has held since 1965, but in order to do so, chip manufacturers have jumped from one technology to another. Gordon Moore himself has predicted that, if restricted to CMOS silicon, his law will fail sometime around 2020. The discovery of this 7-atom transistor gives new life to Moore's Law—and we suspect that Gordon Moore is breathing a sigh of relief over its discovery. However, noted physicist Stephen Hawking has explained that chip manufacturers are limited in their quest to "enforce" Moore's Law by two fundamental constraints: the speed of light and the atomic nature of matter, implying that Moore's Law will eventually fail, regardless of the technology being used.

1.9 NON–VON NEUMANN MODELS

Until recently, almost all general-purpose computers followed the von Neumann design. That is, the architecture consisted of a CPU, memory, and I/O devices, and they had single storage for instructions and data, as well as a single bus used for fetching instructions and transferring data. von Neumann computers execute instructions sequentially and are therefore extremely well suited to sequential processing. However, the von Neumann bottleneck continues to baffle engineers looking for ways to build fast systems that are inexpensive and compatible with the vast body of commercially available software.

Engineers who are not constrained by the need to maintain compatibility with von Neumann systems are free to use many different models of computing. Non–von Neumann architectures are those in which the model of computation varies from the characteristics listed for the von Neumann architecture. For example, an architecture that does not store programs and data in memory or does not process a program sequentially would be considered a non–von Neumann machine. Also, a computer that has two buses, one for data and a separate one for instructions, would be considered a non–von Neumann machine. Computers designed using the **Harvard architecture** have two buses, thus allowing data and instructions to be transferred simultaneously, but also have separate storage for data and instructions. Many modern general-purpose computers use a modified version of the Harvard architecture in which they have separate pathways for data and instructions but not separate storage. Pure Harvard architectures are typically used in microcontrollers (an entire computer system on a chip), such as those found in embedded systems, as in appliances, toys, and cars.

Many non–von Neumann machines are designed for special purposes. The first recognized non–von Neumann processing chip was designed strictly for image processing. Another example is a **reduction machine** (built to perform combinatory logic calculations using graph reduction). Other non–von Neumann computers include **digital signal processors** (DSPs) and **media processors**, which can execute a single instruction on a set of data (instead of executing a single instruction on a single piece of data).

A number of different subfields fall into the non–von Neumann category, including **neural networks** (using ideas from models of the brain as a computing paradigm) implemented in silicon, **cellular automata**, **cognitive computers** (machines that learn by experience rather than through programming, including IBM's SyNAPSE computer, a machine that models the human brain), **quantum computation** (a combination of computing and quantum physics), **dataflow computation**, and **parallel computers**. These all have something in common—the computation is distributed among different processing units that act in parallel. They differ in how weakly or strongly the various components are connected. Of these, parallel computing is currently the most popular.

1.10   PARALLEL PROCESSORS AND PARALLEL COMPUTING

Today, parallel processing solves some of our biggest problems in much the same way that settlers of the Old West solved their biggest problems using parallel oxen. If they were using an ox to move a tree and the ox was not big enough or strong enough, they certainly didn't try to grow a bigger ox—they used two oxen. If our computer isn't fast enough or powerful enough, instead of trying to develop a faster, more powerful computer, why not simply use multiple computers? This is precisely what parallel computing does. The first parallel processing systems were built in the late 1960s and had only two processors. The 1970s saw the introduction of supercomputers with as many as 32 processors, and the 1980s brought the first systems with more than 1000 processors. Finally, in 1999, IBM announced funding for the development of a supercomputer architecture called the **Blue Gene** series. The first computer in this series, the **Blue Gene/L**, is a massively parallel computer containing 131,000 dual-core processors, each with its own dedicated memory. In addition to allowing researchers to study the behavior of protein folding (by using large simulations), this computer has also allowed researchers to explore new ideas in parallel architectures and software for those architectures. IBM has continued to add computers to this series. The **Blue Gene/P** appeared in 2007 and has quad-core processors. The latest computer designed for this series, the **Blue Gene/Q**, uses 16-core processors, with 1024 compute nodes per rack, scalable up to 512 racks. Installations of the Blue Gene/Q computer include Nostromo (being used for biomedical data in Poland), Sequoia (being used at Lawrence Livermore National Laboratory for nuclear simulations and scientific research), and Mira (used at Argonne National Laboratory).

Dual-core and quad-core processors (and higher, as we saw in Blue Gene/Q) are examples of **multicore processors**. But what is a multicore processor? Essentially, it is a special type of parallel processor. Parallel processors are often classified as either "shared memory" processors (in which processors all share the same global memory) or "distributed memory" computers (in which each processor has its own private memory). Chapter 9 covers parallel processors in detail. The following discussion is limited to shared memory multicore architectures—the type used in personal computers.

Multicore architectures are parallel processing machines that allow for multiple processing units (often called **cores**) on a single chip. Dual core means 2 cores; quad core machines have 4 cores; and so on. But what is a core? Instead of a single processing unit in an integrated circuit (as found in typical von Neumann machines), independent multiple cores are "plugged in" and run in parallel. Each processing unit has its own ALU and set of registers, but all processors share memory and some other resources. "Dual core" is different from "dual processor." Dual-processor machines, for example, have two processors, but each processor plugs into the motherboard separately. The important distinction to note is that all cores in multicore machines are integrated into the same chip. This means that you could, for example, replace a single-core (uniprocessor) chip in your computer with, for example, a dual-core processor chip (provided your computer had the appropriate socket for the new chip). Many computers today are advertised as dual core, quad core, or higher. Dual core is generally considered the standard in today's computers. Although most desktop and laptop computers have limited cores (fewer than 8), machines with hundreds of cores are available for the right price, of course.

Just because your computer has multiple cores does not mean it will run your programs more quickly. Application programs (including operating systems) must be written to take advantage of multiple processing units (this statement is true for parallel processing in general). Multicore computers are very useful for **multitasking**—when users are doing more than one thing at a time. For example, you may be reading email, listening to music, browsing the Web, and burning a DVD all at the same time. These "multiple tasks" can be assigned to different processors and carried out in parallel, provided the operating system is able to manipulate many tasks at once.

In addition to multitasking, **multithreading** can also increase the performance of any application with inherent parallelism. Programs are divided into

threads, which can be thought of as mini-processes. For example, a Web browser is multithreaded; one thread can download text, while each image is controlled and downloaded by a separate thread. If an application is multithreaded, separate threads can run in parallel on different processing units. We should note that even on uniprocessors, multithreading can improve performance, but this is a discussion best left for another time. For more information, see Stallings (2012).

To summarize, parallel processing refers to a collection of different architectures, from multiple separate computers working together, to multiple processors sharing memory, to multiple cores integrated onto the same chip. Parallel processors are technically not classified as von Neumann machines because they do not process instructions sequentially. However, many argue that parallel processing computers contain CPUs, use program counters, and store both programs and data in main memory, which makes them more like an extension to the von Neumann architecture rather than a departure from it; these people view parallel processing computers as sets of cooperating von Neumann machines. In this regard, perhaps it is more appropriate to say that parallel processing exhibits "non–von Neumannness." Regardless of how parallel processors are classified, parallel computing allows us to multitask and to solve larger and more complex problems, and is driving new research in various software tools and programming.

Even parallel computing has its limits, however. As the number of processors increases, so does the overhead of managing how tasks are distributed to those processors. Some parallel processing systems require extra processors just to manage the rest of the processors and the resources assigned to them. No matter how many processors we place in a system, or how many resources we assign to them, somehow, somewhere, a bottleneck is bound to develop. The best we can do, however, is make sure the slowest parts of the system are the ones that are used the least. This is the idea behind **Amdahl's Law**. This law states that the performance enhancement possible with a given improvement is limited by the amount that the improved feature is used. The underlying premise is that every algorithm has a sequential part that ultimately limits the speedup that can be achieved by multiprocessor implementation.

If parallel machines and other non–von Neumann architectures give such huge increases in processing speed and power, why isn't everyone using them everywhere? The answer lies in their programmability. Advances in operating systems that can utilize multiple cores have put these chips in laptops and desktops that we can buy today; however, true multiprocessor programming is more complex than both uniprocessor and multicore programming and requires people to think about problems in a different way, using new algorithms and programming tools.

One of these programming tools is a set of new programming languages. Most of our programming languages are von Neumann languages, created for the von Neumann architecture. Many common languages have been extended with special libraries to accommodate parallel programming, and many new languages have been designed specifically for the parallel programming environment. We have very few programming languages for the remaining (nonparallel) non–von Neumann platforms, and fewer people who really understand how to program in these environments efficiently. Examples of non–von Neumann languages include Lucid (for dataflow) and QCL (Quantum Computation Language) for quantum computers, as well as VHDL or Verilog (languages used to program FPGAs). However, even with the inherent difficulties in programming parallel machines, we see in the next section that significant progress is being made.

1.11 PARALLELISM: ENABLER OF MACHINE INTELLIGENCE—DEEP BLUE AND WATSON

It is evident by our sidebar on the Mechanical Turk that chess playing has long been considered the ultimate demonstration of a "thinking machine." The chessboard is a battlefield where human can meet machine on more-or-less equal terms—with the human always having the edge, of course. Real chess-playing computers have been around since the late 1950s. Over the decades, they gradually improved their hardware and software to eventually become formidable opponents for reasonably skilled players. The problem of *championship* chess playing, however, had long been considered so hard that many believed a machine could never beat a human Grandmaster. On May 11, 1997, a machine called Deep Blue did just that.

Deep Blue's principal designers were IBM researchers Feng-hsiung Hsu, Thomas Anantharaman, and Murray Campbell. Reportedly costing more than $6 million and taking six years to build, Deep Blue was a massively parallel system consisting of 30 RS/6000-based nodes supplemented with 480 chips built especially to play chess. Deep Blue included a database of 700,000 complete games with separate systems for opening and endgames. It evaluated 200 million positions per second on average. This enabled Deep Blue to produce a 12-move look ahead.

Having soundly beat an earlier version of Deep Blue, world chess champion Garry Kasparov was overwhelmingly favored to win a rematch starting May 3, 1997. At the end of five games, Kasparov and Deep Blue were tied, 2½ to 2½. Then Deep Blue quickly seized upon an error that Kasparov made early in the sixth game. Kasparov had no choice but to concede, thus making Deep Blue the first machine to ever defeat a chess Grandmaster.

With Deep Blue's stunning win over Kasparov now in the history books, IBM Research manager Charles Lickel began looking for a new challenge. In 2004, Lickel was among the millions mesmerized by Ken Jennings's unprecedented 74-game winning streak on the American quiz show, *Jeopardy*! As he watched Jennings win one match after another, Lickel dared to think that it was possible to build a machine that could win at *Jeopardy*! Moreover, he believed that IBM Research had the talent to build such a machine. He tapped Dr. David Ferrucci to lead the effort.

IBM scientists were in no rush to sign on to Lickel's audacious project. They doubted—with good reason—that such a machine could be built. After all, creating Deep Blue was hard enough. Playing *Jeopardy*! is enormously more difficult than playing chess. In chess, the problem domain is clearly defined with fixed, unambiguous rules, and a finite (although very large) solution space. *Jeopardy!* questions, on the other hand, cover a nearly infinite problem space compounded by the vagaries of human language, odd relations between concepts, puns, and vast amounts of unstructured factual information. For example, a *Jeopardy!* category could be titled "Doozy Twos" and relate to an African leader, an article of clothing, an Al Jolson song, and an ammunition size (Benjamin Tutu, tutu skirt, "Toot Toot Tootsie," and .22 caliber). Whereas a human being has little trouble seeing the relationship (especially once the answer is revealed), computers are utterly baffled.

To make the game fair, Watson had to emulate a human player as closely as possible. No connection to the Internet or any other computers was permitted, and Watson was required to physically press a plunger to "buzz in" with an answer. However, Watson wasn't programmed to process sound or images, so visual and strictly audio clues—such as musical selections—were not used during the match.

Once a clue was read, Watson initiated several parallel processes. Each process examined different aspects of the clue, narrowed the solution space, and formulated a hypothesis as to the answer. The hypothesis included a probability of its being correct. Watson selected the most likely of the hypotheses, or selected no hypothesis at all if the probability of correctness didn't reach a predetermined threshold. Watson's designers determined that if Watson were to attempt just 70% of the questions and respond correctly just 85% of the time, it would win the contest. No human players had ever done as well.

Using Watson's algorithms, a typical desktop computer would need about two hours to come up with a good hypothesis. Watson had to do it in less than *three seconds*. It achieved this feat through a massively parallel architecture dubbed **DeepQA** (Deep Question and Answer). The system relied on 90 IBM POWER 750 servers. Each server was equipped with four POWER7 processors, and each POWER7 processor had eight cores, giving a total of 2880 processor cores. While playing *Jeopardy!*, each core had access to 16TB of main memory and 4TB of clustered storage.

Unlike Deep Blue, Watson could not be programmed to solve problems through brute force: The problem space was much too large. Watson's designers, therefore, approached the situation just as a human being would: Watson "learned" by consuming terabytes of unstructured data from thousands of news sources, journals, and books. The DeepQA algorithms provided Watson with the ability to synthesize information—in a humanlike manner—from this universe of raw data. Watson drew inferences and made assumptions using hard facts and incomplete information. Watson could see information in context: The same question, in a different context, might well produce a different answer.

On the third day of its match, February 16, 2011, Watson stunned the world by soundly beating both reigning *Jeopardy!* champs, Ken Jennings and Brad Rutter. Watson's winnings were donated to charity, but Watson's service to humanity was only beginning. Watson's ability to absorb and draw inferences from pools of unstructured data made it a perfect candidate for medical school. Beginning in 2011, IBM, WellPoint, and Memorial Sloan-Kettering Cancer Center set Watson to work absorbing more than 600,000 pieces of medical evidence, and two million pages of text from 42 medical journals and oncology research documents. Watson's literature assimilation was supplemented with 14,700 hours of live training provided by WellPoint nurses. Watson was then given 25,000 test case scenarios and 1500 real-life cases from which it demonstrated that it had gained the ability to derive meaning from the mountain of complex medical data, some of which was in informal natural language—such as doctors' notes, patient records, medical annotations, and clinical feedback. Watson's *Jeopardy*! success has now been matched by its medical school success. Commercial products based on Watson technology, including "Interactive Care Insights for Oncology" and "Interactive Care Reviewer," are now available. They hold the promise to improve the speed and accuracy of medical care for cancer patients.

Although Watson's applications and abilities have been growing, Watson's footprint has been shrinking. In the span of only a few years, system performance has improved by 240% with a 75% reduction in physical resources. Watson can now be run on a single POWER 750 server, leading some to claim that "Watson on a chip" is just around the corner.

In Watson, we have not merely seen an amazing *Jeopardy*! player or crack oncologist. What we have seen is the future of computing. Rather than people being trained to use computers, computers will train themselves to interact with people—with all their fuzzy and incomplete information. Tomorrow's systems will meet humans on human terms. As Dr. Ferrucci puts it, there simply is no other future for computers except to become like Watson. It just *has to* be this way.

CHAPTER SUMMARY

In this chapter, we have presented a brief overview of computer organization and computer architecture and shown how they differ. We also have introduced some terminology in the context of a fictitious computer advertisement. Much of this terminology will be expanded on in later chapters.

Historically, computers were simply calculating machines. As computers became more sophisticated, they became general-purpose machines, which necessitated viewing each system as a hierarchy of levels instead of one gigantic machine. Each layer in this hierarchy serves a specific purpose, and all levels help minimize the semantic gap between a high-level programming language or application and the gates and wires that make up the physical hardware. Perhaps the single most important development in computing that affects us as programmers is the introduction of the stored-program concept of the von Neumann machine. Although there are other architectural models, the von Neumann architecture is predominant in today's general-purpose computers.

FURTHER READING

We encourage you to build on our brief presentation of the history of computers. We think you will find this subject intriguing because it is as much about people as it is about machines. You can read about the "forgotten father of the computer," John Atanasoff, in Mollenhoff (1988). This book documents the odd relationship between Atanasoff and John Mauchly, and recounts the open court battle of two computer giants, Honeywell and Sperry Rand. This trial ultimately gave Atanasoff his proper recognition.

For a lighter look at computer history, try the book by Rochester and Gantz (1983). Augarten's (1985) illustrated history of computers is a delight to read and contains hundreds of hard-to-find pictures of early computers and computing devices. For a complete discussion of the historical development of computers, you can check out the three-volume dictionary by Cortada (1987). A particularly thoughtful account of the history of computing is presented in Ceruzzi (1998). If you are interested in an excellent set of case studies about historical computers, see Blaauw and Brooks (1997).

You will also be richly rewarded by reading McCartney's (1999) book about the ENIAC, Chopsky and Leonsis's (1988) chronicle of the development of the IBM PC, and Toole's (1998) biography of Ada, Countess of Lovelace. Polachek's (1997) article conveys a vivid picture of the complexity of calculating ballistic firing tables. After reading this article, you will understand why the army would gladly pay for anything that promised to make the process faster or more accurate. The Maxfield and Brown book (1997) contains a fascinating look at the origins and history of computing as well as in-depth explanations of how a computer works.

For more information on Moore's Law, we refer the reader to Schaller (1997). For detailed descriptions of early computers as well as profiles and reminiscences of industry pioneers, you may wish to consult the *IEEE Annals of the History of Computing*, which is published quarterly. The Computer Museum History Center can be found online at www.computerhistory.org. It contains various exhibits, research, timelines, and collections. Many cities now have computer museums and allow visitors to use some of the older computers.

A wealth of information can be found at the websites of the standards-making bodies discussed in this chapter (as well as sites not discussed in this chapter). The IEEE can be found at www.ieee.org; ANSI at www.ansi.org; the ISO at www.iso.ch; the BSI at www.bsi-global.com; and the ITU-T at www.itu.int. The ISO site offers a vast amount of information and standards reference materials.

The WWW Computer Architecture Home Page at www.cs.wisc.edu/~arch/www/ contains a comprehensive index to computer architecture–related information. Many USENET newsgroups are devoted to these topics as well, including comp.arch and comp.arch.storage.

The entire May–June 2000 issue of MIT's *Technology Review* magazine is devoted to architectures that may be the basis of tomorrow's computers. Reading this issue will be time well spent. In fact, we could say the same of every issue.

For a truly unique account of human computers, we invite you to read Grier's *When Computers Were Human*. Among other things, he presents a stirring account of the human computers who drove the mathematical tables project under the Depression-era Works Progress Administration (WPA). The contributions made by these "table factories" were crucial to America's victory in World War II. A shorter account of this effort can also be found in Grier's 1998 article that appears in the *IEEE Annals of the History of Computing*.

The entire May–June 2012 issue of the *IBM Journal of Research and Development* is dedicated to the building of Watson. The two articles by Ferrucci and Lewis give great insight into the challenges and triumphs of this groundbreaking machine. The IBM whitepaper, "Watson—A System Designed for Answers," provides a nice summary of Watson's hardware architecture. Feng-hsiung Hsu gives his first-person account of the building of Deep Blue in *Behind Deep Blue: Building the Computer that Defeated the World Chess Champion*. Readers interested in the Mechanical Turk can find more information in the book of the same name by Tom Standage.

REFERENCES

Augarten, S. *Bit by Bit: An Illustrated History of Computers.* London: Unwin Paperbacks, 1985.

Blaauw, G., & Brooks, F. *Computer Architecture: Concepts and Evolution.* Reading, MA: Addison-Wesley, 1997.

Ceruzzi, P. E. *A History of Modern Computing.* Cambridge, MA: MIT Press, 1998.

Chopsky, J., & Leonsis, T. *Blue Magic: The People, Power and Politics Behind the IBM Personal Computer.* New York: Facts on File Publications, 1988.

Cortada, J. W. *Historical Dictionary of Data Processing*, Volume 1: *Biographies*; Volume 2: *Organization*; Volume 3: *Technology*. Westport, CT: Greenwood Press, 1987.

Ferrucci, D. A., "Introduction to 'This is Watson.'" *IBM Journal of Research and Development* 56:3/4, May–June 2012, pp. 1:1–1:15.

Grier, D. A. "The Math Tables Project of the Work Projects Administration: The Reluctant Start of the Computing Era." *IEEE Annals of the History of Computing 20*:3, July–Sept. 1998, pp. 33–50.

Grier, D. A. *When Computers Were Human.* Princeton, NJ: Princeton University Press, 2007.

Hsu, F.-h. *Behind Deep Blue: Building the Computer that Defeated the World Chess Champion.* Princeton, NJ: Princeton University Press, 2006.

IBM. "Watson—A System Designed for Answers: The future of workload optimized systems design." February 2011. ftp://public.dhe.ibm.com/common/ssi/ecm/en/pow03061usen/POW-03061USEN.PDF. Retrieved June 4, 2013.

Lewis, B. L. "In the game: The interface between Watson and *Jeopardy!*" *IBM Journal of Research and Development* 56:3/4, May–June 2012, pp. 17:1–17:6.

Maguire, Y., Boyden III, E. S., & Gershenfeld, N. "Toward a Table-Top Quantum Computer." *IBM Systems Journal 39*:3/4, June 2000, pp. 823–839.

Maxfield, C., & Brown, A. *Bebop BYTES Back (An Unconventional Guide to Computers).* Madison, AL: Doone Publications, 1997.

McCartney, S. *ENIAC: The Triumphs and Tragedies of the World's First Computer.* New York: Walker and Company, 1999.

Mollenhoff, C. R. *Atanasoff: The Forgotten Father of the Computer.* Ames, IA: Iowa State University Press, 1988.

Polachek, H. "Before the ENIAC." *IEEE Annals of the History of Computing 19*:2, June 1997, pp. 25–30.

Rochester, J. B., & Gantz, J. *The Naked Computer: A Layperson's Almanac of Computer Lore, Wizardry, Personalities, Memorabilia, World Records, Mindblowers, and Tomfoolery.* New York: William A. Morrow, 1983.

Schaller, R. "Moore's Law: Past, Present, and Future." *IEEE Spectrum*, June 1997, pp. 52–59.

Stallings, W. *Operating Systems: Internals and Design Principles,* 7th ed. Upper Saddle River, NJ: Prentice Hall, 2012.

Standage, T. *The Turk: The Life and Times of the Famous Eighteenth-Century Chess-Playing Machine.* New York: Berkley Trade, 2003.

Tanenbaum, A. *Structured Computer Organization,* 6th ed. Upper Saddle River, NJ: Prentice Hall, 2013.

Toole, B. A. *Ada, the Enchantress of Numbers: Prophet of the Computer Age.* Mill Valley, CA: Strawberry Press, 1998.

Waldrop, M. M. "Quantum Computing." *MIT Technology Review 103*:3, May/June 2000, pp. 60–66.

REVIEW OF ESSENTIAL TERMS AND CONCEPTS

1. What is the difference between computer organization and computer architecture?
2. What is an ISA?
3. What is the importance of the Principle of Equivalence of Hardware and Software?
4. Name the three basic components of every computer.
5. To what power of 10 does the prefix giga- refer? What is the (approximate) equivalent power of 2?
6. To what power of 10 does the prefix micro- refer? What is the (approximate) equivalent power of 2?
7. What unit is typically used to measure the speed of a computer clock?
8. What are the distinguishing features of tablet computers?
9. Name two types of computer memory.
10. What is the mission of the IEEE?
11. What is the full name of the organization that uses the initials ISO? Is ISO an acronym?
12. ANSI is the acronym used by which organization?
13. What is the name of the Swiss organization that devotes itself to matters concerning telephony, telecommunications, and data communications?
14. Who is known as the father of computing, and why?
15. What was the significance of the punched card?

16. Name two driving factors in the development of computers.

17. What is it about the transistor that made it such a great improvement over the vacuum tube?

18. How does an integrated circuit differ from a transistor?

19. Explain the differences between SSI, MSI, LSI, and VLSI.

20. What technology spawned the development of microcomputers? Why?

21. What is meant by an "open architecture"?

22. State Moore's Law.

23. How is Rock's Law related to Moore's Law?

24. Name and explain the seven commonly accepted layers of the Computer Level Hierarchy. How does this arrangement help us to understand computer systems?

25. How does the term *abstraction* apply to computer organization and architecture?

26. What was it about the von Neumann architecture that distinguished it from its predecessors?

27. Name the characteristics present in von Neumann architecture.

28. How does the fetch-decode-execute cycle work?

29. What is a multicore processor?

30. What are the key characteristics of Cloud computing?

31. What are the three types of Cloud computing platforms?

32. What are the main challenges of Cloud computing from a provider perspective as well as a consumer perspective?

33. What are the advantages and disadvantages of service-oriented computing?

34. What is meant by parallel computing?

35. What is the underlying premise of Amdahl's Law?

36. What makes Watson so different from traditional computers?

EXERCISES

◆ 1. In what ways are hardware and software different? In what ways are they the same?

2. a) How many milliseconds (ms) are in 1 second?

   b) How many microseconds (μs) are in 1 second?

   c) How many nanoseconds (ns) are in 1 millisecond?

   d) How many microseconds are in 1 millisecond?

   e) How many nanoseconds are in 1 microsecond?

   f) How many kilobytes (KB) are in 1 gigabyte (GB)?

   g) How many kilobytes are in 1 megabyte (MB)?

    h) How many megabytes are in 1 gigabyte?

    i) How many bytes are in 20 megabytes?

    j) How many kilobytes are in 2 gigabytes?

◆**3.** By what order of magnitude is something that runs in nanoseconds faster than something that runs in milliseconds?

4. Pretend you are ready to buy a new computer for personal use. First, take a look at ads from various magazines and newspapers and list terms you don't quite understand. Look up these terms and give a brief written explanation. Decide what factors are important in your decision as to which computer to buy and list them. After you select the system you would like to buy, identify which terms refer to hardware and which refer to software.

5. Makers of tablet computers continually work within narrow constraints on cost, power consumption, weight, and battery life. Describe what you feel would be the perfect tablet computer. How large would the screen be? Would you rather have a longer-lasting battery, even if it means having a heavier unit? How heavy would be too heavy? Would you rather have low cost or fast performance? Should the battery be consumer replaceable?

6. Pick your favorite computer language and write a small program. After compiling the program, see if you can determine the ratio of source code instructions to the machine language instructions generated by the compiler. If you add one line of source code, how does that affect the machine language program? Try adding different source code instructions, such as an add and then a multiply. How does the size of the machine code file change with the different instructions? Comment on the result.

7. Respond to the idea presented in Section 1.5: If invented today, what name do you think would be given to the computer? Give at least one good reason for your answer.

8. Briefly explain two breakthroughs in the history of computing.

9. Would it be possible to fool people with an automaton like the Mechanical Turk today? If you were to try to create a Turk today, how would it differ from the eighteenth-century version?

◆**10.** Suppose a transistor on an integrated circuit chip were 2 microns in size. According to Moore's Law, how large would that transistor be in 2 years? How is Moore's Law relevant to programmers?

11. What circumstances helped the IBM PC become so successful?

12. List five applications of personal computers. Is there a limit to the applications of computers? Do you envision any radically different and exciting applications in the near future? If so, what?

13. In the von Neumann model, explain the purpose of the:

    a) processing unit

    b) program counter

14. Under the von Neumann architecture, a program and its data are both stored in memory. It is therefore possible for a program, thinking that a memory location holds a piece of data when it actually holds a program instruction, to accidentally (or on purpose) modify itself. What implications does this present to you as a programmer?

15. Explain why modern computers consist of multiple levels of virtual machines.

16. Explain the three main types of Cloud computing platforms.

17. What are the challenges facing organizations that wish to move to a Cloud platform? What are the risks and benefits?

18. Does Cloud computing eliminate all of an organization's concerns about its computing infrastructure?

19. Explain what it means to "fetch" an instruction.

20. Read a popular local newspaper and search through the job openings. (You can also check some of the more popular online career sites.) Which jobs require specific hardware knowledge? Which jobs imply knowledge of computer hardware? Is there any correlation between the required hardware knowledge and the company or its location?

21. List and describe some common uses and some not-so-common uses of computers in business and other sectors of society.

22. The technologist's notion of Moore's Law is that the number of transistors per chip doubles approximately every 18 months. In the 1990s, Moore's Law started to be described as the doubling of microprocessor power every 18 months. Given this new variation of Moore's Law, answer the following:

    a) After successfully completing your computer organization and architecture class, you have a brilliant idea for a new chip design that would make a processor six times faster than the fastest ones on the market today. Unfortunately, it will take you four and a half years to save the money, create the prototype, and build a finished product. If Moore's Law holds, should you spend your money developing and producing your chip or invest in some other venture?

    b) Suppose we have a problem that currently takes 100,000 hours of computer time using current technology to solve. Which of the following would give us the solution first: (1) Replace the algorithm used in the current solution with one that runs twice as fast and run it on the current technology, or (2) Wait 3 years, assuming Moore's Law doubles the performance of a computer every 18 months, and find the solution using the current algorithm with the new technology?

23. What are the limitations of Moore's Law? Why can't this law hold forever? Explain.

24. What are some technical implications of Moore's Law? What effect does it have on your future?

25. Do you share Dr. Ferrucci's opinion that all computers will become like Watson someday? If you had a tablet-sized Watson, what would you do with it?

There are 10 kinds of people in the world—those who understand binary and those who don't.

—Anonymous

CHAPTER 2

Data Representation in Computer Systems

2.1 INTRODUCTION

The organization of any computer depends considerably on how it represents numbers, characters, and control information. The converse is also true: Standards and conventions established over the years have determined certain aspects of computer organization. This chapter describes the various ways in which computers can store and manipulate numbers and characters. The ideas presented in the following sections form the basis for understanding the organization and function of all types of digital systems.

The most basic unit of information in a digital computer is called a **bit**, which is a contraction of **binary digit**. In the concrete sense, a bit is nothing more than a state of "on" or "off" (or "high" and "low") within a computer circuit. In 1964, the designers of the IBM System/360 mainframe computer established a convention of using groups of 8 bits as the basic unit of addressable computer storage. They called this collection of 8 bits a **byte**.

Computer **words** consist of two or more adjacent bytes that are sometimes addressed and almost always are manipulated collectively. The **word size** represents the data size that is handled most efficiently by a particular architecture. Words can be 16 bits, 32 bits, 64 bits, or any other size that makes sense in the context of a computer's organization (including sizes that are not multiples of eight). An 8-bit byte can be divided into two 4-bit halves called **nibbles** (or **nybbles**). Because each bit of a byte has a value within a positional numbering system, the nibble containing the least-valued binary digit is called the low-order nibble, and the other half the high-order nibble.

57

2.2 POSITIONAL NUMBERING SYSTEMS

At some point during the middle of the sixteenth century, Europe embraced the decimal (or base 10) numbering system that the Arabs and Hindus had been using for nearly a millennium. Today, we take for granted that the number 243 means two hundreds, plus four tens, plus three units. Notwithstanding the fact that zero means "nothing," virtually everyone knows that there is a substantial difference between having 1 of something and having 10 of something.

The general idea behind positional numbering systems is that a numeric value is represented through increasing powers of a **radix** (or base). This is often referred to as a **weighted numbering system** because each position is weighted by a power of the radix.

The set of valid numerals for a positional numbering system is equal in size to the radix of that system. For example, there are 10 digits in the decimal system, 0 through 9, and 3 digits for the ternary (base 3) system, 0, 1, and 2. The largest valid number in a radix system is one smaller than the radix, so 8 is not a valid numeral in any radix system smaller than 9. To distinguish among numbers in different radices, we use the radix as a subscript, such as in 33_{10} to represent the decimal number 33. (In this text, numbers written without a subscript should be assumed to be decimal.) Any decimal integer can be expressed exactly in any other integral base system (see Example 2.1).

$\equiv$ **EXAMPLE 2.1**   Three numbers represented as powers of a radix.

$$243.51_{10} = 2 \times 10^2 + 4 \times 10^1 + 3 \times 10^0 + 5 \times 10^{-1} + 1 \times 10^{-2}$$
$$212_3 = 2 \times 3^2 + 1 \times 3^1 + 2 \times 3^0 = 23_{10}$$
$$10110_2 = 1 \times 2^4 + 0 \times 2^3 + 1 \times 2^2 + 1 \times 2^1 + 0 \times 2^0 = 22_{10}$$

The two most important radices in computer science are binary (base two), and hexadecimal (base 16). Another radix of interest is octal (base 8). The binary system uses only the digits 0 and 1; the octal system, 0 through 7. The hexadecimal system allows the digits 0 through 9 with A, B, C, D, E, and F being used to represent the numbers 10 through 15. Table 2.1 shows some of the radices.

2.3 CONVERTING BETWEEN BASES

Gottfried Leibniz (1646–1716) was the first to generalize the idea of the (positional) decimal system to other bases. Being a deeply spiritual person, Leibniz attributed divine qualities to the binary system. He correlated the fact that any integer could be represented by a series of ones and zeros with the idea that God (1) created the universe out of nothing (0). Until the first binary digital computers were built in the late 1940s, this system remained nothing more than

Powers of 2
$2^{-2} = \frac{1}{4} = 0.25$
$2^{-1} = \frac{1}{2} = 0.5$
$2^0 = 1$
$2^1 = 2$
$2^2 = 4$
$2^3 = 8$
$2^4 = 16$
$2^5 = 32$
$2^6 = 64$
$2^7 = 128$
$2^8 = 256$
$2^9 = 512$
$2^{10} = 1024$
$2^{15} = 32,768$
$2^{16} = 65,536$

Decimal	4-Bit Binary	Hexadecimal
0	0000	0
1	0001	1
2	0010	2
3	0011	3
4	0100	4
5	0101	5
6	0110	6
7	0111	7
8	1000	8
9	1001	9
10	1010	A
11	1011	B
12	1100	C
13	1101	D
14	1110	E
15	1111	F

TABLE 2.1   Some Numbers to Remember

a mathematical curiosity. Today, it lies at the heart of virtually every electronic device that relies on digital controls.

Because of its simplicity, the binary numbering system translates easily into electronic circuitry. It is also easy for humans to understand. Experienced computer professionals can recognize smaller binary numbers (such as those shown in Table 2.1) at a glance. Converting larger values and fractions, however, usually requires a calculator or pencil and paper. Fortunately, the conversion techniques are easy to master with a little practice. We show a few of the simpler techniques in the sections that follow.

2.3.1   Converting Unsigned Whole Numbers

We begin with the base conversion of unsigned numbers. Conversion of signed numbers (numbers that can be positive or negative) is more complex, and it is important that you first understand the basic technique for conversion before continuing with signed numbers.

Conversion between base systems can be done by using either repeated subtraction or a division-remainder method. The subtraction method is cumbersome and requires a familiarity with the powers of the radix being used. Because it is the more intuitive of the two methods, however, we will explain it first.

As an example, let's say we want to convert 104_{10} to base 3. We know that $3^4 = 81$ is the highest power of 3 that is less than 104, so our base 3 number will be 5 digits wide (one for each power of the radix: 0 through 4). We make note that 81 goes once into 104 and subtract, leaving a difference of 23. We know that the next power of 3, $3^3 = 27$, is too large to subtract, so we note the zero "placeholder" and look for how many times $3^2 = 9$ divides 23. We see that it goes twice and subtract 18. We are left with 5, from which we subtract $3^1 = 3$, leaving 2, which is 2×3^0. These steps are shown in Example 2.2.

EXAMPLE 2.2   Convert 104_{10} to base 3 using subtraction.

$$
\begin{aligned}
104 & \\
\underline{-81} &= 3^4 \times 1 \\
23 & \\
\underline{-0} &= 3^3 \times 0 \\
23 & \\
\underline{-18} &= 3^2 \times 2 \\
5 & \\
\underline{-3} &= 3^1 \times 1 \\
2 & \\
\underline{-2} &= 3^0 \times 2 \\
0 &
\end{aligned}
$$

$$104_{10} = 10212_3$$

The division-remainder method is faster and easier than the repeated subtraction method. It employs the idea that successive divisions by the base are in fact successive subtractions by powers of the base. The remainders that we get when we sequentially divide by the base end up being the digits of the result, which are read from bottom to top. This method is illustrated in Example 2.3.

EXAMPLE 2.3   Convert 104_{10} to base 3 using the division-remainder method.

$$
\begin{array}{rl}
3\,\lfloor 104 & \quad 2 \quad \text{3 divides 104 34 times with a remainder of 2} \\
3\,\lfloor 34 & \quad 1 \quad \text{3 divides 34 11 times with a remainder of 1} \\
3\,\lfloor 11 & \quad 2 \quad \text{3 divides 11 3 times with a remainder of 2} \\
3\,\lfloor 3 & \quad 0 \quad \text{3 divides 3 1 time with a remainder of 0} \\
3\,\lfloor 1 & \quad 1 \quad \text{3 divides 1 0 times with a remainder of 1} \\
0 &
\end{array}
$$

Reading the remainders from bottom to top, we have: $104_{10} = 10212_3$.

This method works with any base, and because of the simplicity of the calculations, it is particularly useful in converting from decimal to binary. Example 2.4 shows such a conversion.

≡   **EXAMPLE 2.4**   Convert 147_{10} to binary.

2 ⌊147   1   2 divides 147 73 times with a remainder of 1
  2 ⌊73   1   2 divides 73 36 times with a remainder of 1
   2 ⌊36   0   2 divides 36 18 times with a remainder of 0
    2 ⌊18   0   2 divides 18 9 times with a remainder of 0
     2 ⌊9   1   2 divides 9 4 times with a remainder of 1
      2 ⌊4   0   2 divides 4 2 times with a remainder of 0
       2 ⌊2   0   2 divides 2 1 time with a remainder of 0
        2 ⌊1   1   2 divides 1 0 times with a remainder of 1
         0

Reading the remainders from bottom to top, we have: $147_{10} = 10010011_2$.

A binary number with N bits can represent unsigned integers from 0 to $2^N - 1$. For example, 4 bits can represent the decimal values 0 through 15, whereas 8 bits can represent the values 0 through 255. The range of values that can be represented by a given number of bits is extremely important when doing arithmetic operations on binary numbers. Consider a situation in which binary numbers are 4 bits in length, and we wish to add 1111_2 (15_{10}) to 1111_2. We know that 15 plus 15 is 30, but 30 cannot be represented using only 4 bits. This is an example of a condition known as **overflow**, which occurs in unsigned binary representation when the result of an arithmetic operation is outside the range of allowable precision for the given number of bits. We address overflow in more detail when discussing signed numbers in Section 2.4.

2.3.2   Converting Fractions

Fractions in any base system can be approximated in any other base system using negative powers of a radix. **Radix points** separate the integer part of a number from its fractional part. In the decimal system, the radix point is called a decimal point. Binary fractions have a binary point.

Fractions that contain repeating strings of digits to the right of the radix point in one base may not necessarily have a repeating sequence of digits in another base. For instance, ⅔ is a repeating decimal fraction, but in the ternary system, it terminates as 0.2_3 ($2 \times 3^{-1} = 2 \times ⅓$).

We can convert fractions between different bases using methods analogous to the repeated subtraction and division-remainder methods for converting integers. Example 2.5 shows how we can use repeated subtraction to convert a number from decimal to base 5.

☰ **EXAMPLE 2.5** Convert 0.4304_{10} to base 5.

$$
\begin{array}{ll}
0.4304 & \\
\underline{-0.4000} & = 5^{-1} \times 2 \\
0.0304 & \\
\underline{-0.0000} & = 5^{-2} \times 0 \qquad \text{(A placeholder)}\\
0.0304 & \\
\underline{-0.0240} & = 5^{-3} \times 3 \\
0.0064 & \\
\underline{-0.0064} & = 5^{-4} \times 4 \\
0.0000 &
\end{array}
$$

Reading from top to bottom, we have: $0.4304_{10} = 0.2034_5$.

Because the remainder method works with positive powers of the radix for conversion of integers, it stands to reason that we would use multiplication to convert fractions, because they are expressed in negative powers of the radix. However, instead of looking for remainders, as we did above, we use only the integer part of the product after multiplication by the radix. The answer is read from top to bottom instead of bottom to top. Example 2.6 illustrates the process.

☰ **EXAMPLE 2.6** Convert 0.4304_{10} to base 5.

$$
\begin{array}{l}
.4304 \\
\underline{\times \quad 5} \\
2.1520 \qquad \text{The integer part is 2. Omit from subsequent multiplication.} \\
\\
.1520 \\
\underline{\times \quad 5} \\
0.7600 \qquad \text{The integer part is 0. We'll need it as a placeholder.} \\
\\
.7600 \\
\underline{\times \quad 5} \\
3.8000 \qquad \text{The integer part is 3. Omit from subsequent multiplication.} \\
\\
.8000 \\
\underline{\times \quad 5} \\
4.0000 \qquad \text{The fractional part is now zero, so we are done.}
\end{array}
$$

Reading from top to bottom, we have $0.4304_{10} = 0.2034_5$.

This example was contrived so that the process would stop after a few steps. Often things don't work out quite so evenly, and we end up with repeating fractions. Most computer systems implement specialized rounding algorithms to provide a predictable degree of accuracy. For the sake of clarity, however, we will simply discard (or truncate) our answer when the desired accuracy has been achieved, as shown in Example 2.7.

EXAMPLE 2.7 Convert 0.34375_{10} to binary with 4 bits to the right of the binary point.

$$
\begin{array}{r}
.34375 \\
\times \quad 2 \\
\hline
0.68750 \\
\end{array}
$$ (Another placeholder)

$$
\begin{array}{r}
.68750 \\
\times \quad 2 \\
\hline
1.37500 \\
\end{array}
$$

$$
\begin{array}{r}
.37500 \\
\times \quad 2 \\
\hline
0.75000 \\
\end{array}
$$

$$
\begin{array}{r}
.75000 \\
\times \quad 2 \\
\hline
1.50000 \\
\end{array}
$$ (This is our fourth bit. We will stop here.)

Reading from top to bottom, $0.34375_{10} = 0.0101_2$ to four binary places.

The methods just described can be used to directly convert any number in any base to any other base, say from base 4 to base 3 (as in Example 2.8). However, in most cases, it is faster and more accurate to first convert to base 10 and then to the desired base. One exception to this rule is when you are working between bases that are powers of two, as you'll see in the next section.

EXAMPLE 2.8 Convert 3121_4 to base 3.

First, convert to decimal:

$$
\begin{aligned}
3121_4 &= 3 \times 4^3 + 1 \times 4^2 + 2 \times 4^1 + 1 \times 4^0 \\
&= 3 \times 64 + 1 \times 16 + 2 \times 4 + 1 = 217_{10}
\end{aligned}
$$

Then convert to base 3:

$$
\begin{array}{rl}
3\,\lfloor 217 & \quad 1 \\
3\,\lfloor 72 & \quad 0 \\
3\,\lfloor 24 & \quad 0 \\
3\,\lfloor 8 & \quad 2 \\
3\,\lfloor 2 & \quad 2 \\
\hline
0 & \quad \text{We have } 3121_4 = 22001_3.
\end{array}
$$

2.3.3   Converting Between Power-of-Two Radices

Binary numbers are often expressed in hexadecimal—and sometimes octal—to improve their readability. Because $16 = 2^4$, a group of 4 bits (called a **hextet**) is easily recognized as a hexadecimal digit. Similarly, with $8 = 2^3$, a group of 3 bits (called an **octet**) is expressible as one octal digit. Using these relationships, we can therefore convert a number from binary to octal or hexadecimal by doing little more than looking at it.

≡   **EXAMPLE 2.9**   Convert 110010011101_2 to octal and hexadecimal.

$\underline{110}\ \underline{010}\ \underline{011}\ \underline{101}$ Separate into groups of 3 for the octal conversion.
  6   2   3   5

$$110010011101_2 = 6235_8$$

$\underline{1100}\ \underline{1001}\ \underline{1101}$ Separate into groups of 4 for the hexadecimal conversion.
  C   9   D

$$110010011101_2 = C9D_{16}$$

If there are too few bits, leading zeros can be added.

2.4   SIGNED INTEGER REPRESENTATION

We have seen how to convert an unsigned integer from one base to another. Signed numbers require that additional issues be addressed. When an integer variable is declared in a program, many programming languages automatically allocate a storage area that includes a sign as the first bit of the storage location. By convention, a "1" in the high-order bit indicates a negative number. The storage location can be as small as an 8-bit byte or as large as several words, depending on the programming language and the computer system. The remaining bits (after the sign bit) are used to represent the number itself.

How this number is represented depends on the method used. There are three commonly used approaches. The most intuitive method, signed magnitude, uses the remaining bits to represent the magnitude of the number. This method and the other two approaches, which both use the concept of **complements**, are introduced in the following sections.

2.4.1   Signed Magnitude

Up to this point, we have ignored the possibility of binary representations for negative numbers. The set of positive and negative integers is referred to as the set of **signed integers**. The problem with representing signed integers as binary values is the sign—how should we encode the actual sign of the number?

Signed-magnitude representation is one method of solving this problem. As its name implies, a signed-magnitude number has a sign as its leftmost bit (also referred to as the high-order bit or the most significant bit) whereas the remaining bits represent the magnitude (or absolute value) of the numeric value. For example, in an 8-bit word, -1 would be represented as 10000001, and $+1$ as 00000001. In a computer system that uses signed-magnitude representation and 8 bits to store integers, 7 bits can be used for the actual representation of the magnitude of the number. This means that the largest integer an 8-bit word can represent is $2^7 - 1$, or 127 (a zero in the high-order bit, followed by 7 ones). The smallest integer is 8 ones, or -127. Therefore, N bits can represent $-(2^{(N-1)} - 1)$ to $2^{(N-1)} - 1$.

Computers must be able to perform arithmetic calculations on integers that are represented using this notation. Signed-magnitude arithmetic is carried out using essentially the same methods that humans use with pencil and paper, but it can get confusing very quickly. As an example, consider the rules for addition: (1) If the signs are the same, add the magnitudes and use that same sign for the result; (2) If the signs differ, you must determine which operand has the larger magnitude. The sign of the result is the same as the sign of the operand with the larger magnitude, and the magnitude must be obtained by subtracting (not adding) the smaller one from the larger one. If you consider these rules carefully, this is the method you use for signed arithmetic by hand.

We arrange the operands in a certain way based on their signs, perform the calculation without regard to the signs, and then supply the sign as appropriate when the calculation is complete. When modeling this idea in an 8-bit word, we must be careful to include only 7 bits in the magnitude of the answer, discarding any carries that take place over the high-order bit.

EXAMPLE 2.10 Add 01001111_2 to 00100011_2 using signed-magnitude arithmetic.

```
            1 1 1 1      ⇐ carries
  0    1 0 0 1 1 1 1         (79)
  0 +  0 1 0 0 0 1 1       + (35)
  0    1 1 1 0 0 1 0        (114)
```

The arithmetic proceeds just as in decimal addition, including the carries, until we get to the seventh bit from the right. If there is a carry here, we say that we have an overflow condition and the carry is discarded, resulting in an incorrect sum. There is no overflow in this example.

We find that $01001111_2 + 00100011_2 = 01110010_2$ in signed-magnitude representation.

Sign bits are segregated because they are relevant only after the addition is complete. In this case, we have the sum of two positive numbers, which is positive.

Overflow (and thus an erroneous result) in signed numbers occurs when the sign of the result is incorrect.

In signed magnitude, the sign bit is used only for the sign, so we can't "carry into" it. If there is a carry emitting from the seventh bit, our result will be truncated as the seventh bit overflows, giving an incorrect sum. (Example 2.11 illustrates this overflow condition.) Prudent programmers avoid "million-dollar" mistakes by checking for overflow conditions whenever there is the slightest possibility they could occur. If we did not discard the overflow bit, it would carry into the sign, causing the more outrageous result of the sum of two positive numbers being negative. (Imagine what would happen if the next step in a program were to take the square root or log of that result!)

EXAMPLE 2.11   Add 01001111_2 to 01100011_2 using signed-magnitude arithmetic.

Last carry	1 ←				1 1 1 1	⇐ carries
overflows and	0		1 0 0 1 1 1 1			(79)
is discarded.	0 +		1 1 0 0 0 1 1			+ (99)
	0		0 1 1 0 0 1 0			(50)

We obtain the erroneous result of 79 + 99 = 50.

Dabbling on the Double

The fastest way to convert a binary number to decimal is a method called **double-dabble** (or **double-dibble**). This method builds on the idea that a subsequent power of two is double the previous power of two in a binary number. The calculation starts with the leftmost bit and works toward the rightmost bit. The first bit is doubled and added to the next bit. This sum is then doubled and added to the following bit. The process is repeated for each bit until the rightmost bit has been used.

EXAMPLE 1

Convert 10010011_2 to decimal.

Step 1:   Write down the binary number, leaving space between the bits.

    1   0   0   1   0   0   1   1

Step 2:   Double the high-order bit and copy it under the next bit.

    1   0   0   1   0   0   1   1
         2
    × 2
    ‾‾‾‾
      2

Step 3:   Add the next bit and double the sum. Copy this result under the next bit.

```
    1       0    0    1    0    0    1    1
            2    4
          + 0
            2
      × 2   × 2
        2    4
```

Step 4:   Repeat Step 3 until you run out of bits.

```
   1     0     0     1     0     0     1     1
   2     4     8    18    36    72   146
 + 0   + 0   + 1   + 0   + 0   + 1   + 1
   2     4     9    18    36    73   147      ⇐ The answer: $10010011_2 = 147_{10}$
 × 2   × 2   × 2   × 2   × 2   × 2   × 2
   2     4     8    18    36    72   146
```

When we combine hextet grouping (in reverse) with the double-dabble method, we find that we can convert hexadecimal to decimal with ease.

EXAMPLE 2

Convert $02CA_{16}$ to decimal.

First, convert the hex to binary by grouping into hextets.

```
   0      2      C      A
 0000   0010   1100   1010
```

• • •

Then apply the double-dabble method on the binary form:

```
   1     0     1     1     0     0     1     0     1     0
         2     4    10    22    44    88   178   356   714
       + 0   + 1   + 1   + 0   + 0   + 1   + 0   + 1   + 0
         2     5    11    22    44    89   178   357   714
       × 2   × 2   × 2   × 2   × 2   × 2   × 2   × 2   × 2
         2     4    10    22    44    88   178   356   714
```

$02CA_{16} = 1011001010_2 = 714_{10}$

As with addition, signed-magnitude subtraction is carried out in a manner similar to pencil-and-paper decimal arithmetic, where it is sometimes necessary to borrow from digits in the **minuend**.

≡ **EXAMPLE 2.12** Subtract 01001111_2 from 01100011_2 using signed-magnitude arithmetic.

$$
\begin{array}{llllllll}
 & 0 & 1 & 1 & 2 & & \Leftarrow \text{borrows} \\
0 & \;\; 1 & \cancel{+}\; \cancel{0} & \cancel{0} & \cancel{0} & 1 & 1 & (99) \\
0 & - 1 & 0 & 0 & 1 & 1 & 1 & - (79) \\
\hline
0 & \;\; 0 & 0 & 1 & 0 & 1 & 0 \; 0 & (20)
\end{array}
$$

We find that $01100011_2 - 01001111_2 = 00010100_2$ in signed-magnitude representation.

≡ **EXAMPLE 2.13** Subtract 01100011_2 (99) from 01001111_2 (79) using signed-magnitude arithmetic.

By inspection, we see that the subtrahend, 01100011, is larger than the minuend, 01001111. With the result obtained in Example 2.12, we know that the difference of these two numbers is 0010100_2. Because the subtrahend is larger than the minuend, all we need to do is change the sign of the difference. So we find that $01001111_2 - 01100011_2 = 10010100_2$ in signed-magnitude representation.

We know that subtraction is the same as "adding the opposite," which equates to negating the value we wish to subtract and then adding instead (which is often much easier than performing all the borrows necessary for subtraction, particularly in dealing with binary numbers). Therefore, we need to look at some examples involving both positive and negative numbers. Recall the rules for addition: (1) If the signs are the same, add the magnitudes and use that same sign for the result; (2) If the signs differ, you must determine which operand has the larger magnitude. The sign of the result is the same as the sign of the operand with the larger magnitude, and the magnitude must be obtained by subtracting (not adding) the smaller one from the larger one.

≡ **EXAMPLE 2.14** Add 10010011_2 (−19) to 00001101_2 (+13) using signed-magnitude arithmetic.

The first number (the augend) is negative because its sign bit is set to 1. The second number (the addend) is positive. What we are asked to do is in fact a subtraction. First, we determine which of the two numbers is larger in magnitude and use that number for the augend. Its sign will be the sign of the result.

```
          0  1  2        ⇐ borrows
 1     0  0  1̶  0̶  0̶  1  1      (−19)
 0  −  0  0  0  1  1  0  1      + (13)
 1     0  0  0  0  1  1  0      (−6)
```

With the inclusion of the sign bit, we see that $10010011_2 - 00001101_2 = 10000110_2$ in signed-magnitude representation.

≡ **EXAMPLE 2.15** Subtract 10011000_2 (-24) from 10101011_2 (-43) using signed-magnitude arithmetic.

We can convert the subtraction to an addition by negating -24, which gives us 24, and then we can add this to -43, giving us a new problem of $-43 + 24$. However, we know from the addition rules above that because the signs now differ, we must actually subtract the smaller magnitude from the larger magnitude (or subtract 24 from 43) and make the result negative (because 43 is larger than 24).

```
       0  2
    0  1̶  0  1  0  1  1     (43)
 −  0  0  1  1  0  0  0   − (24)
    0  0  1  0  0  1  1     (19)
```

Note that we are not concerned with the sign until we have performed the subtraction. We know the answer must be negative. So we end up with $10101011_2 - 10011000_2 = 10010011_2$ in signed-magnitude representation.

While reading the preceding examples, you may have noticed how many questions we had to ask ourselves: Which number is larger? Am I subtracting a negative number? How many times do I have to borrow from the minuend? A computer engineered to perform arithmetic in this manner must make just as many decisions (though a whole lot faster). The logic (and circuitry) is further complicated by the fact that signed magnitude has two representations for zero, 10000000 and 00000000 (and mathematically speaking, this simply shouldn't happen!). Simpler methods for representing signed numbers would allow simpler and less expensive circuits. These simpler methods are based on radix complement systems.

2.4.2 Complement Systems

Number theorists have known for hundreds of years that one decimal number can be subtracted from another by adding the difference of the subtrahend from all nines and adding back a carry. This is called taking the nine's complement of the subtrahend or, more formally, finding the **diminished radix complement** of the subtrahend. Let's say we wanted to find $167 - 52$. Taking the difference of 52 from 999, we have 947. Thus, in nine's complement arithmetic, we have $167 - 52 = 167 + 947 = 1114$. The "carry" from the hundreds column is added back to the units place, giving us a correct $167 - 52 = 115$. This method was commonly called "casting out 9s" and has been extended to binary operations to simplify computer arithmetic. The advantage that complement systems give us over signed magnitude is that there is no need to process sign bits separately, but we can still easily check the sign of a number by looking at its high-order bit.

Another way to envision complement systems is to imagine an odometer on a bicycle. Unlike cars, when you go backward on a bike, the odometer will go backward as well. Assuming an odometer with three digits, if we start at zero and end with 700, we can't be sure whether the bike went forward 700 miles or backward 300 miles! The easiest solution to this dilemma is simply to cut the number space in half and use 001–500 for positive miles and 501–999 for negative miles. We have, effectively, cut down the distance our odometer can measure. But now if it reads 997, we know the bike has backed up 3 miles instead of riding forward 997 miles. The numbers 501–999 represent the **radix complements** (the second of the two methods introduced below) of the numbers 001–500 and are being used to represent negative distance.

One's Complement

As illustrated above, the diminished radix complement of a number in base 10 is found by subtracting the subtrahend from the base minus one, which is 9 in decimal. More formally, given a number N in base r having d digits, the diminished radix complement of N is defined to be $(r^d - 1) - N$. For decimal numbers, $r = 10$, and the diminished radix is $10 - 1 = 9$. For example, the nine's complement of 2468 is $9999 - 2468 = 7531$. For an equivalent operation in binary, we subtract from one less the base (2), which is 1. For example, the one's complement of 0101_2 is $1111_2 - 0101 = 1010$. Although we could tediously borrow and subtract as discussed above, a few experiments will convince you that forming the one's complement of a binary number amounts to nothing more than switching all of the 1s with 0s and vice versa. This sort of bit-flipping is very simple to implement in computer hardware.

It is important to note at this point that although we can find the nine's complement of any decimal number or the one's complement of any binary number, we are most interested in using complement notation to represent negative numbers. We know that performing a subtraction, such as $10 - 7$, can also be thought of as "adding the opposite," as in $10 + (-7)$. Complement notation allows us to simplify subtraction by turning it into addition, but it also gives us a method to represent negative numbers. Because we do not wish to use a special bit to represent the sign (as we did in signed-magnitude representation), we need to remember that if a number is negative, we should convert it to its complement. The result should have a 1 in the leftmost bit position to indicate that the number is negative.

Although the one's complement of a number is technically the value obtained by subtracting that number from a large power of two, we often refer to a computer using one's complement for negative numbers as a one's complement system, or a computer that uses one's complement arithmetic. This can be somewhat misleading, as positive numbers do not need to be complemented; we only complement negative numbers so we can get them into a format the computer will understand. Example 2.16 illustrates these concepts.

EXAMPLE 2.16 Express 23_{10} and -9_{10} in 8-bit binary, assuming a computer is using one's complement representation.

$$23_{10} = + (00010111_2) = 00010111_2$$
$$-9_{10} = -(00001001_2) = 11110110_2$$

Unlike signed magnitude, in one's complement addition there is no need to maintain the sign bit separate from the other bits. The sign takes care of itself. Compare Example 2.17 with Example 2.10.

EXAMPLE 2.17 Add 01001111_2 to 00100011_2 using one's complement addition.

```
          1 1 1 1      ⇐ carries
    0 1 0 0 1 1 1 1        (79)
  + 0 0 1 0 0 0 1 1      + (35)
    0 1 1 1 0 0 1 0       (114)
```

Suppose we wish to subtract 9 from 23. To carry out a one's complement subtraction, we first express the subtrahend (9) in one's complement, then add it to the minuend (23); we are effectively now adding −9 to 23. The high-order bit will have a 1 or a 0 carry, which is added to the low-order bit of the sum. (This is called **end carry-around** and results from using the diminished radix complement.)

EXAMPLE 2.18 Add 23_{10} to -9_{10} using one's complement arithmetic.

```
      1 ← 1 1 1    1 1      ⇐ carries
        0 0 0 1 0 1 1 1        (23)
      + 1 1 1 1 0 1 1 0      + (−9)
        0 0 0 0 1 1 0 1
                      + 1
        0 0 0 0 1 1 1 0       14₁₀
```

The last carry is added to the sum.

≡ **EXAMPLE 2.19** Add 9_{10} to -23_{10} using one's complement arithmetic.

The last	$0 \leftarrow 0\ 0\ 0\ 0\ 1\ 0\ 0\ 1$	(9)
carry is zero	$+\ 1\ 1\ 1\ 0\ 1\ 0\ 0\ 0$	$+\ (-23)$
so we are done.	$1\ 1\ 1\ 1\ 0\ 0\ 0\ 1$	-14_{10}

How do we know that 11110001_2 is actually -14_{10}? We simply need to take the one's complement of this binary number (remembering it must be negative because the leftmost bit is negative). The one's complement of 11110001_2 is 00001110_2, which is 14.

The primary disadvantage of one's complement is that we still have two representations for zero: 00000000 and 11111111. For this and other reasons, computer engineers long ago stopped using one's complement in favor of the more efficient two's complement representation for binary numbers.

Two's Complement

Two's complement is an example of a radix complement. Given a number N in base r having d digits, the radix complement of N is defined as $r^d - N$ for $N \neq 0$ and 0 for $N = 0$. The radix complement is often more intuitive than the diminished radix complement. Using our odometer example, the ten's complement of going forward 2 miles is $10^3 - 2 = 998$, which we have already agreed indicates a negative (backward) distance. Similarly, in binary, the two's complement of the 4-bit number 0011_2 is $2^4 - 0011_2 = 10000_2 - 0011_2 = 1101_2$.

Upon closer examination, you will discover that two's complement is nothing more than one's complement incremented by 1. To find the two's complement of a binary number, simply flip bits and add 1. This simplifies addition and subtraction as well. Because the subtrahend (the number we complement and add) is incremented at the outset, however, there is no end carry-around to worry about. We simply discard any carries involving the high-order bits. Just as with one's complement, two's complement refers to the complement of a number, whereas a computer using this notation to represent negative numbers is said to be a two's complement system, or uses two's complement arithmetic. As before, positive numbers can be left alone; we only need to complement negative numbers to get them into their two's complement form. Example 2.20 illustrates these concepts.

≡ **EXAMPLE 2.20** Express 23_{10}, -23_{10}, and -9_{10} in 8-bit binary, assuming a computer is using two's complement representation.

$$23_{10} = +\ (00010111_2) = 00010111_2$$
$$-23_{10} = -\ (00010111_2) = 11101000_2 + 1 = 11101001_2$$
$$-9_{10} = -\ (00001001_2) = 11110110_2 + 1 = 11110111_2$$

Because the representation of positive numbers is the same in one's complement and two's complement (as well as signed-magnitude), the process of adding two positive binary numbers is the same. Compare Example 2.21 with Example 2.17 and Example 2.10.

≡   **EXAMPLE 2.21**   Add 01001111_2 to 00100011_2 using two's complement addition.

$$
\begin{array}{r}
1\ 1\ 1\ 1 \quad \Leftarrow \text{carries} \\
0\ 1\ 0\ 0\ 1\ 1\ 1\ 1 \qquad (79) \\
\underline{0\ 0\ 1\ 0\ 0\ 0\ 1\ 1} \qquad +\ (35) \\
+\ 0\ 1\ 1\ 1\ 0\ 0\ 10 \qquad (114)
\end{array}
$$

Suppose we are given the binary representation for a number and want to know its decimal equivalent. Positive numbers are easy. For example, to convert the two's complement value of 00010111_2 to decimal, we simply convert this binary number to a decimal number to get 23. However, converting two's complement negative numbers requires a reverse procedure similar to the conversion from decimal to binary. Suppose we are given the two's complement binary value of 11110111_2, and we want to know the decimal equivalent. We know this is a negative number but must remember it is represented using two's complement. We first flip the bits and then add 1 (find the one's complement and add 1). This results in the following: $00001000_2 + 1 = 00001001_2$. This is equivalent to the decimal value 9. However, the original number we started with was negative, so we end up with -9 as the decimal equivalent to 11110111_2.

The following two examples illustrate how to perform addition (and hence subtraction, because we subtract a number by adding its opposite) using two's complement notation.

≡   **EXAMPLE 2.22**   Add 9_{10} to -23_{10} using two's complement arithmetic.

$$
\begin{array}{r}
0\ 0\ 0\ 0\ 1\ 0\ 0\ 1 \qquad (9) \\
+\ \underline{1\ 1\ 1\ 0\ 1\ 0\ 0\ 1} \qquad +\ (-23) \\
1\ 1\ 1\ 1\ 0\ 0\ 1\ 0 \qquad -14_{10}
\end{array}
$$

It is left as an exercise for you to verify that 11110010_2 is actually -14_{10} using two's complement notation.

≡   **EXAMPLE 2.23**   Find the sum of 23_{10} and -9_{10} in binary using two's complement arithmetic.

$$
\begin{array}{r}
1\leftarrow 1\ 1\ 1 \quad\ 1\ 1\ 1 \quad \Leftarrow \text{carries} \\
\text{Discard} \qquad 0\ 0\ 0\ 1\ 0\ 1\ 1\ 1 \qquad (23) \\
\text{carry.} \qquad +\ \underline{1\ 1\ 1\ 1\ 0\ 1\ 1\ 1} \qquad +\ (-9) \\
0\ 0\ 0\ 0\ 1\ 1\ 1\ 0 \qquad 14_{10}
\end{array}
$$

In two's complement, the addition of two negative numbers produces a negative number, as we might expect.

≡   **EXAMPLE 2.24**   Find the sum of 11101001_2 (-23) and 11110111_2 (-9) using two's complement addition.

$$
\begin{array}{rll}
 & 1 \leftarrow 1\ 1\ 1\ 1\ 1\ 1\ 1 & \Leftarrow \text{carries} \\
\text{Discard} & \quad 1\ 1\ 1\ 0\ 1\ 0\ 0\ 1 & (-23) \\
\text{carry.} & +\ 1\ 1\ 1\ 1\ 0\ 1\ 1\ 1 & +\ (-9) \\
\hline
 & \quad 1\ 1\ 1\ 0\ 0\ 0\ 0\ 0 & (-32)
\end{array}
$$

Notice that the discarded carries in Examples 2.23 and 2.24 did not cause an erroneous result. An overflow occurs if two positive numbers are added and the result is negative, or if two negative numbers are added and the result is positive. It is not possible to have overflow when using two's complement notation if a positive and a negative number are being added together.

INTEGER MULTIPLICATION AND DIVISION

Unless sophisticated algorithms are used, multiplication and division can consume a considerable number of computation cycles before a result is obtained. Here, we discuss only the most straightforward approach to these operations. In real systems, dedicated hardware is used to optimize throughput, sometimes carrying out portions of the calculation in parallel. Curious readers will want to investigate some of these advanced methods in the references cited at the end of this chapter.

The simplest multiplication algorithms used by computers are similar to traditional pencil-and-paper methods used by humans. The complete multiplication table for binary numbers couldn't be simpler: zero times any number is zero, and one times any number is that number.

To illustrate simple computer multiplication, we begin by writing the multiplicand and the multiplier to two separate storage areas. We also need a third storage area for the product. Starting with the low-order bit, a pointer is set to each digit of the multiplier. For each digit in the multiplier, the multiplicand is "shifted" one bit to the left. When the multiplier is 1, the "shifted" multiplicand is added to a running sum of partial products. Because we shift the multiplicand by one bit for each bit in the multiplier, a product requires double the working space of either the multiplicand or the multiplier.

There are two simple approaches to binary division: We can either iteratively subtract the denominator from the divisor, or we can use the same trial-and-error method of long division that we were taught in grade school. As with multiplication, the most efficient methods used for binary division are beyond the scope of this text and can be found in the references at the end of this chapter.

Regardless of the relative efficiency of any algorithms that are used, division is an operation that can always cause a computer to crash. This is the

Simple computer circuits can easily detect an overflow condition using a rule that is easy to remember. You'll notice in both Examples 2.23 and 2.24 that the carry going into the sign bit (a 1 is carried from the previous bit position into the sign bit position) is the same as the carry going out of the sign bit (a 1 is carried out and discarded). When these carries are equal, no overflow occurs. When they differ, an overflow indicator is set in the arithmetic logic unit, indicating the result is incorrect.

A Simple Rule for Detecting an Overflow Condition in Signed Numbers: *If the carry into the sign bit equals the carry out of the bit, no overflow has occurred. If the carry into the sign bit is different from the carry out of the sign bit, overflow (and thus an error) has occurred.*

The hard part is getting programmers (or compilers) to consistently check for the overflow condition. Example 2.25 indicates overflow because the carry into the sign bit (a 1 is carried in) is not equal to the carry out of the sign bit (a 0 is carried out).

case particularly when division by zero is attempted or when two numbers of enormously different magnitudes are used as operands. When the divisor is much smaller than the dividend, we get a condition known as **divide underflow**, which the computer sees as the equivalent of division by zero, which is impossible.

Computers make a distinction between integer division and floating-point division. With integer division, the answer comes in two parts: a quotient and a remainder. Floating-point division results in a number that is expressed as a binary fraction. These two types of division are sufficiently different from each other as to warrant giving each its own special circuitry. Floating-point calculations are carried out in dedicated circuits called **floating-point units**, or **FPUs**.

EXAMPLE   Find the product of 00000110_2 and 00001011_2.

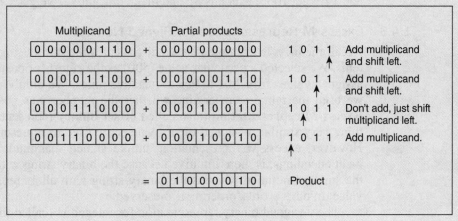

≡   **EXAMPLE 2.25**   Find the sum of 126_{10} and 8_{10} in binary using two's complement arithmetic.

$$
\begin{array}{rll}
0\leftarrow\ 1\ \ 1\ \ 1\ \ 1 & & \Leftarrow \text{carries} \\
\text{Discard last} \quad\quad 0\ 1\ 1\ 1\ 1\ 1\ 1\ 0 & & (126) \\
\text{carry.} \quad\quad\quad\ + \underline{0\ 0\ 0\ 0\ 1\ 0\ 0\ 0} & & \underline{+(8)} \\
1\ 0\ 0\ 0\ 0\ 1\ 1\ 0 & & (-122???)
\end{array}
$$

A one is carried into the leftmost bit, but a zero is carried out. Because these carries are not equal, an overflow has occurred. (We can easily see that two positive numbers are being added but the result is negative.) We return to this topic in Section 2.4.6.

Two's complement is the most popular choice for representing signed numbers. The algorithm for adding and subtracting is quite easy, has the best representation for 0 (all 0 bits), is self-inverting, and is easily extended to larger numbers of bits. The biggest drawback is in the asymmetry seen in the range of values that can be represented by N bits. With signed-magnitude numbers, for example, 4 bits allow us to represent the values -7 through $+7$. However, using two's complement, we can represent the values -8 through $+7$, which is often confusing to anyone learning about complement representations. To see why $+7$ is the largest number we can represent using 4-bit two's complement representation, we need only remember that the first bit must be 0. If the remaining bits are all 1s (giving us the largest magnitude possible), we have 0111_2, which is 7. An immediate reaction to this is that the smallest negative number should then be 1111_2, but we can see that 1111_2 is actually -1 (flip the bits, add one, and make the number negative). So how do we represent -8 in two's complement notation using 4 bits? It is represented as 1000_2. We know this is a negative number. If we flip the bits (0111), add 1 (to get 1000, which is 8), and make it negative, we get -8.

2.4.3   Excess-M Representation for Signed Numbers

Recall the bicycle example that we discussed when introducing complement systems. We selected a particular value (500) as the cutoff for positive miles, and we assigned values from 501 to 999 to negative miles. We didn't need signs because we used the range to determine whether the number was positive or negative. **Excess-M representation** (also called **offset binary** representation) does something very similar; unsigned binary values are used to represent signed integers. However, excess-M representation, unlike signed magnitude and the complement encodings, is more intuitive because the binary string with all 0s represents the smallest number, whereas the binary string with all 1s represents the largest value; in other words, ordering is preserved.

The unsigned binary representation for integer M (called the **bias**) represents the value 0, whereas all zeros in the bit pattern represents the integer $-M$. Essentially, a decimal integer is "mapped" (as in our bicycle example) to an unsigned binary integer, but interpreted as positive or negative depending on where it falls in the range. If we are using n bits for the binary representation, we need to select the bias in such a manner that we split the range equally. We typically do this by choosing a bias of $2^{n-1} - 1$. For example, if we were using 4-bit representation, the bias should be $2^{4-1} - 1 = 7$. Just as with signed magnitude, one's complement, and two's complement, there is a specific range of values that can be expressed in n bits.

The unsigned binary value for a signed integer using excess-M representation is determined simply by adding M to that integer. For example, assuming that we are using excess-7 representation, the integer 0_{10} would be represented as $0 + 7 = 7_{10} = 0111_2$; the integer 3_{10} would be represented as $3 + 7 = 10_{10} = 1010_2$; and the integer -7 would be represented as $-7 + 7 = 0_{10} = 0000_2$. Using excess-7 notation and given the binary number 1111_2, to find the decimal value it represents, we simply subtract 7: $1111_2 = 15_{10}$, and $15 - 7 = 8$; therefore, the value 1111_2, using excess-7 representation, is $+8_{10}$.

Let's compare the encoding schemes we have seen so far, assuming 8-bit numbers:

Integer		Binary Strings Representing the Signed Integer			
Decimal	Binary (for absolute value)	Signed Magnitude	One's Complement	Two's Complement	Excess-127
2	00000010	00000010	00000010	00000010	10000001
−2	00000010	10000010	11111101	11111110	01111101
100	01100100	01100100	01100100	01100100	11100011
−100	01100100	11100100	10011011	10011100	00011011

Excess-M representation allows us to use unsigned binary values to represent signed integers; it is important to note, however, that two parameters must be specified: the number of bits being used in the representation and the bias value itself. In addition, a computer is unable to perform addition on excess-M values using hardware designed for unsigned numbers; special circuits are required. Excess-M representation is important because of its use in representing integer exponents in floating-point numbers, as we will see in Section 2.5.

2.4.4 Unsigned Versus Signed Numbers

We introduced our discussion of binary integers with unsigned numbers. Unsigned numbers are used to represent values that are guaranteed not to be negative. A good example of an unsigned number is a memory address. If the 4-bit binary value 1101 is unsigned, then it represents the decimal value 13, but as a signed two's complement number, it represents −3. Signed numbers are used to represent data that can be either positive or negative.

A computer programmer must be able to manage both signed and unsigned numbers. To do so, the programmer must first identify numeric values as either signed or unsigned numbers. This is done by declaring the value as a specific type.

For instance, the C programming language has `int` and `unsigned int` as possible types for integer variables, defining signed and unsigned integers, respectively. In addition to different type declarations, many languages have different arithmetic operations for use with signed and unsigned numbers. A language may have one subtraction instruction for signed numbers and a different subtraction instruction for unsigned numbers. In most assembly languages, programmers can choose from a signed comparison operator or an unsigned comparison operator.

It is interesting to compare what happens with unsigned and signed numbers when we try to store values that are too large for the specified number of bits. Unsigned numbers simply wrap around and start over at zero. For example, if we are using 4-bit unsigned binary numbers, and we add 1 to 1111, we get 0000. This "return to zero" wraparound is familiar—perhaps you have seen a high-mileage car in which the odometer has wrapped back around to zero. However, signed numbers devote half their space to positive numbers and the other half to negative numbers. If we add 1 to the largest positive 4-bit two's complement number 0111 (+7), we get 1000 (−8). This wraparound with the unexpected change in sign has been problematic to inexperienced programmers, resulting in multiple hours of debugging time. Good programmers understand this condition and make appropriate plans to deal with the situation before it occurs.

2.4.5 Computers, Arithmetic, and Booth's Algorithm

Computer arithmetic as introduced in this chapter may seem simple and straightforward, but it is a field of major study in computer architecture. The basic focus is on the implementation of arithmetic functions, which can be realized in software, firmware, or hardware. Researchers in this area are working toward designing superior central processing units (CPUs), developing high-performance arithmetic circuits, and contributing to the area of embedded systems application-specific circuits. They are working on algorithms and new hardware implementations for fast addition, subtraction, multiplication, and division, as well as fast floating-point operations. Researchers are looking for schemes that use nontraditional approaches, such as the **fast carry look-ahead** principle, **residue arithmetic**, and **Booth's algorithm**. Booth's algorithm is a good example of one such scheme and is introduced here in the context of signed two's complement numbers to give you an idea of how a simple arithmetic operation can be enhanced by a clever algorithm.

Although Booth's algorithm usually yields a performance increase when multiplying two's complement numbers, there is another motivation for introducing this algorithm. In Section 2.4.2, we covered examples of two's complement addition and saw that the numbers could be treated as unsigned values. We simply perform "regular" addition, as the following example illustrates:

$$
\begin{array}{rl}
1001 & (-7) \\
+\ \ 0011 & (+3) \\
\hline
1100 & (-4)
\end{array}
$$

The same is true for two's complement subtraction. However, now consider the standard pencil-and-paper method for multiplying the following two's complement numbers:

$$
\begin{array}{r}
1011 \quad (-5) \\
\times \; 1100 \quad (-4) \\
\hline
0000 \\
0000 \\
1011 \\
1011 \\
\hline
10000100 \quad (-124)
\end{array}
$$

"Regular" multiplication clearly yields the incorrect result. There are a number of solutions to this problem, such as converting both values to positive numbers, performing conventional multiplication, and then remembering if one or both values were negative to determine whether the result should be positive or negative. Booth's algorithm not only solves this dilemma, but also speeds up multiplication in the process.

The general idea of Booth's algorithm is to increase the speed of a multiplication when there are consecutive zeros or ones in the multiplier. It is easy to see that consecutive zeros help performance. For example, if we use the tried and true pencil-and-paper method and find 978×1001, the multiplication is much easier than if we take 978×999. This is because of the two zeros found in 1001. However, if we rewrite the two problems as follows:

$$978 \times 1001 = 978 \times (1000 + 1) = 978 \times 1000 + 978$$
$$978 \times 999 = 978 \times (1000 - 1) = 978 \times 1000 - 978$$

we see that the problems are in fact equal in difficulty.

Our goal is to use a string of ones in a binary number to our advantage in much the same way that we use a string of zeros to our advantage. We can use the rewriting idea from above. For example, the binary number 0110 can be rewritten $1000 - 0010 = -0010 + 1000$. The two ones have been replaced by a "subtract" (determined by the rightmost 1 in the string) followed by an "add" (determined by moving one position left of the leftmost 1 in the string).

Consider the following standard multiplication example:

$$
\begin{array}{r}
0011 \\
\times \; 0110 \\
\hline
+ \; 0000 \\
+ \; 0011 \\
+ \; 0011 \\
+ \; 0000 \\
\hline
00010010
\end{array}
$$

+ 0000	(0 in multiplier means simple shift)
+ 0011	(1 in multiplier means add multiplicand and shift)
+ 0011	(1 in multiplier means add multiplicand and shift)
+ 0000	(0 in multiplier means simple shift)

The idea of Booth's algorithm is to replace the string of ones in the multiplier with an initial subtract when we see the rightmost 1 of the string (or subtract

0011) and then later add for the bit after the last 1 (or add 001100). In the middle of the string, we can now use simple shifting:

```
        0011
    ×  0110
    +  0000     (0 in multiplier means shift)
    −  0011     (first 1 in multiplier means subtract multiplicand and shift)
    +  0000     (middle of string of 1s means shift)
    +  0011     (prior step had last 1 so add multiplicand)
      00010010
```

In Booth's algorithm, if the multiplicand and multiplier are n-bit two's complement numbers, the result is a $2n$-bit two's complement value. Therefore, when we perform our intermediate steps, we must extend our n-bit numbers to $2n$-bit numbers. If a number is negative and we extend it, we must extend the sign. For example, the value 1000 (-8) extended to 8 bits would be 11111000. We continue to work with bits in the multiplier, **shifting each time we complete a step**. However, we are interested in *pairs* of bits in the multiplier and proceed according to the following rules:

1. If the current multiplier bit is 1 and the preceding bit was 0, we are at the beginning of a string of ones, so subtract the multiplicand from the product (or add the opposite).

2. If the current multiplier bit is 0 and the preceding bit was 1, we are at the end of a string of ones, so add the multiplicand to the product.

3. If it is a 00 pair, or a 11 pair, do no arithmetic operation (we are in the middle of a string of zeros or a string of ones). Simply shift. The power of the algorithm is in this step: We can now treat a string of ones as a string of zeros and do nothing more than shift.

Note: The first time we pick a pair of bits in the multiplier, we should assume a mythical 0 as the "previous" bit. Then we simply move left one bit for our next pair.

Example 2.26 illustrates the use of Booth's algorithm to multiply -3×5 using signed 4-bit two's complement numbers.

EXAMPLE 2.26   Negative 3 in 4-bit two's complement is 1101. Extended to 8 bits, it is 11111101. Its complement is 00000011. When we see the rightmost 1 in the multiplier, it is the beginning of a string of 1s, so we treat it as if it were the string 10:

```
           1101     (for subtracting, we will add −3's complement, or 00000011)
        ×  0101
     +00000011      (10 = subtract 1101 = add 00000011)
     +11111101      (01 = add 11111101 to product—note sign extension)
     +00000011      (10 = subtract 1101 = add 00000011)
     +11111101      (01 = add multiplicand 11111101 to product)
     100111110001   (using the 8 rightmost bits, we have −3 × 5 = −15)
        ⌣
```

Ignore extended sign bits that go beyond $2n$.

≡ **EXAMPLE 2.27** Let's look at the larger example of 53 × 126:

00110101	(for subtracting, we will add the complement of 53, or
× 01111110	11001011)
+000000000000000	(00 = simple shift)
+111111111001011	(10 = subtract = add 11001011, extend sign)
+00000000000000	(11 = simple shift)
+0000000000000	(11 = simple shift)
+000000000000	(11 = simple shift)
+00000000000	(11 = simple shift)
+0000000000	(11 = simple shift)
+000110101	(01 = add)
10001101000010110	(53 × 126 = 6678)

Note that we have not shown the extended sign bits that go beyond what we need and use only the 16 rightmost bits. The entire string of ones in the multiplier was replaced by a subtract (adding 11001011) followed by an add. Everything in the middle is simply shifting—something that is very easy for a computer to do (as we will see in Chapter 3). If the time required for a computer to do an add is sufficiently larger than that required to do a shift, Booth's algorithm can provide a considerable increase in performance. This depends somewhat, of course, on the multiplier. If the multiplier has strings of zeros and/or ones, the algorithm works well. If the multiplier consists of an alternating string of zeros and ones (the worst case), using Booth's algorithm might very well require more operations than the standard approach.

Computers perform Booth's algorithm by adding and shifting values stored in registers. A special type of shift called an **arithmetic shift** is necessary to preserve the sign bit. Many books present Booth's algorithm in terms of arithmetic shifts and add operations on registers only, and may appear quite different from the preceding method. We have presented Booth's algorithm so that it more closely resembles the pencil-and-paper method with which we are all familiar, although it is equivalent to the computer algorithms presented elsewhere.

There have been many algorithms developed for fast multiplication, but many do not hold for signed multiplication. Booth's algorithm not only allows multiplication to be performed faster in most cases, but it also has the added bonus in that it works correctly on signed numbers.

2.4.6 Carry Versus Overflow

The wraparound referred to in the preceding section is really overflow. CPUs often have flags to indicate both carry and overflow. However, the overflow flag is used only with signed numbers and means nothing in the context of unsigned numbers, which use the carry flag instead. If carry (which means *carry out of the leftmost bit*) occurs in unsigned numbers, we know we have overflow (the new value is too large to be stored in the given number of bits) but the overflow bit is not set. Carry out can occur in signed numbers as well; however, its occurrence in signed numbers is neither sufficient nor necessary for overflow. We have already seen that overflow in signed numbers can be determined if the

Expression	Result	Carry?	Overflow?	Correct Result?
0100(+4)+0010(+2)	0110(+6)	No	No	Yes
0100(+4)+0110(+6)	1010(-6)	No	Yes	No
1100(-4)+1110(-2)	1010(-6)	Yes	No	Yes
1100(-4)+1010(-6)	0110(+6)	Yes	Yes	No

TABLE 2.2   Examples of Carry and Overflow in Signed Numbers

carry in to the leftmost bit and the carry out of the leftmost bit differ. However, carry out of the leftmost bit in unsigned operations always indicates overflow.

To illustrate these concepts, consider 4-bit unsigned and signed numbers. If we add the two unsigned values 0111 (7) and 0001 (1), we get 1000 (8). There is no carry (out), and thus no error. However, if we add the two unsigned values 0111 (7) and 1011 (11), we get 0010 with a carry, indicating that there is an error (indeed, 7 + 11 is not 2). This wraparound would cause the carry flag in the CPU to be set. Essentially, carry out in the context of unsigned numbers means an overflow has occurred, even though the overflow flag is not set.

We said carry (out) is neither sufficient nor necessary for overflow in signed numbers. Consider adding the two's complement integers 0101 (+5) and 0011 (+3). The result is 1000 (−8), which is clearly incorrect. The problem is that we have a carry in to the sign bit, but no carry out, which indicates that we have an overflow (therefore, carry is not necessary for overflow). However, if we now add 0111 (+7) and 1011 (−5), we get the correct result: 0010 (+2). We have both a carry in to and a carry out of the leftmost bit, so there is no error (so carry is not sufficient for overflow). The carry flag would be set, but the overflow flag would not be set. Thus carry out does not necessarily indicate an error in signed numbers, nor does the lack of carry out indicate that the answer is correct.

To summarize, the rule of thumb used to determine when carry indicates an error depends on whether we are using signed or unsigned numbers. For unsigned numbers, a carry (out of the leftmost bit) indicates the total number of bits was not large enough to hold the resulting value, and overflow has occurred. For signed numbers, if the carry in to the sign bit and the carry (out of the sign bit) differ, then overflow has occurred. The overflow flag is set only when overflow occurs with signed numbers.

Carry and overflow clearly occur independently of each other. Examples using signed two's complement representation are given in Table 2.2. Carry in to the sign bit is not indicated in the table.

2.4.7   Binary Multiplication and Division Using Shifting

Shifting a binary number simply means moving the bits left or right by a certain amount. For example, the binary value 00001111 shifted left one place results in 00011110 (if we fill with a zero on the right). The first number is equivalent to decimal value 15; the second is decimal 30, which is exactly double the first value. This is no coincidence!

When working with signed two's complement numbers, we can use a special type of shift, called an arithmetic shift, to perform quick and easy multiplication and division by 2. Recall that the leftmost bit in a two's complement number determines its sign, so we must be careful when shifting these values that we don't change the sign bit, as multiplying or dividing by 2 should not change the sign of the number.

We can perform a left arithmetic shift (which multiples a number by 2) or a right arithmetic shift (which divides a number by 2). Assuming that bits are numbered right to left beginning with zero, we have the following definitions for left and right arithmetic shifts.

A **left arithmetic shift** inserts a 0 in for bit b_0, and shifts all other bits left one position, resulting in bit b_{n-1} being replaced by bit b_{n-2}. Because bit b_{n-1} is the sign bit, if the value in this bit changes, the operation has caused overflow. Multiplication by 2 always results in a binary number with the rightmost bit equal to 0, which is an even number, and thus explains why we pad with a zero on the right. Consider the following examples:

≡ **EXAMPLE 2.28** Multiply the value 11 (expressed using 8-bit signed two's complement representation) by 2.

We start with the binary value for 11:

00001011

and we shift left one place, resulting in:

00010110

which is decimal 2 = 11 × 2. No overflow has occurred, so the value is correct.

≡ **EXAMPLE 2.29** Multiply the value 12 (expressed using 8-bit signed two's complement representation) by 4.

We start with the binary value for 12:

00001100

and we shift left two places (each shift multiplies by 2, so two shifts is equivalent to multiplying by 4), resulting in:

00110000

which is decimal 48 = 12 × 4. No overflow has occurred, so the value is correct.

≡ **EXAMPLE 2.30** Multiply the value 66 (expressed using 8-bit signed two's complement representation) by 2.

We start with the binary value for 66:

01000010

and we shift left one place, resulting in:

10000100

but the sign bit has changed, so overflow has occurred (66 × 2 = 132, which is too large to be expressed using 8 bits in signed two's complement notation).

A **right arithmetic shift** moves all bits to the right, but carries (copies) the sign bit from bit b_{n-1} to b_{n-2}. Because we copy the sign bit from right to left, overflow is not a problem. However, division by 2 may have a remainder of 1; division using this method is strictly integer division, so the remainder is not stored in any way. Consider the following examples:

≡ **EXAMPLE 2.31** Divide the value 12 (expressed using 8-bit signed two's complement representation) by 2.
We start with the binary value for 12:

00001100

and we shift right one place, copying the sign bit of 0, resulting in:

00000110

which is decimal 6 = 12 ÷ 2.

≡ **EXAMPLE 2.32** Divide the value 12 (expressed using 8-bit signed two's complement representation) by 4.
We start with the binary value for 12:

00001100

and we shift right two places, resulting in:

00000011

which is decimal 3 = 12 ÷ 4.

≡ **EXAMPLE 2.33** Divide the value −14 (expressed using 8-bit signed two's complement representation) by 2.
We start with the two's complement representation for −14:

11110010

and we shift right one place (carrying across the sign bit), resulting in:

11111001

which is decimal −7 = −14 ÷ 2.

Note that if we had divided −15 by 2 (in Example 2.33), the result would be 11110001 shifted one to the left to yield 11111000, which is −8. Because we are doing integer division, −15 divided by 2 is indeed equal to −8.

2.5 FLOATING-POINT REPRESENTATION

If we wanted to build a real computer, we could use any of the integer representations that we just studied. We would pick one of them and proceed with our design tasks. Our next step would be to decide the word size of our system. If we want our system to be really inexpensive, we would pick a small word size, say, 16 bits. Allowing for the sign bit, the largest integer this system could store is 32,767. So now what do we do to accommodate a potential customer who wants to keep a tally of the number of spectators paying admission to professional sports events in a given year? Certainly, the number is larger than 32,767. No problem. Let's just make the word size larger. Thirty-two bits ought to do it. Our word is now big enough for just about anything that anyone wants to count. But what if this customer also needs to know the amount of money each spectator spends per minute of playing time? This number is likely to be a decimal fraction. Now we're really stuck.

The easiest and cheapest approach to this problem is to keep our 16-bit system and say, "Hey, we're building a cheap system here. If you want to do fancy things with it, get yourself a good programmer." Although this position sounds outrageously flippant in the context of today's technology, it was a reality in the earliest days of each generation of computers. There simply was no such thing as a floating-point unit in many of the first mainframes or microcomputers. For many years, clever programming enabled these integer systems to act as if they were, in fact, floating-point systems.

If you are familiar with scientific notation, you may already be thinking of how you could handle floating-point operations—how you could provide **floating-point emulation**—in an integer system. In scientific notation, numbers are expressed in two parts: a fractional part and an exponential part that indicates the power of ten to which the fractional part should be raised to obtain the value we need. So to express 32,767 in scientific notation, we could write 3.2767×10^4. Scientific notation simplifies pencil-and-paper calculations that involve very large or very small numbers. It is also the basis for floating-point computation in today's digital computers.

2.5.1 A Simple Model

In digital computers, floating-point numbers consist of three parts: a sign bit, an exponent part (representing the exponent on a power of 2), and a fractional part (which has sparked considerable debate regarding appropriate terminology). The term **mantissa** is widely accepted when referring to this fractional part. However, many people take exception to this term because it also denotes the fractional part of a logarithm, which is not the same as the fractional part of a floating-point number. The Institute of Electrical and Electronics Engineers (IEEE) introduced the term **significand** to refer to the fractional part of a floating-point number combined with the implied binary point and implied 1 (which we discuss at the end of this section). Regrettably, the two terms *mantissa* and *significand* have become interchangeable when referring to the fractional part of a floating-point number, even though they are not technically equivalent. Throughout this text, we refer to the fractional part as the significand, regardless of whether it includes the implied 1 as intended by IEEE.

The number of bits used for the exponent and significand depends on whether we would like to optimize for range (more bits in the exponent) or precision

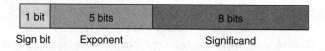

1 bit	5 bits	8 bits
Sign bit	Exponent	Significand

FIGURE 2.1   Simple Model Floating-Point Representation

(more bits in the significand). (We discuss range and precision in more detail in Section 2.5.7.) For the remainder of this section, we will use a 14-bit model with a 5-bit exponent, an 8-bit significand, and a sign bit (see Figure 2.1). More general forms are described in Section 2.5.2.

Let's say that we wish to store the decimal number 17 in our model. We know that $17 = 17.0 \times 10^0 = 1.7 \times 10^1 = 0.17 \times 10^2$. Analogously, in binary, $17_{10} = 10001_2 \times 2^0 = 1000.1_2 \times 2^1 = 100.01_2 \times 2^2 = 10.001_2 \times 2^3 = 1.0001_2 \times 2^4 = 0.10001_2 \times 2^5$. If we use this last form, our fractional part will be 10001000 and our exponent will be 00101, as shown here:

0	0 0 1 0 1	1 0 0 0 1 0 0 0

Using this form, we can store numbers of much greater magnitude than we could using a **fixed-point** representation of 14 bits (which uses a total of 14 binary digits plus a binary, or radix, point). If we want to represent $65536 = 0.1_2 \times 2^{17}$ in this model, we have:

0	1 0 0 0 1	1 0 0 0 0 0 0 0

One obvious problem with this model is that we haven't provided for negative exponents. If we wanted to store 0.25, we would have no way of doing so because 0.25 is 2^{-2} and the exponent -2 cannot be represented. We could fix the problem by adding a sign bit to the exponent, but it turns out that it is more efficient to use a **biased** exponent, because we can use simpler integer circuits designed specifically for unsigned numbers when comparing the values of two floating-point numbers.

Recall from Section 2.4.3 that the idea behind using a bias value is to convert every integer in the range into a nonnegative integer, which is then stored as a binary numeral. The integers in the desired range of exponents are first adjusted by adding this fixed bias value to each exponent. The bias value is a number near the middle of the range of possible values that we select to represent zero. In this case, we would select 15 because it is midway between 0 and 31 (our exponent has 5 bits, thus allowing for 2^5 or 32 values). Any number larger than 15 in the exponent field represents a positive value. Values less than 15 indicate negative values. This is called an **excess-15** representation because we have to subtract 15 to get the true value of the exponent. Note that exponents of all zeros or all ones are typically reserved for special numbers (such as zero or infinity). In our simple model, we allow exponents of all zeros and ones.

Returning to our example of storing 17, we calculated $17_{10} = 0.10001_2 \times 2^5$. The biased exponent is now $15 + 5 = 20$:

0	1	0	1	0	0	1	0	0	0	1	0	0	0

If we wanted to store $0.25 = 0.1 \times 2^{-1}$, we would have:

0	0	1	1	1	0	1	0	0	0	0	0	0	0

There is still one rather large problem with this system: We do not have a unique representation for each number. All of the following are equivalent:

0	1	0	1	0	1	1	0	0	0	1	0	0	0	=

0	1	0	1	1	0	0	1	0	0	0	1	0	0	=

0	1	0	1	1	1	0	0	1	0	0	0	1	0	=

0	1	1	0	0	0	0	0	0	1	0	0	0	1

Because synonymous forms such as these are not well-suited for digital computers, floating-point numbers must be **normalized**—that is, the leftmost bit of the significand must always be 1. This process is called **normalization**. This convention has the additional advantage that if the 1 is implied, we effectively gain an extra bit of precision in the significand. Normalization works well for every value except zero, which contains no nonzero bits. For that reason, any model used to represent floating-point numbers must treat zero as a special case. We will see in the next section that the IEEE-754 floating-point standard makes an exception to the rule of normalization.

EXAMPLE 2.34 Express 0.03125_{10} in normalized floating-point form using the simple model with excess-15 bias.

$0.03125_{10} = 0.00001_2 \times 2^0 = 0.0001 \times 2^{-1} = 0.001 \times 2^{-2} = 0.01 \times 2^{-3} = 0.1 \times 2^{-4}$. Applying the bias, the exponent field is $15 - 4 = 11$.

0	0	1	0	1	1	1	0	0	0	0	0	0	0

Note that in our simple model we have not expressed the number using the normalization notation that implies the 1, which is introduced in Section 2.5.4.

2.5.2 Floating-Point Arithmetic

If we wanted to add two decimal numbers that are expressed in scientific notation, such as $1.5 \times 10^2 + 3.5 \times 10^3$, we would change one of the numbers so that both of them are expressed in the same power of the base. In our example, $1.5 \times 10^2 + 3.5 \times 10^3 = 0.15 \times 10^3 + 3.5 \times 10^3 = 3.65 \times 10^3$. Floating-point addition and subtraction work the same way, as illustrated below.

EXAMPLE 2.35 Add the following binary numbers as represented in a normalized 14-bit format, using the simple model with a bias of 15.

| 0 | 1 | 0 | 0 | 0 | 1 | 1 | 1 | 0 | 0 | 1 | 0 | 0 | 0 | + |

| 0 | 0 | 1 | 1 | 1 | 1 | 1 | 0 | 0 | 1 | 1 | 0 | 1 | 0 |

We see that the addend is raised to the second power and that the augend is to the zero power. Alignment of these two operands on the binary point gives us:

$$
\begin{array}{r}
11.001000 \\
+\ 0.10011010 \\
\hline
11.10111010
\end{array}
$$

Renormalizing, we retain the larger exponent and truncate the low-order bit. Thus, we have:

| 0 | 1 | 0 | 0 | 0 | 1 | 1 | 1 | 1 | 0 | 1 | 1 | 1 | 0 |

However, because our simple model requires a normalized significand, we have no way to represent zero. This is easily remedied by allowing the string of all zeros (a zero sign, a zero exponent, and a zero significand) to represent the value zero. In the next section, we will see that IEEE-754 also reserves special meaning for certain bit patterns.

Multiplication and division are carried out using the same rules of exponents applied to decimal arithmetic, such as $2^{-3} \times 2^4 = 2^1$, for example.

EXAMPLE 2.36 Assuming a 15-bit bias, multiply:

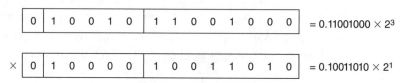

Multiplication of 0.11001000 by 0.10011010 yields a product of 0.0111100001010000, and then multiplying by $2^3 \times 2^1 = 2^4$ yields 111.10000101. Renormalizing and supplying the appropriate exponent, the floating-point product is:

0	1	0	0	1	0	1	1	1	1	0	0	0	0

2.5.3 Floating-Point Errors

When we use pencil and paper to solve a trigonometry problem or compute the interest on an investment, we intuitively understand that we are working in the system of real numbers. We know that this system is infinite, because given any pair of real numbers, we can always find another real number that is smaller than one and greater than the other.

Unlike the mathematics in our imaginations, computers are finite systems, with finite storage. When we call upon our computers to carry out floating-point calculations, we are modeling the infinite system of real numbers in a finite system of integers. What we have, in truth, is an *approximation* of the real number system. The more bits we use, the better the approximation. However, there is always some element of error, no matter how many bits we use.

Floating-point errors can be blatant, subtle, or unnoticed. The blatant errors, such as numeric overflow or underflow, are the ones that cause programs to crash. Subtle errors can lead to wildly erroneous results that are often hard to detect before they cause real problems. For example, in our simple model, we can express normalized numbers in the range of $-.11111111_2 \times 2^{16}$ through $+.11111111 \times 2^{16}$. Obviously, we cannot store 2^{-19} or 2^{128}; they simply don't fit. It is not quite so obvious that we cannot accurately store 128.5, which is well within our range. Converting 128.5 to binary, we have 10000000.1, which is 9 bits wide. Our significand can hold only eight. Typically, the low-order bit is dropped or rounded into the next bit. No matter how we handle it, however, we have introduced an error into our system.

We can compute the relative error in our representation by taking the ratio of the absolute value of the error to the true value of the number. Using our example of 128.5, we find:

$$\frac{128.5 - 128}{128.5} = 0.00389105 \approx 0.39\%.$$

If we are not careful, such errors can propagate through a lengthy calculation, causing substantial loss of precision. Table 2.3 illustrates the error propagation as we iteratively multiply 16.24 by 0.91 using our 14-bit simple model. Upon converting these numbers to 8-bit binary, we see that we have a substantial error from the outset.

As you can see, in six iterations, we have more than tripled the error in the product. Continued iterations will produce an error of 100% because the product eventually goes to zero. Although this 14-bit model is so small that it exaggerates

Multiplier		Multiplicand	14-Bit Product	Real Product	Error
10000.001 (16.125)	×	0.11101000 = (0.90625)	1110.1001 (14.5625)	14.7784	1.46%
1110.1001 (14.5625)	×	0.11101000 =	1101.0011 (13.1885)	13.4483	1.94%
1101.0011 (13.1885)	×	0.11101000 =	1011.1111 (11.9375)	12.2380	2.46%
1011.1111 (11.9375)	×	0.11101000 =	1010.1101 (10.8125)	11.1366	2.91%
1010.1101 (10.8125)	×	0.11101000 =	1001.1100 (9.75)	10.1343	3.79%
1001.1100 (9.75)	×	0.11101000 =	1000.1101 (8.8125)	8.3922	4.44%

TABLE 2.3 Error Propagation in a 14-Bit Floating-Point Number

the error, all floating-point systems behave the same way. There is always some degree of error involved when representing real numbers in a finite system, no matter how large we make that system. Even the smallest error can have cata-strophic results, particularly when computers are used to control physical events such as in military and medical applications. The challenge to computer scientists is to find efficient algorithms for controlling such errors within the bounds of per-formance and economics.

2.5.4   The IEEE-754 Floating-Point Standard

The floating-point model we have been using in this section is designed for simplic-ity and conceptual understanding. We could extend this model to include whatever number of bits we wanted. Until the 1980s, these kinds of decisions were purely arbitrary, resulting in numerous incompatible representations across various manu-facturers' systems. In 1985, the IEEE published a floating-point standard for both single- and double-precision floating-point numbers. This standard is officially known as IEEE-754 (1985) and includes two formats: **single precision** and **double precision**. The IEEE-754 standard not only defines binary floating-point represen-tations, but also specifies basic operations, exception conditions, conversions, and arithmetic. Another standard, IEEE 854-1987, provides similar specifications for decimal arithmetic. In 2008, IEEE revised the 754 standard, and it became known as IEEE 754-2008. It carried over the single and double precision from 754, and added support for decimal arithmetic and formats, superseding both 754 and 854. We discuss only the single and double representation for floating-point numbers.

The IEEE-754 single-precision standard uses an excess 127 bias over an 8-bit exponent. The significand assumes an implied 1 *to the left* of the radix point and

FIGURE 2.2 IEEE-754 Single-Precision Floating-Point Representation

is 23 bits. This implied 1 is referred to as the **hidden bit** or **hidden 1** and allows an actual significand of $23 + 1 = 24$ bits. With the sign bit included, the total word size is 32 bits, as shown in Figure 2.2.

We mentioned earlier that IEEE-754 makes an exception to the rule of normalization. Because this standard assumes an implied 1 to the left of the radix point, the leading bit in the significand can indeed be zero. For example, the number $5.5 = 101.1 = .1011 \times 2^3$. IEEE-754 assumes an implied 1 to the left of the radix point and thus represents 5.5 as 1.011×2^2. Because the 1 is implied, the significand is 011 and does not begin with a 1.

Table 2.4 shows the single-precision representation of several floating-point numbers, including some special ones. One should note that zero is not directly representable in the given format, because of a required hidden bit in the significand. Therefore, zero is a special value denoted using an exponent of all zeros and a significand of all zeros. IEEE-754 does allow for both -0 and $+0$, although they are equal values. For this reason, programmers should use caution when comparing a floating-point value to zero.

Floating-Point Number	Single-Precision Representation
1.0	0 01111111 00000000000000000000000
0.5	0 01111110 00000000000000000000000
19.5	0 10000011 00111000000000000000000
−3.75	1 10000000 11100000000000000000000
Zero	0 00000000 00000000000000000000000
± Infinity	0/1 11111111 00000000000000000000000
NaN	0/1 11111111 any nonzero significand
Denormalized Number	0/1 00000000 any nonzero significand

TABLE 2.4 Some Example IEEE-754 Single-Precision Floating-Point Numbers

When the exponent is 255, the quantity represented is ± infinity (which has a zero significand) or "not a number" (which has a nonzero significand). "Not a number," or NaN, is used to represent a value that is not a real number (such as the square root of a negative number) or as an error indicator (such as in a "division by zero" error).

Under the IEEE-754 standard, most numeric values are normalized and have an implicit leading 1 in their significands (that is assumed to be to the left of

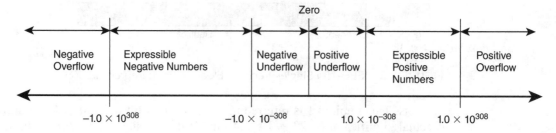

FIGURE 2.3   Range of IEEE-754 Double-Precision Numbers

the radix point). Another important convention is when the exponent is all zeros but the significand is nonzero. This represents a **denormalized** number in which there is no hidden bit assumed.

The largest magnitude value we can represent (forget the sign for the time being) with the single-precision floating-point format is $2^{127} \times 1.1111111111$ 1111111111111_2 (let's call this value MAX). We can't use an exponent of all ones because that is reserved for NaN. The smallest magnitude number we can represent is $2^{-127} \times .00000000000000000000001_2$ (let's call this value MIN). We can use an exponent of all zeros (which means the number is denormalized) because the significand is nonzero (and represents 2^{-23}). Due to the preceding special values and the limited number of bits, there are four numerical ranges that single-precision floating-point numbers cannot represent: negative numbers less than −MAX (negative overflow); negative numbers greater than −MIN (negative underflow); positive numbers less than +MIN (positive underflow); and positive numbers greater than +MAX (positive overflow).

Double-precision numbers use a signed 64-bit word consisting of an 11-bit exponent and a 52-bit significand. The bias is 1023. The range of numbers that can be represented in the IEEE double-precision model is shown in Figure 2.3. NaN is indicated when the exponent is 2047. Representations for zero and infinity correspond to the single-precision model.

At a slight cost in performance, most FPUs use only the 64-bit model so that only one set of specialized circuits needs to be designed and implemented.

Virtually every recently designed computer system has adopted the IEEE-754 floating-point model. Unfortunately, by the time this standard came along, many mainframe computer systems had established their own floating-point systems. Changing to the newer system has taken decades for well-established architectures such as IBM mainframes, which now support both their traditional floating-point system and IEEE-754. Before 1998, however, IBM systems had been using the same architecture for floating-point arithmetic that the original System/360 used in 1964. One would expect that both systems will continue to be supported, owing to the substantial amount of older software that is running on these systems.

2.5.5   Range, Precision, and Accuracy

When discussing floating-point numbers it is important to understand the terms *range, precision,* and *accuracy.* Range is very straightforward, because it represents the interval from the smallest value in a given format to the largest value in that same format. For example, the range of 16-bit two's complement integers is −32768 to +32767. The range of IEEE-754 double-precision floating-point numbers is given in Figure 2.3. Even with this large range, we know there are infinitely many numbers that do not exist within the range specified by IEEE-754. The reason floating-point numbers work at all is that there will always be a number in this range that is *close to* the number you want.

People have no problem understanding range, but accuracy and precision are often confused with each other. Accuracy refers to how close a number is to its true value; for example, we can't represent 0.1 in floating point, but we can find a number in the range that is relatively close, or reasonably accurate, to 0.1. Precision, on the other hand, deals with how much information we have about a value and the amount of information used to represent the value. 1.666 is a number with four decimal digits of precision; 1.6660 is the same exact number with five decimal digits of precision. The second number is not more accurate than the first.

Accuracy must be put into context—to know how accurate a value is, one must know how close it is to its intended target or "true value." We can't look at two numbers and immediately declare that the first is more accurate than the second simply because the first has more digits of precision.

Although they are separate, accuracy and precision are related. Higher precision often allows a value to be more accurate, but that is not always the case. For example, we can represent the value 1 as an integer, a single-precision floating point, or a double-precision floating point, but each is equally (exactly) accurate. As another example, consider 3.13333 as an estimate for pi. It has 6 digits of precision, yet is accurate to only two digits. Adding more precision will do nothing to increase the accuracy.

On the other hand, when multiplying 0.4×0.3, our accuracy depends on our precision. If we allow only one decimal place for precision, our result is 0.1 (which is close to, but not exactly, the product). If we allow two decimal places of precision, we get 0.12, which accurately reflects the answer.

2.5.6 Additional Problems with Floating-Point Numbers

We have seen that floating-point numbers can overflow and underflow. In addition, we know that a floating-point number may not exactly represent the value we wish, as is the case with the rounding error that occurs with the binary floating-point representation for the decimal number 0.1. As we have seen, these rounding errors can propagate, resulting in substantial problems.

Although rounding is undesirable, it is understandable. In addition to this rounding problem, however, floating-point arithmetic differs from real number arithmetic in two relatively disturbing, and not necessarily intuitive, ways. First, floating-point arithmetic is not always associative. This means that for three floating-point numbers a, b, and c,

$$(a + b) + c \neq a + (b + c)$$

The same holds true for associativity under multiplication. Although in many cases the left-hand side will equal the right-hand side, there is no guarantee. Floating-point arithmetic is also not distributive:

$$a \times (b + c) \neq ab + ac$$

Although results can vary depending on compiler (we used Gnu C), declaring the doubles $a = 0.1$, $b = 0.2$, and $c = 0.3$ illustrates the above inequalities nicely. We encourage you to find three additional floating-point numbers to illustrate that floating-point arithmetic is neither associative nor distributive.

What does this all mean to you as a programmer? Programmers should use extra care when using the equality operator on floating-point numbers. This implies that they should be avoided in controlling looping structures such as do...while and for loops. It is good practice to declare a "nearness to x" epsilon (e.g., epsilon = 1.0×10^{-20}) and then test an absolute value.

For example, instead of using:

```
if x = 2 then...
```

it is better to use:

```
if(abs(x - 2) < epsilon) then...\\ It's close enough if we've
                                 \\ defined epsilon correctly!
```

Floating-Point Ops or Oops?

In this chapter, we have introduced floating-point numbers and the means by which computers represent them. We have touched upon floating-point rounding errors (studies in numerical analysis will provide further depth on this topic) and the fact that floating-point numbers don't obey the standard associative and distributive laws. But just how serious are these issues? To answer this question, we introduce three major floating-point blunders.

In 1994, when Intel introduced the Pentium microprocessor, number crunchers around the world noticed something weird was happening. Calculations involving double-precision divisions and certain bit patterns were producing incorrect results. Although the flawed chip was slightly inaccurate for some pairs of numbers, other instances were more extreme. For example, if $x = 4,195,835$ and $y = 3,145,727$, finding $z = x - (x /y) \times y$ should produce a z of 0. The Intel 286, 386, and 486 chips gave exactly that result. Even taking into account the possibility of floating-point round-off error, the value of z should have been about 9.3×10^{-10}. But on the new Pentium, z was equal to 256!

Once Intel was informed of the problem, research and testing revealed the flaw to be an omission in the chip's design. The Pentium was using the radix-4 SRT algorithm for speedy division, which necessitated a 1066-element table. Once implemented in silicon, 5 of those table entries were 0 and should have been +2.

Although the Pentium bug was a public relations debacle for Intel, it was not a catastrophe for those using the chip. In fact, it was a minor thing compared to the programming mistakes with floating-point numbers that have resulted in disasters in areas from off-shore oil drilling, to stock markets, to missile defense. The list of actual disasters that resulted from floating-point errors is very long. The following two instances are among the worst of them.

During the Persian Gulf War of 1991, the United States relied on Patriot missiles to track and intercept cruise missiles and Scud missiles. One of these missiles failed to track an incoming Scud missile, allowing the Scud to hit an American army barracks, killing 28 people and injuring many more. After an investigation, it was determined that the failure of the Patriot missile was due to using too little precision to allow the missile to accurately determine the incoming Scud velocity.

The Patriot missile uses radar to determine the location of an object. If the internal weapons control computer identifies the object as something that should be intercepted, calculations are performed to predict the air space in which the object should be located at a specific time. This prediction is based on the object's known velocity and time of last detection.

The problem was in the clock, which measured time in tenths of seconds. But the time since boot was stored as an integer number of seconds (determined by multiplying the elapsed time by 1/10). For predicting where an object would be at a specific time, the time and velocity needed to be real numbers. It was no problem to convert the integer to a real number; however, using 24-bit registers for its calculations, the Patriot was limited in the precision of this operation. The potential problem is easily seen when one realizes 1/10 in binary is:

```
0.00011001100110011001100110011001100 . . .
```

When the elapsed time was small, this "chopping error" was insignificant and caused no problems. The Patriot was designed to be on for only a few minutes at a time, so this limit of 24-bit precision would be of no consequence. The problem was that during the Gulf War, the missiles were on for days. The longer a missile was on, the larger the error became, and the more probable that the inaccuracy of the prediction calculation would cause an unsuccessful interception. And this is precisely what happened on February 25, 1991, when a failed interception resulted in 28 people killed—a failed interception caused by loss of precision (required for accuracy) in floating-point numbers. It is estimated that the Patriot missile had been operational about 100 hours, introducing a rounding error in the time conversion of about 0.34 seconds, which translates to approximately half a kilometer of travel for a Scud missile.

Designers were aware of the conversion problem well before the incident occurred. However, deploying new software under wartime conditions is anything but trivial. Although the new software would have fixed the bug, field personnel could have simply rebooted the systems at specific intervals to keep the clock value small enough so that 24-bit precision would have been sufficient.

One of the most famous examples of a floating-point numeric disaster is the explosion of the Ariane 5 rocket. On June 4, 1996, the unmanned Ariane 5 was launched by the European Space Agency. Forty seconds after liftoff, the rocket exploded, scattering a $500 million cargo across parts of French Guiana. Investigation revealed perhaps one of the most devastatingly careless but efficient software bugs in the annals of computer science—a floating-point conversion error. The rocket's inertial reference system converted a 64-bit floating-point number (dealing with the horizontal velocity of the rocket) to a 16-bit signed integer. However, the particular 64-bit floating-point number to be converted was larger than 32,767 (the largest integer that can be stored in 16-bit signed representation), so the conversion process failed. The rocket tried to make an abrupt course correction for a wrong turn that it had never taken, and the guidance system shut down. Ironically, when the guidance system shut down, control reverted to a backup unit installed in the rocket in case of just such a failure, but the backup system was running the same flawed software.

It seems obvious that a 64-bit floating-point number could be much larger than 32,767, so how did the rocket programmers make such a glaring error? They decided the velocity value would never get large enough to be a problem. Their reasoning? It had never gotten too large before. Unfortunately, this rocket was faster than all previous rockets, resulting in a larger velocity value than the programmers expected. One of the most serious mistakes a programmer can make is to accept the old adage "But we've always done it that way."

Computers are everywhere—in our washing machines, our televisions, our microwaves, even our cars. We certainly hope the programmers who work on computer software for our cars don't make such hasty assumptions. With approximately 15 to 60 microprocessors in all new cars that roll off the assembly line and innumerable processors in commercial aircraft and medical equipment, a deep understanding of floating-point anomalies can quite literally be a lifesaver.

2.6 CHARACTER CODES

We have seen how digital computers use the binary system to represent and manipulate numeric values. We have yet to consider how these internal values can be converted to a form that is meaningful to humans. The manner in which this is done depends on both the coding system used by the computer and how the values are stored and retrieved.

2.6.1 Binary-Coded Decimal

For many applications, we need the exact binary equivalent of the decimal system, which means we need an encoding for individual decimal digits. This is precisely the case in many business applications that deal with money—we can't afford the rounding errors that occur when we convert real numbers to floating point when making financial transactions!

Binary-coded decimal (BCD) is very common in electronics, particularly those that display numerical data, such as alarm clocks and calculators. BCD encodes each digit of a decimal number into a 4-bit binary form. Each decimal digit is individually converted to its binary equivalent, as seen in Table 2.5. For example, to encode 146, the decimal digits are replaced by 0001, 0100, and 0110, respectively.

Because most computers use bytes as the smallest unit of access, most values are stored in 8 bits, not 4. That gives us two choices for storing 4-bit BCD digits. We can ignore the cost of extra bits and pad the high-order nibbles with zeros (or ones), forcing each decimal digit to be replaced by 8 bits. Using this approach, padding with zeros, 146 would be stored as 00000001 00000100 00000110. Clearly, this approach is quite wasteful. The second approach, called **packed BCD**, stores two digits per byte. Packed decimal format allows numbers to be signed, but instead of putting the sign at the beginning, the sign is stored at the end. The standard values for this "sign digit" are 1100 for +, 1101 for −, and 1111 to indicate that the value is unsigned (see Table 2.5). Using packed decimal format, +146 would be stored as 00010100 01101100. Padding would still be required for an even number of digits. Note that if a number has a decimal point (as with monetary values), this is not stored in the BCD representation of the number and must be retained by the application program.

Another variation of BCD is **zoned decimal format**. Zoned decimal representation stores a decimal digit in the low-order nibble of each byte, which is exactly the same as unpacked decimal format. However, instead of padding the high-order nibbles with zeros, a specific pattern is used. There are two choices for the high-order nibble, called the numeric **zone**. **EBCDIC zoned decimal format** requires the zone to be all ones (hexadecimal F). **ASCII zoned decimal format** requires the zone to be 0011 (hexadecimal 3). (See the next two sections for detailed explanations of EBCDIC and ASCII.) Both formats allow for signed numbers (using the

Digit	BCD
0	0000
1	0001
2	0010
3	0011
4	0100
5	0101
6	0110
7	0111
8	1000
9	1001
Zones	
1111	Unsigned
1100	Positive
1101	Negative

TABLE 2.5 Binary-Coded Decimal

sign digits found in Table 2.5) and typically expect the sign to be located in the high-order nibble of the least significant byte (although the sign could be a completely separate byte). For example, +146 in EBCDIC zoned decimal format is 11110001 11110100 11000110 (note that the high-order nibble of the last byte is the sign). In ASCII zoned decimal format, +146 is 00110001 00110100 11000110.

Note from Table 2.5 that six of the possible binary values are not used—1010 through 1111. Although it may appear that nearly 40% of our values are going to waste, we are gaining a considerable advantage in accuracy. For example, the number 0.3 is a repeating decimal when stored in binary. Truncated to an 8-bit fraction, it converts back to 0.296875, giving us an error of approximately 1.05%. In EBCDIC zoned decimal BCD, the number is stored directly as 1111 0011 (we are assuming the decimal point is implied by the data format), giving no error at all.

≡ **EXAMPLE 2.37** Represent −1265 using packed BCD and EBCDIC zoned decimal.

The 4-bit BCD representation for 1265 is:

0001 0010 0110 0101

Adding the sign after the low-order digit and padding the high-order bit with 0000, we have:

0000	0001	0010	0110	0101	1101

The EBCDIC zoned decimal representation requires 4 bytes:

1111	0001	1111	0010	1111	0110	1101	0101

The sign bit is shaded in both representations.

2.6.2 EBCDIC

Before the development of the IBM System/360, IBM had used a 6-bit variation of BCD for representing characters and numbers. This code was severely limited in how it could represent and manipulate data; in fact, lowercase letters were not part of its repertoire. The designers of the System/360 needed more information processing capability as well as a uniform manner in which to store both numbers and data. To maintain compatibility with earlier computers and peripheral equipment, the IBM engineers decided that it would be best to simply expand BCD from 6 bits to 8 bits. Accordingly, this new code was called **Extended Binary Coded Decimal Interchange Code (EBCDIC)**. IBM continues to use EBCDIC in IBM mainframe and midrange computer systems; however, IBM's AIX operating system (found on the RS/6000 and its successors) and operating systems for the IBM PC use ASCII. The EBCDIC code is shown in Table 2.6 in zone-digit form. Characters are represented by appending digit bits to zone bits. For example, the character *a* is 1000 0001 and the digit 3 is 1111 0011 in EBCDIC. Note that the only difference between uppercase and lowercase characters is in bit position 2, making a translation from uppercase to lowercase (or vice versa) a simple matter of flipping one bit. Zone bits also make it easier for a programmer to test the validity of input data.

2.6.3   ASCII

While IBM was busy building its iconoclastic System/360, other equipment makers were trying to devise better ways for transmitting data between systems. The **American Standard Code for Information Interchange (ASCII)** is one outcome of those efforts. ASCII is a direct descendant of the coding schemes used for decades by teletype (telex) devices. These devices used a 5-bit (Murray) code that was derived from the Baudot code, which was invented in the 1880s. By the early 1960s, the limitations of the 5-bit codes were becoming apparent. The International Organization for Standardization devised a 7-bit coding scheme that it called International Alphabet Number 5. In 1967, a derivative of this alphabet became the official standard that we now call ASCII.

As you can see in Table 2.7, ASCII defines codes for 32 control characters, 10 digits, 52 letters (uppercase and lowercase), 32 special characters (such as $ and #), and the space character. The high-order (eighth) bit was intended to be used for parity.

Parity is the most basic of all error-detection schemes. It is easy to implement in simple devices like teletypes. A parity bit is turned "on" or "off" depending on whether the sum of the other bits in the byte is even or odd. For example, if we decide to use even parity and we are sending an ASCII *A*, the lower 7 bits are 100 0001. Because the sum of the bits is even, the parity bit would be set to *off* and we would transmit 0100 0001. Similarly, if we transmit an ASCII *C*, 100 0011, the parity bit would be set to *on* before we sent the 8-bit byte, 1100 0011. Parity can be used to detect only single-bit errors. We will discuss more sophisticated error-detection methods in Section 2.7.

To allow compatibility with telecommunications equipment, computer manufacturers gravitated toward the ASCII code. As computer hardware became more reliable, however, the need for a parity bit began to fade. In the early 1980s, microcomputer and microcomputer-peripheral makers began to use the parity bit to provide an "extended" character set for values between 128_{10} and 255_{10}.

Depending on the manufacturer, the higher-valued characters could be anything from mathematical symbols to characters that form the sides of boxes to foreign-language characters such as ñ. Unfortunately, no number of clever tricks can make ASCII a truly international interchange code.

2.6.4   Unicode

Both EBCDIC and ASCII were built around the Latin alphabet. As such, they are restricted in their abilities to provide data representation for the non-Latin alphabets used by the majority of the world's population. As all countries began using computers, each was devising codes that would most effectively represent their native languages. None of these was necessarily compatible with any others, placing yet another barrier in the way of the emerging global economy.

Zone	0000	0001	0010	0011	0100	0101	0110	0111	1000	1001	1010	1011	1100	1101	1110	1111
0000	NUL	SOH	STX	ETX	PF	HT	LC	DEL		RLF	SMM	VT	FF	CR	SO	SI
0001	DLE	DC1	DC2	TM	RES	NL	BS	IL	CAN	EM	CC	CU1	IFS	IGS	IRS	IUS
0010	DS	SOS	FS		BYP	LF	ETB	ESC			SM	CU2		ENQ	ACK	BEL
0011			SYN		PN	RS	UC	EOT				CU3	DC4	NAK		SUB
0100	SP										[	.	<	(	+	!
0101	&										]	$	*	)	;	^
0110	–	/									|	,	%	_	>	?
0111										'	:	#	@	'	=	"
1000		a	b	c	d	e	f	g	h	i						
1001		j	k	l	m	n	o	p	q	r						
1010		~	s	t	u	v	w	x	y	z						
1011																
1100	{	A	B	C	D	E	F	G	H	I						
1101	}	J	K	L	M	N	O	P	Q	R						
1110	\		S	T	U	V	W	X	Y	Z						
1111	0	1	2	3	4	5	6	7	8	9						

Digit

Abbreviations

NUL	Null	TM	Tape mark	ETB	End of transmission block
SOH	Start of heading	RES	Restore	ESC	Escape
STX	Start of text	NL	New line	SM	Set mode
ETX	End of text	BS	Backspace	CU2	Customer use 2
PF	Punch off	IL	Idle	ENQ	Enquiry
HT	Horizontal tab	CAN	Cancel	ACK	Acknowledge
LC	Lowercase	EM	End of medium	BEL	Ring the bell (beep)
DEL	Delete	CC	Cursor control	SYN	Synchronous idle
RLF	Reverse linefeed	CU1	Customer use 1	PN	Punch on
SMM	Start manual message	IFS	Interchange file separator	RS	Record separator
VT	Vertical tab	IGS	Interchange group separator	UC	Uppercase
FF	Form feed	IRS	Interchange record separator	EOT	End of transmission
CR	Carriage return	IUS	Interchange unit separator	CU3	Customer use 3
SO	Shift out	DS	Digit select	DC4	Device control 4
SI	Shift in	SOS	Start of significance	NAK	Negative acknowledgment
DLE	Data link escape	FS	Field separator	SUB	Substitute
DC1	Device control 1	BYP	Bypass	SP	Space
DC2	Device control 2	LF	Line feed		

TABLE 2.6   The EBCDIC Code (Values Given in Binary Zone-Digit Format)

0 NUL	16 DLE	32	48 0	64 @	80 P	96 `	112 p
1 SOH	17 DC1	33 !	49 1	65 A	81 Q	97 a	113 q
2 STX	18 DC2	34 "	50 2	66 B	82 R	98 b	114 r
3 ETX	19 DC3	35 #	51 3	67 C	83 S	99 c	115 s
4 EOT	20 DC4	36 $	52 4	68 D	84 T	100 d	116 t
5 ENQ	21 NAK	37 %	53 5	69 E	85 U	101 e	117 u
6 ACK	22 SYN	38 &	54 6	70 F	86 V	102 f	118 v
7 BEL	23 ETB	39 '	55 7	71 G	87 W	103 g	119 w
8 BS	24 CAN	40 (	56 8	72 H	88 X	104 h	120 x
9 HT	25 EM	41)	57 9	73 I	89 Y	105 i	121 y
10 LF	26 SUB	42 *	58 :	74 J	90 Z	106 j	122 z
11 VT	27 ESC	43 +	59 ;	75 K	91 [	107 k	123 {
12 FF	28 FS	44 ,	60 <	76 L	92 \	108 l	124	
13 CR	29 GS	45 -	61 =	77 M	93]	109 m	125 }
14 SO	30 RS	46 .	62 >	78 N	94 ^	110 n	126 ~
15 SI	31 US	47 /	63 ?	79 O	95 _	111 o	127 DEL

Abbreviations

NUL	Null		DLE	Data link escape
SOH	Start of heading		DC1	Device control 1
STX	Start of text		DC2	Device control 2
ETX	End of text		DC3	Device control 3
EOT	End of transmission		DC4	Device control 4
ENQ	Enquiry		NAK	Negative acknowledge
ACK	Acknowledge		SYN	Synchronous idle
BEL	Bell (beep)		ETB	End of transmission block
BS	Backspace		CAN	Cancel
HT	Horizontal tab		EM	End of medium
LF	Line feed, new line		SUB	Substitute
VT	Vertical tab		ESC	Escape
FF	Form feed, new page		FS	File separator
CR	Carriage return		GS	Group separator
SO	Shift out		RS	Record separator
SI	Shift in		US	Unit separator
			DEL	Delete/idle

TABLE 2.7 The ASCII Code (Values Given in Decimal)

In 1991, before things got too far out of hand, a consortium of industry and public leaders was formed to establish a new international information exchange code called Unicode. This group is appropriately called the Unicode Consortium.

Unicode is a 16-bit alphabet that is downward compatible with ASCII and the Latin-1 character set. It is conformant with the ISO/IEC 10646-1 international alphabet. Because the base coding of Unicode is 16 bits, it has the capacity to encode the majority of characters used in every language of the world. If this weren't enough, Unicode also defines an extension mechanism that will allow for the coding of an additional million characters. This is sufficient to provide codes for every written language in the history of civilization.

The Unicode codespace consists of five parts, as shown in Table 2.8. A full Unicode-compliant system will also allow formation of composite characters from the individual codes, such as the combination of ´ and A to form Á. The algorithms used for these composite characters, as well as the Unicode extensions, can be found in the references at the end of this chapter.

Although Unicode has yet to become the exclusive alphabet of American computers, most manufacturers are including at least some limited support for it in their systems. Unicode is currently the default character set of the Java programming language. Ultimately, the acceptance of Unicode by all manufacturers

Character Types	Character Set Description	Number of Characters	Hexadecimal Values
Alphabets	Latin, Cyrillic, Greek, etc.	8192	0000 to 1FFF
Symbols	Dingbats, mathematical, etc.	4096	2000 to 2FFF
CJK	Chinese, Japanese, and Korean phonetic symbols and punctuation	4096	3000 to 3FFF
Han	Unified Chinese, Japanese, and Korean	40,960	4000 to DFFF
	Expansion or spillover from Han	4096	E000 to EFFF
User defined		4095	F000 to FFFE

TABLE 2.8 Unicode Codespace

will depend on how aggressively they wish to position themselves as international players and how inexpensively disk drives can be produced to support an alphabet with double the storage requirements of ASCII or EBCDIC.

2.7 ERROR DETECTION AND CORRECTION

No communications channel or storage medium can be completely error-free. It is a physical impossibility. As transmission rates are increased, bit timing gets tighter. As more bits are packed per square millimeter of storage, magnetic flux densities increase. Error rates increase in direct proportion to the number of bits per second transmitted, or the number of bits per square millimeter of magnetic storage.

In Section 2.6.3, we mentioned that a parity bit could be added to an ASCII byte to help determine whether any of the bits had become corrupted during transmission. This method of error detection is limited in its effectiveness: Simple parity can detect only an odd number of errors per byte. If two errors occur, we are helpless to detect a problem. Nonsense could pass for good data. If such errors occur in sending financial information or program code, the effects can be disastrous.

As you read the sections that follow, you should keep in mind that just as it is impossible to create an error-free medium, it is also impossible to detect or correct 100% of all errors that *could* occur in a medium. Error detection and correction is yet another study in the trade-offs that one must make in designing computer systems. The well-constructed error control system is therefore a system where a "reasonable" number of the "reasonably" expected errors can be detected or corrected within the bounds of "reasonable" economics. (Note: The word *reasonable* is implementation-dependent.)

2.7.1 Cyclic Redundancy Check

Checksums are used in a wide variety of coding systems, from bar codes to International Standard Book Numbers. These are self-checking codes that will quickly indicate whether the preceding digits have been misread. A **cyclic redundancy check (CRC)** is a type of checksum used primarily in data communications that determines whether an error has occurred within a large block or stream of information bytes. The larger the block to be checked, the larger the checksum must be to provide adequate protection. Checksums and CRCs are types of **systematic error detection** schemes, meaning that the error-checking bits are appended to the original information byte. The group of error-checking bits is called a **syndrome**. The original information byte is unchanged by the addition of the error-checking bits.

The word *cyclic* in cyclic redundancy check refers to the abstract mathematical theory behind this error control system. Although a discussion of this theory is beyond the scope of this text, we can demonstrate how the method works to aid in your understanding of its power to economically detect transmission errors.

Arithmetic Modulo 2

You may be familiar with integer arithmetic taken over a modulus. Twelve-hour clock arithmetic is a modulo 12 system that you use every day to tell time. When we add 2 hours to 11:00, we get 1:00. Arithmetic modulo 2 uses two binary operands with no borrows or carries. The result is likewise binary and is also a member of the modulus 2 system. Because of this closure under addition, and the existence of identity elements, mathematicians say that this modulo 2 system forms an **algebraic field**.

The addition rules are as follows:

$$0 + 0 = 0$$
$$0 + 1 = 1$$
$$1 + 0 = 1$$
$$1 + 1 = 0$$

≡   **EXAMPLE 2.38**   Find the sum of 1011_2 and 110_2 modulo 2.

$$
\begin{array}{r}
1011 \\
+110 \\
\hline
1101_2 \ (\text{mod } 2)
\end{array}
$$

This sum makes sense only in modulo 2.

Modulo 2 division operates through a series of partial sums using the modulo 2 addition rules. Example 2.39 illustrates the process.

≡   **EXAMPLE 2.39**   Find the quotient and remainder when 1001011_2 is divided by 1011_2.

$$
\begin{array}{r}
1011\overline{)1001011} \\
1011 \\
\hline
0010 \\
\\
001001 \\
1011 \\
\hline
0010 \\
00101
\end{array}
$$

1. Write the divisor directly beneath the first bit of the dividend.
2. Add these numbers using modulo 2.
3. Bring down bits from the dividend so that the first 1 of the difference can align with the first 1 of the divisor.
4. Copy the divisor as in Step 1.
5. Add as in Step 2.
6. Bring down another bit.
7. 101_2 is not divisible by 1011_2, so this is the remainder.

The quotient is 1010_2.

Arithmetic operations over the modulo 2 field have polynomial equivalents that are analogous to polynomials over the field of integers. We have seen how positional number systems represent numbers in increasing powers of a radix, for example,

$$1011_2 = 1 \times 2^3 + 0 \times 2^2 + 1 \times 2^1 + 1 \times 2^0.$$

By letting $X = 2$, the binary number 1011_2 becomes shorthand for the polynomial:

$$1 \times X^3 + 0 \times X^2 + 1 \times X^1 + 1 \times X^0.$$

The division performed in Example 2.39 then becomes the polynomial operation:

$$\frac{X^6 + X^3 + X + 1}{X^3 + X + 1}$$

Calculating and Using CRCs

With that lengthy preamble behind us, we can now proceed to show how CRCs are constructed. We will do this by example:

1. Let the information byte $I = 1001011_2$. (Any number of bytes can be used to form a message block.)

2. The sender and receiver agree upon an arbitrary binary pattern, say, $P = 1011_2$. (Patterns beginning and ending with 1 work best.)

3. Shift I to the left by one less than the number of bits in P, giving a new $I = 1001011000_2$.

4. Using I as a dividend and P as a divisor, perform the modulo 2 division (as shown in Example 2.39). We ignore the quotient and note that the remainder is 100_2. The remainder is the actual CRC checksum.

5. Add the remainder to I, giving the message M:

$$1001011000_2 + 100_2 = 1001011100_2$$

6. M is decoded and checked by the message receiver using the reverse process. Only now P divides M exactly:

```
               1010100
      1011 ) 1001011100
             1011
             001001
               1011
               0010
               001011
                 1011
                 0000
```

Note: The reverse process would include appending the remainder.

A remainder other than zero indicates that an error has occurred in the transmission of M. This method works best when a large prime polynomial is used. There are four standard polynomials used widely for this purpose:

- CRC-CCITT (ITU-T): $X^{16} + X^{12} + X^5 + 1$
- CRC-12: $X^{12} + X^{11} + X^3 + X^2 + X + 1$
- CRC-16 (ANSI): $X^{16} + X^{15} + X^2 + 1$
- CRC-32: $X^{32} + X^{26} + X^{23} + X^{22} + X^{16} + X^{12} + X^{11} + X^{10} + X^8 + X^7 + X^5 + X^4 + X + 1$

CRC-CCITT, CRC-12, and CRC-16 operate over pairs of bytes; CRC-32 uses four bytes, which is appropriate for systems operating on 32-bit words. It has been proven that CRCs using these polynomials can detect more than 99.8% of all single-bit errors.

CRCs can be implemented effectively using lookup tables as opposed to calculating the remainder with each byte. The remainder generated by each possible input bit pattern can be "burned" directly into communications and storage electronics. The remainder can then be retrieved using a 1-cycle lookup as compared to a 16- or 32-cycle division operation. Clearly, the trade-off is in speed versus the cost of more complex control circuitry.

2.7.2 Hamming Codes

Data communications channels are simultaneously more error-prone and more tolerant of errors than disk systems. In data communications, it is sufficient to have only the ability to detect errors. If a communications device determines that a message contains an erroneous bit, all it has to do is request retransmission. Storage systems and memory do not have this luxury. A disk can sometimes be the sole repository of a financial transaction or other collection of nonreproducible real-time data. Storage devices and memory must therefore have the ability to not only detect but to correct a reasonable number of errors.

Error-recovery coding has been studied intensively over the past century. One of the most effective codes—and the oldest—is the Hamming code. **Hamming codes** are an adaptation of the concept of parity, whereby error detection and correction capabilities are increased in proportion to the number of parity bits added to an information word. Hamming codes are used in situations where random errors are likely to occur. With random errors, we assume each bit failure has a fixed probability of occurrence independent of other bit failures. It is common for computer memory to experience such errors, so in our following discussion, we present Hamming codes in the context of memory bit error detection and correction.

We mentioned that Hamming codes use parity bits, also called **check bits** or **redundant bits**. The memory word itself consists of m bits, but r redundant bits are added to allow for error detection and/or correction. Thus, the final word, called a **code word**, is an n-bit unit containing m data bits and r check bits. There exists a unique code word consisting of $n = m + r$ bits for each data word as follows:

m bits	r bits

The number of bit positions in which two code words differ is called the **Hamming distance** of those two code words. For example, if we have the following two code words:

$$1\ 0\ 0\ 0\ 1\ 0\ 0\ 1$$
$$1\ 0\ 1\ 1\ 0\ 0\ 0\ 1$$
$$*\quad*\quad*$$

we see that they differ in 3 bit positions (marked by *), so the Hamming distance of these two code words is 3. (Please note that we have not yet discussed how to create code words; we will do that shortly.)

The Hamming distance between two code words is important in the context of error detection. If two code words are a Hamming distance d apart, d single-bit errors are required to convert one code word to the other, which implies that this type of error would not be detected. Therefore, if we wish to create a code that guarantees detection of all single-bit errors (an error in only 1 bit), all pairs of code words must have a Hamming distance of at least 2. If an n-bit word is not recognized as a legal code word, it is considered an error.

Given an algorithm for computing check bits, it is possible to construct a complete list of legal code words. The smallest Hamming distance found among all pairs of the code words in this code is called the **minimum Hamming distance** for the code. The minimum Hamming distance of a code, often signified by the notation **D(min)**, determines its error detecting and correcting capability. Stated succinctly, for any code word X to be received as another valid code word Y, at least $D(min)$ errors must occur in X. So, to detect k (or fewer) single-bit errors, the code must have a Hamming distance of $D(min) = k + 1$. Hamming codes can always detect $D(min) - 1$ errors and correct $\lfloor (D(min) - 1)/2 \rfloor$ errors.[1] Accordingly, the Hamming distance of a code must be at least $2k + 1$ in order for it to be able to correct k errors.

Code words are constructed from information words using r parity bits. Before we continue the discussion of error detection and correction, let's consider a simple example. The most common error detection uses a single parity bit appended to the data (recall the discussion on ASCII character representation). A single-bit error in any bit of the code word produces the wrong parity.

---

[1]The $\lfloor \ \rfloor$ brackets denote the integer floor function, which is the largest integer that is smaller than or equal to the enclosed quantity. For example, $\lfloor 8.3 \rfloor = 8$ and $\lfloor 8.9 \rfloor = 8$.

≡   **EXAMPLE 2.40**   Assume a memory with 2 data bits and 1 parity bit (appended at the end of the code word) that uses even parity (so the number of 1s in the code word must be even). With 2 data bits, we have a total of 4 possible words. We list here the data word, its corresponding parity bit, and the resulting code word for each of these 4 possible words:

Data Word	Parity Bit	Code Word
00	0	000
01	1	011
10	1	101
11	0	110

The resulting code words have 3 bits. However, using 3 bits allows for 8 different bit patterns, as follows (valid code words are marked with an *):

000*	100
001	101*
010	110*
011*	111

If the code word 001 is encountered, it is invalid and thus indicates that an error has occurred somewhere in the code word. For example, suppose the correct code word to be stored in memory is 011, but an error produces 001. This error can be detected, but it cannot be corrected. It is impossible to determine exactly how many bits have been flipped and exactly which ones are in error. Error-correcting codes require more than a single parity bit, as we see in the following discussion.

What happens in the above example if a valid code word is subject to two-bit errors? For example, suppose the code word 011 is converted into 000. This error is not detected. If you examine the code in the above example, you will see that $D(min)$ is 2, which implies that this code is guaranteed to detect only single-bit errors.

We have already stated that the error detecting and correcting capabilities of a code are dependent on $D(min)$, and from an error detection point of view, we have seen this relationship exhibited in Example 2.40. Error correction requires the code to contain additional redundant bits to ensure a minimum Hamming distance $D(min) = 2k + 1$ if the code is to detect and correct k errors. This Hamming distance guarantees that all legal code words are far enough apart that even with k changes, the original invalid code word is closer to one unique valid code word. This is important because the method used in error correction is to change the invalid code word into the valid code word that differs in the fewest number of bits. This idea is illustrated in Example 2.41.

≡ **EXAMPLE 2.41** Suppose we have the following code (do not worry at this time about how this code was generated; we will address this issue shortly):

```
0 0 0 0 0
0 1 0 1 1
1 0 1 1 0
1 1 1 0 1
```

First, let's determine $D(min)$. By examining all possible pairs of code words, we discover that the minimum Hamming distance $D(min) = 3$. Thus, this code can detect up to two errors and correct one single-bit error. How is correction handled? Suppose we read the invalid code word 10000. There must be at least one error because this does not match any of the valid code words. We now determine the Hamming distance between the observed code word and each legal code word: It differs in 1 bit from the first code word, 4 from the second, 2 from the third, and 3 from the last, resulting in a **difference vector** of [1,4,2,3]. To make the correction using this code, we automatically correct to the legal code word closest to the observed word, resulting in a correction to 00000. Note that this "correction" is not necessarily correct! We are assuming that the minimum number of possible errors has occurred, namely, 1. It is possible that the original code word was supposed to be 10110 and was changed to 10000 when two errors occurred.

Suppose two errors really did occur. For example, assume we read the invalid code word 11000. If we calculate the distance vector of [2,3,3,2], we see there is no "closest" code word, and we are unable to make the correction. The minimum Hamming distance of 3 permits correction of one error only, and cannot ensure correction, as evidenced in this example, if more than one error occurs.

In our discussion up to this point, we have simply presented you with various codes, but have not given any specifics as to how the codes are generated. There are many methods that are used for code generation; perhaps one of the more intuitive is the Hamming algorithm for code design, which we now present. Before explaining the actual steps in the algorithm, we provide some background material.

Suppose we wish to design a code with words consisting of m data bits and r check bits, which allows for single-bit errors to be corrected. This implies that there are 2^m legal code words, each with a unique combination of check bits. Because we are focused on single-bit errors, let's examine the set of invalid code words that are a distance of 1 from all legal code words.

Each valid code word has n bits, and an error could occur in any of these n positions. Thus, each valid code word has n illegal code words at a distance of 1. Therefore, if we are concerned with each legal code word and each invalid code word consisting of one error, we have $n + 1$ bit patterns associated with each code word (1 legal word and n illegal words). Because each code word consists of n bits, where $n = m + r$, there are 2^n total bit patterns possible. This results in the following inequality:

$$(n + 1) \times 2^m \leq 2^n$$

where $n + 1$ is the number of bit patterns per code word, 2^m is the number of legal code words, and 2^n is the total number of bit patterns possible. Because $n = m + r$, we can rewrite the inequality as:

$$(m + r + 1) \times 2^m \leq 2^{m+r}$$

or

$$(m + r + 1) \leq 2^r$$

This inequality is important because it specifies the lower limit on the number of check bits required (we always use as few check bits as possible) to construct a code with m data bits and r check bits that corrects all single-bit errors.

Suppose we have data words of length $m = 4$. Then:

$$(4 + r + 1) \leq 2^r$$

which implies that r must be greater than or equal to 3. We choose $r = 3$. This means to build a code with data words of 4 bits that should correct single-bit errors, we must add 3 check bits.

The Hamming Algorithm

The Hamming algorithm provides a straightforward method for designing codes to correct single-bit errors. To construct error-correcting codes for any size memory word, we follow these steps:

1. Determine the number of check bits, r, necessary for the code and then number the n bits (where $n = m + r$), right to left, starting with 1 (not 0).

2. Each bit whose bit number is a power of 2 is a parity bit—the others are data bits.

3. Assign parity bits to check bit positions as follows: Bit b is checked by those parity bits $b_1, b_2, \ldots, b_j$ such that $b_1 + b_2 + \ldots + b_j = b$ (where "+" indicates the modulo 2 sum).

We now present an example to illustrate these steps and the actual process of error correction.

EXAMPLE 2.42 Using the Hamming code just described and even parity, encode the 8-bit ASCII character K. (The high-order bit will be zero.) Induce a single-bit error and then indicate how to locate the error.

We first determine the code word for K.

Step 1: Determine the number of necessary check bits, add these bits to the data bits, and number all n bits.

Because $m = 8$, we have: $(8 + r + 1) \leq 2^r$, which implies that r must be greater than or equal to 4. We choose $r = 4$.

Step 2: Number the n bits right to left, starting with 1, which results in:

| $\overline{12}$ | $\overline{11}$ | $\overline{10}$ | $\overline{9}$ | $\underline{\square}$ $\overline{8}$ | $\overline{7}$ | $\overline{6}$ | $\overline{5}$ | $\underline{\square}$ $\overline{4}$ | $\underline{\square}$ $\overline{3}$ | $\underline{\square}$ $\overline{2}$ | $\underline{\square}$ $\overline{1}$ |

The parity bits are marked by boxes.

Step 3: Assign parity bits to check the various bit positions.

To perform this step, we first write all bit positions as sums of those numbers that are powers of 2:

$1 = 1$	$5 = 1 + 4$	$9 = 1 + 8$
$2 = 2$	$6 = 2 + 4$	$10 = 2 + 8$
$3 = 1 + 2$	$7 = 1 + 2 + 4$	$11 = 1 + 2 + 8$
$4 = 4$	$8 = 8$	$12 = 4 + 8$

The number 1 contributes to 1, 3, 5, 7, 9, and 11, so this parity bit will reflect the parity of the bits in these positions. Similarly, 2 contributes to 2, 3, 6, 7, 10, and 11, so the parity bit in position 2 reflects the parity of this set of bits. Bit 4 provides parity for 4, 5, 6, 7, and 12, and bit 8 provides parity for bits 8, 9, 10, 11, and 12. If we write the data bits in the nonboxed blanks, and then add the parity bits, we have the following code word as a result:

$$\underset{12}{0} \ \underset{11}{1} \ \underset{10}{0} \ \underset{9}{0} \ \underset{8}{\boxed{1}} \ \underset{7}{1} \ \underset{6}{0} \ \underset{5}{1} \ \underset{4}{\boxed{0}} \ \underset{3}{1} \ \underset{2}{\boxed{1}} \ \underset{1}{\boxed{0}}$$

Therefore, the code word for K is 010011010110.

Let's introduce an error in bit position b_9, resulting in the code word 010111010110. If we use the parity bits to check the various sets of bits, we find the following:

Bit 1 checks 1, 3, 5, 7, 9, and 11: With even parity, this produces an error.

Bit 2 checks 2, 3, 6, 7, 10, and 11: This is ok.

Bit 4 checks 4, 5, 6, 7, and 12: This is ok.

Bit 8 checks 8, 9, 10, 11, and 12: This produces an error.

Parity bits 1 and 8 show errors. These two parity bits both check 9 and 11, so the single-bit error must be in either bit 9 or bit 11. However, because bit 2 checks bit 11 and indicates no error has occurred in the subset of bits it checks, the error must occur in bit 9. (We know this because we created the error; however, note that even if we have no clue where the error is, using this method allows us to determine the position of the error and correct it by simply flipping the bit.)

Because of the way the parity bits are positioned, an easier method to detect and correct the error bit is to add the positions of the parity bits that indicate an error. We found that parity bits 1 and 8 produced an error, and $1 + 8 = 9$, which is exactly where the error occurred.

EXAMPLE 2.43 Use the Hamming algorithm to find all code words for a 3-bit memory word, assuming odd parity.

We have 8 possible words: 000, 001, 010, 011, 100, 101, 110, and 111. We first need to determine the required number of check bits. Because $m = 3$, we have: $(3 + r + 1) \leq 2^r$, which implies that r must be greater than or equal to 3.

We choose $r = 3$. Therefore, each code word has 6 bits, and the check bits are in positions 1, 2, and 4, as shown here:

$$\overline{}\ \overline{}\ \boxed{}\ \overline{}\ \boxed{}\ \boxed{}$$
$$6\ \ 5\ \ 4\ \ 3\ \ 2\ \ 1$$

From our previous example, we know that:

- bit 1 checks the parity over bits 1, 3, and 5
- bit 2 check the parity over bits 2, 3, and 6
- bit 4 checks the parity over bits 4, 5, and 6

Therefore, we have the following code words for each memory word:

Memory Word	Code Word

Memory Word | **Code Word**

000

	0	0	1	0	1	1
Bit Position	6	5	4	3	2	1

001

	0	0	1	1	0	0
Bit Position	6	5	4	3	2	1

010

	0	1	0	0	1	0
Bit Position	6	5	4	3	2	1

011

	0	1	0	1	0	1
Bit Position	6	5	4	3	2	1

100

	1	0	0	0	0	1
Bit Position	6	5	4	3	2	1

101

	1	0	0	1	1	0
Bit Position	6	5	4	3	2	1

110

	1	1	1	0	0	0
Bit Position	6	5	4	3	2	1

111

	1	1	1	1	1	1
Bit Position	6	5	4	3	2	1

Our set of code words is 001011, 001100, 010010, 010101, 100001, 100110, 111000, 111111. If a single bit in any of these words is flipped, we can determine exactly which one it is and correct it. For example, to send 111, we actually send the code word 111111 instead. If 110111 is received, parity bit 1 (which checks bits 1, 3, and 5) is ok, and parity bit 2 (which checks bits 2, 3, and 6) is ok, but parity bit 4 shows an error, as only bits 5 and 6 are ones, violating odd parity. Bit 5 cannot be incorrect, because parity bit 1 checked out ok. Bit 6 cannot be wrong because parity bit 2 checked out ok. Therefore, it must be bit 4 that is wrong, so it is changed from a 0 to a 1, resulting in the correct code word 111111.

In the next chapter, you will see how easy it is to implement a Hamming code using simple binary circuits. Because of its simplicity, Hamming code protection can be added inexpensively and with minimal effect on performance.

2.7.3 Reed-Solomon

Hamming codes work well in situations where one can reasonably expect errors to be rare events. Fixed magnetic disk drives have error ratings on the order of 1 bit in 100 million. The 3-bit Hamming code that we just studied will easily correct this type of error. However, Hamming codes are useless in situations where there is a likelihood that multiple adjacent bits will be damaged. These kinds of errors are called **burst errors**. Because of their exposure to mishandling and environmental stresses, burst errors are common on removable media such as magnetic tapes and compact discs.

If we expect errors to occur in blocks, it stands to reason that we should use an error-correcting code that operates at a block level, as opposed to a Hamming code, which operates at the bit level. A **Reed-Solomon (RS)** code can be thought of as a CRC that operates over entire characters instead of only a few bits. RS codes, like CRCs, are systematic: The parity bytes are appended to a block of information bytes. RS(n, k) codes are defined using the following parameters:

- s = The number of bits in a character (or "symbol")
- k = The number of s-bit characters comprising the data block
- n = The number of bits in the code word

RS(n, k) can correct $\dfrac{(n - k)}{2}$ errors in the k information bytes.

The popular RS(255, 223) code, therefore, uses 223 8-bit information bytes and 32 syndrome bytes to form 255-byte code words. It will correct as many as 16 erroneous bytes in the information block.

The generator polynomial for an RS code is given by a polynomial defined over an abstract mathematical structure called a **Galois field**. (A lucid discussion of Galois mathematics is beyond the scope of this text. See the references at the end of the chapter.) The RS-generating polynomial is:

$$g(x) = (x - a^i)(x - a^{i+1}) \ldots (x - a^{i+2t})$$

where $t = n - k$ and x is an entire byte (or symbol) and $g(x)$ operates over the field $GF(2^s)$. (Note: This polynomial expands over the Galois field, which is considerably different from the integer fields used in ordinary algebra.)

The n-byte RS code word is computed using the equation:

$$c(x) = g(x) \times i(x)$$

where $i(x)$ is the information block.

Despite the daunting algebra behind them, RS error-correction algorithms lend themselves well to implementation in computer hardware. They are implemented in high-performance disk drives for mainframe computers as well as compact discs used for music and data storage. These implementations will be described in Chapter 7.

CHAPTER SUMMARY

We have presented the essentials of data representation and numerical operations in digital computers. You should master the techniques described for base conversion and memorize the smaller hexadecimal and binary numbers. This knowledge will be beneficial to you as you study the remainder of this text. Your knowledge of hexadecimal coding will be useful if you are ever required to read a core (memory) dump after a system crash or if you do any serious work in the field of data communications.

You have also seen that floating-point numbers can produce significant errors when small errors are allowed to compound over iterative processes. There are various numerical techniques that can be used to control such errors. These techniques merit detailed study but are beyond the scope of this text.

You have learned that most computers use ASCII or EBCDIC to represent characters. It is generally of little value to memorize any of these codes in their entirety, but if you work with them frequently, you will find yourself learning a number of "key values" from which you can compute most of the others that you need.

Unicode is the default character set used by Java and recent versions of Windows. It is likely to replace EBCDIC and ASCII as the basic method of character representation in computer systems; however, the older codes will be with us for the foreseeable future, owing both to their economy and their pervasiveness.

Error detecting and correcting codes are used in virtually all facets of computing technology. Should the need arise, your understanding of the various error control methods will help you to make informed choices among the various options available. The method that you choose will depend on a number of factors including computational overhead and the capacity of the storage and transmission media available to you.

FURTHER READING

A brief account of early mathematics in Western civilization can be found in Bunt et al. (1988).

Knuth (1998) presents a delightful and thorough discussion of the evolution of number systems and computer arithmetic in Volume 2 of his series on computer algorithms. (*Every* computer scientist should own a set of the Knuth books.)

A definitive account of floating-point arithmetic can be found in Goldberg (1991). Schwartz et al. (1999) describe how the IBM System/390 performs floating-point operations in both the older form and the IEEE standard. Soderquist and Leeser (1996) provide an excellent and detailed discussion of the problems surrounding floating-point division and square roots.

Detailed information about Unicode can be found at the Unicode Consortium website, www.unicode.org, as well as in the *Unicode Standard, Version 4.0* (2003).

The International Standards Organization website can be found at www.iso.ch. You will be amazed at the span of influence of this group. A similar trove of information can be found at the American National Standards Institute website: www.ansi.org.

After you master the concepts of Boolean algebra and digital logic, you will enjoy reading Arazi's book (1988). This well-written book shows how error detection and correction are achieved using simple digital circuits. Arazi's appendix gives a remarkably lucid discussion of the Galois field arithmetic that is used in Reed-Solomon codes.

If you'd prefer a rigorous and exhaustive study of error-correction theory, Pretzel's (1992) book is an excellent place to start. The text is accessible, well-written, and thorough.

Detailed discussions of Galois fields can be found in the (inexpensive!) books by Artin (1998) and Warner (1990). Warner's much larger book is a clearly written and comprehensive introduction to the concepts of abstract algebra. A study of abstract algebra will be helpful to you should you delve into the study of mathematical cryptography, a fast-growing area of interest in computer science.

REFERENCES

Arazi, B. *A Commonsense Approach to the Theory of Error Correcting Codes.* Cambridge, MA: The MIT Press, 1988.

Artin, E. *Galois Theory.* New York: Dover Publications, 1998.

Bunt, L. N. H., Jones, P. S., & Bedient, J. D. *The Historical Roots of Elementary Mathematics.* New York: Dover Publications, 1988.

Goldberg, D. "What Every Computer Scientist Should Know about Floating-Point Arithmetic." *ACM Computing Surveys 23*:1, March 1991, pp. 5–47.

Knuth, D. E. *The Art of Computer Programming,* 3rd ed. Reading, MA: Addison-Wesley, 1998.

Pretzel, O. *Error-Correcting Codes and Finite Fields.* New York: Oxford University Press, 1992.

Schwartz, E. M., Smith, R. M., & Krygowski, C. A. "The S/390 G5 Floating-Point Unit Supporting Hex and Binary Architectures." *IEEE Proceedings from the 14th Symposium on Computer Arithmetic,* 1999, pp. 258–265.

Soderquist, P., & Leeser, M. "Area and Performance Tradeoffs in Floating-Point Divide and Square-Root Implementations." *ACM Computing Surveys 28*:3, September 1996, pp. 518–564.

The Unicode Consortium. *The Unicode Standard, Version 4.0.* Reading, MA: Addison-Wesley, 2003.

Warner, S. *Modern Algebra.* New York: Dover Publications, 1990.

REVIEW OF ESSENTIAL TERMS AND CONCEPTS

1. The word *bit* is a contraction for what two words?
2. Explain how the terms *bit*, *byte*, *nibble*, and *word* are related.
3. Why are binary and decimal called positional numbering systems?
4. Explain how base 2, base 8, and base 16 are related.
5. What is a radix?
6. How many of the "numbers to remember" (in all bases) from Table 2.1 can you remember?
7. What does overflow mean in the context of unsigned numbers?
8. Name the four ways in which signed integers can be represented in digital computers, and explain the differences.
9. Which one of the four representations for signed integers is used most often by digital computer systems?
10. How are complement systems similar to the odometer on a bicycle?
11. Do you think that double-dabble is an easier method than the other binary-to-decimal conversion methods explained in this chapter? Why?
12. With reference to the previous question, what are the drawbacks of the other two conversion methods?
13. What is overflow, and how can it be detected? How does overflow in unsigned numbers differ from overflow in signed numbers?
14. If a computer is capable only of manipulating and storing integers, what difficulties present themselves? How are these difficulties overcome?
15. What are the goals of Booth's algorithm?
16. How does carry differ from overflow?
17. What is arithmetic shifting?
18. What are the three component parts of a floating-point number?
19. What is a biased exponent, and what efficiencies can it provide?
20. What is normalization, and why is it necessary?
21. Why is there always some degree of error in floating-point arithmetic when performed by a binary digital computer?
22. How many bits long is a double-precision number under the IEEE-754 floating-point standard?
23. What is EBCDIC, and how is it related to BCD?
24. What is ASCII, and how did it originate?
25. Explain the difference between ASCII and Unicode.
26. How many bits does a Unicode character require?
27. Why was Unicode created?
28. How do cyclic redundancy checks work?

29. What is systematic error detection?
30. What is a Hamming code?
31. What is meant by Hamming distance, and why is it important? What is meant by minimum Hamming distance?
32. How is the number of redundant bits necessary for code related to the number of data bits?
33. What is a burst error?
34. Name an error-detection method that can compensate for burst errors.

EXERCISES

◆1. Perform the following base conversions using subtraction or division-remainder:
  ◆ a) $458_{10} = \underline{\hspace{2cm}}_3$
  ◆ b) $677_{10} = \underline{\hspace{2cm}}_5$
  ◆ c) $1518_{10} = \underline{\hspace{2cm}}_7$
  ◆ d) $4401_{10} = \underline{\hspace{2cm}}_9$

2. Perform the following base conversions using subtraction or division-remainder:
  a) $588_{10} = \underline{\hspace{2cm}}_3$
  b) $2254_{10} = \underline{\hspace{2cm}}_5$
  c) $652_{10} = \underline{\hspace{2cm}}_7$
  d) $3104_{10} = \underline{\hspace{2cm}}_9$

3. Perform the following base conversions using subtraction or division-remainder:
  a) $137_{10} = \underline{\hspace{2cm}}_3$
  b) $248_{10} = \underline{\hspace{2cm}}_5$
  c) $387_{10} = \underline{\hspace{2cm}}_7$
  d) $633_{10} = \underline{\hspace{2cm}}_9$

4. Perform the following base conversions:
  a) $20101_3 = \underline{\hspace{2cm}}_{10}$
  b) $2302_5 = \underline{\hspace{2cm}}_{10}$
  c) $1605_7 = \underline{\hspace{2cm}}_{10}$
  d) $687_9 = \underline{\hspace{2cm}}_{10}$

5. Perform the following base conversions:
  a) $20012_3 = \underline{\hspace{2cm}}_{10}$
  b) $4103_5 = \underline{\hspace{2cm}}_{10}$
  c) $3236_7 = \underline{\hspace{2cm}}_{10}$
  d) $1378_9 = \underline{\hspace{2cm}}_{10}$

6. Perform the following base conversions:

   a) $21200_3 =$ _____ $_{10}$

   b) $3244_5 =$ _____ $_{10}$

   c) $3402_7 =$ _____ $_{10}$

   d) $7657_9 =$ _____ $_{10}$

◆**7.** Convert the following decimal fractions to binary with a maximum of six places to the right of the binary point:

   ◆ **a)** 26.78125

   ◆ **b)** 194.03125

   ◆ **c)** 298.796875

   ◆ **d)** 16.1240234375

8. Convert the following decimal fractions to binary with a maximum of six places to the right of the binary point:

   a) 25.84375

   b) 57.55

   c) 80.90625

   d) 84.874023

9. Convert the following decimal fractions to binary with a maximum of six places to the right of the binary point:

   a) 27.59375

   b) 105.59375

   c) 241.53125

   d) 327.78125

10. Convert the following binary fractions to decimal:

   a) 10111.1101

   b) 100011.10011

   c) 1010011.10001

   d) 11000010.111

11. Convert the following binary fractions to decimal:

   a) 100001.111

   b) 111111.10011

   c) 1001100.1011

   d) 10001001.0111

12. Convert the following binary fractions to decimal:

   a) 110001.10101

   b) 111001.001011

   c) 1001001.10101

   d) 11101001.110001

13. Convert the hexadecimal number AC12$_{16}$ to binary.

14. Convert the hexadecimal number 7A01$_{16}$ to binary.

15. Convert the hexadecimal number DEAD BEEF$_{16}$ to binary.

16. Represent the following decimal numbers in binary using 8-bit signed magnitude, one's complement, two's complement, and excess-127 representations.

◆ **a)** 77

◆ **b)** −42

 c) 119

 d) −107

17. Represent the following decimal numbers in binary using 8-bit signed magnitude, one's complement, two's complement, and excess-127 representations:

 a) 60

 b) −60

 c) 20

 d) −20

18. Represent the following decimal numbers in binary using 8-bit signed magnitude, one's complement, two's complement, and excess-127 representations:

 a) 97

 b) −97

 c) 44

 d) −44

19. Represent the following decimal numbers in binary using 8-bit signed magnitude, one's complement, two's complement, and excess-127 representations:

 a) 89

 b) −89

 c) 66

 d) −66

20. What decimal value does the 8-bit binary number 10011110 have if:

 a) it is interpreted as an unsigned number?

 b) it is on a computer using signed-magnitude representation?

 c) it is on a computer using one's complement representation?

 d) it is on a computer using two's complement representation?

 e) it is on a computer using excess-127 representation?

21. What decimal value does the 8-bit binary number 00010001 have if:

 a) it is interpreted as an unsigned number?

 b) it is on a computer using signed-magnitude representation?

 c) it is on a computer using one's complement representation?

 d) it is on a computer using two's complement representation?

 e) it is on a computer using excess-127 representation?

22. What decimal value does the 8-bit binary number 10110100 have if:

    a) it is interpreted as an unsigned number?

    b) it is on a computer using signed-magnitude representation?

    c) it is on a computer using one's complement representation?

    d) it is on a computer using two's complement representation?

    e) it is on a computer using excess-127 representation?

23. Given the following two binary numbers: 11111100 and 01110000.

    a) Which of these two numbers is the larger unsigned binary number?

    b) Which of these two is the larger when it is being interpreted on a computer using signed two's complement representation?

    c) Which of these two is the smaller when it is being interpreted on a computer using signed-magnitude representation?

24. Using a "word" of 3 bits, list all the possible signed binary numbers and their decimal equivalents that are representable in:

    a) Signed magnitude

    b) One's complement

    c) Two's complement

25. Using a "word" of 4 bits, list all the possible signed binary numbers and their decimal equivalents that are representable in:

    a) Signed magnitude

    b) One's complement

    c) Two's complement

26. From the results of the previous two questions, generalize the range of values (in decimal) that can be represented in any given x number of bits using:

    a) Signed magnitude

    b) One's complement

    c) Two's complement

27. Fill in the following table to indicate what each binary pattern represents using the various formats.

Unsigned Integer	4-Bit Binary Value	Signed Magnitude	One's Complement	Two's Complement	Excess-7
0	0000				
1	0001				
2	0010				
3	0011				
4	0100				
5	0101				
6	0110				
7	0111				

8	1000				
9	1001				
10	1010				
11	1011				
12	1100				
13	1101				
14	1110				
15	1111				

28. Given a (very) tiny computer that has a word size of 6 bits, what are the smallest negative numbers and the largest positive numbers that this computer can represent in each of the following representations?

   ◆ **a)** One's complement

   b) Two's complement

29. To add 2 two's complement numbers together, what must be true?

30. What is the most common representation used in most computers to store signed integer values and why?

31. You have stumbled on an unknown civilization while sailing around the world. The people, who call themselves Zebronians, do math using 40 separate characters (probably because there are 40 stripes on a zebra). They would very much like to use computers, but would need a computer to do Zebronian math, which would mean a computer that could represent all 40 characters. You are a computer designer and decide to help them. You decide the best thing is to use BCZ, Binary-Coded Zebronian (which is like BCD except it codes Zebronian, not Decimal). How many bits will you need to represent each character if you want to use the minimum number of bits?

◆ **32.** Add the following unsigned binary numbers as shown.

   a) 01110101   **b)**   00010101   **c)**   01101111
       +00111011   +00011011   +00010001

33. Add the following unsigned binary numbers as shown.

   a) 01000100   **b)**   01011011   **c)**   10101100
      +10111011   +00011111   +00100100

◆ **34.** Subtract the following signed binary numbers as shown using two's complement arithmetic.

   a) 01110101   **b)**   00110101   **c)**   01101111
      −00111011   −00001011   −00010001

35. Subtract the following signed binary numbers as shown using two's complement arithmetic.

   a) 11000100   **b)**   01011011   **c)**   10101100
      −00111011   −00011111   −00100100

36. Perform the following binary multiplications, assuming unsigned integers:

   ◆ **a)** $\quad$ 1100
$$\underline{\times 101}$$

    b) $\quad$ 10101
$$\underline{\times 111}$$

    c) $\quad$ 11010
$$\underline{\times 1100}$$

37. Perform the following binary multiplications, assuming unsigned integers:

    a) $\quad$ 1011
$$\underline{\times 101}$$

    b) $\quad$ 10011
$$\underline{\times 1011}$$

    c) $\quad$ 11010
$$\underline{\times 1011}$$

38. Perform the following binary divisions, assuming unsigned integers:

   ◆ **a)** $101101 \div 101$

    b) $10000001 \div 101$

    c) $1001010010 \div 1011$

39. Perform the following binary divisions, assuming unsigned integers:

    a) $11111101 \div 1011$

    b) $110010101 \div 1001$

    c) $1001111100 \div 1100$

◆ **40.** Use the double-dabble method to convert 10212_3 directly to decimal. (Hint: You have to change the multiplier.)

41. Using signed-magnitude representation, complete the following operations:

$$+ 0 + (-0) =$$
$$(-0) + 0 =$$
$$0 + 0 =$$
$$(-0) + (-0) =$$

◆ **42.** Suppose a computer uses 4-bit one's complement representation. Ignoring overflows, what value will be stored in the variable *j* after the following pseudocode routine terminates?

```
0 → j    // Store 0 in j.
-3 → k   // Store -3 in k.
while k ≠ 0
  j = j + 1
  k = k - 1
end while
```

43. Perform the following binary multiplications using Booth's algorithm, assuming signed two's complement integers:

a) 1011
 ×0101

b) 0011
 ×1011

c) 1011
 ×1100

44. Using arithmetic shifting, perform the following:

a) double the value 00010101_2

b) quadruple the value 01110111_2

c) divide the value 11001010_2 in half

45. If the floating-point number representation on a certain system has a sign bit, a 3-bit exponent, and a 4-bit significand:

a) What is the largest positive and the smallest positive number that can be stored on this system if the storage is normalized? (Assume that no bits are implied, there is no biasing, exponents use two's complement notation, and exponents of all zeros and all ones are allowed.)

b) What bias should be used in the exponent if we prefer all exponents to be non-negative? Why would you choose this bias?

♦ **46.** Using the model in the previous question, including your chosen bias, add the following floating-point numbers and express your answer using the same notation as the addend and augend:

0	1	1	1	1	0	0	0
0	1	0	1	1	0	0	1

Calculate the relative error, if any, in your answer to the previous question.

47. Assume we are using the simple model for floating-point representation as given in the text (the representation uses a 14-bit format, 5 bits for the exponent with a bias of 15, a normalized mantissa of 8 bits, and a single sign bit for the number):

a) Show how the computer would represent the numbers 100.0 and 0.25 using this floating-point format.

b) Show how the computer would add the two floating-point numbers in part a by changing one of the numbers so they are both expressed using the same power of 2.

c) Show how the computer would represent the sum in part b using the given floating-point representation. What decimal value for the sum is the computer actually storing? Explain.

48. What causes divide underflow, and what can be done about it?

49. Why do we usually store floating-point numbers in normalized form? What is the advantage of using a bias as opposed to adding a sign bit to the exponent?

50. Let $a = 1.0 \times 2^9$, $b = -1.0 \times 2^9$ and $c = 1.0 \times 2^1$. Using the simple floating-point model described in the text (the representation uses a 14-bit format, 5 bits for the exponent with a bias of 15, a normalized mantissa of 8 bits, and a single sign bit for the number), perform the following calculations, paying close attention to the order of operations. What can you say about the algebraic properties of floating-point arithmetic in our finite model? Do you think this algebraic anomaly holds under multiplication as well as addition?

$$b + (a + c) =$$
$$(b + a) + c =$$

51. Show how each of the following floating-point values would be stored using IEEE-754 single precision (be sure to indicate the sign bit, the exponent, and the significand fields):

    a) 12.5   **b)** −1.5   **c)** 0.75   **d)** 26.625

52. Show how each of the following floating-point values would be stored using IEEE-754 double precision (be sure to indicate the sign bit, the exponent, and the significand fields):

    a) 12.5   **b)** −1.5   **c)** 0.75   **d)** 26.625

53. Suppose we have just found yet another representation for floating-point numbers. Using this representation, a 12-bit floating-point number has 1 bit for the sign of the number, 4 bits for the exponent, and 7 bits for the mantissa, which is normalized as in the Simple Model so that the first digit to the right of the radix points must be a 1. Numbers in the exponent are in signed two's complement representation. No bias is used, and there are no implied bits. Show the representation for the smallest positive number this machine can represent using the following format (simply fill in the squares provided). What decimal number does this equate to?

SIGN   EXPONENT   MANTISSA

54. Find three floating-point values to illustrate that floating-point addition is not associative. (You will need to run a program on specific hardware with a specific compiler.)

55. **a)** Given that the ASCII code for A is 1000001, what is the ASCII code for J?

    b) Given that the EBCDIC code for A is 1100 0001, what is the EBCDIC code for J?

56. **a)** The ASCII code for the letter A is 1000001, and the ASCII code for the letter a is 1100001. Given that the ASCII code for the letter G is 1000111, without looking at Table 2.7, what is the ASCII code for the letter g?

    b) The EBCDIC code for the letter A is 1100 0001, and the EBCDIC code for the letter a is 1000 0001. Given that the EBCDIC code for the letter G is 1100 0111, without looking at Table 2.6, what is the EBCDIC code for the letter g?

    c) The ASCII code for the letter A is 1000001, and the ASCII code for the letter a is 1100001. Given that the ASCII code for the letter Q is 1010001, without looking at Table 2.7, what is the ASCII code for the letter q?

    d) The EBCDIC code for the letter J is 1101 0001, and the EBCDIC code for the letter j is 1001 0001. Given that the EBCDIC code for the letter Q is 1101 1000, without looking at Table 2.6, what is the EBCDIC code for the letter q?

e) In general, if you were going to write a program to convert uppercase ASCII characters to lowercase, how would you do it? Looking at Table 2.6, could you use the same algorithm to convert uppercase EBCDIC letters to lowercase?

f) If you were tasked with interfacing an EBCDIC-based computer with an ASCII or Unicode computer, what would be the best way to convert the EBCDIC characters to ASCII characters?

◆ **57.** Assume a 24-bit word on a computer. In these 24 bits, we wish to represent the value 295.

◆ **a)** How would the computer represent the decimal value 295?

◆ **b)** If our computer uses 8-bit ASCII and even parity, how would the computer represent the string 295?

◆ **c)** If our computer uses packed BCD with zero padding, how would the computer represent the number +295?

58. Decode the following ASCII message, assuming 7-bit ASCII characters and no parity:
1001010 1001111 1001000 1001110 0100000 1000100 1001111 1000101

59. Why would a system designer wish to make Unicode the default character set for their new system? What reason(s) could you give for not using Unicode as a default? (Hint: Think about language compatibility versus storage space.)

60. Assume we wish to create a code using 3 information bits, 1 parity bit (appended to the end of the information), and odd parity. List all legal code words in this code. What is the Hamming distance of your code?

61. Suppose we are given the following subset of code words, created for a 7-bit memory word with one parity bit: 11100110, 00001000, 10101011, and 11111110. Does this code use even or odd parity? Explain.

62. Are the error-correcting Hamming codes systematic? Explain.

63. Compute the Hamming distance of the following code:
0011010010111100
0000011110001111
0010010110101101
0001011010011110

64. Compute the Hamming distance of the following code:
0000000101111111
0000001010111111
0000010011011111
0000100011101111
0001000011110111
0010000011111011
0100000011111101
1000000011111110

65. In defining the Hamming distance for a code, we choose to use the minimum (Hamming) distance between any two encodings. Explain why it would not be better to use the maximum or average distance.

66. Suppose we want an error-correcting code that will allow all single-bit errors to be corrected for memory words of length 10.

    a) How many parity bits are necessary?

    b) Assuming we are using the Hamming algorithm presented in this chapter to design our error-correcting code, find the code word to represent the 10-bit information word:

    1 0 0 1 1 0 0 1 1 0.

67. Suppose we want an error-correcting code that will allow all single-bit errors to be corrected for memory words of length 12.

    a) How many parity bits are necessary?

    b) Assuming we are using the Hamming algorithm presented in this chapter to design our error-correcting code, find the code word to represent the 12-bit information word:

    1 0 0 1 0 0 0 1 1 0 1 0.

♦ 68. Suppose we are working with an error-correcting code that will allow all single-bit errors to be corrected for memory words of length 7. We have already calculated that we need 4 check bits, and the length of all code words will be 11. Code words are created according to the Hamming algorithm presented in the text. We now receive the following code word:

    1 0 1 0 1 0 1 1 1 1 0

    Assuming even parity, is this a legal code word? If not, according to our error-correcting code, where is the error?

69. Repeat exercise 68 using the following code word:

    0 1 1 1 1 0 1 0 1 0 1

70. Suppose we are working with an error-correcting code that will allow all single-bit errors to be corrected for memory words of length 12. We have already calculated that we need 5 check bits, and the length of all code words will be 17. Code words are created according to the Hamming algorithm presented in the text. We now receive the following code word:

    0 1 1 0 0 1 0 1 0 0 1 0 0 1 0 0 1

    Assuming even parity, is this a legal code word? If not, according to our error-correcting code, where is the error?

71. Name two ways in which Reed-Solomon coding differs from Hamming coding.

72. When would you choose a CRC code over a Hamming code? A Hamming code over a CRC?

◆ **73.** Find the quotients and remainders for the following division problems modulo 2.

    ◆ **a)** $1010111_2 \div 1101_2$

    ◆ **b)** $1011111_2 \div 11101_2$

    ◆ **c)** $1011001101_2 \div 10101_2$

    ◆ **d)** $111010111_2 \div 10111_2$

74. Find the quotients and remainders for the following division problems modulo 2.

    a) $1111010_2 \div 1011_2$

    b) $1010101_2 \div 1100_2$

    c) $1101101011_2 \div 10101_2$

    d) $1111101011_2 \div 101101_2$

75. Find the quotients and remainders for the following division problems modulo 2.

    a) $11001001_2 \div 1101_2$

    b) $1011000_2 \div 10011_2$

    c) $11101011_2 \div 10111_2$

    d) $111110001_2 \div 1001_2$

76. Find the quotients and remainders for the following division problems modulo 2.

    a) $1001111_2 \div 1101_2$

    b) $1011110_2 \div 1100_2$

    c) $1001101110_2 \div 11001_2$

    d) $111101010_2 \div 10011_2$

◆ **77.** Using the CRC polynomial 1011, compute the CRC code word for the information word, 1011001. Check the division performed at the receiver.

78. Using the CRC polynomial 1101, compute the CRC code word for the information word, 01001101. Check the division performed at the receiver.

79. Using the CRC polynomial 1101, compute the CRC code word for the information word, 1100011. Check the division performed at the receiver.

80. Using the CRC polynomial 1101, compute the CRC code word for the information word, 01011101. Check the division performed at the receiver.

81. Pick an architecture (such as 80486, Pentium, Pentium IV, SPARC, Alpha, or MIPS). Do research to find out how your architecture approaches the concepts introduced in this chapter. For example, what representation does it use for negative values? What character codes does it support?

82. We have seen that floating-point arithmetic is neither associative nor distributive. Why do you think this is the case?

FOCUS ON CODES FOR DATA RECORDING AND TRANSMISSION

ASCII, EBCDIC, and Unicode are represented unambiguously in computer memories. (Chapter 3 describes how this is done using binary digital devices.) Digital switches, such as those used in memories, are either "off " or "on" with nothing in between. However, when data are written to some sort of recording medium (such as tape or disk), or transmitted over long distances, binary signals can become blurred, particularly when long strings of ones and zeros are involved. This blurring is partly attributable to timing drifts that occur between senders and receivers. Magnetic media, such as tapes and disks, can also lose synchronization owing to the electrical behavior of the magnetic material from which they are made. Signal transitions between the "high" and "low" states of digital signals help to maintain synchronization in data recording and communications devices. To this end, ASCII, EBCDIC, and Unicode are translated into other codes before they are transmitted or recorded. This translation is carried out by control electronics in data recording and transmission devices. Neither the user nor the host computer is ever aware that this translation has taken place.

Bytes are sent and received by telecommunications devices by using "high" and "low" pulses in the transmission media (copper wire, for example). Magnetic storage devices record data using changes in magnetic polarity called **flux reversals**. Certain coding methods are better suited for data communications than for data recording. New codes are continually being invented to accommodate evolving recording methods and improved transmission and recording media. We will examine a few of the more popular recording and transmission codes to show how some of the challenges in this area have been overcome. For the sake of brevity, we will use the term **data encoding** to mean the process of converting a simple character code such as ASCII to some other code that better lends itself to storage or transmission. **Encoded data** will be used to refer to character codes so encoded.

2A.1 NON-RETURN-TO-ZERO CODE

The simplest data encoding method is the **non-return-to-zero (NRZ)** code. We use this code implicitly when we say that "highs" and "lows" represent ones and zeros: ones are usually high voltage, and zeroes are low voltage. Typically, high voltage is positive 3 or 5 volts; low voltage is negative 3 or 5 volts. (The reverse is logically equivalent.)

For example, the ASCII code for the English word *OK* with even parity is 11001111 01001011. This pattern in NRZ code is shown in its signal form as well as in its magnetic flux form in Figure 2A.1. Each of the bits occupies an arbitrary slice of time in a transmission medium or an arbitrary speck of space on a disk. These slices and specks are called **bit cells**.

a)

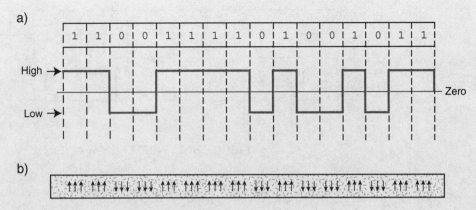

b)

FIGURE 2A.1 NRZ Encoding of *OK* as
a) Transmission Waveform
b) Magnetic Flux Pattern (The direction of the arrows indicates the magnetic polarity.)

As you can see by the figure, we have a long run of ones in the ASCII O. If we transmit the longer form of the word *OK*, *OKAY*, we would have a long string of zeros as well as a long string of ones: 11001111 01001011 01000001 01011001. Unless the receiver is synchronized precisely with the sender, it is not possible for either to know the exact duration of the signal for each bit cell. Slow or out-of-phase timing within the receiver might cause the bit sequence for *OKAY* to be received as: 10011 0100101 010001 0101001, which would be translated back to ASCII as *<ETX>()*, bearing no resemblance to what was sent. (*<ETX>* is used here to mean the single ASCII End-of-Text character, 26 in decimal.)

A little experimentation with this example will demonstrate to you that if only one bit is missed in NRZ code, the entire message can be reduced to gibberish.

2A.2 NON-RETURN-TO-ZERO-INVERT CODE

The **non-return-to-zero-invert (NRZI)** method addresses part of the problem of synchronization loss. NRZI provides a transition—either high-to-low or low-to-high—for each binary one, and no transition for binary zero. The NRZI coding for *OK* (with even parity) is shown in Figure 2A.2.

Although NRZI eliminates the problem of dropping binary ones, we are still faced with the problem of long strings of zeros causing the receiver or reader to drift out of phase, potentially dropping bits along the way.

The obvious approach to solving this problem is to inject sufficient transitions into the transmitted waveform to keep the sender and receiver synchronized, while preserving the information content of the message. This is the essential idea behind all coding methods used today in the storage and transmission of data.

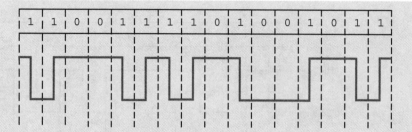

FIGURE 2A.2   NRZI Encoding of *OK*

2A.3   PHASE MODULATION (MANCHESTER CODE)

The coding method known commonly as **phase modulation (PM)**, or **Manchester coding**, deals with the synchronization problem head-on. PM provides a transition for each bit, whether a one or a zero. In PM, each binary one is signaled by an "up" transition, and binary zeros with a "down" transition. Extra transitions are provided at bit cell boundaries when necessary. The PM coding of the word *OK* is shown in Figure 2A.3.

Phase modulation is often used in data transmission applications such as local area networks. It is inefficient for use in data storage, however. If PM were used for tape and disk, phase modulation would require twice the bit density of NRZ. (One flux transition for each half bit cell, depicted in Figure 2A.3b.) However, we have

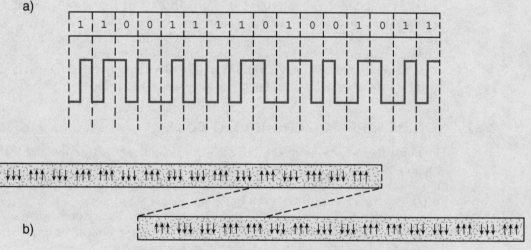

FIGURE 2A.3   Phase Modulation (Manchester Coding) of the Word *OK* as:
a)   Transmission Waveform
b)   Magnetic Flux Pattern

just seen how using NRZ might result in unacceptably high error rates. We could therefore define a "good" encoding scheme as a method that most economically achieves a balance between "excessive" storage volume requirements and "excessive" error rates. A number of codes have been created in trying to find this middle ground.

2A.4 FREQUENCY MODULATION

As used in digital applications, **frequency modulation (FM)** is similar to phase modulation in that at least one transition is supplied for each bit cell. These synchronizing transitions occur at the beginning of each bit cell. To encode a binary 1, an additional transition is provided in the center of the bit cell. The FM coding for *OK* is shown in Figure 2A.4.

As you can readily see from the figure, FM is only slightly better than PM with respect to its storage requirements. FM, however, lends itself to a coding method called **modified frequency modulation (MFM)**, whereby bit cell boundary transitions are provided only between consecutive zeros. With MFM, then, at least one transition is supplied for every pair of bit cells, as opposed to each cell in PM or FM.

With fewer transitions than PM and more transitions than NRZ, MFM is a highly effective code in terms of economy and error control. For many years, MFM was virtually the only coding method used for rigid disk storage. The MFM coding for *OK* is shown in Figure 2A.5.

2A.5 RUN-LENGTH-LIMITED CODE

Run-length-limited (RLL) is a coding method in which block character code words such as ASCII or EBCDIC are translated into code words specially designed to limit the number of consecutive zeros appearing in the code. An **RLL(*d*, *k*) code** allows a minimum of *d* and a maximum of *k* consecutive zeros to appear between any pair of consecutive ones.

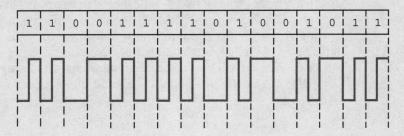

FIGURE 2A.4 Frequency Modulation Coding of *OK*

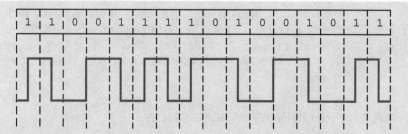

FIGURE 2A.5 Modified Frequency Modulation Coding of *OK*

Clearly, RLL code words must contain more bits than the original character code. However, because RLL is coded using NRZI on the disk, RLL-coded
data actually occupy less space on magnetic media because fewer flux transitions are involved. The code words employed by RLL are designed to prevent a
disk from losing synchronization as it would if a "flat" binary NRZI code were
used.

Although there are many variants, RLL(2, 7) is the predominant code used
by magnetic disk systems. It is technically a 16-bit mapping of 8-bit ASCII or
EBCDIC characters. However, it is nearly 50% more efficient than MFM in
terms of flux reversals. (Proof of this is left as an exercise.)

Theoretically speaking, RLL is a form of data compression called **Huffman coding** (discussed in Chapter 7), where the most likely information
bit patterns are encoded using the shortest code word bit patterns. (In our
case, we are talking about the fewest number of flux reversals.) The theory is based on the assumption that the presence or absence of a 1 in any
bit cell is an equally likely event. From this assumption, we can infer that
the probability is 0.25 of the pattern 10 occurring within any pair of adja-
cent bit cells. ($P(b_i = 1) = \frac{1}{2}$; $P(b_j = 0) = \frac{1}{2}$; $\Rightarrow P(b_i b_j = 10) = \frac{1}{2} \times \frac{1}{2} = \frac{1}{4}$.)
Similarly, the bit pattern 011 has a probability of 0.125 of occurring.
Figure 2A.6 shows the probability tree for the bit patterns used in RLL(2, 7).
Table 2A.1 gives the bit patterns used by RLL(2, 7).

As you can see by the table, it is impossible to have more than seven consecutive 0s, whereas at least two 0s will appear in any possible combination of bits.

Figure 2A.7 compares the MFM coding for *OK* with its RLL(2, 7) NRZI coding. MFM has 12 flux transitions to 8 transitions for RLL. If the limiting factor
in the design of a disk is the number of flux transitions per square millimeter, we
can pack 50% more *OK*s in the same magnetic area using RLL than we could
using MFM. For this reason, RLL is used almost exclusively in high-capacity
disk drives.

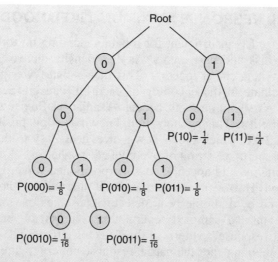

FIGURE 2A.6   The Probability Tree for RLL(2, 7) Coding

Character Bit Pattern	RLL(2, 7) Code
10	0100
11	1000
000	000100
010	100100
011	001000
0010	00100100
0011	00001000

TABLE 2A.1   RLL(2, 7) Coding

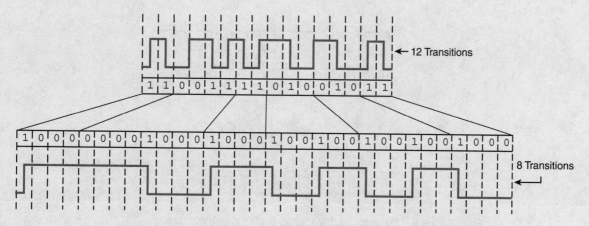

FIGURE 2A.7   MFM (top) and RLL(2, 7) Coding (bottom) for *OK*

2A.6 PARTIAL RESPONSE MAXIMUM LIKELIHOOD CODING

RLL by itself is insufficient for reliable encoding on today's ultra-high-capacity magnetic disk and tape media. As data density increases, encoded bits are necessarily written closer together. This means that fewer grains of magnetic material participate in the encoding of each bit, causing decreased magnetic signal strength. As signal strength decreases, adjacent flux reversals begin to interfere with each other. This phenomenon, known as **superpositioning**, is characterized in Figure 2A.8, which shows how a nice, neat, easy-to-detect magnetic sine wave starts looking like a string of overcooked spaghetti.

Despite its wild appearance, superpositioned waveforms are well defined and understood. However, unlike traditional sine waves, their characteristics cannot be captured by a simple peak detector that takes one measurement per bit cell. They are instead sampled several times across the bit cell waveform, giving a "partial response" pattern to the detector circuit. The detector circuit (Viterbi detector) then matches the partial response pattern to a relatively small set of possible response patterns and the closest match (the pattern with the "maximum likelihood" of being correct) is passed to the digital decoder. Thus, this encoding scheme is called **partial response maximum likelihood**, or **PRML**. (After you read Chapter 3, you will understand how a Viterbi detector decides which pattern is the most likely.)

PRML is a generic designation for a family of encoding methods that are distinguished from one another by the number of samples taken per bit cell. More

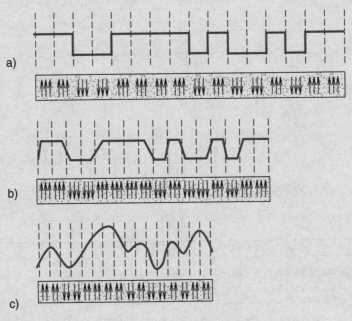

FIGURE 2A.8 Magnetic Behaviors as Bit Density Increases
In a), b), and c), magnetic flux changes are pushed increasingly closer together.

frequent sampling permits greater data density. Along with improvements in magnetic head technology, PRML has been a fundamental enabler of the geometric increase in disk and tape densities since 2000, and it is indeed possible that this technology has not yet been fully exploited.

2A.7 SUMMARY

Your knowledge of how bytes are stored on disks and tape will help you to understand many of the concepts and problems relating to data storage. Your familiarity with error control methods will aid you in your study of both data storage and data communications. The best information pertinent to data encoding for magnetic storage can be found in electrical engineering books. They contain a trove of fascinating information regarding the behavior of physical media, and how this behavior is employed by various coding methods. You will learn more about data storage in Chapter 7. Chapter 12 presents topics relating to data communications.

EXERCISES

1. Why is non-return-to-zero coding avoided as a method for writing data to a magnetic disk?

2. Why is Manchester coding not a good choice for writing data to a magnetic disk?

3. Explain how run-length-limited encoding works.

4. Write the 7-bit ASCII code for the character *4* using the following encoding:

   a) Non-return-to-zero

   b) Non-return-to-zero-invert

   c) Manchester code

   d) Frequency modulation

   e) Modified frequency modulation

   f) Run-length-limited

   (Assume 1 is "high" and 0 is "low.")

CHAPTER 3
Boolean Algebra and Digital Logic

3.1 INTRODUCTION

George Boole lived in England during the first half of the nineteenth century. The firstborn son of a cobbler, Boole taught himself Greek, Latin, French, German, and the language of mathematics. Just before he turned 16, Boole accepted a position teaching at a small Methodist school, providing his family with much-needed income. At the age of 19, Boole returned home to Lincoln, England, and founded his own boarding school to better provide support for his family. He operated this school for 15 years, until he became Professor of Mathematics at Queen's College in Cork, Ireland. His social status as the son of a tradesman prevented Boole's appointment to a more prestigious university, despite his authoring of more than a dozen highly esteemed papers and treatises. His most famous monograph, *The Laws of Thought*, published in 1854, created a branch of mathematics known as **symbolic logic** or **Boolean algebra**.

Nearly 85 years later, John Vincent Atanasoff applied Boolean algebra to computing. He recounted the moment of his insight to Linda Null. At the time, Atanasoff was attempting to build a calculating machine based on the same technology used by Pascal and Babbage. His aim was to use this machine to solve systems of linear equations. After struggling with repeated failures, Atanasoff was so frustrated that he decided to take a drive. He was living in Ames, Iowa, at the time, but found himself 200 miles away in Illinois before he suddenly realized how far he had driven.

Atanasoff had not intended to drive that far, but because he was in Illinois, where it was legal to buy a drink in a tavern, he sat down and ordered a bourbon. He chuckled to himself when he realized that he had driven such a distance for a drink! Even more ironic is the fact that he never touched the drink. He felt he

137

needed a clear head to write down the revelations that came to him during his long, aimless journey. Exercising his physics and mathematics backgrounds and focusing on the failures of his previous computing machine, he made four critical breakthroughs necessary in the machine's new design:

1. He would use electricity instead of mechanical movements (vacuum tubes would allow him to do this).

2. Because he was using electricity, he would use base 2 numbers instead of base 10 (this correlated directly with switches that were either "on" or "off"), resulting in a digital, rather than an analog, machine.

3. He would use capacitors (condensers) for memory because they store electrical charges with a regenerative process to avoid power leakage.

4. Computations would be done by what Atanasoff termed "direct logical action" (which is essentially equivalent to Boolean algebra) and not by enumeration as all previous computing machines had done.

It should be noted that at the time, Atanasoff did not recognize the application of Boolean algebra to his problem and that he devised his own direct logical action by trial and error. He was unaware that in 1938, Claude Shannon proved that two-valued Boolean algebra could describe the operation of two-valued electrical switching circuits. Today, we see the significance of Boolean algebra's application in the design of modern computing systems. It is for this reason that we include a chapter on Boolean logic and its relationship to digital computers.

This chapter contains a brief introduction to the basics of logic design. It provides minimal coverage of Boolean algebra and this algebra's relationship to logic gates and basic digital circuits. You may already be familiar with the basic Boolean operators from your previous programming experience. It is a fair question, then, to ask why you must study this material in more detail. The relationship between Boolean logic and the actual physical components of any computer system is strong, as you will see in this chapter. As a computer scientist, you may never have to design digital circuits or other physical components—in fact, this chapter will not prepare you to design such items. Rather, it provides sufficient background for you to understand the basic motivation underlying computer design and implementation. Understanding how Boolean logic affects the design of various computer system components will allow you to use, from a programming perspective, any computer system more effectively. If you are interested in delving deeper, there are many resources listed at the end of the chapter to allow further investigation into these topics.

3.2 BOOLEAN ALGEBRA

Boolean algebra is an algebra for the manipulation of objects that can take on only two values, typically true and false, although it can be any pair of values. Because computers are built as collections of switches that are either "on" or "off," Boolean algebra is a natural way to represent digital information. In reality, digital circuits use low and high voltages, but for our level of understanding, 0 and 1 will suffice. It is common to interpret the digital value 0 as *false* and the digital value 1 as *true*.

3.2.1 Boolean Expressions

In addition to binary objects, Boolean algebra also has operations that can be performed on these objects, or variables. Combining the variables and operators yields **Boolean expressions**. A **Boolean function** typically has one or more input values and yields a result, based on the input values, in the set $\{0,1\}$.

Three common Boolean operators are **AND, OR**, and **NOT**. To better understand these operators, we need a mechanism to allow us to examine their behaviors. A Boolean operator can be completely described using a table that lists the inputs, all possible values for these inputs, and the resulting values of the operation for all possible combinations of these inputs. This table is called a **truth table**. A truth table shows the relationship, in tabular form, between the input values and the result of a specific Boolean operator or function on the input variables. Let's look at the Boolean operators AND, OR, and NOT to see how each is represented, using both Boolean algebra and truth tables.

The logical operator AND is typically represented by either a dot or no symbol at all. For example, the Boolean expression xy is equivalent to the expression $x \cdot y$ and is read "x and y." The expression xy is often referred to as a **Boolean product**. The behavior of this operator is characterized by the truth table shown in Table 3.1.

The result of the expression xy is 1 only when both inputs are 1, and 0 otherwise. Each row in the table represents a different Boolean expression, and all possible combinations of values for x and y are represented by the rows in the table.

The Boolean operator OR is typically represented by a plus sign. Therefore, the expression $x + y$ is read "x or y." The result of $x + y$ is 0 only when both of its input values are 0. The expression $x + y$ is often referred to as a **Boolean sum**. The truth table for OR is shown in Table 3.2.

The remaining logical operator, NOT, is represented typically by either an overscore or a prime. Therefore, both $\bar{x}$ and x' are read "not x." The truth table for NOT is shown in Table 3.3.

Inputs		Outputs
x	y	xy
0	0	0
0	1	0
1	0	0
1	1	1

TABLE 3.1 Truth Table for AND

Inputs		Outputs
x	y	x + y
0	0	0
0	1	1
1	0	1
1	1	1

TABLE 3.2 Truth Table for OR

Inputs	Outputs
x	x'
0	1
1	0

TABLE 3.3 Truth Table for NOT

We now understand that Boolean algebra deals with binary variables and logical operations on those variables. Combining these two concepts, we can examine Boolean expressions composed of Boolean variables and multiple logic operators. For example, the Boolean function

$$F(x,y,z) = x + y'z$$

is represented by a Boolean expression involving the three Boolean variables *x, y,* and *z* and the logical operators OR, NOT, and AND. How do we know which operator to apply first? The rules of precedence for Boolean operators give NOT top priority, followed by AND, and then OR. For our previous function *F*, we would negate *y* first, then perform the AND of *y'* and *z*, and finally OR this result with *x*.

We can also use a truth table to represent this expression. It is often helpful, when creating a truth table for a more complex function such as this, to build the table representing different pieces of the function, one column at a time, until the final function can be evaluated. The truth table for our function *F* is shown in Table 3.4.

The last column in the truth table indicates the values of the function for all possible combinations of *x, y,* and *z*. We note that the real truth table for our function *F* consists of only the first three columns and the last column. The shaded columns show the intermediate steps necessary to arrive at our final answer. Creating truth tables in this manner makes it easier to evaluate the function for all possible combinations of the input values.

3.2.2   Boolean Identities

Frequently, a Boolean expression is not in its simplest form. Recall from algebra that an expression such as $2x + 6x$ is not in its simplest form; it can be reduced (represented by fewer or simpler terms) to $8x$. Boolean expressions can also be simplified, but we need new **identities**, or laws, that apply to Boolean algebra instead of regular algebra. These identities, which apply to single Boolean variables as well as Boolean expressions, are listed in Table 3.5. Note that each relationship (with the exception of the last one) has both an AND (or product) form and an OR (or sum) form. This is known as the **duality principle**.

Inputs			Outputs
x y z	y'	y'z	x + y'z = F
0 0 0	1	0	0
0 0 1	1	1	1
0 1 0	0	0	0
0 1 1	0	0	0
1 0 0	1	0	1
1 0 1	1	1	1
1 1 0	0	0	1
1 1 1	0	0	1

TABLE 3.4   Truth Table for $F(x,y,z) = x + y'z$

Identity Name	AND Form	OR Form
Identity Law	$1x = x$	$0 + x = x$
Null (or Dominance) Law	$0x = 0$	$1 + x = 1$
Idempotent Law	$xx = x$	$x + x = x$
Inverse Law	$xx' = 0$	$x + x' = 1$
Commutative Law	$xy = yx$	$x + y = y + x$
Associative Law	$(xy)z = x(yz)$	$(x + y) + z = x + (y + z)$
Distributive Law	$x + (yz) = (x + y)(x + z)$	$x(y + z) = xy + xz$
Absorption Law	$x(x + y) = x$	$x + xy = x$
DeMorgan's Law	$(xy)' = x' + y'$	$(x + y)' = x'y'$
Double Complement Law	$x'' = x$	

TABLE 3.5   Basic Identities of Boolean Algebra

The Identity Law states that any Boolean variable ANDed with 1 or ORed with 0 simply results in the original variable (1 is the identity element for AND; 0 is the identity element for OR). The Null Law states that any Boolean variable ANDed with 0 is 0, and a variable ORed with 1 is always 1. The Idempotent Law states that ANDing or ORing a variable with itself produces the original variable. The Inverse Law states that ANDing or ORing a variable with its complement produces the identity for that given operation. Boolean variables can be reordered (commuted) and regrouped (associated) without affecting the final result. You should recognize these as the Commutative and Associative Laws from algebra. The Distributive Law shows how OR distributes over AND and vice versa.

The Absorption Law and DeMorgan's Law are not so obvious, but we can prove these identities by creating a truth table for the various expressions: If the right-hand side is equal to the left-hand side, the expressions represent the same function and result in identical truth tables. Table 3.6 depicts the truth table for both the left- and right-hand sides of DeMorgan's Law for AND. It is left as exercises to prove the validity of the remaining laws, in particular, the OR form of DeMorgan's Law and both forms of the Absorption Law.

The Double Complement Law formalizes the idea of the double negative, which evokes rebuke from high school English teachers. The Double Complement Law can be useful in digital circuits as well as in your life. For example, let $x = 1$ represent the idea that you have a positive quantity of cash. If you have no cash, you have x'. When an untrustworthy acquaintance asks to borrow some cash, you can truthfully say that you don't have no money. That is, $x = (x)''$ even if you just got paid.

x	y	(xy)	$(xy)'$	x'	y'	$x' + y'$
0	0	0	1	1	1	1
0	1	0	1	1	0	1
1	0	0	1	0	1	1
1	1	1	0	0	0	0

TABLE 3.6   Truth Table for the AND Form of DeMorgan's Law

One of the most common errors that beginners make when working with Boolean logic is to assume the following: $(xy)' = x'y'$. **Please note that this is not a valid equality!** DeMorgan's Law clearly indicates that this statement is incorrect. Instead, $(xy)' = x' + y'$. This is a very easy mistake to make, and one that should be avoided. Care must be taken with other expressions involving negation as well.

3.2.3 Simplification of Boolean Expressions

The algebraic identities we studied in algebra class allow us to reduce algebraic expressions (such as $10x + 2y - x + 3y$) to their simplest forms ($9x + 5y$). The Boolean identities can be used to simplify Boolean expressions in a similar manner. We apply these identities in the following examples.

EXAMPLE 3.1 Suppose we have the function $F(x,y) = xy + xy$. Using the OR form of the Idempotent Law and treating the expression xy as a Boolean variable, we simplify the original expression to xy. Therefore, $F(x,y) = xy + xy = xy$.

EXAMPLE 3.2 Given the function $F(x,y,z) = x'yz + x'yz' + xz$, we simplify as follows:

$$
\begin{aligned}
F(x,y,z) &= x'yz + x'yz' + xz \\
&= x'y(z + z') + xz &&\text{(Distributive)} \\
&= x'y(1) + xz &&\text{(Inverse)} \\
&= x'y + xz &&\text{(Identity)}
\end{aligned}
$$

EXAMPLE 3.3 Given the function $F(x,y) = y + (xy)'$, we simplify as follows:

$$
\begin{aligned}
F(x,y) &= y + (xy)' \\
&= y + (x' + y') &&\text{(DeMorgan's)} \\
&= y + (y' + x') &&\text{(Commutative)} \\
&= (y + y') + x' &&\text{(Associative)} \\
&= 1 + x' &&\text{(Inverse)} \\
&= 1 &&\text{(Null)}
\end{aligned}
$$

EXAMPLE 3.4 Given the function $F(x,y) = (xy)'(x' + y)(y' + y)$, we simplify as follows:

$$
\begin{aligned}
F(x,y) &= (xy)'(x' + y)(y' + y) \\
&= (xy)'(x' + y)(1) &&\text{(Inverse)} \\
&= (xy)'(x' + y) &&\text{(Identity)} \\
&= (x' + y')(x' + y) &&\text{(DeMorgan's)} \\
&= x' + y'y &&\text{(Distributive over AND)} \\
&= x' + 0 &&\text{(Inverse)} \\
&= x' &&\text{(Idempotent)}
\end{aligned}
$$

At times, the simplification is reasonably straightforward, as in the preceding examples. However, using the identities can be tricky, as we see in the next two examples.

EXAMPLE 3.5 Given the function $F(x,y) = x'(x + y) + (y + x)(x + y')$, we simplify as follows:

$$
\begin{aligned}
F(x,y) &= x'(x + y) + (y + x)(x + y') \\
&= x'(x + y) + (x + y)(x + y') && \text{(Commutative)} \\
&= x'(x + y) + (x + yy') && \text{(Distributive over AND)} \\
&= x'(x + y) + (x + 0) && \text{(Inverse)} \\
&= x'(x + y) + x && \text{(Identity)} \\
&= x'x + x'y + x && \text{(Distributive)} \\
&= 0 + x'y + x && \text{(Inverse)} \\
&= x'y + x && \text{(Identity)} \\
&= x + x'y && \text{(Commutative)} \\
&= (x + x')(x + y) && \text{(Distributive over AND)} \\
&= 1(x + y) && \text{(Inverse)} \\
&= x + y && \text{(Identity)}
\end{aligned}
$$

EXAMPLE 3.6 Given the function $F(x,y,z) = xy + x'z + yz$, we simplify as follows:

$$
\begin{aligned}
F(x,y,z) &= xy + x'z + yz \\
&= xy + x'z + yz(1) && \text{(Identity)} \\
&= xy + x'z + yz(x + x') && \text{(Inverse)} \\
&= xy + x'z + (yz)x + (yz)x' && \text{(Distributive)} \\
&= xy + x'z + x(yz) + x'(zy) && \text{(Commutative)} \\
&= xy + x'z + (xy)z + (x'z)y && \text{(Associative twice)} \\
&= xy + (xy)z + x'z + (x'z)y && \text{(Commutative)} \\
&= xy(1 + z) + x'z(1 + y) && \text{(Distributive)} \\
&= xy(1) + x'z(1) && \text{(Null)} \\
&= xy + x'z && \text{(Identity)}
\end{aligned}
$$

Example 3.6 illustrates what is commonly known as the **Consensus Theorem**.

How did we know to insert additional terms to simplify the function in Example 3.6? Unfortunately, there is no defined set of rules for using these identities to minimize a Boolean expression; it is simply something that comes with experience. There are other methods that can be used to simplify Boolean expressions; we mention these later in this section.

We can also use these identities to prove Boolean equalities, as we see in Example 3.7.

≡ **EXAMPLE 3.7** Prove that $(x + y)(x' + y) = y$

$$
\begin{aligned}
(x + y)(x' + y) &= xx' + xy + yx' + yy && \text{(Distributive)} \\
&= 0 + xy + yx' + yy && \text{(Inverse)} \\
&= 0 + xy + yx' + y && \text{(Idempotent)} \\
&= xy + yx' + y && \text{(Identity)} \\
&= yx + yx' + y && \text{(Commutative)} \\
&= y(x + x') + y && \text{(Distributive)} \\
&= y(1) + y && \text{(Inverse)} \\
&= y + y && \text{(Identity)} \\
&= y && \text{(Idempotent)}
\end{aligned}
$$

To prove the equality of two Boolean expressions, you can also create the truth tables for each and compare. If the truth tables are identical, the expressions are equal. We leave it as an exercise to find the truth tables for the equality proven in Example 3.7.

3.2.4 Complements

As you saw in Example 3.1, the Boolean identities can be applied to Boolean expressions, not simply Boolean variables (we treated xy as a Boolean variable and then applied the Idempotent Law). The same is true for the Boolean operators. The most common Boolean operator applied to more complex Boolean expressions is the NOT operator, resulting in the **complement** of the expression. Quite often, it is cheaper and less complicated to implement the complement of a function rather than the function itself. If we implement the complement, we must invert the final output to yield the original function; this is accomplished with one simple NOT operation. Therefore, complements are quite useful.

To find the complement of a Boolean function, we use DeMorgan's Law. The OR form of this law states that $(x + y)' = x'y'$. We can easily extend this to three or more variables as follows:

Given the function:

$F(x,y,z) = (x + y + z)$. Then $F'(x,y,z) = (x + y + z)'$.

Let $w = (x + y)$. Then $F'(x,y,z) = (w + z)' = w'z'$.

Now, applying DeMorgan's Law again, we get:

$w'z' = (x + y)'z' = x'y'z' = F'(x,y,z)$

Therefore, if $F(x,y,z) = (x + y + z)$, then $F'(x,y,z) = x'y'z'$. Applying the principle of duality, we see that $(xyz)' = x' + y' + z'$.

It appears that, to find the complement of a Boolean expression, we simply replace each variable by its complement (x is replaced by x') and interchange ANDs and ORs. In fact, this is exactly what DeMorgan's Law tells us to do. For example, the complement of $x' + yz'$ is $x(y' + z)$. We have to add the parentheses to ensure the correct precedence.

You can verify that this simple rule of thumb for finding the complement of a Boolean expression is correct by examining the truth tables for both the expression and its complement. The complement of any expression, when represented as a truth table, should have 0s for output everywhere the original function has 1s, and 1s in those places where the original function has 0s. Table 3.7 depicts the truth tables for $F(x,y,z) = x' + yz'$ and its complement, $F'(x,y,z) = x(y' + z)$. The shaded portions indicate the final results for F and F'.

3.2.5 Representing Boolean Functions

We have seen that there are many different ways to represent a given Boolean function. For example, we can use a truth table, or we can use one of many different Boolean expressions. In fact, there are an infinite number of Boolean expressions that are **logically equivalent** to one another. Two expressions that can be represented by the same truth table are considered logically equivalent (see Example 3.8).

EXAMPLE 3.8 Suppose $F(x,y,z) = x + xy'$. We can also express F as $F(x,y,z) = x + x + xy'$ because the Idempotent Law tells us these two expressions are the same. We can also express F as $F(x,y,z) = x(1 + y')$ using the Distributive Law.

To help eliminate potential confusion, logic designers specify a Boolean function using a **canonical**, or **standardized**, form. For any given Boolean function, there exists a unique standardized form. However, there are different "standards" that designers use. The two most common are the sum-of-products form and the product-of-sums form.

The **sum-of-products form** requires that the expression be a collection of ANDed variables (or product terms) that are ORed together. The function $F_1(x,y,z) = xy + yz' + xyz$ is in sum-of-products form. The function $F_2(x,y,z) = xy' + x(y + z')$ is not in sum-of-products form. We apply the Distributive Law to distribute the x variable in F_2, resulting in the expression $xy' + xy + xz'$, which is now in sum-of-products form.

x	y	z	yz'	x' + yz'	y' + z	x(y' + z)
0	0	0	0	1	1	0
0	0	1	0	1	1	0
0	1	0	1	1	0	0
0	1	1	0	1	1	0
1	0	0	0	0	1	1
1	0	1	0	0	1	1
1	1	0	1	1	0	0
1	1	1	0	0	1	1

TABLE 3.7 Truth Table Representation for a Function and Its Complement

Boolean expressions stated in **product-of-sums form** consist of ORed variables (sum terms) that are ANDed together. The function $F_1(x,y,z) = (x + y)$ $(x + z')(y + z')(y + z)$ is in product-of-sums form. The product-of-sums form is often preferred when the Boolean expression evaluates true in more cases than it evaluates false. This is not the case with the function F_1, so the sum-of-products form is appropriate. Also, the sum-of-products form is usually easier to work with and to simplify; we therefore use this form exclusively in the sections that follow.

Any Boolean expression can be represented in sum-of-products form. Because any Boolean expression can also be represented as a truth table, we conclude that any truth table can also be represented in sum-of-products form. Example 3.9 shows us that it is a simple matter to convert a truth table into sum-of-products form.

EXAMPLE 3.9   Consider a simple majority function. This is a function that, when given three inputs, outputs a 0 if less than half of its inputs are 1, and a 1 if at least half of its inputs are 1. Table 3.8 depicts the truth table for this majority function over three variables.

To convert the truth table to sum-of-products form, we start by looking at the problem in reverse. If we want the expression $x + y$ to equal 1, then either x or y (or both) must be equal to 1. If $xy + yz = 1$, then either $xy = 1$ or $yz = 1$ (or both).

Using this logic in reverse and applying it to our majority function, we see that the function must output a 1 when $x = 0$, $y = 1$, and $z = 1$. The product term that satisfies this is $x'yz$ (clearly, this is equal to 1 when $x = 0$, $y = 1$, and $z = 1$). The second occurrence of an output value of 1 is when $x = 1$, $y = 0$, and $z = 1$. The product term to guarantee an output of 1 is $xy'z$. The third product term we need is xyz', and the last is xyz. In summary, to generate a sum-of-products expression using the truth table for any Boolean expression, we must generate a product term of the input variables corresponding to each row where the value of the output variable in that row is 1. In each product term, we must then complement any variables that are 0 for that row.

Our majority function can be expressed in sum-of-products form as $F(x,y,z)$ $= x'yz + xy'z + xyz' + xyz$.

x	y	z	F
0	0	0	0
0	0	1	0
0	1	0	0
0	1	1	1
1	0	0	0
1	0	1	1
1	1	0	1
1	1	1	1

TABLE 3.8   Truth Table Representation for the Majority Function

Please note that the expression for the majority function in Example 3.9 may not be in simplest form; we are only guaranteeing a standard form. The sum-of-products and product-of-sums standard forms are equivalent ways of expressing a Boolean function. One form can be converted to the other through an application of Boolean identities. Whether using sum-of-products or product-of-sums, the expression must eventually be converted to its simplest form, which means reducing the expression to the minimum number of terms. Why must the expressions be simplified? A one-to-one correspondence exists between a Boolean expression and its implementation using electrical circuits, as shown in the next section. Unnecessary terms in the expression lead to unnecessary components in the physical circuit, which in turn yield a suboptimal circuit.

3.3 LOGIC GATES

The logical operators AND, OR, and NOT that we have discussed have been represented thus far in an abstract sense using truth tables and Boolean expressions. The actual physical components, or **digital circuits**, such as those that perform arithmetic operations or make choices in a computer, are constructed from a number of primitive elements called **gates**. Gates implement each of the basic logic functions we have discussed. These gates are the basic building blocks for digital design. Formally, a gate is a small, electronic device that computes various functions of two-valued signals. More simply stated, a gate implements a simple Boolean function. To physically implement each gate requires from one to six or more transistors (described in Chapter 1), depending on the technology being used. To summarize, the basic physical component of a computer is the transistor; the basic logic element is the gate.

3.3.1 Symbols for Logic Gates

We initially examine the three simplest gates. These correspond to the logical operators AND, OR, and NOT. We have discussed the functional behavior of each of these Boolean operators. Figure 3.1 depicts the graphical representation of the gate that corresponds to each operator.

Note the circle at the output of the NOT gate. Typically, this circle represents the complement operation.

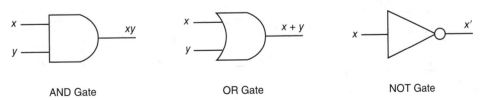

| AND Gate | OR Gate | NOT Gate |

FIGURE 3.1 The Three Basic Gates

x	y	x XOR y
0	0	0
0	1	1
1	0	1
1	1	0

a)   b)

FIGURE 3.2   a) The Truth Table for XOR

b) The Logic Symbol for XOR

Another common gate is the exclusive-OR (XOR) gate, represented by the Boolean expression: $x \oplus y$. XOR is false if both of the input values are equal and true otherwise. Figure 3.2 illustrates the truth table for XOR as well as the logic diagram that specifies its behavior.

3.3.2 Universal Gates

Two other common gates are NAND and NOR, which produce complementary output to AND and OR, respectively. Each gate has two different logic symbols that can be used for gate representation. (It is left as an exercise to prove that the symbols are logically equivalent. Hint: Use DeMorgan's Law.) Figures 3.3 and 3.4 depict the logic diagrams for NAND and NOR along with the truth tables to explain the functional behavior of each gate.

The NAND gate is commonly referred to as a **universal gate**, because any electronic circuit can be constructed using only NAND gates. To prove this, Figure 3.5 depicts an AND gate, an OR gate, and a NOT gate using only NAND gates.

Why not simply use the AND, OR, and NOT gates we already know exist? There are two reasons for using only NAND gates to build any given circuit. First,

x	y	x NAND y
0	0	1
0	1	1
1	0	1
1	1	0

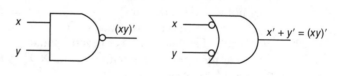

FIGURE 3.3   Truth Table and Logic Symbols for NAND

x	y	x NOR y
0	0	1
0	1	0
1	0	0
1	1	0

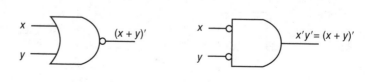

FIGURE 3.4   Truth Table and Logic Symbols for NOR

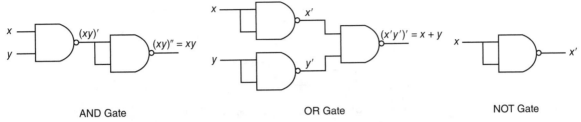

AND Gate   OR Gate   NOT Gate

FIGURE 3.5 Three Circuits Constructed Using Only NAND Gates

NAND gates are cheaper to build than the other gates. Second, complex integrated circuits (which are discussed in the following sections) are often much easier to build using the same building block (i.e., several NAND gates) rather than a collection of the basic building blocks (i.e., a combination of AND, OR, and NOT gates).

Please note that the duality principle applies to universality as well. One can build any circuit using only NOR gates. NAND and NOR gates are related in much the same way as the sum-of-products form and the product-of-sums form presented. One would use NAND for implementing an expression in sum-of-products form and NOR for those in product-of-sums form.

3.3.3 Multiple Input Gates

In our examples thus far, all gates have accepted only two inputs. Gates are not limited to two input values, however. There are many variations in the number and types of inputs and outputs allowed for various gates. For example, we can represent the expression $x + y + z$ using one OR gate with three inputs, as in Figure 3.6. Figure 3.7 represents the expression $xy'z$.

We shall see later in this chapter that it is sometimes useful to depict the output of a gate as Q along with its complement Q' as shown in Figure 3.8.

Note that Q always represents the actual output.

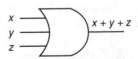

FIGURE 3.6 A Three-Input OR Gate Representing $x + y + z$

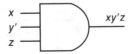

FIGURE 3.7 A Three-Input AND Gate Representing $xy'z$

FIGURE 3.8 AND Gate with Two Inputs and Two Outputs

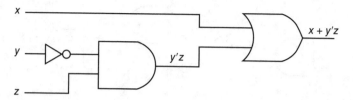

FIGURE 3.9   Logic Diagram for $F(x,y,z) = x + y'z$

3.4   DIGITAL COMPONENTS

Upon opening a computer and looking inside, one would realize that there is a lot to know about all of the digital components that make up the system. Every computer is built using collections of gates that are all connected by way of wires acting as signal pathways. These collections of gates are often quite standard, resulting in a set of building blocks that can be used to build the entire computer system. Surprisingly, these building blocks are all constructed using the basic AND, OR, and NOT operations. In the next few sections, we discuss digital circuits, their relationship to Boolean algebra, the standard building blocks, and examples of the two different categories, combinational logic and sequential logic, into which these building blocks can be placed.

3.4.1   Digital Circuits and Their Relationship to Boolean Algebra

What is the connection between Boolean functions and digital circuits? We have seen that a simple Boolean operation (such as AND or OR) can be represented by a simple logic gate. More complex Boolean expressions can be represented as combinations of AND, OR, and NOT gates, resulting in a logic diagram that describes the entire expression. This logic diagram represents the physical implantation of the given expression, or the actual digital circuit. Consider the function $F(x,y,z) = x + y'z$ (which we looked at earlier). Figure 3.9 represents a logic diagram that implements this function.

Recall our discussion of sum-of-products form. This form lends itself well to implementation using digital circuits. For example, consider the function $F(x,y,z) = xy + yz' + xyz$. Each term corresponds to an AND gate, and the sum is implemented by a single OR gate, resulting in the following circuit:

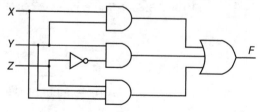

We can build logic diagrams (which in turn lead to digital circuits) for any Boolean expression. At some level, every operation carried out by a computer is an implementation of a Boolean expression. This may not be obvious to high-level language programmers because the semantic gap between the high-level programming level and the Boolean logic level is so wide. Assembly language programmers, being much closer to the hardware, use Boolean tricks to accelerate program performance. A good example is the use of the XOR operator to clear a storage location, as in A XOR A. The XOR operator can also be used to exchange the values of two storage locations. The same XOR statement applied three times to two variables, say A and B, swaps their values:

$$A = A \text{ XOR } B$$

$$B = A \text{ XOR } B$$

$$A = A \text{ XOR } B$$

One operation that is nearly impossible to perform at the high-level language level is bit masking, where individual bits in a byte are stripped off (set to 0) according to a specified pattern. Boolean bit masking operations are indispensable for processing individual bits in a byte. For example, if we want to find out whether the 4's position of a byte is set, we AND the byte with 04_{16}. If the result is nonzero, the bit is equal to 1. Bit masking can strip off any pattern of bits. Place a 1 in the position of each bit that you want to keep, and set the others to 0. The AND operation leaves behind only the bits that are of interest.

Boolean algebra allows us to analyze and design digital circuits. Because of the relationship between Boolean algebra and logic diagrams, we simplify our circuit by simplifying our Boolean expression. Digital circuits are implemented with gates, but gates and logic diagrams are not the most convenient forms for representing digital circuits during the design phase. Boolean expressions are much better to use during this phase because they are easier to manipulate and simplify.

The complexity of the expression representing a Boolean function has a direct effect on the complexity of the resulting digital circuit: The more complex the expression, the more complex the resulting circuit. We should point out that we do not typically simplify our circuits using Boolean identities; we have already seen that this can sometimes be quite difficult and time consuming. Instead, designers use a more automated method to do this. This method involves the use of **Karnaugh maps** (or **Kmaps**). Refer to the focus section following this chapter to learn how Kmaps are used to simplify digital circuits.

3.4.2 Integrated Circuits

Computers are composed of various digital components, connected by wires. Like a good program, the actual hardware of a computer uses collections of gates to create larger modules, which, in turn, are used to implement various functions. The number of gates required to create these "building blocks" depends on the technology being used. Because the circuit technology is beyond the scope of this text, you are referred to the reading list at the end of this chapter for more information on this topic.

Typically, gates are not sold individually; they are sold in units called **integrated circuits (ICs)**. A chip (a silicon semiconductor crystal) is a small electronic device consisting of the necessary electronic components (transistors, resistors, and capacitors) to implement various gates. As already explained, components are etched directly on the chip, allowing them to be smaller and to require less power for operation than their discrete component counterparts. This

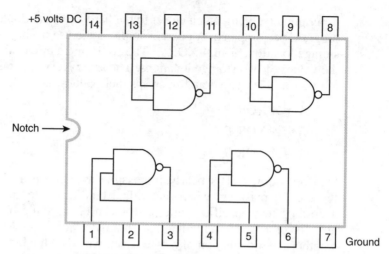

FIGURE 3.10   Simple SSI Integrated Circuit

chip is then mounted in a ceramic or plastic container with external pins. The necessary connections are welded from the chip to the external pins to form an IC. The first ICs contained very few transistors. As we learned, the first ICs were called SSI chips and contained up to 100 electronic components per chip. We now have ultra-large-scale integration (ULSI) with more than 1 million electronic components per chip. Figure 3.10 illustrates a simple SSI IC.

We have seen that we can represent any Boolean function as (1) a truth table, (2) a Boolean expression (in sum-of-products form), or (3) a logic diagram using gate symbols. Consider the function represented by the following truth table:

x	y	z	F
0	0	0	0
0	0	1	0
0	1	0	1
0	1	1	1
1	0	0	0
1	0	1	0
1	1	0	0
1	1	1	0

This function is expressed in sum-of-products form as $F(x,y,z) = x'yz' + x'yz$. This simplifies to $F(x,y,z) = x'y$ (the simplification is left as an exercise). We can now express this using a logic diagram as follows:

$$ x \longrightarrow \quad y \longrightarrow \quad x'y $$

Using only NAND gates, we can redraw the logic diagram as follows:

$$ x \longrightarrow \quad x' \quad (x'y)' = x + y' \quad y \longrightarrow \quad (x + y')'\ (x + y')' = (x + y')' = x'y $$

We can implement this in hardware using the SSI circuit from Figure 3.10 as follows:

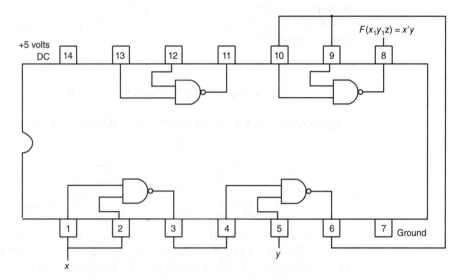

3.4.3   Putting It All Together: From Problem Description to Circuit

We now understand how to represent a function by a Boolean expression, how to simplify a Boolean expression, and how to represent a Boolean expression using a logic diagram. Let's combine these skills to design a circuit from beginning to end.

≡   **EXAMPLE 3.10**   Suppose we are given the task of designing a logic circuit to help us determine the best time to plant our garden. We investigate three possible factors: (1) time, where 0 represents day and 1 represents evening; (2) moon phase, where 0 represents not full and 1 represents full; and (3) temperature, where 0 represents 45°F and below, and 1 represents over 45°F. These three items represent our inputs. After significant research, we determine that the best time to plant a garden is during the evening with a full moon (temperature does not appear to matter). This results in the following truth table:

Time (x)	Moon (y)	Temperature (z)	Plant?
0	0	0	0
0	0	1	0
0	1	0	0
0	1	1	0
1	0	0	0
1	0	1	0
1	1	0	1
1	1	1	1

We have placed 1s in the output column when the inputs indicated "evening" and "full moon," and 0s everywhere else. By converting our truth table to a Boolean function F, we see that $F(x,y,z) = xyz' + xyz$ (we use a process similar to that presented in Example 3.9: We include terms where the function evaluates to 1). We now simplify F:

$$F(x,y,z) = xyz' + xyz$$

$$= xy \text{ (using the absorption law)}$$

Therefore, this function evaluates to one AND gate using x and y as input.

The steps to design a Boolean circuit are as follows: (1) read the problem carefully to determine the input and output values; (2) establish a truth table that shows the output for all possible inputs; (3) convert the truth table into a Boolean expression; and (4) simplify the Boolean expression.

≡ **EXAMPLE 3.11** Assume you are responsible for designing a circuit that will allow the president of your college to determine whether to close campus due to weather conditions. If the highway department has not salted the area roads, and there is ice on the roads, campus should be closed. Regardless of whether there is ice or salt on the roads, if there is more than 8 in. of snow, campus should be closed. In all other situations, campus should remain open.

There are three inputs: ice (or no ice), salt (or not salt), and snow of more than 8 in. on the roads (or not), resulting in the following truth table:

Ice (x)	Salt (y)	Snow (z)	Close?
0	0	0	0
0	0	1	1
0	1	0	0
0	1	1	1
1	0	0	1
1	0	1	1
1	1	0	0
1	1	1	1

The truth table yields the Boolean expression $F(x,y,z) = x'y'z + x'yz + xy'z' + xy'z + xyz$. We can simplify this expression using Boolean identities as follows:

$$
\begin{aligned}
F(x,y,z) &= x'y'z + x'yz + xy'z' + xy'z + xyz \\
&= x'y'z + x'yz + xy'z + xyz + xy'z' && \text{(Commutative)} \\
&= x'(y'z + yz) + x(y'z + yz) + xy'z' && \text{(Distributive} \times 2) \\
&= (x' + x)(y'z' + yz) + xy'z' && \text{(Distributive)} \\
&= (y'z' + yz) + xy'z' && \text{(Inverse/Identity)} \\
&= (y' + y)z + xy'z' && \text{(Distributive)} \\
&= z + xy'z' && \text{(Inverse/Identity)}
\end{aligned}
$$

We leave it to the reader to draw the logic diagram corresponding to $z + xy'z'$. Once the circuit has been implemented in hardware, all the college president has to do is set the inputs to indicate the current conditions, and the output will tell her whether to close campus.

3.5 COMBINATIONAL CIRCUITS

Digital logic chips are combined to give us useful circuits. These logic circuits can be categorized as either **combinational logic** or **sequential logic**. This section introduces combinational logic. Sequential logic is covered in Section 3.6.

3.5.1 Basic Concepts

Combinational logic is used to build circuits that contain basic Boolean operators, inputs, and outputs. The key concept in recognizing a combinational circuit is that an output is always based entirely on the given inputs (as we saw in Examples 3.10 and 3.11). Thus, the output of a combinational circuit is a function of its inputs, and the output is uniquely determined by the values of the inputs at any given moment. A given combinational circuit may have several outputs. If so, each output represents a different Boolean function.

3.5.2 Examples of Typical Combinational Circuits

Let's begin with a very simple combinational circuit called a **half-adder**.

EXAMPLE 3.12 Consider the problem of adding two binary digits together. There are only three things to remember: $0 + 0 = 0$, $0 + 1 = 1 + 0 = 1$, and $1 + 1 = 10$. We know the behavior this circuit exhibits, and we can formalize this behavior using a truth table. We need to specify two outputs, not just one, because we have a sum and a carry to address. The truth table for a half-adder is shown in Table 3.9.

A closer look reveals that *Sum* is actually an XOR. The *Carry* output is equivalent to that of an AND gate. We can combine an XOR gate and an AND gate, resulting in the logic diagram for a half-adder shown in Figure 3.11.

Inputs		Outputs	
x	y	Sum	Carry
0	0	0	0
0	1	1	0
1	0	1	0
1	1	0	1

TABLE 3.9   Truth Table for a Half-Adder

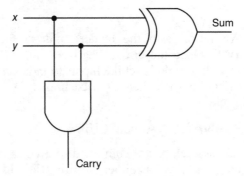

FIGURE 3.11   Logic Diagram for a Half-Adder

The half-adder is a very simple circuit and not really very useful because it can only add two bits together. However, we can extend this adder to a circuit that allows the addition of larger binary numbers. Consider how you add base 10 numbers: You add up the rightmost column, note the units digit, and carry the tens digit. Then you add that carry to the current column and continue in a similar manner. We can add binary numbers in the same way. However, we need a circuit that allows three inputs (x, y, and Carry In) and two outputs (Sum and Carry Out). Figure 3.12 illustrates the truth table and corresponding logic diagram for a **full-adder**. Note that this full-adder is composed of two half-adders and an OR gate.

Given this full-adder, you may be wondering how this circuit can add binary numbers; it is capable of adding only three bits. The answer is, it can't. However, we can build an adder capable of adding two 16-bit words, for example, by replicating the above circuit 16 times, feeding the Carry Out of one circuit into the Carry In of the circuit immediately to its left. Figure 3.13 illustrates this idea. This type of circuit is called a **ripple-carry adder** because of the sequential generation of carries that "ripple" through the adder stages. Note that instead of drawing all the gates that constitute a full-adder, we use a **black box** approach to depict our adder. A black box approach allows us to ignore the details of the actual gates. We concern ourselves only with the inputs and outputs of the circuit. This is typically done with most circuits, including decoders, multiplexers, and adders, as we shall see very soon.

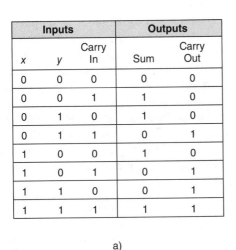

Inputs			Outputs	
x	y	Carry In	Sum	Carry Out
0	0	0	0	0
0	0	1	1	0
0	1	0	1	0
0	1	1	0	1
1	0	0	1	0
1	0	1	0	1
1	1	0	0	1
1	1	1	1	1

a)

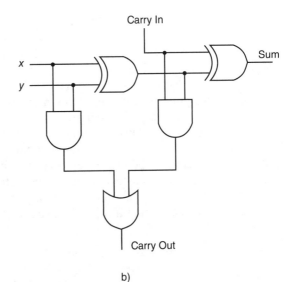

b)

FIGURE 3.12   a) Truth Table for a Full-Adder

b) Logic Diagram for a Full-Adder

FIGURE 3.13   Logic Diagram for a Ripple-Carry Adder

Because this adder is very slow, it is not normally implemented. However, it is easy to understand and should give you some idea of how addition of larger binary numbers can be achieved. Modifications made to adder designs have resulted in the carry-look-ahead adder, the carry-select adder, and the carry-save adder, as well as others. Each attempts to shorten the delay required to add two binary numbers. In fact, these newer adders achieve speeds of 40–90% faster than the ripple-carry adder by performing additions in parallel and reducing the maximum carry path. Adders are very important circuits—a computer would not be very useful if it could not add numbers.

An equally important operation that all computers use frequently is decoding binary information from a set of n inputs to a maximum of 2^n outputs. A **decoder** uses the inputs and their respective values to select one specific output line. What do we mean by "select an output line"? It simply means that one unique output line is asserted, or set to 1, whereas the other output lines are set to 0. Decoders are normally defined by the number of inputs and the number of outputs. For example, a decoder that has 3 inputs and 8 outputs is called a 3-to-8 decoder.

We mentioned that this decoder is something the computer uses frequently. At this point, you can probably name many arithmetic operations the computer must be able to perform, but you might find it difficult to propose an example of decoding. If so, it is because you are not familiar with how a computer accesses memory.

All memory addresses in a computer are specified as binary numbers. When a memory address is referenced (whether for reading or for writing), the computer first has to determine the actual address. This is done using a decoder. Example 3.13 should clarify any questions you may have about how a decoder works and what it might be used for.

≡   **EXAMPLE 3.13**   A 3-to-8 decoder circuit

Imagine memory consisting of 8 chips, each containing 8K bytes. Let's assume chip 0 contains memory addresses 0–8191 (or 1FFF in hex), chip 1 contains memory addresses 8192–16,383 (or 2000–3FFF in hex), and so on. We have a total of 8K × 8, or 64K (65,536) addresses available. We will not write down all 64K addresses as binary numbers; however, writing a few addresses in binary form (as we illustrate in the following paragraphs) will illustrate why a decoder is necessary.

Given $64 = 2^6$ and $1K = 2^{10}$, then $64K = 2^6 \times 2^{10} = 2^{16}$, which indicates that we need 16 bits to represent each address. If you have trouble understanding this, start with a smaller number of addresses. For example, if you have four addresses—addresses 0, 1, 2, and 3, the binary equivalent of these addresses is 00, 01, 10, and 11, requiring two bits. We know $2^2 = 4$. Now consider eight addresses. We have to be able to count from 0 to 7 in binary. How many bits does that require? The answer is 3. You can either write them all down, or you recognize that $8 = 2^3$. The exponent tells us the minimum number of bits necessary to represent the addresses. (We will see this idea again later in this chapter, as well as in Chapters 4 and 6.)

All addresses on chip 0 have the format: 000xxxxxxxxxxxxx. Because chip 0 contains the addresses 0–8191, the binary representation of these addresses is in the range 0000000000000000 to 0001111111111111. Similarly, all addresses on chip 1 have the format 001xxxxxxxxxxxxx, and so on for the remaining chips. The leftmost 3 bits determine on which chip the address is actually located. We need 16 bits to represent the entire address, but on each chip, we only have 2^{13} addresses. Therefore, we need only 13 bits to uniquely identify an address on a given chip. The rightmost 13 bits give us this information.

When a computer is given an address, it must first determine which chip to use; then it must find the actual address on that specific chip. In our example, the computer would use the 3 leftmost bits to pick the chip and then find the address on the chip using the remaining 13 bits. These 3 high-order bits are actually used as the inputs to a decoder so the computer can determine which chip to activate for reading or writing. If the first 3 bits are 000, chip 0 should be activated. If the first 3 bits are 111, chip 7 should be activated. Which chip would be activated if the first 3 bits were 010? It would be chip 2. Turning on a specific wire activates a chip. The output of the decoder is used to activate one, and only one, chip as the addresses are decoded.

Figure 3.14 illustrates the physical components in a decoder and the symbol often used to represent a decoder. We will see how a decoder is used in memory in Section 3.6.

Another common combinational circuit is a **multiplexer**. This circuit selects binary information from one of many input lines and directs it to a single output line. Selection of a particular input line is controlled by a set of selection variables, or control lines. At any given time, only one input (the one selected) is routed through the circuit to the output line. All other inputs are "cut off." If the values on the control lines change, the input actually routed through changes as well. Figure 3.15 illustrates the physical components in a multiplexer and the symbol often used to represent a multiplexer. S_0 and S_1 are the control lines; $I_0 - I_3$ are the input values.

Another useful set of combinational circuits to study includes a parity generator and a parity checker (recall we studied parity in Chapter 2). A **parity generator** is a circuit that creates the necessary parity bit to add to a word; a **parity checker** checks to make sure proper parity (odd or even) is present in the word, detecting an error if the parity bit is incorrect.

Typically, parity generators and parity checkers are constructed using XOR functions. Assuming we are using odd parity, the truth table for a parity generator for a 3-bit word is given in Table 3.10. The truth table for a parity checker to be used on a 4-bit word with 3 information bits and 1 parity bit is given in

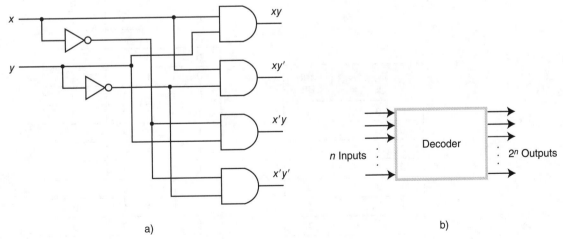

a)

b)

FIGURE 3.14   a) A Look Inside a Decoder
b) A Decoder Symbol

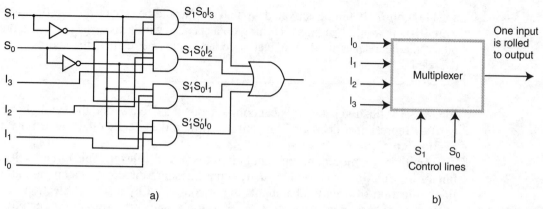

FIGURE 3.15   a) A Look Inside a Multiplexer
b) A Multiplexer Symbol

Table 3.11. The parity checker outputs a 1 if an error is detected and 0 otherwise. We leave it as an exercise to draw the corresponding logic diagrams for both the parity generator and the parity checker.

Bit shifting, moving the bits of a word or byte one position to the left or right, is a very useful operation. Shifting a bit to the left takes it to the position of the next higher power of two. When the bits of an unsigned integer are shifted to

x	y	z	Parity Bit
0	0	0	1
0	0	1	0
0	1	0	0
0	1	1	1
1	0	0	0
1	0	1	1
1	1	0	1
1	1	1	0

TABLE 3.10   Parity Generator

x	y	z	P	Error detected?
0	0	0	0	1
0	0	0	1	0
0	0	1	0	0
0	0	1	1	1
0	1	0	0	0
0	1	0	1	1
0	1	1	0	1
0	1	1	1	0
1	0	0	0	0
1	0	0	1	1
1	0	1	0	1
1	0	1	1	0
1	1	0	0	1
1	1	0	1	0
1	1	1	0	0
1	1	1	1	1

TABLE 3.11   Parity Checker

the left by one position, it has the same effect as multiplying that integer by 2, but using significantly fewer machine cycles to do so. The leftmost or rightmost bit is lost after a left or right shift (respectively). Left shifting the nibble, 1101, changes it to 1010, and right shifting it produces 0110. Some buffers and encoders rely on shifters to produce a bit stream from a byte so that each bit can be processed in sequence. A 4-bit shifter is illustrated in Figure 3.16. When the control line, S, is low (i.e., zero), each bit of the input (labeled I_0 through I_3) is shifted left by one position into the outputs (labeled O_0 through O_3). When the control line is high, a right shift occurs. This shifter can easily be expanded to any number of bits, or combined with memory elements to create a shift register.

There are far too many combinational circuits for us to be able to cover them all in this brief chapter. The references at the end of this chapter provide much more information on combinational circuits than we can give here. However, before we finish the topic of combinational logic, there is one more combinational circuit we need to introduce. We have covered all of the components necessary to build an **arithmetic logic unit (ALU)**.

Figure 3.17 illustrates a simple ALU with four basic operations—AND, OR, NOT, and addition—carried out on two machine words of 2 bits each. The control lines, f_0 and f_1, determine which operation is to be performed by the CPU. The signal 00 is used for addition ($A + B$); 01 for NOT A; 10 for A OR B, and 11 for A AND B. The input lines A_0 and A_1 indicate 2 bits of one word, and B_0 and B_1 indicate the second word. C_0 and C_1 represent the output lines.

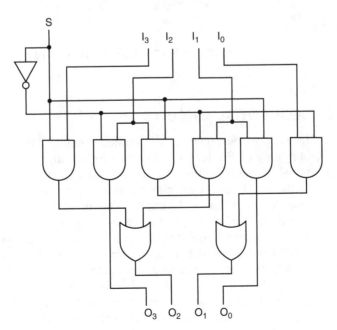

FIGURE 3.16   4-Bit Shifter

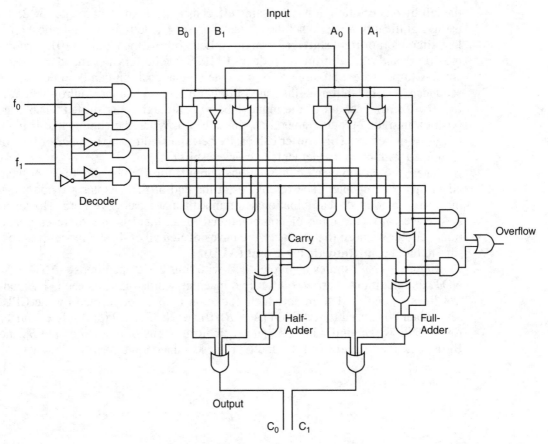

FIGURE 3.17 A Simple Two-Bit ALU

3.6 SEQUENTIAL CIRCUITS

In the previous section, we studied combinational logic. We have approached our study of Boolean functions by examining the variables, the values for those variables, and the function outputs that depend solely on the values of the inputs to the functions. If we change an input value, this has a direct and immediate effect on the value of the output. The major weakness of combinational circuits is that there is no concept of storage—they are memoryless. This presents us with a dilemma. We know that computers must have a way to remember values. Consider a much simpler digital circuit needed for a soda machine. When you put money into a soda machine, the machine remembers how much you have put in at any given instant. Without this ability to remember, it would be very difficult to use. A soda machine cannot be built using only combinational circuits. To understand how a soda machine works, and ultimately how a computer works, we must study sequential logic.

3.6.1 Basic Concepts

A sequential circuit defines its output as a function of both its current inputs and its previous inputs. Therefore, the output depends on past inputs. To remember previous inputs, sequential circuits must have some sort of storage element. We typically refer to this storage element as a **flip-flop**. The state of this flip-flop is a function of the previous inputs to the circuit. Therefore, pending output depends on both the current inputs and the current state of the circuit. In the same way that combinational circuits are generalizations of gates, sequential circuits are generalizations of flip-flops.

3.6.2 Clocks

Before we discuss sequential logic, we must first introduce a way to order events. (The fact that a sequential circuit uses past inputs to determine present outputs indicates that we must have event ordering.) Some sequential circuits are **asynchronous**, which means they become active the moment any input value changes. **Synchronous** sequential circuits use clocks to order events. A **clock** is a circuit that emits a series of pulses with a precise pulse width and a precise interval between consecutive pulses. This interval is called the **clock cycle time**. Clock speed is generally measured in megahertz or gigahertz.

A clock is used by a sequential circuit to decide when to update the state of the circuit (i.e., when do "present" inputs become "past" inputs?). This means that inputs to the circuit can only affect the storage element at given, discrete instances of time. In this chapter, we examine synchronous sequential circuits because they are easier to understand than their asynchronous counterparts. From this point, when we refer to "sequential circuit," we are implying "synchronous sequential circuit." Most sequential circuits are edge triggered (as opposed to being level triggered). This means they are allowed to change their states on either the rising or falling edge of the clock signal, as seen in Figure 3.18.

3.6.3 Flip-Flops

A level-triggered circuit is allowed to change state whenever the clock signal is either high or low. Many people use the terms *latch* and *flip-flop* interchangeably. Technically, a latch is level triggered, whereas a flip-flop is edge triggered. In this text, we use the term **flip-flop**. William Eccles and F. W. Jordan invented the first flip-flop (from vacuum tubes) in 1918, so these circuits have been around for some time. However, they have not always been called flip-flops. Like so many

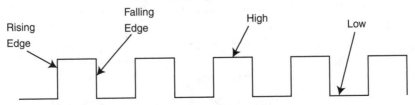

FIGURE 3.18   A Clock Signal Indicating Discrete Instances of Time

other inventions, they were originally named after the inventors and were called Eccles–Jordan trigger circuits. So where did "flip-flop" come from? Some say it was the sound the circuit made (as produced on a speaker connected to one of the components in the original circuit) when it was triggered; others believe it came from the circuit's ability to flip from one state to another and back again.

To "remember" a past state, sequential circuits rely on a concept called **feedback**. This simply means the output of a circuit is fed back as an input to the same circuit. A very simple feedback circuit uses two NOT gates, as shown in Figure 3.19. In this figure, if Q is 0, it will always be 0. If Q is 1, it will always be 1. This is not a very interesting or useful circuit, but it allows you to see how feedback works.

A more useful feedback circuit is composed of two NOR gates resulting in the most basic memory unit called an **SR flip-flop**. SR stands for "set/reset." The logic diagram for the SR flip-flop is given in Figure 3.20.

We can describe any flip-flop by using a characteristic table, which indicates what the next state should be based on the inputs and the current state, Q. The notation $Q(t)$ represents the current state, and $Q(t + 1)$ indicates the next state, or the state the flip-flop should enter after the clock has been pulsed. We can also specify a timing diagram, which indicates the relationship of signals from the clock to changes in a flip-flop's output. Figure 3.21a shows the actual implementation of the SR sequential circuit; Figure 3.21b adds a clock to the flip-flop; Figure 3.21c specifies its characteristic table; and Figure 3.21d shows an example timing diagram. We are interested in exploring only clocked flip-flops.

An SR flip-flop exhibits interesting behavior. There are three inputs: S, R, and the current output $Q(t)$. We create the truth table shown in Table 3.12 to further illustrate how this circuit works.

For example, if S is 0 and R is 0, and the current state, $Q(t)$, is 0, then the next state, $Q(t + 1)$, is also 0. If S is 0 and R is 0, and $Q(t)$ is 1, then $Q(t + 1)$ is **set** to 1. Actual inputs of (0, 0) for (S, R) result in no change when the clock is

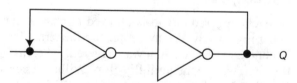

FIGURE 3.19   Example of Simple Feedback

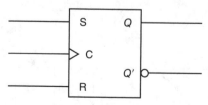

FIGURE 3.20   SR Flip-Flop Logic Diagram

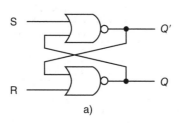

S

R

a)

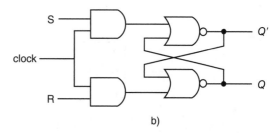

S

clock

R

Q'

Q

b)

S	R	Q(t+1)
0	0	Q(t) (no change)
0	1	0 (reset to 0)
1	0	1 (set to 1)
1	1	undefined

c)

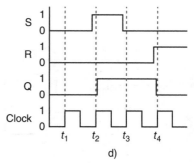

d)

FIGURE 3.21   a) SR Flip-Flop

b) Clocked SR Flip-Flop

c) Characteristic Table for the SR Flip-Flop

d) Timing Diagram for the SR Flip-Flop (assuming initial
state of Q is 0)

S	R	Present State Q(t)	Next State Q(t+1)
0	0	0	0
0	0	1	1
0	1	0	0
0	1	1	0
1	0	0	1
1	0	1	1
1	1	0	Undefined
1	1	1	Undefined

TABLE 3.12   Truth Table for SR Flip-Flop

pulsed. Following a similar argument, we can see that inputs $(S, R) = (0,1)$ force
the next state, $Q(t + 1)$, to 0 regardless of the current state (thus forcing a **reset**
on the circuit output). When $(S, R) = (1, 0)$, the circuit output is **set** to 1.

Looking at the example timing diagram in Figure 3.21d, we see that at time t_1,
the clock ticks, but because $S = R = 0$, Q does not change. At t_2, S has changed
to 1, and R is still 0, so when the clock ticks, Q is **set** to 1. At t_3, $S = R = 0$,

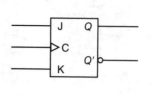

a)

J	K	Q(t +1)
0	0	Q(t) (no change)
0	1	0 (reset to 0)
1	0	1 (set to 1)
1	1	Q'(t)

b)

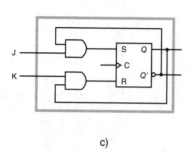

c)

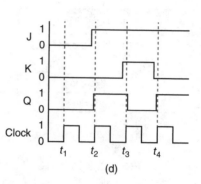

(d)

FIGURE 3.22   a) JK Flip-Flop
   b) JK Characteristic Table
   c) JK Flip-Flop as a Modified SR Flip-Flop
   d) Timing Diagram for JK Flip-Flop (assuming initial state of Q is 0)

so Q does not change. By t_4, because R has changed to 1, when the clock ticks, $S = 0, R = 1$, and Q is **reset** to 0.

There is one oddity with this particular flip-flop. What happens if both S and R are set to 1 at the same time? If we examine the unclocked flip-flop in Figure 3.21a, this forces a final state in which both Q and Q' are 0, but how can $Q = 0 = Q'$? Let's look at what happens when $S = R = 1$ using the clocked flip-flop in Figure 3.21b. When the clock pulses, the S and R values are input into the flip-flop. This forces both Q and Q' to 0. When the clock pulse is removed, the final state of the flip-flop cannot be determined, as once the clock pulse ends, both the S and R inputs are killed, and the resulting state depends on which one actually terminated first (this situation is often called a "race condition"). Therefore, this combination of inputs is not allowed in an SR flip-flop.

We can add some conditioning logic to our SR flip-flop to ensure that the illegal state never arises—we simply modify the SR flip-flop as shown in Figure 3.22. This results in a **JK flip-flop**. A JK flip-flop is basically the same thing as an SR flip-flop except when both inputs are 1, this circuit negates the current state. The timing diagram in Figure 3.22d illustrates how this circuit works. At time t_1, $J = K = 0$, resulting in no change to Q. At t_2, $J = 1$ and $K = 0$, so Q is set to 1. At t_3, $K = J = 1$, which causes Q to be negated, changing it from 1 to 0. At t_4, $K = 0$ and $J = 1$, forcing Q to be set to 1.

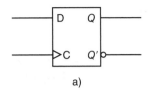

D	Q(t + 1)
0	0
1	1

a)   b)

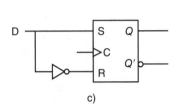

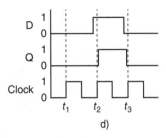

c)   d)

FIGURE 3.23   a) D Flip-Flop
b) D Flip-Flop Characteristic Table
c) D Flip-Flop as a Modified SR Flip-Flop
d) Timing Diagram for D Flip-Flop

There appears to be significant disagreement regarding where the "*JK*" came from. Some believe it was named after Jack Kilby, inventor of the integrated circuit. Others believe it is named after John Kardash, who is often credited as its inventor (as specified in his biographical data on his current company's website). Still others believe it was coined by workers at Hughes Aircraft who labeled circuits input using letters, and *J* and *K* just happened to be next on the list (as detailed in a letter submitted to the electronics magazine *EDN* in 1968).

Another variant of the SR flip-flop is the **D (data) flip-flop**. A D flip-flop is a true representation of physical computer memory. This sequential circuit stores one bit of information. If a 1 is asserted on the input line *D*, and the clock is pulsed, the output line *Q* becomes a 1. If a 0 is asserted on the input line and the clock is pulsed, the output becomes 0. Remember that output *Q* represents the current state of the circuit. Therefore, an output value of 1 means the circuit is currently "storing" a value of 1. Figure 3.23 illustrates the D flip-flop, lists its characteristic table and timing diagram, and reveals that the D flip-flop is actually a modified SR flip-flop.

3.6.4   Finite State Machines

Characteristic tables and timing diagrams allow us to describe the behavior of flip-flops and sequential circuits. An equivalent graphical depiction is provided by a **finite state machine** (**FSM**). Finite state machines typically use circles to represent machine states and directed arcs to represent transitions from one state to another. Each circle is labeled with the state it represents, and each arc is labeled with the input and/or output for that state transition. FSMs can be in only one state at a time. We are interested in synchronous FSMs (those allowing state transitions only when the clock ticks).

A real-world example that can be modeled with state machines is a common traffic light. It has three states: green, yellow, and red. Transitions among states occur as timers in the hardware expire. An FSM for a traffic light appears below:

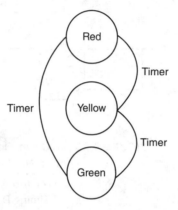

There are a number of different kinds of finite state machines, each suitable for a different purpose. Figure 3.24 shows a **Moore machine** representation of a JK flip-flop. The circles represent the two states of the flip-flop, which we have labeled A and B. The output, Q, is indicated in brackets, and the arcs illustrate the transitions between the states. We can see in this figure exactly how a JK flip-flop goes from state 0 to state 1 when $J = 1$ and $S = 0$, or when $J = K = 1$, and how it goes from state 1 to state 0 when $J = K = 1$, or when $J = 1$ and $K = 0$. This finite state machine is a Moore-type machine because each of the states is associated with the output of the machine. In fact, the reflexive arcs shown in the figure are not required because the output of the machine changes only when the state changes, and the state does not change through a reflexive arc. We can therefore draw a simplified Moore machine (Figure 3.25). Moore machines are named for Edward F. Moore, who invented this type of FSM in 1956.

A contemporary of Edward Moore, George H. Mealy, independently invented another type of FSM that has also been named after its inventor. Like

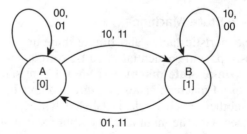

FIGURE 3.24   JK Flip-Flop Represented as a Moore Machine

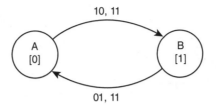

FIGURE 3.25   Simplified Moore Machine for the JK Flip-Flop

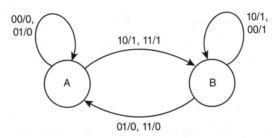

FIGURE 3.26   JK Flip-Flop Represented as a Mealy Machine

a Moore machine, a **Mealy machine** consists of a circle for each state, and the circles are connected by arcs for each transition. Unlike a Moore machine, which associates an output with each state (indicated in the Moore machine example by putting a 0 or 1 in square brackets), a Mealy machine associates an output with each transition. This implies that a Mealy machine's outputs are a function of its current state and its input, and a Moore machine's output is a function only of its current state. Each transition arc is labeled with its input and output separated by a slash. Reflexive arcs cannot be removed from Mealy machines because they depict an output of the machine. A Mealy machine for our JK flip-flop is shown in Figure 3.26.

In the actual implementation of either a Moore or Mealy machine, two things are required: a memory (register) to store the current state and combinational logic components that control the output and transitions from one state to another. Figure 3.27 illustrates this idea for both machines.

The graphical models and the block diagrams that we have presented for the Moore and Mealy machines are useful for high-level conceptual modeling of the behavior of circuits. However, once a circuit reaches a certain level of complexity, Moore and Mealy machines become unwieldy and only with great difficulty capture the details required for implementation. Consider, for example, a microwave oven. The oven will be in the "on" state only when the door is closed, the control dial is set to "cook" or "defrost," and there is time on the timer. The "on" state means that the magnetron is producing microwaves, the light in the

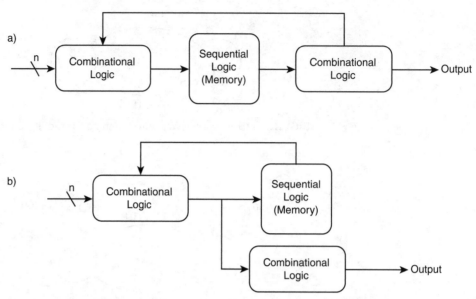

FIGURE 3.27 a) Block Diagram for Moore Machines
b) Block Diagram for Mealy Machines

oven compartment is lit, and the carousel is rotating. If the time expires, the door opens, or the control is turned from "cook" to "off," the oven moves to the "off" state. The dimension provided by the timer, along with the numerous signals that define a state, is hard to capture in the Moore and Mealy models. For this reason, Christopher R. Clare invented the **algorithmic state machine (ASM)**. As its name implies, an algorithmic state machine is directed at expressing the algorithms that advance an FSM from one state to another.

An algorithmic state machine consists of blocks that contain a state box, a label, and optionally condition and output boxes (Figure 3.28). Each ASM block has exactly one entry point and at least one exit point. Moore type outputs (the circuit signals) are indicated inside the state block; Mealy-type outputs are indicated in the oval output "box." If a signal is asserted when "high," it is prefixed with an H; otherwise, it is prefixed with an L. If the signal is asserted immediately, it is also prefixed with an I; otherwise, the signal asserts at the next clock cycle. The input conditions that cause changes in state (this is the algorithmic part) are expressed by elongated, six-sided polygons called condition boxes. Any number of condition boxes can be placed inside an ASM block, and the order in which they are shown is unimportant. An ASM for our microwave oven example is shown in Figure 3.29.

As implied, ASMs can express the behavior of either a Moore or Mealy machine. Moore and Mealy machines are probably equivalent and can be

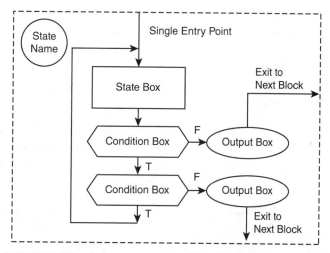

FIGURE 3.28 Components of an Algorithmic State Machine

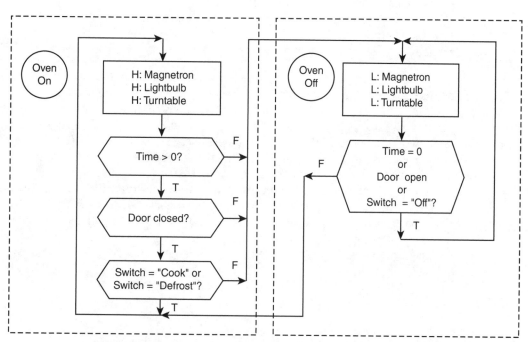

FIGURE 3.29 Algorithmic State Machine for a Microware Oven

used interchangeably. However, it is sometimes easier to use one rather than the other, depending on the application. In most cases, Moore machines require more states (memory) but result in simpler implementations than Mealy machines, because there are fewer transitions to account for in Moore machines.

Hardware-Free Machines

Moore and Mealy machines are only two of many different types of finite state machines that you will encounter in computer science literature. An understanding of FSMs is essential in the study of programming languages, compilers, the theory of computation, and automata theory. We refer to these abstractions as *machines* because machines are devices that respond to a set of stimuli (events) by generating predictable responses (actions) based on a history of prior events (current state). One of the most important of these is the **deterministic finite automata (DFA)** computational model. Formally speaking, a DFA, M, is completely described by the quintuple $M = (Q, S, \Sigma, \delta, F)$ where

- Q is a finite set of states that represents every configuration the machine can assume;
- S is an element of Q that represents the start state, which is the initial state of the machine before it receives any inputs;
- Σ is the input alphabet or set of events that the machine will recognize;
- δ is a transition function that maps a state in Q and a letter from the input alphabet to another (possibly the same) state in Q; and
- F is a set of states (elements of Q) designated as the final (or accepting) states.

DFAs are particularly important in the study of programming languages; they are used to recognize grammars or languages. To use a DFA, you begin in the Start state and process an input string, one character at a time, changing states as you go. Upon processing the entire string, if you are in a final accepting state, a legal string is "accepted" by that DFA. Otherwise, the string is rejected.

We can use this DFA definition to describe a machine—as in a compiler— that extracts variable names (character strings) from a source code file. Suppose our computer language accepts variable names that must start with a letter, can contain an infinite stream of letters or numbers following the initial letter, and is terminated by a whitespace character (tab, space, linefeed, etc.). The initial state of the variable name is the null string, because no input has been read. We indicate this starting state in the figure below with an exaggerated arrowhead (there are several other notations).

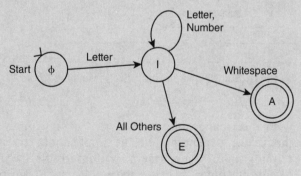

Finite State Machine for Accepting a Variable Name

When the machine recognizes an alphabetic character, it transitions to State *I*, where it stays as long as a letter or number is input. Upon accepting a whitespace character, the machine transitions to State *A*, its final accepting state, which we indicate with a double circle. If a character other than a number, letter, or whitespace is entered, the machine enters its error state, which is a final state that rejects the string.

Of more interest to us (because we are discussing hardware) are Moore and Mealy FSMs that have output states. The basic difference between these FSMs and DFAs is that—in addition to the transition function moving us from state to state—Moore and Mealy machines also generate an output symbol. Furthermore, no set of final states is defined because circuits have no concept of halting or accepting strings; they instead generate output. Both the Moore and Mealy machines, *M*, can be completely described by the quintuple $M = (Q, S, \Sigma, \Gamma, \delta)$ where

- *Q* is a finite set of states that represents each configuration of the machine;
- *S* is an element of *Q* that represents the Start state, the state of the machine before it has received any inputs;
- Σ is the input alphabet or set of events that the machine will recognize;
- Γ is the finite output alphabet; and
- δ is a transition function that maps a state from *Q* and a letter from the input alphabet to a state from *Q*.

We note that the input and output alphabets are usually identical, but they don't have to be. The way in which output is produced is the distinguishing element between the Moore and Mealy machines. Hence, the output function of the Moore machine is embedded in its definition of *S*, and the output function for the Mealy machine is embedded in the transition function, δ.

If any of this seems too abstract, just remember that a computer can be thought of as a universal finite state machine. It takes the description of one machine plus its input and then produces output that is as (usually) expected. Finite state machines are just a different way of thinking about the computer and computation.

3.6.5 Examples of Sequential Circuits

Latches and flip-flops are used to implement more complex sequential circuits. Registers, counters, memories, and shift registers all require the use of storage and are therefore implemented using sequential logic.

EXAMPLE 3.14 Our first example of a sequential circuit is a simple 4-bit register implemented using four D flip-flops. (To implement registers for larger words, we would need to add flip-flops.) There are four input lines, four output lines, and a clock signal line. The clock is very important from a timing standpoint; the registers must all accept their new input values and change their storage elements at the same time. Remember that a synchronous sequential circuit

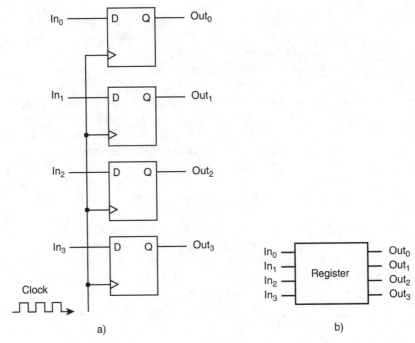

FIGURE 3.30 a) 4-Bit Register
b) Block Diagram for a 4-Bit Register

cannot change state unless the clock pulses. The same clock signal is tied into all four D flip-flops, so they change in unison. Figure 3.30 depicts the logic diagram for our 4-bit register, as well as a block diagram for the register. In reality, physical components have additional lines for power and for ground, as well as a clear line (which gives the ability to reset the entire register to all zeros). However, in this text, we are willing to leave those concepts to the computer engineers and focus on the actual digital logic present in these circuits.

EXAMPLE 3.15 Another useful sequential circuit is a binary counter, which goes through a predetermined sequence of states as the clock pulses. In a straight binary counter, these states reflect the binary number sequence. If we begin counting in binary 0000, 0001, 0010, 0011, ..., we can see that as the numbers increase, the low-order bit is complemented each time. Whenever it changes state from 1 to 0, the bit to the left is then complemented. Each of the other bits changes state from 0 to 1 when all bits to the right are equal to 1. Because of this concept of complementing states, our binary counter is best implemented using a JK flip-flop (recall that when *J* and *K* are both equal to 1, the flip-flop

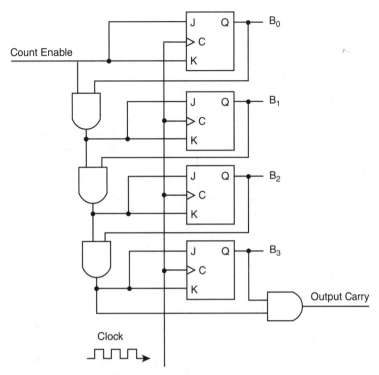

FIGURE 3.31   4-Bit Synchronous Counter Using JK Flip-Flops

complements the present state). Instead of independent inputs to each flip-flop, there is a **count enable line** that runs to each flip-flop. The circuit counts only when the clock pulses and this count enable line is set to 1. If count enable is set to 0 and the clock pulses, the circuit does not change state. Examine Figure 3.31 very carefully, tracing the circuit with various inputs to make sure you understand how this circuit outputs the binary numbers from 0000 to 1111. Note: B_0, B_1, B_2, and B_3 are the outputs of this circuit, and they are always available regardless of the values of the count enable and clock signals. Also check to see which state the circuit enters if the current state is 1111 and the clock is pulsed.

We have looked at a simple register and a binary counter. We are now ready to examine a very simple memory circuit.

EXAMPLE 3.16   The memory depicted in Figure 3.32 holds four 3-bit words (this is typically denoted as a 4×3 memory). Each column in the circuit represents one 3-bit word. Notice that the flip-flops storing the bits for each word are synchronized via the clock signal, so a read or write operation always reads or writes a complete word. The inputs In_0, In_1, and In_2 are the lines used to store, or

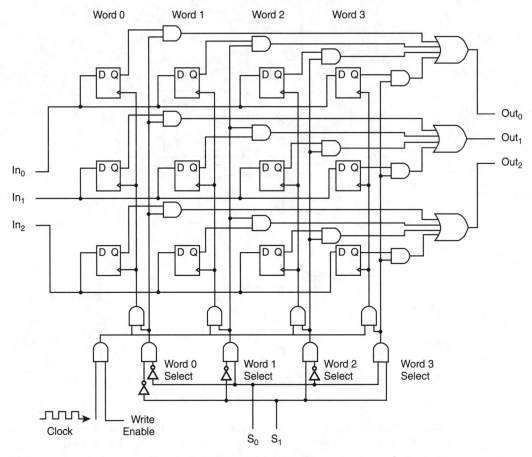

FIGURE 3.32 4 x 3 Memory

write, a 3-bit word to memory. The lines S_0 and S_1 are the address lines used to select which word in memory is being referenced. (Notice that S_0 and S_1 are the input lines to a 2-to-4 decoder that is responsible for selecting the correct memory word.) The three output lines (Out_0, Out_1, and Out_2) are used when reading words from memory.

You should notice another control line as well. The *write enable* control line indicates whether we are reading or writing. Note that in this chip, we have separated the input and output lines for ease of understanding. In practice, the input lines and output lines are the same lines.

To summarize our discussion of this memory circuit, here are the steps necessary to write a word to memory:

1. An address is asserted on S_0 and S_1.

2. Write enable (WE) is set to high.

3. The decoder using S_0 and S_1 enables only one AND gate, selecting a given word in memory.

4. The line selected in Step 3 combines with the clock and Write Enable select only one word.

5. The write gate enabled in Step 4 drives the clock for the selected word.

6. When the clock pulses, the word on the input lines is loaded into the D flip-flops.

We leave it as an exercise to create a similar list of the steps necessary to read a word from this memory. Another interesting exercise is to analyze this circuit and determine what additional components would be necessary to extend the memory from, say, a 4×3 memory to an 8×3 memory or a 4×8 memory.

Logically Speaking, How'd They Do That?

In this chapter, we introduced logic gates. But exactly what goes on inside these gates to carry out the logic functions? How do these gates physically work? It's time to open the hood and take a peek at the internal composition of digital logic gates.

The implementation of the logic gates is accomplished using different types of logic devices belonging to different production technologies. These devices are often classified into **logic families**. Each family has its advantages and disadvantages, and each differs from the others in its capabilities and limitations. The logic families currently of interest include TTL, NMOS/PMOS, CMOS, and ECL.

TTL (transistor–transistor logic) replaces all the diodes originally found in integrated circuits with bipolar transistors. (See the sidebar on transistors in Chapter 1 for more information.) TTL defines binary values as follows: 0 to 0.8 V is logic 0, and 2–5 V is logic 1. Virtually any gate can be implemented using TTL. Not only does TTL offer the largest number of logic gates (from the standard combinational and sequential logic gates to memory), but this technology also offers superior speed of operation. The problem with these relatively inexpensive integrated circuits is that they draw considerable power.

TTL was used in the first integrated circuits that were widely marketed. However, the most commonly used type of transistor used in integrated circuits today is called a **MOSFET (metal-oxide semiconductor field effect transistor). Field effect transistors (FETs)** are simply transistors whose output fields are controlled by a variable electric field. The phrase *metal-oxide semiconductor* is actually a reference to the process used to make the chip, and even though polysilicon is used today instead of metal, the name continues to be used.

NMOS (N-type metal-oxide semiconductors) and **PMOS (P-type metal-oxide semiconductors)** are the two basic types of MOS transistors. NMOS transistors are faster than PMOS transistors, but the real advantage of NMOS over PMOS is that of higher component density (more NMOS transistors can be put on a single chip). NMOS circuits have lower power consumption than their bipolar relatives. The main disadvantage of NMOS technology is its sensitivity to damage from electrical discharge. In addition, not as many gate implementations are available with NMOS as with TTL. Despite NMOS circuits using less power than TTL, increased NMOs circuit densities caused a resurgence in power consumption problems.

CMOS (complementary metal-oxide semiconductor) chips were designed as low-power alternatives to TTL and NMOS circuits, providing more TTL equivalents than NMOS in addition to addressing the power issues. Instead of using bipolar transistors, this technology uses a complementary pair of FETs, an NMOS and a PMOS FET (hence the name "complementary"). CMOS differs from NMOS because when the gate is in a static state, CMOS uses virtually no power. Only when the gate switches states does the circuit draw power. Lower power consumption translates to reduced heat dissipation.

For this reason, CMOS is extensively used in a wide variety of computer systems. In addition to low power consumption, CMOS chips operate within a wide range of supply voltages (typically from 3 to 15 V)—unlike TTL, which requires a power supply voltage of plus or minus 0.5 V. However, CMOS technology is extremely sensitive to static electricity, so extreme care must be taken when handling circuits. Although CMOS technology provides a larger selection of gates than NMOS, it still does not match that of its bipolar relative, TTL.

ECL (emitter-coupled logic) gates are used in situations that require extremely high speeds. Whereas TTL and MOS use transistors as digital switches (the transistor is either saturated or cut off), ECL uses transistors to guide current through gates, resulting in transistors that are never completely turned off or completely saturated. Because they are always in an active status, the transistors can change states very quickly. However, the trade-off for this high speed is substantial power requirements. Therefore, ECL is used only rarely, in very specialized applications.

A newcomer to the logic family scene, **BiCMOS (bipolar CMOS)** integrated circuits use both the bipolar and CMOS technologies. Despite the fact that BiCMOS logic consumes more power than TTL, it is considerably faster. Although not currently used in manufacturing, BiCMOS appears to have great potential.

3.6.6 An Application of Sequential Logic: Convolutional Coding and Viterbi Detection

Several coding methods are employed in data storage and communication. One of them is the partial response maximum likelihood (PRML) encoding method. Our previous discussion (which isn't prerequisite for understanding this section) concerned the "partial response" component of PRML. The "maximum likelihood" component derives from the way that bits are encoded and decoded. The salient feature of the decoding process is that only certain bit patterns are valid. These patterns are produced using a convolutional code. A **Viterbi decoder** reads the bits that have been output by a convolutional encoder and compares the symbol

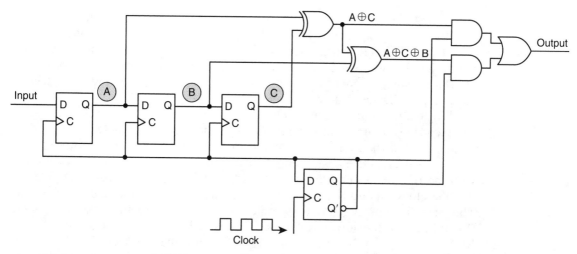

FIGURE 3.33 Convolutional Encoder for PRML

stream read with a set of "probable" symbol streams. The one with the least error is selected for output. We present this discussion because it brings together a number of concepts from this chapter as well as from Chapter 2. We begin with the encoding process.

The Hamming code introduced in Chapter 2 is a type of forward error correction that uses blocks of data (or block coding) to compute the necessary redundant bits. Some applications require a coding technique suitable for a continuous stream of data, such as that from a satellite television transmitter. **Convolutional coding** is a method that operates on an incoming serial bit stream, generating an encoded serial output stream (including redundant bits) that enables it to correct errors continuously. A **convolutional code** is an encoding process whereby the output is a function of the input and some number of bits previously received. Thus, the input is overlapped, or *convoluted*, over itself to form a stream of output symbols. In a sense, a convolutional code builds a context for accurate decoding of its output. Convolutional encoding combined with Viterbi decoding has become an accepted industry standard for encoding and decoding data stored or transmitted over imperfect (**noisy**) media.

The convolutional coding mechanism used in PRML is illustrated in Figure 3.33. Careful examination of this circuit reveals that two output bits are written for each input bit. The first output bit is a function of the input bit and the second previous input bit: A XOR C. The second bit is a function of the input bit and the two previous bits: A XOR C XOR B. The two AND gates at the right-hand side of the diagram alternatively select one of these functions during each pulse of the clock. The input is shifted through the D flip-flops on every second clock pulse. We note that the leftmost flip-flop serves only as a buffer for the input and isn't strictly necessary.

At first glance, it may not be easy to see how the encoder produces two output bits for every input bit. The trick has to do with the flip-flop situated between the clock and the other components of the circuit. When the complemented output of this flip-flop is fed back to its input, the flip-flop alternately stores 0s and 1s. Thus, the output goes high on every other clock cycle, enabling and disabling the correct AND gate with each cycle.

We step through a series of clock cycles in Figure 3.34. The initial state of the encoder is assumed to contain all 0s in the flip-flops labeled A, B, and C. A couple of clock cycles are required to move the first input into the A flip-flop (buffer), and the encoder outputs two zeros. Figure 3.34a shows the encoder with the first input (1) after it has passed to the output of flip-flop A. We see that the clock on flip-flops A, B, and C is enabled, as is the upper AND gate. Thus, the function A XOR C is routed to the output. At the next clock cycle (Figure 3.34b), the lower AND gate is enabled, which routes the function A XOR C XOR B to the output. However, because the clock on flip-flops A, B, and C is disabled, the input bit does not propagate from flip-flop A to flip-flop B. This prevents the next input bit from being consumed while the second output bit is written. At clock cycle 3 (Figure 3.34c), the input has propagated through flip-flop A, and the bit that was in flip-flop A has propagated to flip-flop B. The upper AND gate on the output is enabled and the function A XOR C is routed to the output.

The characteristic table for this circuit is given in Table 3.13. As an example, consider the stream of input bits, 11010010. The encoder initially contains all 0s, so $B = 0$ and $C = 0$. We say that the encoder is in State 0 (00_2). When the leading 1 of the input stream exits the buffer, A, $B = 0$ and $C = 0$, giving (A XOR C XOR B) = 1 and (A XOR C) = 1. The output is 11 and the encoder transitions to State 2 (10_2). The next input bit is 1, and we have $B = 1$ and $C = 0$ (in State 2), giving (A XOR C XOR B) = 0 and (A XOR C) = 1. The output is 01 and the encoder transitions to State 1 (01_2). Following this process over the remaining six bits, the completed function is:

$$F(1101\ 0010) = 11\ 01\ 01\ 00\ 10\ 11\ 11\ 10$$

The encoding process is made a little clearer using the Mealy machine (Figure 3.35). This diagram informs us at a glance as to which transitions are possible and which are not. You can see the correspondence between the Figure 3.35 machine and the characteristic table by reading the table and tracing the arcs or vice versa. The fact that there is a limited set of allowable transitions is crucial to the error-correcting properties of this code and to the operation of the Viterbi decoder, which is responsible for decoding the stream of bits correctly. By reversing the inputs with the outputs on the transition arcs, as shown in Figure 3.36, we place bounds around the set of possible decoding inputs.

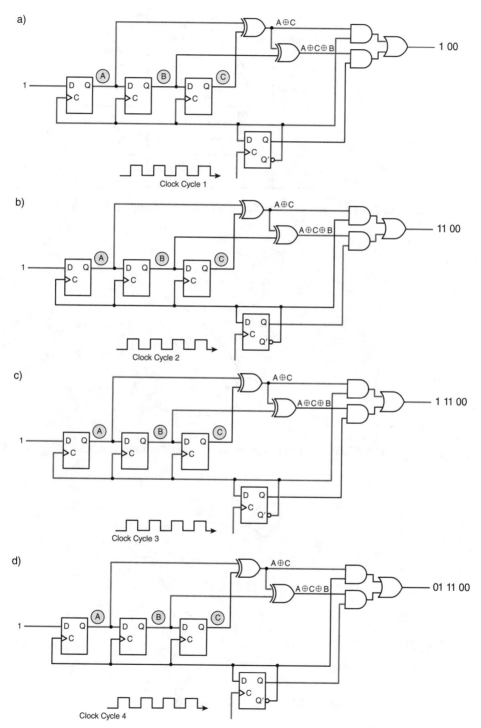

FIGURE 3.34 Stepping through Four Clock Cycles of a Convolutional Encoder

Input A	Current State B C	Next State B C	Output
0	00	00	00
1	00	10	11
0	01	00	11
1	01	10	00
0	10	01	10
1	10	11	01
0	11	01	01
1	11	11	10

TABLE 3.13 Characteristic Table for the Convolutional Encoder in Figure 3.33

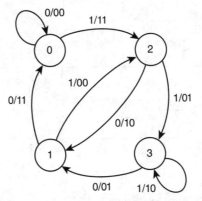

FIGURE 3.35 Mealy Machine for the Convolutional Encoder in Figure 3.33

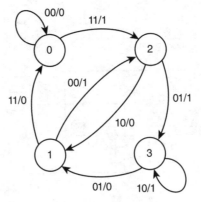

FIGURE 3.36 Mealy Machine for a Convolutional Decoder

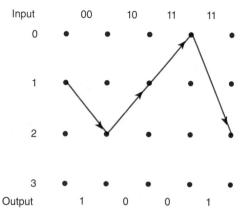

FIGURE 3.37 Trellis Diagram Illustrating State Transitions for the Sequence 00 10 11 11

For example, suppose the decoder is in State 1 and sees the pattern 00 01. The decoded bit values returned are 1 1, and the decoder ends up in State 3. (The path traversed is $1 \rightarrow 2 \rightarrow 3$.) If, on the other hand, the decoder is in State 2 and sees the pattern 00 11, an error has occurred because there is no outbound transition on State 2 for 00. The outbound transitions on State 2 are 01 and 10. Both of these have a Hamming distance of 1 from 00. If we follow both (equally likely) paths out of State 2, the decoder ends up in either State 1 or State 3. We see that there is no outbound transition on State 3 for the next pair of bits, 11. Each outbound transition from State 3 has a Hamming distance of 1 from 11. This gives an accumulated Hamming distance of 2 for both paths: $2 \rightarrow 3 \rightarrow 1$ and $2 \rightarrow 3 \rightarrow 2$. However, State 1 has a valid transition on 11. By taking the path $2 \rightarrow 1 \rightarrow 0$, the accumulated error is only 1, so this is the most likely sequence. The input therefore decodes to 00 with **maximum likelihood**.

An equivalent (and probably clearer) way of expressing this idea is through the trellis diagram, shown in Figure 3.37. The four states are indicated on the left side of the diagram. The transition (or time) component reads from left to right. Every code word in a convolutional code is associated with a unique path in the trellis diagram. A Viterbi detector uses the logical equivalent of paths through this diagram to determine the most likely bit pattern. In Figure 3.37, we show the state transitions that occur when the input sequence 00 10 11 11 is encountered with the decoder starting in State 1. You can compare the transitions in the trellis diagram with the transitions in the Mealy diagram in Figure 3.36.

Suppose we introduce an error in the first pair of bits in our input, giving the erroneous string 10 10 11 11. With our decoder starting in State 1 as before, Figure 3.38 traces the possible paths through the trellis. The accumulated Hamming distance is shown on each of the transition arcs. The correct path that correctly assumes that the string should be 00 10 11 11 is the one having the smallest accumulated error, so it is accepted as the correct sequence.

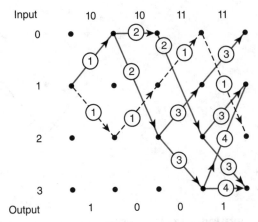

FIGURE 3.38 Trellis Diagram Illustrating Hamming Errors for the Sequence
10 10 11 11

In most cases where it is applied, the Viterbi decoder provides only one level of error correction. Additional error-correction mechanisms such as cyclic redundancy checking and Reed-Solomon coding (discussed in Chapter 2) are applied after the Viterbi algorithm has done what it can to produce a clean stream of symbols. All these algorithms are usually implemented in hardware for utmost speed using the digital building blocks described in this chapter.

We hope that our discussion in this section has helped you to see how digital logic and error-correction algorithms fit together. The same can be done with any algorithm that can be represented using one of the finite state machines described. In fact, the convolutional code just described is also referred to as a (2, 1) convolutional code because two symbols are output for every one symbol input. Other convolutional codes provide somewhat deeper error correction, but they are too complex for economical hardware implementation.

3.7 DESIGNING CIRCUITS

In the preceding sections, we introduced many different components used in computer systems. We have, by no means, provided enough detail to allow you to start designing circuits or systems. Digital logic design requires someone not only familiar with digital logic, but also well versed in **digital analysis** (analyzing the relationship between inputs and outputs), **digital synthesis** (starting with a truth table and determining the logic diagram to implement the given logic function), and the use of computer-aided design (CAD) software. Recall from our previous discussions that great care needs to be taken when designing the circuits to ensure that they are minimized. A circuit designer faces many problems, including finding efficient Boolean functions, using the smallest number of gates, using an inexpensive combination of gates, organizing the gates of a circuit board to use the smallest surface area and minimal power requirements, and attempting to do all of this using a standard set of modules for implementation. Add to this the many problems we have not discussed, such as signal propagation, fan out, synchronization issues, and external interfacing, and you can see that digital circuit design is quite complicated.

Up to this point, we have discussed how to design registers, counters, memory, and various other digital building blocks. Given these components, a circuit designer can implement any given algorithm in hardware (recall the Principle of Equivalence of Hardware and Software from Chapter 1). When you write a program, you are specifying a sequence of Boolean expressions. Typically, it is much easier to write a program than it is to design the hardware necessary to implement the algorithm. However, there are situations in which the hardware implementation is better (e.g., in a real-time system, the hardware implementation is faster, and faster is definitely better.) However, there are also cases in which a software implementation is better. It is often desirable to replace a large number of digital components with a single programmed microcomputer chip, resulting in an **embedded system**. Your microwave oven and your car most likely contain embedded systems. This is done to replace additional hardware that could present mechanical problems. Programming these embedded systems requires design software that can read input variables and send output signals to perform such tasks as turning a light on or off, emitting a beep, sounding an alarm, or opening a door. Writing this software requires an understanding of how Boolean functions behave.

CHAPTER SUMMARY

The main purpose of this chapter is to acquaint you with the basic concepts involved in logic design and to give you a general understanding of the basic circuit configurations used to construct computer systems. This level of familiarity will not enable you to design these components; rather, it gives you a much better understanding of the architectural concepts discussed in the following chapters.

In this chapter, we examined the behaviors of the standard logical operators AND, OR, and NOT and looked at the logic gates that implement them. Any Boolean function can be represented as a truth table, which can then be transformed into a logic diagram, indicating the components necessary to implement the digital circuit for that function. Thus, truth tables provide us with a means to express the characteristics of Boolean functions as well as logic circuits. In practice, these simple logic circuits are combined to create components such as adders, ALUs, decoders, multiplexers, registers, and memory.

There is a one-to-one correspondence between a Boolean function and its digital representation. Boolean identities can be used to reduce Boolean expressions, and thus, to minimize both combinational and sequential circuits. Minimization is extremely important in circuit design. From a chip designer's point of view, the two most important factors are speed and cost; minimizing circuits helps to both lower the cost and increase performance.

Digital logic is divided into two categories: combinational logic and sequential logic. Combinational logic devices, such as adders, decoders, and multiplexers, produce outputs that are based strictly on the current inputs. The AND, OR, and NOT gates are the building blocks for combinational logic circuits, although universal gates, such as NAND and NOR, could also be used. Sequential logic devices, such as registers, counters, and memory, produce outputs based on the combination of current inputs and the current state of the circuit. These circuits are built using SR, D, and JK flip-flops.

You have seen that sequential circuits can be represented in a number of different ways, depending on the particular behavior that we want to emphasize. Clear pictures can be rendered by Moore, Mealy, and algorithmic state machines. A lattice diagram expresses transitions as a function of time. These finite state machines differ from DFAs in that, unlike DFAs, they have no final state because circuits produce output rather than accept strings.

These logic circuits are the building blocks necessary for computer systems. In Chapter 4, we put these blocks together and take a closer, more detailed look at how a computer actually functions.

If you are interested in learning more about Kmaps, there is a special section that focuses on Kmaps located at the end of this chapter, after the exercises.

FURTHER READING

Most computer organization and architecture books have a brief discussion of digital logic and Boolean algebra. The books by Stallings (2013), Tanenbaum (2012), and Patterson and Hennessy (2011) contain good synopses of digital logic. Mano (1993) presents a good discussion on using Kmaps for circuit simplification (discussed in the focus section of this chapter) and programmable logic devices, as well as an introduction to the various circuit technologies. For more in-depth information on digital logic, see the Wakerly (2000), Katz (1994), or Hayes (1993) books.

Davis (2000) traces the history of computer theory, including biographies of all the seminal thinkers, in his *Universal Computer* book. This book is a joy to read. For a good discussion of Boolean algebra in lay terms, check out the book by Gregg (1998). The book by Maxfield (1995) is an absolute delight to read and contains informative and sophisticated concepts on Boolean logic, as well as a trove of interesting and enlightening bits of trivia (including a wonderful recipe for seafood gumbo!). For a straightforward and easy-to-read book on gates and flip-flops (as well as a terrific explanation of what computers are and how they work), see Petzold (1989). Davidson (1979) presents a method of decomposing NAND-based circuits (of interest because NAND is a universal gate).

Moore, Mealy, and algorithmic state machines were first proposed in papers by Moore (1956), Mealy (1955), and Clare (1973). Cohen's (1991) computer theory book is one of the most easily understandable on this topic. In it you will find excellent presentations of Moore, Mealy, and finite state machines in general, including DFAs. Forney's (1973) well-written tutorial on the Viterbi algorithm in a paper by that same name explains the concept and the mathematics behind this convolutional decoder. Fisher's (1996) article explains how PRML is used in disk drives.

If you are interested in actually designing some circuits, there are several nice simulators freely available. One set of tools is called the Chipmunk System. It performs a wide variety of applications, including electronic circuit simulation, graphics editing, and curve plotting. It contains four main tools, but for circuit simulation, *Log* is the program you need. The *Diglog* portion of Log allows you to create and actually test digital circuits. If you are interested in downloading the program and running it on your machine, the general Chipmunk distribution can be found at www.cs.berkeley.edu/~lazzaro/chipmunk/. The distribution is available for a wide variety of platforms (including PCs and Unix machines).

Another nice package is Multimedia Logic (MMLogic) by Softronix, but it is currently available for Windows platforms only. This fully functional package has a nice GUI with drag-and-drop components and comprehensive online help. It includes not only the standard complement of devices (such as ANDs, ORs, NANDs, NORs, adders, and counters), but also special multimedia devices (including bitmap, robot, network, and buzzer devices). You can create logic circuits and interface them to real devices (keyboards, screens, serial ports, etc.) or other computers. The package is advertised for use by beginners but allows users to build quite complex applications (such as games that run over the Internet). MMLogic can be found at www.softronix.com/logic.html, and the distribution includes not only the executable package, but also the source code so users can modify or extend its capabilities.

A third digital logic simulator is Logisim, an open-source software package available at http://ozark.hendrix.edu/~burch/logisim/. This software is compact, easy to install, and easy to use, and it requires only that Java 5 or later be installed; therefore, it is available for Windows, Mac, and Linux platforms. The interface is intuitive, and unlike most simulators, Logisim allows the user to modify a circuit during simulation. The application allows the user to build larger circuits from smaller ones, draw bundles of wires (with multi-bit width) in one mouse action, and use a tree view to see the library of components that can be utilized for building circuits. Like MMLogic, the package was designed as an educational tool to help beginners experiment with digital logic circuits, but also allows the user to build fairly complex circuits.

Any of these simulators can be used to build the MARIE architecture discussed next in Chapter 4.

REFERENCES

Clare, C. R. *Designing Logic Systems Using State Machines.* New York: McGraw-Hill, 1973.

Cohen, D. I. A. *Introduction to Computer Theory*, 2nd ed. New York: John Wiley & Sons, 1991.

Davidson, E. S. "An Algorithm for NAND Decomposition under Network Constraints." *IEEE Transactions on Computing C-18*, 1979, p. 1098.

Davis, M. *The Universal Computer: The Road from Leibniz to Turing.* New York: W. W. Norton, 2000.

Fisher, K. D., Abbott, W. L., Sonntag, J. L., & Nesin, R. "PRML Detection Boosts Hard-Disk Drive Capacity." *IEEE Spectrum*, November 1996, pp. 70–76.

Forney, G. D. "The Viterbi Algorithm." *Proceedings of the IEEE 61*, March 1973, pp. 268–278.

Gregg, J. *Ones and Zeros: Understanding Boolean Algebra, Digital Circuits, and the Logic of Sets.* New York: IEEE Press, 1998.

Hayes, J. P. *Digital Logic Design.* Reading, MA: Addison-Wesley, 1993.

Katz, R. H. *Contemporary Logic Design.* Redwood City, CA: Benjamin Cummings, 1994.

Mano, M. M. *Computer System Architecture*, 3rd ed. Englewood Cliffs, NJ: Prentice Hall, 1993.

Maxfield, C. *Bebop to the Boolean Boogie.* Solana Beach, CA: High Text Publications, 1995.

Mealy, G. H. "A Method for Synthesizing Sequential Circuits." *Bell System Technical Journal 34*, September 1955, pp. 1045–1079.

Moore, E. F. "Gedanken Experiments on Sequential Machines," in *Automata Studies*, edited by C. E. Shannon and John McCarthy. Princeton, NJ: Princeton University Press, 1956, pp. 129–153.

Patterson, D. A., & Hennessy, J. L. *Computer Organization and Design, The Hardware/Software Interface*, 4th ed. San Mateo, CA: Morgan Kaufmann, 2011.

Petzold, C. *Code: The Hidden Language of Computer Hardware and Software.* Redmond, WA: Microsoft Press, 1989.

Stallings, W. *Computer Organization and Architecture*, 9th ed. Upper Saddle River, MJ: Prentice Hall, 2013.

Tanenbaum, A. *Structured Computer Organization*, 6th ed. Upper Saddle River, NJ: Prentice Hall, 2012.

Wakerly, J. F. *Digital Design Principles and Practices.* Upper Saddle River, NJ: Prentice Hall, 2000.

REVIEW OF ESSENTIAL TERMS AND CONCEPTS

1. Why is an understanding of Boolean algebra important to computer scientists?

2. Which Boolean operation is referred to as a Boolean product?

3. Which Boolean operation is referred to as a Boolean sum?

4. Create truth tables for the Boolean operators OR, AND, and NOT.

5. What is the Boolean duality principle?

6. Why is it important for Boolean expressions to be minimized in the design of digital circuits?

7. What is the relationship between transistors and gates?

8. What is the difference between a gate and a circuit?

9. Name the four basic logic gates.

10. What are the two universal gates described in this chapter? Why are these universal gates important?

11. Describe the basic construction of a digital logic chip.

12. Describe the operation of a ripple-carry adder. Why are ripple-carry adders not used in most computers today?

13. What are the three methods we can use to express the logical behavior of Boolean functions?

14. What are the necessary steps one must take when designing a logic circuit from a description of the problem?

15. What is the difference between a half-adder and a full-adder?

16. What do we call a circuit that takes several inputs and their respective values to select one specific output line? Name one important application for these devices.

17. What kind of circuit selects binary information from one of many input lines and directs it to a single output line?

18. How are sequential circuits different from combinational circuits?

19. What is the basic element of a sequential circuit?

20. What do we mean when we say that a sequential circuit is edge triggered rather than level triggered?

21. In the context of digital circuits, what is feedback?

22. How is a JK flip-flop related to an SR flip-flop?

23. Why are JK flip-flops often preferred to SR flip-flops?

24. Which flip-flop gives a true representation of computer memory?

25. How is a Mealy machine different from a Moore machine?

26. What does an algorithmic state machine offer that is not provided by either a Moore or a Mealy machine?

EXERCISES

◆**1.** Construct a truth table for the following:

 ◆ **a)** $yz + z(xy)'$

 ◆ **b)** $x(y' + z) + xyz$

   c) $(x + y)(x' + y)$ (Hint: This is from Example 3.7.)

2. Construct a truth table for the following:

   a) $xyz + x(yz)' + x'(y + z) + (xyz)'$

   b) $(x + y')(x' + z')(y' + z')$

◆**3.** Using DeMorgan's Law, write an expression for the complement of F if $F(x,y,z) = xy'(x + z)$.

4. Using DeMorgan's Law, write an expression for the complement of F if $F(x,y,z) = (x' + y)(x + z)(y' + z)'$.

◆**5.** Using DeMorgan's Law, write an expression for the complement of F if $F(w,x,y,z) = xz'(x'yz + x) + y(w'z + x')$.

6. Using DeMorgan's Law, write an expression for the complement of F if $F(x,y,z) = xz'(xy + xz) + xy'(wz + y)$.

7. Prove DeMorgan's Laws are valid.

◆ **8.** Is the following distributive law valid or invalid? Prove your answer.

x XOR $(y + z) = (x$ XOR $y) + (x$ XOR $z)$

9. Is the following true or false? Prove your answer.

$(x$ XOR $y)' = xy + (x + y)'$

10. Show that $x = xy + xy'$

a) Using truth tables

b) Using Boolean identities

11. Use only the first seven Boolean identities to prove the Absorption Laws.

12. Show that $xz = (x + y)(x + y')(x' + z)$

a) Using truth tables

b) Using Boolean identities

13. Use any method to prove the following either true or false.

$xz + x'y' + y'z' = xz + y'$

14. Simplify the following functional expressions using Boolean algebra and its identities. List the identity used at each step.

a) $F(x,y,z) = y(x' + (x + y)')$

b) $F(x,y,z) = x'yz + xz$

c) $F(x,y,z) = (x' + y + z')' + xy'z' + yz + xyz$

◆ **15.** Simplify the following functional expressions using Boolean algebra and its identities. List the identity used at each step.

a) $x(yz + y'z) + xy + x'y + xz$

b) $xyz'' + (y + z)' + x'yz$

c) $z(xy' + z)(x + y')$

16. Simplify the following functional expressions using Boolean algebra and its identities. List the identity used at each step.

a) $z(w + x)' + w'xz + wxyz' + wx'yz'$

b) $y'(x'z' + xz) + z(x + y)'$

c) $x(yz' + x)(y' + z)$

17. Simplify the following functional expressions using Boolean algebra and its identities. List the identity used at each step.

◆ a) $x(y + z)(x' + z')$

b) $xy + xyz + xy'z + x'y'z$

c) $xy'z + x(y + z')' + xy'z'$

18. Simplify the following functional expressions using Boolean algebra and its identities. List the identity used at each step.

a) $y(xz' + x'z) + y'(xz' + x'z)$

b) $x(y'z + y) + x'(y + z')'$

c) $x[y'z + (y + z')'](x'y + z)$

◆ **19.** Using the basic identities of Boolean algebra, show that

$$x(x' + y) = xy$$

* **20.** Using the basic identities of Boolean algebra, show that

$$x + x'y = x + y$$

21. Using the basic identities of Boolean algebra, show that

$$xy + x'z + yz = xy + x'z$$

◆ **22.** The truth table for a Boolean expression is shown below. Write the Boolean expression in sum-of-products form.

x	y	z	F
0	0	0	1
0	0	1	0
0	1	0	1
0	1	1	0
1	0	0	0
1	0	1	1
1	1	0	1
1	1	1	1

23. The truth table for a Boolean expression is shown below. Write the Boolean expression in sum-of-products form.

x	y	z	F
0	0	0	1
0	0	1	1
0	1	0	1
0	1	1	0
1	0	0	1
1	0	1	1
1	1	0	0
1	1	1	0

24. Which of the following Boolean expressions is not logically equivalent to all the rest?

    a) $wx' + wy' + wz$

    b) $w + x' + y' + z$

    c) $w(x' + y' + z)$

    d) $wx'yz' + wx'y' + wy'z' + wz$

◆ **25.** Draw the truth table and rewrite the expression below as the complemented sum of two products:

$$xy' + x'y + xz + y'z$$

26. Given the Boolean function, $F(x,y,z) = x'y + xyz'$

    a) Derive an algebraic expression for the complement of F. Express in sum-of-products form.

    b) Show that $FF' = 0$.

    c) Show that $F + F' = 1$.

27. Given the function, $F(x,y,z) = y(x'z + xz') + x(yz + yz')$

   a) List the truth table for F.

   b) Draw the logic diagram using the original Boolean expression.

   c) Simplify the expression using Boolean algebra and identities.

   d) List the truth table for your answer in part c.

   e) Draw the logic diagram for the simplified expression in part c.

28. Construct the XOR operator using only AND, OR, and NOT gates.

29. Construct the XOR operator using only NAND gates.

   Hint: x XOR $y = ((x'y)'(xy')')'$

30. Draw a half-adder using only NAND gates.

31. Draw a full-adder using only NAND gates.

32. Design a circuit with three inputs x, y, and z representing the bits in a binary number, and three outputs (a, b, and c) also representing bits in a binary number. When the input is 0, 1, 6, or 7, the binary output will be the complement of the input. When the binary input is 2, 3, 4, or 5, the output is the input shifted left with rotate. (For example, $3 = 011_2$ outputs 110; $4 = 100_2$ outputs 001.) Show your truth table, all computations for simplification, and the final circuit.

◆33. Draw the combinational circuit that directly implements the Boolean expression:

   $F(x,y,z) = xyz + (y' + z)$

34. Draw the combinational circuit that directly implements the following Boolean expression:

   $F(x,y,z) = x + xy + y'z$

35. Draw the combinational circuit that directly implements the Boolean expression:

   $F(x,y,z) = (x(y \text{ XOR } z)) + (xz)'$

◆36. Find the truth table that describes the following circuit:

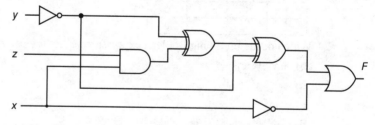

37. Find the truth table that describes the following circuit:

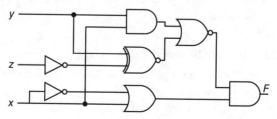

38. Find the truth table that describes the following circuit:

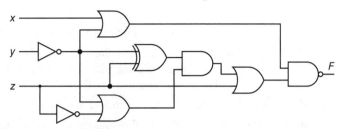

39. How many inputs does a decoder have if it has 64 outputs?

40. How many control lines does a multiplexer have if it has 32 inputs?

41. Draw circuits to implement the parity generator and parity checker shown in Tables 3.10 and 3.11, respectively.

42. Assume you have the following truth tables for functions $F_1(x,y,z)$ and $F_2(x,y,z)$:

x	y	z	F_1	F_2
0	0	0	1	0
0	0	1	1	0
0	1	0	1	1
0	1	1	0	1
1	0	0	0	0
1	0	1	0	0
1	1	0	0	1
1	1	1	0	1

a) Express F_1 and F_2 in sum-of-products form.

b) Simplify each function.

c) Draw one logic circuit to implement the above *two* functions.

43. Assume you have the following truth tables for functions $F_1(w,x,y,z)$ and $F_2(w,x,y,z)$:

w	x	y	z	F_1	F_2
0	0	0	0	0	0
0	0	0	1	1	1
0	0	1	0	0	0
0	0	1	1	1	1
0	1	0	0	0	0
0	1	0	1	0	0
0	1	1	0	0	0
0	1	1	1	0	0
1	0	0	0	0	0
1	0	0	1	1	0
1	0	1	0	0	0
1	0	1	1	1	0
1	1	0	0	1	1
1	1	0	1	1	1
1	1	1	0	1	1
1	1	1	1	1	1

     a) Express F_1 and F_2 in sum-of-products form.

     b) Simplify each function.

     c) Draw one logic circuit to implement the above *two* functions.

44. Design a truth table for a combinational circuit that detects an error in the representation of a decimal digit encoded in BCD. (This circuit should output a 1 when the input is one of the six unused combinations for BCD code.)

45. Simplify the function from exercise 44 and draw the logic circuit.

46. Describe how each of the following circuits works and indicate typical inputs and outputs. Also provide a carefully labeled "black box" diagram for each.

     a) Decoder

     b) Multiplexer

47. Little Susie is trying to train her new puppy. She is trying to figure out when the puppy should get a dog biscuit as a reward. She has concluded the following:

     1. Give the puppy a biscuit if it sits and wiggles but does not bark.

     2. Give the puppy a biscuit if it barks and wiggles but does not sit.

     3. Give the puppy a biscuit if it sits but does not wiggle or bark.

     4. Give the puppy a biscuit if it sits, wiggles, and barks.

     5. Don't give the puppy a treat otherwise.

     Use the following:

     S: Sit (0 for not sitting; 1 for sitting)

     W: Wiggles (0 for not wiggling; 1 for wiggling)

     B: Barking (0 for not barking; 1 for barking)

     F: Biscuit function (0, don't give the puppy a biscuit; 1, give the puppy a biscuit)

     Construct a truth table and find the minimized Boolean function to implement the logic telling Susie when to give her dog a biscuit.

48. Tyrone Shoelaces has invested a huge amount of money into the stock market and doesn't trust just anyone to give him buying and selling information. Before he will buy a certain stock, he must get input from three sources. His first source is Pain Webster, a famous stock broker. His second source is Meg A. Cash, a self-made millionaire in the stock market, and his third source is Madame LaZora, world-famous psychic. After several months of receiving advice from all three, he has come to the following conclusions:

     a) Buy if Pain and Meg both say yes and the psychic says no.

     b) Buy if the psychic says yes.

     c) Don't buy otherwise.

     Construct a truth table and find the minimized Boolean function to implement the logic telling Tyrone when to buy.

◆*49. A very small company has hired you to install a security system. The brand of system that you install is priced by the number of bits encoded on the proximity cards that allow access to certain locations in a facility. Of course, this small company wants to use the fewest bits possible (spending the least amount of money possible) yet have all of its security needs met. The first thing you need to do is to determine how many bits each card requires. Next, you have to program card readers in each secured location so that they respond appropriately to a scanned card.

This company has four types of employees and five areas that they wish to restrict to certain employees. The employees and their restrictions are as follows:

a) The Big Boss needs access to the executive lounge and the executive washroom.

b) The Big Boss's secretary needs access to the supply closet, employee lounge, and executive lounge.

c) Computer room employees need access to the server room and the employee lounge.

d) The janitor needs access to all areas in the workplace.

Determine how each class of employee will be encoded on the cards and construct logic diagrams for the card readers in each of the five restricted areas.

◆50. Complete the truth table for the following sequential circuit:

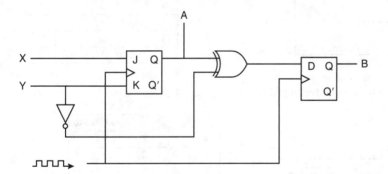

			Next State	
X	Y	A	A	B
0	0	0		
0	0	1		
0	1	0		
0	1	1		
1	0	0		
1	0	1		
1	1	0		
1	1	1		

51. Complete the truth table for the following sequential circuit:

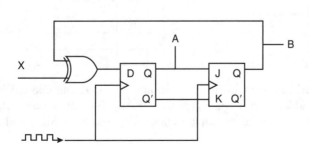

			Next State	
A	B	X	A	B
0	0	0		
0	0	1		
0	1	0		
0	1	1		
1	0	0		
1	0	1		
1	1	0		
1	1	1		

52. Complete the truth table for the following sequential circuit:

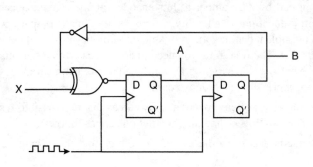

			Next State	
A	B	X	A	B
0	0	0		
0	0	1		
0	1	0		
0	1	1		
1	0	0		
1	0	1		
1	1	0		
1	1	1		

53. Complete the truth table for the following sequential circuit:

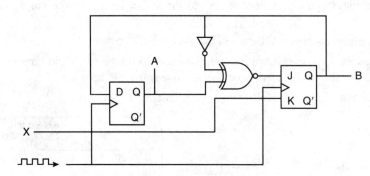

			Next State	
A	B	X	A	B
0	0	0		
0	0	1		
0	1	0		
0	1	1		
1	0	0		
1	0	1		
1	1	0		
1	1	1		

◆**54.** Complete the truth table for the following sequential circuit:

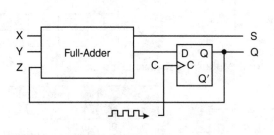

			Next State	
X	Y	Z	S	Q
0	0	0		
0	0	1		
0	1	0		
0	1	1		
1	0	0		
1	0	1		
1	1	0		
1	1	1		

55. A sequential circuit has one flip-flop; two inputs, X and Y; and one output, S. It consists of a full-adder circuit connected to a JK flip-flop, as shown. Fill in the truth table for this sequential circuit by completing the Next State and Output columns.

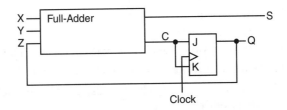

Present State Q(t)	Inputs X Y		Next State Q(t+1)	Output S
0	0	0		
0	0	1		
0	1	0		
0	1	1		
1	0	0		
1	0	1		
1	1	0		
1	1	1		

56. True or false: When a JK flip-flop is constructed from an SR flip-flop, $S = JQ'$ and $R = KQ$.

◆*57. Investigate the operation of the following circuit. Assume an initial state of 0000. Trace the outputs (the Qs) as the clock ticks and determine the purpose of the circuit. You must show the trace to complete your answer.

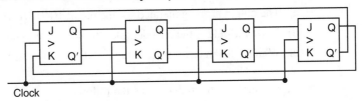

58. A Null–Lobur flip-flop (NL flip-flop) behaves as follows: If $N = 0$, the flip-flop does not change state. If $N = 1$, the next state of the flip-flop is equal to the value of L.

a) Derive the characteristic table for the NL flip-flop.

b) Show how an SR flip-flop can be converted to an NL flip-flop by adding gate(s) and inverter(s). (Hint: What values must S and R have so that the flip-flop will be set and reset at the proper time when $N = 1$? How can you prevent the flip-flop from changing state when $N = 0$?)

*59. A Mux-Not flip-flop (MN flip-flop) behaves as follows: If $M = 1$, the flip-flop complements the current state. If $M = 0$, the next state of the flip-flop is equal to the value of N.

a) Derive the characteristic table for the flip-flop.

b) Show how a JK flip-flop can be converted to an MN flip-flop by adding gate(s) and and inverter(s).

60. List the steps necessary to read a word from memory in the 4 × 3 memory circuit shown in Figure 3.32.

61. Construct Moore and Mealy machines that complement their input.

62. Construct a Moore machine that counts modulo 5.

63. Construct two parity checkers using a Moore machine for one and a Mealy machine for the other.

64. Using the lemma that two FSMs are equivalent if and only if they produce the same output from the same input strings, show that Moore and Mealy machines are equivalent.

65. Using the convolutional code and Viterbi algorithm described in this chapter, assuming that the encoder and decoder always start in State 0, determine the following:

    a) The output string generated for the input: 10010110.

    b) In which state is the encoder after the sequence in part a is read?

    c) Which bit is in error in the string, 11 01 10 11 11 11 10? What is the probable value of the string?

66. Repeat question 65 to determine the following:

    a) The output string generated for the input: 00101101.

    b) In which state is the encoder after the sequence in part a is written?

    c) Which bit is in error in the string, 00 01 10 11 00 11 00? What is the probable value of the string?

67. Repeat question 65 to determine the following:

    a) The output string generated for the input: 10101010.

    b) In which state is the encoder after the sequence in part a is written?

    c) Which bit is in error in the string, 11 10 01 00 00 11 01? What is the probable value of the string?

68. Repeat question 65 to determine the following:

    a) The output string generated for the input: 01000111.

    b) In which state is the encoder after the sequence in part a is written?

    c) Which bit is in error in the string, 11 01 10 11 01 00 01? What is the probable value of the string?

FOCUS ON KARNAUGH MAPS

3A.1   INTRODUCTION

In this chapter, we focused on Boolean expressions and their relationship to digital circuits. Minimizing these circuits helps reduce the number of components in the actual physical implementation. Having fewer components allows the circuitry to operate faster.

Reducing Boolean expressions can be done using Boolean identities; however, using identities can be difficult because no rules are given on how or when to use the identities, and there is no well-defined set of steps to follow. In one respect, minimizing Boolean expressions is very much like doing a proof: You know when you are on the right track, but getting there can sometimes be frustrating and time consuming. In this focus section, we introduce a systematic approach for reducing Boolean expressions.

3A.2   DESCRIPTION OF KMAPS AND TERMINOLOGY

Karnaugh maps, or **Kmaps**, are a graphical way to represent Boolean functions. A map is simply a table used to enumerate the values of a given Boolean expression for different input values. The rows and columns correspond to the possible values of the function's inputs. Each cell represents the outputs of the function for those possible inputs.

If a product term includes all of the variables exactly once, either complemented or not complemented, this product term is called a **minterm**. For example, if there are two input values, x and y, there are four minterms, $x'y'$, $x'y$, xy', and xy, which represent all of the possible input combinations for the function. If the input variables are x, y, and z, then there are eight minterms: $x'y'z'$, $x'y'z$, $x'yz'$, $x'yz$, $xy'z'$, $xy'z$, xyz', and xyz.

As an example, consider the Boolean function $F(x,y) = xy + x'y$. Possible inputs for x and y are shown in Figure 3A.1. The minterm $x'y'$ represents the input pair (0, 0). Similarly, the minterm $x'y$ represents (0, 1), the minterm xy' represents (1, 0), and xy represents (1, 1).

The minterms for three variables, along with the input values they represent, are shown in Figure 3A.2.

Minterm	x	y
$x'y'$	0	0
$x'y$	0	1
xy'	1	0
xy	1	1

FIGURE 3A.1   Minterms for Two Variables

Minterm	x	y	z
x'y'z'	0	0	0
x'y'z	0	0	1
x'yz'	0	1	0
x'yz	0	1	1
xy'z'	1	0	0
xy'z	1	0	1
xyz'	1	1	0
xyz	1	1	1

FIGURE 3A.2 Minterms for Three Variables

A Kmap is a table with a cell for each minterm, which means it has a cell for each line of the truth table for the function. Consider the function $F(x,y) = xy$ and its truth table, as seen in Example 3A.1.

EXAMPLE 3A.1 $F(x,y) = xy$

x	y	xy
0	0	0
0	1	0
1	0	0
1	1	1

The corresponding Kmap is

Notice that the only cell in the map with a value of 1 occurs when $x = 1$ and $y = 1$, the same values for which $xy = 1$. Let's look at another example, $F(x,y) = x + y$.

EXAMPLE 3A.2 $F(x,y) = x + y$

x	y	x + y
0	0	0
0	1	1
1	0	1
1	1	1

Three of the minterms in Example 3A.2 have a value of 1, exactly the minterms for which the input to the function gives us a 1 for the output. To assign 1s in the Kmap, we simply place 1s where we find corresponding 1s in the truth table. We can express the function $F(x,y) = x + y$ as the logical OR of all minterms for which the minterm has a value of 1. Then $F(x,y)$ can be represented by the expression $x'y + xy' + xy$. Obviously, this expression is not minimized (we already know this function is simply $x + y$). We can minimize using Boolean identities.

$$\begin{aligned}
F(x,y) &= x'y + xy' + xy \\
&= x'y + xy + xy' + xy \qquad \text{(remember, } xy + xy = xy) \\
&= y(x' + x) + x(y' + y) \\
&= y + x \\
&= x + y
\end{aligned}$$

How did we know to add an extra xy term? Algebraic simplification using Boolean identities can be tricky. This is where Kmaps can help.

3A.3 KMAP SIMPLIFICATION FOR TWO VARIABLES

In the previous reduction for the function $F(x,y)$, the goal was to group the terms so we could factor out variables. We added the xy to give us a term to combine with the $x'y$. This allowed us to factor out the y, leaving $x' + x$, which reduces to 1. However, if we use Kmap simplification, we won't have to worry about which terms to add or which Boolean identity to use. The maps take care of that for us.

Let's look at the Kmap for $F(x,y) = x + y$ again in Figure 3A.3.

To use this map to reduce a Boolean function, we simply need to group 1s. This grouping is similar to how we grouped terms when we reduced using Boolean identities, except we must follow specific rules. First, we group only 1s. Second, we can group 1s in the Kmap if the 1s are in the same row or in the same column, but they cannot be on the diagonal (i.e., they must be adjacent cells). Third, we can group 1s if the total number in the group is a power of 2. The fourth rule specifies that we must make the groups as large as possible. As a fifth and final rule, all 1s must be in a group (even if some are in a group of one). Let's examine some correct and incorrect groupings, as shown in Figures 3A.4 through 3A.7.

Notice in Figures 3A.6b and 3A.7b that one 1 belongs to two groups. This is the map equivalent of adding the term xy to the Boolean function, as we did when we were performing simplification using identities. The xy term in the map is used twice in the simplification procedure.

	y	
x	0	1
0	0	1
1	1	1

FIGURE 3A.3   Kmap for $F(x,y) = x + y$

FIGURE 3A.4   Groups Contain Only 1s   **FIGURE 3A.5**   Groups Cannot Be Diagonal

FIGURE 3A.6   Groups Must Be Powers of 2   **FIGURE 3A.7**   Groups Must Be as Large
                                                                                                as Possible

To simplify using Kmaps, first create the groups as specified by the rules above. After you have found all groups, examine each group and discard the variable that differs within each group. For example, Figure 3A.7b shows the correct grouping for $F(x,y) = x + y$. Let's begin with the group represented by the second row (where $x = 1$). The two minterms are xy' and xy. This group represents the logical OR of these two terms, or $xy' + xy$. These terms differ in y, so y is discarded, leaving only x. (We can see that if we use Boolean identities, this would reduce to the same value. The Kmap allows us to take a shortcut, helping us to automatically discard the correct variable.) The second group represents $x'y + xy$. These differ in x, so x is discarded, leaving y. If we OR the results of the first group and the second group, we have $x + y$, which is the correct reduction of the original function, F.

3A.4 KMAP SIMPLIFICATION FOR THREE VARIABLES

Kmaps can be applied to expressions of more than two variables. In this focus section, we show three- and four-variable Kmaps. These can be extended for situations that have five or more variables. We refer you to Maxfield (1995) in the "Further Reading" section of this chapter for thorough and enjoyable coverage of Kmaps.

You already know how to set up Kmaps for expressions involving two variables. We simply extend this idea to three variables, as indicated by Figure 3A.8.

The first difference you should notice is that two variables, y and z, are grouped together in the table. The second difference is that the numbering for the columns is not sequential. Instead of labeling the columns as 00, 01, 10, 11 (a normal binary progression), we have labeled them 00, 01, 11, 10. The input values for the Kmap must be ordered so that each minterm differs in only one variable from each neighbor. By using this order (for example, 01 followed by 11), the corresponding minterms, $x'y'z$ and $x'yz$ differ only in the y variable. Remember,

yz x	00	01	11	10
0	X'Y'Z'	X'Y'Z	X'YZ	X'YZ'
1	XY'Z'	XY'Z	XYZ	XYZ'

FIGURE 3A.8 Minterms and Kmap Format for Three Variables

to reduce, we need to discard the variable that is different. Therefore, we must ensure that each group of two minterms differs in only one variable.

The largest groups we found in our two-variable examples were composed of two 1s. It is possible to have groups of four or even eight 1s, depending on the function. Let's look at a couple of examples of map simplification for expressions of three variables.

≡ **EXAMPLE 3A.3** $F(x,y,z) = x'y'z + x'yz + xy'z + xyz$

yz x	00	01	11	10
0	0	1	1	0
1	0	1	1	0

We again follow the rules for making groups. You should see that you can make groups of two in several ways. However, the rules stipulate that we must create the largest groups whose sizes are powers of two. There is one group of four, so we group these as follows:

yz x	00	01	11	10
0	0	1	1	0
1	0	1	1	0

It is not necessary to create additional groups of two. The fewer groups you have, the fewer terms there will be. Remember, we want to simplify the expression, and all we have to do is guarantee that every 1 is in some group.

How, exactly, do we simplify when we have a group of four 1s? Two 1s in a group allowed us to discard one variable. Four 1s in a group allows us to discard two variables: The two variables in which all four terms differ. In the group of four from the preceding example, we have the following minterms: $x'y'z$, $x'yz$, $xy'z$, and xyz. These all have z in common, but the x and y variables differ. So we discard x and y, leaving us with $F(x,y,z) = z$ as the final reduction. To see how this parallels simplification using Boolean identities, consider the same reduction using identities. Note that the function is represented originally as the logical OR of the minterms with a value of 1.

$$F(x,y,z) = x'y'z + x'yz + xy'z + xyz$$
$$= x'(y'z + yz) + x(y'z + yz)$$
$$= (x' + x)(y'z + yz)$$
$$= y'z + yz$$
$$= (y' + y)z$$
$$= z$$

The end result using Boolean identities is exactly the same as the result using map simplification.

From time to time, the grouping process can be a little tricky. Let's look at an example that requires more scrutiny.

EXAMPLE 3A.4 $F(x,y,z) = x'y'z' + x'y'z + x'yz + x'yz' + xy'z' + xyz'$

x \ yz	00	01	11	10
0	1	1	1	1
1	1	0	0	1

This is a tricky problem for two reasons: We have overlapping groups, and we have a group that "wraps around." The leftmost 1s in the first column can be grouped with the rightmost 1s in the last column, because the first and last columns are logically adjacent (envision the map as being drawn on a cylinder). The first and last rows of a Kmap are also logically adjacent, which becomes apparent when we look at four-variable maps in the next section.

The correct groupings are as follows:

x \ yz	00	01	11	10
0	1	1	1	1
1	1	0	0	1

The first group reduces to x (this is the only term the four have in common), and the second group reduces to z, so the final minimized function is $F(x,y,z) = x' + z$.

EXAMPLE 3A.5   Suppose we have a Kmap with all 1s:

x \ yz	00	01	11	10
0	1	1	1	1
1	1	1	1	1

The largest group of 1s we can find is a group of eight, which puts all of the 1s in the same group. How do we simplify this? We follow the same rules we have been following. Remember, groups of two allowed us to discard one variable,

wx \ yz	00	01	11	10
00	$W'X'Y'Z'$	$W'X'Y'Z$	$W'X'YZ$	$W'X'YZ'$
01	$W'XY'Z'$	$W'XY'Z$	$W'XYZ$	$W'XYZ'$
11	$WXY'Z'$	$WXY'Z$	$WXYZ$	$WXYZ'$
10	$WX'Y'Z'$	$WX'Y'Z$	$WX'YZ$	$WX'YZ'$

FIGURE 3A.9   Minterms and Kmap Format for Four Variables

and groups of four allowed us to discard two variables; therefore, groups of eight should allow us to discard three variables. But that's all we have! If we discard all the variables, we are left with $F(x,y,z) = 1$. If you examine the truth table for this function, you see that we do indeed have a correct simplification.

3A.5   KMAP SIMPLIFICATION FOR FOUR VARIABLES

We now extend the map simplification techniques to four variables. Four variables give us 16 minterms, as shown in Figure 3A.9. Notice that the special order of 11 followed by 10 applies for the rows as well as the columns.

Example 3A.6 illustrates the representation and simplification of a function with four variables. We are only concerned with the terms that are 1s, so we omit entering the 0s into the map.

≡   **EXAMPLE 3A.6** $F(w,x,y,z) = w'x'y'z' + w'x'y'z + w'x'yz' + w'xyz' + wx'y'z' + wx'y'z + wx'yz'$

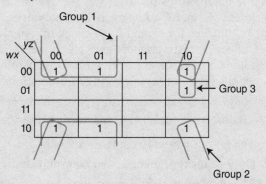

Group 1 is a "wraparound" group, as we saw previously. Group 3 is easy to find as well. Group 2 represents the ultimate wraparound group: It consists of the 1s in the four corners. Remember, these corners are logically adjacent. The final result is that F reduces to three terms, one from each group: $x'y'$ (from Group 1), $x'z'$ (from Group 2), and $w'yz'$ (from Group 3). The final reduction for F is then $F(w,x,y,z) = x'y' + x'z' + w'yz'$.

Occasionally, there are choices to make when performing map simplification. Consider Example 3A.7.

≡ **EXAMPLE 3A.7** A choice of groups

wx \ yz	00	01	11	10
00	1		1	
01	1		1	1
11	1			
10	1			

The first column should clearly be grouped. Also, the $w'x'yz$ and $w'xyz$ terms should be grouped. However, we have a choice as to how to group the $w'xyz'$ term. It could be grouped with $w'xyz$ or with $w'xy'z'$ (as a wraparound). These two solutions are as follows.

wx \ yz	00	01	11	10
00	1		1	
01	1		1	1
11	1			
10	1			

wx \ yz	00	01	11	10
00	1		1	
01	1		1	1
11	1			
10	1			

The first map simplifies to $F(w,x,y,z) = F_1 = y'z' + w'yz + w'xy$. The second map simplifies to $F(w,x,y,z) = F_2 = y'z' + w'yz + w'xz'$. The last terms are different. F_1 and F_2, however, are equivalent. We leave it up to you to produce the truth tables for F_1 and F_2 to check for equality. They both have the same number of terms and variables as well. If we follow the rules, Kmap minimization results in a minimized function (and thus a minimal circuit), but these minimized functions need not be unique in representation.

Before we move on to the next section, here are the rules for Kmap simplification.

1. The groups can only contain 1s, no 0s.

2. Only 1s in adjacent cells can be grouped; diagonal grouping is not allowed.

3. The number of 1s in a group must be a power of 2.

4. The groups must be as large as possible while still following all rules.

5. All 1s must belong to a group, even if it is a group of one.

6. Overlapping groups are allowed.

7. Wraparounds are allowed.

8. Use the fewest number of groups possible.

Using these rules, let's complete one more example for a four-variable function. Example 3A.8 shows several applications of the various rules.

≡ **EXAMPLE 3A.8**

$$F(w,x,y,z) = w'x'y'z' + w'x'yz + w'xy'z + w'xyz$$

$$+ wxy'z + wxyz + wx'yz + wx'yz'$$

yz wx	00	01	11	10
00	①		1	
01		1	1	
11		1	1	
10			1	1

In this example, we have one group with a single element. Note that there is no way to group this term with any others if we follow the rules. The function represented by this Kmap simplifies to $F(w,x,y,z) = yz + xz + w'x'y'z' + wx'y$.

If you are given a function that is not written as a sum of minterms, you can still use Kmaps to help minimize the function. However, you have to use a procedure that is somewhat the reverse of what we have been doing to set up the Kmap before reduction can occur. Example 3A.9 illustrates this procedure.

≡ **EXAMPLE 3A.9** A function not represented as a sum of minterms

Suppose you are given the function $F(w,x,y,z) = w'xy + w'x'yz + w'x'yz'$. The last two terms are minterms, and we can easily place 1s in the appropriate positions in the Kmap. However, the term $w'xy$ is not a minterm. Suppose this term were the *result* of a grouping you had performed on a Kmap. The term that was discarded was the z term, which means this term is equivalent to the two terms $w'xyz' + w'xyz$. You can now use these two terms in the Kmap, because they are both minterms. We now get the following Kmap:

yz wx	00	01	11	10
00			1	1
01			1	1
11				
10				

So we know the function $F(w,x,y,z) = w'xy + w'x'yz + w'x'yz'$ simplifies to $F(w,x,y,z) = w'y$.

3A.6 DON'T CARE CONDITIONS

There are certain situations where a function may not be completely specified, meaning there may be some inputs that are undefined for the function. For example, consider a function with four inputs that act as bits to count, in binary, from 0 to 10 (decimal). We use the bit combinations 0000, 0001, 0010, 0011, 0100, 0101, 0110, 0111, 1000, 1001, and 1010. However, we do not use the combinations 1011, 1100, 1101, 1110, and 1111. These latter inputs would be invalid, which means if we look at the truth table, these values wouldn't be either 0 or 1. They should not be in the truth table at all.

We can use these **don't care** inputs to our advantage when simplifying Kmaps. Because they are input values that should not matter (and should never occur), we can let them have values of either 0 or 1, depending on which helps us the most. The basic idea is to set these don't care values in such a way that they either contribute to make a larger group, or they don't contribute at all. Example 3A.10 illustrates this concept.

≡ **EXAMPLE 3A.10** Don't care conditions

Don't care values are typically indicated with an "X" in the appropriate cell. The following Kmap shows how to use these values to help with minimization. We treat the don't care values in the first row as 1s to help form a group of four. The don't care values in rows 01 and 11 are treated as 0s. This reduces to $F_1(w,x,y,z) = w'x' + yz$.

wx \ yz	00	01	11	10
00	X	1	1	X
01		X	1	
11	X		1	
10			1	

There is another way these values can be grouped:

wx \ yz	00	01	11	10
00	X	1	1	X
01		X	1	
11	X		1	
10			1	

Using these groupings, we end up with a simplification of $F_2(w,x,y,z) = w'z + yz$. Notice that in this case, F_1 and F_2 are not equal. However, if you create the truth tables for both functions, you should see that they are not equal only in those values for which we "don't care."

3A.7 SUMMARY

In this section, we have given a brief introduction to Kmaps and map simplification. Using Boolean identities for reduction is awkward and can be very difficult. Kmaps, on the other hand, provide a precise set of steps to follow to find the minimal representation of a function, and thus the minimal circuit that function represents.

=== EXERCISES ===

1. Write a simplified expression for the Boolean function defined by each of the following Kmaps:

   ◆ a)

x \ yz	00	01	11	10
0	0	1	1	0
1	1	0	0	1

   ◆ b)

x \ yz	00	01	11	10
0	0	1	1	1
1	1	0	0	0

   c)

x \ yz	00	01	11	10
0	1	1	1	0
1	1	1	1	1

2. Write a simplified expression for the Boolean function defined by each of the following Kmaps:

   a)

x \ yz	00	01	11	10
0	1	1	1	1
1	1	0	0	0

   b)

x \ yz	00	01	11	10
0	1	0	0	1
1	1	0	0	0

   c)

x \ yz	00	01	11	10
0	1	0	0	1
1	1	0	1	1

3. Create the Kmaps and then simplify for the following functions:

a) $F(x,y,z) = x'y'z' + x'yz + x'yz'$

b) $F(x,y,z) = x'y'z' + x'yz' + xy'z' + xyz'$

c) $F(x,y,z) = y'z' + y'z + xyz'$

4. Write a simplified expression for the Boolean function defined by each of the following Kmaps:

◆a)

wx \ yz	00	01	11	10
00	1	0	0	1
01	1	0	0	1
11	0	0	1	0
10	1	0	1	0

◆b)

wx \ yz	00	01	11	10
00	1	1	1	1
01	0	0	1	1
11	1	1	1	1
10	1	0	0	1

c)

wx \ yz	00	01	11	10
00	0	1	0	1
01	0	1	1	1
11	1	1	0	0
10	1	1	0	1

5. Write a simplified expression for the Boolean function defined by each of the following Kmaps (leave in sum-of-products form):

a)

wx \ yz	00	01	11	10
00	1	1	0	1
01	1	1	0	1
11	0	0	0	0
10	1	1	1	1

b)

wx \ yz	00	01	11	10
00	0	1	1	0
01	1	1	1	1
11	0	0	1	1
10	0	1	1	0

c)

wx \ yz	00	01	11	10
00	0	1	0	0
01	1	1	1	1
11	1	1	1	1
10	0	1	0	1

6. Create the Kmaps and then simplify for the following functions (leave in sum-of-products form):

◆ **a)** $F(w,x,y,z) = w'x'y'z' + w'x'yz' + w'xy'z + w'xyz + w'xyz' + wx'y'z' + wx'yz'$

◆ **b)** $F(w,x,y,z) = w'x'y'z' + w'x'y'z + wx'y'z + wx'yz' + wx'y'z'$

c) $F(w,x,y,z) = y'z + wy' + w'xy + w'x'yz' + wx'yz'$

7. Create the Kmaps and then simplify for the following functions (leave in sum-of-products form):

a) $F(w,x,y,z) = w'x'y'z + w'x'yz' + w'xy'z + w'xyz + w'xyz' + wxy'z + wxyz$
$+ wx'y'z$

b) $F(w,x,y,z) = w'x'y'z' + w'z + w'x'yz' + w'xy'z' + wx'y$

c) $F(w,x,y,z) = w'x'y' + w'xz + wxz + wx'y'z'$

◆ **8.** Given the following Kmap, show algebraically (using Boolean identities) how the four terms reduce to one term.

x \ yz	00	01	11	10
0	0	1	1	0
1	0	1	1	0

◆ **9.** Write a simplified expression for the Boolean function defined by each of the following Kmaps:

a)

x \ yz	00	01	11	10
0	1	1	0	X
1	1	1	1	1

b)

wx\yz	00	01	11	10
00	1	1	1	1
01	0	X	1	X
11	0	0	X	0
10	1	0	X	1

10. Write a simplified expression for the Boolean function defined by each of the following Kmaps:

a)

x\yz	00	01	11	10
0	X	0	0	1
1	1	1	X	1

b)

wx\yz	00	01	11	10
00	1	1	1	1
01	X	0	1	X
11	0	0	0	0
10	0	1	X	0

11. Write a simplified expression for the Boolean function defined by each of the following Kmaps:

a)

x\yz	00	01	11	10
0	1	X	0	1
1	0	0	1	1

b)

wx\yz	00	01	11	10
00	0	0	1	0
01	X	0	0	X
11	X	1	0	0
10	1	X	0	0

12. Find the minimized Boolean expression for the functions defined by each of the following truth tables:

a)

x	y	z	F
0	0	0	X
0	0	1	X
0	1	0	1
0	1	1	0
1	0	0	0
1	0	1	1
1	1	0	0
1	1	1	1

b)

w	x	y	z	F
0	0	0	0	0
0	0	0	1	1
0	0	1	0	0
0	0	1	1	0
0	1	0	0	X
0	1	0	1	0
0	1	1	0	X
0	1	1	1	0
1	0	0	0	1
1	0	0	1	X
1	0	1	0	X
1	0	1	1	X
1	1	0	0	X
1	1	0	1	1
1	1	1	0	X
1	1	1	1	X

CHAPTER 4

MARIE: An Introduction to a Simple Computer

4.1 INTRODUCTION

Designing a computer nowadays is a job for a computer engineer with plenty of training. It is impossible in an introductory textbook such as this (and in an introductory course in computer organization and architecture) to present everything necessary to design and build a working computer such as those we can buy today. However, in this chapter, we first look at a very simple computer called MARIE: a **M**achine **A**rchitecture that is **R**eally **I**ntuitive and **E**asy. We then provide brief overviews of Intel and MIPs machines, two popular architectures reflecting the CISC and RISC design philosophies. The objective of this chapter is to give you an understanding of how a computer functions. We have, therefore, kept the architecture as uncomplicated as possible, following the advice in the opening quote by Leonardo da Vinci.

4.2 CPU BASICS AND ORGANIZATION

From our studies in Chapter 2 (data representation), we know that a computer must manipulate binary-coded data. We also know from Chapter 3 that memory is used to store both data and program instructions (also in binary). Somehow, the program must be executed and the data must be processed correctly. The **central processing unit** (CPU) is responsible for fetching program instructions, decoding each instruction that is fetched, and performing the indicated sequence of operations on the correct data. To understand how computers work, you must first become familiar with their various components and the interaction among

215

these components. To introduce the simple architecture in the next section, we first examine, in general, the microarchitecture that exists at the control level of modern computers.

All computers have a CPU that can be divided into two pieces. The first is the **datapath**, which is a network of storage units (registers) and arithmetic and logic units (for performing various operations on data) connected by buses (capable of moving data from place to place) where the timing is controlled by clocks. The second CPU component is the **control unit**, a module responsible for sequencing operations and making sure the correct data are where they need to be at the correct time. Together, these components perform the tasks of the CPU: fetching instructions, decoding them, and finally performing the indicated sequence of operations. The performance of a machine is directly affected by the design of the datapath and the control unit. Therefore, we cover these components of the CPU in detail in the following sections.

4.2.1 The Registers

Registers are used in computer systems as places to store a wide variety of data, such as addresses, program counters, and data necessary for program execution. Put simply, a **register** is a hardware device that stores binary data. Registers are located on the processor so information can be accessed very quickly. We saw in Chapter 3 that D flip-flops can be used to implement registers. One D flip-flop is equivalent to a 1-bit register, so a collection of D flip-flops is necessary to store multi-bit values. For example, to build a 16-bit register, we need to connect 16 D flip-flops together. We saw in our binary counter figure from Chapter 3 that these collections of flip-flops must be clocked to work in unison. At each pulse of the clock, input enters the register and cannot be changed (and thus is stored) until the clock pulses again.

Data processing on a computer is usually done on fixed-size binary words stored in registers. Therefore, most computers have registers of a certain size. Common sizes include 16, 32, and 64 bits. The number of registers in a machine varies from architecture to architecture, but is typically a power of 2, with 16, 32, and 64 being most common. Registers contain data, addresses, or control information. Some registers are specified as "special purpose" and may contain only data, only addresses, or only control information. Other registers are more generic and may hold data, addresses, and control information at various times.

Information is written to registers, read from registers, and transferred from register to register. Registers are not addressed in the same way memory is addressed (recall that each memory word has a unique binary address beginning with location 0). Registers are addressed and manipulated by the control unit itself.

In modern computer systems, there are many types of specialized registers: registers to store information, registers to shift values, registers to compare values, and registers that count. There are "scratchpad" registers that store temporary values, index registers to control program looping, stack pointer registers to manage stacks of information for processes, status (or flag) registers to hold the status or mode of operation (such as overflow, carry, or zero conditions), and general-purpose registers that are the registers available to the programmer. Most computers have register sets, and each set is used in a specific way. For example, the Pentium architecture has a data register set and an address register set. Certain architectures have very large sets of registers that can be used in quite novel ways to speed up execution of instructions. (We discuss this topic when we cover advanced architectures in Chapter 9.)

4.2.2 The ALU

The **arithmetic logic unit** (**ALU**) carries out the logic operations (such as comparisons) and arithmetic operations (such as add or multiply) required during the program execution. You saw an example of a simple ALU in Chapter 3. Generally, an ALU has two data inputs and one data output. Operations performed in the ALU often affect bits in the **status register** (bits are set to indicate actions such as whether an overflow has occurred). The ALU knows which operations to perform because it is controlled by signals from the control unit.

4.2.3 The Control Unit

The **control unit** is the "policeman" or "traffic manager" of the CPU. It monitors the execution of all instructions and the transfer of all information. The control unit extracts instructions from memory, decodes these instructions, making sure data are in the right place at the right time, tells the ALU which registers to use, services interrupts, and turns on the correct circuitry in the ALU for the execution of the desired operation. The control unit uses a **program counter** register to find the next instruction for execution and a status register to keep track of overflows, carries, borrows, and the like. Section 4.13 covers the control unit in more detail.

4.3　THE BUS

The CPU communicates with the other components via a bus. A **bus** is a set of wires that acts as a shared but common datapath to connect multiple subsystems within the system. It consists of multiple lines, allowing the parallel movement of bits. Buses are low cost but very versatile, and they make it easy to connect new devices to each other and to the system. At any one time, only one device (be it a register, the ALU, memory, or some other component) may use the bus. However, this sharing often results in a communications bottleneck. The speed of the bus is affected by its length as well as by the number of devices sharing it. Quite often, devices are divided into **master** and **slave** categories; a master device is one that initiates actions and a slave is one that responds to requests by a master.

A bus can be **point-to-point**, connecting two specific components (as seen in Figure 4.1a) or it can be a **common pathway** that connects a number of devices,

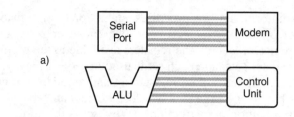

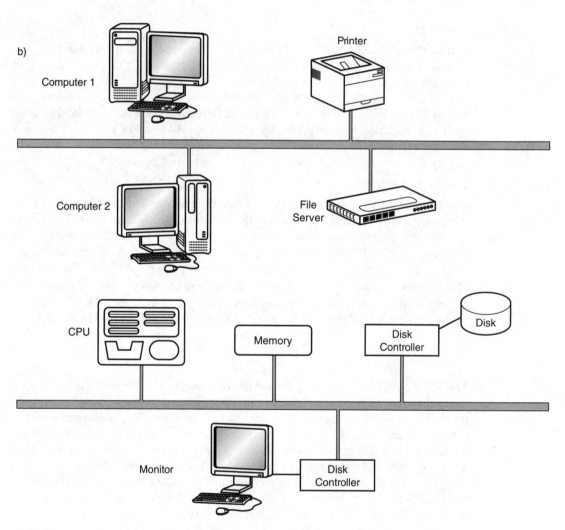

FIGURE 4.1 a) Point-to-Point Buses
b) Multipoint Buses

requiring these devices to share the bus (referred to as a **multipoint** bus and shown in Figure 4.1b).

Because of this sharing, the **bus protocol** (set of usage rules) is very important. Figure 4.2 shows a typical bus consisting of data lines, address lines, control lines, and power lines. Often the lines of a bus dedicated to moving data are called the **data bus**. These data lines contain the actual information that must be moved from one location to another. **Control lines** indicate which device has permission to use the bus and for what purpose (reading or writing from memory or from an input/output [I/O] device, for example). Control lines also transfer acknowledgments for bus requests, interrupts, and clock synchronization signals. **Address lines** indicate the location (e.g., in memory) that the data should be either read from or written to. The **power lines** provide the electrical power necessary. Typical bus transactions include sending an address (for a read or write), transferring data from memory to a register (a memory read), and transferring data to the memory from a register (a memory write). In addition, buses are used for I/O reads and writes from peripheral devices. Each type of transfer occurs within a **bus cycle**, the time between two ticks of the bus clock.

Because of the different types of information buses transport and the various devices that use the buses, buses themselves have been divided into different types. **Processor-memory buses** are short, high-speed buses that are closely matched to the memory system on the machine to maximize the bandwidth (transfer of data) and are usually design specific. **I/O buses** are typically longer than processor-memory buses and allow for many types of devices with varying bandwidths. These buses are compatible with many different architectures. A **backplane bus** (Figure 4.3) is actually built into the chassis of the machine and

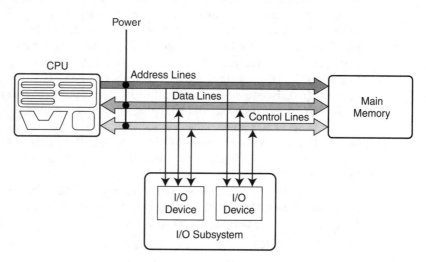

FIGURE 4.2   The Components of a Typical Bus

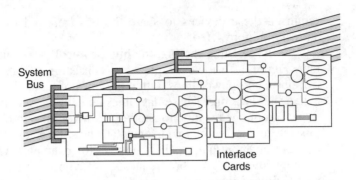

System
Bus

Interface
Cards

FIGURE 4.3   Backplane Bus

connects the processor, the I/O devices, and the memory (so all devices share one bus). Many computers have a hierarchy of buses, so it is not uncommon to have two buses (e.g., a processor-memory bus and an I/O bus) or more in the same system. High-performance systems often use all three types of buses.

Personal computers have their own terminology when it comes to buses. They have an internal bus (called the **system bus**) that connects the CPU, memory, and all other internal components. External buses (sometimes referred to as **expansion buses**) connect external devices, peripherals, expansion slots, and I/O ports to the rest of the computer. Most PCs also have **local buses**, data buses that connect a peripheral device directly to the CPU. These high-speed buses can be used to connect only a limited number of similar devices. Expansion buses are slower but allow for more generic connectivity. Chapter 7 deals with these topics in great detail.

Buses are physically little more than bunches of wires, but they have specific standards for connectors, timing, and signaling specifications and exact protocols for use. **Synchronous buses** are clocked, and things happen only at the clock ticks (a sequence of events is controlled by the clock). Every device is synchronized by the rate at which the clock ticks, or the **clock rate**. The bus cycle time mentioned is the reciprocal of the bus clock rate. For example, if the bus clock rate is 133MHz, then the length of the bus cycle is 1/133,000,000 or 7.52 nanoseconds (ns). Because the clock controls the transactions, any **clock skew** (drift in the clock) has the potential to cause problems, implying that the bus must be kept as short as possible so the clock drift cannot get overly large. In addition, the bus cycle time must not be shorter than the length of time it takes information to traverse the bus. The length of the bus, therefore, imposes restrictions on both the bus clock rate and the bus cycle time.

With **asynchronous buses**, control lines coordinate the operations, and a complex **handshaking protocol** must be used to enforce timing. To read a word of data from memory, for example, the protocol would require steps similar to the following:

1. ReqREAD: This bus control line is activated and the data memory address is put on the appropriate bus lines at the same time.

2. ReadyDATA: This control line is asserted when the memory system has put the required data on the data lines for the bus.

3. ACK: This control line is used to indicate that the ReqREAD or the ReadyDATA has been acknowledged.

Using a protocol instead of the clock to coordinate transactions means that asynchronous buses scale better with technology and can support a wider variety of devices.

To use a bus, a device must reserve it, because only one device can use the bus at a time. As mentioned, bus masters are devices that are allowed to initiate transfer of information (control bus), and bus slaves are modules that are activated by a master and respond to requests to read and write data (so only masters can reserve the bus). Both follow a communications protocol to use the bus, working within very specific timing requirements. In a very simple system (such as the one we present in the next section), the processor is the only device allowed to become a bus master. This is good in terms of avoiding chaos, but bad because the processor now is involved in every transaction that uses the bus.

In systems with more than one master device, **bus arbitration** is required. Bus arbitration schemes must provide priority to certain master devices and, at the same time, make sure lower priority devices are not starved out. Bus arbitration schemes fall into four categories:

1. Daisy chain arbitration: This scheme uses a "grant bus" control line that is passed down the bus from the highest priority device to the lowest priority device. (Fairness is not ensured, and it is possible that low-priority devices are "starved out" and never allowed to use the bus.) This scheme is simple but not fair.

2. Centralized parallel arbitration: Each device has a request control line to the bus and a centralized arbiter selects who gets the bus. Bottlenecks can result using this type of arbitration.

3. Distributed arbitration using self-selection: This scheme is similar to centralized arbitration but instead of a central authority selecting who gets the bus, the devices themselves determine who has highest priority and who should get the bus.

4. Distributed arbitration using collision detection: Each device is allowed to make a request for the bus. If the bus detects any collisions (multiple simultaneous requests), the device must make another request. (Ethernet uses this type of arbitration.)

Chapter 7 contains more detailed information on buses and their protocols.

4.4   CLOCKS

Every computer contains an internal clock that regulates how quickly instructions can be executed. The clock also synchronizes all of the components in the system. As the clock ticks, it sets the pace for everything that happens in the system, much like a metronome or a symphony conductor. The CPU uses this clock to regulate its progress, checking the otherwise unpredictable speed of the digital logic gates. The CPU requires a fixed number of clock ticks to execute each instruction. Therefore, instruction performance is often measured in **clock cycles**—the time between clock ticks—instead of seconds. The **clock frequency** (sometimes called the clock rate or clock speed) is measured in megahertz (MHz) or gigahertz (GHz), as we saw in Chapter 1. The **clock cycle time** (or clock period) is simply the reciprocal of the clock frequency. For example, an 800MHz machine has a clock cycle time of 1/800,000,000 or 1.25ns. If a machine has a 2ns cycle time, then it is a 500MHz machine.

Most machines are synchronous: there is a master clock signal, which ticks (changing from 0 to 1 to 0 and so on) at regular intervals. Registers must wait for the clock to tick before new data can be loaded. It seems reasonable to assume that if we speed up the clock, the machine will run faster. However, there are limits on how short we can make the clock cycles. When the clock ticks and new data are loaded into the registers, the register outputs are likely to change. These changed output values must propagate through all the circuits in the machine until they reach the input of the next set of registers, where they are stored. The clock cycle must be long enough to allow these changes to reach the next set of registers. If the clock cycle is too short, we could end up with some values not reaching the registers. This would result in an inconsistent state in our machine, which is definitely something we must avoid. Therefore, the minimum clock cycle time must be at least as great as the maximum propagation delay of the circuit, from each set of register outputs to register inputs. What if we "shorten" the distance between registers to shorten the propagation delay? We could do this by adding registers between the output registers and the corresponding input registers. But recall that registers cannot change values until the clock ticks, so we have, in effect, increased the number of clock cycles. For example, an instruction that would require two clock cycles might now require three or four (or more, depending on where we locate the additional registers).

Most machine instructions require one or two clock cycles, but some can take 35 or more. We present the following formula to relate seconds to cycles:

$$\text{CPU time} = \frac{\text{seconds}}{\text{program}} = \frac{\text{instructions}}{\text{program}} \times \frac{\text{average cycles}}{\text{instruction}} \times \frac{\text{seconds}}{\text{cycle}}$$

It is important to note that the architecture of a machine has a large effect on its performance. Two machines with the same clock speed do not necessarily execute instructions in the same number of cycles. For example, a multiply operation on an older Intel 286 machine required 20 clock cycles, but on a new Pentium, a multiply operation can be done in 1 clock cycle, which implies that the newer machine would be 20 times faster than the 286, even if they both had the same internal system clock. In general, multiplication requires more time than addition, floating-point operations require more cycles than integer ones, and accessing memory takes longer than accessing registers.

Generally, when we mention the **clock**, we are referring to the **system clock**, or the master clock that regulates the CPU and other components. However, certain buses also have their own clocks. **Bus clocks** are usually slower than CPU clocks, causing bottleneck problems.

System components have defined performance bounds, indicating the maximum time required for the components to perform their functions. Manufacturers guarantee that their components will run within these bounds in the most extreme circumstances. When we connect all of the components together serially, where one component must complete its task before another can function properly, it is important to be aware of these performance bounds so we are able to synchronize the components properly. However, many people push the bounds of certain system components in an attempt to improve system performance. **Overclocking** is one method people use to achieve this goal.

Although many components are potential candidates, one of the most popular components for overclocking is the CPU. The basic idea is to run the CPU at clock and/or bus speeds above the upper bound specified by the manufacturer. Although this can increase system performance, one must be careful not to create system timing faults or, worse yet, overheat the CPU. The system bus can also be overclocked, which results in overclocking the various components that communicate via the bus. Overclocking the system bus can provide considerable performance improvements, but can also damage the components that use the bus or cause them to perform unreliably.

4.5   THE INPUT/OUTPUT SUBSYSTEM

Input and output (I/O) devices allow us to communicate with the computer system. I/O is the transfer of data between primary memory and various I/O peripherals. Input devices such as keyboards, mice, card readers, scanners, voice recognition systems, and touch screens allow us to enter data into the computer. Output devices such as monitors, printers, plotters, and speakers allow us to get information from the computer.

These devices are not connected directly to the CPU. Instead, there is an **interface** that handles the data transfers. This interface converts the system bus signals to and from a format that is acceptable to the given device. The CPU communicates to these external devices via I/O registers. This exchange of data is performed in two ways. In **memory-mapped I/O**, the registers in the interface appear in the computer's memory map and there is no real difference between accessing memory and accessing an I/O device. Clearly, this is advantageous from the perspective of speed, but it uses up memory space in the system. With **instruction-based I/O**, the CPU has specialized instructions that perform the input and output. Although this does not use memory space, it requires specific I/O instructions, which implies that it can be used only by CPUs that can execute these specific instructions. Interrupts play a very important part in I/O, because they are an efficient way to notify the CPU that input or output is available for use. We explore these I/O methods in detail in Chapter 7.

4.6 MEMORY ORGANIZATION AND ADDRESSING

We saw an example of a rather small memory in Chapter 3. In this chapter, we continue to refer to very small memory sizes (so small that any reasonable person today would consider them to be ridiculously small in any modern computing device). However, smaller memories make the numbers manageable, and the principles we discuss in this chapter apply to small and large memories alike. These principles include how memory is laid out and how it is addressed. It is important that you have a good understanding of these concepts before we continue.

You can envision memory as a matrix of bits. Each row, implemented by a register, has a length typically equivalent to the addressable unit size of the machine. Each register (more commonly referred to as a **memory location**) has a unique address; memory addresses usually start at zero and progress upward. Figure 4.4 illustrates this concept.

An address is typically represented by an unsigned integer. Recall from Chapter 2 that four bits are a nibble and eight bits are a byte. Normally, memory is **byte addressable**, which means that each individual byte has a unique address. Some machines may have a word size that is larger than a single byte. For example, a computer might handle 32-bit words (which means it can manipulate 32 bits at a time through various instructions and it uses 32-bit registers) but still employ a byte-addressable architecture. In this situation, when a word uses multiple bytes, the byte with the lowest address determines the address of the entire word. It is also possible that a computer might be **word addressable**, which means each word (not necessarily each byte) has its own address, but most current machines are byte addressable (even though they have 32-bit or larger words). A memory address is typically stored in a single machine word.

If all this talk about machines using byte addressing with words of different sizes has you somewhat confused, the following analogy may help. Memory is similar to a street full of apartment buildings. Each building (word) has multiple apartments (bytes), and each apartment has its own address. All of the apartments are numbered sequentially (addressed), from 0 to the total number of apartments in the complex minus one. The buildings themselves serve to group the apartments. In computers, words do the same thing. Words are the basic unit of size used in various instructions. For example, you may read a word from or write a word to memory, even on a byte-addressable machine.

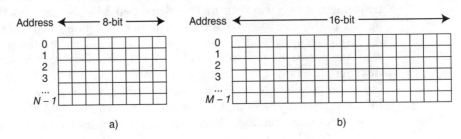

FIGURE 4.4 a) *N* 8-Bit Memory Locations
b) *M* 16-Bit Memory Locations

If an architecture is byte addressable, and the instruction set architecture word is larger than 1 byte, the issue of **alignment** must be addressed. For example, if we wish to read a 32-bit word on a byte-addressable machine, we must make sure that (1) the word is stored on a natural alignment boundary, and (2) the access starts on that boundary. This is accomplished, in the case of 32-bit words, by requiring the address to be a multiple of 4. Some architectures allow certain instructions to perform unaligned accesses, where the desired address does not have to start on a natural boundary.

Memory is built from random access memory (RAM) chips. (We cover memory in detail in Chapter 6.) Memory is often referred to using the notation length $\times$ width (L $\times$ W). For example, 4M $\times$ 8 means the memory is 4M long (it has 4M $= 2^2 \times 2^{20} = 2^{22}$ items) and each item is 8 bits wide (which means that each item is a byte). To address this memory (assuming byte addressing), we need to be able to uniquely identify 2^{22} different items, which means we need 2^{22} different addresses. Because addresses are unsigned binary numbers, we need to count from 0 to $(2^{22} - 1)$ in binary. How many bits does this require? Well, to count from 0 to 3 in binary (for a total of four items), we need 2 bits. To count from 0 to 7 in binary (for a total of eight items), we need 3 bits. To count from 0 to 15 in binary (for a total of 16 items), we need 4 bits. Do you see a pattern emerging here? Can you fill in the missing value for Table 4.1?

The correct answer to the missing table entry is 5 bits. What is actually important when calculating how many bits a memory address must contain is not the length of the addressable unit but rather the number of addressable units. The number of bits required for our 4M memory is 22. Because most memories are *byte* addressable, we say we need N bits to uniquely address each *byte*. In general, if a computer has 2^N addressable units of memory, it requires N bits to uniquely address each unit.

To better illustrate the difference between words and bytes, suppose the 4M $\times$ 8 memory referred to in the previous example were word addressable instead of byte addressable and each word were 16 bits long. There are 2^{22} unique bytes, which implies there are $2^{22} \div 2 = 2^{21}$ total words, which would require 21, not 22, bits per address. Each word would require two bytes, but we express the address of the entire word by using the lower byte address.

Although most memory is byte addressable and 8 bits wide, memory can vary in width. For example, a 2K $\times$ 16 memory holds $2^{11} = 2048$ 16-bit items. This type of memory is typically used on a word-addressable architecture with 16-bit words.

Main memory is usually larger than one RAM chip. Consequently, these chips are combined into a single memory of the desired size. For example, suppose you need to build a 32K $\times$ 8 byte-addressable memory and all you have are 2K $\times$ 8 RAM chips. You could connect 16 rows of chips together as shown in Figure 4.5.

Total Items	2	4	8	16	32
Total as a Power of 2	2^1	2^2	2^3	2^4	2^5
Number of Address Bits	1	2	3	4	??

TABLE 4.1 Calculating the Address Bits Required

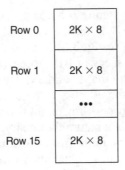

FIGURE 4.5 Memory as a Collection of RAM Chips

Each chip addresses 2K bytes. Addresses for this memory must have 15 bits (there are $32K = 2^5 \times 2^{10}$ bytes to access). But each chip requires only 11 address lines (each chip holds only 2^{11} bytes). In this situation, a decoder is needed to decode either the leftmost or rightmost 4 bits of the address to determine which chip holds the desired data. Once the proper chip has been located, the remaining 11 bits are used to determine the offset on that chip. Whether we use the 4 leftmost or 4 rightmost bits depends on how the memory is interleaved. (Note: We could also build a $16K \times 16$ memory using 8 rows of 2 RAM chips each. If this memory were word addressable, assuming 16-bit words, an address for this machine would have only 14 bits.)

A single memory module causes sequentialization of access (only one memory access can be performed at a time). **Memory interleaving**, which splits memory across multiple memory modules (or banks), in which multiple banks can be accessed simultaneously, can be used to help relieve this. The number of banks is determined solely by how many addressable items we have, not by the size of each addressable item. Each bank, when accessed, will return a word the size of the addressable unit for that architecture. If memory is **8-way interleaved**, the memory is implemented using 8 modules, numbered 0 through 7. With **low-order interleaving**, the low-order bits of the address are used to select the bank; in **high-order interleaving**, the high-order bits of the address are used.

Suppose we have a byte-addressable memory consisting of 8 modules of 4 bytes each, for a total of 32 bytes of memory. We need 5 bits to uniquely identify each byte. Three of these bits are used to determine the module (we have $2^3 = 8$ modules), and the remaining two are used to determine the offset within that module. High-order interleaving, the most intuitive organization, distributes the addresses so that each module contains consecutive addresses, as we see with the 32 addresses in Figure 4.6a. Module 0 contains the data stored at addresses 0, 1, 2, and 3; module 1 contains the data stored at addresses 4, 5, 6, and 7; and so on. We see the address structure for an address in this memory using high-order interleaving in Figure 4.6b. This tells us that the first three bits of an address should be used to determine the memory module, whereas the two

Module 0   Module 1   Module 2   Module 3   Module 4   Module 5   Module 6   Module 7

0	4	8	12	16	20	24	28
1	5	9	13	17	21	25	29
2	6	10	14	18	22	26	30
3	7	11	15	19	23	27	31

a)

3 bits   2 bits

| Module number | Offset in module |

b)   ←————————— 5 bits —————————→

Module	Decimal Word Address	Binary Address	Address Split per Given Structure	Module Number	Offset in Module
Module 0	0	00000	000 00	0	0
	1	00001	000 01	0	1
	2	00010	000 10	0	2
	3	00011	000 11	0	3
Module 1	4	00100	001 00	1	0
	5	00101	001 01	1	1
	6	00110	001 10	1	2
	7	00111	001 11	1	3

c)

FIGURE 4.6   a)   High-Order Memory Interleaving
b)   Address Structure
c)   First Two Modules

remaining bits are used to determine the offset within the module. Figure 4.6c shows us a more detailed view of what the first two modules of this memory look like for high-order interleaving. Consider address 3, which in binary (using our required 5 bits), is 00011. High-order interleaving uses the leftmost three bits (000) to determine the module (so the data at address 3 is in module 0). The remaining two bits (11) tell us that the desired data is at offset 3 (11_2 is decimal value 3), the last address in module 0.

Low-order interleaved memory places consecutive addresses of memory in different memory modules. Figure 4.7 shows low-order interleaving on 32 addresses. We see the address structure for an address in this memory using low-order interleaving in Figure 4.7b. The first two modules of this memory are shown in Figure 4.7c. In this figure, we see that module 0 now contains the data stored at addresses 0, 8, 16, and 24. To locate address 3 (00011), low-order interleaving uses the rightmost 3 bits to determine the module (which points us to module 3), and the remaining two bits, 00, tell us to look at offset zero within that module. If you check module 3 in Figure 4.7, this is precisely where we find address 3.

For both low- and high-order interleaving, there is a relationship between k (the number of bits used to identify the module) and the order of interleaving: 4-way interleaving uses $k = 2$; 8-way interleaving uses $k = 3$; 16-way interleaving uses

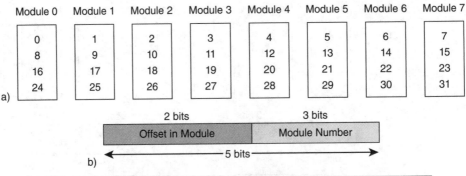

a)

b)

c)

FIGURE 4.7   a)   Low-Order Memory Interleaving

b)   Address Structure

c)   First Two Modules

$k = 4$; and in general, for *n*-way interleaving, we note that $n = 2^k$. (This relationship is reinforced in Chapter 6.)

With the appropriate buses using low-order interleaving, a read or write using one module can be started before a read or write using another module actually completes. (Reads and writes can be overlapped.) For example, if an array of length 4 is stored in the example of memory using high-order interleaving (stored at addresses 0, 1, 2, and 3), we are forced to access each array element sequentially, as the entire array is stored in one module. If, however, low-order interleaving is used (and the array is stored in modules 0, 1, 2, and 3 at offset 0 in each), we can access the array elements in parallel because each array element is in a different module.

EXAMPLE 4.1 Suppose we have a 128-word memory that is 8-way low-order interleaved (please note that the *size* of a word is not important in this example), which means it uses 8 memory banks; $8 = 2^3$, so we use the low-order 3 bits to identify the bank. Because we have 128 words, we need 7 bits for each address ($128 = 2^7$). Therefore, an address in this memory has the following structure:

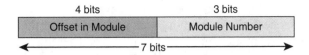

Note that each module must be of size 2^4. We can reach this conclusion two ways. First, if memory is 128 words, and we have 8 modules, then $128/8 = 2^7/2^3 = 2^4$ (so each module holds 16 words). We can also see from the address structure that the offset in the module required 4 bits, allowing for $2^4 = 16$ words per module.

What would change if Example 4.1 used high-order interleaving instead? We leave this as an exercise.

Let's return to the memory shown in Figure 4.5, a 32K $\times$ 8 memory consisting of 16 chips (modules) of size 2K $\times$ 8 each. Memory is 32K $= 2^5 \times 2^{10} = 2^{15}$ addressable units (in this case, bytes), which means we need 15 bits for each address. Each chip holds 2K $= 2^{11}$ bytes, so 11 bits are used to determine the offset on the chip. There are $16 = 2^4$ chips, so we need 4 bits to determine the chip. Consider the address 001000000100111. Using high-order interleaving, we use the 4 leftmost bits to determine the chip, and the remaining 11 as the offset:

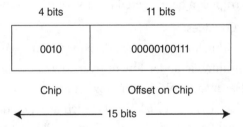

The data at address 001000000100111 is stored on chip 2 (0010_2) at offset 39 (00000100111_2). If we use low-order interleaving, the rightmost 4 bits are used to determine the chip:

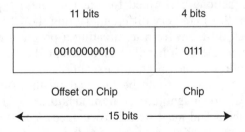

So the data, using low-order interleaving, is stored on chip 7 (0111_2) at offset 258 (00100000010_2).

Although low-order interleaving allows for concurrent access of data stored sequentially in memory (such as an array or the instructions in a program), high-order interleaving is more intuitive. Therefore, for the remainder of the text, we assume high-order interleaving is being used.

The memory concepts we have covered are very important and appear in various places in the remaining chapters, in particular in Chapter 6, which discusses memory in detail. The key concepts to focus on are: (1) Memory addresses are unsigned binary values (although we often view them as hex values because it is easier), and (2) The number of items to be addressed, **NOT** the size of the item, determines the numbers of bits that occur in the address. Although we could always use more bits for the address than required, that is seldom done because minimization is an important concept in computer design.

4.7   INTERRUPTS

We have introduced the basic hardware information required for a solid understanding of computer architecture: the CPU, buses, control unit, registers, clocks, I/O, and memory. However, there is one more concept we need to cover that deals with how these components interact with the processor: **Interrupts** are events that alter (or interrupt) the normal flow of execution in the system. An interrupt can be triggered for a variety of reasons, including:

- I/O requests
- Arithmetic errors (e.g., division by 0)
- Arithmetic underflow or overflow
- Hardware malfunction (e.g., memory parity error)
- User-defined break points (such as when debugging a program)
- Page faults (this is covered in detail in Chapter 6)
- Invalid instructions (usually resulting from pointer issues)
- Miscellaneous

The actions performed for each of these types of interrupts (called **interrupt handling**) are very different. Telling the CPU that an I/O request has finished is much different from terminating a program because of division by 0. But these actions are both handled by interrupts because they require a change in the normal flow of the program's execution.

An interrupt can be initiated by the user or the system, can be **maskable** (disabled or ignored) or **nonmaskable** (a high-priority interrupt that cannot be disabled and must be acknowledged), can occur within or between instructions, may be synchronous (occurs at the same place every time a program is executed) or asynchronous (occurs unexpectedly), and can result in the program terminating or continuing execution once the interrupt is handled. Interrupts are covered in more detail in Section 4.9.2 and in Chapter 7.

Now that we have given a general overview of the components necessary for a computer system to function, we proceed by introducing a simple, yet functional, architecture to illustrate these concepts.

4.8   MARIE

MARIE, a **M**achine **A**rchitecture that is **R**eally **I**ntuitive and **E**asy, is a simple architecture consisting of memory (to store programs and data) and a CPU (consisting of an ALU and several registers). It has all the functional components necessary to be a real working computer. MARIE will help to illustrate the concepts in this and the preceding three chapters. We describe MARIE's architecture in the following sections.

4.8.1   The Architecture

MARIE has the following characteristics:

- Binary, two's complement
- Stored program, fixed word length
- Word (but not byte) addressable
- 4K words of main memory (this implies 12 bits per address)
- 16-bit data (words have 16 bits)
- 16-bit instructions: 4 for the opcode and 12 for the address
- A 16-bit accumulator (AC)
- A 16-bit instruction register (IR)
- A 16-bit memory buffer register (MBR)
- A 12-bit program counter (PC)
- A 12-bit memory address register (MAR)
- An 8-bit input register
- An 8-bit output register

Figure 4.8 shows the architecture for MARIE.

Before we continue, we need to stress one important point about memory. In Chapter 3, we presented a simple memory built using D flip-flops. We emphasize again that each location in memory has a unique address (represented in binary) and each location can hold a value. These notions of the address versus what is actually stored at that address tend to be confusing. To help avoid confusion, visualize a post office. There are post office boxes with various "addresses" or numbers. Inside the post office box, there is mail. To get the mail, the number of the post office box must be known. The same is true for data or instructions that need to be fetched from memory. The contents of any memory address are manipulated by specifying the address of that memory location. We shall see that there are many different ways to specify this address.

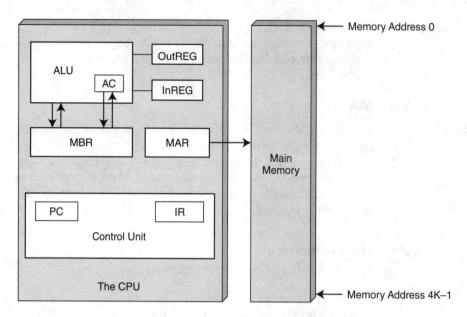

FIGURE 4.8 MARIE's Architecture

4.8.2 Registers and Buses

Registers are storage locations within the CPU (as illustrated in Figure 4.8). The ALU portion of the CPU performs all of the processing (arithmetic operations, logic decisions, etc.). The registers are used for very specific purposes when programs are executing: They hold values for temporary storage, data that is being manipulated in some way, or results of simple calculations. Many times, registers are referenced implicitly in an instruction, as we see when we describe the instruction set for MARIE in Section 4.8.3.

In MARIE, there are seven registers, as follows:

- **AC:** The **accumulator**, which holds data values. This is a **general-purpose register,** and it holds data that the CPU needs to process. Most computers today have multiple general-purpose registers.
- **MAR:** The **memory address register**, which holds the memory address of the data being referenced.
- **MBR:** The **memory buffer register**, which holds either the data just read from memory or the data ready to be written to memory.
- **PC:** The **program counter**, which holds the address of the next instruction to be executed in the program.
- **IR:** The **instruction register**, which holds the next instruction to be executed.
- **InREG:** The **input register**, which holds data from the input device.
- **OutREG:** The **output register**, which holds data for the output device.

The MAR, MBR, PC, and IR hold very specific information and cannot be used for anything other than their stated purposes. For example, we could not store an arbitrary data value from memory in the PC. We must use the MBR or the AC to store this arbitrary value. In addition, there is a **status** or **flag register** that holds information indicating various conditions, such as an overflow in the ALU, whether or not the result of an arithmetic or logical operation is zero, if a carry bit should be used in a computation, and when a result is negative. However, for clarity, we do not include that register explicitly in any figures.

MARIE is a very simple computer with a limited register set. Modern CPUs have multiple general-purpose registers, often called **user-visible registers**, that perform functions similar to those of the AC. Today's computers also have additional registers; for example, some computers have registers that shift data values and other registers that, if taken as a set, can be treated as a list of values.

MARIE cannot transfer data or instructions into or out of registers without a bus. In MARIE, we assume a common bus scheme. Each device connected to the bus has a number, and before the device can use the bus, it must be set to that identifying number. We also have some pathways to speed up execution. We have a communication path between the MAR and memory (the MAR provides the inputs to the address lines for memory so the CPU knows where in memory to read or write), and a separate path from the MBR to the AC. There is also a special path from the MBR to the ALU to allow the data in the MBR to be used in arithmetic operations. Information can also flow from the AC through the ALU and back into the AC without being put on the common bus. The advantage gained using these additional pathways is that information can be put on the common bus in the same clock cycle in which data are put on these other pathways, allowing these events to take place in parallel. Figure 4.9 shows the datapath (the path that information follows) in MARIE.

4.8.3 Instruction Set Architecture

MARIE has a very simple, yet powerful, instruction set. The **instruction set architecture (ISA)** of a machine specifies the instructions that the computer can perform and the format for each instruction. The ISA is essentially an interface between the software and the hardware. Some ISAs include hundreds of instructions. We mentioned previously that each instruction for MARIE consists of 16 bits. The most significant 4 bits, bits 12 through 15, make up the **opcode** that specifies the instruction to be executed (which allows for a total of 16 instructions). The least significant 12 bits, bits 0 through 11, form an address, which allows for a maximum memory address of $2^{12} - 1$. The instruction format for MARIE is shown in Figure 4.10.

Most ISAs consist of instructions for processing data, moving data, and controlling the execution sequence of the program. MARIE's instruction set consists of the instructions shown in Table 4.2.

The Load instruction allows us to move data from memory into the CPU (via the MBR and the AC). All data (which includes anything that is *not* an instruction) from memory must move first into the MBR and then into either the AC or the ALU; there are no other options in this architecture. Notice that the Load instruction does not have to name the AC as the final destination; this register is *implicit*

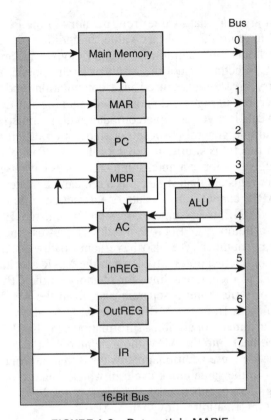

FIGURE 4.9 Datapath in MARIE

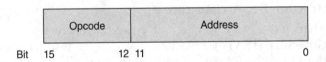

| Opcode | Address |

Bit   15   12 11   0

FIGURE 4.10 MARIE's Instruction Format

Instruction Number			
Bin	**Hex**	**Instruction**	**Meaning**
0001	1	Load X	Load the contents of address X into AC.
0010	2	Store X	Store the contents of AC at address X.
0011	3	Add X	Add the contents of address X to AC and store the result in AC.
0100	4	Subt X	Subtract the contents of address X from AC and store the result in AC.
0101	5	Input	Input a value from the keyboard into AC.
0110	6	Output	Output the value in AC to the display.
0111	7	Halt	Terminate the program.
1000	8	Skipcond	Skip the next instruction on condition.
1001	9	Jump X	Load the value of X into PC.

TABLE 4.2 MARIE's Instruction Set

in the instruction. Other instructions reference the AC register in a similar fashion. The `Store` instruction allows us to move data from the CPU back to memory. The `Add` and `Subt` instructions add and subtract, respectively, the data value found at address *X* to or from the value in the AC. The data located at address *X* is copied into the MBR where it is held until the arithmetic operation is executed. `Input` and `Output` allow MARIE to communicate with the outside world.

Input and output are complicated operations. In modern computers, input and output are done using ASCII bytes. This means that if you type in the number 32 on the keyboard as input, it is actually read in as the ASCII characters "3" followed by "2." These two characters must be converted to the numeric value 32 before they are stored in the AC. Because we are focusing on how a computer works, we are going to assume that a value input from the keyboard is "automatically" converted correctly. We are glossing over a very important concept: How does the computer know whether an I/O value is to be treated as numeric or ASCII, if everything that is input or output is actually ASCII? The answer is that the computer knows through the context of how the value is used. In MARIE, we assume numeric input and output only. We also allow values to be input as decimal and assume there is a "magic conversion" to the actual binary values that are stored. In reality, these are issues that must be addressed if a computer is to work properly.

The `Halt` command causes the current program execution to terminate. The `Skipcond` instruction allows us to perform **conditional branching** (as is done with "while" loops or "if" statements). When the `Skipcond` instruction is executed, the value stored in the AC must be inspected. Two of the address bits (let's assume we always use the two address bits closest to the opcode field, bits 10 and 11) specify the condition to be tested. If the two address bits are 00, this translates to "skip if the AC is negative." If the two address bits are 01 (bit eleven is 0 and bit ten is 1), this translates to "skip if the AC is equal to 0." Finally, if the two address bits are 10 (or 2), this translates to "skip if the AC is greater than 0." By "skip" we simply mean jump over the next instruction. This is accomplished by incrementing the PC by 1, essentially ignoring the following instruction, which is never fetched. The `Jump` instruction, an **unconditional branch**, also affects the PC. This instruction causes the contents of the PC to be replaced with the value of *X*, which is the address of the next instruction to fetch.

We wish to keep the architecture and the instruction set as simple as possible and yet convey the information necessary to understand how a computer works. Therefore, we have omitted several useful instructions. However, you will see shortly that this instruction set is still quite powerful. Once you gain familiarity with how the machine works, we will extend the instruction set to make programming easier.

Let's examine the instruction format used in MARIE. Suppose we have the following 16-bit instruction:

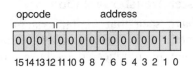

The leftmost four bits indicate the opcode, or the instruction to be executed. 0001 is binary for 1, which represents the Load instruction. The remaining 12 bits indicate the address of the value we are loading, which is address 3 in main memory. This instruction causes the data value found in main memory, address 3, to be copied into the AC. Consider another instruction:

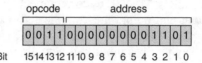

The leftmost four bits, 0011, are equal to 3, which is the Add instruction. The address bits indicate address 00D in hex (or 13 decimal). We go to main memory, get the data value at address 00D, and add this value to the AC. The value in the AC would then change to reflect this sum. One more example follows:

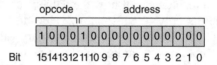

The opcode for this instruction represents the Skipcond instruction. Bits ten and eleven (read left to right, or bit eleven followed by bit ten) are 10, indicating a value of 2. This implies a "skip if AC greater than 0." If the value in the AC is less than or equal to zero, this instruction is ignored and we simply go on to the next instruction. If the value in the AC is greater than zero, this instruction causes the PC to be incremented by 1, thus causing the instruction immediately following this instruction in the program to be ignored (keep this in mind as you read the following section on the instruction cycle).

These examples bring up an interesting point. We will be writing programs using this limited instruction set. Would you rather write a program using the commands Load, Add, and Halt, or their binary equivalents 0001, 0011, and 0111? Most people would rather use the instruction name, or **mnemonic**, for the instruction, instead of the binary value for the instruction. Our binary instructions are called **machine instructions**. The corresponding mnemonic instructions are what we refer to as **assembly language instructions**. There is a one-to-one correspondence between assembly language and machine instructions. When we type in an assembly language program (i.e., using the instructions listed in Table 4.2), we need an assembler to convert it to its binary equivalent. We discuss assemblers in Section 4.11.

4.8.4   Register Transfer Notation

We have seen that digital systems consist of many components, including arithmetic logic units, registers, memory, decoders, and control units. These units are interconnected by buses to allow information to flow through the system. The instruction set presented for MARIE in the preceding section constitutes a set of machine-level instructions used by these components to execute a program. Each instruction appears to be very simplistic; however, if you examine what actually happens at the component level, each instruction involves multiple operations. For example, the Load instruction loads the contents of the given memory location into the AC register. But if we observe what is happening at the component level, we see that multiple "mini-instructions" are being executed. First, the address from the instruction must be loaded into the MAR. Then the data in memory at this location must be loaded into the MBR. Then the MBR must be loaded into the AC. These mini-instructions are called **microoperations** and specify the elementary operations that can be performed on data stored in registers.

The symbolic notation used to describe the behavior of microoperations is called **register transfer notation** (**RTN**) or **register transfer language** (**RTL**). We use the notation $M[X]$ to indicate the actual data stored at location X in memory, and $\leftarrow$ to indicate a transfer of information. In reality, a transfer from one register to another always involves a transfer onto the bus from the source register, and then a transfer off the bus into the destination register. However, for the sake of clarity, we do not include these bus transfers, assuming that you understand that the bus must be used for data transfer.

We now present the register transfer notation for each of the instructions in the ISA for MARIE.

Load *X*

Recall that this instruction loads the contents of memory location X into the AC. However, the address X must first be placed into the MAR. Then the data at location M[MAR] (or address X) is moved into the MBR. Finally, this data is placed in the AC.

```
MAR ← X
MBR ← M[MAR]
AC ← MBR
```

Because the IR must use the bus to copy the value of X into the MAR, before the data at location X can be placed into the MBR, this operation requires two bus cycles. Therefore, these two operations are on separate lines to indicate that they cannot occur during the same cycle. However, because we have a special connection between the MBR and the AC, the transfer of the data from the MBR to the AC can occur immediately after the data is put into the MBR, without waiting for the bus.

Store *X*

This instruction stores the contents of the AC in memory location X:

```
MAR ← X, MBR ← AC
M[MAR] ← MBR
```

Add *X*

The data value stored at address *X* is added to the AC. This can be accomplished as follows:

```
MAR ← X
MBR ← M[MAR]
AC ← AC + MBR
```

Subt *X*

Similar to Add, this instruction subtracts the value stored at address *X* from the accumulator and places the result back in the AC:

```
MAR ← X
MBR ← M[MAR]
AC ← AC - MBR
```

Input

Any input from the input device is first routed into the InREG. Then the data is transferred into the AC.

```
AC ← InREG
```

Output

This instruction causes the contents of the AC to be placed into the OutREG, where it is eventually sent to the output device.

```
OutREG ← AC
```

Halt

No operations are performed on registers; the machine simply ceases execution of the program.

Skipcond

Recall that this instruction uses the bits in positions 10 and 11 in the address field to determine what comparison to perform on the AC. Depending on this bit combination, the AC is checked to see whether it is negative, equal to 0, or greater than 0. If the given condition is true, then the next instruction is skipped. This is performed by incrementing the PC register by 1.

```
If IR[11-10] = 00 then        {if bits 10 and 11 in the IR are both 0}
    If AC < 0 then PC ← PC + 1
else If IR[11-10] = 01 then   {if bit 11 = 0 and bit 10 = 1}
    If AC = 0 then PC ← PC + 1
else If IR[11-10] = 10 then   {if bit 11 = 1 and bit 10 = 0}
    If AC > 0 then PC ← PC + 1
```

If the bits in positions ten and eleven are both ones, an error condition results. However, an additional condition could also be defined using these bit values.

Jump *X*

This instruction causes an unconditional branch to the given address, *X*. Therefore, to execute this instruction, *X* must be loaded into the PC.

```
PC ← X
```

In reality, the lower or least significant 12 bits of the instruction register (or IR[11–0]) reflect the value of *X*. So this transfer is more accurately depicted as:

```
PC ← IR[11-0]
```

However, we feel that the notation PC ← *X* is easier to understand and relate to the actual instructions, so we use this instead.

Register transfer notation is a symbolic means of expressing what is happening in the system when a given instruction is executing. RTN is sensitive to the datapath, in that if multiple microoperations must share the bus, they must be executed in a sequential fashion, one following the other.

4.9 INSTRUCTION PROCESSING

Now that we have a basic language with which to communicate ideas to our computer, we need to discuss exactly how a specific program is executed. All computers follow a basic machine cycle: the fetch, decode, and execute cycle.

4.9.1 The Fetch–Decode–Execute Cycle

The **fetch–decode–execute cycle** represents the steps that a computer follows to run a program. The CPU fetches an instruction (transfers it from main memory to the instruction register), decodes it (determines the opcode and fetches any data necessary to carry out the instruction), and executes it (performs the operation[s] indicated by the instruction). Notice that a large part of this cycle is spent copying data from one location to another. When a program is initially loaded, the address of the first instruction must be placed in the PC. The steps in this cycle, which take place in specific clock cycles, are listed below. Note that Steps 1 and 2 make up the fetch phase, Step 3 makes up the decode phase, and Step 4 is the execute phase.

1. Copy the contents of the PC to the MAR: MAR ← PC.
2. Go to main memory and fetch the instruction found at the address in the MAR, placing this instruction in the IR; increment PC by 1 (PC now points to the next instruction in the program): IR ← M[MAR] and then PC ← PC + 1. (*Note:* Because MARIE is word addressable, the PC is incremented by 1, which results in the next word's address occupying the PC. If MARIE were byte addressable, the PC would need to be incremented by 2 to point to the

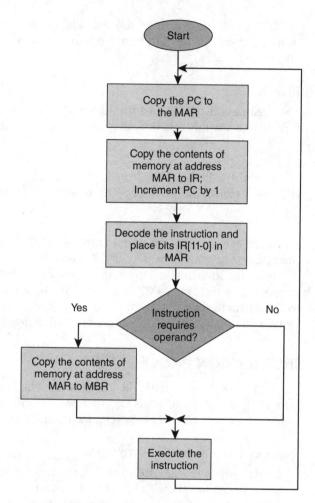

FIGURE 4.11   The Fetch–Decode–Execute Cycle

address of the next instruction, because each instruction would require 2 bytes. On a byte-addressable machine with 32-bit words, the PC would need to be incremented by 4.)

3. Copy the rightmost 12 bits of the IR into the MAR; decode the leftmost 4 bits to determine the opcode, MAR ← IR[11-0], and decode IR[15–12].

4. If necessary, use the address in the MAR to go to memory to get data, placing the data in the MBR (and possibly the AC), and then execute the instruction MBR ← M[MAR] and execute the actual instruction.

This cycle is illustrated in the flowchart in Figure 4.11.

Note that computers today, even with large instruction sets, long instructions, and huge memories, can execute millions of these fetch–decode–execute cycles in the blink of an eye.

4.9.2 Interrupts and the Instruction Cycle

All computers provide a means for the normal fetch–decode–execute cycle to be interrupted. These interruptions may be necessary for many reasons, including a program error (such as division by 0, arithmetic overflow, stack overflow, or attempting to access a protected area of memory); a hardware error (such as a memory parity error or power failure); an I/O completion (which happens when a disk read is requested and the data transfer is complete); a user interrupt (such as hitting Ctrl-C or Ctrl-Break to stop a program); or an interrupt from a timer set by the operating system (such as is necessary when allocating virtual memory or performing certain bookkeeping functions). All of these have something in common: they interrupt the normal flow of the fetch–decode–execute cycle and tell the computer to stop what it is currently doing and go do something else. They are, naturally, called **interrupts**.

The speed with which a computer processes interrupts plays a key role in determining the computer's overall performance. **Hardware interrupts** can be generated by any peripheral on the system, including memory, the hard drive, the keyboard, the mouse, or even the modem. Instead of using interrupts, processors could poll hardware devices on a regular basis to see if they need anything done. However, this would waste CPU time as the answer would more often than not be "no." Interrupts are nice because they let the CPU know the device needs attention at a particular moment without requiring the CPU to constantly monitor the device. Suppose you need specific information that a friend has promised to acquire for you. You have two choices: call the friend on a regular schedule (polling) and waste his or her time and yours if the information is not ready, or wait for a phone call from your friend once the information has been acquired. You may be in the middle of a conversation with someone else when the phone call "interrupts" you, but the latter approach is by far the more efficient way to handle the exchange of information.

Computers also employ **software interrupts** (also called **traps** or **exceptions**) used by various software applications. Modern computers support both software and hardware interrupts by using **interrupt handlers.** These handlers are simply routines (procedures) that are executed when their respective interrupts are detected. The interrupts, along with their associated **interrupt service routines (ISRs)**, are stored in an **interrupt vector table**.

How do interrupts fit into the fetch–decode–execute cycle? The CPU finishes execution of the current instruction and checks, at the beginning of every fetch–decode–execute cycle, to see if an interrupt has been generated, as shown in Figure 4.12. Once the CPU acknowledges the interrupt, it must then process the interrupt.

The details of the "Process the Interrupt" block are given in Figure 4.13. This process, which is the same regardless of what type of interrupt has been invoked, begins with the CPU detecting the interrupt signal. Before doing anything else, the system suspends whatever process is executing by saving the program's state and variable information. The device ID or interrupt request number of the device causing the interrupt is then used as an index into the interrupt vector

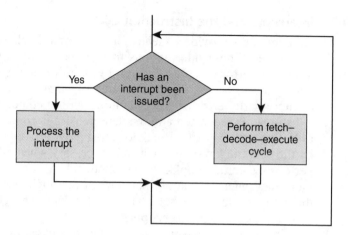

FIGURE 4.12   Fetch–Decode–Execute Cycle with Interrupt Checking

table, which is kept in very low memory. The address of the interrupt service routine (known as its **address vector**) is retrieved and placed into the program counter, and execution resumes (the fetch–decode–execute cycle begins again) within the service routine. After the interrupt service has completed, the system restores the information it saved from the program that was running when the interrupt occurred, and program execution may resume—unless another interrupt is detected, whereupon the interrupt is serviced as described.

It is possible to suspend processing of noncritical interrupts by use of a special interrupt mask bit found in the flag register. This is called **interrupt masking**, and interrupts that can be suspended are called **maskable** interrupts. **Nonmaskable** interrupts cannot be suspended, because to do so, it is possible that the system would enter an unstable or unpredictable state.

Assembly languages provide specific instructions for working with hardware and software interrupts. When writing assembly language programs, one of the most common tasks is dealing with I/O through software interrupts (see Chapter 7 for additional information on interrupt-driven I/O). Indeed, one of the more complicated functions for the novice assembly language programmer is reading input and writing output, specifically because this must be done using interrupts. MARIE simplifies the I/O process for the programmer by avoiding the use of interrupts for I/O.

4.9.3   MARIE's I/O

I/O processing is one of the most challenging aspects of computer system design and programming. Our model is necessarily simplified, and we provide it at this point only to complete MARIE's functionality.

MARIE has two registers to handle input and output. One, the input register, holds data being transferred from an input device into the computer; the other, the

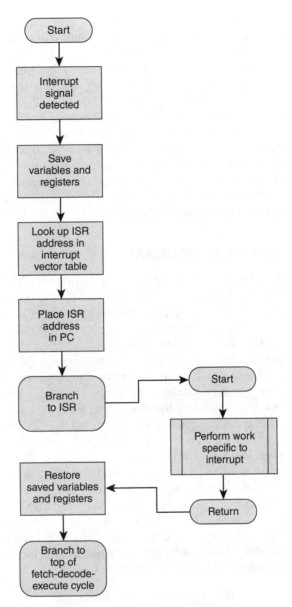

FIGURE 4.13 Processing an Interrupt

output register, holds information ready to be sent to an output device. The timing used by these two registers is very important. For example, if you are entering input from the keyboard and type very fast, the computer must be able to read each character that is put into the input register. If another character is entered into that register before the computer has a chance to process the current character, the current character is lost. It is more likely, because the processor is very fast and keyboard input is very slow, that the processor might read the same character from the input register multiple times. We must avoid both of these situations.

To get around problems like these, MARIE employs a modified type of programmed I/O (discussed in Chapter 7) that places all I/O under the direct control of the programmer. MARIE's output action is simply a matter of placing a value into the OutREG. This register can be read by an output controller that sends it to an appropriate output device, such as a terminal display, printer, or disk. For input, MARIE, being the simplest of simple systems, places the CPU into a wait state until a character is entered into the InREG. The InREG is then copied to the accumulator for subsequent processing as directed by the programmer. We observe that this model provides no concurrency. The machine is essentially idle while waiting for input. Chapter 7 explains other approaches to I/O that make more efficient use of machine resources.

4.10 A SIMPLE PROGRAM

We now present a simple program written for MARIE. In Section 4.12, we present several additional examples to illustrate the power of this minimal architecture. It can even be used to run programs with procedures, various looping constructs, and different selection options.

Our first program adds two numbers together (both of which are found in main memory), storing the sum in memory. (We forgo I/O for now.)

Table 4.3 lists an assembly language program to do this, along with its corresponding machine language program. The list of instructions under the Instruction column constitutes the actual assembly language program. We know that the fetch–decode–execute cycle starts by fetching the first instruction of the program, which it finds by loading the PC with the address of the first instruction when the program is loaded for execution. For simplicity, let's assume our programs in MARIE are always loaded starting at address 100 (in hex).

The list of instructions under the Binary Contents of Memory Address column constitutes the actual machine language program. It is often easier for humans to read hexadecimal as opposed to binary, so the actual contents of memory are displayed in hexadecimal. **To avoid using a subscript of 16, we use the standard "0x" notation to distinguish a hexadecimal number.** For example, instead of saying 123_{16}, we write 0x123.

Hex Address	Instruction		Binary Contents of Memory Address	Hex Contents of Memory
100	Load	104	0001000100000100	1104
101	Add	105	0011000100000101	3105
102	Store	106	0010000100000110	2106
103	Halt		0111000000000000	7000
104	0023		0000000000100011	0023
105	FFE9		1111111111101001	FFE9
106	0000		0000000000000000	0000

TABLE 4.3 A Program to Add Two Numbers

This program loads 0x0023 (or decimal value 35) into the AC. It then adds 0xFFE9 (decimal −23) that it finds at address 0x105. This results in a value of 0x000C, or 12, in the AC. The `Store` instruction stores this value at memory location 0x106. When the program is done, the binary contents of location 0x106 change to 0000000000001100, which is hex 000C, or decimal 12. Figure 4.14 indicates the contents of the registers as the program executes.

a) Load 104

Step	RTN	PC	IR	MAR	MBR	AC
(initial values)		100	------	------	------	------
Fetch	MAR ⟵ PC	100	------	100	------	------
	IR ⟵ M[MAR]	100	1104	100	------	------
	PC ⟵ PC + 1	101	1104	100	------	------
Decode	MAR ⟵ IR[11-0]	101	1104	104	------	------
	(Decode IR[15-12])	101	1104	104	------	------
Get operand	MBR ⟵ M[MAR]	101	1104	104	0023	------
Execute	AC ⟵ MBR	101	1104	104	0023	0023

b) Add 105

Step	RTN	PC	IR	MAR	MBR	AC
(initial values)		101	1104	104	0023	0023
Fetch	MAR ⟵ PC	101	1104	101	0023	0023
	IR ⟵ M[MAR]	101	3105	101	0023	0023
	PC ⟵ PC + 1	102	3105	101	0023	0023
Decode	MAR ⟵ IR[11-0]	102	3105	105	0023	0023
	(Decode IR[15-12])	102	3105	105	0023	0023
Get operand	MBR ⟵ M[MAR]	102	3105	105	FFE9	0023
Execute	AC ⟵ AC + MBR	102	3105	105	FFE9	000C

c) Store 106

Step	RTN	PC	IR	MAR	MBR	AC
(initial values)		102	3105	105	FFE9	000C
Fetch	MAR ⟵ PC	102	3105	102	FFE9	000C
	IR ⟵ M[MAR]	102	2106	102	FFE9	000C
	PC ⟵ PC + 1	103	2106	102	FFE9	000C
Decode	MAR ⟵ IR[11-0]	103	2106	106	FFE9	000C
	(Decode IR[15-12])	103	2106	106	FFE9	000C
Get operand	(not necessary)	103	2106	106	FFE9	000C
Execute	MBR ⟵ AC	103	2106	106	000C	000C
	M[MAR] ⟵ MBR	103	2106	106	000C	000C

FIGURE 4.14   A Trace of the Program to Add Two Numbers

The last RTN instruction in Figure 4.14c places the sum at the proper memory location. The statement "decode IR[15–12]" simply means the instruction must be decoded to determine what is to be done. This decoding can be done in software (using a microprogram) or in hardware (using hardwired circuits). These two concepts are covered in more detail in Section 4.13.

Note that there is a one-to-one correspondence between the assembly language and the machine language instructions. This makes it easy to convert assembly language into machine code. Using the instruction tables given in this chapter, you should be able to hand assemble any of our example programs. For this reason, we look at only the assembly language code from this point on. Before we present more programming examples, however, a discussion of the assembly process is in order.

4.11   A DISCUSSION ON ASSEMBLERS

In the program shown in Table 4.3, it is a simple matter to convert from the assembly language instruction Load 104, for example, to the machine language instruction 0x1104. But why bother with this conversion? Why not just write in machine code? Although it is very efficient for computers to see these instructions as binary numbers, it is difficult for human beings to understand and program in sequences of 0s and 1s. We prefer words and symbols over long numbers, so it seems a natural solution to devise a program that does this simple conversion for us. This program is called an **assembler**.

4.11.1   What Do Assemblers Do?

An assembler's job is to convert assembly language (using mnemonics) into machine language (which consists entirely of binary values, or strings of 0s and 1s). Assemblers take a programmer's assembly language program, which is really a symbolic representation of the binary numbers, and convert it into binary instructions, or the machine code equivalent. The assembler reads a **source file** (assembly program) and produces an **object file** (the machine code).

Substituting simple alphanumeric names for the opcodes makes programming much easier. We can also substitute **labels** (simple names) to identify or name particular memory addresses, making the task of writing assembly programs even simpler. For example, in our program to add two numbers, we can use labels to indicate the memory addresses, thus making it unnecessary to know the exact memory address of the operands for instructions. Table 4.4 illustrates this concept.

When the address field of an instruction is a label instead of an actual physical address, the assembler still must translate it into a real, physical address in main memory. Most assembly languages allow for labels. Assemblers typically specify formatting rules for their instructions, including those with labels. For example, a label might be limited to three characters and may also be required to occur as the first field in the instruction. MARIE requires labels to be followed by a comma.

Hex Address		Instruction	
100		Load	X
101		Add	Y
102		Store	Z
103		Halt	
104	X,	0023	
105	Y,	FFE9	
106	Z,	0000	

TABLE 4.4   An Example Using Labels

Labels are nice for programmers. However, they make more work for the assembler. It must make two passes through a program to do the translation. This means the assembler reads the program twice, from top to bottom each time. On the first pass, the assembler builds a set of correspondences called a **symbol table**. For the above example, it builds a table with three symbols: *X*, *Y*, and *Z*. Because an assembler goes through the code from top to bottom, it cannot translate the entire assembly language instruction into machine code in one pass; it does not know where the data portion of the instruction is located if it is given only a label. But after it has built the symbol table, it can make a second pass and "fill in the blanks."

In the above program, the first pass of the assembler creates the following symbol table:

X	0x104
Y	0x105
Z	0x106

It also begins to translate the instructions. After the first pass, the translated instructions would be incomplete as follows:

1			X
3			Y
2			Z
7	0	0	0

On the second pass, the assembler uses the symbol table to fill in the addresses and create the corresponding machine language instructions. Thus, on the second pass, it would know that *X* is located at address 0x104, and would then substitute 0x104 for the *X*. A similar procedure would replace the *Y* and *Z*, resulting in:

1	1	0	4
3	1	0	5
2	1	0	6
7	0	0	0

Because most people are uncomfortable reading hexadecimal, most assembly languages allow the data values stored in memory to be specified as binary, hexadecimal, or decimal. Typically, some sort of **assembler directive** (an instruction

Hex Address		Instruction	
100		Load	X
101		Add	Y
102		Store	Z
103		Halt	
104	X,	DEC	35
105	Y,	DEC	-23
106	Z,	HEX	0000

TABLE 4.5   An Example Using Directives for Constants

specifically for the assembler that is not supposed to be translated into machine code) is given to the assembler to specify which base is to be used to interpret the value. We use DEC for decimal and HEX for hexadecimal in MARIE's assembly language. For example, we rewrite the program in Table 4.4 as shown in Table 4.5.

Instead of requiring the actual binary data value (written in HEX), we specify a decimal value by using the directive DEC. The assembler recognizes this directive and converts the value accordingly before storing it in memory. Again, directives are not converted to machine language; they simply instruct the assembler in some way.

Another kind of directive common to virtually every programming language is the **comment delimiter**. Comment delimiters are special characters that tell the assembler (or compiler) to ignore all text following the special character. MARIE's comment delimiter is a front slash ("/"), which causes all text between the delimiter and the end of the line to be ignored.

4.11.2   Why Use Assembly Language?

Our main objective in presenting MARIE's assembly language is to give you an idea of how the language relates to the architecture. Understanding how to program in assembly goes a long way toward understanding the architecture (and vice versa). Not only do you learn basic computer architecture, but you also can learn exactly how the processor works and gain significant insight into the particular architecture on which you are programming. There are many other situations where assembly programming is useful.

Most programmers agree that 10% of the code in a program uses approximately 90% of the CPU time. In time-critical applications, we often need to optimize this 10% of the code. Typically, the compiler handles this optimization for us. The compiler takes a high-level language (such as C++) and converts it into assembly language (which is then converted into machine code). Compilers have been around a long time, and in most cases they do a great job. Occasionally, however, programmers must bypass some of the restrictions found in high-level languages and manipulate the assembly code themselves. By doing this, programmers can make the program more efficient in terms of time (and space). This hybrid approach (most of the program written in a high-level language, with part rewritten in assembly) allows the programmer to take advantage of the best of both worlds.

Are there situations in which entire programs should be written in assembly language? If the overall size of the program or response time is critical, assembly language often becomes the language of choice. This is because compilers tend to obscure information about the cost (in time) of various operations and programmers often find it difficult to judge exactly how their compiled programs will perform. Assembly language puts the programmer closer to the architecture and, thus, in firmer control. Assembly language might actually be necessary if the programmer wishes to accomplish certain operations not available in a high-level language.

A perfect example, in terms of both response performance and space-critical design, is found in **embedded systems**. These are systems in which the computer is integrated into a device that is typically not a computer. Embedded systems must be reactive and often are found in time-constrained environments. These systems are designed to perform either a single instruction or a very specific set of instructions. Chances are you use some type of embedded system every day. Consumer electronics (such as cameras, camcorders, cellular phones, PDAs, and interactive games), consumer products (such as washers, microwave ovens, and washing machines), automobiles (particularly engine control and antilock brakes), medical instruments (such as CAT scanners and heart monitors), and industry (for process controllers and avionics) are just a few of the examples of where we find embedded systems.

The software for an embedded system is critical. An embedded software program must perform within very specific response parameters and is limited in the amount of space it can consume. These are perfect applications for assembly language programming. We delve deeper into this topic in Chapter 10.

4.12   EXTENDING OUR INSTRUCTION SET

Even though MARIE's instruction set is sufficient to write any program we wish, there are a few instructions we can add to make programming much simpler. We have 4 bits allocated to the opcode, which implies that we can have 16 unique instructions, and we are using only 9 of them. Surely, we can make many programming tasks much easier by adding a few well-chosen instructions to our instruction set. Our new instructions are summarized in Table 4.6.

The JnS (jump-and-store) instruction allows us to store a pointer to a return instruction and then proceeds to set the PC to a different instruction. This enables us to call procedures and other subroutines, and then return to the calling point in our code once the subroutine has finished. The Clear instruction moves all 0s into the accumulator. This saves the machine cycles that would otherwise be expended in loading a 0 operand from memory.

With the AddI, JumpI, LoadI, and StoreI instructions, we introduce a different **addressing mode**. All previous instructions assume that the value in the data portion of the instruction is the **direct address** of the operand required for the instruction. These instructions use the **indirect addressing mode**. Instead of using the value found at location X as the actual address, we use the value found in X as a pointer to a new memory location that contains the data we wish to use in the instruction. For example, to execute the instruction AddI 400, we first go to location 0x400. If we find the value 0x240 stored at location 0x400, we would go to location 0x240 to get the actual operand for the instruction. We have essentially allowed for pointers in our language,

Instruction Number (hex)	Instruction	Meaning
0	JnS X	Store the PC at address X and jump to X + 1.
A	Clear	Put all zeros in AC.
B	AddI X	Add indirect: Go to address X. Use the value at X as the actual address of the data operand to add to AC.
C	JumpI X	Jump indirect: Go to address X. Use the value at X as the actual address of the location to jump to.
D	LoadI X	Load indirect: Go to address X. Use the value at X as the actual address of the operand to load into the AC.
E	StoreI X	Store indirect: Go to address X. Use the value at X as the destination address for storing the value in the accumulator.

TABLE 4.6 MARIE's Extended Instruction Set

giving us tremendous power to create advanced data structures and manipulate strings. (We delve more deeply into addressing modes in Chapter 5.)

Our six new instructions are detailed below using register transfer notation.

JnS

MBR ← PC

MAR ← X

M[MAR] ← MBR

MBR ← X

AC ← 1

AC ← AC + MBR

PC ← AC

Clear

AC ← 0

AddI X

MAR ← X

MBR ← M[MAR]

MAR ← MBR

MBR ← M[MAR]

AC ← AC + MBR

JumpI X

MAR ← X

MBR ← M[MAR]

PC ← MBR

LoadI X

MBR ← X

MBR ← M[MAR]

MAR ← MBR

MBR ← M[MAR]

AC ← MBR

StoreI X

MBR ← X

MBR ← M[MAR]

MAR ← MBR

MBR ← AC

M[MAR] ← MBR

Table 4.7 summarizes MARIE's entire instruction set.
Let's look at some examples using the full instruction set.

≡   **EXAMPLE 4.2**   Here is an example using a loop to add five numbers:

```
Hex
Address          Instruction
100              Load     Addr    /Load address of first number to be added
101              Store    Next    /Store this address as our Next pointer
102              Load     Num     /Load the number of items to be added
103              Subt     One     /Decrement
104              Store    Ctr     /Store this value in Ctr to control looping
105     Loop,    Load     Sum     /Load the Sum into AC
106              AddI     Next    /Add the value pointed to by location Next
107              Store    Sum     /Store this sum
108              Load     Next    /Load Next
109              Add      One     /Increment by one to point to next address
10A              Store    Next    /Store in our pointer Next
10B              Load     Ctr     /Load the loop control variable
10C              Subt     One     /Subtract one from the loop control variable
10D              Store    Ctr     /Store this new value in loop control variable
10E              Skipcond 000     /If control variable < 0, skip next
                                  /instruction
10F              Jump     Loop    /Otherwise, go to Loop
110              Halt             /Terminate program
111     Addr,    Hex      117     /Numbers to be summed start at location 117
112     Next,    Hex      0       /A pointer to the next number to add
113     Num,     Dec      5       /The number of values to add
114     Sum,     Dec      0       /The sum
115     Ctr,     Hex      0       /The loop control variable
116     One,     Dec      1       /Used to increment and decrement by 1
117              Dec      10      /The values to be added together
118              Dec      15
119              Dec      20
11A              Dec      25
11B              Dec      30
```

Note: Line numbers in program are given for information only and are not used in the MarieSim environment.

Although the comments are reasonably explanatory, let's walk through Example 4.2. Recall that the symbol table stores [label, location] pairs. The Load Addr instruction becomes Load 111, because Addr is located at physical memory address 0x111. The value of 0x117 (the value stored at Addr) is then stored in Next. This is the pointer that allows us to "step through" the five values we are

Opcode	Instruction	RTN
0000	JnS X	MBR ← PC MAR ← X M[MAR] ← MBR MBR ← X AC ← 1 AC ← AC + MBR PC ← AC
0001	Load X	MAR ← X MBR ← M[MAR] AC ← MBR
0010	Store X	MAR ← X, MBR ← AC M[MAR] ← MBR
0011	Add X	MAR ← X MBR ← M[MAR] AC ← AC + MBR
0100	Subt X	MAR ← X MBR ← M[MAR] AC ← AC - MBR
0101	Input	AC ← InREG
0110	Output	OutREG ← AC
0111	Halt	
1000	Skipcond	If IR[11–10] = 00 then If AC < 0 then PC ← PC + 1 Else If IR[11-10] = 01 then If AC = 0 then PC ← PC + 1 Else If IR[11-10] = 10 then If AC > 0 then PC ← PC + 1
1001	Jump X	PC ← IR[11-0]
1010	Clear	AC ← 0
1011	AddI X	MAR ← X MBR ← M[MAR] MAR ← MBR MBR ← M[MAR] AC ← AC + MBR
1100	JumpI X	MAR ← X MBR ← M[MAR] PC ← MBR
1101	LoadI X	MAR ← X MBR ← M[MAR] MAR ← MBR MBR ← M[MAR] AC ← MBR
1110	StoreI X	MAR ← X MBR ← M[MAR] MAR ← MBR MBR ← AC M[MAR] ← MBR

TABLE 4.7 MARIE's Full Instruction Set

adding (located at hex addresses 117, 118, 119, 11A, and 11B). The Ctr variable keeps track of how many iterations of the loop we have performed. Because we are checking to see if Ctr is negative to terminate the loop, we start by subtracting one from Ctr. Sum (with an initial value of 0) is then loaded in the AC. The loop begins, using Next as the address of the data we wish to add to the AC. The Skipcond statement terminates the loop when Ctr is negative by skipping the unconditional branch to the top of the loop. The program then terminates when the Halt statement is executed.

Example 4.3 shows how you can use the Skipcond and Jump instructions to perform selection. Although this example illustrates an if/else construct, you can easily modify this to perform an if/then structure, or even a case (or switch) structure.

≡ **EXAMPLE 4.3** This example illustrates the use of an if/else construct to allow for selection. In particular, it implements the following:

```
if X = Y then
    X = X × 2
else
    Y = Y − X;
```

Hex Address		Instruction		
100	If,	Load	X	/Load the first value
101		Subt	Y	/Subtract the value of Y, store result in AC
102		Skipcond	400	/If AC = 0, skip the next instruction
103		Jump	Else	/Jump to Else part if AC is not equal to 0
104	Then,	Load	X	/Reload X so it can be doubled
105		Add	X	/Double X
106		Store	X	/Store the new value
107		Jump	Endif	/Skip over the false, or else, part to end of /if
108	Else,	Load	Y	/Start the else part by loading Y
109		Subt	X	/Subtract X from Y
10A		Store	Y	/Store Y - X in Y
10B	Endif,	Halt		/Terminate program (it doesn't do much!)
10C	X,	Dec	12	/Load the loop control variable
10D	Y,	Dec	20	/Subtract one from the loop control variable

≡ **EXAMPLE 4.4** This program demonstrates the use of indirect addressing to traverse and output a string. The string is terminated with a null.

```
Hex
Address    Instruction
100    Getch,  LoadI    Chptr        /Load the character found at address Chptr.
101            Skipcond 400          /If AC = 0, skip next instruction.
102            Jump     Outp         /Otherwise, proceed with operation.
103            Halt
104    Outp,   Output                /Output the character.
105            Load     Chptr        /Move pointer to next character.
106            Add      One
107            Store    Chptr
108            Jump     Getch         /Process next character.
109    One,    Hex      0001
10A    Chptr,  Hex      10B           /Pointer to "current" character.
10B    String, Dec      072   /H      /String definition starts here.
10C            Dec      101   /e
10D            Dec      108   /l
10E            Dec      108   /l
10F            Dec      111   /o
110            Dec      032   /[space]
111            Dec      119   /w
112            Dec      111   /o
113            Dec      114   /r
114            Dec      108   /l
115            Dec      100   /d
116            Dec      033   /!
117            Dec      000   /[null]
END
```

Example 4.4 demonstrates the use of the LoadI and StoreI instructions by printing a string. Readers who understand the C and C++ programming languages will recognize the pattern: We start by declaring the memory location of the first character of the string and read it until we find a null character. Once the LoadI instruction places a null in the accumulator, Skipcond 400 evaluates to true, and the Halt instruction is executed. You will notice that to process each character of the string, we increment the "current character" pointer, Chptr, so that it points to the next character to print.

Example 4.5 demonstrates how JnS and JumpI are used to allow for subroutines. This program includes an END statement, another example of an assembler directive. This statement tells the assembler where the program ends. Other potential directives include statements to let the assembler know where to find the first program instruction, how to set up memory, and whether blocks of code are procedures.

≡   **EXAMPLE 4.5** This example illustrates the use of a simple subroutine to double the value stored at *X*.

Hex Address		Instruction		
100		Load	X	/Load the first number to be doubled
101		Store	Temp	/Use Temp as a parameter to pass value to Subr
102		JnS	Subr	/Store return address, jump to procedure
103		Store	X	/Store first number, doubled
104		Load	Y	/Load the second number to be doubled
105		Store	Temp	/Use Temp as a parameter to pass value to Subr
106		JnS	Subr	/Store return address, jump to procedure
107		Store	Y	/Store second number, doubled
108		Halt		/End program
109	X,	Dec	20	
10A	Y,	Dec	48	
10B	Temp,	Dec	0	
10C	Subr,	Hex	0	/Store return address here
10D		Load	Temp	/Subroutine to double numbers
10E		Add	Temp	
10F		JumpI	Subr	
		END		

Note: Line numbers in program are given for information only and are not used in the MarieSim environment.

Using MARIE's simple instruction set, you should be able to implement any high-level programming language construct, such as loop statements and while statements. These are left as exercises at the end of the chapter.

4.13 A DISCUSSION ON DECODING: HARDWIRED VERSUS MICROPROGRAMMED CONTROL

How does the control unit really function? We have done some hand waving and simply assumed that everything works as described, with a basic understanding that, for each instruction, the control unit causes the CPU to execute a sequence of steps correctly. In reality, there must be control signals to assert lines on various digital components to make things happen as described (recall the various digital components from Chapter 3). For example, when we perform an Add instruction in MARIE in assembly language, we assume the addition takes place because the control signals for the ALU are set to "add" and the result is put into the AC. The ALU has various control lines that determine which operation to perform. The question we need to answer is, "How do these control lines actually become asserted?"

The control unit, driven by the processor's clock, is responsible for decoding the binary value in the instruction register and creating all necessary control signals; essentially, the control unit takes the CPU through a sequence of "control" steps for each program instruction. Each control step results in the control unit creating a set of signals (called a **control word**) that executes the appropriate microoperation.

There are two methods by which control lines can be set. The first approach, **hardwired control**, directly connects the control lines to the actual machine instructions. The instructions are divided into fields, and bits in the fields are connected to input lines that drive various digital logic components. The second approach, **microprogrammed control**, employs software consisting of micro-instructions that carry out an instruction's microoperations. We look at both of these control methods in more detail after we describe machine control in general.

4.13.1 Machine Control

In Sections 4.8 and 4.12, we provided register transfer language for each of MARIE's instructions. The microoperations described by the register transfer language actually define the operation of the control unit. Each microoperation is associated with a distinctive signal pattern. The signals are fed to combinational circuits within the control unit that carry out the logical operations appropriate to the instruction.

A schematic of MARIE's data path is shown in Figure 4.9. We see that each register and main memory has an address (0 through 7) along the datapath. These addresses, in the form of signal patterns, are used by the control unit to enable the flow of bytes through the system. For the sake of example, we define two sets of signals: P_2, P_1, P_0 that can enable reading from memory or a register and P_5, P_4, P_3 that can enable writing to a register or memory. The control lines that convey these signals are connected to registers through combinational logic circuits.

A close-up view of the connection of MARIE's MBR (with address 3) to the datapath is shown in Figure 4.15. Because each register is connected to the datapath in a similar manner, we have to make sure that they are not all "competing" with the bus. This is done by introducing a **tri-state** device. This circuit, the triangle with three inputs, uses one input to allow the circuit to act as a switch; if the input is 1, the device is closed and a value can "flow through." If the input is 0, the switch is open and doesn't allow any values to flow through. The input used to control these devices comes from the decoder AND gate that gets its inputs from P_0, P_1, and P_2.

In Figure 4.15, we see that if P_1 and P_0 are high, this AND gate computes $P_2'P_1P_0$, which outputs a 1 precisely when the MBR is selected for reading (which means the MBR is writing to the bus, or $D_{15} - D_0$). Any other registers are disconnected from the bus wires because their tri-state devices are receiving the value of 0 from this decoder AND gate. We can also see in Figure 4.15 how values are written to the MBR (read from the bus). When P_4 and P_3 are high, the decoder AND gate for P_3, P_4, and P_5 outputs a 1, resulting in the D flipflops being

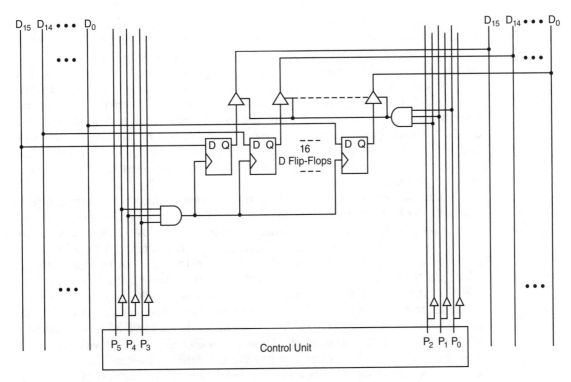

FIGURE 4.15 Connection of MARIE's MBR to the Datapath

ALU Control Signals		ALU Response
A_1	A_0	
0	0	Do Nothing
0	1	AC ← AC + MBR
1	0	AC ← AC − MBR
1	1	AC ← 0 (Clear)

TABLE 4.8 ALU Control Signals and Response

clocked and storing the values from the bus in the MBR. (The combinational logic that enables the other entities on the datapath is left as an exercise.)

If you study MARIE's instruction set, you will see that the ALU has only three operations: add, subtract, and clear. We also need to consider the case where the ALU is not involved in an instruction, so we'll define "do nothing" as a fourth ALU state. Thus, with only four operations, MARIE's ALU can be controlled using only two control signals that we'll call A_0 and A_1. These control signals and the ALU response are given in Table 4.8.

A computer's clock sequences microoperations by raising the right signals at the right time. MARIE's instructions vary in the number of clock cycles each requires. The activities taking place during each clock cycle are coordinated with signals from a cycle counter. One way of doing this is to connect the clock to a synchronous counter, and the counter to a decoder. Suppose that the largest number of clock cycles required by any instruction is eight. Then we need a 3-bit counter and a 3×8 decoder. The output of the decoder, signals T_0 through T_7, is ANDed with combinational components and registers to produce the behavior required by the instruction. If fewer than eight clock cycles are needed for an instruction, the cycle counter reset signal, C_r, is asserted to get ready for the next machine instruction.

Before we continue, we need to discuss two additional concepts, beginning with the RTN instruction: PC ← PC + 1. We have seen this in the Skipcond instruction as well as in the fetch portion of the fetch–decode–execute cycle. This is a more complicated instruction than it first appears. The constant 1 must be stored somewhere, both this constant and the contents of the PC must be input into the ALU, and the resulting value must be written back to the PC. Because the PC, in this context, is essentially a counter, we can implement the PC using a circuit similar to the counter in Figure 3.31. However, we cannot use the simple counter as shown because we must also be able to store values directly in the PC (for example, when executing a JUMP statement). Therefore, we need a counter with additional input lines allowing us to overwrite any current values with new ones. To increment the PC, we introduce a new control signal **IncrPC** for this new circuit; when this signal is asserted and the clock ticks, the PC is incremented by 1.

The second issue we need to address becomes clear if one examines Figure 4.9, the MARIE datapath, in more detail. Note that the AC can not only read a value from the bus, but it can also receive a value from the ALU. The MBR has a similar alternative source, as it can read from the bus or get a value directly from the AC. Multiplexers can be added to Figure 4.15, using a control line L_{ALT}, to select which value each register should load: the default bus value ($L_{ALT} = 0$), or the alternative source ($L_{ALT} = 1$).

To pull all of this together, consider MARIE's Add instruction. The RTN is:

```
MAR ← X
MBR ← M[MAR]
AC ← AC + MBR
```

After the Add instruction is fetched, X is in the rightmost 12 bits of the IR and the IR's datapath address is 7, so we need to raise all three datapath read signals, $P_2P_1P_0$, to place IR bits 0 through 11 on the bus. The MAR, with an address of 1, is activated for writing by raising only P_3. In the next statement, we must go to memory and retrieve the data stored at the address in the MAR and write it to the MBR. Although it appears that the MAR must be read to first get this value, in MARIE, we assume that the MAR is hardwired directly to memory. Because the memory we depicted in Figure 3.32 has only a write enable line (we denote this control line as M_W), memory, by default, can be read without any further control lines being set. Let us now modify that memory to include a read enable line (M_R) as well. This allows MARIE to deal with any competition for the data bus that memory might introduce, similar to the reason we added tri-state devices to Figure 4.15. To retrieve the value fetched from memory, we assert P_4 and P_3 to write to the MBR. Finally, we add the value in the MBR to the value in the AC, writing the result in the AC. Because the MBR and AC are directly connected to the ALU, the only control required is to: (1) assert A_0 to perform an addition; (2) assert P_5 to allow the AC to change; and (3) assert L_{ALT} to force the AC to read its value from the ALU instead of the bus. Using the signals as we have just defined them, we can add the signal patterns to our RTN as follows:

```
P₃P₂P₁P₀T₃:        MAR ← X
P₄P₃T₄M_R:         MBR ← M[MAR]
C_rA₀P₅T₅L_ALT:    AC ← AC + MBR [reset the clock cycle counter]
```

Note that we start the clock cycle at T_3, as the fetch uses T_0, T_1, and T_2 (to copy the value of the PC to the MAR, to copy the specified memory value to the IR, and to increment the PC). The first line listed above is actually the "get operand" operation (as it copies the value in IR[12-0] to the MAR). The last line contains the control signal C_r, which resets the clock cycle counter.

All signals, except for data signals ($D_0 . . .D_{15}$), are assumed to be low unless specified in the RTN. Figure 4.16 is a timing diagram that illustrates the sequence of signal patterns just described. As you can see, at clock cycle C_3, all signals except P_0, P_1, P_2, P_3, and T_3 are low. Enabling P_0, P_1, and P_2 allows the IR to be read from, and asserting P_3 allows the MAR to be written to. This action occurs only when T_3 is asserted. At clock cycle C_4, all signals except P_3, P_4, M_R, and T_4 are low. This machine state, occurring at time T_4, connects the bytes read from main memory (address zero) to the inputs on the MBR. The last microinstruction of the Add sequence occurs at clock cycle T_5, when the sum is placed into the AC (so L_{ALT} is high) and the clock cycle counter is reset.

4.13.2 Hardwired Control

Hardwired control uses the bits in the instruction register to generate control signals by feeding these bits into basic logic gates. There are three essential components common to all hardwired control units: the instruction decoder, the cycle counter, and the control matrix. Depending on the complexity of the system, specialized registers and sets of status flags may be provided as well. Figure 4.17 illustrates a simplified control unit. Let us look at it in detail.

The first essential component is the **instruction decoder**. Its job is to raise the unique output signal corresponding to the opcode in the instruction register. If we have a four-bit opcode, the instruction decoder could have as many as 16 output signal lines. (Why?) A partial decoder for MARIE's instruction set is shown in Figure 4.18.

The next important component is the control unit's **cycle counter**. It raises a single, distinct timing signal, T_0, T_1, T_2, ... , T_n, for each tick of the system

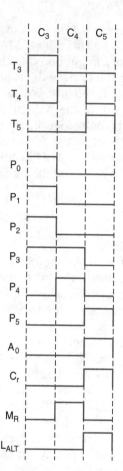

FIGURE 4.16   Timing Diagram for the Microoperations of MARIE's Add Instruction

clock. After T_n is reached, the counter cycles back to T_0. The maximum number of microoperations required to carry out any of the instructions in the instruction set determines the number of distinct signals (i.e., the value of n in T_n). MARIE's timer needs to count only up to 7 (T_0 through T_6) to accommodate the JnS instruction. (You can verify this statement with a close inspection of Table 4.7.)

The sequential logic circuit that provides a repeated series of timing signals is called a ring counter. Figure 4.19 shows one implementation of a ring counter using D flip-flops. Initially, all of the flip-flop inputs are low except for the input to D_0 (because of the inverted OR gate on the other outputs). Thus, in the counter's initial state, output T_0 is energized. At the next tick of the clock, the output of D_0 goes high, causing the input of D_0 to go low (because of the inverted OR gate). T_0 turns off and T_1 turns on. As you can readily see, we have effectively moved a "timing bit" from D_0 to D_1. This bit circulates through the ring of flip-flops until it reaches D_n, unless the ring is first reset by way of the clock reset signal, C_r.

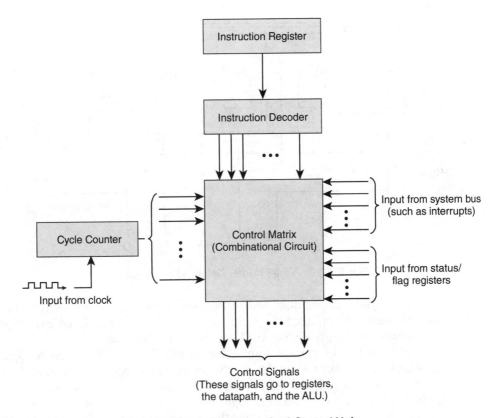

FIGURE 4.17   Hardwired Control Unit

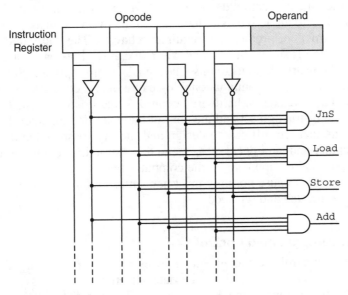

FIGURE 4.18   Partial Instruction Decoder for MARIE's Instruction Set

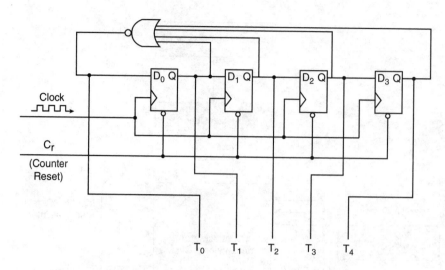

FIGURE 4.19 Ring Counter Using D Flip-Flops

Signals from the counter and instruction decoder are combined within the **control matrix** to produce the series of signals that result in the execution of microoperations involving the ALU, registers, and datapath.

The sequence of control signals for MARIE's Add instruction is identical regardless of whether we employ hardwired or microprogrammed control. If we use hardwired control, the bit pattern in the machine instruction (Add = 0011) feeds directly into combinational logic within the control unit. The control unit initiates the sequence of signal events that we just described. Consider the control unit in Figure 4.17. The most interesting part of this diagram is the connection between the instruction decoder and the logic inside the control unit. With timing being key to all activities in the system, the timing signals, along with the bits in the instruction, produce the required behavior. The hardwired logic for the Add instruction is shown in Figure 4.20. You can see how each clock cycle is ANDed with the instruction bits to raise the signals as appropriate. With each clock tick, a different group of combinational logic circuits is activated.

The advantage of hardwired control is that it is very fast. The disadvantage is that the instruction set and the control logic are tied together directly by complex circuits that are difficult to design and modify. If someone designs a hardwired computer and later decides to extend the instruction set (as we did with MARIE), the physical components in the computer must be changed. This is prohibitively expensive, because not only must new chips be fabricated, but the old ones must also be located and replaced.

4.13.3 Microprogrammed Control

Signals control the movement of bytes (which are actually signal patterns that we *interpret* as bytes) along the datapath in a computer system. The manner in which these control signals are produced is what distinguishes hardwired control

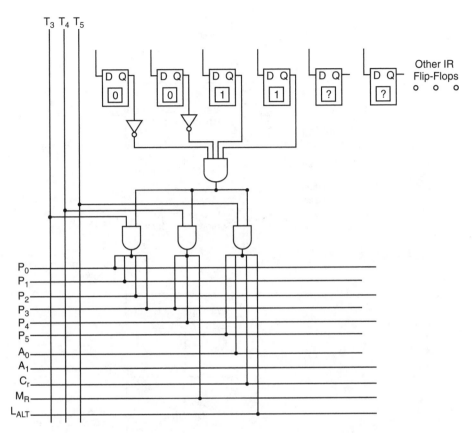

FIGURE 4.20   Combinational Logic for Signal Controls of MARIE's Add Instruction

from microprogrammed control. In hardwired control, timing signals from the clock are ANDed using combinational logic circuits to raise and lower signals. Hardwired control results in very complex logic, in which basic logic gates are responsible for generating all control words. For a computer with a large instruction set, it might be virtually impossible to implement hardwired control. In microprogrammed control, instruction **microcode** produces the necessary control signals. A generic block diagram of a microprogrammed control unit is shown in Figure 4.21.

All machine instructions are input into a special program, the **microprogram**, that converts machine instructions of 0s and 1s into control signals. The microprogram is essentially an interpreter, written in microcode, that is stored in **firmware** (ROM, PROM, or EPROM), which is often referred to as the **control store**. A microcode microinstruction is retrieved during each clock cycle. The particular instruction retrieved is a function of the current state of the machine and the value of the **microsequencer**, which is somewhat like a program counter that selects the next instruction from the control store. If MARIE were microprogrammed, the microinstruction format might look like the one shown in Figure 4.22.

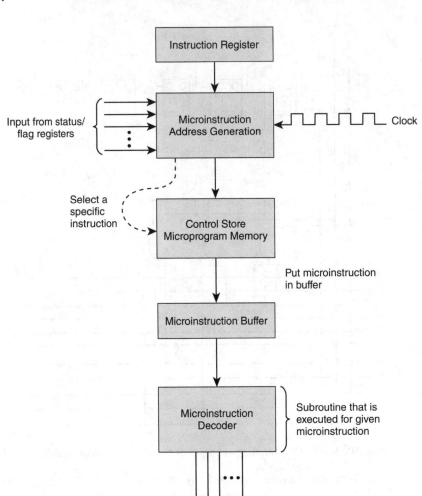

FIGURE 4.21 Microprogrammed Control Unit

Field Name	MicroOp1	MicroOp2	Jump	Dest
Meaning	First Microoperation	Second Microoperation	Boolean: Set to indicate a jump	Destination address for jump
Bit	17 13	12 8	7	6 0

FIGURE 4.22 MARIE's Microinstruction Format

Each microoperation corresponds to specific control lines being either active or not active. For example, the microoperation MAR ← PC must assert the controls signals to put the contents of the PC on the datapath and then transfer them to the MAR (which would include raising the clock signal for the MAR to accept the new value). The microoperation AC ← AC + MBR generates the ALU control signals for add, while also asserting the clock for the AC to receive the new value. The microoperation MBR ← M[MAR] generates control signals to enable the correct memory chip for the address stored in the MAR (this would include multiple control signals for the appropriate decoders), set memory to READ, place the memory data on the data bus, and put the data into the MBR (which, again, requires that sequential circuit to be clocked). One microinstruction might require tens (or even hundreds or thousands in a more complex architecture) of control lines to be asserted. These control signals are all quite complicated; therefore, we will center our discussion on the microoperations that create the control signals, rather than the control signals themselves, assuming the reader understands that executing these microoperations, in reality, translates into generating all required control signals. Another way to visualize what is happening is to associate, with each microoperation, a control word with one bit for every control line in the system (decoders, multiplexers, ALUs, memory, shifters, clocks, etc.). Instead of "executing" the microoperation, a microprogrammed control unit simply locates the control word associated with that microoperation and outputs it to the hardware.

MicroOp1 and MicroOp2 are binary codes for each unique microoperation specified in the RTN for MARIE's instruction set. A comprehensive list of this RTN (as given in Table 4.7) along with the RTN for the fetch–decode–execute cycle reveals that there are only 22 unique microoperations required to implement MARIE's entire instruction set. Two additional microoperations are also necessary. One of these codes, NOP, indicates "no operation." NOP is useful when the system must wait for a set of signals to stabilize, when waiting for a value to be fetched from memory, or when we need a placeholder. Second, and most important, we need a microoperation that compares the bit pattern in the first 4 bits of the instruction register (IR[15–12]) to a literal value that is in the first 4 bits of the MicroOp2 field. This instruction is crucial to the execution control of MARIE's microprogram. Each of MARIE's microoperations is assigned a binary code, as shown in Table 4.9.

MARIE's entire microprogram consists of fewer than 128 statements, so each statement can be uniquely identified by seven bits. This means that each microinstruction has a seven-bit address. When the Jump bit is set, it indicates that the Dest field contains a valid address. This address is then moved to the microsequencer. Control then branches to the address found in the Dest field.

MARIE's control store memory holds the entire microprogram in contiguous space. This program consists of a jump table and blocks of code that correspond to each of MARIE's operations. The first nine statements (in RTL form) of MARIE's microprogram are given in Figure 4.23 (we have used the RTL for clarity; the microprogram is actually stored in binary). When MARIE is booted up, hardware sets the microsequencer to point to address 0000000 of the

MicroOp Code	Microoperation	MicroOp Code	Microoperation
00000	NOP	01101	MBR ← M[MAR]
00001	AC ← 0	01110	OutREG ← AC
00010	AC ← MBR	01111	PC ← IR[11-0]
00011	AC ← AC - MBR	10000	PC ← MBR
00100	AC ← AC + MBR	10001	PC ← PC + 1
00101	AC ← InREG	10010	If AC = 00
00110	IR ← M[MAR]	10011	If AC > 0
00111	M[MAR] ← MBR	10100	If AC < 0
01000	MAR ← IR[11-0]	10101	If IR[11-10] = 00
01001	MAR ← MBR	10110	If IR[11-10] = 01
01010	MAR ← PC	10111	If IR[11-10] = 10
01011	MAR ← X	11000	If IR[15-12] =
01100	MBR ← AC		MicroOp2[4-1]

TABLE 4.9 Microoperation Codes and Corresponding MARIE RTL

Address	MicroOp1	MicroOp2	Jump	Dest
0000000	MAR ← PC	NOP	0	0000000
0000001	IR ← M[MAR]	NOP	0	0000000
0000010	PC ← PC + 1	NOP	0	0000000
0000011	MAR ←IR[11-0]	NOP	0	0000000
0000100	If IR[15-12] = MicroOP2[4-1]	00000	1	0100000
0000101	If IR[15-12] = MicroOP2[4-1]	00010	1	0100111
0000110	If IR[15-12] = MicroOP2[4-1]	00100	1	0101010
0000111	If IR[15-12] = MicroOP2[4-1]	00110	1	0101100
0001000	If IR[15-12] = MicroOP2[4-1]	01000	1	0101111
. . .	. . .	. . .	. . .	. . .
. . .	. . .	. . .	. . .	. . .
0101010	MAR ← X	MBR ← AC	0	0000000
0101011	M[MAR]← MBR	NOP	1	0000000
0101100	MAR ← X	NOP	0	0000000
0101101	MBR ←M[MAR]	NOP	0	0000000
0101110	AC ←AC + MBR	NOP	1	0000000
0101111	MAR ←MAR	NOP	0	0000000
. . .	. . .	. . .	. . .	. . .

FIGURE 4.23 Selected Statements in MARIE's Microprogram

microprogram. Execution commences from this entry point. We see that the first four statements of the microprogram are the first four statements of the fetch–decode–execute cycle. The statements starting at address 0000100 that contain "ifs" are the jump table containing the addresses of the statements that carry out the machine instructions. They effectively decode the instruction by branching to the code block that sets the control signals to carry out the machine instruction.

At line number 0000111, the statement If IR[15-12] = MicroOp2[4-1] compares the value in the leftmost 4 bits of the second microoperation field with the value in the opcode field of the instruction that was fetched in the first three lines of the microprogram. In this particular statement, we are comparing the opcode against MARIE's binary code for the Add operation, 0011. If we have a match, the Jump bit is set to true and control branches to address 0101100.

At address 0101100, we see the microoperations (RTN) for the Add instruction. As these microoperations are executed, control lines are set exactly as described in Section 4.13.1. The last instruction for Add, at 0101110, has the Jump bit set once again. The setting of this bit causes the value of all 0s (the jump Dest) to be moved to the microsequencer. This effectively branches back to the start of the fetch cycle at the top of the program.

We must emphasize that a microprogrammed control unit works like a system in miniature. To fetch an instruction from the control store, a certain set of signals must be raised. The microsequencer points at the instruction to retrieve and is subsequently incremented. This is why microprogrammed control tends to be slower than hardwired control—all instructions must go through an additional level of interpretation. But performance is not everything. Microprogramming is flexible, simple in design, and lends itself to very powerful instruction sets. The great advantage of microprogrammed control is that if the instruction set requires modification, only the microprogram needs to be updated to match: No changes to the hardware are required. Thus, microprogrammed control units are less costly to manufacture and maintain. Because cost is critical in consumer products, microprogrammed control dominates the personal computer market.

4.14 REAL-WORLD EXAMPLES OF COMPUTER ARCHITECTURES

The MARIE architecture is designed to be as simple as possible so that the essential concepts of computer architecture would be easy to understand without being completely overwhelming. Although MARIE's architecture and assembly language are powerful enough to solve any problems that could be carried out on a modern architecture using a high-level language such as C++, Ada, or Java, you probably wouldn't be happy with the inefficiency of the architecture or with how difficult the program would be to write and to debug! MARIE's performance could be significantly improved if more storage were incorporated into the CPU by adding more registers. Making things easier for the programmer is a different matter. For example, suppose a MARIE programmer wants to use procedures with parameters. Although MARIE allows for subroutines (programs can branch to various sections of code, execute the code, and then return), MARIE has no mechanism to support the passing of parameters. Programs can be written without parameters, but we know that using them not only makes the program more efficient (particularly in the area of reuse), but also makes the program easier to write and debug.

To allow for parameters, MARIE would need a **stack**, a data structure that maintains a list of items that can be accessed from only one end. A pile of plates in your kitchen cabinet is analogous to a stack: You put plates on the top and you take plates off the top (normally). For this reason, stacks are often called **last-in-first-out** structures. (Please see Appendix A at the end of this book for a brief overview of the various data structures.)

We can emulate a stack using certain portions of main memory if we restrict the way data is accessed. For example, if we assume that memory locations 0000 through 00FF are used as a stack, and we treat 0000 as the top, then **pushing** (adding) onto the stack must be done from the top, and **popping** (removing) from the stack must be done from the top. If we push the value 2 onto the stack, it would be placed at location 0000. If we then push the value 6, it would be placed at location 0001. If we then performed a pop operation, the 6 would be removed. A **stack pointer** keeps track of the location to which items should be pushed or popped.

MARIE shares many features with modern architectures, but is not an accurate depiction of them. In the next two sections, we introduce two contemporary computer architectures to better illustrate the features of modern architectures that, in an attempt to follow Leonardo da Vinci's advice, were excluded from MARIE. We begin with the Intel architecture (the x86 and the Pentium families) and then follow with the MIPS architecture. We chose these architectures because, although they are similar in some respects, they are built on fundamentally different philosophies. Each member of the x86 family of Intel architectures is known as a **CISC (complex instruction set computer)** machine, whereas the Pentium family and the MIPS architectures are examples of **RISC (reduced instruction set computer)** machines.

CISC machines have a large number of instructions, of variable length, with complex layouts. Many of these instructions are quite complicated, performing multiple operations when a single instruction is executed (e.g., it is possible to do loops using a *single* assembly language instruction). The basic problem with CISC machines is that a small subset of complex CISC instructions slows the systems down considerably. Designers decided to return to a less complicated architecture and to hardwire a small (but complete) instruction set that would execute extremely quickly. This meant it would be the compiler's responsibility to produce efficient code for the ISA. Machines utilizing this philosophy are called RISC machines.

RISC is something of a misnomer. It is true that the number of instructions is reduced. However, the main objective of RISC machines is to simplify instructions so they can execute more quickly. Each instruction performs only one operation, they are all the same size, they have only a few different layouts, and all arithmetic operations must be performed between registers (data in memory cannot be used as operands). Virtually all new instruction sets (for any architectures) since 1982 have been RISC, or some sort of combination of CISC and RISC. We cover CISC and RISC in detail in Chapter 9.

4.14.1   Intel Architectures

The Intel Corporation has produced many different architectures, some of which may be familiar to you. Intel's first popular chip, the **8086**, was introduced in 1979 and was used in the IBM PC. It handled 16-bit data and worked with 20-bit addresses; thus it could address a million bytes of memory. (A close cousin of the 8086, the 8-bit 8088, was used in many personal computers to lower the cost.) The 8086 CPU was split into two parts: the **execution unit**, which included the general registers and the ALU, and the **bus interface unit**, which included the instruction queue, the segment registers, and the instruction pointer.

The 8086 had four 16-bit general-purpose registers named AX (the primary accumulator), BX (the base register used to extend addressing), CX (the count register), and DX (the data register). Each of these registers was divided into two pieces: The most significant half was designated the "high" half (denoted by AH, BH, CH, and DH), and the least significant was designated the "low" half (denoted by AL, BL, CL, and DL). Various 8086 instructions required the use of a specific register, but the registers could be used for other purposes as well. The 8086 also had three pointer registers: the stack pointer (SP), which was used as an offset into the stack; the base pointer (BP), which was used to reference parameters pushed onto the stack; and the instruction pointer (IP), which held the address of the next instruction (similar to MARIE's PC). There were also two index registers: the SI (source index) register, used as a source pointer for string operations, and the DI (destination index) register, used as a destination pointer for string operations. The 8086 also had a **status flags register**. Individual bits in this register indicated various conditions, such as overflow, parity, carry interrupt, and so on.

An 8086 assembly language program was divided into different **segments**, special blocks or areas to hold specific types of information. There was a code segment (for holding the program), a data segment (for holding the program's data), and a stack segment (for holding the program's stack). To access information in any of these segments, it was necessary to specify that item's offset from the beginning of the corresponding segment. Therefore, segment pointers were necessary to store the addresses of the segments. These registers included the code segment (CS) register, the data segment (DS) register, and the stack segment (SS) register. There was also a fourth segment register, called the extra segment (ES) register, which was used by some string operations to handle memory addressing. Addresses were specified using segment/offset addressing in the form: *xxx:yyy*, where *xxx* was the value in the segment register and *yyy* was the offset.

In 1980, Intel introduced the 8087, which added floating-point instructions to the 8086 machine set as well as an 80-bit-wide stack. Many new chips were introduced that used essentially the same ISA as the 8086, including the 80286 in 1982 (which could address 16 million bytes) and the 80386 in 1985 (which could address up to 4 billion bytes of memory). The 80386 was a 32-bit chip, the first in a family of chips often called **IA-32** (for Intel Architecture, 32-bit). When Intel moved from the 16-bit 80286 to the 32-bit 80386, designers wanted these architectures to be **backward compatible**, which means that programs written for a less powerful and older processor should run on the newer, faster processors. For example, programs that ran on the 80286 should also run on the 80386. Therefore,

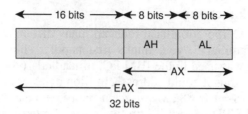

FIGURE 4.24 EAX Register, Broken into Parts

Intel kept the same basic architecture and register sets. (New features were added to each successive model, so forward compatibility was not guaranteed.)

The naming convention used in the 80386 for the registers, which had gone from 16 to 32 bits, was to include an "E" prefix (which stood for "extended"). So instead of AX, BX, CX, and DX, the registers became EAX, EBX, ECX, and EDX. This same convention was used for all other registers. However, the programmer could still access the original registers, AX, AL, and AH, for example, using the original names. Figure 4.24 illustrates how this worked, using the AX register as an example.

The 80386 and 80486 were both 32-bit machines, with 32-bit data buses. The 80486 added a high-speed **cache** memory (see Chapter 6 for more details on cache and memory), which improved performance significantly.

The **Pentium** series (see sidebar "What's in a Name?" to find out why Intel stopped using numbers and switched to the name "Pentium") started with the Pentium processor, which had 32-bit registers and a 64-bit data bus and employed a **superscalar** design. This means the CPU had multiple ALUs and could issue more than one instruction per clock cycle (i.e., run instructions in parallel). The Pentium Pro added branch prediction, and the Pentium II added MMX technology (which most will agree was not a huge success) to deal with multimedia. The Pentium III added increased support for 3D graphics (using floating-point instructions). Historically, Intel used a classic CISC approach throughout its processor series. The more recent Pentium II and III used a combined approach, employing CISC architectures with RISC cores that could translate from CISC to RISC instructions. Intel was conforming to the current trend by moving away from CISC and toward RISC.

The seventh-generation family of Intel CPUs introduced the Intel **Pentium IV** (also known as the **Pentium 4**) processor. This processor differs from its predecessors in several ways, many of which are beyond the scope of this text. Suffice it to say that the Pentium IV processor has clock rates of 1.4 and 1.7GHz, uses no less than 42 million transistors for the CPU, and implements a **NetBurst microarchitecture**. (The processors in the Pentium family, up to this point, had all been based on the same **microarchitecture**, a term used to describe the architecture below the instruction set.) This type of architecture includes four salient improvements: hyperpipelining, a wider instruction pipeline (pipelining is covered in Chapter 5) to handle more instructions concurrently; a rapid execution engine (the Pentium IV has two arithmetic logic units); an execution trace cache, a cache that holds decoded instructions so if they are used again, they do not have to be decoded again; and a 400MHz bus. This has made the Pentium IV an extremely useful processor for multimedia applications.

The Pentium IV processor also introduced **hyperthreading (HT)**. **Threads** are tasks that can run independently of one another within the context of the same process. A thread shares code and data with the parent process but has its own resources, including a stack and instruction pointer. Because multiple child threads share with their parent, threads require fewer system resources than if each were a separate process. Systems with more than one processor take advantage of thread processing by splitting instructions so that multiple threads can execute on the processors in parallel. However, Intel's HT enables a single physical processor to simulate two logical (or virtual) processors—the operating system actually sees two processors where only one exists. (To take advantage of HT, the operating system must recognize thread processing.) HT does this through a mix of shared, duplicated, and partitioned chip resources, including registers, math units, counters, and cache memory.

HT duplicates the architectural state of the processor but permits the threads to share main execution resources. This sharing allows the threads to utilize resources that might otherwise be idle (e.g., on a cache miss), resulting in up to a 40% improvement in resource utilization and potential performance gains as high as 25%. Performance gains depend on the application, with computationally intensive applications seeing the most significant gain. Commonplace programs, such as word processors and spreadsheets, are mostly unaffected by HT technology.

What's in a Name?

Intel Corporation makes approximately 80% of the CPUs used in today's microcomputers. It all started with the 4-bit 4004, which in 1971 was the first commercially available microprocessor, or "CPU on a chip." Four years later, Intel's 8-bit 8080 with 6000 transistors was put into the first personal computer, the Altair 8800. As technology allowed more transistors per chip, Intel kept pace by introducing the 16-bit 8086 in 1978 and the 8088 in 1979 (both with approximately 29,000 transistors). These two processors truly started the personal computer revolution, as they were used in the IBM personal computer (later dubbed the XT) and became the industry standard.

The 80186 was introduced in 1980, and although buyers could choose from an 8-bit or a 16-bit version, the 80186 was never used in personal computers. In 1982, Intel introduced the 80286, a 16-bit processor with 134,000 transistors. In fewer than 5 years, more than 14 million personal computers were using the 80286 (which most people shortened to simply "286"). In 1985, Intel came out with the first 32-bit microprocessor, the 80386. The 386 multitasking chip was an immediate success, with its 275,000 transistors and 5 million instructions-per-second operating speed. Four years later, Intel introduced the 80486, which had an amazing 1.2 million transistors per chip and operated at 16.9 million instructions per second! The 486, with its built-in math coprocessor, was the first microprocessor to truly rival mainframe computers.

With such huge success and name recognition, why then did Intel suddenly stop using the 80x86 moniker and switch to *Pentium* in 1993? By that time, many companies were copying Intel's designs and using the same numbering scheme. One of the most successful of these was Advanced Micro Device (AMD). The AMD486 processor had already found its way into many portable and desktop computers. Another was Cyrix with its 486SLC chip. Before introducing its next processor, Intel asked the U.S. Patent and Trademark Office if the company could trademark the name "586." In the United States, numbers cannot be trademarked. (Other countries do allow numbers as trademarks, such as Peugeot's trademark three-digit model numbers with a central zero.) Intel was denied its trademark request and switched the name to *Pentium*. (The astute reader will recognize that *pent* means five, as in *pentagon*.)

It is interesting to note that all of this happened at about the same time as Intel began using its ubiquitous "Intel inside" stickers. It is also interesting that AMD introduced what it called the PR rating system, a method of comparing its x86 processor to Intel's processor. PR stands for "Performance Rating" (not "Pentium Rating" as many people believe) and was intended to guide consumers regarding a particular processor's performance as compared to that of a Pentium.

Intel has continued to manufacture chips using the Pentium naming scheme. The first Pentium chip had 3 million transistors, operated at 25 million instructions per second, and had clock speeds from 60 to 200MHz. Intel produced many different name variations of the Pentium, including the Pentium MMX in 1997, which improved multimedia performance using the MMX instruction set.

Other manufacturers have also continued to design chips to compete with the Pentium line. AMD introduced the AMD5x86, and later the K5 and K6, to compete with Pentium MMX technology. AMD gave its 5x86 processor a "PR75" rating, meaning this processor was as fast as a Pentium running at 75MHz. Cyrix introduced the 6x86 chip (or M1) and MediaGX, followed by the Cyrix 6x86MX (M2), to compete with the Pentium MMX.

Intel moved on to the Pentium Pro in 1995. This processor had 5.5 million transistors but had only a slightly larger die than the 4004, which was introduced almost 25 years earlier. The Pentium II (1997) was a cross between the Pentium MMX and the Pentium Pro and contained 7.5 million transistors. AMD continued to keep pace and introduced the K6-2 in 1998, followed by the K6-3. In an attempt to capture more of the low-end market, Intel introduced the Celeron, an entry-level version of the Pentium II with less cache memory.

Intel released the Pentium III in 1999. This chip, housing 9.5 million transistors, used the SSE instruction set (which is an extension to MMX). Intel continued with improvements to this processor by placing cache directly on the core, making caching considerably faster. AMD released the Athlon line of chips in 1999 to compete with the Pentium III. (AMD continues to manufacture the Athlon line to this day.) In 2000, Intel released the Pentium IV, and depending on the particular core, this chip has from 42 to 55 million transistors. The Itanium 2, in 2002, had 220 million transistors, and the new Itanium in 2004 had 592 million transistors. By 2008, Intel had created the Core i7 with 731 million transistors. By 2010, the number of transistors on the Core i7 had topped a billion! In 2011, the Xeon was released and consisted of more than 2 billion transistors, followed in 2012 by the Itanium with more than 3 billion transistors and the Xeon with more than 5 billion transistors!

Clearly, changing the name of its processors from the x86 designation to the Pentium-based series has had no negative effects on Intel's success. However, because Pentium is one of the most recognized trademarks in the processor world, industry watchers were surprised when Intel introduced its 64-bit Itanium processor without including *Pentium* as part of the name. Some people believe that this chip name has backfired, and their comparison of this chip to a sinking ship has prompted some to call it the *Itanic*.

Although this discussion has given a timeline of Intel's processors, it also shows that, for the past 30 years, Moore's law has held with remarkable accuracy. And we have looked at only Intel and Intel clone processors. There are many other microprocessors we have not mentioned, including those made by Motorola, Zilog, TI, and RCA, to name only a few. With continually increasing power and decreasing costs, there is little wonder that microprocessors have become the most prevalent type of processor in the computer market. Even more amazing is that there is no sign of this trend changing at any time in the near future.

The introduction of the **Itanium** processor in 2001 marked Intel's first 64-bit chip (**IA-64**). Itanium includes a register-based programming language and a very rich instruction set. It also employs a hardware emulator to maintain backward compatibility with IA-32/x86 instruction sets. This processor has four integer units, two floating-point units, a significant amount of cache memory at four different levels (we study cache levels in Chapter 6), 128 floating-point registers, 128 integer registers, and multiple miscellaneous registers for dealing with efficient loading of instructions in branching situations. Itanium can address up to 16 GB of main memory. Intel introduced its popular "core" micro architecture in 2006.

The assembly language of an architecture reveals significant information about that architecture. To compare MARIE's architecture to Intel's architecture, let's return to Example 4.2, the MARIE program that used a loop to add five numbers. Let's rewrite the program in x86 assembly language, as seen in Example 4.6. Note the addition of a `Data` segment directive and a `Code` segment directive.

≡   **EXAMPLE 4.6**   A program using a loop to add five numbers written to run on a Pentium.

```
        .DATA
Num1    DD    10              ; Num1 is initialized to 10
        DD    15              ; Each word following Num1 is initialized
        DD    20
        DD    25
        DD    30
Num     DB    5               ; Initialize the loop counter
Sum     DB    0               ; Initialize the Sum
```

```
        .CODE
        LEA   EBX, Num1        ; Load the address of Num1 into EBX
        MOV   ECX, Num         ; Set the loop counter
        MOV   EAX, 0           ; Initialize the sum
        MOV   EDI, 0           ; Initialize the offset (of which number to add)
Start:  ADD   EAX, [EBX+EDI*4] ; Add the EBXth number to EAX
        INC   EDI              ; Increment the offset by 1
        DEC   ECX              ; Decrement the loop counter by 1
        JG    Start            ; If counter is greater than 0, return to Start
        MOV   Sum, EAX         ; Store the result in Sum
```

We can make this program easier to read (which also makes it look less like MARIE's assembly language) by using the loop statement. Syntactically, the loop instruction resembles a jump instruction, in that it requires a label. This loop can be rewritten as follows:

```
        MOV   ECX, Num          ; Set the counter
Start:  ADD   EAX, [EBX + EDI * 4]
        INC   EDI
        LOOP  Start
        MOV   Sum, EAX
```

The loop statement in x86 assembly is similar to the do...while construct in C, C++, or Java. The difference is that there is no explicit loop variable—the ECX register is assumed to hold the loop counter. Upon execution of the loop instruction, the processor decreases ECX by one, and then tests ECX to see if it is equal to 0. If it is not 0, control jumps to Start; if it is 0, the loop terminates. The loop statement is an example of the types of instructions that can be added to make the programmer's job easier, but aren't necessary for getting the job done.

4.14.2 MIPS Architectures

The MIPS family of CPUs has been one of the most successful and flexible designs of its class. The MIPS R3000, R4000, R5000, R8000, and R10000 are some of the many registered trademarks belonging to MIPS Technologies, Inc. MIPS chips are used in embedded systems, in addition to computers (such as Silicon Graphics machines) and various computerized toys (Nintendo and Sony use the MIPS CPU in many of their products). Cisco, a very successful manufacturer of Internet routers, uses MIPS CPUs as well.

The first MIPS ISA was MIPS I, followed by MIPS II through MIPS V. The current ISAs are referred to as MIPS32 (for the 32-bit architecture) and MIPS64 (for the 64-bit architecture). Our discussion in this section focuses on MIPS32. It is important to note that MIPS Technologies made a decision similar to that of Intel—as the ISA evolved, backward compatibility was maintained. And, like Intel, each new version of the ISA included operations and instructions to improve efficiency and handle floating-point values. The new MIPS32 and MIPS64 architectures have significant improvements in VLSI technology and CPU organization. The end result is notable cost and performance benefits over traditional architectures.

Like IA-32 and IA-64, the MIPS ISA embodies a rich set of instructions, including arithmetic, logical, comparison, data transfer, branching, jumping, shifting, and multimedia instructions. MIPS is a **load/store architecture**, which means that all instructions (other than the load and store instructions) must use registers as operands (no memory operands are allowed). MIPS32 has 168 32-bit instructions, but many are similar. For example, there are six different add instructions, all of which add numbers, but they vary in the operands and registers used. This idea of having multiple instructions for the same operation is common in assembly language instruction sets. Another common instruction is the MIPS NOP instruction, which does nothing except eat up time (NOPs are used in pipelining, as we see in Chapter 5).

The CPU in a MIPS32 architecture has thirty-two 32-bit general-purpose registers numbered r0, through r31. (Two of these have special functions: r0 is hardwired to a value of 0, and r31 is the default register for use with certain instructions, which means it does not have to be specified in the instruction itself.) In MIPS assembly, these 32 general-purpose registers are designated $0, $1, . . . , $31. Register 1 is reserved, and registers 26 and 27 are used by the operating system kernel. Registers 28, 29, and 30 are pointer registers. The remaining registers can be referred to by number, using the naming convention shown in Table 4.10. For example, you can refer to register 8 as $8 or as $t0.

There are two special-purpose registers, HI and LO, which hold the results of certain integer operations. Of course, there is a PC register as well, giving a total of three special-purpose registers.

MIPS32 has thirty-two 32-bit floating-point registers that can be used in single-precision floating-point operations (with double-precision values being stored in even–odd pairs of these registers). There are four special-purpose floating-point control registers for use by the floating-point unit.

Let's continue our comparison by writing the programs from Examples 4.2 and 4.6 in MIPS32 assembly language.

≡ **EXAMPLE 4.7**

. . .

```
            .data
    # $t0 = sum
    # $t1 = loop counter Ctr
Value:      .word 10,15,20,25,30
            Sum = 0
            Ctr = 5
```

Naming Convention	Register Number	Value Put in Register
$v0-$v1	2-3	Results, expressions
$a0-$a3	4-7	Arguments
$t0-$t7	8-15	Temporary values
$s0-$s7	16-23	Saved values
$t8-$t9	24-25	More temporary values

TABLE 4.10   MIPS32 Register Naming Convention

```
        .text
        .global main            # Declaration of main as a global variable
main:   lw $t0, Sum             # Initialize register containing sum to zero
        lw $t1, Ctr             # Copy Ctr value to register
        la $t2, value           # $t2 is a pointer to current value
while:  blez $t1, end_while     # Done with loop if counter <= 0
        lw $t3, 0($t2)          # Load value offset of 0 from pointer
        add $t0, $t0, $t3       # Add value to sum
        addi $t2, $t2, 4        # Go to next data value
        sub $t1, $t1, 1         # Decrement Ctr
        b while                 # Return to top of loop
        la $t4, sum             # Load the address of sum into register
        sw $t0, 0($t4)          # Write the sum into memory location sum

        . . .
```

This is similar to the Intel code in that the loop counter is copied into a register, decremented during each interation of the loop, and then checked to see if it is less than or equal to 0. The register names may look formidable, but they are actually easy to work with once you understand the naming conventions.

If you have enjoyed working with the MARIE simulator and are ready to try your hand at a more complex machine, you will surely find the **MIPS Assembler and Runtime Simulator**, **MARS**, to your liking. MARS is a Java-based MIPS R2000 and R3000 simulator designed especially for undergraduate education by Kenneth Vollmar and Pete Sanderson. It provides all the essential MIPS machine functions in a useful and inviting graphical interface. **SPIM** is another popular MIPS simulator widely used by students and professionals alike. Both of these simulators are freely downloadable and can run on Windows XP and Windows Vista, Mac OS X, Unix, and Linux. For more information, see the references at the end of this chapter.

If you examine Examples 4.2, 4.6, and 4.7, you can see that the instructions are quite similar. Registers are referenced in different ways and have different names, but the underlying operations are basically the same. Some assembly languages have larger instruction sets, allowing the programmer more choices for coding various algorithms. But, as we have seen with MARIE, a large instruction set is not absolutely necessary to get the job done.

CHAPTER SUMMARY

This chapter presented a simple architecture, MARIE, as a means to understand the basic fetch–decode–execute cycle and how computers actually operate. This simple architecture was combined with an ISA and an assembly language, with emphasis given to the relationship between these two, allowing us to write programs for MARIE.

The CPU is the principal component in any computer. It consists of a datapath (registers and an ALU connected by a bus) and a control unit responsible for sequencing the operations and data movement and creating the timing signals. All components use these timing signals to work in unison. The I/O subsystem accommodates getting data into the computer and back out to the user.

MARIE is a very simple architecture designed specifically to illustrate the concepts in this chapter without getting bogged down in too many technical details. MARIE has 4K 16-bit words of main memory, uses 16-bit instructions, and has seven registers. There is only one general-purpose register, the AC. Instructions for MARIE use 4 bits for the opcode and 12 bits for an address. Register transfer notation was introduced as a symbolic means for examining what each instruction does at the register level.

The fetch–decode–execute cycle consists of the steps a computer follows to run a program. An instruction is fetched and then decoded, any required operands are then fetched, and finally the instruction is executed. Interrupts are processed at the beginning of this cycle, returning to normal fetch–decode–execute status when the interrupt handler is finished.

A machine language is a list of binary numbers representing executable machine instructions, whereas an assembly language program uses symbolic instructions to represent the numerical data from which the machine language program is derived. Assembly language *is* a programming language, but does not offer a large variety of data types or instructions for the programmer. Assembly language programs represent a lower-level method of programming.

You would probably agree that programming in MARIE's assembly language is, at the very least, quite tedious. We saw that most branching must be explicitly performed by the programmer, using jump and branch statements. It is also a large step from this assembly language to a high-level language such as C++ or Ada. However, the assembler is one step in the process of converting source code into something the machine can understand. We have not introduced assembly language with the expectation that you will rush out and become an assembly language programmer. Rather, this introduction should serve to give you a better understanding of machine architecture and how instructions and architectures are related. Assembly language should also give you a basic idea of what is going on behind the scenes in high-level C++, Java, or Ada programs. Although assembly language programs are easier to write for x86 and MIPS than for MARIE, all are more difficult to write and debug than high-level language programs.

Intel and MIPS assembly languages and architectures were introduced (but by no means covered in detail) for two reasons. First, it is interesting to compare the various architectures, starting with a very simple architecture and continuing with much more complex and involved architectures. You should focus on the differences as well as the similarities. Second, although the Intel and MIPS assembly languages looked different from MARIE's assembly language, they are actually quite comparable. Instructions access memory and registers, and there are instructions for moving data, performing arithmetic and logic operations, and branching. MARIE's instruction set is very simple and lacks many of the "programmer friendly" instructions that are present in both Intel and MIPS instruction sets. Intel and MIPS also have more registers than MARIE. Aside from the number of instructions and the number of registers, the languages function almost identically.

FURTHER READING

A MARIE assembly simulator is available on this text's home page. This simulator assembles and executes your MARIE programs.

For more detailed information on CPU organization and ISAs, you are referred to the Tanenbaum (2013) and Stallings (2013) books. Mano and Ciletti (2006) contains instructional examples of microprogrammed architectures. Wilkes, Renwick, and Wheeler (1958) is an excellent reference on microprogramming.

For more information regarding Intel assembly language programming, check out the Abel (2001), Dandamudi (1998), and Jones (2001) books. The Jones book takes a straightforward and simple approach to assembly language programming, and all three books are quite thorough. If you are interested in other assembly languages, you might refer to Struble (1975) for IBM assembly; Gill, Corwin, and Logar (1987) for Motorola; and SPARC International (1994) for SPARC. For a gentle introduction to embedded systems, try Williams (2000).

If you are interested in MIPS programming, Patterson and Hennessy (2008) give a very good presentation, and their book has a separate appendix with useful information. Donovan (1972) and Goodman and Miller (1993) also have good coverage of the MIPS environment. Kane and Heinrich (1992) wrote the definitive text on the MIPS instruction set and assembly language programming on MIPS machines. The MIPS home page also has a wealth of information.

To read more about Intel architectures, please refer to Alpert and Avnon (1993), Brey (2003), Dulon (1998), and Samaras (2001). Perhaps one of the best books on the subject of the Pentium architecture is Shanley (1998). Motorola, UltraSparc, and Alpha architectures are discussed in Circello and colleagues (1995), Horel and Lauterbach (1999), and McLellan (1995), respectively. For a more general introduction to advanced architectures, see Tabak (1994).

If you wish to learn more about the SPIM simulator for MIPS, see Patterson and Hennessy (2008) or the SPIM home page, which has documentation, manuals, and various other downloads. The excellent MARS MIPS Simulator can be downloaded from Vollmar's page at Missouri State University, at http://courses .missouristate.edu/KenVollmar/MARS/. Waldron (1999) is an excellent introduction to RISC assembly language programming and MIPS as well.

REFERENCES

Abel, P. *IBM PC Assembly Language and Programming,* 5th ed. Upper Saddle River, NJ: Prentice Hall, 2001.

Alpert, D., & Avnon, D. "Architecture of the Pentium Microprocessor." *IEEE Micro 13,* April 1993, pp. 11–21.

Brey, B. *Intel Microprocessors 8086/8088, 80186/80188, 80286, 80386, 80486 Pentium, and Pentium Pro Processor, Pentium II, Pentium III, and Pentium IV: Architecture, Programming, and Interfacing*, 6th ed. Englewood Cliffs, NJ: Prentice Hall, 2003.

Circello, J., Edgington, G., McCarthy, D., Gay, J., Schimke, D., Sullivan, S., Duerden, R., Hinds, C., Marquette, D., Sood, L., Crouch, A., & Chow, D. "The Superscalar Architecture of the MC68060." *IEEE Micro 15,* April 1995, pp. 10–21.

Dandamudi, S. P. *Introduction to Assembly Language Programming—From 8086 to Pentium Processors.* New York: Springer Verlag, 1998.

Donovan. J. J. *Systems Programming.* New York: McGraw-Hill, 1972.

Dulon, C. "The IA-64 Architecture at Work." *COMPUTER 31,* July 1998, pp. 24–32.

Gill, A., Corwin, E., & Logar, A. *Assembly Language Programming for the 68000.* Upper Saddle River, NJ: Prentice Hall, 1987.

Goodman, J., & Miller, K. *A Programmer's View of Computer Architecture.* Philadelphia: Saunders College Publishing, 1993.

Horel, T., & Lauterbach, G. "UltraSPARC III: Designing Third Generation 64-Bit Performance." *IEEE Micro 19,* May/June 1999, pp. 73–85.

Jones, W. *Assembly Language for the IBM PC Family,* 3rd ed. El Granada, CA: Scott Jones, Inc., 2001.

Kane, G., & Heinrich, J. *MIPS RISC Architecture,* 2nd ed. Englewood Cliffs, NJ: Prentice Hall, 1992.

Mano, M., & Ciletti, M. *Digital Design,* 3rd ed. Upper Saddle River, NJ: Prentice Hall, 2006.

McLellan, E. "The Alpha AXP Architecture and 21164 Alpha Microprocessor." *IEEE Micro 15,* April 1995, pp. 33–43.

MIPS home page: *www.mips.com.*

Patterson, D. A., & Hennessy, J. L. *Computer Organization and Design: The Hardware/Software Interface*, 4th ed. San Mateo, CA: Morgan Kaufmann, 2008.

Samaras, W. A., Cherukuri, N., & Venkataraman, S. "The IA-64 Itanium Processor Cartridge." *IEEE Micro 21*, Jan/Feb 2001, pp. 82–89.

Shanley, T. *Pentium Pro and Pentium II System Architecture.* Reading, MA: Addison-Wesley, 1998.

SPARC International, Inc. *The SPARC Architecture Manual: Version 9.* Upper Saddle River, NJ: Prentice Hall, 1994.

SPIM home page: *www.cs.wisc.edu/~larus/spim.html.*

Stallings, W. *Computer Organization and Architecture*, 9th ed. Upper Saddle River, NJ: Prentice Hall, 2013.

Struble, G. W. *Assembler Language Programming: The IBM System/360 and 370*, 2nd ed. Reading, MA: Addison Wesley, 1975.

Tabak, D. *Advanced Microprocessors.* 2nd ed. New York: McGraw-Hill, 1994.

Tanenbaum, A. *Structured Computer Organization*, 6th ed. Upper Saddle River, NJ: Prentice Hall, 2013.

Waldron, J. *Introduction to RISC Assembly Language.* Reading, MA: Addison Wesley, 1999.

Wilkes, M. V., Renwick, W., & Wheeler, D. J. "The Design of the Control Unit of an Electronic Digital Computer." *Proceedings of IEEE 105,* 1958, pp. 121–128.

Williams, A. *Microcontroller Projects with Basic Stamps.* Gilroy, CA: R&D Books, 2000.

REVIEW OF ESSENTIAL TERMS AND CONCEPTS

1. What is the function of a CPU?

2. What purpose does a datapath serve?

3. What does the control unit do?

4. Where are registers located, and what are the different types?

5. How does the ALU know which function to perform?

6. Why is a bus often a communications bottleneck?

7. What is the difference between a point-to-point bus and a multipoint bus?

8. Why is a bus protocol important?

9. Explain the differences between data buses, address buses, and control buses.

10. What is a bus cycle?

11. Name three different types of buses and where you would find them.

12. What is the difference between synchronous buses and nonsynchronous buses?

13. What are the four types of bus arbitration?

14. Explain the difference between clock cycles and clock frequency.

15. How do system clocks and bus clocks differ?

16. What is the function of an I/O interface?

17. Explain the difference between memory-mapped I/O and instruction-based I/O.

18. What is the difference between a byte and a word? What distinguishes each?

19. Explain the difference between byte addressable and word addressable.

20. Why is address alignment important?

21. List and explain the two types of memory interleaving and the differences between them.

22. Describe how an interrupt works, and name four different types.

23. How does a maskable interrupt differ from a nonmaskable interrupt?

24. Why is it that if MARIE has 4K words of main memory, addresses must have 12 bits?

25. Explain the functions of all of MARIE's registers.

26. What is an opcode?

27. Explain how each instruction in MARIE works.

28. How does a machine language differ from an assembly language? Is the conversion one-to-one (one assembly instruction equals one machine instruction)?

29. What is the significance of RTN?

30. Is a microoperation the same thing as a machine instruction?

31. How does a microoperation differ from a regular assembly language instruction?

32. Explain the steps of the fetch–decode–execute cycle.

33. How does interrupt-driven I/O work?

34. Explain how an assembler works, including how it generates the symbol table, what it does with source and object code, and how it handles labels.

35. What is an embedded system? How does it differ from a regular computer?

36. Provide a trace (similar to the one in Figure 4.14) for Example 4.1.

37. Explain the difference between hardwired control and microprogrammed control.

38. What is a stack? Why is it important for programming?

39. Compare CISC machines to RISC machines.

40. How does Intel's architecture differ from MIPS?

41. Name four Intel processors and four MIPS processors.

EXERCISES

1. What are the main functions of the CPU?

2. How is the ALU related to the CPU? What are its main functions?

3. Explain what the CPU should do when an interrupt occurs. Include in your answer the method the CPU uses to detect an interrupt, how it is handled, and what happens when the interrupt has been serviced.

◆ **4.** How many bits would you need to address a 2M × 32 memory if

   a) the memory is byte addressable?

   b) the memory is word addressable?

5. How many bits are required to address a 4M × 16 main memory if

   a) main memory is byte addressable?

   b) main memory is word addressable?

6. How many bits are required to address a 1M × 8 main memory if

   a) main memory is byte addressable?

   b) main memory is word addressable?

7. Redo Example 4.1 using high-order interleaving instead of low-order interleaving.

8. Suppose we have 4 memory modules instead of 8 in Figures 4.6 and 4.7. Draw the memory modules with the addresses they contain using:

   a) High-order interleaving

   b) Low-order interleaving

9. How many 256x8 RAM chips are needed to provide a memory capacity of 4096 bytes?

   a) How many bits will each address contain?

   b) How many lines must go to each chip?

   c) How many lines must be decoded for the chip select inputs? Specify the size of the decoder.

◆ **10.** Suppose that a 2M × 16 main memory is built using 256K × 8 RAM chips and memory is word addressable.

   a) How many RAM chips are necessary?

   b) If we were accessing one full word, how many chips would be involved?

   c) How many address bits are needed for each RAM chip?

   d) How many banks will this memory have?

   e) How many address bits are needed for all memory?

   f) If high-order interleaving is used, where would address 14 (which is E in hex) be located?

   g) Repeat exercise 9f for low-order interleaving.

11. Redo exercise 10 assuming a 16M × 16 memory built using 512K × 8 RAM chips.

12. Suppose we have 1G × 16 RAM chips that make up a 32G × 64 memory that uses high interleaving. (Note: This means that each word is 64 bits in size and there are 32G of these words.)

   a) How many RAM chips are necessary?

   b) Assuming four chips per bank, how many banks are required?

   c) How many lines must go to each chip?

   d) How many bits are needed for a memory address, assuming it is word addressable?

e) For the bits in part d, draw a diagram indicating how many and which bits are used for chip select, and how many and which bits are used for the address on the chip.

f) Redo this problem assuming that low-order interleaving is being used instead.

13. A digital computer has a memory unit with 24 bits per word. The instruction set consists of 150 different operations. All instructions have an operation code part (opcode) and an address part (allowing for only one address). Each instruction is stored in one word of memory.

a) How many bits are needed for the opcode?

b) How many bits are left for the address part of the instruction?

c) What is the maximum allowable size for memory?

d) What is the largest unsigned binary number that can be accommodated in one word of memory?

14. A digital computer has a memory unit with 32 bits per word. The instruction set consists of 110 different operations. All instructions have an operation code part (opcode) and two address fields: one for a memory address and one for a register address. This particular system includes eight general-purpose, user-addressable registers. Registers may be loaded directly from memory, and memory may be updated directly from the registers. Direct memory-to-memory data movement operations are not supported. Each instruction is stored in one word of memory.

a) How many bits are needed for the opcode?

b) How many bits are needed to specify the register?

c) How many bits are left for the memory address part of the instruction?

d) What is the maximum allowable size for memory?

e) What is the largest unsigned binary number that can be accommodated in one word of memory?

15. Assume a 2^{20} byte memory.

◆ a) What are the lowest and highest addresses if memory is byte addressable?

◆ b) What are the lowest and highest addresses if memory is word addressable, assuming a 16-bit word?

c) What are the lowest and highest addresses if memory is word addressable, assuming a 32-bit word?

16. Suppose the RAM for a certain computer has 256M words, where each word is 16 bits long.

a) What is the capacity of this memory expressed in bytes?

b) If this RAM is byte addressable, how many bits must an address contain?

c) If this RAM is word addressable, how many bits must an address contain?

17. You and a colleague are designing a brand new microprocessor architecture. Your colleague wants the processor to support 509 different instructions. You do not agree, and would like to have many fewer instructions. Outline the argument for a position paper to present to the management team that will make the final decision. Try to anticipate the argument that could be made to support the opposing viewpoint.

18. Given a memory of 2048 bytes consisting of several 64 × 8 RAM chips, and assuming byte-addressable memory, which of the following seven diagrams indicates the correct way to use the address bits? Explain your answer.

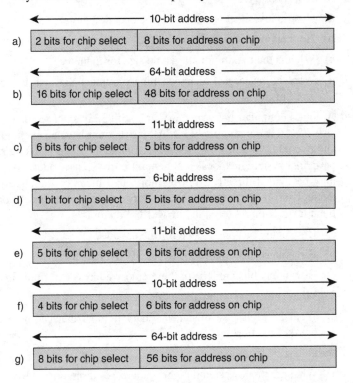

19. Explain the steps in the fetch–decode–execute cycle. Your explanation should include what is happening in the various registers.

20. Combine the flowcharts that appear in Figures 4.11 and 4.12 so that the interrupt checking appears at a suitable place.

21. Explain why, in MARIE, the MAR is only 12 bits wide and the AC is 16 bits wide. (Hint: Consider the difference between data and addresses.)

22. List the hexadecimal code for the following program (hand assemble it).

```
Hex Address    Label    Instruction
100                     LOAD A
101                     ADD ONE
102                     JUMP S1
103            S2,      ADD ONE
```

```
104                    STORE A
105                    HALT
106          S1,       ADD A
107                    JUMP S2
108          A,        HEX 0023
109          One,      HEX 0001
```

◆ **23.** What are the contents of the symbol table for the preceding program?

24. Consider the MARIE program below.

    a) List the hexadecimal code for each instruction.

    b) Draw the symbol table.

    c) What is the value stored in the AC when the program terminates?

```
Hex Address    Label     Instruction
100            Start,    LOAD A
101                      ADD B
102                      STORE D
103                      CLEAR
104                      OUTPUT
105                      ADDI D
106                      STORE B
107                      HALT
108            A,        HEX 00FC
109            B,        DEC 14
10A            C,        HEX 0108
10B            D,        HEX 0000
```

25. Consider the MARIE program below.

    a) List the hexadecimal code for each instruction.

    b) Draw the symbol table.

    c) What is the value stored in the AC when the program terminates?

```
Hex Address    Label     Instruction
200            Begin,    LOAD Base
201                      ADD Offs
202            Loop,     SUBT One
203                      STORE Addr
204                      SKIPCOND 800
205                      JUMP Done
206                      JUMPI Addr
207                      CLEAR
208            Done,     HALT
209            Base,     HEX 200
20A            Offs,     DEC 9
20B            One,      HEX 0001
20C            Addr,     HEX 0000
```

26. Given the instruction set for MARIE in this chapter, do the following.

Decipher the following MARIE machine language instructions (write the assembly language equivalent):

◆ **a)** `0010000000000111`

b) `1001000000001011`

c) `0011000000001001`

27. Write the assembly language equivalent of the following MARIE machine language instructions:

a) `0111000000000000`

b) `1011001100110000`

c) `0100111101001111`

28. Write the assembly language equivalent of the following MARIE machine language instructions:

a) `0000010111000000`

b) `0001101110010010`

c) `1100100101101011`

29. Write the following code segment in MARIE's assembly language:

```
if X > 1 then
   Y = X + X;
   X = 0;
endif;
Y = Y + 1;
```

30. Write the following code segment in MARIE's assembly language:

```
if x <= y then
   y = y + 1;
else if x != z
   then y = y - 1;
else z = z + 1;
```

31. What are the potential problems (perhaps more than one) with the following assembly language code fragment (implementing a subroutine) written to run on MARIE? The subroutine assumes the parameter to be passed is in the AC and should double this value. The Main part of the program includes a sample call to the subroutine. You can assume this fragment is part of a larger program.

```
Main,   Load   X
        Jump   Sub1
Sret,          Store X

        . . .

Sub1,   Add    X
        Jump   Sret
```

32. Write a MARIE program to evaluate the expression A × B + C × D.

33. Write the following code segment in MARIE assembly language:

```
X = 1;
while X < 10 do
    X = X + 1;
endwhile;
```

34. Write the following code segment in MARIE assembly language. (Hint: Turn the `for` loop into a `while` loop.)

```
Sum = 0;
for X = 1 to 10 do
    Sum = Sum + X;
```

35. Write a MARIE program using a loop that multiplies two positive numbers by using repeated addition. For example, to multiply 3 × 6, the program would add 3 six times, or 3 + 3 + 3 + 3 + 3 + 3.

36. Write a MARIE subroutine to subtract two numbers.

37. A linked list is a linear data structure consisting of a set of nodes, where each one except the last one points to the next node in the list. (Appendix A provides more information about linked lists.) Suppose we have the set of 5 nodes shown in the illustration below. These nodes have been scrambled up and placed in a MARIE program as shown below. Write a MARIE program to traverse the list and print the data in order as stored in each node.

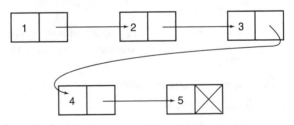

MARIE program fragment:

```
Address    Label
(Hex)
00D        Addr,  Hex ????   / Top of list pointer:
                             / You fill in the address of Node1
00E        Node2, Hex 0032   / Node's data is the character "2"
00F               Hex ????   / Address of Node3
010        Node4, Hex 0034   / Character "4"
011               Hex ????
012        Node1, Hex 0031   / Character "1"
013               Hex ????
014        Node3, Hex 0033   / Character "3"
015               Hex ????
016        Node5, Hex 0035   / Character "5"
017               Hex 0000   / Indicates terminal node
```

38. More registers appear to be a good thing, in terms of reducing the total number of memory accesses a program might require. Give an arithmetic example to support this statement. First, determine the number of memory accesses necessary using MARIE and the two registers for holding memory data values (AC and MBR). Then perform the same arithmetic computation for a processor that has more than three registers to hold memory data values.

39. MARIE saves the return address for a subroutine in memory, at a location designated by the JnS instruction. In some architectures, this address is stored in a register, and in many it is stored on a stack. Which of these methods would best handle recursion? Explain your answer. (Hint: Recursion implies many subroutine calls.)

40. Write a MARIE program that performs the three basic stack operations: push, peek, and pop (in that order). In the peek operation, output the value that's on the top of the stack. (If you are unfamiliar with stacks, see Appendix A for more information.)

41. Provide a trace (similar to the one in Figure 4.14) for Example 4.3.

42. Provide a trace (similar to the one in Figure 4.14) for Example 4.4.

43. Suppose we add the following instruction to MARIE's ISA:

IncSZ Operand

This instruction increments the value with effective address "Operand," and if this newly incremented value is equal to 0, the program counter is incremented by 1. Basically, we are incrementing the operand, and if this new value is equal to 0, we skip the next instruction. Show how this instruction would be executed using RTN.

44. Suppose we add the following instruction to MARIE's ISA:

JumpOffset X

This instruction will jump to the address calculated by adding the given address, X, to the contents of the accumulator. Show how this instruction would be executed using RTN.

45. Suppose we add the following instruction to MARIE's ISA:

JumpIOffset X

This instruction will jump to the address calculated by going to address X, then adding the value found there to the value in the AC. Show how this instruction would be executed using RTN.

46. Draw the connection of MARIE's PC to the datapath using the format shown in Figure 4.15.

47. The table below provides a summary of MARIE's datapath control signals. Using this information, Table 4.9, and Figure 4.20 as guides, draw the control logic for MARIE's Load instruction.

Register	Memory	MAR	PC	MBR	AC	IN	OUT	IR
Signals								
$P_2P_1P_0$ (Read) $P_5P_4P_3$ (Write)	000	001	010	011	100	101	110	111

48. The table in exercise 47 provides a summary of MARIE's datapath control signals. Using this information, Table 4.9, and Figure 4.20 as guides, draw the control logic for MARIE's JumpI instruction.

49. The table in exercise 47 provides a summary of MARIE's datapath control signals. Using this information, Table 4.9, and Figure 4.20 as guides, draw the control logic for MARIE's StoreI instruction.

50. Suppose some hypothetical system's control unit has a ring (cycle) counter consisting of some number of D flip-flops. This system runs at 1GHz and has a maximum of 10 microoperations/instruction.

   a) What is the maximum frequency of the output (number of signal pulses) output by each flip-flop?

   b) How long does it take to execute an instruction that requires only 4 micro-operations?

51. Suppose you are designing a hardwired control unit for a very small computerized device. This system is so revolutionary that the system designers have devised an entirely new ISA for it. Because everything is so new, you are contemplating including one or two extra flip-flops and signal outputs in the cycle counter. Why would you want to do this? Why would you not want to do this? Discuss the trade-offs.

52. Building on the idea presented in exercise 51, suppose that MARIE has a hardwired control unit and we decide to add a new instruction that requires 8 clock cycles to execute. (This is one cycle longer than the longest instruction, JnS.) Briefly discuss the changes that we would need to make to accommodate this new instruction.

53. Draw the timing diagram for MARIE's Load instruction using the format of Figure 4.16.

54. Draw the timing diagram for MARIE's Subt instruction using the format of Figure 4.16.

55. Draw the timing diagram for MARIE's AddI instruction using the format of Figure 4.16.

56. Using the coding given in Table 4.9, translate into binary the mnemonic microcode instructions given in Figure 4.23 for the fetch–decode cycle (the first nine lines of the table).

57. Continuing from exercise 56, write the microcode for the jump table for the MARIE instructions for Jump X, Clear, and AddI X. (Use all 1s for the Destination value.)

58. Using Figure 4.23 as a guide, write the binary microcode for MARIE's Load instruction. Assume that the microcode begins at instruction line number 0110000_2.

59. Using Figure 4.23 as a guide, write the binary microcode for MARIE's Add instruction. Assume that the microcode begins at instruction line number 0110100_2.

60. Would you recommend a synchronous bus or an asynchronous bus for use between the CPU and the memory? Explain your answer.

* **61.** Pick an architecture (other than those covered in this chapter). Do research to find out how your architecture deals with the concepts introduced in this chapter, as was done for Intel and MIPS.

62. Which control signals should contain a 1 for each step in executing the JumpI instruction?

Step	RTN	Time	P₅	P₄	P₃	P₂	P₁	P₀	Cᵣ	IncrPC	Mᵣ	M_w	L_ALT
Fetch	MAR ← PC	T_0											
	IR ← M[MAR]	T_1											
Decode IR[15-12]	PC ← PC + 1	T_2											
Get operand	MAR ← IR[11-0]	T_3											
Execute	MBR ← M[MAR]	T_4											
	PC ← MBR	T_5											

63. Which control signals should contain a 1 for each step in executing the StoreI instruction?

Step	RTN	Time	P₅	P₄	P₃	P₂	P₁	P₀	Cᵣ	IncrPC	Mᵣ	M_w	L_ALT
Fetch	MAR ← PC	T_0											
	IR ← M[MAR]	T_1											
	PC ← PC + 1	T_2											
Decode IR[15-12]	MAR ← IR[11-0]	T_3											
Get operand	MBR ← M[MAR]	T_4											
Execute	MAR ← MBR	T_5											
	MBR ← AC	T_6											
	M[MAR] ← MBR	T_7											
		T_8											

64. The PC ← PC + 1 microoperation is executed at the end of every fetch cycle (to prepare for the next instruction to be fetched). However, if we execute a Jump or a JumpI instruction, the PC overwrites the value in the PC with a new one, thus voiding out the microoperation that incremented the PC. Explain how the microprogram for MARIE might be modified to be more efficient in this regard.

TRUE OR FALSE

1. If a computer uses hardwired control, the microprogram determines the instruction set for the machine. This instruction set can never be changed unless the architecture is redesigned.

2. A branch instruction changes the flow of information by changing the PC.

3. Registers are storage locations within the CPU itself.

4. A two-pass assembler generally creates a symbol table during the first pass and finishes the complete translation from assembly language to machine instructions on the second.

5. The MAR, MBR, PC, and IR registers in MARIE can be used to hold arbitrary data values.

6. MARIE has a common bus scheme, which means a number of entities share the bus.

7. An assembler is a program that accepts a symbolic language program and produces the binary machine language equivalent, resulting in a one-to-one correspondence between the assembly language source program and the machine language object program.

8. If a computer uses microprogrammed control, the microprogram determines the instruction set for the machine.

9. The length of a word determines the number of bits necessary in a memory address.

10. If memory is 16-way interleaved, it means memory is implemented using 4 banks (because $2^4 = 16$).

CHAPTER 5

A Closer Look at Instruction Set Architectures

5.1 INTRODUCTION

We saw in Chapter 4 that machine instructions consist of opcodes and operands. The opcodes specify the operations to be executed; the operands specify register or memory locations of data. Why, when we have languages such as C++, Java, and Ada available, should we be concerned with machine instructions? When programming in a high-level language, we frequently have little awareness of the topics discussed in Chapter 4 (or in this chapter) because high-level languages hide the details of the architecture from the programmer. Employers frequently prefer to hire people with assembly language backgrounds not because they need an assembly language programmer, but because they need someone who can understand computer architecture to write more efficient and more effective programs.

In this chapter, we expand on the topics presented in the last chapter, the objective being to provide you with a more detailed look at machine instruction sets. We look at different instruction types and operand types, and how instructions access data in memory. You will see that the variations in instruction sets are integral in distinguishing different computer architectures. Understanding how instruction sets are designed and how they function can help you understand the more intricate details of the architecture of the machine itself.

5.2 INSTRUCTION FORMATS

We know that a machine instruction has an opcode and zero or more operands. In Chapter 4, we saw that MARIE had an instruction length of 16 bits and could have, at most, 1 operand. Encoding an instruction set can be done in a variety of ways. Architectures are differentiated from one another by the number of bits allowed per instruction (16, 32, and 64 are the most common), by the number of operands allowed per instruction, and by the types of instructions and data each can process. More specifically, instruction sets are differentiated by the following features:

- Operand storage (data can be stored in a stack structure or in registers or both)
- Number of explicit operands per instruction (zero, one, two, and three being the most common)
- Operand location (instructions can be classified as register-to-register, register-to-memory, or memory-to-memory, which simply refer to the combinations of operands allowed per instruction)
- Operations (including not only types of operations but also which instructions can access memory and which cannot)
- Type and size of operands (operands can be addresses, numbers, or even characters)

5.2.1   Design Decisions for Instruction Sets

When a computer architecture is in the design phase, the instruction set format must be determined before many other decisions can be made. Selecting this format is often quite difficult because the instruction set must match the architecture, and the architecture, if well designed, could last for decades. Decisions made during the design phase have long-lasting ramifications.

Instruction set architectures are measured by several different factors, including (1) the amount of space a program requires; (2) the complexity of the instruction set, in terms of the amount of decoding necessary to execute an instruction, and the complexity of the tasks performed by the instructions; (3) the length of the instructions; and (4) the total number of instructions. Things to consider when designing an instruction set include the following:

- Short instructions are typically better because they take up less space in memory and can be fetched quickly. However, this limits the number of instructions, because there must be enough bits in the instruction to specify the number of instructions we need. Shorter instructions also have tighter limits on the size and number of operands.
- Instructions of a fixed length are easier to decode but waste space.
- Memory organization affects instruction format. If memory has, for example, 16- or 32-bit words and is not byte addressable, it is difficult to access a single character. For this reason, even machines that have 16-, 32-, or 64-bit words are often byte addressable, meaning every byte has a unique address even though words are longer than 1 byte.
- A fixed-length instruction does not necessarily imply a fixed number of operands. We could design an ISA with fixed overall instruction length, but allow the number of bits in the operand field to vary as necessary. (This is called an **expanding opcode** and is covered in more detail in Section 5.2.5.)

- There are many different types of addressing modes. In Chapter 4, MARIE used two addressing modes: direct and indirect; however, we see in this chapter that a large variety of addressing modes exist.

- If words consist of multiple bytes, in what order should these bytes be stored on a byte-addressable machine? Should the least significant byte be stored at the highest or lowest byte address? This little versus big endian debate is discussed in the following section.

- How many registers should the architecture contain, and how should these registers be organized? How should operands be stored in the CPU?

The little versus big endian debate, expanding opcodes, and CPU register organization are examined further in the following sections. In the process of discussing these topics, we also touch on the other design issues listed.

5.2.2 Little Versus Big Endian

The term **endian** refers to a computer architecture's "byte order," or the way the computer stores the bytes of a multiple-byte data element. Virtually all computer architectures today are byte addressable and must, therefore, have a standard for storing information requiring more than a single byte. Some machines store a two-byte integer, for example, with the least significant byte first (at the lower address), followed by the most significant byte. Therefore, a byte at a lower address has lower significance. These machines are called **little endian** machines. Other machines store this same two-byte integer with the most significant byte first, followed by the least significant byte. These are called **big endian** machines because they store the most significant bytes at the lower addresses. Most UNIX machines are big endian, whereas most PCs are little endian machines. Most newer RISC architectures are also big endian.

These two terms, little and big endian, are from the book *Gulliver's Travels*. You may remember the story in which the Lilliputians (the tiny people) were divided into two camps: those who ate their eggs by opening the "big" end (big endians) and those who ate their eggs by opening the "little" end (little endians). CPU manufacturers are also divided into two factions. For example, Intel has always done things the "little endian" way, whereas Motorola has always done things the "big endian" way. (It is also worth noting that some CPUs can handle both little and big endian.)

For example, consider an integer requiring 4 bytes:

Byte 3	Byte 2	Byte 1	Byte 0

On a little endian machine, this is arranged in memory as follows:

```
Base Address + 0 = Byte0
Base Address + 1 = Byte1
Base Address + 2 = Byte2
Base Address + 3 = Byte3
```

Address ⟶	00	01	10	11
Big Endian	12	34	56	78
Little Endian	78	56	34	12

FIGURE 5.1 The Hex Value 12345678 Stored in Both Big and Little Endian Formats

On a big endian machine, this long integer would then be stored as:

```
Base Address + 0 = Byte3
Base Address + 1 = Byte2
Base Address + 2 = Byte1
Base Address + 3 = Byte0
```

Let's assume that on a byte-addressable machine, the 32-bit hex value 12345678 is stored at address 0. Each digit requires a nibble, so one byte holds two digits. This hex value is stored in memory as shown in Figure 5.1, where the shaded cells represent the actual contents of memory. Example 5.1 shows multiple consecutive numbers stored in both formats.

EXAMPLE 5.1 Assume that a computer has 32-bit integers. Let's show how each of the values 0xABCD1234, 0x00FE4321, and 0x10 would be stored sequentially in memory, starting at address 0x200, assuming that each address holds 1 byte.

	Byte Order	
Address	Big Endian	Little Endian
0x200	AB	34
0x201	CD	12
0x202	12	CD
0x203	34	AB
0x204	00	21
0x205	FE	43
0x206	43	FE
0x207	21	00
0x208	00	10
0x209	00	00
0x20A	00	00
0x20B	10	00

We notice when using big endian representation that the number 0xABCD1234 reads "normally" when we start at address 0x200; we see the byte AB, which is the high-order byte of the value, followed by CD, then 12, then 34. However, for the little endian representation of this number, address 0x200 holds the least significant byte, or 34. Note that we do NOT store the little endian number as 43, then 21, then DC, then BA; this is a reversal of the *digits*, not the bytes. Again, little and big endian refer to the *byte* ordering, not the digit ordering. Also note that we padded the final value with zeros to get 0x00000010; this was necessary to use the required 32 bits (or 8 hex digits).

There are advantages and disadvantages to each method, although one method is not necessarily better than the other. Big endian is more natural to most people and thus makes it easier to read hex dumps. By having the high-order byte come first, you can always test whether the number is positive or negative by looking at the byte at offset zero. (Compare this to little endian, where you must know how long the number is and then must skip over bytes to find the one containing the sign information.) Big endian machines store integers and strings in the same order and are faster in certain string operations. Most bitmapped graphics are mapped with a "most significant bit on the left" scheme, which means working with graphical elements larger than one byte can be handled by the architecture itself. This is a performance limitation for little endian computers because they must continually reverse the byte order when working with large graphical objects. When decoding compressed data encoded with such schemes as Huffman and LZW (discussed in Chapter 7), the actual codeword can be used as an index into a lookup table if it is stored in big endian (this is also true for encoding).

However, big endian also has disadvantages. Conversion from a 32-bit integer address to a 16-bit integer address requires a big endian machine to perform addition. High-precision arithmetic on little endian machines is faster and easier. Most architectures using the big endian scheme do not allow words to be written on nonword address boundaries (for example, if a word is 2 or 4 bytes, it must always begin on an even-numbered byte address). This wastes space. Little endian architectures, such as Intel, allow odd address reads and writes, which makes programming on these machines much easier. If a programmer writes an instruction to read a nonzero value of the wrong word size, on a big endian machine it is always read as an incorrect value; on a little endian machine, it can sometimes result in the correct data being read. (Note that Intel finally has added an instruction to reverse the byte order within registers.)

Computer networks are big endian, which means that when little endian computers are going to pass integers over the network (network device addresses, for example), they need to convert them to network byte order. Likewise, when they receive integer values over the network, they need to convert them back to their own native representation.

Although you may not be familiar with this little versus big endian debate, it is important to many current software applications. Any program that writes data to or reads data from a file must be aware of the byte ordering on the particular machine. For example, the Windows BMP graphics format was developed on a little endian machine, so to view BMPs on a big endian machine, the application used to view them must first reverse the byte order. Software designers of popular software are well aware of these byte-ordering issues. For example, Adobe Photoshop uses big endian, GIF is little endian, JPEG is big endian, MacPaint is big endian, PC Paintbrush is little endian, RTF by Microsoft is little endian, and Sun raster files are big endian. Some applications support both formats: Microsoft WAV and AVI files, TIF files, and XWD (X Windows Dump) support both, typically by encoding an identifier into the file.

5.2.3 Internal Storage in the CPU: Stacks Versus Registers

Once byte ordering in memory is determined, the hardware designer must make some decisions on how the CPU should store data. This is the most basic means to differentiate ISAs. There are three choices:

1. A stack architecture

2. An accumulator architecture

3. A general-purpose register (GPR) architecture

Stack architectures use a stack to execute instructions, and the operands are (implicitly) found on top of the stack. Even though stack-based machines have good code density and a simple model for evaluation of expressions, a stack cannot be accessed randomly, which makes it difficult to generate efficient code. In addition, the stack becomes a bottleneck during execution. **Accumulator architectures** such as MARIE, with one operand implicitly in the accumulator, minimize the internal complexity of the machine and allow for very short instructions. But because the accumulator is only temporary storage, memory traffic is very high. **General-purpose register architectures**, which use sets of general-purpose registers, are the most widely accepted models for machine architectures today. These register sets are faster than memory, easy for compilers to deal with, and can be used very effectively and efficiently. In addition, hardware prices have decreased significantly, making it possible to add a large number of registers at a minimal cost. If memory access is fast, a stack-based design may be a good idea; if memory is slow, it is often better to use registers. These are the reasons most computers over the past 10 years have been general-register based. However, because all operands must be named, using registers results in longer instructions, causing longer fetch and decode times. (A very important goal for ISA designers is short instructions.) Designers choosing an ISA must decide which will work best in a particular environment and examine the trade-offs carefully.

The general-purpose architecture can be broken into three classifications, depending on where the operands are located. **Memory-memory** architectures may have two or three operands in memory, allowing an instruction to perform an operation without requiring any operand to be in a register. **Register-memory** architectures require a mix, where at least one operand is in a register and one is in memory. **Load-store** architectures require data to be moved into registers before any operations on those data are performed. Intel and Motorola are examples of register-memory architectures; Digital Equipment's VAX architecture allows memory-memory operations; and SPARC, MIPS, Alpha, and the PowerPC are all load-store machines.

Given that most architectures today are GPR based, we now examine two major instruction set characteristics that divide general-purpose register architectures. Those two characteristics are the number of operands and how the operands are addressed. In Section 5.2.4, we look at the instruction length and number of operands an instruction can have. (Two or three operands are the most common for GPR architectures, and we compare these to zero- and one-operand architectures.) We then investigate instruction types. Finally, in Section 5.4, we investigate the various addressing modes available.

5.2.4   Number of Operands and Instruction Length

The traditional method for describing a computer architecture is to specify the maximum number of operands, or addresses, contained in each instruction. This has a direct effect on the length of the instruction itself. MARIE uses a fixed-length instruction with a 4-bit opcode and a 12-bit operand. Instructions on current architectures can be formatted in two ways:

- **Fixed length**—Wastes space but is fast and results in better performance when instruction-level pipelining is used, as we see in Section 5.5.
- **Variable length**—More complex to decode but saves storage space.

Typically, the real-life compromise involves using two to three instruction lengths, which provides bit patterns that are easily distinguishable and simple to decode. The instruction length must also be compared to the word length on the machine. If the instruction length is exactly equal to the word length, the instructions align perfectly when stored in main memory. Instructions always need to be word aligned for addressing reasons. Therefore, instructions that are half, quarter, double, or triple the actual word size can waste space. Variable length instructions are clearly not the same size and need to be word aligned, resulting in loss of space as well.

The most common instruction formats include zero, one, two, or three operands. We saw in Chapter 4 that some instructions for MARIE have no operands, whereas others have one operand. Arithmetic and logic operations typically have two operands, but can be executed with one operand (as we saw in MARIE), if the accumulator is implicit. We can extend this idea to three operands if we consider the final destination as a third operand. We can also use a stack that allows us to have zero-operand instructions. The following are some common instruction formats:

- **OPCODE only** (zero addresses)
- **OPCODE + 1 Address** (usually a memory address)
- **OPCODE + 2 Addresses** (usually registers, or one register and one memory address)
- **OPCODE + 3 Addresses** (usually registers, or combinations of registers and memory)

All architectures have a limit on the maximum number of operands allowed per instruction. For example, in MARIE, the maximum was one, although some instructions had no operands (Halt and Skipcond). We mentioned that zero-, one-, two-, and three-operand instructions are the most common. One-, two-, and even three-operand instructions are reasonably easy to understand; an entire ISA built on zero-operand instructions can, at first, be somewhat confusing.

Machine instructions that have no operands must use a stack (the last-in, first-out data structure, introduced in Chapter 4 and described in detail in Appendix A, where all insertions and deletions are made from the top) to perform those operations that logically require one or two operands (such as an Add). Instead of using general-purpose registers, a stack-based architecture stores the operands on the top of the stack, making the top element accessible to the CPU. (Note that one of the most important data structures in machine architectures is the stack. Not only does this structure provide an efficient means of storing intermediate data values during complex calculations, but it also provides an efficient method for passing parameters during procedure calls as well as a means to save local block structure and define the scope of variables and subroutines.)

In architectures based on stacks, most instructions consist of opcodes only; however, there are special instructions (those that add elements to and remove elements from the stack) that have just one operand. Stack architectures need a push instruction and a pop instruction, each of which is allowed one operand. Push X places the data value found at memory location X onto the stack; Pop X removes the top element in the stack and stores it at location X. Only certain instructions are allowed to access memory; all others must use the stack for any operands required during execution.

For operations requiring two operands, the top two elements of the stack are used. For example, if we execute an Add instruction, the CPU adds the top two elements of the stack, popping them both and then pushing the sum onto the top of the stack. For noncommutative operations such as subtraction, the top stack element is subtracted from the next-to-the-top element, both are popped, and the result is pushed onto the top of the stack.

This stack organization is very effective for evaluating long arithmetic expressions written in **reverse Polish notation** (**RPN**), a mathematical notation made possible by logician Jan Lukasiewicz, a Polish mathematician who invented this notation in 1924. This representation places the operator after the operands in what is known as **postfix notation**, as compared to **infix notation**, which places the operator between operands, and **prefix notation** (**Polish**), which places the operator before the operands. For example:

$$X + Y \text{ is in infix notation}$$

$$+ \, X \, Y \text{ is in prefix notation}$$

$$X \, Y + \text{ is in postfix notation}$$

When using postfix (or RPN) notation, every operator follows its operands in any expression. If the expression contains more than one operation, the operator is given immediately after its second operand. The infix expression "3 + 4" is equivalent to the postfix expression "3 4 +"; the + operator is applied to the two operands 3 and 4. If the expression is more complex, we can still use this idea to convert from infix to postfix. We simply need to examine the expression and determine operator precedence.

$\equiv$ **EXAMPLE 5.2** Consider the infix expression $12/(4 + 2)$. We convert this to postfix as follows:

Expression	Explanation
12 / 4 2 +	The sum 4 + 2 is in parentheses and takes precedence; we replace it with 4 2 +
12 4 2 + /	The two new operands are 12 and the sum of 4 and 2; we place the first operand followed by the second, followed by the division operator

Therefore, the postfix expression 12 4 2 + / is equivalent to the infix expression $12/(4 + 2)$. Notice that there was no need to change the order of operands, and the need for parentheses to preserve precedence for the addition operator is eliminated.

$\equiv$ **EXAMPLE 5.3** Consider the following infix expression $(2 + 3) - 6/3$. We convert this to postfix as follows:

Expression	Explanation
2 3 + − 6/3	The sum 2 + 3 is in parentheses and takes precedence; we replace it with 2 3 +
2 3 + − 6 3 /	The division operator takes precedence, so we replace 6/3 with 6 3 /
2 3 + 6 3 / −	We wish to subtract the quotient of 6/3 from the sum of 2 + 3, so we move the − operator to the end

Therefore, the postfix expression 2 3 + 6 3 / − is equivalent to the infix expression $(2 + 3) - 6/3$.

All arithmetic expressions can be written using any of these representations. However, postfix representation combined with a stack of registers is the most efficient means to evaluate arithmetic expressions. In fact, some electronic calculators (such as Hewlett-Packard) require the user to enter expressions in postfix notation. With a little practice on these calculators, it is possible to rapidly evaluate long expressions containing many nested parentheses without ever stopping to think about how terms are grouped.

The algorithm to evaluate an RPN expression using a stack is quite simple: The expression is scanned from left to right, each operand (variable or constant) is pushed onto the stack, and when a binary operator is encountered, the top two operands are popped from the stack, the specified operation is performed on those operands, and then the result is pushed onto the stack.

≡ **EXAMPLE 5.4** Consider the RPN expression 10 2 3 + /. Using a stack to evaluate the expression and scanning left to right, we would first push 10 onto the stack, followed by 2, and then 3, to get:

```
 3 ◄──── Stack top
 2
10
```

The "+" operator is next, which pops 3 and 2 from the stack, performs the operation (2 + 3), and pushes 5 onto the stack, resulting in:

```
 5 ◄──── Stack top
10
```

The "/" operator then causes 5 and 10 to be popped from the stack, 10 is divided by 5, and then the result 2 is pushed onto the stack. (Note: For noncommutative operations such as subtraction and division, the top stack element is always the second operand.)

≡ **EXAMPLE 5.5** Consider the following infix expression:

$$(X + Y) \times (W - Z) + 2$$

This expression, written in RPN notation, is:

$$X\,Y + W\,Z - \times 2 +$$

To evaluate this expression using a stack, we push X and Y, add them (which pops them from the stack), and store the sum $(X + Y)$ on the stack. Then we push W and Z, subtract (which pops them both from the stack), and store the difference $(W - Z)$ on the stack. The $\times$ operator multiplies $(X + Y)$ by $(W - Z)$, removes both of these expressions from the stack, and places the product on the stack. We push 2 onto the stack, resulting in:

```
         2          ◄──── Stack top
(X + Y) × (W − Z)
```

The + operator adds the top two stack elements, pops them from the stack, and pushes the sum onto the stack, resulting in $(X + Y) \times (W - Z) + 2$ stored on the top of the stack.

≡ **EXAMPLE 5.6** Convert the RPN expression:

$$8\,6 + 4\,2 - /$$

to infix notation.

Recall that each operator follows its operands. Therefore, the "+" operator has operands 8 and 6, and the "−" operator has operands 4 and 2. The "/" operator must use the sum of 8 and 6 as the first operand and the difference of 4 and 2 as the second. We must use parentheses to express this in infix notation (to ensure that the addition and subtraction are performed before the division), resulting in the infix expression:

$$(8 + 6) / (4 - 2)$$

To illustrate the concepts of zero, one, two, and three operands, let's write a simple program to evaluate an arithmetic expression, using each of these formats.

EXAMPLE 5.7   Suppose we wish to evaluate the following expression:

$$Z = (X \times Y) + (W \times U)$$

Typically, when three operands are allowed, at least one operand must be a register, and the first operand is normally the destination. Using three-address instructions, the code to evaluate the expression for Z is written as follows:

```
Mult     R1, X, Y
Mult     R2, W, U
Add      Z, R2, R1
```

When using two-address instructions, normally one address specifies a register (two-address instructions seldom allow for both operands to be memory addresses). The other operand could be either a register or a memory address. Using two-address instructions, our code becomes:

```
Load     R1, X
Mult     R1, Y
Load     R2, W
Mult     R2, U
Add      R1, R2
Store    Z, R1
```

Note that it is important to know whether the first operand is the source or the destination. In the above instructions, we assume it is the destination. (This tends to be a point of confusion for those programmers who must switch between Intel assembly language and Motorola assembly language—Intel assembly specifies the first operand as the destination, whereas in Motorola assembly, the first operand is the source.)

Using one-address instructions (as in MARIE), we must assume that a register (normally the accumulator) is implied as the destination for the result of the instruction. To evaluate Z, our code now becomes:

```
Load    X
Mult    Y
Store   Temp
Load    W
Mult    U
Add     Temp
Store   Z
```

Note that as we reduce the number of operands allowed per instruction, the number of instructions required to execute the desired code increases. This is an example of a typical space/time trade-off in architecture design—shorter instructions but longer programs.

What does this program look like on a stack-based machine with zero-address instructions? Stack-based architectures use no operands for instructions such as Add, Subt, Mult, or Divide. We need a stack and two operations on that stack: Pop and Push. Operations that communicate with the stack must have an address field to specify the operand to be popped or pushed onto the stack (all other operations are zero address). Push places the operand on the top of the stack. Pop removes the stack top and places it in the operand. This architecture results in the longest program to evaluate our equation. Assuming that arithmetic operations use the two operands on the stack top, pop them, and push the result of the operation, our code is as follows:

```
Push    X
Push    Y
Mult
Push    W
Push    U
Mult
Add
Pop     Z
```

The instruction length is certainly affected by the opcode length and by the number of operands allowed in the instruction. If the opcode length is fixed, decoding is much easier. However, to provide for backward compatibility and flexibility, opcodes can have variable length. Variable length opcodes present the same problems as variable versus constant length instructions. A compromise used by many designers is expanding opcodes.

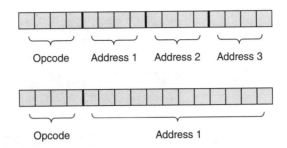

FIGURE 5.2   Two Possibilities for a 16-Bit Instruction Format

5.2.5   Expanding Opcodes

We have seen how the number of operands in an instruction is dependent on the instruction length; we must have enough bits for the opcode and for the operand addresses. However, not all instructions require the same number of operands.

Expanding opcodes represent a compromise between the need for a rich set of opcodes and the desire to have short opcodes, and thus short instructions. The idea is to make some opcodes short, but have a means to provide longer ones when needed. When the opcode is short, a lot of bits are left to hold operands (which means we could have two or three operands per instruction). When you don't need any space for operands (for an instruction such as Halt or because the machine uses a stack), all the bits can be used for the opcode, which allows for many unique instructions. In between, there are longer opcodes with fewer operands as well as shorter opcodes with more operands.

Consider a machine with 16-bit instructions and 16 registers. Because we now have a register set instead of one simple accumulator (as in MARIE), we need to use 4 bits to specify a unique register. We could encode 16 instructions, each with three register operands (which implies that any data to be operated on must first be loaded into a register), or use 4 bits for the opcode and 12 bits for a memory address (as in MARIE, assuming a memory of size 4K). However, if all data in memory is first loaded into a register in this register set, the instruction can select that particular data element using only 4 bits (assuming 16 registers). These two choices are illustrated in Figure 5.2.

But why limit the opcode to only 4 bits? If we allow the length of the opcode to vary, that changes the number of remaining bits that can be used for operand addresses. Using expanding opcodes, we could allow for opcodes of 8 bits that require two register operands; or we could allow opcodes of 12 bits that operate on one register; or we could allow for 16-bit opcodes that require no operands. These formats are illustrated in Figure 5.3.

The only issue is that we need a method to determine when the instruction should be interpreted as having a 4-bit, 8-bit, 12-bit, or 16-bit opcode. The trick is to use an "escape opcode" to indicate which format should be used. This idea is best illustrated with an example.

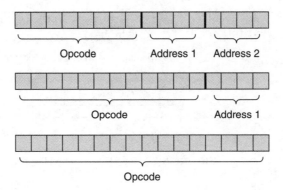

FIGURE 5.3 Three More Possibilities for a 16-Bit Instruction Format

≡ **EXAMPLE 5.8** Suppose we wish to encode the following instructions:

- 15 instructions with three addresses
- 14 instructions with two addresses
- 31 instructions with one address
- 16 instructions with zero addresses

Can we encode this instruction set in 16 bits? The answer is yes, as long as we use expanding opcodes. The encoding is as follows:

```
0000 R1    R2    R3    ⎫
...                    ⎬  15 three-address codes
1110 R1    R2    R3    ⎭
1111 - escape opcode

1111 0000 R1    R2     ⎫
...                    ⎬  14 two-address codes
1111 1101 R1    R2     ⎭
1111 1110 - escape opcode

1111 1110 0000 R1      ⎫
...                    ⎬  31 one-address codes
1111 1111 1110 R1      ⎭
1111 1111 1111 - escape opcode

1111 1111 1111 0000    ⎫
...                    ⎬  16 zero-address codes
1111 1111 1111 1111    ⎭
```

We can see the use of the escape opcode in the first group of three-address instructions. When the first 4 bits are 1111, that indicates that the instruction does not have three operands, but instead has two, one or none (which of these depends on the following groups of 4 bits). For the second group of two-address instructions, the escape opcode is 11111110 (any instruction with this opcode or higher cannot have more than one operand). For the third group of one-address instructions, the escape opcode is 111111111111 (instructions having this sequence of 12 bits have zero operands).

Although allowing for a wider variety of instructions, this expanding opcode scheme also makes the decoding more complex. Instead of simply looking at a bit pattern and deciding which instruction it is, we need to decode the instruction something like this:

```
if (leftmost four bits != 1111 ) {
    Execute appropriate three-address instruction}
else if (leftmost seven bits != 1111 111 ) {
    Execute appropriate two-address instruction}
else if (leftmost twelve bits != 1111 1111 1111 ) {
    Execute appropriate one-address instruction }
else {
    Execute appropriate zero-address instruction
}
```

At each stage, one spare code—the escape code—is used to indicate that we should now look at more bits. This is another example of the types of trade-offs hardware designers continually face: Here, we trade opcode space for operand space.

How do we know if the instruction set we want is possible when using expanding opcodes? We must first determine if we have enough bits to create the desired number of bit patterns. Once we determine this is possible, we can create the appropriate escape opcodes for the instruction set.

EXAMPLE 5.9 Refer back to the instruction set given in Example 5.8. To show that there are enough overall bit patterns, we need to calculate the number of bit patterns each instruction format requires.

- The first 15 instructions account for $15 * 2^4 * 2^4 * 2^4 = 15 * 2^{12} = 61440$ bit patterns. (Each register address can be one of 16 different bit patterns.)
- The next 14 instructions account for $14 * 2^4 * 2^4 = 14 * 2^8 = 3584$ bit patterns.
- The next 31 instructions account for $31 * 2^4 = 496$ bit patterns.
- The last 16 instructions account for 16 bit patterns.

If we add these up, we have $61440 + 3584 + 496 + 16 = 65536$. We have a total of 16 bits, which means we can create $2^{16} = 65536$ total bit patterns (an exact match with no wasted bit patterns).

≡ **EXAMPLE 5.10** Is it possible to design an expanding opcode to allow the following to be encoded in a 12-bit instruction? Assume that a register operand requires 3 bits and this instruction set does not allow memory addresses to be directly used in an instruction.

- 4 instructions with three registers
- 255 instructions with one register
- 16 instructions with zero registers

The first 4 instructions would account for $4 * 2^3 * 2^3 * 2^3 = 2^{11} = 2048$ bit patterns. The next 255 instructions would account for $255 * 2^3 = 2040$ bit patterns. The last 16 instructions would account for 16 bit patterns.

12 bits allow for a total of $2^{12} = 4096$ bit patterns. If we add up what each instruction format requires, we get $2048 + 2040 + 16 = 4104$. We need 4104 bit patterns to create this instruction set, but with 12 bits we only have 4096 bit patterns possible. Therefore, we cannot design an expanding opcode instruction set to meet the specified requirements.

Let's look at one last example, from start to finish.

≡ **EXAMPLE 5.11** Given 8-bit instructions, is it possible to use expanding opcodes to allow the following to be encoded? If so, show the encoding.

- 3 instructions with two 3-bit operands
- 2 instructions with one 4-bit operand
- 4 instructions with one 3-bit operand

First, we must determine if the encoding is possible.

- $3 * 2^3 * 2^3 = 3 * 2^6 = 192$
- $2 * 2^4 = 32$
- $4 * 2^3 = 32$

If we sum the required number of bit patterns, we get $192 + 32 + 32 = 256$. 8 bits in the instruction means a total of $2^8 = 56$ bit patterns, so we have an exact match (which means the encoding is possible, but every bit pattern will be used in creating it).

The encoding we can use is as follows:

```
00 xxx xxx  ⎫
            ⎬  3 instructions with two 3-bit operands
01 xxx xxx  ⎪
            ⎬
10 xxx xxx  ⎭

11 - escape opcode
```

```
1100 xxxx  ⎫
           ⎬  2 instructions with one 4-bit operand
1101 xxxx  ⎭

1110 - escape opcode

1111 - escape opcode

11100 xxx  ⎫
11101 xxx  ⎪
           ⎬  4 instructions with one 3-bit operand
11110 xxx  ⎪
11111 xxx  ⎭
```

5.3   INSTRUCTION TYPES

Most computer instructions operate on data; however, there are some that do not. Computer manufacturers regularly group instructions into the following categories: data movement, arithmetic, Boolean, bit manipulation (shift and rotate), I/O, transfer of control, and special purpose.

We discuss each of these categories in the following sections.

5.3.1   Data Movement

Data movement instructions are the most frequently used instructions. Data is moved from memory into registers, from registers to registers, and from registers to memory, and many machines provide different instructions depending on the source and destination. For example, there may be a MOVER instruction that always requires two register operands, whereas a MOVE instruction allows one register and one memory operand. Some architectures, such as RISC, limit the instructions that can move data to and from memory in an attempt to speed up execution. Many machines have variations of load, store, and move instructions to handle data of different sizes. For example, there may be a LOADB instruction for dealing with bytes and a LOADW instruction for handling words. Data movement instructions include MOVE, LOAD, STORE, PUSH, POP, EXCHANGE, and multiple variations on each of these.

5.3.2   Arithmetic Operations

Arithmetic operations include those instructions that use integers and floating-point numbers. Many instruction sets provide different arithmetic instructions for various data sizes. As with the data movement instructions, there are sometimes different instructions for providing various combinations of register and memory accesses in different addressing modes. Instructions may exist for arithmetic operations on both signed and unsigned numbers, as well as for operands in different bases. Many times, operands are implied in arithmetic instructions. For example, a multiply instruction may assume that the multiplicand is resident in a specific register so it need not be explicitly given in the instruction. This class of instructions also affects the flag register, setting the zero, carry, and overflow bits (to name only a few). Arithmetic instructions include ADD, SUBTRACT, MULTIPLY, DIVIDE, INCREMENT, DECREMENT, and NEGATE (to change the sign).

5.3.3 Boolean Logic Instructions

Boolean logic instructions perform Boolean operations, much in the same way that arithmetic operations work. These instructions allow bits to be set, cleared, and complemented. Logic operations are commonly used to control I/O devices. As with arithmetic operations, logic instructions affect the flag register, including the carry and overflow bits. There are typically instructions for performing AND, NOT, OR, XOR, TEST, and COMPARE.

5.3.4 Bit Manipulation Instructions

Bit manipulation instructions are used for setting and resetting individual bits (or sometimes groups of bits) within a given data word. These include both arithmetic and logical SHIFT instructions and ROTATE instructions, each to the left and to the right. Logical shift instructions simply shift bits to either the left or the right by a specified number of bits, shifting in zeros on the opposite end. For example, if we have an 8-bit register containing the value 11110000, and we perform a logical shift left by one bit, the result is 11100000. If our register contains 11110000 and we perform a logical shift right by one bit, the result is 01111000.

Arithmetic shift instructions, commonly used to multiply or divide by 2, treat data as signed two's complement numbers, and do not shift the leftmost bit, because this represents the sign of the number. On a right arithmetic shift, the sign bit is replicated into the bit position(s) to its right: If the number is positive, the leftmost bits are filled by zeros; if the number is negative, the leftmost bits are filled by ones. A right arithmetic shift is equivalent to division by 2. For example, if our value is 00001110 (+14) and we perform an arithmetic shift right by one bit, the result is 00000111 (+7). If the value is negative, such as 11111110 (−2), the result is 11111111 (−1). On a left arithmetic shift, bits are shifted left, and zeros are shifted in, but the sign bit does not participate in the shifting. An arithmetic shift left is equivalent to multiplication by 2. For example, if our register contains 00000011 (+3) and we perform an arithmetic shift left by one bit, the result is 00000110 (+6). If the register contains a negative number, such as 11111111 (−1), performing an arithmetic shift left by one bit yields 11111110 (−2). If the last bit shifted out (excluding the sign bit) does not match the sign, overflow or underflow occurs. For example, if the number is 10111111 (−65) and we do an arithmetic shift left by one bit, the result is 11111110 (−2), but the bit that was "shifted out" is a zero and does not match the sign; hence we have overflow.

Rotate instructions are simply shift instructions that shift in the bits that are shifted out—a circular shift basically. For example, on a rotate left one bit, the leftmost bit is shifted out and rotated around to become the rightmost bit. If the value 00001111 is rotated left by one bit, we have 00011110. If 00001111 is rotated right by one bit, we have 10000111. With rotate, we do not worry about the sign bit.

In addition to shifts and rotates, some computer architectures have instructions for clearing specific bits, setting specific bits, and toggling specific bits.

5.3.5 Input/Output Instructions

I/O instructions vary greatly from architecture to architecture. The input (or read) instruction transfers data from a device or port to either memory or a specific register. The output (or write) instruction transfers data from a register or memory to a specific port or device. There may be separate I/O instructions for numeric data and character data. Generally, character and string data use some type of block I/O instruction, automating the input of a string. The basic schemes for handling I/O are programmed I/O, interrupt-driven I/O, and DMA devices. These are covered in more detail in Chapter 7.

5.3.6 Instructions for Transfer of Control

Control instructions are used to alter the normal sequence of program execution. These instructions include branches, skips, procedure calls, returns, and program termination. Branching can be unconditional (such as jump) or conditional (such as jump on condition). Skip instructions (which can also be conditional or unconditional) are basically branch instructions with implied addresses. Because no operand is required, skip instructions often use bits of the address field to specify different situations (recall the Skipcond instruction used by MARIE). Some languages include looping instructions that automatically combine conditional and unconditional jumps.

Procedure calls are special branch instructions that automatically save the return address. Different machines use different methods to save this address. Some store the address at a specific location in memory, and others store it in a register, whereas still others push the return address on a stack.

5.3.7 Special-Purpose Instructions

Special-purpose instructions include those used for string processing, high-level language support, protection, flag control, word/byte conversions, cache management, register access, address calculation, no-ops, and any other instructions that don't fit into the previous categories. Most architectures provide instructions for string processing, including string manipulation and searching. No-op instructions, which take up space and time but reference no data and basically do nothing, are often used as placeholders for insertion of useful instructions at a later time, or in pipelines (see Section 5.5).

5.3.8 Instruction Set Orthogonality

Regardless of whether an architecture is hard-coded or microprogrammed, it is important that the architecture have a complete instruction set. However, designers must be careful not to add redundant instructions, as each instruction translates either to a circuit or a procedure. Therefore, each instruction should perform a unique function without duplicating any other instruction. Some people refer to this characteristic as **orthogonality**. In actuality, orthogonality goes one step further. Not only must the instructions be independent, but the instruction set must be consistent. For example, orthogonality addresses the degree to which operands and addressing modes are uniformly (and consistently) available with various operations. This means the addressing modes of the operands must be independent from the operands (addressing modes are discussed in detail in Section 5.4.2). Under orthogonality, the operand/opcode relationship cannot be restricted (there are no special registers for particular instructions). In addition, an instruction set with a multiply command and no divide instruction would not be orthogonal. Therefore, orthogonality encompasses both independence and consistency in the instruction set. An orthogonal instruction set makes writing a language compiler much easier; however, orthogonal instruction sets typically have quite long instruction words (the operand fields are long because of the consistency requirement), which translates to larger programs and more memory use.

5.4 ADDRESSING

Although addressing is an instruction design issue and is technically part of the instruction format, there are so many issues involved with addressing that it merits its own section. We now present the two most important of these addressing issues: the types of data that can be addressed and the various addressing modes. We cover only the fundamental addressing modes; more specialized modes are built using the basic modes in this section.

5.4.1 Data Types

Before we look at how data is addressed, we will briefly mention the various types of data an instruction can access. There must be hardware support for a particular data type if the instruction is to reference that type. In Chapter 2, we discussed data types, including numbers and characters. Numeric data consist of integers and floating-point values. Integers can be signed or unsigned and can be declared in various lengths. For example, in C++ integers can be *short* (16 bits), *int* (the word size of the given architecture), or *long* (32 bits). Floating-point numbers have lengths of 32, 64, or 128 bits. It is not uncommon for ISAs to have special instructions to deal with numeric data of varying lengths, as we have seen earlier. For example, there might be a MOVE for 16-bit integers and a different MOVE for 32-bit integers.

Nonnumeric data types consist of strings, Booleans, and pointers. String instructions typically include operations such as copy, move, search, or modify. Boolean operations include AND, OR, XOR, and NOT. Pointers are actually addresses in memory. Even though they are, in reality, numeric in nature, pointers are treated differently than integers and floating-point numbers. MARIE allows for this data type by using the indirect addressing mode. The operands in the instructions using this mode are actually pointers. In an instruction using a pointer, the operand is essentially an address and must be treated as such.

5.4.2 Address Modes

We saw in Chapter 4 that the 12 bits in the operand field of a MARIE instruction can be interpreted in two different ways: The 12 bits represent either the memory address of the operand or a pointer to a physical memory address. These 12 bits can be interpreted in many other ways, thus providing us with several different **addressing modes**. Addressing modes allow us to specify where the instruction operands are located. An addressing mode can specify a constant, a register, or a location in memory. Certain modes allow shorter addresses, and some allow us to determine the location of the actual operand, often called the **effective address** of the operand, dynamically. We now investigate the most basic addressing modes.

Immediate addressing is so named because the value to be referenced immediately follows the operation code in the instruction. That is to say, the data to be operated on is part of the instruction. For example, if the addressing mode of the operand is immediate and the instruction is Load 008, the numeric value 8 is loaded into the AC. The 12 bits of the operand field do not specify an address; they specify the actual operand the instruction requires. Immediate addressing is fast because the value to be loaded is included in the instruction. However, because the value to be loaded is fixed at compile time, it is not very flexible.

Direct addressing is so named because the value to be referenced is obtained by specifying its memory address directly in the instruction. For example, if the addressing mode of the operand is direct and the instruction is Load 008, the data value found at memory address 008 is loaded into the AC. Direct addressing is typically quite fast because, although the value to be loaded is not included in the instruction, it is quickly accessible. It is also much more flexible than immediate addressing because the value to be loaded is whatever is found at the given address, which may be variable.

In **register addressing**, a register, instead of memory, is used to specify the operand. This is similar to direct addressing, except that instead of a memory address, the address field contains a register reference. The contents of that register are used as the operand.

Indirect addressing is a powerful addressing mode that provides an exceptional level of flexibility. In this mode, the bits in the address field specify a memory address that is to be used as a pointer. The effective address of the operand is found by going to this memory address. For example, if the addressing mode of the operand is indirect and the instruction is Load 008, the data value found at memory address 0x008 is actually the effective address of the desired operand. Suppose we find the value 0x2A0 stored in location 0x008. 0x2A0 is the "real" address of the value we want. The value found at location 0x2A0 is then loaded into the AC.

In a variation on this scheme, the operand bits specify a register instead of a memory address. This mode, known as **register indirect addressing**, works exactly the same way as indirect addressing mode, except that it uses a register instead of a memory address to point to the data. For example, if the instruction is Load R1 and we are using register indirect addressing mode, we would find the effective address of the desired operand in R1.

In **indexed addressing** mode, an index register (either explicitly or implicitly designated) is used to store an offset (or displacement), which is added to the operand, resulting in the effective address of the data. For example, if the operand X of the instruction Load X is to be addressed using indexed addressing, assuming that R1 is the index register and holds the value 1, the effective address of the operand is actually $X + 1$. **Based addressing** mode is similar, except a base address register, rather than an index register, is used. In theory, the difference between these two modes is in how they are used, not how the operands are computed. An index register holds an index that is used as an offset, relative to the address given in the address field of the instruction. A base register holds a base address, where the address field represents a displacement from this base. These two addressing modes are quite useful for accessing array elements as well as characters in strings. In fact, most assembly languages provide special index registers that are implied in many string operations. Depending on the instruction-set design, general-purpose registers may also be used in this mode.

If **stack addressing mode** is used, the operand is assumed to be on the stack. We have already seen how this works in Section 5.2.4.

Many variations on the above schemes exist. For example, some machines have **indirect indexed addressing**, which uses both indirect and indexed addressing at the same time. There is also **base/offset addressing**, which adds an offset to a specific base register and then adds this to the specified operand, resulting in the effective address of the actual operand to be used in the instruction. There are also **auto-increment** and **auto-decrement** modes. These modes automatically increment or decrement the register used, thus reducing the code size, which can be extremely important in applications such as embedded systems. **Self-relative addressing** computes the address of the operand as an offset from the current instruction. Additional modes exist; however, familiarity with immediate, direct, register, indirect, indexed, and stack addressing modes goes a long way in understanding any addressing mode you may encounter.

Let's look at an example to illustrate these various modes. Suppose we have the instruction Load 800 and the memory and register R1 shown in Figure 5.4. Applying the various addressing modes to the operand field containing the 0x800, and assuming that R1 is implied in the indexed addressing mode, the value actually loaded into AC is seen in Table 5.1. The instruction Load R1, using register addressing mode, loads 0x800 into the accumulator and, using register indirect addressing mode, loads 0x900 into the accumulator.

We summarize the addressing modes in Table 5.2.

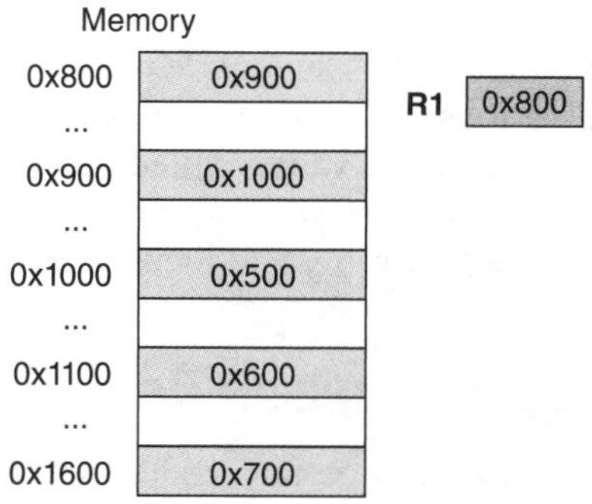

Memory

FIGURE 5.4   Contents of Memory When Load 800 Is Executed

Mode	Value Loaded into AC
Immediate	0x800
Direct	0x900
Indirect	0x1000
Indexed	0x700

TABLE 5.1   Results of Using Various Addressing Modes on Memory in Figure 5.4

Addressing Mode	To Find Operand
Immediate	Operand value present in the instruction
Direct	Effective address of operand in address field
Register	Operand value located in register
Indirect	Address field points to address of the actual operand
Register Indirect	Register contains address of actual operand
Indexed or Based	Effective address of operand generated by adding value in address field to contents of a register
Stack	Operand located on stack

TABLE 5.2   A Summary of the Basic Addressing Modes

How does the computer know which addressing mode is supposed to be used for a particular operand? We have already seen one way to deal with this issue. In MARIE, there are two JUMP instructions—a JUMP and a JUMPI. There are also two add instructions—an ADD and an ADDI. The instruction itself contains information the computer uses to determine the appropriate addressing mode. Many languages have multiple versions of the same instruction, where each variation indicates a different addressing mode and/or a different data size.

Encoding the address mode in the opcode itself works well if there is a small number of addressing modes. However, if there are many addressing modes, it is better to use a separate address specifier, a field in the instruction with bits to indicate which addressing mode is to be applied to the operands in the instruction.

The various addressing modes allow us to specify a much larger range of locations than if we were limited to using one or two modes. As always, there are trade-offs. We sacrifice simplicity in address calculation and limited memory references for flexibility and increased address range.

5.5 INSTRUCTION PIPELINING

By now you should be reasonably familiar with the fetch–decode–execute cycle presented in Chapter 4. Conceptually, each pulse of the computer's clock is used to control one step in the sequence, but sometimes additional pulses can be used to control smaller details within one step. Some CPUs break down the fetch–decode–execute cycle into smaller steps, where some of these smaller steps can be performed in parallel. This overlapping speeds up execution. This method, used by all current CPUs, is known as **pipelining**. Instruction pipelining is one method used to exploit **instruction-level parallelism (ILP)**. (Other methods include superscalar and VLIW.) We include it in this chapter because the ISA of a machine affects how successful instruction pipelining can be.

Suppose the fetch–decode–execute cycle were broken into the following "ministeps":

1. Fetch instruction
2. Decode opcode
3. Calculate effective address of operands
4. Fetch operands
5. Execute instruction
6. Store result

Pipelining is analogous to an automobile assembly line. Each step in a computer pipeline completes a part of an instruction. Like the automobile assembly line, different steps are completing different parts of different instructions in parallel. Each of the steps is called a **pipeline stage**. The stages are connected to form a pipe. Instructions enter at one end, progress through the various stages, and exit at the other end. The goal is to balance the time taken by each pipeline stage (i.e., more or less the same as the time taken by any other pipeline stage). If the stages are not balanced in time, after awhile, faster stages will be waiting on slower ones. To see an example of this imbalance in real life, consider the stages of doing laundry. If you have only one washer and one dryer, you usually end up waiting on the dryer. If you consider washing as the first stage and drying as the next, you can see that the longer drying stage causes clothes to pile up between the two stages. If you add folding clothes as a third stage, you soon realize that this stage would consistently be waiting on the other, slower stages.

Figure 5.5 provides an illustration of computer pipelining with overlapping stages. We see each clock cycle and each stage for each instruction (where S1

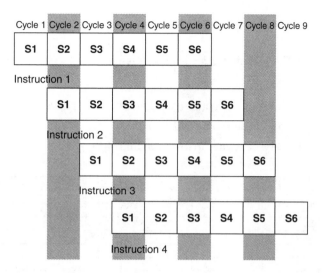

FIGURE 5.5 Four Instructions Going through a 6-Stage Pipeline

represents the fetch, S2 represents the decode, S3 is the calculate state, S4 is the operand fetch, S5 is the execution, and S6 is the store).

We see from Figure 5.5 that once instruction 1 has been fetched and is in the process of being decoded, we can start the fetch on instruction 2. When instruction 1 is fetching operands, and instruction 2 is being decoded, we can start the fetch on instruction 3. Notice that these events can occur in parallel, very much like an automobile assembly line.

Suppose we have a k-stage pipeline. Assume that the clock cycle time is t_p; that is, it takes t_p time per stage. Assume also that we have n instructions (often called **tasks**) to process. Task 1 (T_1) requires $k \times t_p$ time to complete. The remaining $n - 1$ tasks emerge from the pipeline one per cycle, which implies a total time for these tasks of $(n - 1)t_p$. Therefore, to complete n tasks using a k-stage pipeline requires:

$$(k \times t_p) + (n - 1)t_p = (k + n - 1)t_p$$

or $k + (n - 1)$ clock cycles.

Let's calculate the speedup we gain using a pipeline. Without a pipeline, the time required is nt_n cycles, where $t_n = k \times t_p$. Therefore, the speedup (time without a pipeline divided by the time using a pipeline) is:

$$\text{Speedup } S = \frac{nt_n}{(k + n - 1)t_p}$$

If we take the limit of this as n approaches infinity, we see that $(k + n - 1)$ approaches n, which results in a theoretical speedup of:

$$\text{Speedup} = \frac{k \times t_p}{t_p} = k$$

The theoretical speedup, k, is the number of stages in the pipeline.

Let's look at an example.

≡ **EXAMPLE 5.12** Suppose we have a 4-stage pipeline, where:

- S1 = fetch instruction
- S2 = decode and calculate effective address
- S3 = fetch operand
- S4 = execute instruction and store results

Time Period →	1	2	3	4	5	6	7	8	9	10	11	12	13
Instruction: 1	S1	S2	S3	S4									
2		S1	S2	S3	S4								
(branch) 3			S1	S2	S3	S4							
4				S1	S2	S3							
5					S1	S2							
6						S1							
8								S1	S2	S3	S4		
9									S1	S2	S3	S4	
10										S1	S2	S3	S4

FIGURE 5.6 Example Instruction Pipeline with Conditional Branch

We must also assume that the architecture provides a means to fetch data and instructions in parallel. This can be done with separate instruction and data paths; however, most memory systems do not allow this. Instead, they provide the operand in cache, which, in most cases, allows the instruction and operand to be fetched simultaneously. Suppose, also, that instruction I3 is a conditional branch statement that alters the execution sequence (so that instead of I4 running next, it transfers control to I8). This results in the pipeline operation shown in Figure 5.6.

Note that I4, I5, and I6 are fetched and proceed through various stages, but after the execution of I3 (the branch), I4, I5, and I6 are no longer needed. Only after time period 6, when the branch has executed, can the next instruction to be executed (I8) be fetched, after which the pipe refills. From time periods 6 through 9, only one instruction has executed. In a perfect world, for each time period after the pipe originally fills, one instruction should flow out of the pipeline. However, we see in this example that this is not necessarily true.

Please note that not all instructions must go through each stage of the pipe. If an instruction has no operand, there is no need for stage 3. To simplify pipelining hardware and timing, all instructions proceed through all stages, whether necessary or not.

From our preceding discussion of speedup, it might appear that the more stages that exist in the pipeline, the faster everything will run. This is true to a point. There is a fixed overhead involved in moving data from memory to registers. The amount of control logic for the pipeline also increases in size proportional to the number of stages, thus slowing down total execution. In addition, there are several conditions that result in "pipeline conflicts," which keep us from reaching the goal of executing one instruction per clock cycle. These include:

- Resource conflicts
- Data dependencies
- Conditional branch statements

Resource conflicts (also called **structural hazards**) are a major concern in instruction-level parallelism. For example, if one instruction is storing a value to memory while another is being fetched from memory, both need access to memory. Typically this is resolved by allowing the instruction execute to continue, while forcing the instruction fetch to wait. Certain conflicts can also be resolved by providing two separate pathways: one for data coming from memory and another for instructions coming from memory.

Data dependencies arise when the result of one instruction, not yet available, is to be used as an operand to a following instruction.

For example, consider the two sequential statements $X = Y + 3$ and $Z = 2 * X$.

Time Period →	1	2	3	4	5
$X = Y + 3$	fetch instruction	decode	fetch Y	execute & store X	
$Z = 2 * X$		fetch instruction	decode	fetch X	

The problem arises at time period 4. The second instruction needs to fetch X, but the first instruction does not store the result until the execution is finished, so X is not available at the beginning of the time period.

There are several ways to handle these types of pipeline conflicts. Special hardware can be added to detect instructions whose source operands are destinations for instructions farther up the pipeline. This hardware can insert a brief delay (typically a no-op instruction that does nothing) into the pipeline, allowing enough time to pass to resolve the conflict. Specialized hardware can also be used to detect these conflicts and route data through special paths that exist between various stages of the pipeline. This reduces the time necessary for the instruction to access the required operand. Some architectures address this problem by letting the compiler resolve the conflict. Compilers have been designed that reorder instructions, resulting in a delay of loading any conflicting data but having no effect on the program logic or output.

Branch instructions allow us to alter the flow of execution in a program, which, in terms of pipelining, causes major problems. If instructions are fetched one per clock cycle, several can be fetched and even decoded before a preceding instruction, indicating a branch, is executed. Conditional branching is particularly difficult to deal with. Many architectures offer **branch prediction**, using logic to make the best guess as to which instructions will be needed next (essentially, they are predicting the outcome of a conditional branch). Compilers try to resolve branching issues by rearranging the machine code to cause a **delayed branch**.

An attempt is made to reorder and insert useful instructions, but if that is not possible, no-op instructions are inserted to keep the pipeline full. Another approach used by some machines given a conditional branch is to start fetches on both paths of the branch and save them until the branch is actually executed, at which time the "true" execution path will be known.

In an effort to squeeze even more performance out of the chip, modern CPUs employ superscalar design (introduced in Chapter 4), which is one step beyond pipelining. Superscalar chips have multiple ALUs and issue more than one instruction in each clock cycle. The clock cycles per instruction can actually go below one. But the logic to keep track of hazards becomes even more complex; more logic is needed to schedule operations than to do them. Even with complex logic, it is hard to schedule parallel operations "on the fly."

The limits of dynamic scheduling have led machine designers to consider a very different architecture, **explicitly parallel instruction computers (EPIC)**, exemplified by the Itanium architecture discussed in Chapter 4. EPIC machines have very large instructions (recall that the instructions for the Itanium are 128 bits), which specify several operations to be done in parallel. Because of the parallelism inherent in the design, the EPIC instruction set is heavily compiler dependent (which means a user needs a sophisticated compiler to take advantage of the parallelism to gain significant performance advantages). The burden of scheduling operations is shifted from the processor to the compiler, and much more time can be spent in developing a good schedule and analyzing potential pipeline conflicts.

To reduce the pipelining problems caused by conditional branches, the IA-64 introduced **predicated** instructions. Comparison instructions set predicate bits, much like they set condition codes on the x86 machine (except that there are 64 predicate bits). Each operation specifies a predicate bit; it is executed only if the predicate bit equals 1. In practice, all operations are performed, but the result is stored into the register file only if the predicate bit equals 1. The result is that more instructions are executed, but we don't have to stall the pipeline waiting for a condition.

There are several levels of parallelism, varying from the simple to the more complex. All computers exploit parallelism to some degree. Instructions use words as operands (where words are typically 16, 32, or 64 bits in length), rather than acting on single bits at a time. More advanced types of parallelism require more specific and complex hardware and operating system support.

Although an in-depth study of parallelism is beyond the scope of this text, we would like to take a brief look at what we consider the two extremes of parallelism: program-level parallelism (PLP) and instruction-level parallelism (ILP). PLP actually allows parts of a program to run on more than one computer. This may sound simple, but it requires coding the algorithm correctly so that this parallelism is possible, in addition to providing careful synchronization between the various modules.

ILP involves the use of techniques to allow the execution of overlapping instructions. Essentially, we want to allow more than one instruction within a single program to execute concurrently. There are two kinds of ILP. The first type decomposes an instruction into stages and overlaps these stages. This is exactly what pipelining does. The second kind of ILP allows individual instructions to overlap (that is, instructions can be executed at the same time by the processor itself).

In addition to pipelined architectures, superscalar, superpipelining, and very long instruction word (VLIW) architectures exhibit ILP. Superscalar architectures (as you may recall from Chapter 4) perform multiple operations at the same time by employing parallel pipelines. Examples of superscalar architectures include IBM's PowerPC, Sun's UltraSparc, and DEC's Alpha. **Superpipelining** architectures combine superscalar concepts with pipelining, by dividing the pipeline stages into smaller pieces. The IA-64 architecture exhibits a **VLIW** architecture, which means each instruction can specify multiple scalar operations (the compiler puts multiple operations into a single instruction). Superscalar and VLIW machines fetch and execute more than one instruction per cycle.

5.6 REAL-WORLD EXAMPLES OF ISAS

Let's look at the two architectures we discussed in Chapter 4, Intel and MIPS, to see how the designers of these processors chose to deal with the issues introduced in this chapter: instruction formats, instruction types, number of operands, addressing, and pipelining. We'll also introduce the Java Virtual Machine to illustrate how software can create an ISA abstraction that completely hides the real ISA of the machine. Finally, we introduce the ARM architecture, one you may not have heard of but most likely use every day.

5.6.1 Intel

Intel uses a little endian, two-address architecture, with variable-length instructions. Intel processors use a register-memory architecture, which means all instructions can operate on a memory location, but the other operand must be a register. This ISA allows variable-length operations, operating on data with lengths of 1, 2, or 4 bytes.

The 8086 through the 80486 are single-stage pipeline architectures. The architects reasoned that if one pipeline was good, two would be better. The Pentium had two parallel five-stage pipelines, called the U pipe and the V pipe, to execute instructions. Stages for these pipelines include prefetch, instruction decode, address generation, execute, and write back. To be effective, these pipelines must be kept filled, which requires instructions that can be issued in parallel. It is the compiler's responsibility to make sure this parallelism happens. The Pentium II increased the number of stages to 12, including prefetch, length decode, instruction decode, rename/resource allocation, UOP scheduling/dispatch, execution, write back, and retirement. Most of the new stages were added to address Intel's MMX technology, an extension to the architecture that handles multimedia data. The Pentium III increased the stages to 14, and the Pentium IV to 24. Additional stages (beyond those introduced in this chapter) included stages for determining the length of the instruction, stages for creating microoperations, and stages to "commit" the instruction (make sure it executes and the results become permanent). The Itanium contains only a 10-stage instruction pipeline: Instruction pointer generation, fetch, rotate, expand, rename, word-line decode, register read, execute, exception detect, and write back.

Intel processors allow for the basic addressing modes introduced in this chapter, in addition to many combinations of those modes. The 8086 provided 17 different ways to access memory, most of which were variants of the basic modes. Intel's more current Pentium architectures include the same addressing modes as their predecessors, but also introduce new modes, mostly to help with maintaining backward compatibility. The IA-64 is surprisingly lacking in memory-addressing modes. It has only one: register indirect (with optional post-increment). This seems unusually limiting but follows the RISC philosophy. Addresses are calculated and stored in general-purpose registers. The more complex addressing modes require specialized hardware; by limiting the number of addressing modes, the IA-64 architecture minimizes the need for this specialized hardware.

5.6.2   MIPS

The MIPS architecture (which originally stood for "Microprocessor without Interlocked Pipeline Stages") is a little endian, word-addressable, three-address, fixed-length ISA. This is a load and store architecture, which means that only the load and store instructions can access memory. All other instructions must use registers for operands, which implies that this ISA needs a large register set. MIPS is also limited to fixed-length operations (those that operate on data with the same number of bytes).

Some MIPS processors (such as the R2000 and R3000) have five-stage pipelines (fetch, instruction decode, execute, memory access, and write back). The R4000 and R4400 have 8-stage superpipelines (instruction fetch first half, instruction fetch second half, register fetch, execution, data fetch first half, data fetch second half, tag check, and write back). The R10000 is quite interesting in that the number of stages in the pipeline depends on the functional unit through which the instruction must pass: there are five stages for integer instructions, six for load/store instructions, and seven for floating-point instructions. Both the MIPS 5000 and 10000 are superscalar.

MIPS has a straightforward ISA with five basic types of instructions: simple arithmetic (add, XOR, NAND, shift), data movement (load, store, move), control (branch, jump), multicycle (multiply, divide), and miscellaneous instructions (save PC, save register on condition). MIPS programmers can use immediate, register, direct, indirect register, base, and indexed addressing modes. However, the ISA itself provides for only one (base addressing). The remaining modes are provided by the assembler. The MIPS64 has two additional addressing modes for use in embedded systems optimizations.

The MIPS instructions in Chapter 4 have up to four fields: an opcode, two operand addresses, and one result address. Essentially three instruction formats are available: the I type (immediate), the R type (register), and the J type (jump).

R-type instructions have a 6-bit opcode, a 5-bit source register, a second 5-bit source register, a 5-bit target register, a 5-bit shift amount, and a 6-bit function. I-type instructions have a 6-bit operand, a 5-bit source register, a 5-bit target register or branch condition, and a 16-bit immediate branch displacement or address displacement. J-type instructions have a 6-bit opcode and a 26-bit target address.

The MIPS ISA is different from the Intel ISA partially because the design philosophies between the two are so different. Intel created its ISA for the 8086 when memory was very expensive, which meant designing an instruction set that would allow for extremely compact code. This is the main reason Intel uses variable-length instructions. The small set of registers used in the 8086 did not allow for much data to be stored in these registers; hence the two-operand instructions (as opposed to three as in MIPS). When Intel moved to the IA32 ISA, backward compatibility was a requirement for its large customer base.

5.6.3 Java Virtual Machine

Java, a language that is becoming quite popular, is very interesting in that it is platform independent. This means that if you compile code on one architecture (say a Pentium) and you wish to run your program on a different architecture (say a Sun workstation), you can do so without modifying or even recompiling your code.

The Java compiler makes no assumptions about the underlying architecture of the machine on which the program will run, such as the number of registers, memory size, or I/O ports, when you first compile your code. After compilation, however, to execute your program, you will need a **Java Virtual Machine** (**JVM**) for the architecture on which your program will run. (A **virtual machine** is a software emulation of a real machine.) The JVM is essentially a "wrapper" that goes around the hardware architecture and is very platform dependent. The JVM for a Pentium is different from the JVM for a Sun workstation, which is different from the JVM for a Macintosh, and so on. But once the JVM exists on a particular architecture, that JVM can execute any Java program compiled on any ISA platform. It is the JVM's responsibility to load, check, find, and execute bytecodes at run time. The JVM, although virtual, is a nice example of a well-designed ISA.

The JVM for a particular architecture is written in that architecture's native instruction set. It acts as an interpreter, taking Java bytecodes and interpreting them into explicit underlying machine instructions. **Bytecodes** are produced when a Java program is compiled. These bytecodes then become input for the JVM. The JVM can be compared to a giant switch (or case) statement, analyzing one bytecode instruction at a time. Each bytecode instruction causes a jump to a specific block of code, which implements the given bytecode instruction.

This differs significantly from other high-level languages with which you may be familiar. For example, when you compile a C++ program, the object code produced is for that particular architecture. (Compiling a C++ program results in an assembly language program that is translated to machine code.) If you want to run your C++ program on a different platform, you must recompile it for the target architecture. Compiled languages are translated into runnable files of the binary machine code by the compiler. Once this code has been generated, it can be run only on the target architecture. Compiled languages typically exhibit excellent performance and give very good access to the operating system. Examples of compiled languages include C, C++, Ada, FORTRAN, and COBOL.

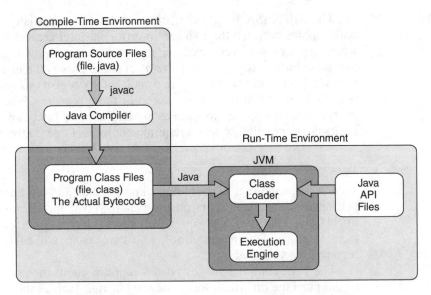

FIGURE 5.7 The Java Programming Environment

Some languages, such as LISP, PhP, Perl, Python, Tcl, and most BASIC languages, are interpreted. The source must be reinterpreted each time the program is run. The trade-off for the platform independence of interpreted languages is slower performance—usually by a factor of 100 times. (We will have more to say on this topic in Chapter 8.)

Languages that are a bit of both (compiled and interpreted) exist as well. These are often called **P-code languages**. The source code written in these languages is compiled into an intermediate form, called P-code, and the P-code is then interpreted. P-code languages typically execute from 5 to 10 times more slowly than compiled languages. Python, Perl, and Java are actually P-code languages, even though they are typically referred to as interpreted languages.

Figure 5.7 presents an overview of the Java programming environment.

Perhaps more interesting than Java's platform independence, particularly in relationship to the topics covered in this chapter, is the fact that Java's bytecode is a stack-based language, partially composed of zero-address instructions. Each instruction consists of a one-byte opcode followed by zero or more operands. The opcode itself indicates whether it is followed by operands and the form the operands (if any) take. Many of these instructions require zero operands.

Java uses two's complement to represent signed integers but does not allow for unsigned integers. Characters are coded using 16-bit Unicode. Java has four registers that provide access to five different main memory regions. All references to memory are based on offsets from these registers; pointers or absolute memory addresses are never used. Because the JVM is a stack machine, no general registers are provided. This lack of general registers is detrimental to performance, as more memory references are generated. We are trading performance for portability.

Let's take a look at a short Java program and its corresponding bytecode. Example 5.13 shows a Java program that finds the maximum of two numbers.

≡   **EXAMPLE 5.13**   Here is a Java program to find the maximum of two numbers.

```
public class Maximum {

  public static void main (String[] Args)
  { int X,Y,Z;
    X = Integer.parseInt(Args[0]);
    Y = Integer.parseInt(Args[1]);
    Z = Max(X,Y);
    System.out.println(Z);
  }

  public static int Max (int A, int B)
  { int C;
    if (A > B) C = A;
    else C = B;
    return C;
  }
}
```

After we compile this program (using `javac`), we can disassemble it to examine the bytecode, by issuing the following command:

```
javap -c Maximum
```

You should see the following:

```
Compiled from Maximum.java
public class Maximum extends java.lang.Object {
    public Maximum();
    public static void main(java.lang.String[]);
    public static int Max(int, int);
}
Method Maximum()
   0 aload_0
   1 invokespecial #1 <Method java.lang.Object()>
   4 return
Method void main(java.lang.String[])
   0 aload_0
   1 iconst_0
   2 aaload
   3 invokestatic #2 <Method int parseInt(java.lang.String)>
   6 istore_1
   7 aload_0
   8 iconst_1
```

```
 9 aaload
10 invokestatic #2 <Method int parseInt(java.lang.String)>
13 istore_2
14 iload_1
15 iload_2
16 invokestatic #3 <Method int Max(int, int)>
19 istore_3
20 getstatic #4 <Field java.io.PrintStream out>
23 iload_3
24 invokevirtual #5 <Method void println(int)>
27 return
```

```
Method int Max(int, int)
    0 iload_0
    1 iload_1
    2 if_icmple 10
    5 iload_0
    6 istore_2
    7 goto 12
   10 iload_1
   11 istore_2
   12 iload_2
   13 ireturn
```

Each line number represents an offset (or the number of bytes that an instruction is from the beginning of the current method). Notice that

```
Z = Max (X,Y);
```

gets compiled to the following bytecode:

```
14 iload_1
15 iload_2
16 invokestatic #3 <Method int Max(int, int)>
19 istore_3
```

It should be obvious that Java bytecode is stack based. For example, the `iadd` instruction pops two integers from the stack, adds them, and then pushes the result back to the stack. There is no such thing as "add r0, r1, f2" or "add AC, X". The `iload_1` (integer load) instruction also uses the stack by pushing slot 1 onto the stack (slot 1 in main contains *X*, so *X* is pushed onto the stack). *Y* is pushed onto the stack by instruction 15. The `invokestatic` instruction actually performs the `Max` method call. When the method has finished, the `istore_3` instruction pops the top element of the stack and stores it in *Z*.

We will explore the Java language and the JVM in more detail in Chapter 8.

5.6.4 ARM

ARM is a family of RISC-like (reduced instruction set computer) processor cores found in many portable devices today. In fact, it is the most widely used 32-bit instruction architecture, found in more than 95% of smartphones, 80% of digital cameras, and more than 40% of all digital television sets. Founded in 1990, ARM (Advanced RISC Machine) was originally funded by Apple, Acorn, and VLSI and is now licensed by ARM Holdings in Britain. ARM Holdings does not manufacture these processors; it sells the licenses, and the cores are developed independently by companies that have an architectural license from ARM. This allows developers to extend the chip in any way that best fits their needs.

There are multiple ARM families, including ARM1, ARM2, up through ARM11, with ARM7, ARM9, and ARM10 being the main families currently available for licensing. The ARM processor has three architectural profiles, or series: Cortex-A (designed for full operating systems in third-party applications); Cortex-R (designed for embedded and real-time applications); and Cortex-M (designed for microcontroller situations). Implementations for ARM processors vary significantly. For example, many of these processors use a standard von Neumann architecture, such as the ARM7, whereas others use a Harvard architecture, like the ARM9. Although the latest ARM architecture supports 64-bit computing, our discussion focuses on the most common 32-bit processors.

ARM is a load/store architecture in which all data processing must be performed on values in registers, not in memory. It uses fixed-length, three-operand instructions and simple addressing modes, although its indexed (base plus offset) addressing mode is very powerful. These characteristics, combined with a large register file of 16 32-bit general-purpose registers, facilitate pipelining. All ARM processors have a minimum of a three-stage pipeline (consisting of fetch, decode, and execute); newer processors have deeper pipelines (more stages). For example, the very popular ARM9 typically has a five-stage pipeline (similar to MIPS); certain implementations of the ARM8 have 13-stage integer pipelines (where the fetch is broken into two stages, the decode into five stages, and the execute into six stages.)

There are actually 37 total registers in the ARM architecture; however, because these are shared among the different processor modes, some are only visible (usable) when the processor is in a specific mode. A processor mode places rules and restrictions on the types of operations that can be performed and on the scope of data that can be accessed; the mode a processor is running in basically determines its operating environment. Privileged modes give direct access to hardware and memory; nonprivileged modes place restrictions on which registers and other hardware can be utilized. ARM processors support a variety of different processor modes, depending on the version of the architecture. These modes typically include (1) supervisor mode, a protected mode for the operating system; (2) FIQ mode, a privileged mode that supports high-speed data transfer, used to process high-priority interrupts; (3) IRQ mode, a privileged mode used for general-purpose interrupts; (4) Abort, a privileged mode that deals with memory access violations; (5) Undefined, a privileged mode used when undefined or illegal instructions are encountered; (6) System, a privileged mode that runs privileged operating system tasks; and (7) User, a nonprivileged mode and the mode in which most applications run.

Several of the restrictions associated with the various modes determine how registers are to be utilized. Registers 0 through 7 are treated the same in all processor modes. However, there are multiple copies, called *banks*, of certain registers, and the copy that is actually used is determined by the current mode. For example, registers 13 and 14 are "banked" in most privileged modes; this means that each mode has its own copy of register 13 and register 14. These registers, in addition to register 15, essentially serve dual purposes; while registers 13, 14, and 15 can be accessed directly, in the appropriate mode register 13 can be used as the stack pointer, register 14 as a link register, and register 15 as the program counter.

All ARM processors perform bit-wise logic and comparison operations, as well as addition, subtraction, and multiplication; only a few include instructions for division. ARM processors provide the standard data transfer instructions, including those that move data from memory to register, register to memory, and register to register. In addition to the usual single register transfer, ARM also allows multiple register transfers. ARM can *simultaneously* load or store any subset of the 16 general-purpose registers from/to sequential memory addresses. Control flow instructions include unconditional and conditional branching and procedure calls (using a branch and link instruction that saves the return address in register 14).

Most ARM instructions execute in a single cycle, provided there are no pipeline hazards or instructions that must access memory. To minimize the number of cycles, ARM utilizes various techniques. For example, when branch statements are encountered, branching is typically conditionally executed. ARM also supports auto-indexing mode, which allows the value of the index register to change while a load/store instruction is being executed. In addition, ARM has several "specialty" instructions and registers. For example, if an instruction specifies register 15 as its destination, the result of an ALU operation is automatically used as the next instruction address. If the PC is used in a memory access instruction, the next instruction is automatically fetched from memory.

A sample ARM program to store the larger of two integers in register 1 can be seen below. The compare instruction (cmp) basically subtracts register 1 from register 2, but instead of storing the result, it uses the difference to set flags in the status register that are later utilized by the branch instruction. The branch statement (bge) jumps only if the value in register 2 is greater than or equal to the value in register 1. Note how similar this assembly language is to that of MARIE, Intel, and MIPS (as seen in Chapter 4).

```
        ldr    r1,Num1   ; load the first number into register 1
        ldr    r2,Num2   ; load the second number into register 2
        cmp    r1,r2     ; compare the two numbers
        bge    end       ; if r1 has the larger value we are finished
        mov    r1, r2    ; if not, r2 has the larger value so copy it
                         ; into register 1
        end
Num1 dcd   &13579246
Num2 dcd   &13578246
        end
```

Most ARM architectures implement two different instruction sets: the normal 32-bit ARM instruction set and the 16-bit Thumb instruction set. Those chips supporting Thumb carry a "T" in the name. (Some cores are equipped with Jazelle, which allows them to execute Java bytecode; these processors have a "J" appended to the CPU name). Although ARM has instructions that execute in a single clock cycle, these shorter instructions result in longer programs, thus requiring more memory. In all but those situations where speed is critical, the cost of memory outweighs the execution speed of the processor. Thumb was added as an option to many ARM chips to improve code density and thus reduce the amount of storage space required. We should note that ARM processors actually contain only one instruction set; when a processor is operating in Thumb mode, the processor (via dedicated hardware on the chip) expands a Thumb instruction into an equivalent ARM 32-bit instruction. In Thumb mode, there are no longer 16 general-purpose registers available; that number is reduced to 8 (in addition to the PC, stack pointer, and link pointer registers).

There are actually two variations of the Thumb instruction set: Thumb, which includes 16-bit fixed-length instructions, and Thumb-2 (introduced in the latest cores), which is backward compatible with Thumb but allows for 32-bit instructions. Although Thumb is a compact and condensed language (it requires roughly 40% less space than ARM instructions) and allows for shorter opcodes and better code density, its performance does not match that of the ARM instruction set. Thumb-2 gives roughly 25% better performance than Thumb, while still offering good code density and energy efficiency.

ARM is small and thus requires few transistors, which in turn means it requires less power. This gives it a good performance-to-watts ratio and makes it a perfect processor for portable devices. ARM processors are currently used in smartphones, digital cameras, GPS devices, exercise machines, book readers, MP3 players, intelligent toys, appliances, vending machines, printers, game consoles, tablets, wireless LAN boxes, USB controllers, Bluetooth controllers, medical scanners, routers, and automobiles, just to name a few. Although other companies have designed mobile processors that are currently being used in portable devices (most notably Intel's Atom x86 processor), we predict that ARM will continue to dominate the mobile market for quite some time.

CHAPTER SUMMARY

The core elements of an instruction set architecture include the memory model (word size and how the address space is split), registers, data types, instruction formats, addressing, and instruction types. Even though most computers today have general-purpose register sets and specify operands by combinations of memory and register locations, instructions vary in size, type, format, and the number of operands allowed. Instructions also have strict requirements for the locations of these operands. Operands can be located on the stack, in registers, in memory, or a combination of the three.

Many decisions must be made when ISAs are designed. Larger instruction sets mandate longer instructions, which means a longer fetch and decode time. Instructions having a fixed length are easier to decode but can waste space. Expanding opcodes represent a compromise between the need for large instruction sets and the desire to have short instructions. Perhaps the most interesting debate is that of little versus big endian byte ordering.

There are three choices for internal storage in the CPU: stacks, an accumulator, or general-purpose registers. Each has its advantages and disadvantages, which must be considered in the context of the proposed architecture's applications. The internal storage scheme has a direct effect on the instruction format, particularly the number of operands the instruction is allowed to reference. Stack architectures use zero operands, which fits well with RPN notation.

Instructions are classified into the following categories: data movement, arithmetic, Boolean, bit manipulation, I/O, transfer of control, and special purpose. Some ISAs have many instructions in each category, others have very few in each category, and many have a mix of each. Orthogonal instruction sets are consistent, with no restrictions on the operand/opcode relationship.

The advances in memory technology, resulting in larger memories, have prompted the need for alternative addressing modes. The various addressing modes introduced included immediate, direct, indirect, register, indexed, and stack. Having these different modes provides flexibility and convenience for the programmer without changing the fundamental operations of the CPU.

Instruction-level pipelining is one example of instruction-level parallelism. It is a common but complex technique that can speed up the fetch–decode–execute cycle. With pipelining, we can overlap the execution of instructions, thus executing multiple instructions in parallel. However, we also saw that the amount of parallelism can be limited by conflicts in the pipeline. Whereas pipelining performs different stages of multiple instructions at the same time, superscalar architectures allow us to perform multiple operations at the same time. Super-pipelining, a combination of superscalar and pipelining, in addition to VLIW, was also briefly introduced. There are many types of parallelism, but at the computer organization and architecture level, we are really concerned mainly with ILP.

Intel and MIPS have interesting ISAs, as we have seen in this chapter as well as in Chapter 4. However, the Java Virtual Machine is a unique ISA because the ISA is built-in software, thus allowing Java programs to run on any machine that supports the JVM. Chapter 8 covers the JVM in great detail. ARM is an example of an architecture that supports multiple ISAs.

FURTHER READING

Instruction sets, addressing, and instruction formats are covered in detail in almost every computer architecture book. The books by Patterson and Hennessy (2009), Stallings (2013), and Tanenbaum (2013) all provide excellent coverage in these areas. Many books, such as Brey (2003), Messmer (2001), Abel (2001) and Jones (2001) are devoted to the Intel x86 architecture. For those interested in the Motorola 68000 series, we suggest Wray, Greenfield, and Bannatyne (1999) or Miller (1992).

Sohi (1990) gives a very nice discussion of instruction-level pipelining. Kaeli and Emma (1991) provide an interesting overview of how branching affects pipeline performance. For a nice history of pipelining, see Rau and Fisher (1993). To get a better idea of the limitations and problems with pipelining, see Wall (1993).

We investigated specific architectures in Chapter 4, but there are many important instruction set architectures worth mentioning. Atanasoff's ABC computer (Burks and Burks [1988]), Von Neumann's EDVAC, and Mauchly and Eckert's UNIVAC (Stern [1981] for information on both) had very simple instruction set architectures but required programming to be done in machine language. The Intel 8080 (a one-address machine) was the predecessor to the 80x86 family of chips introduced in Chapter 4. See Brey (2003) for a thorough and readable introduction to the Intel family of processors. Hauck and Dent (1968) provide good coverage of the Burroughs zero-address machine. Struble (1984) has a nice presentation of IBM's 360 family. Brunner (1991) gives details about DEC's VAX systems, which incorporated two-address architectures with more sophisticated instruction sets. SPARC (1994) provides a great overview of the SPARC architecture. Meyer and Downing (1991), Lindholm and Yellin (1999), and Venners (2000) provide very interesting coverage of the JVM.

For an interesting article that charts the historical development from 32 to 64 bits, see Mashey (2009). The author shows how architectural decisions can have unexpected and lasting consequences.

REFERENCES

Abel, P. *IBM PC Assembly Language and Programming*, 5th ed. Upper Saddle River, NJ: Prentice Hall, 2001.

Brey, B. *Intel Microprocessors 8086/8088, 80186/80188, 80286, 80386, 80486 Pentium, and Pentium Pro Processor, Pentium II, Pentium III, and Pentium IV: Architecture, Programming, and Interfacing*, 6th ed. Englewood Cliffs, NJ: Prentice Hall, 2003.

Brunner, R. A. *VAX Architecture Reference Manual*, 2nd ed. Herndon, VA: Digital Press, 1991.

Burks, A., & Burks, A. *The First Electronic Computer: The Atanasoff Story*. Ann Arbor, MI: University of Michigan Press, 1988.

Hauck, E. A., & Dent, B. A. "Burroughs B6500/B7500 Stack Mechanism." *Proceedings of AFIPS SJCC 32,* 1968, pp. 245–251.

Jones, W. *Assembly Language Programming for the IBM PC Family*, 3rd ed. El Granada, CA: Scott/Jones Publishing, 2001.

Kaeli, D., & Emma, P. "Branch History Table Prediction of Moving Target Branches Due to Subroutine Returns." *Proceedings of the 18th Annual International Symposium on Computer Architecture*, May 1991.

Lindholm, T., & Yellin, F. *The Java Virtual Machine Specification*, 2nd ed., 1999. Online at java.sun.com/docs/books/jvms/index.html.

Mashey, J. "The Long Road to 64 Bits." *CACM 52*:1, January 2009, pp. 45–53.

Messmer, H. *The Indispensable PC Hardware Book*. 4th ed. Reading, MA: Addison-Wesley, 2001.

Meyer, J., & Downing, T. *Java Virtual Machine*. Sebastopol, CA: O'Reilly & Associates, 1991.

Miller, M. A. *The 6800 Microprocessor Family: Architecture, Programming, and Applications*, 2nd ed. Columbus, OH: Charles E. Merrill, 1992.

Patterson, D. A., & Hennessy, J. L. *Computer Organization and Design, The Hardware/Software Interface*, 4th ed. San Mateo, CA: Morgan Kaufmann, 2009.

Rau, B. R., & Fisher, J. A. "Instruction-Level Parallel Processing: History, Overview and Perspective." *Journal of Supercomputing* 7:1, January 1993, pp. 9–50.

Sohi, G. "Instruction Issue Logic for High-Performance Interruptible, Multiple Functional Unit, Pipelined Computers." *IEEE Transactions on Computers*, March 1990.

SPARC International, Inc. *The SPARC Architecture Manual: Version 9*. Upper Saddle River, NJ: Prentice Hall, 1994.

Stallings, W. *Computer Organization and Architecture*, 9th ed. Upper Saddle River, NJ: Prentice Hall, 2013.

Stern, N. *From ENIAC to UNIVAC: An Appraisal of the Eckert-Mauchly Computers*. Herndon, VA: Digital Press, 1981.

Struble, G. W. *Assembler Language Programming: The IBM System/360 and 370*, 3rd ed. Reading, MA: Addison-Wesley, 1984.

Tanenbaum, A. *Structured Computer Organization*, 6th ed. Upper Saddle River, NJ: Prentice Hall, 2013.

Venners, B. *Inside the Java 2 Virtual Machine*, 2000. Online at www.artima.com.

Wall, D. W. *Limits of Instruction-Level Parallelism*. DEC-WRL Research Report 93/6, November 1993.

Wray, W. C., Greenfield, J. D., & Bannatyne, R. *Using Microprocessors and Microcomputers, the Motorola Family*, 4th ed. Englewood Cliffs, NJ: Prentice Hall, 1999.

REVIEW OF ESSENTIAL TERMS AND CONCEPTS

1. Explain the difference between register-to-register, register-to-memory, and memory-to-memory instructions.

2. Several design decisions exist with regard to instruction sets. Name four and explain.

3. What is an expanding opcode?

4. If a byte-addressable machine with 32-bit words stores the hex value 98765432, indicate how this value would be stored on a little endian machine and on a big endian machine. Why does "endian-ness" matter?

5. We can design stack architectures, accumulator architectures, or general-purpose register architectures. Explain the differences between these choices and give some situations where one might be better than another.

6. How do memory-memory, register-memory, and load-store architectures differ? How are they the same?

7. What are the pros and cons of fixed-length and variable-length instructions? Which is currently more popular?

8. How does an architecture based on zero operands ever get any data values from memory?

9. Which is likely to be longer (have more instructions): a program written for a zero-address architecture, a program written for a one-address architecture, or a program written for a two-address architecture? Why?

10. Why might stack architectures represent arithmetic expressions in reverse Polish notation?

11. Name the seven types of data instructions and explain each.

12. What is the difference between an arithmetic shift and a logical shift?

13. Explain what it means for an instruction set to be orthogonal.

14. What is an address mode?

15. Give examples of immediate, direct, register, indirect, register indirect, and indexed addressing.

16. How does indexed addressing differ from based addressing?

17. Why do we need so many different addressing modes?

18. Explain the concept behind instruction pipelining.

19. What is the theoretical speedup for a 4-stage pipeline with a 20ns clock cycle if it is processing 100 tasks?

20. What are the pipeline conflicts that can cause a slowdown in the pipeline?

21. What are the two types of ILP, and how do they differ?

22. Explain superscalar, superpipelining, and VLIW architectures.

23. List several ways in which the Intel and MIPS ISAs differ. Name several ways in which they are the same.

24. Explain Java bytecodes.

25. Give an example of a current stack-based architecture and a current GPR-based architecture. How do they differ?

EXERCISES

1. Assume you have a byte-addressable machine that uses 32-bit integers and you are storing the hex value 1234 at address 0:

   ◆ **a)** Show how this is stored on a big endian machine.

   ◆ **b)** Show how this is stored on a little endian machine.

   c) If you wanted to increase the hex value to 123456, which byte assignment would be more efficient, big or little endian? Explain your answer.

2. Show how the following values would be stored by byte-addressable machines with 32-bit words, using little endian and then big endian format. Assume that each value starts at address 10_{16}. Draw a diagram of memory for each, placing the appropriate values in the correct (and labeled) memory locations.

   a) 0x456789A1

   b) 0x0000058A

   c) 0x14148888

3. Fill in the following table to show how the given integers are represented, assuming that 16 bits are used to store values and the machine uses two's complement notation.

Integer	Binary	Hex	4 Byte Big Endian (Hex value as seen in memory)	4 Byte Little Endian (Hex value as seen in memory)
28				
2216				
−18675				
−12				
31456				

4. Assume a computer that has 32-bit integers. Show how each of the following values would be stored sequentially in memory, starting at address 0x100, assuming that each address holds 1 byte. Be sure to extend each value to the appropriate number of bits. You will need to add more rows (addresses) to store all given values.

Byte Order

Address	Big Endian	Little Endian
0x100		
0x101		
0x102		
0x103		
0x104		
0x105		
0x106		
0x107		

   a) 0xAB123456
   b) 0x2BF876
   c) 0x8B0A1
   d) 0x1
   e) 0xFEDC1234

5. Consider a 32-bit hexadecimal number stored in memory as follows:

Address	Value
100	2A
101	C2
102	08
103	1B

   a) If the machine is big endian and uses two's complement representation for integers, write the 32-bit integer number stored at address 100 (you may write the number in hex).
   b) If the machine is big endian and the number is an IEEE single-precision floating-point value, is the number positive or negative?
   c) If the machine is big endian and the number is an IEEE single-precision floating-point value, determine the decimal equivalent of the number stored at address 100 (you may leave your answer in scientific notation form, as a number times a power of two).

d) If the machine is little endian and uses two's complement representation for integers, write the 32-bit integer number stored at address 100 (you may write the number in hex).

e) If the machine is little endian and the number is an IEEE single-precision floating-point value, is the number positive or negative?

f) If the machine is little endian and the number is an IEEE single-precision floating-point value, determine the decimal equivalent of the number stored at address 100 (you may leave your answer in scientific notation form, as a number times a power of two).

◆**6.** The first two bytes of a 2M × 16 main memory have the following hex values:

- Byte 0 is FE
- Byte 1 is 01

If these bytes hold a 16-bit two's complement integer, what is its actual decimal value if:

a) memory is big endian?

b) memory is little endian?

7. What kinds of problems do you think endian-ness can cause if you wished to transfer data from a big endian machine to a little endian machine? Explain.

8. The Population Studies Institute monitors the population of the United States. In 2008, this institute wrote a program to create files of the numbers representing populations of the various states, as well as the total population of the United States. This program, which runs on a Motorola processor, projects the population based on various rules, such as the average numbers of births and deaths per year. The institute runs the program and then ships the output files to state agencies so the data values can be used as input into various applications. However, one Pennsylvania agency, running all Intel machines, encountered difficulties, as indicated by the following problem. When the 32-bit unsigned integer $1D2F37E8_{16}$ (representing the overall U.S. population prediction for 2013) is used as input, and the agency's program simply outputs this input value, the U.S. population forecast for 2014 is far too large. Can you help this Pennsylvania agency by explaining what might be going wrong? (Hint: They are run on different processors.)

9. There are reasons for machine designers to want all instructions to be the same length. Why is this not a good idea on a stack machine?

◆**10.** A computer has 32-bit instructions and 12-bit addresses. Suppose there are 250 two-address instructions. How many one-address instructions can be formulated? Explain your answer.

11. Convert the following expressions from infix to reverse Polish (postfix) notation.

a) $(8 - 6)/2$

b) $(2 + 3) \times 8/10$

c) $(5 \times (4 + 3) \times 2 - 6)$

12. Convert the following expressions from infix to reverse Polish (postfix) notation.

◆**a)** $X \times Y + W \times Z + V \times U$

b) $W \times X + W \times (U \times V + Z)$

c) $(W \times (X + Y \times (U \times V)))/(U \times (X + Y))$

13. Convert the following expressions from reverse Polish notation to infix notation.

    a) 12 8 3 1 + − /

    b) 5 2 + 2 × 1 + 2 ×

    c) 3 5 7 + 2 1 − × 1 + +

14. Convert the following expressions from reverse Polish notation to infix notation.

    a) $W\,X\,Y\,Z - + \times$

    b) $U\,V\,W\,X\,Y\,Z + \times + \times +$

    c) $X\,Y\,Z + V\,W - \times Z + +$

15. Explain how a stack is used to evaluate the RPN expressions from exercise 13.

16. a) Write the following expression in postfix (reverse Polish) notation. Remember the rules of precedence for arithmetic operators!

$$X = \frac{A - B + C \times (D \times E - F)}{G + H \times K}$$

   b) Write a program to evaluate the above arithmetic statement using a stack-organized computer with zero-address instructions (so only Pop and Push can access memory).

17. a) In a computer instruction format, the instruction length is 11 bits and the size of an address field is 4 bits. Is it possible to have

    5   two-address instructions

    45   one-address instructions

    32   zero-address instructions

    using the specified format? Justify your answer.

   b) Assume that a computer architect has already designed 6 two-address and 24 zero-address instructions using the instruction format above. What is the maximum number of one-address instructions that can be added to the instruction set?

18. Suppose a computer has an instruction format with space for an opcode and either three register values or one register value and an address. What are the various instruction formats that could be used for an ADD instruction on this machine?

19. Given 16-bit instructions, is it possible to use expanding opcodes to allow the following to be encoded assuming we have a total of 32 registers? If so, show the encoding. If not, explain why is it not possible.

    • 60 instructions with two register operands

    • 30 instructions with one register operand

    • 3 instructions with one 10-bit address

    • 26 instructions with zero operands

20. What is the difference between using direct and indirect addressing? Give an example.

◆ **21.** Suppose we have the instruction `Load 1000`. Given that memory and register R1 contain the values below:

Memory

0x1000	0x1400
...	
0x1100	0x400
...	
0x1200	0x1000
...	
0x1300	0x1100
...	
0x1400	0x1300

R1 | 0x200

and assuming that R1 is implied in the indexed addressing mode, determine the actual value loaded into the accumulator and fill in the table below:

Mode	Value Loaded into AC
Immediate	
Direct	
Indirect	
Indexed	

22. Suppose we have the instruction `Load 500`. Given that memory and register R1 contain the values below:

Memory

0x100	0x600
...	
0x400	0x300
...	
0x500	0x100
...	
0x600	0x500
...	
0x700	0x800

R1 | 0x200

and assuming that R1 is implied in the indexed addressing mode, determine the actual value loaded into the accumulator and fill in the table below:

Mode	Value Loaded into AC
Immediate	
Direct	
Indirect	
Indexed	

23. A nonpipelined system takes 200ns to process a task. The same task can be processed in a five-segment pipeline with a clock cycle of 40ns. Determine the speedup ratio of the pipeline for 200 tasks. What is the maximum speedup that could be achieved with the pipeline unit over the nonpipelined unit?

24. A nonpipelined system takes 100ns to process a task. The same task can be processed in a five-stage pipeline with a clock cycle of 20ns. Determine the speedup ratio of the pipeline for 100 tasks. What is the theoretical speedup that could be achieved with the pipeline system over a nonpipelined system?

25. Assuming the same stages as in Example 5.12, explain the potential pipeline hazards (if any) in each of the following code segments.

    a) $X = R2 + Y$
        $R4 = R2 + X$
    b) $R1 = R2 + X$
        $X = R3 + Y$
        $Z = R1 + X$

26. Write code to implement the expression $A = (B + C) \times (D + E)$ on three-, two-, one-, and zero-address machines. In accordance with programming language practice, computing the expression should not change the values of its operands.

♦27. A digital computer has a memory unit with 24 bits per word. The instruction set consists of 150 different operations. All instructions have an operation code part (opcode) and an address part (allowing for only one address). Each instruction is stored in one word of memory.

    a) How many bits are needed for the opcode?
    b) How many bits are left for the address part of the instruction?
    c) What is the maximum allowable size for memory?
    d) What is the largest unsigned binary number that can be accommodated in one word of memory?

28. The memory unit of a computer has 256K words of 32 bits each. The computer has an instruction format with four fields: an opcode field; a mode field to specify one of seven addressing modes; a register address field to specify one of 60 registers; and a memory address field. Assume an instruction is 32 bits long. Answer the following:

    a) How large must the mode field be?
    b) How large must the register field be?
    c) How large must the address field be?
    d) How large is the opcode field?

29. Suppose an instruction takes four cycles to execute in a nonpipelined CPU: one cycle to fetch the instruction, one cycle to decode the instruction, one cycle to perform the ALU operation, and one cycle to store the result. In a CPU with a four-stage pipeline, that instruction still takes four cycles to execute, so how can we say the pipeline speeds up the execution of the program?

* **30.** Pick an architecture (other than those covered in this chapter). Do research to find out how your architecture approaches the concepts introduced in this chapter, as was done for Intel, MIPS, and Java.

TRUE OR FALSE

1. Most computers typically fall into one of three types of CPU organization: (1) general register organization; (2) single accumulator organization; or (3) stack organization.

2. The advantage of zero-address instruction computers is that they have short programs; the disadvantage is that the instructions require many bits, making them very long.

3. An instruction takes less time to execute on a processor using an instruction pipeline than on a processor without an instruction pipeline.

4. The term "endian" refers to an architecture's byte ordering.

5. Stack architectures have good code density and a simple model for evaluation of expressions, but do not allow random access, which can cause a problem with the generation of efficient code.

6. Most architectures today are accumulator based.

7. Fixed-length instruction format typically results in better performance than variable-length instruction format.

8. Expanding opcodes make instruction decoding much easier than when it is not used.

9. Instruction set orthogonality refers to the characteristic in an instruction set architecture where each instruction has a "backup" instruction that performs the same operation.

10. The effective address of an operand is the value of its actual address in memory.

11. Resource conflicts occur in a pipeline when there are multiple instructions that require the same resource.

12. Data dependencies occur in a pipeline when multiple instructions need the CPU.

CHAPTER 6 Memory

6.1 INTRODUCTION

Most computers are built using the Von Neumann model, which is centered on memory. The programs that perform the processing are stored in memory. We examined a small 4 × 3-bit memory in Chapter 3, and we learned how to address memory in Chapters 4 and 5. We know memory is logically structured as a linear array of locations, with addresses from 0 to the maximum memory size the processor can address. In this chapter, we examine the various types of memory and how each is part of the memory hierarchy system. We then look at cache memory (a special high-speed memory) and a method that utilizes memory to its fullest by means of virtual memory implemented via paging.

6.2 TYPES OF MEMORY

A common question many people ask is, "Why are there so many different types of computer memory?" The answer is that new technologies continue to be introduced in an attempt to match the improvements in CPU design—the speed of memory has to, somewhat, keep pace with the CPU, or the memory becomes a bottleneck. Although we have seen many improvements in CPUs over the past few years, improving main memory to keep pace with the CPU is actually not as critical because of the use of **cache memory**. Cache memory is a small, high-speed (and thus high-cost) type of memory that serves as a buffer for frequently accessed data. The additional expense of using very fast technologies for memory cannot always be justified because slower memories can often be "hidden" by

341

high-performance cache systems. However, before we discuss cache memory, we will explain the various memory technologies.

Even though a large number of memory technologies exist, there are only two basic types of memory: **RAM (random access memory)** and **ROM (read-only memory)**. RAM is somewhat of a misnomer; a more appropriate name is read-write memory. RAM is the memory to which computer specifications refer; if you buy a computer with 128 megabytes of memory, it has 128MB of RAM. RAM is also the "main memory" we have continually referred to throughout this text. Often called primary memory, RAM is used to store programs and data that the computer needs when executing programs, but RAM is volatile and loses this information once the power is turned off. There are two general types of chips used to build the bulk of RAM in today's computers: SRAM and DRAM (static and dynamic random access memory).

Dynamic RAM is constructed of tiny capacitors that leak electricity. DRAM requires a recharge every few milliseconds to maintain its data. **Static RAM** technology, in contrast, holds its contents as long as power is available. SRAM consists of circuits similar to the D flip-flops we studied in Chapter 3. SRAM is faster and much more expensive than DRAM; however, designers use DRAM because it is much denser (can store many bits per chip), uses less power, and generates less heat than SRAM. For these reasons, both technologies are often used in combination: DRAM for main memory and SRAM for cache. The basic operation of all DRAM memories is the same, but there are many flavors, including **Multibank DRAM (MDRAM)**, **Fast-Page Mode (FPM) DRAM**, **Extended Data Out (EDO) DRAM**, **Burst EDO DRAM (BEDO DRAM)**, **Synchronous Dynamic Random Access Memory (SDRAM)**, **Synchronous-Link (SL) DRAM**, **Double Data Rate (DDR) SDRAM**, **Rambus DRAM (RDRAM)**, and **Direct Rambus (DR) DRAM**. The different types of SRAM include asynchronous SRAM, synchronous SRAM, and pipeline burst SRAM. For more information about these types of memory, refer to the references listed at the end of the chapter.

In addition to RAM, most computers contain a small amount of ROM that stores critical information necessary to operate the system, such as the program necessary to boot the computer. ROM is not volatile and always retains its data. This type of memory is also used in embedded systems or any systems where the programming does not need to change. Many appliances, toys, and most automobiles use ROM chips to maintain information when the power is shut off. ROMs are also used extensively in calculators and peripheral devices such as laser printers, which store their fonts in ROMs. There are five basic types of ROM: ROM, PROM, EPROM, EEPROM, and flash memory. **PROM (programmable read-only memory)** is a variation on ROM. PROMs can be programmed by the user with the appropriate equipment. Whereas ROMs are hardwired, PROMs have fuses that can be blown to program the chip. Once programmed, the data and instructions in PROM cannot be changed. **EPROM (erasable PROM)** is programmable with the added advantage of being reprogrammable (erasing an EPROM requires a special tool that emits ultraviolet light). To reprogram an EPROM, the entire chip must first be erased. **EEPROM (electrically erasable PROM)** removes many of the disadvantages of EPROM: No special tools are required for erasure (this is performed by applying an electric field) and you can erase only portions of the chip, one byte at a time. **Flash memory** is essentially EEPROM with the added benefit that data can be written or erased in blocks, removing the one-byte-at-a-time limitation. This makes flash memory faster than EEPROM. Flash memory has become a very popular type of storage and is used in many different devices, including cell phones, digital cameras, and music players. It is also being used in solid-state disk drives. (Chapter 7 contains more information on flash memory devices.)

6.3   THE MEMORY HIERARCHY

One of the most important considerations in understanding the performance capabilities of a modern processor is the memory hierarchy. Unfortunately, as we have seen, not all memory is created equal, and some types are far less efficient and thus cheaper than others. To deal with this disparity, today's computer systems use a combination of memory types to provide the best performance at the best cost. This approach is called **hierarchical memory**. As a rule, the faster memory is, the more expensive it is per bit of storage. By using a hierarchy of memories, each with different access speeds and storage capacities, a computer system can exhibit performance above what would be possible without a combination of the various types. The base types that normally constitute the hierarchical memory system include registers, cache, main memory, secondary memory, and off-line bulk memory.

Registers are storage locations available on the processor itself. **Cache memory** is a very-high-speed memory where data from frequently used memory locations may be temporarily stored. This cache is connected to a much larger **main memory**, which is typically a medium-speed memory. This memory is complemented by a very large **secondary memory**, typically composed of hard disk drives containing data not directly accessible by the CPU; instead, secondary memory must have its contents transferred to main memory when the data is needed. Hard drives can either be magnetic or **solid state** (flash-based hard drives that are faster and sturdier than rotating magnetic disks). **Off-line bulk memory** (which includes **tertiary memory** and **off-line storage**) requires either human or robotic intervention before any data can be accessed; the data must be transferred from the storage media to secondary memory. Tertiary memory includes things such as optical jukeboxes and tape libraries, which are typically under robotic control (a robotic arm mounts and dismounts the tapes and disks). It is used for enterprise storage in large systems and networks and is not something an average computer user sees often. These devices typically have nonuniform access times, as the time to retrieve data depends on whether the device is mounted. Off-line storage includes those devices that are connected, loaded with data, and then disconnected from the system, such as floppy disks, flash memory devices, optical disks, and even removable hard drives. By using such a hierarchical scheme, one can improve the effective access speed of the memory, using only a small number of fast (and expensive) chips. This allows designers to create a computer with acceptable performance at a reasonable cost.

We classify memory based on its "distance" from the processor, with distance measured by the number of machine cycles required for access. The closer memory is to the processor, the faster it should be. As memory gets farther from the main processor, we can afford longer access times. Thus, slower technologies are used for these memories, and faster technologies are used for memories closer to the CPU. The better the technology, the faster and more expensive the memory becomes. Thus, faster memories tend to be smaller than slower ones, because of cost.

The following terminology is used when referring to this memory hierarchy:

- **Hit**—The requested data resides in a given level of memory (typically, we are concerned with the hit rate only for upper levels of memory).
- **Miss**—The requested data is not found in the given level of memory.
- **Hit rate**—The percentage of memory accesses found in a given level of memory.
- **Miss rate**—The percentage of memory accesses not found in a given level of memory. Note: Miss Rate = 1 − Hit Rate.
- **Hit time**—The time required to access the requested information in a given level of memory.
- **Miss penalty**—The time required to process a miss, which includes replacing a block in an upper level of memory, plus the additional time to deliver the requested data to the processor. (The time to process a miss is typically significantly larger than the time to process a hit.)

The memory hierarchy is illustrated in Figure 6.1. This is drawn as a pyramid to help indicate the relative sizes of these various memories. Memories closer to the top tend to be smaller in size. However, these smaller memories have better performance and thus a higher cost (per bit) than memories found lower in the pyramid. The numbers given to the left of the pyramid indicate typical access times, which generally increase as we progress from top to bottom. Register accesses typically require one clock cycle.

There is one exception to access times increasing as we move down the hierarchy, in part because of new technologies. The off-line memory devices typically have faster access times than most tertiary devices. Of particular interest are USB flash drives. Both solid-state drives and USB flash drives use the same technology; thus both exhibit similar access times regarding accessing the data on the device. However, USB flash drives have slower access times than solid-state hard drives because of the USB interface. Even so, USB flash drives are faster

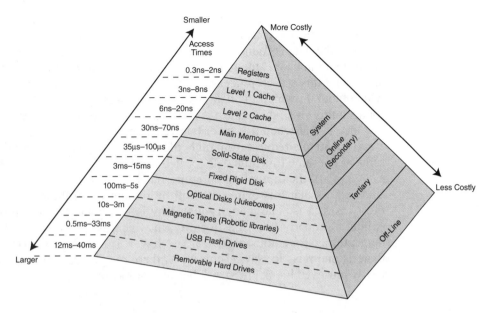

FIGURE 6.1 The Memory Hierarchy

than the other nonsolid-state types of off-line storage. Removable magnetic hard drives have access times of 12–40ms, and USB flash drives have access times of 0.5–33.8ms. Based only on access times, these latter devices do not belong at the bottom of our pyramid.

Figure 6.1 represents not only a memory hierarchy, but also a storage hierarchy. We are most interested in the memory hierarchy that involves registers, cache, main memory, and **virtual memory** (nonsystem memory that acts as an extension to main memory—this is discussed in detail later in this chapter). Virtual memory is typically implemented using a hard drive; it gives the impression that a program may have a large, contiguous working main memory, when in fact the program may exist, in fragments, in main memory, and on disk. Virtual memory increases the available memory your computer can use by extending the address space from RAM to the hard drive. Ordinarily, the memory hierarchy would stop at the hard drive level. However, with the advent of solid-state technology, the definition of virtual memory is changing. We previously mentioned that USB flash drives have very fast access times. They are so fast, in fact, that some operating systems (including some versions of Unix and Windows XP and later) allow a user to utilize a USB flash drive as virtual memory. The Windows operating systems that are mentioned come with software called ReadyBoost that allows various types of removable solid-state devices, such as USB flash drives and SD cards, to augment virtual memory by acting as disk cache. These solid-state devices service requests up to 100 times faster than traditional hard drives; although they are not a replacement for hard drives, they are quickly becoming an interesting enhancement.

For any given data, the processor sends its request to the fastest, smallest partition of memory (typically cache, because registers tend to be more special purpose). If the data is found in cache, it can be loaded quickly into the CPU. If it is not resident in cache, the request is forwarded to the next lower level of the hierarchy, and this search process begins again. If the data is found at this level, the whole block in which the data resides is transferred into cache. If the data is not found at this level, the request is forwarded to the next lower level, and so on. The key idea is that when the lower (slower, larger, and cheaper) levels of the hierarchy respond to a request from higher levels for the content of location X, they also send, at the same time, the data located "around" X ($\ldots, X - 2, X - 1, X, X + 1, X + 2, \ldots$), thus returning an entire block of data to the higher-level memory. The hope is that this extra data will be referenced in the near future, which, in most cases, it is. The memory hierarchy is functional because programs tend to exhibit a property known as **locality**, in which the processor tends to access the data returned for addresses $X - 2, X - 1, X + 1, X + 2$, and so on. Thus, although there is one miss to, say, cache for X, there may be several hits in cache on the newly retrieved block afterward, because of locality.

6.3.1   Locality of Reference

In practice, processors tend to access memory in a patterned way. For example, in the absence of branches, the PC in MARIE is incremented by one after each instruction fetch. Thus, if memory location X is accessed at time t, there is a high probability that memory location $X + 1$ will also be accessed in the near future. This clustering of memory references into groups is an example of **locality of reference**. This locality can be exploited by implementing the memory as a hierarchy; when a miss is processed, instead of simply transferring the requested data to a higher level, the entire block containing the data is transferred. Because of locality of reference, it is likely that the additional data in the block will be needed in the near future, and if so, this data can be loaded quickly from the faster memory.

There are three basic forms of locality:

- **Temporal locality**—Recently accessed items tend to be accessed again in the near future.

- **Spatial locality**—Accesses tend to be clustered in the address space (for example, as in arrays or loops).

- **Sequential locality**—Instructions tend to be accessed sequentially.

The locality principle provides the opportunity for a system to use a small amount of very fast memory to effectively accelerate the majority of memory accesses. Typically, only a small amount of the entire memory space is being accessed at any given time, and values in that space are being accessed repeatedly. Therefore, we can copy those values from a slower memory to a smaller but faster memory that resides higher in the hierarchy. This results in a memory system that can store a large amount of information in a large but low-cost memory, yet provide nearly the same access speeds that would result from using very fast but expensive memory.

6.4   CACHE MEMORY

A computer processor is very fast and is constantly reading information from memory, which means it often has to wait for the information to arrive, because the memory access times are slower than the processor speed. A cache memory is a small, temporary, but fast memory that the processor uses for information it is likely to need again in the very near future.

Noncomputer examples of caching are all around us. Keeping them in mind will help you to understand computer memory caching. Think of a homeowner with a very large tool chest in the garage. Suppose you are this homeowner and have a home improvement project to work on in the basement. You know this project will require drills, wrenches, hammers, a tape measure, several types of saws, and many different types and sizes of screwdrivers. The first thing you want to do is measure and then cut some wood. You run out to the garage, grab the tape measure from a huge tool storage chest, run down to the basement, measure the wood, run back out to the garage, leave the tape measure, grab the saw, and then return to the basement with the saw and cut the wood. Now you decide to bolt some pieces of wood together. So you run to the garage, grab the drill set, go back down to the basement, drill the holes to put the bolts through, go back to the garage, leave the drill set, grab one wrench, go back to the basement, find out the wrench is the wrong size, go back to the tool chest in the garage, grab another wrench, run back downstairs . . . wait! Would you really work this way? No! Being a reasonable person, you think to yourself, "If I need one wrench, I will probably need another one of a different size soon anyway, so why not just grab the whole set of wrenches?" Taking this one step further, you reason, "Once I am done with one certain tool, there is a good chance I will need another soon, so why not just pack up a small toolbox and take it to the basement?" This way, you keep the tools you need close at hand, so access is faster. You have just cached some tools for easy access and quick use! The tools you are less likely to use remain stored in a location that is farther away and requires more time to access. This is all that cache memory does: It stores data that has been accessed and data that might be accessed by the CPU in a faster, closer memory.

Another cache analogy is found in grocery shopping. You seldom, if ever, go to the grocery store to buy one single item. You buy any items you require immediately in addition to items you will most likely use in the future. The grocery store is similar to main memory, and your home is the cache. As another example, consider how many of us carry around an entire phone book. Most of us have a small address book instead. We enter the names and numbers of people we tend to call more frequently; looking up a number in our address book is much quicker than finding a phone book, locating the name, and then getting the number. We tend to have the address book close at hand, whereas the phone book is probably located in our home, hidden in an end table or bookcase somewhere. The phone book is something we do not use frequently, so we can afford to store it in a little more out-of-the-way location. Comparing the size of our address book to the telephone book, we see that the address book "memory" is much smaller than that of a telephone book. But the probability is high that when we make a call, it is to someone in our address book.

Students doing research offer another commonplace cache example. Suppose you are writing a paper on quantum computing. Would you go to the library, check out one book, return home, get the necessary information from that book, go back to the library, check out another book, return home, and so on? No; you would go to the library and check out all the books you might need and bring them all home. The library is analogous to main memory, and your home is, again, similar to cache.

And as a last example, consider how one of your authors uses her office. Any materials she does not need (or has not used for a period of more than six months) get filed away in a large set of filing cabinets. However, frequently used "data" remains piled on her desk, close at hand, and easy (sometimes) to find. If she needs something from a file, she more than likely pulls the entire file, not simply one or two papers from the folder. The entire file is then added to the pile on her desk. The filing cabinets are her "main memory," and her desk (with its many unorganized-looking piles) is the cache.

Cache memory works on the same basic principles as the preceding examples, by copying frequently used data into the cache rather than requiring an access to main memory to retrieve the data. Cache can be as unorganized as your author's desk or as organized as your address book. Either way, however, the data must be accessible (locatable). Cache memory in a computer differs from our real-life examples in one important way: The computer really has no way to know, *a priori*, what data is most likely to be accessed, so it uses the locality principle and transfers an entire block from main memory into cache whenever it has to make a main memory access. If the probability of using something else in that block is high, then transferring the entire block saves on access time. The cache location for this new block depends on two things: the cache mapping policy (discussed in the next section) and the cache size (which affects whether there is room for the new block).

The size of cache memory can vary enormously. A typical personal computer's level 2 (L2) cache is 256K or 512K. Level 1 (L1) cache is smaller, typically 8K to 64K. L1 cache resides on the processor, whereas L2 cache often resides between the CPU and main memory. L1 cache is, therefore, faster than L2 cache. The relationship between L1 and L2 cache can be illustrated using our grocery store example: If the store is main memory, you could consider your refrigerator the L2 cache, and the actual dinner table the L1 cache. We note that with newer processors, instead of incorporating L2 cache into the motherboard, some CPUs actually incorporate L2 cache as well as L1 cache. In addition, many systems employ L3 cache; L3 cache is specialized to work in unison with L1 and L2 caches.

The purpose of cache is to speed up memory accesses by storing recently used data closer to the CPU, instead of storing it in main memory. Although cache is not as large as main memory, it is considerably faster. Whereas main memory is typically composed of DRAM with, say, a 50ns access time, cache is typically composed of SRAM, providing faster access with a much shorter cycle time than DRAM (a typical cache access time is 10ns). Cache does not need to be very large to perform well. A general rule of thumb is to make cache small enough so that the overall average cost per bit is close to that of main memory, but large enough to be beneficial. Because this fast memory is quite expensive, it is not feasible to use the technology found in cache memory to build all of main memory.

What makes cache "special"? Cache is not accessed by address; it is accessed by content. For this reason, cache is sometimes called **content addressable memory** or **CAM**. Under most cache mapping schemes, the cache entries must be checked or searched to see if the value being requested is stored in cache. To simplify this process of locating the desired data, various cache mapping algorithms are used.

6.4.1 Cache Mapping Schemes

For cache to be functional, it must store useful data. However, this data becomes useless if the CPU can't find it. When accessing data or instructions, the CPU first generates a main memory address. If the data has been copied to cache, the address of the data in cache is not the same as the main memory address. For example, data located at main memory address 0x2E3 could be located in the very first location in cache. How, then, does the CPU locate data when it has been copied into cache? The CPU uses a specific mapping scheme that "converts" the main memory address into a cache location.

This address conversion is done by giving special significance to the bits in the main memory address. We first divide the bits into distinct groups we call **fields**. Depending on the mapping scheme, we may have two or three fields. How we use these fields depends on the particular mapping scheme being used. The mapping scheme determines where the data is placed when it is originally copied into cache and also provides a method for the CPU to find previously copied data when searching cache. The mapping schemes include direct mapping, fully associative mapping, and set associative mapping.

Before we discuss these mapping schemes, it is important to understand how data is copied into cache. Main memory and cache are both divided into the same size blocks (the size of these blocks varies). When a memory address is generated, cache is searched first to see if the required data at that address exists there. When the requested data is not found in cache, the entire main memory block in which the requested memory address resides is loaded into cache. As previously mentioned, this scheme is successful because of the principle of locality—if an address was just referenced, there is a good chance addresses in the same general vicinity will soon be referenced as well. Therefore, one missed address often results in several found addresses. For example, when you are in the basement and you first need tools, you have a "miss" and must go to the garage. If you gather up a set of tools that you might need and return to the basement, you hope that you'll have several "hits" while working on your home improvement project and don't have to make many more trips to the garage. Because accessing data in cache (a tool already in the basement) is faster than accessing data in main memory (going to the garage yet again!), cache memory speeds up the overall access time.

So how do we use fields in the main memory address? One field of the main memory address points us to a location in cache in which the data resides if it is resident in cache (this is called a **cache hit**), or where it is to be placed if it is not resident (which is called a **cache miss**). (This is slightly different for associative mapped cache, which we discuss shortly.) The cache block referenced is then checked to see if it is valid. This is done by associating a **valid bit** with each cache block. A valid bit of 0 means the cache block is not valid (we have a cache miss), and we must access main memory. A valid bit of 1 means it is valid (we may have a cache hit, but we need to complete one more step before we know for sure). We then compare the tag in the cache block to the **tag field** of our address. (The tag is a special group of bits derived from the main memory address that is stored with its corresponding block in cache.) If the tags are the same, then we have found the desired cache block (we have a cache hit). At this point, we need to locate the desired data in the block; this can be done using a different portion of the main memory address called the **offset field**. All cache mapping schemes require an offset field; however, the remaining fields are determined by the mapping scheme. We now discuss the three main cache mapping schemes. In these examples, we assume that if the cache block is empty, it is not valid; if it contains data, it is valid. Therefore, we do not include the valid bit in our discussions.

Before we discuss the mapping schemes, we mention one very important point. Some computers are byte addressable; others are word addressable. Key in determining how the mapping schemes work is knowing how many addresses are contained in main memory, in cache, and in each block. If a machine is byte addressable, we are concerned with the number of bytes; if it is word addressable, we are concerned with the number of words, regardless of the size of the word.

Direct Mapped Cache

Direct mapped cache assigns cache mappings using a modular approach. Because there are more main memory blocks than there are cache blocks, it should be clear that main memory blocks compete for cache locations. Direct mapping maps block X of main memory to block Y of cache, mod N, where N is the total number of blocks in cache. For example, if cache contains 4 blocks, then main memory block 0 maps to cache block 0, main memory block 1 maps to cache block 1, main memory block 2 maps to cache block 2, main memory block 3 maps to cache block 3, main memory block 4 maps to cache block 0, and so on. This is illustrated in Figure 6.2. In Figure 6.2a, we see 8 main memory blocks mapping to 4 cache blocks, resulting in 2 memory blocks mapping to each cache block. In Figure 6.2b, there are 16 memory blocks mapping to 4 cache blocks; we have doubled the size of memory and doubled the contention for each cache block. (We will soon see that this contention is one of the major disadvantages of direct mapped cache.)

You may be wondering, if main memory blocks 0 and 4 both map to cache block 0, how does the CPU know which block actually resides in cache block 0 at any given time? The answer is that each block is copied to cache and identified by the tag previously described. This means the tag for a particular block must be stored in cache with that block, as we shall see shortly.

To perform direct mapping, the binary main memory address is partitioned into the fields shown in Figure 6.3.

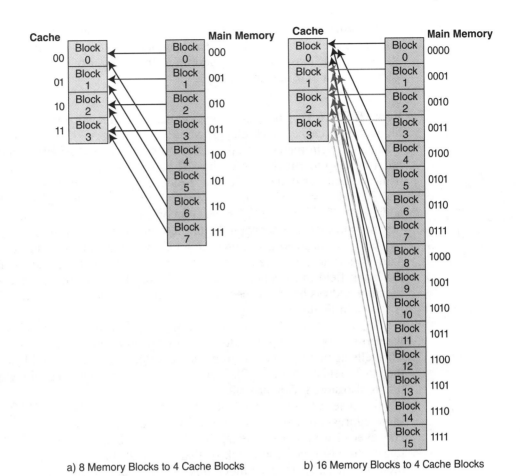

a) 8 Memory Blocks to 4 Cache Blocks   b) 16 Memory Blocks to 4 Cache Blocks

FIGURE 6.2   Direct Mapping of Main Memory Blocks to Cache Blocks

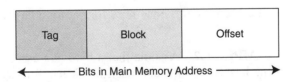

FIGURE 6.3   The Format of a Main Memory Address Using Direct Mapping

The size of each field depends on the physical characteristics of main memory and cache. The **offset** field uniquely identifies an address within a specific block; therefore, it must contain the appropriate number of bits to do this. The number of bytes (if the machine is byte addressable) or words (if the machine is word addressable) in each block dictates the number of bits in the offset field. This is also true of the **block** field—it must select a unique block of cache. (The number of blocks in cache dictates the number of bits in the block field.) The **tag** field is whatever is left over. When a block of main memory is copied to cache, this tag is stored with the block and uniquely identifies this block. The total of all three fields must, of course, add up to the number of bits in a main memory address. Let's look at some examples.

EXAMPLE 6.1 Consider a byte-addressable main memory consisting of 4 blocks, and a cache with 2 blocks, where each block is 4 bytes. This means Block 0 and 2 of main memory map to Block 0 of cache, and Blocks 1 and 3 of main memory map to Block 1 of cache. (This is easy for us to determine simply by using modular arithmetic, because 0 mod 2 = 0, 1 mod 2 = 1, 2 mod 2 = 0, and 3 mod 2 = 1. However, the computer must use the fields in the memory address itself.) Using the tag, block, and offset fields, we can see how main memory maps to cache, as shown in Figure 6.4 and explained as follows.

First, we need to determine the address format for mapping. Each block is 4 bytes, so the offset field must contain 2 bits; there are 2 blocks in cache, so the block field must contain 1 bit; this leaves 1 bit for the tag (because a main memory address has 4 bits because there are a total of $2^4 = 16$ bytes). The format is shown in Figure 6.4a.

Suppose we need to access main memory address 0x03 (0011 in binary). If we partition 0011 using the address format from Figure 6.4a, we get Figure 6.4b. This tells us that the main memory address 0011 maps to cache block 0 (because the block field evaluates to 0). Figure 6.4c shows this mapping, along with the tag that is also stored with the data.

Suppose we now access main memory address 0x0A = 1010_2. Using the same address format, we see that it maps to cache block 0 (see Figure 6.4d). However, if we compare the tag from address 1010 (the tag is 1) to what is currently stored in cache at block 0 (that tag is 0), they do not match. Therefore, the data currently in cache block 0 is removed, and the data from main memory block 3 replaces it and changes the tag, resulting in Figure 6.4e.

Let's consider the memory format for a larger example.

EXAMPLE 6.2 Assume that a byte-addressable memory consists of 2^{14} bytes, cache has 16 blocks, and each block has 8 bytes. From this, we determine that memory $\frac{2^{14}}{2^3} = 2^{11}$ blocks. We know that each main memory address requires 14 bits. Of this 14-bit address field, the rightmost 3 bits reflect the offset field (we need 3 bits to uniquely identify one of 8 bytes in a block). We need 4 bits to select a specific block in cache, so the block field consists of the middle 4 bits. The remaining 7 bits make up the tag field. The fields with sizes are illustrated in Figure 6.5.

As mentioned previously, the tag for each block is stored with that block in the cache. In this example, because main memory blocks 0 and 16 both map to cache block 0, the tag field would allow the system to differentiate between block

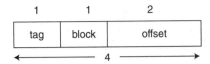

a) Main Memory Format

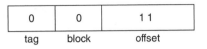

b) The Address 0011 Partitioned into Fields

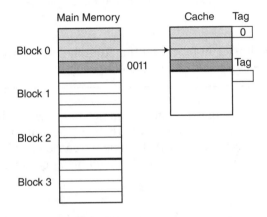

c) Mapping of Block Containing
Address 0011 = 0x3

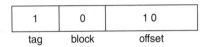

d) The Address 1010 Partitioned into Fields

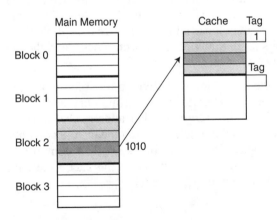

e) Mapping of Block Containing
Address 1010 = 0xA

FIGURE 6.4 Diagrams for Example 6.1

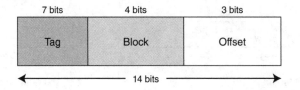

FIGURE 6.5 The Main Memory Address Format for Example 6.2

0 and block 16. The binary addresses in block 0 differ from those in block 16 in the upper leftmost 7 bits, so the tags are different and unique.

EXAMPLE 6.3 Let's look at a slightly larger example. Suppose we have a byte-addressable system using direct mapping with 16 bytes of main memory divided into 8 blocks (so each block has 2 bytes). Assume the cache is 4 blocks in size (for a total of 8 bytes). Figure 6.6 shows how the main memory blocks map to cache.

We know:

- A main memory address has 4 bits (because there are 2^4 or 16 bytes in main memory).

- This 4-bit main memory address is divided into three fields: The offset field is 1 bit (we need only 1 bit to differentiate between the two words in a block); the block field is 2 bits (we have 4 blocks in cache memory and need 2 bits to uniquely identify each block); and the tag field has 1 bit (this is all that is left over).

The main memory address is divided into the fields shown in Figure 6.7.

Suppose we generate the main memory address 0x9. We can see from the mapping listing in Figure 6.6 that address 0x9 is in main memory block 4 and should map to cache block 0 (which means the contents of main memory block 4 should be copied into cache block 0). The computer, however, uses the actual main memory address to determine the cache mapping block. This address, in binary, is represented in Figure 6.8.

Main Memory	Maps To	Cache
(000) Block 0 (addresses 0x0, 0x1)	⟶	Block 0 (00)
(001) Block 1 (addresses 0x2, 0x3)	⟶	Block 1 (01)
(010) Block 2 (addresses 0x4, 0x5)	⟶	Block 2 (10)
(011) Block 3 (addresses 0x6, 0x7)	⟶	Block 3 (11)
(100) Block 4 (addresses 0x8, 0x9)	⟶	Block 0 (00)
(101) Block 5 (addresses 0xA, 0xB)	⟶	Block 1 (01)
(110) Block 6 (addresses 0xC, 0xD)	⟶	Block 2 (10)
(111) Block 7 (addresses 0xE, 0xF)	⟶	Block 3 (11)

FIGURE 6.6 The Memory from Example 6.3 Mapped to Cache

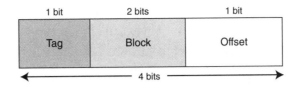

FIGURE 6.7   The Main Memory Address Format for Example 6.3

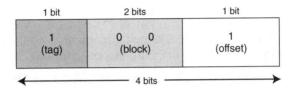

FIGURE 6.8   The Main Memory Address $9 = 1001_2$ Split into Fields

When the CPU generates this address, it first takes the block field bits 00 and uses these to direct it to the proper block in cache. 00 indicates that cache block 0 should be checked. If the cache block is valid, it then compares the tag field value of 1 (in the main memory address) to the tag associated with cache block 0. If the cache tag is 1, then block 4 currently resides in cache block 0. If the tag is 0, then block 0 from main memory is located in block 0 of cache. (To see this, compare main memory address $0x9 = 1001_2$, which is in block 4, to main memory address $0x1 = 0001_2$, which is in block 0. These two addresses differ only in the leftmost bit, which is the bit used as the tag by the cache.) Assuming that the tags match, which means that block 4 from main memory (with addresses 0x8 and 0x9) resides in cache block 0, the offset field value of 1 is used to select one of the two bytes residing in the block. Because the bit is 1, we select the byte with offset 1, which results in retrieving the data copied from main memory address 0x9.

Suppose the CPU now generates address $0x4 = 0100_2$. The middle two bits (10) direct the search to cache block 2. If the block is valid, the leftmost tag bit (0) would be compared to the tag bit stored with the cache block. If they match, the first byte in that block (of offset 0) would be returned to the CPU. To make sure you understand this process, perform a similar exercise with the main memory address $0xC = 1100_2$.

Let's move on to a larger example.

EXAMPLE 6.4   Suppose we have a byte-addressable system using 16-bit main memory addresses and 64 blocks of cache. If each block contains 8 bytes, we know that the main memory 16-bit address is divided into a 3-bit offset field, a 6-bit block field, and a 7-bit tag field. If the CPU generates the main memory address:

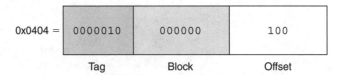

$$0\text{x}0404 =$$

0000010	000000	100
Tag	Block	Offset

it would look in block 0 of cache, and if it finds a tag of 0000010, the byte at offset 4 in this block would be returned to the CPU.

So, to summarize, direct mapped cache implements a mapping scheme that results in main memory blocks being mapped in a modular fashion to cache blocks. To determine how the mapping works, you must know several things:

• How many bits are in the main memory address (which is determined by how many addresses exist in main memory)

• How many blocks are in cache (which determines the size of the block field)

• How many addresses are in a block (which determines the size of the offset field)

Once you know these values, you can use the direct mapping address format to locate the block in cache to which a main memory block maps. Once you find the cache block, you can determine if the block currently in cache is the one you want by checking the tag. If the tags match (the tag from the memory address field and the tag in cache), use the offset field to find the desired data in the cache block.

Fully Associative Cache

Direct mapped cache is not as expensive as other caches because the mapping scheme does not require any searching. Each main memory block has a specific location to which it maps in cache; when a main memory address is converted to a cache address, the CPU knows exactly where to look in the cache for that memory block by simply examining the bits in the block field. This is similar to your address book: The pages often have an alphabetic index, so if you are searching for "Joe Smith," you would look under the "S" tab.

Instead of specifying a unique location for each main memory block, we can look at the opposite extreme: allowing a main memory block to be placed anywhere in cache. The only way to find a block mapped this way is to search all of cache. (This is similar to your author's desk!) This requires the entire cache to be built from **associative memory** so it can be searched in parallel. That is, a single search must compare the requested tag to *all* tags in cache to determine whether the desired data block is present in cache. Associative memory requires special hardware to allow associative searching and is, thus, quite expensive.

Let's look at associative memory in more detail so we can better understand why it is so expensive. We have already mentioned that fully associative cache allows a memory block to be placed anywhere in cache, which means we now have to search to find it, and to make this searching efficient, we search in parallel. But how do we do this in hardware? First, there must be a comparator circuit for each block in cache; this circuit outputs a 1 if the two input values match.

MEMORY   ADDRESS

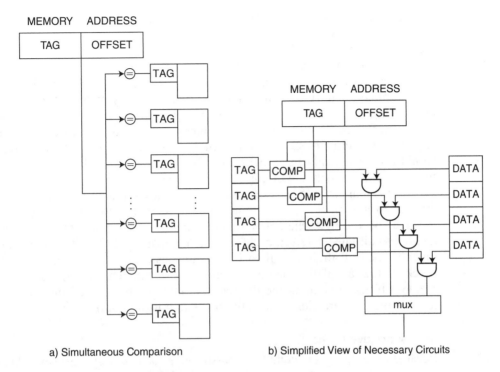

a) Simultaneous Comparison   b) Simplified View of Necessary Circuits

FIGURE 6.9   Associative Cache

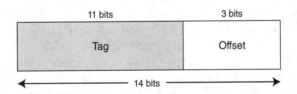

FIGURE 6.10   The Main Memory Address Format for Associative Mapping

The tag field from the main memory address is compared, simultaneously, to each tag from every cache block, as we see in Figure 6.9a. This memory is expensive because it requires not only a set of multiplexers to select the appropriate data once the correct cache block is identified but also the additional circuitry to implement the comparators. Figure 6.9b shows a simplified view of the circuits required for fully associative memory.

Using associative mapping, the main memory address is partitioned into two pieces, the tag and the offset. Recall Example 6.2, which had a memory with 2^{14} bytes, a cache with 16 blocks, and blocks of 8 bytes. Using fully associative mapping instead of direct mapping, we see from Figure 6.10 that the offset field is still 3 bits, but now the tag field is 11 bits. This tag must be stored with each block in cache. When the cache is searched for a specific main memory block, the tag field of the main memory address is compared to all the valid tag fields in cache; if a match is found, the block is found. (Remember, the tag uniquely identifies a main memory block.) If there is no match, we have a cache miss and the block must be transferred from main memory.

With direct mapping, if a block already occupies the cache location where a new block must be placed, the block currently in cache is removed (it is written back to main memory if it has been modified or simply overwritten if it has not been changed). With fully associative mapping, when cache is full, we need a replacement algorithm to decide which block we wish to throw out of cache (we call this our **victim block**). A simple first-in, first-out algorithm would work, as would a least recently used algorithm. There are many replacement algorithms that can be used; these are discussed in Section 6.4.2.

So, to summarize, fully associative cache allows a main memory block to be mapped to *any* block in cache. Once a main memory block resides in cache, to locate a specific byte, the computer compares the tag field of the main memory address to all tags stored in cache (in one comparison). Once the specific cache block is located, the offset field is used to locate the required data within that block. If the tag of the memory address doesn't match any tags in cache, the memory block containing the desired data must be transferred into cache. This transfer may require picking a victim block to transfer out of cache.

Set Associative Cache

Because of its speed and complexity, associative cache is very expensive. Although direct mapping is inexpensive, it is very restrictive. To see how direct mapping limits cache usage, suppose we are running a program on the architecture described in Example 6.3. Suppose the program is using block 0, then block 4, then 0, then 4, and so on as it executes instructions. Blocks 0 and 4 both map to the same location, which means the program would repeatedly throw out 0 to bring in 4, then throw out 4 to bring in 0, even though there are additional blocks in cache not being used. Fully associative cache remedies this problem by allowing a block from main memory to be placed anywhere. However, it requires a larger tag to be stored with the block (which results in a larger cache) in addition to requiring special hardware for searching of all blocks in cache simultaneously (which implies a more expensive cache). We need a scheme somewhere in the middle.

The third mapping scheme we introduce is *N*-**way set associative cache mapping**, a combination of these two approaches. This scheme is similar to direct mapped cache, in that we use the address to map the block to a certain cache location. The important difference is that instead of mapping to a single cache block, an address maps to a **set** of several cache blocks. All sets in cache must be the same size. This size can vary from cache to cache. For example, in a 2-way set associative cache, there are 2 cache blocks per set, as seen in Figure 6.11. It is easiest to view set associative cache logically as a two-dimensional cache. In Figure 6.11a, we see a 2-way set associative cache, where each set contains 2 blocks, thus giving us rows and columns in cache. However, cache memory is actually linear. In Figure 6.11b, we see how set associative cache is implemented in a linear memory. A 4-way set associative cache has 4 blocks per set; an 8-way

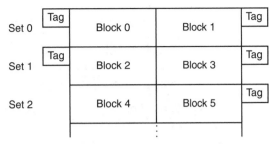

a) Logical View of 2-Way Set Associative Cache

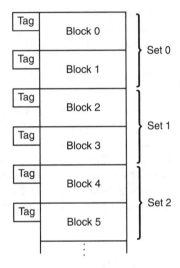

b) Linear View of 2-Way Set Associative Cache

FIGURE 6.11   A 2-Way Set Associative Cache

has 8 blocks per set, and so on. Once the desired set is located, the cache is treated as associative memory; the tag of the main memory address must be compared to the tags of each block in the set. Instead of requiring a comparator circuit for each block in cache, set associative cache only needs a comparator for each block in a set. For example, if there are 64 total cache blocks, using 4-way set associative mapping, the cache needs only 4 total comparators, not 64. Direct mapped cache is a special case of N-way set associative cache mapping where the set size is one. Fully associative cache, where cache has n blocks, is a special case of set associative mapping in which there is only one set of size n.

In set associative cache mapping, the main memory address is partitioned into three pieces: the tag field, the set field, and the offset field. The tag and offset fields assume the same roles as before; the set field indicates into which cache set the main memory block maps, as we see in the following example.

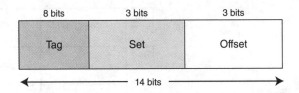

FIGURE 6.12   Format for Set Associative Mapping for Example 6.5

≡   **EXAMPLE 6.5**   Suppose we are using 2-way set associative mapping with a byte-addressable main memory of 2^{14} bytes and a cache with 16 blocks, where each block contains 8 bytes. If cache consists of a total of 16 blocks, and each set has 2 blocks, then there are 8 sets in cache. Therefore, the set field is 3 bits, the offset field is 3 bits, and the tag field is 8 bits. This is illustrated in Figure 6.12.

The set field of a main memory address specifies a unique set in cache for the given main memory block. All blocks in that cache set are then searched for a matching tag. An associative search must be performed, but the search is restricted to the specified set instead of the entire cache. This significantly reduces the cost of the specialized hardware. For example, in a 2-way set associative cache, the hardware searches only 2 blocks in parallel.

Let's look at an example to illustrate the differences among the various mapping schemes.

≡   **EXAMPLE 6.6**   Suppose a byte-addressable memory contains 1MB and cache consists of 32 blocks, where each block contains 16 bytes. Using direct mapping, fully associative mapping, and 4-way set associative mapping, determine where the main memory address 0x326A0 maps to in cache by specifying either the cache block or cache set.

First, we note that a main memory address has 20 bits. The main memory format for direct mapped cache is shown in Figure 6.13:

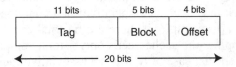

FIGURE 6.13   Direct Mapped Memory Format for Example 6.6

If we represent our main memory address 0x326A0 in binary and place the bits into the format, we get the fields shown in Figure 6.14:

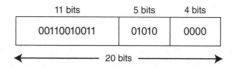

FIGURE 6.14   The Address 0x326A0 from Example 6.6 Divided into Fields for Direct Mapping

This tells us that memory address 0x326A0 maps to cache block 01010 (or block 10).

If we are using fully associative cache, the memory address format is:

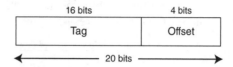

FIGURE 6.15   Fully Associative Memory Format for Example 6.6

However, dividing the main memory address into these fields won't help us determine the mapping location for the main memory block containing this address because with fully associative cache, the block can map anywhere. If we are using 4-way set associative mapping, the memory address format is shown is Figure 6.16:

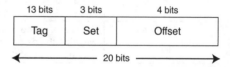

FIGURE 6.16   4-Way Set Associative Mapped Memory Format for Example 6.6

The set field has 3 bits because there are only 8 sets in cache (where each set holds 4 blocks). If we divide our main memory address into these fields, we get:

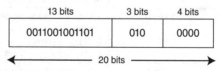

FIGURE 6.17   The Address 0x326A0 from Example 6.6 Divided into Fields for Set Associative Mapping

which tells us that main memory address 0x326A0 maps to cache set $010_2 = 2$. However, the set would still need to be searched (by comparing the tag in the address to all the tags in cache set 2) before the desired data could be found.

Let's look at one more example to reinforce the concepts of cache mapping.

EXAMPLE 6.7   Suppose we have a byte-addressable computer with a cache that holds 8 blocks of 4 bytes each. Assuming that each memory address has 8 bits and cache is originally empty, for each of the cache mapping techniques, direct mapped, fully associative, and 2-way set associative, trace how cache is used when a program accesses the following series of addresses in order: 0x01, 0x04, 0x09, 0x05, 0x14, 0x21, and 0x01.

We start with direct mapped. First, we must determine the address format. Each block has 4 bytes, which requires 2 bits in the offset field. Cache has a total of 8 blocks, so we need 3 bits in the block field. An address has 8 bits, so that leaves 3 bits for the tag field, resulting in:

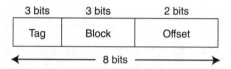

Now that we know the address format, we can begin tracing the program.

Address Reference	Binary Address (divided into fields)	Hit or Miss	Comments
0x01	000 000 01	Miss	If we check cache block 000 for the tag 000, we find that it is not there. So we copy the data from addresses 0x00, 0x01, 0x02, and 0x03 into cache block 0 and store the tag 000 for that block.
0x04	000 001 00	Miss	We check cache block 001 for the tag 000, and on finding it missing, we copy the data from addresses 0x04, 0x05, 0x06, and 0x07 into cache block 1 and store the tag 000 for that block.
0x09	000 010 01	Miss	A check of cache block 010 (2) for the tag 000 reveals a miss, so we copy the data from addresses 0x08, 0x09, 0x0A, and 0x0B into cache block 2 and store the tag 000 for that block.
0x05	000 001 01	Hit	We check cache block 001 for the tag 000, and we find it. We then use the offset value 01 to get the exact byte we need.
0x14	000 101 00	Miss	We check cache block 101 (5) for the tag 000, but it is not present. We copy addresses 0x14, 0x15, 0x16, and 0x17 to cache block 5 and store the tag 000 with that block.
0x21	001 000 01	Miss	We check cache block 000 for the tag 001; we find tag 000 (which means this is not the correct block), so we overwrite the existing contents of this cache block by copying the data from addresses 0x20, 0x21, 0x22, and 0x23 into cache block 0 and storing the tag 001.
0x01	000 000 01	Miss	Although we have already fetched the block that contains address 0x01 once, it was overwritten when we fetched the block containing address 0x21 (if we look at block 0 in cache, we can see that its tag is 001, not 000). Therefore, we must overwrite the contents of block 0 in cache with the data from addresses 0x00, 0x01, 0x02, and 0x03, and store a tag of 000.

A few things to note: We always copy an entire block from memory to cache any time there is a miss. We don't take 4 bytes beginning with the address we missed; we must take the 4-byte block that contains the address we missed. For example, when we missed for memory address 0x09, we brought in 4 bytes of data beginning with address 0x08. Because 0x09 is at an offset of 1 in the block, we know the block begins with address 0x08. Also note the contention for block 0 of cache; this is a typical problem for direct mapped cache. The final contents of cache are:

Block	Cache Contents (represented by address)	Tag
0	0x00, 0x01, 0x02, 0x03	000
1	0x04, 0x05, 0x06, 0x07	000
2	0x08, 0x09, 0x0A, 0x0B	000
3		
4		
5	0x14, 0x15, 0x16, 0x17	000
6		
7		

How do things change if we use fully associative cache? First, the address format becomes:

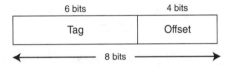

With fully associative cache, the block from memory can be stored anywhere. Let's assume we will store it in the first available location; if all locations are full, we will "roll over" to the beginning and start again.

Address Reference	Binary Address (divided into fields)	Hit or Miss	Comments
0x01	000000 01	Miss	We search all of cache for the tag 000000, and we don't find it. So we copy the data from addresses 0x00, 0x01, 0x02, and 0x03 into cache block 0 and store the tag 000000 for that block.
0x04	000001 00	Miss	We search all of cache for the tag 000001, and on finding it missing, we copy the data from addresses 0x04, 0x05, 0x06, and 0x07 into cache block 1 and store the tag 000001 for that block.
0x09	000010 01	Miss	We don't find the tag 000010 in cache, so we copy the data from addresses 0x08, 0x09, 0x0A, and 0x0B into cache block 2 and store the tag 000010 for that block.
0x05	000001 01	Hit	We search all of cache for the tag 000001, and we find it stored with cache block 1. We then use the offset value 01 to get the exact byte we need.
0x14	000101 00	Miss	We search all of cache for the tag 000101, but it is not present. We copy addresses 0x14, 0x15, 0x16, and 0x17 to cache block 3 and store the tag 000101 with that block.
0x21	001000 01	Miss	We search all of cache for the tag 001000; we don't find it, so we copy the data from addresses 0x20, 0x21, 0x22, and 0x23 into cache block 4 and store the tag 001000.
0x01	000000 01	Hit	We search cache for the tag 000000 and find it with cache block 0. We use the offset of 1 to find the data we want.

The final contents of cache are:

Block	Cache Contents (represented by address)	Tag
0	0x00, 0x01, 0x02, 0x03	000000
1	0x04, 0x05, 0x06, 0x07	000001
2	0x08, 0x09, 0x0A, 0x0B	000010
3	0x14, 0x15, 0x16, 0x17	000101
4	0x20, 0x21, 0x22, 0x23	001000
5		
6		
7		

Now let's take a look at using 2-way set associative cache. Because cache is 8 blocks, and each set contains 2 blocks, cache has 4 sets. The address format for 2-way set associative cache is:

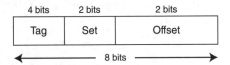

If we trace through the memory references, we get the following:

Address Reference	Binary Address (divided into fields)	Hit or Miss	Comments
0x01	0000 00 01	Miss	We search in set 0 of cache for a block with the tag 0000, and we find it is not there. So we copy the data from addresses 0x00, 0x01, 0x02, and 0x03 into set 0 (so now set 0 has one used block and one free block) and store the tag 0000 for that block. It does not matter which set we use; for consistency, we put the data in the first set.
0x04	0000 01 00	Miss	We search set 1 for a block with the tag 0000, and on finding it missing, we copy the data from addresses 0x04, 0x05, 0x06, and 0x07 into set 1, and store the tag 0000 for that block.
0x09	0000 10 01	Miss	We search set 2 (10) for a block with the tag 0000, but we don't find one, so we copy the data from addresses 0x08, 0x09, 0x0A, and 0x0B into set 2 and store the tag 0000 for that block.
0x05	0000 01 01	Hit	We search set 1 for a block with the tag 0000, and we find it. We then use the offset value 01 within that block to get the exact byte we need.
0x14	0001 01 00	Miss	We search set 1 for a block with the tag 0001, but it is not present. We copy addresses 0x14, 0x15, 0x16, and 0x17 to set 1 and store the tag 0001 with that block. Note that set 1 is now full.
0x21	0010 00 01	Miss	We search cache set 0 for a block with the tag 0010; we don't find it, so we copy the data from addresses 0x20, 0x21, 0x22, and 0x23 into set 0 and store the tag 0010. Note that set 0 is now full.
0x01	0000 00 01	Hit	We search cache set 0 for a block with the tag 0000, and we find it. We use the offset of 1 within that block to find the data we want.

Set	Block	Cache Contents (represented by address)	Tag
0	First	0x00, 0x01, 0x02, 0x03	0000
	Second	0x20, 0x21, 0x22, 0x23	0010
1	First	0x04, 0x05, 0x06, 0x07	0000
	Second	0x14, 0x15, 0x16, 0x17	0001
2	First	0x08, 0x09, 0x0A, 0x0B	0000
	Second		
3	First		
	Second		

Set associative cache mapping is a good compromise between direct mapped and fully associative cache. Studies indicate that it exhibits good performance, and that 2-way up to 16-way caches perform almost as well as fully associative cache at a fraction of the cost. Therefore, most modern computer systems use some form of set associative cache mapping, with 4-way set associative being one of the most common.

6.4.2 Replacement Policies

In a direct-mapped cache, if there is contention for a cache block, there is only one possible action: The existing block is kicked out of cache to make room for the new block. This process is called **replacement**. With direct mapping, there is no need for a replacement policy because the location for each new block is predetermined. However, with fully associative cache and set associative cache, we need a replacement algorithm to determine the "victim" block to be removed from cache. When using fully associative cache, there are K possible cache locations (where K is the number of blocks in cache) to which a given main memory block may map. With N-way set associative mapping, a block can map to any of N different blocks within a given set. How do we determine which block in cache should be replaced? The algorithm for determining replacement is called the **replacement policy**.

There are several popular replacement policies. One that is not practical but that can be used as a benchmark by which to measure all others is the **optimal** algorithm. We like to keep values in cache that will be needed again soon, and throw out blocks that won't be needed again, or that won't be needed for some time. An algorithm that could look into the future to determine the precise blocks to keep or eject based on these two criteria would be best. This is what the optimal algorithm does. We want to replace the block that will not be used for the longest period of time in the future. For example, if the choice for the victim block is between block 0 and block 1, and block 0 will be used again in 5 seconds, whereas block 1 will not be used again for 10 seconds, we would throw out block 1. From a practical standpoint, we can't look into the future—but we can run a program and then rerun it, so we effectively *do* know the future. We can then apply the optimal algorithm on the second run. The optimal algorithm guarantees the lowest possible miss rate. Because we cannot see the future on every single program we run, the optimal algorithm is used only as a metric to determine how good or bad another algorithm is. The closer an algorithm performs to the optimal algorithm, the better.

We need algorithms that best approximate the optimal algorithm. We have several options. For example, we might consider temporal locality. We might guess that any value that has not been used recently is unlikely to be needed again soon. We can keep track of the last time each block was accessed (assign a timestamp to the block) and select as the victim block the block that has been used least recently. This is the **least recently used** (**LRU**) algorithm. Unfortunately, LRU requires the system to keep a history of accesses for every cache block, which requires significant space and slows down the operation of the cache. There are ways to approximate LRU, but that is beyond the scope of this text. (Refer to the references at the end of the chapter for more information.)

First-in, first-out (**FIFO**) is another popular approach. With this algorithm, the block that has been in cache the longest (regardless of how recently it has been used) would be selected as the victim to be removed from cache memory.

Another approach is to select a victim at **random**. The problem with LRU and FIFO is that there are degenerate referencing situations in which they can be made to **thrash** (constantly throw out a block, then bring it back, then throw it out, then bring it back, repeatedly). Some people argue that random replacement, although it sometimes throws out data that will be needed soon, never thrashes. Unfortunately, it is difficult to have truly random replacement, and it can decrease average performance.

The algorithm selected often depends on how the system will be used. No single (practical) algorithm is best for all scenarios. For that reason, designers use algorithms that perform well under a wide variety of circumstances.

6.4.3   Effective Access Time and Hit Ratio

The performance of a hierarchical memory is measured by its **effective access time** (**EAT**), or the average time per access. EAT is a weighted average that uses the hit ratio and the relative access times of the successive levels of the hierarchy. The actual access time for each level depends on the technology and method used for access.

Before we can determine the average access time, we have to know something about how cache and memory work. When data is needed from cache, there are two options for retrieving that data. We could start an access to cache and, at the same time, start an access to main memory (in parallel). If the data is found in cache, the access to main memory is terminated, at no real cost because the accesses were overlapped. If the data is not in cache, the access to main memory is already well on its way. This overlapping helps reduce the cost (in time) for a cache miss. The alternative is to perform everything sequentially. First, cache is checked; if the data is found, we're done. If the data is not found in cache, then an access is started to retrieve the data from main memory. The method used affects the average (effective) access time, as we see below.

For example, suppose the cache access time is 10ns, main memory access time is 200ns, and the cache hit rate is 99%. Using overlapped (parallel) access, the average time for the processor to access an item in this two-level memory would then be:

$$\text{EAT} = \underbrace{0.99(10\text{ns})}_{\text{cache hit}} + \underbrace{0.01(200\text{ns})}_{\text{cache miss}} = 9.9\text{ns} + 2\text{ns} = 11\text{ns}$$

Using nonoverlapped (sequential) access, the average access time would change to:

$$\text{EAT} = \underbrace{0.99(10\text{ns})}_{\text{cache hit}} + 0.01(\overbrace{10\text{ns}}^{\text{check cache}} + \overbrace{200\text{ns}}^{\text{go to main memory}}) = 9.9\text{ns} + 2.1\text{ns} = 12\text{ns}$$

What, exactly, does this mean? If we look at the access times over a long period of time, this system performs as if it had a single large memory with an 11ns or 12ns access time. A 99% cache hit rate allows the system to perform very well, even though most of the memory is built using slower technology with an access time of 200ns.

The formula for calculating effective access time for a two-level memory consisting of cache and main memory is given by:

$$\text{EAT} = H \times \text{Access}_C + (1 - H) \times \text{Access}_{MM}$$

where H = cache hit rate, Access_C = cache access time, and Access_{MM} = main memory access time.

This formula can be extended to apply to three- or even four-level memories, as we will see shortly.

6.4.4 When Does Caching Break Down?

When programs exhibit locality, caching works quite well. However, if programs exhibit bad locality, caching breaks down and the performance of the memory hierarchy is poor. In particular, object-oriented programming can cause programs to exhibit less than optimal locality. Another example of bad locality can be seen in two-dimensional array access. Arrays are typically stored in row-major order. Suppose, for purposes of this example, that one row fits exactly in one cache block and cache can hold all but one row of the array. Assume, also, that cache uses a first-in, first-out replacement policy. If a program accesses the array one row at a time, the first row access produces a miss, but once the block is transferred into cache, all subsequent accesses to that row are hits. So a 5 × 4 array would produce 5 misses and 15 hits over 20 accesses (assuming that we are accessing each element of the array). If a program accesses the array in column-major order, the first access to the column, entry (1,1), results in a miss, after which an entire row is transferred in. However, the second access to the column, entry (2,1), results in another miss. The access to entry (3,1) produces a miss, as does the access to entry (4,1). Reading entry (5,1) produces a miss, but bringing in the fifth row requires us to throw out the first row. Because we have removed the first row, our next access to entry (1,2) causes a miss as well. This continues throughout the entire array access; the data being transferred in for each row is not being used because the array is being accessed by column. Because cache is not large enough, this would produce 20 misses on 20 accesses. A third example would be a program that loops through a linear array that does not fit in cache. There would be a significant reduction in the locality when memory is used in this manner.

6.4.5 Cache Write Policies

In addition to determining which victim to select for replacement, designers must also decide what to do with so-called **dirty blocks** of cache, or blocks that have been modified. When the processor writes to main memory, the data may be written to the cache instead under the assumption that the processor will probably read it again soon. If a cache block is modified, the cache **write policy** determines when the actual main memory block is updated to match the cache block. There are two basic write policies:

- **Write-through**—A write-through policy updates both the cache and the main memory simultaneously on every write. This is slower than write-back, but ensures that the cache is consistent with the main system memory. The obvious disadvantage here is that every write now requires a main memory access. Using a write-through policy means every write to the cache necessitates a main memory write, thus slowing the system (if all accesses are write, this essentially slows down the system to main memory speed). However, in real applications, the majority of accesses are reads, so this slow-down is negligible.

- **Write-back**—A write-back policy (also called **copyback**) only updates blocks in main memory when the cache block is selected as a victim and must be removed from cache. This is normally faster than write-through because time is not wasted writing information to memory on each write to cache. Memory traffic is also reduced. The disadvantage is that main memory and cache may not contain the same value at a given instant of time, and if a process terminates (crashes) before the write to main memory is done, the data in cache may be lost.

To improve the performance of cache, one must increase the hit ratio by using a better mapping algorithm (up to roughly a 20% increase), better strategies for write operations (potentially a 15% increase), better replacement algorithms (up to a 10% increase), and better coding practices, as we saw in the earlier example of row versus column-major access (up to a 30% increase in hit ratio). Simply increasing the size of cache may improve the hit ratio by roughly 1–4% but is not guaranteed to do so.

Caching and Hashing and Bits, Oh My!

Suppose you have a large set of data, and you are writing a program to search that data set. You could store the data in an array, at which point you have two options. If the array is unsorted, a linear search could be used to locate a particular piece of information. If the data is sorted, a binary search could be used. However, the running times of both types of searches are dependent on the data set size with which you are working.

Hashing is a process that allows us to store and retrieve data in an average time that does not depend on the size of the data set we are searching. Hashing is simply the process of putting an item into a structure by transforming a key value into an address. Typically, a **hash table** is used to store the hashed values, and a **hashing function** performs the key-to-address transformation. When we want to look up a value, the key for the value is input into the hash function, and the output is the address in the table at which the value is stored. Hash tables were invented by compiler writers in the 1960s to maintain symbol tables (as discussed in Chapter 4).

Suppose you are tired of looking up names in an extremely large phone book. Even though the names are sorted, with so many pages, it takes you a long time to find a particular phone number. You could create a hash function to store those names and numbers in a hash table on your computer. When you want a phone number, all you would need to do is input the name into the hash function and it would point you to the correct location of the corresponding phone number in the hash table. Computerized dictionaries often use hash tables for storing words and definitions because the lookup time is much faster than it would be with binary search.

Hashing works because of good hash functions—good hash functions give a uniform distribution even if the key values are not distributed well. A perfect hash function is a one-to-one mapping of the values into the table. However, perfect hash functions are difficult to construct. Hash functions that map most values to unique locations are acceptable, provided that the number of **collisions** (cases in which two values map to the same location) are minimal. Collisions are handled in several different ways, the easiest of which is chaining. **Chaining** is simply the process of creating a list of items that map to a particular location. When a key value maps to a list, more time is required to find the item because we have to search the entire list.

Hash functions can be simple or complex. Examples of simple hash functions with numeric keys include (1) modulo arithmetic, in which the number of items in the table is estimated, that number is used as a divisor into the key, and the remainder is the hashed value; (2) radix transformation, a process in which the digital key's number base is changed, resulting in a different sequence of digits, and a specific "substring" of those digits is used as the hash value; (3) key transposition, in which the digits in the portion of the key are simply scrambled, and the new scrambled value is used as the hash value; and (4) folding, a method in which the key is portioned into several parts, the parts are added together, and a portion of the result is used as the hash value. For the above phone book example, we could substitute a character's ASCII value for each letter in the name, and use a radix transformation by selecting some base, multiplying each ASCII value by a power of that base, and adding the results to yield the hash value. For example, if the name is "Tim" and the base is 8, the hash value would be $(84 \times 8^2) + (105 \times 8^1) + (109 \times 8^0) = 6325$, meaning we could find Tim in location 6325 of our hash table.

Hashing is used in many computer science applications. For example, web browsers use a hashed cache to store recently viewed web pages. Hashing is used to store and retrieve items in indexed database systems. There are several well-known hash functions used in cryptography, message authentication, and error checking. In large file systems, both caching and hashing (to determine file location) are used to increase performance.

You should notice a similarity between hashing and the cache mapping schemes discussed in this chapter. The "key" used for cache mapping is the middle field of the address, which is the block field for direct mapped cache and the set field for set associative cache. The hash function used by direct mapping and set associative mapping is simple modulo arithmetic (fully associative mapping uses no hashing and requires a full search of the cache to find the desired data element). In direct mapping, if we have a collision, the value currently in cache is replaced by the incoming value. With set associative cache, the set is similar to a list in chaining—if there is a collision, depending on the size of the set, multiple values that hash to the same location can coexist. To retrieve a value in set associative cache, once the middle bits determine the location (or set) in cache, the set must be searched for the desired value. Recall that a tag is stored with each value and is used to identify the correct item.

Different items can be used as keys for hashing. We use the middle bits of the physical address of a desired value as the key in cache mapping. But why use the middle bits? The lower bits (in the rightmost word field) are used to determine the offset within the block. However, the higher bits (in the leftmost tag field) could be used as the key instead of the middle bits (and the middle bits could, correspondingly, be used as the tag). Why did designers choose the middle bits?

There are two options for memory interleaving: high-order interleaving and low-order memory interleaving. High-order interleaving uses the high-order bits to determine the memory module location and places consecutive memory addresses in the same module. This is precisely what would happen if we used the high-order bits of the memory address to determine the cache location—values from consecutive memory addresses would map to the same location in cache. Spatial locality tells us that memory locations close to each other tend to be referenced in clusters. If values from adjacent memory locations are mapped to the same cache block or set, spatial locality implies that there will be collisions (larger sets result in fewer collisions). However, if the middle bits are used as the key instead, adjacent memory locations are mapped to different cache locations, resulting in fewer collisions, and, ultimately, better hit ratios.

6.4.6   Instruction and Data Caches

In our discussion of cache, we have focused mainly on what is called a **unified** or **integrated cache**, that is, cache that holds the more recently used data *and* instructions. However, many modern computers employ a **Harvard cache**, which means they have separate data and instruction caches.

A **data cache** is reserved for storing data only. When a request is made for data from memory, this cache is checked first. If the data is found, it is retrieved from data cache and the execution continues. If not found, the data is retrieved from memory and placed in the data cache. Data that exhibits good locality yields higher hit rates. For example, data accessed from an array exhibits better locality than data accessed from a linked list. Thus, the way in which you program can affect the data cache hit rate.

Just as high data cache hit rates are desirable, high **instruction cache** hit rates are imperative for good performance. Most program instructions are executed sequentially, branching only occasionally for procedure calls, loops, and conditional statements. Therefore, program instructions tend to have high locality. Even when a procedure is called or a loop is executed, these modules are often small enough to fit in one block of an instruction cache (a good motivator for small procedures!), thus increasing performance.

Separating instructions from data in cache allows the accesses to be less random and more clustered. However, some designers prefer an integrated cache; to get the same performance as a system with separate data and instruction caches, the integrated cache must be larger, thus introducing more latency in retrieving values. In addition, a unified cache has only one port for data and instructions, resulting in conflicts between the two.

Some processors also have what is known as a **victim cache**, a small, associative cache used to hold blocks that have been thrown out of the CPU cache due to conflicts. The idea is that if the victim block is used in the near future, it can be retrieved from the victim cache with less penalty than going to memory. This basically gives the data that was evicted from cache a "second chance" to be used before being sent to memory. Another type of specialized cache, **trace cache**, is a variant of an instruction cache. Trace caches are used to store instruction sequences that have already been decoded, so that if the instructions are needed again, no decoding is required. In addition, the processor can deal with blocks of instructions and not worry about branches in the execution flow of the program. This cache is so named because it stores traces of the dynamic instruction stream, making noncontiguous instructions appear to be contiguous. The Intel Pentium 4 uses this type of cache to increase performance.

6.4.7   Levels of Cache

Clearly, caching provides an increase in performance, provided the hit rate is satisfactory. Increasing the size of cache might be your first thought to produce a higher hit rate; however, larger caches are slower (the access time is larger). For years, manufacturers have been trying to balance the higher latency in larger caches with the increase in hit rates by selecting just the right size cache. However, many designers are applying the concepts of levels of memory to cache itself, and they are now using a **multilevel cache hierarchy** in most systems—caches are using caching for increased performance!

As we have seen, Level 1 (L1) cache is the term used for cache that is resident on the chip itself, and it is the fastest, smallest cache. L1 cache, often referred to as "internal cache," typically ranges in size from 8KB to 64KB. When a memory access is requested, L1 is checked first, with typical access speeds of approximately 4ns. If the data is not found in L1, the Level 2 (L2) cache is checked. The L2 cache is typically located external to the processor, and it has access speeds of 15–20ns. L2 cache can be located on the system motherboard, on a separate chip, or on an expansion board. L2 cache is larger, but slower than L1 cache. Typical sizes for L2 cache range from 64KB to 2MB. If data is missing from L1, but found in L2, it is loaded into L1 cache (in some architectures, the data being replaced in L1 is swapped with the requested data in L2). More manufacturers have begun to include L2 cache in their architectures by building L2 cache onto the same die as the CPU itself so the cache runs at CPU speed (but not on the same circuit with the CPU, such as is the case with L1 cache). This reduces the access speed of L2 cache to approximately 10ns. **L3 cache** is the term now used to refer to the extra cache between the processor and memory (that used to be called L2 cache) on processors that include L2 cache as part of their architecture. L3 caches range in size from 256MB to 8MB.

Inclusive caches are caches at different levels that allow the data to be present at multiple levels concurrently. For example, in the Intel Pentium family, data found in L1 may also exist in L2. A **strictly inclusive cache** guarantees that all data at one level is also found in the next lower level. **Exclusive caches** guarantee the data to be in, at most, one level of cache.

We discussed separate data and instruction caches in the previous section. Typically, architectures use integrated caches at levels L2 and L3. However, many have separate instruction and data caches at L1. For example, the Intel Celeron uses two separate L1 caches, one for instructions and one for data. In addition to this nice design feature, Intel uses **nonblocking cache** for its L2 caches. Most caches can process only one request at a time (so on a cache miss, the cache has to wait for memory to provide the requested value and load it into cache). Nonblocking caches can process up to four requests concurrently.

6.5 VIRTUAL MEMORY

You now know that caching allows a computer to access frequently used data from a smaller but faster cache memory. Cache is found near the top of our memory hierarchy. Another important concept inherent in the hierarchy is **virtual memory**. The purpose of virtual memory is to use the hard disk as an extension of RAM, thus increasing the available address space a process can use. Most personal computers have a relatively small amount (typically around 4GB) of main memory. This is usually not enough memory to hold multiple applications concurrently, such as a word processing application, an email program, and a graphics program, in addition to the operating system itself. Using virtual memory, your computer addresses more main memory than it actually has, and it uses the hard drive to hold the excess. This area on the hard drive is called a **page file**, because it holds chunks of main memory on the hard drive. The easiest way to think about virtual memory is to conceptualize it as an imaginary memory location in which all addressing issues are handled by the operating system.

The most common way to implement virtual memory is by using **paging**, a method in which main memory is divided into fixed-size blocks and programs are divided into the same size blocks. Typically, chunks of the program are brought into memory as needed. It is not necessary to store contiguous chunks of the program in contiguous chunks of main memory. Because pieces of the program can be stored out of order, program addresses, once generated by the CPU, must be translated to main memory addresses. Remember, in caching, a main memory address had to be transformed into a cache location. The same is true when using virtual memory; every virtual address must be translated into a physical address. How is this done? Before delving further into an explanation of virtual memory, let's define some frequently used terms for virtual memory implemented through paging:

- **Virtual address**—The logical or program address that the process uses. Whenever the CPU generates an address, it is always in terms of virtual address space.
- **Physical address**—The real address in physical memory.
- **Mapping**—The mechanism by which virtual addresses are translated into physical ones (very similar to cache mapping)
- **Page frames**—The equal-size chunks or blocks into which main memory (physical memory) is divided.
- **Pages**—The chunks or blocks into which virtual memory (the logical address space) is divided, each equal in size to a page frame. Virtual pages are stored on disk until needed.
- **Paging**—The process of copying a virtual page from disk to a page frame in main memory.
- **Fragmentation**—Memory that becomes unusable.
- **Page fault**—An event that occurs when a requested page is not in main memory and must be copied into memory from disk.

Because main memory and virtual memory are divided into equal-size pages, pieces of the process address space can be moved into main memory but need not be stored contiguously. As previously stated, we need not have all of the process in main memory at once; virtual memory allows a program to run when only specific pieces are present in memory. The parts not currently being used are stored in the page file on disk.

Virtual memory can be implemented with different techniques, including paging, segmentation, or a combination of both, but paging is the most popular. (This topic is covered in great detail in the study of operating systems.) The success of paging, like that of cache, is dependent on the locality principle. When data is needed that does not reside in main memory, the entire block in which it resides is copied from disk to main memory, in hopes that other data on the same page will be useful as the program continues to execute.

6.5.1 Paging

The basic idea behind paging is quite simple: Allocate physical memory to processes in fixed-size chunks (page frames) and keep track of where the various pages of the process reside by recording information in a **page table**. Every process has its own page table that typically resides in main memory, and the page table stores the physical location of each virtual page of the process. The page table has N rows, where N is the number of virtual pages in the process. If there are pages of the process currently not in main memory, the page table indicates this by setting a **valid bit** to 0; if the page is in main memory, the valid bit is set to 1. Therefore, each entry of the page table has two fields: a valid bit and a frame number.

Additional fields are often added to relay more information. For example, a **dirty bit** (or a **modify bit**) could be added to indicate whether the page has been changed. This makes returning the page to disk more efficient, because if it is not modified, it does not need to be rewritten to disk. Another bit (the **usage bit**) can be added to indicate the page usage. This bit is set to 1 whenever the page is accessed. After a certain time period, the usage bit is set to 0. If the page is referenced again, the usage bit is set to 1. However, if the bit remains 0, this indicates that the page has not been used for a period of time, and the system might benefit by sending this page out to disk. By doing so, the system frees up this page's location for another page that the process eventually needs (we discuss this in more detail when we introduce replacement algorithms).

Virtual memory pages are the same size as physical memory page frames. Process memory is divided into these fixed-size pages, resulting in potential **internal fragmentation** when the last page is copied into memory. The process may not actually need the entire page frame, but no other process may use it. Therefore, the unused memory in this last frame is effectively wasted. It might happen that the process itself requires less than one page in its entirety, but it must occupy an entire page frame when copied to memory. Internal fragmentation is unusable space *within* a given partition (in this case, a page) of memory.

Now that you understand what paging is, we will discuss how it works. When a process generates a virtual address, the operating system must dynamically translate this virtual address into the physical address in memory at which the data actually resides. (For purposes of simplicity, let's assume that we have no cache memory for the moment.) For example, from a program viewpoint, we see the final byte of a 10-byte program as address 0x09, assuming 1-byte instructions and 1-byte addresses, and a starting address of 0x00. However, when actually loaded into memory, the logical address 0x09 (perhaps a reference to the label X in an assembly language program) may actually reside in physical memory location 0x39, implying that the program was loaded starting at physical address 0x30. There must be an easy way to convert the logical, or virtual, address 0x09 to the physical address 0x39.

To accomplish this address translation, a virtual address is divided into two fields: a **page field** and an **offset field**, to represent the offset within that page where the requested data is located. This address translation process is similar to the process we used when we divided main memory addresses into fields for the cache mapping algorithms. And similar to cache blocks, page sizes are usually powers of 2; this simplifies the extraction of page numbers and offsets from virtual addresses.

To access data at a given virtual address, the system performs the following steps:

1. Extract the page number from the virtual address.

2. Extract the offset from the virtual address.

3. Translate the page number into a physical page frame number by accessing the page table.

   A. Look up the page number in the page table (using the virtual page number as an index).

   B. Check the valid bit for that page.

       1. If the valid bit = 0, the system generates a page fault and the operating system must intervene to

           a. Locate the desired page on disk.

           b. Find a free page frame (this may necessitate removing a "victim" page from memory and copying it back to disk if memory is full).

           c. Copy the desired page into the free page frame in main memory.

           d. Update the page table. (The virtual page just brought in must have its frame number and valid bit in the page table modified. If there was a "victim" page, its valid bit must be set to zero.)

           e. Resume execution of the process causing the page fault, continuing to Step B2.

       2. If the valid bit = 1, the page is in memory.

           a. Replace the virtual page number with the actual frame number.

           b. Access data at offset in physical page frame by adding the offset to the frame number for the given virtual page.

Please note that if a process has free frames in main memory when a page fault occurs, the newly retrieved page can be placed in any of those free frames. However, if the memory allocated to the process is full, a victim page must be selected. The replacement algorithms used to select a victim are quite similar to those used in cache. FIFO, random, and LRU are all potential replacement algorithms for selecting a victim page. (For more information on replacement algorithms, see the references at the end of this chapter.)

Let's look at an example.

≡ **EXAMPLE 6.8** Suppose that we have a virtual address space of 2^8 bytes for a given process (this means the program generates addresses in the range 0x00 to 0xFF, which is 0 to 255 in base 10), and physical memory of 4 page frames (no cache). Assume also that pages are 32 bytes in length. Virtual addresses contain 8 bits, and physical addresses contain 7 bits (4 frames of 32 bytes each is 128 bytes, or 2^7). Suppose, also, that some pages from the process have been brought into main memory. Figure 6.18 illustrates the current state of the system.

Each virtual address has 8 bits and is divided into 2 fields: the page field has 3 bits, indicating that there are 2^3 pages of virtual memory, $\left(\dfrac{2^8}{2^5}\right) = 2^3$. Each page is $2^5 = 32$ bytes in length, so we need 5 bits for the page offset (assuming a byte-addressable memory). Therefore, an 8-bit virtual address has the format shown in Figure 6.19.

Suppose the system now generates the virtual address 0x0D = 00001101_2. Dividing the binary address into the page and offset fields (see Figure 6.20), we see the page field P = 000_2 and the offset field equals 01101_2. To continue the translation process, we use the 000 value of the page field as an index into the page table. Going to the 0th entry in the page table, we see that virtual page 0 maps to physical page frame 2 = 10_2. Thus the translated physical address becomes page frame 2, offset 13. Note that a physical address has only 7 bits (2 for the frame, because there are 4 frames, and 5 for the offset). Written in binary, using the two fields, this becomes 1001101_2, or address 0x4D, and is shown in Figure 6.21.

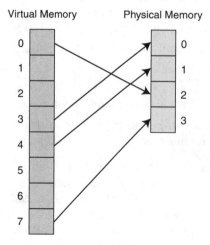

Virtual Memory	Physical Memory	Page	Page Table	
			Frame #	Valid Bit
0	0	0	2	1
1	1	1	-	0
		2	-	0
2	2	3	0	1
		4	1	1
3	3	5	-	0
		6	-	0
4		7	3	1
5				
6				
7				

FIGURE 6.18 Current State Using Paging and the Associated Page Table

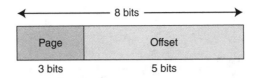

FIGURE 6.19 Format for an 8-Bit Virtual Address with 2^5 = 32-Byte Page Size

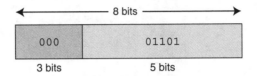

FIGURE 6.20 Format for Virtual Address 00001101_2 = 0x0D

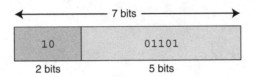

FIGURE 6.21 Format for Physical Address 1001101_2 = $4D_{16}$

Let's look at a complete example in a real (but small) system (again, with no cache).

EXAMPLE 6.9 Suppose a program is 16 bytes long, has access to an 8-byte memory that uses byte addressing, and a page is 2 bytes in length. As the program executes, it generates the following address reference string: 0x0, 0x1, 0x2, 0x3, 0x6, 0x7, 0xA, 0xB. (This address reference string indicates that address 0x0 is referenced first, then address 0x1, then address 0x2, and so on.) Originally, memory contains no pages for this program. When address 0x0 is needed, both address 0x0 and address 0x1 (in page 0) are copied to page frame 2 in main memory. (It could be that frames 0 and 1 of memory are occupied by another process and thus unavailable.) This is an example of a page fault, because the desired page of the program had to be fetched from disk. When address 0x1 is referenced, the data already exists in memory (so we have a page hit). When address 0x2 is referenced, this causes another page fault, and page 1 of the program is copied to frame 0 in memory. This continues, and after these addresses are referenced and pages are copied from disk to main memory, the state of the system is as shown in Figure 6.22a. We see that address 0x0 of the program, which contains the data value "A," currently resides in memory address 0x4 = 100_2. Therefore, the CPU must translate from virtual address 0x0 to physical address 0x4, and uses

a) Program Address Space

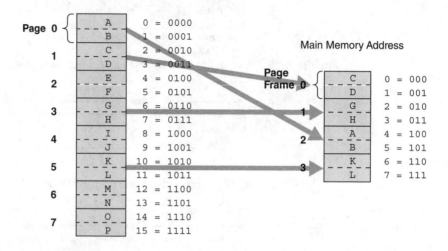

b) Page Table

Page	Frame	Valid Bit
0	2	1
1	0	1
2	-	0
3	1	1
4	-	0
5	3	1
6	-	0
7	-	0

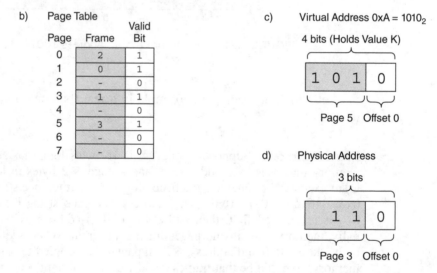

c) Virtual Address 0xA = 1010_2

4 bits (Holds Value K)

| 1 | 0 | 1 | 0 |

Page 5   Offset 0

d) Physical Address

3 bits

| 1 | 1 | 0 |

Page 3   Offset 0

FIGURE 6.22 A Small Memory from Example 6.9 Using Paging

the translation scheme described previously to do this. Note that main memory addresses contain 3 bits (there are 8 bytes in memory), but virtual addresses (from the program) must have 4 bits (because there are 16 bytes in the virtual address). Therefore, the translation must also convert a 4-bit address into a 3-bit address.

Figure 6.22b depicts the page table for this process after the given pages have been accessed. We can see that pages 0, 1, 3, and 5 of the process are valid, and thus reside in memory. Pages 2, 6, and 7 are not valid and would each cause page faults if referenced.

Let's take a closer look at the translation process. Using the architecture from Example 6.9, suppose the CPU now generates program, or virtual, address $0xA = 1010_2$ for a second time. We see in Figure 6.22a that the data at this location, "K," resides in main memory address $0x6 = 0110_2$. However, the computer must perform a specific translation process to find the data. To accomplish this, the virtual address, 1010_2, is divided into a page field and an offset field. The page field is 3 bits long because there are 8 pages in the program. This leaves 1 bit for the offset, which is correct because there are only 2 words on each page. This field division is illustrated in Figure 6.22c.

Once the computer sees these fields, it is a simple matter to convert to the physical address. The page field value of 101_2 is used as an index into the page table. Because $101_2 = 5$, we use 5 as the offset into the page table (Figure 6.22b) and see that virtual page 5 maps to physical frame 3. We now replace the $5 = 101_2$ with $3 = 11_2$, but keep the same offset. The new physical address is 110_2, as shown in Figure 6.22d. This process successfully translates from virtual addresses to physical addresses and reduces the number of bits from four to three as required.

Now that we have worked with a small example, we are ready for a larger, more realistic example.

≡ **EXAMPLE 6.10**   Suppose we have a virtual address space of 8K bytes, a physical memory size of 4K bytes that uses byte addressing, and a page size of 1K bytes. (There is no cache on this system either, but we are getting closer to understanding how memory works and eventually will use both paging and cache in our examples.) A virtual address has a total of 13 bits ($8K = 2^{13}$), with 3 bits used for the page field (there are $\frac{2^{13}}{2^{10}} = 2^3$ virtual pages), and 10 used for the offset (each page has 2^{10} bytes). A physical memory address has only 12 bits ($4K = 2^{12}$), with the first 2 bits as the page field (there are 2^2 page frames in main memory) and the remaining 10 bits as the offset within the page. The formats for the virtual address and physical address are shown in Figure 6.23a.

For purposes of this example, let's assume we have the page table indicated in Figure 6.23b. Figure 6.23c shows a table indicating the various main memory addresses that is useful for illustrating the translation.

Suppose the CPU now generates virtual address $0x1553 = 1010101010011_2$. Figure 6.23d illustrates how this address is divided into the page and offset fields and how it is converted to the physical address $0x553 = 010101010011_2$. Essentially, the page field 101 of the virtual address is replaced by the frame number 01, because page 5 maps to frame 1 (as indicated in the page table). Figure 6.23e illustrates how virtual address $0x802$ is translated to physical address $0x002$. Figure 6.23f shows virtual address $0x1004$ generating a page fault; page $4 = 100_2$ is not valid in the page table.

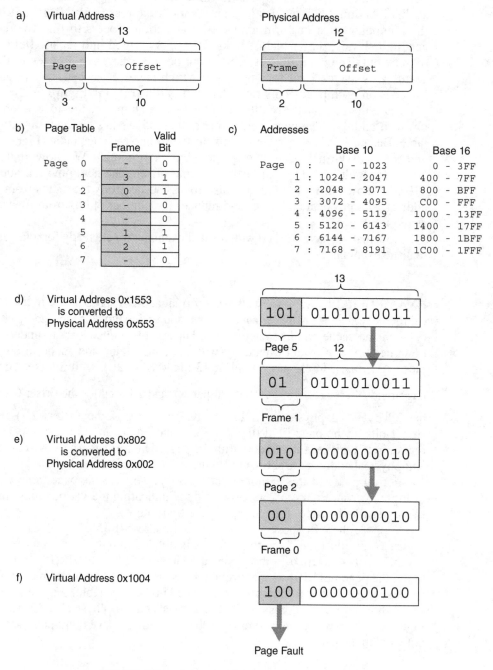

Virtual Address Space: 8K = 2^{13}
Physical Memory: 4K = 2^{12}
Page Size: 1K = 2^{10}

a)   Virtual Address

13

Page	Offset

3   10

Physical Address

12

Frame	Offset

2   10

b)   Page Table

		Frame	Valid Bit
Page	0	–	0
	1	3	1
	2	0	1
	3	–	0
	4	–	0
	5	1	1
	6	2	1
	7	–	0

c)   Addresses

		Base 10	Base 16
Page	0 :	0 - 1023	0 - 3FF
	1 :	1024 - 2047	400 - 7FF
	2 :	2048 - 3071	800 - BFF
	3 :	3072 - 4095	C00 - FFF
	4 :	4096 - 5119	1000 - 13FF
	5 :	5120 - 6143	1400 - 17FF
	6 :	6144 - 7167	1800 - 1BFF
	7 :	7168 - 8191	1C00 - 1FFF

d)   Virtual Address 0x1553
      is converted to
      Physical Address 0x553

13

| 101 | 0101010011 |

Page 5   12

| 01 | 0101010011 |

Frame 1

e)   Virtual Address 0x802
      is converted to
      Physical Address 0x002

| 010 | 0000000010 |

Page 2

| 00 | 0000000010 |

Frame 0

f)   Virtual Address 0x1004

| 100 | 0000000100 |

Page Fault

FIGURE 6.23   A Larger Memory Example Using Paging

Page Table

Page	Frame	Valid
0000	00000	1
...	...	...
00111	0A121	1
00112	3F00F	1
00113	2AC11	1
...	...	...

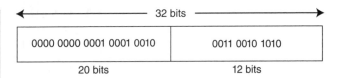

FIGURE 6.24 Format for Virtual Address 0x1211232A

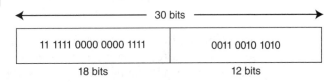

FIGURE 6.25 Format for Physical Address 0x3F00F32A

EXAMPLE 6.11 Suppose a computer has 32-bit virtual addresses, pages of size 4K, and 1GB of byte-addressable main memory. Given the partial page table above, convert virtual address 0x0011232A to a physical address. The page number and frame number values for this example are in hexadecimal.

The format for virtual memory address 0x0011232A is shown in Figure 6.24. There are 32 bits in a virtual address, and 12 of those must refer to the offset within a page (because pages are of size 4K = 2^{12}). The remaining 20 bits are used to determine the virtual page number: 0000 0000 0001 0001 0010$_2$ = 0x00112. The format for a physical address is shown in Figure 6.25. The offset field must still contain 12 bits, but a physical address only has 30 bits (1GB = 2^{30}), so the frame field has only 18 bits. If we check the page table for virtual page 00112, we see that it is valid and mapped to frame number 3F00F. If we substitute 3F00F into the frame field, we end up with the physical address of 11 1111 0000 0000 1111$_2$ = 0x3F00F32A, as shown in Figure 6.25.

It is worth mentioning that selecting an appropriate page size is very difficult. The larger the page size is, the smaller the page table is, thus saving space in main memory. However, if the page is too large, the internal fragmentation becomes worse. Larger page sizes also mean fewer actual transfers from disk to main memory because the chunks being transferred are larger. However, if they are too large, the principle of locality begins to break down and we are wasting resources by transferring data that may not be necessary.

6.5.2 Effective Access Time Using Paging

When we studied cache, we introduced the notion of effective access time. We also need to address EAT while using virtual memory. There is a time penalty associated with virtual memory: For each memory access that the processor generates, there must now be *two* physical memory accesses—one to reference the

Virtual Page Number	Physical Page Number
-	-
5	1
2	0
-	-
-	-
1	3
6	2

FIGURE 6.26   Current State of the TLB for Figure 6.23

page table and one to reference the actual data we wish to access. It is easy to see how this affects the effective access time. Suppose a main memory access requires 200ns and the page fault rate is 1% (that is, 99% of the time we find the page we need in memory). Assume that it costs us 10ms to access a page not in memory. (This time of 10ms includes the time necessary to transfer the page into memory, update the page table, and access the data.) The effective access time for a memory access is now:

$$EAT = .99(200ns + 200ns) + .01(10ms) = 100.396ns$$

Even if 100% of the pages were in main memory, the effective access time would be:

$$EAT = 1.00(200ns + 200ns) = 400ns,$$

which is double the access time of memory. Accessing the page table costs us an additional memory access because the page table itself is stored in main memory.

We can speed up the page table lookup by storing the most recent page lookup values in a page table cache called a **translation look-aside buffer** (**TLB**). Each TLB entry consists of a virtual page number and its corresponding frame number. A possible state of the TLB for the page table from Example 6.10 is indicated in Figure 6.26.

Typically, the TLB is implemented as associative cache, and the virtual page/ frame pairs can be mapped anywhere. Here are the steps necessary for an address lookup when using a TLB (see Figure 6.27):

1. Extract the page number from the virtual address.
2. Extract the offset from the virtual address.
3. Search for the virtual page number in the TLB using parallel searching.
4. If the (virtual page #, page frame #) pair is found in the TLB, add the offset to the physical frame number and access the memory location.
5. If there is a TLB miss, go to the page table to get the necessary frame number. If the page is in memory, use the corresponding frame number and add the off-set to yield the physical address.

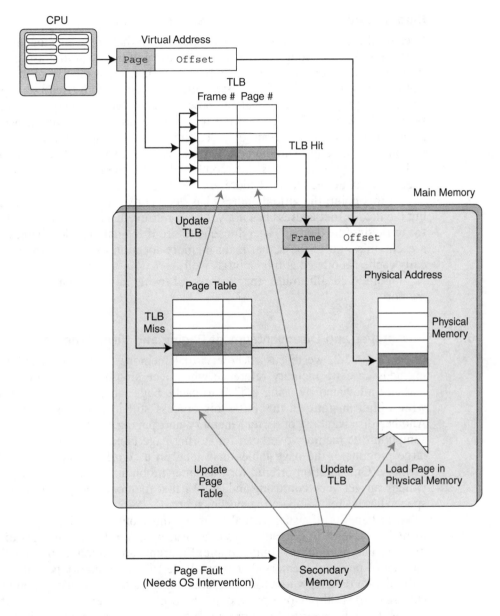

FIGURE 6.27 Using the TLB

6. If the page is not in main memory, generate a page fault and restart the access when the page fault is complete.

In Section 6.4, we presented cache memory. In our discussion of paging, we have introduced yet another type of cache—the TLB, which caches page table entries. TLBs use associative mapping. As is the case with L1 cache, computers often have two separate TLBs—one for instructions and another for data.

6.5.3 Putting It All Together: Using Cache, TLBs, and Paging

Because the TLB is essentially a cache, putting all these concepts together can be confusing. A walkthrough of the entire process will help you to grasp the overall idea. When the CPU generates an address, it is an address relative to the program itself, or a virtual address. This virtual address must be converted into a physical address before the data retrieval can proceed. There are two ways this is accomplished: (1) use the TLB to find the frame by locating a recently cached (page, frame) pair; or (2) in the event of a TLB miss, use the page table to find the corresponding frame in main memory (typically the TLB is updated at this point as well). This frame number is then combined with the offset given in the virtual address to create the physical address.

At this point, the virtual address has been converted into a physical address but the data at that address has not yet been retrieved. There are two possibilities for retrieving the data: (1) search cache to see if the data resides there; or (2) on a cache miss, go to the actual main memory location to retrieve the data (typically cache is updated at this point as well).

Figure 6.28 illustrates the process of using a TLB, paging, and cache memory.

6.5.4 Advantages and Disadvantages of Paging and Virtual Memory

In Section 6.5.2, we discussed how virtual memory implemented through paging adds an extra memory reference when accessing data. This time penalty is partially alleviated by using a TLB to cache page table entries. However, even with a high hit ratio in the TLB, this process still incurs translation overhead. Another disadvantage of virtual memory and paging is the extra resource consumption (the memory overhead for storing page tables). In extreme cases (very large programs), the page tables may take up a significant portion of physical memory. One solution offered for this latter problem is to page the page tables, which can get very confusing indeed! Virtual memory and paging also require special hardware and operating system support.

The benefits of using virtual memory must outweigh these disadvantages to make it useful in computer systems. But what are the advantages of virtual memory and paging? It is quite simple: Programs are no longer restricted by the amount of physical memory that is available. Virtual memory permits us to run individual programs whose virtual address space is larger than physical memory. (In effect, this allows one process to share physical memory with itself.) This makes it much easier to write programs because the programmer no longer has to worry about the physical address space limitations. Because each program requires less physical memory, virtual memory also permits us to run more programs at the same time. This allows us to share the machine among processes whose total address space sizes exceed the physical memory size, resulting in an increase in CPU utilization and system throughput.

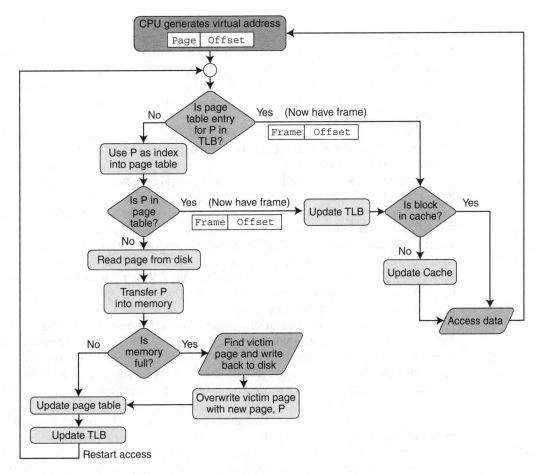

FIGURE 6.28 Putting It All Together: The TLB, Page Table, Cache, and Main Memory

The fixed size of frames and pages simplifies both allocation and placement from the perspective of the operating system. Paging also allows the operating system to specify protection ("this page belongs to User X and you can't access it") and sharing ("this page belongs to User X but you can read it") on a per page basis.

6.5.5 Segmentation

Although it is the most common method, paging is not the only way to implement virtual memory. A second method employed by some systems is **segmentation**. Instead of dividing the virtual address space into equal, fixed-size pages, and the physical address space into equal-size page frames, the virtual address space is divided into logical, variable-length units, or **segments**. Physical memory isn't really divided or partitioned into anything. When a segment needs to be copied into physical memory, the operating system looks for a chunk of free memory large enough to store the entire segment. Each segment has a base address, indicating where it is located in memory, and a bounds limit, indicating its size. Each program, consisting of multiple segments, now has an associated **segment table** instead of a page table. This segment table is simply a collection of the base/bounds pairs for each segment.

Memory accesses are translated by providing a segment number and an offset within the segment. Error checking is performed to make sure the offset is within the allowable bound. If it is, then the base value for that segment (found in the segment table) is added to the offset, yielding the actual physical address. Because paging is based on a fixed-size block and segmentation is based on a logical block, protection and sharing are easier using segmentation. For example, the virtual address space might be divided into a code segment, a data segment, a stack segment, and a symbol table segment, each of a different size. It is much easier to say, "I want to share all my data, so make my data segment accessible to everyone" than it is to say, "OK, in which pages does my data reside, and now that I have found those four pages, let's make three of the pages accessible, but only half of that fourth page accessible."

As with paging, segmentation suffers from fragmentation. Paging creates internal fragmentation because a frame can be allocated to a process that doesn't need the entire frame. Segmentation, on the other hand, suffers from **external fragmentation**. As segments are allocated and deallocated, the free chunks that reside in memory become broken up. Eventually, there are many small chunks, but none large enough to store an entire segment. The difference between external and internal fragmentation is that, with external fragmentation, enough total memory space may exist to allocate to a process, but this space is not contiguous—it exists as a large number of small, unusable holes. With internal fragmentation, the memory simply isn't available because the system has overallocated memory to a process that doesn't need it. To combat external fragmentation, systems use some sort of **garbage collection**. This process simply shuffles occupied chunks of memory to coalesce the smaller, fragmented chunks into larger, usable chunks. If you have ever defragmented a disk drive, you have witnessed a similar process, collecting the many small free spaces on the disk and creating fewer, larger ones.

6.5.6   Paging Combined with Segmentation

Paging is not the same as segmentation. Paging is based on a purely physical value: The program and main memory are divided up into chunks of the same physical size. Segmentation, on the other hand, allows for logical portions of the program to be divided into variable-sized partitions. With segmentation, the user is aware of the segment sizes and boundaries; with paging, the user is unaware of the partitioning. Paging is easier to manage: Allocation, freeing, swapping, and relocating are easy when everything's the same size. However, pages are typically smaller than segments, which means more overhead (in terms of resources to both track and transfer pages). Paging eliminates external fragmentation, whereas segmentation eliminates internal fragmentation. Segmentation has the ability to support sharing and protection, both of which are very difficult to do with paging.

Paging and segmentation both have their advantages; however, a system does not have to use one or the other—these two approaches can be combined, in an effort to get the best of both worlds. In a combined approach, the virtual address space is divided into segments of variable length, and the segments are divided into fixed-size pages. Main memory is divided into the same size frames.

Each segment has a page table, which means every program has multiple page tables. The physical address is divided into three fields. The first field is the segment field, which points the system to the appropriate page table. The second field is the page number, which is used as an offset into this page table. The third field is the offset within the page.

Combined segmentation and paging is advantageous because it allows for segmentation from the user's point of view and paging from the system's point of view.

6.6   A REAL-WORLD EXAMPLE OF MEMORY MANAGEMENT

Because the Pentium exhibits fairly characteristic traits of modern memory management, we present a short overview of how this processor deals with memory.

The Pentium architecture allows for 32-bit virtual addresses and 32-bit physical addresses. It uses either 4KB or 4MB page sizes when using paging. Paging and segmentation can be applied in different combinations, including unsegmented, unpaged memory; unsegmented, paged memory; segmented, unpaged memory; and segmented, paged memory.

The Pentium has two caches, L1 and L2, both utilizing a 32-byte block size. L1 is next to the processor, whereas L2 is between the processor and memory. The L1 cache is actually two caches; the Pentium (like many other machines) separates L1 cache into cache used to hold instructions (called the **I-cache**) and cache used to hold data (called the **D-cache**). Both L1 caches utilize an LRU bit for dealing with block replacement. Each L1 cache has a TLB; the D-cache TLB has 64 entries and the I-cache has only 32 entries. Both TLBs are 4-way set associative and use a pseudo-LRU replacement. The L1 D-cache and I-cache both use 2-way set associative mapping. The L2 cache can be from 512KB (for earlier models) up to 1MB (in later models). The L2 cache, like both L1 caches, uses 2-way set associative mapping.

To manage access to memory, the Pentium I-cache and the L2 cache use the MESI cache coherency protocol. Each cache line has two bits that store one of the following MESI states: (1) M: modified (cache is different from main memory); (2) E: exclusive (cache has not been modified and is the same as memory); (3) S: shared (this line/block may be shared with another cache line/block); and (4) I: invalid (the line/block is not in cache). Figure 6.29 presents an overview of the Pentium memory hierarchy.

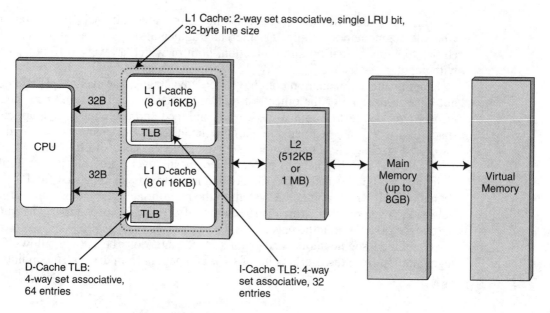

FIGURE 6.29   Pentium Memory Hierarchy

We have given only a brief and basic overview of the Pentium and its approach to memory management. If you are interested in more details, please check the "Further Reading" section.

CHAPTER SUMMARY

Memory is organized as a hierarchy, with larger memories being cheaper but slower, and smaller memories being faster but more expensive. In a typical memory hierarchy, we find a cache, main memory, and secondary memory (usually a disk drive). The principle of locality helps bridge the gap between successive layers of this hierarchy, and the programmer gets the impression of a very fast and very large memory without being concerned about the details of transfers among the various levels of this hierarchy.

Cache acts as a buffer to hold the most frequently used blocks of main memory and is close to the CPU. One goal of the memory hierarchy is for the processor to see an effective access time very close to the access time of the cache. Achieving this goal depends on the behavioral properties of the programs being executed, the size and organization of the cache, and the cache replacement policy. Processor references that are found in cache are called cache hits; if not found, they are cache misses. On a miss, the missing data is fetched from main memory, and the entire block containing the data is loaded into cache. A unified cache holds both data and instructions, whereas a Harvard cache uses a separate cache for data and a separate cache for instructions. A multilevel cache hierarchy is used to increase cache performance.

The organization of cache determines the method the CPU uses to search cache for different memory addresses. Cache can be organized in different ways: direct mapped, fully associative, or set associative. Direct mapped cache needs no replacement algorithm; however, fully associative and set associative must use FIFO, LRU, or some other placement policy to determine the block to remove from cache to make room for a new block, if cache is full. LRU gives very good performance but is difficult to implement.

Another goal of the memory hierarchy is to extend main memory by using the hard disk itself, also called virtual memory. Virtual memory allows us to run programs whose virtual address space is larger than physical memory. It also allows more processes to run concurrently. The disadvantages of virtual memory implemented with paging include extra resource consumption (storing the page table) and extra memory accesses (to access the page table), unless a TLB is used to cache the most recently used virtual/physical address pairs. Virtual memory also incurs a translation penalty to convert the virtual address to a physical one as well as a penalty for processing a page fault should the requested page currently reside on disk instead of main memory. The relationship between virtual memory and main memory is similar to the relationship between main memory and cache. Because of this similarity, the concepts of cache memory and the TLB are often confused. In reality, the TLB *is* a cache. It is important to realize that virtual addresses must be translated to physical ones first, before anything else can be done, and this is what the TLB does. Although cache and paged memory appear to be similar, the objectives are different: Cache improves the effective access time to main memory, whereas paging extends the size of main memory.

FURTHER READING

Mano (2007) has a nice explanation of RAM. Stallings (2013) also gives a very good explanation of RAM. Hamacher, Vranesic, and Zaky (2002) contains an extensive discussion of cache. For good coverage of virtual memory, see Stallings (2012), Tanenbaum (2013), or Tanenbaum and Woodhull (2006). For more information on memory management in general, check out the books by Flynn and McHoes (2010), Stallings (2013), Tanenbaum and Woodhull (2006), or Silberschatz, Galvin, and Gagne (2013). Hennessy and Patterson (2012) discuss issues involved with determining cache performance. For an online tutorial on memory technologies, see www.kingston.com/tools/umg. George Mason University also has a set of workbenches on various computer topics. The workbench for virtual memory is located at cs.gmu.edu/cne/workbenches/vmemory.html.

REFERENCES

Flynn, I. M., & McHoes, A. M. *Understanding Operating Systems*, 6th ed. Boston, MA: Thomson Course Technology, 2010.

Hamacher, V. C., Vranesic, Z. G., & Zaky, S. G. *Computer Organization*, 5th ed. New York: McGraw-Hill, 2002.

Hennessy, J. L., & Patterson, D. A. *Computer Architecture: A Quantitative Approach*, 5th ed. San Francisco: Morgan Kaufmann, 2012.

Mano, M. *Digital Design*, 4th ed. Upper Saddle River, NJ: Prentice Hall, 2007.

Silberschatz, A., Galvin, P., & Gagne, G. *Operating System Concepts*, 9th ed. New York, NY: John Wiley & Sons, 2013.

Stallings, W. *Computer Organization and Architecture*, 9th ed. Upper Saddle River, NJ: Prentice Hall, 2013.

Stallings, W. *Operating Systems*, 7th ed. Upper Saddle River, NJ: Prentice Hall, 2012.

Tanenbaum, A. *Structured Computer Organization*, 6th ed. Englewood Cliffs, NJ: Prentice Hall, 2013.

Tanenbaum, A., & Woodhull, S. *Operating Systems, Design and Implementation*, 3rd ed. Englewood Cliffs, NJ: Prentice Hall, 2006.

REVIEW OF ESSENTIAL TERMS AND CONCEPTS

1. Which is faster, SRAM or DRAM?
2. What are the advantages of using DRAM for main memory?
3. Name three different applications where ROMs are often used.
4. Explain the concept of a memory hierarchy. Why did your authors choose to represent it as a pyramid?
5. Explain the concept of locality of reference, and state its importance to memory systems.
6. What are the three forms of locality?
7. Give two noncomputer examples of the concept of cache.
8. Which of L1 or L2 cache is faster? Which is smaller? Why is it smaller?
9. Cache is accessed by its _____, whereas main memory is accessed by its _____.
10. What are the three fields in a direct mapped cache address? How are they used to access a word located in cache?
11. How does associative memory differ from regular memory? Which is more expensive and why?
12. Explain how fully associative cache is different from direct mapped cache.
13. Explain how set associative cache combines the ideas of direct and fully associative cache.

14. Direct mapped cache is a special case of set associative cache where the set size is 1. So fully associative cache is a special case of set associative cache where the set size is ___.

15. What are the three fields in a set associative cache address, and how are they used to access a location in cache?

16. Explain the four cache replacement policies presented in this chapter.

17. Why is the optimal cache replacement policy important?

18. What is the worst-case cache behavior that can develop using LRU and FIFO cache replacement policies?

19. What, exactly, is effective access time (EAT)?

20. Explain how to derive an effective access time formula.

21. When does caching behave badly?

22. What is a dirty block?

23. Describe the advantages and disadvantages of the two cache write policies.

24. Explain the difference between a unified cache and a Harvard cache.

25. What are the advantages of a Harvard cache?

26. Why would a system contain a victim cache? A trace cache?

27. Explain the differences among L1, L2, and L3 cache.

28. Explain the differences between inclusive and exclusive cache.

29. What is the advantage to a nonblocking cache?

30. What is the difference between a virtual memory address and a physical memory address? Which is larger? Why?

31. What is the objective of paging?

32. Discuss the pros and cons of paging.

33. What is a page fault?

34. What causes internal fragmentation?

35. What are the components (fields) of a virtual address?

36. What is a TLB, and how does it improve EAT?

37. What are the advantages and disadvantages of virtual memory?

38. When would a system ever need to page its page table?

39. What causes external fragmentation, and how can it be fixed?

EXERCISES

◆ **1.** Suppose a computer using direct mapped cache has 2^{20} bytes of byte-addressable main memory and a cache of 32 blocks, where each cache block contains 16 bytes.

   a) How many blocks of main memory are there?

   b) What is the format of a memory address as seen by the cache; that is, what are the sizes of the tag, block, and offset fields?

   c) To which cache block will the memory address 0x0DB63 map?

2. Suppose a computer using direct mapped cache has 2^{32} bytes of byte-addressable main memory and a cache of 1024 blocks, where each cache block contains 32 bytes.

   a) How many blocks of main memory are there?

   b) What is the format of a memory address as seen by the cache; that is, what are the sizes of the tag, block, and offset fields?

   c) To which cache block will the memory address 0x000063FA map?

3. Suppose a computer using direct mapped cache has 2^{32} bytes of byte-addressable main memory and a cache size of 512 bytes, and each cache block contains 64 bytes.

   a) How many blocks of main memory are there?

   b) What is the format of a memory address as seen by cache; that is, what are the sizes of the tag, block, and offset fields?

   c) To which cache block will the memory address 0x13A4498A map?

♦4. Suppose a computer using fully associative cache has 2^{16} bytes of byte-addressable main memory and a cache of 64 blocks, where each cache block contains 32 bytes.

   a) How many blocks of main memory are there?

   b) What is the format of a memory address as seen by the cache; that is, what are the sizes of the tag and offset fields?

   c) To which cache block will the memory address 0xF8C9 map?

5. Suppose a computer using fully associative cache has 2^{24} bytes of byte-addressable main memory and a cache of 128 blocks, where each cache block contains 64 bytes.

   a) How many blocks of main memory are there?

   b) What is the format of a memory address as seen by the cache; that is, what are the sizes of the tag and offset fields?

   c) To which cache block will the memory address 0x01D872 map?

6. Suppose a computer using fully associative cache has 2^{24} bytes of byte-addressable main memory and a cache of 128 blocks, where each block contains 64 bytes.

   a) How many blocks of main memory are there?

   b) What is the format of a memory address as seen by cache; that is, what are the sizes of the tag and offset fields?

   c) To which cache block will the memory address 0x01D872 map?

♦7. Assume that a system's memory has 128M bytes. Blocks are 64 bytes in length, and the cache consists of 32K blocks. Show the format for a main memory address assuming a 2-way set associative cache mapping scheme and byte addressing. Be sure to include the fields as well as their sizes.

8. A 2-way set associative cache consists of 4 sets. Main memory contains 2K blocks of 8 bytes each and byte addressing is used.

   a) Show the main memory address format that allows us to map addresses from main memory to cache. Be sure to include the fields as well as their sizes.

   b) Compute the hit ratio for a program that loops 3 times from addresses 0x8 to 0x33 in main memory. You may leave the hit ratio in terms of a fraction.

9. Suppose a byte-addressable computer using set associative cache has 2^{16} bytes of main memory and a cache of 32 blocks, and each cache block contains 8 bytes.

   a) If this cache is 2-way set associative, what is the format of a memory address as seen by the cache; that is, what are the sizes of the tag, set, and offset fields?

   b) If this cache is 4-way set associative, what is the format of a memory address as seen by the cache?

10. Suppose a byte-addressable computer using set associative cache has 2^{21} bytes of main memory and a cache of 64 blocks, where each cache block contains 4 bytes.

   a) If this cache is 2-way set associative, what is the format of a memory address as seen by the cache; that is, what are the sizes of the tag, set, and offset fields?

   b) If this cache is 4-way set associative, what is the format of a memory address as seen by the cache?

* 11. Suppose we have a computer that uses a memory address word size of 8 bits. This computer has a 16-byte cache with 4 bytes per block. The computer accesses a number of memory locations throughout the course of running a program.

   Suppose this computer uses direct-mapped cache. The format of a memory address as seen by the cache is shown here:

Tag 4 bits	Block 2 bits	Offset 2 bits

   The system accesses memory addresses in this exact order: 0x6E, 0xB9, 0x17, 0xE0, 0x4E, 0x4F, 0x50, 0x91, 0xA8, 0xA9, 0xAB, 0xAD, 0x93, and 0x94. The memory addresses of the first four accesses have been loaded into the cache blocks as shown below. (The contents of the tag are shown in binary, and the cache "contents" are simply the address stored at that cache location.)

	Tag Contents	Cache Contents (represented by address)
Block 0	1110	0xE0
		0xE1
		0xE2
		0xE3
Block 2	1011	0xB8
		0xB9
		0xBA
		0xBB

	Tag Contents	Cache Contents (represented by address)
Block 1	0001	0x14
		0x15
		0x16
		0x17
Block 3	0110	0x6C
		0x6D
		0x6E
		0x6F

   a) What is the hit ratio for the entire memory reference sequence given above, assuming that we count the first four accesses as misses?

   b) What memory blocks will be in the cache after the last address has been accessed?

12. Given a byte-addressable memory with 256 bytes, suppose a memory dump yields the results shown below. The address of each memory cell is determined by its row and column. For example, memory address 0x97 is in the 9th row, 7th column, and contains the hexadecimal value 43. Memory location 0xA3 contains the hexadecimal value 58.

	0	1	2	3	4	5	6	7	8	9	A	B	C	D	E	F
0	DC	D5	9C	77	C1	99	90	AC	33	D1	37	74	B5	82	38	E0
1	49	E2	23	FD	D0	A6	98	BB	DE	9A	9E	EB	04	AA	86	E5
2	3A	14	F3	59	5C	41	B2	6D	18	3C	9D	1F	2F	78	44	1E
3	4E	B7	29	E7	87	3D	B8	E1	EF	C5	CE	BF	93	CB	39	7F
4	6B	69	02	56	7E	DA	2A	76	89	20	85	88	72	92	E9	5B
5	B9	16	A8	FA	AE	68	21	25	34	24	B6	48	17	83	75	0A
6	40	2B	C4	1D	08	03	0E	0B	B4	C2	53	FB	E3	8C	0C	9B
7	31	AF	30	9F	A4	FE	09	60	4F	D7	D9	97	2E	6C	94	BC
8	CD	80	64	B3	8D	81	A7	DB	F1	BA	66	BE	11	1A	A1	D2
9	61	28	5D	D4	4A	10	A2	43	CC	07	7D	5A	C0	D3	CF	67
A	52	57	A3	58	55	0F	E8	F6	91	F0	C3	19	F9	BD	8B	47
B	26	51	1C	C6	3B	ED	7B	EE	95	12	7C	DF	B1	4D	EC	42
C	22	0D	F5	2C	62	B0	5E	DD	8E	96	A0	C8	27	3E	EA	01
D	50	35	A9	4C	6A	00	8A	D6	5F	7A	FF	71	13	F4	F8	46
E	1B	4B	70	84	6E	F7	63	3F	CA	45	65	73	79	C9	FC	A5
F	AB	E6	2D	54	E4	8F	36	6F	C7	05	D8	F2	AD	15	32	06

The system from which this memory dump was produced contains 4 blocks of cache, where each block consists of 8 bytes. Assume that the following sequence of memory addresses takes place: 0x2C, 0x6D, 0x86, 0x29, 0xA5, 0x82, 0xA7, 0x68, 0x80, and 0x2B.

a) How many blocks of main memory are there?

b) Assuming a direct mapped cache:

   i. Show the format for a main memory address assuming that the system uses direct mapped cache. Specify field names and sizes.

   ii. What does cache look like after the 10 memory accesses have taken place? Draw the cache and show contents and tags.

   iii. What is the hit rate for this cache on the given sequence of memory accesses?

c) Assuming a fully associative cache:

   i. Show the format for a main memory address. Specify field names and sizes.

   ii. Assuming that all cache blocks are initially empty, blocks are loaded into the first available empty cache location, and cache uses a first-in, first-out replacement policy, what does cache look like after the 10 memory accesses have taken place?

   iii. What is the hit rate for this cache on the given sequences of memory accesses?

d) Assuming a 2-way set associative cache:

   i. Show the format for a main memory address. Specify field names and sizes.

   ii. What does cache look like after the 10 memory accesses have taken place?

iii. What is the hit ratio for this cache on the given sequence of memory accesses?

iv. If a cache hit retrieves a value in 5ns, and retrieving a value from main memory requires 25ns, what is the average effective access time for this cache, assuming that all memory accesses exhibit the same hit rate as the sequence of 10 given, and assuming that the system uses a nonoverlapped (sequential) access strategy?

13. A direct mapped cache consists of 8 blocks. Byte-addressable main memory contains 4K blocks of 8 bytes each. Access time for the cache is 22ns, and the time required to fill a cache slot from main memory is 300ns. (This time allows us to determine that the block is missing and bring it into cache.) Assume that a request is always started in parallel to both cache and to main memory (so if it is not found in cache, we do not have to add this cache search time to the memory access). If a block is missing from cache, the entire block is brought into the cache and the access is restarted. Initially, the cache is empty.

a) Show the main memory address format that allows us to map addresses from main memory to cache. Be sure to include the fields as well as their sizes.

b) Compute the hit ratio for a program that loops 4 times from addresses 0x0 to 0x43 in memory.

c) Compute the effective access time for this program.

14. Consider a byte-addressable computer with 24-bit addresses, a cache capable of storing a total of 64KB of data, and blocks of 32 bytes. Show the format of a 24-bit memory address for:

a) direct mapped

b) associative

c) 4-way set associative

* 15. Suppose a byte-addressable computer using 4-way set associative cache has 2^{16} words of main memory (where each word is 32 bits) and a cache of 32 blocks, where each block is 4 words. Show the main memory address format for this machine. (Hint: Because this architecture is byte addressable, and the number of addresses is critical in determining the address format, you must convert everything to bytes.)

16. Assume a direct mapped cache that holds 4096 bytes, in which each block is 16 bytes. Assuming that an address is 32 bits and that cache is initially empty, complete the table that follows. (You should use hexadecimal numbers for all answers.) Which, if any, of the addresses will cause a collision (forcing the block that was just brought in to be overwritten) if they are accessed one right after the other?

Address	TAG	Cache Location (block)	Offset within Block
0x0FF0FABA			
0x00000011			
0x0FFFFFFE			
0x23456719			
0xCAFEBABE			

17. Redo exercise 16, assuming now that cache is 16-way set associative.

Address	TAG	Cache Location (set)	Offset within Block
0x0FF0FABA			
0x00000011			
0x0FFFFFFE			
0x23456719			
0xCAFEBABE			

18. Suppose a process page table contains the entries shown below. Using the format shown in Figure 6.17a, indicate where the process pages are located in memory.

Frame	Valid Bit
1	1
-	0
0	1
3	1
-	0
-	0
2	1
-	0

♦ **19.** Suppose a process page table contains the entries shown below. Using the format shown in Figure 6.22a, indicate where the process pages are located in memory.

Frame	Valid Bit
-	0
3	1
-	0
-	0
2	1
0	1
-	0
1	1

20. Suppose you have a byte-addressable virtual address memory system with eight virtual pages of 64 bytes each, and four page frames. Assuming the following page table, answer the questions below:

Page #	Frame #	Valid Bit
0	1	1
1	3	0
2	-	0
3	0	1
4	2	1
5	-	0
6	-	0
7	-	0

a) How many bits are in a virtual address?

b) How many bits are in a physical address?

c) What physical address corresponds to the following virtual addresses? (If the address causes a page fault, simply indicate this is the case.)

   i. 0x0

   ii. 0x44

   iii. 0xC2

   iv. 0x80

21. Suppose we have 2^{10} bytes of virtual memory and 2^8 bytes of physical main memory. Suppose the page size is 2^4 bytes.

a) How many pages are there in virtual memory?

b) How many page frames are there in main memory?

c) How many entries are in the page table for a process that uses all of virtual memory?

* 22. You have a byte-addressable virtual memory system with a two-entry TLB, a 2-way set associative cache, and a page table for a process P. Assume cache blocks of 8 bytes and page size of 16 bytes. In the system below, main memory is divided into blocks, where each block is represented by a letter. Two blocks equal one frame.

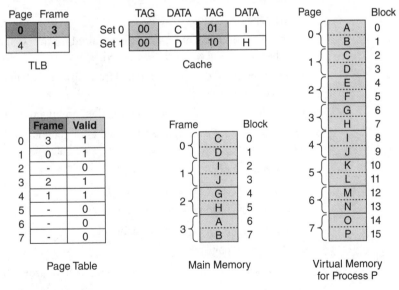

Given the system state as depicted above, answer the following questions:

a) How many bits are in a virtual address for process P? Explain.

b) How many bits are in a physical address? Explain.

c) Show the address format for virtual address 0x12 (specify field name and size) that would be used by the system to translate to a physical address and then translate this virtual address into the corresponding physical address. (Hint: Convert the address to its binary equivalent and divide it into the appropriate fields.) Explain how these fields are used to translate to the corresponding physical address.

    d) Given virtual address 0x06 converts to physical address 0x36. Show the format for a physical address (specify the field names and sizes) that is used to determine the cache location for this address. Explain how to use this format to determine where physical address 0x36 would be located in cache. (Hint: Convert 0x36 to binary and divide it into the appropriate fields.)

    e) Given virtual address 0x19 is located on virtual page 1, offset 9. Indicate exactly how this address would be translated to its corresponding physical address and how the data would be accessed. Include in your explanation how the TLB, the page table, cache, and memory are used.

23. Given a virtual memory system with a TLB, a cache, and a page table, assume the following:

- A TLB hit requires 5ns.
- A cache hit requires 12ns.
- A memory reference requires 25ns.
- A disk reference requires 200ms (this includes updating the page table, cache, and TLB).
- The TLB hit ratio is 90%.
- The cache hit rate is 98%.
- The page fault rate is .001%.
- On a TLB or cache miss, the time required for access includes a TLB and/or cache update, but the access is *not* restarted.
- On a page fault, the page is fetched from disk, and all updates are performed, but the access *is* restarted.
- All references are sequential (no overlap, nothing done in parallel).

For each of the following, indicate whether or not it is possible. If it is possible, specify the time required for accessing the requested data.

    a) TLB hit, cache hit

    b) TLB miss, page table hit, cache hit

    c) TLB miss, page table hit, cache miss

    d) TLB miss, page table miss, cache hit

    e) TLB miss, page table miss

Write down the equation to calculate the effective access time.

24. Does a TLB miss always indicate that a page is missing from memory? Explain.

25. A system implements a paged virtual address space for each process using a one-level page table. The maximum size of virtual address space is 16MB. The page table for the running process includes the following valid entries (the $\rightarrow$ notation indicates that a virtual page maps to the given page frame; that is, it is located in that frame):

Virtual page 2 $\rightarrow$ Page frame 4	Virtual page 4 $\rightarrow$ Page frame 9
Virtual page 1 $\rightarrow$ Page frame 2	Virtual page 3 $\rightarrow$ Page frame 16
Virtual page 0 $\rightarrow$ Page frame 1	

The page size is 1024 bytes and the maximum physical memory size of the machine is 2MB.

a) How many bits are required for each virtual address?

b) How many bits are required for each physical address?

c) What is the maximum number of entries in a page table?

d) To which physical address will the virtual address 0x5F4 translate?

e) Which virtual address will translate to physical address 0x400?

26. a) If you are a computer builder trying to make your system as price-competitive as possible, what features and organization would you select for its memory hierarchy?

b) If you are a computer buyer trying to get the best performance from a system, what features would you look for in its memory hierarchy?

* 27. Consider a system that has multiple processors where each processor has its own cache, but main memory is shared among all processors.

a) Which cache write policy would you use?

b) **The Cache Coherency Problem**. With regard to the system just described, what problems are caused if a processor has a copy of memory block *A* in its cache and a second processor, also having a copy of *A* in its cache, then updates main memory block *A*? Can you think of a way (perhaps more than one) of preventing this situation, or lessening its effects?

* 28. Pick a specific architecture (other than the one covered in this chapter). Do research to find out how your architecture approaches the concepts introduced in this chapter, as was done for Intel's Pentium.

29. Name two ways that, as a programmer, you can improve cache performance.

30. Look up a specific vendor's specifications for memory, and report the memory access time, cache access time, and cache hit rate (and any other data the vendor provides).

CHAPTER 7

Input/Output and Storage Systems

7.1 INTRODUCTION

One could easily argue that computers are more useful to us as appliances for information storage and retrieval than they are as instruments of computation. Indeed, without having some means of getting data into the computer and information out of it, we have little use at all for a CPU and memory. We interact with these components only through the I/O devices connected to them.

With personal systems, for example, a keyboard and mouse are the primary user input devices. A standard monitor is an output-only device that presents results to the user. Although most printers provide device status information to the host system to which they are connected, they are still considered output-only devices. Disk drives are called input/output devices because data can be written to and read from them. I/O devices also exchange control and status information with the host system. We observe that the term **I/O** is commonly used both as an adjective and as a noun: Computers have I/O devices connected to them, and to achieve good performance, one endeavors to keep disk I/O to a minimum.

After reading this chapter, you will understand the details of how input, output, and I/O devices interact with their host systems, and the various ways in which I/O is controlled. We also discuss the internals of mass storage devices and some of the ways in which they are put to work in large-scale computer systems. Enterprise-class storage systems incorporate many of the ideas presented in this chapter, but they also rely on data network infrastructures. We therefore defer our discussion of storage systems until Chapter 13.

7.2   I/O AND PERFORMANCE

We expect our computer systems to be able to efficiently store and retrieve data, and to quickly carry out the commands we give them. When processing time exceeds user "think time," we complain that the computer is "slow." Sometimes this slowness can have a substantial productivity impact, measured in hard currency. More often than not, the root cause of the problem is not in the processor or the memory but in how the system processes its input and output (I/O).

I/O is more than just file storage and retrieval. A poorly functioning I/O system can have a ripple effect, dragging down the entire computer system. In the preceding chapter, we described virtual memory, that is, how systems page blocks of memory to disk to make room for more user processes in main memory. If the disk system is sluggish, process execution slows down, causing backlogs in CPU and disk queues. The easy solution to the problem is to simply throw more resources at the system. Buy more main storage. Buy a faster processor. If we're in a particularly Draconian frame of mind, we could simply limit the number of concurrent processes!

Such measures are wasteful, if not plain irresponsible. If we really understand what's happening in a computer system, we can make the best use of the resources available, adding costly resources only when absolutely necessary. There are a number of tools we can use to determine the most effective way performance can be improved. Amdahl's Law is one of them.

7.3   AMDAHL'S LAW

Each time a (particular) microprocessor company announces its latest and greatest CPU, headlines sprout across the globe heralding this latest leap forward in technology. Cyberphiles the world over would agree that such advances are laudable and deserving of fanfare. However, when similar advances are made in I/O technology, the story is apt to appear on page 29 of some obscure trade magazine. Under the glare of media hype, it is easy to lose sight of the integrated nature of computer systems. A 40% speedup for one component certainly will not make the entire system 40% faster, despite media implications to the contrary.

In 1967, Gene Amdahl recognized the interrelationship of all components with the overall efficiency of a computer system. He quantified his observations in a formula, which is now known as Amdahl's Law. In essence, Amdahl's Law states that the overall **speedup** of a computer system depends on both the speedup in a particular component and how much that component is used by the system. In symbols:

$$S = \frac{1}{(1 - f) + f/k}$$

where

S is the overall system speedup;

f is the fraction of work performed by the faster component; and

k is the speedup of a new component.

Let's say that most of your daytime processes spend 70% of their time running in the CPU and 30% waiting for service from the disk. Suppose also that someone is trying to sell you a processor array upgrade that is 50% faster than what you have and costs $10,000. The day before, someone called offering you a set of disk drives for $7,000. These new disks promise to be 150% faster than your existing disks. You know that the system performance is starting to degrade, so you need to do something. Which would you choose to yield the best performance improvement for the least amount of money?

For the processor option, we have:

$$f = .70, \ k = 1.5, \text{ so } S = \frac{1}{(1 - 0.7) + 0.7/5} = 1.30$$

We therefore appreciate a total speedup of 1.3 times, or 30%, with the new processor for $10,000.

For the disk option, we have:

$$f = .30, \ k = 2.5, \text{ so } S = \frac{1}{(1 - 0.3) + 0.3/2.5} \approx 1.22$$

The disk upgrade gives us a speedup of 1.22 times, or 22%, for $7,000.

All things being equal, it is a close decision. Each 1% of performance improvement resulting from the processor upgrade costs about $333. Each 1% with the disk upgrade costs about $318. This makes the disk upgrade a slightly better choice, based solely on dollars spent per performance improvement percentage point. Certainly, other factors would influence your decision. For example, if your disks are nearing the end of their expected lives, or if you're running out of disk space, you might consider the disk upgrade even if it were to cost more than the processor upgrade.

What Do We Really Mean by "Speedup"?

Amdahl's Law uses the variable *K* to represent the speedup of a particular component. But what do we really mean by "speedup"?

There are many different ways to discuss the notion of "speedup." For example, one person may say A is twice as fast as B; another may say A is 100%

faster than B. It is important to understand the difference if you want to use Amdahl's Law.

It is a common misconception to believe that if A is twice as fast as B that A is 200% faster than B. However, this is not accurate. It is easy to see that if A is twice as fast as B, that a multiple of 2 is involved. For example, if Bob runs a race in 15 seconds, but it takes Sue 30 seconds, clearly Bob is twice as fast as Sue. If Bob is running an average of 4mph, then Sue must be running an average of 2mph. The error occurs when converting it to "percentage" terminology. Bob's speed does not represent a 200% increase over Sue's speed; it is only a 100% increase. This becomes clearer when we look at the definition for "% faster."

$$\text{A is N\% faster than B if } \frac{time \, B}{time \, A} = 1 + \frac{N}{100}$$

Bob is 100% faster than Sue because $30/15 = 1 + 100/100$ (*N* must be 100). The ratio of Bob's time to Sue's time (30/15) represents the speedup (Bob is 2 times faster than Sue). It is this notion of speedup that must be used for *k* in Amdahl's' equation; it is also this notion of speedup that results from applying Amdahl's Law.

Suppose we wish to use Amdahl's Law to find the overall speedup for a system, assuming we replace the CPU. We know that the CPU is used 80% of the time and that the new CPU we are considering is 50% faster than the current one in the system. Amdahl's Law requires us to know the speedup of the newer component. The variable *k* in this case is not 50 or 0.5; instead, it is 1.5 (because the newer CPU is 1.5 times faster than the old one):

$$\frac{time \, old \, CPU}{time \, new \, CPU} = 1 + \frac{50}{100} = 1.5$$

So, applying Amdahl's Law, we get:

$$S = \frac{1}{(1 - 0.8) + 8/1.5} = 1.36$$

which means we have an overall speedup of 1.36; with the new CPU, the system will be 1.36 times faster. The new system is 36% faster.

In addition to being used for hardware speedup, Amdahl's Law can be used in programming. It is well known that, on average, a program spends a majority of its time in a small percentage of its code. Programmers will often focus on increasing the performance of that small segment of code. They can use Amdahl's Law to determine the overall effect on the program's running time.

Suppose you have written a program and determined that 80% of the time is spent in one segment of code. You examine the code and determine that you can decrease the running time in that segment of code by half (i.e., a speedup of 2). If we apply Amdahl's Law, we see that the overall effect on the entire program is:

$$S = \frac{1}{(1 - .8) + .8/2} = 1.67$$

which means the program, as a whole, will run 1.67 times faster with the new code.

Consider one last example. As a programmer, you have an option of making a segment of code that is used 10% of the time 100 times faster. You estimate the cost at one month (time and wages) to rewrite the code. You could also make it 1,000,000 times faster but estimate that it will cost you 6 months. What should you do? If we use Amdahl's Law, we see that a speedup of 100 times yields:

$$S = \frac{1}{(1 - .1) + .1/100} = 1.1098$$

so the overall program is sped up 1.1 times (roughly 11%). If we spend 6 months to increase the performance 1,000,000 times, the overall program execution speedup is:

$$S = \frac{1}{(1 - .1) + 1/1.000.000} = 1.1111$$

The speedup is minimal at best. So it is clear that spending the additional time and wages to speed up that section of code is not worth the effort. Programmers working on parallel programs often apply Amdahl's Law to determine the benefit of parallelizing code.

Amdahl's Law is used in many areas of computer hardware and software, including programming in general, memory hierarchy design, hardware replacement, processor set design, instruction set design, and parallel programming. However, Amdahl's Law is important to *any* activity subject to the notion of diminishing returns; even business managers are applying Amdahl's Law when developing and comparing various business processes.

Before you make that disk decision, however, you need to know your options. The sections that follow will help you to gain an understanding of general I/O architecture, with special emphasis on disk I/O. Disk I/O follows closely behind the CPU and memory in determining the overall effectiveness of a computer system.

7.4 I/O ARCHITECTURES

We will define input/output as a subsystem of components that moves coded data between external devices and a host system, consisting of a CPU and main memory. I/O subsystems include, but are not limited to:

- Blocks of main memory that are devoted to I/O functions
- Buses that provide the means of moving data into and out of the system
- Control modules in the host and in peripheral devices
- Interfaces to external components such as keyboards and disks
- Cabling or communications links between the host system and its peripherals

Figure 7.1 shows how all of these components can fit together to form an integrated I/O subsystem. The I/O modules take care of moving data between main memory and a particular device interface. Interfaces are designed specifically to communicate with certain types of devices, such as keyboards, disks, or printers. Interfaces handle the details of making sure that devices are ready for the next batch of data, or that the host is ready to receive the next batch of data coming in from the peripheral device.

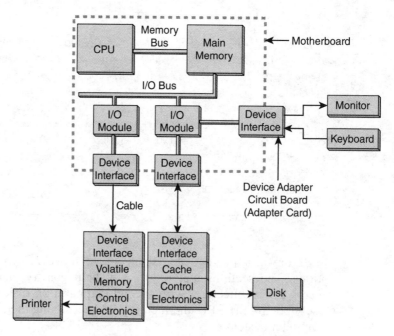

FIGURE 7.1 A Model I/O Configuration

The exact form and meaning of the signals exchanged between a sender and a receiver is called a **protocol**. Protocols include command signals, such as "Printer reset"; status signals, such as "Tape ready"; or data-passing signals, such as "Here are the bytes you requested." In most data-exchanging protocols, the receiver must acknowledge the commands and data sent to it or indicate that it is ready to receive data. This type of protocol exchange is called a **handshake**.

External devices that handle large blocks of data (such as printers, and disk and tape drives) are often equipped with buffer memory. Buffers allow the host system to send large quantities of data to peripheral devices in the fastest manner possible, without having to wait until slow mechanical devices have actually written the data. Dedicated memory on disk drives is usually of the fast cache variety, whereas printers are usually provided with slower RAM.

Device control circuits take data to or from on-board buffers and ensure that it gets where it's going. In the case of writing to disks, this involves making certain that the disk is positioned properly so that the data is written to a particular location. For printers, these circuits move the print head or laser beam to the next character position, fire the head, eject the paper, and so forth.

Disk and tape are forms of **durable storage**, so called because data recorded on them lasts longer than it would in volatile main memory. However, no storage method is permanent. The expected life of data on these media is approximately 5 to 30 years for magnetic media and as much as 100 years for optical media.

7.4.1 I/O Control Methods

Because of the great differences in control methods and transmission modes among various kinds of I/O devices, it is infeasible to try to connect them directly to the system bus. Instead, dedicated I/O modules serve as interfaces between the CPU and its peripherals. These modules perform many functions, including controlling device actions, buffering data, performing error detection, and communicating with the CPU. In this section, we are most interested in the method by which these I/O modules communicate with the CPU, thus controlling I/O. Computer systems employ any of five general I/O control methods, including **programmed I/O**, **interrupt-driven I/O**, **memory-mapped I/O**, **direct memory access**, and **channel-attached I/O**. Although one method isn't necessarily better than another, the manner in which a computer controls its I/O greatly influences overall system design and performance. The objective is to know when the I/O method employed by a particular computer architecture is appropriate to how that system will be used.

Programmed I/O

The simplest way for a CPU to communicate with an I/O device is through **programmed I/O**, sometimes called **polled I/O** (or **port I/O**). The CPU continually monitors (**polls**) a control register associated with each I/O port. When a byte arrives in the port, a bit in the control register is also set. The CPU eventually polls the port and notices that the "data ready" control bit is set. The CPU resets the control bit, retrieves the byte, and processes it according to instructions programmed for that particular port. When the processing is complete, the CPU resumes polling the control registers as before.

The benefit of using this approach is that we have programmatic control over the behavior of each device. By modifying a few lines of code, we can adjust the number and types of devices in the system, as well as their polling priorities and intervals. Constant register polling, however, is a problem. The CPU is in a continual "busy wait" loop until it starts servicing an I/O request. It doesn't do any useful work until there is I/O to process. Another problem is in deciding how frequently to poll; some devices might need to be polled more frequently than others. Because of these limitations, programmed I/O is best suited for special-purpose systems such as automated teller machines and embedded systems that control or monitor environmental events.

Interrupt-Driven I/O

A more common and efficient control method is **interrupt-driven I/O**. Interrupt-driven I/O can be thought of as the converse of programmed I/O. Instead of the CPU continually asking its attached devices whether they have any input, the devices tell the CPU when they have data to send. The CPU proceeds with other tasks until a device requesting service sends an interrupt to the CPU. These interrupts are typically generated for every word of information that is transferred. In most interrupt-driven I/O implementations, this communication takes place through an intermediary interrupt controller. This circuit handles interrupt signals from all I/O devices in the system. Once this circuit recognizes an interrupt signal from any of its attached devices, it raises a single interrupt signal that activates a control line on the system bus. The control line typically feeds directly into a pin on the CPU chip. An example configuration is shown in Figure 7.2. Every peripheral device in the system has access to an interrupt request line. The interrupt control chip has an input for each interrupt line. Whenever an interrupt line is asserted, the controller decodes the interrupt and raises the `Interrupt (INT)` input on the CPU. When the CPU is ready to process the interrupt, it asserts the

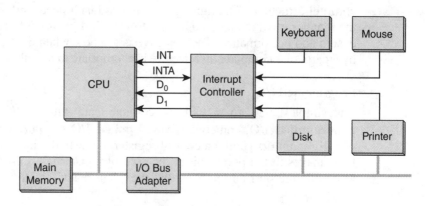

FIGURE 7.2   An I/O Subsystem Using Interrupts

Interrupt Acknowledge (INTA) signal. Once the interrupt controller gets this acknowledgment, it can lower its INT signal. When two or more I/O interrupts occur simultaneously, the interrupt controller determines which one should take precedence, based on the time-criticality of the device requesting the I/O. Keyboard and mouse I/O are usually the least critical.

System designers determine which devices should take precedence over the others when more than one device raises an interrupt simultaneously. The interrupt priorities are then hardwired into the I/O controller, making them practically impossible to change. Each computer that uses the same operating system and interrupt controller connects low-priority devices (such as a keyboard) to the same interrupt request line. The number of interrupt request lines is necessarily limited, and in some cases, the interrupt can be shared. Shared interrupts cause no problems when it is clear that no two devices will need the same interrupt at the same time. For example, a scanner and a printer can usually coexist peacefully using the same interrupt. This is not always the case with serial mice and modems, which often do try to share the same interrupt, causing bizarre behavior in both.

In Chapter 4, we described how interrupt processing changes the fetch–decode–execute cycle. We have reproduced Figure 4.12 in Figure 7.3, which shows how the CPU finishes execution of the current instruction and checks the status of its interrupt pins (not just I/O) at the beginning of every fetch–decode–execute cycle. Once the CPU acknowledges the interrupt, it saves its current state and processes the interrupt (as shown in Figure 7.4, also taken from Chapter 4).

Interrupt-driven I/O is similar to programmed I/O in that the service routines can be modified to accommodate hardware changes. Because vectors for the various types of hardware are usually kept in the same locations in systems running the same type and level of operating system, these vectors are easily changed to point to vendor-specific code. For example, if someone comes up with a new type of disk drive that is not yet supported by a popular operating system, the disk's

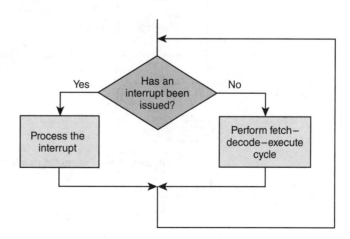

FIGURE 7.3   The Fetch–Decode–Interrupt Cycle with Interrupt Checking

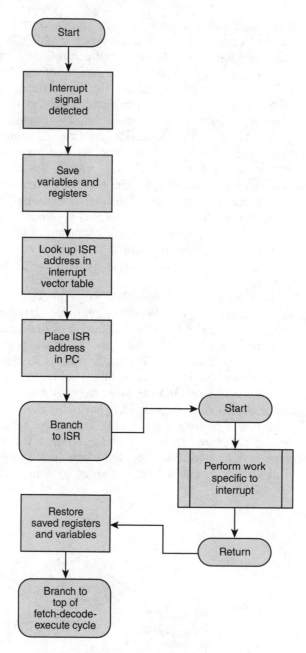

FIGURE 7.4 Processing an Interrupt

manufacturer may provide a specialized **device driver** program to be kept in memory along with code for the standard devices. Installation of the device driver code involves updating the disk I/O vector to point to code particular to the disk drive.

We mentioned in Chapter 4 that I/O interrupts are usually maskable, and an I/O device can generate a nonmaskable interrupt if it encounters an error that it cannot handle, such as the removal or destruction of an I/O medium. We return to this topic later in the context of embedded systems in Chapter 10.

Memory-Mapped I/O

The design decisions made with regard to a system's I/O control method are enormously influential in determining the overall system architecture. If we decide to use programmed I/O, it is to our advantage to establish separate buses for memory traffic and I/O traffic so that the continued polling doesn't interfere with memory access. In this case, the system requires a set of distinct instructions for I/O control. Specifically, the system needs to know how to check the status of a device, transfer bytes to and from the device, and verify that the transfer has executed correctly. This approach has some serious limitations. For one, adding a new device type to the system may require changes to the processor's control store or hardwired control matrix.

A simpler and more elegant approach is **memory-mapped I/O** in which I/O devices and main memory share the same address space. Thus, each I/O device has its own reserved block of memory. Data transfers to and from the I/O device involve moving bytes to or from the memory address that is mapped to the device. Memory-mapped I/O therefore looks just like a memory access from the point of view of the CPU. This means we can use the same instructions to move data to and from both I/O and memory, greatly simplifying system design.

In small systems, the low-level details of the data transfers are offloaded to the I/O controllers built into the I/O devices themselves, as shown in Figure 7.1. The CPU does not need to concern itself with whether a device is ready, or counting the bytes in a transfer, or calculating error-correcting codes.

Direct Memory Access

With both programmed I/O and interrupt-driven I/O, the CPU moves data to and from the I/O device. During I/O, the CPU runs instructions similar to the following pseudocode:

```
WHILE More-input AND NOT (Error or Timeout)
        ADD 1 TO Byte-count
        IF Byte-count > Total-bytes-to-be-transferred THEN
          EXIT
        ENDIF
        Place byte in destination buffer
        Raise byte-ready signal
        Initialize timer
```

```
                        REPEAT
                         WAIT
                        UNTIL Byte-acknowledged, Timeout, OR Error
                  ENDWHILE
```

Clearly, these instructions are simple enough to be programmed in a dedicated chip. This is the idea behind **direct memory access (DMA)**. When a system uses DMA, the CPU offloads execution of tedious I/O instructions. To effect the transfer, the CPU provides the DMA controller with the location of the bytes to be transferred, the number of bytes to be transferred, and the destination device or memory address. This communication usually takes place through special I/O registers on the CPU. A sample DMA configuration is shown in Figure 7.5. In this configuration, I/O and memory share the same address space, so it is one type of memory-mapped I/O.

Once the proper values are placed in memory, the CPU signals the DMA subsystem and proceeds with its next task, while the DMA takes care of the details of the I/O. After the I/O is complete (or ends in error), the DMA subsystem signals the CPU by sending it another interrupt.

As you can see in Figure 7.5, the DMA controller and the CPU share the bus. Only one of them at a time can have control of the bus, that is, be the **bus master**. Generally, I/O takes priority over CPU memory fetches for program instructions and data because many I/O devices operate within tight timing parameters. If they detect no activity within a specified period, they **timeout** and abort the I/O process. To avoid device timeouts, the DMA uses memory cycles that would otherwise be used by the CPU. This is called **cycle stealing**. Fortunately, I/O tends to create **bursty** traffic on the bus: data is sent in blocks, or

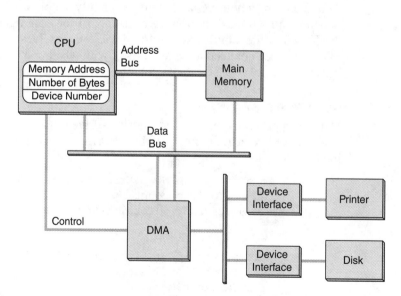

FIGURE 7.5   A Sample DMA Configuration

clusters. The CPU should be granted access to the bus between bursts, though this access may not be of long enough duration to spare the system from accusations of "crawling during I/O."

Figure 7.6 shows the activities of the CPU and the DMA. This swimlane diagram emphasizes how the DMA offloads I/O processing from the CPU.

Channel I/O

Programmed I/O transfers data one byte at a time. Interrupt-driven I/O can handle data one byte at a time or in small blocks, depending on the type of device participating in the I/O. Slower devices such as keyboards generate more interrupts per number of bytes transferred than disks or printers. DMA methods are all block-oriented, interrupting the CPU only after completion (or failure) of transferring a group of bytes. After the DMA signals the I/O completion, the CPU may give it the address of the next block of memory to be read from or written to. In the event of failure, the CPU is solely responsible for taking appropriate action. Thus, DMA I/O requires only a little less CPU participation than does interrupt-driven I/O. Such overhead is fine for small, single-user systems; however, it does not scale well to large, multiuser systems such as mainframe computers. Most large computer systems use an intelligent type of DMA interface known as an **I/O channel**. Although channel I/O is traditionally used on mainframe computers, it is becoming common on file servers and storage networks. Storage networks and other high-performance I/O implementations are presented in Chapter 13.

With **channel I/O**, one or more I/O processors control various I/O pathways called **channel paths**. Channel paths for "slow" devices such as terminals and printers can be combined (**multiplexed**), allowing management of several of these devices through only one controller. On IBM mainframes, a multiplexed channel path is called a **multiplexor channel**. Channels for disk drives and other "fast" devices are called **selector channels**.

I/O channels are driven by small CPUs called **I/O processors** (**IOPs**), which are optimized for I/O. Unlike DMA circuits, IOPs have the ability to execute programs that include arithmetic-logic and branching instructions. Figure 7.7 shows a simplified channel I/O configuration.

IOPs execute programs that are placed in main system memory by the host processor. These programs, consisting of a series of **channel command words** (**CCWs**), include not only the actual transfer instructions, but also commands that control the I/O devices. These commands include such things as device initializations, printer page ejects, and tape rewind commands, to name a few. Once the I/O program has been placed in memory, the host issues a **start subchannel** (**SSCH**) command, informing the IOP of the location in memory where the program can be found. After the IOP has completed its work, it places completion information in memory and sends an interrupt to the CPU. The CPU then obtains the completion information and takes action appropriate to the return codes.

The principal distinction between standalone DMA and channel I/O lies in the intelligence of the IOP. The IOP negotiates protocols, issues device commands, and translates storage coding to memory coding, and can transfer entire

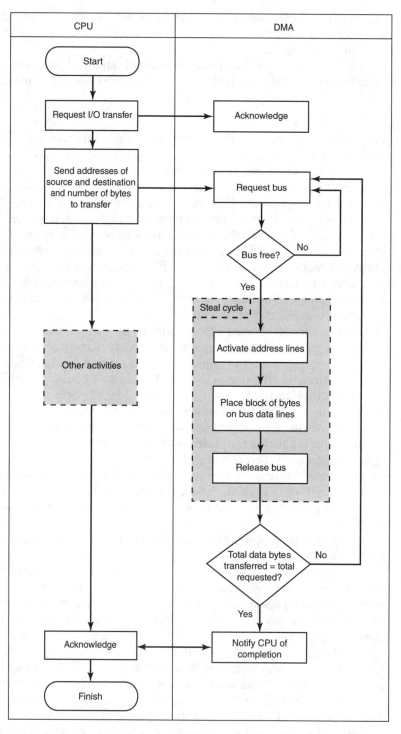

FIGURE 7.6   Swimlane Diagram Showing the Interaction of a CPU and a DMA

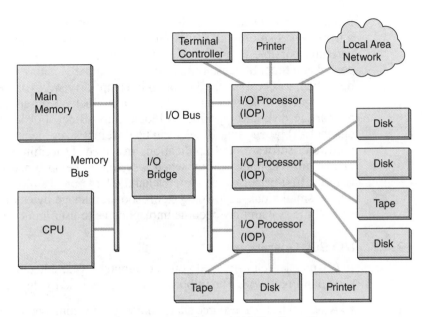

FIGURE 7.7 A Channel I/O Configuration

files or groups of files independent of the host CPU. The host has only to create the program instructions for the I/O operation and tell the IOP where to find them.

Like standalone DMA, an IOP must steal memory cycles from the CPU. Unlike standalone DMA, channel I/O systems are equipped with separate I/O buses, which help to isolate the host from the I/O operation. Thus, channel I/O is a type of **isolated I/O**. When copying a file from disk to tape, for example, the IOP uses the system memory bus only to fetch its instructions from main memory. The remainder of the transfer is effected using only the I/O bus. Because of its intelligence and bus isolation, channel I/O is used in high-throughput transaction processing environments, where its cost and complexity can be justified.

7.4.2 Character I/O Versus Block I/O

Pressing a key on a computer keyboard sets in motion a sequence of activities that process the keystroke as a single event (no matter how fast you type!). The reason for this is found within the mechanics of the keyboard. Each key controls a small switch that closes a connection in a matrix of conductors that runs horizontally and vertically beneath the keys. When a key switch closes, a distinct **scan code** is read by the keyboard circuitry. The scan code is then passed to a serial interface circuit, which translates the scan code into a character code. The interface places the character code in a keyboard buffer that is maintained in low memory. Immediately afterward, an I/O interrupt signal is raised. The characters wait patiently in the buffer until they are retrieved—one at a time—by a program (or until the buffer is reset). The keyboard circuits are able to process a new keystroke only after the old one is on its way to the buffer. Although it is certainly possible to press two keys at once, only one of the strokes can be processed at a time. Because of the random, sequential nature of character I/O as just described, it is best handled through interrupt-driven I/O processing.

Magnetic disks and tapes store data in blocks. Consequently, it makes sense to manage disk and tape I/O in block units. Block I/O lends itself to DMA or channel I/O processing. Blocks can be different sizes, depending on the particular hardware, software, and applications involved. Determining an ideal block size can be an important activity when a system is being tuned for optimum performance. High-performance systems handle large blocks more efficiently than they handle small blocks. Slower systems should manage bytes in smaller blocks; otherwise, the system may become unresponsive to user input during I/O.

7.4.3 I/O Bus Operation

In Chapter 1, we introduced you to computer bus architecture using the schematic shown in Figure 7.8. The important ideas conveyed by this diagram are:

- A system bus is a resource shared among many components of a computer system.
- Access to this shared resource must be controlled. This is why a control bus is required.

From our discussions in the preceding sections, it is evident that the memory bus and the I/O bus can be separate entities. In fact, it is often a good idea to separate them. One good reason for having memory on its own bus is that memory transfers can be **synchronous**, using some multiple of the CPU's clock cycles to retrieve data from main memory. In a properly functioning system, there is never an issue of the memory being offline or sustaining the same types of errors that afflict peripheral equipment, such as a printer running out of paper.

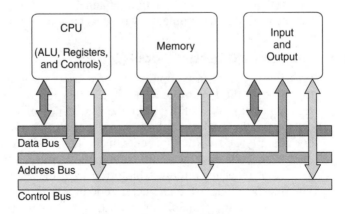

FIGURE 7.8 High-Level View of a System Bus

I/O buses, on the other hand, cannot operate synchronously. They must take into account the fact that I/O devices cannot always be ready to process an I/O transfer. I/O control circuits placed on the I/O bus and within the I/O devices negotiate with each other to determine the moment when each device may use the bus. Because these handshakes take place every time the bus is accessed, I/O buses are called **asynchronous**. We often distinguish synchronous from asynchronous transfers by saying that a synchronous transfer requires both the sender and the receiver to share a common clock for timing. But asynchronous bus protocols also require a clock for bit timing and to delineate signal transitions. This idea will become clear after we look at an example.

Consider, once again, the configuration shown in Figure 7.5. The connection between the DMA circuit and the device interface circuits is detailed in Figure 7.9, which shows the individual component buses.

Figure 7.10 gives the details of how the disk interface connects to all three buses. The address and data buses consist of a number of individual conductors, each of which carries one bit of information. The number of data lines determines the **width** of the bus. A data bus having eight data lines carries one byte at a time. The address bus has a sufficient number of conductors to uniquely identify each device on the bus.

The group of control lines shown in Figure 7.10 is the minimum that we need for our illustrative purpose. Real I/O buses typically have more than a dozen control lines. (The original IBM PC had more than 20!) Control lines coordinate the activities of the bus and its attached devices. To write data to the disk drive, our example bus executes the following sequence of operations:

1. The DMA circuit places the address of the disk controller on the address lines, and raises (asserts) the `Request` and `Write` signals.

2. With the `Request` signal asserted, decoder circuits in the controller interrogate the address lines.

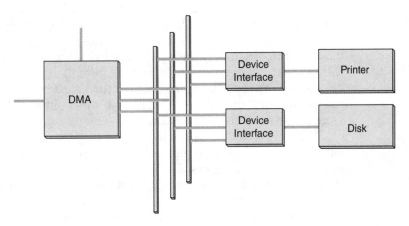

FIGURE 7.9   DMA Configuration Showing Separate Address, Data, and Control Lines

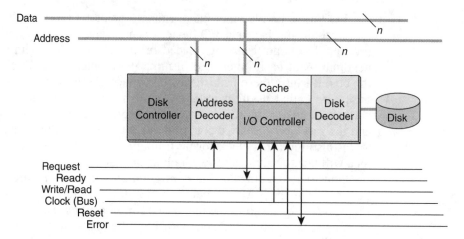

FIGURE 7.10 A Disk Controller Interface with Connections to the I/O Bus

3. Upon sensing its own address, the decoder enables the disk control circuits. If the disk is available for writing data, the controller asserts a signal on the Ready line. At this point, the handshake between the DMA and the controller is complete. With the Ready signal raised, no other devices may use the bus.

4. The DMA circuits then place the data on the lines and lower the Request signal.

5. When the disk controller sees the Request signal drop, it transfers the byte from the data lines to the disk buffer, and then lowers its Ready signal.

To make this picture clearer and more precise, engineers describe bus operation through **timing diagrams**. The timing diagram for our disk write operation is shown in Figure 7.11. The vertical lines, marked t_0 through t_{10}, specify the duration of the various signals. In a real timing diagram, an exact duration would be assigned to the timing intervals, usually in the neighborhood of 50ns. Signals on the bus can change only during a clock cycle transition. Notice that the signals shown in the diagram do not rise and fall instantaneously. This reflects the physical reality of the bus. A small amount of time must be allowed for the signal level to stabilize, or "settle down." This **settle time**, although small, contributes to a large delay over long I/O transfers.

The address and data lines in a timing diagram are rarely shown individually, but usually as a group. In our diagram, we imply the group by the use of a pair of lines. When the address and data lines transition from an active to an inactive state, we show the lines crossing. When the lines are inactive, we shade the space between them to make it clear that their state is undefined.

Many real I/O buses, unlike our example, do not have separate address and data lines. Because of the asynchronous nature of an I/O bus, the data lines can

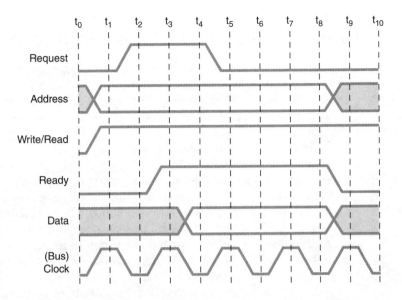

Time	Salient Bus Signal	Meaning
t_0	Assert Write	Bus is needed for writing (not reading)
t_0	Assert Address	Indicates where bytes will be written
t_1	Assert Request	Request write to address on address lines
t_2	Assert Ready	Acknowledges write request, bytes placed on data lines
t_3–t_7	Data Lines	Write data (requires several cycles)
t_8	Lower Ready	Release bus

FIGURE 7.11　A Bus Timing Diagram

be used to hold the device address. All we need to do is add another control line that indicates whether the signals on the data lines represent an address or data. This approach contrasts to a memory bus, where the address and data must be simultaneously available.

7.5　DATA TRANSMISSION MODES

Bytes can be transmitted between a host and a peripheral device by sending one bit at a time or one byte at a time. These are called, respectively, **serial** and **parallel** transmission modes. Each transmission mode establishes a particular communication protocol between the host and the device interface.

BYTES, DATA, **AND** *INFORMATION* . . . **FOR THE RECORD**

Far too many people use the word *information* as a synonym for *data*, and *data* as a synonym for *bytes*. In fact, we have often used data as a synonym for bytes in this text for readability, hoping that the context makes the meaning clear. We are compelled, however, to point out that there is indeed a world of difference in the meanings of these words.

In its most literal sense, the word *data* is plural. It comes from the Latin singular *datum*. Hence, to refer to more than one datum, one properly uses the word *data*. It is in fact easy on our ears when someone says, "The recent mortality data *indicate* that people are now living longer than they did a century ago." But we are at a loss to explain why we wince when someone says something like, "A page fault occurs when data *are* swapped from memory to disk." When we are using *data* to refer to something stored in a computer system, we really are conceptualizing data as an "indistinguishable mass" in the same sense that we think of air and water. Air and water consist of various d iscrete elements called molecules. Similarly, a mass of data consists of discrete elements called data. No educated person who is fluent in English would say that she breathes *airs* or takes a bath in *waters*. So it seems reasonable to say, ". . . data *is* swapped from memory to disk." Most scholarly sources (including the *American Heritage Dictionary*) now recognize *data* as a singular collective noun when used in this manner.

Strictly speaking, computer storage media don't store data. They store bit patterns called bytes. For example, if you were to use a binary sector editor to examine the contents of a disk, you might see the pattern 01000100. So what knowledge have you gained on seeing it? For all you know, this bit pattern could be the binary code of a program, part of an operating system structure, a photograph, or even someone's bank balance. If you know for a fact that the bits represent some numeric quantity (as opposed to program code or an image file, for example) and

7.5.1 Parallel Data Transmission

Parallel communication systems operate in a manner analogous to the operation of a host memory bus. They require at least eight data lines (one for each bit) and one line for synchronization, sometimes called a **strobe**.

Parallel connections are effective over short distances—usually less than 30 feet—depending on the strength of the signal, the frequency of the signal, and the quality of the cable. At longer distances, signals in the cable begin to weaken, because of the internal resistance of the conductors. Electrical signal loss over time or distance is called **attenuation**. The problems associated with attenuation become clear by studying an example.

that it is stored in two's complement binary, you can safely say that it is the decimal number 68. But you still don't have a datum. Before you can have a datum, someone must ascribe some context to this number. Is it a person's age or height? Is it the model number of a can opener? If you learn that 01000100 comes from a file that contains the temperature output from an automated weather station, then you have yourself a datum. The file on the disk can then be correctly called a *data file*.

By now, you've probably surmised that the weather data is expressed in degrees Fahrenheit, because no place on Earth has ever reached 68° Celsius. But you still don't have information. The datum is meaningless: Is it the current temperature in Amsterdam? Is it the temperature that was recorded at 2:00 AM three years ago in Miami? The *datum* 68 becomes *information* only when it has meaning to a human being.

Another plural Latin noun that has recently become recognized in singular usage is the word *media*. Formerly, educated people used this word only when they wished to refer to more than one *medium*. Newspapers are one kind of communication medium. Television is another. Collectively, they are media. But now some editors accept the singular usage, as in, "At this moment, the news media *is* gathering at the Capitol."

Inasmuch as artists can paint using a watercolor medium or an oil paint medium, computer data recording equipment can write to an electronic medium such as tape or disk. Collectively, these are electronic media. But rarely will you find a practitioner who intentionally uses the term properly. It is much more common to encounter statements like, "Volume 2 ejected. Please place new *media* into the tape drive." In this context, it's debatable whether most people would even understand the directive ". . . place a new *medium* into the tape drive."

Semantic arguments such as these are symptomatic of the kinds of problems computer professionals face when they try to express human ideas in digital form, and vice versa. There is bound to be something lost in the translation.

Figure 7.12 renders a simplified timing diagram for a parallel printer interface. The lines marked nStrobe and nAck are strobe and acknowledgment signals that are asserted when they carry low voltage. The Busy and Data signals are asserted when they carry high voltage. In other words, Busy and Data are positive logic signals, whereas nStrobe and nAck are negative logic signals. The data signal represents eight different lines. Each of these lines can be either high or low (signal 1 or 0). The signals on these lines are meaningless (shaded in diagram) before the nStrobe signal is asserted and after nAck is asserted. Arbitrary

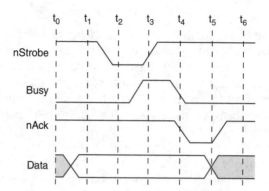

FIGURE 7.12 A Simplified Timing Diagram for a Parallel Printer

reference times are listed across the top of the diagram, t_0 through t_6. The difference between two consecutive times, Δt, determines the speed of transmission. Typically Δt will range between 1ms and 5ms.

The signals illustrated in Figure 7.12 comprise the handshake that takes place between a printer interface circuit (on a host) and the host interface of a parallel printer. The process starts when a bit is placed on each of the eight data lines. Next, the busy line is checked to see that it is low. Once the busy line is low, the strobe signal is asserted so the printer will know that there is data on the data lines. As soon as the printer detects the strobe, it reads the data lines while raising the busy signal to prevent the host from placing more data on the data lines. After the printer has read the data lines, it lowers the busy signal and asserts the acknowledgment signal, nAck, to let the host know that the data has been received.

Notice that although the data signals are acknowledged, there is no guarantee of their correctness. Both the host and the printer assume that the signals received are the same as the signals that were sent. Over short distances, this is a fairly safe assumption. Over longer distances, this may not be the case.

Let's say that the bus operates on a voltage of ±5 volts. Anything between 0 and +5 volts is considered "high" and anything between 0 and −5 volts is considered "low." The host places voltages of +5 and −5 volts on the data lines, respectively, for each 1 and 0 of the data byte. Then it sets the strobe line to −5 volts.

With a case of "mild" attenuation, the printer could be slow to detect the nStrobe signal or the host could be slow to detect the nAck signal. This kind of sluggishness is hardly noticeable when printers are involved, but horrendously slow over a parallel disk interface, where we typically expect an instantaneous response.

Over a very long cable, we could end up with entirely different voltages at the printer end. By the time the signals arrive, "high" could be +1 volt and "low" could be -3 volts. If 1 volt is not sufficiently above the voltage threshold for a logical 1, we could end up with a 0 where a 1 should be, scrambling the output in the process. Also, over long distances, it is possible that the strobe signal gets to the printer before the data bits do. The printer then prints whatever is on the data lines at the time it detects the assertion of nStrobe. (The extreme case is when a text character is mistaken for a control character. This can cause remarkably bizarre printer behavior and the death of many trees.)

7.5.2   Serial Data Transmission

We have seen how a parallel data transmission moves one byte at a time along a data bus. A data line is required for each bit, and the data lines are activated by pulses in a separate strobe line. Serial data transmission differs from parallel data transmission in that only one conductor is used for sending data, one bit at a time, as pulses in a single data line. Other conductors can be provided for special signals, as defined in particular protocols. RS-232-C is one such serial protocol that requires separate signaling lines; the data, however, is sent over only one line (see Chapter 12). Serial storage interfaces incorporate these special signals into protocol frames exchanged along the data path. We will examine some serial storage protocols in Chapter 13. Generally speaking, serial data streams can be reliably sent faster over longer distances than parallel data. This makes serial transmission the method of choice for high-performance interfaces.

Serial transfer methods can also be used for time-sensitive **isochronous** data transfers. Isochronous protocols are used with real-time data such as voice and video signals. Because voice and video are intended for consumption by human senses, occasional transmission errors bear little notice. The approximate nature of the data permits less error control; hence, data can flow with minimal protocol-induced latency from its source to its destination.

7.6   MAGNETIC DISK TECHNOLOGY

Before the advent of disk drive technology, sequential media such as punched cards and magnetic or paper tape were the only kinds of durable storage available. If the data that someone needed were written at the trailing end of a tape reel, the entire volume had to be read—one record at a time. Sluggish readers and small system memories made this an excruciatingly slow process. Tape and cards were not only slow, but they also degraded rather quickly because of the physical and environmental stresses to which they were exposed. Paper tape often stretched and broke. Open reel magnetic tape not only stretched, but also was subject to mishandling by operators. Cards could tear, get lost, and warp.

In this technological context, it is easy to see how IBM fundamentally changed the computer world in 1956 when it deployed the first commercial disk-based computer called the **Random Access Method of Accounting and Control** computer, or **RAMAC** for short. By today's standards, the disk in this early machine was incomprehensibly huge and slow. Each disk platter was 24 inches in diameter, containing only 50,000 7-bit characters of data on each surface. Fifty two-sided platters were mounted on a spindle that was housed in a flashy glass enclosure about the size of a small garden shed. The total storage capacity per spindle was a mere 5 million characters, and it took one full second, on average, to access data on the disk. The drive weighed more than a ton and cost millions of dollars to lease. (One could not *buy* equipment from IBM in those days.)

By contrast, in early 2000, IBM began marketing a high-capacity disk drive for use in palmtop computers and digital cameras. These disks were 1 inch (2.5cm) in diameter, held 1GB of data, and provided an average access time of 15ms. The drive weighed less than an ounce and retailed for less than $300! Since then, other manufacturers have produced 1-inch drives that are even less expensive and hold more data.

Disk drives are called **random** (sometimes **direct**) access devices because each unit of storage on a disk, the **sector**, has a unique address that can be accessed independently of the sectors around it. As shown in Figure 7.13, sectors are divisions of concentric circles called **tracks**. On most systems, every track contains

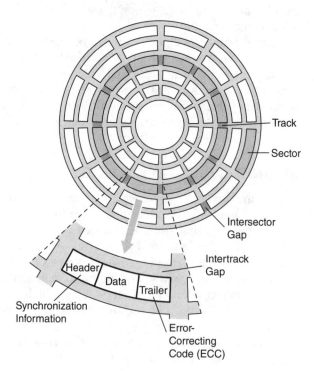

FIGURE 7.13   Disk Sectors Showing Intersector Gaps and Logical Sector Format

exactly the same number of sectors. Each sector contains the same number of bytes. Hence, the data is written more "densely" at the center of the disk than at the outer edge. Some manufacturers pack more bytes onto their disks by making all sectors approximately the same size, placing more sectors on the outer tracks than on the inner tracks. This is called **zoned-bit** recording. Zoned-bit recording is rarely used because it requires more sophisticated drive control electronics than traditional systems.

Disk tracks are consecutively numbered starting with track 0 at the outermost edge of the disk. Sectors, however, may not be in consecutive order around the perimeter of a track. They sometimes "skip around" to allow time for the drive circuitry to process the contents of a sector prior to reading the next sector. This is called **interleaving**. Interleaving varies according to the speed of rotation of the disk as well as the speed of the disk circuitry and its buffers. Most of today's fixed disk drives read disks a track at a time, not a sector at a time, so interleaving is becoming less common.

7.6.1 Rigid Disk Drives

Rigid ("hard" or fixed) disks contain control circuitry and one or more metal or glass disks called **platters** to which a thin film of magnetizable material is bonded. Disk platters are stacked on a spindle, which is turned by a motor located within the drive housing. Disks can rotate as fast as 15,000 revolutions per minute (rpm), the most common speeds being 5,400rpm and 7,200rpm. Read/write heads are typically mounted on a rotating **actuator arm** that is positioned in its proper place by magnetic fields induced in coils surrounding the axis of the actuator arm (see Figure 7.14). When the actuator is energized, the entire comb of read/write heads moves toward or away from the center of the disk.

Despite continual improvements in magnetic disk technology, it is still impossible to mass-produce a completely error-free medium. Although the probability of error is small, errors must, nevertheless, be expected. Two mechanisms are used to reduce errors on the surface of the disk: special coding of the data itself and error-correcting algorithms. (This special coding and some error-correcting codes were discussed in Chapter 2.) These tasks are handled by circuits built into the disk controller hardware. Other circuits in the disk controller take care of head positioning and disk timing.

In a stack of disk platters, all of the tracks directly above and below each other form a **cylinder**. A comb of read/write heads accesses one cylinder at a time. Cylinders describe circular areas on each disk.

Typically, there is one read/write head per usable surface of the disk. (Older disks—particularly removable disks—did not use the top surface of the top platter or the bottom surface of the bottom platter.) Fixed disk heads never touch the surface of the disk. Instead, they float above the disk surface on a cushion of air only a few microns thick. When the disk is powered down, the

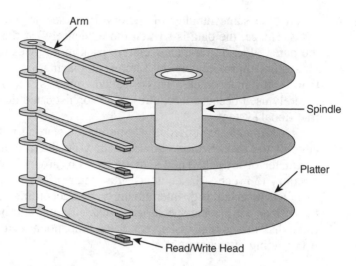

FIGURE 7.14 Rigid Disk Actuator (with Read/Write Heads) and Disk Platters

heads retreat to a safe place. This is called **parking the heads**. If a read/write head were to touch the surface of the disk, the disk would become unusable. This condition is known as a **head crash**.

Head crashes were common during the early years of disk storage. First-generation disk drive mechanical and electronic components were costly with respect to the price of disk platters. To provide the most storage for the least money, computer manufacturers made disk drives with removable disks called **disk packs**. When the drive housing was opened, airborne impurities, such as dust and water vapor, would enter the drive housing. Consequently, large head-to-disk clearances were required to prevent these impurities from causing head crashes. (Despite these large head-to-disk clearances, frequent crashes persisted, with some companies experiencing as much downtime as uptime.) The price paid for the large head-to-disk clearance was substantially lower data density. The greater the distance between the head and the disk, the stronger the charge in the flux coating of the disk must be for the data to be readable. Stronger magnetic charges require more particles to participate in a flux transition, resulting in lower data density for the drive.

Eventually, cost reductions in controller circuitry and mechanical components permitted widespread use of sealed disk units. IBM invented this technology, which was developed under the code name "Winchester." **Winchester** soon became a generic term for any sealed disk unit. Today, with removable-pack drives no longer being manufactured, we have little need to make the distinction. Sealed drives permit closer head-to-disk clearances, increased data densities, and faster rotational speeds. These factors constitute the performance characteristics of a rigid disk drive.

Seek time is the time it takes for a disk arm to position itself over the required track. Seek time does not include the time that it takes for the head to read the disk directory. The **disk directory** maps logical file information, for example, my_story.doc, to a physical sector address, such as cylinder 7, surface 3, sector 72. Some high-performance disk drives practically eliminate seek time by providing a read/write head for each track of each usable surface of the disk. With no movable arms in the system, the only delays in accessing data are caused by rotational delay.

Rotational delay is the time it takes for the required sector to position itself under a read/write head. The sum of the rotational delay and seek time is known as the **access time**. If we add to the access time the time it takes to actually read the data from the disk, we get a quantity known as **transfer time**, which, of course, varies depending on how much data is read. **Latency** is a direct function of rotational speed. It is a measure of the amount of time it takes for the desired sector to move beneath the read/write head after the disk arm has positioned itself over the desired track. Usually cited as an average, it is calculated as:

$$\frac{\dfrac{60 \text{ seconds}}{\text{disk rotation speed}} \times \dfrac{1000 \text{ ms}}{\text{second}}}{2}$$

To help you appreciate how all of this terminology fits together, we have provided a typical disk specification as Figure 7.15.

Because the disk directory must be read prior to every data read or write operation, the location of the directory can have a significant effect on the overall performance of the disk drive. Outermost tracks have the lowest bit density per areal measure; hence, they are less prone to bit errors than the innermost tracks. To ensure the best reliability, disk directories can be placed at the outermost track, track 0. This means, for every access, the arm has to swing out to track 0 and then back to the required data track. Performance therefore suffers from the wide arc made by the access arms.

Improvements in recording technology and error-correction algorithms permit the directory to be placed in the location that gives the best performance: at the innermost track. This substantially reduces arm movement, giving the best possible throughput. Some, but not all, modern systems take advantage of center track directory placement.

Directory placement is one of the elements of the logical organization of a disk. A disk's logical organization is a function of the operating system that uses it. A major component of this logical organization is the way in which sectors are mapped. Fixed disks contain so many sectors that keeping tabs on each one is infeasible. Consider the disk described in our data sheet. Each track contains 746 sectors. There are 48,000 tracks per surface and 8 surfaces on the disk. This means there are more than 286 million sectors on the disk. An allocation table listing the status of each sector (the status being recorded in 1 byte) would therefore consume more than 200MB of disk space. Not only is this a lot of disk space spent for overhead, but reading this data structure would consume an inordinate

CONFIGURATION:		RELIABILITY AND MAINTENANCE:	
Formatted Capacity, GB	1500	MTTF	300,000 hours
Integrated Controller	SATA	Start/Stop Cycles	50,000
Encoding Method	EPRML	Design Life	5 years (minimum)
Buffer Size	32MB	Data Errors	
Platters	8	(nonrecoverable)	<1 per 10^{15} bits read
Data Surfaces	16	PERFORMANCE:	
Tracks per Surface	16,383	Seek Times	
Track Density	190,000tpi	Track to Track	
Recording Density	1,462Kbpi	Read	0.3ms
Bytes per Sector	512	Write	0.5ms
Sectors per Track	63	Average	
PHYSICAL:		Read	4.5ms
Height	26.1mm	Write	5.0ms
Length	147.0mm	Average Latency	4.17ms
Width	101.6mm	Rotational Speed	
Weight	720g	(+/−0.20%)	7,200rpm
Temperature (°C)		Data Transfer Rate:	
Operating	5°C to 55°C	From Disk	1.2MB/sec
Nonoperating/Storage	−40°C to 71°C	To Disk	3GB/sec
Relative Humidity	5% to 95%	Start Time	
Acoustic Noise	33dBA, idle	(0 to Drive Ready)	9 sec

POWER REQUIREMENTS

Mode	+5VDC +5% − 10%	Power +5.0VDC
Spin-up	500mA	16.5W
Read/write	1,080mA	14.4W
Idle	730mA	9.77W
Standby	270mA	1.7W
Sleep	250mA	1.6W

FIGURE 7.15 A Typical Rigid Disk Specification as Provided by a Disk Drive Manufacturer

amount of time whenever we needed to check the status of a sector. (This is a frequently executed task.) For this reason, operating systems address sectors in groups, called **blocks** or **clusters**, to make file management simpler. The number of sectors per block determines the size of the allocation table. The smaller the size of the allocation block, the less wasted space there is when a file doesn't fill the entire block; however, smaller block sizes make the allocation tables larger and slower. We will look deeper into the relationship between directories and file allocation structures in our discussion of floppy disks in the next section.

One final comment about the disk specification shown in Figure 7.15: You can see that it also includes estimates of disk reliability under the heading of "Reliability and Maintenance." According to the manufacturer, this particular disk drive is designed to operate for five years and tolerate being stopped and started 50,000 times. Under the same heading, the **mean time to failure** (**MTTF**) is given as 300,000 hours. Surely this figure cannot be taken to mean that the expected value of the disk life is 300,000 hours—this is just over 34 years if the disk runs continuously. The specification states that the drive is designed to last only five years. This apparent anomaly owes its existence to statistical quality control methods commonly used in the manufacturing industry. Unless the disk is manufactured under a government contract, the exact method used for calculating the MTTF is at the discretion of the manufacturer. Usually the process involves taking random samples from production lines and running the disks under less-than-ideal conditions for a certain number of hours, typically more than 100. The number of failures are then plotted against probability curves to obtain the resulting MTTF figure. In short, the "design life" number is much more credible and understandable.

7.6.2 Solid State Drives

The limitations of magnetic disks are many. To begin with, it takes a lot longer to retrieve data from a magnetic disk than from main memory—around a million times longer. Magnetic disks are fragile. Even "ruggedized" models can break under extreme shock. Their many moving parts are susceptible to wear and failure. And—particularly problematic for mobile devices—magnetic disks are power hungry.

The clear solution to these problems is to replace the hard disk with non-volatile RAM. Indeed, this switch happened decades ago in ultra-high-performance computers. Only recently has the price of memory become low enough to make this an attractive option for industrial, military, and consumer products.

Solid state drives (**SSDs**) consist of a microcontroller and a type of NAND- or NOR-based memory arrays called flash memory. Flash memory is distinguished from standard memory by the fact that it must be first erased ("in a flash") before it can be written to. NOR-based flash is byte addressable, making it more costly than NAND-based flash memory, which is instead organized in blocks (called pages), much like a magnetic disk.

Certainly we all enjoy our pocket-sized memory sticks, thumb drives, and jump drives. We are scarcely awed by the fact that these small devices can store an entire library on our key rings. Because of their low power consumption and durability, flash drives are now routinely replacing standard magnetic disks in portable devices. These applications also benefit from a performance boost: Access times and transfer rates of SSDs are typically 100 times faster than traditional disk drives. SSD accesses, however, are still slower than RAM by a factor of 100,000.

Although the data capacity of SSDs is nearing that of magnetic disks, SSDs tend to be roughly 2 to 3 times as costly. One would expect that the price gap will close considerably with the continued advances in SSD technology. For data centers, the increased cost of large arrays of SSDs may be offset by reduced electricity and air-conditioning costs.

Besides cost, another disadvantage of SSDs versus magnetic disks is that the bit cells of flash storage wear out after 30,000 to 1,000,000 updates to a page. This may seem like a long duty cycle, except that SSDs can store highly volatile data, such as virtual memory pagefiles. Standard magnetic disks tend to reuse the same disk sectors repeatedly, gradually filling up the disk. If this approach is used with an SSD, parts of the drive will eventually wear out and become unusable. So to extend the life of the disk, a technique called **wear leveling** is used to distribute data and erase/write cycles evenly over the entire disk. The drive's built-in microcontroller manages the free space on the disk to ensure that pages are reused in a round-robin-type rotation. This approach does offer a slight performance advantage; since a page must be erased before it can be written to, so the erasing and writing can occur simultaneously if the same page is not reused.

SSDs that are designed for use in servers are called **enterprise-grade SSDs.** These SSDs include cache memory for optimal performance and a small backup power source so that cache contents can be committed to flash in the event of a power failure. Figure 7.16 is a photograph of an Intel 910 800GB SSD. The microcontroller and flash memory chips dominate the card's real estate. The drive mounts in a server as simply as any other bus-attached card.

SSD specifications share many common elements with HDDs. Figure 7.17 is an example of a data sheet for an enterprise-grade SSD. In comparing the specifications in Figure 7.17 with those in Figure 7.15, you can see that there is no reference to platters, or rotational speed, or anything else having to do with the

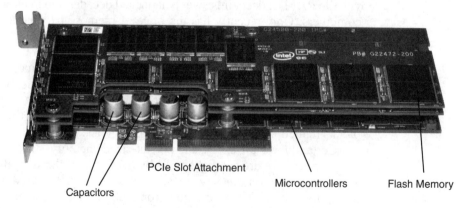

FIGURE 7.16 Intel 910 800GB SSD
Courtesy Intel Corporation.

CONFIGURATION:		RELIABILITY AND MAINTENANCE:	
Capacity, GB	800	MTTF	2,000,000 hours
Integrated Controller	SATA 3.0	Endurance	450 TBW
Encryption	AES 256-bit	Data Retention	3 months
Cache Size	1GB	Data Errors (UBER)	<1 per 10^{17} sector read
Bytes per Sector	512	PERFORMANCE:	
PHYSICAL:		Average Latency	(Sequential)
Height	7mm	Read	50µs
Length	100mm	Write	65µs
Width	70mm	I/O Operations/Sec (IOPS)	(Random)
Weight	170g	8KB Reads	47,500 IOPS
Temperature (°C)		8KB Writes	5,500 IOPS
Operating	0°C to 70°C	Data Transfer Rate:	
Nonoperating/Storage	−55°C to 95°C	Read	500MB/sec
Relative Humidity	5% − 95%	Write	450MB/sec
Acoustic Noise	0dB	Start Time	
		(0 to Drive Ready)	3 sec

POWER REQUIREMENTS

Mode	+3.3VDC +5% − 10%	Power +3.3VDC
Active	1,500mA	5W
Idle	106mA	0.350W

FIGURE 7.17 An SSD Data Sheet

spinning disk form factor. However, the drive's physical characteristics, access time, transfer rate, and power consumption are still significant metrics.

The **Joint Electron Devices Engineering Council (JEDEC)** sets standards for SSD performance and reliability metrics. Two of the most important of these are **Unrecoverable Bit Error Ratio (UBER)** and **terabytes written (TBW)**. UBER is calculated by dividing the number of data errors by the number of bits read using a simulated lifetime workload. TBW is the number of terabytes that can be written to the disk before the disk fails to meet specifications for speed and error rates. TBW is a measure of disk endurance (or service life) and UBER is a measure of disk reliability.

The cost of enterprise-grade SSDs makes sense where fast data retrieval is crucial. It is now common practice to push HDD performance to its limits through a practice known as **short stroking**. Short stroking involves the installation of many extra disk drives, each of which utilizes only a small percentage of its cylinders, thus keeping arm motion to a minimum. With less arm motion, access time decreases, saving a few milliseconds on each disk access. Thus, cost comparisons between HDDs and SSDs in the enterprise must take into account the number of gigabytes of useful storage, general reliability, and the low power consumption of enterprise SDDs.

As drive prices continue to plummet, SSDs are sure to start showing up in less demanding business environments. By some estimates, SSD costs will reach parity with HDDs well before the end of the 2010s.

7.7   OPTICAL DISKS

Optical storage systems offer (practically) unlimited data storage at a cost that is competitive with tape. Optical disks come in a number of formats, the most popular format being the ubiquitous **CD-ROM (compact disc-read only memory)**, which can hold more than 0.5GB of data. CD-ROMs are a read-only medium, making them ideal for software and data distribution. **CD-R (CD-recordable)**, **CD-RW (CD-rewritable)**, and **WORM (write once read many)** disks are optical storage devices often used for long-term data archiving and high-volume data output. CD-R and WORM offer unlimited quantities of tamper-resistant storage for documents and data. For long-term archival storage of data, some computer systems send output directly to optical storage rather than paper or microfiche. This is called **computer output laser disc (COLD)**. Robotic storage libraries called **optical jukeboxes** provide direct access to myriad optical disks. Jukeboxes can store dozens to hundreds of disks, for total capacities of 50GB to 1,200GB and beyond. Proponents of optical storage claim that optical disks, unlike magnetic media, can be stored for 100 years without noticeable degradation. (Who could possibly challenge this claim?)

7.7.1   CD-ROM

CD-ROMs are polycarbonate (plastic) disks 120mm (4.8 inches) in diameter to which a reflective aluminum film is applied. The aluminum film is sealed with a protective acrylic coating to prevent abrasion and corrosion. The aluminum layer reflects light that emits from a green laser diode situated beneath the disk. The reflected light passes through a prism, which diverts the light into a photodetector. The photodetector converts pulses of light into electrical signals, which it sends to decoder electronics in the drive (see Figure 7.18).

Compact discs are written from the center to the outside edge using a single spiraling track of bumps in the polycarbonate substrate. These bumps are called **pits** because they look like pits when viewed from the top surface of the CD. Lineal spaces between the pits are called **lands**. Pits measure 0.5μm wide and are between 0.83μm and 3.56μm long. (The edges of the pits correspond to binary 1s.) The bump formed by the underside of a pit is as high as one-quarter of the wavelength of the light produced by the laser diode. This means that the bump interferes with the reflection of the laser beam in such a way that the light bouncing off the bump exactly cancels out light incident from the laser. This results in pulses of light and dark, which are interpreted by drive circuitry as binary digits.

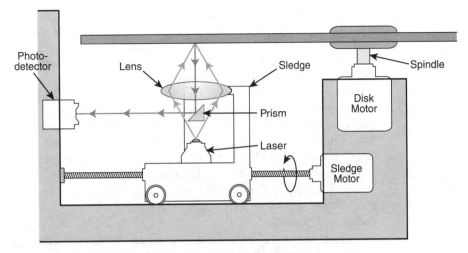

FIGURE 7.18   The Internals of a CD-ROM Drive

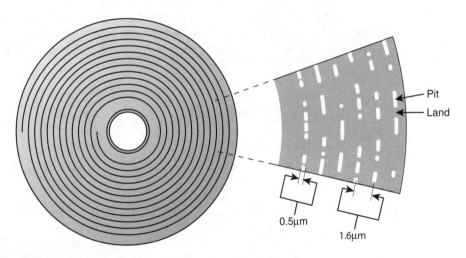

FIGURE 7.19   CD Track Spiral and Track Enlargement

The distance between adjacent turns of the spiral track, the **track pitch**, must be at least 1.6μm (see Figure 7.19). If you could "unravel" a CD-ROM or audio CD track and lay it on the ground, the string of pits and lands would extend nearly 5 miles (8km). (Being only 0.5μm wide—less than half the thickness of a human hair—it would be barely visible to the unaided eye.)

Although a CD has only one track, a string of pits and lands spanning 360° of the disk is referred to as a track in most optical disk literature. Unlike magnetic storage, tracks at the center of the disk have the same bit density as tracks at the outer edge of the disk.

CD-ROMs were designed for storing music and other sequential audio signals. Data storage applications were an afterthought, as you can see by the data sector format in Figure 7.20. Data is stored in 2,352-byte chunks called sectors that lie along the length of the track. Sectors are made up of 98 588-bit primitive units called **channel frames**. As shown in Figure 7.21, channel frames consist of synchronizing information, a header, and 33 17-bit symbols for a payload. The 17-bit symbols are encoded using an RLL(2, 10) code called **EFM** (**eight-to-fourteen modulation**). The disk drive electronics read and interpret (**demodulate**) channel frames to create yet another data structure called a **small frame**. Small frames are 33 bytes wide, 32 bytes of which are occupied by user data. The remaining byte is used for **subchannel** information. There are eight subchannels, named P, Q, R, S, T, U, V, and W. All except P (which denotes starting and stopping times) and Q (which contains control information) have meaning only for audio applications.

Most compact discs operate at **constant linear velocity** (**CLV**), which means that the rate at which sectors pass over the laser remains constant regardless of whether those sectors are at the beginning or the end of the disk. The constant velocity is achieved by spinning the disk slower when accessing the outermost tracks than the innermost. A sector number is addressable by the number of minutes and seconds of track that lie between it and the beginning (the center) of the disk. These "minutes and seconds" are calibrated under the assumption that

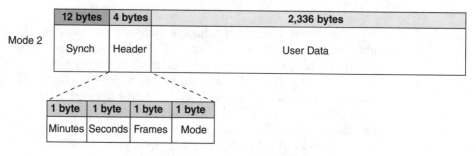

FIGURE 7.20 CD Data Sector Formats

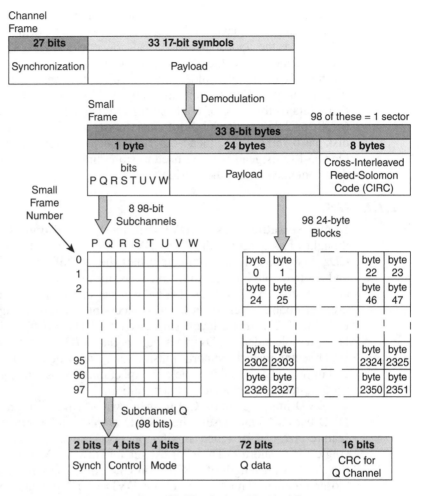

FIGURE 7.21   CD Physical and Logical Formats

the CD player processes 75 sectors per second. Computer CD-ROM drives are much faster than that with speeds up to 52 times (52×) the speed of audio CDs, 7.8MBps (with faster speeds sure to follow). To locate a particular sector, the sledge moves perpendicular to the disk track, taking its best guess as to where a particular sector may be. After an arbitrary sector is read, the head follows the track to the desired sector.

Sectors can have one of three different formats, depending on which mode is used to record the data. There are three different modes. Modes 0 and 2, intended for music recording, have no error-correction capabilities. Mode 1, intended for data recording, sports two levels of error detection and correction. These formats are shown in Figure 7.20. The total capacity of a CD recorded in Mode 1 is 650MB. Modes 0 and 2 can hold 742MB, but cannot be used reliably for data recording.

The track pitch of a CD can be more than 1.6µm when multiple **sessions** are used. Audio CDs have songs recorded in sessions, which, when viewed from below, give the appearance of broad concentric rings. When CDs began to be used for data storage, the idea of a music "recording session" was extended (without modification) to include data recording sessions. There can be as many as 99 sessions on CDs. Sessions are delimited by a 4,500-sector (1-minute) **lead-in** that contains the table of contents for the data contained in the session and by a 6,750- or 2,250-sector **lead-out** (or **runout**) at the end. (The first session on the disk has 6,750 sectors of lead-out. Subsequent sessions have the shorter lead-out.) On CD-ROMs, lead-outs are used to store directory information pertaining to the data contained within the session.

7.7.2 DVD

Digital versatile discs, or **DVD**s (formerly called **digital video discs**), can be thought of as quad-density CDs. DVDs rotate at about three times the speed of CDs. DVD pits are approximately half the size of CD pits (0.4µm to 2.13µm), and the track pitch is 0.74µm. Like CDs, they come in recordable and nonrecordable varieties. Unlike CDs, DVDs can be single sided or double sided, single layer or double layer. Each layer is accessible by refocusing the laser, as shown in Figure 7.22. Single-layer, single-sided DVDs can store 4.78GB, and double-layer, double-sided DVDs can accommodate 17GB of data. The same 2,048-byte DVD sector format supports music, data, and video. With greater data density and improved access time, one can expect that DVDs will eventually replace CDs for long-term data storage and distribution.

DVD improves upon CD in many ways. One of the most important is that DVD uses a 650nm laser whereas CD employs a 780nm laser. This means the feature size can be much smaller on DVD, so the linear space occupied by a single bit is shorter. The shortest pit length on DVD is 0.4µm as opposed to the shortest pit length of 0.83µm on CD. And DVD tracks can be placed much closer together. The track pitch on DVD is 0.74µm, as opposed to 1.6µm for CD. This means the spiral track is longer on DVD. Remember, the track length

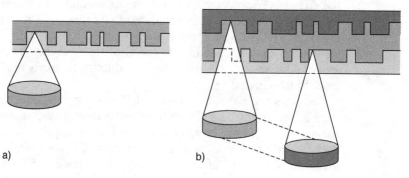

a)   b)

FIGURE 7.22   A Laser Focusing on a) a Single-Layer DVD and b) a Double-Layer
                 DVD One Layer at a Time

of a CD—if it could be unwound from its spiral—is about 5 miles (8km). By comparison, if you were to unwind the track of a DVD, it would span about 7.35 miles (11.8km).

A second great improvement is that DVD's track format is much leaner than CD's track format. Furthermore, DVD has a much more efficient error-correction algorithm than CD. DVD's error correction provides better protection using a greatly reduced number of redundant bits over CD.

With its greater data density and improved access times, DVD might be an ideal medium for long-term data storage and retrieval. There are, however, many other media in the running.

7.7.3   Blue-Violet Laser Discs

If DVD's 650nm laser provides more than twice the recording density of CD's 750nm laser, then the 405nm wavelength of the blue-violet laser breaks all barriers. Recent advances in laser technology have given us inexpensive blue-violet laser disc drives that can be incorporated in a variety of consumer products. Two incompatible blue-violet disc formats, **Blu-Ray** and **HD-DVD**, fought for market dominance in the mid-2000s. Each brought its own distinct advantage: HD-DVD is backward compatible with traditional DVDs, but Blu-Ray's storage capacity is greater.

The Blu-Ray Disc format was developed by the Blu-Ray Disc Association, a consortium of nine consumer electronic manufacturers. The group, led by MIT, includes such major companies as Sony, Samsung, and Pioneer. A Blu-Ray disk consists of a 120mm polycarbonate disk with data written in a single spiral track. The minimum pit length on a track is 0.13nm, and the track pitch is 0.32nm. The total recording capacity of a single layer disk is 25GB. Multiple layers can be "stacked" on a disk (up to six as of this writing), although only double-layer disks are available for in-home use. Blu-Ray ended up winning the blue-violet disk format battle because of the dominance of Sony in the movie industry and, above all, the release of Sony's enormously popular PlayStation 3, which used Blu-Ray disks for data storage.

For industrial-grade data storage, both Sony and the Plasmon Corporation released a blue laser medium designed especially for archival data storage. Both products are intended for use in large data centers, and thus are optimized for transfer speed (upwards of 6MB/s with verification). Sony's **Professional Disc for Data** (**PDD**) and Plasmon's second-generation **Ultra Density Optical** (**UDO-2**) disks can store up to 23GB and 60GB, respectively.

7.7.4   Optical Disk Recording Methods

Various technologies are used to enable recording on CDs and DVDs. The most inexpensive—and most pervasive—method uses heat-sensitive dye. The dye is sandwiched between the polycarbonate substrate and the reflective coating on the CD. When struck by light emitting from the laser, this dye creates a pit in the polycarbonate substrate. This pit affects the optical properties of the reflective layer.

Rewritable optical media, such as CD-RW, replace the dye and reflective coating layers of a CD-R disk with a metallic alloy that includes such exotic elements as indium, tellurium, antimony, and silver. In its unaltered state, this metallic coating is reflective to the laser light. When heated by a laser to about 500°C, it undergoes a molecular change, making it less reflective. (Chemists and physicists call this a **phase change**.) The coating reverts to its original reflective state when heated to only 200°C, thus allowing the data to be changed any number of times. (Industry experts have cautioned that phase-change CD recording may work for "only" 1,000 cycles.)

WORM drives, commonly found on large systems, employ higher-powered lasers than can be reasonably attached to systems intended for individual use. Lower-powered lasers are subsequently used to read the data. The higher-powered lasers permit different—and more durable—recording methods. Three of these methods are:

- **Ablative:** A high-powered laser melts a pit in a reflective metal coating sandwiched between the protective layers of the disk.

- **Bimetallic Alloy:** Two metallic layers are encased between protective coatings on the surfaces of the disk. Laser light fuses the two metallic layers together, causing a reflectance change in the lower metallic layer. Bimetallic Alloy WORM disk manufacturers claim that this medium will maintain its integrity for 100 years.

- **Bubble-Forming:** A single layer of thermally sensitive material is pressed between two plastic layers. When hit by high-powered laser light, bubbles form in the material, causing a reflectance change.

Despite their ability to use the same frame formats as CD-ROM, CD-R and CD-RW disks may not be readable in some CD-ROM drives. The incompatibility arises from the notion that CD-ROMs would be recorded (or pressed) in a single session. CD-Rs and CD-RWs, on the other hand, are most useful when they can be written incrementally like floppy disks. The first CD-ROM specification, ISO 9660, assumed single-session recording and has no provisions for allowing more than 99 sessions on the disk. Cognizant that the restrictions of ISO 9660 were inhibiting wider use of their products, a group of leading CD-R/CD-RW manufacturers formed a consortium to address the problem. The result of their efforts is the **Universal Disk Format Specification**, which allows an unlimited number of recording sessions for each disk. Key to this new format is the idea of replacing the table of contents associated with each session by a floating table of contents. This floating table of contents, called a **virtual allocation table** (**VAT**), is written to the lead-out following the last sector of user data written on the disk. As data is appended to what had been recorded in a previous session, the VAT is rewritten at the end of the new data. This process continues until the VAT reaches the last usable sector on the disk.

7.8   MAGNETIC TAPE

Magnetic tape is the oldest and most cost-effective of all mass-storage devices. First-generation magnetic tapes were made of the same material used by analog tape recorders. A cellulose-acetate film one-half inch wide (1.25cm) was coated on one side with a magnetic oxide. Twelve hundred feet of this material were wound onto a reel, which then could be hand-threaded on a tape drive. These tape drives were approximately the size of a small refrigerator. Early tapes had capacities under 11MB and required nearly half an hour to read or write the entire reel.

Data was written across the tape one byte at a time, creating one track for each bit. An additional track was added for parity, making the tape nine tracks wide, as shown in Figure 7.23. Nine-track tape used phase modulation coding with odd parity. The parity was odd to ensure that at least one "opposite" flux transition took place during long runs of zeros (nulls), characteristic of database records.

The evolution of tape technology over the years has been remarkable, with manufacturers constantly packing more bytes onto each linear inch of tape. Higher-density tapes are not only more economical to purchase and store, but they also allow backups to be made more quickly. This means that if a system must be taken offline while its files are being copied, downtime is reduced. Further economies can be realized when data is compressed before being written to the tape. (See "Focus on Data Compression" at the end of this chapter.)

The price paid for all of these innovative tape technologies is that a plethora of standards and proprietary techniques have emerged. Cartridges of various sizes and capacities have replaced nine-track open-reel tapes. Thin film coatings similar to those found on digital recording tape have replaced oxide coatings. Tapes support various track densities and employ serpentine or helical scan recording methods.

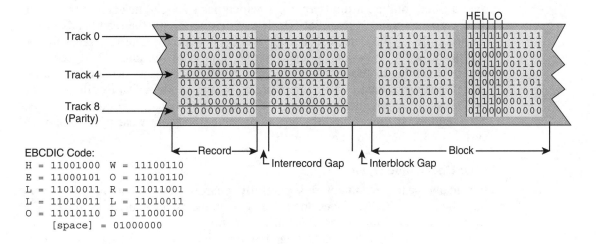

FIGURE 7.23   A Nine-Track Tape Format

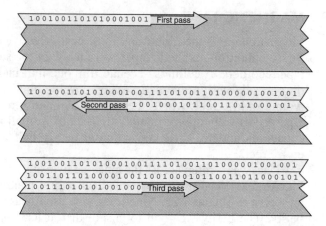

FIGURE 7.24 Three Recording Passes on a Serpentine Tape

Serpentine recording methods place bits on the tape in series. Instead of the bytes being perpendicular to the edges of the tape, as in the nine-track format, they are written "lengthwise," with each byte aligning in parallel with the edge of the tape. A stream of data is written along the length of the tape until the end is reached; then the tape reverses and the next track is written beneath the first one (see Figure 7.24). This process continues until the track capacity of the tape has been reached. **Digital linear tape** (**DLT**) and **Quarter Inch Cartridge** systems use serpentine recording with 50 or more tracks per tape.

Digital audio tape (**DAT**) and 8mm tape systems use **helical scan** recording. In other recording systems, the tape passes straight across a fixed magnetic head in a manner similar to a tape recorder. DAT systems pass tape over a tilted rotating drum (**capstan**), which has two read heads and two write heads, as shown in Figure 7.25. (During write operations, the read heads verify the integrity of the data just after it has been written.) The capstan spins at 2,000rpm in the direction opposite of the motion of the tape. (This configuration is similar to the mechanism used by VCRs.) The two read/write head assemblies write data at 40-degree angles to one another. Data written by the two heads overlaps, thus increasing the recording density. Helical scan systems tend to be slower, and the tapes are subject to more wear than serpentine systems with their simpler tape paths.

LTO: Linear Tape Open

For many years, manufacturers carefully guarded the technology that went into their tape drives. Tapes made for one brand of tape drive could not be read in another. Sometimes even different models of the same brand of tape drive were incompatible. Realizing that this situation was benefiting no one,

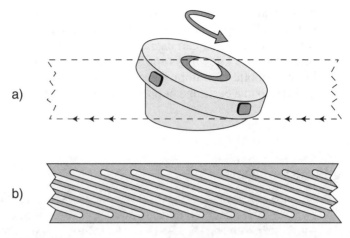

FIGURE 7.25   A Helical Scan Recording
a) The Read /Write Heads on Capstan
b) Pattern of Data Written on the Tape

Hewlett-Packard, IBM, and Seagate Technologies came together in 1997 to formulate an open specification for a best-of-breed tape format called **Linear Tape Open**, or simply **LTO**. In a rare display of collaboration and cooperation among competing vendors, LTO's track format, cartridge design, error-correction algorithm, and compression method incorporated the best ideas presented by each manufacturer. LTO was designed so that it could be refined through a series of "generations," with each generation doubling the capability of the one before it. Generation 5 was released in 2010. These tapes can hold up to 1.4TB with a transfer rate of 280MB per second without compression. Up to 2:1 compression is possible, thus doubling both the capacity and the transfer rate.

The reliability and manageability of LTO far surpass all formats that came before it. Deep error-correction algorithms ensure that burst errors as well as single-bit errors are recoverable. The tape cartridge contains memory circuits that store historical information including the number of times the cartridge has been used, the locations and types of errors in the tape, and a table of contents for the data stored on the volume. Like DAT, LTO ensures data readability through simultaneous read/write operations. Errors discovered during this process are noted in cartridge memory and also on the tape itself. The data is then rewritten to a good segment of the tape. With its superb reliability, high data density, and transfer rates, LTO has found wide acceptance by and support from manufacturers and buyers alike.

Tape storage has been a staple of mainframe environments from the beginning. Tapes appear to offer "infinite" storage at bargain prices. They continue to be the primary medium for making file and system backups on large systems. Although the medium itself is inexpensive, cataloging and handling costs can be substantial, especially when the tape library consists of thousands of tape volumes. Recognizing this problem, several vendors have produced a variety of robotic devices that can catalog, fetch, and load tapes in seconds. **Robotic tape libraries,** also known as **tape silos,** can be found in many large data centers. The largest robotic tape library systems have capacities in the hundreds of terabytes and can load a cartridge at user request in less than half a minute.

The Long Future of Tape

Because tape is perceived as "old technology," some people think that it has no place in the contemporary computing landscape. Moreover, with the cost of some tape cartridges exceeding US $100 each, it's increasingly easy to argue that disk storage is cheaper than tape in terms of dollars per megabyte. The "obvious" conclusion is that a good deal of money can be saved using disk-to-disk backups instead of disk-to-tape configurations.

Indeed, disk-to-disk backup, in the form of "hot" mirroring, is the only solution for ultra-high-availability configurations. Such configurations consist of a set of backup disk drives that is updated in tandem with an identical set of primary disks. The mirrored disks can even be placed in a secure location miles from the main data center. If disaster strikes the data center, a copy of the important data will survive.

The biggest problem in relying exclusively on disk-to-disk backups is that there is no provision for archival copies of the data. Tape backups generally follow a rotation schedule. Two or three sets of monthly backups are taken and rotated offsite, along with several sets of weekly and daily backups. Each installation determines the rotation schedule based on a number of factors including the importance of the data, how often the data is updated (its **volatility**), and the amount of time required to copy the data to tape. Therefore, the oldest offsite backup may be an image taken months earlier.

Such "ancient" copies of data can rescue a database from human and programming errors. For example, it is possible that a damaging error will be discovered only after a program has been misbehaving for days or weeks. A mirror copy of the database would contain the same erroneous data as the primary set, and it would be no help in repairing the damage. If backups have been managed properly, chances are good that at least some of the data can be recovered from an old backup tape.

Some people complain that it takes too long to write data to tape and that there is no time in which transactional activity can be stopped long enough to copy the data to tape: the **backup window** is insufficient. One can't help but think that if the backup window is insufficient for a disk-to-disk backup, it is probably also insufficient for a tape backup as well. However, tape drives have transfer rates that are competitive with disk transfer rates; when the data is compressed as it is written to tape, tape transfer rates exceed those of disk. If the backup window is too small for either disk or tape backups, then a mirroring approach—with backups taken from the mirror set—should be used. This is known as a **disk-to-disk-to-tape** (**D2D2T**) backup method.

Another consideration is the idea of **information lifecycle management** (**ILM**), which seeks to match the cost of a storage medium with the value of the data that is stored on it. The most important data should be stored on the most accessible and reliable media. Government regulations such as the Sarbanes-Oxley Act of 2002 and Internal Revenue Service codes in the United States require retention of large amounts of data over long periods of time. If there is no compelling business need for instant access to the data, why should it be kept online? ILM practices tell us that at some point the data should be encrypted, removed from primary storage, and placed in a vault. Most corporate installations would be wise to resist shipping a $10,000 disk array offsite for indefinite storage.

For these reasons, tape will continue to be the archival medium of choice for many years to come. Its costs are well justified the moment you retrieve data that would have been long ago overwritten on disk storage.

7.9   RAID

In the 30 years following the introduction of IBM's RAMAC computer, only the largest computers were equipped with disk storage systems. Early disk drives were enormously costly and occupied a large amount of floor space in proportion to their storage capacity. They also required a strictly controlled environment: Too much heat would damage control circuitry, and low humidity caused static buildup that could scramble the magnetic flux polarizations on disk surfaces. Head crashes, or other irrecoverable failures, took an incalculable toll on business, scientific, and academic productivity. A head crash toward the end of the business day meant that all data input had to be redone to the point of the last backup, usually the night before.

Clearly, this situation was unacceptable and promised to grow even worse as everyone became increasingly reliant on electronic data storage. A permanent remedy was a long time coming. After all, weren't disks as reliable as we could make them? It turns out that making disks more reliable was only part of the solution.

In their 1988 paper, "A Case for Redundant Arrays of Inexpensive Disks," David Patterson, Garth Gibson, and Randy Katz of the University of California at Berkeley coined the acronym **RAID**. They showed how mainframe disk systems could realize both reliability and performance improvements if they would employ some number of "inexpensive" small disks (such as those used by microcomputers) instead of the **single large expensive disks** (**SLEDs**) typical of large systems. Because the term *inexpensive* is relative and can be misleading, the proper meaning of the acronym is now generally accepted as Redundant Array of *Independent* Disks.

In their paper, Patterson, Gibson, and Katz defined five types (called **levels**) of RAID, each having different performance and reliability characteristics. These original levels were numbered 1 through 5. Definitions for RAID levels 0 and 6 were later recognized. Various vendors have invented other levels, which may in the future become standards also. These are usually combinations of the generally accepted RAID levels. In this section, we briefly examine each of the seven RAID levels as well as a few hybrid systems that combine different RAID levels to meet particular performance or reliability objectives.

Every vendor of enterprise-class storage systems offers at least one type of RAID implementation. But not all storage systems are automatically protected by RAID. Those systems are often referred to as **just a bunch of disks (JBOD)**.

7.9.1   RAID Level 0

RAID Level 0, or RAID-0, places data blocks in stripes across several disk surfaces so that one record occupies sectors on several disk surfaces, as shown in Figure 7.26. This method is also called **drive spanning**, block interleave data striping, or **disk striping**. (Striping is simply the segmentation of logically sequential data so that segments are written across multiple physical devices. These segments can be as small as a single bit, as in RAID-0, or blocks of a specific size.)

Because it offers no redundancy, of all RAID configurations, RAID-0 offers the best performance, particularly if separate controllers and caches are used for each disk. RAID-0 is also very inexpensive. The problem with RAID-0 lies in the fact that the overall reliability of the system is only a fraction of what would be expected with a single disk. Specifically, if the array consists of five disks, each with a design life of 50,000 hours (about six years), the entire system has an expected design life of 50,000 / 5 = 10,000 hours (about 14 months). As the number of disks increases, the probability of failure increases to the point where it approaches certainty. RAID-0 offers no-fault tolerance because there is no redundancy. Therefore, the only advantage offered by RAID-0 is in performance. Its lack of reliability is downright scary. RAID-0 is recommended for noncritical data

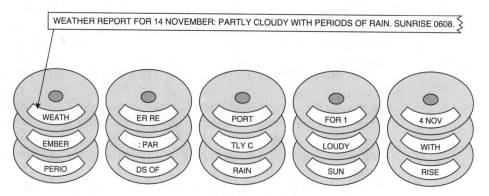

FIGURE 7.26   A Record Written Using RAID-0, Block Interleave Data Striping with No Redundancy

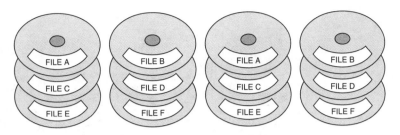

FIGURE 7.27   RAID-1, Disk Mirroring

(or data that changes infrequently and is backed up regularly) that requires high-speed reads and writes, is low cost, is used in applications such as video or image editing.

7.9.2   RAID Level 1

RAID Level 1, or RAID-1 (also known as **disk mirroring**), gives the best failure protection of all RAID schemes. Each time data is written, it is duplicated onto a second set of drives called a **mirror set**, or **shadow set** (as shown in Figure 7.27). This arrangement offers acceptable performance, particularly when the mirror drives are synchronized 180° out of rotation with the primary drives. Although performance on writes is slower than that of RAID-0 (because the data has to be written twice), reads are much faster, because the system can read from the disk arm that happens to be closer to the target sector. This cuts rotational latency in half on reads. RAID-1 is best suited for transaction-oriented, high-availability environments and other applications requiring high-fault tolerance, such as accounting or payroll.

7.9.3   RAID Level 2

The main problem with RAID-1 is that it is costly: You need twice as many disks to store a given amount of data. A better way might be to devote one or more disks to storing information about the data on the other disks. RAID-2 defines one of these methods.

RAID-2 takes the idea of data striping to the extreme. Instead of writing data in blocks of arbitrary size, RAID-2 writes one bit per strip (as shown in Figure 7.28). This requires a minimum of eight surfaces just to accommodate the data. Additional drives are used for error-correction information generated using a Hamming code. The number of Hamming code drives needed to correct single-bit errors is proportionate to the log of the number of data drives to be protected. If any one of the drives in the array fails, the Hamming code words can be used to reconstruct the failed drive. (Obviously, the Hamming drive can be reconstructed using the data drives.)

Because one bit is written per drive, the entire RAID-2 disk set acts as though it were one large data disk. The total amount of available storage is the sum of the storage capacities of the data drives. All of the drives—including the Hamming

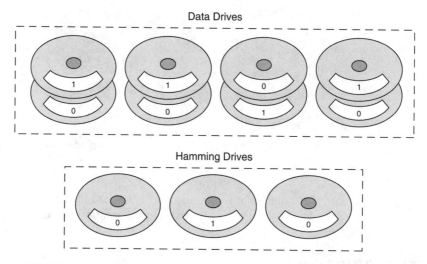

Data Drives

Hamming Drives

FIGURE 7.28 RAID-2, Bit Interleave Data Striping with a Hamming Code

drives—must be synchronized exactly, otherwise the data becomes scrambled and the Hamming drives do no good. Hamming code generation is time-consuming; thus RAID-2 is too slow for most commercial implementations. In fact, most hard drives today have built-in CRC error correction. RAID-2, however, forms the theoretical bridge between RAID-1 and RAID-3, both of which are used in the real world.

7.9.4 RAID Level 3

Like RAID-2, RAID-3 stripes (interleaves) data one bit at a time across all of the data drives. Unlike RAID-2, however, RAID-3 uses only one drive to hold a simple parity bit, as shown in Figure 7.29. The parity calculation can be done quickly in hardware using an exclusive OR (XOR) operation on each data bit (shown as b_n) as follows (for even parity):

$$\text{Parity} = b_0 \text{ XOR } b_1 \text{ XOR } b_2 \text{ XOR } b_3 \text{ XOR } b_4 \text{ XOR } b_5 \text{ XOR } b_6 \text{ XOR } b_7$$

Equivalently,

$$\text{Parity} = (b_0 + b_1 + b_2 + b_3 + b_4 + b_5 + b_6 + b_7) \bmod 2$$

A failed drive can be reconstructed using the same calculation. For example, assume that drive number 6 fails and is replaced. The data on the other seven data drives and the parity drive are used as follows:

$$b_6 = b_0 \text{ XOR } b_1 \text{ XOR } b_2 \text{ XOR } b_3 \text{ XOR } b_4 \text{ XOR } b_5 \text{ XOR Parity XOR } b_7$$

RAID-3 requires the same duplication and synchronization as RAID-2, but is more economical than either RAID-1 or RAID-2 because it uses only one drive for data protection. RAID-3 has been used in some commercial systems over the years, but it is not well suited for transaction-oriented applications. RAID-3 is most useful for environments where large blocks of data would be read or written, such as with image or video processing.

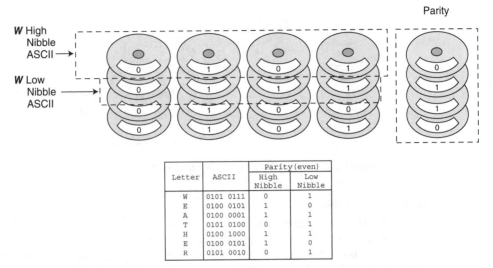

Letter	ASCII	Parity (even)	
		High Nibble	Low Nibble
W	0101 0111	0	1
E	0100 0101	1	0
A	0100 0001	1	1
T	0101 0100	0	1
H	0100 1000	1	1
E	0100 0101	1	0
R	0101 0010	0	1

FIGURE 7.29   RAID-3: Bit Interleave Data Striping with Parity Disk

7.9.5   RAID Level 4

RAID-4 is another "theoretical" RAID level (like RAID-2). RAID-4 would offer poor performance if it were implemented as Patterson et al. describe. A RAID-4 array, like RAID-3, consists of a group of data disks and a parity disk. Instead of writing data one bit at a time across all of the drives, RAID-4 writes data in strips of uniform size, creating a stripe across all of the drives, as described in RAID-0. Bits in the data strip are XORed with each other to create the parity strip.

You could think of RAID-4 as being RAID-0 with parity. However, adding parity results in a substantial performance penalty caused by contention with the parity disk. For example, suppose we want to write to Strip 3 of a stripe spanning five drives (four data, one parity), as shown in Figure 7.30. First we must read the data currently occupying Strip 3 as well as the parity strip. The old data is XORed with the new data to give the new parity. The data strip is then written along with the updated parity.

Imagine what happens if there are write requests waiting while we are twiddling the bits in the parity block, say one write request for Strip 1 and one for Strip 4. If we were using RAID-0 or RAID-1, both of these pending requests could have been serviced concurrently with the write to Strip 3. Thus, the parity drive becomes a bottleneck, robbing the system of all potential performance gains offered by multiple disk systems.

Some writers have suggested that the performance of RAID-4 can be improved if the size of the stripe is optimized with the record size of the data being written. Again, this might be fine for applications (such as voice or video processing) where the data occupy records of uniform size. However, most database applications involve records of widely varying size, making it impossible to find an "optimum" size for any substantial number of records in the database. Because of its expected poor performance, RAID-4 is not considered suitable for commercial implementations.

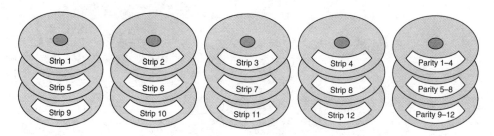

PARITY 1–4 = (Strip 1) XOR (Strip 2) XOR (Strip 3) XOR (Strip 4)

FIGURE 7.30 RAID-4, Block Interleave Data Striping with One Parity Disk

7.9.6 RAID Level 5

Most people agree that RAID-4 would offer adequate protection against single-disk failure. The bottleneck caused by the parity drives, however, makes RAID-4 unsuitable for use in environments that require high-transaction throughput. Certainly, throughput would be better if we could effect some sort of load balancing, writing parity to several disks instead of just one. This is what RAID-5 is all about. RAID-5 is RAID-4 with the parity disks spread throughout the entire array, as shown in Figure 7.31.

Because some requests can be serviced concurrently, RAID-5 provides the best read throughput of all the parity models and gives acceptable throughput on write operations. For example, in Figure 7.31, the array could service a write to drive 4 Strip 6 concurrently with a write to drive 1 Strip 7 because these requests involve different sets of disk arms for both parity and data. However, RAID-5 requires the most complex disk controller of all levels.

Compared with other RAID systems, RAID-5 offers the best protection for the least cost. As such, it has been a commercial success, having the largest installed base of any of the RAID systems. Recommended applications include file and application servers, email and news servers, database servers, and Web servers.

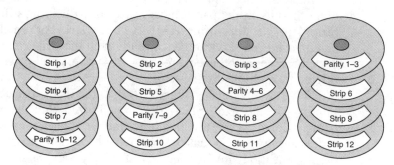

PARITY 1–3 = (Strip 1) XOR (Strip 2) XOR (Strip 3)

FIGURE 7.31 RAID-5, Block Interleave Data Striping with Distributed Parity

7.9.7   RAID Level 6

Most of the RAID systems just discussed can tolerate at most one disk failure at a time. The trouble is that disk drive failures in large systems tend to come in clusters. There are two reasons for this. First, disk drives manufactured at approximately the same time reach the end of their expected useful lives at approximately the same time. So if you are told that your new disk drives have a useful life of about six years, you can expect problems in year six, possibly concurrent failures.

Second, disk drive failures are often caused by a catastrophic event such as a power surge. A power surge hits all the drives at the same instant, the weakest one failing first, followed closely by the next weakest, and so on. Sequential disk failures like these can extend over days or weeks. If they happen to occur within the Mean Time To Repair (MTTR), including call time and travel time, a second disk could fail before the first one is replaced, thereby rendering the whole array unserviceable and useless.

Systems that require high availability must be able to tolerate more than one concurrent drive failure, particularly if the MTTR is a large number. If an array can be designed to survive the concurrent failure of two drives, we effectively double the MTTR. RAID-1 offers this kind of survivability; in fact, as long as a disk and its mirror aren't both wiped out, a RAID-1 array could survive the loss of half its disks.

RAID-6 provides an economical answer to the problem of multiple disk failures. It does this by using two sets of error-correction strips for every **rank** (or horizontal row) of drives. A second level of protection is added with the use of Reed-Solomon error-correcting codes in addition to parity. Having two error-detecting strips per stripe does increase storage costs. If unprotected data could be stored on N drives, adding the protection of RAID-6 requires $N + 2$ drives. Because of the two-dimensional parity, RAID-6 offers very poor write performance. A RAID-6 configuration is shown in Figure 7.32.

Until recently, there were no commercial deployments of RAID-6. There are two reasons for this. First, there is a sizable overhead penalty involved in generating the Reed-Solomon code. Second, twice as many read/write operations are required

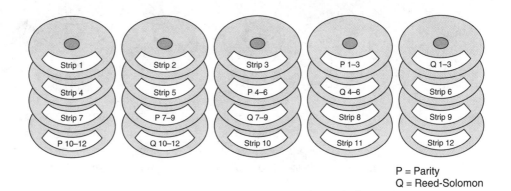

P = Parity
Q = Reed-Solomon

FIGURE 7.32   RAID-6, Block Interleave Data Striping with Dual Error Protection

to update the error-correcting codes resident on the disk. IBM was first to bring RAID-6 to the marketplace with its RAMAC RVA 2 Turbo disk array. The RVA 2 Turbo array eliminates the write penalty of RAID-6 by keeping running "logs" of disk strips within cache memory on the disk controller. The log data permits the array to handle data one stripe at a time, calculating all parity and error codes for the entire stripe before it is written to the disk. Data is never rewritten to the same stripe it occupied prior to the update. Instead, the formerly occupied stripe is marked as free space, once the updated stripe has been written elsewhere.

7.9.8   RAID DP

A relatively new RAID technique employs a pair of parity blocks that protect overlapping sets of data blocks. This method goes by different names depending on the drive manufacturer (there are slight differences among the implementations). The most popular name at this writing seems to be **double parity RAID (RAID DP)**. Others that crop up in the literature include **EVENODD**, **diagonal parity RAID** (also **RAID DP**), **RAID 5DP**, **advanced data guarding RAID (RAID ADG)**, and—erroneously!—RAID 6.

The general idea is that any single-disk data block is protected by two linearly independent parity functions. Like RAID-6, RAID DP can tolerate the simultaneous loss of two disk drives without loss of data. In the schematic in Figure 7.33, observe that the contents of each of the RAID surfaces on disk P1 is a function of all the horizontal surfaces to its immediate left. For example, AP1 is a function of A1, A2, A3, and A4. The contents of P2 are functions of diagonal patterns of the surfaces. For example, BP2 is a function of A2, B3, C4, and DP1. Note that AP1 and BP2 overlap on A2. This overlap allows any two drives to be reconstructed by iteratively restoring the overlapped surfaces. This process is illustrated in Figure 7.34.

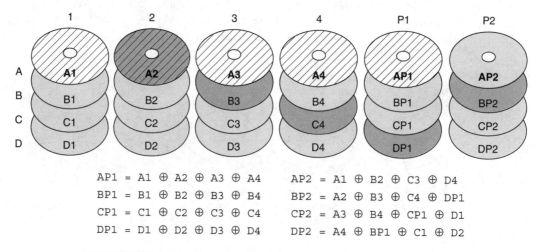

$$AP1 = A1 \oplus A2 \oplus A3 \oplus A4 \qquad AP2 = A1 \oplus B2 \oplus C3 \oplus D4$$
$$BP1 = B1 \oplus B2 \oplus B3 \oplus B4 \qquad BP2 = A2 \oplus B3 \oplus C4 \oplus DP1$$
$$CP1 = C1 \oplus C2 \oplus C3 \oplus C4 \qquad CP2 = A3 \oplus B4 \oplus CP1 \oplus D1$$
$$DP1 = D1 \oplus D2 \oplus D3 \oplus D4 \qquad DP2 = A4 \oplus BP1 \oplus C1 \oplus D2$$

FIGURE 7.33   Error Recovery Pattern for RAID DP
The recovery of A2 is provided by the overlap of equations AP1 and BP2.

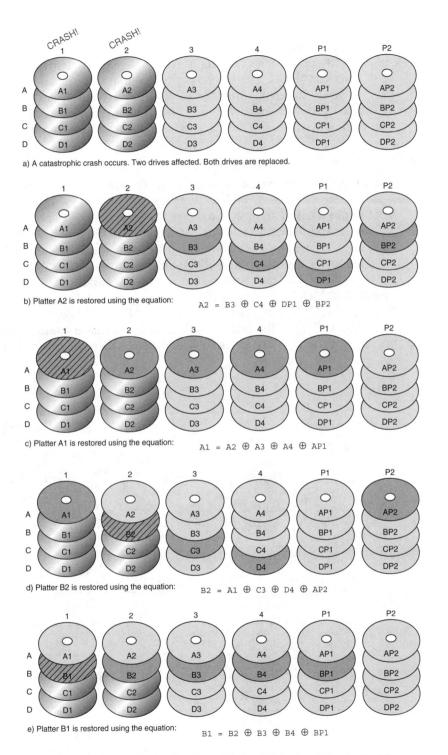

a) A catastrophic crash occurs. Two drives affected. Both drives are replaced.

b) Platter A2 is restored using the equation: A2 = B3 $\oplus$ C4 $\oplus$ DP1 $\oplus$ BP2

c) Platter A1 is restored using the equation: A1 = A2 $\oplus$ A3 $\oplus$ A4 $\oplus$ AP1

d) Platter B2 is restored using the equation: B2 = A1 $\oplus$ C3 $\oplus$ D4 $\oplus$ AP2

e) Platter B1 is restored using the equation: B1 = B2 $\oplus$ B3 $\oplus$ B4 $\oplus$ BP1

FIGURE 7.34 Restoring Two Crashed Spindles Using RAID DP

Owing to the dual parity functions, RAID DP can be used over arrays that contain many more physical disks than can be reliably protected using only the simple parity protection of RAID 5. At the choice of the manufacturer, data can be in stripes or blocks. The simple parity function gives much better performance than the Reed-Solomon correction of RAID-6. However, the write performance of RAID DP is still somewhat degraded from RAID 5 because of the need for dual reads and writes, but the trade-off is in having much-improved reliability.

7.9.9 Hybrid RAID Systems

Many large systems are not limited to using only one type of RAID. In some cases, it makes sense to balance high availability with economy. For example, we might want to use RAID-1 to protect the drives that contain our operating system files, whereas RAID-5 is sufficient for data files. RAID-0 would be good enough for "scratch" files used only temporarily during long processing runs and could potentially reduce the execution time of those runs because of the faster disk access.

Sometimes RAID schemes can be combined (or nested) to form a "new" kind of RAID. RAID-10, shown in Figure 7.35a is one such system. It combines the striping of RAID-0 with the mirroring of RAID-1. Although enormously expensive, RAID-10 gives the best possible read performance while providing the best possible availability. Another hybrid level is RAID 0+1, or RAID 01 (not to be

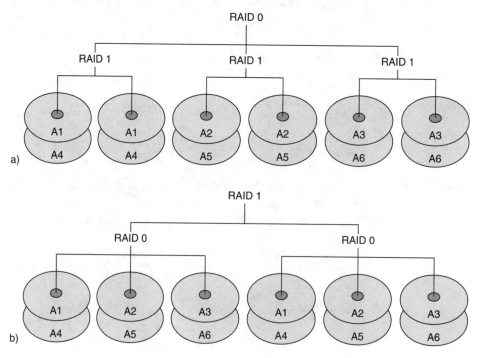

FIGURE 7.35 Hybrid RAID Levels
a) RAID 10, Stripe of Mirrors
b) RAID 01, Mirror of Stripes

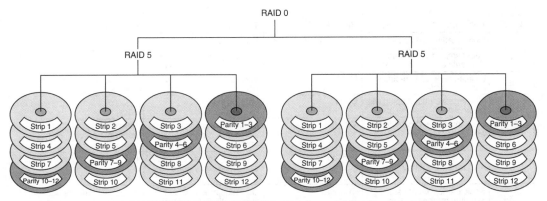

FIGURE 7.36 RAID 50, Striping and Parity

confused with RAID 1), which is used for both sharing and replicating data. Like RAID 10, it also combines mirroring and striping, but in a reversed configuration as shown in Figure 7.35b. RAID 01 allows the disk array to continue operating if more than one drive fails in the same mirrored set, and offers substantially improved read and write performance. RAID 50, shown in Figure 7.36, is a combination of striping and distributed parity. This RAID configuration is good in situations that need good fault tolerance with high capacity. RAID levels can be combined in just about any configuration; although nesting is typically limited to two levels, triple-nested RAID configurations are being explored as viable candidates.

After reading the foregoing sections, it should be clear to you that higher-numbered RAID levels are not necessarily "better" RAID systems. Nevertheless, many people have a natural tendency to think that a higher number of something always indicates something better than a lower number of something. For this reason, various attempts have been made to reorganize and rename the RAID systems that we have just presented. We have chosen to retain the "Berkeley" nomenclature in this book because it is still the most widely recognized. Table 7.1 summarizes the RAID levels just described.

7.10 THE FUTURE OF DATA STORAGE

No one has yet been so bold as to assert a Moore's Law–like prediction for disk storage. In fact, just the opposite is true: Over the years, experts have periodically pronounced that the limits of disk storage have been reached, only to have their predictions shattered when a manufacturer subsequently announces a product exceeding the latest "theoretical storage limit." In the 1970s, the density limit for disk storage was thought to be around 2MB/in^2. Today's disks typically support more than 20GB/in^2. Thus, the "impossible" has been achieved ten thousand times over. These gains have been made possible through advances in several different technologies, including magnetic materials sciences, magneto-optical recording heads, and the invention of more efficient error-correcting codes. But as data

RAID Level	Description	Reliability	Throughput	Pro and Con
0	Block interleave data striping	Worse than single disk	Very good	Least cost, no protection
1	Data mirrored on second identical set	Excellent	Better than single disk on reads, worse on writes	Excellent protection, high cost
2	Bit interleave data striping with Hamming code	Good	Very good	Good performance, high cost, not used in practice
3	Bit interleave data striping with parity disk	Good	Very good	Good performance, reasonable cost
4	Block interleave data striping with one parity disk	Very good	Much worse on writes as single disk, very good on reads	Reasonable cost, poor performance, not used in practice
5	Block interleave data striping with distributed parity	Very good	On writes not as good as single disk, very good on reads	Good performance, reasonable cost
6	Block interleave data striping with dual error protection	Excellent	On writes much worse than single disk, very good on reads	Good performance, reasonable cost, complex to implement
10	Mirrored disk striping	Excellent	Better than single disk on reads, not as good as single disk on writes	Good performance, high cost, excellent protection
50	Parity with striping	Excellent	Excellent read performance. Better than RAID 5; not as good as RAID 10	Good performance, high cost, good protection
DP	Block interleave data striping with dual parity disks	Excellent	Better than single disk on reads, not as good as single disk on writes	Good performance, reasonable cost, excellent protection

TABLE 7.1   Summary of RAID Capabilities

densities increase, there's no getting around the fact that fewer magnetic grains are available within the boundaries of each bit cell. The smallest possible bit cell area is reached when the thermal properties of the disk cause encoded magnetic grains to spontaneously change their polarity, causing a 1 to change to a 0 or a 0 to a 1. This behavior is called **superparamagnetism**, and the bit density at which it occurs is called the **superparamagnetic limit**. At this writing, the superparamagnetic limit is thought to be between $150GB/in^2$ and $200GB/in^2$. Even if this figure is in error by a few orders of magnitude, it is likely that the greatest increases in magnetic data density have already been achieved. Future exponential gains in data densities will almost certainly be realized by using entirely new storage technologies. With this in mind, research is under way to invent biological, holographic, or mechanical replacements for magnetic disks.

Biological materials can store data in many different ways. Of course, the ultimate data storage is found in DNA, where trillions of different messages can be encoded in a small strand of genetic material. But creating a practical DNA storage device is decades away. Less ambitious approaches combine inorganic magnetic materials (such as iron) with biologically produced materials (such as oils or proteins). Successful prototypes have encouraged the expectation that biological materials will be capable of supporting data densities of $1Tb/in^2$. Mass-produced biological storage devices might be brought to market in the second or third decade of the twenty-first century.

A **hologram** is a three-dimensional image rendered by the manipulation of laser beams. Credit cards and some copyrighted CDs and DVDs are emblazoned with iridescent holograms to deter counterfeiting. For at least 50 years, the notion of holographic data storage has ignited the imaginations of fiction writers and computer researchers alike. Thanks to advances in polymer science, holographic storage is finally poised to leap from the pages of pulp magazines and into the data center.

In **holographic data storage**, as shown in Figure 7.37, a laser beam is divided into two separate beams, an object beam and a reference beam. The **object beam** passes through a modulator to produce a coded data pattern. The modulated object beam then intersects with the **reference beam** to produce an interference pattern in the polymer recording medium. Data is recovered from the medium when it is illuminated by the reference beam, thereby reproducing the original coded object beam.

Holographic data storage is exciting for a number of reasons. Foremost is the enormous data density made possible by the use of a three-dimensional medium. Initial experimental systems provide more than $30GB/in^2$ with transfer rates of around 1GBps. Holographic data storage is also unique in its ability to provide mass storage that is content addressable. This implies that holographic storage would not necessarily require a directory system as we find on magnetic disks today. All accesses

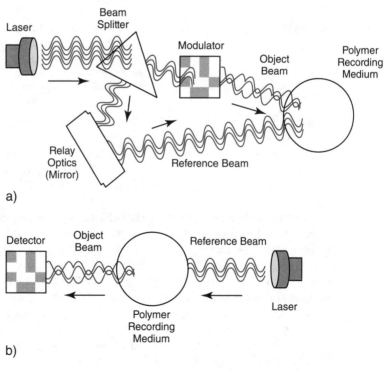

FIGURE 7.37 Holographic Storage
a) Writing Data
b) Reading Data

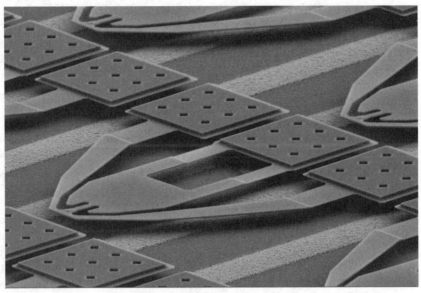

FIGURE 7.38   A Scanning Electron Microscope Image of the Three-Terminal
Integrated Cantilevers of IBM's "Millipede" Storage Device
The cantilevers are 70 µm long and 75 µm wide. The outer arms of the cantile-
vers are just 10 µm wide. Reprint Courtesy of International Business Machines
Corporation © 2006 International Business Machines Corporation.

would go directly to where a file is placed, without any need to first consult any file
allocation tables.

The greatest challenge in bringing holographic data storage to commercial
production has been in the creation of a suitable polymer medium. Although great
progress has been made, inexpensive, rewriteable, stable media still seem to be
several years away.

Micro-electro-mechanical (MEMS) devices offer another approach to tran-
scending the limits of magnetic storage. One such device is IBM's Millipede. Millipede consists of thousands of microscopic cantilevers that record a binary 1 by
pressing a heated microscopic tip into a polymer substrate. The tip reads a binary 1
when it dips into the imprint in the polymer. Laboratory prototypes have achieved
densities of more than $100GB/in^2$, with $1Tb/in^2$ expected as the technology is
refined. An electron micrograph of a Millipede cantilever is shown in Figure 7.38.

Even using traditional magnetic disks, enterprise-class storage continues to
grow in size and complexity. Terabyte-sized storage systems are now commonplace. It is increasingly likely that the storage problem of the future is not in having sufficient capacity, but in finding the useful information after the data has
been stored. This problem may prove to be the most intractable of all.

Carbon nanotubes (CNTs) are among many recent discoveries in the
field of nanotechnology. As the name suggests, CNTs are a cylindrical form of

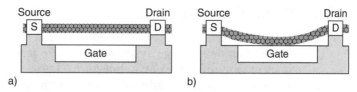

FIGURE 7.39 Carbon Nanotube Bit Storage
a) Set to 0
b) Set to 1

elemental carbon where the walls of the cylinders are one atom thick. Carbon nanotubes can be made to act like switches, opening and closing to store bits. Scientists have devised a number of different nanotube memory configurations. Figure 7.39 is a schematic of the configuration that Nantero, Inc., uses in its NRAM product. The nanotube is suspended over a conductor called a gate (Figure 7.39a). This represents the zero state. To set the gate to 1, voltage that is sufficient to attract the nanotube is applied to the gate (Figure 7.39b). The tube stays in place until a release voltage is applied. Thus, the bit cell consumes no power at all until it is read from or written to.

With access times measured in the neighborhood of 3ns, CNTs have been billed as a nonvolatile replacement for volatile RAM as well as a replacement for flash memory. Although not yet in mass production as of this writing, the manufacturability of CNT memories has been demonstrated. It is easy to see that if large-capacity CNT memories can be manufactured economically, they will effectively flatten the storage hierarchy and might all but eliminate the need for at least one level of cache memory in large computer systems.

Like CNTs, **memristor memories** are a type of nonvolatile RAM. Memristors are a rather recently discovered electronic component that combines the properties of a resistor with memory. This is to say, the component's resistance to current flow can be controlled so that states of "high" and "low" can effectively store data bits. These states of high resistance and low resistance are controlled by the application of certain threshold currents that change the physical properties of the underlying semiconductive materials. Like CNTs, memristor memories promise to replace flash memory and flatten the storage hierarchy. This goal can be achieved only if large-capacity devices can be manufactured economically.

Corporations and governments are investing tremendous amounts of research money to bring new storage technologies to market. There seems no end to our thirst for data—accessible data—with which we can infer all kinds of trends and predictions of human behavior, known as **big data**. Big data, however, is becoming increasingly expensive as terabytes of disk storage spin 24 hours a day, consuming gigawatts of electrical power in the process. Even with billions of investment dollars flowing into these new technologies, the payoff is expected to be even greater—by orders of magnitude.

CHAPTER SUMMARY

This chapter has given you a broad overview of many aspects of computer input/output and storage systems. You have learned that different classes of machines require different I/O architectures. Large systems store and access data in ways that are fundamentally different from the methods used by smaller computers. For the very smallest computers—such as embedded processors—programmed I/O is most suitable. It is flexible, but it doesn't offer good performance in general-purpose systems. For single-user systems, interrupt-driven I/O is the best choice, particularly when multitasking is involved. Single-user and medium-sized systems usually employ DMA I/O, in which the CPU offloads I/O to the DMA circuits. Channel I/O is best for high-performance systems. It allocates separate high-capacity paths to facilitate large data transfers.

I/O can be processed character by character or in blocks. Character I/O is best for serial data transfers. Block I/O can be used in serial or parallel data transmission. The original articles that describe IBM's RAMAC system can be found in Lesser & Haanstra (2000) and Noyes & Dickinson (2000).

You have seen how data is stored on a variety of media, including magnetic tape and disk and optical media. Your understanding of magnetic disk operations will be particularly useful to you if you are ever in a position to analyze disk performance in the context of programming, system design, or problem diagnosis.

Our discussion of RAID systems should help you to understand how RAID can provide both improved performance and increased availability for systems upon which we all depend. The most important RAID implementations are given in Table 7.1.

We hope that throughout our discussions, you have gained an appreciation for the trade-offs that are involved with virtually every system decision. You have seen how we must often make choices between "better" and "faster," and "faster" and "cheaper," in so many of the areas that we have just studied. As you assume leadership in systems projects, you must be certain that your customers understand these trade-offs as well. Often you need the tact of a diplomat to thoroughly convince your clients that there is no such thing as a free lunch.

FURTHER READING

You can learn more about Amdahl's Law by reading his original paper (Amdahl, 1967). Hennessy and Patterson (2011) provide additional coverage of Amdahl's Law. Gustavson's tutorial (1984) on computer buses is well worth reading.

Rosch (1997) contains a wealth of detail relevant to many of the topics described in this chapter, although it focuses primarily on small computer systems. It is well organized, and its style is clear and readable. Anderson's article (2003) takes a slightly different point of view of topics discussed in this chapter.

Rosch (1997) also presents a good overview of CD storage technology. More complete coverage, including CD-ROM's physical, mathematical, and electrical engineering underpinnings, can be found in Stan (1998) and Williams (1994).

Patterson, Gibson, and Katz (1988) provide the foundation paper for the RAID architecture. RAID DP is nicely explained in papers by Blaum et al. (1994) and Corbett et al. (2004).

The IBM Corporation hosts what is by far the best website for detailed technical information. IBM stands alone in making prodigious quantities of excellent documentation available for all seekers. Its home page can be found at www.ibm.com. IBM also has a number of sites devoted to specific areas of interest, including storage systems (www.storage.ibm.com), in addition to its server product lines (www.ibm.com/eservers). IBM's research and development pages contain the latest information relevant to emerging technologies (www.research.ibm.com). High-quality scholarly research journals can be found through this site at www.research.ibm.com/journal. Jaquette's LTO article (2003) explains this topic well.

Holographic storage has been discussed with varying intensity over the years. Two recent articles are Ashley et al. (2000) and Orlov (2000). Visitors to IBM's Zurich Research Laboratory website (www.zurich.ibm.com/st) will be rewarded with fascinating photographs and detailed descriptions of the MEMS storage system. Two good articles on the same subject are Carley, Ganger, & Nagle (2000) and Vettiger (2000).

Michael Cornwell's (2012) article on solid state drives gives the reader some good general information. The websites of various manufacturers are loaded with technical documentation regarding these devices. SanDisk (http://www.sandisk.com), Intel (http://www.intel.com), and Hewlett-Packard (http://www.hp.com/) are three such sites.

The article by Kryder and Kim (2009) is a look forward into some of the storage technologies that were discussed in this chapter as well as some interesting ones that were not. More information about memristor storage can be found in papers by Anthes (2011) and Ohta (2011). You can explore the amazing world of CNTs in the papers by Bichoutskaia et al. (2008), Zhou et al. (2007), and Paulson (2004). We encourage you to keep alert for breaking news in the areas of memristor and CNT storage. Both of these technologies are well positioned to make the spinning disk obsolete.

REFERENCES

Amdahl, G. M. "Validity of the Single Processor Approach to Achieving Large Scale Computing Capabilities." *Proceedings of AFIPS 1967 Spring Joint Computer Conference 30,* April 1967, Atlantic City, NJ, pp. 483–485.

Anderson, D. "You Don't Know Jack about Disks." *ACM Queue,* June 2003, pp. 20–30.

Anthes, G. "Memristors: Pass or Fail?" *Communications of the ACM 54*:3, March 2011, pp. 22–23.

Ashley, J., et al. "Holographic Data Storage." *IBM Journal of Research and Development 44*:3, May 2000, pp. 341–368.

Bichoutskaia, E., Popov, A. M., & Lozovik, Y. E. "Nanotube-Based Data Storage Devices." *Materials Today 11*:6, June 2008, pp. 38–43.

Blaum, M., Brady, J., Bruck, J., & Menon, J. "EVENODD: An Optimal Scheme for Tolerating Double Disk Failures in RAID Architectures." *ACM SIGARCH Computer Architecture News 22*:2, April 1994, pp. 245–254.

Carley, R. L., Ganger, G. R., & Nagle, D. F. "MEMS-Based Integrated-Circuit Mass-Storage Systems." *Communications of the ACM 43*:11, November 2000, pp. 72–80.

Corbett, P., et al. "Row-Diagonal Parity for Double Disk Failure Correction." *Proceedings of the Third USENIX Conference on File and Storage Technologies.* San Francisco, CA, 2004.

Cornwell, M. "Anatomy of a Solid-State Drive." *CACM 55*:12, December 2012, pp. 59–63.

Gustavson, D. B. "Computer Buses—A Tutorial." *IEEE Micro,* August 1984, pp. 7–22.

Hennessy, J. L., & Patterson, D. A. *Computer Architecture: A Quantitative Approach*, 5th ed. San Francisco, CA: Morgan Kaufmann Publishers, 2011.

Jaquette, G. A. "LTO: A Better Format for Midrange Tape." *IBM Journal of Research and Development 47*:4, July 2003, pp. 429–443.

Kryder, M. H. & Kim, C. S. "After Hard Drives—What Comes Next?" *IEEE Transactions on Magnetics 45*:10, October 2009, pp. 3406–3413.

Lesser, M. L., & Haanstra, J. W. "The Random Access Memory Accounting Machine: I. System Organization of the IBM 305." *IBM Journal of Research and Development 1*:1, January 1957. Reprinted in Vol. 44, No. 1/2, January/March 2000, pp. 6–15.

Noyes, T., & Dickinson, W. E. "The Random Access Memory Accounting Machine: II. System Organization of the IBM 305." *IBM Journal of Research and Development 1*:1, January 1957. Reprinted in Vol. 44, No. 1/2, January/March 2000, pp. 16–19.

Ohta, T. "Phase Change Memory and Breakthrough Technologies." *IEEE Transactions on Magnetics 47*:3, March 2011, pp. 613–619.

Orlov, S. S. "Volume Holographic Data Storage." *Communications of the ACM 43*:11, November 2000, pp. 47–54.

Patterson, D. A., Gibson, G., & Katz, R. "A Case for Redundant Arrays of Inexpensive Disks (RAID)." *Proceedings of the ACM SIGMOD Conference on Management of Data,* June 1988, pp. 109–116.

Paulson, L. D. "Companies Develop Nanotech RAM Chips." *IEEE Computer.* August 2004, p. 28.

Rosch, W. L. *The Winn L. Rosch Hardware Bible.* Indianapolis: Sams Publishing, 1997.

Stan, S. G. *The CD-ROM Drive: A Brief System Description.* Boston: Kluwer Academic Publishers, 1998.

Vettiger, P., et al. "The 'Millipede'—More than One Thousand Tips for Future AFM Data Storage." *IBM Journal of Research and Development 44*:3, May 2000, pp. 323–340.

Williams, E. W. *The CD-ROM and Optical Recording Systems.* New York: Oxford University Press, 1994.

Zhou, C., Kumar, A., & Ryu, K. "Small Wonder." *IEEE Nanotechnology Magazine 1*:1, September 2007, pp. 13, 17.

REVIEW OF ESSENTIAL TERMS AND CONCEPTS

1. State Amdahl's Law in words.
2. What is speedup?
3. What is a protocol, and why is it important in I/O bus technology?
4. Name three types of durable storage.
5. Explain how programmed I/O is different from interrupt-driven I/O.
6. What is polling?
7. How are address vectors used in interrupt-driven I/O?
8. How does direct memory access (DMA) work?
9. What is a bus master?
10. Why does DMA require cycle stealing?
11. What does it mean when someone refers to I/O as bursty?
12. How is channel I/O different from interrupt-driven I/O?
13. How is channel I/O similar to DMA?
14. What is multiplexing?
15. What distinguishes an asynchronous bus from a synchronous bus?
16. What is settle time, and what can be done about it?
17. Why are magnetic disks called direct access devices?
18. Explain the relationship among disk platters, tracks, sectors, and clusters.
19. What are the major physical components of a rigid disk drive?
20. What is zoned-bit recording?
21. What is seek time?
22. What is the sum of rotational delay and seek time called?
23. Explain the differences between an SSD and a magnetic disk.
24. By how much is an SSD faster than a magnetic disk?
25. What is short stroking, and how does it affect the relative cost per gigabyte of SSDs?
26. How do enterprise SSDs differ from SSDs intended for laptop computers?
27. What is wear leveling, and why is it needed for SSDs?
28. What is the name for robotic optical disk library devices?
29. What is the acronym for computer output that is written directly to optical media rather than paper or microfiche?
30. Magnetic disks store bytes by changing the polarity of a magnetic medium. How do optical disks store bytes?
31. How is the format of a CD that stores music different from the format of a CD that stores data? How are the formats alike?

32. Why are CDs especially useful for long-term data storage?

33. Do CDs that store data use recording sessions?

34. How do DVDs store so much more data than regular CDs?

35. Explain why Blu-Ray discs hold so much more data than regular DVDs.

36. Name the three methods for recording WORM disks.

37. Why is magnetic tape a popular storage medium?

38. Explain how serpentine recording differs from helical scan recording.

39. What are two popular tape formats that use serpentine recording?

40. Which RAID levels offer the best performance?

41. Which RAID levels offer the best economy while providing adequate redundancy?

42. Which RAID level uses a mirror (shadow) set?

43. What are hybrid RAID systems?

44. What is the significance of the superparamagnetic limit?

45. What does the superparamagnetic limit mean for disk drives?

46. Explain how holographic storage works.

47. What is the general idea behind MEMS storage?

48. How does CNT storage work?

49. What is a memristor, and how does it store data?

EXERCISES

◆ 1. Calculate the overall speedup of a system that spends 65% of its time on I/O with a disk upgrade that provides for 50% greater throughput.

2. Calculate the overall speedup of a system that spends 40% of its time in calculations with a processor upgrade that provides for 100% greater throughput.

3. Suppose your company has decided that it needs to make certain busy servers 50% faster. Processes in the workload spend 60% of their time using the CPU and 40% on I/O. In order to achieve an overall system speedup of 25%:

   a) How much faster does the CPU need to be?

   b) How much faster does the disk need to be?

4. Suppose your company has decided that it needs to make certain busy servers 30% faster. Processes in the workload spend 70% of their time using the CPU and 30% on I/O. In order to achieve an overall system speedup of 30%:

   a) How much faster does the CPU need to be?

   b) How much faster does the disk need to be?

5. Suppose that you are designing a game system that responds to players' pressing buttons and toggling joysticks. The prototype system is failing to react in time to these input events, causing noticeable annoyance to the gamers. You have calculated that

you need to improve overall system performance by 50%. This is to say that the entire system needs to be 50% faster than it is now. You know that these I/O events account for 75% of the system workload. You figure that a new I/O interface card should do the trick. If the system's existing I/O card runs at 10kHz (pulses per second), what is the speed of the I/O card that you need to order from the supplier?

6. Suppose that you are designing an electronic musical instrument. The prototype system occasionally produces off-key notes, causing listeners to wince and grimace. You have determined that the cause of the problem is that the system becomes overwhelmed in processing the complicated input. You are thinking that if you could boost overall system performance by 12% (making it 12% faster than it is now), you could eliminate the problem. One option is to use a faster processor. If the processor accounts for 25% of the workload of this system, and you need to boost performance by 12%, how much faster does the new processor need to be?

7. Your friend has just bought a new personal computer. She tells you that her new system runs at 1GHz, which makes it more than three times faster than her old 300MHz system. What would you tell her? (Hint: Consider how Amdahl's Law applies.)

8. Suppose the daytime processing load consists of 60% CPU activity and 40% disk activity. Your customers are complaining that the system is slow. After doing some research, you learn that you can upgrade your disks for $8,000 to make them 2.5 times as fast as they are currently. You have also learned that you can upgrade your CPU to make it 1.4 times as fast for $5,000.

   a) Which would you choose to yield the best performance improvement for the least amount of money?

   b) Which option would you choose if you don't care about the money, but want a faster system?

   c) What is the break-even point for the upgrades? That is, what price would we need to charge for the CPU (or the disk—change only one) so the result was the same cost per 1% increase for both?

◆ 9. How would you answer exercise 8 if the system activity consists of 55% processor time and 45% disk activity?

10. Amdahl's Law is as applicable to software as it is to hardware. An oft-cited programming truism states that a program spends 90% of its time executing 10% of its code. Thus, tuning a small amount of program code can often have an enormous effect on the overall performance of a software product. Determine the overall system speedup if:

   a) 90% of a program is made to run 10 times as fast (900% faster).

   b) 80% of a program is made to run 20% faster.

11. Name the four types of I/O architectures. Where are each of these typically used, and why are they used there?

◆ 12. A CPU with interrupt-driven I/O is busy servicing a disk request. While the CPU is midway through the disk-service routine, another I/O interrupt occurs.

   a) What happens next?

    b) Is it a problem?

    c) If not, why not? If so, what can be done about it?

13. A generic DMA controller consists of the following components:

    • Address generator

    • Address bus interface

    • Data bus interface

    • Bus requestor

    • Interrupt signal circuits

    • Local peripheral controller

    The local peripheral controller is the circuitry that the DMA uses to select among the peripherals connected to it. This circuit is activated right after the bus is requested. What is the purpose of each of the other components listed above, and when are they active? (Use Figure 7.6 as a guide.)

14. Of programmed I/O, interrupt-driven I/O, DMA, or channel I/O, which is most suitable for processing the I/O of a:

    a) Mouse

    b) Game controller

    c) CD

    d) Thumb drive or memory stick

    Explain your answers.

15. Why are I/O buses provided with clock signals?

16. If an address bus needs to be able to address eight devices, how many conductors will be required? What if each of those devices also needs to be able to talk back to the I/O control device?

17. The protocol for a certain data bus is shown in the table below. Draw the corresponding timing diagram. You may refer to Figure 7.11.

Time	Salient Bus Signal	Meaning
t_0	Assert Read	Bus is needed for reading (not writing)
t_1	Assert Address	Indicates where bytes will be written
t_2	Assert Request	Request read to address on address lines
t_3–t_7	Data Lines	Read data (requires several cycles)
t_4	Assert Ready	Acknowledges read request, bytes placed on data lines
t_4	Lower Request	Request signal no longer needed
t_8	Lower Ready	Release bus

18. With regard to Figure 7.11 and exercise 17, we have not provided for any type of error handling, such as if the address on the address lines were invalid, or the memory couldn't be read because of a hardware error. What could we do with our bus model to provide for such events?

19. We pointed out that I/O buses do not need separate address lines. Construct a timing diagram similar to Figure 7.11 that describes the handshake between an I/O controller and a disk controller for a write operation. (Hint: You will need to add a control signal.)

* **20.** If each interval shown in Figure 7.11 is 50ns, how long would it take to transfer 10 bytes of data? Devise a bus protocol, using as many control lines as you need, that would reduce the time required for this transfer to take place. What happens if the address lines are eliminated and the data bus is used for addressing instead? (Hint: An additional control line may be needed.)

21. Define the terms *seek time*, *rotational delay*, and *transfer time*. Explain their relationship.

◆ **22.** Why do you think the term *random access device* is something of a misnomer for disk drives?

23. Why do differing systems place disk directories in different track locations on the disk? What are the advantages of using each location that you cited?

◆ **24.** Verify the average latency rate cited in the disk specification of Figure 7.15. Why is the calculation divided by 2?

25. By inspection of the disk specification in Figure 7.15, what can you say about whether the disk drive uses zoned-bit recording?

26. The disk specification in Figure 7.15 gives a data transfer rate of 60MB per second when reading from the disk, and 320MB per second when writing to the disk. Why are these numbers different? (Hint: Think about buffering.)

27. Do you trust disk drive MTTF figures? Explain.

◆ **28.** Suppose a disk drive has the following characteristics:

- 4 surfaces
- 1,024 tracks per surface
- 128 sectors per track
- 512 bytes/sector
- Track-to-track seek time of 5ms
- Rotational speed of 5,000 rpm

   a) What is the capacity of the drive?

   b) What is the access time?

29. Suppose a disk drive has the following characteristics:

- 5 surfaces
- 1,024 tracks per surface
- 256 sectors per track
- 512 bytes/sector
- Track-to-track seek time of 8ms
- Rotational speed of 7,500 rpm

    a) What is the capacity of the drive?

    b) What is the access time?

    c) Is this disk faster than the one described in exercise 28? Explain.

30. Suppose a disk drive has the following characteristics:
    - 6 surfaces
    - 16,383 tracks per surface
    - 63 sectors per track
    - 512 bytes/sector
    - Track-to-track seek time of 8.5ms
    - Rotational speed of 7,200 rpm

    a) What is the capacity of the drive?

    b) What is the access time?

31. Suppose a disk drive has the following characteristics:
    - 6 surfaces
    - 953 tracks per surface
    - 256 sectors per track
    - 512 bytes/sector
    - Track-to-track seek time of 6.5ms
    - Rotational speed of 5,400 rpm

    a) What is the capacity of the drive?

    b) What is the access time?

    c) Is this disk faster than the one described in exercise 30? Explain.

♦ 32. Transfer rate of a disk drive can be no faster than the bit density (bits/track) times the rotational speed of the disk. Figure 7.15 gives a data transfer rate of 112GB/sec. Assume that the average track length of the disk is 5.5 inches. What is the average bit density of the disk?

33. What are the advantages and disadvantages of having a small number of sectors per disk cluster? (Hint: You may want to think about retrieval time and the required lifetime of the archives.)

34. How does the organization of an optical disk differ from the organization of a magnetic disk?

35. How does the organization of an SSD differ from a magnetic disk? How are they similar to a disk?

36. In Section 7.6.2, we said that magnetic disks are power hungry as compared to main memory. Why do you think this is the case?

37. Explain wear leveling and why it is needed for SSDs. We said that wear-leveling is important for the continual updating of virtual memory pagefiles. What problem does wear-leveling aggravate for pagefiles?

38. Compare the disk specifications for the HDD and SSD in Figures 7.15 and 7.17, respectively. Which items are the same? Why? Which items are different? Why?

◆ **39.** If 800GB server-grade HDDs cost $300, electricity costs $0.10 per kilowatt hour, and facilities cost $0.01 per GB per month, use the disk specification in Figure 7.15 to determine how much it costs to store 8TB of data online for 5 years. Assume that the HDD is active 25% of the time. What can be done to reduce this cost? Hint: Use the "Read/Write" and "Idle" power requirements in Figure 7.15. Use the tables below as a guide.

Specifications	
Hours/year	8,760
Cost per kWh	0.1
Active percentage	0.25
Active watts	
Idle percentage	
Idle watts	

Hours active/yr	0.25 × 8,760 = 2,190	
kWatts consumed active		
Hours idle/yr		
kWatts consumed idle		

Total kWatts	
Energy cost/yr	
× 5 disks	
× 5 years	
+ disk costs $300 × 10	

Facilities	
Fixed cost per GB per month	0.01
Number of GB	× 8,000
Total cost per month	
Number of months	
Total facilities cost	

Grand total:	

40. The disk drives connected to the servers in your company's server farm are nearing the end of their useful lives. Management is considering replacing 8TB of disk capacity with SSDs. Someone is making the argument that the difference in the cost between the SSDs and traditional magnetic disks will be offset by the cost of electricity saved by the SSDs. The 800GB SSDs cost $900. The 800GB server-grade HDDs cost $300. Use the disk specifications in Figures 7.15 and 7.17 to confirm or refute this claim. Assume that both the HDD and the SSD are active 25% of the time and that the cost of electricity is $0.10 per kilowatt hour. Hint: Use the "Read/Write" and "Idle" power requirements in Figure 7.15.

41. A company that has engaged in a business that requires fast response times has just received a bid for a new system that includes much more storage than was specified in the requirements document. When the company questioned the vendor about the increased storage, the vendor said he was bidding a set of the smallest-capacity disk drives that the company makes. Why didn't the vendor just bid fewer disks?

42. Discuss the difference between how DLT and DAT record data. Why would you say that one is better than the other?

43. How would the error-correction requirements of an optical document storage system differ from the error-correction requirements of the same information stored in textual form? What are the advantages offered by having different levels of error correction for optical storage devices?

44. You have a need to archive a large amount of data. You are trying to decide whether to use tape or optical storage methods. What are the characteristics of this data and how it is used that will influence your decision?

45. Discuss the pros and cons of using disk versus tape for backups.

46. Suppose you have a 100GB database housed on a disk array that supports a transfer rate of 60MBps and a tape drive that supports 200GB cartridges with a transfer rate of 80MBps. How long will it take to back up the database? What is the transfer time if 2:1 compression is possible?

* 47. A particular high-performance computer system has been functioning as an e-business server on the Web. This system supports $10,000 per hour in gross business volume. It has been estimated that the net profit per hour is $1,200. In other words, if the system goes down, the company will lose $1,200 every hour until repairs are made. Furthermore, any data on the damaged disk would be lost. Some of this data could be retrieved from the previous night's backups, but the rest would be gone forever. Conceivably, a poorly timed disk crash could cost your company hundreds of thousands of dollars in immediate revenue loss, and untold thousands in permanent business loss. The fact that this system is not using any type of RAID is disturbing to you.

   Although your chief concern is data integrity and system availability, others in your group are obsessed with system performance. They feel that more revenue would be lost in the long run if the system slowed down after RAID is installed. They have stated specifically that a system with RAID performing at half the speed of the current system would result in gross revenue dollars per hour declining to $5,000 per hour.

   In total, 80% of the system e-business activity involves a database transaction. The database transactions consist of 60% reads and 40% writes. On average, disk access time is 20ms.

   The disks on this system are nearly full and are nearing the end of their expected lives, so new ones must be ordered soon. You feel that this is a good time to try to install RAID, even though you'll need to buy extra disks. The disks that are suitable for your system cost $2,000 for each 10GB spindle. The average access time of these new disks is 15ms with an MTTF of 20,000 hours and an MTTR of 4 hours. You have projected that you will need 60GB of storage to accommodate the existing data as well as the expected data growth over the next 5 years. (All of the disks will be replaced.)

   a) Are the people who are against adding RAID to the system correct in their assertion that 50% slower disks will result in revenues declining to $5,000 per hour? Justify your answer.

   b) What would be the average disk access time on your system if you decide to use RAID-1?

c) What would be the average disk access time on your system using a RAID-5 array with two sets of four disks if 25% of the database transactions must wait behind one transaction for the disk to become free?

d) Which configuration has a better cost justification, RAID-1 or RAID-5? Explain your answer.

48. a) Which of the RAID systems described in this chapter cannot tolerate a single disk failure?

b) Which can tolerate more than one simultaneous disk failure?

49. Our discussion of RAID is biased toward consideration of standard rotating magnetic disks. Is RAID necessary for SSD storage? If not, does this make SSD storage slightly more affordable for the enterprise? If it is necessary, do the redundant disks necessarily also need to be SSD?

FOCUS ON DATA COMPRESSION

7A.1 INTRODUCTION

No matter how cheap storage gets, no matter how much of it we buy, we never seem to be able to get enough of it. New huge disks fill rapidly with all the things we wish we could have put on the old disks. Before long, we are in the market for another set of new disks. Few people or corporations have access to unlimited resources, so we must make optimal use of what we have. One way to do this is to make our data more compact, compressing it before writing it to disk. (In fact, we could even use some kind of compression to make room for a parity or mirror set, adding RAID to our system for "free"!)

Data compression can do more than just save space. It can also save time and help to optimize resources. For example, if compression and decompression are done in the I/O processor, less time is required to move the data to and from the storage subsystem, freeing the I/O bus for other work.

The advantages offered by data compression in sending information over communication lines are obvious: less time to transmit and less storage on the host. Although a detailed study is beyond the scope of this text (see the references section for some resources), you should understand a few basic data compression concepts to complete your understanding of I/O and data storage.

When we evaluate various compression algorithms and compression hardware, we are often most concerned with how fast a compression algorithm executes and how much smaller a file becomes after the compression algorithm is applied. The **compression factor** (sometimes called **compression ratio**) is a statistic that can be calculated quickly and is understandable by virtually anyone who would care. There are a number of different methods used to compute a compression factor. We will use the following:

$$\text{Compression factor} = 1 - \left[\frac{\text{compressed size}}{\text{uncompressed size}} \right] \times 100\%$$

For example, suppose we start with a 100KB file and apply some kind of compression to it. After the algorithm terminates, the file is 40KB in size. We can say that the algorithm achieved a compression factor of $(1 - (\frac{40}{100})) \times 100\% = 60\%$ for this particular file. An exhaustive statistical study should be undertaken before inferring that the algorithm would *always* produce 60% file compression. We can, however, determine an expected compression ratio for particular messages or message types once we have a little theoretical background.

The study of data compression techniques is a branch of a larger field of study called **information theory**. Information theory concerns itself with the way in which information is stored and coded. It was born in the late 1940s through the work of Claude Shannon, a scientist at Bell Laboratories. Shannon established a number of information metrics, the most fundamental of which is **entropy**. Entropy is the measure of information content in a message. Messages with higher entropy carry more information than messages with lower entropy. This definition implies that a message with lower information content would compress to a smaller size than a message with a higher information content.

Determining the entropy of a message requires that we first determine the frequency of each symbol within the message. It is easiest to think of the symbol frequencies in terms of probability. For example, in the famous program output statement:

HELLO WORLD!

the probability of the letter L appearing is $\frac{3}{12}$, or $\frac{1}{4}$. In symbols, we have $P(L) = 0.25$. To map this probability to bits in a code word, we use the base-2 log of this probability. Specifically, the minimum number of bits required to encode the letter L is $-\log_2 P(L)$, or 2. The entropy of the message is the weighted average of the number of bits required to encode each of the symbols in the message. If the probability of a symbol x appearing in a message is $P(x)$, then the entropy, H, of the symbol x is:

$$H = -P(x) \times \log_2 P(x)$$

The average entropy over the entire message is the sum of the weighted probabilities of all n symbols of the message:

$$\sum_{i=1}^{n} -P(x_i) \times \log_2 P(x_i)$$

Entropy establishes a lower bound on the number of bits required to encode a message. Specifically, if we multiply the number of characters in the entire message by the weighted entropy, we get the theoretical minimum of the number of bits that are required to encode the message without loss of information. Bits in addition to this lower bound do not add information. They are therefore **redundant**. The objective of data compression is to remove redundancy while preserving information content. We can quantify the average redundancy for each character contained in a coded message of length n containing code words of length l by the formula:

$$\sum_{i=1}^{n} -P(x_i) \times l_i - \sum_{i=1}^{n} - P(x_i) \times \log_2 P(x_i)$$

This formula is most useful when we are comparing the effectiveness of one coding scheme over another for a given message. The code producing the message with the least amount of redundancy is the better code in terms of data compression. (Of course, we must also consider such things as speed and computational complexity as well as the specifics of the application before we can say that one method is *better* than another.)

Finding the entropy and redundancy for a text message is a straightforward application of the formula above. With a fixed-length code, such as ASCII or EBCDIC, the left-hand sum above is exactly the length of the code, usually 8 bits. In our *HELLO WORLD!* example (using the right-hand sum), we find the average symbol entropy is about 3.022. This means that if we reached the theoretical maximum entropy, we would need only 3.022 bits per character × 12 characters = 36.26, or 37 bits, to encode the entire message. The 8-bit ASCII version of the message, therefore, carries 96 − 37, or 59, redundant bits.

7A.2   STATISTICAL CODING

The entropy metric just described can be used as a basis for devising codes that minimize redundancy in the compressed message. Generally, any application of statistical compression is a relatively slow and I/O-intensive process, requiring two passes to read the file before it is compressed and written.

Two passes over the file are needed because the first pass is used for tallying the number of occurrences of each symbol. These tallies are used to calculate probabilities for each different symbol in the source message. Values are assigned to each symbol in the source message according to the calculated probabilities. The newly assigned values are subsequently written to a file along with the information required to decode the file. If the encoded file—along with the table of values needed to decode the file—is smaller than the original file, we say that data compression has occurred.

Huffman and arithmetic coding are two fundamental statistical data compression methods. Variants of these methods can be found in a large number of popular data compression programs. We examine each of these in the next sections, starting with Huffman coding.

7A.2.1   Huffman Coding

Suppose that after we determine probabilities for each of the symbols in the source message, we create a variable-length code that assigns the most frequently used symbols to the shortest code words. If the code words are shorter than the information words, it stands to reason that the resulting compressed message will be shorter as well. David A. Huffman formalized this idea in a paper published in 1952. Interestingly, one form of **Huffman coding**, Morse code, has been around since the early 1800s.

A •–	J •–––	S •••	1 •––––
B –•••	K –•–	T –	2 ••–––
C –•–•	L •–••	U ••–	3 •••––
D –••	M ––	V •••–	4 ••••–
E •	N –•	W •––	5 •••••
F ••–•	O –––	X –••–	6 –••••
G ––•	P •––•	Y –•––	7 ––•••
H ••••	Q ––•–	Z ––••	8 –––••
I ••	R •–•	0 –––––	9 ––––•

FIGURE 7A.1 The International Morse Code

Morse code was designed using typical letter frequencies found in English writing. As you can see in Figure 7A.1, the shorter codes represent the more frequently used letters in the English language. These frequencies clearly cannot apply to every single message. A notable exception would be a telegram from Uncle Zachary vacationing in Zanzibar, requesting a few quid so he can quaff a quart of quinine! Thus, the most accurate statistical model would be individualized for each message. To accurately assign code words, the Huffman algorithm builds a binary tree using symbol probabilities found in the source message. A traversal of the tree gives the bit pattern assignments for each symbol in the message. We illustrate this process using a simple nursery rhyme. For clarity, we render the rhyme in all uppercase with no punctuation, as follows:

HIGGLETY PIGGLETY POP
THE DOG HAS EATEN THE MOP
THE PIGS IN A HURRY THE CATS IN A FLURRY
HIGGLETY PIGGLETY POP

We start by tabulating all occurrences of each letter in the rhyme. We will use the abbreviation <ws> (white space) for the space characters between each word as well as the newline characters (see Table 7A.1).

Letter	Count	Letter	Count
A	5	N	3
C	1	O	4
D	1	P	8
E	10	R	4
F	1	S	3
G	10	T	10
H	8	U	2
I	7	Y	6
L	5	<ws>	21
M	1		

TABLE 7A.1 Letter Frequencies

These letter frequencies are associated with each letter using two nodes of a tree. The collection of these trees (a **forest**) is placed in a line ordered by the letter frequencies like this:

We begin building the binary tree by joining the nodes with the two smallest frequencies. Because we have a four-way tie for the smallest, we arbitrarily select the leftmost two nodes. The sum of the combined frequencies of these two nodes is two. We create a parent node labeled with this sum and place it back into the forest in the location determined by the label on the parent node, as shown:

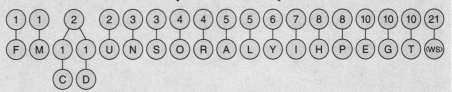

We repeat the process for the nodes now having the lowest frequencies:

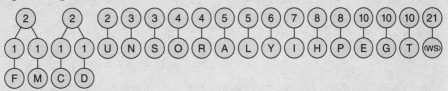

The two smallest nodes are the parents of F, M, C, and D. Taken together, they sum to a frequency of 4, which belongs in the fourth position from the left:

The leftmost nodes add up to 5. They are moved to their new position in the tree as shown:

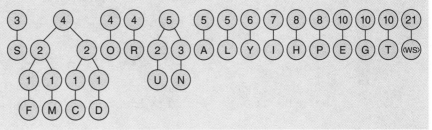

The two smallest nodes now add up to 7. Create a parent node and move the subtree to the middle of the forest with the other node with frequency 7:

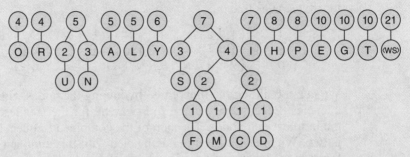

The leftmost pair combine to create a parent node with a frequency of 8. It is placed back in the forest as shown:

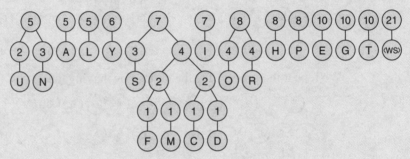

After several more iterations, the completed tree looks like this:

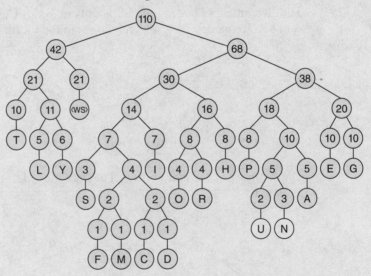

This tree establishes the framework for assigning a Huffman value to each symbol in the message. We start by labeling every right branch with a binary 1, then

Letter	Code	Letter	Code
<ws>	01	O	10100
T	000	R	10101
L	0010	A	11011
Y	0011	U	110100
I	1001	N	110101
H	1011	F	1000100
P	1100	M	1000101
E	1110	C	1000110
G	1111	D	1000111
S	10000		

TABLE 7A.2 The Coding Scheme

each left branch with a binary 0. The result of this step is shown below. (The frequency nodes have been removed for clarity.)

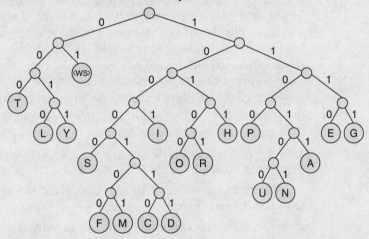

All we need to do now is traverse the tree from its root to each leaf node, keeping track of the binary digits encountered along the way. The completed coding scheme is shown in Table 7A.2.

As you can see, the symbols with the highest frequencies end up having the fewest bits in their code. The entropy of this message is approximately 3.82 bits per symbol. The theoretical lower bound compression for this message is therefore 110 symbols × 3.82 bits = 421 bits. This Huffman code renders the message in 426 bits, or about 1% more than is theoretically necessary.

7A.2.2 Arithmetic Coding

Huffman coding cannot always achieve theoretically optimal compression because it is restricted to using an integral number of bits in the resulting code. In the nursery rhyme in the previous section, the entropy of the symbol S is approximately 1.58. An optimal code would use 1.58 bits to encode each occurrence of S. With Huffman coding, we are restricted to using at least 2 bits for this purpose.

Symbol	Probability	Interval	Symbol	Probability	Interval
D	$\frac{1}{12}$	[0.0 ... 0.083)	R	$\frac{1}{12}$	[0.667 ... 0.750)
E	$\frac{1}{12}$	[0.083 ... 0.167)	W	$\frac{1}{12}$	[0.750 ... 0.833)
H	$\frac{1}{12}$	[0.167 ... 0.250)	<space>	$\frac{1}{12}$	[0.833 ... 0.917)
L	$\frac{3}{12}$	[0.250 ... 0.500)	!	$\frac{1}{12}$	[0.917 ... 1.0)
O	$\frac{2}{12}$	[0.500 ... 0.667)			

TABLE 7A.3 Probability Interval Mapping for HELLO WORLD!

This lack of precision cost us a total of 5 redundant bits in the end. Not too bad, but it seems we could do better.

Huffman coding falls short of optimality because it is trying to map probabilities—which are elements of the set of real numbers—to elements of a small subset of the set of integers. We are bound to have problems! So why not devise some sort of real-to-real mapping to achieve data compression? In 1963, Norman Abramson conceived of such a mapping, which was subsequently published by Peter Elias. This real-to-real data compression method is called **arithmetic coding**.

Conceptually, arithmetic coding partitions the real number line in the interval between 0 and 1 using the probabilities in the symbol set of the message. More frequently used symbols get a larger chunk of the interval.

Returning to our favorite program output, *HELLO WORLD!*, we see that there are 12 characters in this imperative statement. The lowest probability among the symbols is $\frac{1}{12}$. All other probabilities are a multiple of $\frac{1}{12}$. Thus, we divide the $0 - 1$ interval into 12 parts. Each of the symbols except *L* and *O* are assigned $\frac{1}{12}$ of the interval. *L* and *O* get $\frac{3}{12}$ and $\frac{2}{12}$, respectively. Our probability-to-interval mapping is shown in Table 7A.3.

We encode a message by successively dividing a range of values (starting with 0.0 through 1.0) proportionate to the interval assigned to the symbol. For example, if the "current interval" is $\frac{1}{8}$ and the letter *L* gets $\frac{1}{4}$ of the current interval, as shown above, then to encode the *L*, we multiply $\frac{1}{8}$ by $\frac{1}{4}$, giving $\frac{1}{32}$ as the new current interval. If the next character is another *L*, $\frac{1}{32}$ is multiplied by $\frac{1}{4}$, yielding $\frac{1}{128}$ for the current interval. We proceed in this vein until the entire message is encoded. This process becomes clear after studying the pseudocode below. A trace of the pseudocode for *HELLO WORLD!* is given in Figure 7A.2.

```
ALGORITHM Arith_Code (Message)
    HiVal ← 1.0                        /* Upper limit of interval. */
    LoVal ← 0.0                        /* Lower limit of interval. */
    WHILE (more characters to process)
        Char ← Next message character
        Interval ← HiVal - LoVal
        CharHiVal ← Upper interval limit for Char
        CharLoVal ← Lower interval limit for Char
        HiVal ← LoVal +  Interval * CharHiVal
        LoVal ← LoVal +  Interval * CharLoVal
```

Symbol	Interval	CharLoVal	CharHiVal	LoVal	HiVal
				0.0	1.0
H	1.0	0.167	0.25	0.167	0.25
E	0.083	0.083	0.167	0.173889	0.180861
L	0.006972	0.25	0.5	0.1756320	0.1773750
L	0.001743	0.25	0.5	0.17606775	0.17650350
O	0.00043575	0.5	0.667	0.176285625	0.176358395
<sp>	0.00007277025	0.833	0.917	0.1763462426	0.1763523553
W	0.00000611270	0.75	0.833	0.1763508271	0.1763513345
O	0.00000050735	0.5	0.667	0.1763510808	0.1763511655
R	0.00000008473	0.667	0.75	0.1763511373	0.1763511444
L	0.00000000703	0.25	0.5	0.1763511391	0.1763511409
D	0.00000000176	0	0.083	0.1763511391	0.1763511392
!	0.00000000015	0.917	1	0.176351139227	0.176351139239
				0.176351139227	

FIGURE 7A.2 Encoding HELLO WORLD! with Arithmetic Coding

```
    ENDWHILE
    OUTPUT (LoVal)
END Arith_Code
```

The message is decoded using the same process in reverse, as shown by the pseudocode that follows. A trace of the pseudocode is given in Figure 7A.3.

```
ALGORITHM Arith_Decode (CodedMsg)
    Finished ← FALSE
    WHILE NOT Finished
        FoundChar ← FALSE            /* We could do this search much more    */
        WHILE NOT FoundChar          /* efficiently in a real implementation. */
            PossibleChar ← next symbol from the code table
            CharHiVal ← Upper interval limit for PossibleChar
            CharLoVal ← Lower interval limit for PossibleChar
            IF CodedMsg < CharHiVal AND CodedMsg > CharLoVal THEN
                FoundChar ← TRUE
            ENDIF                     / * We now have a character whose interval */
        ENDWHILE                     /* surrounds the current message value.    */
        OUTPUT(Matching Char)
        Interval ← CharHiVal - CharLoVal
    CodedMsgInterval ← CodedMsg - CharLoVal
    CodedMsg ← CodedMsgInterval / Interval
    IF CodedMsg = 0.0 THEN
        Finished ← TRUE
    ENDIF
END WHILE
END Arith_Decode
```

Symbol	LowVal	HiVal	Interval	CodedMsg-Interval	CodedMsg
					0.176351139227
H	0.167	0.25	0.083	0.009351139227	0.112664328032
E	0.083	0.167	0.084	0.029664328032	0.353146762290
L	0.25	0.5	0.250	0.103146762290	0.412587049161
L	0.25	0.5	0.250	0.162587049161	0.650348196643
O	0.5	0.667	0.167	0.15034819664	0.90028860265
<sp>	0.833	0.917	0.084	0.0672886027	0.8010547935
W	0.75	0.833	0.083	0.051054793	0.615117994
O	0.5	0.667	0.167	0.11511799	0.6893293
R	0.667	0.75	0.083	0.0223293	0.2690278
L	0.25	0.5	0.250	0.019028	0.076111
D	0	0.083	0.083	0.0761	0.917
!	0.917	1	0.083	0.000	0.000

FIGURE 7A.3   A Trace of Decoding HELLO WORLD!

You may have noticed that neither of the arithmetic coding/decoding algorithms contains any error checking. We have done this for the sake of clarity. Real implementations must guard against floating-point underflow in addition to making sure that the number of bits in the result are sufficient for the entropy of the information.

Differences in floating-point representations can also cause the algorithm to miss the zero condition when the message is being decoded. In fact, an end-of-message character is usually inserted at the end of the message during the coding process to prevent such problems during decoding.

7A.3   ZIV-LEMPEL (LZ) DICTIONARY SYSTEMS

Although arithmetic coding can produce nearly optimal compression, it is even slower than Huffman coding because of the floating-point operations that must be performed during both the encoding and decoding processes. If speed is our first concern, we might wish to consider other compression methods, even if it means that we can't achieve a perfect code. Surely, we would gain considerable speed if we could avoid scanning the input message twice. This is what dictionary methods are all about.

Jacob Ziv and Abraham Lempel pioneered the idea of building a dictionary during the process of reading information and writing encoded bytes. The output of dictionary-based algorithms contains either literals or pointers to information that has previously been placed in the dictionary. Where there is substantial "local" redundancy in the data, such as long strings of spaces or zeros, dictionary-based techniques work exceptionally well. Although referred to as LZ dictionary systems, the name "Ziv-Lempel" is preferred to "Lempel-Ziv" when using the authors' full names.

Ziv and Lempel published their first algorithm in 1977. This algorithm, known as the **LZ77 compression algorithm**, uses a text window in conjunction with a look-ahead buffer. The look-ahead buffer contains the information to be encoded. The text window serves as the dictionary. If any characters inside the look-ahead buffer can be found in the dictionary, the location and length of the text in the window is written to the output. If the text cannot be found, the unencoded symbol is written with a flag indicating that the symbol should be used as a literal.

There are many variants of LZ77, all of which build on one basic idea. We will explain this basic version through an example, using another nursery rhyme. We have replaced all spaces by underscores for clarity:

STAR_LIGHT_STAR_BRIGHT_

FIRST_STAR_I_SEE_TONIGHT_

I_WISH_I_MAY_I_WISH_I_MIGHT_

GET_THE_WISH_I_WISH_TONIGHT

For illustrative purposes, we will use a 32-byte text window and a 16-byte look-ahead buffer. (In practice, these two areas usually span several kilobytes.) The text is first read into the look-ahead buffer. Having nothing in the text window yet, the *S* is placed in the text window and a triplet composed of:

1. The offset to the text in the text window

2. The length of the string that has been matched

3. The first symbol in the look-ahead buffer that follows the phrase

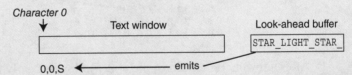

In the example above, there is no match in the text, so the offset and string length are both zeros. The next character in the look-ahead buffer also has no match, so it is also written as a literal with index and length both zero.

We continue writing literals until a *T* appears as the first character of the look-ahead buffer. This matches the *T* that is in position 1 of the text window. The

character following the *T* in the look-ahead buffer is an underscore, which is the third item in the triplet that is written to the output.

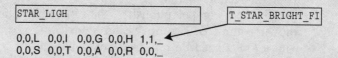

The look-ahead buffer now shifts by two characters. *STAR_* is now at the beginning of the look-ahead buffer. It has a match at the first character position (position 0) of the text window. We write 0, 5, B because *B* is the character following *STAR_* in the buffer.

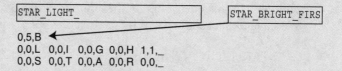

We shift the look-ahead buffer by six characters and look for a match on the *R*. We find one at position 3 of the text, writing 3, 1, I.

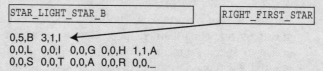

GHT is now at the beginning of the buffer. It matches four characters in the text starting at position 7. We write 7, 4, F.

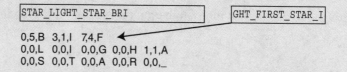

After a few more iterations, the text window is nearly full:

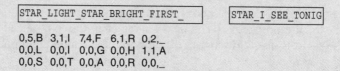

After we match *STAR_* with the characters at position 0 of the text, the six characters, *STAR_I*, shift out of the buffer and into the text window. In order to accommodate all six characters, the text window must shift to the right by three characters after we process *STAR_*.

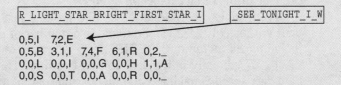

```
STAR_LIGHT_STAR_BRIGHT_FIRST_        STAR_I_SEE_TONIG

0,5,I  ◄
0,5,B  3,1,I  7,4,F  6,1,R  0,2,_
0,0,L  0,0,I  0,0,G  0,0,H  1,1,A
0,0,S  0,0,T  0,0,A  0,0,R  0,0,_
```

After writing the code for *STAR_I* and shifting the windows, *_S* is at the beginning of the buffer. These characters match with the text at position 7.

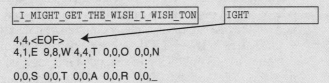

```
R_LIGHT_STAR_BRIGHT_FIRST_STAR_I     _SEE_TONIGHT_I_W

0,5,I  7,2,E  ◄
0,5,B  3,1,I  7,4,F  6,1,R  0,2,_
0,0,L  0,0,I  0,0,G  0,0,H  1,1,A
0,0,S  0,0,T  0,0,A  0,0,R  0,0,_
```

Continuing in this manner, we ultimately come to the end of the text. The last characters to be processed are *IGHT*. These match the text at position 4. Because there are no characters after *IGHT* in the buffer, the last triple written is tagged with an end of file character, *<EOF>*.

```
_I_MIGHT_GET_THE_WISH_I_WISH_TON     IGHT

4,4,<EOF>  ◄
4,1,E  9,8,W  4,4,T  0,0,O  0,0,N
 ⋮      ⋮      ⋮      ⋮      ⋮
0,0,S  0,0,T  0,0,A  0,0,R  0,0,_
```

A total of 36 triples are written to the output in this example. Using a text window of 32 bytes, the index needs only 5 bits to point to any text character. Because the look-ahead buffer is 16 bytes wide, the longest string that we can match is 16 bytes, so we require a maximum of 4 bits to store the length. Using 5 bits for the index, 4 bits for the string length, and 7 bits for each ASCII character, each triple requires 16 bits, or 2 bytes. The rhyme contains 103 characters, which would have been stored in 103 uncompressed bytes on disk. The compressed message requires only 72 bytes, giving us a compression factor of $\left(1 - \left(\frac{72}{103}\right)\right) \times 100 = 30\%$.

It stands to reason that if we make the text window larger, we increase the likelihood of finding matches with the characters in the look-ahead buffer. For example, the string *_TONIGHT* occurs at the forty-first position of the rhyme and again at position 96. Because there are 48 characters between the two occurrences of *_TONIGHT*, the first occurrence cannot possibly be used as a dictionary entry for the second occurrence if we use a 32-character text window. Enlarging the text window to 64 bytes allows the first *_TONIGHT* to be used to encode the second one, and it would add only one bit to each coded triple. In this example, however, an expanded 64-byte text window decreases the output by only two triples: from 36 to 34. Because the text window requires 7 bits for the index, each triple would consist of 17 bits. The compressed message then occupies a total of $17 \times 34 = 578$ bits, or about 73 bytes. Therefore, the larger text window actually costs us a few bits in this example.

A degenerate condition occurs when there are no matches whatsoever between the text and the buffer during the compression process. For instance, if we would have used a 36-character string consisting of all the letters of the alphabet and the digits 0 through 9, ABC . . . XYZ012 . . . 9, we would have had no matches in our example. The output of the algorithm would have been 36 triples of the form, 0,0,?. We would have ended up with an output triple the size of the original string, or an *expansion* of 200%.

Fortunately, exceptional cases like the one just cited happen rarely in practice. Variants of LZ77 can be found in a number of popular compression utilities, including the ubiquitous PKZIP. Several brands of tape and disk drives implement LZ77 directly in the disk control circuitry. This compression takes place at hardware speeds, making it completely transparent to users.

Dictionary-based compression has been an active area of research since Ziv and Lempel published their algorithm in 1977. One year later, Ziv and Lempel improved on their own work when they published their second dictionary-based algorithm, now known as LZ78. LZ78 differs from LZ77 in that it removes the limitation of the fixed-size text window. Instead, it creates a special tree data structure called a **trie**, which is populated by tokens as they are read from the input. (Each interior node of the tree can have as many children as it needs.) Instead of writing characters to the disk as in LZ77, LZ78 writes pointers to the tokens in the trie. The entire trie is written to disk following the encoded message, and read first before decoding the message. (See Appendix A for more information regarding tries.)

7A.4   GIF AND PNG COMPRESSION

Efficient management of the trie of tokens is the greatest challenge for LZ78 implementations. If the dictionary gets too large, the pointers can become larger than the original data. A number of solutions to this problem have been found, one of which has been the source of acrimonious debate and legal action.

In 1984, Terry Welsh, an employee of the Sperry Computer Corporation (now Unisys), published a paper describing an effective algorithm for managing an LZ78-style dictionary. His solution, which involves controlling the sizes of the tokens used in the trie, is called **LZW data compression**, for Lempel-Ziv-Welsh. LZW compression is the fundamental algorithm behind the **graphics interchange format**, **GIF** (pronounced "jiff"), developed by CompuServe engineers and popularized by the World Wide Web. Because Welsh devised his algorithm as part of his official duties at Sperry, Unisys exercised its right to place a patent on it. It has subsequently requested small royalties each time a GIF is used by service providers or high-volume users.[1] LZW is not specific to GIF. It is also used in the tagged image file format (TIFF), other compression programs (including Unix Compress), various software applications (such as PostScript and PDF), and hardware devices (most notably modems). Not surprisingly, the royalty request of

---

[1] The U.S. patent on Gif expired in 2003.

Unisys has not been well received within the Web community, some sites blazing with vows to boycott GIFs in perpetuity. Cooler heads have simply circumvented the issue by producing better (or at least different) algorithms, one of which is **PNG, portable network graphics**.

Royalty disputes alone did not "cause" PNG (pronounced "ping") to come into being, but they undoubtedly hastened its development. In a matter of months in 1995, PNG went from a draft to an accepted international standard. Amazingly, the PNG specification has had only two minor revisions as of 2005.

PNG offers many improvements over GIF, including:

- User-selectable compression modes: "Faster" or "better" on a scale of 0 to 3, respectively
- Improved compression ratios over GIF, typically 5% to 25% better
- Error detection provided by a 32-bit CRC (ISO 3309/ITU-142)
- Faster initial presentation in progressive display mode
- An open international standard, freely available and sanctioned by the World Wide Web Consortium (W3C) and many other organizations and businesses

PNG uses two levels of compression: First, information is reduced using Huffman coding. The Huffman code is then followed by LZ77 compression using a 32KB text window.

GIF can do one thing that PNG cannot: support multiple images in the same file, giving the illusion of animation (albeit stiffly). To correct this limitation, the Internet community produced the **multiple-image network graphics** algorithm (or **MNG**, pronounced "ming"). MNG is an extension of PNG that allows multiple images to be compressed into one file. These files can be of any type, such as gray-scale, true color, or even JPEGs (see the next section). Version 1.0 of MNG was released in January 2001, with refinements and enhancements sure to follow. With PNG and MNG both freely available (with source code!) over the Internet, one is inclined to think it is only a matter of time before the GIF issue becomes passé.

7A.5 JPEG COMPRESSION

When we see a graphic image such as a photograph on a printed page or computer screen, what we are really looking at is a collection of small dots called **pixels** or **picture elements**. Pixels are particularly noticeable in low-image-quality media like newspapers and comic books. When pixels are small and packed closely together, our eyes perceive a "good quality" image. "Good quality," being a subjective measure, starts at about 300 pixels per inch (120 pixels/cm). On the high end, most people would agree that an image of 1600 pixels per inch (640 pixels/cm) is "good," if not excellent.

Pixels contain the binary coding for the image in a form that can be interpreted by display and printer hardware. Pixels can be coded using any number of bits. If, for example, we are producing a black-and-white line drawing, we can do so using one bit per pixel. The bit is either black (pixel = 0) or white (pixel = 1). If we decide that we'd rather have a grayscale image, we need to think about how many shades of gray will suffice. If we want to have eight shades of gray, we need three bits per pixel. Black would be 000, white 111. Anything in between would be some shade of gray.

Color pixels are produced using a combination of red, green, and blue components. If we want to render an image using eight different shades each of red, green, and blue, we must use three bits for *each color component*. Hence, we need nine bits per pixel, giving $2^9 - 1$ different colors. Black would still be all zeros: R = 000, G = 000, B = 000; white would still be all ones: R = 111, G = 111, B = 111. "Pure" green would be R = 000, G = 111, B = 000. R = 011, G = 000, B = 101 would give us some shade of purple. Yellow would be produced by R = 111, G = 111, B = 000. The more bits we use to represent each color, the closer we get to the "true color" that we see around us. Many computer systems approximate true color using eight bits per color—rendering 256 different shades of each. These 24-bit pixels can display about 16 million different colors.

Let's say that we wish to store a 4in. × 6in. (10cm × 15cm) photographic image in such a way as to give us "reasonably" good quality when it is viewed or printed. Using 24 bits (3 bytes) per pixel at 300 pixels per inch, we need 300 × 300 × 6 × 4 × 3 = 6.48MB to store the image. If this 4in. × 6in. photo is part of a sales brochure posted on the Web, we would risk losing customers with dial-up modems once they realize that 20 minutes have passed and they still have not completed downloading the brochure. At 1,600 pixels per inch, storage balloons to just under 1.5GB, which is practically impossible to download and store.

JPEG is a compression algorithm designed specifically to address this problem. Fortunately, photographic images contain a considerable amount of redundant information. Furthermore, some of the information having high theoretical entropy is often of no consequence to the integrity of the image. With these ideas in mind, the ISO and ITU together commissioned a group to formulate an international image compression standard. This group is called the **Joint Photographic Experts Group**, or **JPEG**, pronounced "jay-peg." The first JPEG standard, 10928-1, was finalized in 1992. Major revisions and enhancements to this standard were begun in 1997. The new standard is called JPEG2000 and was finalized in December 2000.

JPEG is a collection of algorithms that provides excellent compression at the expense of some image information loss. Up to this point, we have been describing **lossless data compression**: The data restored from the compressed sequence is precisely the same as it was before compression, barring any computational or media errors. Sometimes we can achieve much better compression if a little information loss can be tolerated. Photographic images lend themselves particularly well to **lossy data compression** because of the human eye's ability to compensate for minor imperfections in graphical images. Of course, some images carry real information and should be subjected to lossy compression only after "quality" has been carefully defined. Medical diagnostic images such as x-rays and electrocardiograms fall into this class. Family album and sales brochure photographs, however, are the kinds of images that can lose considerable "information," while retaining their illusion of visual "quality."

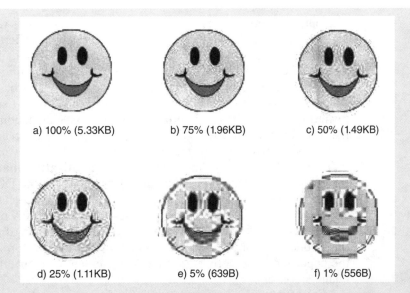

a) 100% (5.33KB)   b) 75% (1.96KB)   c) 50% (1.49KB)

d) 25% (1.11KB)   e) 5% (639B)   f) 1% (556B)

FIGURE 7A.4 JPEG Compression Using Different Quantizations on a 7.14KB Bitmap File

One of the salient features of JPEG is that the user can control the amount of information loss by supplying parameters prior to compressing the image. Even at 100% fidelity, JPEG produces remarkable compression. At 75%, the "lost" information is barely noticeable and the image file is a small fraction of its original size. Figure 7A.4 shows a grayscale image compressed using different quality parameters. (The original 7.14KB bitmap was used as input with the stated quality parameters.)

As you can see, the lossiness of JPEG becomes problematic only when using the lowest quality factors. You'll also notice how the image takes on the appearance of a crossword puzzle when it is at its highest compression. The reason for this becomes clear once you understand how JPEG works.

When compressing color images, the first thing that JPEG does is to convert the RGB components to the domain of **luminance** and **chrominance**, where luminance is the brightness of the color and chrominance is the color itself. The human eye is less sensitive to chrominance than luminance, so the resulting code is constructed so that the luminance component is least likely to be lost during the subsequent compression steps. Grayscale images do not require this step.

Next, the image is divided into square blocks of eight pixels on each side. These 64-pixel blocks are converted from the spatial domain (x, y) to a frequency domain (i, j) using a discrete cosine transform (DCT) as follows:

$$\text{DCT}\,(i, j) = \frac{1}{4}\,C(i) \times C(j) \sum_{x=0}^{7} \sum_{y=0}^{7} \text{pixel}(x, y) \times \cos\left[\frac{(2x + 1)i\pi}{16}\right] \times \cos\left[\frac{(2y + 1)j\pi}{16}\right]$$

where

$$C(a) = \begin{cases} \frac{1}{\sqrt{2}} & \text{if } a = 0, \\ 1 & \text{otherwise.} \end{cases}$$

The output of this transform is an 8×8 matrix of integers ranging from $-1,024$ to $1,023$. The pixel at $i = 0, j = 0$ is called the **DC coefficient**, and it contains a weighted average of the values of the 64 pixels in the original block. The other 63 values are called **AC coefficients**. Because of the behavior of the cosine function $(\cos 0 = 1)$, the resulting frequency matrix, the (i, j) matrix, has a concentration of low numbers and zeros in the lower right-hand corner. Larger numbers collect toward the upper left-hand corner of the matrix. This pattern lends itself well to many different compression methods, but we're not quite ready for that step.

Before the frequency matrix is compressed, each value in the matrix is divided by its corresponding element in a **quantization matrix**. The purpose of the quantization step is to reduce the 11-bit output of the DCT to an 8-bit value. This is the lossy step in JPEG, the degree of which is selectable by the user. The JPEG specification gives several quantization matrices, any of which may be used at the discretion of the implementer. All of these standard matrices ensure that the frequency matrix elements containing the most information (those toward the upper left-hand corner) lose the least amount of their information during the quantization step.

Following the quantization step, the frequency matrix is **sparse**—containing more zero than nonzero entries—in the lower right-hand corner. Large blocks of identical values can be compressed easily using **run-length coding**.

Run-length coding is a simple compression method where instead of coding XXXXX, we code 5,X to indicate a run of five Xs. When we store 5,X instead of XXXXX, we save three bytes, not including any delimiters that the method might require. Clearly, the most effective way of doing this is to try to align everything so that we get as many of the zero values adjacent to each other as we can. JPEG achieves this by doing a **zig-zag scan** of the frequency matrix. The result of this step is a one-dimensional matrix (a vector) that usually contains a long run of zeros. Figure 7A.5 illustrates how the zig-zag scan works.

Each of the AC coefficients in the vector is compressed using run-length coding. The DC coefficient is coded as the arithmetic difference between its original value and the DC coefficient of the previous block, if there is one.

The resulting run-length encoded vector is further compressed using either Huffman or arithmetic coding. Huffman coding is the preferred method because of a number of patents on the arithmetic algorithms.

Figure 7A.6 summarizes the steps we have just described for the JPEG algorithm. Decompression is achieved by reversing this process.

JPEG2000 offers a number of improvements over the JPEG standard of 1997. The underlying mathematics are more sophisticated, which permits greater flexibility with regard to quantization parameters and the incorporation of multiple images into one JPEG file. One of the most striking features of JPEG2000 is its ability to allow user definition of **regions of interest**. A region of interest is an area within an image that serves as a focal point, and would not be subjected to the same degree of lossy compression as the rest of the image. If, for example, you had a photograph of a friend standing on the shore of a lake, you would tell JPEG2000 that your friend is a region of interest. The background of the lake and

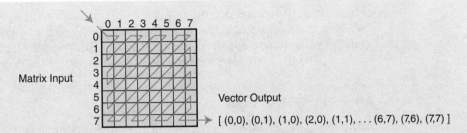

FIGURE 7A.5   A Zig-Zag Scan of a JPEG Frequency Matrix

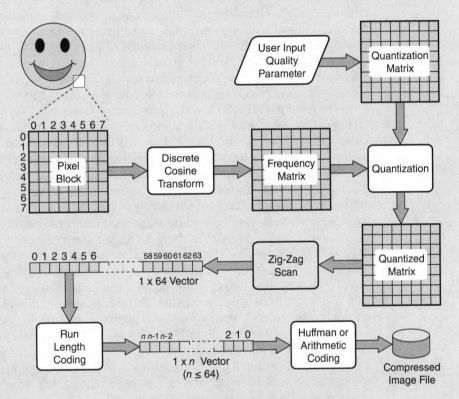

FIGURE 7A.6   The JPEG Compression Algorithm

the trees could be compressed to a great degree before they would lose definition. The image of your friend, however, would remain clear—if not enhanced—by a lower-quality background.

JPEG2000 replaces the discrete cosine transform of JPEG with a wavelet transform. (Wavelets are a different way of sampling and encoding an image or any set of signals.) Quantization in JPEG2000 uses a sine function rather than the simple division of the earlier version. These more sophisticated mathematical manipulations require substantially more processor resources than JPEG, causing noticeable performance degradation in some applications. Legal concerns have been raised about patent rights to some of the JPEG2000 component algorithms. Thus, many software suppliers are reluctant to incorporate JPEG2000 into their products. It will surely take time for JPEG2000 to realize the popularity of JPEG.

7A.6 MP3 COMPRESSION

Although there are many more powerful audio file compression algorithms, such as AAC, OGG, and WMA, MP3 is universally used and supported. MP3 employs several different compression techniques as well as a bit of human physiology. Although many others helped in its refinement and implementation, German doctoral student, Karlheinz Brandenburg at Erlangen-Nuremberg University is widely recognized as the chief architect of MP3. In 1987, the University and the Fraunhofer Institute for Integrated Circuits formed an alliance to implement Brandenburg's ideas in electronic circuits. Fraunhofer-Gesellschaft's refinements of Brandenburg's work were subsequently adopted by the **Moving Picture Experts Group** (**MPEG**) for compression of the audio component of motion pictures. One of several related audio compression standards, **MP3** is officially known as **MPEG-1 Audio Layer III** or **MPEG-1 Part 3**. It was adopted in 1993 by the International Organization for Standardization as **ISO/IEC 11172-3-1993**. It is important to note that the standard describes only the compression methods. Its implementation—the electronics of the coders and decoders—is left to the creativity of the manufacturers. To fully appreciate the power of MP3 compression, we must first understand how audio signals are recorded onto digital media.

Sound is produced by disturbing air in some way to create a vibration that is ultimately detected by small structures in the human ear. These vibrations are analog waves that have both frequency and amplitude. Converting analog waves to a digital format is achieved by sampling the analog waves at specified intervals. The more frequent the sampling, and the greater number of bits used for the encoding, the more accurately the sound approximates the analog wave.

We illustrate this concept in Figure 7A.7a–c. The y-axes in the figures consist of eight values so that the amplitude of the wave can be encoded—modulated to a digital signal—using 3 bits. You can see that the axis is not evenly divided, but has more divisions in the middle of the range. The analog waveform is matched, or quantized, to its nearest integral value. Thus, we get better resolution, or a closer fit to the waveform in areas where most sound occurs. This manner of converting an analog signal to digital is known as **pulse code modulation** (**PCM**). Standard audio pulse code modulation uses 16 bits along the y-axis.

The next matter to address is the sampling rate. In Figure 7A.7a, the vertical bars represent the sampling intervals taken over the example waveform. It is easy to see that a great deal of the waveform lies outside the rectangles. If we double the sampling rate, as in Figure 7A.7b, we get closer to the waveform. With tripling the sampling rate, we get even closer, as in Figure 7A.7c. As any student of calculus knows, we can keep making these rectangles smaller (by increasing the sampling rate) until the difference between the digital signal and the analog signal

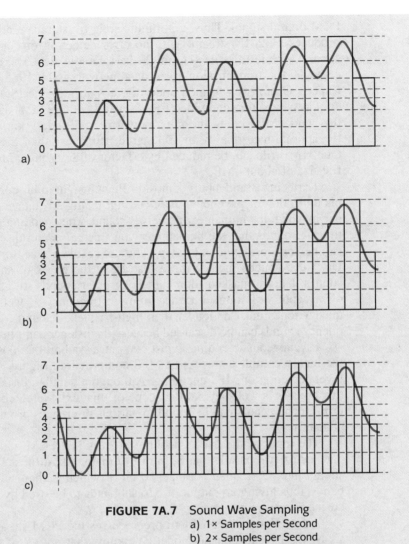

FIGURE 7A.7 Sound Wave Sampling
a) 1× Samples per Second
b) 2× Samples per Second
c) 3× Samples per Second

becomes too small to measure. However, this "perfection" is costly, as each rectangle requires 2 bytes to encode in PCM. At some point, the encoded audio file becomes too large to be of any practical use.

In the late 1970s, digital recording established a sampling rate of 44,100 samples per second (44.1kHz). At 44.1kHz, an audio signal can be conveyed with sufficient accuracy using electronic circuits that are practical to implement. Using a 44.1kHz sampling rate, and encoding each pulse using 2 bytes, the resulting bit rate is 44,100 samples/s × 16 bits/sample = 705,600 bits/s for each stereo channel. This gives us a total of 705,600 × 2 = 1.41Mb/s for a standard

PCM digital signal. Thus, a 3-minute song (in stereo) rendered as a PCM signal produces a 32MB stream (with no error detection or correction applied to the stream). While this file size might be tolerable for CDs, it is completely unacceptable for transmission over data networks. In 1988, the Moving Picture Experts Group was formed under the auspices of the ISO to find a method for compressing audio and video files. Several compression standards emerged from this work, MP3 being the most powerful and widely known. MP3 can provide the approximate quality of CD stereo using less than 2 bits per PCM sample. Our 31MB file can be reduced by a factor of 8, giving a much more manageable file size of about 4MB.[2]

Karlheinz Brandenburg's most brilliant insight in his compression algorithm is his utilization of **psychoacoustic coding**: taking advantage of the imperfect manner in which the human ear perceives sound. The encoding process needs to identify the sounds that the human ear won't perceive and discard them. Thus, MP3 can be very lossy without having any noticeable effects to the untrained listener. Discarded sounds include those that are at the edges of auditory perception and sounds that are masked (dominated) by other sounds. In addition, the thresholds of perception of sound vary according to frequency as well as volume. Low-frequency tones must be louder than high-frequency sounds. Low-volume, low-frequency sounds can be discarded because the listener can't hear them anyway.

Psychoacoustic coding is just one piece—albeit the most powerful piece—of the highly complex process of MP3 compression. Figure 7A.8 provides a high-level depiction of MP3 encoding. Although a detailed discussion of each step of this process is well beyond the scope of this text, we can describe each in broad terms. (The details can be found in various references provided at the end of this chapter.)

The input to the MP3 encoding process is a PCM audio stream that is dispatched on two parallel paths. In one of them, a **bandpass filterbank** divides the stream into 32 frequency ranges, each of which is then subdivided into 18 subbands, thus giving an output of 576 subbands to be used by the modified discrete cosine transform process.

A **fast Fourier transform** preprocesses the PCM stream to facilitate analysis by the psychoacoustic model. We know that not all of the 576 subbands are necessary for producing good-quality sound; only a subset of them thus needs to be processed. The **psychoacoustic model** determines which sounds fall outside the range of human hearing and which are masked by other sounds in nearby frequency bands. (The masking thresholds are a function of frequency: The thresholds are higher at the middle ranges of audible sound.) The psychoacoustic model is subsequently used both by a modified discrete cosine transform and by the quantization process.

The **modified discrete cosine transform** (MDCT) process applies the psychoacoustic model to the 576 subbands output by the bandpass filterbank. Generally

---

[2] Reductions in sampling rate can make the MP3 file even smaller, but the sound quality is reduced. Popular sampling rates for digital audio include 8,000Hz, 11,025Hz, 16,000Hz, 22,050Hz, 44,100Hz, 48,000Hz, and 96,000Hz.

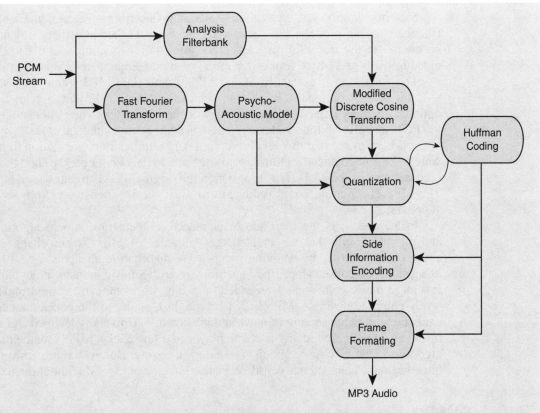

FIGURE 7A.8   Generalized MP3

speaking, the purpose of a discrete cosine transform (DCT) is to map an input in the form of image intensity or sound amplitude to the frequency domain expressed in terms of the cosine function. The DCT of MP3 is called *modified* because, unlike a "pure" DCT, it processes the 576 subband filterbank output through a set of overlapping windows. This overlapping prevents the noise that occurs at window boundaries later in the encoding process.

The output of the MDCT in the form of cosine functions is passed to a quantization function that maps the real-valued cosine function into the integer domain. Such quantization always involves the loss of data because, as discussed in Chapter 2, real values cannot map precisely into the integer domain. MP3 can use 64 bits or 128 bits per second in its quantization, with 128 bits giving better resolution. The psychoacoustic model helps the quantizer find the best fit onto the integer domain, thus reducing the loss of important sounds. Instead of using a fixed quantization, as in the creation of the PCM code shown above, MP3 uses variable **scalefactor bands** that quantize different parts of the sound differently depending on the sensitivity of the human ear to the sound. Less sensitivity allows a wider scalefactor band. The scalefactors are compressed along with the quantized sound using a type of Huffman coding to ensure that the sound is decompressed using the same scalefactor.

Side information is a type of MP3 metadata describing the particulars of the Huffman coding process, the scalefactor bands, and other information that will be crucial to the decoding process. This information is compressed and organized into 17- or 32-byte frames for mono or stereo streams, respectively.

The final step is assembly of the MP3 frame. The MP3 frame consists of a 32-bit header, optional CRC block, side information, MP3 data payload, and optional ancillary data. The actual length of the MP3 frame varies depending on the PCM sampling bitrate and scalefactors used to quantize the data.

It is easy to see that this level of complexity requires implementation in hardware to be able to encode audio in real time and to decode it quickly enough as to render output at the 44.1kHz rate at which the original PCM stream was sampled. The MP3 encoder–decoders (**codecs**) are available inexpensively from several suppliers.

In the end, it is the marriage of advanced mathematics, superb algorithms, and digital circuits that has created the "miracle" of MP3. It has changed the entire music industry by enabling inexpensive distribution channels for all types of music. As a consequence, the hegemony over the music industry enjoyed by a few large music companies was ended, as many other companies could inexpensively enter the business. MP3 has also brought ubiquity to the podcast medium, enabling worldwide sharing of news and information. University lectures and seminars can be delivered to any portable player in a few clicks. MP3's mathematics, algorithms, and electronic circuits are indeed amazing. But even more amazing is how they have changed our world. We can't imagine our world without them.

7A.7 SUMMARY

This special section has presented you with a brief survey of information theory and data compression. We have seen that compression seeks to remove redundant information from data so that only its information content is stored. This saves storage space and improves data transfer speeds for archival storage. Several popular data compression methods were presented; including statistical Huffman coding, Ziv-Lempel dictionary coding, and the compression methods of the Internet, JPG, GIF, and MP3. Dictionary systems compress data in one pass; other methods require at least two: one pass to gather information about the data to be compressed, and the second to carry out the compression process. Most importantly, you now have a sufficient foundation in each type of data compression so that you can select the best method for any particular application.

FURTHER READING

Definitive sources for the theory and application of data compression include works by Salomon (2006), Lelewer and Hirschberg (1987), and Sayood (2012). Sayood's work provides an in-depth description of the entire suite of MPEG compression algorithms. Nelson and Gailly's (1996) thorough treatment—with source code—is clear and easy to read. They make learning the arcane art of data compression a truly pleasurable experience. A wealth of information relevant to data compression can be found on the Web as well. Any good search engine will point you to hundreds of links when you search any of the key data compression terms introduced in this chapter. Wavelet theory is gaining importance in the area of data compression and data communications. If you want to delve into this heady area, you may wish to start with Vetterli and Kovačević (1995). This book also contains an exhaustive account of image compression, including JPEG and, of course, the wavelet theory behind JPEG2000.

We barely scratched the surface of the complexity of MP3 in this section. If you would like to understand the details, the master's thesis by Sripada (2006) contains a wonderfully readable account of the process. The articles by Pan (1995) and Noll (1997) also give a detailed treatment of the subject. A great deal of information concerning all manner of MPEG coding can be found at http://www .mpeg.org/MPEG/audio.htm1. The definitive history of MP3 is posted at http:// www.mp3-history.com. It is well worth your time to see how the story unfolds!

REFERENCES

Lelewer, D. A. and Hirschberg, D. S. "Data Compression." *ACM Computing Surveys 19:*3, 1987, pp. 261–297.

Nelson, M., & Gailly, J. *The Data Compression Book,* 2nd ed. New York: M&T Books, 1996.

Noll, P. "MPEG Digital Audio Coding," *IEEE Signal Processing Magazine 14:*5, September 1997, pp. 59–81.

Pan, D. "A Tutorial on MPEG/Audio Compression." *IEEE Multimedia 2:*2, Summer 1995, pp. 60–74.

Salomon, D. *Data Compression: The Complete Reference*, 4th ed. New York: Springer, 2006.

Sayood, K. *Introduction to Data Compression*, 4th ed. San Mateo, CA: Morgan Kaufmann, 2012.

Sripada, P. "MP3 Decoder in Theory and Practice." Master's Thesis: MEE06:09, Blekinge Tekniska Högskola, March 2006. Available at http://sea-mist.se/fou/cuppsats.nsf/all/857e49 b9bfa2d753c125722700157b97/$file/Thesis%20report-%20MP3%20Decoder.pdf. Retrieved September 1, 2013.

Vetterli, M., & Kovačević, J. *Wavelets and Subband Coding*. Englewood Cliffs, NJ: Prentice Hall PTR, 1995.

Welsh, T. "A Technique for High-Performance Data Compression." *IEEE Computer 17:*6, June 1984, pp. 8–19.

Ziv, J., & Lempel, A. "A Universal Algorithm for Sequential Data Compression." *IEEE Transactions on Information Theory 23:*3, May 1977, pp. 337–343.

Ziv, J., & Lempel, A. "Compression of Individual Sequences via Variable-Rate Coding." *IEEE Transactions on Information Theory 24:*5, September 1978, pp. 530–536.

EXERCISES

1. Who was the founder of the science of information theory? During which decade did he do his work?

2. What is information entropy, and how does it relate to information redundancy?

3. **a)** Name two types of statistical coding.

   b) Name an advantage and a disadvantage of statistical coding.

4. Use arithmetic coding to compress your name. Can you get it back after you have compressed it?

5. Compute the compression factors for each of the JPEG images in Figure 7A.4.

6. Create a Huffman tree and assign Huffman codes for the "Star Bright" rhyme used in Section 7A.3. Use <ws> for whitespace instead of underscores.

7. Complete the LZ77 data compression illustrated in Section 7A.3.

8. JPEG is a poor choice for compressing line drawings, such as the one shown in Figure 7A.4. Why do you think this is the case? What other compression methods would you suggest? Give justification for your choice(s).

9. **a)** The LZ77 compression algorithm falls into which class of data compression algorithms?

   b) Name an advantage of Huffman coding over LZ77.

   c) Name an advantage of LZ77 over Huffman coding.

   d) Which is better?

10. State one feature of PNG that you could use to convince someone that PNG is a better algorithm than GIF.

CHAPTER 8

System Software

8.1 INTRODUCTION

O ver the course of your career, you may find yourself in a position where you are compelled to buy "suboptimal" computer hardware because a certain system is the only one that runs a particular software product needed by your employer. Although you may be tempted to see this situation as an insult to your better judgment, you have to recognize that a complete system requires software as well as hardware. Software is the window through which users see a system. If the software can't deliver services in accordance with users' expectations, they see the entire system as inadequate, regardless of the quality of its hardware.

In Chapter 1, we introduced a computer organization that consists of six machine levels, with each level above the gate level providing an abstraction for the layer below it. In Chapter 4, we discussed assemblers and the relationship of assembly language to the architecture. In this chapter, we study software found at the third level and tie these ideas to software at the fourth and fifth levels. The collection of software at these three levels runs below application programs and just above the instruction set architecture level. These are the software components, the "machines," with which your application source code interacts. Programs at these levels work together to grant access to the hardware resources that carry out the commands contained in application programs. But to look at a computer system as if it were a single thread running from application source code down to the gate level is to limit our understanding of what a computer system is. We would be ignoring the rich set of services provided at each level.

Although our model of a computer system places only the operating system in the "system software" level, the study of system software often includes compilers and other utilities, as well as a category of complex programs sometimes called **middleware**. Generally speaking, middleware is a broad classification for software that provides services above the operating system layer, but below the application program layer. You may recall that in Chapter 1 we discussed the semantic gap that exists between physical components and high-level languages and applications. We know this semantic gap must not be perceptible to the user, and middleware is the software that provides the necessary invisibility. Because the operating system is the foundation for all system software, virtually all system software interacts with the operating system to some extent. We start with a brief introduction to the inner workings of operating systems, and then we move on to the higher software layers.

8.2 OPERATING SYSTEMS

Originally, the main role of an operating system was to help various applications interact with the computer hardware. Operating systems provide a necessary set of functions allowing software packages to control the computer's hardware. Without an operating system, each program you run would need its own driver for the video card, the sound card, the hard drive, and so on.

Although modern operating systems still perform this function, users' expectations of operating systems have changed considerably. They assume that an operating system will make it easy for them to manage the system and its resources. This expectation has begotten "drag and drop" file management, as well as "plug and play" device management. From the programmer's perspective, the operating system obscures the details of the system's lower architectural levels, permitting greater focus on high-level problem solving. We have seen that it is difficult to program at the machine level or the assembly language level. The operating system works with numerous software components, creating a friendlier environment in which system resources are utilized effectively and efficiently and where programming in machine code is not required. The operating system not only provides this interface to the programmer, but it also acts as a layer between application software and the actual hardware of the machine. Whether looked at through the eyes of the user or the lines of code of an application, the operating system is, in essence, a virtual machine that provides an interface from hardware to software. It deals with real devices and real hardware so the application programs and users don't have to.

The operating system itself is little more than an ordinary piece of software. It differs from most other software in that it is loaded by booting the computer and is then executed directly by the processor. The operating system must have control of the processor (as well as other resources), because one of its many tasks is scheduling the processes that use the CPU. It relinquishes control of the CPU to various application programs during the course of their execution. The operating system is dependent on the processor to regain control when the application either no longer requires the CPU or gives up the CPU as it waits for other resources.

As we have mentioned, the operating system is an important interface to the underlying hardware, both for users and for application programs. In addition to its role as an interface, it has three principal tasks. Process management is perhaps the most interesting of these three. The other two are system resource management and protection of those resources from errant processes. Before we discuss these duties, let's look at a short history of operating systems development to see how it parallels the evolution of computer hardware.

8.2.1 Operating Systems History

Today's operating systems strive for optimum ease of use, providing an abundance of graphical tools to assist both novice and experienced users. But this wasn't always the case. A scant generation ago, computer resources were so precious that every machine cycle had to do useful work. Because of the enormously high cost of computer hardware, computer time was allotted with utmost care. In those days, if you wished to use a computer, your first step was to sign up for time on the machine. When your time arrived, you fed in a deck of punched cards yourself, running the machine in single-user, interactive mode. Before loading your program, however, you had to first load the compiler. The initial set of cards in the input deck included the bootstrap loader, which caused the rest of the cards to be loaded. At this point, you could compile your program. If there was an error in your code, you had to find it quickly, repunch the offending card (or cards) and feed the deck into the computer again in another attempt to compile your program. If you couldn't quickly locate the problem, you had to sign up for more time and try again later. If your program compiled, the next step was to link your object code with library code files to create the executable file that would actually be run. This was a terrible waste of expensive computer—and human—time. In an effort to make the hardware usable by more people, **batch processing** was introduced.

With batch processing, professional operators combined decks of cards into batches, or bundles, with the appropriate instructions, allowing them to be processed with minimal intervention. These batches were usually programs of similar types. For example, there might be a batch of Fortran programs and then a batch of COBOL programs. This allowed the operator to set up the machine for Fortran programs, read and execute them all, and then switch to COBOL. A program called a **resident monitor** allowed programs to be processed without human interaction (other than placing the decks of cards into the card reader).

Monitors were the precursors of modern-day operating systems. Their role was straightforward. The monitor started the job, gave control of the computer to the job, and when the job was done, the monitor resumed control of the machine. The work originally done by people was being done by the computer, thus increasing efficiency and utilization. As your authors remember, however, the turnaround time for batch jobs was quite large. (We recall the good old days of dropping off decks of assembly language cards for processing at the data center. We were thrilled if we had to wait less than 24 hours before getting results back!) Batch processing made debugging difficult or, more correctly, very time consuming. An infinite loop in a program could wreak havoc in a system. Eventually, timers were added to monitors to prevent one process from monopolizing the system. However, monitors had a severe limitation in that they provided no additional protection. Without protection, a batch job could affect pending jobs. (For example, a "bad" job might read too many cards, thus rendering the next program incorrect.) Moreover, it was even possible for a batch job to affect the monitor code! To fix this problem, computer systems were provided with specialized hardware, allowing the computer to operate in either monitor mode or user mode. Programs were run in user mode, switching to monitor mode when certain system calls were necessary.

Increases in CPU performance made punched card batch processing increasingly less efficient. Card readers simply could not keep the CPU busy. Magnetic tape offered one way to process decks faster. Card readers and printers were connected to smaller computers, which were used to read decks of cards onto tape. One tape might contain several jobs. This allowed the mainframe CPU to continually switch among processes without reading cards. A similar procedure was followed for output. The output was written to tape, which was then removed and put on a smaller computer that performed the actual printing. It was necessary for the monitor to periodically check whether an I/O operation was needed. Timers were added to jobs to allow for brief interruptions so the monitor could send pending I/O to the tape units. This allowed I/O and CPU computations to occur in parallel. This process, prevalent in the late 1960s to late 1970s, was known as **Simultaneous Peripheral Operation Online**, or **SPOOLing**, and it is the simplest form of multiprogramming. The word has stuck in the computer lexicon, but its contemporary meaning refers to printed output that is written to disk prior to being sent to the printer.

Multiprogramming systems (established in the late 1960s and continuing to the present day) extend the idea of spooling and batch processing to allow several executing programs to be in memory concurrently. This is achieved by cycling through processes, allowing each one to use the CPU for a specific slice of time. Monitors were able to handle multiprogramming to a certain extent. They could start jobs, spool operations, perform I/O, switch between user jobs, and give some protection between jobs. It should be clear, however, that the monitor's job was becoming more complex, necessitating software that was more elaborate. It was at this point that monitors evolved into the software we now know as **operating systems**.

Although operating systems relieved programmers (and operators) of a significant amount of work, users wanted closer interaction with computers. In particular, the concept of batch jobs was unappealing. Wouldn't it be nice if users could submit their own jobs, interactively, and get immediate feedback? **Time-sharing systems** allowed exactly this. Terminals were connected to systems that allowed access by multiple concurrent users. Batch processing was soon outmoded, as interactive programming facilitated timesharing (also known as **timeslicing**). In a timesharing system, the CPU switches between user sessions very quickly, giving each user a small slice of processor time. This procedure of switching between processes is called **context switching**. The operating system performs these context switches quickly, in essence giving the user a personal virtual machine.

Timesharing permits many users to share the same CPU. By extending this idea, a system can allow many users to share a single application. Large interactive systems, such as airline reservation systems, service thousands of simultaneous users. As with timesharing systems, large interactive system users are unaware of the other users on the system.

The introduction of multiprogramming and timesharing required more complex operating system software. During a context switch, all pertinent information about the currently executing process must be saved, so that when the process is scheduled to use the CPU again, it can be restored to the exact state in which it was interrupted. This requires that the operating system know all the details of the hardware. Recall from Chapter 6 that virtual memory and paging are used in today's systems. Page tables and other information associated with virtual memory must be saved during a context switch. CPU registers must also be saved when a context switch occurs because they contain the current state of the executing process. These context switches are not cheap in terms of resources or time. To make them worthwhile, the operating system must deal with them quickly and efficiently.

It is interesting to note the close correlation between the advances in architecture and the evolution of operating systems. First-generation computers used vacuum tubes and relays and were quite slow. There was no need, really, for an operating system, because the machines could not handle multiple concurrent tasks. Human operators performed the required task management chores. Second-generation computers were built with transistors. This resulted in an increase in speed and CPU capacity. Although CPU capacity had increased, it was still costly and had to be utilized to the maximum possible extent. Batch processing was introduced as a means to keep the CPU busy. Monitors helped with the processing, providing minimal protection and handling interrupts. The third generation of computers was marked by the use of integrated circuits. This, again, resulted in an increase in speed. Spooling alone could not keep the CPU busy, so timesharing was introduced. Virtual memory and multiprogramming necessitated a more sophisticated monitor, which evolved into what we now call an operating system. Fourth-generation technology, VLSI, allowed for the personal computing market to flourish. Network operating systems and distributed systems are an outgrowth of this technology. Minimization of circuitry also saved on chip real estate, allowing more room for circuits that manage pipelining, array processing, and multiprocessing.

Early operating systems were divergent in design. Vendors frequently produced one or more operating systems specific to a given hardware platform. Operating systems from the same vendor designed for different platforms could vary radically both in their operation and in the services they provided. It wasn't uncommon for a vendor to introduce a new operating system when a new model of computer was introduced. IBM put an end to this practice in the mid-1960s when it introduced the 360 series of computers. Although each computer in the 360 family of machines differed greatly in performance and intended audience, all computers ran the same basic operating system, OS/360.

Unix is another operating system that exemplifies the idea of one operating system spanning many hardware platforms. Ken Thompson, of AT&T's Bell Laboratories, began working on Unix in 1969. Thompson originally wrote Unix in assembly language. Because assembly languages are hardware specific, any code written for one platform must be rewritten and assembled for a different platform. Thompson was discouraged by the thought of rewriting his Unix code for different machines. With the intention of sparing future labor, he created a new interpreted high-level language called **B**. It turned out that B was too slow to support operating system activities. Dennis Ritchie subsequently joined Thompson to develop the **C** programming language, releasing the first C compiler in 1973. Thompson and Ritchie rewrote the Unix operating system in C, forever dispelling the belief that operating systems must be written in assembly language. Because it was written in a high-level language and could be compiled for different platforms, Unix was highly portable. This major departure from tradition has allowed Unix to become extremely popular, and although it found its way into the market slowly, it is currently the operating system of choice for millions of users. The hardware neutrality exhibited by Unix allows users to select the best hardware for their applications, instead of being limited to a specific platform. There are literally hundreds of different flavors of Unix available today, including Sun's Solaris, IBM's AIX, Hewlett-Packard's HP-UX, and Linux for PCs and servers.

Real-Time, Multiprocessor, and Distributed/Networked Systems

Perhaps the biggest challenge to operating system designers in recent years has been the introduction of real-time, multiprocessor, and distributed/networked systems. **Real-time systems** are used for process control in manufacturing plants, assembly lines, robotics, and complex physical systems such as the space station, to name only a few. Real-time systems have severe timing constraints. If specific deadlines are not met, physical damage or other undesirable effects to persons or property can occur. Because these systems must respond to external events, correct process scheduling is critical. Imagine a system controlling a nuclear power plant that couldn't respond quickly enough to an alarm signaling critically high temperatures in the core! In **hard real-time systems** (with potentially fatal results if deadlines aren't met), there can be no errors. In **soft real-time systems**, meeting deadlines is desirable, but does not result in catastrophic results if deadlines are missed. QNX is an excellent example of a **real-time operating system** (**RTOS**) designed to meet strict scheduling requirements. QNX is also suitable for embedded systems because it is powerful yet has a small footprint (requires very little memory) and tends to be secure and reliable.

Multiprocessor systems present their own set of challenges, because they have more than one processor that must be scheduled. The manner in which the operating system assigns processes to processors is a major design consideration. Typically, in a multiprocessing environment, the CPUs cooperate with each other to solve problems, working in parallel to achieve a common goal. Coordination of processor activities requires that they have some means of communicating with one another. System synchronization requirements determine whether the processors are designed using tightly coupled or loosely coupled communication methods.

Tightly coupled multiprocessors share a single centralized memory, which requires that an operating system must synchronize processes carefully to ensure protection. This type of coupling is typically used for multiprocessor systems consisting of 16 or fewer processors. **Symmetric multiprocessors (SMPs)** are a popular form of tightly coupled architecture. These systems have multiple processors that share memory and I/O devices. All processors perform the same functions, with the processing load being distributed among all of them.

Loosely coupled multiprocessors have a physically distributed memory and are also known as **distributed systems**. Distributed systems can be viewed in two different ways. A distributed collection of workstations on a LAN, each with its own operating system, is typically referred to as a **networked system**. These systems were motivated by a need for multiple computers to share resources. A network operating system includes the necessary provisions, such as remote command execution, remote file access, and remote login, to attach machines to the network. User processes also have the ability to communicate over the network with processes on other machines. Network file systems are one of the most important applications of networked systems. These allow multiple machines to share one logical file system, although the machines are located in different geographical locations and may have different architectures and unrelated operating systems. Synchronization among these systems is an important issue, but communication is even more important, because this communication may occur over large networked distances. Although networked systems may be distributed over geographical areas, they are not considered true distributed systems. We will have more to say about distributed systems in Chapter 9.

A truly distributed system differs from a network of workstations in one significant way: A distributed operating system runs concurrently on all the machines, presenting to the user an image of one single machine. In contrast, in a networked system, the user is aware of the existence of different machines. Transparency, therefore, is an important issue in distributed systems. The user should not be required to use different names for files simply because they reside in different locations, provide different commands for different machines, or perform any other interaction dependent solely upon machine location.

For the most part, operating systems for multiprocessors need not differ significantly from those for uniprocessor systems. Scheduling is one of the main differences, however, because multiple CPUs must be kept busy. If scheduling is not done properly, the inherent advantages of the multiprocessor parallelism are not fully realized. In particular, if the operating system does not provide the proper tools to exploit parallelism, performance will suffer.

Real-time systems, as we have mentioned, require specially designed operating systems. Real-time and embedded systems require an operating system of minimal size and minimal resource utilization. Wireless networks, which combine the compactness of embedded systems with issues characteristic of networked systems, have also motivated innovations in operating systems design.

Operating Systems for Personal Computers

Operating systems for personal computers have a different goal than those for larger systems. Whereas larger systems want to provide for excellent performance and hardware utilization (while still making the system easy to use), operating systems for personal computers have one main objective: Make the system user friendly.

When Intel came out with the 8080 microprocessor in 1974, the company asked Gary Kildall to write an operating system. Kildall built a controller for a floppy disk, hooked the disk to the 8080, and wrote the software for the operating system to control the system. Kildall called this disk-based operating system **CP/M (Control Program for Microcomputers)**. The **BIOS (basic input/output system)** allowed CP/M to be exported to different types of PCs easily because it provided the necessary interactions with input/output devices. Because the I/O devices are the most likely components to vary from system to system, by packaging the interfaces for these devices into one module, the actual operating systems could remain the same for various machines. Only the BIOS had to be altered.

Intel erroneously assumed that disk-based machines had a bleak future. After deciding not to use this new operating system, Intel gave Kildall the rights to CP/M. In 1980, IBM needed an operating system for the IBM PC. Although IBM approached Kildall first, the deal ended up going to Microsoft, which had purchased a disk-based operating system named **QDOS (Quick and Dirty Operating System)** from the Seattle Computer Products Company for $15,000. The software was renamed **MS-DOS**, and the rest is history.

Operating systems for early personal computers operated on commands typed from the keyboard. Alan Key, inventor of the **GUI (graphical user interface)**, and Doug Engelbart, inventor of the mouse, both of the Xerox Palo Alto Research Center, changed the face of operating systems forever when their ideas were incorporated into operating systems. Through their efforts, command prompts were replaced by windows, icons, and dropdown menus. Microsoft popularized these ideas (but did not invent them) through its Windows series of operating systems: Windows 1.x, 2.x, 3.x, 95, 98, ME, NT, 2000, XP, Windows 7, and Windows 8. The Macintosh graphical operating system, **MacOS**, which preceded the Windows GUI by several years, has gone through numerous versions as well. Unix is gaining popularity in the personal computer world through Linux and OpenBSD. There are many other disk operating systems (such as DR DOS, PC DOS, and OS/2), but none are as popular as Windows and the numerous variants of Unix.

8.2.2 Operating System Design

Because the single most important piece of software used by a computer is its operating system, considerable care must be given to its design. The operating system controls the basic functions of the computer, including memory management and I/O, not to mention the "look and feel" of the interface. An operating system differs from most other software in that it is **event driven**, meaning it performs tasks in response to commands, application programs, I/O devices, and interrupts.

Four main factors drive operating system design: performance, power, cost, and compatibility. By now, you should have a feeling for what an operating system is, but there are many differing views regarding what an operating system should be, as evidenced by the various operating systems available today. Most operating systems have similar interfaces, but vary greatly in how tasks are carried out. Some operating systems are minimalistic in design, choosing to cover only the most basic functions, whereas others try to include every conceivable feature. Some have superior interfaces but lack in other areas, whereas others are superior in memory management and I/O, but fall short in the area of user friendliness. No single operating system is superior in all respects.

Two components are crucial in operating system design: the kernel and the system programs. The **kernel** is the core of the operating system. It is used by the process manager, the scheduler, the resource manager, and the I/O manager. The kernel is responsible for scheduling, synchronization, protection/security, memory management, and dealing with interrupts. It has primary control of system hardware, including interrupts, control registers, status words, and timers. It loads all device drivers, provides common utilities, and coordinates all I/O activity. The kernel must know the specifics of the hardware to combine all of these pieces into a working system.

The two extremes of kernel design are **microkernel** architectures and **monolithic** kernels. Microkernels provide rudimentary operating system functionality, relying on other modules to perform specific tasks, thus moving many typical operating system services into user space. This permits many services to be restarted or reconfigured without restarting the entire operating system. Microkernels provide security, because services running at the user level have restricted access to system resources. Microkernels can be customized and ported to other hardware more easily than monolithic kernels. However, additional communication between the kernel and the other modules is necessary, often resulting in a slower and less efficient system. Key features of microkernel design are its smaller size, easy portability, and the array of services that run a layer above the kernel instead of in the kernel itself. Microkernel development has been significantly encouraged by the growth in SMP and other multiprocessor systems. Examples of microkernel operating systems include MINIX, Mach, and QNX.

Monolithic kernels provide all their essential functionality through a single process. Consequently, they are significantly larger than microkernels. Typically targeted for specific hardware, monolithic kernels interact directly with the hardware, so they can be optimized more easily than can microkernel operating systems. It is for this reason that monolithic kernels are not easily portable. Examples of monolithic kernel operating systems include Linux, MacOS, and DOS.

Because an operating system consumes resources, in addition to managing them, designers must consider the overall size of the finished product. For example, Ubuntu 12.04, a very popular Linux distribution, requires 5MB of disk space for a full installation; both Windows 7 and Windows 8 require more than 3 times that amount. These statistics attest to the explosion of operating system functionality over the past two decades. MS-DOS 1.0 fit comfortably on a single 100KB floppy diskette.

8.2.3 Operating System Services

Throughout the preceding discussion of operating system architecture, we mentioned some of the most important services that operating systems provide. The operating system oversees all critical system management tasks, including memory management, process management, protection, and interaction with I/O devices. In its role as an interface, the operating system determines how the user interacts with the computer, serving as a buffer between the user and the hardware. Each of these functions is an important factor in determining overall system performance and usability. In fact, sometimes we are willing to accept reduced performance if the system is easy to use. Nowhere is this trade-off more apparent than in the area of graphical user interfaces.

The Human Interface

The operating system provides a layer of abstraction between the user and the hardware of the machine. Neither users nor applications see the hardware directly, because the operating system provides an interface to hide the details of the bare machine. Operating systems provide three basic interfaces, each providing a different view for a particular individual. Hardware developers are interested in the operating system as an interface to the hardware. Applications developers view the operating system as an interface to various application programs and services. Ordinary users are most interested in the graphical interface, which is the interface most commonly associated with the term *interface*.

Operating system user interfaces can be divided into two general categories: **command line interfaces** and **graphical user interfaces** (**GUIs**). Command line interfaces provide a prompt at which the user enters various commands, including those for copying files, deleting files, providing a directory listing, and manipulating the directory structure. Command line interfaces require the user to know the syntax of the system, which is often too complicated for the average user. However, for those who have mastered a particular command vocabulary, tasks are performed more efficiently with direct commands as opposed to using a graphical interface. GUIs, on the other hand, provide a more accessible interface for the casual user. Modern GUIs consist of windows placed on desktops. They include features such as icons and other graphical representations of files that are manipulated using a mouse. Examples of command line interfaces include Unix shells and DOS. Examples of GUIs include the various flavors of Microsoft Windows and MacOS. The decreasing cost of equipment, especially processors and memory, has made it practical to add GUIs to many other operating systems. Of particular interest is the generic X Window System provided with many Unix operating systems.

The user interface is a program, or small set of programs, that constitutes the **display manager**. This module is normally separate from the core operating system functions found in the kernel of the operating system. Most modern operating systems create an overall operating system package with modules for interfacing, handling files, and other applications that are tightly bound with the kernel. The manner in which these modules are linked with one another is a defining characteristic of today's operating systems.

Process Management

Process management rests at the heart of operating system services. It includes everything from creating processes (setting up the appropriate structures to store information about each one), to scheduling processes' use of various resources, to deleting processes and cleaning up after their termination. The operating system keeps track of each process, its status (which includes the values of variables, the contents of CPU registers, and the actual state—running, ready, or waiting—of the process), the resources it is using, and those that it requires. The operating system maintains a watchful eye on the activities of each process to prevent **synchronization problems**, which arise when concurrent processes have access to shared resources. These activities must be monitored carefully to avoid inconsistencies in the data and accidental interference.

At any given time, the kernel is managing a collection of processes, consisting of user processes and system processes. Most processes are independent of each other. However, in the event that they need to interact to achieve a common goal, they rely on the operating system to facilitate their interprocess communication tasks.

Process scheduling is a large part of the operating system's normal routine. First, the operating system must determine which processes to admit to the system (often called **long-term scheduling**). Then it must determine which process will be granted the CPU at any given instant (**short-term scheduling**). To perform short-term scheduling, the operating system maintains a list of ready processes, so it can differentiate between processes that are waiting on resources and those that are ready to be scheduled and run. If a running process needs I/O or other resources, it voluntarily relinquishes the CPU and places itself in a waiting list, and another process is scheduled for execution. This sequence of events constitutes a **context switch**.

During a context switch, all pertinent information about the currently executing process is saved, so that when that process resumes execution, it can be restored to the exact state in which it was interrupted. Information saved during a context switch includes the contents of all CPU registers, page tables, and other information associated with virtual memory. Once this information is safely tucked away, a previously interrupted process (the one preparing to use the CPU) is restored to its exact state prior to its interruption. (New processes, of course, have no previous state to restore.)

A process can give up the CPU in two ways. In **nonpreemptive scheduling**, a process relinquishes the CPU voluntarily (possibly because it needs another unscheduled resource). However, if the system is set up with time slicing, the process might be taken from a running state and placed into a waiting state by the operating system. This is called **preemptive scheduling** because the process is preempted and the CPU is taken away. Preemption also occurs when processes are scheduled and interrupted according to priority. For example, if a low-priority job is running and a high-priority job needs the CPU, the low-priority job is placed in the ready queue (a context switch is performed), allowing the high-priority job to run immediately.

The operating system's main task in process scheduling is to determine which process should be next in line for the CPU. Factors affecting scheduling decisions include CPU utilization, throughput, turnaround time, waiting time, and response time. Short-term scheduling can be done in a number of ways. The approaches include first-come, first-served (FCFS), shortest job first (SJF), round-robin, and priority scheduling. In **first-come**, **first-served scheduling**, processes are allocated processor resources in the order in which they are requested. Control of the CPU is relinquished when the executing process terminates. FCFS scheduling is a nonpreemptive algorithm that has the advantage of being easy to implement. However, it is unsuitable for systems that support multiple users because there is a high variance in the average time a process must wait to use the CPU. In addition, a process could monopolize the CPU, causing inordinate delays in the execution of other pending processes.

In **shortest job first scheduling**, the process with the shortest execution time takes priority over all others in the system. SJF is a provably optimal scheduling algorithm. The main trouble with it is that there is no way of knowing in advance exactly how long a job is going to run. Systems that employ SJF apply some heuristics in making "guesstimates" of job run time, but these heuristics are far from perfect. SJF can be nonpreemptive or preemptive. (The preemptive version is often called **shortest remaining time first**.)

Round-robin scheduling is an equitable and simple preemptive scheduling scheme. Each process is allocated a certain slice of CPU time. If the process is still running when its timeslice expires, it is swapped out through a context switch. The next process waiting in line is then awarded its own slice of CPU time. Round-robin scheduling is used extensively in timesharing systems. When the scheduler employs sufficiently small timeslices, users are unaware that they are sharing the resources of the system. However, the timeslices should not be so small that the context switch time is large by comparison.

Priority scheduling associates a priority with each process. When the short-term scheduler selects a process from the ready queue, the process with the highest priority is chosen. FCFS gives equal priority to all processes. SJF gives priority to the shortest job. The foremost problem with priority scheduling is the potential for starvation, or indefinite blocking. Can you imagine how frustrating it would be to try to run a large job on a busy system when users continually submit shorter jobs that run before yours? Folklore has it that when a mainframe in a large university was halted, a job was found in the ready queue that had been trying to run for several years!

Some operating systems offer a combination of scheduling approaches. For example, a system might use a preemptive, priority-based, first-come, first-served algorithm. Highly complex operating systems that support enterprise class systems allow some degree of user control over timeslice duration, the number of allowable concurrent tasks, and assignment of priorities to different job classes.

Multitasking (allowing multiple processes to run concurrently) and **multi-threading** (allowing a process to be subdivided into different threads of control) provide interesting challenges for CPU scheduling. A **thread** is the smallest schedulable unit in a system. Threads share the same execution environment as their parent process, including its CPU registers and page table. Because of this, context switching among threads generates less overhead so they can occur much faster than a context switch involving the entire process. Depending on the degree of concurrency required, it is possible to have one process with one thread, one process with multiple threads, multiple single-threaded processes, or multiple multithreaded processes. An operating system that supports multithreading must be able to handle all combinations.

Resource Management

In addition to process management, the operating system manages system resources. Because these resources are relatively expensive, it is preferable to allow them to be shared. For example, multiple processes can share one processor, multiple programs can share physical memory, and multiple users and files can share one disk. There are three resources that are of major concern to the operating system: the CPU, memory, and I/O. Access to the CPU is controlled by the scheduler. Memory and I/O access require a different set of controls and functions.

Recall from Chapter 6 that most modern systems have some type of virtual memory that extends RAM. This implies that parts of several programs may coexist in memory, and each process must have a page table. Originally, before operating systems were designed to deal with virtual memory, the programmer implemented virtual memory using the **overlay** technique. If a program was too large to fit into memory, the programmer divided it into pieces, loading only the data and instructions necessary to run at a given moment. If new data or instructions were needed, it was up to the programmer (with some help from the compiler) to make sure the correct pieces were in memory. The programmer was responsible for managing memory. Now, operating systems have taken over that chore. The operating system translates virtual addresses to physical addresses, transfers pages to and from disk, and maintains memory page tables. The operating system also determines main memory allocation and tracks free frames. As it deallocates memory space, the operating system performs "garbage collection," which is the process of coalescing small portions of free memory into larger, more usable chunks.

In addition to processes sharing a single finite memory, they also share I/O devices. Most input and output is done at the request of an application. The operating system provides the necessary services to allow input and output to occur. It's possible for applications to handle their own I/O without using the operating system, but in addition to duplicating effort, this presents protection and access issues. If several different processes try to use the same I/O device simultaneously, the requests must be mediated. It falls on the operating system to perform this task. The operating system provides a generic interface to

I/O through various system calls. These calls allow an application to request an I/O service through the operating system. The operating system then calls upon device drivers that contain software implementing a standard set of functions relevant to particular I/O devices.

The operating system also manages disk files. The operating system takes care of file creation, file deletion, directory creation, and directory deletion, and also provides support for primitives that manipulate files and directories and their mapping onto secondary storage devices. Although I/O device drivers take care of many of the particular details, the operating system coordinates device driver activities that support I/O system functions.

Security and Protection

In its role as a resource and process manager, the operating system has to make sure that everything works correctly, fairly, and efficiently. Resource sharing, however, creates a multitude of exposures, such as the potential for unauthorized access or modification of data. Therefore, the operating system also serves as a resource protector, making sure "bad guys" and buggy software don't ruin things for everyone else. Concurrent processes must be protected from each other, and operating system processes must be protected from all user processes. Without this protection, a user program could potentially wipe out the operating system code for dealing with, say, interrupts. Multiuser systems require additional security services to protect both shared resources (such as memory and I/O devices) and nonshared resources (such as personal files). Memory protection safeguards against a bug in one user's program affecting other programs or a malicious program taking control of the entire system. CPU protection makes sure user programs don't get stuck in infinite loops, consuming CPU cycles needed by other jobs.

The operating system provides security services in a variety of ways. First, active processes are limited to execution within their own memory space. All requests for I/O or other resources from the process pass through the operating system, which then processes the request. The operating system executes most commands in user mode and others in kernel mode. In this way, the resources are protected against unauthorized use. The operating system also provides facilities to control user access, typically through login names and passwords. Stronger protection can be effected by restricting processes to a single subsystem or partition.

8.3 PROTECTED ENVIRONMENTS

To provide protection, multiuser operating systems guard against processes running amok in the system. Process execution must be isolated from both the operating system and other processes. Access to shared resources must be controlled and mediated to avoid conflicts. There are a number of ways in which protective barriers can be erected in a system. In this section, we examine three of them: virtual machines, subsystems, and partitions.

8.3.1   Virtual Machines

The timesharing systems of the 1950s and 1960s continually wrestled with problems relating to shared resources such as memory, magnetic storage, card readers, printers, and processor cycles. The hardware of this era could not support the solutions that were on the minds of many computer scientists. In a better world, each user process would have its own machine—an imaginary machine that would peacefully coexist with many other imaginary machines inside the real machine. In the late 1960s and early 1970s, hardware had finally become sufficiently sophisticated to deliver these "virtual machines" to general-purpose time-sharing computers.

Virtual machines are, in concept, quite simple. The real hardware of the real computer is under the exclusive command of a **controlling program** (or kernel). The controlling program creates an arbitrary number of virtual machines that execute under the kernel as if they were ordinary user processes, subject to the same restrictions as any program that runs in user space. The controlling program presents each virtual machine with an image resembling the hardware of the real machine. Each virtual machine then "sees" an environment consisting of a CPU, registers, I/O devices, and (virtual) memory as though these resources were dedicated to the exclusive use of the virtual machine. Thus, virtual machines are imaginary machines reflecting the resources of full-fledged systems. As illustrated in Figure 8.1, a user program executing within the confines of the virtual machine can access any system resource that is defined to it. When a program invokes a system service to write data to a disk, for example, it executes the same call as it would if it were running on the real machine. The virtual machine receives the I/O request and passes it on to the control program for execution on the real hardware.

It is entirely possible for a virtual machine to be running an operating system that differs from the kernel's operating system. It is also possible for each virtual machine to run an operating system that is different from the operating systems run by other virtual machines in the system. In fact, this is often the case.

If you have ever opened an "MS-DOS" command prompt on a Microsoft Windows (95 through XP) system, you have instantiated a virtual machine environment. The controlling program for these Windows versions is called a Windows **Virtual Machine Manager** (**VMM**). The VMM is a 32-bit protected-mode subsystem (see the next section) that creates, runs, monitors, and terminates virtual machines. The VMM is loaded into memory at boot time. When invoked through the command interface, the VMM creates an "MS-DOS" machine running under a virtual image of a 16-bit Intel 8086/8088 processor. Although the real system has many more registers (which are 32 bits wide), tasks executing within the DOS environment see only the limited number of 16-bit registers characteristic of an

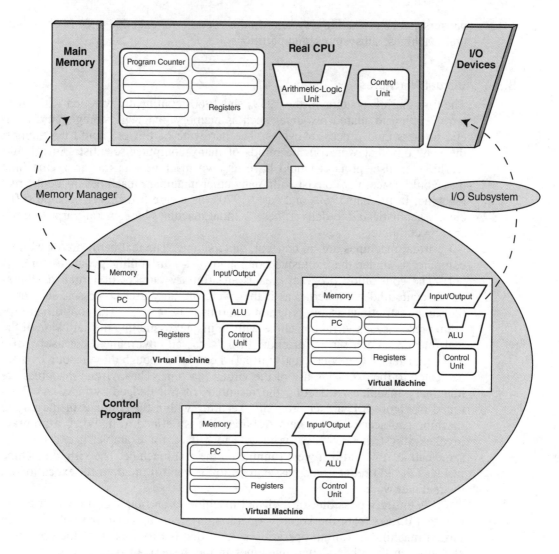

FIGURE 8.1   Virtual Machine Images Running under a Control Program

8086/8088 processor. The VMM controlling program converts (or, in virtual machine jargon, **thunks**) the 16-bit instructions to 32-bit instructions before they are executed on the real system processor.

To service hardware interrupts, the VMM loads a defined set of **virtual device drivers** (**VxDs**) whenever Windows is booted. A VxD can simulate external hardware, or it can simulate a programming interface accessed through privileged instructions. The VMM works with 32-bit protected-mode dynamic link libraries (explained in Section 8.4.3), allowing virtual devices to intercept interrupts and faults. In this way, it controls an application's access to hardware devices and system software.

Of course, virtual machines use virtual memory, which must coexist with the memory of the operating system and with other virtual machines running in the system. A diagram of the Windows 95 memory address allocation is shown in Figure 8.2. Each process is given between 1MB and 1GB of private address space. This private address space is inaccessible by other processes. If an unauthorized process attempts to use the protected memory of another process or the operating system, a **protection fault** occurs (rudely announced by way of a message on a plain blue screen). The shared memory region is provided to allow data and program code sharing among processes. The upper region holds components of the system virtual machine in addition to the DLLs accessible to all processes. The lower region is not addressable, which serves as a way to detect pointer errors.

When modern systems support virtual machines, they are better able to provide the protection, security, and manageability required by large enterprise-class computers. Virtual machines also provide compatibility across innumerable hardware platforms. One such machine, the Java Virtual Machine, is described in Section 8.5.

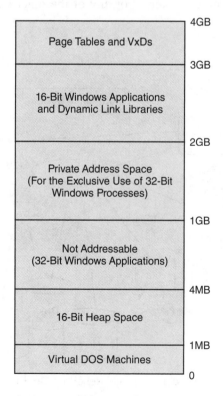

FIGURE 8.2 Windows 95 Memory Map

8.3.2 Subsystems and Partitions

The Windows VMM is a **subsystem** that starts when Windows is booted. Windows also starts other special-purpose subsystems for file management, I/O, and configuration management. Subsystems establish logically distinct environments that can be individually configured and managed. Subsystems run on top of the operating system kernel, which provides them with access to fundamental system resources, such as the CPU scheduler, that must be shared among several subsystems.

Each subsystem must be defined within the context of the controlling system. These definitions include resource descriptions such as disk files, input and output queues, and various other hardware components such as terminal sessions and printers. The resources defined to a subsystem are not always seen directly by the underlying kernel, but are visible through the subsystem for which they are defined. Resources defined to a subsystem may or may not be shareable among peer subsystems. Figure 8.3 is a conceptual rendering of the relationship of subsystems to other system resources.

Subsystems assist in management of the activities of large, highly complex computer systems. Because each subsystem is its own discrete controllable entity, system administrators can start and stop each subsystem individually, without disturbing the kernel or any of the other subsystems that happen to be running.

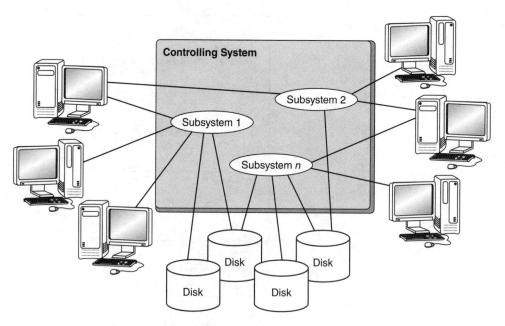

FIGURE 8.3 A Single Resource Can Be Defined to Multiple Subsystems

Each subsystem can be tuned individually by reallocating system resources, such as adding or removing disk space or memory. Moreover, if a process goes out of control within a subsystem—or crashes the subsystem itself—usually only the subsystem in which the process is running is affected. Thus, subsystems not only make systems more manageable, but also make them more robust.

In very large computer systems, subsystems do not go far enough in segmenting the machine and its resources. Sometimes a more sophisticated barrier is required to facilitate security and resource management. In these instances, a system may be broken up into **logical partitions**, sometimes called **LPAR**s, as illustrated in Figure 8.4. LPARs create distinct machines within one physical system, with nothing implicitly shared between them. The resources of one partition are no more accessible to another partition than if the partitions were running on physically separate systems. For example, if a system has two partitions, *A* and *B*, partition *A* can read a file from partition *B* only if both partitions agree to establish a mutually shared resource, such as a pipe or message queue. Generally speaking, files can be copied between partitions only through the use of a file transfer protocol or a utility written for this purpose by the system vendor.

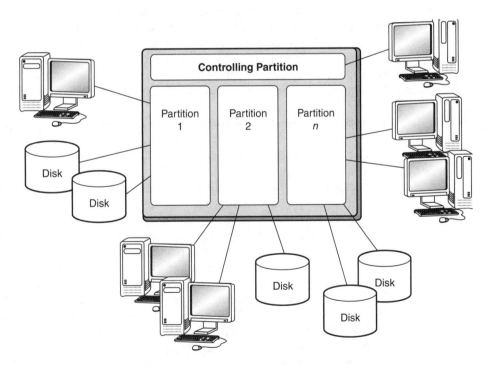

FIGURE 8.4   Logical Partitions and Their Controlling System: Resources Cannot Be Shared Easily between the Partitions

Logical partitions are especially useful in creating "sandbox" environments for user training or testing new programs. Sandbox environments get their name from the idea that anyone using these environments is free to "play around" to his or her heart's content, as long as this playing is done within the confines of the sandbox. Sandbox environments place strict limits on the accessibility of system resources. Processes running in one partition can never intentionally or inadvertently access data or processes resident in other partitions. Partitions thus raise the level of security in a system by isolating resources from processes that are not entitled to use them.

Although subsystems and partitions are different from each other in how they define their constituent resources, you can think of both as being mini-models of the layered system architecture of a computer system. In the case of a partitioned environment, the levels would look like adjacent layered birthday cakes, extending from the hardware level to the application level. Subsystems, on the other hand, are not so distinct from one another, with most of the differences taking place at the system software level.

8.3.3 Protected Environments and the Evolution of Systems Architectures

Until recently, virtual machines, subsystems, and logical partitions were considered artifacts of "old technology" mainframe systems. Throughout the 1990s, smaller machines were widely believed to be more cost-effective than mainframe systems. The "client-server" paradigm was thought to be more user friendly and responsive to dynamic business conditions. Application development for small systems quickly conscripted programming talent. Office automation programs, such as word processing and calendar management, found homes that are much more comfortable in collaborative, networked environments supported by small file servers. Print servers controlled network-enabled laser printers that produced crisp, clean output on plain paper faster than mainframe line printers could produce smudgy output on special forms. By any measure, desktop and small server platforms provide raw computing power and convenience at a fraction of the cost of equivalent raw mainframe computing power. Raw computing power, however, is only one part of an enterprise computing system.

When office automation moved to the desktop, office networks were built to connect the desktop systems to each other and to file servers that were repositories for documents and other vital business records. Application servers hosted programs that performed core business management functions. When companies became Internet-enabled, email and Web servers were added to the network. If any of the servers became bogged down with activity, the simple solution was to add another server to distribute the load. By the end of the 1990s, large enterprises were owners of huge **server farms** supporting hundreds of individual servers in environmentally controlled, secure facilities. Server farms soon became voracious consumers of manpower, each server occasionally demanding considerable attention. The contents of each server had to be backed up onto tape, and the tapes were subsequently rotated offsite for security. Each server was a potential source of failure, with problem diagnosis and software patch application becoming daily tasks. Before long, it became evident that the smaller, cheaper systems weren't quite the bargain they were once thought to be. This is particularly true for enterprises that find themselves supporting hundreds of small server systems.

Every major enterprise computer manufacturer is now offering a **server consolidation** product. Different vendors take different approaches to the problem. One of the most interesting of these is the idea of creating logical partitions containing numerous virtual machines within a single very large computer. The many advantages of server consolidation include the following:

- Managing one large system is easier than managing a multitude of smaller ones.
- A single large system consumes less electricity than a group of smaller systems having equivalent computational power.
- With less electrical power usage, less heat is generated, which economizes on air-conditioning.
- Larger systems can provide greater failover protection. (Hot spare disks and processors are often included with the systems.)
- A single system is easier to back up and recover.
- Single systems occupy less floor space, reducing real estate costs.
- Software licensing fees *may* be lower for a single large system than for a large number of small ones.
- Less labor is involved in applying system and user program software upgrades to one system rather than many.

Large system vendors, such as IBM, Unisys, and Hewlett-Packard (to name a few), were quick to pounce on server consolidation opportunities. IBM's mainframe and midrange lines have been recast as eSeries Servers. The System/390 mainframe has been reincarnated as the zSeries Server. zSeries Servers can support as many as 60 logical partitions. Each partition that runs IBM's Virtual Machine operating system can define *thousands* of virtual Linux systems. Figure 8.5 shows a model zSeries/Linux configuration. Each virtual Linux system is equally capable of sustaining enterprise applications and e-commerce activities as a freestanding Linux system, but without the management overhead. Thus, a football field–sized server farm can be replaced by one zSeries "box," which is slightly larger than a household refrigerator. One could say that the server consolidation movement epitomizes operating system evolution. Systems makers, by applying the evolving resources of the machine, continue to make their systems easier to manage even as they become increasingly powerful.

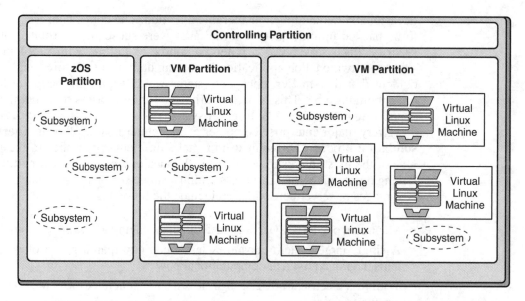

FIGURE 8.5 Linux Machines within Logical Partitions of an IBM zSeries Server

8.4 PROGRAMMING TOOLS

The operating system and its collection of applications provide an interface between the user who is writing the programs and the system that is running them. Other utilities, or programming tools, are necessary to carry out the more mechanical aspects of software creation. We discuss them in the sections below.

8.4.1 Assemblers and Assembly

In our layered system architecture, the level that sits directly on the operating system layer is the assembly language layer. In Chapter 4, we presented a simple, hypothetical machine architecture, which we called MARIE. The architecture is so simple, in fact, that no real machine would ever use it. For one thing, the continual need to fetch operands from memory would make the system very slow. Real systems minimize memory fetches by providing a sufficient number of addressable on-chip registers. Furthermore, the instruction set architecture of any real system would be much richer than MARIE's is. Many microprocessors have more than a thousand different instructions in their repertoires.

Although the machine we presented is quite different from a real machine, the assembly process we described is not. Virtually every assembler in use today passes twice through the source code. The first pass assembles as much code as it can, while building a symbol table; the second pass completes the binary instructions using address values retrieved from the symbol table built during the first pass.

The final output of most assemblers is a stream of **relocatable** binary instructions. Binary code is relocatable when the addresses of the operands are relative to the location where the operating system has loaded the program in memory, and the operating system is free to load this code wherever it wants. Take, for example, the following MARIE code from Table 4.5:

```
    Load x
    Add y
    Store z
    Halt
x, DEC 35
y, DEC -23
z, HEX 0000
```

The assembled code output could look similar to this:

```
1+004
3+005
2+006
7000
0023
FFE9
0000
```

The "+" sign in our example is not to be taken literally. It signals the program loader (component of the operating system) that the 004 in the first instruction is relative to the starting address of the program. Consider what happens if the loader happens to put the program in memory at address 0x250. The image in memory would appear as shown in Table 8.1.

If the loader happened to think that memory at address 0x400 was a better place for the program, the memory image would look like Table 8.2.

In contrast to relocatable code, **absolute code** is executable binary code that must always be loaded at a particular location in memory. Nonrelocatable code is used for specific purposes on some computer systems. Usually these applications

Address	Memory Contents
0x250	1254
0x251	3255
0x252	2256
0x253	7000
0x254	0023
0x255	FFE9
0x256	0000

TABLE 8.1 Memory If Program Is Loaded Starting at Address 0x250

Address	Memory Contents
0x400	1404
0x401	3405
0x402	2406
0x403	7000
0x404	0023
0x405	FFE9
0x406	0000

TABLE 8.2   Memory If Program Is Loaded Starting at 0x400

involve explicit control of attached devices or manipulation of system software, in which particular software routines can always be found in clearly defined locations.

Of course, binary machine instructions cannot be provided with "+" signs to distinguish between relocatable and nonrelocatable code. The specific manner in which the distinction is made depends on the design of the operating system that will be running the code. One of the simplest ways to distinguish between the two is to use different file types (extensions) for this purpose. The MS-DOS operating system uses a .COM (a COMmand file) extension for nonrelocatable code and .EXE (an EXEcutable file) extension for relocatable code. COM files always load at address 0x100. EXE files can load anywhere, and they don't even have to occupy contiguous memory space. Relocatable code can also be distinguished from nonrelocatable code by prepending all executable binary code with prefix or preamble information that lets the loader know its options while it is reading the program file from disk.

When relocatable code is loaded into memory, special registers usually provide the base address for the program. All addresses in the program are then considered to be offsets from the base address stored in the register. In Table 8.1, where we showed the loader placing the code at address 0x0250, a real system would simply store 0x0250 in the program base address register and use the program without modification, as in Table 8.3, where the address of each operand

Address	Memory Contents
0x250	1004
0x251	3005
0x252	2006
0x253	7000
0x254	0023
0x255	FFE9
0x256	0000

TABLE 8.3   Memory If Program Is Loaded at Address 0x250 Using Base Address Register

becomes an effective address after it has been augmented by the 0x250 stored in the base address register.

Whether we have relocatable code or nonrelocatable code, a program's instructions and data must be **bound** to actual physical addresses. The binding of instructions and data to memory addresses can happen at compile time, load time, or execution time. Absolute code is an example of **compile-time binding**, where the instruction and data references are bound to physical addresses when the program is compiled. Compile-time binding works only if the load memory location for a process image is known in advance. However, under compile-time binding, if the starting location of the process image changes, the code must be recompiled. If the load memory location for a process image is not known at compile time, relocatable code is generated, which can be bound either at load time or at run time. **Load-time binding** adds the starting address of the process image to each reference as the binary module is loaded into memory. However, the process image cannot be moved during execution, because the starting address for the process must remain the same. **Run-time binding** (or **execution-time binding**) delays binding until the process is actually running. This allows the process image to be moved from one memory location to another as it executes. Run-time binding requires special hardware support for **address mapping**, or translating from a logical process address to a physical address. A special base register stores the starting address of the program. This address is added to each reference generated by the CPU. If the process image is moved, the base register is updated to reflect the new starting address of the process. Additional virtual memory hardware is necessary to perform this translation quickly.

8.4.2 Link Editors

On most systems, program compiler output must pass through a **link editor** (or **linker**) before it can be executed on the target system. Linking is the process of matching the external symbols of a program with all exported symbols from other files, producing a single binary file with no unresolved external symbols. The principal job of a link editor, as shown in Figure 8.6, is to combine related program files into a unified loadable module. (The example in the figure uses file extensions characteristic of a DOS/Windows environment.) The constituent binary files can be entirely user-written, or they can be combined with standard system routines, depending on the needs of the application. Moreover, the binary linker input can be produced by any compiler. Among other things, this permits various sections of a program to be written in different languages, so part of a program could be written in C++, for ease of coding, and another part might be written in assembly language to speed up execution in a particularly slow section of the code.

As with assemblers, most link editors require two passes to produce a complete load module comprising all of the external input modules. During its first pass, the linker produces a global external symbol table containing the names of each of the external modules and their relative starting addresses with respect to the beginning of the total linked module. During the second pass, all references

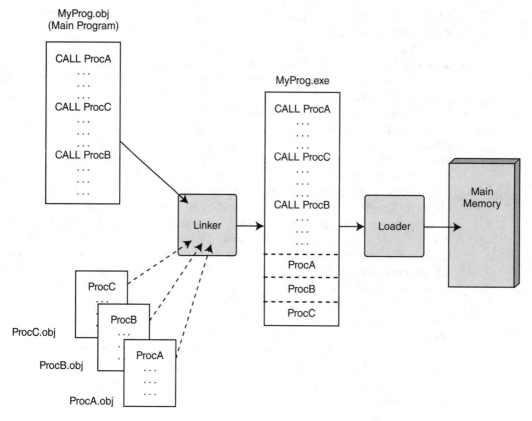

FIGURE 8.6 Linking and Loading Binary Modules

between the (formerly separate and external) modules are replaced with displacements for those modules from the symbol table. During the second pass of the linker, platform-dependent code can also be added to the combined module, producing a unified and loadable binary program file.

8.4.3 Dynamic Link Libraries

Some operating systems, notably Microsoft Windows, do not require link editing of all procedures used by a program before creating an executable module. With proper syntax in the source program, certain external modules can be linked at run time. These external modules are called **dynamic link libraries** (**DLLs**), because the linking is done only when the program or module is first invoked. The dynamic linking process is shown schematically in Figure 8.7. As each procedure is loaded, its address is placed in a cross-reference table within the main program module.

This approach has many advantages. First, if an external module is used repeatedly by several programs, static linking would require that each of these programs include a copy of the module's binary code. Clearly, it is a waste of

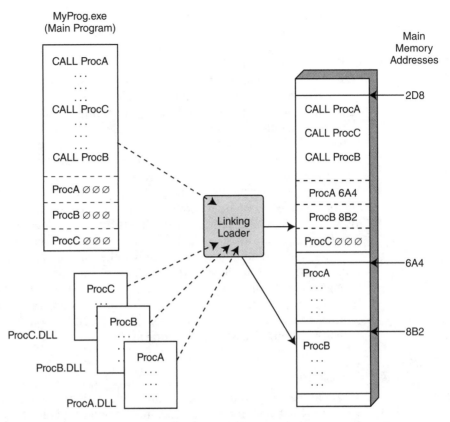

FIGURE 8.7 Dynamic Linking with Load-Time Address Resolution

disk space to have multiple copies of the same code hanging around, so we save space by linking at run time. The second advantage of dynamic linking is that if the code in one of the external modules changes, then each module that has been linked with it does not need to be relinked to preserve the integrity of the program. Moreover, keeping track of which modules employ which particular external modules can be difficult—perhaps impossible—for large systems. Thirdly, dynamic linking provides the means whereby third parties can create common libraries, the presence of which can be assumed by anyone writing programs for a particular system. In other words, if you are writing a program for a particular brand of operating system, you can take for granted that certain specific libraries will be available on every computer running that operating system. You need not concern yourself with the operating system's version number, or patch level, or anything else that is prone to frequent changes. As long as the library is never deleted, it can be used for dynamic linking.

Dynamic linking can take place either when a program is loaded or when an unlinked procedure is first called by a program while it is running. Dynamic linking at load time causes program startup delays. Instead of simply reading the program's binary code from the disk and running it, the operating system not only loads the main program, but also loads the binaries for all modules that the program uses. The loader provides the load addresses of each module to the main program prior to the execution of the first program statement. The time lag between the moment the user invokes the program and when program execution actually commences may be unacceptable for some applications. On the other hand, run-time linking does not incur the startup penalties of load-time linking, because a module is linked only if it is called. This saves a considerable amount of work when relatively few of a program's modules are actually invoked. However, some users object to perceived erratic response times when a running program frequently halts to load library routines.

A less obvious problem with dynamic linking is that the programmer writing the module has no direct control over the contents of the dynamic link library routine. Hence, if the authors of the link library code decide to change its functionality, they can do so without the knowledge or consent of the people who use the library. In addition, as anyone who has written commercial programs can tell you, the slightest changes in these library routines can cause rippling effects throughout an entire system. These effects can be disruptive and hard to track down to their source. Fortunately, such surprises are rare, so dynamic linking continues to be an approach favored for the distribution of commercial binary code across entire classes of operating systems.

8.4.4 Compilers

Assembly language programming can do many things that higher-level languages can't do. First and foremost, assembly language gives the programmer direct access to the underlying machine architecture. Programs used to control and/or communicate with peripheral devices are typically written in assembly because of the special instructions available in assembly that are customarily not available in higher-level languages. A programmer doesn't have to rely on operating system services to control a communications port, for example. Using assembly language, you can get the machine to do anything, even those things for which operating system services are not provided. In particular, programmers often use assembly language to take advantage of specialized hardware, because compilers for higher-level languages aren't designed to deal with uncommon or infrequently used devices. Also, well-written assembly code is blazingly fast. Each primitive instruction can be honed so that it produces the most timely and effective action upon the system.

These advantages, however, are not sufficiently compelling reasons to use assembly language for general application development. The fact remains that programming in assembly language is difficult and error-prone. It is even more difficult to maintain than it is to write, especially if the maintenance programmer is not the original author of the program. Most importantly, assembly languages are not portable to different machine architectures. For these reasons, most general-purpose system software contains very few, if any, assembly instructions. Assembly code is used only when it is absolutely necessary to do so.

Today, virtually all system and application programs use higher-level languages almost exclusively. Of course, "higher-level" is a relative term, subject to misunderstanding. One accepted taxonomy for programming languages starts by calling binary machine code the "first-generation" computer language (**1GL**). Programmers of this 1GL formerly entered program instructions directly into the machine using toggle switches on the system console! More "privileged" users punched binary instructions onto paper tape or cards. Programming productivity vaulted upward when the first assemblers were written in the early 1950s. These "second-generation" languages (**2GLs**) eliminated the errors introduced when instructions were translated to machine code by hand. The next productivity leap came with the introduction of compiled symbolic languages, or "third-generation" languages (**3GLs**), in the late 1950s. Fortran (*Form*ula *Trans*lation) was the first of these, released by John Backus and his IBM team in 1957. In the years since, a veritable alphabet soup of 3GLs has poured onto the programming community. Their names are sometimes snappy acronyms, such as COBOL, SNOBOL, and COOL. Sometimes they are named after people, as with Pascal and Ada. Not infrequently, 3GLs are called whatever their designers feel like calling them, as in the cases of C, C++, and Java.

Each "generation" of programming languages gets closer to how people think about problems and more distant from how machinery solves them. Some fourth- and fifth-generation languages are so easy to use that programming tasks formerly requiring a trained professional programmer can easily be done by end users, the key idea being that the user simply tells the computer what to do, not how to do it: The compiler figures out the rest. In making things simpler for the user, these latter-generation languages place substantial overhead on computer systems. Ultimately, all instructions must be pushed down through the language hierarchy, because the digital hardware that actually does the work can execute only binary instructions.

In Chapter 4, we pointed out that there is a one-to-one correspondence between assembly language statements and the binary code that the machine actually runs. In compiled languages, this is a one-to-many relationship. For example, allowing for variable storage definitions, the high-level language statement, $x = 3*y$, would require at least 12 program statements in MARIE's assembly language. The ratio of source code instructions to binary machine instructions becomes smaller in proportion to the sophistication of the source language. The "higher" the language, the more machine instructions each program line typically generates. This relationship is shown in the programming language hierarchy of Figure 8.8.

The science of compiler writing has continued to improve since the first compilers were written in the late 1950s. Through its achievements in compiler construction, the science of software engineering proved its ability to convert seemingly intractable problems into routine programming tasks. The intractability of the problem lies in bridging the semantic gap between statements that make sense to people and statements that make sense to machines.

Most compilers effect this transformation using a six-phase process, as shown in Figure 8.9. The first step in code compilation, called **lexical analysis**, aims to extract meaningful language primitives, or **tokens**, from a stream of textual

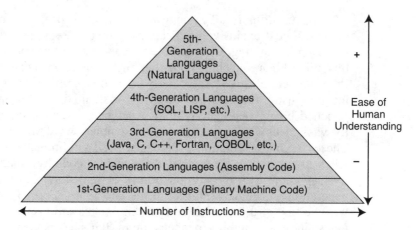

FIGURE 8.8 A Programming Language Hierarchy

source code. These tokens consist of reserved words particular to a language (e.g., if, else), Boolean and mathematical operators, literals (e.g., 12.27), and programmer-defined variables. While the lexical analyzer is creating the token stream, it is also building the framework for a symbol table. At this point, the symbol table most likely contains user-defined tokens (variables and procedure names), along with annotations as to their location and data type. Lexical errors

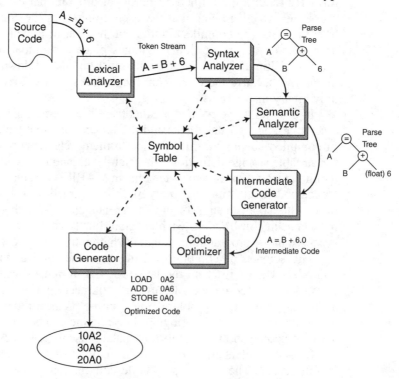

FIGURE 8.9 The Six Phases of Program Compilation

occur when characters or constructs foreign to the language are discovered in the source code. The programmer-defined variable 1DaysPay, for example, would produce a lexical error in most languages because variable names typically cannot begin with a digit. If no lexical errors are found, the compiler proceeds to analyze the syntax of the token stream.

Syntax analysis, or **parsing**, of the token stream involves creation of a data structure called a **parse tree** or **syntax tree**. The inorder traversal of a parse tree usually gives the expression just parsed. Consider, for example, the following program statement:

```
monthPrincipal = payment - (outstandingBalance * interestRate)
```

One correct syntax tree for this statement is shown in Figure 8.10.

The parser checks the symbol table for the presence of programmer-defined variables that populate the tree. If the parser encounters a variable for which no description exists in the symbol table, it issues an error message. The parser also detects illegal constructions such as $A = B + C = D$. What the parser does not do, however, is check that the $=$ or $+$ operators are valid for the variables A, B, C, and D. The **semantic analyzer** does this in the next phase. It uses the parse tree as input and checks it for appropriate data types using information from the symbol table. The semantic analyzer also makes appropriate data type promotions, such as changing an integer to a floating-point value or variable, if such promotions are supported by the language rules.

After the compiler has completed its analysis functions, it begins its synthesis phase using the syntax tree from the semantic analysis phase. The first step in code synthesis is to create a pseudo-assembly code from the syntax tree. This code is often referred to as **three-address code**, because it supports statements such as $A = B + C$, which most assembly languages do not support. This intermediate code enables compilers to be portable to many different kinds of computers.

Once all of the tokenizing, tree-building, and semantic analyses are done, it becomes a relatively easy task to write a three-address code translator that produces output for a number of different instruction sets. Most systems' ISAs use two-address code, so the addressing mode differences have to be resolved during

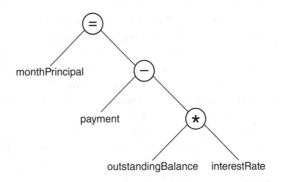

FIGURE 8.10 A Syntax Tree

the translation process. (Recall that the MARIE instruction set is a one-address architecture.) The final compiler phase, however, often does more than just translate intermediate code to assembly instructions. Good compilers make some attempt at code optimization, which can take into account different memory and register organizations and can supply the most powerful instructions needed to carry out the task. Code optimization also involves removing unnecessary temporary variables, collapsing repeated expressions into single expressions, and flagging dead (unreachable) code.

After all the instructions have been generated and optimizations have been made where possible, the compiler creates binary object code, suitable for linking and execution on the target system.

8.4.5 Interpreters

Like compiled languages, interpreted languages also have a one-to-many relationship between the source code statements and executable machine instructions. However, unlike compilers, which read the entire source code file before producing a binary stream, interpreters process one source statement at a time.

With so much work being done "on the fly," interpreters are typically much slower than compilers. At least five of the six steps required of compilers must also be carried out in interpreters, and these steps are carried out in "real time." This approach affords no opportunity for code optimization. Furthermore, error detection in interpreters is usually limited to language syntax and variable type checking. For example, very few interpreters detect possible illegal arithmetic operations before they happen or warn the programmer before exceeding the bounds of an array.

Some early interpreters provided syntax checking within custom-designed editors. For instance, if a user were to type "esle" instead of "else", the editor would immediately issue a remark to that effect. Other interpreters allow use of general-purpose text editors, delaying syntax checking until execution time. The latter approach is particularly risky when used for business-critical application programs. If the application program happens to execute a branch of code that has not been checked for proper syntax, the program crashes, leaving the hapless user staring at an odd-looking system prompt, with his files perhaps only partially updated.

Despite the sluggish execution speed and delayed error checking, there are good reasons for using an interpreted language. Foremost among these is that interpreted languages allow source-level debugging, making them ideal for beginning programmers and end users. This is why, in 1964, two Dartmouth professors, John G. Kemeny and Thomas E. Kurtz, invented **BASIC**, the **Beginners All-purpose Symbolic Instruction Code**. At that time, students' first programming experiences involved punching Fortran instructions on 80-column cards. The cards were then run through a mainframe compiler, which often had a turnaround time measured in hours. Sometimes days would elapse before a clean compilation and execution could be achieved. In its dramatic departure from compiling statements in batch mode, BASIC allowed students to type program statements during an interactive terminal session. The BASIC interpreter, which was continually running on the mainframe, gave students immediate feedback. They could quickly correct syntax and logic errors, thus creating a more positive and effective learning experience.

For these same reasons, BASIC was the language of choice on the earliest personal computer systems. Many first-time computer buyers were not experienced programmers, so they needed a language that would make it easy for them to learn programming on their own. BASIC was ideal for this purpose. Moreover, on a single-user, personal system, very few people cared that interpreted BASIC was much slower than a compiled language.

8.5 JAVA: ALL OF THE ABOVE

In the early 1990s, Dr. James Gosling and his team at Sun Microsystems set out to create a programming language that would run on any computing platform. The mantra was to create a "write once, run anywhere" computer language. In 1995, Sun released the first version of the Java programming language. Because of its portability and open specifications, Java has become enormously popular. Java code is runnable on virtually all computer platforms, from the smallest handheld devices to the largest mainframes. The timing of Java's arrival couldn't have been better: It is a cross-platform language that was deployable at the inception of wide-scale Internet-based commerce, the perfect model of cross-platform computing. Although Java and some of its features were briefly introduced in Chapter 5, we now go into more detail.

If you have ever studied the Java programming language, you know that the output from the Java compiler is a binary **class** file. This class file is executable by a **Java Virtual Machine (JVM)**, which resembles a real machine in many respects. It has private memory areas addressable only by processes running within the machine. It also has its own *bona fide* instruction set architecture. This ISA is stack based to keep the machine simple and portable to practically any computing platform.

Of course, a Java Virtual Machine isn't a real machine. It is a layer of software that sits between the operating system and the application program: a binary class file. Class files include variables as well as the **methods** (procedures) for manipulating those variables.

Figure 8.11 illustrates how the JVM is a computing machine in miniature with its own memory and method area. Notice that the memory heap, method code, and "native method interface" areas are shared among all processes running within the machine.

The memory **heap** is main memory space that is allocated and deallocated as data structures are created and destroyed through thread execution. Java's deallocation of heap memory is (indelicately) referred to as **garbage collection**, which the JVM (instead of the operating system) does automatically. The Java **native method area** provides workspace for binary objects external to Java, such as compiled C++ or assembly language modules. The JVM **method area** contains the binary code required to run each application thread living in the JVM. This is

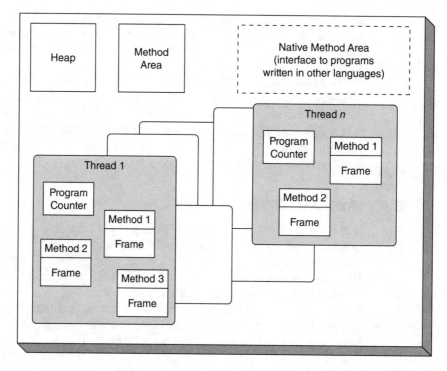

FIGURE 8.11   The Java Virtual Machine

where the class variable data structures and program statements required by the class reside. Java's executable program statements are stored in an intermediate code called **bytecode**, also introduced in Chapter 5.

Java method bytecode is executed in various thread processes. Several thread processes are started automatically by the JVM, the main program thread being one of them. Only one method can be active at a time in each thread, and programs may spawn additional threads to provide concurrency. When a thread invokes a method, it creates a memory frame for the method. Part of this memory frame is used for the method's local variables, and another part for its private stack. After the thread has defined the method stack, it pushes the method's parameters and points its program counter to the first executable statement of the method.

Each Java class contains a type of symbol table called a **constant pool**, which is an array that contains information about the data type of each of the variables of a class and the initial value of the variable, as well as access flags for the variable (e.g., whether it is public or private to the class). The constant pool also contains several structures other than those defined by the programmer. This is why Sun Microsystems calls entries in the constant pool (the array elements) **attributes**. Among the attributes of every Java class, one finds housekeeping items such as the name of the Java source file, part of its inheritance hierarchy, and pointers to other JVM internal data structures.

```
public class Simple {
  public static void main (String[ ] args) {
    int i = 0;
    double j = 0;
    while (i < 10) {
     i = i + 1;
     j = j + 1.0;
     } // while
  } // main()
} // Simple()
```

FIGURE 8.12   A Simple Java Program

To illustrate how the JVM executes method bytecode, consider the Java program shown in Figure 8.12.

Java requires the source code for this class to be stored in a text file named `Simple.java`. The Java compiler reads `Simple.java` and does all the things that other compilers do. Its output is a binary stream of bytecode named `Simple.class`. The `Simple.class` file can be run by any JVM of equal or later version than that of the compiler that created the class. These steps are shown in Figure 8.13.

At execution time, a Java Virtual Machine must be running on the host system. When the JVM loads a class file, the first thing it does is verify the integrity of the bytecode by checking the class file format, checking the format of the bytecode instructions, and making sure that no illegal references are made. After this preliminary verification is successfully completed, the loader performs a number of run-time checks as it places the bytecode in memory.

After all verification steps have been completed, the loader invokes the bytecode interpreter. This interpreter has six phases in which it will:

1. Perform a link edit of the bytecode instructions by asking the loader to supply all referenced classes and system binaries, if they are not already loaded.

2. Create and initialize the main stack frame and local variables.

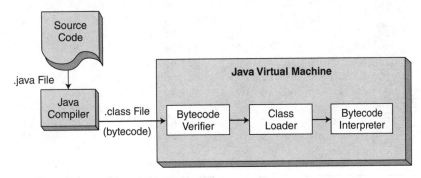

FIGURE 8.13   Java Class Compilation and Execution

3. Create and start execution thread(s).

4. While the threads are executing, manage heap storage by deallocating unused storage.

5. As each thread dies, deallocate its resources.

6. Upon program termination, kill any remaining threads and terminate the JVM.

Figure 8.14 shows the hexadecimal image of the bytecode for `Simple.class`. The address of each byte can be found by adding the value in the first (shaded) column to the row offset in the first (shaded) row. For convenience, we have translated the bytecode into characters where the binary value has a meaningful 7-bit ASCII value. You can see the name of the source file, `Simple.java`, beginning at address 0x06D. The name of the class starts at 0x080. Readers familiar with Java are aware that the `Simple` class is also known as `.this` class, and its superclass is `java.lang.Object`, the name of which starts at address 0x089.

Notice that our class file begins with the hex number CAFEBABE. It is the **magic number** indicating the start of a class file (and yes, it *is* politically incorrect!). An 8-byte sequence indicating the language version of the class file follows the magic number. If this sequence number is greater than the version that the interpreting JVM can support, the verifier terminates the JVM.

The executable bytecode begins at address 0x0E6. The hex digits, 16, at address 0x0E5 let the interpreter know that the executable method bytecode is 22 bytes long. As in assembly languages, each executable bytecode has a corresponding mnemonic. Java currently defines 204 different bytecode instructions.

	+0	+1	+2	+3	+4	+5	+6	+7	+8	+9	+A	+B	+C	+D	+E	+F	Characters
000	CA	FE	BA	BE	00	03	00	2D	00	0F	0A	00	03	00	0C	07	-
010	00	0D	07	00	0E	01	00	06	3C	69	6E	69	74	3E	01	00	<init>
020	03	28	29	56	01	00	04	43	6F	64	65	01	00	0F	4C	69	()V Code Li
030	6E	65	4E	75	6D	62	65	72	54	61	62	6C	65	01	00	04	neNumberTable
040	6D	61	69	6E	01	00	16	28	5B	4C	6A	61	76	61	2F	6C	main ([Ljava/l
050	61	6E	67	2F	53	74	72	69	6E	67	3B	29	56	01	00	0A	ang/String;)V
060	53	6F	75	72	63	65	46	69	6C	65	01	00	0B	53	69	6D	SourceFile Sim
070	70	6C	65	2E	6A	61	76	61	0C	00	04	00	05	01	00	06	ple.java
080	53	69	6D	70	6C	65	01	00	10	6A	61	76	61	2F	6C	61	Simple java/la
090	6E	67	2F	4F	62	6A	65	63	74	00	21	00	02	00	03	00	ng/Object !
0A0	00	00	00	00	02	00	01	00	04	00	05	00	01	00	06	00	
0B0	00	00	1D	00	01	00	01	00	00	00	05	2A	B7	00	01	B1	*
0C0	00	00	00	01	00	07	00	00	00	06	00	01	00	00	00	01	
0D0	00	09	00	08	00	09	00	01	00	06	00	00	00	46	00	04	F
0E0	00	04	00	00	00	16	03	3C	0E	49	A7	00	0B	1B	04	60	< I `
0F0	3C	28	0F	63	49	1B	10	0A	A1	FF	F5	B1	00	00	00	01	<(cI
100	00	07	00	00	00	1E	00	07	00	00	00	03	00	02	00	04	
110	00	04	00	05	00	07	00	06	00	0B	00	07	00	0F	00	05	
120	00	15	00	09	00	01	00	0A	00	00	00	02	00	0B	00	3D	=

FIGURE 8.14 Binary Image of `Simple.class`

Hence, only one byte is needed for the entire range of opcodes. These small opcodes help to keep classes small, making them fast to load and easily convertible to binary instructions on the host system.

Because certain small constants are used so frequently in computer programs, bytecodes have been defined especially to provide these constants where needed. For example, the mnemonic iconst_5 pushes the integer 5 onto the stack. In order to push larger constants onto the stack, two bytecodes are required, the first for the operation, the second for the operand. As we mentioned above, local variables for each class are kept in an array. Characteristically, the first few elements of this array are the most active, so there are bytecodes particular to addressing these initial local array elements. Access to other positions in the array requires a 2-byte instruction: one for the opcode and the second for the offset of the array element.

That being said, let us look at the bytecode for the main() method of Simple.class. We have extracted the bytecode from Figure 8.14 and listed it in Figure 8.15 along with mnemonics and some commentary. The leftmost column gives the relative address of each instruction. The thread-specific program counter uses this relative address to control program flow. We now trace the execution of this bytecode so you can see how it works.

When the interpreter begins running this code, the PC is initially set to zero and the iconst_0 instruction is executed. This is the execution of the int i = 0; statement in the third line of the Simple.java source code. The PC is incremented by one and subsequently executes each initialization instruction until it encounters the goto statement at instruction 4. This instruction adds a decimal 11 to the program counter, so its value becomes 0x0F, which points to the load_1 instruction.

At this point, the JVM has assigned initial values to i and j and now proceeds to check the initial condition of the while loop to see whether the loop body should be executed. To do this, it places the value of i (from the local variable array) onto the stack, and then it pushes the comparison value 0x0A. Note that this is a little bit of code optimization that has been done for us by the compiler. By default, Java stores integer values in 32 bits, thus occupying 4 bytes. However, the compiler is smart enough to see that the decimal constant 10 is small enough to store in 1 byte, so it wrote code to push a single byte rather than 4 bytes onto the stack.

The comparison operation instruction, if_icmplt, pops i and 0x0A and compares their values (the lt at the end of the mnemonic means that it is looking for the **less than** condition). If i is less than 10, 0x0B is subtracted from the PC, giving 7, which is the starting address for the body of the loop. When the instructions within the loop body have been completed, execution falls through to the conditional processing at address 0x0F. Once this condition becomes false, the interpreter returns control to the operating system, after doing some cleanup.

Java programmers who have wondered how the interpreter knows which source line has caused a program crash will find their answer starting at address 0x108 in the binary class file image of Figure 8.14. This is the beginning of the line number table that associates the program counter value with a particular line in the

Offset (PC value)	Bytecode	Mnemonic	Meaning
– – – – – – – – –			Variable initialization
0	03	iconst_0	Push integer 0 onto data stack.
1	3C	istore_1	Remove integer from top of stack and place into local variable array at address 1.
2	0E	dconst_0	Push double precision constant 0 onto the stack.
3	A7	goto	Skip number of bytes as given in following two bytes.
	00		This means we'll skip next 11 bytes.
	0B		This means add 0B to the program counter.
– – – – – – – – –			Loop body
7	1B	iload_1	Push an integer value from local array onto stack.
8	04	iconst_1	Push integer constant 1.
9	60	iadd	Add two integer operands that are at top of stack. (Sum is pushed.)
A	3C	istore_1	Remove integer from top of stack and place into local variable array at address 1.
B	28	dload_2	Load double variable from local array and place it on the stack.
C	0F	dconst_1	Push double precision constant 1 onto the stack.
D	63	dadd	Add the double precision values that are at the top of the stack.
E	49	dstore_2	Store the double sum from the top of the stack to local variable array position 2.
– – – – – – – – –			Loop condition
F	1B	iload_1	Load integer from local variable array position 1.
10	10	bipush	Push the following byte value onto the stack. (10 decimal)
	0A		
12	A1	if_icmplt	Compare two integer values at the top of stack for "less than" condition.
	FF		If true (i < 10), add the following value to the program counter.
	F5		Note: FFF5 = −11 decimal.
15	B1	return	Otherwise, return.

FIGURE 8.15 Annotated Bytecode for Simple.class

PC	Source Line #	
	1	public class Simple {
	2	public static void main (String[] args) {
00	3	int i = 0;
02	4	double j = 0;
04	5	while (i < 10) {
07	6	i = i + 1;
0B	7	j = j + 1.0;
0F	8	} // while
15	9	} // main()
	A	} // Simple()

FIGURE 8.16 A Program Counter–to–Source Line Cross-Reference for `Simple.class`

source program. The two bytes starting at address 0x106 tell the JVM that there are seven entries in the line number table that follows. By filling in a few details, we can build the cross-reference shown in Figure 8.16.

Notice that if the program crashes when the PC = 9, for example, the offending source program line would be line 6. Interpretation of the bytecode generated for source code line number 7 begins when the PC is greater than or equal to 0x0B, but less than 0x0F.

Because the JVM does so much as it loads and executes its bytecode, its performance cannot possibly match the performance of a compiled language. This is true even when speedup software like Java's Just-In-Time (JIT) compiler is used. The trade-off, however, is that class files can be created and stored on one platform and executed on a completely different platform. For example, we can write and compile a Java program on an Alpha RISC server and it will run just as well on CISC Pentium–class clients that download the class file bytecode. This "write-once, run-anywhere" paradigm is of enormous benefit for enterprises with disparate and geographically separate systems. Java applets (bytecode that runs in browsers) are essential for Web-based transactions and e-commerce. Ultimately, all that is required of the user is to be running (reasonably) current browser software. Given its portability and relative ease of use, the Java language and its virtual machine environment are the ideal middleware platform.

8.6 DATABASE SOFTWARE

By far, the most precious assets of an enterprise are not its offices or its factories, but its data. Regardless of the nature of the enterprise—be it a private business, an educational institution, or a government agency—the definitive record of its history and current state is imprinted on its data. If the data is inconsistent with the state of the enterprise, or if the data is inconsistent with itself, its usefulness is questionable, and problems are certain to arise.

Any computer system supporting an enterprise is the platform for interrelated application programs. These programs perform updates on the data in accordance with changes to the state of the enterprise. Groups of interrelated programs are often referred to as **application systems**, because they work together as an integrated whole: Few pieces are very useful standing on their own. Application system components share the same set of data and typically, but not necessarily, share the same computing environment. Today, application systems use many platforms: desktop microcomputers, file servers, and mainframes. With cooperative Web-based computing coming into vogue, sometimes we don't know or even care where the application is running. Although each platform brings its unique benefits and challenges to the science of data management, the fundamental concepts of database management software have been unchanged for more than three decades.

Early application systems recorded data using magnetic tape or punched cards. By their sequential nature, tape and punched card updates had to be run as a group, in batch processing mode, for efficiency. Because any data element on magnetic disks can be accessed directly, batch processing of updates against **flat files** was no longer forced by the systems architecture. However, old habits are hard to break, and programs are costly to rewrite. Hence, flat file processing persisted years after most card readers became museum pieces.

In flat file systems, each application program is free to define whatever data objects it needs. For this reason, a consistent view of the system is hard to enforce. For example, let's say we have an accounts receivable system, which is an application system that keeps track of who owes us how much money and for how long it has been owed. The program that produces monthly invoices may post monthly transactions to a 6-digit field (or data element) called CUST_OWE. Now, the person doing the monthly reconciliations could just as well call this field CUST_BAL, and may be expecting it to be five digits wide. It is almost certain that somewhere along the line, information will be lost and confusion will reign. Sometime during the month, after several thousand dollars are "unaccounted for," the debuggers will eventually figure out that CUST_OWE is the same data element as CUST_BAL, and that the problem was caused by truncation or a field overflow condition.

Database management systems (**DBMSs**) were created to prevent these predicaments. They enforce order and consistency on file-based application systems. With database systems, no longer are programmers free to describe and access a data element in any manner they please. There is one—and only one—definition of the data elements in a database management system. This definition is a system's **database schema**. In some systems, a distinction is made between the programmer's view of the database, its **logical schema**, and the computer system's view of the database, called its **physical schema**. The database management system integrates the physical and logical views of the database. Application programs employ the logical schema presented by the database management system to read and update data within the physical schema, under control of the database management system and the operating system. Figure 8.17 illustrates this relationship.

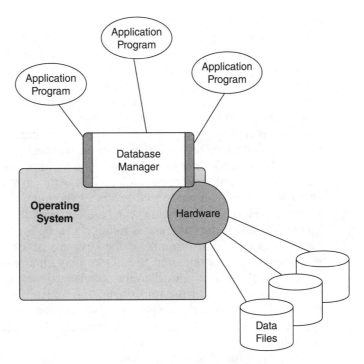

FIGURE 8.17   The Relationship of a Database Management System to Other
System Components

The individual data elements defined by a database schema are organized into logical structures called **records**, which are grouped together into **files**. Related files collectively form the database.

Database architects are mindful of application needs as well as performance when they create logical and physical schemas. The general objective is to minimize redundancy and wasted space while maintaining a desired level of performance, usually measured in terms of application response time. A banking system, for example, would not place the customer's name and address on every canceled check record in the database. This information would be kept in an account master file that uses an account number as its **key field**. Each canceled check, then, would have to bear only the account number along with information particular to the check itself.

Database management systems vary widely in how data is physically organized. Virtually every database vendor has invented proprietary methods for managing and indexing files. Most systems use a variant of the B+ tree data structure. (See Appendix A for details.) Database management systems typically manage disk storage independent of the underlying operating system. By removing the operating system layer from the process, database systems can optimize reads and writes according to the database schema and index design.

In Chapter 7, we studied disk file organization. We learned that most disk systems read data in chunks from the disk, the smallest addressable unit being a sector. Most large systems read an entire track at a time. As an index structure becomes very deep, the likelihood increases that we will need more than one read operation to traverse the index tree. So how do we organize the tree to keep disk I/O as infrequent as we can? Is it better to create very large internal index nodes so that more record values can be spanned per node? This would make the number of nodes per level smaller, and perhaps permit an entire tree level to be accessed in one read operation. Or is it better to keep the internal node sizes small so that we can read more layers of the index in one read operation? The answers to all of these questions can be found only in the context of the particular system on which the database is running. An optimal answer may even depend on the data itself. For example, if the keys are **sparse**, that is, if there are many possible key values that aren't used, we may choose one particular index organization scheme. But with densely populated index structures, we may choose another. Regardless of the implementation, database tuning is a nontrivial task that requires an understanding of the database management software, the storage architecture of the system, and the particulars of the data population managed by the system.

Database files often carry more than one index. For example, if you have a customer database, it would be a good idea if you could locate records by the customer's account number as well as his name. Each index, of course, adds overhead to the system, both in terms of space (for storing the index) and in time (because all indices must be updated at once when records are added or deleted). One of the major challenges facing systems designers is in making sure that there are sufficient indices to allow fast record retrieval in most circumstances, but not so many as to burden the system with an inordinate amount of housekeeping.

The goal of database management systems is to provide timely and easy access to large amounts of data, but to do so in ways that ensure that database integrity is always preserved. This means that a database management system must allow users to define and manage rules, or **constraints**, placed on certain critical data elements. Sometimes these constraints are just simple rules such as, "The customer number can't be null." More complex rules dictate which particular users can see which data elements and how files with interrelated data elements will be updated. The definition and enforcement of security and data integrity constraints are critical to the usefulness of any database management system.

Another core component of a database management system is its transaction manager. A **transaction manager** controls updates to data objects in such a way as to ensure that the database is always in a consistent state. Formally, a transaction manager controls changes to the state of data so that each transaction has the following properties:

- **Atomicity**—All related updates take place within the bounds of the transaction or no updates are made at all.

- **Consistency**—All updates comply with the constraints placed on all data elements.
- **Isolation**—No transaction can interfere with the activities or updates of another transaction.
- **Durability**—Successful transactions are written to "durable" media (e.g., magnetic disk) as soon as possible.

These four items are known as the **ACID properties** of transaction management. The importance of the ACID properties can be understood easily through an example.

Suppose you've made your monthly credit card payment and, soon after mailing it, you go to a nearby store to make another purchase with your card. Suppose also that at the exact moment that the sales clerk is swiping your plastic across a magnetic reader, an accounting clerk at the bank is entering your payment into the bank's database. Figure 8.18 illustrates one way in which a central computer system could process these transactions.

In the figure, the accounting clerk finishes his update before the sales clerk finishes hers, leaving you with a $300 unpaid balance. The transaction could just as easily occur as shown in Figure 8.19, where the sales clerk finishes her update first, so the account then ends up with a $0.00 balance and you've just gotten your stuff for free!

Although getting free stuff probably would make you happy, it is equally likely that you would end up paying your bill twice (or hassling with the accounting clerk until your records were corrected). The situation we have just described is called a **race condition**, because the final state of the database depends not on the correctness of the updates, but on which transaction happens to finish last.

Transaction managers prevent race conditions through their enforcement of atomicity and isolation. They do this by placing various types of locks on data records. In our example in Figure 8.18, the accounting clerk should be granted

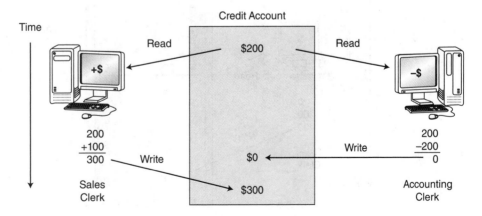

FIGURE 8.18 One Transaction Scenario

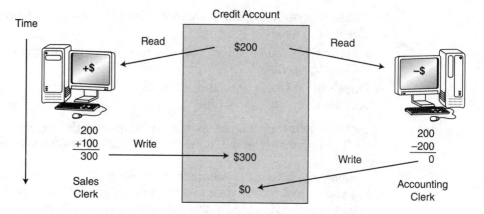

FIGURE 8.19 Another Transaction Scenario

an "exclusive" lock on your credit card record. The lock is released only after the updated balance is written back to the disk. While the accounting clerk's transaction is running, the sales clerk gets a message saying that the system is busy. When the update has been completed, the transaction manager releases the accounting clerk's lock and immediately places another for the sales clerk. The corrected transaction is shown in Figure 8.20.

There is some risk with this approach. Anytime an entity is locked in a complex system, there is a potential for deadlock. Systems can cleverly manage their

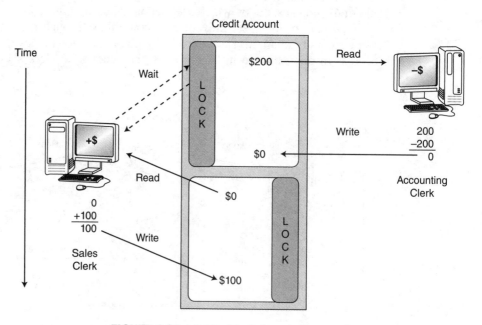

FIGURE 8.20 An Isolated, Atomic Transaction

locks to reduce the risk of deadlock, but each measure taken to prevent or detect deadlock places more overhead on the system. With too much lock management, transaction performance suffers. In general, deadlock prevention and detection are secondary to performance considerations. Deadlock situations happen rarely, whereas performance is a factor in every transaction.

Another performance impediment is data logging. During the course of updating records (which includes record deletion), database transaction managers write images of the transaction to a **log file**. Hence, each update requires at least two writes: one to the primary file, and one to the log file. The log file is important because it helps the system maintain transaction integrity if the transaction must be aborted due to an error. If, for example, the database management system captures an image of the record being updated before the update is made, this old image can be quickly written back to disk, thereby erasing all subsequent updates to the record. In some systems, both "before" and "after" images are captured, making error recovery relatively easy.

Database logs are also useful as **audit trails** to show who has updated which files at what time and exactly which data elements were changed. Some cautious systems administrators keep these log files for years in vaulted tape libraries.

Log files are particularly important tools for data backup and recovery. Some databases are simply too large to be backed up to tape or optical disk every night—it takes too much time. Instead, full backups of the database files are taken only once or twice a week, but the log files are saved nightly. Should disaster strike sometime between these full backups, the log files from the other days' transactions would be used for **forward recovery**, rebuilding each day's transactions as if they were rekeyed by the users onto the full database images taken days earlier.

The database access controls that we have just discussed—security, index management, and lock management—consume tremendous system resources. In fact, this overhead was so great on early systems that some people argued successfully to continue using their file-based systems, because their host computers could not handle the database management load. Even with today's enormously powerful systems, throughput can suffer severely if the database system isn't properly tuned and maintained. High-volume transaction environments are often attended to by systems programmers and database analysts whose sole job is to keep the system working at optimal performance.

8.7 TRANSACTION MANAGERS

One way to improve database performance is to simply ask the database to do less work by moving some of its functions to other system components. Transaction management is one database component often partitioned from the core data management functions of a database management system. Standalone transaction managers also typically incorporate load balancing and other optimization features that are unsuitable for inclusion in core database software, thus improving the effectiveness of the entire system. Transaction managers are particularly useful when business transactions span two or more separate databases. None of the participating databases can be responsible for the integrity of their peer databases, but an external transaction manager can keep all of them in synch.

One of the earliest and most successful transaction managers was IBM's Customer Information and Control System (CICS). CICS has been around for well over four decades, coming on the market in 1968. CICS is noteworthy because it was the first system to integrate transaction processing (TP), database management, and communications management within a single applications suite. Yet the components of CICS were (and still are) loosely coupled to enable tuning and management of each component as a separate entity. The communications management component of CICS controls interactions, called **conversations**, between dumb terminals and a host system. Freed from the burdens of protocol management, the database and the application programs do their jobs more effectively.

CICS was one of the first application systems to employ remote procedure calls within a client-server environment. In its contemporary incarnation, CICS can manage transaction processing between thousands of Internet users and large host systems. But even today, CICS strongly resembles its 1960s-vintage architecture, which has become the paradigm for virtually every transaction processing system invented since. The modern CICS architecture is shown schematically in Figure 8.21.

As you see from the diagram, a program called the **transaction processing monitor** (**TP monitor**) is the pivotal component of the system. It accepts input from the telecommunications manager and authenticates the transaction against data files containing lists of which users are authorized to which transactions. Sometimes this security information includes specific information such as defining which locations can run particular transactions (intranet versus Internet, for example). Once the monitor has authenticated the transaction, it initiates the application program requested by the user. When data is needed by the application, the TP monitor sends a request to the database management software. It does all of this while maintaining atomicity and isolation among many concurrent application processes.

You may already be thinking that there should be no reason that all of these TP software components would have to reside on the same host computer. Indeed, there is no reason to keep them together. Some distributed architectures dedicate groups of small servers to running TP monitors. These systems are physically distinct from the systems containing the database management software. There is also no need for systems running the TP monitors to be the same class of system as the systems running the database software. For example, you could have Sun Unix RISC systems for communications management and a Unisys ES/7000 running the database software under the Windows Datacenter operating system. Transactions would be entered through desktop or mobile personal computers. This configuration is known as a **3-tiered architecture**, with each platform representing one of the tiers, with the general case being an *n*-tiered, or **multitiered, architecture**. With the advent of Web computing and e-commerce, *n*-tiered TP architectures are becoming increasingly popular. Many vendors, including Microsoft, Netscape, Sybase, SAP AG, and IBM's CICS, have been successful in supporting various *n*-tiered transaction systems. Of course, it is impossible

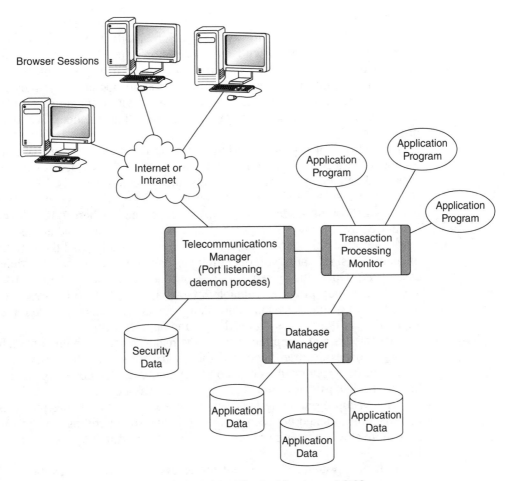

FIGURE 8.21 The Architecture of CICS

to say which of these is "better" for a particular enterprise, each having its own advantages and disadvantages. The prudent systems architect keeps all cost and reliability factors in mind when designing a TP system before deciding which architecture makes the most sense for any particular environment.

CHAPTER SUMMARY

This chapter has described the mutual dependence of computer hardware and software. System software works in concert with system hardware to create a functional and efficient system. System software, including operating systems and application software, is an interface between the user and the hardware, allowing the low-level architecture of a computer to be treated abstractly. This gives users an environment in which they can concentrate on problem solving rather than system operations.

The interaction and deep interdependence between hardware and software is most evident in operating system design. In their historical development, operating systems started with an "open shop" approach, then changed to an operator-driven batch approach, and then evolved to support interactive multiprogramming and distributed computing. Modern operating systems provide a user interface in addition to an assortment of services, including memory management, process management, general resource management, scheduling, and protection.

Knowledge of operating system concepts is critical to every computer professional. Virtually all system activity ties back to the services of the operating system. When the operating system fails, the entire system fails. You should realize, however, that not all computers have or need operating systems. This is particularly true of embedded systems, as we shall see in Chapter 10. The computer in your car or microwave has such simple tasks to perform that an operating system is not necessary. However, for computers that go beyond the simplistic task of running a single program, operating systems are mandatory for efficiency and ease of use. Operating systems are one of many examples of large software systems. Their study provides valuable lessons applicable to software development in general. For these reasons and many others, we heartily encourage further exploration of operating systems design and development.

Assemblers and compilers provide the means by which human-readable computer languages are translated into the binary form suitable for execution by a computer. Interpreters also produce binary code, but the code is generally not as fast or efficient as that which is generated by an assembler.

The Java programming language produces code that is interpreted by a virtual machine situated between its bytecode and the operating system. Java code runs more slowly than binary programs, but it is portable to a wide array of platforms.

Database system software controls access to data files, often through the services of a transaction processing system. The ACID properties of a database system ensure that the data is always in a consistent state.

Building large, reliable systems is a major challenge facing computer science today. By now, you understand that a computer system is much more than hardware and programs. Enterprise-class systems are aggregations of interdependent processes, each with its own purpose. The failure or poor performance of any of these processes will have a damaging effect on the entire system—if only in the perception of its users. As you continue along in your career and education, you will study many of the topics of this chapter in more detail. If you are a systems administrator or systems programmer, you will master these ideas as they apply in the context of a particular operating environment.

No matter how clever we are in writing our programs, we can do little to compensate for the poor performance of any of the system components on which our programs rely. We invite you to delve into Chapter 11, where we present a more detailed study of system performance issues.

FURTHER READING

The most interesting material in the area of system software is that which accompanies certain vendor products. In fact, you can often judge the quality of a vendor's product by the quality and care with which the documentation is prepared. A visit to a vendor's website may sometimes reward you with a first-rate presentation of the theoretical basis for their products. Two of the best vendor websites at this writing are those of IBM and Sun: www.software.ibm.com and java.sun.com. If you persevere, undoubtedly, you will find others.

Hall's (1994) book on client-server systems provides an excellent introduction to client-server theory. It explores a number of products that were popular when the book was written.

Stallings (2012), Tanenbaum and Woodhull (2006), and Silberschatz, Galvin, and Gagne (2009) all provide excellent coverage of the operating systems concepts introduced in this chapter, as well as more advanced topics. Stallings includes detailed examples of various operating systems and their relationship to the actual hardware of the machine. An illuminating account of the development of OS/360 can be found in Brooks (1995).

Gorsline's (1988) assembly book offers one of the better treatments of how assemblers work. He also delves into the details of linking and macro assembly. Aho, Sethi, and Ullman (1986) wrote "the definitive" compiler book. Often called "The Dragon Book" because of its cover illustration, it has remained in print for nearly two decades because of its clear, comprehensive coverage of compiler theory. Every serious computer scientist should have this book nearby.

The May 2005 issue of *IEEE Computer* is devoted to virtualization technologies. The article by Smith and Nair is especially recommended. Rosenblum and Garfinkel provide an interesting discussion of the challenges faced in the design of virtual machine monitors from a historical viewpoint.

There are very few server farms that haven't adopted some manner of consolidation and virtualization. Virtualized server operating systems is a lucrative niche market. To learn more, you can visit the websites of the leading VM software providers, including Citrix (Citrix.com), VMWare (vmware.com), Microsoft (microsoft.com/hyper-v-server), and IBM (ibm.com).

Sun Microsystems is the primary source for anything concerning the Java language. Addison-Wesley publishes a series of books detailing Java's finer points. *The Java Virtual Machine Specification* by Lindholm and Yellin (1999) is one of the books in the series. It will supply you with some of the specifics of class file construction that we glossed over in this introductory material. Lindholm and Yellin's book also includes a complete listing of Java bytecode instructions with their binary equivalents. A careful study of this work will certainly give you a new perspective on the language.

Although somewhat dated, Gray and Reuter's (1993) transaction processing book is comprehensive and easy to read. It will give you a good foundation for further studies in this area. A highly regarded and comprehensive treatment of database theory and applications can be found in Silberschatz, Korth, and Sudarshan (2010).

REFERENCES

Aho, A. V., Sethi, R., & Ullman, J. D. *Compilers: Principles, Techniques, and Tools.* Reading, MA: Addison-Wesley, 1986.

Brooks, F. *The Mythical Man-Month.* Reading, MA: Addison-Wesley, 1995.

Gorsline, G. W. *Assembly and Assemblers: The Motorola MC68000 Family.* Englewood Cliffs, NJ: Prentice Hall, 1988.

Gray, J., & Reuter, A. *Transaction Processing: Concepts and Techniques.* San Mateo, CA: Morgan Kaufmann, 1993.

Hall, C. *Technical Foundations of Client/Server Systems.* New York: Wiley, 1994.

Lindholm, T., & Yellin, F. *The Java Virtual Machine Specification*, 2nd ed. Reading, MA: Addison-Wesley, 1999.

Rosenblum, M., & Garfinkel, T. "Virtual Machine Monitors: Current Technology and Future Trends." *IEEE Computer 38*:5, May 2005, pp. 39–47.

Silberschatz, A., Galvin, P., & Gagne, G. *Operating System Concepts*, 8th ed. Reading, MA: Addison-Wesley, 2009.

Silberschatz, A., Korth, H. F., & Sudarshan, S. *Database System Concepts*, 6th ed. Boston, MA: McGraw-Hill, 2010.

Smith, J. E., & Nair, R. "The Architecture of Virtual Machines." *IEEE Computer 38*:5, May 2005, pp. 32–38.

Stallings, W. *Operating Systems*, 7th ed. New York: Macmillan Publishing Company, 2012.

Tanenbaum, A., & Woodhull, A. *Operating Systems, Design and Implementation*, 3rd ed. Englewood Cliffs, NJ: Prentice Hall, 2006.

REVIEW OF ESSENTIAL TERMS AND CONCEPTS

1. What was the main objective of early operating systems as compared to the goals of today's systems?
2. What improvements to computer operations were brought about by resident monitors?
3. With regard to printer output, how was the word *spool* derived?
4. Describe how multiprogramming systems differ from timesharing systems.
5. What is the most critical factor in the operation of hard real-time systems?
6. Multiprocessor systems can be classified by the way in which they communicate. How are they classified in this chapter?
7. How is a distributed operating system different from a networked operating system?
8. What is meant by transparency?
9. Describe the two divergent philosophies concerning operating system kernel design.

10. What are the benefits and drawbacks to a GUI operating system interface?

11. How is long-term process scheduling different from short-term process scheduling?

12. What is meant by preemptive scheduling?

13. Which method of process scheduling is most useful in a timesharing environment?

14. Which process scheduling method is provably optimal?

15. Describe the steps involved in performing a context switch.

16. Besides process management, what are the other two important functions of an operating system?

17. What is an overlay? Why are overlays no longer needed in large computer systems?

18. The operating system and a user program hold two different perceptions of a virtual machine. Explain how they differ.

19. What is the difference between a subsystem and a logical partition?

20. Name some advantages of server consolidation. Is server consolidation a good idea for every enterprise?

21. Describe the programming language hierarchy. Why is a triangle a suitable symbol for representing this hierarchy?

22. How does absolute code differ from relocatable code?

23. What is the purpose of a link editor? How is it different from a dynamic link library?

24. Describe the purpose of each phase of a compiler.

25. How does an interpreter differ from a compiler?

26. What is the salient feature of the Java programming language that provides for its portability across disparate hardware environments?

27. Assemblers produce machine code that is executable after it has been link edited. Java compilers produce _____ that is interpreted during its execution.

28. What is a magic number that identifies a Java class file?

29. How is a logical database schema different from a physical database schema?

30. Which data structure is most commonly used to index databases?

31. Why are database reorganizations necessary?

32. Explain the ACID properties of a database system.

33. What is a race condition?

34. Database logs serve two purposes. What are they?

35. What services do transaction managers provide?

EXERCISES

1. What do you feel are the limitations of a computer that has no operating system? How would a user load and execute a program?

2. Microkernels attempt to provide as small a kernel as possible, putting much of the operating system support into additional modules. What do you feel are the minimum services that the kernel must provide?

3. If you were writing code for a real-time operating system, what restrictions might you want to impose on the system? Hint: Think about the types of things that cause unpredictable reaction times. (How might a memory access be delayed, for example?)

4. What is the difference between multiprogramming and multiprocessing? Multiprogramming and multithreading?

♦5. Under what circumstances is it desirable to collect groups of processes and programs into subsystems running on a large computer? What advantages would there be to creating logical partitions on this system?

6. What advantages would there be to using both subsystems and logical partitions on the same machine?

♦7. When is it appropriate to use nonrelocatable binary program code? Why is relocatable code preferred?

8. Suppose there were no such thing as relocatable program code. How would the process of memory paging be made more complex?

♦9. Discuss the advantages and disadvantages of dynamic linking.

10. What problems does an assembler have to overcome in order to produce complete binary code in one pass over the source file? How would code written for a one-pass assembler be different from code written for a two-pass assembler?

11. Why should assembly language be avoided for general application development? Under what circumstances is assembly language preferred or required?

12. Under what circumstances would you argue in favor of using assembly language code for developing an application program?

13. What are the advantages of using a compiled language over an interpreted one? Under what circumstances would you choose to use an interpreted language?

14. Discuss the following questions relative to compilers:

    a) Which phase of a compiler would give you a syntax error?

    b) Which phase complains about undefined variables?

    c) If you try to add an integer to a character string, which compiler phase would emit the error message?

15. Why is the execution environment of a Java class called a virtual machine? How does this virtual machine compare to a real machine running code written in C?

16. Why do you suppose the method area of a JVM is global to all of the threads running in the virtual machine environment?

17. We stated that only one method at a time can be active within each thread running in the JVM. Why do you think this is the case?

18. The Java bytecode for access to the local variable array for a class is at most two bytes long. One byte is used for the opcode; the other indicates the offset into the array. How many variables can be held in the local variable array? What do you think happens when this number is exceeded?

♦19. Java is called an interpreted language, yet Java is a compiled language that produces a binary output stream. Explain how this language can be both compiled and interpreted.

20. We stated that the performance of a Java program running in the JVM cannot possibly match that of a regular compiled language. Explain why this is so.

◆21. Answer the following with respect to database processing:

   a) What is a race condition? Give an example.

   b) How can race conditions be prevented?

   c) What are the risks in race condition prevention?

22. In what ways are *n*-tiered transaction processing architectures superior to single-tiered architectures? Which usually costs more?

23. To improve performance, your company has decided to replicate its product database across several servers so that not all transactions go through a single system. What sorts of issues will need to be considered?

24. We said that the risk of deadlock is always present anytime a system resource is locked. Describe a way in which deadlock can occur.

* 25. Research various command line interfaces (such as Unix, MS-DOS, and VMS) and different windows interfaces (such as any Microsoft Windows product, MacOS, and KDE).

   a) Consider some of the major commands, such as getting a directory listing, deleting a file, or changing directories. Explain how each of these commands is implemented on the various operating systems you studied.

   b) List and explain some of the commands that are easier using a command line interface versus using a GUI. List and explain some of the commands that are easier using a GUI versus using a command line interface.

   c) Which type of interface do you prefer? Why?

Quality is never an accident; it is always the result of intelligent effort.

—John Ruskin

It would appear that we have reached the limits of what it is possible to achieve with computer technology, although one should be careful with such statements, as they tend to sound pretty silly in 5 years.

—John von Neumann, 1949.
Reprinted by permission
of Marina von Neumann Whitman.

CHAPTER 9 Alternative Architectures

9.1 INTRODUCTION

Our previous chapters have featured excursions into the background of computing technology. The presentations have been distinctly focused on uniprocessor systems from a computer science practitioner's point of view. We hope you have gained an understanding of the functions of various hardware components and can see how each contributes to overall system performance. This understanding is vital not only to hardware design, but also to efficient algorithm implementation. Most people gain familiarity with computer hardware through their experiences with personal computers and workstations. This leaves one significant area of computer architecture untouched: that of alternative architectures. Therefore, the focus of this chapter is to introduce you to a few of the architectures that transcend the classical von Neumann approach.

This chapter discusses RISC machines, architectures that exploit instruction-level parallelism, and multiprocessing architectures (with a brief introduction to parallel processing). We begin with the notorious RISC-versus-CISC debate to give you an idea of the differences between these two ISAs and their relative advantages and disadvantages. We then provide a taxonomy by which the various architectures may be classified, with a view as to how the parallel architectures fit into the classification. Next, we consider topics relevant to instruction-level parallel architectures, emphasizing superscalar architectures and reintroducing EPIC (explicitly parallel instruction computers). We then look at alteratives to RISC and CISC by revisting VLIW (which uses instruction-level parallelism) and introducing vector processors. Finally, we provide a brief introduction to multiprocessor systems and some alternative approaches to parallelism, including systolic arrays, dataflow computing, neural networks, and quantum computing.

Computer hardware designers began to reevaluate various architectural principles in the early 1980s. The first target of this reevaluation was the instruction set architecture. The designers wondered why a machine needed an extensive set of complex instructions when only about 20% of the instructions were used most of the time. This question led to the development of RISC machines, which we first introduced in Chapters 4 and 5, and to which we now devote an entire section of this chapter. The pervasiveness of RISC designs has led to a unique marriage of CISC and RISC. Many architectures now employ RISC cores to implement CISC architectures.

Chapters 4 and 5 described how new architectures, such as VLIW, EPIC, and multiprocessors, are taking over a large percentage of the hardware market. The invention of architectures exploiting instruction-level parallelism has led to techniques that accurately predict the outcome of branches in program code before the code is executed. Prefetching instructions based on these predictions has greatly increased computer performance. In addition to predicting the next instruction to fetch, high degrees of instruction-level parallelism have given rise to ideas such as speculative execution, where the processor guesses the value of a result before it has actually been calculated.

The subject of alternative architectures also includes multiprocessor systems. For these architectures, we return to the lesson we learned from our ancestors and the friendly ox. If we are using an ox to pull out a tree, and the tree is too large, we don't try to grow a bigger ox. Instead, we use two oxen. Multiprocessing architectures are analogous to the oxen. We need them if we are to budge the stumps of intractable problems. However, multiprocessor systems present us with unique challenges, particularly with respect to cache coherence and memory consistency.

We note that although some of these alternative architectures are taking hold, their real advancement is dependent on their incremental cost. Currently, the relationship between the performance delivered by advanced systems and their cost is nonlinear, with the cost far exceeding performance gains in most situations. This makes it cost-prohibitive to integrate these architectures into mainstream applications. Alternative architectures do have their place in the market, however. Highly numerical science and engineering applications demand machines that outperform standard uniprocessor systems. For computers in this league, cost is usually not an issue.

As you read this chapter, keep in mind the previous computer generations introduced in Chapter 1. Many people believe we have entered a new generation based on these alternative architectures, particularly in the area of parallel processing.

9.2   RISC MACHINES

We introduced RISC architectures in the context of some example systems in Chapter 4. RISC is not so much an architecture as it is a design philosophy. Recall that RISC machines are so named because they originally offered a smaller instruction set as compared to CISC machines. As RISC machines were being developed, the term "reduced" became somewhat of a misnomer, and is even more so now. The original idea was to provide a set of minimal instructions that could carry out all essential operations: data movement, ALU operations, and branching. Only explicit `load` and `store` instructions were permitted access to memory.

Complex instruction set designs were motivated by the high cost of memory. Having more complexity packed into each instruction meant that programs could be smaller, thus occupying less storage. When memory was small, it was important to have small programs, so CISC dominated as a natural outgrowth of computer technology at the time. CISC ISAs employ variable-length instructions, keeping the simple instructions short, while also allowing for longer, more complicated instructions. Additionally, CISC architectures include a large number of instructions that directly access memory. So what we have at this point is a dense, powerful, variable-length set of instructions, which results in a varying number of clock cycles per instruction. Some complex instructions, particularly those instructions that access memory, require hundreds of cycles. In certain circumstances, computer designers have found it necessary to slow down the system clock (making the interval between clock ticks larger) to allow sufficient time for instructions to complete. This all adds up to longer execution time.

Human languages exhibit some of the qualities of RISC and CISC and serve as a good analogy to understand the differences between the two. Suppose you have a Chinese pen pal. Let's assume that each of you speak and write fluently in both English and Chinese. You both wish to keep the cost of your correspondence at a minimum, although you both enjoy sharing long letters. You have a choice between using expensive airmail paper, which will save considerable postage, or using plain paper and paying extra for stamps. A third alternative is to pack more information onto each written page.

As compared to the Chinese language, English is simple but verbose. Chinese characters are more complex than English words, and what might require 200 English letters might require only 20 Chinese characters. Corresponding in Chinese requires fewer symbols, saving on both paper and postage. However, reading and writing Chinese requires more effort, because each symbol contains more information. The English words are analogous to RISC instructions, whereas the Chinese symbols are analogous to CISC instructions. For most English-speaking people, "processing" the letter in English would take less time, but would also require more physical resources.

Although many sources tout RISC as a new and revolutionary design, its seeds were sown in the mid-1970s through the work of IBM's John Cocke. Cocke started building his experimental Model 801 mainframe in 1975. This system initially received little attention, its details being disclosed only many years later. In the interim, David Patterson and David Ditzel published their widely acclaimed "Case for a Reduced Instruction Set Computer" in 1980. This paper gave birth to a radically new way of thinking about computer architecture and brought the acronyms **CISC** and **RISC** into the lexicon of computer science. The new architecture proposed by Patterson and Ditzel advocated simple instructions, all of the same length. Each instruction would perform less work, but the time required for instruction execution would be constant and predictable.

Support for RISC machines came by way of programming observations on CISC machines. These studies revealed that data movement instructions accounted for approximately 45% of all instructions, ALU operations (including arithmetic, comparison, and logical) accounted for 25%, and branching (or flow control) amounted to 30%. Although many complex instructions existed, few were used. This finding, coupled with the advent of cheaper and more plentiful memory, and the development of VLSI technology, led to a different type of architecture. Cheaper memory meant that programs could use more storage. Larger programs consisting of simple, predictable instructions could replace shorter programs consisting of complicated and variable-length instructions. Simple instructions would allow the use of shorter clock cycles. In addition, having fewer instructions would mean that fewer transistors were needed on the chip. Fewer transistors translated to cheaper manufacturing costs and more chip real estate available for other uses. Instruction predictability coupled with VLSI advances would allow various performance-enhancing tricks, such as pipelining, to be implemented in hardware. CISC does not provide this diverse array of performance-enhancement opportunities.

We can quantify the differences between RISC and CISC using the basic computer performance equation as follows:

$$\frac{\text{time}}{\text{program}} = \frac{\text{time}}{\text{cycle}} \times \frac{\text{cycles}}{\text{instruction}} \times \frac{\text{instructions}}{\text{program}}$$

Computer performance, as measured by program execution time, is directly proportional to clock cycle time, the number of clock cycles per instruction, and the number of instructions in the program. Shortening the clock cycle, when possible, results in improved performance for RISC as well as CISC. Otherwise, CISC machines increase performance by reducing the number of instructions per program. RISC computers minimize the number of cycles per instruction. Yet both architectures can produce identical results in approximately the same amount of time. At the gate level, both systems perform an equivalent quantity of work. So what's going on between the program level and the gate level?

CISC machines rely on microcode to tackle instruction complexity. Microcode tells the processor how to execute each instruction. For performance reasons, microcode is compact and efficient, and it certainly must be correct. Microcode efficiency, however, is limited by variable-length instructions, which slow the decoding process, and a varying number of clock cycles per instruction, which makes it difficult to implement instruction pipelines. Moreover, microcode interprets each instruction as it is fetched from memory. This additional translation process takes time. The more complex the instruction set, the more time it takes to look up the instruction and engage the hardware suitable for its execution.

RISC architectures take a different approach. Most RISC instructions execute in one clock cycle. To accomplish this speedup, microprogrammed control is replaced by hardwired control, which is faster at executing instructions. This makes it easier to do instruction pipelining, but more difficult to deal with complexity at the hardware level. In RISC systems, the complexity removed from the instruction set is pushed up a level into the domain of the compiler.

To illustrate, let's look at an instruction. Suppose we want to compute the product, 5×10. The code on a CISC machine might look like this:

```
mov ax, 10
mov bx, 5
mul bx, ax
```

A minimalistic RISC ISA has no multiplication instructions. Thus, on a RISC system, our multiplication problem would look like this:

```
       mov ax, 0
       mov bx, 10
       mov cx, 5
Begin: add ax, bx
       loop Begin    ;causes a loop cx times
```

The CISC code, although shorter, requires more clock cycles to execute. Suppose that on each architecture, register-to-register moves, addition, and loop operations each consume one clock cycle. Suppose also that a multiplication operation requires 30 clock cycles.[1] Comparing the two code fragments, we have:

CISC instructions:

Total clock cycles = (2 `movs` $\times$ 1 clock cycle) + (1 `mul` $\times$ 30 clock cycles)

= 32 clock cycles

RISC instructions:

Total clock cycles = (3 `movs` $\times$ 1 clock cycle) + (5 `adds` $\times$ 1 clock cycle)

+ (5 `loops` $\times$ 1 clock cycle)

= 13 clock cycles

Add to this the fact that RISC clock cycles are often shorter than CISC clock cycles, and it should be clear that even though there are more instructions, the actual execution time is less for RISC than for CISC. This is the main inspiration behind the RISC design.

We have mentioned that reducing instruction complexity results in simpler chips. Transistors formerly employed in the execution of CISC instructions are used for pipelines, cache, and registers. Of these three, registers offer the greatest potential for improved performance, so it makes sense to increase the number of registers and to use them in innovative ways. One such innovation is the use of **register window sets**. Although not as widely accepted as other innovations associated with RISC architectures, register windowing is nevertheless an interesting idea and is briefly introduced here.

---

[1]This is not an unrealistic number—a multiplication on an Intel 8088 requires 133 clock cycles for two 16-bit numbers.

High-level languages depend on modularization for efficiency. Procedure calls and parameter passing are natural side effects of using these modules. Calling a procedure is not a trivial task. It involves saving a return address, preserving register values, passing parameters (either by pushing them on a stack or using registers), branching to the subroutine, and executing the subroutine. Upon subroutine completion, parameter value modifications must be saved, and previous register values must be restored before returning execution to the calling program. Saving registers, passing parameters, and restoring registers involves considerable effort and resources. With RISC chips having the capacity for hundreds of registers, the saving and restoring sequence can be reduced to simply changing register environments.

To fully understand this concept, try to envision all registers as being divided into sets. When a program is executing in one environment, only one certain register set is visible. If the program changes to a different environment (say a procedure is called), the visible set of registers for the new environment changes. For example, while the main program is running, perhaps it sees only registers 0 through 9. When a certain procedure is called, perhaps it will see registers 10 through 19. Typical values for real RISC architectures include 16 register sets (or **windows**) of 32 registers each. The CPU is restricted to operating in only one single window at any given time. Therefore, from the programmer's perspective, there are only 32 registers available.

Register windows, by themselves, do not necessarily help with procedure calls or parameter passing. However, if these windows are overlapped carefully, the act of passing parameters from one module to another becomes a simple matter of shifting from one register set to another, allowing the two sets to overlap in exactly those registers that must be shared to perform the parameter passing. This is accomplished by dividing the register window set into distinct partitions, including **global registers** (common to all windows), **local registers** (local to the current window), **input registers** (which overlap with the preceding window's output registers), and **output registers** (which overlap with the next window's input registers). When the CPU switches from one procedure to the next, it switches to a different register window, but the overlapping windows allow parameters to be "passed" simply by changing from output registers in the calling module to input registers in the called module. A **current window pointer (CWP)** points to the register window set to be used at any given time.

Consider a scenario in which Procedure One is calling Procedure Two. Of the 32 registers in each set, assume that 8 are global, 8 are local, 8 are for input, and 8 are for output. When Procedure One calls Procedure Two, any parameters that need to be passed are put into the output register set of Procedure One. Once Procedure Two begins execution, these registers become the input register set for Procedure Two. This process is illustrated in Figure 9.1.

One more important piece of information to note regarding register windows on RISC machines is the circular nature of the set of registers. For programs having a high degree of nesting, it is possible to exhaust the supply of registers. When this happens, main memory takes over, storing the lowest numbered windows, which contain values from the oldest procedure activations. The highest

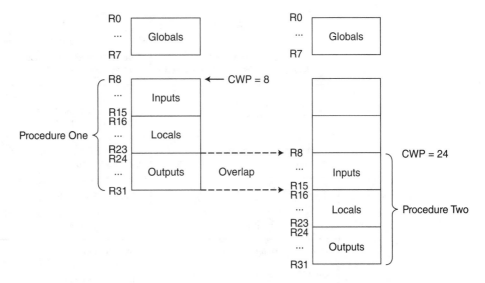

FIGURE 9.1   Overlapping Register Windows

numbered register locations (the most recent activations) then wrap around to the lowest numbered registers. As returns from procedures are executed, the level of nesting decreases, and register values from memory are restored in the order in which they were saved.

In addition to simple, fixed-length instructions, efficient pipelines in RISC machines have provided these architectures with an enormous increase in speed. Simpler instructions have freed up chip real estate, resulting in not only more usable space, but also in chips that are easier and less time consuming to design and manufacture.

You should be aware that it is becoming increasingly difficult to categorize today's processors as either RISC or CISC, as most CPU architectures have evolved into combinations of the two. The lines separating these architectures have blurred. Some current architectures use both approaches. If you browse some of the newer chip manuals, you will see that today's RISC machines have more extravagant and more complex instructions than some CISC machines. The RISC PowerPC, for example, has a larger instruction set than the CISC Pentium. Most RISC processors today have added multiplication and division instructions, utilizing microcode to execute these instructions. On the other hand, most recent CISC processors are, to some extent, RISC based; Intel's x86 architecture is a prime example. The x86's CISC instructions are converted to an internal RISC format, before being executed, by using microcode to convert complex instructions into simpler ones that are then executed via hardware. As VLSI technology continues to make transistors smaller and cheaper, the expansiveness of the instruction set is now becoming less of an issue in the CISC-versus-RISC debate, whereas register usage and the load/store architecture are becoming more prominent.

With that being said, we cautiously provide Table 9.1 as a summary of the classical differences between RISC and CISC.

RISC	CISC
Multiple register sets, often consisting of more than 256 registers	Single register set, typically 6 to 16 registers total
Three register operands allowed per instruction (e.g., `add R1, R2, R3`)	One or two register operands allowed per instruction (e.g., `add R1, R2`)
Parameter passing through efficient on-chip register windows	Parameter passing through inefficient off-chip memory
Single-cycle instructions (except for `load` and `store`)	Multiple-cycle instructions
Hardwired control	Microprogrammed control
Highly pipelined	Less pipelined
Simple instructions that are few in number	Many complex instructions
Fixed-length instructions	Variable-length instructions
Complexity in compiler	Complexity in microcode
Only load and store instructions can access memory	Many instructions can access memory
Few addressing modes	Many addressing modes

TABLE 9.1 The Characteristics of RISC Machines versus CISC Machines

We have stated that RISC is somewhat of a misnomer. Although the original goal was to reduce the instruction set, the RISC design philosophy has evolved. As stated by Paul DeMone, the major focus of RISC can now be summarized as follows: "No instruction or addressing mode whose function can be implemented by a sequence of other instructions should be included in the ISA unless its inclusion can be quantitatively shown to improve performance by a non-trivial amount, even after accounting for the new instruction's negative impact on likely hardware implementations in terms of increased data path and control complexity, reduction in clock rate, and conflict with efficient implementation of existing instructions." A secondary design philosophy mandates that RISC processors should not execute anything at run time via hardware that can be done at compile time via software.

We have indicated that although the two architectures, CISC and RISC, originally had clear-cut distinctions, they have evolved toward each other to such an extent that computer architectures of today no longer fit precisely into either category. In fact, the terms *RISC* and *CISC* had essentially lost most of their significance—until the advent of embedded systems, most notably mobile computing. Phones and tablets need processors that can efficiently utilize memory,

CPU cycles, and power, in addition to being relatively inexpensive to make; the RISC design philosophy is a perfect fit for this environment.

When the RISC-versus-CISC debate first began, the focus was on chip area and processor design complexity, but now energy and power are the focal points. There are two competitors worth mentioning who are vying for control of the market: ARM and Intel. Whereas Intel has typically focused on performance, giving it the lead in the server market, ARM has focused on efficiency, giving it the lead in the mobile and embedded systems market. (In fact, ARM's new 64-bit processor is given significant credit for bringing relevance back to the RISC-versus-CISC debate.) Intel is attempting to take the lead in the mobile market with its Atom processor. However, the Atom is suffering from its CISC legacy (in particular, its bloated ISA), which is why RISC architectures such as ARM and MIPS are preferred choices in this market. Even though Intel is employing a few other tricks to speed up execution, cumbersome decode hardware and an instruction set filled with unused instructions are still issues.

As we have mentioned, although many sources praise the revolutionary innovations of RISC design, many of the ideas used in RISC machines (including pipelining and simple instructions) were implemented on mainframes in the 1960s and 1970s. There are many so-called new designs that aren't really new, but are simply recycled. Innovation does not necessarily mean inventing a new wheel; it may be a simple case of figuring out the best way to use a wheel that already exists. This is a lesson that will serve you well in your career in the computing field.

9.3 FLYNN'S TAXONOMY

Over the years, several attempts have been made to find a satisfactory way to categorize computer architectures. Although none of them are perfect, today's most widely accepted taxonomy is the one proposed by Michael Flynn in 1972. **Flynn's taxonomy** considers two factors: the number of instructions and the number of data streams that flow into the processor. A machine can have either one or multiple streams of data, and can have either one or multiple processors working on this data. This gives us four possible combinations: **SISD (single instruction stream, single data stream), SIMD (single instruction stream, multiple data streams), MISD (multiple instruction streams, single data stream)**, and **MIMD (multiple instruction streams, multiple data streams)**.

Uniprocessors are SISD machines. SIMD machines, which have a single point of control, execute the same instruction simultaneously on multiple data values. The SIMD category includes array processors, vector processors, and systolic arrays. MISD machines have multiple instruction streams operating on the same data stream. MIMD machines, which employ multiple control points, have independent instruction and data streams. Multiprocessors and most current parallel systems are MIMD machines. SIMD computers are simpler to design than MIMD machines, but they are also considerably less flexible. All of the SIMD multiprocessors must execute the *same* instruction simultaneously. If you think about this, executing something as simple as conditional branching could quickly become very expensive.

Flynn's taxonomy falls short in several areas. For one, there seem to be very few (if any) applications for MISD machines. Secondly, Flynn assumed that parallelism was homogeneous. A collection of processors can be homogeneous or heterogeneous. A machine could conceivably have four separate floating-point adders, two multipliers, and a single integer unit. This machine could therefore execute seven operations in parallel, but it does not readily fit into Flynn's classification system.

Another problem with this taxonomy is with the MIMD category. An architecture with multiple processors falls into this category without consideration for how the processors are connected or how they view memory. There have been several attempts to refine the MIMD category. Suggested changes include subdividing MIMD to differentiate systems that share memory from those that don't, as well as categorizing processors according to whether they are bus based or switched.

Shared memory systems are those in which all processors have access to a global memory and communicate through shared variables, just as processes do on a uniprocessor. If multiple processors do not share memory, each processor must own a portion of memory. Consequently, all processors must communicate by way of message passing, which can be expensive and inefficient. The issue some people have with using memory as a determining factor for classifying hardware is that shared memory and message passing are actually programming models, not hardware models. Thus, they more properly belong in the domain of system software.

The two major parallel architectural paradigms, **symmetric multiprocessors (SMPs)** and **massively parallel processors (MPPs)**, are both MIMD architectures, but differ in how they use memory. SMP machines, such as a dual-processor Intel PC and the Silicon Graphics Origin 3900 (that scales up to 512 processors), share memory, whereas MPP processors, such as the nCube, CM5, and Cray T3E, do not. These particular MPP machines typically house thousands of CPUs in a single large cabinet connected to hundreds of gigabytes of memory. The price of these systems can run into millions of dollars.

Originally, the term *MPP* described tightly coupled SIMD multiprocessors, such as the Connection Machine and Goodyear's MPP. Today, however, the term *MPP* is used to refer to parallel architectures that have multiple self-contained nodes with private memories, all of which have the ability to communicate via a network. An easy way to differentiate SMP and MPP (by today's definition) is the following:

MPP = many processors + distributed memory + communication via network

and

SMP = few processors + shared memory + communication via memory

MPP computers are harder to program because the programmer must make sure that the pieces of the program running on separate CPUs can communicate with each other. However, SMP machines suffer from a serious bottleneck when all processors attempt to access the same memory at the same time. The decision to use MPP or SMP depends on the application—if the problem is easily partitioned, MPP is a good option. Large companies frequently use MPP systems to store customer data (data warehousing) and to perform data mining on that data.

Distributed computing is another example of the MIMD architecture. **Distributed computing** (covered in more detail in Section 9.4.5) is typically defined as a set of networked computers that work collaboratively to solve a problem. This collaboration, however, can occur in many different ways.

A **network of workstations (NOW)** is a collection of distributed workstations that works in parallel only while the nodes are not being used as regular workstations. NOWs typically consist of heterogeneous systems, with different processors and software, that communicate via the Internet. Individual users must establish the appropriate connection to the network before joining the parallel computation. NOWs are often deployed in organizations using building or corporate intranets, in which all the workstations can be controlled. A **cluster of workstations (COW)** is a collection similar to a NOW, but it requires that a single entity be in charge. Nodes typically have common software, and a user that can access one node can usually access all nodes. A **dedicated cluster parallel computer (DCPC)** is a collection of workstations specifically collected to work on a given parallel computation. The workstations have common software and file systems, are managed by a single entity, communicate via the Internet, and aren't used as workstations. A **pile of PCs (PoPC)** is a cluster of dedicated heterogeneous hardware used to build a parallel system out of mass market commodity components, or COTs. Whereas a DCPC has relatively few but expensive and fast components, a PoPC uses a large number of slow but relatively cheap nodes. NOWs, COWs, DCPCs, and PoPCs are all examples of **cluster computing**, distributed computing in which the resources are all within the same administrative domain, working on group tasks.

The BEOWULF project, introduced in 1994 by Thomas Sterling and Donald Becker of the Goddard Space Flight Center, is a PoPC architecture that has successfully bundled various hardware platforms with specially designed software, resulting in an architecture that has the look and feel of a unified parallel machine. A BEOWULF cluster has three defining characteristics: off-the-shelf personal computers, fast data switching, and open source software. The nodes on a BEOWULF network are always connected via a private Ethernet or fiber network. If you have an old Sun SPARC, a couple of 486 machines, a DEC Alpha (or simply a large collection of dusty Intel machines!), and a means to connect them into a network, you can install the BEOWULF software and create your own personal, but extremely powerful, parallel computer.

Flynn's taxonomy has recently been expanded to include **SPMD (single program multiple data)** architectures. An SPMD consists of multiprocessors, each with its own data set and program memory. The same program is executed on each processor, with synchronization at various global control points. Although each processor loads the same program, each may execute different instructions. For example, a program may have code that resembles:

```
If myNodeNum = 1 do this, else do that
```

In this way, different nodes execute different instructions within the same program. SPMD is actually a programming paradigm used on MIMD machines and differs from SIMD in that the processors can do different things at the same time. Supercomputers often use an SPMD design.

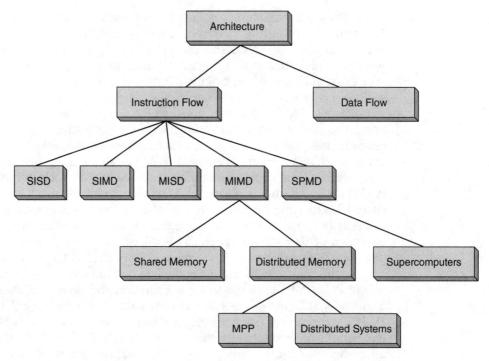

FIGURE 9.2 A Taxonomy of Computer Architectures

At a level above where Flynn begins his taxonomy, we need to add one more characteristic, and that is whether the architecture is instruction driven or data driven. The classic von Neumann architecture is instruction driven. All processor activities are determined by a sequence of program code. Program instructions act *on* the data. Data-driven, or **dataflow**, architectures do just the opposite. The characteristics of the data determine the sequence of processor events. We explore this idea in more detail in Section 9.5.

With the addition of dataflow computers and some refinements to the MIMD classification, we obtain the taxonomy shown in Figure 9.2. You may wish to refer to it as you read the sections that follow. We begin on the left-hand branch of the tree, with topics relevant to SIMD and MIMD architectures.

9.4 PARALLEL AND MULTIPROCESSOR ARCHITECTURES

Since the beginning of computing, scientists have endeavored to make machines solve problems better and faster. Miniaturization technology has resulted in improved circuitry, and more of it on a chip. Clocks have become faster, leading to CPUs in the gigahertz range. However, we know that there are physical barriers that control the extent to which single-processor performance can be improved. Heat and electromagnetic interference limit chip transistor density. Even if (when?) these problems are solved, processor speeds will always be constrained by the speed of light. On top of these physical limitations, there are also economic limitations. At some point, the cost of making a processor incrementally faster will exceed the price that anyone is willing to pay. Ultimately, we will be left with no feasible way of improving processor performance except to distribute the computational load among several processors. For these reasons, parallelism is becoming increasingly popular.

It is important to note, however, that not all applications can benefit from parallelism. For example, multiprocessing parallelism adds cost (such as process synchronization and other aspects of process administration). If an application isn't amenable to a parallel solution, generally it is not cost-effective to port it to a multiprocessing parallel architecture.

Implemented correctly, parallelism results in higher throughput, better fault tolerance, and a more attractive price/performance ratio. Although parallelism can result in significant speedup, this speedup can never be perfect. Given n processors running in parallel, perfect speedup would imply that a computational job could complete in $\frac{1}{n}$ time, leading to an n-fold increase in power (or a run-time decrease by a factor of n).

We need only recall Amdahl's Law to realize why perfect speedup is not possible. If two processing components run at two different speeds, the slower speed will dominate. This law also governs the speedup attainable using parallel processors on a problem. No matter how well you parallelize an application, there will always be a small portion of work done by one processor that must be done serially. Additional processors can do nothing but wait until the serial processing is complete. The underlying premise is that every algorithm has a sequential part that ultimately limits the speedup achievable through a multiprocessor implementation. The greater the sequential processing, the less cost-effective it is to employ a multiprocessing parallel architecture.

Using multiple processors on a single task is only one of many different types of parallelism. In earlier chapters, we introduced a few of these including pipelining, VLIW, and instruction-level parallelism (ILP), giving motivations for each particular type. Other parallel architectures deal with multiple (or parallel) data. Examples include SIMD machines such as vector, neural, and systolic processors. There are many architectures that allow for multiple or parallel processes, characteristic of all MIMD machines. It is important to note that "parallel" can have many different meanings, and it is equally important to be able to differentiate among them.

We begin this section with a discussion of examples of ILP architectures, and then move on to SIMD and MIMD architectures. The last section introduces alternative (less mainstream) parallel processing approaches, including systolic arrays, neural networks, and dataflow computing.

9.4.1 Superscalar and VLIW

In this section, we revisit the concept of superscalar architectures and compare them to VLIW architectures. Superscalar and VLIW architectures both exhibit instruction-level parallelism, but differ in their approach. To set the stage for our discussion, we start with a definition of superpipelining. Recall that pipelining divides the fetch–decode–execute cycle into stages, in which a set of instructions is in different stages at the same time. In a perfect world, one instruction would exit the pipe every clock cycle. However, because of branching instructions and data dependencies in the code, the goal of one instruction per cycle is never quite achieved.

Superpipelining occurs when a pipeline has stages that require less than half a clock cycle to execute. An internal clock can be added that, when running at double the speed of the external clock, can complete two tasks per external clock cycle. Although superpipelining is equally applicable to both RISC and CISC architectures, it is most often incorporated in RISC processors. Superpipelining is one aspect of superscalar design, and for this reason, there is often confusion regarding which is which.

So, what exactly is a superscalar processor? We know that the Pentium processor is superscalar, but have yet to discuss what this really means. **Superscalar** is a design methodology that allows multiple instructions to be executed simultaneously in each cycle. Although superscalar differs from pipelining in several ways that will be discussed shortly, the net effect is the same. The way in which superscalar designs achieve speedup is similar to the idea of adding another lane to a busy single-lane highway. Additional "hardware" is required, but in the end, more cars (instructions) can get from point A to point B in the same amount of time.

The superscalar components analogous to our additional highway lanes are called **execution units**. Execution units consist of floating-point adders and multipliers, integer adders and multipliers, and other specialized components. Although the units may also work independently, it is important that the architecture have a sufficient number of these specialized units to process several instructions in parallel. It is not uncommon for execution units to be duplicated; for example, a system could have a pair of identical floating-point units. Often, the execution units are pipelined, providing even better performance.

A critical component of this architecture is a specialized **instruction fetch unit**, which can retrieve multiple instructions simultaneously from memory. This unit, in turn, passes the instructions to a complex **decoding unit** that determines whether the instructions are independent (and can thus be executed simultaneously) or whether a dependency of some sort exists (in which case not all instructions can be executed at the same time).

As an example, consider the IBM RS/6000. This processor had an instruction fetch unit and two processors, each containing a 6-stage floating-point unit and a 4-stage integer unit. The instruction fetch unit was set up with a 2-stage pipeline, where the first stage fetched packets of four instructions each, and the second stage delivered the instructions to the appropriate processing unit.

Superscalar computers are architectures that exhibit parallelism through pipelining and replication. Superscalar design includes superpipelining, simultaneous fetching of multiple instructions, a complex decoding unit capable of determining instruction dependencies and dynamically combining instructions to ensure that no dependencies are violated, and sufficient quantities of resources for parallel execution of multiple instructions. We note that although this type of parallelism requires very specific hardware, a superscalar architecture also requires a sophisticated compiler to schedule operations that make the best use of machine resources.

Whereas superscalar processors rely on both the hardware (to arbitrate dependencies) and the compiler (to generate approximate schedules), VLIW processors rely *entirely* on the compiler. VLIW processors pack independent instructions into one long instruction, which, in turn, tells the execution units what to do. Many argue that because the compiler has a better overall picture of dependencies in the code, this approach results in better performance. However, the compiler cannot have an overall picture of the run-time code, so it is compelled to be conservative in its scheduling.

As a VLIW compiler creates very long instructions, it also arbitrates all dependencies. These long instructions, which are fixed at compile time, typically contain four to eight regular instructions. Because the instructions are fixed, any modification that could affect scheduling of instructions (such as changing memory latency) requires a recompilation of the code, potentially causing a multitude of problems for software vendors. VLIW supporters point out that this technology simplifies the hardware by moving complexity to the compiler. Superscalar supporters counter with the argument that VLIW can, in turn, lead to significant increases in the amount of code generated. For example, when program control fields are not used, memory space and bandwidth are wasted. In fact, a typical Fortran program explodes to double and sometimes triple its normal size when compiled on a VLIW machine.

Intel's Itanium, IA-64, is one example of a VLIW processor. Recall that the IA-64 uses an EPIC style of VLIW processor. An EPIC architecture holds some advantages over an ordinary VLIW processor. Like VLIW, EPIC bundles its instructions for delivery to various execution units. However, unlike VLIW, these bundles need not be the same length. A special delimiter indicates where one bundle ends and another begins. Instruction words are prefetched by hardware, which identifies and then schedules the bundles in independent groups for parallel execution. This is an attempt to overcome the limitations introduced by the compiler's lack of total knowledge of the run-time code. Instructions within bundles may be executed in parallel with no concern for dependencies, and thus no concern for ordering. By most people's definition, EPIC is really VLIW. Although Intel might argue the point, and die-hard architects would cite the minor differences mentioned above (as well as a few others), EPIC is, in reality, an enhanced version of VLIW.

9.4.2 Vector Processors

Often referred to as supercomputers, **vector processors** are specialized, heavily pipelined SIMD processors that perform efficient operations on entire vectors and matrices at once. This class of processor is suited for applications that can benefit from a high degree of parallelism, such as weather forecasting, medical diagnosing, and image processing.

To understand vector processing, one must first understand vector arithmetic. A vector is a fixed-length, one-dimensional array of values, or an ordered series of scalar quantities. Various arithmetic operations are defined over vectors, including addition, subtraction, and multiplication.

Vector computers are highly pipelined so that arithmetic operations can be overlapped. Each instruction specifies a set of operations to be carried over an entire vector. For example, let's say we want to add vectors V1 and V2 and place the results in V3. On a traditional processor, our code would include the following loop:

```
for i = 0 to VectorLength
    V3[i] = V1[i] + V2[i];
```

However, on a vector processor, this code becomes

```
LDV   V1, R1        ;load vector1 into vector register R1
LDV   V2, R2
ADDV  R3, R1, R2
STV   R3, V3        ;store vector register R3 in vector V3
```

Vector registers are specialized registers that can hold several vector elements at one time. The register contents are sent one element at a time to a vector pipeline, and the output from the pipeline is sent back to the vector registers one element at a time. These registers are, therefore, FIFO queues capable of holding many values. Vector processors generally have several of these registers. The instruction set for a vector processor contains instructions for loading these registers, performing operations on the elements within the registers, and storing the vector data back to memory.

Vector processors are often divided into two categories according to how the instructions access their operands. **Register-register vector processors** require that all operations use registers as source and destination operands. **Memory-memory vector processors** allow operands from memory to be routed directly to the arithmetic unit. The results of the operation are then streamed back to memory. Register-to-register processors are at a disadvantage in that long vectors must be broken into fixed-length segments that are small enough to fit into the registers. However, memory-to-memory machines have a large startup time because of memory latency. (Startup time is the time between initializing the instruction and the first result emerging from the pipeline.) After the pipeline is full, however, this disadvantage disappears.

Vector instructions are efficient for two reasons. First, the machine fetches significantly fewer instructions, which means there is less decoding, control unit overhead, and memory bandwidth usage. Second, the processor knows it will have a continuous source of data and can begin prefetching corresponding pairs of values. If interleaved memory is used, one pair can arrive per clock cycle. The most famous vector processors are the Cray series of supercomputers. Their basic architecture has changed little over the past 25 years.

9.4.3 Interconnection Networks

In parallel MIMD systems, such as shared memory multiprocessors and distributed computing, communication is essential for synchronized processing and data sharing. The manner in which messages are passed among system components determines the overall system design. The two choices are to use shared memory or an interconnection network model. Shared memory systems have one large memory that is accessed identically by all processors. In interconnected systems, each processor has its own memory, but processors are allowed to access other processors' memories via the network. Both, of course, have their strengths and weaknesses.

Interconnection networks are often categorized according to topology, routing strategy, and switching technique. The **network topology**, the way in which the components are interconnected, is a major determining factor in the overhead cost of message passing. Message passing efficiency is limited by:

- **Bandwidth**—The information-carrying capacity of the network.
- **Message latency**—The time required for the first bit of a message to reach its destination.
- **Transport latency**—The time the message spends in the network.
- **Overhead**—Message-processing activities in the sender and receiver.

Accordingly, network designs attempt to minimize both the number of messages required and the distances over which they must travel.

Interconnection networks can be either **static** or **dynamic**. Dynamic networks allow the path between two entities (either two processors or a processor and a memory) to change from one communication to the next, whereas static networks do not. Interconnection networks can also be **blocking** or **nonblocking**. Nonblocking networks allow new connections in the presence of other simultaneous connections, whereas blocking networks do not.

Static interconnection networks are used mainly for message passing and include a variety of types, many of which may be familiar to you. Processors are typically interconnected using static networks, whereas processor-memory pairs usually employ dynamic networks.

Completely connected networks are those in which all components are connected to all other components. These are very expensive to build, and as new entities are added, they become difficult to manage. **Star-connected networks** have a central hub through which all messages must pass. Although a hub can be a central bottleneck, it provides excellent connectivity. **Linear array** or **ring networks** allow any entity to directly communicate with its two neighbors, but any other communication has to go through multiple entities to arrive at its destination. (The ring is just a variation of a linear array in which the two end entities are directly connected.) A **mesh network** links each entity to four or six neighbors (depending on whether it is two-dimensional or three-dimensional). Extensions of this network include those that wrap around, similar to how a linear network can wrap around to form a ring.

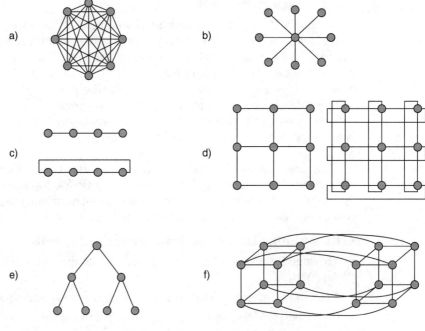

FIGURE 9.3 Static Network Topologies
a) Completely Connected
b) Star
c) Linear and Ring
d) Mesh and Mesh Ring
e) Tree
f) Four-Dimensional Hypercube

Tree networks arrange entities in noncyclic structures, which have the potential for communication bottlenecks forming at the roots. **Hypercube networks** are multidimensional extensions of mesh networks in which each dimension has two processors. (Hypercubes typically connect processors, not processor-memory sets.) Two-dimensional hypercubes consist of pairs of processors that are connected by a direct link if, and only if, the binary representation of their labels differ in exactly one bit position. In an n-dimensional hypercube, each processor is directly connected to n other processors. It is interesting to note that the total number of bit positions at which two labels of a hypercube differ is called their **Hamming distance**, which is also the term used to indicate the number of communication links in the shortest path between two processors. Figure 9.3 illustrates the various types of static networks.

Dynamic networks allow for dynamic configuration of the network in one of two ways: either by using a bus or by using a switch that can alter the routes through the network. **Bus-based networks**, illustrated in Figure 9.4, are the simplest and most efficient when cost is a concern and the number of entities is

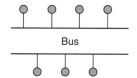

FIGURE 9.4 A Bus-Based Network

moderate. Clearly, the main disadvantage is the bottleneck that can result from bus contention as the number of entities grows large. Parallel buses can alleviate this problem, but their cost is considerable.

Switching networks use switches to dynamically alter routing. There are two types of switches: crossbar switches and 2×2 switches. **Crossbar switches** are simply switches that are either open or closed. Any entity can be connected to any other entity by closing the switch (making a connection) between them. Networks consisting of crossbar switches are fully connected because any entity can communicate directly with any other entity, and simultaneous communications between different processor/memory pairs are allowed. (A given processor can have at most one connection at a time, however.) No transfer is ever prevented because of a switch being closed. Therefore, the crossbar network is a nonblocking network. However, if there is a single switch at each crosspoint, n entities require n^2 switches. In reality, many multiprocessors require many switches at each crosspoint. Thus, managing numerous switches quickly becomes difficult and costly. Crossbar switches are practical only in high-speed multiprocessor vector computers. A crossbar switch configuration is shown in Figure 9.5. The blue switches indicate closed switches. A processor can be connected to only one memory at a time, so there will be at most one closed switch per column.

The second type of switch is the **2×2 switch**. It is similar to a crossbar switch, except that it is capable of routing its inputs to different destinations, whereas the crossbar simply opens or closes the communications channel. A 2×2 interchange switch has two inputs and two outputs. At any given moment, a 2×2 switch can be in one of four states: **through**, **cross**, **upper broadcast**, and **lower broadcast**, as shown in Figure 9.6. In the `through` state, the upper input is directed to the upper output and the lower input is directed to the lower output.

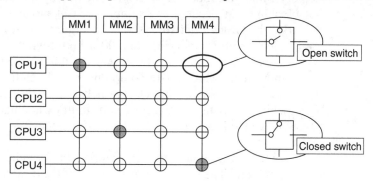

FIGURE 9.5 A Crossbar Network

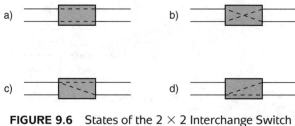

FIGURE 9.6   States of the 2 × 2 Interchange Switch
a) Through
b) Cross
c) Upper Broadcast
d) Lower Broadcast

More simply, the input is directed through the switch. In the cross state, the upper input is directed to the lower output, and the lower input is directed to the upper output. In upper broadcast, the upper input is broadcast to both the upper and lower outputs. In lower broadcast, the lower input is broadcast to both the upper and lower outputs. The through and cross states are the ones relevant to interconnection networks.

The most advanced class of networks, **multistage interconnection networks**, is built using 2 × 2 switches. The idea is to incorporate stages of switches, typically with processors on one side and memories on the other, with a series of switching elements as the interior nodes. These switches dynamically configure themselves to allow a path from any given processor to any given memory. The number of switches and the number of stages contribute to the path length of each communication channel. A slight delay may occur as the switch determines the configuration required to pass a message from the specified source to the desired destination. These multistage networks are often called **shuffle networks**, alluding to the pattern of the connections between the switches.

Many topologies have been suggested for multistage switching networks. These networks can be used to connect processors in loosely coupled distributed systems, or they can be used in tightly coupled systems to control processor-to-memory communications. A switch can be in only one state at a time, so it is clear that blocking can occur. For example, consider one simple topology for these networks, the **Omega network** shown in Figure 9.7. It is possible for CPU 00 to communicate with Memory Module 00 if both Switch 1A and Switch 2A are set to through. At the same time, however, it is impossible for CPU 10 to communicate with Memory Module 01. To do this, both Switch 1A and Switch 2A would need to be set to cross. This Omega network is, therefore, a blocking network. Nonblocking multistage networks can be built by adding more switches and more stages. In general, an Omega network of n nodes requires $\log_2 n$ stages with $\frac{n}{2}$ switches per stage.

It is interesting to note that configuring the switches is not really as difficult as it might seem. The binary representation of the destination module can be used to program the switches as the message travels the network. Using one bit of the

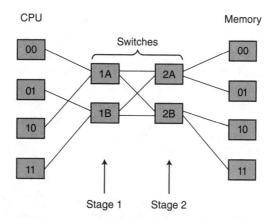

CPU   Memory

FIGURE 9.7   A Two-Stage Omega Network

destination address for each stage, each switch can be programmed based on the value of that bit. If the bit is a 0, the input is routed to the upper output. If the bit is a 1, the input is routed to the lower output. For example, suppose CPU 00 wishes to communicate with Memory Module 01. We can use the first bit of the destination (0) to set Switch 1A to `through` (which routes the input to the upper output), and the second bit (1) to set Switch 2A to `cross` (which routes the input to the lower output). If CPU 11 wishes to communicate with Memory Module 00, we would set Switch 1B to `cross`, and Switch 2A to `cross` (because both inputs must be routed to the upper outputs).

Another interesting method for determining the switch setting is to compare the corresponding bits of the source and destination. If the bits are equal, the switch is set to `through`. If the bits are different, the switch is set to `cross`. For example, suppose CPU 00 wishes to communicate with Memory Module 01. We compare the first bits of each (0 to 0), setting Switch 1A to `through`, and compare the second bits of each (0 to 1), setting Switch 2A to `cross`.

Each method for interconnecting multiprocessors has its advantages and disadvantages. For example, bus-based networks are the simplest and most efficient solution when a moderate number of processors are involved. However, the bus becomes a bottleneck if many processors make memory requests simultaneously. We compare bus-based, crossbar, and multistage interconnection networks in Table 9.2.

Property	Bus	Crossbar	Multistage
Speed	Low	High	Moderate
Cost	Low	High	Moderate
Reliability	Low	High	High
Configurability	High	Low	Moderate
Complexity	Low	High	Moderate

TABLE 9.2   Properties of the Various Interconnection Networks

9.4.4 Shared Memory Multiprocessors

We have mentioned that multiprocessors are classified by how memory is organized. Tightly coupled systems use the same memory and are thus known as **shared memory processors**. This does not mean that all processors must share one large memory. Each processor could have a local memory, but it must be shared with other processors. It is also possible that local caches could be used with a single global memory. These three ideas are illustrated in Figure 9.8.

The concept of a shared memory multiprocessor (SMM) dates back to the 1970s. The first SMM machine was built at Carnegie-Mellon University using

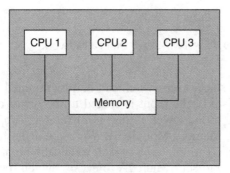

a) Global shared memory

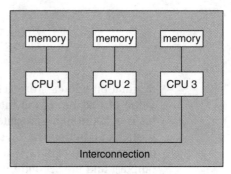

b) Distributed shared memory

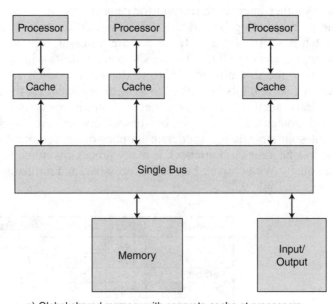

c) Global shared memory with separate cache at processors

FIGURE 9.8 Shared Memory Configurations

crossbar switches to connect 16 processors to 16 memory modules. The most widely acclaimed of the early SMM machines was the cm* system with its 16 PDP-11 processors and 16 memory banks, all of which were connected using a tree network. The global shared memory was divided equally among the processors. If a processor generated an address, it would first check its local memory. If the address was not found in local memory, it was passed on to a controller. The controller would try to locate the address within the processors that occupied the subtree for which it was the root. If the required address still could not be located, the request was passed up the tree until the data was found or the system ran out of places to look.

There are some commercial SMMs in existence, but they are not extremely popular. One of the first commercial SMM computers was the BBN (Bolt, Beranek, and Newman) Butterfly, which used 256 Motorola 68000 processors. The KSR-1 (from Kendall Square Research) has recently become available and should prove quite useful for computational science applications. Each KSR-1 processor contains a cache, but the system has no primary memory. Data is accessed through cache directories maintained in each processor. The KSR-1 processing elements are connected in a unidirectional ring topology, as shown in Figure 9.9. Messages and data travel around the rings in only one direction. Each first-level ring can connect from 8 to 32 processors. A second-level ring can connect up to 34 first-level rings, for a maximum of 1,088 processors. When a processor references an item in, say, location x, the processor cache that contains address x places the requested cache slot on the ring. The cache entry (containing the data) migrates through the rings until it reaches the processor that made the request. Distributed shared memory systems of this type are called **shared virtual memory systems**.

Shared memory MIMD machines can be divided into two categories according to how they synchronize their memory operations. In **Uniform Memory Access (UMA)** systems, all memory accesses take the same amount of time. A UMA machine has one pool of shared memory that is connected to a group of processors through a bus or switch network. All processors have equal access to memory, according to the established protocol of the interconnection network. As the number of processors increases, a switched interconnection network (requiring 2^n connections) quickly becomes very expensive in a UMA machine. Bus-based UMA systems saturate when the bandwidth of the bus becomes insufficient for the number of processors in the system. Multistage networks run into wiring constraints and significant latency if the number of processors becomes very large. Thus the scalability of UMA machines is limited by the properties of interconnection networks. Symmetric multiprocessors are well-known UMA architectures. Specific examples of UMA machines include Sun's Ultra Enterprise, IBM's iSeries and pSeries servers, the Hewlett-Packard 900, and DEC's AlphaServer.

Nonuniform memory access (NUMA) machines get around the problems inherent in UMA architectures by providing each processor with its own piece of memory. The memory space of the machine is distributed across all of the processors, but the processors see this memory as a contiguous addressable entity.

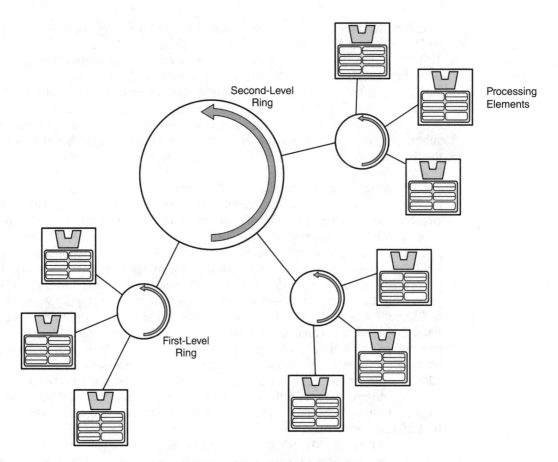

FIGURE 9.9   KSR-1 Hierarchical Ring Topology

Although NUMA memory constitutes a single addressable entity, its distributed nature is not completely transparent. Nearby memory takes less time to read than memory that is farther away. Thus, memory access time is inconsistent across the address space of the machine. An example of NUMA architectures include Sequent's NUMA-Q and the Origin2000 by Silicon Graphics.

NUMA machines are prone to **cache coherence** problems. To reduce memory access time, each NUMA processor maintains a private cache. However, when a processor modifies a data element that is in its local cache, other copies of the data become inconsistent. For example, suppose Processor A and Processor B both have a copy of data element x in their cache memories. Let's say x has a value of 10. If Processor A sets x to 20, Processor B's cache (which still contains a value of 10) has an old, or **stale**, value of x. Inconsistencies in data such as this cannot be allowed, so mechanisms must be provided to ensure cache coherence. Specially designed hardware units known as **snoopy cache controllers** monitor all caches on the system. They implement the system's cache consistency protocol. NUMA machines that employ snoopy caches and maintain cache consistency are referred to as **cache coherent NUMA (CC-NUMA)** architectures.

The easiest approach to cache consistency is to ask the processor having the stale value to either void x from its cache or to update x to the new value. When this is done immediately after the value of x is changed, we say that the system uses a **write-through** cache update protocol. With this approach, the data is written to cache and memory concurrently. If the **write-through with update** protocol is used, a message containing the new value of x is broadcast to all other cache controllers so that they can update their caches. If the **write-through with invalidation** protocol is used, the broadcast contains a message asking all cache controllers to remove the stale value of x from their caches. Write-invalidate uses the network only the first time x is updated, thus keeping bus traffic light. Write-update keeps all caches current, which reduces latency; however, it increases communications traffic.

A second approach to maintaining cache coherency is the use of a **write-back** protocol that changes only the data in cache at the time of modification. Main memory is not modified until the modified cache block must be replaced and thus written to memory. With this protocol, data values are read in the normal manner, but before data can be written, the processor performing the modification must obtain exclusive rights to the data. It does so by requesting ownership of the data. When ownership is granted, any copies of the data at other processors are invalidated. If other processors wish to read the data, they must request the value from the processor that owns it. The processor with ownership then relinquishes its rights and forwards the current data value to main memory.

9.4.5 Distributed Computing

Distributed computing is another form of multiprocessing. Although it has become an increasingly popular source of computational power, it means different things to different people. In a sense, all multiprocessor systems are also distributed systems because the processing load is divided among a group of processors that work collectively to solve a problem. When most people use the term **distributed system**, they are referring to a very loosely coupled multicomputer system. Recall that multiprocessors can be connected using local buses (as in Figure 9.8c), or they can be connected through a network, as indicated in Figure 9.10. Loosely coupled distributed computers depend on a network for communication among processors.

This idea is exemplified by the recent practice of using individual microcomputers and NOWs for distributed computing systems. These systems allow idle PC processors to work on small pieces of large problems. A recent cryptographic problem was solved through the resources of thousands of personal computers, each performing brute-force cryptanalysis using a small set of possible message keys.

Grid computing is a great example of distributed computing. Grid computing uses the resources of many computers connected by a network (generally the Internet) to solve computation problems that are too large for any single

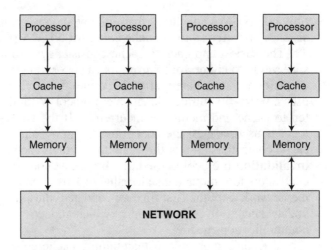

FIGURE 9.10   Multiprocessors Connected by a Network

supercomputer. Grid computers make use of unused heterogeneous resources (typically either CPU cycles or disk storage) located in different places and belonging to different administrative domains. Essentially, grid computing *virtualizes* computing resources. The major difference between grid computing and the cluster computing discussed earlier is that the grid resources are not all within the same administrative domain, which means that the grid must support computation across domains owned and controlled by different entities. The real challenge is establishing and enforcing the proper authorization techniques to allow remote users to control computing resources out of their domains.

Public-resource computing, also known as **global computing**, is a specialization of grid computing where the computing power is supplied by volunteers, many of whom may be anonymous. It endeavors to harness idle computer time from millions of PCs, workstations, and servers to solve intractable problems. The University of California at Berkeley has created open source software that makes it easy for the scientific community to use donated processor and disk resources from all over the world. The **Berkeley Open Infrastructure for Network Computing** (or **BOINC**) is an outgrowth of Berkeley's famous SETI@Home project. SETI@Home (which stands for Search for Extra Terrestrial Intelligence at Home) analyzed data from radiotelescopes to try to discern patterns that could be indicative of intelligent communication. To help with this project, PC users installed a SETI screen saver on their home computers. The screen saver was part of a program that analyzed signal data during the processor's normal idle time. When the PC was idle, the SETI screen saver downloaded data from the SETI server (using disk space), analyzed the data searching for patterns (using CPU cycles), reported the results to the server, and requested more data. If, during this process, the PC became active, the screen saver paused, picking up where it left off the next time the PC became idle. This way, the processing did not conflict with user applications. The project has been highly successful, with two million years of CPU time and 50TB of data being accumulated in its six-year run. On December 15, 2005, SETI@Home was discontinued, with the SETI initiative now completely under the auspices of BOINC. In addition to continuing SETI work, BOINC projects include climate prediction and biomedical research.

Other global and grid computing efforts have focused on other tasks, including protein folding, cancer research, weather models, molecular modeling, financial modeling, earthquake simulations, and mathematical problems. Most of these projects employ screen savers that use idle processor time to analyze data that would otherwise require enormously expensive computing power to crack. For example, SETI has millions of hours of radiotelescope data to analyze, whereas cancer research has millions of combinations of chemicals for potential cancer treatment methods. Without using grid computing, these problems would require years to solve, even on the fastest supercomputers.

For general-use computing, the concept of transparency is very important in distributed systems. Whenever possible, details about the distributed nature of the network should be hidden. Using remote system resources should require no more effort than using the local system. This transparency is most obvious in **ubiquitous computing** (also called **pervasive computing**) systems that are totally embedded in the environment, simple to use, completely connected, typically mobile, and often invisible. Mark Weiser, considered the father of ubiquitous computing, said of this topic:

> Ubiquitous computing names the third wave in computing, just now
> beginning. First were mainframes, each shared by lots of people. Now
> we are in the personal computing era, person and machine staring
> uneasily at each other across the desktop. Next comes ubiquitous
> computing, or the age of calm technology, when technology recedes into
> the background of our lives.

Weiser envisioned an individual interacting with hundreds of computers at a time, each computer invisible to the user, and communicating wirelessly with the others. Access to the Internet might be via your telephone or a household appliance, instead of your desktop, with no need to actively connect to the Internet—the device will do that for you. Weiser compared devices such as servo motors to computers: Not too long ago, these motors were very large and required dedicated care. However, these devices are now so small and common that we basically ignore their existence. The goal of ubiquitous computing is precisely that—embed many small, highly specialized computers in our environment in such a way that they become transparent. Examples of ubiquitous computing include wearable devices, smart classrooms, and environmentally aware homes and offices. Ubiquitous computing is distributed computing, albeit quite different from the systems previously discussed.

Distributed computing is supported by a large distributed computing infrastructure. **Remote procedure calls (RPCs)** extend the concept of distributed computing and help provide the necessary transparency for resource sharing. Using

RPCs, a computer can invoke a procedure to use the resources available on another computer. The procedure itself resides on the remote machine, but the invocation is done as if the procedure were local to the calling system. RPCs are used by Microsoft's Distributed Component Object Model (DCOM), the Open Group's Distributed Computing Environment (DCE), the Common Object Request Broker Architecture (CORBA), and Java's Remote Method Invocation (RMI). Today's software designers are leaning toward an object-oriented view of distributed computing, which has fostered the popularity of DCOM, CORBA, RMI, and now SOAP. SOAP (originally an acronym for Simple Object Access Protocol, but dropped in recent revisions of the protocol) uses XML (extensible markup language) to encapsulate data that is sent to and received from remote procedures. Although any mode of transport can be used for a SOAP call, HTTP is proving to be the most popular.

An emerging variant of distributed computing is Cloud computing, as mentioned in Chapter 1. Cloud computing concerns computing services provided by a collection of loosely coupled systems connected to service consumers via the Internet "cloud." The consumer of the computing service, the client, theoretically has no knowledge or interest in the particular piece of hardware providing the service at any given time. Thus, the client sees the Cloud only in terms of the services it provides. Inside a particular Cloud, which is actually at a server farm somewhere, the first available system handles each service request as it arrives. Well-engineered Clouds provide redundancy and scalability among the systems, hence, good failover protection and response time.

Cloud computing differs from classical distributed computing because the Cloud defines itself only in terms of the services it provides, rather than by a fixed hardware architecture upon which applications are deployed. The Cloud provides separation between the service provider and the service consumer. Thus, it facilitates outsourcing of common business services such as accounting and payroll. Enterprises that have embraced this approach have done so because it means that the company does not need to worry about buying and maintaining its own servers for the applications that it puts in the Cloud. It pays only for the services that it actually uses. Businesses that have shunned outsourced Cloud computing cite concerns over security and privacy, which loom large when the Internet becomes a strategic part of a computing infrastructure.

9.5 ALTERNATIVE PARALLEL PROCESSING APPROACHES

Entire books have been devoted to particular alternative and advanced architectures. Although we cannot discuss all of them in this brief section, we can introduce you to a few of the more notable systems that diverge from the traditional von Neumann architecture. These systems implement new ways of thinking about computers and computation. They include dataflow computing, neural networks, and systolic processing.

9.5.1   Dataflow Computing

von Neumann machines exhibit sequential control flow. A program counter determines the next instruction to execute. Data and instructions are segregated. The only way in which data may alter the execution sequence is if the value in the program counter is changed according to the outcome of a statement that references a data value.

In **dataflow** computing, the control of the program is directly tied to the data itself. It is a simple approach: An instruction is executed when the data necessary for execution becomes available. Therefore, the actual order of instructions has no bearing on the order in which they are eventually executed. Execution flow is completely determined by data dependencies. There is no concept of shared data storage in these systems, and there are no program counters to control execution. Data flows continuously and is available to multiple instructions at the same time. Each instruction is considered to be a separate process. Instructions do not reference memory; instead, they reference other instructions. Data is passed from one instruction to the next.

We can understand the computation sequence of a dataflow computer by examining its **dataflow graph**. In a dataflow graph, nodes represent instructions, and arcs indicate data dependencies between instructions. Data flows through this graph in the form of **data tokens**. When an instruction has all of the data tokens it needs, the node **fires**. When a node fires, it consumes the data tokens, performs the required operation, and places the resulting data token on an output arc. This idea is illustrated in Figure 9.11.

The dataflow graph shown in Figure 9.11 is an example of a **static** dataflow architecture in which the tokens flow through the graph in a staged pipelined fashion. In **dynamic** dataflow architectures, tokens are tagged with context information and are stored in a memory. During every clock cycle, memory is searched for the set of tokens necessary for a node to fire. Nodes fire only when they find a complete set of input tokens in the same context.

Programs for dataflow machines must be written in languages that are specifically designed for this type of architecture; these include VAL, Id, SISAL,

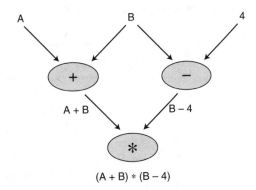

$$(A + B) * (B - 4)$$

FIGURE 9.11   Dataflow Graph Computing $N = (A + B) * (B - 4)$

and LUCID. Compilation of a dataflow program results in a dataflow graph much like the one illustrated in Figure 9.11. The tokens propagate along the arcs as the program executes.

Consider the sample code that calculates *N*!:

```
(initial j <- n; k <- 1
  while j > 1 do
    new k <- k * j;
    new j <- j - 1;
return k)
```

The corresponding dataflow graph is shown in Figure 9.12. The two values, *N* and 1, are fed into the graph. *N* becomes token *j*. When *j* is compared to 1, if it is greater than 1, the *j* token is passed through and doubled, with one copy of the token passed to the "−1 node" and one copy passed to the multiply node. If *j* is not greater than 1, the value of *k* is passed through as the output of the program. The multiply node can only fire when both a new *j* token and a new *k* token are available. The "right-facing" triangles that *N* and 1 feed into are "merge" nodes and fire whenever either input is available. Once *N* and 1 are fed into the graph, they are "used up" and the new *j* and new *k* values cause the merge nodes to fire.

Al Davis, of the University of Utah, built the first dataflow machine in 1977. The first multiprocessor dataflow system (containing 32 processors) was developed at CERT-ONERA in France in 1979. The University of Manchester created the first tagged-token dataflow computer in 1981. The commercially available **Manchester tagged dataflow model** is a powerful dataflow paradigm based on dynamic tagging. This particular architecture is described as tagged because data values (tokens) are tagged with unique identifiers to specify the current iteration level. The tags are required because programs can be **reentrant**, meaning the same code can be used with different data. By comparing the tags, the system determines which data to use during each iteration. Tokens that have matching tags for the same instruction cause the node to fire.

A loop serves as a good example to explain the concept of tagging. A higher level of concurrency can be achieved if each iteration of the loop is executed in a separate instance of a subgraph. This subgraph is simply a copy of the graph.

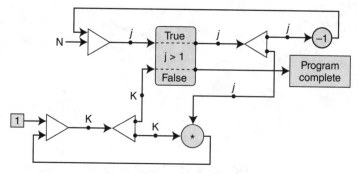

FIGURE 9.12 Dataflow Graph Corresponding to the Program to Calculate *N*!

However, if there are many iterations of the loop, there will be many copies of the graph. Rather than copying the graph, it would be more efficient to share the nodes among different instances of a graph. The tokens for each instance must be identifiable, and this is done by giving each of them a tag. The tag for each token identifies the instance to which it belongs. That way, tokens intended for, say, the third iteration, cannot cause nodes for the fourth iteration to fire.

The architecture of a dataflow machine consists of a number of processing elements that must communicate with each other. Each processing element has an **enabling unit** that sequentially accepts tokens and stores them in memory. If the node to which this token is addressed fires, the input tokens are extracted from memory and are combined with the node itself to form an executable packet. The processing element's **functional unit** computes any necessary output values and combines them with destination addresses to form more tokens. These tokens are then sent back to the enabling unit, at which time they may enable other nodes. In a tagged-token machine, the enabling unit is split into two separate stages: the **matching unit** and the **fetching unit**. The matching unit stores tokens in its memory and determines whether an instance of a given destination node has been enabled. In tagged architectures, there must be a match of both the destination node address and the tag. When all matching tokens for a node are available, they are sent to the fetching unit, which combines these tokens with a copy of the node into an executable packet, which is then passed on to the functional unit.

Because data drives processing on dataflow systems, dataflow multiprocessors do not suffer from the contention and cache coherency problems that are so vexing to designers of control-driven multiprocessors. It is interesting to note that von Neumann, whose name is given to the von Neumann bottleneck in traditional computer architectures, studied the possibility of data-driven architectures similar in nature to dataflow machines. In particular, he studied the feasibility of neural networks, which are data driven by nature and discussed in the next section.

9.5.2 Neural Networks

Traditional architectures are quite good at fast arithmetic and executing deterministic programs. However, they are not so good at massively parallel applications, fault tolerance, or adapting to changing circumstances. Neural networks, on the other hand, are useful in dynamic situations where we can't formulate an exact algorithmic solution, and where processing is based on an accumulation of previous behavior.

Whereas von Neumann computers are based on the processor/memory structure, **neural networks** are based on the parallel architecture of human brains. They attempt to implement simplified versions of biological neural networks. Neural networks represent an alternative form of multiprocessor computing with a high degree of connectivity and simple processing elements. They can deal with imprecise and probabilistic information and have mechanisms that allow for adaptive interaction between the processing elements. Neural networks (or neural nets), like biological networks, can learn from experience.

Neural network computers are composed of a large number of simple processing elements that individually handle one piece of a much larger problem. Simply stated, a neural net consists of **processing elements (PEs)**, which multiply inputs by various sets of weights, yielding a single output value. The actual computation involved is deceptively easy; the true power of a neural network comes from the parallel processing of the interconnected PEs and the adaptive nature of the sets of weights. The difficulties in creating neural networks lie in determining which neurons (PEs) should be connected to which, what weights should be placed on the edges, and the various thresholds that should be applied to these weights. Furthermore, as a neural network is learning, it can make a mistake. When it does, weights and thresholds must be changed to compensate for the error. The network's **learning algorithm** is the set of rules that governs how these changes are to be made.

Neural networks are known by many different names, including **connectionist systems**, **adaptive systems**, and **parallel distributed processing systems**. These systems are particularly powerful when a large database of previous examples can be used by the neural net to learn from prior experiences. They have been used successfully in a multitude of real-world applications including quality control, weather forecasting, financial and economic forecasting, speech and pattern recognition, oil and gas exploration, healthcare cost reduction, bankruptcy prediction, machine diagnostics, securities trading, and targeted marketing. It is important to note that each of these neural nets has been specifically designed for a certain task, so we cannot take a neural network designed for weather forecasting and expect it to do a good job for economic forecasting.

The simplest example of a neural net is the **perceptron**, a single trainable neuron. A perceptron produces a Boolean output based on the values that it receives from several inputs. A perceptron is trainable because its threshold and input weights are modifiable. Figure 9.13 shows a perceptron with inputs x_1, x_2, ..., x_n, which can be Boolean or real values. Z is the Boolean output. The w_i's represent the weights of the edges and are real values. T is the real-valued threshold. In this example, the output Z is true (1) if the net input, $w_1x_1 + w_2x_2 + \cdots + w_nx_n$, is greater than the threshold T. Otherwise, Z is zero.

A perceptron produces outputs for specific inputs according to how it is trained. If the training is done correctly, we should be able to give it any input and get reasonably correct output. The perceptron should be able to determine a

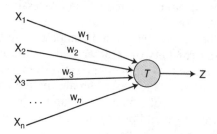

FIGURE 9.13 A Perceptron

reasonable output even if it has never before seen a particular set of inputs. The "reasonableness" of the output depends on how well the perceptron is trained.

Perceptrons are trained by use of either supervised or unsupervised learning algorithms. **Supervised learning** assumes prior knowledge of correct results, which are fed to the neural net during the training phase. While it is learning, the neural net is told whether its final state is correct. If the output is incorrect, the network modifies input weights to produce the desired results. **Unsupervised learning** does not provide the correct output to the network during training. The network adapts solely in response to its inputs, learning to recognize patterns and structure in the input sets. We assume supervised learning in our examples.

The best way to train a neural net is to compile a wide range of examples that exhibit the very characteristics in which you are interested. A neural network is only as good as the training data, so great care must be taken to select a sufficient number of correct examples. For example, you would not expect a small child to be able to identify all birds if the only bird he had ever seen was a chicken. Training takes place by giving the perceptron inputs and then checking the output. If the output is incorrect, the perceptron is notified to change its weights and possibly the threshold value to avoid the same mistake in the future. Moreover, if we show a child a chicken, a sparrow, a duck, a hawk, a pelican, and a crow, we cannot expect the child to remember the similarities and differences after seeing them only once. Similarly, the neural net must see the same examples many times in order to infer the characteristics of the input data that you seek.

A perceptron can be trained to recognize the logical AND operator quite easily. Assuming there are n inputs, the output should be 1 only if all inputs are equal to 1. If the threshold of the perceptron is set to n, and the weights of all edges are set to 1, the correct output is given. On the other hand, to compute the logical OR of a set of inputs, the threshold simply needs to be set to 1. In this way, if at least one of the inputs is 1, the output will be 1.

For both the AND and OR operators, we know what the values for the threshold and weights should be. For complex problems, these values are not known. If we had not known the weights for AND, for example, we could start the weights at 0.5 and give various inputs to the perceptron, modifying the weights as incorrect outputs were generated. This is how neural net training is done. Typically, the network is initialized with random weights between -1 and 1. Correct training requires thousands of steps. The training time itself depends on the size of the network. As the number of perceptrons increases, the number of possible "states" also increases.

Let's consider a more sophisticated example, that of determining whether a tank is hiding in a photograph. A neural net can be configured so that each output value correlates to exactly one pixel. If the pixel is part of the image of a tank, the net should output a one; otherwise, the net should output a zero. The input information would most likely consist of the color of the pixel. The network would be trained by feeding it many pictures with and without tanks. The training would continue until the network correctly identified whether the photos included tanks.

The U.S. military conducted a research project exactly like the one we just described. One hundred photographs were taken of tanks hiding behind trees and in bushes, and another 100 photographs were taken of ordinary landscape with no tanks. Fifty photos from each group were kept "secret," and the rest were used to train the neural network. The network was initialized with random weights before being fed one picture at a time. When the network was incorrect, it adjusted its input weights until the correct output was reached. Following the training period, the 50 "secret" pictures from each group of photos were fed into the network. The neural network correctly identified the presence or absence of a tank in each photo.

The real question at this point has to do with the training: Had the neural net actually learned to recognize tanks? The Pentagon's natural suspicion led to more testing. Additional photos were taken and fed into the network, and to the researchers' dismay, the results were quite random. The neural net could not correctly identify tanks in photos. After some investigation, the researchers determined that in the original set of 200 photos, all photos with tanks had been taken on a cloudy day, whereas the photos with no tanks had been taken on a sunny day. The neural net had properly separated the two groups of pictures, but had done so using the color of the sky to do this rather than the existence of a hidden tank. The government was now the proud owner of a very expensive neural net that could accurately distinguish between sunny and cloudy days!

This is a great example of what many consider the biggest issue with neural networks. If there are more than 10 to 20 neurons, it is impossible to understand how the network is arriving at its results. One cannot tell if the net is making decisions based on correct information or, as in the above example, something totally irrelevant. Neural networks have a remarkable ability to derive meaning and extract patterns from data that are too complex to be analyzed by human beings. However, some people trust neural networks to be experts in their area of training. Neural nets are used in such areas as sales forecasting, risk management, customer research, undersea mine detection, facial recognition, and data validation. Although neural networks are promising, and the progress made in the past several years has led to significant funding for neural net research, many people are hesitant to put confidence in something that no human being can completely understand.

9.5.3 Systolic Arrays

Systolic array computers derive their name from drawing an analogy to how blood rhythmically flows through a biological heart. They are a network of processing elements that rhythmically compute data by circulating it through the system. Systolic arrays are a variation of SIMD computers that incorporates large arrays of simple processors that use vector pipelines for data flow, as shown in Figure 9.14b. Since their introduction in the 1970s, they have had a significant effect on special-purpose computing. One well-known systolic array is CMU's iWarp processor, which was manufactured by Intel in 1990. This system consists of a linear array of processors connected by a bidirectional data bus.

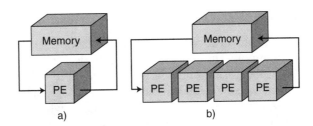

a)   b)

FIGURE 9.14   a) A Simple Processing Element (PE)
b) A Systolic Array Processor

Although Figure 9.14b illustrates a one-dimensional systolic array, two-dimensional arrays are not uncommon. Three-dimensional arrays are becoming more prevalent with the advances in VLSI technology.

Systolic arrays employ a high degree of parallelism (through pipelining) and can sustain a very high throughput. Connections are typically short, and the design is simple and thus highly scalable. They tend to be robust, highly compact, efficient, and cheap to produce. On the down side, they are highly specialized and thus inflexible as to the types and sizes of problems they can solve.

A good example of using systolic arrays can be found in polynomial evaluation. To evaluate the polynomial $y = a_0 + a_1x + a_2x^2 + \ldots + a_kx^k$, we can use Horner's Rule:

$$y = ((((a_nx + a_{n-1}) \times x + a_{n-2}) \times x + a_{n-3}) \times x \ldots a_1) \times x + a_0$$

A **linear systolic array**, in which the processors are arranged in pairs, can be used to evaluate a polynomial using Horner's Rule, as shown in Figure 9.15. One processor multiplies its input by x, which is then passed to the right (to the other processor in the pair). This processor adds the appropriate a_j and passes this sum to the right (to the next processor pair). This continues until all processors are busy. After an initial latency of $2n$ cycles to get started, a polynomial is computed in every cycle.

Systolic arrays are typically used for repetitive tasks, including Fourier transformations, image processing, data compression, shortest path problems, sorting, signal processing, and various matrix computations (such as inversion and multiplication). In short, systolic array computers are suitable for computational problems that lend themselves to a parallel solution using a large number of simple processing elements.

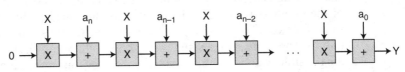

FIGURE 9.15   Using a Systolic Array to Evaluate a Polynomial

9.6 QUANTUM COMPUTING

All the classical computer architectures presented up to this point have one thing in common: They all use Boolean logic, dealing with bits that are either on or off. From the basic von Neumann architecture to the most complicated parallel processing systems, all are based on binary mathematics. In addition, each is based on transistor technology. Moore's Law, which states that the number of transistors on a single chip doubles every 18 months, cannot hold forever. The law of physics suggests that eventually transistors will become so tiny that distances between them will permit electrons to jump from one to the other, causing fatal short circuits. This suggests that we need to look in the direction of other technologies for answers.

One possible answer is **optical** or **photonic computing**. Rather than using electrons to perform logic in a computer, optical computers use photons of laser light. The speed of light in photonic circuits could approach the speed of light in a vacuum, with the added advantage of no heat dissipation. The fact that light beams can travel in parallel would suggest an additional increase in speed and performance. It may be many years before we see an optical computer on our desktops, if at all—many people believe optical computing will be reserved only for special-purpose applications.

One very promising technology is **biological computing**, computing that uses components from living organisms instead of inorganic silicon ones. One such project is the "leech-ulator," a computer created by U.S. scientists that was made of neurons from leeches. Another example is **DNA computing**, which uses DNA as software and enzymes as hardware. DNA can be replicated and programmed to perform massively parallel tasks, one of the first of which was the traveling salesman problem, limited in parallelism only by the number of DNA strands. DNA computers (also called **molecular computers**) are essentially collections of specially selected DNA strands that test all solutions at once and output the correct answer. Scientists are also experimenting with certain bacteria that can turn genes on or off in predictable ways. Researchers have already successfully programmed *E. coli* bacteria to emit red or green (i.e., 0 or 1) fluorescent light.

Perhaps the most interesting technology currently being studied is **quantum computing**. Whereas classical computers use bits that are either on or off, quantum computers use **quantum bits (qubits)** that can be in multiple states simultaneously. Recall from physics that in a magnetic field, an electron can be in two possible states: The spin can be aligned with the field or opposite to the field. When we measure this spin, we find the electron to be in one of these two states. However, it is possible for the particle to be in a **superposition** of the two states, where each exists simultaneously. Three qubits could evaluate to any one of the numbers 0 to 7 simultaneously because each qubit can be in a superposition of states. (To get a single value output, we must take a measurement of the qubit.) Therefore, processing with three qubits can perform calculations using all possible values simultaneously, working on eight calculations at the same time, resulting in **quantum parallelism**. A system with 600 qubits represents a quantum superpositioning of 2^{600} states, something impossible to simulate on a classical architecture. In addition to being close to a billion times faster than their silicon-based relatives, quantum computers could theoretically operate utilizing no energy.

Superpositioning is not new; it simply refers to the ability of two things to overlap. In Chapter 3, when we introduced clocks, we overlapped (or superpositioned) multiple clocks to create a clock with multiple stages. Sine waves can be superpositioned to create a new wave representing a combination of its components. A doubly linked list could be traversed by performing an exclusive OR on the current pointer and the pointer on the left (or right, depending on the desired direction), resulting in a superposition that gives the address of the next desired node. The superpositioning of clock signals and sine waves and node pointers is exactly how qubits are able to maintain multiple states simultaneously.

D-Wave Computers is the first company in the world to manufacture and sell what it identifies as a quantum computer. (Some believe this particular computer has not yet reached quantum status; see the reference article by Jones for more on this debate.) The company's goal is to push the limits of science and build computers that exploit the newest research in physics. By utilizing quantum mechanics, D-Wave is building effective and efficient computers, with hopes of accelerating computing beyond what is possible in normal transistor-based technology. Instead of processors, these computers use qubits (also known as **sqids**—superconducting quantum interference devices). In these machines, a qubit is essentially a metal superconducting loop, cooled to almost absolute zero, in which quantizised current can run both clockwise and counterclockwise at once. By allowing current to flow in both directions around the loop, the system loses the ability to distinguish between them and can thus be in two states at once. Qubits interact with other objects, ultimately choosing a final state.

The first machine that D-Wave sold was to the University of Southern California for its USC Lockheed Martin Quantum Computation Center. The focus of this lab is to research how quantum computing works. USC has been using this computer for basic research to determine answers to questions such as what causes quantum computing errors when unexpected results are obtained, how the computer's architecture affects how programmers reason about computation, and how increasing the size of a problem relates to how much harder is it for the machine to find a solution. USC's quantum computer originally consisted of 128 qubits; it has since been upgraded to 512 qubits.

In 2013, Google purchased a D-Wave computer for its new NASA-hosted lab, the Quantum Artificial Intelligence Lab. Unlike the USC lab, this lab is used mostly for running machine learning algorithms. This D-Wave quantum computer contains 512 superconducting qubits. To program this computer, a user assigns it a task; the computer then utilizes algorithms to map a calculation across the qubits. The ability to be in multiple states concurrently makes the D-Wave computer very useful in solving combinatorial optimization problems, such as risk analysis, vehicle routing and mapping, traffic light synchronization, and train schedules, to name a few.

This raises an interesting question: What algorithms *can* be run on a quantum computer? The answer: Anything that can be run on a typical von Neumann machine (i.e., a "classical machine" as this architecture is known in the quantum computer community) can be run on a quantum computer; after all, as any physicist can verify, classical is a subset of quantum. Another popular question deals with how much more powerful a quantum computer actually is when compared to a classical one. Although this depends on the specifics of the problem, the complete answer to this question has evaded researchers, as much of what quantum computers can do is beyond the limits of empirical testing; these computers are basically "too quantum" for any meaningful theoretical analysis. What we do know, however, is that the true power of quantum computers lies in their ability to successfully run **quantum algorithms**. These are algorithms—including those that exploit quantum parallelism—that do not lend themselves to being run on a classical computer, but do exceptionally well on a quantum computer.

An example of such an algorithm is Shor's algorithm for factoring products of prime numbers, which is useful for cryptography and coding. Peter Shor at Bell Labs created an algorithm that exploits quantum parallelism to factor large prime numbers, a problem so difficult that it is used as the basis for RSA encryption, the most popular form of public key encryption today. This is unfortunate news for RSA, because a quantum computer could break the encryption in a matter of seconds, rendering all current encryption software that is based on this method completely useless. To break a code, a programmer simply asks the quantum machine to simulate every possible state of the problem set (i.e., every possible key for a cipher) and it "collapses" on the correct solution. In addition to uses in quantum cryptography, quantum computers could yield super-dense communications and improved error correction and detection.

An application for quantum computing, perhaps more relevant to everyday programming, is the ability to generate truly random numbers. Classical computers can generate only pseudorandom numbers, because the process is based on an algorithm that always contains a cycle or repetition of some type. In a quantum computer, the superpositioning of states of qubits is always measured with a certain probability (i.e., each state has a numerical coefficient representing its probability). In our example using three qubits, each of the eight numbers has an equal probability of being measured, thus resulting in the ultimate random number generator.

The reason these computers perform well on hard problems such as those we have discussed is that the quantum computer programmer has access to operations that are basically prohibited by classical physics. The process of programming on these machines requires a completely different way of thinking, as there is no sense of a clock or a fetch–decode–execute cycle. In addition, there is no real notion of gates; although a quantum computer could be built using the gate model, doing so appears to be more because it has always been done that way, and less about creating an efficient machine. Quantum computers have the freedom to choose from many different architectures. It is interesting to note that, similar to Moore's Law (which has predicted the transistor density on integrated circuits), quantum computing has **Rose's Law** (named after Geordie Rose, D-Wave's founder and chief technology officer). Rose's Law states that the number of qubits that can be assembled to successfully perform computations will double every 12 months; this has been precisely the case for the past nine years.

There are a significant number of difficulties that must be overcome before quantum computers become common desktop machines. One obstacle is the tendency for qubits to decay into a single incoherent state (called **decoherence**), resulting in a breakdown of information and unavoidable and uncorrectable errors; recent research efforts have made remarkable strides in error-correcting quantum coding. Perhaps the greatest limiting factor regarding the development of quantum computing is that the ability to fabricate to scale simply does not exist. This is a similar problem to the one faced by Charles Babbage so long ago: We have the vision; we just don't have the necessary means to build the machine. If these obstacles can be overcome, quantum computers will do to silicon what transistors did to vacuum tubes, rendering them quaint artifacts of a bygone era.

The realization of quantum computing has prompted many to consider what is known as the **technological singularity**, a theoretical point in time when human technology has progressed to the point when it will fundamentally and irreversibly alter human development—a point when civilization changes to such an extent that its technology is incomprehensible to previous generations. John von Neumann first coined the term *singularity* when he spoke of an "ever accelerating progress of technology and changes in the mode of human life, which gives the appearance of approaching some essential singularity in the history of the race beyond which human affairs, as we know them, could not continue"… or the moment in time when "technological progress became incomprehensibly rapid and complicated." In the early 1980s, Vernor Vinge (a computer science professor and author) introduced the term *technological singularity* and defined it as that point in time when we create intelligence greater than our own—essentially a point representing that moment in time when machines replace humans as the dominant force on the planet. Since then, many have modified this definition. Ray Kurzwell (an author and popular singularitarian) defines the technological singularity as "a future period during which the pace of technological change will be so rapid, its impact so deep, that human life will be irreversibly transformed." James Martin (a computer scientist and author) defines the singularity as "a break in human evolution that will be caused by the staggering speed of technological evolution." Kevin Kelly (co-founder of *Wired Magazine*) defines it as the point when "all the change in the last million years will be superseded by the change in the next five minutes." No matter which definition is used, many believe the singularity is a long way off; some (such as D-Wave's Geordie Rose) feel that point in technological development has already occurred.

Quantum computing is a field that presents both immense challenges and enormous promise. The field is in its infancy, but it is progressing much faster than people anticipated. Significant funding has been given for research in this area, and many algorithms suitable for use on a quantum computer have already been developed. We are in a unique situation to watch as these systems mature and become a practical reality, significantly changing what we know about computers and how we program them. If you are interested in trying your hand at quantum computing, you can contact either the USC lab or the Google lab and apply for time on either of their quantum computers.

CHAPTER SUMMARY

This chapter has presented an overview of some important aspects of multiprocessor and multicomputer systems. These systems provide a means of solving otherwise unmanageable problems in an efficient manner.

The RISC-versus-CISC debate is becoming increasingly more a comparison of chip architectures, not ISAs. What really matters is program execution time, and both RISC and CISC designers will continue to improve performance.

Flynn's taxonomy categorizes architectures depending on the number of instructions and data streams. MIMD machines should be further divided into those that use shared memory and those that do not.

The power of today's digital computers is truly astounding. Internal processor parallelism has contributed to this increased power through superscalar and superpipelined architectures. Originally, processors did one thing at a time, but it is now common for them to perform multiple concurrent operations. Vector processors support vector operations, whereas MIMD machines incorporate multiple processors.

SIMD and MIMD processors are connected through interconnection networks. Shared memory multiprocessors treat the collection of physical memories as a single entity, whereas distributed memory architectures allow a processor sole access to its memory. Either approach allows the common user to have supercomputing capability at an affordable price. The most popular multiprocessor architectures are MIMD, shared memory, bus-based systems.

Some highly complex problems cannot be solved using our traditional model of computation. Alternative architectures are necessary for specific applications. Dataflow computers allow data to drive computation, rather than the other way around. Neural networks learn to solve problems of the highest complexity. Systolic arrays harness the power of small processing elements, pushing data throughout the array until the problem is solved. The departure from silicon-based computers to biological, optical, and quantum computers may very well usher in a new generation of computing technology.

FURTHER READING

For more information on the current RISC-versus-CISC debate, see Blem et al. (2013).

There have been several attempts at modifying Flynn's taxonomy. Hwang (1987), Bell (1989), Karp (1987), and Hockney and Jesshope (1988) have all extended this taxonomy to varying degrees.

There are many good textbooks on advanced architectures, including Hennessy and Patterson (2006), Hwang (1993), and Stone (1993). Stone has very detailed explanations of pipelining and memory organization, in addition to vector machines and parallel processing. For a detailed explanation of superscalar execution in a modern RISC processor, see Grohoski (1990). For a thorough discussion of RISC principles with a good explanation of instruction pipelines, see Patterson (1985) and Patterson and Ditzel (1980).

For an excellent article on the interaction between VLSI technology and computer processor design, see Hennessy (1984). Leighton (1982) has a dated but very good view of architectures and algorithms and is a good reference for interconnection networks. Omondi (1999) provides an authoritative treatment of the implementation of computer microarchitecture.

For excellent survey papers on dataflow architectures, as well as comparisons of various dataflow machines, see Dennis (1980), Hazra (1982), Srini (1986), Treleaven et al. (1982), and Vegdahl (1984).

Foster and Kesselman (2003) provide detailed information on grid computing, as does Anderson (2004, 2005). For more information on BOINC, see http://boinc.berkeley.edu. For readers interested in quantum computing, Brown (2000) provides a wonderful introduction to quantum computing, quantum physics, and nanotechnology. Williams and Clearwater (1998) provide good coverage for the beginner, as does Johnson (2003).

For additional coverage on the topics in this chapter, see Stallings (2009), Goodman and Miller (1993), Patterson and Hennessy (2008), and Tanenbaum (2005). For a historical perspective and performance information on interconnection networks, see Byuyan, et al. (1989), Reed and Grunwald (1987), and Siegel (1985). Circello, et al. (1995) contains an overview of the superscalar architecture used by Motorola for the MC68060 chip.

Architectural decisions, challenges, and trade-offs for 64-bit machines are discussed in Horel and Lauterback (1999); the IA-64 architecture, and its use of instruction-level parallelism, is explained well in Dulong (1998). A thorough discussion of pipelined computers can be found in Kogge (1981), which is considered the first formal treatise on pipelining. Trew and Wilson (1991) provide an older, yet still interesting, survey of parallel machines, as well as discussions on the various form of parallelism. Silc, et al. (1999) offers a survey of the various architectural approaches and implementation techniques that can be used to exploit parallelism in microprocessors.

REFERENCES

Amdahl, G. "The Validity of the Single Processor Approach to Achieving Large Scale Computing Capabilities." *AFIPS Conference Proceedings 30*, 1967, pp. 483–485.

Anderson, D. P. "BOINC: A System for Public-Resource Computing and Storage." *5th IEEE/ACM International Workshop on Grid Computing,* November 8, 2004, Pittsburgh, PA, pp. 4–10.

Anderson, D. P., Korpela, E., & Walton, R. "High-Performance Task Distribution for Volunteer Computing." IEEE International Conference on e-Science and Grid Technologies, 5–8 December 2005, Melbourne.

Bell, G. "The Future of High Performance Computers in Science and Engineering." *Communications of the ACM 32,* 1989, pp. 1091–1101.

Bhuyan, L., Yang, Q., & Agrawal, D. "Performance of Multiprocessor Interconnection Networks." *Computer*, 22:2, 1989, pp. 25–37.

Blem, E., Menon, J., & Sankaralingam, K. "Power Struggles: Revisting the RISC vs. CISC Debate on Contemporary ARM and x86 Architectures." 19th IEEE International Symposium on High Performance Computer Architecture (HPCA), February 23–27, 2013, pp. 1–12.

Brown, J. *Minds, Machines, and the Multiverse: The Quest for the Quantum Computer.* New York: Simon & Schuster, 2000.

Circello, J., et al. "The Superscalar Architecture of the MC68060." *IEEE Micro, 15*:2, April 1995, pp. 10–21.

DeMone, P. "RISC vs CISC Still Matters." Real World Technologies, February 13, 2000. Last accessed September 1, 2013, at http://www.realworld tech.com/risc-vs-cisc/

Dennis, J. B. "Dataflow Supercomputers." *Computer 13*:4, November 1980, pp. 48–56.

Dulong, C. "The IA-64 Architecture at Work." *Computer 31*:7, July 1998, pp. 24–32.

Flynn, M. "Some Computer Organizations and Their Effectiveness." *IEEE Transactions on Computers* C-21, 1972, p. 94.

Foster, I., & Kesselman, C. *The Grid 2: Blueprint for a New Computing Infrastructure.* San Francisco: Morgan-Kaufmann Publishers, 2003.

Goodman, J., & Miller, K. *A Programmer's View of Computer Architecture.* Philadelphia: Saunders College Publishing, 1993.

Grohoski, G. F. "Machine Organization of the IBM RISC System/6000 Processor." *IBM J. Res. Develop. 43*:1, January 1990, pp. 37–58.

Hazra, A. "A Description Method and a Classification Scheme for Dataflow Architectures." *Proceedings of the 3rd International Conference on Distributed Computing Systems,* October 1982, pp. 645–651.

Hennessy, J. L. "VLSI Processor Architecture." *IEEE Trans. Comp. C-33*:12, December 1984, pp. 1221–1246.

Hennessy, J. L., & Patterson, D. A. *Computer Architecture: A Quantitative Approach,* 4th ed. San Francisco: Morgan Kaufmann, 2006.

Hockney, R., & Jesshope, C. *Parallel Computers 2.* Bristol, UK: Adam Hilger, Ltd., 1988.

Horel, T., & Lauterbach, G. "UltraSPARC III: Designing Third Generation 64-Bit Performance." *IEEE Micro 19*:3, May/June 1999, pp. 73–85.

Hwang, K. *Advanced Computer Architecture.* New York: McGraw-Hill, 1993.

Hwang, K. "Advanced Parallel Processing with Supercomputer Architectures." *Proc. IEEE 75,* 1987, pp. 1348–1379.

Johnson, G. *A Shortcut Through Time—The Path to a Quantum Computer.* New York: Knopf, 2003.

Jones, N. & Nature Magazine. "D-Wave's Quantum Computer Courts Controversy." *Scientific American,* June 19, 2013.

Karp, A. "Programming for Parallelism." *IEEE Computer 20*:5, 1987, pp. 43–57.

Kogge, P. *The Architecture of Pipelined Computers.* New York: McGraw-Hill, 1981.

Leighton, F. T. *Introduction to Parallel Algorithms and Architectures.* New York: Morgan Kaufmann, 1982.

MIPS home page: *www.mips.com.*

Omondi, A. *The Microarchitecture of Pipelined and Superscalar Computers.* Boston: Kluwer Academic Publishers, 1999.

Patterson, D. A. "Reduced Instruction Set Computers." *Communications of the ACM 28*:1, January 1985, pp. 8–20.

Patterson, D., & Ditzel, D. "The Case for the Reduced Instruction Set Computer." *ACM SIGARCH Computer Architecture News*, October 1980, pp. 25–33.

Patterson, D. A., & Hennessy, J. L. *Computer Organization and Design: The Hardware/Software Interface*, 4th ed. San Mateo, CA: Morgan Kaufmann, 2008.

Reed, D., & Grunwald, D. "The Performance of Multicomputer Interconnection Networks." *IEEE Computer*, June 1987, pp. 63–73.

Siegel, H. *Interconnection Networks for Large Scale Parallel Processing: Theory and Case Studies*. Lexington, MA: Lexington Books, 1985.

Silc, J., Robic, B., & Ungerer, T. *Processor Architecture: From Dataflow to Superscalar and Beyond*. New York: Springer-Verlag, 1999.

SPIM home page: *www.cs.wisc.edu/~larus/spim.html.*

Srini, V. P. "An Architectural Comparison of Dataflow Systems." *IEEE Computer*, March 1986, pp. 68–88.

Stallings, W. *Computer Organization and Architecture*, 8th ed. Upper Saddle River, NJ: Prentice Hall, 2009.

Stone, H. S. *High Performance Computer Architecture,* 3rd ed. Reading, MA: Addison-Wesley, 1993.

Tanenbaum, A. *Structured Computer Organization*, 5th ed. Upper Saddle River, NJ: Prentice Hall, 2005.

Treleaven, P. C., Brownbridge, D. R., & Hopkins, R. P. "Data-Driven and Demand-Driven Computer Architecture." *Computing Surveys 14*:1, March 1982, pp. 93–143.

Trew, A., & Wilson, A., Eds. *Past, Present, Parallel: A Survey of Available Parallel Computing Systems*. New York: Springer-Verlag, 1991.

Vegdahl, S. R. "A Survey of Proposed Architectures for the Execution of Functional Languages." *IEEE Transactions on Computers C-33*:12, December 1984, pp. 1050–1071.

Williams, C., & Clearwater, S. *Explorations in Quantum Computing*. New York: Springer-Verlag, 1998.

REVIEW OF ESSENTIAL TERMS AND CONCEPTS

1. Why was the RISC architecture concept proposed?

2. Why is a RISC processor easier to pipeline than a CISC processor?

3. Describe how register windowing makes procedure calls more efficient.

4. Flynn's taxonomy classifies computer architectures based on two properties. What are they?

5. What is the difference between MPP and SMP processors?

6. We propose adding a level to Flynn's taxonomy. What is the distinguishing characteristic of computers at this higher level?

7. Do all programming problems lend themselves to parallel execution? What is the limiting factor?

8. Define *superpipelining.*

9. How is a superscalar design different from a superpipelined design?

10. In what way does a VLIW design differ from a superpipelined design?

11. What are the similarities and differences between EPIC and VLIW?

12. Explain the limitation inherent in a register-register vector processing architecture.

13. Give two reasons for the efficiency of vector processors.

14. Draw pictures of the six principal interconnection network topologies.

15. There are three types of shared memory organizations. What are they?

16. Describe one of the cache consistency protocols discussed in this chapter.

17. Describe grid computing and some applications for which it is suitable.

18. What is SETI, and how does it use the distributed computing model?

19. What is ubiquitous computing?

20. What differentiates dataflow architectures from "traditional" computational architectures?

21. What is reentrant code?

22. What is the fundamental computing element of a neural network?

23. Describe how neural networks "learn."

24. Through what metaphor do systolic arrays get their name? Why is the metaphor fairly accurate?

25. What kinds of problems are suitable for solution by systolic arrays?

26. How does a quantum computer differ from a classical computer? What are the obstacles that must be overcome in quantum computing?

EXERCISES

♦ 1. Why do RISC machines operate on registers?

2. Which characteristics of RISC systems could be directly implemented in CISC systems? Which characteristics of RISC machines could not be implemented in CISC machines (based on the defining characteristics of both architectures as listed in Table 9.1)?

♦ 3. What does the "reduced" in *reduced instruction set computer* really mean?

4. Suppose a RISC machine uses overlapping register windows with:

   • 10 global registers
   • 6 input parameter registers
   • 10 local registers
   • 6 output parameter registers

   How large is each overlapping register window?

♦ 5. A RISC processor has 8 global registers and 10 register windows. Each window has 4 input registers, 8 local registers, and 4 output registers. How many total registers are in this CPU? (Hint: Remember, because of the circular nature of the windows, the output registers of the last window are shared as the input registers of the first window.)

6. A RISC processor has 152 total registers, with 12 designated as global registers. The 10 register windows each have 6 input registers and 6 output registers. How many local registers are in each register window set?

7. A RISC processor has 186 total registers, with 18 globals. There are 12 register windows, each with 10 locals. How many input/output registers are in each register window?

8. Suppose a RISC machine uses overlapping register windows for passing parameters between procedures. The machine has 298 registers. Each register window has 32 registers, of which 10 are global variables and 10 are local variables. Answer the following:

   a) How many registers would be available for use by input parameters?

   b) How many registers would be available for use by output parameters?

   c) How many register windows would be available for use?

   d) By how much would the current window pointer (CWP) be incremented at each procedure call?

◆ 9. Recall our discussions from Chapter 8 regarding context switches. These occur when one process stops using the CPU and another process begins. In this sense, register windows could be viewed as a potential weakness of RISC. Explain why this is the case.

10. Suppose that a RISC machine uses 5 register windows.

   a) How deep can the procedure calls go before registers must be saved in memory? (That is, what is the maximum number of "active" procedure calls that can be made before we need to save any registers in memory?)

   b) Suppose two more calls are made after the maximum value from part (a) is reached. How many register windows must be saved to memory as a result?

   c) Now suppose that the most recently called procedure returns. Explain what occurs.

   d) Now suppose one more procedure is called. How many register windows need to be stored in memory?

11. In Flynn's taxonomy:

   ◆ a) What does SIMD stand for? Give a brief description and an example.

   b) What does MIMD stand for? Give a brief description and an example.

12. Flynn's taxonomy consists of four primary models of computation. Briefly describe each of the categories and give an example of a high-level problem for which each of these models might be used.

◆ 13. Explain the difference between loosely coupled and tightly coupled architectures.

14. Describe the characteristics of MIMD multiprocessors that distinguish them from multicomputer systems or computer networks.

15. How are SIMD and MIMD similar? How are they different? Note: You are not to define the terms, but instead compare the models.

16. What is the difference between SIMD and SPMD?

◆ 17. For what type of program-level parallelism (data or control) is SIMD best suited? For what type of program-level parallelism is MIMD best suited?

18. Describe briefly and compare the VLIW and superscalar models with respect to instruction-level parallelism.

◆ **19.** Which model, VLIW or superscalar, presents the greater challenge for compilers? Why?

◆ **20.** Compare and contrast the superscalar architecture to the VLIW architecture.

◆ **21.** Why are distributed systems desirable?

22. What is the difference between UMA and NUMA?

◆ **23.** What are the main problems with using crossbars for interconnection networks? What problems do buses present in interconnection networks?

24. Given the following Omega network, which allows 8 CPUs (P0 through P7) to access 8 memory modules (M0 through M7):

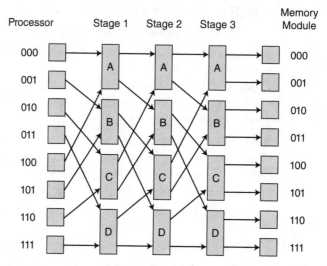

a) Show how the following connections through the network are achieved (explain how each switch must be set). Refer to the switches as 1A, 2B, etc.:

   i) P0 → M2

   ii) P4 → M4

   iii) P6 → M3

b) Can these connections occur simultaneously, or do they conflict? Explain.

c) List a processor-to-memory access that conflicts (is blocked) by the access P0 → M2 and is not listed in part (a).

d) List a processor-to-memory access that is not blocked by the access P0 → M2 and is not listed in part (a).

◆ **25.** Describe write-through and write-back cache modification as they are used in shared memory systems, and the advantages and disadvantages of both approaches.

26. Should the memory of a dataflow system be associative or address based? Explain.

◆ **27.** Do neural networks process information sequentially? Explain.

28. Compare and contrast supervised learning and unsupervised learning with regard to neural networks.

◆ 29. Describe the process of supervised learning in neural networks from a mathematical perspective.

30. These two questions deal with a single perceptron of a neural network.

    a) The logical NOT is a little trickier than AND or OR, but can be done. In this case, there is only one Boolean input. What would the weight and threshold be for this perceptron to recognize the logical NOT operator?

    b) Show that it is not possible to solve the binary XOR problem for two inputs, x_1 and x_2, using a single perceptron.

31. Explain the differences between SIMD and systolic array computing when the systolic array is one-dimensional.

32. With respect to Flynn's taxonomy, where do systolic arrays fit? What about clusters of workstations?

33. Indicate whether each of the following applies to CISC or RISC by placing either a **C** (for CISC) or an **R** (for RISC) in the blank.

    _____ 1. Simple instructions averaging one clock cycle to execute.

    _____ 2. Single register set.

    _____ 3. Complexity is in the compiler.

    _____ 4. Highly pipelined.

    _____ 5. Any instruction can reference memory.

    _____ 6. Instructions are interpreted by the microprogram.

    _____ 7. Fixed length, easily decoded instruction format.

    _____ 8. Highly specialized, infrequently used instructions.

    _____ 9. Use of overlapping register windows.

    _____ 10. Relatively few addressing modes.

34. Research quantum computing and provide a summary of a recent article on the topic.

CHAPTER 10 Topics in Embedded Systems

10.1 INTRODUCTION

Greg Papadopoulos is among many who believe that embedded processors are the next big thing in computer hardware. Proponents of general-purpose microprocessors may find this statement provocative—if not downright inflammatory. It is, however, easy to see how someone could come to this conclusion, given that practically every device that interacts with the physical world includes some sort of computerized control. As we conduct our daily activities, we encounter literally scores of embedded processors, whereas we might use only one or two general-purpose systems.

An exact definition of *embedded systems* is hard to come by. In every sense, they are real computers, having a CPU, memory, and some sort of I/O capabilities. But they differ from general-purpose computers because they carry out a limited set of tasks within the domain of a larger system. Most often, the larger system is something other than a computer. Embedded systems can be found in devices as simple and innocuous as coffeemakers and tennis shoes, and as complex and critical as commercial aircraft. Many of today's automobiles contain dozens of embedded processors, each of which manages a particular subsystem. These subsystems include fuel injection, emissions control, antilock brakes, and cruise control, to name only a few. Moreover, automotive processors communicate with one another so that their efforts are coordinated and appropriate to the state of the automobile. For example, the cruise control disengages when the antilock brakes engage. Embedded systems are also found in other computers. A disk drive controller is an example of a computer within a computer. The controller positions the disk arm and encodes and decodes data as it is written and read from the disk surface.

The design and programming of embedded systems requires us to think in new dimensions. We see first that the distinction between hardware and software is fuzzy and mutable. In general-purpose computing, we know in advance the capabilities of the hardware that run the programs we write. In embedded systems design, this is not always the case. The capabilities of the hardware can change while the system is under development. The principle of equivalence of hardware and software becomes a profound guiding tenet of system development. The functional partitioning of the hardware and software is a major—and sometimes contentious—issue.

The second way in which embedded system development differs greatly from general-purpose computing is that a deep comprehension of the underlying hardware is required. A person who writes application programs in high-level languages such as Java or C++ may never know or care about the endianness of a system's data storage, or whether an interrupt occurs at any particular time. Yet these considerations are paramount in the mind of an embedded systems programmer.

Along these same lines are the tremendous constraints under which many embedded systems must function. These constraints include limited CPU speed, limited memory, weight restrictions, limited power consumption, uncontrolled and often harsh operating environments, limited physical space, and unforgiving requirements as to the responsiveness demanded of the embedded system. Moreover, embedded systems designers constantly struggle under the burden of stringent cost requirements for both design and implementation! Enhancements or bug fixes made to an embedded system's programming may cause the entire system to go over budget with respect to power consumption or memory footprint. Today's embedded systems programmer, much like his or her grandfather who programmed a mainframe in the 1950s, may spend a good part of the day counting machine cycles—because every machine cycle counts.

Of the aforementioned constraints, limited power consumption is often at the forefront during the design process. Low power consumption means lower heat dissipation, which in turn means fewer heat sinks—which means less money for components and a smaller overall size. Lower power consumption also means battery backup is more feasible, thus providing uninterruptible and reliable operation.

Most embedded systems can be divided into three categories, based on their power requirements: battery-operated, fixed power, and high-density systems. Battery-operated systems, such as those found in portable audio devices, need to maximize battery life but minimize size. Fixed power systems, such as those found in payphones and caller ID boxes, have limited power supplies (such as phone lines), and the goal is to offer maximal performance within the constraints of the limited power available. High-density systems (high-performance and multiprocessor systems) are more concerned with power efficiency primarily because of heat dissipation issues. For example, voice over IP (VOIP) systems integrate data with voice signals and require a significant number of components, and this translates into significant heat generation. These systems often have unlimited power supplies, but must limit power consumption so they do not overheat.

The fourth, and possibly most difficult, aspect of embedded systems is the matter of signal timing. Embedded systems designers hold a precise and unambiguous awareness of the interrelationship between signals generated by events in the outside world and signals routinely taking place within the embedded system. Any set of events can take place at any time and in any order. Moreover, the reactions to these events often take place within milliseconds. In hard real-time systems, a late reaction is tantamount to failure.

Embedded systems must be functional and flexible, yet small and inexpensive (both to develop and to manufacture). Power consumption is always a major concern. We expand on all these ideas in the sections that follow, beginning with a look at embedded hardware.

10.2 AN OVERVIEW OF EMBEDDED HARDWARE

The embedded processors that control airliner telemetry are radically different from those that control the quality of a cup of coffee produced by a sophisticated coffeemaker. These applications differ in both their complexity and their timing models. Accordingly, they require vastly divergent hardware solutions. For the simplest control applications, off-the-shelf microcontrollers are often quite suitable. Applications of higher complexity can exceed the capabilities of standard components in terms of performance, power consumption, or cost. Possibly, a configurable manufactured circuit might be adapted to the task. In cases where the application is highly specialized, or responsiveness is critical, a chip must be designed from scratch. We therefore place embedded processors into three broad classifications: standardized processors, configurable processors, and full-custom processors. After describing each type, we will examine the trade-offs that are considered in selecting one approach over another.

10.2.1 Off-the-Shelf Embedded System Hardware

Advances in VLSI technology are most obvious to us when we think about the ever-increasing power available to us in desktop, laptop, and PDA systems. The computing power of yesteryear's million-dollar water-cooled mainframe fits into a shirt pocket today, and this computational power costs less than a good business suit. But some of the most striking applications of VLSI technology go practically unnoticed, despite being quite literally under our noses every day.

Microcontrollers

Many of the embedded processors that we routinely (and unwittingly) rely on for our daily convenience and safety are derivatives of yesterday's leading-edge general-purpose processors. Although these early processors are not powerful enough to run today's common desktop software, they possess more than enough power for simple control applications. Furthermore, these processors are now sold at a fraction of their original prices, because their makers long ago recovered the costs of developing them when they were widely used in personal computers. Motorola's enormously popular 68HC12 shares common ancestry with its 6800, the chip that was at the heart of the first Apple computers. Motorola has sold billions of the 68HC12 and its less-sophisticated predecessors. In large quantities, the MC68H12 can today be purchased for less money than the first Apple users shelled out for a decent printer cable. Intel's 8051 is an offspring of the 8086, the processor that was the heart of the first IBM PC.

Microcontrollers have a great deal in common with general-purpose processors. Like a general-purpose processor, a microcontroller is programmable and can access a variety of peripherals. Unlike a general-purpose processor, a microcontroller runs at a much slower clock speed, has much smaller memory address space, and its software cannot be changed by the consumer.

A simplified example of a microcontroller is shown in Figure 10.1. It consists of a CPU core, memory for programs and data, I/O ports, controllers for I/O and the system bus, a clock, and a watchdog timer. Of these components, the watchdog timer is the only one that we haven't discussed at length in earlier chapters.

As the name implies, **watchdog timers** keep an eye on things within the microcontroller. They provide a fail-safe mechanism that engages when a problem is detected. General-purpose computers do not need watchdog timers because they interact directly with human beings. If the system hangs or crashes, a human being corrects the situation, usually by rebooting the computer. It is impossible for humans to pay such close attention to the myriad embedded systems all around us. Moreover, embedded systems are often installed in places

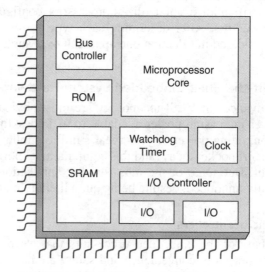

FIGURE 10.1   A Simplified Microcontroller

where we cannot get to them. Who can hit the reset button of a deep space probe? How would one reset a cardiac pacemaker? Might it take too long to realize such action is necessary?

Conceptually, the design and operation of watchdog timers are simple. The timer is initialized with an integer value from which 1 is subtracted after a given number of milliseconds elapse. The application program running in the microcontroller periodically "kicks" or "tickles" the timer, causing the count to revert to its initial value. Should the timer ever reach zero, the watchdog circuit may issue a system reset signal. Timer tickling is the responsibility of the application program running in the microcontroller. The program may have a structure that resembles the following:

```
main() {
    boolean error = false;
    do while not (error) {
        resetWatchdog();        // Reinitialize watchdog timer count
        error = function1();    // Perform first user function
        if (error)
            exit while;
        endif;
        resetWatchdog();        // Tell the timer we are still alive
        error = function2();    // Perform second user function
        if (error)
            exit while;
        endif;
        resetWatchdog();
        error = function3();    // Perform third user function
    }
}
```

If any one of the functions, function1 through function3, becomes stuck in an infinite loop, or just hangs, the watchdog timer count will run out. One of the tricks involved in this type of programming is to ensure that no function runs longer than the watchdog timeout interval, including any interrupts that might take place along the way.

There are literally hundreds of different kinds of microcontrollers, some of which are built with specific applications in mind. Some of the most popular are Intel's 8051; Microchip's 16F84A, one of the PIC (Programmable Intelligent Computer) family; and Motorola's 68HC12, one of the many chips in the so-called 68000 (68K) series. Microcontrollers can have analog interfaces that are suitable for nondiscrete physical control applications and I/O buffers designed for continuous high-volume throughput. Microcontroller I/O control may be through any of the methods described in Chapter 7. Unlike general-purpose systems, however, programmed I/O control is feasible for embedded control applications.

Microcontroller CPUs can be as small as 4 bits and as large as 64 bits, with memory ranging from a few kilobytes to several megabytes. To make their circuitry as small and as fast as possible, microcontroller ISAs are generally stack based and can be optimized for a particular area of specialization. Despite their "old technology," microcontrollers continue to be widely used in a vast array of consumer products and industrial machinery. One has every reason to believe that this will continue to be the case for many years to come.

Watchdog Timer Engineering Decisions

Embedded systems designers may spend a good amount of time debating whether an expired watchdog timer should immediately issue a reset or whether it should instead invoke an interrupt routine. If an interrupt is issued, valuable debugging information can be captured prior to issuing the reset. Debugging information often exposes the root cause of the timeout, permitting the problem to be analyzed and corrected. If the system is simply reset, most of the diagnostic information is lost.

On the other hand, it is possible for a failing system to become so hobbled that it cannot reliably execute any code, including interrupt processing code. Thus, the reset might never be issued by the interrupt routine. Such irrecoverable errors can be caused by something as simple as a corrupted stack pointer, or an errant signal in an I/O port. If we simply issue a reset, we are certain that—barring a catastrophic hardware failure—the system will return to a consistent state within milliseconds.

Unlike personal computer reboots, embedded controller resets take very little time. In fact, resets can happen so quickly that it is not always possible to know whether a reset has occurred. This problem lends weight to the argument that the interrupt approach is superior to the reset approach. The other side of the argument is that there is a hardware solution: Prudent engineers connect a latch and a light-emitting diode (LED) to the processor's reset line. After a reset, the LED will stay illuminated to indicate that a problem has occurred. Assuming that the LED is situated in a location where a human can see it, the reset event will sooner or later be noticed.

It is, of course, possible to combine both approaches. We might initialize the timer with a small value prior to invoking the debugging interrupt. If the count expires, it is certain that the system is in trouble, and a reset would subsequently be issued by the watchdog. A company that seeks to deliver a "quality" product would do well to give this technique some consideration.

However, a company that seeks to go beyond delivering a "quality" product to produce a "high-reliability" system has to think a little deeper. Watchdog timers usually share the silicon space and resources of the systems they are supposed to be watching. What happens if a catastrophic hardware failure occurs in the chip itself? What if the system clock stops? Engineers plan for this contingency by providing a backup watchdog timer on a separate chip. The extra circuit adds only a few dollars to the cost of a system, but may save thousands of dollars—or human lives—if it is ever needed. So now the discussion moves to whether the backup watchdog timer should issue a reset or whether it should instead process the timeout through an interrupt routine.

Systems on a Chip

We have observed that microcontrollers are computer systems in miniature. They consist of a CPU, memory, and I/O ports. They are not, however, called systems on a chip. That designation is usually reserved for devices that are much more complex.

Systems on a chip (**SOCs**) are distinguished from microcontrollers by their complexity and increased on-chip resources. Microcontrollers often require supporting circuits such as signal processors, decoders, and signal converters, to name only a few. A system on a chip is a single piece of silicon that contains all circuits required to deliver a set of functions. A system on a chip can even consist of more than one processor. These loosely coupled processors do not necessarily share the same clock or memory space. The individual processor functions can be specialized to the extent that they are provided with ISAs designed specifically for efficient programming in a particular application domain. For example, an Internet router may have several RISC processors that handle communications traffic, and a CISC processor for configuration and management of the router itself. Although microcontroller memory is usually measured in kilobytes, SOCs can include memory on the order of megabytes. With their larger memories, SOCs accommodate full-featured real-time operating systems (which we discuss in Section 10.3.2). The great advantage of SOCs is that they are faster, smaller, more reliable, and consume less power than the several chips they replace.

Although there are many off-the-shelf SOCs available, customization is sometimes required to support a particular application. Rather than absorb the cost of designing an SOC from scratch, a semicustom chip may be assembled from intellectual property (IP) circuits licensed from companies that specialize in creating and testing circuit designs. Licensed IP module designs are combined with customized circuits to produce a circuit mask. The completed mask is subsequently sent to a circuit fabrication facility (a fab) to be etched in silicon. This process is very expensive. Mask costs are now approaching $1 million (US). The economic benefits of this approach must therefore be considered carefully. If a standard SOC provides the same functionality—even with lesser performance—the $1 million expenditure is not justifiable. We return to this idea in a later section.

10.2.2 Configurable Hardware

Some applications are so specialized that no off-the-shelf microcontroller can do the job. When designers find themselves in this situation, they can choose between two alternatives: They can elect to create a chip from scratch, or they can employ a **programmable logic device** (**PLD**). When speed and die size are not primary concerns, a PLD may be a good choice. PLDs come in three general varieties: programmable array logic, programmable logic arrays, and field-programmable gate arrays. Any of these three types of circuits can be used as **glue logic**, or customized circuits that interconnect prefabricated IP circuit elements. Programmable logic devices are usually presented along with the

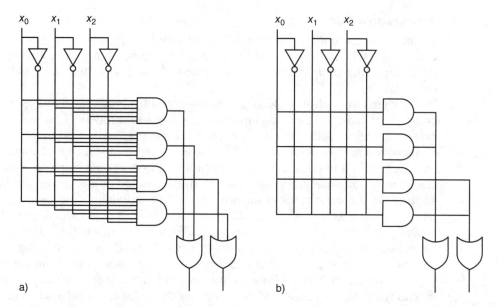

FIGURE 10.2 Programmable Array Logic (PAL)
a) Detailed logic diagram for a PAL
b) A shorthand version of the same PAL

combinational logic components we described in Chapter 3. We have deferred this discussion until now because it is helpful to understand the functional context in which these chips are most useful.

Programmable Array Logic

Programmable Array Logic (PAL) chips were the first logic devices that could be configured to provide a variety of logic functions. PALs consist of a set of inputs and a set of outputs that are connected by an array of programmable AND gates and a fixed array of OR gates, as shown in Figure 10.2. A PAL chip's outputs give a sum-of-products function of its inputs. The circuit is programmed by blowing fuses or throwing switches within a conductor grid that interconnects the inputs and the AND gates. When a PAL fuse is blown, the AND gate input to which it is connected becomes a logical 0.[1] OR gates collect the outputs from the AND gates to complete the function.

Figure 10.3 illustrates a 3-input, 2-output PAL. Standard commercial PALs provide several inputs and dozens of outputs. In the figure, it is easy to see that

---

[1] There are two types of PLD fuses. The first type requires a higher than normal voltage on the fuse that causes it to blow, severing any connection. The second type of fuse is sometimes referred to as an antifuse because its initial state is open. When an antifuse is blown, a conductive path is created by melting a thin insulating layer between two conducting lines, thus completing a circuit. This is the opposite behavior that we normally expect from a fuse. In our discussions in this chapter, we refer to the first type of technology—so blowing a fuse indicates severing the connection.

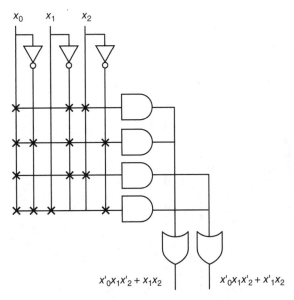

FIGURE 10.3 A Programmed PAL

it is not possible to provide an output for every possible function of the inputs. It is also not possible to use the same product term in more than one OR gate, so a product term may have to be repeated across more than one OR gate.

Figure 10.3 shows a PAL programmed to provide the functions $x_0' x_1 x_2' + x_1 x_2$ and $x_0' x_1 x_2' + x_1' x_2$. The connections between the logic devices are indicated as "blown" using an $\times$. (Sometimes we see PAL illustrations use $\times$ to indicate a connection, that is, a fuse that is *not* blown.) As you can see, the minterm $x_0' x_1 x_2'$ is repeated. It would seem that we could make more efficient use of our gates if arbitrary connections were also allowed between the OR gates. Programmable logic arrays are devices that provide this additional level of configurability.

Programmable Logic Arrays (PLAs)

It is easy to see that the outputs of a PAL are always the logical sum of all the logical products provided by the AND gates in the array. In our illustration above, each output function consists of two minterms, regardless of whether we need them both. PLAs remove this restriction by providing fuses or switches for the OR gates and the AND gates, as shown in Figure 10.4. The blown fuses or thrown switches provide logical 0s as inputs to the AND gates and to the OR gates.

PLAs are more flexible than PALs, but they also tend to be slower and more costly than PALs. Thus, the occasional redundancy among PAL minterms is only a minor inconvenience when speed and cost are important considerations. To maximize functionality and flexibility, PLA and PAL chips usually include several arrays on one silicon die. Both types are referred to as **complex programmable logic devices (CPLDs)**.

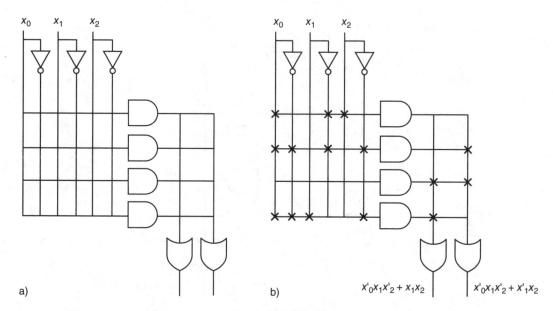

FIGURE 10.4   a) A programmable logic array
b) A PLA reusing a minterm

Field-Programmable Gate Arrays

A third type of PLD, the **field-programmable gate array** (**FPGA**), provides programmable logic using lookup tables instead of changing the wiring of the chip.

Figure 10.5 shows a typical FPGA logic element consisting of memory cells and multiplexers. The inputs of the multiplexers (labeled MUX) are selected according to the values of the logic function inputs, x and y. These inputs trigger multiplexer selection of the appropriate memory cell, labeled "?" in the diagram. The value stored in the memory cell is then raised on the appropriate output of the multiplexer.

As a simple example, consider the XOR function discussed in Chapter 3. The truth table for a two-input XOR is shown at the left in Figure 10.6a. The table has been programmed into the FPGA as shown at the right. You can see the direct correspondence between the values in the truth table and the values in the memory cells. For example, when the y signal is high (logical 1), the lower memory cell value of each pair is selected by the leftmost pair of multiplexers. When the x value is high, the input from the lower y multiplexer is selected, giving a logical 0 for the value on the output of the x multiplexer. This agrees with the truth table: 1 XOR 1 = 0. Figure 10.6b shows FPGA programming for the AND function.

FPGA logic elements are interconnected through a routing architecture that consists of switches and connection multiplexers. A typical configuration, called an **island architecture**, is shown in Figure 10.7. Each connection multiplexer and

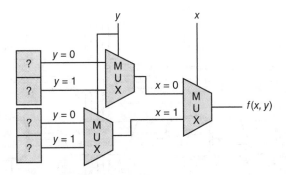

FIGURE 10.5 Logic Diagram for a Field Programmable Gate Array Logic Element

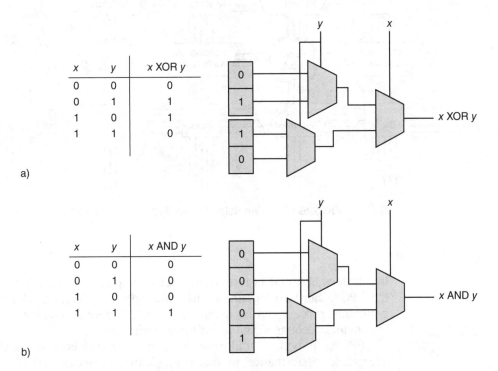

x	y	x XOR y
0	0	0
0	1	1
1	0	1
1	1	0

a)

x	y	x AND y
0	0	0
0	1	0
1	0	0
1	1	1

b)

FIGURE 10.6 Logic Diagram for a Field Programmable Gate Array

switch block is programmed to connect the outputs of one logic element to the inputs of another. A good portion of the chip area, usually about 70%, is devoted to connection and routing functions. This is one of the many things that make FPGAs slow and costly.

To help reduce cost and improve speed and functionality, some FPGAs are also equipped with microprocessor cores. It would seem that such chips give designers the best of everything: The microprocessor can carry out the functions

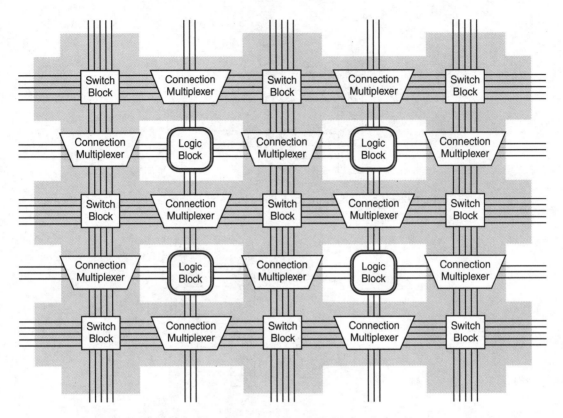

FIGURE 10.7 An "Island Style" FPGA Configuration

that it does best and fastest. Where the microprocessor functionality falls short, the FPGA can be programmed to make up the difference. Moreover, the programming process can be iterative. An FPGA permits continual changes while the circuit is debugged and tuned for performance.

FPGAs provide a multitude of logic functions at a reasonable cost with acceptable performance in many applications. Because they can be reprogrammed as many times as needed, FPGAs are especially useful for prototyping customized circuit designs. In fact, FPGAs can even be programmed to reprogram themselves! Because of this, FPGA-based systems are considered by many to be the first of a new breed of computers that can dynamically reconfigure themselves in response to variations in workload or component failures. They have the potential to bring new levels of reliability to critical embedded processors that operate in hostile or safety-critical environments. They can repair themselves whenever a human can't get to them—or can't get to them quickly enough to avert catastrophe.

Reconfigurable Computers

It hardly escapes anyone's notice that our world is awash in electronic gizmos and gadgets. The well-equipped college student is laden with a notebook computer, a cellular telephone, a personal digital assistant, a CD player, and possibly an electronic book reader. So how does one deal with having so much electronic stuff to lug around?

Clothing manufacturers have addressed the problem by providing clothing and backpacks with ample specialized pockets. At least one clothier has gone so far as to create garments having built-in "personal area networks"!

The "engineering solution" to the problem of the gadget glut is just to make fewer gadgets, giving each greater functionality. The greatest challenges lie in overcoming the barriers presented by the power and cost constraints of portable consumer electronics. Certainly, a notebook computer can do just about anything we want it to, but it all happens at the expense of weight and high power consumption. Thus, we have the Holy Grail of reconfigurable electronics: a single, affordable, electronic device that can be a cell phone, a PDA, a camera, and even a music playback device, with sufficient battery life to be useful.

There is no doubt that this vision lies far past today's horizons. The reconfigurable devices of today consist mainly of FPGAs. Today's FPGAs are too slow, too power hungry, and much too expensive for wide deployment in consumer electronics. Research in this area is following several tracks. The first approach concerns the routing architecture of FPGA chips. Different topologies have been found to be more effective than others in certain applications. Most notably, linear configurations are better for shifters, because bit shifting is inherently a linear operation. A three-dimensional approach is also under study by several companies. This topology places the control elements beneath the logic elements, making the entire package denser and the routes shorter.

Another concern related to topology is inconsistent signal response within the chip. Signals traveling a longer distance through the routing structure take longer to get where they're going than signals traveling only a short distance. This tends to slow down the whole chip, because there seems no way to know in advance whether an operation will use a logic element that is nearby or one that is far away. Clock speed is limited by the worst case. Electronic design language compilers (see below) optimized for FPGA implementations are helping to make progress in this area.

Logic cell memory power consumption is an active area of FPGA research. This memory is usually SRAM, which is volatile. This means that the FPGA must be configured each time it is powered on, and the configuration has to be stored in ROM or flash. Various nonvolatile memories have been created from materials that are (for now) too exotic for the general market. If these new memories show promise in the general market, mass production will eventually drive down their cost.

It is also possible to create hybrid FPGA chips that contain islands of generic circuits (such as adders or shifters) that are common to all functions served by the device. The rest of the chip is then available for function-specific logic that can be paged on and off the circuit as needed.

In the short term, reconfigurable circuits may be incorporated in specialized applications such as cell phone communications protocol modules. Cell phones equipped with flexible modules could operate efficiently across areas that employ differing protocols within a national (or international) cell phone network. Although this idea is certainly appealing to the consumer's wallet, it also means fewer discarded phones ending up in solid waste landfills, ameliorating an environmental problem of growing importance.

10.2.3   Custom-Designed Embedded Hardware

To command the largest market for their products, embedded processor manufacturers load their chips with as many features as possible. The chief disadvantage in purchasing these complex, ready-made processors is that some of the functionality of the chip may not be needed. Unused circuits not only cause the chip to run slower, but they also generate heat and waste precious power. In a tightly constrained application, programmable logic devices are not much help because they tend to be slow and power hungry. In short, there are situations where the only reasonable approach is to create a fully customized **application-specific integrated circuit** (**ASIC**).

Designing full-custom ASICs requires thinking of the chip from three perspectives: From a behavioral perspective, we define exactly what the chip is supposed to do. How do we produce the desired outputs as functions of the inputs? From a structural perspective, we determine which logic components provide the desired behavior. From a physical perspective, we think of how the components should be placed on the silicon die to make the best use of chip real estate and minimize connection distances between the components.

Each perspective is a unique problem domain requiring a distinct set of tools. The interrelationship of these ideas is made clear by the logic synthesis Y-chart developed by Daniel Gajski, shown in Figure 10.8.

Each of the three axes in Gajski's chart is labeled to show the levels of detail for each dimension of chip design. As an example, consider a binary counter. At the highest behavioral level (the algorithmic level), we know that the counter increments its current value, producing a new value. At the next lower level, we understand that to carry out this function, some sort of register is needed to hold the value of the counter. We can state this idea using a register transfer statement such as $AC \leftarrow AC + 1$.

On the structural side, we specify how large the register will be. The register consists of gates and flip-flops, which themselves consist of transistors. To make a silicon chip that contains the counter, each storage cell is positioned and connected to make the best use of die space.

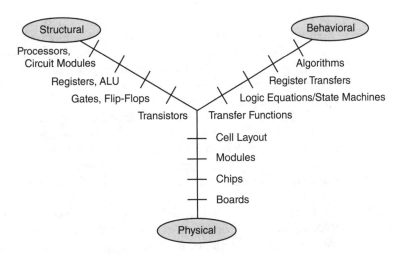

FIGURE 10.8 Gajski's Logic Synthesis Y-Chart

Direct manual synthesis of logic components is feasible only for very small circuits. Today's ASICs consist of hundreds of thousands of gates and millions of transistors. The complexity of these chips escapes human comprehension. Various tools and design languages help manage the complexity, but the constantly increasing gate densities are forcing the design process to a higher plane of abstraction. One of the tools used in dealing with this complexity is the **hardware definition language (HDL)**. Hardware definition languages allow a designer to specify circuit behavior on an algorithmic level. Instead of thinking about the circuit in terms of gates and wires, a designer works with variables and control structures in a manner similar to working with a second- or third-generation programming language. Instead of creating a stream of binary machine code, the HDL source code produces a specification for gates and wires called a **netlist**. The netlist is suitable input for the software that ultimately produces the silicon die layout.

HDLs have been around for a few decades. The earliest of these were proprietary languages supplied by chip fabricators. One of these languages, **Verilog**, created by Gateway Design Automation in 1983, became one of the two leading design languages by the end of the twentieth century. In 1989, Cadence Design Systems bought Gateway, and in the next year, it released Verilog into the public domain. Verilog became an IEEE standard in 1995, the latest version of which is IEEE 1364-2001.

Because it was patterned after the C programming language, Verilog is considered an easy language to learn. With C being a popular language for writing embedded systems software, engineers can shift between writing software and designing hardware with relative ease. Verilog produces netlists at two levels of abstraction. The highest level, the register transfer level (RTL), uses constructs akin to any C language program, with variables replaced by registers and signals. When necessary, Verilog can also model circuits at the gate and transistor levels.

The second dominant HDL is **VHDL**, which is an abbreviation for Very (high-speed integrated circuit) Hardware Design Language. VHDL came into existence under a U.S. Defense Advanced Research Program Agency (DARPA) contract awarded in 1983 to Intermetrics, IBM, and Texas Instruments. The language was released in August 1985, and it became an IEEE standard in 1987. Its latest revision is IEEE 1097-2002.

VHDL syntax is similar to the Ada programming language, which was once the only language authorized for use in any Defense Department projects. VHDL models circuits at a higher level than Verilog. Like Ada, it is a strongly typed language that permits user-defined types. Unlike Verilog, VHDL supports concurrent procedure calls, which are essential for multiprocessor designs.

Increasingly, VHDL and Verilog are strained to keep up with advances in VLSI technology. Modeling and testing the latest multimillion-gate circuits with these languages is tedious, error prone, and costly. It has become evident that the level of abstraction in chip design must be raised once again to allow designers to think in terms of functions, processes, and systems, as opposed to worrying about gates, signals, and wires. Several system-level design languages have been proposed to fill this need. Two competing languages have emerged as leaders of the pack: SystemC and SpecC.

SystemC is an extension of C++ that includes classes and libraries geared specifically for modeling timing, events, reactive behavior, and concurrency in embedded systems. It was the product of the combined efforts of several electronic design automation (EDA) and embedded software companies. Among its strongest proponents were Synopsys, CoWare, and Frontier Design. They garnered support from virtually every other major player in the industry. A consortium of business and academic experts, the Open SystemC Initiative, oversees the evolution and promotion of the language.

The principal aim for the invention of SystemC was to create an architecture-independent specification language that would be widely disseminated and supported within the electronic design community. To this end, anyone agreeing to the terms of the SystemC license may download the language source code and its requisite class libraries. Any ANSI-compliant C++ compiler can produce executable SystemC modules.

SystemC models designs at two levels of abstraction. At the highest level, only the circuit functionality is specified. This specification is sufficient for production of simulation test suites and netlists. If finer granularity is required, SystemC can produce a system or module at the hardware implementation level using either a functional or an RTN style.

SpecC is another system-level design language arousing some interest in the EDA industry. SpecC was originally developed at the University of California at Irvine by Daniel Gajski, Jianwen Zhu, Rainer Dömer, Andreas Gerstlauer, and Shuqing Zhao. It has since been placed under the control of the SpecC Open Consortium, which consists of a number of academic and industry leaders. The SpecC compiler and its related tools and documentation are available from the SpecC website.

The SpecC language differs from SystemC in two fundamental ways. First, SpecC is a modification of the C programming language that is tailored to the needs of embedded system design. Designers of SpecC found that their objectives could not be met through the simple addition of libraries (as is the case with SystemC).

The second—and most remarkable—difference between SpecC and SystemC is that SpecC includes a design methodology as part of the package. The methodology guides engineers through four facets of system development: its specification, architecture, communication channels, and implementation.

Indeed, using any of the several system-level specification languages requires some degree of departure from the embedded system design methodologies that have been in use for decades. The traditional approach typically follows the paths shown in Figure 10.9. The process flows as follows:

- A detailed specification is derived from a functional description articulated by the designers of the product in which the embedded system will be installed. Product improvement ideas based on customer feedback can be put forth by the marketing department at this stage.

- Based on the specification and sales estimates, engineers decide whether an off-the-shelf processor is suitable, or whether creating a custom-designed processor makes more sense.

- The next step is to partition the system into a hardware component and a software component. Consideration is given to the availability of intellectual property designs and to the footprint and power requirements of the proposed processor.

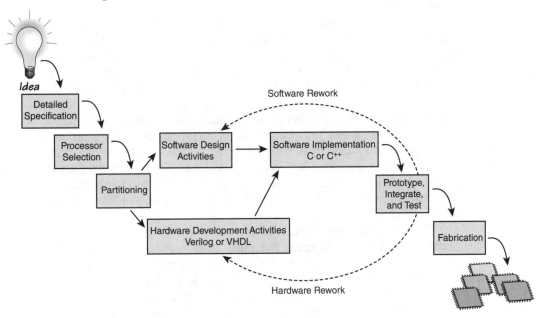

FIGURE 10.9 A Traditional Embedded System Design Cycle

- With the system partitioning complete, general software and detailed hardware design begins. Software design proceeds to the point where the underlying machine architecture of the finished product makes a difference. After the underlying machine structure is finalized, the programming can be completed.

- A hardware prototype may be created allowing the software to be tested in the prototype. If for some reason a prototype cannot be created, a software simulation of the completed processor is produced. Integration testing usually involves creating test vectors that contain the binary state of the signals on each pin of the processor as it executes its program. Simulation testing consumes many hours of execution time in the simulator, because each clock tick of the new processor must be simulated using the test vectors as inputs and outputs of a complex program.

- When testing is completed to everyone's satisfaction, the finalized design is sent to a fabrication facility, which produces the finished microprocessor.

At any rate, this is how things are supposed to work. However, this is not always the case. The reverse arrows in the diagram are two of the paths that can be taken when an error is discovered. Because hardware and software are developed by two different teams, it is easy for a critical function to be overlooked or for a requirement to be misunderstood. Misunderstandings in requirements can, in fact, ripple back through the whole process, causing redesign after the fabrication step has been completed. In the worst case, a design flaw would be detected after the processor is placed in the finished product. Errors found this late in the process are enormously costly to correct, both in terms of retooling the hardware or software (or both), and in terms of lost opportunity in the marketplace.

Today's chip complexity is exponentially greater than it was when Verilog and VHDL were invented. The traditional model for embedded system development is increasingly error prone and unsuited for today's shrinking product development time frames. The potential competitive edge offered by processor-enabled consumer products is lost when the time to market increases because of protracted processor design time frames. This gives similar products without complex processors command of the market until the more sophisticated product is introduced. In order for manufacturers of processor-enabled products to stay competitive, it is clear that the embedded systems methodology must change. System-level languages like SystemC and SpecC are the facilitators of this change. Not only do these languages raise the level of design abstraction, but they also remove many of the barriers that are so vexing in traditional embedded processor development projects.

The first limitation inherent in the traditional design life cycle is that development teams do not all speak the same language. The "idea people" state their requirements in plain English. A structured system-level design is then derived from their requirements. The specification is next translated into Verilog or VHDL for the hardware design. The hardware design is then "thrown over the wall" to the software designers, who are usually doing their work in C, C++, or assembly. Multiple iterations through this disjointed process can result in reworking the design in at least two different languages.

How much simpler life would be if everyone spoke the same language, and if everyone were working on the same models throughout the design life of the processor! Indeed, one of the greatest benefits offered by SystemC or SpecC is that they both present a uniform, high-level view of the system. Such consistency permits **codevelopment**, where hardware and software are designed simultaneously. The product design life cycle can thus be shortened appreciably while improving processor design quality.

A streamlined codesign methodology life cycle is shown in Figure 10.10. As you can see, fewer distinct steps are involved:

- A system-level processor simulation is drawn up in SpecC or SystemC, using the inputs, outputs, and other constraints derived from the detailed specification. This is the **behavioral model** of the system. The behavioral model validates the designers' understanding of the functions of the processor. This model will also be used to validate the behavior of the completed design.

- Next, during the system **codesign phase**, software development and virtual hardware development proceed concurrently through stepwise decomposition and refinement of the system specification. Partitioning decisions take into consideration the usual array of concerns, including time–space trade-offs. However, because the hardware design is only simulated at this point, partitioning becomes a dynamic activity instead of one where the objective is to force the software to work in a (fairly) static hardware prototype.

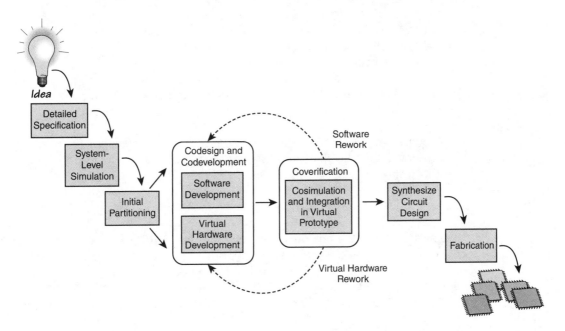

FIGURE 10.10 Embedded Processor Codevelopment

- Through each refinement step, the behavioral model of the system is checked against the simulated processor in a process called **coverification**. Design corrections are expedited because the hardware design is only a computer simulation of the final product. Additionally, because of the close proximity of the development teams, the number of iterations is usually decreased.

- Once the programming and virtual hardware models are complete, their functions are tested simultaneously using a virtual model of the processor. This activity is called **cosimulation**.

- With the functionality of both the hardware and software verified against the original behavioral model, a netlist can be synthesized and sent for layout and fabrication.

Although they were the first, neither SystemC nor SpecC is the last word on system-level development languages. Efforts are also under way to adapt Java and UML for this purpose. Support-tool vendors and their customers will determine which of these wins out. Clearly, the sun is setting on the era when circuits are designed exclusively with VHDL or Verilog. Moreover, if a standard language could be agreed upon, intellectual property designs could be exchanged economically. Vendors should be relieved of the risk in choosing a single design language, or the costs of supporting several of them. Intellectual effort could be spent in developing better designs, rather than translating designs from one language to another.

Embedded System Trade-offs

The costly task of designing a full-custom die is undertaken only when no off-the-shelf chip has the desired functionality, power consumption profile, or speed—or, if such a chip is available, the cost of using it cannot be justified.

Because embedded systems are sold as an unnoticed part of some other product, the decision to build or buy is rarely made without considerable market analysis. Two questions weigh heavily in the decision: What is the expected market demand for the product, and how long will it take to bring the product to market if a custom processor is built?

Although it is enormously expensive to design and fabricate a processor, in very large quantities, the economics may favor a customized solution. This idea is captured by the following processor cost formula:

Total processor cost = Fixed cost + (unit cost × number of units)

Fixed costs are the **non-recurring engineering** (**NRE**) expenses that include designing and testing the processor, producing the masks, and production setup. Unit cost is the amount of money required to produce each unit after all the setup is complete.

As an example, suppose we are in the video game business. Let's say that the hottest new game is expected to be spawned by a movie version of *Gulliver's Travels* to be released in June. (One plays the game by controlling the antics of the Lilliputians.) Our marketing staff believes that with timely release of our game, we can sell 50,000 units, which will be priced to give us a profit of $12 per unit. From previous experience, we know that our total NRE expenses for such a product would be $750,000, and each processor would cost $10 to produce. Thus, the total cost for the game unit processors is:

Game unit processor cost = $750,000 + (50,000 × $10) = $1,250,000

The alternative is to purchase a processor that is a little slower and more expensive (per unit) than the custom processor. If such processors cost $30 each in lots of 10,000, the total cost for the processors in the game is:

Game unit processor cost = $0 + (50,000 × $30) = $1,500,000

Thus, the custom-design approach would save $250,000 in processor costs. This means we could charge the customer less per unit, or increase our per-unit profit, or have some combination of both.

Clearly, our cost model rests on the assumption that we will sell 50,000 units. If that assumption holds true, the choice seems obvious. One thing we have not considered, however, is the length of time it will take to build the processor.

Suppose that the marketing department has come up with monthly sales projections as shown in the chart below. Based on their experience with movie-themed games, the marketing staff knows that some units will be sold before the movie is released. Sales will peak the month following the movie release and will then decline steadily over the subsequent six months.

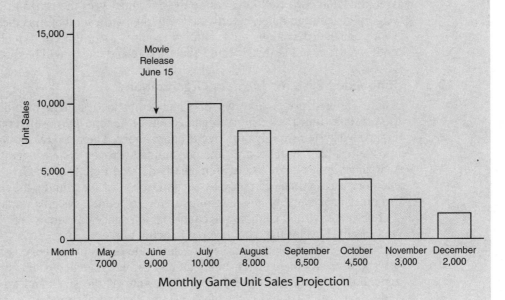

Monthly Game Unit Sales Projection

To sell 50,000 units, the product must be on store shelves by May 1. If the design and manufacture of the customized processor causes us to miss the May product release by three months or more, the best choice becomes one of using an off-the-shelf processor despite its higher unit cost and lower performance.

Our (greatly) simplified example illustrates the trade-offs that take place when the timing of product release is essential to profitability. Another reason for choosing an off-the-shelf processor or an FPGA might also be when sales data are unclear. In other words, if market demand is uncertain, it makes sense to minimize the initial investment by using a standard part rather than incur the NRE expenses of a customized processor. If the product proves to be a hot seller, the NRE expenses would be justified in releasing a subsequent "new and improved" model of the product (containing a faster, customized processor) that would generate even more sales.

10.3 AN OVERVIEW OF EMBEDDED SOFTWARE

Thanks to virtual memory and gigahertz processor clocks, a general applications programmer typically doesn't have to give much thought to the hardware that runs the programs. Moreover, when he or she writes an application program, perhaps in C or Java, performance problems are usually addressed only after several user complaints have been made. Sometimes the problem is solved by an adjustment to the program code; sometimes it is solved by adding hardware components to the machine that is running the slow application. The embedded systems programmer typically writes programs exclusively in assembly language and does not have the luxury of after-the-fact performance tuning. Performance problems must be identified and corrected long before the consumer sees the program in operation. Algorithms are intimately intertwined with the hardware that runs the program. In short, embedded systems programming requires us to think differently about the code we write, and to think deeply about where and how it will be run.

10.3.1 Embedded Systems Memory Organization

There are two principal ways in which embedded system memory organization differs from the memory organization of general-purpose computers. First, embedded systems rarely employ virtual memory. The main reason for this is that most embedded systems are time constrained. Proper system operation requires that all activities take place within clearly defined time frames. Given that virtual memory access times can vary by several orders of magnitude, the timing model becomes unacceptably nondeterministic for embedded systems implementations. Furthermore, virtual memory page table maintenance consumes precious memory and machine cycles that could be put to better use.

The second distinctive aspect of embedded system memory is the variability and diversity of memory architectures. Unlike general systems programmers, embedded programmers are continually aware of the sizes and types of available memory. A single embedded system can contain random access memory

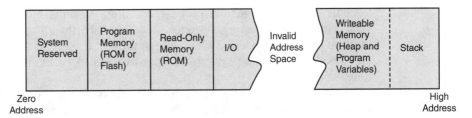

FIGURE 10.11 An Embedded System Memory Model

(RAM), ROM, and flash memory. Memory space is not always continuous, so some memory addresses may be invalid. Figure 10.11 shows a model execution environment, consisting of several predefined address blocks. The reserved system memory space contains interrupt vectors that hold interrupt service routine (ISR) addresses. ISR programs are invoked in response to various signals as they are raised on the pins of the processor. (The programmer has no control over which pins are connected to which vector.)

You will also notice that our memory space distinguishes between program memory, writeable data memory, and read-only memory. Read-only memory contains constants and literals used by the embedded program. Because small embedded systems usually run only one program, constants can be stored in ROM, thus protecting them from accidental overwrites. In many embedded systems, the designer determines the placement of program code, and whether the code will reside in RAM, ROM, or flash memory. The stack and the heap are often implemented in static RAM to eliminate the need for DRAM refresh cycles. An embedded system may or may not use a heap. Some programmers avoid dynamic memory allocation altogether for the same reasons that virtual memory is avoided: Memory cleanup incurs overhead that can cause unpredictable access delays. More importantly, memory cleanup should be performed routinely to avoid the risk of running out of heap space. Embedded systems memory leaks are serious business because some systems may operate for months or years without rebooting. Without explicit cleanup or restarts, even the smallest memory leak will eventually consume the entire heap, causing a system crash that could be catastrophic.

10.3.2 Embedded Operating Systems

Simple microcontrollers typically run a single application that tends to be of low to medium complexity. As such, microcontrollers require no task or resource management beyond that which is provided by its program. As the capabilities of embedded hardware continue to grow, embedded applications become more diverse and complex. Today's high-end embedded processors are capable of supporting multiple concurrent programs. As we explained in Chapter 8, it is difficult to exploit the capabilities of today's powerful processors without sophisticated multitasking and other resource management that is routinely provided by an operating system—but not just *any* operating system. Embedded operating systems differ from general-purpose operating systems in two important ways. First, embedded operating systems allow direct hardware access, unlike general-purpose operating systems, which aim to prevent it. Second and more importantly, an embedded operating system's responsiveness to events is clearly defined and understood.

Embedded operating systems are not necessarily real-time operating systems. In Chapter 8, we mentioned that there are two types of real-time systems. "Hard" real-time means that system responses take place within strictly defined timing parameters. "Soft" real-time systems have more lenient timing constraints, but a soft real-time system is still reactive to its environment within clearly defined bounds.

Embedded devices that carry out activities based solely on human interactions with them are no stricter in their timing requirements than ordinary desktop computers. A sluggish response from a cell phone or PDA is an annoyance, but usually not a crisis. In a real-time system, however, responsiveness is an essential factor in determining its correct behavior. In short, if the response from a real-time system is late, it's wrong.

Two of the most important metrics in the evaluation of real-time operating systems are context switch time and interrupt latency. **Interrupt latency** is the elapsed time between the occurrence of an interrupt and the execution of the first instruction of the interrupt service routine.

Interrupt handling lies at the heart of real-time systems design. Programmers must be continually mindful of the fact that interrupts can occur at any time, even while other critical activities are taking place. Thus, if the highest-priority user thread is executing when a high-priority interrupt occurs, what should the operating system do? Some systems continue to process the user thread while keeping the interrupt in queue until the user thread processing is complete. This approach may or may not present a problem depending on the application and the speed of the hardware.

In hard real-time applications, the system must quickly respond to external events. Therefore, a hard real-time scheduler must be preemptive. The best real-time embedded operating systems allow a wide range of values in the assignment of task and interrupt priorities. However, priority inversion can be problematic. Thread priority inversion occurs when a higher-priority task needs the services provided by a task that runs at a lower priority, or when a lower-priority task holds a resource that a higher-priority task requires in order to complete. When one of these conditions exists, the higher-priority task can do nothing but wait for the lower-priority task to complete. Conceivably, the system could deadlock. Some embedded operating systems deal with priority inversion through priority inheritance: Once the situation is recognized, the priorities are equalized so that all competing tasks can complete.

The second type of priority inversion pertains to interrupts. Interrupts can be disabled during interrupt processing. This avoids a situation called **interrupt nesting**, where interrupt service routines are interrupted to process other interrupts, potentially causing stack overflow in the extreme case. The problem arises with this approach whenever a high-priority interrupt occurs while a low-priority interrupt is being serviced. When interrupts are disabled, the high-priority interrupt ends up sitting in the queue until the lower-priority interrupt service routine completes. High-quality systems allow interrupt nesting and will recognize the occurrence of a high-priority interrupt, subsequently preempting the lower-priority interrupt service routine.

After responsiveness, the next most important consideration in operating system selection is usually memory footprint. Using a small, efficient operating system kernel means that less memory has to be installed in each device. This gives us a cost model that pits operating system license fees against memory chip prices. If memory is expensive, you can afford to pay more for a small, optimized operating system. If memory is very expensive, or most of it is needed for the application program, the effort of hand coding a totally customized operating system may be justified. With cheap memory, a larger operating system with good tool support may be the better choice.

Embedded operating systems vendors aim to strike a balance between offering a variety of features and small footprint by making their systems as modular as possible. The kernel typically consists of little more than a scheduler, an interprocess communications manager, primitive I/O facilities, and a collection of protection mechanisms, such as semaphores. All other operating system features, such as file management, network support, and a user interface, are optional. If they are not needed, they aren't installed.

The extent to which an operating system adheres to standards can be critical in selecting one operating system over another. One of the most important standards is the IEEE 1003.1-2001 Portable Operating System Interface, POSIX (pronounced *paw-zicks*), which is a standardized Unix specification that now includes real-time extensions. POSIX real-time specifications include provisions for timers, signals, shared memory, scheduling, and mutexes. A POSIX-compliant real-time operating system must implement these functions through interfaces as specified in the standard. Many major embedded operating systems manufacturers have had their products certified as POSIX compliant by the IEEE. This certification is required for work performed under U.S. government and military contracts.

There are literally dozens of embedded operating systems available. Among the most popular are QNX, Windows 8 Embedded, and Embedded Linux. QNX is the oldest of this group, and at less than 10 kilobytes, it has the smallest memory footprint. QNX is POSIX compliant with installable GUI, file system, and I/O systems, including PCI, SCSI, USB, serial ports, parallel ports, and Internet communications. For more than 20 years, QNX has been running scientific and medical systems on PowerPC, MIPS, and Intel architectures.

Linux was POSIX compliant from the start, but it was unsuitable (without modifications) for hard real-time systems because it did not have a preemptive scheduler. In September 2003, Linus Torvalds and Andrew Morton released version 2.6 of the Linux kernel. This version includes a more efficient scheduling algorithm that is preemptive. Some kernel processes (i.e., "system calls") can also be preempted. Virtual memory is an installable option. (Many embedded systems designers won't install it.) Its minimal footprint for basic functionality is only 250KB. A full-featured installation requires 500KB. Nearly everything outside the Linux kernel is installable—even support for a keyboard, mouse, and display. Embedded Linux distributions are available for every major processor architecture, including several popular microcontrollers.

Microsoft offers several embedded operating systems, each aimed at different classes of embedded systems and mobile devices. In a break with its past, the Windows Embedded suite supports ARM as well as x86-class processors. Adding ARM support was a crucial step in order to keep Microsoft competitive in this arena. Microsoft's enormous investments in the embedded space have brought a dizzying array of products and licensing terms to market. These offerings include the following:

- **Windows Embedded 8 Standard**, a modular version of Windows 8 that allows designers to select only the features that are needed for any particular application. Selectable features include networking, multimedia support, and security.

- **Windows Embedded 8 Pro**, a full Windows 8 version with a modified licensing model suited to the embedded market.

- **Windows Embedded 8 Industry**, a Windows 8 version tailored specifically to the needs of the retail, financial services, and hospitality industries. Enhanced support is provided for point-of-sale (POS) devices, branding, and security.

- **Windows Phone 8**, a lean version of Windows 8 with features specific to supporting the Windows phone platform.

- **Windows Embedded 8 Handheld**, a version of Windows Phone 8 tailored to industrial handheld devices, such as scanners and manufacturing control products.

- **Windows Embedded Compact 2013**, a modular version of Windows 8 that is even more streamlined from Windows 8 Compact. The entire operating system is typically stored in ROM.

- **Windows Embedded Automotive 7**, a specialization of Windows 7 Compact specifically aimed at automotive applications.

When not operating in highly resource-constrained applications, the Windows Embedded 8 series provides traditional software developers an easy transition into the embedded space. The tools, to which developers have become accustomed, such as Visual Studio, can be used for Windows Embedded 8 development without modification. Microsoft has thus opened the door for many traditional applications to be ported to mobile environments, a space that heretofore had been dominated by Android and iOS. In theory, an embedded Windows-based product could be brought to market sooner than competing systems because Windows tools make the programming much easier. Getting to market faster means cash flow starts sooner. This implies that more money is available for memory chips and operating system licensing fees. Of course, cost models are never quite that simple.

Another operating system that is widely used in embedded systems is MS-DOS. Although it was never intended to support real-time hardware, MS-DOS provides access to underlying hardware and responsiveness that is adequate for many applications. If multitasking is not required, its small memory footprint (approximately 64KB) and inexpensive licensing fees make MS-DOS a very attractive embedded operating system option. Additionally, because MS-DOS has been around for so long, tool and driver support is readily available. After all, it stands to reason that if obsolescent desktop processors find new life in embedded systems, there is nothing wrong with bringing their operating systems along for the ride.

10.3.3 Embedded Systems Software Development

The development of general application programs tends to be a highly iterative process. Some of the most successful development methodologies involve prototyping wherein a semifunctional mockup of the application is produced and presented to the system users for their review and comment. In accordance with the user input, the prototype is then modified and presented once again. This process can repeat itself for quite some time. What makes this approach so successful is that it eventually produces a set of unambiguous functional requirements that can be stated in a manner suitable to software implementation.

Although iterative approaches are good for general applications development, embedded systems development requires a much more rigorous and linear path. Functional requirements must be spelled out in great detail before work begins on either the hardware or the software. To this end, formal languages are useful in specifying embedded program behavior, because these languages are unambiguous and testable. Furthermore, unlike general applications, where a little schedule "slippage" is tolerable, embedded development schedules must be carefully planned and monitored to ensure coordination with the hardware development schedule. Unfortunately, even with the most rigorous development efforts, requirements can be overlooked, causing a flurry of last-minute "crunch time" programming activity.

Developing software for complex general applications usually requires the work to be partitioned and delegated to teams of programmers. Without this division of labor, it would be nearly impossible for a large project to meet its deadlines. Assuming that the system and its modules have been properly analyzed and specified, it is usually not too hard to figure out which modules to assign to which teams.

By contrast, embedded software is difficult to partition into team-sized chunks. Many embedded programs "jump to main()" right after the system boots. The programs then run "forever" in a super loop (or grand loop) polling for signals raised by external events.

One area of perennial debate among embedded programmers concerns the use of global variables and unstructured code. As you probably know, global variables are named memory space that is visible from any point in the program. The risk in using global variables is that of side effects: They may be updated in ways that the programmer does not expect through variations in the program's execution path. Global variables make it practically impossible to be certain of the value of a variable at any given time.

The advantage offered by global variables is that of performance. When the scope of a variable is limited to a particular procedure or function, every time the subprogram is invoked, the variable is created in the program's namespace. This activity causes negligible execution delay in a general-purpose system, but when every cycle counts, the overhead of local variable creation can be problematic. This is especially true if a function or subroutine is called frequently, as in processing a routine event.

The same people who advocate the use of global variables are often the same people who condone the use of unstructured ("spaghetti") code in embedded systems. Structured programs consist of a mainline that calls a sequence of procedures or functions, which in turn may call more procedures or functions. The program fragment given in our discussion of microcontrollers in Section 10.2.1 is an example of a structured program mainline. In unstructured code, most—if not all—of the code provided by each of the modules is inside the main loop of the program. Instead of controlling execution by calling modules, unstructured code controls execution using branch (goto) statements.

The problem with unstructured code is that it can be hard to maintain. This is especially true if the program is long and involves a lot of branching. Mistakes are easy to make, especially if there is no obvious way to discern the execution path for any particular block of code. Multiple entrance and exit points can create a debugger's nightmare.

Advocates of unstructured embedded programming point out that subprogram calls involve considerable overhead. The return address is placed on a stack, the subprogram address is retrieved from memory, local variables (if any) are created, and the return address is popped from the stack. Furthermore, if program address space is large, subprogram and return addresses can span two or more bytes, causing multiple stack pushes and pops at both ends of the call. In hearing these arguments, one can't help but wonder that if resources are *that* tight, why wouldn't one just move up to a more powerful processor? Software engineering instinct implores us to find some way other than global variables and spaghetti code to help us to optimize performance.

One of the greatest challenges to the embedded programmer is dealing with events. Events can happen asynchronously and can occur in any order. It is virtually impossible to test all possible sequences of events. There is always the risk that after successfully processing n events, the arrival of event $n + 1$ will cause a failure. Consequently, embedded systems designers carefully craft formal test plans to facilitate rigorous and detailed testing. To the extent possible, proper operation of the product must be ensured before it is released to the field. It is difficult enough to apply patches to standard desktop software, but it is nearly impossible to patch software that conceivably could be running on millions of devices, the whereabouts of which may be unknown and untraceable.

Debugging embedded systems usually requires more than setting a few breakpoints and stepping through code. Indeed, when event timing is suspected as a problem, stepping through code may not be the best way to approach the problem. Many embedded processors are provided with integrated debugging facilities that reveal some of the inner workings of the chip. Motorola provides **Background Debug Mode (BDM)** for its embedded processors. The output of BDM can be connected to a diagnostic system via a special "*n*-wire" connector. The IEEE 1149.1 **Joint Test Action Group (JTAG)** interface samples signals through a serial loop connected to all signals of interest on a chip. **Nexus** (IEEE-5001) is a specialized debugger for automotive systems. People who debug embedded software often find themselves working with oscilloscopes and logic analyzers equally as much as they use traditional debugging tools.

An **in-circuit emulator (ICE)** has helped many embedded system designers out of tight spots. An ICE is a test instrument that integrates microprocessor execution control, memory access (read/write), and real-time trace, among other things. It consists of a microprocessor, shadow memory, and logic that provide control over the emulator's operations. ICE boards vary in their design and capabilities. They can be expensive to buy and build, and hard to learn to use. In the long run, however, they can pay for themselves many times over in the time and frustration they save.

As in general applications development, tool support in the form of compilers, assemblers, and debuggers is important in embedded system work. In fact, tool support can be a major consideration in selecting one processor over another. Because of their varied architectures, each processor offers a unique set of tools that is not necessarily compatible across processor types. Furthermore, simply porting a compiler from one processor to another might not produce a compiler that makes optimal use of the underlying architecture in order to produce optimized code. For example, porting a compiler from a CISC system to a RISC system will probably not result in a compiler that takes advantage of the larger register set of RISC systems.

There may be no tool support at all for custom-developed processors. These systems tend to be the most resource constrained, requiring considerable hand optimization to squeeze maximum work out of every cycle. If the processor is power constrained, its designers will want the clock to run as slowly as possible, thus making optimization even more important to the success of the implementation. Accordingly, creating systems without the benefit of a compiler, assembler, or source-level debugger is the most tedious and costly approach to embedded software development. The results, however, can be magnificently efficient and robust if done properly.

CHAPTER SUMMARY

We encounter hundreds of embedded systems every day. Their diversity defies any effort to define them. The design and programming of these systems require us to think in different ways about hardware, software, and operating systems. The principle of equivalence of hardware and software gives designers maximum flexibility in engineering for performance and economy. Programming embedded systems requires a deep understanding of hardware, and the ability to think in terms of timing and events. Embedded systems designers draw on every aspect of their computer science or engineering education. Mastery of the principles of computer organization and architecture is essential to success in this field. A deep understanding of operating systems concepts helps in resource management and event handling. A good education in the discipline of software engineering provides a foundation for writing solid code and ensuring its quality. A firm foundation in the study of algorithms helps an embedded system designer to write efficient programs without resorting to dangerous shortcuts, such as global variables. Embedded systems require a change in thinking about all aspects of computing, including the division between hardware and software.

Many processors and operating systems long considered "obsolete" for desktop computing continue to live on within embedded systems. They are easy to program and inexpensive. The simplest of these devices is the microcontroller, which usually consists of a CPU core, memory (ROM and RAM), I/O ports, controllers for I/O, and a system bus, clock, and watchdog timer.

More sophisticated embedded processors, called systems on a chip (SOCs), contain more than one CPU. These processors don't necessarily share the same clock or instruction set. Each processor can be specialized to a particular role within the system. Some SOCs are assembled from intellectual property (IP) circuits licensed from companies that specialize in creating and testing special-purpose circuit designs.

The cost of embedded system development and prototyping can be reduced by using programmable logic devices. They come in three general varieties: programmable array logic (PAL), programmable logic arrays (PLAs), and field-programmable gate arrays (FPGAs). PALs and PLAs are programmed by blowing fuses. Their outputs are sum-of-products and product-of-sums functions of their respective inputs. FPGAs, consisting of memory elements and multiplexers, can implement any logic function based on the values supplied in their memory cells. FPGAs can even be programmed to reprogram themselves.

It can be more economical to buy than to build the microcontroller or microprocessor for an embedded system. It usually makes more sense to build rather than buy when large quantities of the chip are required or responsiveness or power constraints are so tight that only a customized ASIC will suffice. Traditionally, hardware and software design activities followed different paths in the development life cycle. Software was designed using C, C++, or assembly. Hardware was designed using Verilog or VHDL. New system-level specification languages are enabling collaborative codesign and coverification by cross-functional teams of hardware and software designers. A dominant system-level language has yet to emerge, although SystemC and SpecC are gaining widespread support.

The memory organization of an embedded system can be quite different from the memory organization of a general-purpose computer. In particular, large blocks of memory addresses may not be valid. Virtual memory is rarely used. Programs and constant values are usually stored in read-only memory.

Not all embedded systems require an operating system. For those that do, the important considerations in operating system selection include memory footprint, responsiveness, licensing fees, and adherence to standards. Hard real-time embedded systems require operating systems with clearly defined responsiveness limits. This implies that they employ preemptive scheduling and make provisions for priority manipulation, particularly with regard to interrupt processing. There are literally dozens of embedded operating systems on the market. Among the most popular are QNX, Windows CE, Windows Embedded 8, and Embedded Linux.

Embedded system software development is typically more controlled and linear than general application software development, and it requires a thorough understanding of the underlying hardware architecture. Embedded systems are subjected to rigorous testing because the costs associated with their failure are so great.

FURTHER READING

Many books provide detailed coverage of embedded design and development. Berger (2002) is an excellent and comprehensive beginner's introduction to embedded design activities. Heath (2003) is strong in its coverage of embedded programming. Vahid and Givargis (2002) is noteworthy in its exacting descriptions of embedded system components, including an entire chapter on embedded control applications (PID controllers) that is remarkably well done.

Embedded Systems Programming magazine published three very good watchdog timer articles. Two were written by Jack Ganssle (2003), and the third is by Niall Murphy (2000). All three are worth reading.

Reconfigurable and adaptive systems loom large in the future of embedded systems as well as the future of general-purpose computers. Among many good articles on this subject are those by Andrews et al. (2004), Compton and Hauck (2002), Prophet (2004), Tredennick and Shimato (2003), and Verkest (2003).

Berger (2002) provides a detailed account of the traditional embedded system design life cycle. His exposition describes the many ways in which the development process can go off track. Later chapters describe testing and debugging activities that are beyond the scope of this chapter. Articles by Goddard (2003), Neville-Neil (2003), Shahri (2003), and Whitney (2003) present clear pictures of two of the most challenging aspects of programming customized processors: hardware-software partitioning and the lack of development tool support. Similarly, Daniel Gajski (1997) provides a great deal of information regarding the details of circuit creation.

Owing to ever-increasing circuit complexity, embedded system codesign and coverification is a growing area of interest. Good introductory papers are those by De Micheli and Gupta (1997) and Ernst (1998). Wolf (2003) traces a ten-year history of hardware/software codesign, and Benini et al. (2003) describe the use of SystemC in codesign. Information on the specifics of the various hardware definition languages can be obtained from the following websites:

SpecC: www.specc.org
SystemC: www.systemc.org
Real-time UML: www.omg.org
Verilog and VHDL: www.accellera.org

Bruce Douglass (1999, 2000) has written the definitive real-time UML books. Reading them will give you a new and deeper understanding of real-time software development and a new perspective on UML. Stephen J. Mellor (2003) describes how Executable and Translatable UML can be used in the development of real-time systems. Lee's (2005) article outlines the ways in which computer science thinking is challenged by embedded systems development.

The best sources for up-to-the-minute embedded systems information is found on vendor websites. Among the best are:

ARM: www.arm.com
Cadence Corporation: www.cadence.com
Ilogix: www.ilogix.com
Mentor Graphics: www.mentor.com
Motorola Corporation: www.motorola.com
Synopsis Corporation: www.synopsis.com
Wind River Systems: www.windriver.com
Xilinx Incorporated: www.xilinx.com

Good general information sites include:

EDN (Electronic Design News): www.edn.com
Embedded Systems Journal: www.embedded.com

Embedded operating systems sites include:

Embedded Linux: www.embeddedlinux.com
Microsoft operating systems: www.embeddedwindows.com and
    www.microsoft.com
POSIX: www.opengroup.org

If you find that the subject of embedded systems sufficiently excites you to pursue it as a career, in his article "Breaking into Embedded," Jack Ganssle (2002) provides a number of steps that you should take to get yourself started along this path. One activity that he stresses as the best way to learn embedded programming is to *do* embedded programming. He urges aspiring embedded system designers to visit www.stampsinclass.com for information on purchasing microcontroller kits and manuals that are designed for educational purposes. A recent addition to their offerings is the Javelin Stamp, which is a PIC microcontroller programmable in Java. (Other languages are also available.)

REFERENCES

Andrews, D., Niehaus, D., & Ashenden, P. "Programming Models for Hybrid CPU/FPGA Chips." *IEEE Computer,* January 2004, pp. 118–120.

Benini, L., Bertozzi, D., Brunni, D., Drago, N., Fummi, F., & Poncino, M. "SystemC Cosimulation and Emulation of Multiprocessor SoC Designs." *IEEE Computer,* April 2003, pp. 53–59.

Berger, A. *Embedded Systems Design: An Introduction to Processes, Tools, & Techniques.* Lawrence, KS: CMP Books, 2002.

Compton, K., & Hauck, S. "Reconfigurable Computing: A Survey of Systems and Software." *ACM Computing Surveys 34*:2, June 2002, pp. 171–210.

De Micheli, G., & Gupta, R. K. "Hardware/Software Co-Design." *Proceedings of the IEEE 85*:3, March 1997, pp. 349–365.

Douglass, B. P. *Real-Time UML: Developing Efficient Objects for Embedded Systems,* 2nd ed. Upper Saddle River, NJ: Addison-Wesley, 2000.

Douglass, B. P. *Doing Hard Time: Developing Real-Time Systems with UML, Objects, Frameworks, and Patterns.* Upper Saddle River, NJ: Addison-Wesley, 1999.

Ernst, E. "Codesign of Embedded Systems: Status and Trends." *IEEE Design and Test of Computers,* April–June 1998, pp. 45–54.

Gajski, D. D. *Principles of Logic Design.* Englewood Cliffs, NJ: Prentice-Hall, 1997.

Ganssle, J. "Breaking into Embedded." *Embedded Systems Programming,* August 2002.

Ganssle, J. "L'il Bow Wow." *Embedded Systems Programming*, January 2003.

Ganssle, J. "Watching the Watchdog." *Embedded Systems Programming*, February 2003.

Goddard, I. "Division of Labor in Embedded Systems." *ACM Queue,* April 2003, pp. 32–41.

Heath, S. *Embedded Systems Design,* 2nd ed. Oxford, England: Newnes, 2003.

Lee, E. A. "Absolutely, Positively on Time: What Would It Take?" *IEEE Computer,* July 2005, pp. 85–87.

Mellor, S. J. "Executable and Translatable UML." *Embedded Systems Programming,* January 2003.

Murphy, N. "Watchdog Timers." *Embedded Systems Programming*, November 2000.

Neville-Neil, G. V. "Programming Without a Net." *ACM Queue,* April 2003, pp. 17–22.

Prophet, G. "Reconfigurable Systems Shape Up for Diverse Application Tasks." *EDN Europe,* January 2004, pp. 27–34.

Shahri, H. "Blurring Lines between Hardware and Software." *ACM Queue,* April 2003, pp. 42–48.

Tredennick, N., & Shimato, B. "Go Reconfigure." *IEEE Spectrum,* December 2003, pp. 37–40.

Vahid, F,, & Givargis, T. *Embedded System Design: A Unified Hardware/Software Introduction.* New York: John Wiley & Sons, 2002.

Verkest, D. "Machine Camelion: A Sneak Peek Inside the Handheld of the Future." *IEEE Spectrum,* December 2003, pp. 41–46.

Whitney, T., & Neville-Neil, G. V. "SoC: Software, Hardware, Nightmare, or Bliss." *ACM Queue,* April 2003, pp. 25–31.

Wolf, W. "A Decade of Hardware/Software Codesign." *IEEE Computer,* April 2003, pp. 38–43.

REVIEW OF ESSENTIAL TERMS AND CONCEPTS

1. In which ways do embedded systems differ from general-purpose computers?

2. How is embedded systems programming different from general applications development?

3. Why are watchdog timers necessary in many embedded systems?

4. What is the difference between a microcontroller and a system-on-a-chip?

5. What is the difference between a PLA and a PAL?

6. How does one program an FPGA?

7. Name the three aspects of digital synthesis as articulated by Gajski.

8. Discuss the reasons that one might choose SystemC over Verilog.

9. In what ways does SpecC differ from SystemC?

10. Why is virtual memory not often used in embedded systems?

11. Why is the prevention of memory leaks so important in embedded systems?

12. How do real-time operating systems differ from non-real-time operating systems?

13. What are the major considerations in selecting an operating system for an embedded system?

14. How is embedded systems software development different from general-purpose software development?

EXERCISES

1. What happens if an infinite loop includes a watchdog timer reset? Name one thing that can be done to guard against this.

◆ 2. In the sidebar concerning watchdog timer engineering decisions, we stated that rebooting an embedded system typically takes less time than rebooting a personal computer. Why do you think this is so?

3. **a)** Show how a two-input XOR gate can be implemented in the PAL shown below.

   b) Show how a two-input NAND gate can be implemented in the PLA shown below.

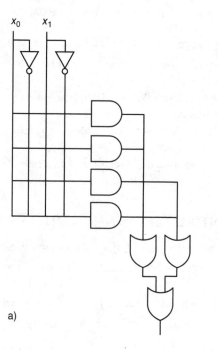

a)

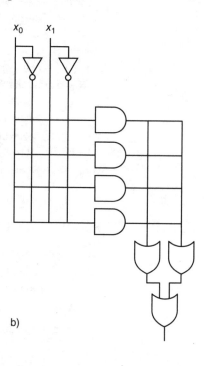

b)

4. Use the FPGA illustrated below to implement a full adder. Label the outputs clearly. Draw lines between the cells to indicate a connection between the logic functions.

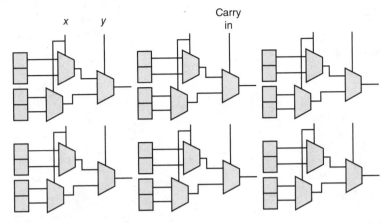

5. Provide a detailed logic diagram for a multiplexer that could be used in an FPGA.

6. Present arguments for and against the use of dynamic memory in embedded systems. Should it be banned for use under all circumstances? Why or why not?

7. We say that in embedded operating systems, if the highest-priority user thread is executing when a high-priority interrupt occurs, most operating systems will continue to process the user thread and keep the interrupt in queue until processing is completed. Under what circumstances would this be and would this not be a problem? Give an example of each.

◆ **8.** Explain interrupt latency. How is it related to context switch time?

9. In an ideal embedded operating system, would all nonkernel threads always execute at lower priority than interrupts?

10. Explain the challenges of embedded software development. How do designers answer these challenges?

If you can't measure it, you can't manage it.

—Peter Drucker

Figures are not always facts.

—American saying

CHAPTER 11

Performance Measurement and Analysis

11.1 INTRODUCTION

The two quotations with which we introduce this chapter highlight the dilemma of computer performance evaluation. One must have quantitative tools with which to gauge performance, but how can one be certain that the tools chosen for the task meet the objectives of the assessment? In fact, one *cannot* always be certain that this is the case. Furthermore, system purveyors are strongly motivated to slant otherwise truthful numbers so that their system looks better than its competitors.

You can defend yourself against most statistical chicanery by cultivating a thorough understanding of the basics of computer performance assessment. The foundation that we present in this chapter will be useful to you whether you are called upon to help select a new system or are trying to improve the performance of an existing system.

This chapter also presents some of the factors that affect the performance of processors, programs, and magnetic disk storage. The ideas presented in these sections are of primary concern in system tuning. Good system performance tools (usually supplied by the manufacturer) are an indispensable aid in keeping a system running at its best. After completing this chapter, you will know what to look for in system tuning reports, and how each piece of information fits into the big picture of overall system performance.

11.2 COMPUTER PERFORMANCE EQUATIONS

You have seen the basic computer performance equation several times in previous chapters. This equation, which is fundamental to measuring computer performance, measures the CPU time:

$$\frac{time}{program} = \frac{time}{cycle} \times \frac{cycles}{instruction} \times \frac{instructions}{program}$$

where the time per program is the required CPU time. Analysis of this equation reveals that CPU optimization can have a dramatic effect on performance. We have already discussed several ways to increase performance based on this equation. RISC machines try to reduce the number of cycles per instruction, and CISC machines try to reduce the number of instructions per program. Vector processors and parallel processors also increase performance by reducing CPU time. Other ways to improve CPU performance are discussed later in this chapter.

CPU optimization is not the only way to increase system performance. Memory and I/O also weigh heavily on system throughput. The contribution of memory and I/O, however, is not accounted for in the basic equation. For increasing the overall performance of a system, we have the following options:

- **CPU optimization**—Maximize the speed and efficiency of operations performed by the CPU (the performance equation addresses this optimization).
- **Memory optimization**—Maximize the efficiency of a code's memory management.
- **I/O optimization**—Maximize the efficiency of input/output operations.

An application whose overall performance is limited by one of the above is said to be **CPU bound, memory bound,** or **I/O bound,** respectively. In this chapter, we address optimization at all three levels.

Before examining optimization techniques, we first ask you to recall Amdahl's Law, which places a limit on the potential speedup one can obtain by any means. The equation states that the performance improvement to be gained from using some faster mode of execution is limited by the fraction of the time that the faster mode is used:

$$S = \frac{1}{(1 - f) + f/k}$$

where S is the overall system speedup; f is the fraction of work performed by the faster component (or the enhancement); and k is the speedup of a new component (or the enhancement).

Accordingly, the most dramatic improvement in system performance is realized when the performance of the most frequently used components is improved. In short, our efforts at improving performance reap the greatest rewards by making the common case faster. Knowing whether a system or application is CPU bound, memory bound, or I/O bound is the first step toward improving system performance. Keep these ideas in mind as you read the discussions on improving performance. We begin with a discussion of the various measures of overall system performance and then describe factors relating to the performance of individual system components. Before beginning any of these topics, however, we first introduce the necessary mathematical concepts for understanding general computer performance measurement.

11.3 MATHEMATICAL PRELIMINARIES

Computer performance assessment is a quantitative science. Mathematical and statistical tools give us many ways in which to rate the overall performance of a system and the performance of its constituent components. In fact, there are so many ways to quantify system performance that selecting the correct statistic becomes a challenge in itself. In this section, we describe the most common measures of "average" computer performance and then provide situations where the use of each is appropriate and inappropriate. In the second part of this section, we present other ways in which quantitative information can be misapplied through erroneous reasoning. Before proceeding, however, a few definitions are in order.

Measures of system performance depend on one's point of view. A computer user is most concerned with **response time**: How long does it take for the system to carry out a task? System administrators are most concerned with **throughput**: How many concurrent tasks can the system carry out without adversely affecting response time? These two points of view are inversely related. Specifically, if a system carries out a task in k seconds, its throughput is $1/k$ of these tasks per second.

In comparing the performance of two systems, we measure the time it takes for each system to perform the same amount of work. If the same program is run on two systems, System A and System B, System A is ***n* times faster than** System B if:

$$\frac{\text{running time on system B}}{\text{running time on system A}} = n$$

System A is $x\%$ faster than System B if:

$$\left| \frac{\text{running time on system B}}{\text{running time on system A}} - 1 \right| \times 100 = x$$

Consider the performance of two race cars. Car A completes a 10-mile run in 3 minutes, and Car B completes the same 10-mile course in 4 minutes. Using our performance formulas, the performance of Car A is 1.33 times faster than Car B:

$$\frac{\text{time for Car B to travel 10 miles}}{\text{time for Car A to travel 10 miles}} = \frac{4}{3} = 1.33.$$

Car A is also 33% faster than Car B:

$$\frac{\text{time for Car B to travel 10 miles}}{\text{time for Car A to travel 10 miles}} = \left(\frac{4}{3} - 1 \right) \times 100 = 33\%.$$

These formulas are useful in comparing the average performance of one system with the average performance of another. However, the number that we end up with is as much dependent on our definition of "average" as it is on the actual performance of the systems.

11.3.1   What the Means Mean

The science of statistics tells us that if we want meaningful information, we must conduct an adequate number of tests in order to justify making inferences based on the results of the tests. The greater the variability in the test, the larger the sample size must be. After we have conducted a "sufficient" number of tests, we are left with the task of combining, or averaging, the data in a way that makes sense, forming a concise **measure of central tendency**. Measures of central tendency indicate to us the expected behavior of the sampled system (population). But not all methods of averaging data are equal. The method we choose depends on the nature of the data itself as well as the statistical distribution of the test results.

The Arithmetic Mean

The arithmetic mean is the one with which everyone is most familiar. If we have five measurements, and we add them together and divide by five, then the result is the **arithmetic mean**. When people refer to the average results of some metric—for example, the cost of gasoline in the past year—they are usually referring to the arithmetic average of the price sampled at some given frequency.

An arithmetic average should not be used when the data are highly variable or skewed toward lower or higher values. Consider the performance numbers for three computers, as shown in Table 11.1. The values given are the running times for five programs as measured on each of the three systems. Looking at the running times, we see that the performance of these three systems is obviously different. This fact is completely hidden if we report only the arithmetic average of the running times.

When it is used properly, the **weighted arithmetic mean** improves on the arithmetic average because it can give us a clear picture of the *expected* behavior

Program	System A Execution Time	System B Execution Time	System C Execution Time
v	50	100	500
w	200	400	600
x	250	500	500
y	400	800	800
z	5,000	4,100	3,500
Average	1,180	1,180	1,180

TABLE 11.1   The Arithmetic Average Running Time in Seconds of Five Programs on Three Systems

of the system. If we have some indication of how frequently each of the five programs is run during the daily processing on these systems, we can use the execution mix to calculate relative expected performance for each of the systems. The weighted average is found by taking the products of the frequency with which the program is run and its running time. Averaging the weighted running times produces the weighted arithmetic mean.

The running times for System A and System C from Table 11.1 are restated in Table 11.2. We have supplemented the running times with execution frequencies for each of the programs. For example, on System A, for every 100 of the combined executions of programs v, w, x, y, and z, program y runs 5 times. The weighted average of the execution times for these five programs running on System A is:

$$(50 \times 0.5) + (200 \times 0.3) + (250 \times 0.1) + (400 \times 0.05) + (5{,}000 \times 0.05) = 380.$$

A similar calculation reveals that the weighted average of the execution times for these five programs running on System B is 695 seconds. Using the weighted average, we now see clearly that System A is about 83% faster than System C for this particular workload.

One of the easiest ways to get into trouble with weighted averages is using assumptions that don't hold over time. Let's assume that the computer workload profile for a particular company exhibits the execution mix shown in Table 11.2. Based on this information, the company purchases System A rather than System C. Suppose a sharp user (we can call him Wally) figures out that Program z will give him the same results as running Program v, and then using its result as an input to Program w. Furthermore, because Program z takes such a long time to run, Wally has a good excuse to take an extra coffee break. Before long, word of Wally's discovery spreads throughout the office and practically everyone in Wally's unit begins capitalizing on his idea. Within days, the workload profile of System A looks like the one shown in Table 11.3. The folks in the executive suite are

Program	Execution Frequency	System A Execution Time	System C Execution Time
v	50%	50	500
w	30%	200	600
x	10%	250	500
y	5%	400	800
z	5%	5,000	3,500
Weighted Average		380 seconds	695 seconds

TABLE 11.2 The Execution Mix for Five Programs on Two Systems and the Weighted Average of the Running Times

Program	Execution Time	Execution Frequency
v	50	25%
w	200	5%
x	250	10%
y	400	5%
z	5,000	55%
Weighted Average	2,817.5 seconds	

TABLE 11.3 The Weighted Average Running Times for System A Using a Revised Execution Mix

certain to be at a loss to explain why their brand new system is suddenly offering such poor performance.

The Geometric Mean

We know from the previous discussion that we cannot use the arithmetic mean if our measurements exhibit a great deal of variability. Furthermore, unless we have a clear view of a static and representative workload, the weighted arithmetic mean is of no help either. The **geometric mean** gives us a consistent number with which to perform comparisons regardless of the distribution of the data.

Formally, the geometric mean is defined as the nth root of the product of the n measurements. It is represented by the following formula:

$$G = \left(x_1 \times x_2 \times x_3 \times \ldots \times x_n\right)^{\frac{1}{n}}$$

The geometric mean is more helpful to us than the arithmetic average when we are comparing the relative performance of two systems. Performance results are easy to compare when they are stated in relation to the performance of a common machine used only as a reference. We say that the systems under evaluation are **normalized** to the reference machine when we take the ratio of the run time of a program on the reference machine to the run time of the same program on the system being evaluated.

To find the geometric mean of the normalized ratios, we take the nth root of the product of the n ratios. The geometric means for System A and System C normalized to System B are calculated as follows:

Geometry Mean for A $= (100 / 50 \times 400 / 200 \times 500 / 250 \times 800 / 400 \times 4{,}100 / 5{,}000)^{\frac{1}{5}}$

≈ 1.6733

Geometry Mean for C $= (100 / 500 \times 400 / 600 \times 500 / 500 \times 800 / 800 \times 4{,}100 / 3{,}500)^{\frac{1}{5}}$

≈ 0.6898

Program	System A Execution Time	Execution Time Normalized to B	System B Execution Time	Execution Time Normalized to B	System C Execution Time	Execution Time Normalized to B
v	50	2	100	1	500	0.2
w	200	2	400	1	600	0.6667
x	250	2	500	1	500	1
y	400	2	800	1	800	1
z	5,000	0.82	4,100	1	3,500	1.1714
Geometric Mean		1.6733		1		0.6898

TABLE 11.4   The Geometric Means for This Sample of Five Programs, Found by Taking the Fifth Root of the Products of the Normalized Execution Times for Each System

Program	System A Execution Time	Execution Time Normalized to C	System B Execution Time	Execution Time Normalized to C	System C Execution Time	Execution Time Normalized to C
v	50	10	100	5	500	1
w	200	3	400	1.5	600	1
x	250	2	500	1	500	1
y	400	2	800	1	800	1
z	5,000	0.7	4,100	0.8537	3,500	1
Geometric Mean		2.4258		1.4497		1

TABLE 11.5   The Geometric Means When System C Is Used as a Reference System

The details of this calculation are shown in Table 11.4.

One of the nice properties of the geometric mean is that we get the same results regardless of which system we pick for a reference. Table 11.5 shows the results when System C is the reference machine. Notice that the ratio of the geometric means is consistent no matter which system we choose for the reference machine:

$$\frac{\text{Geometric Mean A}}{\text{Geometric Mean B}} \approx 1.67 \text{ and}$$

$$\frac{\text{Geometric Mean B}}{\text{Geometric Mean C}} \approx 1.45 \text{ and}$$

$$\frac{\text{Geometric Mean A}}{\text{Geometric Mean C}} \approx 2.43.$$

We would find the same ratios if we used System A as a reference.

The geometric mean bears out our intuition concerning the relative performance of System A and System C. By taking the ratios of their geometric means, we see that System A gives a much poorer result than System B. However, the geometric mean is not linear. Although the ratio of the geometric means of System A to System C is 2.43, this does not imply that System C is 2.43 times as fast as System A. This fact is evident by the raw data. So anyone who buys System C thinking that it will give double the performance of System A is sure to be disappointed. Unlike the weighted arithmetic mean, the geometric mean gives us absolutely no help in formulating a statistical expectation of the actual behavior of the systems.

A second problem with the geometric mean is that small values have a disproportionate influence in the overall result. For example, if the makers of System C improve the performance of the fastest (probably simplest) program in the test set by 20%, so that it runs in 400 seconds instead of 500 seconds, the normalized geometric mean improves by more than 4.5%. If we improve it by 40% (so that it runs in 300 seconds), the normalized geometric mean improves by more than 16%. No matter which program we improve by 20% or 40%, we see the same reduction in the relative geometric mean. One would expect that it's much more difficult to shave 700 seconds from a large, complex program than it is to pare 200 seconds from the execution of a smaller, simpler program. In the real world (by Amdahl's Law), it is our largest, most time-consuming programs that have the greatest influence on system performance.

The Harmonic Mean

Neither the geometric mean nor the arithmetic mean is appropriate when our data are expressed as a rate, such as operations per second. For averaging rates or ratios, the **harmonic mean** should be used. The harmonic mean allows us to form a mathematical expectation of throughput and to compare the relative throughput of systems or system components. To find the harmonic mean, we add the reciprocals of the data and then divide this sum into the number of data elements in the sample. Stated mathematically:

$$H = n \div (1/x_1 + 1/x_2 + 1/x_3 + \ldots + 1/x_n)$$

To see how the harmonic mean applies to rates, consider the simple example of an automobile trip. Suppose we make a 30-mile journey, traveling the first 10 miles at 30 miles per hour, the second 10 miles at 40 miles per hour, and the last 10 miles at 60 miles per hour. Taking the arithmetic mean of these rates, the average speed of the trip is 43.3 miles per hour. This is incorrect. The time required to travel the first 10 miles was $\frac{1}{3}$ hour. The second 10 miles took $\frac{1}{4}$ hour, and the third 10 miles was traveled in $\frac{1}{6}$ hour. The total time of the journey was $\frac{3}{4}$ hour, making the average speed 30 miles $\div \frac{3}{4}$ hour = 40 miles per hour. The harmonic mean gives us the correct answer succinctly:

$$3 \div (1/30 + 1/40 + 1/60) = 40 \text{ miles per hour.}$$

In order for our example to work out with respect to the average speed over a given distance, we had to be careful that the same amount of distance was

Mean	Uniformly Distributed Data	Skewed Data	Data Expressed as a Ratio	Indicator of System Performance under a Known Workload	Data Expressed as a Rate
Arithmetic	X			X	
Weighted Arithmetic		X		X	
Geometric		X	X		
Harmonic				X	X

TABLE 11.6   Data Characteristics and Suitability of Means

covered on each leg of the journey. Otherwise, the harmonic mean would have been the same if the car had traveled 100 miles (instead of 10) at 60 miles per hour. A harmonic mean does not tell us how much work was done, only the average rate at which it was done.

The harmonic mean holds two advantages over the geometric mean. First, a harmonic mean is a suitable predictor of machine behavior. The result, therefore, has usefulness outside the realm of performance comparison. Secondly, more time-consuming programs have greater influence on the harmonic mean than less time-consuming ones. Not only does this fact weigh against "quick fix" optimizations, but it also reflects reality. Large, slow tasks have the potential of eating more machine cycles than smaller, faster ones. Consequently, we have more to gain by improving their performance.

As with the geometric mean, the harmonic mean can be used with relative performance ratios. However, the harmonic mean is more sensitive to the choice of the reference machine. In other words, the ratios of the harmonic means are not as consistent as those of the geometric means. Before the geometric mean can be used to compare machine performance, however, a definition of "work" must be established. Later in this chapter, you will see what a slippery idea this is.

We showed that the arithmetic mean is inappropriate for averaging rates, using an example road trip. It is also incorrect to use the arithmetic mean with results expressed as normalized ratios. The proper application of each of the means that we have presented is summarized in Table 11.6.

Occasionally, misapplied statistics turn up in places where we least expect to find them. Misapplication of the means is only one of several pitfalls that lie in the path of equitable and objective system performance assessment.

11.3.2   The Statistics and Semantics

Human nature impels us to cast ourselves and our beliefs in the best way possible. For persons trying to sell their products to us, their motivations are tied to survival as much as ego. It can be exceedingly difficult to see a product in its true light when it is surrounded by the fog of slick presentations and advertisements—even when the product is very good. Readers who have had some exposure to the concepts of rhetorical logic understand the ways in which fallacious reasoning can be used in sales and advertising. A classic example is where an actor "who plays a doctor on TV" recommends a certain remedy for a vexing ailment. In rhetorical logic, this is called the *argumentum ad verecundiam*, or "appeal to unqualified authority" fallacy. An actor, unless he also has a medical degree, is not qualified to make assertions as to the suitability of any treatment for any malady. Although we don't often see actors "who play computer scientists on TV" recommending mainframes, some computer vendors' sales pitches can be a source of considerable amusement for people who know what to watch for.

Computer buyers are often intimidated by the numbers cited in computer sales literature. We have mentioned how averages can be misapplied. Even when the correct statistics are used, they are not easy for many people to understand. The "quantitative" information supplied by vendors always lends an aura of credibility to the vendors' claims of superior performance. In Section 11.4, we discuss a number of objective measures of computer performance. Reputable vendors cite these measurements without distortion. But even excellent metrics are subject to misuse. In the sections that follow, we present three of the prevalent rhetorical fallacies that you are likely to encounter if you are ever tasked with purchasing new hardware or system software. We supply them as much for your entertainment as for your enlightenment.

Incomplete Information

In early 2002, a full-page advertisement was running in major business and trade magazines. The gist of the ad was, "We ran a test of our product and published the results. Vendor X did not publish results for the same test for his product; therefore, our product is faster." *Huh?* All you really know are the statistics cited in the ad. It says absolutely nothing about the relative performance of the products.

Sometimes, the fallacy of incomplete information takes the form of a vendor citing only the good test results while failing to mention that less favorable test results were also obtained on the same system at the same time. An example of this is the "single figure of merit." Vendors focus on a single performance metric that gives their systems a marketing advantage over the competition when, in reality, these individual metrics are not representative of the actual workloads of the systems in question. Another way incomplete information manifests itself is when a vendor cites only "peak" performance numbers, omitting the average or more commonly expected case.

Vague Information and Inappropriate Measurements

Imprecise words such as "more," "less," "nearly," "practically," "almost," and their synonyms should always raise immediate alarm when cited in the context of assessing the relative performance of systems. If these terms are supported with appropriate data, their use may be justified. However, observant readers may learn that "nearly" can mean "only" a 50% difference in performance between Product A and Product B.

A recent pamphlet extolling a certain brand of system software compounded imprecision with the use of inappropriate and incomparable measurements. The flier said roughly, "Software A and Software B were run using Test X. We have results for Software B running Test Y. We show that Test X is *almost* equivalent to Test Y. From this, we conclude that Software A is faster." And by how much are Tests X and Y *not* equivalent? Is it possible that Test X is contrived to make Software A look better? In this case, not only is the (probably well-paid) writer comparing apples to oranges, he or she can't even say whether the total volume of these fruits amounts to a bushel!

Appeal to Popularity

This fallacy is by far the most common, and usually the hardest to defend against in a crowd (such as a computer procurement committee). The pitch is, "Our product is used by *X*% of the Fortune 500 list of the largest companies in America." This often irrefutable fact shows that the company is well established and is probably trustworthy and stable. These nonquantitative considerations are indeed important factors in systems and software selection. However, just because *X*% of the Fortune 500 companies use the product, it doesn't mean that the product is suitable for *your* business. That is a much more complicated matter.

11.4 BENCHMARKING

Performance benchmarking is the science of making objective assessments of the performance of one system over another. Benchmarks are also useful for assessing performance improvements obtained by upgrading a computer or its components. Good benchmarks enable us to cut through advertising hype and statistical tricks. Ultimately, good benchmarks will identify the systems that provide good performance at the most reasonable cost.

Although the issue of "reasonable" cost is usually self-evident after you've done some careful shopping, the matter of "good" performance is elusive, defying all attempts at definition for decades. Yet good performance is one of those things where you "know it when you see it," and bad performance is certain to make your life miserable until the problem is corrected. In a few words, optimum performance is achieved when a computer system runs *your* application using the least possible amount of elapsed (or **wall clock**) time. That same computer system will not necessarily run someone else's application in the shortest possible time.

Life would be easy for the computer buyer if there were some way to classify systems according to a single performance number, or **metric**. The obvious advantage of this approach is that people with little or no understanding of computers would know when they were getting good value for their money. If we had a simple metric, we could use a **price-performance ratio** to indicate which system was the best buy.

For example, let's define a fictional all-encompassing system metric called a "zing." A $150,000 system offering 150 zings would be a better buy than a $125,000 system offering 120 zings. The price-performance ratio of the first system is:

$$\frac{\$150,000}{150 \text{ zings}} = \frac{\$1,000}{\text{zing}}$$

MIPS . . . OR . . . OOPS?

During the 1970s and 1980s, competition was fierce between two leading computer makers: IBM and Digital Equipment Corporation (DEC). Although DEC did not manufacture huge mainframe systems, its largest systems were suitable for the customers that might be served by IBM's smaller systems.

To help market their brand-new VAX 11/780, DEC engineers ran some small synthetic benchmark programs on an IBM 370/158 and on their VAX. IBM had traditionally marketed the 370/158 as a "1 MIPS" machine. So when the benchmarks ran in the same elapsed time on the VAX 11/780, DEC began selling its system as a competitive "1 MIPS" system.

whereas the second is:

$$\frac{\$125,000}{120 \text{ zings}} = \frac{\$1,042}{\text{zing}}$$

The question becomes whether you can live with 120 zings and save $25,000 or if it is better to buy the "large economy size," knowing it will be a while before you exhaust the system's capacity.

The trouble with this approach is that there can be no universal measure of computer performance, such as "zings," that is applicable to all systems under all types of workloads. So if you are looking for a system to handle heavy (I/O-bound) transaction processing, such as an airline reservation system, you should be more concerned with I/O performance than with CPU speed. Similarly, if your system will be tasked with computationally intense (CPU-bound) applications, such as weather forecasting or computer-aided drafting, your main focus should be on CPU power rather than on I/O.

11.4.1 Clock Rate, MIPS, and FLOPS

CPU speed, by itself, is a misleading metric that (unfortunately) is most often used by computer vendors touting their systems' alleged superiority to all others. In architecturally identical systems, a CPU running at double the clock speed of another is likely to give better CPU throughput. But when comparing offerings from different vendors, the systems will probably not be architecturally identical. (Otherwise, neither could claim a competitive performance edge over another.)

A widely cited metric related to clock rate is the **millions of instructions per second** (**MIPS**) metric. (Many people, however, believe MIPS actually stands for "Meaningless Indicators of Performance for Salesmen"!) This measures the rate at which the system can execute a typical mix of floating-point and integer arithmetic instructions, as well as logical operations. Again, the greatest weakness in

The VAX 11/780 was a commercial success. The system was so popular that it became *the* standard 1 MIPS system. For many years, the VAX 11/780 was the reference system for numerous benchmarks. The results of these benchmarks could be extrapolated to infer an "approximate MIPS" rating for whatever system was tested.

There is no doubt that the VAX 11/780 had comparable computing power to that of the IBM 370/158. But the notion of it being a "1 MIPS" machine didn't hold up under closer scrutiny. It turns out that to run the benchmarks, the VAX 11/780 executed only about 500,000 machine instructions, owing to its particular ISA. Thus, the "1 MIPS standard system" was, in fact, a 0.5 MIPS system, after all. DEC subsequently marketed its machines by specifying VUPs (VAX Units of Performance), which indicates the relative speed of a machine to the VAX 11/780.

this metric is that different machine architectures often require a different number of machine cycles to carry out a given task. The MIPS metric does not take into account the number of instructions necessary to complete a specific task.

The most glaring contrast can be seen when we compare RISC systems to CISC systems. Let's say that we ask both of these systems to perform an integer division operation. The CISC system may carry out 20 binary machine instructions before delivering a final answer. The RISC system may execute 60 instructions. If both of these systems deliver the answer in one second, the MIPS rating of the RISC system would be triple that of the CISC system. Can we honestly say that the RISC system is three times as fast as the CISC system? Of course not: In both cases, we received our answer in one second.

There is a similar problem with the **FLOPS** (floating-point operations per second) metric. Megaflops, or **MFLOPS**, is a metric that was originally used in describing the power of supercomputers but is now cited in personal computer literature. The FLOPS metric is even more vexing than the MIPS metric because there is no agreement as to what constitutes a floating-point operation. In Chapter 2, we explained how computers perform multiplication and division operations through a series of partial products, arithmetic shifts, and additions. During each of these primitive operations, floating-point numbers are manipulated. So can we say that calculating an intermediate partial sum is a floating-point operation? If so, and our metric is FLOPS, then we punish the vendor who uses efficient algorithms. Efficient algorithms arrive at the same result using fewer steps. If the amount of time consumed in finding the answer is the same amount of time consumed using less efficient algorithms, the FLOPS rate of the more efficient system is lower. If we say we're not going to count partial-sum addition steps, then how can we justify counting other floating-point addition operations? Furthermore, some computers use no floating-point instructions at all. (Early Cray supercomputers and IBM PCs emulated floating-point operations using integer routines.) Because the FLOPS metric takes into account only floating-point operations, based solely on this metric, these systems would be utterly worthless! Nevertheless, MFLOPS, like MIPS, is a popular metric with marketing people because it sounds like a "hard" value that represents a simple and intuitive concept.

Despite their shortcomings, clock speed, MIPS, and FLOPS can be useful metrics in comparing relative performance across a line of similar computers offered by the same vendor. So if a vendor offers to upgrade your system from its present x MIPS rating to a $2x$ MIPS rating, you have a fairly good idea of the performance improvement that you will be getting for your money. In fact, a number of manufacturers have their own sets of metrics for this singular purpose. Ethical salespeople will avoid using their companies' proprietary metrics to characterize their competitors' systems. When one manufacturer's proprietary metrics are used to describe the performance of competing systems, potential customers have no way of knowing whether the proprietary metric is contrived to focus on the strong points of a particular type of system, while ignoring its weaknesses.

Clearly, any metric that is dependent on a particular system's organization or its instruction set architecture misses the point of what computer buyers are looking for. They need some objective means of knowing which system offers the maximum throughput for their workloads at the lowest cost.

11.4.2   Synthetic Benchmarks: Whetstone, Linpack, and Dhrystone

Computer researchers have long sought to define a single benchmark that would allow fair and reliable performance comparisons yet be independent of the organization and architecture of any type of system. The quest for the ideal performance measure started in earnest in the late 1980s. The prevailing idea at the time was that one could independently compare the performance of many different systems through a standardized benchmarking application program. It follows that one could write a program using a third-generation language (such as C), compile it and run it on various systems, and then measure the elapsed time for each run of the program on various systems. The resulting execution time would lead to a single performance metric across all of the systems tested. Performance metrics derived in this manner are called **synthetic benchmarks**, because they don't necessarily represent any particular workload or application. Three of the better-known synthetic benchmarks are the Whetstone, Linpack, and Dhrystone metrics.

The **Whetstone** benchmarking program was published in 1976 by Harold J. Curnow and Brian A. Wichman of the British National Physical Laboratory. Whetstone is floating-point intensive, with many calls to library routines for computation of trigonometric and exponential functions. Results are reported in Kilo-Whetstone Instructions per Second or Mega-Whetstone Instructions per Second.

Another source for floating-point performance is the **Linpack** benchmark. Linpack, a contraction of *LINear algebra PACKage*, is a collection of subroutines called **Basic Linear Algebra Subroutines** (BLAS), which solve systems of linear equations using double-precision arithmetic. Jack Dongarra, Jim Bunch, Cleve Moler, and Pete Stewart of the Argonne National Laboratory developed Linpack in 1984 to measure the performance of supercomputers. It was originally written in Fortran 77 and has subsequently been rewritten in C and Java. Although it has some serious shortcomings, one of the good things about Linpack is that it sets a standard measure for FLOPS. A system that has no floating-point circuitry at all can obtain a FLOPS rating if it properly carries out the Linpack benchmark.

High-speed floating-point calculations certainly aren't important to every computer user. Recognizing this, Reinhold P. Weicker of Siemens Nixdorf Information Systems wrote a benchmarking program in 1984 that focused on string manipulation and integer operations. He called his program the **Dhrystone** benchmark, reportedly as a pun on the Whetstone benchmark. The program is CPU bound, performing no I/O or system calls. Unlike WIPS, Dhrystone results are reported simply as Dhrystones per second (the number of times the test program can be run in one second), *not* in DIPS or Mega-DIPS!

With respect to their algorithms and their reported results, the Whetstone, Linpack, and Dhrystone benchmarks have the advantage of being simple and easy to understand. Unfortunately, that is also their major limitation. Because the operations of these programs are so clearly defined, it is easy for compiler writers to equip their products with "Whetstone," "Linpack," or "Dhrystone" compilation switches. When set, these compiler options invoke special code that is optimized for the benchmarks. Furthermore, the compiled objects are so small that the largest portion of the program stays in the cache of today's systems. This just about eliminates any chance of assessing a system's memory management capabilities.

Designing compilers and systems so that they perform optimally when running benchmarking programs is a practice as old as the synthetic benchmarks themselves. So long as there is an economic advantage in being able to report good numbers, manufacturers will do whatever they can to make their numbers look good. When their numbers are better than those of their competition, they waste no time in advertising their "superior" systems. This widespread practice has become known as **benchmarketing**. Of course, no matter how good the numbers are, the only thing that benchmark results really tell you is how well the tested system runs the benchmark, and not necessarily how well it will run anything else—especially *your* particular workload.

11.4.3 Standard Performance Evaluation Corporation Benchmarks

The science of computer performance measurement benefited greatly by the contributions of the Whetstone, Linpack, and Dhrystone benchmarks. For one thing, these programs gave merit to the idea of having a common standard by which all systems could be compared. More importantly, although unintentionally, they demonstrated how easy it is for manufacturers to optimize their products' performance when a contrived benchmark is small and simple. The obvious response to this problem is to devise a more complex benchmark that also produces easily understood results. This is the aim of the SPEC CPU benchmarks.

SPEC (Standard Performance Evaluation Corporation) was founded in 1988 by a consortium of computer manufacturers in cooperation with the *Electrical Engineering Times*. SPEC's main objective is to establish equitable and realistic methods for computer performance measurement. Today, this group encompasses more than 60 member companies and three constituent committees. These committees are the:

- Open Systems Group (OSG), which addresses workstation, file server, and desktop computing environments
- High-Performance Group (HPG), which focuses on enterprise-level multiprocessor systems and supercomputers
- Graphics and Workstation Performance Group (GWPG), which concentrates on development of graphics and workstation benchmarks

These groups work with computer users to identify applications that represent typical workloads, or those applications that can distinguish a superior system from the rest. When I/O routines and other non-CPU-intensive code are pared away from these applications, the resulting program is called a **kernel**. A SPEC committee carefully selects kernel programs from submissions by various application communities. The final collection of kernel programs is called a **benchmark suite**.

The most widely known (and respected) of SPEC's benchmarks is its CPU suite, which measures CPU throughput, cache and memory access speed, and compiler efficiency. The latest version of this benchmark is CPU2006. It consists of two parts: CINT2006, which measures how well a system performs integer processing, and CFP2006, which measures floating-point performance (see Table 11.7). (The "C" in CINT and CFP stands for "component." This designation underscores the fact that the benchmark tests only one component of the system.)

CINT2006 consists of 12 applications, 9 of which are written in C and 3 in C++. The CFP2006 suite consists of 17 applications, 6 of which are written in Fortran, 3 in C, 4 in C++, and 4 in both C and Fortran. The results (system throughput) obtained by running these programs are reported as a ratio of the time it takes the system under test to run the kernel to the time it takes a reference machine to run the same kernel. For CPU2006, the reference machine is a Sun Ultra Enterprise 2 workstation with a 296MHz Ultra SPARC 2 processor. A system under test will almost certainly be faster than the Sun Ultra, so you can expect to see large positive numbers cited by vendors. The larger, the better. A complete run of the entire SPEC CPU2006 suite requires just over two 24-hour days to complete on most systems. The reported CINT2006 and CFP2006 result is a geometric mean of the ratios for all component kernels. (See the sidebar "Calculating the SPEC CPU Benchmark" for details.)

With system sales so heavily dependent on favorable benchmark results, one would expect that computer manufacturers would do everything in their power to find ways of circumventing SPEC's rules for running the benchmark programs. The first trick was the use of compiler "benchmark switches," as had become traditional with the Whetstone, Linpack, and Dhrystone programs. However, finding the perfect set of compiler options to use with the SPEC suite wasn't quite as simple as it was with the earlier synthetic benchmarks. Different settings

SPEC CINT2006 Benchmark Kernels				
Benchmark	**Reference Time**	**Language**	**Application Area**	**Brief Description**
400.perlbench	9,770	C	Programming Language	A scaled-back version Perl V5.8.7 scripting language. Workload includes some third-party modules, such as SpamAssassin, MHonArc (an email indexer), and specdiff (SPEC's tool that checks benchmark outputs), that are executed as part of the test.
401.bzip2	9,650	C	Compression	Julian Seward's bzip2 version 1.0.3, modified to do most work in memory, rather than doing I/O.
403.gcc	8,050	C	C Compiler	Based on gcc Version 3.2, generates code for an AMD Opteron processor.
429.mcf	9,120	C	Combinatorial Optimization	Vehicle scheduling. Uses a network simplex algorithm to schedule public transport.
445.gobmk	10,490	C	Artificial Intelligence: Go	Plays the game of Go, a complex game with simple rules.
456.hmmer	9,330	C	Search Gene Sequence	Protein sequence analysis using profile hidden Markov models (HMMs).
458.sjeng	12,100	C	Artificial Intelligence: Chess	A chess-playing program that includes several chess variants.
462.libquantum	20,720	C	Physics / Quantum Computing	Simulates a quantum computer, running Shor's polynomial-time factorization algorithm.
464.h264ref	22,130	C	Video Compression	A reference implementation of H.264/Advanced Video Coding, encodes a video stream using 2 parameter sets.
471.omnetpp	6,250	C++	Discrete Event Simulation	Models a large Ethernet network using a discrete event simulation.
473.astar	7,020	C++	Path-Finding Algorithms	Uses the A* algorithm (among others) for finding paths on 2D maps.
483.xalancbmk	6,900	C++	XML Processing	Transforms XML documents to other document types.

TABLE 11.7 The Constituent Kernels of the SPEC CPU2006 Benchmark Suite (continued on page 650)

are often necessary to optimize each kernel in the suite, and finding the settings is a time-consuming and tedious chore.

SPEC became aware of the use of "benchmark special" compiler options prior to the release of its CPU95 benchmark suite. It attempted to put an end to the benchmark specials by mandating that all programs in the suite written in the same language must be compiled using the same set of compiler flags. This stance evoked immediate criticism from the vendor community, arguing that their customers were entitled to know the best possible performance attainable from a system. Furthermore, if a customer's application were similar to one of the kernel programs, the customer would have much to gain by knowing the optimal compiler options.

These arguments were sufficiently compelling for SPEC to allow the use of different compiler flags for each program in a suite. In the interest of fairness to all, however, manufacturers report two sets of results for SPEC CPU2006. One set is for tests where all compiler settings are the same for the entire suite (the base metric), and the second set gives results obtained through optimized settings

TABLE 11.7 (continued)

SPEC CFP2006 Benchmark Kernels				
Benchmark	**Reference Time**	**Language**	**Application Area**	**Brief Description**
410.bwaves	13,590	Fortran	Fluid Dynamics	Numerically simulates blast waves in three-dimensional viscous flow within a bounded cube.
416.gamess	19,580	Fortran	Quantum Chemistry	Gamess implements a wide range of quantum chemical computations.
433.milc	9,180	C	Physics / Quantum Chromodynamics	A gauge field-generating program for lattice gauge theory programs with dynamical quarks.
434.zeusmp	9,100	Fortran	Physics / CFD	A computational fluid dynamics code developed at the Laboratory for Computational Astrophysics (NCSA, University of Illinois at Urbana-Champaign) for the simulation of astrophysical phenomena.
435.gromacs	7,140	C, Fortran	Biochemistry / Molecular Dynamics	Molecular dynamics, i.e., simulate Newtonian equations of motion for hundreds to millions of particles.
436.cactusADM	11,950	C, Fortran	Physics / General Relativity	Solves the Einstein evolution equations using a staggered-leapfrog numerical method.
437.leslie3d	9,400	Fortran	Fluid Dynamics	Computational Fluid Dynamics (CFD) using Large-Eddy Simulations with Linear-Eddy Model in 3D. It is the primary solver used to investigate a wide array of turbulence phenomena such as mixing, combustion, acoustics, and general fluid mechanics.
444.namd	8,020	C++	Biology / Molecular Dynamics	Simulates large biomolecular systems. The test case has 92,224 atoms of apolipoprotein A-I.
447.dealII	11,440	C++	Finite Element Analysis	deal.II is a C++ program library targeted at adaptive finite elements and error estimation.
450.soplex	8,340	C++	Linear Programming, Optimization	Solves a linear program using a simplex algorithm and sparse linear algebra. Test cases include railroad planning and military airlift models.
453.povray	5,320	C++	Image Rendering and Ray Tracing	Renders a 1,280x1,024 anti-aliased image of a chessboard with pieces in the starting position.
454.calculix	8,250	C, Fortran	Structural Mechanics	Finite element code for linear and nonlinear 3D structural applications.
459.GemsFDTD	10,610	Fortran	Computational Electromagnetics	Solves the Maxwell equations in 3D using the finite-difference time-domain (FDTD) method.
465.tonto	9,840	Fortran	Quantum Chemistry	The test case places a constraint on a molecular Hartree-Fock wave function calculation to match experimental X-ray diffraction data.
470.lbm	13,740	C	Fluid Dynamics	Simulates incompressible fluids in 3D.
481.wrf	11,170	C, Fortran	Weather	Weather modeling from scales of meters to thousands of kilometers.
482.sphinx3	19,490	C	Speech Recognition	A speech recognition system from Carnegie Mellon University that uses a program called `livepretend` to decode utterances in batch mode, but operates as if it were decoding vocal sounds of a live human.

(the peak metric). Both numbers are reported in the benchmark compilations, along with complete disclosure of the compiler settings for each run.

Users of the SPEC benchmarks pay an administrative fee for the suite's source code and instructions for its installation and compilation. Manufacturers are encouraged (but not required) to submit a report that includes the results of the benchmarks to SPEC for review. After SPEC is satisfied that the tests were run in accordance with its guidelines, it publishes the benchmark results and configuration disclosure reports on its website. SPEC's oversight ensures that the manufacturer has used the benchmark software correctly and that the system's configuration is completely revealed.

Although processor wars generate reams of coverage in the computer trade press, Amdahl's Law tells us that a useful system requires more than simply a fast CPU. Computer buyers are interested in how well an *entire* system will perform under their particular workloads. Toward this end, SPEC has created an array of other metrics, including SPEC Web for Web servers, SPEC Power for electrical power versus performance, and SPEC JVM for client-side Java performance. SPEC JVM is complemented by SPEC JBB (Java Business Benchmark) for Java server performance. Each of these benchmarks adheres to SPEC's philosophy of establishing fair and objective system performance measurements.

11.4.4 Transaction Processing Performance Council Benchmarks

SPEC's CPU benchmarks are helpful to computer buyers whose principal concern is CPU performance. They are not quite so beneficial to buyers of enterprise transaction-processing servers. For systems in this class, buyers are most interested in the server's ability to process a great number of concurrent short-duration activities, where each transaction involves communications and disk I/O to some extent.

Sluggish transaction-processing systems can be enormously costly to businesses, causing far-reaching problems. When a customer-service system is slow, long lines of grumpy customers are detrimental to a retail store's image. Customers standing in slow-moving lines at checkout counters don't care that a credit authorization system is bogging things down. Lethargic automated teller machines and unresponsive point-of-sale debit systems can alienate customers in droves if their waits are too long. Transaction-processing systems aren't merely important to the customer service sector; they are its lifeblood. Wise business leaders are willing to invest small fortunes to keep their customers satisfied. With so much at stake, it is essential to find some method of objectively evaluating the overall performance of systems supporting these critical business processes.

Computer manufacturers have always had ways of gauging the performance of their own systems. These measurements are not intended for public consumption, but are instead for internal use by engineers seeking ways to make their systems (or parts of them) perform better. In the early 1980s, the IBM Corporation invented such a benchmark to help with the design of its mainframe systems. This benchmark, which was called **TP1** (TP for transaction processing), eventually found its way into the public domain. A number of competing vendors began using it and announcing their (amazing) results. Transaction processing experts were critical of this practice because the benchmark wasn't designed to simulate a real transaction-processing environment. For one thing, it ignored network delays and the variability of user "think time." Stated another way, all that TP1 could do was measure peak throughput under ideal conditions. Although this measurement was useful to system designers, it didn't give the computer buyer much to go on.

In 1985, Jim Gray, one of the more vocal critics of TP1, worked with a large group of his fellow dissenters to propose a benchmark that would address the

CALCULATING THE SPEC CPU BENCHMARK

As we stated in the text, the first step in calculating SPEC benchmark results is to normalize the time it takes for a reference machine to run a benchmark kernel to the time it takes for the system under test to run the same kernel program. The kernel is run three times, and the median run time is used in the calculations. For example, suppose a hypothetical system runs the 401.bzip2 kernel in 907, 920, and 928 seconds. The median is 920. The reference machine took 9,650 seconds to run the same program. The normalized ratio is 9,650 ÷ 920 = 10.5 (rounded to one decimal place). The final SPECint result is the geometric mean of all the normalized ratios in the integer program suite. Consider the results shown in the Table 11.8.

Benchmark	Reference Time	Run Time	Ratio to Reference Time
400.perlbench	9,770	739	13.2
401.bzip2	9,650	920	10.5
403.gcc	8,050	814	9.89
429.mcf	9,120	1,161	7.86
445.gobmk	10,490	719	14.6
456.hmmer	9,330	697	13.4
458.sjeng	12,100	870	13.9
462.libquantum	20,720	1,342	15.4
464.h264ref	22,130	995	22.2
471.omnetpp	6,250	659	9.49
473.astar	7,020	732	9.59
483.xalancbmk	6,900	820	8.42

TABLE 11.8   A Set of Hypothetical SPECInt2006 Results

shortcomings of TP1. They called their benchmark **DebitCredit** to emphasize its focus on business transaction processing performance. In addition to specifying how this benchmark would work, Gray and his group proposed that the outcome of the system tests should be reported along with the total cost of the system configuration that was tested. They offered ways in which the benchmark could be scaled proportionately to make the tests fair across various sizes of systems.

DebitCredit was welcomed by the vendor community because it delivered a clear and objective performance measurement. Before long, most vendors were using it, announcing their good results with reckless abandon. Unfortunately, no formal mechanism was in place to verify or refute their claims. In essence,

To determine the geometric mean, first find the product of all 12 normalized benchmark times:

$$13.2 \times 10.5 \times 9.89 \times 7.86 \times 14.6 \times 13.4$$
$$\times 13.9 \times 15.4 \times 22.2 \times 9.49 \times 9.59 \times 8.42 \approx 7.68 \times 10^{12}$$

Then take the twelfth root of this product:

$$(7.68 \times 10^{12})^{1/12} \approx 11.8$$

Thus, the CINT metric for this system is (a fairly impressive) 11.8. If this result were obtained when running benchmarks compiled with standard (conservative) compiler settings, it would be reported as the "base" metric, SPECint_base_2006. Otherwise, it is the SPECint2006 rating for this system.

The CINT 2006 and CFP 2006 suites measure a CPU's capabilities when running only one image of each benchmark at a time. This single-thread model doesn't tell us anything about how well the system handles concurrent processes. SPEC CPU "rate" metrics give us some insight here. Calculation of SPECint_rate metrics is a bit more complicated than calculating single-thread SPECint metrics.

To find a rate metric, a number of identical benchmark kernel processes are started in the host. For the sake of example, let's say we start 4 concurrent 401 .bzip2 processes. After all instances of the 401.bzip2 program terminate, we find the elapsed time by subtracting the time that the first instance starts from the time that the last instance finishes. As with the base metric, we do this three times and use the median result in the calculations. Suppose our median result is 1,049 seconds. We then multiply the number of copies run by the reference time for the benchmark and divide by the median elapsed seconds. The reference time for the 401.bzip2 benchmark is 9,650, so we have:

$$4 \text{ copies} \times 9,650 \div 1,049 \approx 36.8$$

This gives us the rate in jobs per unit time for the 401.bzip2 benchmark.

The SPECint_rate2006 metric that will be reported for this system is the geometric mean of all the component CINT2006 kernels. The same process is used in determining the SPECfp_rate results.

manufacturers could cite whatever results they thought would give them an advantage over their competition. Clearly, some means of independent review and control was desperately needed. To this end, in 1988, Omri Serlin persuaded eight computer manufacturers to join together to form the independent **Transaction Processing Performance Council** (**TPC**). Today, the TPC consists of approximately 30 member companies, including makers of system software as well as hardware.

The first task before the TPC was to release a benchmark suite bearing its official stamp. This benchmark, released in 1990, was called **TPC-A**. In keeping with the pace of technological innovation, as well as the advances of benchmarking science, TPC-A is now in the fifth version of its third major revision, **TPC-C Version 5**.

The TPC-C benchmarking suite models the activities of a wholesale product distribution company. The suite is a controlled mix of five transaction types that are typical of order fulfillment systems. These transactions include new order initiation, stock level inquiries, order status inquiries, goods delivery postings, and payment processing. The most resource-intensive of these transactions is the order initiation transaction, which must constitute at least 45% of the transaction mix.

TPC-C employs remote terminal emulation software that simulates a user's interaction with the system. Each interaction takes place through a formatted data entry screen that would be usable by a human data entry clerk. The emulator program picks its transactions from a menu, just as a real person would do. The choices, however, are statistically randomized so that the correct transaction mix is executed. Input values, such as customer names and part numbers, are also randomized to avoid repeated cache hits on the data values, thus forcing frequent disk I/O.

TPC-C's end-to-end response time is measured from the instant the "user" has completed the required entries to the instant the system presents the required response at the terminal. Under the latest TPC-C rules, 90% of all transactions, except the stock level inquiry, must be accurately completed within five seconds. The stock inquiry is excepted from the five-second rule because stock levels may be checked in a number of different warehouses in a single inquiry transaction. This task is more I/O intensive than the others.

Keeping in mind that the TPC-C suite simulates a real business that uses a real system, every update transaction must support the ACID properties of a production database. (These properties were described in Chapter 8.) TPC-C's ACID properties include record locking and unlocking, as well as the rollback capability provided by logging updates to a database journal file.

The TPC-C metric is the number of new order transactions completed per minute (**tpmC**), while a mix of the other transactions is concurrently executing on the same system. Reported TPC-C results also include a price-performance ratio, which is found by dividing the cost of the system by the throughput metric. Hence, if a $90,000 system provides a throughput of 15,000tpmC, its price-performance ratio is $6tpmC. The system cost includes all hardware, software, and network components that are required to execute the TPC-C transactions. Each component used in the test must be available for sale to the general public at the time the results are reported. This rule is intended to prevent the use of benchmark special components. All the system components involved in producing the reported benchmark results must be listed (in great detail) on a full-disclosure report submitted to the TPC. The disclosed configuration must also include all tuning parameters[1] (e.g., compiler switches) in effect during the test. The full-disclosure report also includes "total cost of ownership" figures that take into account the cost of three years of maintenance and support for the entire system.

---

[1]Tuning information supplied in full-disclosure reports is a valuable resource for system administrators seeking to optimize the performance of a system similar to one covered by a TPC-C report. Because a real workload is not identical to the TPC-C suite, the reported tuning information may not give optimal results, but it's often a good starting point.

The TPC has recently improved (but not yet replaced) the TPC-C benchmark with the **TPC-E** benchmark that simulates an online brokerage. The intention of this new benchmark is to reflect, as realistically as possible, a contemporary OLTP system configuration. The benchmark uses a fictional online brokerage that manages customer accounts and executes stock trades on behalf of those customers. The data tables are preloaded with realistic census data gathered from the United States and Canada, and the American NYSE and NASDAQ stock exchanges. The workload can be varied based on the number of "customers" using the system under test. The resulting metrics are transactions per second E, **tpsE**, the price-performance dollars per tpsE, **\$/tpsE,** and watts (power consumed) per tpsE, **Watts/tpsE**. As with all other TPC benchmarks, the TPC-E results are subject to the strictest auditing and truth-in-reporting requirements.

When a vendor submits its TPC-C or TPC-E results to the TPC, all of the information in the reports is audited by an independent auditing firm to ensure its completeness and accuracy. (Of course, the auditor cannot rerun the test, so the throughput figures are usually taken at face value if the test was performed correctly.) Once the reports are accepted by the TPC, they are published on the Web for inspection by customers and competitors alike. On occasion, a competitor or the TPC itself challenges a manufacturer's results. In these situations, the manufacturer may either withdraw or defend its report. Sometimes the report is quietly withdrawn because the cost of defending the results is prohibitive, even if a manufacturer is well founded in its claims. A vendor may also choose to withdraw its results because the tested configuration is no longer available or the next model of the system is greatly improved over the old one.

TPC-C and TPC-E are just two of several benchmarks sponsored by the Transaction Processing Council. When the TPC was founded, the world of business computation consisted primarily of transaction-processing systems that also supported financial processes such as bookkeeping and payroll. These systems took a clearly defined set of inputs and produced a clearly defined output, usually in the form of printed reports and forms. This deterministic model lacks the flexibility needed to provide deep data analysis tools required in today's business environment. Many companies have replaced their static reports with **decision support** tools. These applications access enormous quantities of input data to produce business intelligence information for marketing guidance and business logistics. In a sense, decision support applications are the complete opposite of transaction-processing applications. They require a different breed of computer system. Whereas transaction-processing environments handle large numbers of short-duration processes, decision support systems handle a small number of long-duration processes.

No one can reasonably expect decision support systems to produce the instantaneous results characteristic of a simple online order status inquiry. However, there are limits to the amount of time one is willing to wait, no matter how useful the end result will be. In fact, if a decision support system is "too slow," executives will be reluctant to use it, thus defeating its purpose. So even in the cases where we are willing to wait "a while" for our answers, performance remains an issue.

TPC BENCHMARKS: A REALITY CHECK

The Transaction Processing Performance Council has made every attempt to model real-world scenarios with its TPC-C, TPC-H, and TPC-R benchmarks. It has taken great pains to ensure that the benchmarks contain a realistic mix of common business transactions and activities. These activities are randomized to generate as much I/O activity as possible. Specifically, data should be fetched most often directly from disk rather than from cache or other fast memory.

The thinking behind this is that the tests shouldn't be biased toward one particular type of architecture. If the data weren't randomized, the benchmark would favor systems with large cache memories that may not perform (proportionately) as well in real environments.

For many years, this idea was unchallenged until a doctoral student intern at IBM, Windsor W. Hsu, conducted a series of empirical studies. Under the auspices of IBM's Almaden Research Center, Hsu and his fellow researchers monitored millions of transactions on systems owned by ten of IBM's largest customers. Hsu's work validated many aspects of the TPC benchmarks, including their workload mix. However, Hsu found that real-world activity differed from the TPC models in two important ways.

First, the TPC benchmarks exhibit a sustained and constant transaction rate. This is what they are designed to do in order to fully stress a system at peak

In response to this relatively new area of computing, the TPC produced two benchmarks, **TPC-H** and **TPC-R**, to describe the performance of decision support systems. Although both of these benchmarks are directed at decision support systems, the TPC-R benchmark measures performance when the reporting parameters of the system are known in advance (the database can be indexed and optimized for the reporting). The TPC-H benchmark measures how well a system can produce ad hoc query results, which are queries where the parameters of the query are not known in advance. Results of TPC-H tests are given in queries per hour, **QphH**, and those of TPC-R as **QphR**. The TPC categorizes these results according to the size of the databases against which the queries were run, because running a query against 100 gigabytes of data is a far different task than running a query against a terabyte of data.

The TPC benchmarks are trustworthy aids in selecting systems to serve the computing needs of the enterprise. The principal pitfall in the use of these metrics is assuming that the benchmarks accurately predict the performance of a system under anyone's particular workload. This is not TPC's claim or intent. Research has shown the ways one particular set of real workloads differs from the TPC workloads (see sidebar). Computer benchmarks, when used correctly, are indispensable tools. Used incorrectly, they can lead us down paths where we would rather not venture.

workload rates. But Hsu found that real workloads are bursty. A flurry of activity occurs, and then there is a lull before the next flurry of activity occurs. What this means to designers is that overall performance could be improved if effective dynamic resource allocation facilities were incorporated into the system software and hardware. Although many vendors do in fact use dynamic resource allocation, their efforts are not rewarded in the TPC benchmarks.

Hsu's second major result challenges the notion of randomizing the data and the workload in the TPC benchmarks. He found that real systems exhibit significantly greater "pseudo-sequentiality" than the TPC programs do. This finding is important because many systems prefetch data from disk and memory. Real workloads benefit greatly when prefetching is used. Furthermore, the pseudo-sequentiality of data access patterns lends itself well to least recently used (LRU) cache and memory page replacement policies. The TPC benchmarks do not.

Hsu's work is not an indictment against the TPC benchmarks. Instead, it amplifies the folly of thinking that one can extrapolate benchmark results into particular real-world situations. Although the TPC benchmarks don't model the real world as well as some would like, they continue to be an honest and fairly reliable yardstick to use when comparing performance among different systems' architectures.

11.4.5 System Simulation

The TPC benchmarks differ from the SPEC benchmarks in that they endeavor to simulate a complete computing environment. Although the purpose of the TPC benchmarks is to measure performance, their simulated environment may also be useful to predict, and hence optimize, performance under various conditions. In general, simulations give us tools that we can use to model and predict aspects of system behavior without the use of the exact live environment that the simulator is modeling.

Simulation is very useful for estimating the performance of systems or system configurations that do not yet exist. Prudent system designers always conduct simulation studies of new hardware and software prior to building commercial versions of their products. The wisdom of this approach was shown dramatically in 1967 by Stanford doctoral candidate Norman R. Nielson in his thesis "The Analysis of General Purpose Computer Time-Sharing Systems." Nielson's thesis documented his simulation study of IBM's yet-to-be-released 360/67 Time-Sharing System (TSS). Using IBM's published specifications, Nielson's work revealed serious flaws in the 360/67 TSS. His findings impelled IBM to improve the system's design prior to its widespread release.

Simulations are models of particular aspects of full systems. They give system designers the luxury of performing "what if" testing in a controlled environment separate from the live system. Suppose, for example, that you are interested in maximizing the number of concurrent tasks a system can sustain. The tuning parameters include the memory allocation for each task and its CPU timeslice duration. Based on what you know about the characteristics of each task, the tuning values could be adjusted until an optimal balance is found. Such tinkering in a live environment having real tasks and real users incurs some real risks, the worst of which might be that no one gets any work done.

One of the major challenges of system simulation lies in determining the characteristics of the workload. The workload mix should correspond to the system components that are modeled. One approach starts by examining system logs to derive a synthetic, yet statistically sound, workload profile. This is the method used by the TPC in producing the workload mix for its TPC-W benchmark.

Capturing the behavior of an entire system or its entire workload will not produce sufficient data granularity if a simulator is focused on only one component of the system. Say, example, a system designer is trying to determine an ideal set-associative memory cache configuration. This configuration includes the sizes of the level 1 and level 2 caches, as well as the set size for each cache block. For this type of simulation, the simulator needs detailed memory access data. This kind of information is usually derived from system traces.

System traces gather detailed behavior information using hardware or software probes into the activity of the component of interest. Probes trace every detail of the component's actual behavior, possibly including binary instructions and memory references. Traces gathered by probes consist of only a few seconds of system activity because the data set output is very large. In producing a statistically meaningful model, several traces are required.

When designing a simulator, a clear definition of the purpose of the simulator must be established. Good engineering judgment is required to separate the important from the unimportant system characteristics. A model that is too detailed is costly and time-consuming to write. Conversely, simulators that are so simplistic that they ignore key factors produce misleading results. System simulation is an excellent tool, but like any tool, we must have some assurance of its suitability for the job. System simulators must be validated to affirm the assumptions around which the model was built. The simplest models are the easiest to validate.

11.5 CPU PERFORMANCE OPTIMIZATION

CPU performance has long been the principal focus of system optimization efforts. There is no single way to enhance CPU performance, because CPU throughput is affected by a multitude of factors. For instance, program code affects the instruction count; the compiler influences both the instruction count and the average clock cycles per instruction; the ISA determines the instruction count and the average clock cycles per instruction; and the actual hardware organization establishes the clock cycles per instruction and the clock cycle time.

Potential CPU optimization techniques include integrated floating-point units, parallel execution units, specialized instructions, instruction pipelining, branch prediction, and code optimization. Because all but the last two items have been addressed in previous chapters, we focus our attention on branch prediction and user code optimization.

11.5.1 Branch Optimization

At this point, you should be very familiar with the fetch–decode–execute cycle. Instruction pipelining has a significant influence on performance and is incorporated in most contemporary architectures. However, branching imposes a penalty on this pipeline. Consider a conditional branching situation in which the address of the next instruction is not known until the current instruction execution is complete. This forces a delay in the flow of instructions through the pipeline because the processor does not know which instruction comes next until it has finished executing the branch instruction. In fact, the longer the pipeline is (the more stages it has), the more time the pipeline must wait before it knows which instruction to feed next into the pipeline.

Modern processors have increasingly longer pipelines. Typically, 20% to 30% of machine instructions involve branching, and studies indicate that approximately 65% of the branches are taken. Additionally, programs average about five instructions between branches, forcing many pipeline stalls, thus creating a growing need to reduce the penalties imposed by branching. The factors contributing to pipeline stalls are called **hazards**. They include such things as data dependencies, resource conflicts, and fetch access delays from memory. Aside from stopping the pipeline upon detection of a hazard, there is little that can be done about them. Branch optimization, however, is within the scope of our control. For this reason, branch prediction has been the focus of recent efforts toward improving CPU performance.

Delayed branching is one method of dealing with the effects branching has on pipelines. When performing a conditional branch, for example, one or more instructions *after* the branch are executed regardless of the outcome of the branching. The idea is to utilize otherwise wasted cycles following a branch. This is accomplished by inserting an instruction behind the branch and then executing it before the branch. The net effect is that the instruction following the branch is executed before the branch takes effect.

This concept is best explained by way of an example. Consider the following program:

```
        Add    R1, R2, R3
        Branch Loop
        Div    R4, R5, R6
Loop: Mult    . . .
```

This results in the following trace for the fetch (F), decode (D), and execute (E) pipeline:

Time Slots:	1	2	3	4	5	6
Add	F	D	E			
Branch		F	D	E		
Div			F			
Mult				F	D	E

The divide instruction represents a wasted instruction slot, because the instruction is fetched but never decoded or executed due to the branch. This slot could be filled with another instruction by reversing the execution sequence of the branch instruction and another instruction that will be executed anyway:

Time Slots:	1	2	3	4	5	6
Branch	F	D	E			
Add		F	D	E		
Mult			F	D	E	

It should be clear that delayed branching, although it uses otherwise wasted branch delay slots, actually reorders the execution sequence of the instructions. The compiler must, therefore, perform a data dependency analysis to determine whether delayed branching is possible. Situations may arise in which no instruction can be moved after the branch (into the delay slot). In this case, a NOP ("no operation" instruction that does nothing) is placed after the branch. Clearly, the penalty for branching in this case is the same as if delayed branching were not employed.

A compiler can choose the instruction to place in the delay slot in a number of ways. The first choice is a useful instruction that executes regardless of whether the branch occurs. The instructions before the branch statement are the prime candidates. Other possibilities include instructions that execute if the branch occurs but do no harm if the branch does not occur. The reverse of this is also considered: statements that execute if the branch does not occur but do no harm if the branch does occur. Candidates also include those statements that do no harm regardless of whether the branch occurs. Delayed branching has the advantage of low hardware cost and is dependent on the compiler to fill the delay slots.

Another approach to minimizing the penalty introduced with branching is branch prediction. **Branch prediction** is the process of attempting to guess the next instruction in the instruction stream, thus avoiding pipeline stalls due to branching. If the prediction is successful, no delay is introduced into the pipeline. If the prediction is unsuccessful, the pipeline must be flushed and all calculations caused by this miscalculation must be discarded. Branch prediction techniques vary depending on the branch characterization: loop control branching, if/then/else branching, or subroutine branching.

To take full advantage of branch prediction, the pipeline must be kept full. Therefore, once a prediction is made, the instruction is fetched and execution begins. This is called **speculative execution**. These instructions are executed before it is known for sure whether they will need to execute. This work must be undone if a prediction is found to be incorrect.

Branch prediction is like a black box into which we feed various input data, getting a predicted target instruction as output. When the code in question is simply fed into this black box, this is known as **static prediction**. If, in addition to the code, we feed in state history (previous information about the branch instruction and its outcomes in the past), the black box is using **dynamic prediction**. **Fixed predictions** are those that are always the same: Either the branch will be taken or it will not, and every time the branch is encountered, the prediction is the same. **True predictions** have two potential outcomes, either "take branch" or "do not take branch."

In fixed prediction, when the assumption is that the branch is not taken, the idea is to assume that the branch will not occur and continue on the normal sequential path. However, processing is done in parallel in case the branch occurs. If the prediction is correct, the preprocessing information is deleted and execution continues. If the prediction is incorrect, the speculative processing is deleted and the preprocessing information is used to continue on the correct path.

In fixed prediction, when the assumption is that the branch is always taken, preparation is also made for an incorrect prediction. State information is saved before the speculative processing begins. If the guess is correct, this saved information is deleted. If the prediction is incorrect, the speculative processing is deleted and the saved information is used to restore the execution environment, at which time the proper path is taken.

Dynamic prediction increases the accuracy of branch prediction by using a recorded history of previous branches. This information is then combined with the code and fed into the branch predictor (our black box). The principal component used for branch prediction is a **branch prediction buffer**. This high-speed buffer is indexed by the lower portion of the address of the branch instruction, with additional bits indicating whether the branch was recently taken. Branch prediction buffers always return a prediction using a small number of bits. **One-bit dynamic prediction** uses a single bit to record whether the last occurrence of the branch was taken. **Two-bit prediction** retains the history of the two previous branches for a given branch instruction. The extra bit helps reduce mispredictions at the end of loops (when the loop exits instead of branching as before). The two branch prediction bits can represent state information in various ways. For example, the four possible bit patterns can indicate the historical probability of taking the branch (11: strongly taken; 10: weakly taken; 01: weakly not taken; and 00: strongly not taken). The probabilities are changed only if a misprediction occurs twice.

Early implementations of branch prediction were almost exclusively of the static variety. Most newer processors (including the Pentium, PowerPC, Ultra-Sparc, and Motorola 68060) use two-bit dynamic branch prediction, which has resulted in higher accuracy and fewer mispredictions. Some superscalar

PROGRAM OPTIMIZATION TIPS

- Give the compiler as much information as possible about what you are doing. Use constants and local variables where possible. If your language permits them, define prototypes and declare static functions. Use arrays instead of pointers when you can.
- Avoid unnecessary typecasting and minimize floating-point-to-integer conversions.
- Avoid overflow and underflow.
- Use a suitable data type (e.g., `float`, `double`, `int`).
- Consider using multiplication instead of division.

processors mandate its use, whereas others offer it as an option. A number of systems offload branch prediction processing to specialized circuits, which produce more timely and accurate predictions.

11.5.2   Use of Good Algorithms and Simple Code

The world's best processor hardware and optimizing compilers can go only so far in making programs faster. They will never be equal to a human who has mastered the science of effective algorithm and coding design. Recall from Chapter 6 the example of accessing an array row major versus column major. The basic idea was that matching the access of the data more closely to how it is stored can increase performance. If an array is stored row major, and you access it in column-major order, the principle of locality is weakened, potentially resulting in degraded performance. Although compilers can improve performance to some extent, their scope is primarily limited to low-level code optimization. Program code can have a monumental effect on all aspects of performance, from pipelining to memory to I/O. This section is devoted to those mechanisms that you, as a programmer, can employ to achieve optimal performance from your computer.

Operation counting is one way to enhance the performance of your program. With this method, you estimate the number of instruction types that are executed in a loop, then determine the number of machine cycles required for each instruction type. This information can then be used to achieve a better instruction balance. The idea is to attempt to write your loops with the best mix of instructions for a given architecture (e.g., loads, stores, integer operations, floating-point operations, system calls). Keep in mind that a good instruction mix for one hardware platform may not be a good mix for a different platform.

- Eliminate all unnecessary branches.
- Use iteration instead of recursion when possible.
- Build conditional statements (e.g., `if`, `switch`, `case`) with the most probable cases first.
- Declare variables in a structure in order of size with the largest ones first.
- When a program is having performance problems, profile the program before beginning optimization procedures. (**Profiling** is the process of breaking your code into small chunks and timing each of these chunks to determine which of them take the most time.)
- Never discard an algorithm based solely on its original performance. A fair comparison can occur only when all algorithms are fully optimized.

Loops are used extensively in programs and are excellent candidates for optimization. In particular, nested loops present a number of interesting optimization opportunities. With some investigation, you can improve memory access patterns and increase instruction-level parallelism. **Loop unrolling** is one approach easily employed by any programmer. Loop unrolling is the process of expanding a loop so that each new iteration contains several of the original iterations, thus performing more computations per loop iteration. In this way, several loop iterations are processed each time through the loop. For example:

```
for (i = 1; i <= 30; i+ +)
    a[i] = a[i] + b[i] * c;
```

when unrolled (twice) becomes:

```
for (i = 1; i <= 30; i+=3){
    a[i] = a[i] + b[i] * c;
    a[i+1] = a[i+1] + b[i+1] * c;
    a[i+2] = a[i+2] + b[i+2] * c; }
```

Upon first inspection, this appears to be a bad way to write code. But it reduces loop overhead (such as the maintenance of the index variable) and helps with control hazards in pipelines. It typically enables operations from different loop iterations to execute in parallel. In addition, it allows for better instruction scheduling due to less data dependence and better register usage. Clearly the amount of code is increased, so this is not a technique that should be employed for every loop in your program. It is best used in sections of code that account for a significant portion of the execution time. Optimization efforts give the greatest reward when applied to those parts of the program that will yield the greatest improvement. This technique is also suitable for `while` loops, although its application is not so straightforward.

Another useful loop optimization technique is loop fusion. **Loop fusion** combines loops that use the same data items. This can result in increased cache performance, increased instruction-level parallelism, and reduced loop overhead. Loop fusion on the following loops:

```
for (i=0; i<N; i++)
   C[i] = A[i] + B[i];
for (i=0; i<N; i++)
   D[i] = E[i] + C[i];
```

results in:

```
for (i=0; i<N; i++)  {
   C[i] = A[i] + B[i];
   D[i] = E[i] + C[i];}
```

Sometimes, the potential for loop fusion is not as obvious as it is in the above code. Given the code segment:

```
for (i=1; i<100; i++)
   A[i] = B[i] + 8;
for (i=1; i<99; i++)
   C[i] = A[i+1] * 4;
```

it isn't clear how to fuse these loops because the second one uses a value from array A that is one ahead of the loop counter. However, we could easily rewrite this code:

```
A[1] = B[1] + 8;
for (i=2; i<100; i++)  {
   A[i] = B[i] + 8;}
for (i=1; i<99; i++)  {
   C[i] = A[i+1] * 4;  }
```

Now we are ready to fuse the loops:

```
i = 1;
A[i] = B[i] + 8;
for (j=0; j<98; j++)  {
   i = j + 2;
   A[i] = B[i] + 8;
   i = j + 1;
   C[i] = A[i+1] * 4;  }
```

Loop fission, splitting large loops into smaller ones, also has a place in loop optimization, because it can eliminate data dependencies and reduce cache delays resulting from conflicts. One example of loop fission is **loop peeling**, the process of removing the beginning or ending statements from a loop. These are the statements that usually contain the loop's boundary conditions. For example, the code:

```
for (i=1; i<N+1; i++)  {
   if (i==1)
      A[i] = 0;
   else if (i= =N)
      A[i] = N;
   else
      A[i] = A[i] + 8;}
```

becomes:

```
A[1] = 0;
for (i=2; i<N; i++)
   A[i] = A[i] + 8;
A[N] = N;
```

This example of loop peeling results in more instruction-level parallelism because it removes branching from the loop.

We have already alluded to **loop interchange**, which is the process of rearranging loops so that memory is accessed more closely to the way in which the data is stored. In most languages, loops are stored in row-major order. Accessing data in row-major versus column-major order results in fewer cache misses and better locality of reference.

Loop optimization is an important tool for improving program performance. It exemplifies how you can use your knowledge of computer organization and architecture to write superior programs. We have provided a sidebar containing a list of things to keep in mind while you are optimizing your program code. We invite you to ponder the ways each of these tips takes various system components into account. You should be able to explain the rationale behind each of them.

The more things you try, the more successful you will be. Keep in mind that often a tweak that should result in increased performance isn't immediately successful. Many times, these ideas must be used in combination for their effects to be apparent.

11.6 DISK PERFORMANCE

Although CPU and memory performance are important factors in system performance, optimal disk performance is crucial to system throughput. The vast majority of user interactions with a system involve some kind of disk input or output. Furthermore, this disk I/O can happen through a page fault, its timing and duration being beyond the control of either the user or the programmer. With a properly functioning I/O subsystem, total system throughput can be an order of magnitude better than when the I/O subsystem is functioning poorly. Because the performance stakes are so high, disk systems must be well designed and well configured from the outset. Throughout the life of the system, disk subsystems must be continually monitored and tuned. In this section, we introduce the principal aspects of I/O system performance. The generic concepts introduced here will be useful to you whether you are selecting a new system or trying to keep an existing system running at its best.

11.6.1   Understanding the Problem

Disk drive performance issues loom large in overall system performance because retrieving an item from a disk takes such a long time, relative to CPU or memory speed. A CPU needs only a few nanoseconds to execute an instruction when all operands are in its registers. When the CPU needs an operand from memory before it can complete a task, the execution time may rise to tens of nanoseconds. But when the operand must be fetched from the disk, the time required to complete the task soars to tens of milliseconds—a millionfold increase! Moreover, because the CPU can dispatch I/O requests much faster than disk drives can keep up with them, disk drives can become throughput bottlenecks. In fact, when a system exhibits "low" CPU utilization, it can be because the CPU is continually waiting for I/O requests to complete. Such a system is I/O bound.

One of the most important metrics of I/O performance is **disk utilization**, the measure of the percentage of time that the disk is busy servicing I/O requests. Stated another way, disk utilization gives the probability that the disk is busy when another I/O request arrives in the disk service queue. Utilization is determined by the speed of the disk and the rate at which requests arrive in the service queue. Stated mathematically:

$$\text{Utilization} = \frac{\text{Request Arrival Rate}}{\text{Disk Service Rate}}$$

where the arrival rate is given in requests per second and the disk service rate is given in I/O operations per second (IOPS).

For example, consider a particular disk drive that can complete an I/O operation in 15ms. This means that its service rate is about 67 I/O operations per second (0.015 seconds per operation = 66.7 operations per second). If this disk gets 33 I/O requests per second, it is about 50% utilized. Utilization of 50% gives good performance on practically any system. But what happens if this system starts seeing a sustained I/O request rate of 60 requests per second? Or 64 requests per second? We can model the effects of the increasing load using a result from queuing theory. Simply stated, the amount of time that a request spends in the queue is directly related to the service time and the probability that the disk is busy, and it is indirectly related to the probability that the disk is idle. In formula form, we have:

$$\text{Time in Queue} = \frac{(\text{Service Time} \times \text{Utilization})}{(1 - \text{Utilization})}$$

By substitution, it is easy to see that when the I/O request arrival rate is 60 requests per second, with a service time of 15ms, the utilization is 90%. Hence, a request will have to wait 135ms in the queue. This brings total service time for the request to 135 + 15 = 150ms. At 64 requests per second (only a 7% increase), completion time soars to 370ms (a 147% increase). At 65 requests per second, service time is more than a half-second . . . from our 15ms disk drive!

The relationship between queue time and utilization (from the formula above) is shown in Figure 11.1. As you can see, the "knee" of the curve (the point at which the slope changes most drastically) is at about 78%. This is why 80% utilization is the rule-of-thumb upper limit for most disk drives.

You can readily see by our model how things could get wildly out of control. If we have a sustained request rate of 68 I/O requests per second, this disk becomes overwhelmed. And what happens if 25% of the requests generate two

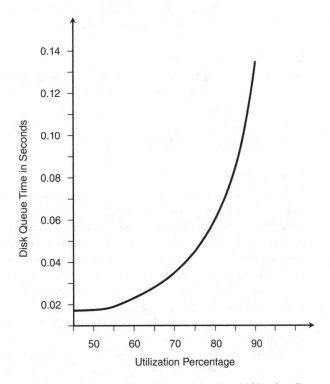

FIGURE 11.1   Disk Queue Time Plotted Against Utilization Percentage

disk operations? These scenarios result in more complex models, but the ultimate solution to the problem lies in finding ways to keep service time at an absolute minimum. This is what disk performance optimization is all about.

11.6.2   Physical Considerations

In Chapter 7, we introduced the metrics that determine the physical performance of a disk. These metrics include rotational delay (a function of the rpm rating of the disk), seek time (the time that it takes for a disk arm to position itself over a particular disk track), and transfer rate (the rate at which the read/write head transfers data from the surface of the disk to the system bus). The sum of rotational delay and seek time represents the access time for the disk.

Lower access time and a higher transfer rate contribute to lower total service time. Service time also can be reduced by adding platters to a disk, or by adding more disks to a system. Doubling the number of disks in an I/O system typically increases throughput by 50%. Replacing existing disks with the same number of faster disks can also result in a marked performance improvement. For example, replacing 7,200rpm disks with 10,000rpm disks can bring a 10% to 50% performance improvement. Physical disk performance metrics are usually disclosed in specification sheets provided by manufacturers. Comparisons between brands, therefore, are usually straightforward. But as the saying goes, your mileage may vary. Performance has as much to do with how a disk is used as it does with its inherent capabilities. Raw speed has its limits.

11.6.3   Logical Considerations

Sometimes the only cure for a slow system is to add or replace disks. But this step should be taken only after all other measures have failed. In the following sections, we discuss a number of the aspects of logical disk performance. Logical considerations in disk performance are those that present us with opportunities for tuning and adjustment, tasks that should be a routine part of system operations.

Disk Scheduling

Disk arm motion is the greatest consumer of service time in most disk configurations. The average rotational delay—the time it takes for the desired sector to move under the read/write head—is about 4ms for a 7,200rpm disk, and about 3ms for a 10,000rpm disk (this delay is calculated as the time required for half a revolution). For this same class of disk, average seek time—the time required to position the read/write head over the desired track—ranges from 5 to 10ms. In many cases, this is twice the rotational latency of the disk. Furthermore, actual seek times can be much worse than the average. As much as 15 to 20ms can be consumed during a **full-stroke seek** (moving the disk arm from the innermost track to the outermost, or vice versa).

Clearly, one road to better disk performance involves finding ways to minimize disk arm motion. This can be done by optimizing the order in which requests for sectors on the disk are serviced. **Disk scheduling** can be a function of either the disk controller or the host operating system, but it should not be done by both, because conflicting schedules will probably result, thus reducing throughput.

The most naïve disk scheduling policy is **first-come, first-served (FCFS)**. As its name implies, all I/O requests are serviced in the order in which they arrive in the disk service queue. The easiest way to see the problem with this approach is through an example. Let's say we have a disk with 100 tracks, numbered 0 through 99. Processes running in the system issue requests to read tracks from the disk in the following order:

28, 35, 52, 6, 46, 62, 19, 75, 21

With the FCFS scheduling policy, assuming we are currently servicing track 40, the disk arm traces the pattern shown in Figure 11.2. As you can see by the diagram, the disk arm changes direction six times and traverses a total of 291 tracks before completing this series of requests.

Surely, arm motion could be reduced substantially if requests were ordered so that the disk arm moves only to the track nearest its current location. This is the idea employed by the **shortest seek time first (SSTF)** scheduling algorithm. Using the same disk track requests as listed above, assuming that the disk arm starts at track 40, the disk schedule using SSTF would be carried out as follows:

35, 28, 21, 19, 6, 46, 52, 62, 75

The pattern for this schedule is shown in Figure 11.3. As you can see, the disk arm changes direction only once and traverses a total of only 103 tracks. One shortcoming of SSTF is that **starvation** is possible: Theoretically, a track requested at a "remote" part of the disk could keep getting shoved to the back of the queue when requests for tracks closer to the present arm position arrive. Interestingly, this problem is at its worst with low disk utilization rates.

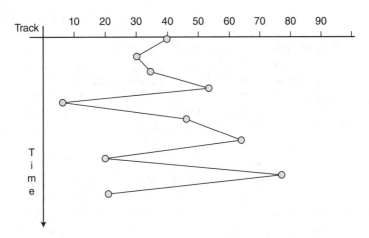

FIGURE 11.2 Disk Track Seeks Using the First-Come, First-Served Disk Scheduling Policy

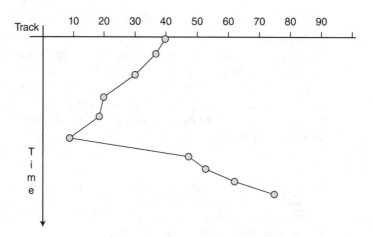

FIGURE 11.3   Disk Arm Motion for the Shortest Seek Time First Scheduling Algorithm

To avoid the starvation risk of SSTF, some fairness mechanism must be designed into the system. An easy way to do this is to have the disk arm continually sweep over the surface of the disk, stopping when it reaches a track for which it has a request in its service queue. This approach is called the **elevator algorithm**, because of its similarity to how skyscraper elevators service their passengers. In the context of disk scheduling, the elevator algorithm is known as **SCAN** (which is *not* an acronym). To illustrate how SCAN works, let's say that in our example, the disk arm happens to be positioned at track 40, and is in the process of sweeping toward the inner, higher-numbered tracks. With the same series of requests as before, SCAN reads the disk tracks in the following order:

46, 52, 62, 75, 35, 28, 21, 19, 6

The disk arm passes over track 99 between reading tracks 75 and 35, and then travels to track zero after reading track 6, as shown in Figure 11.4. SCAN has a variant, called *C-SCAN*, for circular SCAN, in which track zero is treated as if it is adjacent to track 99. In other words, the arm reads in one direction only, as shown in Figure 11.5. Once it passes track 99, it moves to track zero without stopping. Thus, in our example, C-SCAN would read disk tracks as follows:

46, 52, 62, 75, 6, 19, 21, 28, 35

The disk arm motion of SCAN and C-SCAN is reduced even further through the use of the **LOOK** and **C-LOOK** algorithms. In our example, SCAN and C-SCAN continually sweep over all 100 disk tracks. But, in fact, the lowest required track is 6 and the highest is 75. Thus, if the disk arm changes direction only when the highest- and lowest-numbered tracks are read, the arm will traverse only 69 tracks. This gives an arm-motion savings of about 30% over SCAN and C-SCAN.

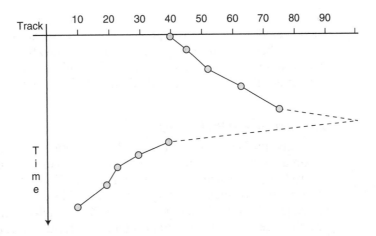

FIGURE 11.4   Disk Arm Motion for the SCAN Disk Scheduling Algorithm

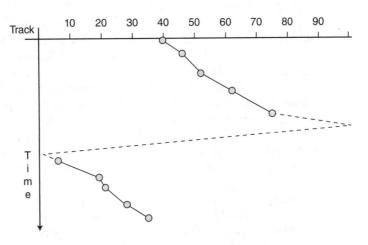

FIGURE 11.5   Disk Arm Motion for the C-SCAN Disk Scheduling Algorithm

Interestingly, at high utilization rates, SSTF performs slightly better than SCAN or LOOK. But the risk of starving an individual request persists. Under very low utilization (under 20%), the performance of any of these algorithms is acceptable.

In light of the preceding discussion of disk scheduling algorithms, a few words concerning file placement are in order. Maximum performance is realized if the most frequently used files are placed at the center of the disk. Of particular importance are the disk directory and memory page (swap) files. A central position provides the least head motion and, hence, the best access time for both SSTF and SCAN/LOOK. A worst-case situation presents itself when files are badly fragmented, that is, when a file is located in more than one contiguous disk location. If SCAN/LOOK is the scheduling method of the disk, it is possible that several full-stroke head movements will occur before the end of the file is encountered. For this reason, disks should be **defragmented**, or reorganized, on a regular basis. Additionally, disks should not be allowed to get too full. Another rule of thumb is that when a disk is 80% full, it is time to start removing some files. If no files can be removed, it's time to get another disk.

Disk Caching and Prefetching

Certainly, the best way to reduce disk arm motion is to avoid using the disk to the maximum extent possible. With this goal in mind, many disk drives, or disk drive controllers, are provided with cache memory. This memory may be supplemented by a number of main memory pages set aside for the exclusive use of the I/O subsystem. Disk cache memory is usually associative. Because associative cache searches are somewhat time-consuming, performance can actually be better with smaller disk caches because hit rates are usually low.

Main memory pages dedicated to the I/O subsystem serve as a second-level cache for the disk. On large servers, the number of pages set aside for this purpose is a tunable system parameter. If main memory utilization is high, the number of pages allocated to the I/O subsystem must be reduced. Otherwise, an excessive number of page faults will result, defeating the whole purpose of using main memory as an I/O cache.

Main memory I/O caches can be managed by operating system software running on the host, or they may be managed by applications that generate the I/O. Application-level cache management usually offers superior performance because it can capitalize on the characteristics particular to the application. The best applications give the user some control over the size of the cache, so that it can be adjusted with respect to the host's memory utilization in an effort to prevent excessive page faulting.

Many disk drive–based caches use **prefetching** techniques to reduce disk accesses. Prefetching is conceptually similar to CPU-to-memory caching: Both leverage the principles of locality for better performance. When using prefetching, a disk reads a number of sectors subsequent to the one requested with the expectation that one or more of the subsequent sectors will be needed "soon." Empirical studies have shown that more than 50% of disk accesses are sequential in nature, and that prefetching increases performance by 40% on average.

The downside of prefetching is the phenomenon of **cache pollution**. Cache pollution occurs when the cache is filled with data that no process needs, leaving less room for useful data. As with main memory caches, various replacement algorithms are employed to help keep the cache clean. These strategies include the same ones used by CPU-to-memory caches (LRU, LFU, and random). Additionally, because disk caches serve as a staging area for data to be written to the disk, some disk cache management schemes simply evict all bytes after they have been written to the disk.

The fundamental difference between reading data from and writing data to the disk gives rise to a number of thorny cache issues. First and foremost is the problem that cache is volatile memory. In the event of a massive system failure, data in the cache is lost. Suppose an application running on the host believes that the data has been committed to the disk, when it really is resident only in the cache. If the cache fails, the data just disappears. This, of course, can lead to serious data inconsistencies, such as an ATM dispensing money without debiting the customer's account.

To defend against power loss to the cache, some disk controller-based caches are **mirrored** and supplied with a battery backup. When a cache is mirrored, the controller contains two identical caches that operate in tandem, both containing the same data at all times. Another approach is to employ the write-through cache discussed in Chapter 6, where a copy of the data is retained in the cache in case it is needed again "soon," but it is simultaneously written to the disk. The operating system is signaled that the I/O is complete only after the data has actually been placed on the disk. Performance is compromised to some extent to provide better reliability.

When throughput is more important than reliability, a system may employ the write-back cache policy. Recall that there are two types of write-back policies. The simplest is where the disk simply reads the cache periodically (usually twice a minute), and writes any dirty blocks that it finds to the disk. If reliability is a concern, the commitment interval can be made shorter (at the expense of performance). A more complex write-back algorithm uses **opportunistic** writes. With this approach, dirty blocks wait in the cache until the arrival of a read request for the same cylinder. The write operation is then "piggybacked" onto the read operation. This approach has the effect of reducing performance on reads, but improving it for writes. Many systems combine periodic and opportunistic write-back policies to try to strike a balance between efficiency and reliability.

The trade-offs involved in optimizing disk performance present difficult choices. Our first responsibility is to ensure data reliability and consistency. But the highest throughput is realized when volatile caches compensate for access time delays. Caches with battery backups are costly. Adding disks to increase throughput is also an expensive option. Removing cache intermediaries from disk write operations may result in performance degradation, particularly if disk utilization rates are high. Users will soon complain of lengthy response times, and financial people will complain when you ask them for money for a disk upgrade. Keep in mind that no matter what its price, upgrading a disk subsystem is always cheaper than replacing lost data.

CHAPTER SUMMARY

This chapter has presented the two aspects of computer performance: performance assessment and performance optimization. You should come away from this chapter knowing the key measurements of computer performance and how to correctly summarize them. Specifically, you should know that arithmetic averages are not appropriate for highly variable data and should not be used with rates or ratios. The geometric mean is useful when data are highly variable, but this mean cannot be used to predict performance. The harmonic mean is appropriate when comparing rates, and it is also useful as a performance predictor. However, when the harmonic mean is used to compare relative system performance, it is more sensitive to the choice of a reference machine than the geometric mean.

We have explained a number of the more popular benchmarking programs and suites in this chapter. The most reliable of these are the benchmarks that are formulated and administered by impartial oversight bodies such as SPEC and the TPC. Regardless of which ones you use, benchmarks should be interpreted in terms of your specific application. Remember, there is no single metric that is universally applicable to all situations.

Computer performance is directly dependent on computer component optimization. We examined the factors that influence the performance of the principal computer system components. Amdahl's Law gives us a tool for determining the potential speedup due to various optimization techniques and places a ceiling on performance enhancements. Areas to consider for optimization include CPU performance, memory performance, and I/O. CPU performance is dependent on the program code, the compiler technology, the ISA, and the underlying technology of the hardware. Branch instructions have a dramatic effect on pipeline performance, which in turn has a significant effect on CPU performance. Branch prediction is one way to offset the complications introduced by branching. Fixed and static methods of branch prediction are less accurate than dynamic techniques, but are attainable at a lower cost.

I/O performance is a function of both the logical and physical characteristics of disk drives. Short of replacing the hardware, we are unable to improve physical disk performance. But many aspects of logical disk performance lend themselves to tuning and optimization. These factors include disk utilization, file placement, and memory cache sizes. Good performance reporting tools not only provide thorough I/O statistics, but they also offer tuning suggestions.

System performance evaluation and optimization are two of the most important tasks of system managers. In this chapter, we have presented only general platform-independent information. Some of the most helpful and interesting information is found in vendor-provided manuals and training seminars. These resources are essential to the continued effectiveness of your system-tuning efforts.

FURTHER READING

In the context of overall computer design, one of the most respected treatments of computer performance is presented in Hennessy and Patterson (2011). Their book integrates performance considerations throughout its exposition of all facets of computer architecture. For a comprehensive text devoted solely to computer performance, Lilja (2005) is readable and thorough in its coverage of the design and analysis of system metrics. Its introduction to the mathematics performance assessment is particularly noteworthy for its clarity. For detailed information on high-performance computing, with excellent coverage of programming and tuning software, as well as benchmarking, see Severance and Dowd (1998). Musumeci and Loukides (2002) also provide excellent coverage of system performance tuning.

In addition to the books cited above, the papers by Fleming and Wallace (1996) and Smith (1998) provide the solid mathematical basis for selection of correct statistical means. They also give some insight into the controversial nature of performance metrics.

In our discussion of statistical pitfalls and fallacies, we did not discuss how graphical representations of statistics can also lead us to incorrect conclusions and assumptions. For an eloquent look at the art of conveying (and obscuring) statistical information through graphical devices, we recommend a thorough reading of Tufte (2001). You will be amazed, delighted, and confounded. We also recommend the classic from Huff (1993). This thin book (originally copyrighted in 1954) has been entertaining readers with its information and illustrations for nearly 60 years.

Price's article (1989) contains a good description of many early synthetic benchmarks, including Whetstone, Dhrystone, and many others not covered in this chapter. Another comprehensive account of early benchmarks can be found in Serlin's article (1986). Weicker (1984) contains the original presentation of his Dhrystone benchmark. Weicker's later work in 1990 also includes LINPACK, Whetstone, and some of the benchmarks that had emerged in the 1980s, including the SPEC suite. Grace (1996) is encyclopedic in its descriptions of practically every major benchmark. His coverage includes all of the ones discussed in this chapter and many others, including benchmarks specific to Windows and Unix environments.

Surprisingly, the MFLOPS figure derived from standard benchmark programs correlated well with the early floating-point SPEC benchmarks. You will find a good discussion of this anomaly in Giladi (1996), which also provides a thorough discussion of the Linpack floating-point benchmark. For a detailed explanation of the SPEC CPU benchmark, see Henning (2006). Current comprehensive information regarding all of the the SPEC benchmarks can be found at SPEC's website: www.spec.org.

The seminal article for the TPC benchmarks was published anonymously by Jim Gray (1985). (He credits *many* others for influencing its final form because he passed the paper to a cast of thousands for their input. He refuses to take sole authorship and published the paper anonymously. Therefore, many people reference this source as "Anon. et al.") It gives the background and philosophy of the Transaction Processing Council. More current information can be found at the TPC website: www.tpc.org.

Hsu, Smith, and Young (2001) provide great detail of an investigation of real workloads in comparison to the TPC benchmarks. This article also illustrates performance data gathering using trace analysis.

There is no shortage of information concerning the performance of I/O systems. Hennessy and Patterson's book (2011) explores this topic in great detail.

An excellent (though dated) investigation of disk scheduling policies can be found in Oney (1975). Karedla, Love, and Wherry (1994) provide a clear, thorough discussion of disk cache performance. Reddy (1992) gives a nice overview of I/O systems architectures.

REFERENCES

Fleming, P. J., & Wallace, J. J. "How Not to Lie with Statistics: The Correct Way to Summarize Benchmark Results." *Communications of the ACM 29*:3, March 1996, pp. 218–221.

Giladi, R. "Evaluating the MFLOPS Measure." *IEEE Micro,* August 1996, pp. 69–75.

Grace, R. *The Benchmark Book.* Upper Saddle River, NJ: Prentice Hall, 1996.

Gray, J., et al. "A Measure of Transaction Processing Power." *Datamation 31*:7, 1985, pp. 112–118.

Hennessy, J. L., & Patterson, D. A. *Computer Architecture: A Quantitative Approach*, 5th ed. San Francisco: Morgan Kaufmann Publishers, 2011.

Henning, J. L. "SPEC CPU 2006 Benchmark Descriptions." ACM SIGARCH News *34*:4, September 2006, pp. 1–17.

Hsu, W. W., Smith, A. J., & Young, H. C. "I/O Reference Behavior of Production Database Workloads and the TPC Benchmarks—An Analysis at the Logical Level." *ACM Transactions on Database Systems 26*:1, March 2001, pp. 96–143.

Huff, D. *How to Lie with Statistics.* New York: W.W. Norton & Company, 1993.

Karedla, R., Love, J. S., & Wherry, B. G. "Caching Strategies to Improve Disk System Performance." *IEEE Computer,* March 1994, pp. 38–46.

Lilja, D. J. *Measuring Computer Performance: A Practitioner's Guide.* New York: Cambridge University Press, 2005.

Musumeci, G.-P., & Loukides, M. *System Performance Tuning*, 2nd ed. Sebastopol, CA: O'Reilly & Associates, Inc., 2002.

Oney, W. C. "Queueing Analysis of the Scan Policy for Moving-Head Disks." *Journal of the ACM 22,* July 1975, pp. 397–412.

Price, W. J. "A Benchmarking Tutorial." *IEEE Microcomputer,* October 1989, pp. 28–43.

Reddy, A. L. N. "A Study of I/O System Organization." *ACM SIGARCH Proceedings of the 19th Annual International Symposium on Computer Architecture 20*:2, April 1992, pp. 308–317.

Serlin, O. "MIPS, Dhrystones, and Other Tales." *Datamation,* June 1 1986, pp. 112–118.

Severance, C., & Dowd, K. *High Performance Computing*, 2nd ed. Sebastopol, CA: O'Reilly & Associates, Inc., 1998.

Smith, J. E. "Characterizing Computer Performance with a Single Number." *Communications of the ACM 32*:10, October 1998, pp. 1202–1206.

Tufte, E. R. *The Visual Display of Quantitative Information*, 2nd ed. Cheshire, CT: Graphics Press, 2001.

Weicker, R. P. "Dhrystone: A Synthetic Systems Programming Benchmark." *Communications of the ACM 27,* October 1984, pp. 1013–1029.

Weicker, R. P. "An Overview of Common Benchmarks." *IEEE Computer,* December 1990, pp. 65–75.

REVIEW OF ESSENTIAL TERMS AND CONCEPTS

1. Explain what is meant when we say that a program or system is memory bound. What other types of bindings have we discussed?
2. What does Amdahl's Law tell us about performance optimization?
3. Which of the means is useful for comparing rates?
4. For what kinds of data is the arithmetic mean inappropriate?
5. Give a definition for *optimum performance*.
6. What is a price-performance ratio? What makes it hard to apply?
7. What is the shortcoming of using MIPS or FLOPS as a measure of system throughput?
8. How is the Dhrystone benchmark different from Whetstone and Linpack?
9. What are the deficiencies in the Whetstone, Dhrystone, and Linpack benchmarks that are addressed by the SPEC CPU benchmarks?
10. Explain the term *benchmarketing*.
11. How is the focus of the TPC different from SPEC?
12. Explain *delayed branching*.
13. What is branch prediction? What is it used for?
14. Give three examples of pipeline hazards.
15. Define the terms *loop fusion*, *loop fission*, *loop peeling*, and *loop interchange*.
16. According to queuing theory, what is the critical disk utilization percentage?
17. What is the risk involved in using the SSTF disk scheduling algorithm?
18. How is LOOK different from SCAN?
19. What is disk prefetching? What are its advantages and disadvantages?
20. What are the advantages and disadvantages of caching disk writes?

EXERCISES

◆ 1. Table 11.2 shows an execution mix and run times for two computers, System A and System C. In this example, System C is 83% faster than System A. Table 11.3 shows run times for System A with a different execution mix. Using the execution mix in Table 11.3, calculate the percentage by which System C would be faster than System A. Using the original statistics from Table 11.2, by how much has the performance of System A degraded under the new execution mix?

2. With regard to the performance data cited for programs v, w, x, y, and z in Section 11.3, find the geometric means of the run times of the programs for System B and System C, using System A as the reference system. Verify that the ratios of the means are consistent with the results obtained using the other two systems as reference systems.

◆ 3. The execution times for three systems running five benchmarks are shown in the following table. Compare the relative performance of each of these systems (i.e., A to B,

B to C, and A to C) using the arithmetic and geometric means. Are there any surprises? Explain.

Program	System A Execution Time	System B Execution Time	System C Execution Time
v	150	200	75
w	200	250	150
x	250	175	200
y	400	800	500
z	1,000	1,200	1,100

4. The execution times for three systems running five benchmarks are shown in the following table. Compare the relative performance of each of these systems (i.e., A to B, B to C, and A to C) using the arithmetic and geometric means. Are there any surprises? Explain.

Program	System A Execution Time	System B Execution Time	System C Execution Time
v	45	125	75
w	300	275	350
x	250	100	200
y	400	300	500
z	800	1,200	700

5. A company that is selling database management optimization software contacts you to pitch its product. The representative claims that the memory management software will reduce page fault rates for your system. She offers you a 30-day free trial of this software. Before you install it, however, you decide to first determine a baseline for your system. At specific times of the day, you sample and record the page fault rate of your system (using the system's diagnostic software). You do the same after the software has been installed. How much of an average performance improvement has the new software provided? (Hint: Use the harmonic mean.)

The fault rates and times of day are shown in the table below.

Time	Fault Rate Before	Fault Rate After
02:00–03:00	35%	45%
10:00–11:00	42%	38%
13:00–14:00	12%	10%
18:00–19:00	20%	22%

6. What are the limitations of synthetic benchmarks such as Whetstone and Dhrystone? Do you think the concept of a synthetic benchmark could be extended to overcome these limitations? Explain your answer.

◆ 7. What would you say to a vendor who tells you that his system runs 50% of the SPEC benchmark kernel programs twice as fast as the leading competitive system? Which statistical fallacy is at work here?

8. Suppose that you are looking into purchasing a new computer system. You have suitable benchmark results for all of the systems that you are considering except for System X Model Q. The benchmark results have been reported for System X Model S, and they are not quite as good as several competing brands. In order to complete your research, you call the people at System X computer company and ask when they plan to publish benchmark results for the Model Q. They tell you that they will not be publishing these results anytime soon, but because the disk drives of Model Q give an average access time of 12ms, whereas Model S had 15ms drives, Model Q will perform better than Model S by 25%. How would you record the performance metrics for System X model Q?

◆ 9. What value do you think there would be in comparing the results of two different SPEC CPU releases, say, SPEC95 and SPEC2000?

10. Besides the retail business sector, what other organizations would need good performance from a transaction-processing system? Justify your answer.

◆ 11. Which of the benchmarks discussed in this chapter would be most helpful to you if you were about to purchase a system to be used in DNA research? Why would you choose this one? Would any of the other benchmarks be of interest to you? Why or why not?

12. Suppose a friend has asked you to help him make a choice as to what kind of computer he should buy for his personal use at home. What would you look for in comparing various makes and models? How is your line of thinking different in this situation than if you were to help your employer purchase a Web server to accept customers' orders over the Internet?

◆ 13. Suppose you have just been assigned to a committee that has been tasked with purchasing a new enterprise file server that will support customer account activity as well as many administrative functions, such as producing a weekly payroll. (Yes, a committee frequently makes these decisions!) One of your committee members has just learned that a particular system has blown out the competition in the SPEC CPU2000 benchmarks. He is now insisting that the committee buy one of these systems. What would be your reaction to this?

*14. We discussed the limitations of the harmonic mean in its application to computer performance assessment. A number of critics have suggested that the SPEC should use the harmonic mean instead. Suggest a unit of "work" that would be appropriate for reformulating the SPEC benchmarks as rate metrics. Test your theory using results from SPEC's website, www.spec.org.

*15. SPEC and the TPC both publish benchmarks for Web server systems. Visit the respective websites of these organizations (www.spec.org and www.tpc.org) to try to find identical (or comparable) systems that have results posted on both sites. Discuss your findings.

16. We mentioned that a large volume of data is gathered during system probe traces. To give you some idea of the actual volume of data involved, suppose plans are being made to install a hardware probe that reports the contents of a system's program counter, instruction register, accumulator, memory address register, and memory buffer register. The system has a clock that runs at 1GHz. During each cycle of the system clock, the status of these five registers is written to nonvolatile memory attached to the probe circuitry. If each register is 64 bits wide, how much storage will the probe require if it is to gather data for 2 seconds?

17. The sidebar in Section 11.5.2 presents ways in which program performance can be improved. For each of the tips in the sidebar, state whether a computer organization and architecture issue is involved. If so, explain the reasoning behind the advice as given. If you feel anything is missing from the sidebar, include your advice in your analysis.

18. In our discussion of the physical aspects of disk performance, we stated that replacing 7,200rpm disks with 10,000rpm disks can bring a 10% to 50% performance improvement. Why would an improvement of only 10% occur? Could it be that no improvement at all would occur? Explain. (Hint: Rotational latency is not the only determining factor of disk performance.)

19. Calculate the number of disk tracks traversed using the FCFS, SSTF, SCAN, and LOOK algorithms for the series of disk track service requests given below. At the time the first request arrives in the disk request queue, the read/write head is at track 50, moving toward the outer (lower-numbered) tracks. (Hint: Each track over which the disk arm passes counts in the total, whether or not the track is read.)

    54, 36, 21, 74, 46, 35, 26, 67

20. Repeat the previous problem using the following tracks:

    82, 97, 35, 75, 53, 47, 17, 11

21. On a particular brand of disk drive, the time that it takes for the disk arm to pass over a single disk track without stopping is 500ns. However, once the head reaches the track for which it has a service request, it needs 2ms to "settle" over the required track before it can start reading or writing. Based on these timings, compare the relative times required for FCFS, SSTF, and LOOK to carry out the schedule given below. You will need to compare SSTF to FCFS, LOOK to FCFS, and LOOK to SSTF.

    As in our previous question, when the first request arrives in the disk request queue, the read/write head is at track 50, moving toward the outer (lower-numbered) tracks. The requested tracks are:

    35, 53, 90, 67, 79, 37, 76, 47

22. Repeat exercise 21 for the following disk tracks (assuming the read/write head is at track 50, moving outward):

    48, 14, 85, 35, 84, 61, 30, 22

*23. In our discussion of the SSTF disk scheduling algorithm, we stated that the problem of starvation "is at its worst with low disk utilization rates." Explain why this is so.

♦ 24. A certain microprocessor requires either 2, 3, 4, 8, or 12 machine cycles to perform various operations. A total of 25% of its instructions require 2 machine cycles, 20% require 3 machine cycles, 17.5% require 4 machine cycles, 12.5% require 8 machine cycles, and 25% require 12 machine cycles.

    ♦ a) What is the average number of machine cycles per instruction for this microprocessor?

    ♦ b) What is the clock rate (machine cycles per second) required for this microprocessor to be a "1 MIPS" processor?

    ♦ c) Suppose this system requires an extra 20 machine cycles to retrieve an operand from memory. It has to go to memory 40% of the time. What is the average number of machine cycles per instruction for this microprocessor, including its memory fetch instructions?

25. A certain microprocessor requires either 2, 4, 8, 12, or 16 machine cycles to perform various operations. A total of 17.5% of its instructions require 2 machine cycles, 12.5% require 4 machine cycles, 35% require 8 machine cycles, 20% require 12 machine cycles, and 15% require 16 machine cycles.

    a) What is the average number of machine cycles per instruction for this microprocessor?

    b) What is the clock rate (machine cycles per second) required for this microprocessor to be a "1 MIPS" processor?

    c) Suppose this system requires an extra 16 machine cycles to retrieve an operand from memory. It has to go to memory 30% of the time. What is the average number of machine cycles per instruction for this microprocessor, including its memory fetch instructions?

26. Herbert Grosch (b. 1918) has been an eminent computer scientist since the 1940s. In 1965, he put forth a claim that he "humbly" called Grosch's Law. This law can be paraphrased as:

    Computer performance increases as the square of the cost. If Computer A costs twice as much as Computer B, you should expect Computer A to be four times as fast as Computer B.

    Use any of the TPC benchmarks to confirm or refute this claim. What happens when you restrict your comparison to similar systems? More specifically, check the price/performance statistics for systems running only the same class of operating system and database software. What happens when you don't restrict the comparison to similar systems? Do these results change when you select a different benchmark, e.g., TPC-W versus TPC-C? Discuss your findings.

CHAPTER 12 Network Organization and Architecture

12.1 INTRODUCTION

Sun Microsystems launched a major advertising campaign in the 1980s with the catchy slogan that opens this chapter. A couple decades ago, its pitch was surely more sizzle than steak, but it was like a voice in the wilderness, heralding today's wired world with the Web at the heart of global commerce. Standalone business computers are now obsolete and irrelevant.

This chapter will introduce you to the vast and complex arena of data communications with a particular focus on the Internet. We will look at architectural models (network protocols) from a historical point of view, a theoretical point of view, and a practical point of view. Once you have an understanding of how a network operates, you will learn about many of the components that constitute network organization. Our intention is to give you a broad view of the technologies and terminology that every computer professional will encounter at some time during his or her career. To understand the computer is to also understand the network.

12.2 EARLY BUSINESS COMPUTER NETWORKS

Today's computer networks evolved along two different paths. One path was directed toward enabling fast and accurate business transactions, whereas the other was aimed at facilitating collaboration and knowledge sharing in the academic and scientific communities.

683

Digital networks of all varieties aspire to share computer resources in the simplest, fastest, and most cost-effective manner possible. The more costly the computer, the stronger the motivation to share it among as many users as possible. In the 1950s, when most computers cost millions of dollars, only the wealthiest companies could afford more than one system. Of course, employees in remote locations had as much need for computer resources as their central office counterparts, so some method of getting them connected had to be devised. And virtually every vendor had a different connectivity solution. The most dominant of these vendors was IBM with its **Systems Network Architecture (SNA)**. This communications architecture, with modifications, has persisted for more than three decades.

IBM's SNA is a specification for end-to-end communication between physical devices (called **physical units**, or **PUs**) over which logical sessions (known as **logical units**, or **LUs**) take place. In the original architecture, the physical components of this system consisted of terminals, printers, communications controllers, multiplexers, and front-end processors. Front-end processors sat between the host (mainframe) system and the communications lines. They managed all of the communications overhead including polling each of the communications controllers, which in turn polled each of their attached terminals. This architecture is shown in Figure 12.1.

IBM's SNA was geared toward high-speed transaction entry and customer service inquiries. Even at the modest line speed of 9,600bps (bits per second), access to data on the host was nearly instantaneous when all network components were functioning properly under normal loads. The speed of this architecture, however, came at the expense of flexibility and interoperability. The human overhead in managing and supporting these networks was enormous, and connections to other vendors' equipment and networks were often laudable feats of software and hardware engineering. Over the past 30 years, SNA has adapted to changing business needs and networking environments, but the underlying concepts are essentially what they were decades ago. In fact, this architecture was so well designed that aspects of it formed the foundation for the definitive international communications architecture, OSI, which we discuss in Section 12.4. Although SNA contributed much to the young science of data communications, the technology has just about run its course. In most installations, it has been replaced by "open" Internet protocols.

12.3 EARLY ACADEMIC AND SCIENTIFIC NETWORKS: THE ROOTS AND ARCHITECTURE OF THE INTERNET

Amid the angst of the Cold War, American scientists at far-flung research institutions toiled under government contracts, seeking to preserve the military ascendancy of the United States. At a time when the country had fallen behind in the technology race, the U.S. government created an organization called the

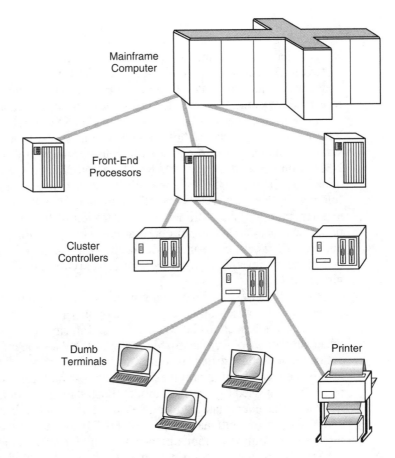

Mainframe
Computer

Front-End
Processors

Cluster
Controllers

Dumb
Terminals

Printer

FIGURE 12.1 A Hierarchical, Polled Network

Advanced Research Projects Agency (ARPA). The sophisticated computers this organization needed to carry out its work, however, were scarce and extremely costly—even by Pentagon standards. Before long, it occurred to someone that by establishing communication links into the few supercomputers that were scattered all over the United States, computational resources could be shared by innumerable like-minded researchers. Moreover, this network would be designed with sufficient redundancy to provide for continuous communication, even if thermonuclear war knocked out a large number of nodes or communication lines. To this end, in December 1968, a Cambridge, Massachusetts, consulting firm called BBN (Bolt, Beranek, and Newman, now Genuity Corporation) was awarded the contract to construct such a network. In December 1969, four nodes, the University of Utah, the University of California at Los Angeles, the University of California at Santa

Barbara, and the Stanford Research Institute, went online. ARPAnet gradually expanded to include more government and research institutions. When President Reagan changed the name of ARPA to the **Defense Advanced Research Projects Network (DARPA)**, ARPAnet became **DARPAnet**. Through the early 1980s, nodes were added at a rate of a little more than one per month. However, military researchers eventually abandoned DARPAnet in favor of more secure channels.

In 1985, the National Science Foundation (NSF) established its own network, **NSFnet**, to support its scientific and academic research. NSFnet and DARPAnet served a similar purpose and a similar user community, but the capabilities of NSFnet outstripped those of DARPAnet. Consequently, when the military abandoned DARPAnet, NSFnet absorbed it and became what we now know as the Internet. By the early 1990s, the NSF had outgrown NSFnet, so it began building a faster, more reliable NSFnet. Administration of the public Internet then fell to private national and regional corporations, such as Sprint, MCI, and PacBell, to name a few. These companies bought the NSFnet trunk lines, called **backbones**, and made money by selling backbone capacity to various **Internet service providers (ISPs)**.

The original DARPAnet (and now the Internet) would have survived thermonuclear war because, unlike all other networks in existence in the 1970s, it had no dedicated connections between systems. Information was instead routed along whatever pathways were available. Parts of the data stream belonging to a single dialogue could take different routes to their destinations. The key to this robustness is the idea of **datagram** message packets, which carry data in chunks instead of the streams used by the SNA model. Each datagram contains addressing information so that every datagram can be routed as a single, discrete unit.

A second revolutionary aspect of DARPAnet was that it created a uniform protocol for communications between dissimilar hosts along networks of differing speeds. Because it connected many different kinds of networks, DARPAnet was said to be an **internetwork**. As originally specified, each host computer connected to DARPAnet by way of an **Interface Message Processor (IMP)**. IMPs took care of protocol translation from the language of DARPAnet to the communications language native to the host system, so any communications protocol could be used between the IMP and the host. Today, routers (discussed in Section 12.6.7) have replaced IMPs, and the communications protocols are less heterogeneous than they were in the 1970s. However, the underlying principles have remained the same, and the generic concept of internetworking has become practically synonymous with the Internet. A modern internetwork configuration is shown in Figure 12.2. The diagram shows how four routers form the heart of the network. They connect many different types of equipment, making decisions on their own as to how datagrams should get to their destinations in the most efficient way possible.

The Internet is much more than a set of good data communication specifications. It is, perhaps, a philosophy. The foremost principle of this philosophy is the idea of a free and open world of information sharing, with the destiny of this world being shaped collaboratively by the people and ideas in it. The epitome of this openness is the manner in which Internet standards are created.

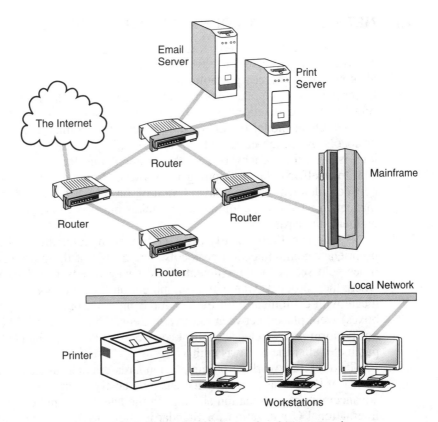

FIGURE 12.2 An Example of an Internetwork

Internet standards are formulated through a democratic process that takes place under the auspices of the **Internet Architecture Board** (**IAB**), which itself operates under the oversight of the not-for-profit **Internet Society** (**ISOC**). The **Internet Engineering Task Force** (**IETF**), operating within the IAB, is a loose alliance of industry experts that develops detailed specifications for Internet protocols. The IETF publishes all proposed standards in the form of **Requests for Comment** (**RFCs**), which are open to anyone's scrutiny and comment. The two most important RFCs—RFC 791 (Internet Protocol Version 4) and RFC 793 (Transmission Control Protocol)—form the foundation of today's global Internet.

The organization of all the ISOC's committees under more committees could have resulted in a tangle of bureaucracy producing inscrutable and convoluted specifications. But owing to the openness of the entire process, as well as the talents of the reviewers, RFCs are among the clearest and most readable documents in the entire body of networking literature. It is little wonder that manufacturers were so quick to adopt Internet protocols. Internet protocols are now running on all sizes of networks, both publicly and privately owned. Formerly, networking standards were handed down by a centralized committee or through an equipment vendor. One such approach resulted in the ISO/OSI protocol model, which we discuss next.

12.4   NETWORK PROTOCOLS I: ISO/OSI PROTOCOL UNIFICATION

In Chapter 13, we show how various data storage interfaces use protocol stacks. The SCSI-3 Architecture Model is one of these. In general, protocol stacks make all kinds of interfaces portable, maintainable, and easy to describe. The most important and comprehensive of these is the ISO/OSI (International Organization for Standardization/Open Systems Interconnect) protocol stack, which is the theoretical model for many storage and data communication interfaces and protocols. Although each protocol differs in implementation details, the general idea is the same: Each layer of the protocol interfaces only with layers adjacent to itself. No layer skipping is allowed. Protocol conversations take place between identical protocol layers running on two different machines. The exact manner in which this communication takes place is clearly defined in the international standards.

By the late 1970s, nearly every computer manufacturer had devised its own proprietary communication protocols. The details of these protocols were sometimes held secret by their inventors as a way to ensure a lock on the markets where their products were sold. Equipment built by Vendor A could not communicate with equipment built by Vendor B unless protocol conversion kits (black boxes) were placed between the two systems. Even then, the black boxes might not perform as expected, usually because a vendor had changed some protocol parameter after the box was built.

Two of the world's premiere standards-making bodies realized that this Tower of Babel was becoming increasingly costly, ultimately working against the advancement of information sharing. In the late 1970s and early 1980s, both the International Organization for Standardization (ISO) and the International Consultative Committee on Telephony and Telegraphy (CCITT) were independently attempting to construct an international standard telecommunications architecture. In 1984, these two entities came together to produce a unified model, now known as the **ISO Open Systems Interconnect Reference Model (ISO/OSI RM)**. (*Open systems*, in this context, means that system connectivity would not be proprietary to any single vendor.) The ISO's work is called a reference model because virtually no commercial system uses all of the features precisely as specified in the model. However, the ISO/OSI model does help us to understand how real protocols and network components fit together in the context of a standard model.

The OSI RM contains seven protocol layers, starting with physical media interconnections at Layer 1, through applications at Layer 7. We must emphasize that the OSI model defines only the functions of each of the seven layers and the interfaces between them. Implementation details are not part of the model. Many different standardization bodies, including the IEEE, the European Computer Manufacturers Association (ECMA), the International Telecommunication Union-Telecommunication Standardization Sector (ITU-T), and the ISO itself (external to the ISO model), have provided such detail. Implementations at the highest layers can be completely user defined.

12.4.1   A Parable

Before we embark on the technicalities of the OSI RM, let us offer a parable to help illustrate how layered protocols work. Suppose you have lost a bet with your sister and the price is to spend the day with your nephew, Billy. Billy is a notorious brat who throws tantrums when he doesn't get his own way. Today he has decided that he wants a roast beef sandwich from Dumpy's Deli down the street. This roast beef sandwich must be dressed with mustard and pickles. Nothing more, nothing less.

Upon entering the deli, you seat Billy and take a number from the dispenser near the counter. There is a cashier taking orders and a second person assembling orders in a food preparation area. The deli is packed with hungry workers on their lunch hours. You remark to yourself that the service seems unusually slow this day. Billy starts to announce loudly that he is hungry, while he thumps his little fists on the table.

Despite how badly you want Billy's sandwich, by waiting for your number to be called, you are obeying a protocol. You know that pushing yourself ahead of the others will get you nowhere. In fact, if you defy the protocol, you could be ejected from the deli, making matters worse.

When you finally get your turn at the counter (Billy by now is yelling quite loudly), you give the cashier your order, adding a tuna sandwich and chips for yourself. The cashier fetches your drinks and tells the food handler to prepare a tuna sandwich and a roast beef sandwich with mustard and pickles. Although the cook could hear every word of Billy's luncheon desires above the din of the crowd, she waited until the cashier told her what to prepare.

Billy, therefore, could not skip over the cashier layer of the deli protocol regardless of how loudly he yelled. Before assembling the sandwiches, the food handler had to know that the order was legitimate and that a customer was willing to pay for it. She could know this only by being told by the cashier.

Once the sandwiches have been prepared, the cook wraps them individually in deli paper, marking the paper to indicate the contents of each. The cashier fetches the sandwiches, placing them both in a brown bag, along with your chips and two cans of cola. She announces that your bill is $6.25, for which you hand her a $10.00 bill. She gives you $4.75 in change. Because she has given you the wrong change, you stand at the counter until you are given the correct change, then you proceed to your table.

Upon unwrapping the sandwich, Billy discovers that his roast beef sandwich is in fact a corned beef sandwich, triggering yet another round of whining. You have no choice but to take another number and wait in line until it is called.

Your refusal to leave the counter when given the wrong change is analogous to error-checking that takes place between the layers of a protocol. The transmission does not proceed until the receiving layer is satisfied with what it has received from the sending layer. Of course, you didn't feel comfortable unwrapping Billy's sandwich while standing at the counter (that would, after all, be icky).

The sandwiches, along with their wrapping, correspond to OSI **Protocol Data Units (PDUs)**. Once data has been encapsulated by an upper-layer protocol, a lower-layer protocol will not examine its contents. Neither you nor the cashier unwrapped the sandwiches. The cashier created yet another PDU when she placed your order in the bag. Because your order was in a bag, you could easily carry it to your table. Juggling two colas, two sandwiches, and a bag of chips through a crowded deli may indeed have had disastrous consequences.

At Dumpy's Deli, you know that if you want something to eat, you can't go directly to the cook, nor can you go to another customer, nor to a maintenance person. For lunch service, you can go only to the cashier after taking a number. The number you pull from the dispenser is analogous to an OSI **Service Access Point (SAP)**. The cashier grants you permission to place your order only when you present the ticket that proves you are the next in line.

12.4.2   The OSI Reference Model

The OSI Reference Model is shown in Figure 12.3. As you can see, the protocol consists of seven layers. Adjacent layers interface with each other through SAPs, and as the protocol data units (PDUs) pass through the stack, each protocol layer adds or removes its own header. Headers are added on the sending end, and they are removed by the receiving end. The contents of the PDUs create a conversation between peer layers on each side of the dialogue. This conversation is their protocol.

Having employed a story to explain the ideas of PDUs and SAPs, we supply another metaphor to help us further explain the OSI Reference Model. In this metaphor, suppose that you are operating your own business. This business, called Super Soups and Tasty Teas, manufactures gourmet soup and tea that is sold all over North America to people of discriminating tastes. In order to get your luscious wares where they are going, you use a private shipping company, Ginger, Lee, and Pronto, also known as GL&P. The system of manufacturing your wares and their ultimate consumption by your epicurean customers spans a series of processes analogous to those carried out by the layers of the OSI Reference Model, as we shall see in the following sections.

The OSI Physical Layer

Many different kinds of media are capable of carrying bits between a communication source (the initiator) and their destination (the responder). Neither the initiator nor the responder need have any concern as to whether their conversation takes place over copper wire, satellite links, or optical cable. The Physical layer of the OSI model assumes the job of carrying a signal from here to there. It receives a stream of bits from the Data Link layer above it, encodes those bits, and places them on the communications medium in accordance with agreed-on protocols and signaling standards.

The function of the OSI Physical layer can be compared to that of the vehicles that the GL&P shipping company uses to move products from your factory to your customer. After giving your parcel to the delivery company, you usually don't care whether the parcel is carried to its destination on a train, a truck, an

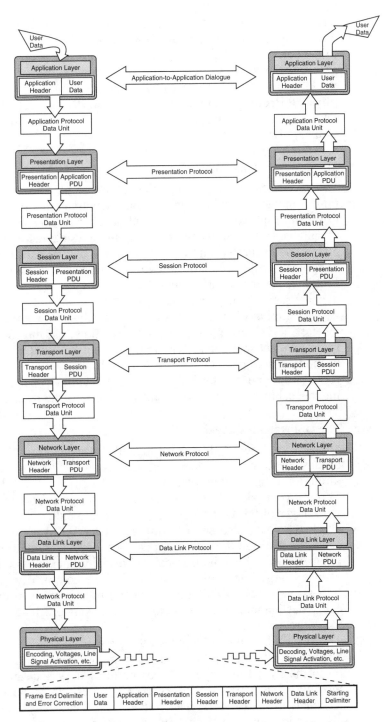

FIGURE 12.3   The OSI Reference Model—Interfaces Operate Vertically;
Protocols Operate Horizontally

airplane, or a ferryboat, as long as it arrives at its destination intact and within a reasonable amount of time. The handlers along the way have no concern as to the contents of the parcel, only as to the address on the box (sometimes even ignoring the word *fragile!*). Similar to how a freight company moves boxes, the OSI Physical layer moves transmission frames, which are sometimes called **physical Protocol Data Units**, or **physical PDUs**. Each physical PDU carries an address and has delimiter signal patterns that surround the **payload**, or contents, of the PDU.

The OSI Data Link Layer

When you send your package, the actions of placing articles in a suitable shipping container and addressing the package are comparable to the function of the OSI Data Link layer. The Data Link layer organizes message bytes into frames of suitable size for transmission along the physical medium. If you were shipping 50kg of soup and tea, and GL&P has a rule that no package can weigh more than 40kg, you would need at least two separate boxes to ship your articles. The Data Link layer does the same thing. It negotiates frame sizes and the speed at which they are sent with the Data Link layer at the other end.

The timing of frame transmission is called **flow control**. If frames are sent too fast, the receiver's buffer could overflow, causing frames to be lost. If the frames are not sent quickly enough, the receiver could time out and drop the connection. In both of these cases, the Data Link layer senses the problem when the receiver does not acknowledge the packets within a specified time interval. Lacking this acknowledgment, the sender retransmits the packet.

The OSI Network Layer

Suppose you could tell GL&P, "Send this package through Newark, New Jersey, because the terminal in New York City is always too crowded to get my package through on time." Stated another way, if you could tell the freight carrier how to route your package, you would be performing the same function as the Network layer of the OSI model. The package handlers at a Philadelphia terminal, however, would also be performing a Network layer function if they decide to route the package through Newark after they've learned of an unusual problem in New York. This kind of localized decision making is critical to the operation of every large internetwork. Because of the complexity of most networks, it is impossible for every end node computer to keep track of every possible route to every destination, so the functions of the Network layer are spread throughout the entire system.

At the originating computers, the Network layer doesn't do much except add addressing information to the PDUs from the Transport layer, and then pass them on to the Data Link layer. It does its most important and complex tasks while moving PDUs across the **intermediate nodes**—those nodes that act like freight terminals in the network. The Network layer not only establishes the route, but also ensures that the size of its PDUs is compatible with all of the equipment between the source and the destination.

The OSI Transport Layer

Let's say that the destination of your parcels, filled with canned soup and packaged teas, is a food distribution warehouse in Quebec. Upon its arrival, a shipping clerk opens the package to make sure that the goods were not damaged in transit. She opens each box, looking for dented cans and ripped tea boxes. She doesn't care whether the soup is too salty or the tea is too tart, only that the products have arrived intact and undamaged. Once the goods pass her inspection, the clerk signs a receipt that GL&P returns to you, letting you know that your products got to their destination.

Similarly, the OSI Transport layer provides quality assurance functions for the layers above it in the protocol stack. It contributes yet another level of end-to-end acknowledgment and error correction through its handshaking with the Transport layer at the other end of the connection. The Transport layer is the lowest layer of the OSI model at which there is any awareness of the network or its protocols. Once the Transport layer peels its protocol information away from the Session PDU, the Session layer can safely assume that there are no network-induced errors in the PDU.

The OSI Session Layer

The Session layer arbitrates the dialogue between two communicating nodes, opening and closing that dialogue as necessary. It controls the direction and mode, which is either **half-duplex** (in one direction at a time) or **full-duplex** (in both directions at once). If the mode is half-duplex, the Session layer determines which node has control of the line. It also supplies recovery checkpoints during file transfers. **Checkpoints** are issued each time a packet, or block of data, is acknowledged as received in good condition. If an error occurs during a large file transfer, the Session layer retransmits all data from the last checkpoint. Without checkpoint processing, the entire file would need to be retransmitted.

If the shipping clerk notices that one of your boxes was smashed in transit, she would notify you (as well as GL&P) that the goods did not arrive intact and that you must send another shipment. If the damaged parcel was a 10kg box of a 50kg shipment, you would replace only the contents of the 10kg box; the other 40kg of merchandise could be sent on its way to the consumer.

The OSI Presentation Layer

What if the consumers of your soup and tea reside in the Quebec market area and the labels on your soup cans are in English only? If you expect to sell your soup to people who speak French, you would certainly want your soup cans to have bilingual labels. If employees of the Quebec food distribution warehouse do this for you, they are doing what the Presentation layer does in the OSI model.

The Presentation layer provides high-level data interpretation services for the Application layer above it. For example, suppose one network node is an IBM zSeries Server that stores and transmits data in EBCDIC. This mainframe server needs to send some data to an ASCII-based microcomputer that has just requested it. The Presentation layers residing on the respective systems decide which of the two will perform the EBCDIC-to-ASCII translation. Either side could do it with equal effectiveness. What is important to remember is that the mainframe is sending EBCDIC to its Application layer and the Application layer on the client is receiving ASCII from the Presentation layer beneath it in the protocol stack. Presentation layer services are also called into play if we use encryption or certain types of data compression during the communication session.

The OSI Application Layer

The Application layer supplies meaningful information and services to users at one end of the communication and interfaces with system resources (programs and data files) at the other end of the communication. Application layers provide a suite of programs that can be invoked as the user sees fit. If none of the applications routinely supplied by the Application layer can do the job, we are free to write our own. With regard to communications, the only thing that these applications need to do is to send messages to the Presentation layer Service Access Points, and the lower layers take care of the hard part.

To enjoy a savory serving of Super Soups, all that the French Canadian soup connoisseur needs to do is open the can, heat, and enjoy. Because GL&P and the regional food distributor have all done their work, your soup is as tasty on the Canadian's table as it was coming out of your kitchen. (*Magnifique!*)

12.5 NETWORK PROTOCOLS II: TCP/IP NETWORK ARCHITECTURE

While the ISO and the CCITT were haggling over the finer points of the perfect protocol stack, TCP/IP was rapidly spreading across the globe. By the sheer weight of its popularity in the academic and scientific communications communities, TCP/IP quietly became the de facto global data communication standard.

Although it didn't start out that way, TCP/IP is now a lean and effective protocol stack. It has three layers that can be mapped to five of the seven layers in the OSI model. These layers are shown in Figure 12.4. Because the IP layer is loosely coupled with OSI's Data Link and Physical layers, TCP/IP can be used with any type of network, even different types of networks within a single session. The singular requirement is that all of the participating networks must be running—at minimum—Version 4 of the Internet Protocol (**IPv4**).

There are two versions of the Internet Protocol in use today: Version 4 and Version 6. IPv6 addresses many of the limitations of IPv4. Despite the many advantages of IPv6, the huge installed base of IPv4 ensures that it will be supported for many years to come. Some of the major differences between IPv4 and IPv6 are outlined in Section 12.5.5. But first, we take a detailed look at IPv4.

12.5.1 The IP Layer for Version 4

The IP layer of the TCP/IP protocol stack provides essentially the same services as the Network and Data Link layers of the OSI Reference Model: It divides TCP packets into protocol data units called datagrams, and then attaches the routing information required to get the datagrams to their destinations. The concept of

Application		FTP, HTTP, Telnet, SMTP, etc.
Presentation		
Session		
Transport		TCP
Network		IP
Data Link		
Physical		

FIGURE 12.4   The TCP/IP Protocol Stack Versus the OSI Protocol Stack

the datagram was fundamental to the robustness of ARPAnet, and now the Internet. Datagrams can take any route available to them without intervention by a human network manager. Take, for example, the network shown in Figure 12.5. If intermediate node X becomes congested or fails, intermediate node Y can route datagrams through node Z until X is back up to full speed. Routers are the Internet's most critical components, and researchers are continually seeking ways to improve their effectiveness and performance. We look at routers in detail in Section 12.6.7.

The bytes that constitute any of the TCP/IP protocol data units are called **octets**. This is because at the time that the ARPAnet protocols were being designed, the word *byte* was thought to be a proprietary term for the 8-bit groups used by IBM mainframes. Most TCP/IP literature uses the word *octet*, but we use *byte* for the sake of clarity.

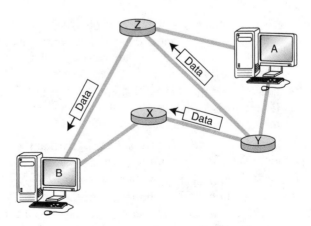

FIGURE 12.5   Datagram Routing in IP

THE IP VERSION 4 DATAGRAM HEADER

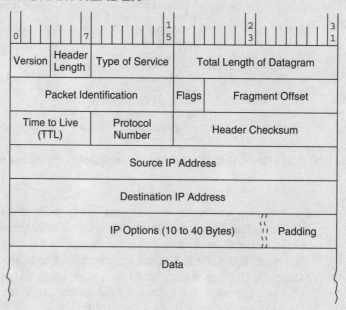

Each IPv4 datagram must contain at least 40 bytes, which include a 24-byte header as shown above. The horizontal rows represent 32-bit words. Upon inspection of the figure, you can see, for example, that the Type of Service field occupies bits 8 through 15, whereas the Packet Identification field occupies bits 32 through 47 of the header. The Padding field shown as the last field of the header ensures that the data that follows the header starts on an even 32-bit boundary. The Padding always contains zeroes. The other fields in the IPv4 header are:

- Version—Specifies the IP protocol version being used. The version number tells all the hardware along the way the length of the datagram and what content to expect in its header fields. For IPv4, this field is always 0100 (because $0100_2 = 4_{10}$).

- Header Length—Gives the length of the header in 32-bit words. The size of the IP header is variable, depending on the value of the IP Options fields, but the minimum value for a correct header is 5.

- Type of Service—Controls the priority that the datagram is given by intermediate nodes. Values can range from "routine" (000) to "critical" (101). Network control datagrams are indicated with 110 and 111.

- Total Length—Gives the length of the entire IP datagram in bytes. As you can see by the layout above, 2 bytes are reserved for this purpose. Hence, the largest allowable IP datagram is $2^{16} - 1$, or 65,535.

- Packet ID—Each datagram is assigned a serial number as it is placed on the network. The combination of Host ID and Packet ID uniquely identifies each IP datagram in existence at any time in the world.
- Flags—Specifies whether the datagram may be fragmented (broken into smaller datagrams) by intermediate nodes. IP networks must be able to handle datagrams of at least 576 bytes. Most IP networks can deal with packets that are about 8KB long. With the "Don't Fragment" bit set, an 8KB datagram will not be routed over a network that says it can handle only 2KB packets, for example.
- Fragment Offset—Indicates the location of a fragment within a certain datagram. That is, it tells which part of the datagram the fragment came from.
- Time to Live (TTL)—TTL was originally intended to measure the number of seconds for which the datagram would remain valid. Should a datagram get caught in a routing loop, the TTL would (theoretically) expire before the datagram could contribute to a congestion problem. In practice, the TTL field is decremented each time it passes through an intermediate network node, so this field does not really measure the number of seconds that a packet lives, but the number of hops it is allowed before it reaches its destination.
- Protocol Number—Indicates which higher-layer protocol is sending the data that follows the header. Some of the important values for this field are:

  0 = Reserved

  1 = Internet Control Message Protocol (ICMP)

  6 = Transmission Control Protocol (TCP)

  17 = User Datagram Protocol (UDP)

  TCP is described in Section 12.5.3.

w_1	w_2
w_3	w_4
$\cdots$	$\cdots$

$\cdots$	$\cdots$
w_{n-1}	w_n

- Header Checksum—This field is calculated by first calculating the one's complement sum of all 16-bit words in the header, and then taking the one's complement of this sum, with the checksum field itself originally set to all zeroes. The one's complement sum is the arithmetic sum of two of the words with the (seventeenth) carry bit added to the lowest bit position of the sum. (See Section 2.4.2.) For example, 11110011 + 10011010 = 110001101 = 10001110 using one's complement arithmetic. What this means is that if we have an IP datagram of the form shown to the right, each w_i is a 16-bit word in the IP datagram. The complete checksum would be computed over two 16-bit words at a time: $w_1 + w_2 = S_1$; $S_1 + w_3 = S_2$; ... $S_k + w_{k-2} = S_{k+1}$.
- Source and Destination Addresses—Tell where the datagram is going. We have much more to say about these 32-bit fields in Section 12.5.2.
- IP Options—Provides diagnostic information and routing controls. IP Options are, well, optional.

12.5.2 The Trouble with IP Version 4

The number of bytes allocated for each field in the IP header reflects the technological era in which IP was designed. Back in the ARPAnet years, no one could have imagined how the network would grow, or even that there would ever be a civilian use for it.

With the slowest networks of today being faster than the fastest networks of the 1960s, IP's packet length limit of 65,536 bytes has become a problem. The packets simply move too fast for certain network equipment to be sure that the packet hasn't been damaged between intermediate nodes. (At gigabit speeds, a 65,535-byte IP datagram passes over a given point in less than 1ms.)

By far the most serious problem with IPv4 headers concerns addressing. Every host and router must have an address that is unique over the entire Internet. To ensure that no Internet node duplicates the address of another Internet node, host IDs are administered by a central authority, the **Internet Corporation for Assigned Names and Numbers** (**ICANN**). ICANN keeps track of groups of IP addresses, which are subsequently allocated or assigned by regional authorities. (The ICANN also coordinates the assignment of parameter values used in protocols so that everyone knows which values evoke which behaviors over the Internet.)

As you can see by looking at the IP header shown in the sidebar, there are 2^{32} or about 4.3 billion host IDs. It would be reasonable to think that there would be plenty of addresses to go around, but this is not the case. The problem lies in the fact that these addresses are not like serial numbers sequentially assigned to the next person who asks for one. It's much more complicated than that.

IP allows for three types, or **classes**, of networks, designated A, B, and C. They are distinguished from each other by the number of nodes (called **hosts**) that each can directly support. Class A networks can support the largest number of hosts; Class C, the least.

The first three bits of an IP address indicate the network class. Addresses for Class A networks always begin with 0, Class B with 10, and Class C with 110. The remaining bits in the address are devoted to the network number and the host ID within that network number, as shown in Figure 12.6.

IP addresses are 32-bit numbers expressed in dotted decimal notation, for example, 18.7.21.69 or 146.186.157.6. Each of these decimal numbers represents 8 bits of binary information and can therefore have a decimal value between 0 and 255. Note that 127.x.x.x is a Class A network that is reserved for **loopback testing**, which checks the TCP/IP protocol processes running on the host. During the loopback test, no datagrams enter the network. The 0.0.0.0 network is typically reserved for use as the default route in the network.

Allowing for the reserved networks 0 and 127, only 126 Class A networks can be defined using a 7-bit network field. Class A networks are the largest networks of all, each able to support about 16.7 million nodes. Although it is unlikely that a Class A network would need all 16 million possible addresses, the Class A addresses, 1.0.0.0 through 126.255.255.255, were long ago assigned

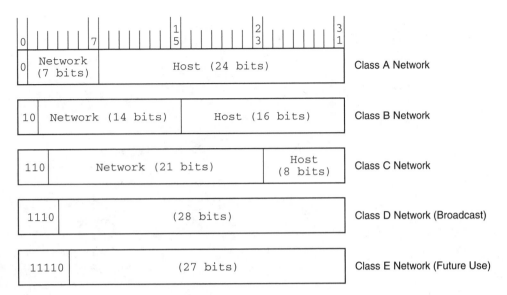

FIGURE 12.6   IP Address Classes

to early Internet adopters such as MIT and the Xerox Corporation. Furthermore, all of the 16,382 Class B network IDs (128.0.0.0 to 191.255.255.255) have also been assigned. Each Class B network can contain 65,534 unique node addresses. Because very few organizations need more than 100,000 addresses, their next choice is to identify themselves as Class C network owners, giving them only 256 addresses within the Class C space of 192.0.0.0 through 233.255.255.255. This is far fewer than would meet the needs of even a moderately sized company or institution. Thus, many networks have been unable to obtain a contiguous block of IP addresses so that each node on the network can have its own address on the Internet. A number of clever workarounds have been devised to deal with this problem, but the ultimate solution lies in reworking the entire IP address structure. (Classes D and E do exist, but they aren't networks at all. Instead, they're groups of reserved addresses. The Class D addresses, 224 through 240, are used for multicasting by groups of hosts that share a common characteristic. The Class E addresses, 241 through 248, are reserved for future use.)

In addition to the eventual depletion of address space, there are other problems with IPv4. Its original designers did not anticipate the growth of the Internet and the routing problems that would result from the address class scheme. There are typically 70,000-plus routes in the routing table of an Internet backbone router. The current routing infrastructure of IPv4 needs to be modified to reduce the number of routes that routers must store. As with cache memory, larger router memories result in slower routing information retrieval. There is also a definite

THE TCP SEGMENT FORMAT

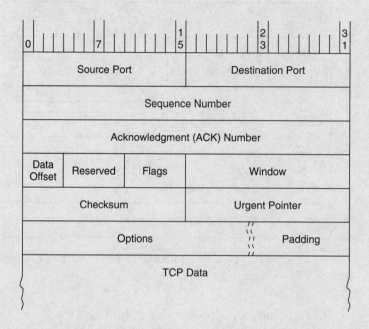

The TCP segment format is shown above. The numbers at the top of the figure are the bit positions spanned by each field. The horizontal rows represent 32-bit words. The fields are defined as follows:

- Source and Destination Ports—Specify interfaces to applications running above TCP. These applications are known to TCP by their port number.
- Sequence Number—Indicates the sequence number of the first byte of data in the payload. TCP assigns each transmitted byte a sequence number. If 100 data bytes will be sent 10 bytes at a time, the sequence number in the first segment might be 0, the second 10, the third 20, and so forth. The starting sequence number is not necessarily 0, so long as the number is unique between the sender and the receiver.
- Acknowledgment Number—Contains the next data sequence number that the receiver is expecting. TCP uses this value to determine whether any datagrams have gotten lost along the way.
- Data Offset—Contains the number of 32-bit words in the header or, equivalently, the relative location of the word where the data starts within the segment. Also known as the header length.

- Reserved—These six bits must be zero until someone comes up with a good use for them.

- Flags—Contains six bits that are used mostly for protocol management. They are set to "true" when their values are nonzero. The TCP flags and their meanings are:

  URG: Indicates that urgent data exists in this segment. The Urgent Pointer field (see below) points to the location of the first byte that follows the urgent information.

  ACK: Indicates whether the Acknowledgment Number field (see above) contains significant information.

  PSH: Tells all TCP processes involved in the connection to clear their buffers, that is, "push" the data to the receiver. This flag should also be set when urgent data exists in the payload.

  RST: Resets the connection. Usually, it forces validation of all packets received and places the receiver back into the "listen for more data" state.

  SYN: Indicates that the purpose of the segment is to synchronize sequence numbers. If the sender transmits [SYN, SEQ# = x], it should subsequently receive [ACK, SEQ# = $x + 1$] from the receiver. At the time that two nodes establish a connection, both exchange their respective initial sequence numbers.

  FIN: This is the "finished" flag. It lets the receiver know that the sender has completed transmission, in effect starting closedown procedures for the connection.

- Window—Allows both nodes to define the size of their respective data windows by stating the number of bytes that each is willing to accept within any single segment. For example, if the sender transmits bytes numbered 0 to 1,023 and the receiver acknowledges with 1,024 in the ACK# field and a window value of 512, the sender should reply by sending data bytes 1,024 through 1,535. (This may happen when the receiver's buffer is starting to fill up so it requests that the sender slow down until the receiver catches up.) Notice that if the receiver's application is running very slowly, say it's pulling data 1 or 2 bytes at a time from its buffer, the TCP process running at the receiver should wait until the application buffer is empty enough to justify sending another segment. If the receiver sends a window size of 0, the effect is acknowledgment of all bytes up to the acknowledgment number, and to stop further data transmission until the same acknowledgment number is sent again with a nonzero window size.

(continued)

THE TCP SEGMENT FORMAT (*continued*)

- Checksum—This field contains the checksum over the fields in the TCP segment (except the data padding and the checksum itself), along with an IP pseudoheader as follows:

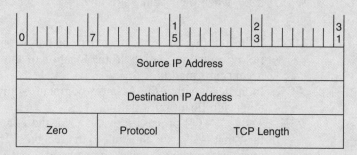

As with the IP checksum explained earlier, the TCP checksum is the 16-bit one's complement of the sum of all 16-bit words in the header and text of the TCP segment.

- Urgent Pointer—Points to the first byte that follows the urgent data. This field is meaningful only when the URG flag is set.

- Options—Concerns, among other things, negotiation of window sizes and whether selective acknowledgment (SACK) can be used. SACK permits retransmission of particular segments within a window as opposed to requiring the entire window to be retransmitted if a segment from somewhere in the middle gets lost. This concept will be clearer to you after our discussion of TCP flow control.

need for security at the IP level. A protocol called **IPSec (Internet Protocol Security)** is currently defined for the IP level. However, it is optional and hasn't been standardized or universally adopted.

12.5.3   Transmission Control Protocol

The sole purpose of IP is to correctly route datagrams across the network. You can think of IP as a courier who delivers packages with no concern as to their contents or the order in which they are delivered. Transmission Control Protocol (TCP) is the consumer of IP services, and it does indeed care about these things and many others.

The protocol connection between two TCP processes is much more sophisticated than the one at the IP layer. Where IP simply accepts or rejects datagrams based only on header information, TCP opens a conversation, called a

connection, with a TCP process running on a remote system. A TCP connection is very much analogous to a telephone conversation, with its own protocol "etiquette." As part of initiating this conversation, TCP also opens a service access point (SAP) in the application running above it. In TCP, this SAP is a numerical value called a **port**. The combination of the port number, the host ID, and the protocol designation becomes a **socket**, which is logically equivalent to a file name (or **handle**) to the application running above TCP. Instead of accessing data by using its disk file name, the application using TCP reads data through the socket. Port numbers 0 through 1,023 are called "well-known" port numbers because they are reserved for particular TCP applications. For example, the TCP/IP File Transfer Protocol (FTP) application uses ports 20 and 21. The Telnet terminal protocol uses port 23. Port numbers 1,024 through 65,535 are available for user-defined implementations.

TCP makes sure that the stream of data it provides to the application is complete, in its proper sequence, and with no duplicated data. TCP also compensates for irregularities in the underlying network by making sure that its **segments** (data packets with headers) aren't sent so fast that they overwhelm intermediate nodes or the receiver. A TCP segment requires at least 20 bytes for its header. The data payload is optional. A segment can be at most 65,515 bytes long, including the header, so that the entire segment fits into an IP payload. If need be, IP can fragment a TCP segment if requested to do so by an intermediate node.

TCP provides a reliable, connection-oriented service. **Connection-oriented** means simply that the connection must be set up before the hosts can exchange any information (much like a telephone call). The reliability is provided by a sequence number assigned to each segment. Acknowledgments are used to verify that segments are received, and must be sent and received within a specific period of time. If no acknowledgment is forthcoming, the data is retransmitted. We provide a brief introduction to how this protocol works in the next section.

12.5.4 The TCP Protocol at Work

So how does all of this fit together to make a solid, sequenced, error-free connection between two (or more) TCP processes running on separate systems? Successful communication takes place in three phases: one to initiate the connection, a second to exchange the data, and a third to tear down the connection. First, the initiator, which we'll call A, transmits an "open" primitive to a TCP process running on the remote system, B. B is assumed to be listening for an "open" request. This "open" primitive has the form:

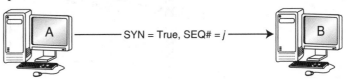

A ———— SYN = True, SEQ# = *j* ————→ B

If B is ready to accept a TCP connection from the sender, it replies with:

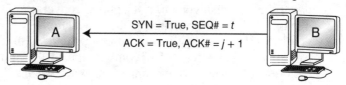

To which A responds:

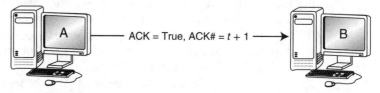

A and B have now acknowledged each other and synchronized the starting sequence numbers. A's next sequence number will be $t + 2$; B's will be $j + 2$. Protocol exchanges like these are often referred to as **three-way handshakes**. Most networking literature displays these sorts of exchanges schematically, as shown in Figure 12.7.

After the connection between A and B is established, they may proceed to negotiate the window size and set other options for their connection. The window tells the sender how much data to send between acknowledgments. For example, suppose A and B negotiate a window size of 500 bytes with a data payload size of 100 bytes, both agreeing not to use selective acknowledgment (discussed below). Figure 12.8 shows how TCP manages the flow of data between the two hosts. Notice what happens when a segment gets lost: The entire window is retransmitted, despite the fact that subsequent segments were delivered without error.

If an acknowledgment gets lost, however, a subsequent acknowledgment can prevent retransmission of the one that got lost, as shown in Figure 12.9. Of course, the acknowledgment must be sent in time to prevent a "timeout" retransmission.

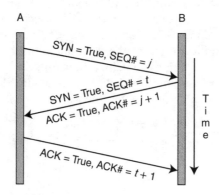

FIGURE 12.7   The TCP 3-Way Handshake

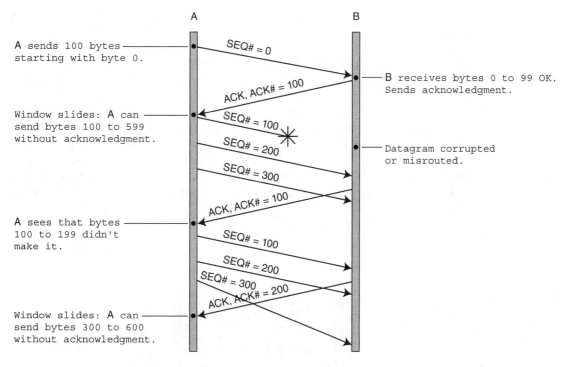

FIGURE 12.8 TCP Data Transfer with a Lost Segment

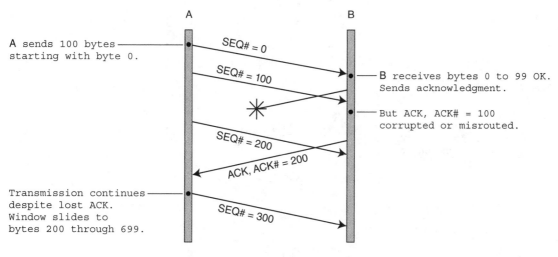

FIGURE 12.9 An Acknowledgment Gets Lost

Using acknowledgment numbers, the receiver can also ask the sender to slow down or halt transmission. It is necessary to do so when the receiver's buffer gets too full. Figure 12.10a illustrates how this is done. Figure 12.10b shows how B keeps the connection alive while it cannot receive any more data.

Upon completion of the data exchange, one or both of the TCP processes gracefully terminates the connection. One side of the connection, say A, may indicate to the other side, B, that it is finished by sending a segment with its FIN flag set to true. This effectively closes down the connection from A to B. B, however, could continue its side of the conversation until it no longer has data to send. Once B is finished, it also transmits a segment with the FIN flag set. If A acknowledges B's FIN, the connection is terminated on both ends. If B receives no acknowledgment for the duration of its timeout interval, it automatically terminates the connection.

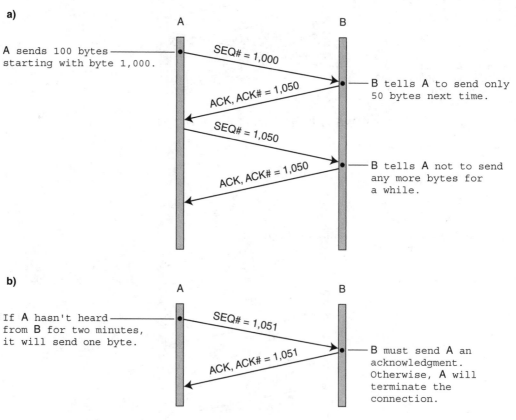

FIGURE 12.10   TCP Flow Control
a) B Tells A to Slow Down
b) B Keeps the Connection Alive while Unable to Receive More Data

As opposed to having hard-and-fast rules, TCP allows the sender and receiver to negotiate a timeout period. The timeout should be set to a greater value if the connection is slower than when it is faster. The sender and receiver can also agree to use selective acknowledgment. When **selective acknowledgment (SACK)** is enabled, the receiver must acknowledge each datagram. In other words, no sliding window is used. SACK can save some bandwidth when an error occurs, because only the segment that has not been acknowledged (instead of the entire window) will be retransmitted. But if the exchange is error-free, bandwidth is wasted by sending acknowledgment segments. For this reason, SACK is chosen only when there is little TCP buffer space on the receiver. The larger the receiver's buffer, the more "wiggle room" it has for receiving segments out of sequence. TCP does whatever it can to provide the applications running above it with an error-free, sequenced stream of data.

12.5.5 IP Version 6

By 1994, it appeared that IP's Class B address problem was a crisis in the making, having the potential to bring the explosive growth of the Internet to an abrupt halt. Spurred by this sense of approaching doom, the IETF began concerted work on a successor to IPv4, now called IPv6. IETF participants released a number of experimental protocols that, over time, became known as IPv5. The corrected and enhanced versions of these protocols became known as IPv6. Experts predict that IPv6 won't be widely implemented until late in the first decade of the twenty-first century. (Every day more Internet applications are being modified to work with IPv6.) In fact, some opponents argue that IPv6 will "never" be completely deployed because so much costly hardware will need to be replaced and because workarounds have been found for the most vexing problems inherent in IPv4. But, contrary to what its detractors would have you believe, IPv6 is much more than a patch for the Class B address shortage problem. It fixes many things that most people don't realize are broken, as we will explain.

The IETF's primary motivation in designing a successor to IPv4 was, of course, to extend IP's address space beyond its current 32-bit limit to 128 bits for both the source and destination host addresses. This is an incredibly large address space, giving 2^{128} possible host addresses. In concrete terms, if each of these addresses were assigned to a network card weighing 28 grams (1 oz), 2^{128} network cards would have a mass 1.61 *quadrillion* times that of the entire Earth! So it would seem that the supply of IPv6 addresses is inexhaustible.

The downside of having such a large address space is that address management becomes critical. If addresses are assigned haphazardly with no organization in mind, effective packet routing would become impossible. Every router on the Internet would eventually require the storage and speed of a supercomputer to deal with the ensuing routing table explosion. To head off this problem, the IETF came up with a hierarchical address organization that it calls the **Aggregatable Global Unicast Address Format** shown in Figure 12.11a. The first 3 bits of the IPv6 address constitute a flag indicating that the address is a Global

THE IP VERSION 6 HEADER

The obvious problem with IPv4, of course, is its 32-bit address fields. IPv6 corrects this shortcoming by expanding the address fields to 128 bits. In order to keep the IPv6 header as small as possible (which speeds routing), many of the rarely used IPv4 header fields are not included in the main header of IPv6. If these fields are needed, a Next Header pointer has been provided. With the Next Header field, IPv6 could conceivably support a large number of header fields. Thus, future enhancements to IP would be much less disruptive than the switch from Version 4 to Version 6. The IPv6 header fields are explained on the next page.

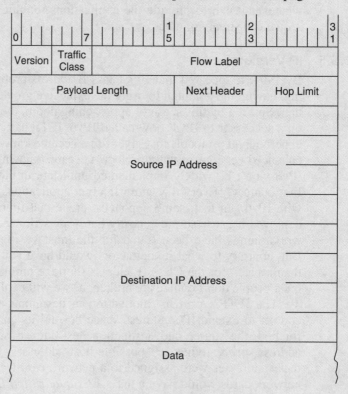

Unicast Address. The next 13 bits form the **Top-Level Aggregation Identifier (TLA ID)**, which is followed by 8 reserved bits that allow either the TLA ID or the 24-bit **Next-Level Aggregation Identifier** (**NLA ID**) to expand, if needed. A TLA entity may be a country or perhaps a major global telecommunications carrier. An NLA entity could be a large corporation, a government, an academic institution, an ISP, or a small telecommunications carrier. The 16 bits following the NLA ID are the **Site-Level Aggregation Identifier** (**SLA ID**). NLA entities

- Version—Always 0110.
- Traffic Class—IPv6 will eventually be able to tell the difference between real-time transmissions (e.g., voice and video) and less time-sensitive data transport traffic. This field will be used to distinguish between these two traffic types.
- Flow Label—This is another field for which specifications are still in progress. A "flow" is a conversation, either broadcast to all nodes or initiated between two particular nodes. The Flow Label field identifies a particular flow stream, and intermediate routers will route the packets in a manner consistent with the code in the flow field.
- Payload Length—Indicates the length of the payload in bytes, which includes the size of additional headers.
- Next Header—Indicates the type of header, if any, that follows the main header. If an IPv6 protocol exchange requires more protocol information than can be carried in a single header, the Next Header field provides for an extension header. These extension headers are placed in the payload of the segment. If there is no IP extension header, then this field will contain the value for "TCP," meaning that the first header data in the payload belongs to TCP, not IP. In general, only the destination node will examine the contents of the extension headers. Intermediate nodes pass them on as if they were common payload data.
- Hop Limit—With 16 bits, this field is much larger than in Version 4, allowing 256 hops. As in Version 4, this field is decremented by each intermediate router. If it ever becomes zero, the packet is discarded and the sender is notified through an ICMP (for IPv6) message.
- Source and Destination Addresses—Much larger, but with the same meaning as in Version 4. See text for a discussion of the format for this address.

can use this field to create their own hierarchy, allowing each NLA entity to have 65,536 subnetworks, each of which can have 2^{64} hosts. This hierarchy is shown graphically in Figure 12.11b.

At first glance, the notion of making allowances for 2^{64} hosts on each subnet seems as wasteful of address space as the IPv4 network class system. However, such a large field is necessary to support **stateless address autoconfiguration**, a new feature in IPv6. In stateless address autoconfiguration, a host uses the 48-bit

a)

3 Bits	13 Bits	8 Bits	24 Bits	16 Bits	64 Bits
Prefix 001	Top-Level Aggregation ID	Reserved	Next-Level Aggregation ID	Site-Level Aggregation ID	Interface ID

b)

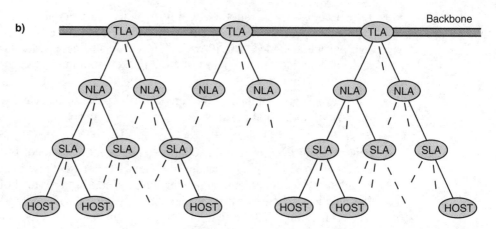

FIGURE 12.11   a) Aggregatable Global Unicast Address Format
b) Aggregatable Global Unicast Hierarchy

address burned into its network interface card (its MAC address, explained in Section 12.6.2), along with the network address information that it retrieves from a nearby router to form its entire IP address. If no problems occur during this process, each host on the network configures its own address information with no intervention by the network administrator. This feature will be a blessing to network administrators if an entity changes its ISP or telecommunications carrier. Network administrators will have to change only the IP addresses of their routers. Stateless address autoconfiguration will automatically update the TLA or SLA fields in every node on the network.

The written syntax of IPv6 addresses also differs from that of IPv4 addresses. Recall that IPv4 addresses are expressed using a dotted decimal notion, as in 146.186.157.6. IPv6 addresses are instead given in hexadecimal, separated by colons, as follows:

```
30FA:505A:B210:224C:1114:0327:0904:0225
```

making it much easier to recognize the binary equivalent of an IP address.

IPv6 addresses can be abbreviated, omitting zeros where possible. If a 16-bit group is 0000, it can be written as 0, or omitted altogether. If more than two consecutive colons result from this omission, they can be reduced to two colons (provided there is only one group of more than two consecutive colons). For example, the IPv6 address:

```
30FA:0000:0000:0000:0010:0002:0300
```

can be written

```
30FA:0:0:0:10:2:300
```

or even

```
30FA::10:2:300
```

However, an address such as 30FA::24D6::12CB is invalid.

The IETF is also proposing two other routing improvements: implementation of **multicasting** (where one message is placed on the network and read by multiple nodes) and **anycasting** (where any one of a logical group of nodes can be the recipient of a message, but no particular receiver is specified by the packet). This feature, along with stateless address autoconfiguration, facilitates support for mobile devices, an increasingly important sector of Internet users, particularly in countries where most telecommunications take place over wireless networks.

As previously mentioned, security is another major area in which IPv6 differs from IPv4. All of IPv4's security features (IPSec) are "optional," meaning that no one is forced to implement any type of security, and most installations don't. In IPv6, IPSec is mandatory. Among the security improvements in IPv6 is a mechanism that prevents **address spoofing**, where a host can engage in communications with another host using a falsified IP address. (IP spoofing is often used to subvert filtering routers and firewalls that are intended to keep outsiders from accessing private intranets, among other things.) IPSec also supports encryption and other measures that make it more difficult for miscreants to sniff out unauthorized information.

Perhaps the best feature of IPv6 is that it provides a transition plan that allows networks to gradually move to the new format. Support for IPv4 is built into IPv6. Devices that use both protocols are called **dual stack** devices, because they support protocol stacks for both IPv4 and IPv6. Most routers on the market today are dual stack devices, with the expectation that IPv6 will become a reality in the not-too-distant future.

The benefits of IPv6 over IPv4 are clear: a greater address space, better and built-in quality of service, and better and more efficient routing. It is not a question of *if* but of *when* we will move to IPv6. The transition will be driven by the business need for IPv6 and development of the necessary applications. Although hardware replacement cost is a significant barrier, technician training and replacement of minor IP devices (such as network fax machines and printers) will contribute to the overall cost of conversion. With the advent of IP-ready automobiles, as well as many other Internet devices, IPv4 no longer meets the needs of many current applications.

Ethernet Then and Now

Ethernet is today's dominant architecture for **local area networks (LANs)**. Ethernet devices can be found on desktops, in data centers, and in living rooms. Its ubiquity was never envisioned by its inventors, Robert Metcalf and David Boggs of the Xerox Corporation, when they developed Ethernet in the early 1970s. In the early 1980s, DEC and Intel were helping to refine Ethernet, and they brought many new and innovative products to market. By the time the IEEE began its Project 802, Ethernet was a well-established networking architecture. As such, its operational theory became part of the IEEE 802.3 standard, but Ethernet is not entirely congruent with the standard, because Ethernet defines Logical Link functionality where IEEE 802.3 does not. (IEEE 802.2 is the Data Link specification.) There are also some slight differences between the Ethernet Protocol Data Unit and the IEEE 802.3 PDU. Because of its wide deployment, our discussion will center on Ethernet.

Ethernet uses a **Carrier Sense Multiple Access / Collision Detection (CSMA/CD)** medium access control. Before placing data on the network, the interface circuit checks to see that the carrier (i.e., the network) is alive; then it listens to see if any other stations are using the line. If the line is silent (quiesced), the interface places its transmission frame on the line. If another station happens to do this at the same instant, the frames will collide. This collision should be detected by both transmitting stations.

Traditional Ethernet networks run at 10Mbps, and they use a bus topology as shown in the figure below. All stations connect directly to the bus (Multiple Access); thus all nodes receive every frame. As each LAN station receives a frame, it checks the (MAC) address information in the frame header. If a station sees its own address, it strips off the framing bits and then passes the PDU to its Logical Link layer.

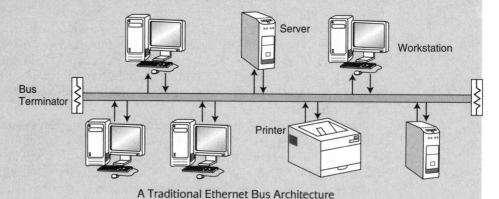

A Traditional Ethernet Bus Architecture

In order to detect collisions, an Ethernet interface card must listen to the line while it is transmitting. If it sees a voltage higher than allowed, that means that another node has begun transmitting at nearly the same time and the frames have collided somewhere along the bus. Once the collision is discovered, the NIC broadcasts a 32-bit jamming signal to notify all stations that a collision has occurred. The stations that were involved in the collision will both cease transmitting and wait a (pseudo) random amount of time before trying once more to transmit. This approach works well when the PDU is long enough to span the distance between the sending node and the destination. Because of this, the maximum speed on a traditional shared-bus CSMA/CD Ethernet system is about 100Mbps. At faster speeds, the traditional Ethernet PDU is too short. (The bit cells are narrower at faster bit rates.) Supporting speeds much beyond that calls for adjustments to Ethernet's architecture. Gigabit speeds require changing the topology of the network from a shared-bus to a switched star-shaped network topology, as shown below. Switches in a star topology funnel one signal at a time from the user nodes onto the backbone of the network. The end nodes connect to the network at 100Mbps, and upstream switches interconnect at 1Gbps or 10Gbps. Medium access management is taken care of at the switch level, so collision detection at the end nodes may be turned off. Switches can be connected to other network components such as hubs and repeaters to further extend the network and provide downward compatibility to slower segments. Gigabit Ethernet competes directly with more radical and costly network solutions such as Fibre Channel. We discuss and Fibre Channel in Chapter 13.

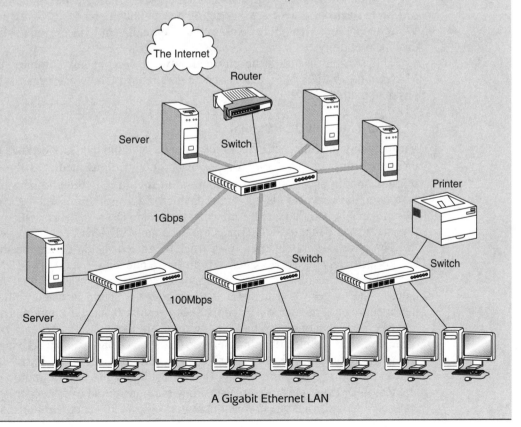

A Gigabit Ethernet LAN

12.6 NETWORK ORGANIZATION

Computer networks are often classified according to their geographic service areas. The smallest networks are **local area networks** (**LANs**). Although they can encompass thousands of nodes, LANs typically are used in a single building, or a group of buildings that are near each other. When a LAN covers more than one building, it is sometimes called a **campus network**. Usually, the region (the property) covered by a LAN is under the same ownership (or control) as the LAN itself. **Metropolitan area networks** (**MANs**) are networks that cover a city and its environs. They often span areas that are not under the ownership of the people who also own the network. **Wide area networks** (**WANs**) can cover multiple cities or span the entire world.

At one time, the protocols employed by LANs, MANs, and WANs differed vastly from one another. MANs and WANs were usually designed for high-speed throughput because they served as backbone systems for multiple slower LANs, or they offered access to large host computers in data centers far away from end users. As network technologies have evolved, however, these networks are now distinguished from each other not so much by their speed or by their protocols, but by their ownership. One person's campus LAN might be another person's MAN. In fact, as LANs are becoming faster and more easily integrated with WAN technology, it is conceivable that eventually the concept of a MAN may disappear entirely.

This section discusses the physical network components common to LANs, MANs, and WANs. We start at the lowest level of network organization, the physical medium level, Layer 1.

12.6.1 Physical Transmission Media

Virtually any medium with the ability to carry a signal can support data communication. There are two general types of communications media: **Guided transmission media** and **unguided transmission media**. Unguided media broadcast data over the airwaves using infrared, microwave, satellite, or broadcast radio carrier signals. Guided media are physical connectors such as copper wire or fiber-optic cable that directly connect to each network node.

The physical and electrical properties of guided media determine their ability to accurately convey signals of given frequencies over various distances. In Chapter 7, we mentioned that signals attenuate (get weaker) over long distances. The longer the distance and the higher the signal frequency, the greater the attenuation. Attenuation in copper wire results from the interactions of several electrical phenomena. Chief among these are the internal resistance of copper conductors and the electrical interference (inductance and capacitance) that occurs when signal-carrying wires are in close proximity to each other. External electrical fields such as those surrounding fluorescent lights and electric motors can also attenuate—or even garble—signals as they are transmitted over copper wire. Collectively, the electrical phenomena that work against the accurate transmission of signals are called **noise**. Signal and noise strengths are both measured in decibels (dB). Cables are rated according to how well they convey signals at different frequencies in the presence of noise. The resulting quantity is the **signal-to-noise** rating for the communications channel, and it is also measured in decibels:

$$\text{Signal-to-Noise Ration (dB)} = 10 \log_{10} \frac{\text{Signal dB}}{\text{Noise dB}}$$

The **bandwidth** of a medium is technically the range of frequencies that it can carry, measured in hertz. The wider the medium's bandwidth, the more information it can carry. In digital communications, bandwidth is the general term for the information-carrying capacity of a medium, measured in bits per second (bps). Another important measure is **bit error rate** (**BER**), which is the ratio of the number of bits received in error to the total number of bits received. If signal frequencies exceed the signal-carrying capacity of the line, the BER may become so extreme that the attached devices will spend more of their time doing error recovery than in doing useful work.

Coaxial Cable

Coaxial cable was once the medium of choice for data communications. It can carry signals up to trillions of cycles per second with low attenuation. Today, it is used mostly for broadcast and closed circuit television applications. Coaxial cable also carries signals for residential Internet services that piggyback on cable television lines.

The heart of a coaxial cable is a thick (12- to 16-gauge) inner conductor surrounded by an insulating layer called a **dielectric**. The dielectric is surrounded by a foil shield to protect it from transient electromagnetic fields. The foil shield is itself wrapped in a steel or copper braid to provide an electrical ground for the cable. The entire cable is then encased in a durable plastic coating (see Figure 12.12).

The coaxial cable employed by cable television services is called **broadband cable** because it has a capacity of at least 2Mbit/sec. Broadband communication provides multiple channels of data, using a form of multiplexing. Computer

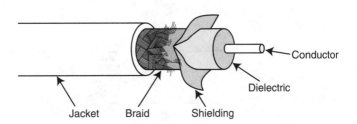

FIGURE 12.12 The Parts of a Coaxial Cable

networks now infrequently use **narrowband cable**, which is optimized for a typical bandwidth of 64kbit/sec, consisting of a single channel.

Twisted Pair

The easiest way to connect two computers is simply to run a pair of copper wires between them. One of the wires is used for sending data, the other for receiving. Of course, the farther apart the two systems are, the stronger the signal has to be to prevent them from attenuating into oblivion over long distances. The distance between the two systems also affects the speed at which data can be transferred. The farther apart they are, the slower the line speed must be to avoid excessive errors. Using thicker conductors (smaller wire gauge numbers) can reduce attenuation. Of course, thick wire is more costly than thin wire.

In addition to attenuation, cable makers are also challenged by an electrical phenomenon known as **inductance**. When two wires lie perfectly flat and adjacent to each other, strong high-frequency signals in the wires create magnetic (inductive) fields around the copper conductors, which interfere with the signals in both lines.

The easiest way to reduce the electrical inductance between conductors is to twist them together. To a point, the more twists that are introduced in a pair of wires per linear foot, the less attenuation is caused by the wires interfering with each other. Twisted wire is more costly to manufacture than untwisted wire because more wire is consumed per linear foot and the twisting must be carefully controlled. **Twisted pair** cabling, with two twisted wire pairs, is used in most LAN installations today (see Figure 12.13). It comes in two varieties: shielded and unshielded. Unshielded twisted pair is the most popular.

Shielded twisted pair cable is suitable for environments having a great deal of electrical interference. Today's business environments are teeming with sources of electromagnetic radiation that can interfere with network signals. These sources can be as seemingly benign as fluorescent lights or as obviously hostile as large, humming power transformers. Any device that produces a magnetic field has the potential for scrambling network communication links. Interference can limit the speed of a network because higher signal frequencies are more sensitive to any kind of signal distortion. As a safeguard against environmental interference (called **electromagnetic interference [EMI]** or **radio-frequency**

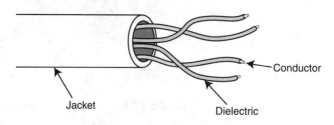

FIGURE 12.13 Twisted Pair Cable

interference [**RFI**]), shielded twisted pair wire can be installed to help maintain the integrity of network communications in hostile environments.

Experts disagree as to whether this shielding is worth the higher material and installation costs. They point out that if the shielding is not properly grounded, it can actually cause more problems than it solves. Specifically, it can act as an antenna that actually attracts radio signals to the conductors!

Whether shielded or unshielded, network conductors must have signal-carrying capacity appropriate to the network technology being used. The Electronic Industries Alliance (EIA), along with the Telecommunications Industry Association (TIA), established a rating system for network cabling in 1991. The latest revision of this rating system is EIA/TIA-568B. The EIA/TIA **category** ratings specify the maximum frequency that the cable can support without excessive attenuation. The ISO rating system, which is not used as often as the EIA/TIA category system, refers to these wire grades as **classes**. These ratings are shown in Table 12.1. Most LANs installed today are equipped with Category 5 or better cabling. Many installations are abandoning copper entirely and installing fiber-optic cable instead (see next Section).

Note that the signal-carrying capacity of the cable grades shown in Table 12.1 is given in terms of megahertz. This is not the same as megabits. As we saw in Chapter 2, Section 2.A, the number of bits carried at any given frequency is a function of the encoding method used in the network. Networks running below 100Mbps could easily afford to use Manchester coding, which requires two signal transitions for every bit transmitted. Networks running at 100Mbps and above use different encoding schemes, one of the most popular being the 4B/5B, 4 bits in 5 baud using NRZI signaling, as shown in Figure 12.14.

Baud is the unit of measure for the number of signal transitions supported by a transmission medium or transmission method over a medium. For networks other than the voice telephone network, the line speed is rated in hertz, but hertz and baud are equivalent with regard to digital signals. As you can see in Figure 12.14, if a network uses 4B/5B encoding, a signal-carrying capacity of 125MHz is required for the line to have a bit rate of 100Mbps.

Fiber-Optic Cable

Optical fiber network media can carry signals faster and farther than either twisted pair or coaxial cable. Fiber-optic cable is theoretically able to support

EIA/TIA	ISO	Maximum Frequency
Category 1		Voice and "low-speed" data (4–9.6kHz)
Category 2	Class A	1Mbps or less
Category 3	Class B	10MHz
Category 4	Class C	20MHz
Category 5	Class D	100MHz
Category 6	Class E	250MHz
Category 7	Class F	600MHz

TABLE 12.1 EIA/TIA-568B and ISO Cable Specifications

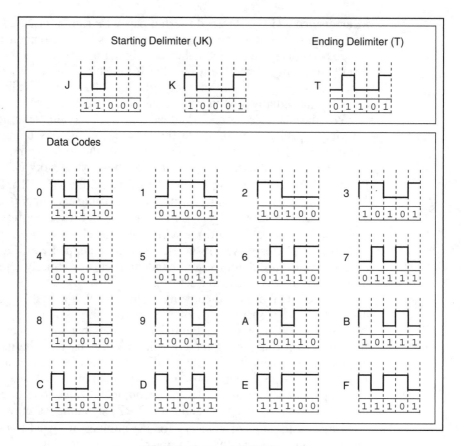

FIGURE 12.14   4B/5B Encoding

frequencies in the terahertz range, but transmission speeds are more commonly in the range of about 2GHz, carried over runs of 10 to 100km (without repeaters). Optical cable consists of bundles of thin (1.5 to 125μm) glass or plastic strands surrounded by a protective plastic sheath. Although the underlying physics is quite different, you can think of a fiber-optic strand as a conductor of light just as copper is a conductor of electricity. The cable is a type of "light guide" that routes the light from one end of the cable to the other. At the sending end, a light emitting diode or laser diode emits pulses of light that travel through the glass strand, much as water goes through a pipe. On the receiving end, photodetectors convert the light pulses into electrical signals for processing by electronic devices.

Optical fiber supports three different transmission modes depending on the type of fiber used. The types of fiber are shown in Figure 12.15. The narrowest fiber, **single-mode** fiber, conveys light at only one wavelength, typically 850, 1,300, or 1,500nm. It allows the fastest data rates over the longest distances.

Multimode fiber can carry several different light wavelengths simultaneously through a larger fiber core. In multimode fiber, the laser light waves bounce off the sides of the fiber core, causing greater attenuation than single-mode fiber. Not only do the light waves scatter, but they also collide with one another to some degree, causing further attenuation.

Multimode graded index fiber also supports multiple wavelengths concurrently, but it does so in a more controlled manner than regular multimode fiber. Multimode graded index fiber consists of concentric layers of plastic or glass, each with refractive properties that are optimized for carrying specific light wavelengths. Like regular multimode fiber, light travels in waves through multimode graded index optical fiber. But unlike multimode fiber, the waves are confined to the area of the optical fiber that is suitable to propagating its particular wavelength. Thus, the different wavelengths concurrently transmitted through the fiber do not interfere with each other.

The fiber-optic medium offers many advantages over copper, the most obvious being its enormous signal-carrying capacity. It is also immune to EMI and RFI, making it ideal for deployment in industrial facilities. Fiber-optic cable is small and lightweight, one fiber being capable of replacing hundreds of pairs of copper wires.

But optical cable is fragile and costly to purchase and install. Because of this, fiber is most often used as network **backbone cable**, which bears the traffic of hundreds or thousands of users. Backbone cable is like an interstate highway. Access to it is limited to specific entrance and exit points, but a large volume of traffic is carried at high speed. For a vehicle to get to its final destination, it has to exit the highway and perhaps drive through a residential street. The network equivalent of a residential street most often takes the form of twisted pair copper wire. This "residential street" copper wire is sometimes called **horizontal cable**, to differentiate it from backbone (**vertical**) cable. Undoubtedly, "fiber to the desktop" will eventually become a reality as costs decrease. At the same time, demand is steadily increasing for the integration of data, voice, and video over the same cable. With the deployment of these new technologies, network media probably will be stretched to their limits before the next generation of high-speed cabling is introduced.

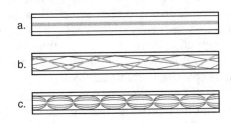

FIGURE 12.15   Optical Fiber
a) Single Mode
b) Multimode
c) Graded Index

Unguided Media—Wireless Data Communications

Bit patterns can be conveyed over any medium capable of supporting a signal. Accordingly, the transmission hardware and methods employed in wireless data communications vary widely. We can't even begin to cover them all here. We will, however, say a few words about the wireless data communications standards that most of us encounter in our daily activities: cellular wireless, Bluetooth, and the 802.11x family of standards.

As their name implies, cellular wireless networks transmit data over the cellular telephone network. Like the early residential telephone network, the cellular system was not intended to be a data network. Consequently, the so-called first- and second-generation cellular data transmission networks have limited features and transmission rates (usually between 0.3 and 1Mbps). There is indeed as much to be gained by establishing broadband cellular service as there was in establishing broadband residential service over guided media (cable and telephone). Fast cellular data communications provides added convenience for people who are already accustomed to fast networking at home and at the office. It also has the potential to reach out to millions of new customers who have been underserved by landlines. With this in mind, the ITU has defined a third-generation wireless communication structure, commonly called **3G**. The features of 3G include data rates up to 2.048Mbps, support for a wide array of equipment, and the integration of low-Earth-orbiting (LEO) satellites into a unified system. Although access speeds may vary, it is possible that with 3G, the World Wide Web will finally be open to the entire world.

Bluetooth, otherwise known as IEEE 802.15.1-2002, was conceived of by Ericsson (Telefonaktiebolaget LM Ericsson) in 1994. Bluetooth is the namesake of a tenth-century king of Denmark and Norway who is famous for ending the hostilities that had been raging among a number of Danish, Norwegian, and Swedish tribes. The analogous aim of Bluetooth is to bring together differing technologies for interconnecting computers and other equipment over very short distances, officially known as **personal area networks (PANs)**, or **piconets**. The first Bluetooth specification was released in 1999 by a consortium consisting of Ericsson, IBM, Intel, Nokia, and Toshiba.

A Bluetooth network consists of a master device and up to seven slave devices, to which the master communicates in round-robin fashion. Data transmission of 720Kbps occurs at very low power (no more than 100mw) over an unregulated frequency of 2.45GHz. Bluetooth is very popular for connecting portable computing devices (such as tablet PCs, PDAs, and cell phones) to a variety of peripheral devices without the need for cables or cable sockets that take up precious space in portable devices.

Wireless local area networks (**WLANs**) are much slower than hardwired LANs, but they provide many other benefits that have contributed to their proliferation. The most important of these is the fact that a network can be set up just about anywhere, and it can be reconfigured with unparalleled ease. The

IEEE Specification	Description
802.11 - 2007	The basic wireless standard includes amendments a – j and the maintenance revision, 802.11.RevMA.
802.11k - 2007	Radio resource measurements to allow remote management of services such as roaming.
802.11n - 2009	Improvements for throughput, up to 600Mbps over the 2.4 and 5GHz bands with a range of around 250ft indoors.
802.11p - 2010	Extensions specifically for automobiles and other vehicles in the 5.9GHz spectrum.
802.11r - 2008	Fast roaming: Allows reliable handoffs between base stations to accommodate wireless devices in motion (e.g., in cars).
802.11s - 2010	Wireless mesh networking
802.11u - 2010	Interworking with non-802 networks, such as 3G cellular.
802.11v - 2010	Wireless network management.
802.11.w - 2009	Wireless LAN management frame protection.
802.11.y - 2008	MAC layer enhancements for the 3,650MHz band for wireless LANs.

TABLE 12.2   IEEE 802.11 Wireless Network Standards

IEEE 802.11 family of WLAN standards has grown steadily since the first standard was published in 1997. We have provided a brief synopsis of the various components of the standard in Table 12.2.

A typical WLAN consists of one or more interconnected (hardwired) **wireless access points** (**WAPs**) that broadcast data to nodes on the network. The node maintains a connection through its assigned frequency for the duration of its session, or until the connection is broken. The range of the WAPs is limited by ambient electromagnetic interference and obstructions such as walls and furniture. In general, the faster a wireless network's data transmission speed, the more susceptible it is to obstructions, and the shorter its range of transmission. Nodes farthest from the WAP will have the lowest throughput, because the transmission speed is stepped down to accommodate the greater distance.

Security is a continual problem in wireless networking. Certain measures can be taken to make unauthorized access difficult, such as the use of the 128-bit encryption mode of **wired equivalent privacy** (**WEP**). Security experts caution, however, that it is impossible to block a determined and sophisticated hacker. If security is a concern, any form of wireless networking should be deployed with extreme care. Even piconets can open the door for malicious access to the entire enterprise network.

12.6.2 Interface Cards

Transmission media are connected to clients, hosts, and other network devices through network interfaces. Because these interfaces are often implemented on removable circuit boards, they are commonly called **network interface cards**, or simply **NICs**. (Please don't say "NIC card"!) A NIC usually embodies the lowest three layers of the OSI protocol stack. It forms the bridge between the physical components of the network and your system. NICs attach directly to a system's main bus or dedicated I/O bus. They convert the parallel data passed on the system bus to the serial signals broadcast on a communications medium. NICs change the encoding of the data from binary to the Manchester or 4B/5B of the network (and vice versa). NICs also provide physical connections and negotiate permission to place signals on the network medium.

Every network card has a unique physical address burned into its circuits. This is called a **Medium Access Control** (**MAC**) address, and it is 6 bytes long. The first 3 bytes are the manufacturer's identification number, which is designated by the IEEE. The last 3 bytes are a unique identifier assigned to the NIC by the manufacturer. No two cards anywhere in the world should ever have the same MAC address. Network protocol layers map this physical MAC address to at least one logical address. The logical address is the name or address by which the node is known to other nodes on the network. It is possible for one computer (logical address) to have two or more NICs, but each NIC will have a distinct MAC address.

12.6.3 Repeaters

A small office LAN installation will have many NICs within a few feet of each other. In an office complex, however, NICs may be separated by hundreds of feet of cable. The longer the cable, the greater the signal attenuation. The effects of attenuation can be mitigated either by reducing transmission speed (usually an unacceptable option) or by adding repeaters to the network. **Repeaters** counteract attenuation by amplifying signals as they are passed through the physical cabling of the network. The number of repeaters required for any network depends on the distance over which the signal is transmitted, the medium used, and the signaling speed of the line. For example, high-frequency copper wire needs more repeaters per kilometer than optical cable operating at a comparable frequency.

Repeaters are part of the network medium. In theory, they are dumb devices functioning entirely without human intervention. As such, they would contain no network-addressable components. However, some repeaters now offer higher-level services to assist with network management and troubleshooting. Figure 12.16 is a representation of how a repeater regenerates an attenuated digital signal.

12.6.4 Hubs

Repeaters are Physical layer devices having one input and one output port. **Hubs** are also Physical layer devices, but they can have many ports for input and output. They receive incoming packets from one or more locations and broadcast the packets to one or more devices on the network. Hubs allow computers to be joined to form **network segments**. The simplest hubs are nothing more than repeaters that connect various branches of a network. Physical network branches stuck together by hubs do not partition the network in any way; they are strictly Layer 1 devices and are not aware of a packet's source or its destination. Every station on the network continues to compete for bandwidth with every other station on the network, regardless of the presence or absence of intervening hubs. Because hubs are Layer 1 devices, the physical medium must be the same on all ports of the hub. You can think of simple hubs as being nothing more than repeaters that provide multiple station access to the physical network. Figure 12.17 shows a network equipped with three hubs.

As hub architectures have evolved, many now have the ability to connect dissimilar physical media. Although such media interconnection is a Layer 2 function, manufacturers continue to call these devices "hubs." **Switching hubs** and **intelligent hubs** are still further removed from the notion of a hub being a "Layer 1 device." These sophisticated components not only connect dissimilar media, but also perform rudimentary routing and protocol conversion, which are all Layer 3 functions.

12.6.5 Switches

A switch is a Layer 2 device that creates a point-to-point connection between one of its input ports and one of its output ports. Although hubs and switches perform the same function, they differ in how they handle the data internally. Hubs broadcast the packets to all computers on the network and handle only one packet at a time. Switches, on the other hand, can handle multiple

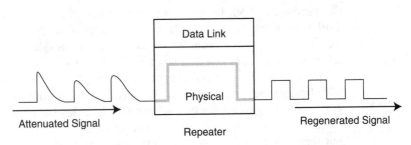

FIGURE 12.16 The Function of a Repeater in the OSI Reference Model

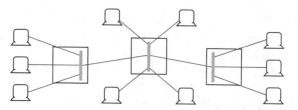

FIGURE 12.17 A Network Connected with Hubs

communications between the computers attached to them. If there were only two computers on the network, a hub and a switch would behave in exactly the same way. If more than two computers were trying to communicate on a network, a switch gives better performance because the full bandwidth of the network is available at both sides of the switch. Therefore, switches are preferred to hubs in most network installations. In Chapter 9, we introduced switches that connect processors to memories or processors to processors. Those switches are the same kind of switches we discuss here. Switches contain some number of buffered input ports, an equal number of output ports, a **switching fabric** (a combination of the switching units, the integrated circuits that they contain, and the programming that allows switching paths to be controlled), and digital hardware that interprets address information encoded on network frames as they arrive in the input buffers.

As with most of the network components we have been discussing, switches have been improved by adding addressability and management features. Most switches today can report on the amount and type of traffic they are handling and can even filter out certain network packets based on user-supplied parameters. Because all switching functions are carried out in hardware, switches are the preferred devices for interconnecting high-performance network components.

12.6.6 Bridges and Gateways

The purpose of both bridges and gateways is to provide a link between two dissimilar network segments. Both can support different media (and network speeds), and they are both "store and forward" devices, holding an entire frame before sending it on. But that's where their similarities end.

Bridges join two similar types of networks so they look like one network. With bridges, all computers on the network belong to the same **subnet** (the network consisting of all devices whose IP addresses have the same prefix). Bridges are relatively simple devices with functionality primarily at Layer 2. This means that they know nothing about protocols, but simply forward data depending on the destination address. Bridges can connect different media having different media access control protocols, but the protocol from the MAC layer through all higher layers in the OSI stack must be identical in both segments. This relationship is shown in Figure 12.18.

Each node connected to any particular bridge must have a unique address. (The MAC address is most often used.) The network administrator must program simple bridges with the addresses and segment numbers of each valid node on the network. The only data that is allowed to cross the bridge is data that is being sent to a valid address on the other side of the bridge. For large networks that change frequently (most networks), this continual reprogramming is tedious, time-consuming, and error prone. **Transparent bridges** were invented to alleviate this problem. They are sophisticated devices that have the ability to learn the address of every device on each segment. Transparent bridges can also supply management information such as throughput reports. Such functionality implies that a bridge is not entirely a Layer 2 device. However, bridges still require identical Network layer protocols and identical interfaces to those protocols on both interconnected segments.

Figure 12.18 shows two different kinds of local area networks connected to each other through a bridge. This is typically how bridges are used. If, however, users on these LANs needed to connect to a system that uses a radically different protocol, for example, a public switched telephone network or a host computer that uses a nonstandard proprietary protocol, then a **gateway** is required. A gateway is a point of entrance to another network. Gateways are full-featured computers that supply communications services spanning all seven OSI layers. Gateway system software converts protocols and character codes, and can provide encryption and decryption services. Because they do so much work in their software, gateways cannot provide the throughput of hardware-based bridges, but they make up for it by providing enormously more functionality. Gateways are often connected directly to switches and routers.

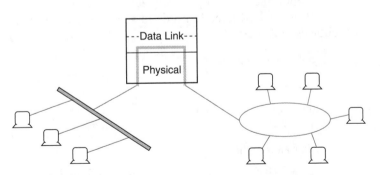

FIGURE 12.18   A Bridge Connecting Two Networks

12.6.7   Routers and Routing

After gateways, routers are the next most complicated components in a network. They are, in fact, small special-purpose computers. A **router** is a device (or a piece of software) connected to at least two networks that determines the destination to which a packet should be forwarded. Routers are normally located at gateways. Operating correctly, routers make the network fast and responsive. Operating incorrectly, one faulty router can bring down the whole system. In this section, we reveal the inner workings of routers and discuss the thorny problems that routers are called upon to solve.

Despite their complexity, routers are usually referred to as Layer 3 devices, because most of their work is done at the Network layer of the OSI Reference Model. However, most routers also provide some network monitoring, management, and troubleshooting services. Because routers are by definition Layer 3 devices, they can bridge different network media types (fiber to copper, for example) and connect different network protocols running at Layer 3 and below. Because of their abilities, routers are sometimes referred to as "intermediate systems" or "gateways" in Internet standards literature. (When the first Internet standards were written, the word *router* hadn't yet been coined.)

Routers are designed specifically to connect two networks together, typically a LAN to a WAN. They are complex devices because not only do they contain buffers and switching logic, but they also have enough memory and processing power to calculate the best way to send a packet to its destination. A conceptual model of the internals of a router is shown in Figure 12.19.

In large networks, routers find an approximate solution to a problem that is fundamentally NP complete. An NP-complete problem is one in which its optimal solution is theoretically impossible within a time period that is short enough for that solution to be useful.

Consider the network shown in Figure 12.20. You may recognize this figure as a complete graph (K_5). There are $n(n - 1) / 2$ edges in a complete graph containing n nodes. In our illustration, we have 5 nodes and 10 edges. The edges represent routes—or **hops**—between each of the nodes.

If Node 1 (Router 1) needs to send a packet to Node 2, it has the following choices of routes:

one route of one hop:

$1 \rightarrow 2$

three routes of two hops:

$1 \rightarrow 3 \rightarrow 2$ $1 \rightarrow 4 \rightarrow 2$ $1 \rightarrow 5 \rightarrow 2$

six routes of three hops:

$1 \rightarrow 3 \rightarrow 4 \rightarrow 2$ $1 \rightarrow 3 \rightarrow 5 \rightarrow 2$ $1 \rightarrow 5 \rightarrow 4 \rightarrow 2$
$1 \rightarrow 4 \rightarrow 3 \rightarrow 2$ $1 \rightarrow 5 \rightarrow 3 \rightarrow 2$ $1 \rightarrow 4 \rightarrow 5 \rightarrow 2$

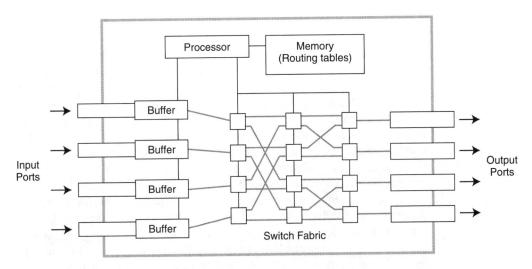

FIGURE 12.19   Anatomy of a Router

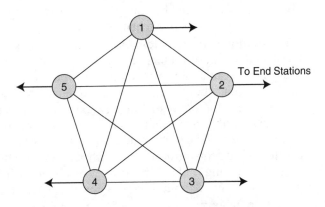

FIGURE 12.20   A Fully Connected Network

six routes of four hops:

$1 \rightarrow 3 \rightarrow 4 \rightarrow 5 \rightarrow 2$ $1 \rightarrow 4 \rightarrow 3 \rightarrow 5 \rightarrow 2$ $1 \rightarrow 5 \rightarrow 4 \rightarrow 3 \rightarrow 2$

$1 \rightarrow 3 \rightarrow 5 \rightarrow 4 \rightarrow 2$ $1 \rightarrow 4 \rightarrow 5 \rightarrow 3 \rightarrow 2$ $1 \rightarrow 5 \rightarrow 3 \rightarrow 4 \rightarrow 2$

When Node 1 and Node 2 are not directly connected, the traffic between them must pass through at least one intermediate node. Considering all options, the number of possible routes is on the algorithmic order of *N!*. This problem is further complicated when costs or weights are applied to the routing paths. Worse yet, the weights can change depending on traffic flow. For example, if the connection between Nodes 1 and 2 were a tariffed **high-latency** (slow) line, we might be a whole lot better off using the $1 \rightarrow 4 \rightarrow 5 \rightarrow 3 \rightarrow 2$ route. Clearly, in a real-world network, with hundreds of routers, the problem becomes enormous. If each router had to come up with the perfect outbound route for each incoming packet by considering all the possibilities, the packets would never get where they were going quickly enough to make anyone happy.

Of course, in a very stable network with only a few nodes, it is possible to program each router so that it always uses the same optimal route. This is called **static routing**, and it is feasible in networks where a large number of users in one location use a centralized host, or gateway, in another location. In the short term, this is an effective way to interconnect systems, but if a problem arises in one of the interconnecting links or routers, users are disconnected from the host. A human being must quickly respond to restore service. Static routing just isn't a reasonable option for networks that change frequently. This is to say that static routing isn't an option for most networks. Conversely, static networks are predictable, because the path (and thus the number of hops) a packet will take is always known and can be controlled. Static routing is also very stable, and it creates no routing protocol exchange traffic.

Dynamic routers automatically set up routes and respond to the changes in the network. These routers can also select an optimal route as well as a backup route should something happen to the route of choice. They do not change routing instructions, but instead allow for dynamic altering of routing tables.

Dynamic routers automatically explore their networks through information exchanges with other routers on the network. The information packets exchanged by the routers reveal their addresses and costs of getting from one point to another. Using this information, each router assembles a table of values in memory. This routing table is, in truth, a reachability list for every node on the network, plus some default values. Typically, each destination node is listed along with the neighboring, or **next-hop**, router to which it is connected.

When creating their tables, dynamic routers consider one of two metrics. They can use either the distance to travel between two nodes or the condition of the network in terms of measured latency. The algorithms using the first metric are **distance vector routing** algorithms. **Link state routing** algorithms use the second metric.

Distance vector routing is derived from a pair of similar algorithms invented in 1957 and 1962 known, respectively, as the **Bellman-Ford** and **Ford-Fulkerson** algorithms. The *distance* in distance vector routing is usually a measure of the number of nodes (hops) through which a packet must pass before reaching its destination, but any metric can be used. For example, suppose we have the network shown in Figure 12.21a. There are 4 routers and 10 nodes connected as indicated. If node B wants to send a packet to node L, there are two choices: One is B → Router 4 → Router 1 → L, with one hop between Router 4 and Router 1. The other routing choice has three hops between the routers: B → Router 4 → Router 3 → Router 2 → Router 1 → L. With distance vector routing, the objective is to always use the shortest route, so our B → Router 4 → Router 1 → L route is the obvious choice.

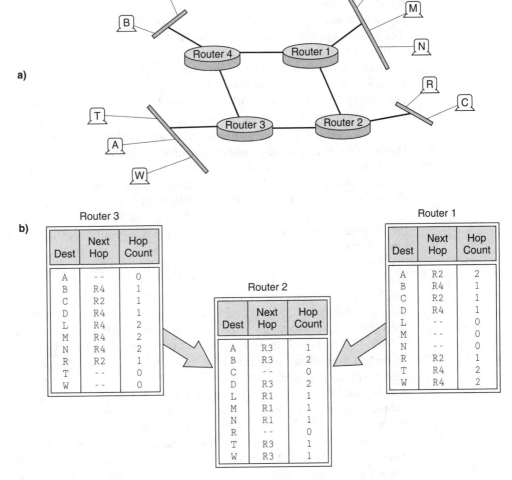

FIGURE 12.21   a) An Example of a Network with 4 Routers and 10 Nodes
b) Routing Tables from Router 1 and Router 3 Are Used for Building the Routing Table for Router 2

Router 3

Dest	Next Hop	Hop Count
A	- -	0
B	R4	1
C	R2	1
D	R4	1
L	R4	2
M	R4	2
N	R4	2
R	R2	1
T	- -	0
W	- -	0

Router 2

Dest	Next Hop	Hop Count
A	R3	1
B	R3	2
C	- -	0
D	R3	2
L	R1	1
M	R1	1
N	R1	1
R	- -	0
T	R3	1
W	R3	1

Router 1

Dest	Next Hop	Hop Count
A	R2	2
B	R4	1
C	R2	1
D	R4	1
L	- -	0
M	- -	0
N	- -	0
R	R2	1
T	R4	2
W	R4	2

In distance vector routing, every router needs to know the identities of each node connected to each router as well as the hop counts between them. To do this efficiently, routers exchange node and hop count information with their adjacent neighbors. For example, using the network shown in Figure 12.21a, Router 1 and Router 3 would have routing tables as shown in Figure 12.21b. These routing tables are then sent to Router 2. As shown in the figure, Router 2 selects the shortest path to any of the nodes considering all of the routes that are reported in the routing tables. The final routing table contains the addresses of nodes directly connected to Router 2 along with a list of destination nodes that are reachable through other routers and a hop count to those nodes. Notice that the hop counts in the final table for Router 2 are increased by 1 to account for the one hop between Router 2 and Router 1, and between Router 2 and Router 3. A real routing table would also contain a default router address that would be used for nodes that are not directly connected to the network, such as stations on a remote LAN or Internet destinations, for example.

Distance vector routing is easy to implement, but it does have a few problems. For one thing, it can take a long time for the routing tables to stabilize (or **converge**) in a large network. Additionally, a considerable amount of traffic is placed on the network as the routing tables are updated. And third, obsolete routes can persist in the routing tables, causing misrouted or lost packets. This last problem is called the **count-to-infinity** problem.

You can understand the count-to-infinity problem by studying the network shown in Figure 12.22a. Notice that there are redundant paths through the network. Note also that the path through the intranet requires 3 hops. For example, if Router 3 goes offline, clients can still get to the mainframe and the Internet, but they won't be able to print anything until Router 3 is again operational.

The paths from all of the routers to the Internet are shown in Figure 12.22b. We call the time that this snapshot was taken $t = 0$. As you can see, Router 1 and Router 2 use Router 3 to get to the Internet. Sometime between $t = 0$ and $t = 1$, the link between Router 3 and Router 4 goes down (say someone unplugs the cable that connects these routers). At $t = 1$, Router 3 discovers this break, but has just received the routing table update from its neighbors, both of which **advertise** themselves as being able to get to the Internet in two hops. Router 3 then assumes that it can get to the Internet using one of these two routers and updates its table accordingly. It picks Router 1 as its next hop to the Internet. (Router 3 is one hop from Router 1, so the total hops from Router 3 to the Internet is $1 + 2 = 3$.) Router 3 then sends its routing table to Router 1 and Router 2 at $t = 2$. At $t = 3$, Router 1 and Router 2 receive Router 3's updated hop count for getting to the Internet, so they add 1 to Router 3's value (because they know that Router 3 is one hop away) and subsequently broadcast their tables. This cycle continues until all of the routers end up with a hop count of infinity, meaning that the registers that hold the hop count eventually overflow, crashing the whole network.

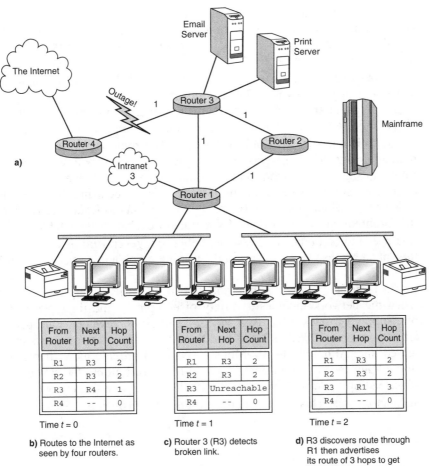

From Router	Next Hop	Hop Count
R1	R3	2
R2	R3	2
R3	R4	1
R4	--	0

Time $t = 0$

b) Routes to the Internet as seen by four routers.

From Router	Next Hop	Hop Count
R1	R3	2
R2	R3	2
R3	Unreachable	
R4	--	0

Time $t = 1$

c) Router 3 (R3) detects broken link.

From Router	Next Hop	Hop Count
R1	R3	2
R2	R3	2
R3	R1	3
R4	--	0

Time $t = 2$

d) R3 discovers route through R1 then advertises its route of 3 hops to get to the Internet.

From Router	Next Hop	Hop Count
R1	R3	4
R2	R3	4
R3	R1	3
R4	--	0

Time $t = 3$

e) The other routers, knowing that they need R3 to get to the Internet, update their tables to reflect the new distance to the Internet as reported by R3.

From Router	Next Hop	Hop Count
R1	R3	5
R2	R3	5
R3	R1	4
R4	--	0

Time $t = 4$

f) R3 now sees that the distance between R1 and the Internet is 5, so it adds 1 to R1's hop count to update its own route to the Internet.

From Router	Next Hop	Hop Count
R1	R3	6
R2	R3	6
R3	R1	5
R4	--	0

Time $t = 5$

g) R1 and R2, upon receiving R3's route advertisement, update their tables with the updated hop count from R3 to the Internet. This process continues until the counters overflow.

FIGURE 12.22   a) An Example of a Network with Redundant Paths
b) The Routing that Router 1, Router 2, and Router 3 would use to get to the Internet
c–g) Routing Table Updates for the Paths to the Internet

Two methods are commonly used to prevent this situation. One is to use a small value for infinity, facilitating early problem detection (before a register overflows), and the other is to somehow prevent short cycles like the one that happened in our example.

Sophisticated routers use a method called **split horizon** routing to keep short cycles out of the network. The idea is simple: No router will use a route given by its neighbor that includes itself in the route. (Similarly, the router could go ahead and use the self-referential route, but set the path value to infinity. This is called **split horizon with poison reverse**. The route is "poisoned" because it is marked as unreachable.) The routing table exchange for our example path to the Internet using split horizon routing would converge as shown in Figure 12.23. Of course, we still have the problem of larger cycles occurring. Say Router 1 points to Router 2, which points to Router 3, which points to Router 1. To some extent, this problem can be remedied if the routers exchange their tables only when a link needs to be updated. (These are called **triggered updates**.) Updates done in this manner cause fewer cycles in the routing graph and also reduce traffic on the network.

In large internetworks, hop counts can be a misleading metric, particularly when the network includes a variety of equipment and line speeds. For example, suppose a packet has two ways of getting somewhere. One path traverses six routers on a 100Mbps LAN, and the other traverses two routers on a 64Kbps leased line. Although the 100Mbps LAN could provide more than ten times the throughput, the hop count metric would force traffic onto the slower leased line. If instead of counting hops we measure the actual line latency, we could prevent such anomalies. This is the idea behind **link state routing**.

From Router	Next Hop	Hop Count
R1	R3	2
R2	R3	2
R3	Unreachable	
R4	--	0

Time $t = 1$

a) R3 detects failed link on its path to the Internet.

From Router	Next Hop	Hop Count
R1	R4	3
R2	R1	4
R3		∞
R4	--	0

Time $t = 2$

b) Because all other routes to the Internet include R3, it advertises its hop count to the Internet as infinity. Upon seeing this, the other routers find a shorter route.

From Router	Next Hop	Hop Count
R1	R4	3
R2	R1	4
R3	R1	4
R4	--	0

Time $t = 3$

c) R3 now sees that its shortest route to the Internet is through R1 and updates its table accordingly.

FIGURE 12.23 Split Horizon with Poison Reverse Routing

As with distance vector routing, link state routing is a self-managing system. Each router discovers the speed of the lines between itself and its neighboring routers by periodically sending out *Hello* packets. At the instant it releases the packet, the router starts a timer. Each router that subsequently receives the packet immediately dispatches a reply. Once the initiator gets a reply, it stops its timer and divides the result by 2, giving the one-way time estimate for the link to the router that replied to the packet. Once all the replies are received, the router assembles the timings into a table of link state values. This table is then broadcast to all other routers, except its adjacent neighbors. Nonadjacent routers then use this information to update all routes that include the sending router. Eventually, all routers within the routing domain end up with identical routing tables. Simply stated, after convergence takes place, a single snapshot of the network exists in the tables of each router. The routers then use this image to calculate the optimal path to every destination in its routing table.

In calculating optimal routes, each router is programmed to think of itself as the root node of a tree with every destination being an internal leaf node of the tree. Using this conceptualization, the router computes an optimal path to each destination using Dijkstra's algorithm.[1] Once found, the router stores only the next hop along the path. It doesn't store the entire path. The next (downstream) router should also have computed the same optimal path—or a better one by the time the packet gets there—so it would use the next link in the optimal path that was computed by its upstream predecessor. After Router 1 in Figure 12.22a has applied Dijkstra's algorithm, it sees the network as shown in Figure 12.24.

Clearly, routers can retain only a finite amount of information. Once a network gets to a size where performance starts to degrade (usually this happens for

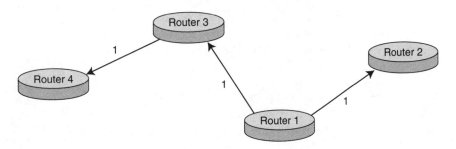

FIGURE 12.24 How Router 1 Sees the Network in Figure 12.22a Using Link State Routing and Dijkstra's Algorithm

---

[1]For an explanation of Dijkstra's algorithm, see Appendix A.

reasons other than routing table saturation), the network must be split into subnetworks, or **segments**. In very large networks, hierarchical topologies that involve a combination of switching and routing technologies are employed to help keep the system manageable. The best network designers know when each technology is called for in the system design. The ultimate aim is to maximize throughput while keeping the network manageable and robust.

What Is a Firewall?

Virtually everyone in government, industry, and academia uses the Internet during the course of daily business. Yet the Internet invites everyone on board—even those persons who would plunder or destroy a company's computing resources. So how do you keep a network open enough for people to do their jobs but sufficiently secure to protect the assets of the business? The preferred solution to this problem is to place a firewall between the internal network and the Internet.

Firewalls get their name by drawing an analogy to the high brick walls that are sometimes placed between adjacent buildings. If a fire erupts in one of the buildings, the adjacent structure has some protection from becoming involved in the blaze. So it is with a network firewall: The internal users are partitioned from external users who may do harm to the internal network structure.

Firewalls come in many varieties. Two types that are most popular are router-based firewalls and host-based—or **proxy server**—firewalls. Both types are programmed with a rule base known as a **policy**. The firewall policy defines which network addresses can have access to which services. A good example of a policy involves file transfers. A firewall could be programmed to allow internal users (on the protected side of the network) to download files from the Internet. Users outside the protected network would be prohibited from downloading files from the internal network. The assumption is that data on the inside of the network may contain sensitive, private information. Any firewall can also be programmed with a list of forbidden addresses. (This is sometimes called a **blacklist.**) Blacklisted addresses often include the websites of groups disseminating objectionable material.

Both types of firewalls also distinguish between inbound and outbound traffic. This prevents the address spoofing that attempts to fool a firewall into thinking that a user is inside the network, when in fact the user is outside the network.

If the firewall were fooled by a spoofed address, an external user would have free run of the internal network.

Both router-based firewalls and proxy servers have the ability to encrypt network traffic. **Encryption** is the process of scrambling a message using an algorithm and a key value so that the only device that can read the message is the device having the corresponding key. Key values are changed periodically, usually daily. This process happens automatically when firewalls are programmed with key exchange routines. Routers tend to use simpler encryption algorithms, usually based on simple bit shifts and logical ANDs using the message and the key value. (One such algorithm is the U.S. federal **Data Encryption Standard** [**DES**]. For more security, the message is sometimes encrypted three times. This is called **Triple-DES**.)

As you might expect, proxy servers are slower and more prone to failure than router-based firewalls, but they also have many more features than router-based firewalls. First among these is their ability to act as an agent for users on the internal network (hence the name *proxy* server). These systems are usually equipped with two network cards, that is, they are **dual homed**. One network card connects to the internal network, and the other connects to the outside network. With this configuration, the server can completely mask the characteristics of the internal network from anyone on the outside. All that the external users can see is the address of the network interface that is connected to the outside.

Server-based firewalls can also maintain extensive network logs. Through these logs, security administrators can detect most invasion attempts by external evildoers. In some cases, logs can provide information regarding the source of a penetration attempt.

12.7 THE FRAGILITY OF THE INTERNET

In a short 35 years, the Cold War's secret DARPANet has been transformed into a crucial resource for civilian business and industry. Although the Internet is obviously our main conduit for information and financial transactions, it not so obviously is the fabric for **supervisory control and data acquisition** (**SCADA**) networks. SCADA systems operate vital portions of our physical infrastructure including power generation facilities, transportation networks, sewage systems, and oil and gas pipelines, to name only a few.

Because of their inherent communication needs, SCADA systems were the first wave of control systems to connect via the Internet. The present wave involves less critical but much more numerous collections of control and sensory nodes known as the **Internet of Things** (**IoT**) or **Machine-to-Machine** (**M2M**) communication. The span of the IoT encompasses everything from the smallest RFID chips, to home appliances, to security systems. One can easily foresee a world in which every object is tagged and able to report its location through the Web. Intelligent nodes might even be able to collaborate with other nodes to make operational decisions. Cisco Systems has estimated that there may be as many as 50 billion M2M devices in use by 2020. It is possible that without the Internet, these devices might be rendered useless—including large portions of our crucial SCADA infrastructure.

As stated earlier in this chapter, the Internet was designed with survivability in mind. If one router fails, another can be used just as easily. And, in fact, this robustness demonstrated itself magnificently in October 2012 when Hurricane Sandy struck the Mid-Atlantic region of the United States. Internet monitoring company Renesys estimated that only 5% of the networks in Manhattan were unreachable between October 29 and October 30, despite a substantial amount of cabling and other equipment being under water or without power. Moreover, the problems were largely limited to Manhattan: The outrages did not propagate throughout the region.

Indeed, if the Internet infrastructure in the northeastern United States could survive Superstorm Sandy, one might be led to believe that the Internet can survive anything. Several Internet observers are becoming increasingly worried, however. Some of the loudest alarms are being heard concerning the possibility of **cyber warfare**—particularly cyber warfare directed at SCADA systems. A well-executed SCADA attack could bring down vast swaths of a country's power systems and transportation networks. But even a less aggressive cyber attack aimed at only a few strategic backbone routers could cause a catastrophic cascading failure. In this scenario, the failed routers overwhelm other routers on the backbone, causing their failure as well.

A second concern is that of the increasing bandwidth demands brought on by the IoT. It is impossible to characterize the type of traffic that these devices will place on the network. Will it consist of billions of short UDP-type bursts? Will it be streams of time-sensitive data? Until now, capacity demands have been met by simply adding more cables and routers to the network. But as more devices are added to the network, the larger the routing tables become, and the more time it takes to select a route and forward a packet. When decisions can't be made timely, packets are lost and need to be retransmitted, putting even more traffic on the network. At its worst, this situation could lead to a condition known as **congestive collapse**, where a significant number of routers go offline because they can no longer handle their incoming traffic, even in defiance of our best efforts at congestion control.

Recognizing that the IoT may push packet traffic past the limits of network scalability, scientists have proposed more intelligent, or cognitive, packet routing. This idea takes advantage of the intelligence of the end nodes in the network. This is to say that end nodes could engage in direct peer-to-peer exchanges, rather than needing to involve a host. As a simple example, consider the process of transferring digital photos from a smartphone to a tablet computer via Wi-Fi. In many cases, the digital photos travel from the phone to a central router and then back through the Internet to the tablet. Despite these devices being inches from each other, the packets may travel hundreds of miles. Indeed, 50 billion transfers like this in a day, and there is no question that congestive collapse is a real concern. The Internet keeps working harder to keep ahead of its many threats. But this hard work leads ultimately to exhaustion. The time has come for the Internet to work smarter. Otherwise, we may be forced to recall how we ever lived without it.

========= **CHAPTER SUMMARY** =========

This chapter has presented an overview of the network components and protocols that are used in building data communications systems. Each network component—each network process—carries out a task at some level within a layered protocol stack. Network engineers use layers of the OSI Reference Model to describe the roles and responsibilities of all network components. When a computer is engaged in communications with another computer, each layer of the protocol stack it is running converses with a corresponding layer running on the remote system. Protocol layers interface with their adjacent layers using service access points.

Most Internet applications rely on TCP/IP, which is by far the most widely deployed data communications protocol. Although often referred to as TCP/IP, this combination is actually two protocols. TCP provides a means for setting up a reliable communications stream on top of the unreliable IP. Version 4 of its IP component is constrained by its 32-bit address fields. Version 6 of IP will solve this problem because its address fields are 128 bits wide. With these larger address fields, routing could be a formidable task. With this in mind, the IETF has devised a hierarchical address scheme, the Aggregatable Global Unicast Address Format, which makes routing of packets both easier and faster.

We have described a number of components common to most data communications networks. The most important of these components are the physical media and the routers. Physical media must be chosen with consideration to the anticipated load and the distance to be covered. Physical media can be extended with repeaters when necessary. Routers are complex devices that monitor the state of the network. Their programming allows them to select nearly optimal paths for network traffic.

As the Internet continues its exponential growth as a vehicle for commerce, routing problems will grow proportionately. The solution to these problems may ultimately reside in rethinking the architecture and some of the assumptions that form the foundation of the Internet as we know it today.

FURTHER READING

There is no shortage of literature on the topic of computer networking. The challenge is in finding *good* networking material these days. Among the best data communications books available are those written by Tanenbaum (2010), Stallings (2013), and Kurose and Ross (2012). Following the OSI protocol stack in its organization, Tanenbaum's work is an easy-to-read introduction to most of the important concepts of data communications and networks. Kurose and Ross discuss most of the topics presented in this chapter with good detail and at a level that is accessible to most interested readers. The book by Stallings covers most of the same material as Tanenbaum's book, but with much more rigor and detail. Sherman (1990) also provides a well-written (but aging) introduction to data communications. The historical perspective that Sherman furnishes is most enjoyable.

The definitive source for information concerning Internet standards (requests for comment, or RFCs) is the Internet Engineering Task Force website at www. ietf.org. The RFCs relevant to material presented in this chapter are:

- RFC 791 "Internet Protocol Version 4 (IPv4)"
- RFC 793 "Transmission Control Protocol (TCP)"
- RFC 1180 "A TCP/IP Tutorial"
- RFC 1887 "An Architecture for IPv6 Unicast Address Allocation"
- RFC 2460 "Internet Protocol, Version 6 (IPv6) Specification"
- RFC 2026 "The Internet Standards Process"
- RFC 1925 "The Fundamental Truths of Networking"

IBM's TCP/IP tutorial Redbook by Rodriguez, Getrell, Karas, and Peschke (2001) is one of the most inexpensive and readable resources outside of the IETF. Unlike the IETF site, it also discusses ways in which a particular vendor's products implement TCP/IP (with no hype). Minoli and Schmidt (1999) discuss the Internet infrastructure, with a particular focus on quality-of-service issues.

Clark (1997) gives us a detailed and comprehensive account of telephone communications (centering in the UK). It relates important aspects of public telephone networks, including their ability to carry data traffic. Burd's (1997) ISDN and de Prycker's (1996) ATM books are both definitive accounts of their subjects. The IBM (1995) Redbook on ATM, though less rigorous than de Prycker, provides excellent, objective detail concerning ATM's salient features.

For more information relevant to the Internet backbone router instability problem, see the papers by Labovitz, Malan, and Jahanian (1998, 1999). The University of Michigan maintains a website devoted to Internet performance issues. It can be found at www.merit.edu/ipma/.

The only way to keep abreast of the latest data networking technologies is to *constantly* read professional and trade periodicals. The most *avant-garde* information can be found in publications by the ACM and IEEE. Outstanding among these are *IEEE/ACM Transactions on Networking* and *IEEE Network*. Trade journals are another source of good information, particularly for understanding how various vendors are implementing the latest in networking technology. Two such magazines published by CMP are *Network Computing* (www.networkcomputing .com) and *Network Magazine* (www.networkmagazine.com). *Network World* is a weekly magazine published by CW Communications that not only provides an excellent print version, but its related website, www.nwfusion.com, teems with information and resources.

Many equipment vendors are gracious enough to post excellent, low-hype tutorial information on their websites. These sites include those by IBM, Cisco Systems, and Corning Glass. Certainly you will discover other great commercial sites as you explore specific technologies related to the topics presented in this chapter. It seems that one can never learn enough when it comes to data communications (no matter how hard one tries!).

REFERENCES

Burd, N. *The ISDN Subscriber Loop.* London: Chapman & Hall, 1997.

Clark, M. P. *Networks and Telecommunications: Design and Operation,* 2nd ed. Chichester, England: John Wiley & Sons, 1997.

Kurose, J. F., & Ross, K. W. *Computer Networking: A Top-Down Approach Featuring the Internet.* Boston, MA: Addison Wesley Longman, 2001.

Labovitz, C., Malan, G. R., & Jahanian, F. "Internet Routing Instability." *IEEE/ACM Transactions on Networking 6*:5, October 1998, pp. 515–528.

Labovitz, C., Malan, G. R., & Jahanian, F. "Origins of Internet Routing Instability." *INFOCOM '99. Eighteenth Annual Joint Conference of the IEEE Computer and Communications Societies. Proceedings. IEEE 1,* 1999, pp. 218–226.

Liotta, A., "The Cognitive NET is Coming," *IEEE Spectrum 50*:8, August 2013, pp. 26–31.

Liu, W., Matthews, C., Parziale L., et al. *TCP/IP Tutorial and Technical Overview*, 8th ed. Armonk, NY: IBM Corporation, 2006.

Minoli, D., & Schmidt, A. *Internet Architectures.* New York: John Wiley & Sons, 1999.

Sherman, K. *Data Communications: A User's Guide*, 3rd ed. Englewood Cliffs, NJ: Prentice Hall, 1990.

Stallings, W. *Data and Computer Communications*, 10th ed. Upper Saddle River, NJ: Prentice Hall, 2013.

Tanenbaum, A. S. *Computer Networks*, 5th ed. Upper Saddle River, NJ: Prentice Hall, 2010.

REVIEW OF ESSENTIAL TERMS AND CONCEPTS

1. How is the organization of a polled network different from that of an internetwork?

2. What protocol device was the key to the robustness of DARPAnet?

3. Who establishes standards for the Internet?

4. What is the formal name given to Internet standards?

5. Which layer of the ISO/OSI Reference Model takes care of negotiating frame size and transmission speed?

6. If a communications session were to employ encryption or compression, which layer of the ISO/OSI Reference Model would perform this service?

7. According to the IPv4 format described in Section 12.5.1, what bit positions does the IP Protocol Number occupy? What is the purpose of this field?

8. Why have certain types of IP addresses become scarce?

9. Explain the general purpose of the TCP protocol.

10. How does IPv6 improve upon IPv4?

11. What is the difference between guided and unguided data transmission media? List some examples of each.

12. What determines the quality of a transmission medium? What metric is used?

13. What are the principal causes of attenuation? What can help reduce it?

14. What is the difference between the baud rate and the bit rate of a line?

15. What are the three types of fiber-optic cable? Which of these can transmit signals the fastest?

16. Where does one find a MAC address? How many bytes are in a MAC address?

17. Briefly describe how repeaters, hubs, switches, and routers differ from one another.

18. What is the difference between a bridge and a gateway? Which one is faster and why?

19. When is it not a very good idea to use static routing?

20. Give two important ways in which link state routing differs from distance vector routing.

21. What are the three main problems that arise from distance vector routing?

22. In what ways does a firewall provide security?

23. What are SCADA systems?

24. In what ways is the Internet threatened?

EXERCISES

1. In what way is the traffic of an early business computer network different from that of an early scientific-academic network? Is there such a distinction between these two types of systems today?

2. Why is the ISO/OSI protocol stack called a reference model? Do you think this will always be the case?

3. How is a Network layer protocol different from a Transport layer protocol?

4. Internet protocol standards are devised through the efforts of thousands of people all over the world—regardless of their having any particular background in data communications. On the other hand, proprietary protocols are created by a much smaller group of people, all of whom are directly or indirectly working for the same employer.

   a) What advantages and disadvantages do you think are offered by each approach? Which would produce a better product? Which would produce a product more quickly?

   b) Why do you think that the IETF approach has achieved ascendancy over the proprietary approach?

◆ 5. In our description of the Window field in the TCP header, we said:

   Notice that if the receiver's application is running very slowly, say it's pulling data 1 or 2 bytes at a time from its buffer, the TCP process running at the receiver should wait until the application buffer is empty enough to justify sending another segment.

   What is the "justification" for sending another segment?

6. The OSI protocol stack includes Session and Presentation layers in addition to its Application layer. TCP/IP applications, such as Telnet and FTP, have no such separate layers defined. Do you think that such a separation should be made? Give some advantages and disadvantages of incorporating the OSI approach into TCP/IP.

7. Why is the length of a TCP segment limited to 65,515 bytes? (Hint: Look at the definition of the Data Offset field of the TCP segment format.)

8. Why does the IETF use the word *octet* instead of *byte*? Do you think this practice should continue?

9. Into which class of networks do the following IP addresses fall?

   a) 180.265.14.3

   b) 218.193.149.222

   c) 92.146.292.7

10. Into which class of networks do the following IP addresses fall?

    a) 223.52.176.62

    b) 127.255.255.2

    c) 191.57.229.163

11. A station running TCP/IP needs to transfer a file to a host. The file contains 1,024 bytes. How many bytes, including all of the TCP/IP overhead, would be sent, assuming a payload size of 128 bytes and that both systems are running IPv4? (Also assume that the three-way handshake and window size negotiation have been completed and that no errors occur during transmission.)

    a) What is the protocol overhead (stated as a percentage)?

    b) Perform the same calculation, this time assuming that both clients are using IPv6.

12. A station running TCP/IP needs to transfer a file to a host. The file contains 2,048 bytes. How many bytes, including all of the TCP/IP overhead, would be sent, assuming a payload size of 512 bytes and that both systems are running IPv4? (Also assume that the three-way handshake and window size negotiation have been completed and that no errors occur during transmission.)

    a) What is the protocol overhead (stated as a percentage)?

    b) Perform the same calculation, this time assuming that both clients are using IPv6.

13. Two stations running TCP/IP are engaged in transferring a file. This file is 100KB long, the payload size is 100 bytes, and the negotiated window size is 300 bytes. The sender receives an ACK 1,500 from the receiver.

    a) Which bytes will be sent next?

    b) What is the last byte number that can be sent without an ACK being sent by the receiver?

14. Two stations running TCP/IP are engaged in transferring a file. This file is 10KB long, the payload size is 100 bytes, and the negotiated window size is 2,000 bytes. The sender receives an ACK 900 from the receiver.

    a) Which bytes will be sent next?

    b) What is the last byte number that can be sent without an ACK being sent by the receiver?

15. What problems would present themselves if TCP did not allow senders and receivers to negotiate a timeout window?

16. IP is a connectionless protocol, whereas TCP is connection-oriented. How can these two protocols coexist in the same protocol stack?

17. Section 12.6.1 states that when using 4B/5B encoding, a signal-carrying capacity of 125MHz is required for a transmission medium to have a bit rate of 100Mbps.

    a) What signal-carrying capacity would be required if Manchester coding were used instead?

    b) What signal-carrying capacity would be required if modified frequency modulation (MFM) coding were used, assuming that the occurrence of a 0 and the occurrance of a 1 are equally likely events?

(Manchester and MFM coding are explained in Chapter 2, Section 2.A.)

18. a) The signal power for a particular class of network wiring is 8,733.26dB, and the noise rating at that particular signal strength at 100MHz is 41.8dB. Find the signal-to-noise ratio for this conductor.

    b) Suppose the noise rating for the network wiring in part a is 9.5dB and the noise rating is 36.9dB when a 200MHz signal is transmitted. What is the signal strength?

♦ **19. ♦ a)** The signal power for a particular class of network wiring is 2,898dB, and the noise rating at that particular signal strength at 100MHz is 40dB. Find the signal-to-noise ratio for this conductor.

    ♦ **b)** Suppose the noise rating for the network wiring in part a is 0.32dB and the noise rating is 35dB when a 200MHz signal is transmitted. What is the signal strength?

20. How big is a physical PDU? The answer to this question determines the number of simultaneous transmissions for many network architectures.

If a signal propagates through copper wire at a rate of 2×10^8 m/s, then on a carrier running at 10Mbps the length of each bit pulse is given by:

$$\frac{\text{Speed of propagation}}{\text{Speed of bus}} = \frac{2 \times 10^8 \text{m/s}}{10 \times 10^6 \text{b/s}} = 20\text{m/bit}$$

If a data frame is 512 bits long, then the entire frame occupies:

(Length of one bit) $\times$ (Frame size) = $20 \times 512 = 10{,}240$ meters.

    a) How big is a 1,024-bit packet if the network runs at 100Mbps?

    b) How big is it if the network speed is increased to 155Mbps?

    c) At 100Mbps, how much time elapses as one of these frames passes a particular point in the network?

21. It looks like the 4B/5B bit cells in Figure 12.14 are fairly small. How long, in reality, is such a bit cell on a 125MHz line? (Use the constants and formulas from the previous question.)

22. With reference to Figure 12.21, suppose Router 4 derives its routing table from the routing tables of Router 1 and Router 3. Complete the routing table for Router 4 using the same format as the routing table of the other three routers.

CHAPTER 13
Selected Storage Systems and Interfaces

13.1 INTRODUCTION

The world's craving for data and passion for information seem to have no upper boundary. If it is at all possible to somehow capture the digital essence of an activity, it seems we are utterly compelled to do so. It's as though the single byte that we fail to lock in our archives will be the only one that's important ten years hence.

Consider a trip to the grocery store, as an example. If you drive there, your automobile may be recording status information from its internal computer systems, while its global positioning system continually relays your location to a satellite. Once inside the store, your picture may be taken several times and recorded in a digital security system. Some of the items you place in your basket might contain embedded radio frequency identification (RFID) tags. Sensors throughout the store constantly record the location of the packages containing the tags while you move from aisle to aisle. As you check out, the purchase of each item is recorded in a computer, whereupon financial and inventory records are updated. When you hand over your "frequent buyer" or "customer loyalty" card, your purchases become associated with your personal information. Paying for your purchases with a credit or debit card generates several more transactions in various computers in the financial processing chain. Days later, some of this data may be extracted by data warehousing, data mining, or decision support systems, creating even more rows in a database table somewhere. Thus, the unremarkable activity of buying one's groceries in the twenty-first century could produce multiple megabytes of data that may persist for years. Whether mere humans can make sense of it all—and what happens if they do—are questions we won't try to

743

address here. We will instead describe the hardware structures that help computer systems deal with this so-called information explosion.

Historically, electronic records in an enterprise were stored on fairly homogeneous, centralized disk and tape storage systems that were directly connected to a large host system. The entire collection of disk drives, tape drives, and the main CPU were under the control of a single operating system (or multiple images of the same operating system). Over the past 20 years, centralized configurations have been replaced or supplemented by myriad smaller servers that offer specialized services including email, e-commerce, end user reporting, and general applications. System management challenges grow proportionately with the number and diversity of server platforms and applications. Not the least of these challenges is enterprise storage management.

A number of storage architectures have recently been put forth to help get things under control. The main purpose of this chapter is to provide you with an overview of various important I/O and storage implementations, with particular attention given to enterprise storage implementations. You will see how these implementations are becoming systems in their own right, having architecture models that are distinct from the host systems to which they attach. We begin by discussing SCSI, one of the most important and enduring I/O interfaces.

13.2   SCSI ARCHITECTURE

The **Small Computer System Interface**, or **SCSI** (pronounced "scuzzy"), was invented in 1981 by a then-premiere disk drive manufacturer, Shugart Associates, and NCR Corporation, formerly also a strong player in the small computer market. This interface was originally called SASI for Shugart Associates Standard Interface. It was so well designed that it became an ANSI standard in 1986. The ANSI committees called the new interface SCSI, thinking it better to refer to the interface in more general terms.

The original standard SCSI interface (which we now call SCSI-1) defined a set of commands, a transport protocol, and the physical connections required to link an unprecedented number of drives (seven) to a CPU at an unprecedented speed of 5 megabytes per second (MBps). The groundbreaking idea was to push intelligence into the interface to make it more or less self-managing. This freed the CPU to work on computational tasks instead of I/O tasks. In the early 1980s, most small computer systems were running at clock rates between 2 and 8.44MHz; this made the throughput of the SCSI bus seem nothing short of dazzling.

Today, SCSI is in its third generation, aptly called SCSI-3. SCSI-3 is more than an interface standard; it is an architecture, officially called the **SCSI Architecture Model-3 (SAM-3)**. This architecture includes the "classic" parallel SCSI interface as well as three serial interfaces and one hybrid interface. We have more to say about SAM in Section 13.2.2.

Ironically, SCSI is no longer the dominant interface for small systems. It has long been supplanted in personal systems by simpler, cheaper disks. However, as of this writing, SCSI is employed in 80% of enterprise-class storage systems. Because of its dominance in this area, it is well worth understanding how it works.

13.2.1 "Classic" Parallel SCSI

Suppose someone says to you, "We just installed a new BackOffice server with three huge SCSI drives," or "My system is screaming since I upgraded to SCSI." The speaker is probably referring to a SCSI-2 or a traditional parallel disk drive system. In the 1980s, these statements would have been quite the techno-brag because of the intractability of connecting and configuring the first generation of SCSI devices. Today, not only are transfer rates a couple of orders of magnitude higher, but intelligence has been built into SCSI devices so as to virtually eliminate the vexations endured by early SCSI adopters.

Parallel SCSI disk drives support a variety of speeds ranging from 10MBps (for downward compatibility with early SCSI-2) to as much as 320MBps for Wide, Fast, and Ultra implementations of the latest SCSI devices. One of the many beauties of SCSI is that a single SCSI bus can support this range of device speeds with no need for recabling or drive replacement. (However, no one will give you any performance guarantees.) Some representative SCSI capabilities are shown in Table 13.1.

Much of the flexibility and robustness of the SCSI parallel architecture can be attributed to the fact that SCSI devices can communicate among themselves. SCSI devices are **daisy-chained** (the input of one drive cabled from the output of another) along one bus. The CPU communicates only with its SCSI host adapter, issuing I/O commands when required. The CPU subsequently goes about its business while the adapter takes care of managing the input or output operation. Figure 13.1 shows this organization for a SCSI-2 system.

"Fast" parallel SCSI cables have 50 conductors. Eight of these are used for data, 11 for various types of control. The remaining conductors are required for

SCSI Designation	Cable Pin Count	Theoretical Maximum Transfer Rate (MBps)	Maximum Number of Devices
SCSI-1	50	5	8
Fast SCSI	50	10	8
Fast and Wide	2 × 68	40	32
Ultra SCSI	2 × 68 or 50 and 68	320	16

TABLE 13.1   A Summary of Various SCSI Capabilities

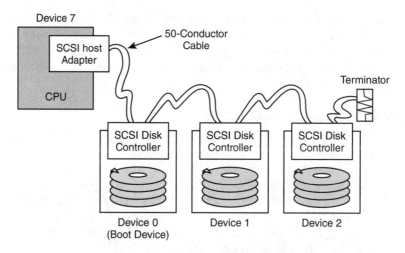

FIGURE 13.1   A SCSI-2 Configuration

the electrical interface. The device selection (SEL) signal is placed on the data bus at the beginning of a transfer or command. Because there are only eight data lines, a maximum of seven devices (in addition to the host adapter) can be supported. "Fast and Wide" SCSI cables have 16-bit data buses, allowing twice as many devices to be supported at (presumably) twice the transfer rate. Some Fast and Wide SCSI systems use two 68-conductor cables, which can support twice the transfer rate and double the number of devices that can be supported by systems using only one 68-conductor cable. Table 13.2 shows the pinouts for a 50-conductor SCSI cable.

Parallel SCSI devices communicate with each other and the host adapter using an asynchronous protocol running in eight phases. Strict timings are defined for each phase. That is, if a phase has not completed within a certain number of milliseconds (depending on the speed of the bus), it is considered an error and the protocol restarts from the beginning of the current phase. The device

Signal	D-Pin Number	Signal	D-Pin Number	Signal	D-Pin Number
Ground	1 → 12	Ground	35	*n* ACKnowledge	44
Termination power	13	Motor power	36	*n* reset	45
12V or 5V power	14	12V or 5V power	37	*n* MeSsaGe	46
12V or 5V (logic)	15	Ground	39, 40	*n* SELect	47
Ground	17 → 25	*n* Attention	41	*n* C/D	48
Data bit 0 → Data bit 7	26 → 33	Synchronization	42	*n* REQuest	49
Parity bit	34	*n* BuSY	43	*n* I/O	50
Negative logic signals are indicated by a leading lowercase *n*. The signal is asserted when the signal is negated.					

TABLE 13.2   SCSI D-Type Connector Pinouts

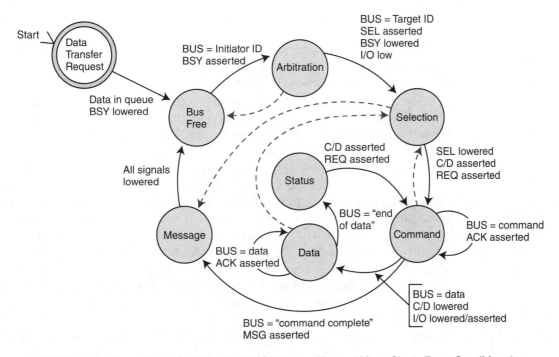

FIGURE 13.2   State Diagram of Parallel SCSI Phases (Dotted Lines Show Error Conditions)

that is sending the data is called the **initiator** and the destination device is called the **target** device. The eight phases of the SCSI protocol are described below. Figure 13.2 illustrates these phases in a state diagram.

- **Bus Free:** Interrogate the "bus busy" (BSY) signaling line to see whether the bus is in use prior to entering the next phase; or lower the BSY signal after data transfer is complete.

- **Arbitration:** The initiator bids for control of the bus by placing its device ID on the bus and raising the busy signal. If two devices do this simultaneously, the one with the highest device ID wins control of the bus. The host must always have the highest device ID. The loser waits for another "Bus Free" state.

- **Selection:** The address of the target device is placed on the data bus, the "selection" (SEL) signal is raised, and the BSY signal is lowered. When the target device sees its own device ID on the bus with SEL raised and BSY and I/O lowered, it raises the BSY signal and stores the ID of the initiator for later use. The initiator knows that the target is ready when it sees the BSY line asserted and responds by lowering the SEL signal.

- **Command:** Once the target detects that the initiator has negated the SEL signal, it indicates that it is ready for a command by asserting the "ready for command" signal on the "command/data" (C/D) line, and requests the command itself by raising the REQ signal. After the initiator senses that the C/D and REQ signals are raised, it places the first command on the data bus and asserts the ACK signal. The target device will respond to the command thus sent and then raise the ACK signal to acknowledge that the command has been received. Subsequent bytes of the command, if any, are exchanged using ACK signals until all command bytes have been transferred.

At this point, the initiator and target could free the bus so that other devices can use it while the disk is being positioned under the read/write head. This allows greater concurrency, but creates more overhead, as control of the bus would have to be renegotiated before the data could be transferred to the initiator.

- **Data:** After the target has received the entire command, it places the bus in "data" mode by lowering the C/D signal. Depending on whether the transfer is an output from the source to the target (say, a disk write) or an input from the source to the target (such as a disk read), the "input/output" line is negated or asserted, respectively. Bytes are then placed on the bus and transferred using the same "REQ/ACK" handshake that is used during the command phase.

- **Status:** Once all the data has been transferred, the target places the bus back into command mode by raising the C/D signal. It then asserts the REQ signal and waits for an acknowledgment from the initiator, which tells it that the initiator is free and ready to accept a command.

- **Message:** When the target senses that the initiator is ready, it places the "command complete" code on the data lines and asserts the "message" line, MSG. When the initiator observes the "command complete" message, it lowers all signals on the bus, thus returning the bus to the "bus free" state.

- **Reselection:** In the event that a transfer was interrupted (such as when the bus is released while waiting for a disk or tape to service a request), control of the bus is renegotiated through an arbitration phase as described above. The initiator determines that it has been reselected when it sees the SEL and I/O lines asserted with the exclusive OR of its own and the ID of the target on the data lines. The protocol then resumes at the Data phase.

Synchronous SCSI data transfers work much the same way as the asynchronous method just described. The primary difference between the two is that no handshaking is required between the transmission of each data byte. Instead, a minimum transfer period is negotiated between the initiator and the target. Data is exchanged for the duration of the negotiated period. A REQ/ACK handshake will then take place before the next block of data will be sent.

It is easy to see why timing is so critical to the effectiveness of SCSI. Upper limits for waiting times prevent the interface from hanging when there is a device error. If this were not the case, the removal of a floppy disk from its drive might prevent access to a fixed disk because the bus could be marked busy "forever" (or at least until the system is restarted). Signal attenuation over long cable runs can cause timeouts, making the entire system slow and unreliable. Serial interfaces are much more tolerant of timing variability.

13.2.2 The SCSI Architecture Model-3

SCSI has evolved from a monolithic system consisting of a protocol, signals, and connectors into a layered interface specification, separating physical connections from transport protocols and interface commands. The new specification, called the **SCSI Architecture Model-3 (SAM-3)**, defines these layers and how they interact with a command-level host architecture called the **SCSI Primary Commands (SPC)** to perform serial and parallel I/O for virtually any type of device that can be connected to a computer system. Layers communicate with adjacent layers using protocol service requests, indications, responses, and confirmations. Loosely coupled protocol stacks such as these allow the greatest flexibility in choices of interface hardware, software, and media. Technical improvements in one layer should have no effect on the operation of the other layers. The flexibility of the SAM has opened a new world of speed and adaptability for disk storage systems.

Figure 13.3 shows how the components of the SAM fit together. Although the architecture retains downward compatibility with SCSI parallel protocols and interfaces, the largest and fastest computer systems are now using serial methods. The SAM-3 serial protocols are **Serial Storage Architecture (SSA)**, **Serial Bus** (also known as **IEEE 1394** or **FireWire**), **Serial Attached SCSI**, **iSCSI**, and **Fibre Channel (FC)**. Because of the speeds of the SCSI buses and the diversity of systems that SCSI can interconnect, the "small" in "Small Computer System Interface" has become a misnomer, with variants of SCSI being used in everything from the smallest personal computer to the largest mainframe systems.

Each of the SCSI serial protocols has its own protocol stack, which conforms to the defined SCSI primary command at the top and clearly defined transport protocols and physical interface systems at the bottom. Serial protocols send data

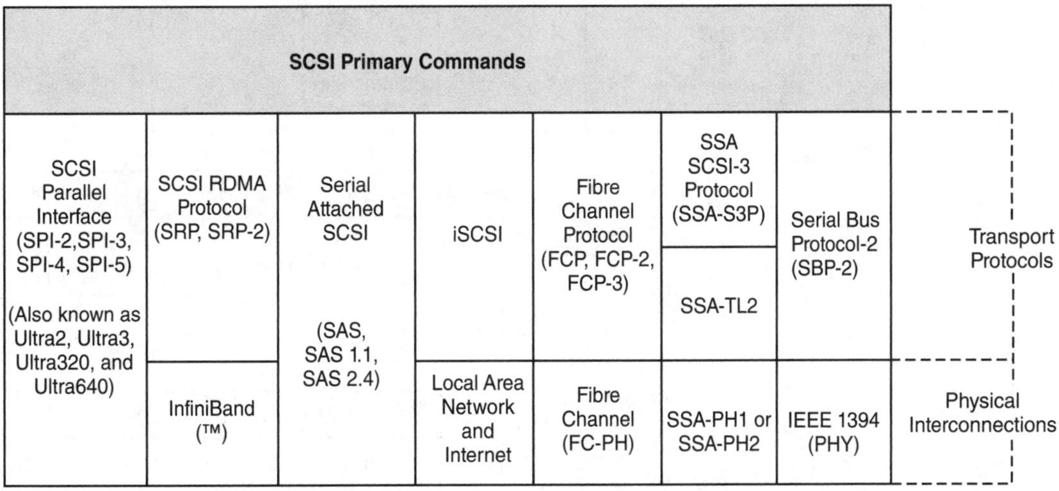

SCSI Primary Commands								
SCSI Parallel Interface (SPI-2,SPI-3, SPI-4, SPI-5) (Also known as Ultra2, Ultra3, Ultra320, and Ultra640)	SCSI RDMA Protocol (SRP, SRP-2)	Serial Attached SCSI (SAS, SAS 1.1, SAS 2.4)	iSCSI	Fibre Channel Protocol (FCP, FCP-2, FCP-3)	SSA SCSI-3 Protocol (SSA-S3P) SSA-TL2	Serial Bus Protocol-2 (SBP-2)	Transport Protocols
	InfiniBand (™)		Local Area Network and Internet	Fibre Channel (FC-PH)	SSA-PH1 or SSA-PH2	IEEE 1394 (PHY)	Physical Interconnections

FIGURE 13.3 The SCSI Architecture Model-3

in packets (or frames). These packets consist of a group of bytes containing identifying information (the packet header), a group of data bytes (called the packet payload), and some sort of trailer delimiting the end of the packet. Error-detection coding is also included in the packet trailer in many of the SAM protocols.

We will examine a few of the more interesting SAM serial protocols in the sections that follow.

IEEE 1394

The interface system now known as **IEEE 1394** had its beginnings at the Apple Computer Company when it saw a need to create a faster and more reliable bus than was provided by the parallel SCSI systems that were dominant in the late 1980s. This interface, which Apple called **FireWire**, today provides bus speeds of 480MBps, with greater speeds expected in the near future.

IEEE 1394 is more than a storage interface; it is a peer-to-peer storage network. Devices are equipped with intelligence that allows them to communicate with each other as well as with the host controller. This communication includes negotiation of transfer speeds and control of the bus. These functions are spread throughout the IEEE 1394 protocol layers, as shown in Figure 13.4.

Not only does IEEE 1394 provide faster data transfer than early parallel SCSI, but it does so using a much thinner cable, with only six conductors—four

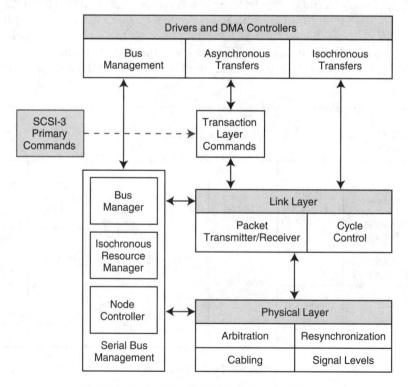

FIGURE 13.4   The IEEE 1394 Protocol Stack

for data and control, two for power. The smaller cable is cheaper and much easier to manage than 50-conductor SCSI-2 cables. Furthermore, IEEE 1394 cables can be extended about 15 feet (4.5 meters) between devices. As many as 63 devices can be daisy-chained on one bus. The IEEE 1394 connector is modular, similar in style to Game Boy connectors.

The entire system is self-configuring, which permits easy **hot-plugging (plug and play)** of a multitude of devices while the system is running. Hot-plugging, however, does not come without a price. The polling required to keep track of devices connected to the interface places overhead on the system, which ultimately limits its throughput. Furthermore, if a connection is busy processing a stream of isochronous data, it may not immediately acknowledge a device being plugged in during the transfer.

Devices can be plugged into extra ports on other devices, creating a tree structure as shown in Figure 13.5. For data I/O purposes, this tree structure is of limited use. Because of its support of isochronous data transfer, IEEE 1394 has gained wide acceptance in consumer electronics. It is also poised to overtake the

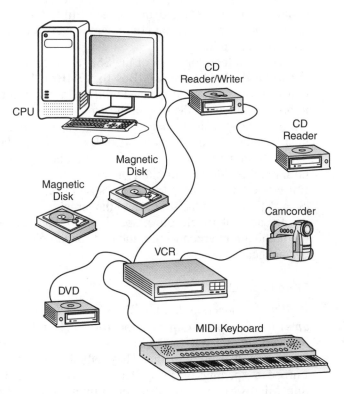

FIGURE 13.5   An IEEE 1394 Tree Configuration, Laden with Consumer Electronics

IEEE 488 **General Purpose Interface Bus** for laboratory data acquisition applications as well. Because of its preoccupation with real-time data handling, it is not likely that IEEE 1394 will endeavor to replace SCSI as a high-capacity data storage interface.

Serial Storage Architecture

Serial Storage Architecture (**SSA**) was the first storage interface to break away from parallel connections. Although it has been superseded by other technologies, SSA was the turning point for industry thinking about storage interfaces. In the early 1990s, IBM was among the many computer manufacturers seeking a fast and reliable alternative to parallel SCSI for use in mainframe disk storage systems. IBM's engineers decided on a serial bus that would offer both compactness and low attenuation for long cable runs. It was required to provide increased throughput and downward compatibility with SCSI-2 protocols. By the end of 1992, SSA was sufficiently refined to warrant IBM proposing it as a standard to ANSI. This standard was approved in late 1996.

SSA's design supports multiple disk drives and multiple hosts in a loop configuration, as shown in Figure 13.6. A four-conductor cable consisting of two twisted pairs of copper wire (or four strands of fiber-optic cable) allows signals to be transmitted in opposite directions in the loop. Because of this redundancy, one drive or host adapter can fail and the rest of the disks will remain accessible.

The dual loop topology of the SSA architecture also allows the base throughput to be doubled from 40MBps to 80MBps. If all nodes are functioning normally, devices can communicate with one another in **full-duplex** mode (data goes in both directions in the loop at the same time).

SSA devices can manage some of their own I/O. For example, in Figure 13.6, host adapter A can be reading disk 0 while host adapter B is writing to disk 3, disk 1 is sending data to a tape unit, and disk 2 is sending data to a printer, with no throughput degradation attributable to the bus itself. IBM calls this idea **spatial reuse** because no parts of the system have to wait for the bus if there is a clear path between the source and the target.

Because of its elegance, speed, and reliability, SSA was poised to become the dominant interconnection method for large computer systems . . . until Fibre Channel came along.

Fibre Channel

In 1991, engineers at the **CERN** (*Conseil Européen pour la Recherche Nucléaire*) (or European Organization for Nuclear Research) laboratory in Geneva, Switzerland, set out to devise a system for transporting Internet communications over fiber-optic media. They called this system **Fibre Channel**, using the European spelling of *fiber*. The following year, Hewlett-Packard, IBM, and Sun Microsystems formed a consortium to adapt Fibre Channel to disk interface systems. This group grew to become the **Fibre Channel Association** (**FCA**), which is working with ANSI to produce a refined and robust model for

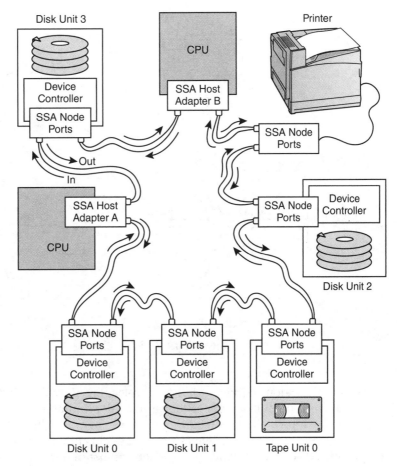

FIGURE 13.6   A Serial Storage Architecture (SSA) Configuration

high-speed interfaces to storage devices. Although originally chartered to define fiber-optic interfaces, Fibre Channel protocols can be used over twisted pair and coaxial copper media as well. Fibre Channel storage systems can have any of three topologies: switched, point-to-point, or loop. The loop topology, called **Fibre Channel Arbitrated Loop (FC-AL)**, is the most widely used—and least costly—of the three Fibre Channel topologies. The Fibre Channel topologies are shown in Figure 13.7.

FC-AL provides 100MBps packet transmission in one direction, with a theoretical maximum of 127 devices in the loop; 60 is considered the practical limit, however.

Notice that Figure 13.7 shows two versions of FC-AL, one with (c) and one without (b) a simple switching device called a **hub**. FC-AL hubs are equipped with port bypass switches that engage whenever one of the FC-AL disks fails. Without some type of port-bypassing ability, the entire loop will fail should only one disk become unusable. (Compare this with SSA.) Thus, adding a hub to the

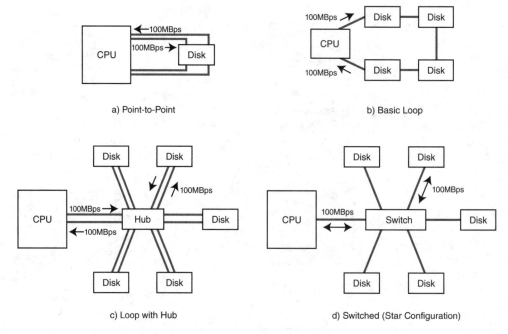

a) Point-to-Point

b) Basic Loop

c) Loop with Hub

d) Switched (Star Configuration)

FIGURE 13.7   Fibre Channel Topologies

configuration introduces failover protection. Because the hub itself can become a single point of failure (although they don't often fail), redundant hubs are provided for installations requiring high system availability.

Switched Fibre Channel storage systems provide much more bandwidth than FC-AL with no practical limit to the number of devices connected to the interface (up to 2^{24}). Each drop between the switch and a node can support a 100MBps connection. Therefore, two disks can be transferring data between each other at 100MBps while the CPU is transferring data to another disk at 100MBps, and so forth. As you might expect, switched Fibre Channel configurations are more costly than loop configurations because of the more sophisticated switching components, which must be redundant to ensure continuous operation.

Fibre Channel is something of an amalgamation of data networks and storage interfaces. It has a protocol stack that fits both the SAM and the internationally accepted network protocol stacks. This protocol stack is shown in Figure 13.8. Because of the higher-level protocol mappings, a Fibre Channel storage configuration does not necessarily require a direct connection to a CPU: The Fibre Channel protocol packets can be encapsulated within a network transmission packet or passed directly as a SCSI command. Layer FC-4 handles the details.

The FC-2 layer produces the protocol packet (or frame) that contains the data or command coming from the upper levels or responses and data coming from the lower levels. This packet, shown in Figure 13.9, has a fixed size of 2,148 bytes, 36 of which are delimiting, routing, and error-control bytes.

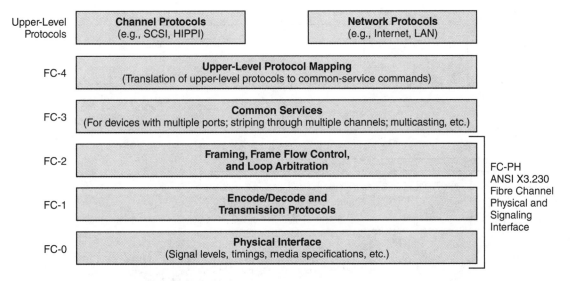

FIGURE 13.8   The Fibre Channel Protocol Stack

The FC-AL loop initializes itself when it is powered up. At that time, participating devices announce themselves, negotiate device (or port) numbers, and select a master device. Data transmissions take place through packet exchanges.

FC-AL is a point-to-point protocol, in some ways similar to SCSI. Only two nodes, the **initiator** and the **responder**, can use the bus at a time. When an initiator wants to use the bus, it places a special signal called ARB(x) on the bus. This means that device *x* wishes to arbitrate for control of the bus. If no other device has control of the bus, each node in the loop forwards the ARB(x) to its next upstream neighbor until the packet eventually gets back to the initiator. When the initiator sees its ARB(x) unchanged on the bus, it knows that it has won control.

If another device has control of the loop, the ARB(x) packet will be changed to an ARB(F0) before it gets back to the initiator. The initiator then tries again. If two devices attempt to get control of the bus at the same instant, the one with the highest node number wins and the other tries again later.

The initiator claims control of the bus by opening a connection with a responder. This is done by sending an OPN(yy) (for full-duplex) or OPN(yx) (for half-duplex) command. Upon receiving the OPN(??) command, the responder enters the "ready" state and notifies the initiator by sending the "receiver ready" (R_RDY) command to the initiator. Once the data transfer is complete, the initiator issues a "close" command (CLS) to relinquish control of the loop.

The specifics of the data transfer protocol depend on what class of service is being used in the loop or fabric. Some classes require that packets be acknowledged (for maximum accuracy) and some do not (for maximum speed).

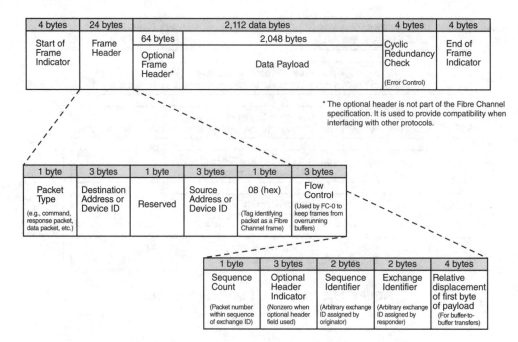

FIGURE 13.9 The Fibre Channel Protocol Packet

At this writing, there are five classes of service defined for Fibre Channel data transfers. Not all of these classes of service have been implemented in real products. Furthermore, some classes of service can be intermixed if there is sufficient bandwidth available. Some implementations allow Class 2 and Class 3 frames to be transmitted when the loop or channel is not being used for Class 1 traffic. Table 13.3 summarizes the various classes of service presently defined for Fibre Channel.

13.3 INTERNET SCSI

Along with its superb performance and expansion capabilities, Fibre Channel comes with major drawbacks: Its hardware components are costly, and the Fibre Channel protocol presents a formidable learning curve. These factors, along with the continuous improvements taking place in less expensive technologies, are providing fertile ground for the growth of several alternatives for high-performance enterprise storage. One of the most widely heralded is **Internet SCSI (iSCSI)**, which capitalizes on well-understood Internet and LAN protocols to provide fast, reliable transport services for SCSI commands and data.

The general idea behind iSCSI is to replace the SCSI bus with the Internet, as shown in Figure 13.10. Although the concept is simple, the protocol overhead is substantial. When a host sends data to an iSCSI disk array, the SCSI data is encapsulated as an iSCSI payload, which in turn is a payload for TCP. The TCP packet is placed inside one or more IP packets, which itself is a payload in one

Class	Description
1	Dedicated connection with acknowledgment of packets. Not supported by many vendors because of the complexity of connection management.
2	Similar to Class 1 except it does not require dedicated connections. Packets may be delivered out of sequence when they are routed through different paths in the network. Class 2 is suitable for low-traffic, infrequent-burst installations.
3	Connectionless unacknowledged delivery. Packet delivery and sequencing are managed by upper-level protocols. In small networks with ample bandwidth, delivery is usually reliable. Well-suited for FC-AL because of temporary paths negotiated by the protocol.
4	Virtual circuits carved out of the full bandwidth of the network. For example, a 100MBps network could support one 75MBps and one 25MBps connection. Each of these virtual circuits would permit different classes of service. In 2002, no commercial Class 4 products had yet been brought to market.
6	Multicasting from one source with acknowledgment delivery to another source. Useful for video or audio broadcasting. To prevent flooding of the broadcasting node (as would happen using Class 3 connections for broadcasting), a separate node would be placed on the network to manage the broadcast acknowledgments. As of 2002, no Class 6 implementations had been brought to market.

TABLE 13.3   Fibre Channel Classes of Service

or more gigabit Ethernet frames, as shown in Figure 13.11. The Ethernet frames are carried across the network (this trip could be measured in meters or kilometers) to an Ethernet interface on the disk array. The payloads are extracted as the packet works its way up the protocol stack, until it is written to a disk (at last). It's important to keep in mind that a data transfer may span many Ethernet frames because of the limitations of TCP, IP, and various hardware components along the way.

Unlike Fibre Channel, iSCSI has no distance limitations. Theoretically, using iSCSI, you could save a file to a disk drive that appears as if it is local storage to you, but the file could end up actually being stored thousands of miles away. This idea ignores the latency characteristic of long-distance file transfers—that a user can't help but notice. To provide tolerable performance, iSCSI requires the fastest possible network connections (at this writing, 10 gigabit Ethernet is recommended) and hardware-based TCP processors called **TCP offload engines** (**TOE**s).

The Internet presents additional challenges of security and transmission integrity that can be largely ignored in an isolated Fibre Channel installation. However, these issues loom large in iSCSI. iSCSI security measures include transmission encryption and firewalls. Transmission integrity is provided at both the outer

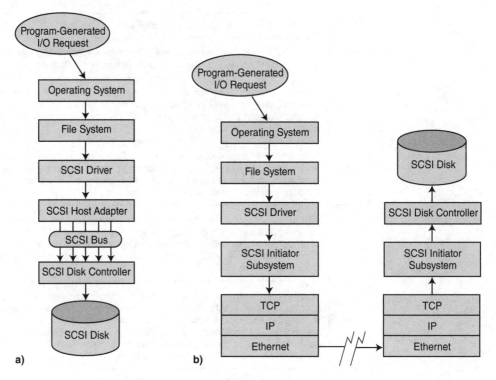

FIGURE 13.10 Replacing the SCSI Bus with the Internet
a) Traditional Parallel SCSI
b) The Protocol Stack of iSCSI

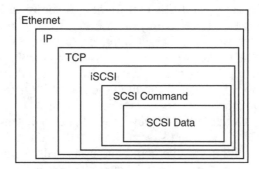

FIGURE 13.11 Internet SCSI Protocol Data Unit (PDU) Encapsulation

protocol levels and inside the iSCSI payload itself, which is protected by a 32-bit CRC. Defective packets are retransmitted unless the TCP or IP session fails, in which case the connection is terminated and reestablished.

An organization does not necessarily have to choose between the exclusive use of iSCSI and Fibre Channel. The two technologies can be combined so that one complements the other. Fibre Channel is best suited for high-throughput applications, and iSCSI for larger pools of less frequently used data. A good use for iSCSI is to provide a cost-effective remote mirror site for a high-availability Fibre Channel installation.

13.4 STORAGE AREA NETWORKS

Fast network connectivity such as provided by Fibre Channel and 10 gigabit Ethernet has enabled construction of dedicated networks built specifically for storage access and management. These networks are called **storage area networks** (**SANs**). SANs logically extend local storage buses, making collections of storage devices accessible to all computer platforms—small, medium, and large. Storage devices can be collocated with the hosts or they can be miles away serving as "hot" backups for a primary processing site.

SANs offer leaner and faster access to large amounts of storage than can be provided by the **network attached storage** (**NAS**) model. In a typical NAS system, all file accesses must pass through a particular file server, incurring all of the protocol overhead and traffic congestion associated with the network. The disk access protocols (SCSI Architecture Model-3 commands) are embedded within the network packets, giving two layers of protocol overhead and two iterations of packet assembly/disassembly.

SANs, sometimes called "the networks behind the network," are isolated from ordinary network traffic. Fibre Channel storage networks (either switched or FC-AL) are potentially much faster than NAS systems because they have only one protocol stack to traverse. They therefore bypass traditional file servers, which can throttle network traffic. NAS and SAN configurations are compared in Figures 13.12 and 13.13.

Because Fibre Channel SANs are independent of any particular network protocols (such as Ethernet) or proprietary host attachments, they are accessible through the SAM upper-level protocols by any platform that can be configured to recognize the SAN storage devices. Even in the most complex SANs, storage management is greatly simplified because all storage is on a single SAN (as opposed to sundry file servers and disk arrays). Data can be vaulted at remote sites through electronic transfer or backed up to tape without interfering with network or host operations. Because of their speed, flexibility, and robustness, SANs are becoming the first choice for providing high-availability, multiterabyte storage to large user communities.

13.5 OTHER I/O CONNECTIONS

A number of I/O architectures lie outside the realm of the SCSI-3 architecture model but can interface with it to some degree. The most popular of these is the **AT Attachment** (**ATA**) used in most low-end computers. Others, designed for computer architectures apart from the Intel paradigm, have found wide application on various platform types. We describe a few of the more popular I/O connections in the sections that follow.

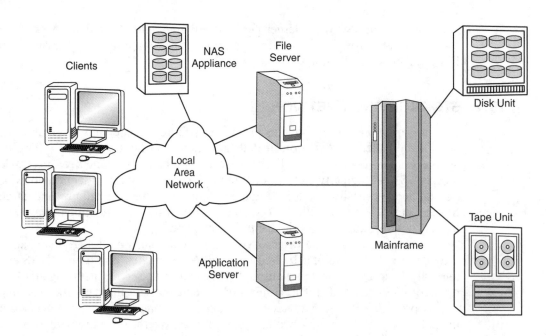

FIGURE 13.12   Network Attached Storage

13.5.1   Parallel Buses: XT to ATA

The first IBM PCs were supported by an 8-bit bus called the PC/XT bus. This bus was accepted by the IEEE and renamed the **Industry Standard Architecture (ISA)** bus. It originally operated at 2.38MBps, and it required two cycles to access a 16-bit memory address because of its narrow width. Because the XT ran at 4.77MHz, the XT bus offered adequate performance. With the introduction of the PC/AT ("AT" for Advanced Technology) with its faster 80286 processor, it was obvious that an 8-bit bus would no longer be useful. The immediate solution was to widen the bus to 16 data lines, increase its clock rate to 8MHz, and call it an "AT bus." It wasn't long, however, before the new AT bus became a serious system bottleneck as microprocessor speeds began exceeding 25MHz.

Several solutions to this problem have been marketed over the years. The most enduring of these is an incarnation of the AT bus—with several variations—known as **AT Attachment (ATA)**, **ATAPI**, **Fast ATA**, and **EIDE**. The latter abbreviation stands for **Enhanced Integrated Drive Electronics**, so-called because much of the controlling function that would normally be placed in a disk drive interface card was moved into the control circuits of the disk drive itself. The ATA offers downward compatibility with 16-bit AT interface cards, while permitting 32-bit interfaces for disk drives and other devices. No external devices can be directly connected to an ATA bus. The number of internal devices is limited to four. Depending on whether programmed I/O or DMA I/O is used, the ATA bus can support 22MBps or 16.7MBps transfer rates with a theoretical

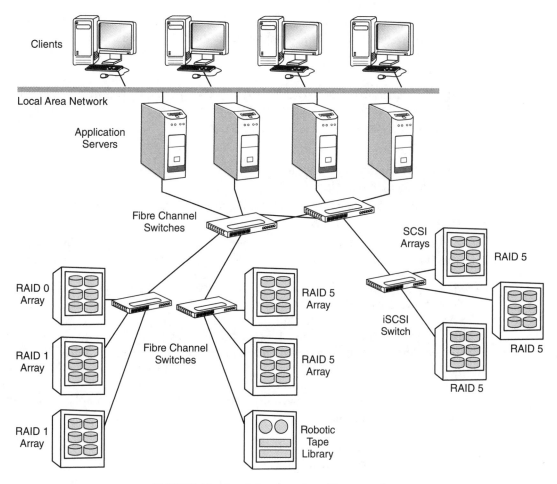

FIGURE 13.13   A Storage Area Network (SAN)

maximum of 100MBps. Ultra ATA provides burst rate transfers of 133MBps. At these speeds, ATA provides one of the most favorable cost-performance ratios for small system buses in the market today.

13.5.2   Serial ATA and Serial Attached SCSI

Notwithstanding its satisfactory performance and low cost, ATA is starting to fade from the small system scene. As processor speeds increase, even Ultra ATA starts to become a bottleneck. Moreover, faster processors generate a great deal of heat, which must be moved away from the processor and other sensitive components. Anything that impedes airflow inside the main system housing is problematic, and the two-inch flat cabling of parallel ATA is certainly no help. With this in mind, the next-generation ATA interface was designed as a serial interface. The **serial ATA**, or **SATA**, interface supports much faster transfer rates than parallel attachments can reliably provide, and it requires only seven conductors (four for data, three for grounding) that fit nicely in a quarter-inch cable.

Besides having thinner cabling, the many attractive features of SATA include:

- Faster data transfer than parallel ATA: 300MBps versus 133MBps (burst rate); faster SATA speeds are expected in the near future
- Lower voltage: 500mV versus 3.0 or 5.0V
- Longer cables: 1m versus 0.5m
- Software compatibility with parallel ATA—no changes to drivers, BIOS, or operating systems required
- Enhanced error checking: 32-bit CRC for all bits, as opposed to data—only CRC for parallel Ultra ATA
- Point-to-point configuration, as opposed to master–slave, enables various devices along the interface to pass data concurrently

Many of these improvements to ATA have also been carried over to a serial version of SCSI called **serial attached SCSI**, or **SAS**. The plugs and cabling of SAS are identical to SATA, and for systems that support both ATA and SCSI, the devices distinguish themselves to the host at power-up time. SAS drives connect through a backplane bus that moves data at rates up to 300MBps (with faster speeds planned). SAS is hugely scalable, with more than 16,000 devices theoretically possible within one domain. With all these advantages, it is clear that it is only a matter of time until SAS and SATA drives completely replace their parallel counterparts.

13.5.3 Peripheral Component Interconnect

By 1992, the AT bus had become the major inhibiting factor with regard to overall small system performance. Fearing that the AT bus had reached the end of its useful life, Intel sponsored an industry group charged with devising a faster and more flexible I/O bus for small systems. The result of their efforts is the **Peripheral Component Interconnect** (**PCI**).

The PCI bus is an extension to the system data bus, supplanting any other I/O bus on the system. PCI runs as fast as 66MHz at the full width of a CPU word. Data throughput is therefore theoretically 264MBps for a 32-bit CPU (66MHz $\times$ (32 bits $\div$ 8 bits/byte) = 264MBps). For a 64-bit bus running at 66MHz, the maximum transfer rate is 528MBps. Although PCI connects to the system bus, it can autonomously negotiate bus speeds and data transfers without CPU intervention. PCI is fast and flexible. Versions of PCI are used in small home computers as well as large, high-performance systems that support data acquisition and scientific research.

13.5.4 A Serial Interface: USB

The **Universal Serial Bus** (**USB**) isn't really a bus, but it is universal. USB is a serial peripheral interface that—in one form or another—is provided on practically every electronic consumer product that is rechargeable or stores data. The family of USB specifications is under the control of a consortium of equipment manufacturers called the **USB Implementers Forum** (**USB-IF**). There have been three major releases of USB starting with USB 1.0 in 1996 to the most current, USB 3.1, in 2013. Speeds have increased from the 12 Mbps offered by USB 1.0 to 10 Gbps for USB 3.1 in *Superspeed+* mode. The 280 Mbps speed provided by the ubiquitous USB 2.0 is sufficient for most everyday file transfers. USB 3.1 is better suited for bulk transfers such as disk backups and isochronous transfers such as video streaming. USB 3.1 is backward compatible with all versions to USB 2.0.

USB requires an adapter card in the host called a **root hub**. The root hub connects to one or more external multiport hubs that can connect directly to a large variety of peripheral devices, including video cameras and telephones. Multiport hubs can be cascaded off one another up to five deep, supporting as many as 127 devices through a single root hub. Properly equipped devices can be daisy-chained and addressed by the host through their respective unique device IDs.

The goal of USB was to make attaching peripheral devices as easy as "plugging a telephone into a wall jack," and it has achieved this goal despite the proliferation of device types that has occurred in the past decade. The joys of USB's plug-and-play capabilities are lost on those who have never known the agony of resolving conflicting interrupt request vectors and rewiring cables that required a few pin swaps. USB achieves its plug-and-play feat through publication of device driver software and a host–device protocol that associates devices with their respective drivers.

Several steps must take place when a device is plugged into a host system:

1. When a device is plugged into a USB port, the electrical state of the port is changed. The host system detects this change and dispatches a reset packet back to the device.

2. The host requests the device's Device Descriptor information. This information includes the device type, device manufacturer's code (assigned by the USB-IF), the manufacturer's product ID, and the USB specification number (e.g., 1.0, 2.0, etc.)

3. As soon as the host is able to do so, it loads the device driver that corresponds to the product ID.

4. The host may request one or more Configuration Descriptors from the device. This step is necessary whenever there is more than one configuration available at the device.

5. Once everything is known about the characteristics of the device and the appropriate driver is loaded, the host dispatches an address assignment to the device. Both the host and the device are now ready to negotiate data transfers.

USB supports four different data transfer modes, each having its respective underlying protocol:

Control transfers—Protocol exchanges between the host and the device, such as plug-and-play, and setups for other transfer types.

Isochronous transfers—Time-sensitive data transfers such as music and video.

Interrupt transfers—Bursty data movement such as the ones generated by mice and keyboards.

Bulk transfers—Transfers between the host and bulk devices such as flash drives, cameras, and scanners.

USB cables require only four conductors: two for data transfer, one for power (+5V), and one for ground. USB 3.0 augments these four with six more: four dedicated for signaling, a signal ground, and one for managing USB on-the-go. **USB On-the-Go** (**USB OTG**), available since USB 1.1, allows a device to act as both a host and a slave device within the same connection. Tablet computers commonly utilize USB OTG, because they can be hosts to external devices like keyboards, or slave devices to desktop computers when files are being transferred.

Portable device manufacturers were quick to exploit the 5V at 500mA power readily available at ubiquitous USB 2.0 ports, and they soon became charging stations for every type of portable device. (USB 3.0 supplies 900mA.) In response, the USB-IF published its *Battery Charging Specification* in 2009. The Forum observed, "USB has evolved from a data interface capable of supplying limited power to a primary provider of power with a data interface." This specification includes a plug-and-play feature to determine the optimal means by which to charge the attached device.

The main objection to USB 1.0 was its slow data transfer rate, so computer manufacturers were slow to adopt it for anything other than keyboards and mice. Since then, data transfer rates have been steadily climbing to 10Gbps for USB 3.1. The evolution of these data rates is shown in Table 13.4.

USB is arguably the most important and successful computer interface. No other type of connectivity has found its way into, such a wide variety of device types, from the smallest MP3 players, to smartphones, to file servers. It has achieved this penetration through its performance and ease of use. It is also a shining example of what can be achieved through standardization and cooperation within the equipment manufacturing industry.

USB Version	Year	Maximum Speed
1.0	1996	12Mbit/s
2.0	2000	480Mbit/s
3.0	2008	5Gbit/s
3.1	2013	10Gbit/s

TABLE 13.4   Data Rates of Several USB Versions

13.6 CLOUD STORAGE

Cloud storage builds on the Cloud computing idea mentioned in Chapters 1 and 9. Cloud storage provides a scalable data storage platform that is accessible via the Internet. Similar to Cloud computing, the idea behind Cloud storage is that one pays only for the storage one uses. Capacity is *elastic*: It can be allocated and deallocated on demand. The servers are configured in redundant clusters to provide failover protection and a scalable architecture.

Cloud storage capabilities vary considerably according to the ways in which it will be used by its customer. Consumer-grade storage provides a convenient platform that subscribers may access from anywhere in the world. Several well-known providers in this area include Amazon Cloud Drive, Apple iCloud, Dropbox, Microsoft SkyDrive, and CX, to name only a few. As of late 2013, prices are between $0.04 and $0.12 per gigabyte per month, depending on features. Most of these providers offer a small amount of storage space for free, only charging after certain thresholds are reached.

Enterprise-class Cloud storage bills itself as a platform suitable for storing an organization's most precious asset: its data. This data must be accessible when needed and must be protected from unauthorized access. The enterprise must be able to control who has access to its data at any given time. Unlike consumer-grade Cloud services, enterprise-grade Cloud storage must meet certain agreed-upon performance requirements. The providers' fees are based on the service parameters and the amount of data stored. For example, one major provider advertised its product with a tenfold price difference between the lowest- and highest-level performance specifications. Because of the wide price variations caused by these performance parameters, service-level agreements (SLAs) can be put in place to make sure the purchaser gets his money's worth. SLAs state specific monetary penalties that the Cloud storage provider incurs when the performance parameters are not met. These parameters typically include (among others) the following:

- **Availability**—Usually stated in terms of percentage of uptime based on 24-hour days in a service month. This category also includes disaster recovery considerations such as the number of disaster drills conducted in a year and the amount of time required to restore service to full capacity.

- **Reliability**—Concerns itself with the number of read and write errors during a service month.

- **Responsiveness**—Typically measured in average seconds per transaction. This metric might also be qualified as to peak- and nonpeak-period response times.

- **Manageability**—Determines to what extent the service consumer can control the configuration and allocation of the storage elements. How difficult is it to expand or contract the amount of storage utilized?

- **Security**—States the types of controls put in place by the Cloud provider and consumer. SLAs can include penalties for data breaches; however, they rarely cover the actual costs of the breach.

In comparing Cloud storage providers, total cost of ownership must be determined. Providers' fees might not be limited to simply costs per gigabyte of storage. Separate charges could be assessed for number of I/O operations per month, bandwidth consumed, and technical support services, as well as "transition fees" that are incurred just for moving data into the providers' Cloud infrastructure.

Nearly every major technology company has some sort of enterprise Cloud storage offering. As of late 2013, the leaders are Amazon's Simple Storage Service (S3), Google, HP, and Microsoft. Even at their highest levels, the prices charged by these companies are a fraction of the total cost of ownership of a data storage facility. Thus, the costs are quite tempting to CIOs under continued pressure to deliver more services for less money.

As with anything, there are downsides to moving to Cloud storage. The greatest of all is that storing one's critical data in the Cloud is fraught with risk. First, there's the risk of availability. Handing over control of one's data infrastructure to an outside company means entering into contracts that include SLAs that must be monitored and enforced. Then there's the risk of the outside company going insolvent. The greatest impediment of all concerns security: It is simply not possible to provide the same security in the Cloud as in a fortified, company-controlled data center. Barriers presented by various government and financial regulations, such as HIPAA and Sarbanes-Oxley, are formidable. Surely, companies will be using the Cloud for storage, but will likely be doing so in small ways for the foreseeable future.

CHAPTER SUMMARY

This chapter has outlined some popular I/O architectures suitable for large and small systems. SCSI-2, ATA, SATA, EIDE, PCI, USB, and IEEE 1394 are suitable for small systems. Fibre Channel and some of the SAM-3 protocols were designed for large, high-capacity systems. The SCSI Architecture Model-3 has defined numerous high-speed interfaces. Aspects of SCSI Architecture Model-3 overlap into the area of data communications because computers and storage systems continue to become more interconnected. For ease of reference, we have provided a summary of the storage interconnections discussed in this chapter in Table 13.5.

Fibre Channel is one of the fastest interface protocols, and it is the first choice for deployment in server farms. However, other protocols are on the horizon, including iSCSI and SATA. It is certain that the industry is replacing parallel interfaces with serial interfaces. This change is driven by the need for speed, the general compatibility of serial protocols with any number of physical interconnection methods, and—in the case of SATA—the need to control heat inside the CPU cabinet.

A new growth industry is emerging around the concepts of "managed storage" and "storage services," where third parties take care of short- and long-term disk storage management for client companies. One can expect that this area of

Interface	Max. Cable Length Between Devices	Maximum Data Rate	Maximum Devices per Controller
ATA	0.9m	133MBps	4
FC-AL	Copper: 50m (165ft) Fiber: 10km (6mi)	25MBps 100MBps	127
IEEE 1394	4.5m (15ft)	480MBps	63
SCSI	12m	320MBps	16
Serial ATA	1m (3ft)	300MBps	15
Serial SCSI	6m (18ft)	300MBps	16,256 (with expanders)
SSA	Copper: 20m (66ft) Fiber: 680m (0.4mi)	40MBps	129
USB 3.1	5m (16.5ft)	10GBps	127

TABLE 13.5   A Summary of Various I/O Interfaces

outsourced services will continue to grow, bringing with it many new ideas, protocols, and architectures to include trustworthy Cloud storage.

FURTHER READING

Because SCSI has been around for such a long time, it is the topic of numerous books, including those by Schmidt (1999) and Field and Ridge (1999). Field and Ridge's SCSI book is noteworthy for its readability. An excellent introduction to SAN and NAS systems is written by Spalding (2003). Tate et al. (2005) contains a good introduction and detailed information about specific products that will improve your understanding of the technology. The books by Clark (1999) and Thornburgh (1999) are very good introductions to Fibre Channel SANs. No-hype introductions to Cloud storage can be found in the papers by Abadi (2009) and Buyya (2009). Goldner (2003) provides a concise discussion of iSCSI. The technical details of iSCSI can be found in Internet RFC 3720 (www.ietf.org). The SCSI Architecture Model-3 is nicely explained by Reidel and Goldner (2003). A great deal of storage and interface information can be found on the InterNational Committee on Information Technology Standards (INCITS) websites: INCITS T10 working group (www.t10.org) is the oversight group for SCSI, T11 (www.t11.org) deals with Fibre Channel and HiPPI, and T13 (www.t13.org) concerns itself with ATA. Other sources of technical information include the SCSI Trade Association (www.scsita.org), the USB Implementers Forum (www.usb.org), the Storage Networking Industry Association (www.snia.org), and the Serial ATA International Organization (www.serialata.org). Good sites for storage news include www.byteandswitch.com, www.wwpi.com (*Computer Technology Review*), and www.storagemagazine.techtarget.com.

Axelson has published an entire series of detailed books on the subject of the USB interface. Her *USB Complete* (2009) is an ideal starting point in the series. It includes a clear and thorough description of USB architecture and protocols. Code samples are provided to aid the reader in interfacing with various types of USB devices. A wealth of information can also be found on the official USB website: www.usb.org.

Intended as a graduate text, Hill et al. (2013) in their *Guide to Cloud Computing* succinctly describe Cloud architectures, including many examples from the major providers. The chapter on data in the Cloud is outstanding in its discussion of the ways in which Cloud data architectures differ from traditional architectures. The authors' presentation of various trade-offs involved with Cloud storage is especially noteworthy. Practitioners may find Erl et al. (2013) useful in its focus on business issues including delivery models, governance, and economics of Cloud. In a similar work, Schultz (2011) describes Cloud storage in the context of the storage hierarchy as well as the computing services hierarchy. The IEEE maintains an educational Cloud computing portal at www.cloudcomputing.ieee.org.

REFERENCES

Abadi, D. "Data Management in the Cloud: Limitations and Opportunities." *IEEE Data Engineering Bulletin, 32*:1, 2009, pp. 3–12.

Axelson, J. *USB Complete: The Developer's Guide*. Madison, WI: Lakeview Research, 2009.

Buyya, R. "Market-Oriented Cloud Computing: Vision, Hype, and Reality of Delivering Computing as the 5th Utility." *Proceedings of the 2009 9th IEEE/ACM International Symposium on Cluster Computing and the Grid* (May 18–21, 2009). CCGRID.IEEE Computer Society, Washington, DC.

Clark, T. *Designing Storage Area Networks: A Practical Guide for Implementing Fibre Channel SANs*. Reading, MA: Addison-Wesley-Longman, 1999.

Erl, T., Ricardo, P., & Zaigham, M. *Cloud Computing: Concepts, Technology & Architecture*. Vancouver, BC: Arcitura, 2013.

Field, G., Ridge, P., et al. *The Book of SCSI: I/O for the New Millennium,* 2nd ed. San Francisco, CA: No Starch Press, 1999.

Goldner, J. S. "The Emergence of iSCSI." *ACM Queue,* June 2003, pp. 44–53.

Hill, R., Hirsch, L., Lake, P., & Moshiri, S. *Guide to Cloud Computing: Principles and Practice*. London: Springer-Verlag, 2013.

Reidel, E., & Goldner, J. S. "Storage Systems: Not Just a Bunch of Disks Anymore." *ACM Queue,* June 2003, pp. 32–41.

Schmidt, F., *The SCSI Bus and IDE Interface,* 2nd ed. Reading, MA: Addison-Wesley, 1999.

Schultz, G. *Cloud and Virtual Data Storage Networking*. Boca Raton, FL: Auerbach Publications, 2011.

Spalding, R. *Storage Networks: The Complete Reference*. Boston, MA: McGraw-Hill, 2003.

Tate, J., Kanth, R., & Telles, A. *Introduction to Storage Area Networks,* 3rd ed. IBM Redbook SG24-5470-02. San Jose, CA: IBM Corporation, International Technical Support, 2005.

Thornburgh, R. H. *Fibre Channel for Mass Storage*. Hewlett-Packard Professional Books series. Upper Saddle River, NJ: Prentice Hall, 1999.

REVIEW OF ESSENTIAL TERMS AND CONCEPTS

1. What does the acronym SCSI stand for? Does the name still make sense?
2. How is SAM-3 different from classic parallel SCSI?
3. What is another name for IEEE 1394?
4. What drawbacks of SCSI-2 does IEEE 1394 improve upon?
5. Define NAS.
6. Define SAN. How is it different from NAS?
7. Under what circumstances would you consider installing a Fibre Channel SAN?
8. What are the advantages and disadvantages of iSCSI?
9. What is ATA? In what ways is SATA an improvement?
10. What two features of USB make it so desirable for portable devices?

EXERCISES

1. Which of the types of storage architectures discussed in this chapter would you expect to find in a large data center or server farm? What would be the problem with using one of the other architectures in the data center environment?
2. How many SCSI devices can be active after the arbitration phase has completed?
3. Suppose during an asynchronous parallel SCSI data transfer someone removes a floppy disk from the drive that is the intended target of the transfer. How would the initiator know that the error has occurred during these phases:

   - Bus-free
   - Selection
   - Command
   - Data
   - Status
   - Message
   - Reselection

   a) During which of the phases is it possible that good data may be written to the floppy if the data transfer is a "write" operation?

   b) If the transfer is a "read," at which point would the system have good data in the buffer? Would the system ever acknowledge this data?

4. Your manager has decided that the throughput of your file server can be improved by replacing your old SCSI-2 host adapter with a Fast and Wide SCSI-3 adapter. She also decides that the old SCSI-2 drives will be replaced with Fast and Wide SCSI-3 drives that are much larger than the old ones. After all the files from the old SCSI-2 disks have been moved to the SCSI-3 drives, you reformat the old drives so they can be used again somewhere. Upon hearing that you did this, your manager tells you to leave the old SCSI-2 drives in the server, because she knows that SCSI-2 is downward compatible with SCSI-3. Being a good employee, you acquiesce to this demand.

A few days later, however, you are not surprised when your manager expresses disappointment that the SCSI-3 upgrade does not seem to be delivering the performance improvement she expected. What happened? How can you fix it?

◆ **5.** You have just upgraded your system to a Fast and Wide SCSI interface. This system has a floppy disk, a CD-ROM, and five 8GB fixed disks. What is the device number of the host adapter? Why?

6. How does SCSI-2 differ from the principles behind the SCSI Architecture Model-3?

7. What benefits does the SCSI Architecture Model-3 provide to computer and peripheral equipment manufacturers?

8. Suppose you wish to devise a video conferencing system by connecting a number of computers and video cameras together. Which interface model would you choose? Will the protocol packet used to transfer the video be identical to the protocol packet used for data transmission? What protocol information would be in one packet and not in the other?

9. How would an SSA bus configuration recover from a single disk failure? Suppose another node fails before the first one can be fixed. How would the system recover?

10. You have been assigned to a work group that has been given the task of placing automated controls in a chemical plant. Hundreds of sensors will be placed in tanks, vats, and hoppers throughout the factory campus. All data from the sensors will be fed into a group of sufficiently high-powered computers so that plant managers and supervisors can control and monitor the various processes taking place.

What type of interface would you use between the sensors and the computers? If all computers are to have access to all of the sensor input, would you use the same type of connection to interconnect the computers among one another? Which I/O control model would you use?

11. One of the engineers who works for you is proposing changes to the bus architecture of the systems that your company manufactures. She claims that if the bus is modified to support network protocols directly, the systems will have no need for network cards. She claims that you could also eliminate your SAN and connect the client computers directly to the disk array. Would you object to this approach? Explain. Hint: Think of other uses for the main bus besides carrying bytes to and from storage devices.

12. Storage systems increasingly rely on the Internet infrastructure as a transport medium. What are the advantages of this approach? What problems are present in terms of security and reliability?

A civilization flourishes when people plant trees under whose shade they will never sit.

—Greek saying

Data Structures and the Computer

A.1 INTRODUCTION

Throughout this text, we take for granted that our readers understand the basics of computer data structures. Such an understanding is not required for overall comprehension of this text, but it is helpful in grasping some of the more subtle points of computer organization and architecture. This appendix is intended as an extended glossary for readers who have yet to experience a formal introduction to data structures. It can also be used as a refresher for those who studied data structures long ago. With this goal in mind, our treatment here is necessarily brief, and it (of course!) is slanted toward hardware considerations. Readers who wish to delve further into this fascinating study are invited to read any of the books cited in the reference list at the end of this appendix. *As you read through this appendix, you should be aware that all of our memory addresses in the examples are given in hexadecimal.* If you haven't already done so, you should read Chapter 2 before proceeding.

A.2 FUNDAMENTAL STRUCTURES

A.2.1 Arrays

The term **data structure** refers to the manner in which related pieces of information are organized so that executing processes can easily access data as needed. Data structures are often independent of their implementation, as the manner of organization is logical, not necessarily physical.

The simplest of all data structures is the linear array. As you probably know from your programming experience, a linear array is a contiguous area of computer memory to which your program has assigned a name. The group of entities stored in this contiguous area must be homogeneous (they must have the same size and type) and can be addressed individually, typically using subscripting. For example, suppose you have the following Java declaration:

```
char[] charArray[10];
```

The operating system assigns a storage value to the variable `charArray` that represents the **base address** (or beginning address) of the array. Access to subsequent characters is provided through offsets from this base location. The offsets are incremented by the size of the primitive data type of the array, in this case, `char`. Characters in Java are 16 bits wide, so the offset for a character array would be 2 bytes per array element. For example, let's say that the `charArray` structure is stored at address 80A2. The program statement:

```
char aChar = charArray[3];
```

would retrieve the 2 bytes found at memory location 80A8. Because Java indexes its arrays starting with zero, we have just stored the fourth element of the array in the character variable `aChar`:

$$80A2 + \frac{2 \text{ bytes}}{\text{character}} \times 3 \text{ characters offset from base address} = 80A2 + 6 = 80A8.$$

Two-dimensional arrays are linear arrays consisting of one-dimensional arrays, so the memory offset value must take the row size into account, along with the size of the primitive data type of the array. Consider, for example, the following Java declaration:

```
char[] charArray[4][10];
```

Here we are defining four linear arrays that have 10 storage locations each. However, it is much easier to think of this structure as a two-dimensional array of 4 rows and 10 columns. If the base address of `charArray` is still 80A2, then element `charArray[1][4]` would be found at address 80BE. This is because row 0 of the array occupies addresses 80A2 through 80B5, row 1 starts at 80B6, and we are accessing the fifth element of row 2:

$$80B6 + \frac{2 \text{ bytes}}{\text{character}} \times 4 \text{ characters offset from base address} = 80B6 + 8 = 80BE.$$

Array storage is a good choice when the problem that our program solves allows us to home in on a small subset of the array's storage locations. This would be the case if we were writing a backgammon game. For example, each "point" would be a location in the "board" array. The program would inspect only those board points that are legal moves for a particular roll of the dice prior to allowing a move.

Another good application for arrays is a data collection task based on times of the day or days of the month. We might, for example, be counting the number of vehicles that pass a particular point on a highway at different times of the day. If someone later asks for the average traffic flow between 9:00 AM and 9:59 AM, all we need to do is average the tenth element of each 24-hour day's array for the period over which we have collected the data. (Midnight to 1:00 AM is the zeroth element.)

A.2.2   Queues and Linked Lists

Arrays are not very helpful when we are processing items in response to requests for service. Requests for service are usually processed according to the time that the request was made. In other words, first-come, first-served.

Consider a Web server that handles Hypertext Transfer Protocol (HTTP) requests from users connected through the Internet. The sequence of incoming requests may resemble the one shown in Table A.1.

Conceivably, we could place each of these requests into an array and then search the array for the lowest timestamp value when we are ready to service the next request. This implementation would be hopelessly inefficient, however, because each element of the array would need to be interrogated every time. Furthermore, we would risk running out of room in the array if we experience a day with an unusually heavy amount of traffic. For these reasons, a **queue** is the appropriate data structure for first-come, first-served applications. The queue data structure requires that elements be removed in the same order in which they are entered. Waiting lines at banks and supermarkets are good examples of queues.

There are different ways to implement queues, but all queue implementations have four components: a memory variable that points to the first item in the queue (the **head** of the queue), a memory variable that points to the end of the queue (its **tail**), memory locations in which to store the queue items, and a set of operations specific to the queue data structure. The pointer to the head of the queue indicates which item is to be serviced next. The tail pointer is useful for adding items to the end of the queue. When the head pointer is null (zero), the queue is empty. The operations on queues typically include adding an entry to the end of the list (enqueue), deleting an entry from the beginning of the list (dequeue), and checking to see whether the queue is empty.

One popular way of implementing a queue is to use a **linked list**. In a linked list, each item in the queue contains a pointer to the next item in the queue. As

Time	Source Address	HTTP Command
07:22:03	10.122.224.5	http://www.spiffywebsite.com/sitemap.html
07:22:04	10.167.14.190	http://www.spiffywebsite.com/shoppingcart.html
07:22:12	10.148.105.67	http://www.spiffywebsite.com/spiffypix.jpg
07:23:09	10.72.99.56	http://www.spiffywebsite.com/userguide.html

TABLE A.1   HTTP Requests for a Web Server

items are dequeued, the head pointer can use the information found in the node that was just deleted to locate the next node. So, in our Web server example above, after Item 1 is serviced (and removed from the queue), the head-of-queue pointer is set to point to Item 2.

In our example from Table A.1, let's say that the head of the queue is at address 7049, which contains the first HTTP request, *www.spiffywebsite.com/sitemap.html*. The head-of-queue pointer is set to the value 7049. At memory address 7049, we will have the entry:

07:22:03, 10.122.224.5, www.spiffywebsite.com/sitemap.html, 70E6,

where 70E6 is the address of the following item:

07:22:04, 10.167.14.190, www.spiffywebsite.com/shoppingcart.html, 712A.

The entire contents of the queue are shown in Table A.2.

The pointer to the head of the queue is set to 7049, and the tail pointer is set to 81B3. If another user request arrives, the system finds a spot for it in memory and updates the last queue item (to point to the new entry) as well as the tail pointer. You should notice that when this kind of pointer structure is used, unlike arrays, there is no requirement that the data elements be contiguous in memory. This is what enables the structure to grow as needed. Moreover, there is no requirement that the addresses be ascending, as we have shown. The queue elements can be located anywhere in memory. The pointers maintain the order of the queue.

The queue architecture that we have described can be modified to create a fixed-size queue (often called a circular queue), or a **priority queue**, where certain types of entries will jump ahead of the others. Even with these added wrinkles, queues are easy data structures to implement.

A.2.3 Stacks

Queues are sometimes called **FIFO (first-in, first-out)** lists, for obvious reasons. Some applications call for the opposite ordering, or **last-in, first-out (LIFO)**. **Stacks** are appropriate data structures for LIFO ordering. They get their name from their similarity to how cafeterias provide plates to their customers. Cafeteria

Memory Address	Queue Data Element			Pointer to Next Element
7049	07:22:03	10.122.224.5	http://www.spiffywebsite.com/sitemap.html	70E6
...	...	...	...	...
70E6	07:22:04	10.167.14.190	http://www.spiffywebsite.com/shoppingcart.html	712A
...	...	...	...	...
712A	07:22:12	10.148.105.67	http://www.spiffywebsite.com/spiffypix.jpg	81B3
...	...	...	...	...
81B3	07:23:09	10.72.99.56	http://www.spiffywebsite.com/userguide.html	null

TABLE A.2 An HTTP Request Queue Implemented in Memory

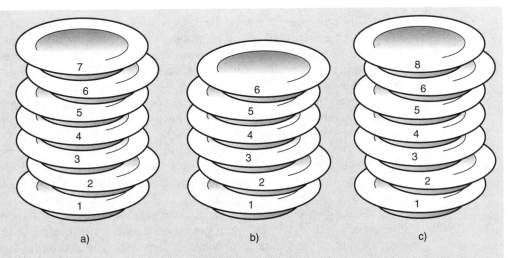

FIGURE A.1   Stacks of Plates
a) The Initial Stack
b) Plate 7 Is Removed (Popped)
c) Plate 8 Is Added (Pushed)

service personnel add hot, wet, clean plates to the top of a spring-loaded tube, pushing the cold, dry plates farther down the tube. The next customer takes a plate from the top of the stack. This sequence is shown in Figure A.1. Figure A.1a shows a stack of plates. The plate numbered 1 was the first one placed on the stack. Plate number 7 was the last. Plate number 7 is the first plate removed, as shown in Figure A.1b. When the next plate arrives, plate number 8, it will go on top of the stack as shown in Figure A.1c. The act of adding an item to a stack is called **push**ing. To remove an item is to **pop** it. To interrogate the top item in a stack, without removing it, is to **peek** at it.

A stack is a useful data structure when you are working your way through a series of nested subroutine calls in a program. If you push the current address on the top of the stack before you branch to the next address, you know that you can return along the same route as you arrived. All you do is pop each address as you need it. As an example from everyday life, say we visit a series of cities in this order:

1. New York, NY
2. Albany, NY
3. Buffalo, NY
4. Erie, PA
5. Pittsburgh, PA
6. Cleveland, OH
7. St. Louis, MO
8. Chicago, IL

From Chicago, how do we get back to New York? A human being would simply pull out a map (and find a more direct route), or would just "know" to find Interstate 80 and head east. Computers certainly aren't as smart as we are. So the easiest thing for a computer to do is to retrace its original route. A stack (like the one shown in Table A.3) is exactly the right data structure for the job. All that the computer needs to do is push the current location on the top of the stack as the route is traversed. The return route is easily found by popping the previous city from the top of the stack.

It is possible to implement stacks in a variety of ways. The most popular software implementations are done via linear arrays and linked lists. System stacks (the hardware versions) are implemented using a fixed memory allocation, which is a block of memory set aside for the exclusive use of the stack. Two memory variables are required to manage the stack. One variable points to the top of the stack (the last item placed on the stack), whereas a second variable keeps count of the number of items in the stack. The maximum stack size (or the highest allowable memory address) is stored as a constant. When an item is pushed onto the stack, the stack pointer (the memory address for the top of the stack) is incremented by the size of the data type that is stored in the stack.

Consider an example where we want to store the last three letters of the alphabet and retrieve them in reverse order. The Java (Unicode) coding for these characters in hexadecimal is:

$$X = 0058, Y = 0059, Z = 005A.$$

Memory addresses 808A through 80CA are reserved for the stack. A constant, MAXSTACK, is set to 20 (hex). Because the stack is initially empty, the stack pointer is set to a null value, and the stack counter is at zero. Table A.4 shows a trace of the stack and its management variables as the three Unicode characters are stored.

To retrieve the data, three pops take place. With each pop, the stack pointer is decremented by two. Of course, with each addition and retrieval, the status of the stack must be checked. We have to be sure that we don't add an item to a stack that is full or try to remove an item from a stack that is empty. Stacks are widely used in computer system firmware and software.

Stack Location	City
7 (top)	St. Louis, MO
6	Cleveland, OH
5	Pittsburgh, PA
4	Erie, PA
3	Buffalo, NY
2	Albany, NY
1	New York, NY

TABLE A.3 A Stack of Visited Cities

Memory Address	Stack Contents
8091	---
8090	---
808F	---
808E	---
808D	---
808C	---
808B	00
808A	58

Top of Stack = 808A
a)

Memory Address	Stack Contents
8091	---
8090	---
808F	---
808E	---
808D	00
808C	59
808B	00
808A	58

Top of Stack = 808C
b)

Memory Address	Stack Contents
8091	---
8090	---
808F	00
808E	5A
808D	00
808C	59
808B	00
808A	58

Top of Stack = 808E
c)

TABLE A.4   Adding the Letters X, Y, and Z to a Stack. (The dashes represent irrelevant memory values.)
   a) X (0058) Is Added and the Stack Pointer Is Incremented by the Size of the Data Element (2 Bytes)
   b) Y (0059) Is Added and the Stack Pointer Is Incremented by 2 Again
   c) Z (005A) Is Added

A.3   TREES

Queues, stacks, and arrays are useful for processing lists of things where the locations of the items in the list (relative to each other) do not change no matter how many items are in the list. Certainly, this is not the nature of many of the data collections that we use in our daily lives. Consider a program that would manage an address book. One useful way of sequencing this data is to keep the list in order by last name. A **binary search** could quickly locate any name in the list, successively limiting the search to half the list. A binary search is shown seeking the name Kleene in the list of famous mathematicians in Figure A.2. We begin by determining the middle of the list (Hilbert) and comparing this value to our key. If they are equal, we have found the desired item. If the key (Kleene) is larger than the item in the middle of the list, we look in the bottom half of the list, as shown in Figure A.2b. (This effectively reduces our search space by half.) Now we determine the new middle (Markov) of the bottom half of the list. If our key (Kleene) is smaller than this new middle, we throw out the bottom half of this list and keep the top half, as in Figure A.2c. If our key has still not been found, we divide the list in half again. In this way, we successively divide the list in half until we find our key (or determine that it is not in the list). This example was contrived to show a worst-case situation. It took 4 operations to locate a key in a list of 16 items. If it happened that we were looking for Hilbert, we'd have found him on the first try. No matter how large the list is, any name could be located in time proportionate to the base 2 logarithm of the number of items in the list.

Clearly, a binary search requires that the data be sequenced by its key values. So what happens when we want to add a name to our address book? We must put

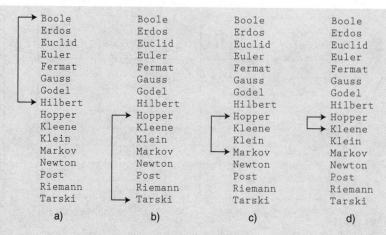

FIGURE A.2   A Binary Search for Kleene

it in its proper place so that we can reliably use the binary search. If the book is stored in a linear array, then we can quite easily figure out where the new element belongs, say at position *k*. But to insert this item, we must make room for it in the array. This means that we must first move all of the items at locations *k* through *n* (the last item in the book) to locations *k* + 1 through *n* + 1. If the address book is large, this shifting process would probably be slower than we would like. Furthermore, if the array can hold only *n* items, we are in big trouble. A new array will have to be defined and then loaded from the old one, consuming even more time.

A linked list implementation won't work very well either, because the midpoint of the list is hard to find. The only way to search a linked list is to follow the chain of list items until you find the spot where the new item should be. If you have a long list, linear searches are operationally infeasible—they won't happen fast enough to make anyone happy.

So a good data structure for keeping ordered, maintainable lists is one that allows us to find things quickly yet add and delete items without excessive overhead. There are several data structures that fit the bill. The simplest of these is the **binary tree**. Like linked lists, binary trees keep track of adjacent data items through the use of pointers to memory locations. And, like linked lists, they can grow arbitrarily large. But this growth is done in such a way that it's easy to retrieve any key from the tree. Binary trees are called *binary* because in their graphical representation, each node (or vertex) has at most two descendant (**child**) nodes. (Trees with more than two descendant nodes are called ***n*-ary trees**.) Some example binary trees are shown in Figure A.3. Don't let it bother you that these graphics look like upside-down trees—they are trees in the mathematical sense. Each node is connected to the graph (meaning that every node is reachable from the first node), and the graph contains no **cycles** (meaning that we can't end up going in circles as we're looking for things).

The topmost node of a tree is its **root**. The root is the only part of a tree that has to be kept track of independently. All other nodes are referenced through the

a)   b)   c)

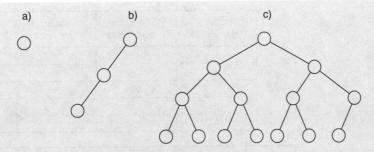

FIGURE A.3   Some Binary Trees

root using two memory pointer values stored in each node. Each pointer indicates where the node's **left child** or **right child** node can be found. The **leaves** of a tree, nodes at the very bottom of the structure, have null values for their child nodes. The distance, the number of *levels*, from the leaves to the root of a tree is called its **height**. Nodes that are not leaves are called **internal nodes** of the tree. Internal nodes have at least one **subtree** (even if it's a leaf).

In addition to pointers, the nodes of a binary tree contain data (or data key values) around which a tree is structured. Binary trees are often organized so that all key values smaller than the key value at a particular node are stored in its left subtree, and all key values greater than or equal to the key value are stored in its right subtree. Figure A.4 shows an example of this idea.

The binary tree shown in Figure A.4 is also a **balanced** binary tree. Formally, when a binary tree is balanced, the depth of the left and right subtree of every node differs by at most 1. What is significant about this is that any data item referenced by the tree can be located in time proportionate to the base 2 logarithm of the number of nodes in the tree. So a tree containing 65,535 data keys requires at most 15 memory operations to find any particular element (or to determine that it's not there). Unlike sorted lists kept in linear arrays (which give the same running time for a search) it is much easier to maintain the set of key values in binary trees. To insert an element, all we do is rearrange a few memory pointers, rather than restructure the entire list. The running time for both inserting and deleting a node from a balanced binary tree is also proportionate to the base 2 logarithm of the number of items in the tree. Thus, this data structure is much better than an array or simple linked list for maintaining a group of sorted data elements.

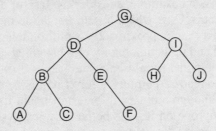

FIGURE A.4   An Ordered Binary Tree with Nondecreasing Key Values

Character (Key value)	ASCII Code (Hexadecimal)	Character (Key value)	ASCII Code (Hexadecimal)
A	41	F	46
B	42	G	47
C	43	H	48
D	44	I	49
E	45	J	4A

	0	1	2	3	4	5	6	7	8	9	A	B	C	D	E	F
0	--	--	--	--	--	--	--	00	46	00	--	--	00	45	07	--
1	00	43	00	--	00	48	00	--	--	--	--	--	--	--	--	--
2	--	00	4A	00	--	2B	44	0C	--	--	--	31	42	10	--	--
3	--	00	41	00	--	--	25	47	3B	--	--	14	49	21	--	--

TABLE A.5   The Memory Map for the Binary Tree in Figure A.4

Although our graphics make it easy to conceptualize the logical structure of a tree, it is good to keep in mind that computer memory is linear, so our picture is only an abstraction. In Table A.5, we have provided a map of 64 bytes of memory that store the tree in Figure A.4. For convenience of reading, we show them in a tabular format. For example, the hex address of the byte located in the column with label 5 (which we will refer to as Column 5) of the row with label 1 (Row 1) is 15. Row 0, Column 0 refers to address 0. The node keys are coded in hexadecimal ASCII, as shown in the table above the memory map.

In our memory map, the root of the tree is located at addresses 36 through 38 (Row 3, Columns 6–8). Its key value is at address 37. The left subtree (child) of the root is found at address 25, and the right subtree at address 3B. If we look at address 3B, we find the key, I, with its left child at address 14 and its right child at address 21. At address 21, we find the leaf node, J, having zeroes for both of its child pointers.

Binary trees are useful in many applications such as compilers and assemblers. (See Chapter 8.) However, when it comes to storing and retrieving key values from very large data sets, several data structures are superior to binary trees. As an example, consider the task of designing an online telephone book for New York City, which has a population of just over 8 million people. Assuming that there are approximately 8 million telephone numbers to put in our book, we would end up with a binary tree having at least 23 levels. Furthermore, more than half the nodes would be at the leaves, meaning that most of the time, we would have to read 22 pointers before finding the desired number.

Although a binary tree design is not totally dreadful for this application, we can improve on it. One better way involves an *n*-ary tree structure called a **trie** (pronounced "try"). Instead of storing an entire key value in each node, tries use fragments of the keys. The key value is assembled as a search proceeds down the trie. Internal nodes contain a sufficient number of pointers to direct a search to the desired key or to the next level of the trie. Tries are particularly suitable for data having variable-length keys, such as our telephone book example. Shorter keys are near the top, whereas longer keys are at the bottom of the data structure.

In Figure A.5, we have depicted a trie containing the names of famous mathematicians. The diagram implies that every internal node contains 26 letters. The nature of our data suggests that there are more efficient trie structures than the one shown. (We observe that it is hard to find a famous mathematician whose name begins with ZQX.) In fact, designing an internal node structure is the hardest part of trie construction. Depending on the key values, more than one character can be used as an index. For example, suppose that instead of containing each letter of the alphabet as a single unit, we could use groups of letters. By changing the multiplicity of the keys in the root node of the trie in Figure A.5, the trie can be made flatter by one level. This modification is shown in Figure A.6. A consequence of flattening the trie is that searching can be done faster, if such flattening is done carefully. In Figure A.6, we chose to roll up only two keys, *ER* and *EU*, to eliminate one level. If we had doubled up every key, the root would

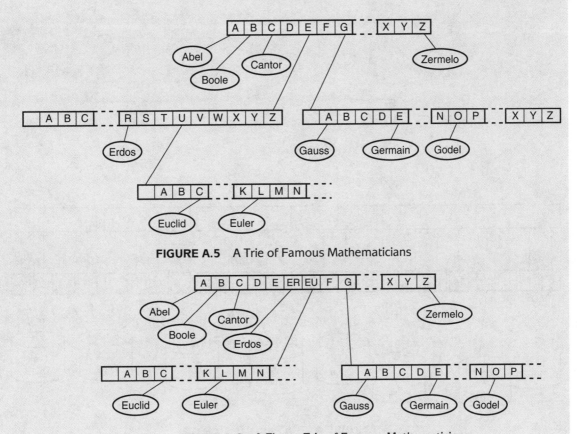

FIGURE A.5 A Trie of Famous Mathematicians

FIGURE A.6 A Flatter Trie of Famous Mathematicians

contain 676 keys (*AA* through *ZZ*), making the data structure unnecessarily large and unwieldy with respect to the amount of data that it stores.

In practice, structures for storage and retrieval of large amounts of data are designed with more consideration to the medium on which they will be stored than to the nature of the data itself. Often, index nodes are contrived so that some integral number of internal nodes at one level of the tree is accessible through one read operation of the disk drive on which the index is stored. One such data structure is a B+ tree, which is used in large database systems.

A **B+ tree** is a hierarchical structure consisting of pointers to index structures or actual data records. As records are added and deleted from the database, leaves in the B+ tree are updated. Additional branches (internal nodes) are spawned when updates to existing leaves are not possible. The internal nodes of a B+ tree are collectively referred to as its **index part**, whereas the leaf nodes are called the **sequence part**, because they will always be in sequential order. A schematic of a portion of a B+ tree is shown in Figure A.7.

The numbers shown in the diagram are record key values. Along with each key value in the leaf node of a B+ tree, the database management system (see

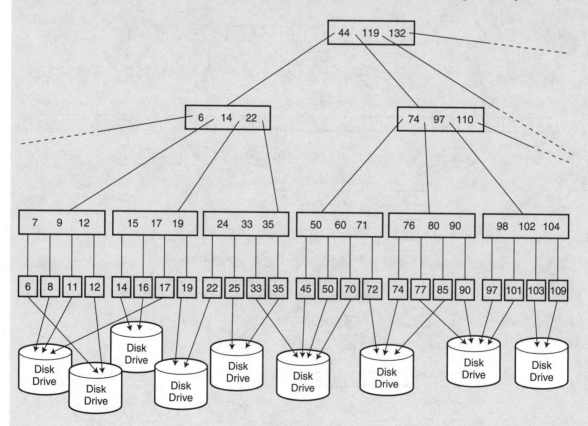

FIGURE A.7   A Partial B+ Tree

Chapter 8) maintains a pointer to the location of the physical record. This pointer value is used by the operating system to retrieve the record from the disk. So the physical record can be located virtually anywhere, but the sequence part of the data structure always stays in order. Traversal of the B+ tree assures us that any record can be located quickly based on its key value.

To locate a key value using the B+ tree shown in Figure A.7, all we need to do is compare the desired value with the values stored in the internal nodes. When a key value is less than the value of a key in an internal node, the tree is traversed to the left. Accordingly, retrieving a value greater than or equal to an internal node's key value requires that we traverse the tree to the right. When an internal node has reached its capacity, and we need to add a record to the database, additional levels are added to the hierarchy. Record deletion, however, does not cause an immediate flattening of the tree, just a movement of pointers. B+ tree hierarchies are flattened during a process called **database reorganization** (or **reorg**). Reorgs can be exceedingly time-consuming in large databases, so they are usually performed only when absolutely necessary.

The best database indexing methods take into account the underlying storage architecture of the systems on which they run. In particular, for best system performance, disk reads must be kept to a minimum. (See Chapter 11.) Unless a substantial part of a data file's index is cached in memory, record accesses require at least two read operations: one to read the index and another to retrieve the record. For B+ tree indices on highly active files, the first few levels of the tree are read from cache memory rather than from disk. Thus, disk reads are required only when retrieving lower index tree levels and the data record itself.

A.4 NETWORK GRAPHS

By definition, tree structures contain no cycles. This makes trees useful for data storage and retrieval, a simple task in terms of computational complexity. Harder problems require more complex structures. Consider, for example, the routing problem that we presented in Section A.2, where we need to find a return path from Chicago to New York. We never said anything about finding the shortest path, only that it was easiest to simply retrace our steps. Finding the shortest path, or an optimal path, requires a different kind of data structure, one that allows cycles.

An n-ary tree can be changed into a more general network graph by allowing leaf nodes to point to each other. But now we have to allow for the fact that it is possible for any node to point to the remaining $n - 1$ nodes in the graph. If we simply extend the binary tree data structure to allow for a network data structure, each node would need $n - 1$ pointers. We can do better.

If the network in question is static, that is, it neither gains nor loses nodes through the execution of our algorithm, it can be represented using an **adjacency matrix**. An adjacency matrix is a two-dimensional array with a row and column for each node. Consider the graph shown in Figure A.8a. It has six interconnected nodes. The connections (**edges**) between the nodes of the graph are indicated by a 1 in the adjacency matrix, where the column of one node and the row of the other intersect. The completed adjacency matrix is shown in Figure A.8b.

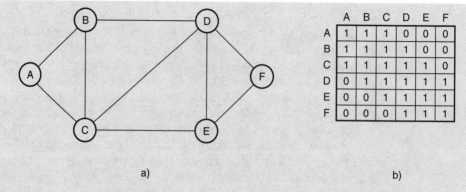

FIGURE A.8   a) A General Graph
b) The Graph's Adjacency Matrix

Let's return to our example of finding an optimal route between two cities. We represent the map as a graph with **weighted** edges. The weights on the edges correspond to the distance, or "cost" of going from one city to another. Instead of entering 1s in the adjacency matrix, these traveling costs are entered where a route between two cities exists.

It is also possible to represent a connected graph as a linked **adjacency list**. The implementation of an adjacency list structure usually involves keeping the nodes of the graph in a linear array that points to a list of nodes to which it is adjacent. The nice part about this arrangement is that we can easily locate any node in the graph, and the cost of moving between one node and another can be kept in the list elements coming off the array. Figure A.9 shows a weighted graph along with its adjacency list data structure.

General graphs, such as the ones we have been describing, are widely used for solving communications routing problems. One of the most important of these algorithms is **Dijkstra's algorithm**, which works on the idea that the least-cost route

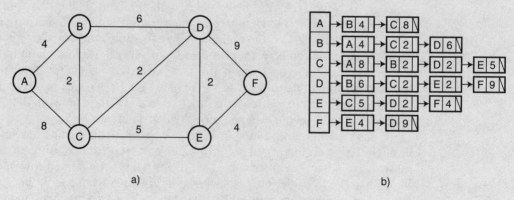

FIGURE A.9   a) A Weighted Graph
b) The Graph's Adjacency List

through the graph consists of the collection of all of the shortest connecting links between all of the nodes. The algorithm starts by inspecting all paths adjacent to the starting node of the graph. It updates each node with the cost of getting there from the starting node. It then inspects each path to adjacent nodes, updating each with the cost of getting to the node. If the node already contains a cost, it is selected as the next destination only if the cost of traveling to that node is smaller than the value already recorded in that node. This process is illustrated in Figure A.10.

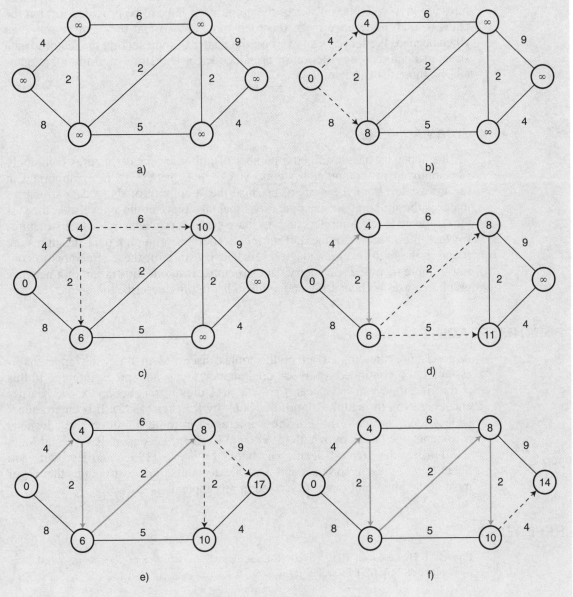

FIGURE A.10 Dijkstra's Algorithm

In Figure A.10a, the value to reach all nodes is set to infinity. Paths from the first node to its adjacent nodes are inspected, and each node is updated with the cost of getting to that node (Figure A.10b). Paths from the node of lesser cost to its neighbors are inspected, updating those nodes with the cost to reach them, if that cost is less than the value that was previously stored in each node. This is what happens to the node at the lower left-hand side of the graph in Figure A.10c. The process repeats until the shortest path is discovered, as shown in Figure A.10f.

One of the tricky parts of Dijkstra's algorithm is that a number of data structures are involved. Not only does the graph itself have to be provided for, but the paths to each node have to be recorded somehow so that they can be retrieved when needed. We leave as an exercise the matter of representing the required data structures and the construction of pseudocode for Dijkstra's algorithm that operates on those data structures.

SUMMARY

This appendix has described a number of important data structures commonly employed by computer systems. Stacks and queues are most important at the lowest levels of the system, because the simplicity of these data structures matches the simplicity of the operations that take place at those levels. At the system software level, compilers and database systems rely heavily on tree structures for fast information storage and retrieval. The most complex data structures are found at the high-level language layer. It is possible for these structures to consist of more than one subsidiary data structure, as in our illustration of a network graph that uses both an array and a linked list to fully describe the graph.

FURTHER READING

A good understanding of all of the topics discussed in this brief appendix is essential for continued study of computer systems and programming. If this is the first time you have seen the data structures in this appendix, we heartily encourage you to read the algorithms book by Rawlins (1992). It is entertaining, well written, and colorful. For those interested in more thorough and advanced treatments, the books by Knuth (1998) and Cormen, Leiserson, Rivest, and Stein (2001) offer the greatest detail. The books by Weiss (1995) and Horowitz and Sahni (1983) present compact and readable accounts of data structures that cover most of the important topics described in this appendix.

REFERENCES

Cormen, T. H., Leiserson, C. E., Rivest, R. L., & Stein, C. *Introduction to Algorithms*, 2nd ed. Cambridge, MA: MIT Press, 2001.

Horowitz, E., & Sahni, S. *Fundamentals of Data Structures*. Rockville, MD: Computer Science Press, 1983.

Knuth, D. E. *The Art of Computer Programming*, 3rd ed. Volumes 1, 2, and 3. Reading, MA: Addison-Wesley, 1998.

Rawlins, G. J. E. *Compared to What? An Introduction to the Analysis of Algorithms*. New York: W. H. Freeman and Company, 1992.

Weiss, M. A. *Data Structures and Algorithm Analysis*, 2nd ed. Redwood City, CA: Benjamin/Cummings Publishing Company, 1995.

EXERCISES

1. Give at least one example of applications where each of the following data structures would be most suitable:

   a) Arrays

   b) Queues

   c) Linked lists

   d) Stacks

   e) Trees

2. As stated in the text, a priority queue is a queue in which certain items are allowed to jump to the head of the line if they meet certain conditions. Devise a data structure and a suitable algorithm to implement a priority queue.

♦ 3. Suppose you didn't want to maintain a set of sorted data elements as a tree, but chose a linked list implementation instead, despite its obvious inefficiencies. The list is ordered by key values in ascending order; that is, the lowest key value is at the head of the list. To locate a data element, you search the list linearly until you find a key value that is greater than the key value of the item's key. If the purpose of this search is to insert another item in the list, how would you achieve this insertion? In other words, give a pseudocode algorithm that lists each step. You can make this algorithm somewhat more efficient by slightly changing the data structure of the list.

4. The memory map shown below describes a binary tree. Draw the tree.

	0	1	2	3	4	5	6	7	8	9	A	B	C	D	E	F
0	--	--	--	--	--	00	45	00	--	--	--	--	--	--	--	--
1	00	41	00	--	--	--	--	--	--	05	46	37	--	--	--	00
2	43	00	--	--	--	--	--	--	--	--	--	--	10	42	1F	--
3	--	--	2C	44	19	--	--	00	47	00	--	--	--	--	--	--

♦ **5.** The memory map shown below describes a binary tree. Draw the tree.

	0	1	2	3	4	5	6	7	8	9	A	B	C	D	E	F
0	--	--	--	--	--	--	--	--	24	46	12	--	--	--	00	42
1	30	--	00	45	00	--	--	--	--	--	--	--	--	--	--	--
2	--	--	--	--	0E	47	00	--	--	--	00	43	00	--	--	--
3	00	44	00	--	--	--	--	--	--	--	--	--	08	41	2A	--

6. The memory map shown below describes a binary tree. The leaves contain the keys *H* (48), *I* (49), *J* (4A), *K* (4B), *L* (4C), *M* (4D), *N* (4E), and *O* (4F). Draw the tree.

	0	1	2	3	4	5	6	7	8	9	A	B	C	D	E	F
0	00	2E	46	39	00	4B	00	48	35	44	04	14	11	41	08	35
1	FF	19	42	22	3F	FF	01	43	3C	00	48	00	48	20	41	00
2	4A	15	00	49	00	42	00	4E	00	47	0C	45	16	08	00	4C
3	00	00	4F	00	43	00	4A	00	45	00	4D	00	26	47	31	41

7. Devise a formula for the maximum number of nodes that can be placed in a binary tree with *n* levels.

8. A graph *traversal* is the act of interrogating (or visiting) every node in the graph. Traversals are useful when nodes are added to a tree in a certain order (perhaps random) and retrieved in some other given order. Three frequently used traversals, *preorder*, *inorder*, and *postorder*, are shown in the diagram below, with diagram (a) illustrating a preorder traversal, (b) an inorder traversal, and (c) a postorder traversal.

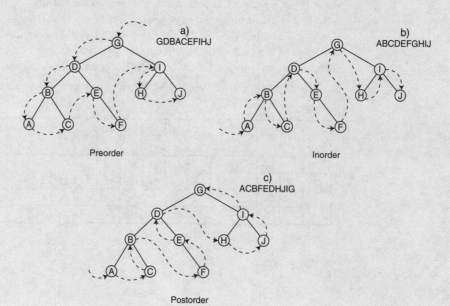

a)
GDBACEFIHJ

Preorder

b)
ABCDEFGHIJ

Inorder

c)
ACBFEDHJIG

Postorder

a) Rearrange the tree above so that a preorder traversal will print the node key values in alphabetical order. Change only the key values in the nodes. Do the same for an inorder traversal.

b) Perform the other two traversals on both of the trees redrawn in exercise 8a.

9. Most books concerning algorithms and data structures present traversal algorithms as recursive procedures. (Recursive procedures are subroutines or functions that call themselves.) However, the *computer* achieves this recursion using iteration! The algorithm below uses a stack to perform an iterative preorder traversal of a tree. (Refer to exercise 8.) As each node is traversed, its key value is printed as in the diagram above.

```
ALGORITHM Preorder
    TreeNode : node
    Boolean : done
    Stack: stack
    Node ← root
    Done ← FALSE
    WHILE NOT done
        WHILE node NOT NULL
            PRINT node
            PUSH node onto stack
            node ← left child node pointer of node
        ENDWHILE
        IF stack is empty
            done ← TRUE
        ELSE
            node ← POP node from stack
            node ← right child node pointer of node
        ENDIF
    ENDWHILE
END Preorder
```

a) Modify the algorithm so that it will perform an inorder traversal.

b) Modify the algorithm so that it will perform a postorder traversal. (Hint: As you leave a node to follow its left subtree, update a value in the node to indicate that the node has been visited.)

10. Regarding the trie root node shown in Figure A.6, what complications arise if we discover a famous mathematician whose name is Ethel? How can we prevent this problem?

11. Using Dijkstra's algorithm, find a shorter route from New York to Chicago using the mileages given in the adjacency matrix below. The value "infinity" (∞) indicates no direct connection between two given cities.

	Albany	Buffalo	Chicago	Cleveland	Erie	New York	Pittsburgh	St. Louis
Albany	0	290	∞	∞	∞	155	450	∞
Buffalo	290	0	∞	∞	100	400	∞	∞
Chicago	∞	∞	0	350	∞	∞	∞	300
Cleveland	∞	∞	350	0	100	∞	135	560
Erie	∞	100	∞	100	0	∞	130	∞
New York	155	400	∞	∞	∞	0	∞	∞
Pittsburgh	450	∞	∞	135	130	∞	0	∞
St. Louis	∞	∞	300	560	∞	∞	∞	0

12. Suggest a way an adjacency matrix could be stored so that it would occupy less main memory space.

13. Design an algorithm, with suitable data structures, that implements Dijkstra's algorithm.

14. Which of the data structures discussed in this appendix would be best for creating a dictionary that would be used by a spelling checker in a word processor?

Glossary

1s Complement Notation See One's Complement Notation.

2s Complement Notation See Two's Complement Notation.

Access Time 1. The sum of the rotational delay and seek time on a hard disk. 2. The time required to find and return a specific piece of information from disk or memory.

Accumulator Architecture An architecture that assumes one operand to be in the accumulator without requiring the accumulator to be explicitly referenced in the instruction.

Accuracy In the context of numeric representation, accuracy refers to how close a number is to its true value.

ACID Properties Four characteristics of a database or transaction-processing system: (1) Atomicity, meaning all related updates take place within the bounds of the transaction or no updates are made at all. (2) Consistency, meaning all updates comply with the constraints placed on all data elements. (3) Isolation, meaning no transaction can interfere with the activities or updates of another transaction. (4) Durability, meaning that successful transactions are written to "durable" media (e.g., magnetic disk) as soon as possible.

Actuator Arm The mechanical component of a disk drive that holds read/write heads.

Addend In an arithmetic addition operation, the addend is increased by the value of the augend to form a sum.

Address Binding The process of mapping symbolic addresses to actual physical memory locations.

Address Bus The part of a bus that transfers the address from which the CPU will read or write.

Address Spoofing   A communications hacking technique where a host engages in communications with another host using a falsified IP address. IP spoofing is often used to subvert filtering routers and firewalls intended to keep outsiders from accessing private intranets, among other things.

Addressing Mode   Specifies where the operand for an instruction is located by how the operand is to be interpreted.

Adjacency List   A data structure that models a directed graph (or network) where a pointer between node elements indicates the existence of a path between two nodes in the graph.

Adjacency Matrix   A two-dimensional array that models a directed graph (or network). If the graph contains n nodes, the adjacency matrix will have n rows and n columns. If there is a path between node x and node y in the graph, then the adjacency matrix will contain a nonzero value in column x of row y. The entry will be zero otherwise.

Aggregatable Global Unicast Address Format   A plan for organizing the 2^{128} possible host addresses under IPv6.

AGP (Accelerated Graphics Port)   A graphics interface designed by Intel specifically for 3D graphics.

Algebraic Field   A set of numbers that is closed under addition and multiplication with identity elements for both operations. Fields also support the associative, commutative, and distributive properties of algebra. The system of real numbers is a field.

Amdahl's Law   A law that states that the performance enhancement possible with a given improvement is limited by the amount that the improved feature is used. More formally, the overall speedup of a computer system depends on both the speedup in a particular component and how much that component is used by the system. Symbolically: $S = 1 \div [(1 - f) + f \div k]$, where S is the speedup; f is the fraction of work performed by the faster component; and k is the speedup of a new component.

American National Standards Institute (ANSI)   The group representing the United States' interests in various international groups for creating standards in the computer industry.

American Standard Code for Information Interchange   See ASCII.

Analytical Engine   A general-purpose machine designed by Charles Babbage in 1833.

Anycasting   A network messaging method that permits any one of a logical group of nodes to receive a message, but no particular receiver is specified in the message.

Application-Specific Integrated Circuit (ASIC)   A customized circuit built to deliver a narrowly defined function or set of functions. The usual motivation for building an ASIC is to deliver better performance than can be achieved by a programmed general-purpose microcontroller or microprocessor. In large batches, ASICs can sometimes be less expensive than programmed general-purpose processors because only the necessary functions are provided for by the hardware on the chip.

Arithmetic Coding   A data compression method that partitions the real number line in the interval between 0 and 1 using the probabilities in the symbol set of the message to be compressed. Symbols with a higher probability of occurrence get a larger chunk of the interval.

Arithmetic Logic Unit (ALU)   The combinational circuit responsible for performing the arithmetic and logic functions in a CPU.

Arithmetic Mean   A measure of central tendency derived by finding the sum of a set of data values and dividing by the number of data values. In commonplace usage, the "average" of a set of values is the arithmetic mean of those values.

Arithmetic Shift   A special type of shift operation that preserves the sign bit.

ARPAnet   See DARPAnet.

ASCII   (American Standard Code for Information Interchange)   A 7-bit character code used to represent numeric, alphabetic, special printable, and control characters.

ASIC   See Application-Specific Integrated Circuit.

Assembler Directive   An instruction specifically for the assembler that is not to be translated into machine code, but rather tells the assembler to perform a specific function, such as generating a page break in a program listing.

Assembly Language   A low-level language using mnemonics that has a one-to-one correspondence with the machine language for a particular architecture.

Associative Memory   Memory whose locations are identified by content, not address, which is specially designed to be searched in parallel.

Asynchronous Circuits   Sequential circuits that become active the moment any input value changes.

AT Attachment   See EIDE.

ATAPI   Abbreviation for AT Attachment Packet Interface, which is an extension of EIDE that supports CR-ROM drives.

Attenuation   Electrical signal loss over time or distance that results in erroneous data at the receiver.

Augend   See Addend.

B+ Tree   An acyclic data structure consisting of pointers to index structures or data records. The internal nodes of a B+ tree are collectively referred to as its index part, whereas the leaf nodes are called the sequence part, because they will always be in sequential order.

Backbone   High-capacity communications (trunk) line that carries digital network traffic.

Backward Compatible   A program is said to be backward compatible if it will run using files and data created for an older version of the same software. A computer is backward compatible if it can run software developed for previous versions of the same architecture.

Bandwidth   The range of frequencies that an analog communications medium can carry, measured in hertz. In digital communications, bandwidth is the general term for the information-carrying capacity of a medium, measured in bits per second (bps).

Base Address   Address of the first element of a data structure. All other elements in the structure are identified as offsets from the base address.

Base/Offset Addressing   An addressing mode in which an offset is added to a specific base register that is then added to the specified operand to yield the effective address of the data.

Based Addressing   An addressing mode that uses a base register (either explicitly or implicitly designated) to store an offset (or displacement), which is added to the operand results in the effective address of the data.

Basic Input/Output System   See BIOS.

Batch Processing   A mode of computation where, under normal conditions, there is no human interaction with the system, aside from initiating a batch processing job. Similar jobs are grouped and executed serially.

Baud   The unit of measure for the number of signal transitions supported by a transmission medium or transmission method over a medium.

BCD   Abbreviation for binary coded decimal. A coding system that uses four bits to express the decimal digits 0 through 9. BCD was the basis for EBCDIC.

Benchmark Suite   A collection of kernel programs intended to measure computer system performance. By using a number of different kernels, it is believed that a system's processing power can be accurately assessed.

Benchmarketing   The widespread practice by computer vendors of advertising their systems' benchmark results when their numbers can be construed to be better than those of their competition.

Benchmarking   The science of making objective assessments of the performance of a hardware or software system. Benchmarks are also useful for determining performance improvements obtained by upgrading a computer or its components.

BER   See Bit Error Rate.

Biased Exponent   The adjustment of the exponent part of a floating-point number that eliminates the need for a sign bit on the exponent. The bias value, which represents zero, is a number near the middle of the range of possible values for the exponent. Values larger than the bias are positive exponents.

Big Endian   Storing multibyte words in memory with the most significant byte at the lowest address.

Binary Coded Decimal   See BCD.

Binary Search   A method of locating a key in a sorted list of values by successively limiting the search to half of the list.

Binary Tree   An acyclic data structure consisting of a root, internal nodes, and leaves. The root and each internal node can have at most two pointers to other nodes (thus, at most, two descendants). Leaves are nodes that have no descendent nodes.

Binding Time   Reference to the operation during which symbolic address binding takes place. Load-time binding provides addresses as the binary module is loaded into memory. Run-time binding (or execution-time binding) delays binding until the process is actually running.

Biological Computer   A computer that uses components from living organisms instead of silicon.

BIOS   Acronym for basic input/output system. A programmable integrated circuit that contains information and programming for the components of a particular system. Microcomputer operating systems perform I/O and other device-specific activities through the system BIOS.

Bit   A contraction of binary digit, the value of which can be 0 or 1.

Bit Cell   The amount of linear or aerial space, or the amount of time occupied by a bit in the storage or transmission of bytes.

Bit Error Rate (BER)   The ratio of the number of erroneous bits received to the total number of bits received.

Black Box   1. A module that performs a function, but the internal details of how the function is performed are not apparent to any person or process external to the black box. 2. In data communications, a device that adapts a device to the protocol of a system for which it was not originally designed.

Block Field   That part of an address that specifies the corresponding cache block.

Blocking Interconnection Network   A network that does not allow new connections in the presence of other simultaneous connections.

Boolean Algebra   An algebra for the manipulation of objects that can take on only two values, typically true and false. Also known as symbolic logic.

Boolean Expressions   The result of combining Boolean variables and Boolean operators.

Boolean Function   A function with one or more Boolean input values that yields a Boolean result.

Boolean Identities   Laws that pertain to Boolean expressions and Boolean variables.

Boolean Product   The result of an AND operation.

Boolean Sum   The result of an OR operation.

Boot   A shortened but most commonly used form of the verb *bootstrapping*, the process by which a small program is invoked to initiate a computer's full operation.

Booth's Algorithm   A fast and efficient method for multiplying signed two's complement numbers that uses a string of ones in a binary number in much the same way as a string of zeros.

Bootstrap Loader   Computer firmware that executes a bootstrapping program.

Bootstrapping   See Boot.

Branch Prediction   The process of guessing the next instruction in the instruction stream prior to its execution, thus avoiding pipeline stalls due to branching. If the prediction is successful, no delay is introduced into the pipeline. If the prediction is unsuccessful, the pipeline must be flushed and all calculations caused by this miscalculation must be discarded.

Bridge   A Layer 2 network component that joins two similar types of networks so they look like one network. A bridge is a "store and forward" device, receiving and holding an entire transmission frame before sending it on its way.

British Standards Institution (BSI)   The group representing Great Britain's interests in various international groups for creating standards in the computer industry.

Broadband Cable   A class of guided network media having a capacity of at least 2Mbps. Broadband communication provides multiple channels of data, using a form of multiplexing.

Burst Error   An error pattern where multiple adjacent bits are damaged.

Bursty Data   An I/O condition where data is sent in blocks, or clusters, as opposed to a steady stream.

Bus   A shared group of wires through which data is transmitted from one part of a computer to another. Synchronous buses are clocked so events occur only at clock ticks. Asynchronous buses use control lines to coordinate the operations and require complex handshaking protocols to enforce timing. See also Address Bus, Control Bus, and Data Bus.

Bus Arbitration   The process used to determine which device should be in control of the bus.

Bus Cycle   The time between one tick of the bus clock and another.

Bus Protocol   A set of usage rules governing how buses are used.

Bus-Based Network   A network that allows processors and memories to communicate via a shared bus.

Byte   A group of eight contiguous bits.

Byte-Addressable   Means each individual byte has a unique address, or the smallest addressable bit string is one byte.

C-LOOK   See LOOK.

C-SCAN   See SCAN.

Cache   Specialized, high-speed storage used to store frequently accessed or recently accessed data. There are two types of cache: memory cache and disk cache. Memory cache (or cache memory) is smaller and faster than main memory. There are two types of memory cache: (1) Level 1 cache (L1) is a small, fast memory cache that is built into the microprocessor chip and helps speed up access to frequently used data; (2) Level 2 cache (L2) is a collection of fast, built-in memory chips situated between the microprocessor and main memory. Disk cache is a specialized buffer used to store data read from disk.

Cache Coherence Problem   The problem that results when the value stored in cache differs from the value stored in memory.

Cache Mapping   The process of converting a memory address into a cache location.

Campus Network   A privately owned data communications network that spans multiple buildings in a small area. Campus networks are typically extensions of LANs and employ LAN protocols.

Canonical Form   With reference to Boolean expressions, this means one of the two standard forms: sum-of-products or product-of-sums.

Carbon Nanotube   A tubular form of elemental carbon that is one atom thick (also known as graphene). Carbon nanotubes possess distinctive electrical properties that make them ideal for nonvolatile bit storage.

CD Recording Mode   Specifies the format used for placing data on a CD-ROM. Modes 0 and 2, intended for music recording, have no error-correction capabilities. Mode 1, intended for data recording, has two levels of error detection and correction. The total capacity of a CD recorded in Mode 1 is 650MB. Modes 0 and 2 can hold 742MB but cannot reliably be used for data recording.

CD-ROM   An acronym for compact disc-read only memory. A type of optical disk capable of storing more than half a gigabyte of data. Other varieties of optical storage include CD-R (CD-Recordable), CD-RW (CD-Rewritable), and WORM (Write Once Read Many).

CEN (Comité Européen de Normalisation)   The European committee for standardization in the computer industry.

Central Processing Unit (CPU)   The computer component responsible for fetching instructions, decoding them, and performing the indicated sequence of operations on the correct data. The CPU consists of an ALU, registers, and a control unit.

Channel I/O   I/O that takes place using an intelligent type of DMA interface known as an I/O channel. I/O channels are driven by small CPUs called I/O processors (IOPs), which are optimized for I/O.

Checkpoint   Issued each time a block of data is correctly processed and committed to durable storage during database updates or network file transfers. If an error occurs during processing, data up to the last checkpoint is considered valid.

Checksum   A group of bits derived through a mathematical operation over one or more data bytes. Checksum bits are often appended to the end of a block of information bytes to maintain the integrity of information in data storage and transmission. One popular checksum is the cyclic redundancy check (CRC).

Chip   A small silicon semiconductor crystal consisting of the necessary electronic components (transistors, resistors, and capacitors) to implement various gates.

CISC (Complex Instruction Set Computer)   A design philosophy in which computers have a large number of instructions, of variable length, with complicated layouts.

Client-Server System   See *n*-Tiered Architecture.

Clock Cycle Time   The reciprocal of the clock frequency. Also called the clock period.

Clock Skew   Clock drift; a situation where coordinated clocks in a system or network gradually lose synchronization.

Clock Speed   The speed of the processor, usually measured in megahertz (millions of pulses per second) or gigahertz (billions of pulses per second). Also called the clock frequency or clock rate.

Cloud Computing   A type of distributed computing where computing services are provided by loosely coupled Web servers. The client computer interacts only with an abstract "cloud" rather than the individual servers.

Cluster Computing   Distributed computing in which all the resources within the same administrative domain work on "group" tasks.

Cluster of Workstations (COW)   A collection of distributed workstations similar to a NOW, but that requires a single entity to be in charge.

CNT   See Carbon Nanotube.

Coaxial Cable   A type of wire that consists of a center wire surrounded by insulation and then a grounded foil shield that is wrapped in steel or copper braid.

Code Word   An n-bit unit containing m data bits and r check bits, used in error detection and error correction.

COLD   An acronym for computer output laser disc. COLD is a computer output method used instead of, or in addition to, paper or microfilm output. COLD provides long-term archival storage of data.

Combinational Circuit   A logic device whose output is always based entirely on the given inputs.

Common Pathway Bus   A bus that is shared by a number of devices (also called a multipoint bus).

Compact Disc-Read Only Memory   See CD-ROM.

Compilation   The process of using a compiler.

Compiler   A program that translates an entire block of source code into object code at one time.

Complement   The negation of a Boolean expression or variable.

Completely Connected Network   A network in which all components are connected to all other components.

Complex Programmable Logic Devices (CPLDs)   Generic name for a class of VLSI chips that contain numerous blocks of programmable array logic or programmable logic array devices.

Compression Factor (Ratio)   Measures the effectiveness of a data compression operation. Mathematically, the compression factor $= 1 -$ (compressed size $\div$ uncompressed size) $\times$ 100%, where the sizes are measured in bytes.

Computer Architecture   Focuses on the structure and behavior of the computer system and refers to the logical aspects of system implementation as seen by the programmer. Includes things such as instruction sets and formats, operation codes, data types, the number and types of registers, addressing modes, and main memory access methods as well as various I/O mechanisms.

Computer Level Hierarchy   An abstract hierarchy that represents most modern computers as a series of levels, starting with the lowest: digital logic level, control level, machine level, system software level, assembly language level, high-level language level, and user level.

Computer Organization   Addresses issues such as control signals and memory types, and encompasses all physical aspects of computer systems.

Computer Output Laser Disc   See COLD.

Context Switch   An operating system procedure of switching from one executing process to another.

Control Bus   The portion of a bus used to transfer control signals.

Control Unit   The part of the CPU that controls execution of instructions, movement of data, and timing. It can be either hardwired (consisting of physical gates that create the control signals) or microprogrammed (consisting of microcode that interprets instructions and translates these instructions to the appropriate control signals).

Convolutional Code   A coding method whereby the output symbol is a function of the current input symbol and some number of symbols previously processed. Convolutional coding is employed in PRML data encoding methods.

CPU Bound   A system performance condition where a process or set of processes spends most of its execution time in the CPU or waiting for CPU resources.

CPU Scheduling   The process of selecting a waiting process for execution. Scheduling approaches include first-come, first-served (pick the next one in line), round-robin (give each process a portion of CPU time), shortest job first (attempt to pick the job with the shortest expected execution time), and priority (base the decision on some predetermined factor, such as a number indicating importance).

CRC   See Cyclic Redundancy Check.

Cycle Stealing   See DMA.

Cyclic Redundancy Check (CRC)   A type of checksum used primarily in data communications that determines whether an error has occurred in a large block or stream of information bytes.

Daisy Chaining   An I/O device connection method where the input of one device is cabled serially from the output of another.

DARPAnet   Acronym for Defense Advanced Research Projects Network. Often referred to as the original Internet. The defense research agency has been named ARPA (Advanced Research Projects Agency) and DARPA at various times, so this original network is known as both ARPAnet and DARPAnet.

DASD   Acronym for direct access storage device. DASD usually refers to a large pool of magnetic disks that attach to very large computer systems. The name DASD derives from the idea that each unit of disk storage on magnetic disks has a unique address that can be accessed independently of the sectors around it.

DAT   See Serpentine Recording.

Data   A numerical value that represents a measurable property. A fact.

Data Bus   The portion of a bus that transfers the actual data.

Data Cache   Cache for holding the most recently used data only (no instructions).

Data Dependency   A situation that arises when the result of one instruction, not yet completely executed, is to be used as an operand to a following instruction. May slow down a pipelined CPU.

Data Structure   The manner in which related pieces of information are organized to facilitate access to data. Data structures are often independent of their implementation, as the manner of organization is logical, not necessarily physical.

Data Token   Unit that represents the data that flows through a dataflow graph. Reception of all data tokens is necessary for nodes in a dataflow graph to fire.

Database Management System (DBMS)   Software that provides management services and enforces order and consistency on a group of related files.

Dataflow Architecture   An architecture in which programs are driven by the availability of data, not by the instruction execution sequence (as in instruction-driven architectures).

Datagram   A network PDU routed as a single, discrete unit. Datagrams are usually components of a dialog or conversation between two communicating entities; thus, they also contain sequencing information to keep them in order and to prevent lost packets.

Datapath   A network of registers, the ALU, and the connections (buses) between them. Indicates the path data must traverse in the system.

DBMS   See Database Management System.

Decoder   A combinational circuit that uses the values of its inputs to select one specific output line.

Decoherence   In quantum computing, the tendency for qubits to decay into an incoherent state.

Dedicated Cluster Parallel Computer (DCPC)   A set of workstations specifically collected to work on a given parallel computation.

Denormalized Number   Any number in IEEE-754 floating-point format that has an exponent of all zeros. Denormalized numbers do not include an implied one.

Deterministic Finite Automaton (DFA)   An abstract computational model consisting of an input alphabet, a finite set of states that represents every configuration the machine can assume, a start state, a final state, and a set of functions that defines transitions between the states. The purpose of a DFA is to accept (or reject) a string. DFAs are useful in computer theory and in the design of compilers.

Dhrystone   A benchmarking program that focuses on string manipulation and integer operations. Reinhold P. Weicker of Siemens Nixdorf Information Systems developed this benchmark in 1984 and named it Dhrystone reportedly as a pun on the Whetstone benchmark, because "Dhrystones don't float."

Difference Engine   A machine designed by Charles Babbage in 1822 to mechanize the solution of polynomial functions.

Digital Circuit   A physical circuit (consisting of gates) that processes signals with two discrete states.

Digital Signal 0   See DS-0.

Digital Subscriber Line   See DSL.

Digital Versatile Disc   See DVD.

Digital-to-Analog Converter (DAC)   Device connected to graphics card and monitor that converts binary images to analog signals that the monitor can understand.

Dijkstra's Algorithm   An algorithm that finds a least-cost path through a network. It works on the idea that the least-cost route through the graph consists of the collection of all of the shortest connecting links between all of the nodes.

Diminished Radix Complement Given a number N in base r having d digits, the diminished radix complement of N is defined to be $(r^d - 1) - N$. For decimal numbers, $r = 10$, and the diminished radix is $10 - 1 = 9$.

Direct Access Storage Device See DASD.

Direct Addressing An addressing mode in which the value to be referenced is obtained by specifying its memory address directly in the instruction.

Direct Mapped Cache A cache-mapping scheme that maps blocks of memory to blocks in cache using a modular approach.

Direct Memory Access See DMA.

Dirty Blocks Blocks in cache that have been modified but not yet copied to main memory.

Disk Scheduling A policy for determining the order in which requests for access to sectors on the disk are serviced. Common disk-scheduling policies are FCFS (first-come, first-served), shortest seek time first (SSTF), SCAN, C-SCAN, LOOK, and C-LOOK.

Disk Striping A type of mapping used in RAID drives in which contiguous blocks of data (strips) are mapped in a round-robin fashion to different disk drives.

Disk Utilization The measure of the percentage of the time that the disk is busy servicing I/O requests. Utilization is determined by the speed of the disk and the rate at which requests arrive in the service queue. Stated mathematically: Utilization = Request Arrival Rate ÷ Disk Service Rate, where the arrival rate is given in requests per second and the disk service rate is given in I/O operations per second.

Distributed Computing A situation in which a set of networked computers work collaboratively to solve a problem.

Divide Underflow The computer equivalent of division by zero, where the divisor value is too small to be stored in the accumulator.

DLL See Dynamic Link Library.

DLT See Serpentine Recording.

DMA Abbreviation for direct memory access, an I/O control method where specialized circuits (other than the CPU) control I/O activity. However, the DMA and the CPU share the memory bus, so the DMA consumes memory cycles that would otherwise be used by the CPU. This is called cycle stealing.

Dot Pitch A measurement that indicates the distance between a dot (or pixel) and the closest dot of the same color on a display monitor. The lower this number is, the crisper the image is.

DRAM (Dynamic RAM) RAM that requires periodic recharging to maintain data (unlike static RAM, which holds its contents as long as power is available).

Dual Stack Communications devices that use two different protocols. Today, most dual stack devices (routers) support protocol stacks for both IPv4 and IPv6.

Duality Principle The principle evident in Boolean identities where the product form and the sum form have similar relationships.

Dump   The act or results of printing the contents of memory (usually in hexadecimal) to facilitate diagnosing a program bug. Old-timers sometimes call this a "core" dump, which dates back to the pre-IC days of ferromagnetic memories.

Durable Storage   Any storage medium that does not rely on the continued supply of electric current to retain data. Magnetic disks, magnetic tape, and optical disks are forms of durable storage.

DVD   Abbreviation for digital versatile disc (formerly called digital *video* disc), a high-density optical storage medium. Single-layer and double-layer 120mm DVDs can accommodate 4.7 and 8.54GB of data, respectively.

Dynamic Interconnection Network   Allows the path between two entities (either two processors or a processor and memory) to change from one communication to the next.

Dynamic Link Library (DLL)   Collection of binary objects usable by a linking (program) loader for the completion of executable modules.

EBCDIC (Extended Binary Coded Decimal Interchange Code)   An 8-bit code invented by the IBM Corporation that supported lowercase as well as uppercase letters and a number of other characters (including customer-defined codes) that were beyond the expressive power of the six- and seven-bit codes in use at the time.

EEPROM (Electronically Erasable PROM)   PROM that can be programmed and erased using an electronic field.

Effective Access Time (EAT)   The weighted average representing the mean access time in a memory hierarchy.

Effective Address   The actual location (in memory) of an operand.

EIDE (Enhanced Integrated Drive Electronics)   A cost-effective hardware interface, which is a newer version of the IDE interface standard, between a computer and its mass storage devices.

Elasticity   The ability to add and remove system resources based on demand from those resources.

Elevator Algorithm   See SCAN.

Embedded System   A microcontroller or microprocessor that controls a device whose primary function is something other than general-purpose computing. Embedded systems serve supporting roles only and are often transparent to the user of the device.

Encoding   The process of converting plain text to a form suitable for digital data storage or transmission.

Encryption   The process of scrambling a message using an algorithm and a key value so that one must have the corresponding key to read the message.

Entropy   In the context of information theory, entropy is a measure of the information content of a message.

EPROM (Erasable PROM)   PROM that can be programmed and erased (using highly specialized equipment) to be programmed again.

Error-Correcting Code   A code constructed in such a way that it can detect the presence of errors and can correct some or all of the errors automatically.

Error-Detecting Code A code constructed in such a way that it can detect the presence of errors.

Ethernet A dominant local area networking technology invented in 1976 that supports data transfer rates up to 100Mbps over coaxial cable. The IEEE 802.3 standard is based on Ethernet but is not identical to it.

Excess-M Representation A representation for floating-point numbers that uses M as a biasing value.

Exclusive Cache A cache that guarantees that data is resident in, at most, one level of one cache.

Expanding Opcodes An instruction design that allows the opcode to vary in length, dependent on the number of operands required for the instruction.

Expansion Bus An external bus that connects peripherals, external devices, expansion slots, and I/O ports to the rest of the computer.

Extended Binary Coded Decimal Interchange Code See EBCDIC.

External Fragmentation Fragmentation that results from many holes in memory that are free to be used but are too small to hold meaningful information. See Fragmentation.

Fab Short for integrated circuit fabrication facility.

Fast ATA Fast AT Attachment. See EIDE.

Fast Fourier Transform Mathematical process for converting discrete, quantized values from one domain to another, such as time or space to frequency.

FC-AL See Fibre Channel.

Fetch–Decode–Execute Cycle The instruction cycle a computer follows to execute a program.

Fiber-Optic Cable See Optical Cable.

Fibre Channel A serial data transfer technology for transmitting data at a rate up to 1Gbps. Fibre Channel Arbitrated Loop (FC-AL) is the most widely used—and least costly—of the three Fibre Channel topologies.

Field-Programmable Gate Array (FPGA) A programmable logic device that provides logic functions using memory and multiplexers instead of connecting or disconnecting gates, as is done in other configurable devices. Memory cells contain the truth table of the desired logic function.

Finite State Machine An abstract computational model consisting of an input alphabet, an output alphabet, a finite set of states that represents every configuration the machine can assume, a start state, and a set of functions that defines transitions between the states. Finite state machines are useful for describing the behavior of sequential logic circuits.

Firewall A Layer 3 network device (together with the corresponding set of programs) that restricts access to a network based on policies programmed into the device. Firewalls protect networks or certain network services from unauthorized access.

FireWire A self-configuring serial I/O connection technology that is now the IEEE 1394 standard. FireWire supports traditional data transfer as well as isochronous input and output at speeds up to 40MBps.

Firmware   Programs stored in read only memory, such as ROM, PROM, or EPROM.

First-In, First-Out (FIFO) Replacement Algorithm   A replacement algorithm that replaces the item that has been resident for the longest period of time.

Flash Memory   EPROM allowing data to be written or erased in blocks.

Flip-Flop   The basic component of sequential circuits that acts as the storage element, which is able to maintain a stable output even after the inputs are made inactive. Also, the simplest type of sequential circuit. Differs from a latch in that a flip-flop is edge-triggered and latch is level-triggered.

Floating-Point Emulation   Programmatic simulation of instructions particular to floating-point operations.

Floating-Point Operations Per Second   See FLOPS.

Floating-Point Unit   Specialized computer circuits that are optimized for the performance of fractional binary computations.

Floppy Disk   Removable, low-density magnetic storage medium consisting of a flexible Mylar substrate coated with a magnetic film.

FLOPS   An acronym for floating-point operations per second. FLOPS is an outmoded measure of computer performance for which there is no clear definition. Several benchmarking programs (such as Whetstone and Linpack) produce megaflops (MFLOPS) rates for the system under test.

Flux Reversal   A change in the polarity of the magnetic coating used in computer tape or disk storage devices. Depending on the encoding method, a flux reversal can indicate a binary 0 or 1.

Flynn's Taxonomy   A scheme for classifying computer architectures based on the number of data streams and the number of instruction streams allowed concurrently. See also MIMD, MISD, SISD, and SIMD.

FM   See Frequency Modulation.

Forest   A collection of one or more disjoint n-ary or binary trees.

FPGA   See Field-Programmable Gate Array.

FPU   See Floating-Point Unit.

Fragmentation   1. Occurs when memory or disk space becomes unusable. See also Internal Fragmentation and External Fragmentation. 2. The process of breaking an IP datagram into smaller pieces to fit the requirements of a given network.

Frame Buffer   RAM located on a graphics card used to store rendered images.

Frequency Division Multiplexing (FDM)   A method whereby a medium carries several communications streams. When FDM is used over long-distance telephone cables, each call is assigned its own frequency band allowing a dozen or more calls to easily travel over the same conductor without interfering with one another.

Frequency Modulation (FM)   As used in digital applications, frequency modulation (FM) is an encoding method for the storage or transmission of information where at least one transition is supplied for each bit cell. These synchronizing transitions occur at the beginning of the bit cell boundary.

Full Duplex   A transfer mode where data travels simultaneously in both directions over a communications medium or data bus.

Full-Adder   A circuit to add three bits, one of which is a carry in, that produces two outputs: a sum and a carry.

Full-Stroke Seek   The act of moving a disk arm from the innermost track to the outermost, or vice versa.

Fully Associative Cache   A cache-mapping scheme that allows blocks of main memory to be mapped to any block in cache. Requires associative memory for cache.

G   Prefix meaning 2^{30}, or approximately one billion.

Galois Field   An algebraic field with a finite number of elements. Commonly used Galois fields are defined through the modulus operation using a prime number, $GF(p) = \{0, 1, \ldots p - 1\}$ for all integers $Z \bmod p$.

Garbage Collection   A process in which chunks of memory are coalesced into larger, usable pieces.

Gate   A small, electronic device that computes various functions of two-valued signals.

Gateway   A point of entrance to a network from external networks.

General-Purpose Register Architecture   An architecture that uses sets of general-purpose registers to hold operands for instructions.

General-Purpose Registers (also User-Visible Registers)   Registers that can be accessed by the programmer and used for different purposes.

Geometric Mean   A measure of central tendency frequently used in computer performance analysis. The geometric mean, G, is the nth root of the product of the n measurements: $G = (x_1 \times x_2 \times x_3 \times \ldots \times x_n)^{1/n}$. The geometric mean provides a consistent number with which to perform comparisons regardless of the distribution of the data.

GIF (Graphics Interchange Format)   See LZW Compression.

Graphics Processing Unit (GPU)   The processor on a graphics card.

Grid Computing   A global effort to use the resources of many computers in different administrative domains, without having to consider where those computer resources are located, to solve large computational problems.

Guided Transmission Media   Physical connectors such as copper wire or fiber-optic cable that have direct physical connections to network components.

Half Duplex   A transfer mode where data can travel in only one direction at a time over a communications medium or data bus.

Half-Adder   A circuit to add two bits that produces two outputs: a sum and a carry.

Hamming Code   An error-correcting code that augments an information byte with check bits (or redundant bits).

Hamming Distance   The number of bit positions in which code words differ. The smallest Hamming distance, D(min), among all pairs of words in a code is its minimum Hamming distance. The minimum Hamming distance determines a code's error-detecting and error-correcting capability.

Handshake   The protocol that requires, before data can be transferred between a sender and a receiver, that the sender contact the receiver to initiate the transfer of bytes. The receiver then must acknowledge the request and indicate that it is able to receive data.

Harmonic Mean   A measure of central tendency frequently used in computer performance analysis for averaging rates or ratios. The harmonic mean is given by $H = n \div (1/x_1 + 1/x_2 + 1/x_3 + \ldots + 1/x_n)$.

Harvard Architecture   A computer architecture that uses two buses: one for data and one for instructions.

Harvard Cache   The name given to a partitioned cache that has separate storage for data and instructions (i.e., a data cache and an instruction cache).

Hazard   A factor contributing to a pipeline stall. Includes such things as data dependencies, resource conflicts, and memory fetch access delays.

Head Crash   A ruinous condition of a rigid magnetic disk caused by a read-write head coming into contact with the surface of the disk.

Heap   Main memory space that is allocated and deallocated as data structures are created and destroyed during process execution.

Helical Scan Recording   A method of placing bits on a magnetic tape where the medium passes over a tilted rotating drum (capstan), which has two read and two write heads.

Hertz   The unit of measurement for clock frequencies as measured in cycles per second. One hertz is one cycle per second.

Hextet   A group of four bits that represents a single hexadecimal digit.

Hierarchical Memory   Memory consisting of a combination of memory types that gives a good cost/performance trade-off, typically including cache, RAM, and virtual memory.

High-Order Interleaving   Memory interleaving that uses the high-order bits of the address to select the memory module.

High-Performance Peripheral Interface   See HiPPI.

HiPPI   Acronym for High-Performance Peripheral Interface, a high-capacity storage interface and backbone protocol for local area networks.

Hit   Occurs when the requested data is found at a particular memory level or a requested page is found in memory.

Hit Rate   The percentage of memory accesses found in a given level of memory.

Hit Time   The time required to access the requested information in a given level of memory.

Hollerith Card   An 80-column punched card developed by Herman Hollerith and used for computer input and output.

Hot Plugging   The ability to add and remove devices while the computer is running.

Hub   An OSI Layer 1 device that has many ports for input and output that broadcasts packets received from one or more locations to one or more devices on the network.

Huffman Coding   A statistical data compression method that creates a binary tree from the symbols in the input. The output is a binary code derived from the frequency of the symbols in the input and a dictionary to decode the binary stream.

Hybrid RAID System A RAID system that uses multiple RAID levels in combination.

Hypercube Networks Multidimensional extensions of mesh networks in which each dimension has two processors.

Hyperthreading Technology that enables a single physical processor to simulate two logical (or virtual) processors.

I/O Bound A system performance condition where a process or set of processes spend most of their execution time executing I/O operations or waiting for I/O resources.

IaaS Abbreviation for Infrastructure-as-a-Service (IaaS) provides only server hardware, secure network access to the servers, and backup and recovery services over the Internet. The customer is responsible for all system software including the operating system and databases. Compare with SaaS and PaaS.

IAB See Internet Engineering Task Force.

ICANN See Internet Corporation for Assigned Names and Numbers.

IEEE-754 Formally known as IEEE Standard for Binary Floating-Point Arithmetic (ANSI/IEEE Std 754-1985), IEEE-754 is a format for representing floating-point numbers. Single-precision numbers have 1 bit for the sign, 8 bits for the exponent (with a bias of 127), and 23 bits for the significand (with an implied 1 to the left of the binary point), for a total of 32 bits. Double-precision numbers have 1 bit for the sign, 11 bits for the exponent (with a bias of 1023), and 52 bits for the significand (with an implied 1 to the left of the binary point), for a total of 64 bits.

IETF See Internet Engineering Task Force.

Immediate Addressing An addressing mode in which the value to be referenced immediately follows the operation code in the instruction.

Inclusive Cache A cache that allows data to exist concurrently at multiple levels in a cache hierarchy.

Indexed Addressing An addressing mode that uses an index register (either explicitly or implicitly designated) to store an offset (or displacement), which is added to the operand and results in the effective address of the data.

Indirect Addressing An addressing mode that uses the bits in the address field to specify a memory address that is to be used as a pointer to the actual operand.

Indirect Indexed Addressing An addressing mode that uses both indirect and indexed addressing at the same time.

Inductance Opposition to changes in current within a conductor. Also, the magnetic field that surrounds a conductor as current passes through it.

Industry Standard Architecture (ISA) Bus The IEEE standardization of the 1980s-generation PC/XT bus.

InfiniBand A 2.5Gbps point-to-point switched fabric interconnection technology developed by Intel. InfiniBand is designed to connect multiple CPUs to multiple peripheral devices simultaneously and with low latency. InfiniBand is a likely replacement for PCI, but requires some improvements before it can replace Fibre Channel.

Infix Notation   One of the orderings of operators and operands that places the operators between operands, such as $2 + 3$.

Information   Data that has meaning to a human being.

Information Theory   A field of study that concerns itself with the way in which information is stored and coded.

Infrastructure-as-a-Service   See IaaS.

Input/Output Devices   Devices that allow users to communicate with the computer or provide read/write access to data.

Input/Output System   A subsystem of components that moves coded data between external devices and a host system, consisting of a CPU and main memory.

Institute of Electrical and Electronic Engineers (IEEE)   An organization dedicated to the advancement of the professions of electronic and computer engineering.

Instruction Cache   Cache used to store the most recently used instructions only (no data).

Instruction Cycle   See Fetch–Decode–Execute cycle.

Instruction Set Architecture (ISA)   The agreed-upon interface between all the software that runs on the machine and the hardware that executes it. It specifies the instructions that the computer can perform and the format for each instruction.

Instruction-Based I/O   I/O method where the CPU has specialized instructions that are used to perform the input and output.

Integrated Cache   See Unified Cache.

Integrated Circuit (IC)   The technology used in the third generation of computers that allows for multiple transistors on a single chip. A chip that has been mounted in a ceramic or plastic container with external pins.

Intellectual Property (IP)   Pretested circuit design modules that are licensed for use in customized circuit-designs. The purchaser typically pays a license fee for the use of the design.

Interconnection Network   The network connecting multiple processors and memories.

Interface   Facility whereby a computer system connects to an outside entity. Hardware interfaces encompass the software, control circuits, and physical connectors required to connect a computer to an I/O device. Also includes the manner in which human beings interact with the machine. The two types of system interfaces are command line interfaces and graphical user interfaces (GUIs).

Interleaving   A method of sector addressing on magnetic disk drives where disk sectors are not in consecutive order around the perimeter of a track. This is an "older" technology invented to compensate for the difference between the rotational speed of a disk drive and the rate at which data can be read from the disk. See also High-order Interleaving, Low-order Interleaving, and Memory Interleaving.

Intermediate Node   Another name for an Internet router.

Internal Fragmentation   Fragmentation internal to a given block and unusable by any process except the process to which the block has been granted.

International Organization for Standardization (ISO)   The entity that coordinates worldwide standards development activities.

International Telecommunications Union (ITU)   An organization concerned with the interoperability of telecommunications systems.

Internet Corporation for Assigned Names and Numbers (ICANN)   A nonprofit corporation that coordinates the assignment of Internet addresses, parameter values used in Internet protocols, and high-level domain names such as .org and .edu.

Internet Engineering Task Force (IETF)   A loose alliance of industry experts that develops detailed specifications for Internet protocols. The IETF operates under the Internet Architecture Board (IAB), which itself operates under the oversight of the not-for-profit Internet Society (ISOC). The IETF publishes all proposed standards in the form of Requests for Comment (RFCs).

Internet of Things (IoT)   A name for the Internet attachment of devices other than traditional host or client computers to the Internet. These devices have varying degrees of intelligence. Thus, the Internet of Things encompasses simple sensors as well as intelligent control devices capable of some degree of self-management. IoT is also known as Machine-to-Machine (M2M) Internet systems.

Internet Protocol   See IP.

Internetwork   A network consisting of subnetworks that use differing protocols.

Interpreter   A program that translates source code into object code by analyzing and executing each line of the source code, one at a time.

Interrupt   An event that alters (or interrupts) the normal fetch–decode–execute cycle of execution in the system.

Interrupt Cycle   The part of the instruction cycle in which the CPU checks to see if an interrupt is pending and, if so, invokes an interrupt-handling routine.

Interrupt Handling   The process of executing a specific routine to process an interrupt.

Interrupt Latency   The elapsed (wall clock) time between the occurrence of an interrupt and the execution of the first instruction of the interrupt service routine. Interrupt latency is an important metric in the evaluation of embedded operating systems.

Interrupt Nesting   An operating system feature that allows suspension of an interrupt service routine to process higher priority interrupts. Interrupt nesting is desirable in real-time operating systems, where event responsiveness is critical to proper system operation.

Interrupt-Driven I/O   An I/O method whereby input devices signal the CPU when they have data ready for processing, thus allowing the CPU to do other, more useful work.

IoT   See Internet of Things.

IP (Internet Protocol)   1. A connectionless Network Layer communications protocol that conveys information in packets called datagrams. Each datagram contains addressing information as well as data. 2. See Intellectual Property.

IR (Instruction Register)   Holds the next instruction to be executed in a program.

ISA Bus   See Industry Standard Architecture (ISA) Bus.

ISO Open Systems Interconnect Reference Model   See ISO/OSI RM.

ISO/OSI RM   A data communications protocol model consisting of seven layers: Application, Presentation, Session, Transport, Network, Data Link, and Physical. The

ISO's work is called a reference model because, owing to its complexity, virtually no commercial system uses all of the features precisely as specified in the model.

ISOC   See Internet Engineering Task Force.

Isochronous Data   Data that is time-sensitive to the extent that if it is delivered too late, much of its meaning (information) is lost. Examples of isochronous are used with real-time data such as voice and video transmission intended for real-time delivery.

JBOD   Acronym for Just a Bunch of Disks. This term is used to contrast an unorganized collection of disk drives from RAID or managed storage, such as a SAN.

Joint Photographic Experts Group   See JPEG.

JPEG   A lossy data compression method devised under the auspices of the Joint Photographic Experts Group. JPEG is an eight-step compression method that allows the user to specify the allowable visual degradation in the compressed image. JPEG 2000 is a more complex and slower version of JPEG.

K   Prefix meaning 2^{10} or 1024 (approximately one thousand). For example, 2Kb means 2048 bits.

Kernel   1. A limited-function program that remains when I/O routines and other non-CPU-intensive code are pared from an application. Kernel programs are used in the creation of benchmark suites. 2. A program module that provides minimal—but critical—functions. In the context of operating systems, a kernel is that portion of the operating system that continuously executes while the system is operational.

Karnaugh map (Kmap)   A method used to simplify Boolean expressions that uses maps, or tables, instead of Boolean algebra identities and equation manipulation.

LAN   An acronym for local area network, a network of computers within a single building. Most LANs currently use Ethernet networking technology at speeds upward of 100Mbps.

Latch   A flip-flop that is level-triggered.

LCD   Liquid crystal display, a common technology used for monitors.

Least Recently Used (LRU) Replacement Algorithm   A replacement algorithm that replaces the item that was used least recently.

Linear Array Network (also Ring Network)   Allows any entity to directly communicate with its two neighbors, but any other communication has to go through multiple entities to arrive at its destination.

Link Editor   See Linking.

Linked List   A data structure where each element contains a pointer that is either null or points to another data element of the same kind.

Linking   The process of matching the external symbols of a program with all exported symbols from other files, producing a single binary file with no unresolved external symbols.

Linpack   A contraction of *LINear algebra PACKage*. Software used to measure floating-point performance. It is a collection of subroutines called Basic Linear Algebra Subroutines (BLAS), which solve systems of linear equations using double-precision arithmetic.

Little Endian   Storing multibyte words with the least significant byte at the lowest address.

Load-Store Architecture   An architecture in which only the load and store instructions of the ISA can access memory. All other instructions must use registers to access data.

Local Area Network   See LAN.

Local Bus   A data bus in a PC that connects the peripheral device directly to the CPU.

Locality (Locality of Reference)   A property in which a program tends to access data or instructions in clusters.

Logical Partition   A nonphysical division of a computer system that gives the illusion that the divisions are physically discrete entities.

Logically Equivalent   In the context of Boolean expressions: two Boolean expressions are logically equivalent if they have the same truth table.

LOOK (C-LOOK)   A disk-scheduling algorithm where the disk arm changes direction only when the highest- and lowest-numbered requested tracks are read or written. LOOK has a variant, called C-LOOK (for circular LOOK), in which track zero is treated as if it were adjacent to the highest-numbered track on the disk.

Loop Fission   The process of splitting large loops into smaller ones. Has a place in loop optimization, because it can eliminate data dependencies, and reduces cache delays resulting from conflicts. See Loop Peeling.

Loop Fusion   The process of combining loops that use the same data items, resulting in increased cache performance, increased instruction-level parallelism, and reduced loop overhead.

Loop Interchange   The process of rearranging loops so that memory is accessed more closely to the way in which the data is stored.

Loop Peeling   A type of loop fission. The process of removing the beginning or ending statements from a loop.

Loop Unrolling   The process of expanding a loop so that each new iteration contains several of the original iterations, thus performing more computations per loop iteration.

Loopback Test   Checks the functions of communications devices and protocols running on a host system. During loopback testing, no data enters the network.

Loosely Coupled Multiprocessors   Multiprocessor systems that have a physically distributed memory. Also known as distributed systems.

Low-Order Interleaving   Memory interleaving that uses the low-order bits of the address to select the correct memory module.

LPAR   See Logical Partition.

LSI (Large-Scale Integration)   Integrated circuits with 1,000 to 10,000 components per chip.

Luminance   Measure of the amount of light an LCD monitor emits.

LZ77 Compression   A data compression method that uses a text window, which serves as a dictionary, in conjunction with a look-ahead buffer, which contains the information to be encoded. If any characters inside the look-ahead buffer can be found in the dictionary, the location and length of the text in the window is written to the output. If the text cannot be found, the unencoded symbol is written with a flag indicating that the symbol should be used as a literal.

LZ78 Compression   Differs from LZ77 in that it removes the limitation of the fixed-size text window. Instead, it populates a trie with tokens from the input. The entire trie is written to disk following the encoded message, and is read first before decoding the message.

LZW Compression   A more efficient implementation of LZ78 compression where the trie size is carefully managed. LZW is the basis for GIF data compression.

M   Prefix meaning 2^{20} or 1,048,576 (approximately one million). For example, 2MB means 2^{21} bytes, or approximately 2 million bytes.

M2M   See Internet of Things.

MAC   See Medium Access Control.

MAC Address   A unique six-byte physical address burned into the circuits of a network interface card (NIC). The first three bytes are the manufacturer's identification number, which is designated by the IEEE. The last three bytes are a unique identifier assigned to the NIC by the manufacturer. No two cards anywhere in the world should ever have the same MAC address. Network protocol layers map this physical MAC address to at least one logical address.

Machine-to-Machine   See Internet of Things.

Main Memory   Storage where program instructions and data are stored. Typically implemented with RAM memory.

MAN   Acronym for metropolitan area network. MANs are high-speed networks that cover a city and its environs.

Manchester Code   Also known as phase modulation (PM), an encoding method used in the transmission or storage of information that provides a transition for each bit, whether a one or a zero. In PM, each binary 1 is signaled by an "up" transition, and each binary zero by a "down" transition. Extra transitions are provided at bit cell boundaries when necessary.

Mantissa   The fractional part of a logarithm, often used to refer to the fractional part of a number expressed in scientific notation, as well as the fractional part of a floating-point number (see Significand).

MAR (Memory Address Register)   Register that holds the memory address of the data being referenced.

Maskable Interrupt   An interrupt that can be ignored or disabled.

MBR (Memory Buffer Register)   Register that holds the data either just read from memory or the data ready to be written to memory.

Mealy Machine   A finite state machine where transitions between the states describe the machine's input and output.

Mean Time to Failure   See MTTF.

Medium Access Control (MAC)   The method by which a node connects to a network. The two dominant approaches to medium access control are token passing and carrier sense/collision detection (CSMA/CD).

Medium Access Control Address   See MAC Address.

Memory Bound   A system performance condition where a process or set of processes spends most of its execution time in main system memory or waiting for memory resources.

Memory Hierarchy (also Hierarchical Memory)   The use of various levels of memory, each with different access speeds and storage capacities, to achieve a better performance/cost ratio than could be achieved using one memory type alone.

Memory Interleaving   A technique that splits memory across multiple memory modules (or banks). See High-Order Interleaving and Low-Order Interleaving.

Memory-Mapped I/O   When registers in an interface appear in the computer's memory map and there is no real difference between accessing memory and accessing an I/O device.

Memory-Memory Architectures   Architectures that allow an instruction to perform an operation without requiring at least one operand to be in a register.

Memristor   An electrical component with discrete states of high resistance and low resistance. The states can be changed through the application of electrical current, thereby making memristors good candidates for nonvolatile bit storage.

Mesh Network   A network that links each entity to four or six (depending on whether they are two-dimensional or three-dimensional) neighbors.

Message Latency   The time required for the first bit of a message to reach its destination.

Metric   A single number that characterizes the performance of a system.

Metropolitan Area Network   See MAN.

MFM   See Modified Frequency Modulation.

Microcomputer   A computer that uses a microprocessor.

Microcontroller   A simple embedded systems processor that consists of a processor, memory, and I/O ports. Memory, consisting of ROM, flash, and RAM, is usually measured in kilobytes.

Microkernel   Operating system component where a relatively small process, the microkernel, provides rudimentary operating system functionality, relying on external modules to perform specific tasks.

Microoperations   "Mini" instructions that specify the elementary operations that can be performed on data stored in registers.

Microprocessor   A processor whose CPU, storage, and I/O capabilities are implemented typically on a single chip.

Microprogram   Software used to interpret instructions into machine language.

Microsequencer   Circuitry that serves as the program counter to control the flow of execution in a microprogram.

Middleware Broad classification for software that provides services above the operating system layer but below the application program layer.

Millions of Instructions per Second See MIPS.

MIMD (Multiple Instruction, Multiple Data) An architecture that employs multiple control points, each with its own instruction and data stream.

Minuend In an arithmetic subtraction, the minuend is decreased by the value of the subtrahend.

MIPS An acronym for millions of instructions per second, an outmoded measure of computer system performance. Mathematically, MIPS = (number of instructions executed) ÷ (execution time × 10^6). MIPS is too architecture-dependent to be useful. As such, the metric has given rise to some creative interpretations of the acronym, for example, "Misleading Indicator of Processor Speed" and "Meaningless Indicators of Performance for Salesmen."

MISD (Multiple Instruction, Single Data) An architecture with multiple instruction streams operating on the same data stream.

Miss Occurs when the requested data is not found in the given level of memory.

Miss Penalty The time required to process a miss, which includes replacing a block in an upper level of memory, plus the additional time to deliver the requested data to the processor.

Miss Rate The percentage of memory accesses not found in a given level of memory.

MNG Multiple-image Network Graphics, MNG, is an extension of PNG that allows multiple images to be compressed into one file. These files can be of any type, such as grayscale, true color, or even JPEGs.

Modified Frequency Modulation (MFM) An encoding method for the storage or transmission of data whereby bit cell boundary transitions are provided only between consecutive zeros. With MFM, then, at least one transition is supplied for every pair of bit cells, as opposed to each cell in PM or FM.

Moore Machine A finite state machine where the states describe the machine's output.

Moore's Law A prediction by Gordon Moore stating that the density of silicon chips doubles every 18 months.

MPP (Massively Parallel Processors) An MIMD distributed memory architecture in which processors do not share memory.

MSI (Medium-Scale Integration) Integrated circuits with 100 to 1,000 components per chip.

MTTF An abbreviation for mean time to failure, MTTF is a mathematical expectation of the life of a component derived through statistical quality control methods commonly used in the manufacturing industry. This is a theoretical quantity that does not necessarily reflect the actual service life of a component.

Multi-Core Processor A multiprocessor with all cores (CPUs) on the same chip.

Multicast A network messaging method that sends a single message that is read by multiple nodes.

Multilevel Cache Hierarchy   A cache memory hierarchy consisting of more than one level.

Multiple-image Network Graphics   See MNG.

Multiplexer   A combinational circuit connecting multiple inputs to one output that selects (using control lines) one of the many input lines and directs it to the single output line.

Multiplexing   Sharing a single communications medium among a number of unrelated, isolated connections. A connection is allocated a channel within a digital carrier through interleaved time slots or, in the case of a broadband carrier, a connection is allocated a particular wavelength (frequency) carried by a broadband medium.

Multipoint Bus   A bus that is shared by a number of devices (also called a common pathway bus).

Multiprocessor System   A computer system containing more than one CPU.

Multiprogramming   Concurrent execution of multiple processes within a single CPU.

Multistage Interconnection Network (Shuffle Network)   Switched network built using 2×2 switches and multiple stages. Examples include the Omega network.

Multitasking   Running multiple processes concurrently. Differs from multiprogramming in that often the processes belong to the same user.

Multithreading   The process of subdividing a process into different threads of control to increase concurrency.

***n*-ary Tree**   An acyclic data structure consisting of a root, internal nodes, and leaves. The root and each internal node can have, at most, n pointers to other nodes (thus, at most, n descendants). Leaves are nodes that have no descendant nodes.

***n*-Tiered Architecture**   Execution environment where processing takes place on more than one computer system. Client-server systems often use a 3-tiered architecture, one tier being a desktop computer, the second an application server, and the third a database server. The application server manages the programs and the interaction between the desktop computer and the database server.

NAP   Acronym for Network Access Point, a switching center used by regional Internet Service Providers (ISPs) to connect to other regional ISPs.

Narrowband Cable   A class of guided network media optimized for a single frequency range.

Network Access Point   See NAP.

Network Interface Card (NIC)   An I/O expansion circuit board that usually encompasses the lowest three layers of the OSI protocol stack. An NIC converts the parallel data passed on the system bus to the serial signals broadcast on a communications medium. NICs convert system data from binary to the coding of the network (and vice versa).

Network of Workstations (NOW)   A collection of distributed workstations that works in parallel only while the nodes are not being used as regular workstations.

Neural Network   A type of computer system composed of large numbers of simple processing elements that individually handle one piece of a much larger problem. The processing elements must undergo training via a specific learning algorithm.

Nibble   One of two 4-bit halves of a byte. Bytes consist of one high-order and one low-order nibble.

NIC   See Network Interface Card.

Noise   The electrical phenomena that work against the accurate transmission of signals. Noise strength is measured in decibels (dB).

Non-Return-to-Zero (NRZ)   A code devised for the transmission of data where 1s are always high and 0s always low, or vice versa. Typically, "high" is +5 or +3 volts and "low" is −5 or −3 volts. This code is ineffective if the sender and receiver are not in exact synchronization. In magnetic storage, the NRZ code is implemented by flux reversals.

Non-Return-to-Zero-Invert (NRZI)   A code for data transmission and storage that provides a transition—either high to low or low to high—for each binary one, and no transition for binary zero. The frequent transitions help to maintain synchronization.

Nonblocking Cache   A cache that can process multiple requests concurrently.

Nonblocking Interconnection Network   A network that allows new connections in the presence of other simultaneous connections.

Nonmaskable Interrupt   A high-priority interrupt that cannot be disabled and must be acknowledged.

Nonrecurring Engineering Costs   See NRE.

Nonuniform Memory Access (NUMA)   A type of shared memory MIMD machine that provides each processor with its own piece of memory, resulting in near-memory accesses taking less time than memory belonging to other processors.

Normalization   1. In the context of computer performance analysis, normalization is the process of expressing a statistical performance measure as a ratio to the performance of a system to which comparisons are made. 2. In the context of floating-point representation, normalizing a number means adjusting the exponent so that the leftmost bit of the significand (fractional part) will be a 1.

NOW   See Network of Workstations.

NRE   Nonrecurring engineering costs involved in the production of a customized integrated circuit. NRE includes the cost of licensing intellectual property designs and creating the circuit mask.

NRZ   See Non-Return-to-Zero.

NRZI   See Non-Return-to-Zero-Invert.

Nybble   See Nibble.

Nyquist's Law   Law from Henry Nyquist that shows no signal can convey information at a rate faster than twice its frequency. Symbolically: $\text{DataRate}_{max} = 2 \times \text{bandwidth} \times \log_2$ (number of signal levels) baud.

Octet   1. A group of three bits that represents a single octal digit. 2. In Internet networking, refers to a group of 8 consecutive bits (otherwise known as a byte).

Offset Binary Representation   See Excess-M Representation.

One's Complement Notation   A method used to represent signed binary values. Positive numbers are simply represented in signed magnitude format; negative numbers are represented by flipping all the bits in the representation of the corresponding positive number.

Opcode   Short for operation code. The part of an instruction that specifies the operation to be executed.

Operating System   Software that controls the overall operation of a computer system to include process scheduling and management, process protection, memory management, I/O, and security.

Operation Counting   The process of estimating the number of instruction types that are executed in a loop, then determining the number of machine cycles required for each instruction type. This information is then used to achieve a better instruction balance and, possibly, increase performance of a program.

Optical Cable   A class of guided network media, often called fiber-optic cable, that consists of bundles of thin (1.5 to 125µm) glass or plastic strands surrounded by a protective plastic sheath. A fiber-optic strand conducts light in a manner comparable to how copper wire conducts electricity and household plumbing "conducts" water.

Optical Computer   A computer that uses photons of laser light to carry out logic functions.

Optical Jukebox   Robotic optical storage libraries that provide direct access to large numbers of optical disks. Jukeboxes can store dozens to hundreds of disks, for total capacities of 50 to 1,200GB and upwards.

Orthogonality   An instruction set is said to be orthogonal if the instructions are independent (there is no overlap in functionality) and consistent (there are no special cases, no special registers, all addressing modes can be used with any data type or instruction type, instructions have the same format, etc.). In the context of programming, an orthogonal instruction set is one in which all instructions have the same format and register usage and can therefore be used interchangeably. (The choice of register to use is orthogonal to the choice of instruction.)

Overclocking   A method used to improve system performance that pushes the bounds of specific system components.

Overflow   A condition where a register is not large enough to contain the result of an arithmetic operation. In signed arithmetic operations, overflow is detectable when the carry in to the sign bit does not equal the carry out from the sign bit.

Overlay   A memory management method where the programmer controls the timing of program submodule loading. Today, this task is usually performed automatically through the system's memory management facilities.

P-Code Languages   Languages that are both compiled and interpreted.

PaaS   Abbreviation for Platform-as-a-Service, where an outside party provides server hardware, operating systems, database services, security components. These facilities are provided over the Internet from a location that is often unknown to the consumer. The consumer of these services also has no concerns regarding the underlying hardware of PaaS. Compare with IaaS and SaaS.

Packed BCD   BCD values that are placed in adjacent nibbles in a byte, allowing one nibble for the sign.

Page Fault   Occurs when a requested page is not in main memory and must be copied to memory from disk.

Page Field   The part of an address that specifies the page (either virtual or physical) in which the requested data resides.

Page Frames   The equal-sized chunks or blocks into which main memory (physical memory) is divided when implementing paged virtual memory.

Page Mapping   The mechanism by which virtual addresses are translated into physical ones.

Page Table   A table that records the physical location of a process's virtual pages.

Pages   The fixed-sized blocks into which virtual memory (the logical address space) is divided, each equal in size to a page frame. Virtual pages are stored on disk until needed.

Paging   1. A method used for implementing virtual memory in which main memory is divided into fixed-sized blocks (frames) and programs are divided into the same size blocks (pages). 2. The process of copying a virtual page from disk to a page frame in main memory.

PAL   See Programmable Array Logic.

Parallel Communication   Communication in which an entire byte (or word) is transmitted at once across the communication medium. The communication medium (data bus or peripheral interface cable) must therefore have one conductor for each bit. Other conductors are needed to manage the data exchange. The presence of a clock signal (or strobe) is critical to the proper handling of parallel data transmission. Compare to Serial Communication.

Parallel Processor   A computer that is capable of carrying out multiple calculations simultaneously.

Parity   The simplest error-detection scheme that is a function of the sum of the 1s in a byte. A parity bit is turned "on" or "off " depending on whether the sum of the other bits in the byte is even or odd.

Parking Heads   Done when a hard disk is powered down. The read/write heads retreat to a safe place to prevent damage to the medium.

Partial Response Maximum Likelihood   See PRML.

PC (Program Counter)   Register that holds the address of the next instruction to be executed in a program.

PCI   See Peripheral Component Interconnect.

PDH   See Plesiochronous Digital Hierarchy.

PDU   See Protocol Data Unit.

Perceptron   A single trainable neuron in a neural network.

Peripheral Component Interconnect (PCI)   A local bus standard from Intel that supports the connection of multiple peripheral devices.

Pervasive Computing   See Ubiquitous Computing.

Phase Modulation (PM)   See Manchester Code.

Photonic Computer   See Optical Computer.

Physical Address   The real address in physical memory.

Pile of PCs (POPC)   A cluster of dedicated heterogeneous hardware used to build a parallel system. BEOWULF is an example of a POPC.

Pipelining   The process of breaking down the fetch–decode–execute cycle into smaller steps (pipeline stages), where some of these smaller steps can be overlapped and performed in parallel.

Platform-as-a-Service   See PaaS.

PLD (Programmable Logic Device)   Any of a general class of logic devices that can be configured (or modified) to provide a desired logic function. PLDs include (but are not limited to) programmable array logic (PAL), programmable logic array (PLA), and Field-Programmable Gate Array (FPGA) devices.

Plug-and-Play   The ability of a computer to configure devices automatically.

PM   See Manchester Code.

PNG (Portable Network Graphics)   Data compression that first encodes the message using Huffman code and then compresses the message again using LZ77 compression.

Point-to-Point Bus   A bus connecting two specific components in a system.

Pointer   A memory address stored as a data value in a register or memory.

Polling   When a system continually monitors registers or communications ports, testing them for the presence of data signals.

POP   See Internet Service Provider.

Port   1. A connection socket (interface) on a computer system that provides access to an I/O bus or controller. 2. In the TCP/IP protocol suite, a port is a numerical value that identifies a particular protocol service.

Portable Network Graphics   See PNG.

POSIX   An acronym for Portable Operating System Interface, an effort by the IEEE to define a "standard" Unix. The current standard is 1003.1-2001, which includes real-time extensions for shared memory, I/O interrupt handling, and priority scheduling. POSIX is pronounced *paw-zicks*.

Postfix Notation   One of the orderings of operators and operands that places the operators after operands, such as 23+. Also known as Reverse Polish Notation.

Precision   In the context of numeric representation, precision deals with how much information we have about a value and the amount of information used to represent the value.

Prefetching   A technique for reducing memory or disk accesses. When using prefetching, multiple pages from memory are read, or a disk reads a number of sectors subsequent to the one requested with the expectation that one or more of the subsequent pages or sectors will be needed "soon."

Prefix Notation   One of the orderings of operators and operands that places the operators before the operands, such as +23.

Price-Performance Ratio   One way of measuring the "value" of a particular system based on its stated performance. Mathematically, a price-performance ratio is found by dividing the price of a system by a meaningful performance metric. A price-performance ratio is only as good as the metric used in the divisor and only as meaningful as the total cost of ownership of the system.

Principle of Equivalence of Hardware and Software   The principle that states that anything that can be done with software can also be done with hardware, and anything that can be done with hardware can also be done with software.

PRML   Partial response maximum likelihood is a widely employed magnetic media encoding method consisting of a convolutional code and a Viterbi detector. While reading a disk (or tape), magnetic detector circuits take several samples across each bit cell. These waveforms are passed to a Viterbi detector that selects the most probable bit pattern. The purpose of PRML is to allow bit cells to be much closer together.

Product-of-Sums Form   A standard form for a Boolean expression that is a collection of sum terms ANDed together.

Profiling   The process of breaking program code into small chunks and timing each of these chunks to determine which chunks take the most time.

Program Counter Register (PC)   A special register that holds the address of the next instruction to be executed.

Programmable Array Logic (PAL)   A configurable logic device that provides a sum-of-products function of its inputs. Connections are made (or broken) between the inputs and AND gates (for the product part) by throwing switches or blowing fuses. The outputs of the AND gates are inputs to OR gates that provide the sum part. Connections between the OR gates and the AND gates are not configurable. PALs are less flexible but faster than PLAs.

Programmable Logic Array (PLA)   A configurable logic device that provides a product-of-sums function of its inputs. Connections are made (or broken) between the inputs and AND gates (for the product part) by throwing switches or blowing fuses. The outputs of the AND gates are inputs to OR gates that provide the sum part. Connections between the OR gates and the AND gates may also be configured using switches or fuses, thus providing greater flexibility than PALs.

Programmed I/O   I/O in which the CPU must wait while the I/O module completes a requested I/O operation.

PROM (Programmable ROM)   ROM that can be programmed with the proper equipment.

Protection Fault   A condition caused by a process attempting to use the protected memory of another process or the operating system.

Protocol   A set of rules to which communicating entities must adhere in order for an information exchange to take place.

Protocol Data Unit (PDU)   A data communications packet that contains protocol information in addition to a data payload.

QIC   See Serpentine Recording.

Quantum Computer   A computer based on the quantum physics of particles that manipulates information as qubits, which can exist in multiple states simultaneously, resulting in quantum parallelism.

Qubit   The basic unit of quantum information, which can represent a 0, a 1, or both. The quantum computing equivalent of a bit.

Queue   A data structure optimized for first-come, first-served (FIFO) element processing. Queue elements are removed in the same order in which they arrived.

Race Condition   A situation where the final state of data depends not on the correctness of the updates, but on the order in which they were accessed.

Radix Complement   Given a number N in base r having d digits, the radix complement of N is defined to be $r^d - N$ for $N \neq 0$ and 0 for $N = 0$.

Radix Point   A separator that distinguishes the integer part of a number from its fractional part.

RAID   A storage system that improves reliability and performance by providing a number of "inexpensive" (or "independent") small disks instead of a single large, expensive disk. The name of this system was initially "redundant array of inexpensive disks." Today, the translation of RAID is properly given as "redundant array of independent disks."

RAID-0   Also known as drive spanning; places data in stripes across several disks. RAID-0 offers no redundancy.

RAID-1   Also known as mirroring; writes two copies of data onto a pair of independent disks.

RAID-10   Combination of the striping of RAID-0 with the mirroring of RAID-1. RAID-10 gives the best possible read performance while providing the best possible availability.

RAID-2   RAID systems that contain a set of data drives and a set of Hamming drives. One bit of data is written to each data drive, with the Hamming drives containing error recovery information for the data drives. RAID-2 is a theoretical RAID design with no commercial implementations.

RAID-3   Popular RAID system that stripes data one bit at a time across all of the data drives and uses one drive to hold a simple parity bit. The parity calculation can be done quickly in hardware using an XOR operation on each data bit.

RAID-4   A theoretical RAID level (like RAID-2). A RAID-4 array, like RAID-3, consists of a group of data disks and a parity disk. Instead of writing data one bit at a time across all of the drives, RAID-4 writes data in strips of uniform size, creating a stripe across all of the drives as described in RAID-0. Bits in the data strip are XORed with each other to create the parity strip. RAID-4 is essentially RAID-0 with parity.

RAID-5   Popular RAID system that builds upon RAID-4 with the parity disks spread throughout the entire array.

RAID-6   RAID system that uses two sets of error-correction strips for every rank (or horizontal row) of drives. A second level of protection is added with the use of Reed-Solomon error-correcting codes in addition to parity.

RAM (Random Access Memory)   Volatile memory that is used to store programs and data on a computer. Each memory location has a unique address.

RAMAC   Acronym for Random Access Method of Accounting and Control. Released by IBM in 1956, RAMAC was the first commercial disk-based computer system.

Range   In the context of numeric representation, the interval from the smallest value in a given format to the largest value in that same format.

Real-Time System   Computer processing that reacts to physical events as they occur, thus requiring rigorous timing constraints. In hard real-time systems (with potentially fatal results if deadlines aren't met), there can be no timing errors. In soft real-time systems, meeting deadlines is desirable, but does not result in catastrophic results if deadlines are missed.

Recording Mode   See CD Recording Mode.

Reed-Solomon (RS)   Code that can be thought of as a CRC that operates over entire characters instead of only a few bits. RS codes, like CRCs, are systematic: the parity bytes are appended to a block of information bytes.

Reentrant Code   Code that can be used with different data.

Register   A hardware circuit that stores binary data. Registers are located on the CPU and are very fast. Some are user-visible; others are not.

Register Addressing   An addressing mode in which the contents of a register are used as the operand.

Register Indirect Addressing   An addressing mode in which the contents of a register are used as a pointer to the actual location of the operand.

Register Transfer Notation (RTN) [also Register Transfer Language (RTL)]   The symbolic notation used to describe the behavior of microoperations.

Register Window Sets (also Overlapping Register Windows)   A technique used by RISC architectures to allow parameter passing to be done by simply changing which registers are visible to the currently executing procedure.

Register-Memory Architecture   An architecture that requires at least one operand to be located in a register and one to be located in memory.

Repeater   An OSI Layer 1 device that amplifies signals sent through long network cabling runs.

Replacement Policy   The policy used to select a victim cache block or page to be replaced. (Necessary for set associative caching, fully associative caching, and paging.)

Request for Comment   See Internet Engineering Task Force.

Resident Monitor   Early type of operating system that allowed programs to be processed without human interaction (other than placing the decks of cards into the card reader). Predecessor to modern operating system.

Resource Conflict   A situation in which two instructions need the same resource. May slow down a pipelined CPU.

Response Time   The amount of time required for a system or one of its components to carry out a task.

Reverse Polish Notation (RPN)   See Postfix Notation.

RISC (Reduced Instruction Set Computer)   A design philosophy in which each computer instruction performs only one operation, instructions are all the same size, they have only a few different layouts, and all arithmetic operations must be performed between registers.

RLL   See Run-Length-Limited.

Robotic Tape Library   Also known as a tape silo, an automated tape library system that can mount, dismount, and keep track of (catalog) great numbers of magnetic tape cartridges. Robotic tape libraries can have total capacities in the hundreds of terabytes and can load a cartridge at user request in less than half a minute.

Rock's Law   A corollary to Moore's Law that states that the cost of capital equipment to build semiconductors will double every four years.

ROM (Read-Only Memory)   Nonvolatile memory that always retains its data.

Rose's Law   A prediction made by Geordie Rose that states that the number of qubits that can be assembled to successfully perform computations will double every 12 months.

Rotational Delay   The time required for a requested sector to position itself under the read/write heads of a hard disk.

Router   A sophisticated hardware device connected to at least two networks that determines the destination to which a packet should be forwarded.

Run-Length-Limited (RLL)   A coding method where block character code words such as ASCII or EBCDIC are translated into code words specially designed to limit the number of consecutive zeros appearing in the code. An RLL(d, k) code allows a minimum of d and a maximum of k consecutive zeros to appear between any pair of consecutive ones.

SaaS   Abbreviation for Software-as-a-Service, which characterizes application software provided over the Internet as a service. SaaS typically has few locally installed components. The consumer of the service has no knowledge of the internals of either the application or its supporting infrastructure. Compare with IaaS and PaaS.

SAS   See Serial Attached SCSI.

SATA   See Serial ATA.

SCADA   Acronym for Supervisory Control and Data Acquisition systems. SCADA systems include those that manage large industrial, manufacturing, transportation, and other physical systems.

SCAN (C-SCAN)   A disk-scheduling algorithm where the disk arm continually sweeps over the surface of the disk, stopping when it reaches a track for which it has a request in its service queue. This approach is called the elevator algorithm because of its similarity to how skyscraper elevators service their passengers. SCAN has a variant, called C-SCAN (for circular SCAN), in which track zero is treated as if it were adjacent to the highest-numbered track on the disk.

SCSI   An acronym for Small Computer System Interface, a disk drive connection technology that allows multiple devices to be daisy-chained and addressed individually through a single host adapter. Has been expanded to include numerous connection methods through the SCSI-3 Architecture Model (SAM), which is a layered system with protocols for communication between the layers. SAM incorporates Serial Storage Architecture (SSA), Serial Bus (also known as IEEE 1394 or FireWire), Fibre Channel, and Generic Packet Protocol (GPP) into a unified architectural model.

SDH See Synchronous Digital Hierarchy.

SDRAM (Synchronous Dynamic Random Access Memory) Memory that is synchronized with the clock speed with which the processor bus is optimized.

Secondary Memory Memory located off the CPU and out of the system itself. Examples include magnetic disk, magnetic tape, and CD-ROM.

Seek Time The time it takes for a disk arm to position itself over a requested track.

Segment Table A table that records the physical locations of a process's segments.

Segmentation Similar to paging except that instead of dividing the virtual address space into equal, fixed-sized pages, and the physical address space into equal-sized page frames, the virtual address space is divided into logical, variable-length units, or *segments*.

Self-Relative Addressing An addressing mode in which the address of the operand is computed as an offset from the current instruction.

Semantic Gap The logical gap that exists between the physical components of a computer and a high-level language.

Sequential Circuit A logic device whose output is defined in terms of its current inputs in addition to its previous outputs.

Serial ATA (SATA) A serial implementation of the ATA interface. Its advantages include much faster speeds (up to 600MBps envisioned) and thinner cables that facilitate airflow inside the main computer cabinets. SATA will eventually replace parallel ATA.

Serial Attached SCSI (SAS) A serial implementation of the SCSI interface. Its advantages include much faster speeds (up to 600MBps envisioned) and thinner cables that facilitate airflow inside the main computer cabinets. SAS supports more than 16,000 devices in a domain. SAS has replaced parallel SCSI in all new equipment.

Serial Communication A method of transmitting data where a data byte is sent one bit at a time. Serial communication is asynchronous: It requires no separate timing signal within the transmission medium. Compare to Parallel Communication.

Serial Storage Architecture See SSA.

Serpentine Recording A method of placing bits on a magnetic tape medium "lengthwise," with each byte aligning in parallel with the long edge of the tape. Popular serpentine tape formats include digital linear tape (DLT) and Quarter-Inch Cartridge (QIC).

Server Consolidation The act of combining numerous (usually small) servers into one (usually larger) system.

Server Farm A large, controlled environment computer facility containing great numbers of small server systems.

Service Access Point (SAP)   A numerical value that identifies the protocol service requested during a communications session. In TCP, this SAP is a numerical value called a port.

Set Associative Cache (also *n*-Way Set Associative Cache)   A cache-mapping scheme that requires cache to be divided into sets of associative memory blocks. Main memory is then modularly mapped to a given set.

Set Field   That part of an address that specifies the corresponding cache set.

Shannon's Law   Articulated in 1948 by Claude Shannon, a measure of the signal-carrying capacity of an imperfect transmission medium. In symbols: $DataRate_{max} =$ Bandwidth $\times \log_2 [1 + (Signal\ dB \div Noise\ dB)]$ baud.

Shared Memory Systems   Systems in which all processors have access to a global memory and communication is via shared variables.

Short Stroking   The practice of placing files on a disk in such a way as to minimize disk arm motion, thus reducing access time.

Shortest Seek Time First (SSTF)   A disk-scheduling algorithm that arranges access requests so that the disk arm services the track nearest its current location.

Shuffle Network   See Multistage Interconnection Network.

Signal-to-Noise Ratio   A measure of the quality of a communications channel. The signal-to-noise ratio varies in proportion to the frequency of the signal carried over the line. (The higher the frequency, the greater the signal-to-noise ratio.) Mathematically: Signal-to-Noise Ratio $(dB) = 10 \log_{10} (Signal\ dB \div Noise\ dB)$.

Signed Magnitude   A binary representation of a number having a sign as its leftmost bit, where the remaining bits comprise its absolute value (or magnitude).

Significand   A term introduced by IEEE to refer to the fractional part of a number expressed in floating-point notation. IEEE's definition includes an implied one to the left of the binary point of a normalized number; however, the term is widely accepted to refer to the fractional part of a floating-point number for any given representation.

SIMD (Single Instruction, Multiple Data)   An architecture with a single point of control that executes the same instruction simultaneously on multiple data values. Examples include vector processors and array processors.

Singularity   See Technical Singularity.

SISD (Single Instruction, Single Data)   An architecture with a single instruction stream and only one data stream. Examples include the von Neumann architecture employed in most current PCs.

SLED (Single Large Expensive Disk)   A term coined along with the concept of RAID. SLED systems are thought to be less reliable and perform poorly as compared to RAID systems.

Small Computer System Interface   See SCSI.

SMP (Symmetric Multiprocessors)   An MIMD shared memory architecture.

SNA   See Systems Network Architecture.

SOC   See System on a Chip.

Software-as-a-Service   See SaaS.

Solid-State Drive   See SSD.

SPEC   Acronym used by the Standard Performance Evaluation Corporation. SPEC's objective is to establish equitable and realistic methods for computer performance measurement. SPEC produces respected benchmarking suites for file server, Web, desktop computing environments, enterprise-level multiprocessor systems and super-computers, and multimedia as well as graphics-intensive systems.

Speculative Execution   The act of fetching an instruction and beginning its execution in the pipeline before it is certain whether the instruction will need to execute. This work must be undone if a prediction is found to be incorrect.

Speedup   See Amdahl's Law.

SPMD (Single Program, Multiple Data)   An extension to Flynn's taxonomy describing systems that consist of multiprocessors, each with its own data set and program memory.

Spooling   Acronym for simultaneous peripheral operation online, a process whereby printed output is written to disk prior to being sent to a printer, helping to compensate for the great difference between CPU speed and printer speed.

SRAM (Static RAM)   RAM that holds its contents as long as power is available (unlike dynamic RAM, which requires recharges to maintain data).

SSA   An abbreviation for Serial Storage Architecture. SSA's design supports multiple disk drives and multiple hosts in a redundant loop configuration. Because of this redundancy, one drive or host adapter can fail and the rest of the disks will remain accessible. The dual loop topology of the SSA architecture also allows the base throughput to be doubled from 40MBps to 80MBps. SSA is losing market share to Fibre Channel.

SSD   Abbreviation for solid-state drive; a mass storage device consisting of a micro-controller and a large array of flash memory. SSDs are more rugged and provide faster access times than conventional magnetic disks.

SSI (Small-Scale Integration)   Integrated circuits with 10 to 100 components per chip.

SSTF   See Shortest Seek Time First.

Stack   A simple data structure optimized for last-in, first-out (LIFO) element process-ing. Stack elements are removed in the reverse order in which they arrived.

Stack Addressing   An addressing mode in which the operand is assumed to be on the system stack.

Stack Architecture   An architecture that uses a stack to execute instructions, where the operands are implicitly found on top of the stack.

Standard Performance Evaluation Corporation   See SPEC.

Star-Connected Network   A network using a central hub through which all messages must pass.

Static Interconnection Network   A network that establishes a fixed path between two entities (either two processors or a processor and a memory) that cannot change from one communication to the next.

Statistical Coding   A data compression method where the frequency of the occurrence of a symbol determines the length of the output symbol. Symbol probabilities are written to a file along with the information required to decode the message. Symbols that occur with greatest frequency in the input become the smallest symbols in the output.

Status Register   A special register that monitors and records special conditions such as overflow, carries, and borrows.

Storage Area Network   Networks built specifically for data storage access and management.

Strictly Inclusive Cache   A cache that guarantees that all data resident in one level is also found in another level of the cache hierarchy.

Subnet   A subdivision of a larger network. Under the TCP/IP protocol, a subnet is a network consisting of all devices whose IP addresses have the same prefix.

Subsystem   A logical computing environment usually established to facilitate management of related applications or processes.

Subtrahend   See Minuend.

Sum-of-Products Form   A standard form for a Boolean expression that is a collection of product terms ORed together.

Superpipelining   The process of combining superscalar concepts with pipelining, by dividing the pipeline stages into many small stages, so more than one stage can be executed during one clock cycle.

Superpositioning   In quantum computing, the phenomenon in which a system exists in more than one state simultaneously.

Superscalar   A design methodology for computer architecture in which the CPU has multiple ALUs and can issue more than one instruction per clock cycle.

Supervised Learning   A type of learning used in training neural networks that assumes prior knowledge of correct results, which are fed to the neural net during the training phase.

Supervisory Control and Data Acquisition   See SCADA.

Switch   A device that provides point-to-point interconnection between system components. In the context of data communications, a switch is a Layer 2 device that creates a point-to-point connection between one of its input ports and one of its output ports.

Switching Network   A network that connects processors and memories via switches (either crossbar or 2×2 switches) that allows for dynamic routing.

Symbol Table   The table built by an assembler that stores the set of correspondences between labels and memory addresses.

Symbolic Logic   See Boolean Algebra.

Synchronous Circuits   Sequential circuits that use clocks to order events. The output values of these circuits can change only when the clock ticks.

Syndrome   A group of error-checking bits.

Synthetic Benchmark   A performance metric derived from a program written to exercise particular system components. By running the synthetic benchmark on various systems, the resulting execution time produces a single performance metric across all of the systems tested. Better-known synthetic benchmarks are the Whetstone, Linpack, and Dhrystone metrics.

System Bus   An internal bus commonly found on PCs that connects the CPU, memory, and all other internal components.

System on a Chip (SOC)   A highly complex embedded system component sometimes consisting of more than one processor and several diverse supporting circuits. SOCs have large memories, enabling them to support full-featured operating systems. When SOCs comprise more than one processor core, they often do not share the same clock and can have different instruction sets and architectures. SOCs get their name from the fact that they etch fully functional systems on a single die, as opposed to socketing several different chips on a printed circuit board.

System Simulation   Software models for predicting aspects of system behavior without the use of the exact live environment that the simulator is modeling. Simulation is useful for estimating the performance of systems or system configurations that do not yet exist.

Systematic Error Detection   An error-detection method where error-checking bits are appended to the original information byte.

Systems Network Architecture (SNA)   An early proprietary network technology invented by IBM. This system originally consisted of dumb terminals that were polled by communications controllers. The communications controllers, in turn, communicated with a communications front-end processor that was connected to a host (mainframe) computer.

Systolic Arrays   A variation of SIMD computers that incorporates large arrays of simple processors that use vector pipelines for data flow and also incorporates a high degree of parallelism.

Tag Field   That part of an address that specifies the cache tag.

Tape Silo   See Robotic Tape Library.

TCM   See Trellis Code Modulation.

TCO   See Total Cost of Ownership.

TCP   A connection-oriented protocol used by the Internet. TCP is a self-managing protocol that ensures the accurate, sequenced delivery of data segments.

Technical Singularity   A theoretical point in time when human technology has progressed to the point where it will fundamentally and irreversibly alter human development.

Thrashing   Occurs when needed blocks or pages are constantly brought into memory but immediately replaced.

Thread   A lightweight or "mini" process.

Throughput   A measure of the number of concurrent tasks that a system can carry out without adversely affecting response time.

Thunking   The process of converting 16-bit instructions to 32-bit instructions in a Microsoft Windows system.

Timesharing   A multiuser computer system where the CPU switches between user processes very quickly, giving each user a small timeslice (portion of processor time).

Timeslice   See Timesharing.

Total Cost of Ownership   The amount of money that a computer system will cost over a given period of time, perhaps over the system's expected life. A useful TCO figure will include, at minimum, the purchase price of the exact configuration to be used including system software, expected expansions and upgrades to the system, hardware and software maintenance fees, and operations staff manpower, as well as facilities costs including floor space, backup power, and air-conditioning.

TPC   An abbreviation for Transaction Processing Performance Council. The TPC produces benchmark suites for servers that support transactions, Web commerce, and data warehouses (decision support systems).

Trace Cache   A variant of an instruction cache that is used to store instruction sequences that have already been decoded.

Transaction Processing Performance Council   See TPC.

Transfer Time   The sum of access time and the time it takes to actually read data from a hard disk. The time varies according to how much data is read.

Transistor   Short for transfer resistor, the solid-state version of the triode, a device that amplifies a signal or opens or closes a circuit. The technology used in the second generation of computers.

Translation Look-aside Buffer (TLB)   A cache for a page table. Entries consist of (virtual page number, physical frame number) pairs.

Transmission Control Performance Protocol   See TCP.

Transparent Bridge   Sophisticated network devices having the ability to learn the address of every device on each segment. Transparent bridges can also supply management information such as throughput reports.

Transport Latency   The time a message spends in the network.

Tree Network   A network that arranges entities in noncyclic tree structures.

Tri-State Device   A circuit that uses an additional input value to determine when current passes through the device and when it does not, thus resulting in three potential outputs: 0, 1, or nothing.

Trie   An acyclic (*n*-ary tree) data structure that stores partial data key values in each of its nodes. The key value is assembled as a search proceeds down the trie. Internal nodes contain a sufficient number of pointers to direct a search to the desired key or to the next level of the trie.

Truth Table   A table that describes a logic function and shows the relationships between all possible values for the input values and the results of those inputs into the function.

Twisted Pair   A pair of insulated wires twisted together and used to transmit electrical signals.

Two's Complement Notation   A method used to represent signed binary values. Positive numbers are simply represented in signed-magnitude representation; negative numbers are represented by flipping all the bits in the representation of the corresponding positive number and adding one.

Ubiquitous Computing   The concept of integrating computers into our environments in such a way that data and network access become transparent but constantly available.

ULSI (Ultra-Large-Scale Integration)   More than 1 million components per chip.

UML   Unified Modeling Language, first released in 1996 by three Rational Software object-oriented design pioneers: Grady Booch, Ivar Jacobson, and James Rumbaugh. UML brought together several object-oriented modeling systems under one standard that now falls under the auspices of the Object Management Group (OMG).

Underflow   See Divide Underflow.

Unguided Transmission Media   Electromagnetic or optical carrier waves that convey data communications signals. This media class includes wireless broadcast, microwave, satellite, and free-space optics.

Unicode   A 16-bit international character code that can express every language in the world. The lower 127 characters of the Unicode character set are identical to the ASCII character set.

Unified Cache   Cache that holds the more recently used data and instructions for an executing program.

Unified Modeling Language   See UML.

Uniform Memory Access (UMA)   Shared memory MIMD machines in which memory accessed by any processor to any memory takes the same amount of time.

Universal Gate   So-called because any electronic circuit can be constructed using only this kind of gate. (NAND and NOR are both examples of universal gates.)

Universal Serial Bus   See USB.

Unsupervised Learning   A type of learning used in training neural networks that does not provide the correct output to the network during training.

USB (Universal Serial Bus)   An external bus standard used in USB ports that supports hot plugging with a variety of devices.

Vacuum Tube   The somewhat undependable technology used in Generation Zero of computers.

Vector Processors   Specialized, heavily pipelined processors that perform efficient operations on entire vectors and matrices at once. Register–register vector processors require all operations to use registers as source and destination operands. Memory–memory vector processors allow operands from memory to be routed directly to the arithmetic unit.

Verilog   A popular hardware definition language used in designing integrated circuits. Verilog was created by Gateway Design Automation in 1983 and released into the public domain in 1990 soon after Cadence Design Systems bought Gateway. Verilog is now standardized as IEEE 1364-2001.

VHDL   An abbreviation for Very (high-speed integrated circuit) Hardware Design Language that enables engineers to create circuit designs using a "higher-level" language similar in syntax to Ada. VHDL was created under a U.S. Defense Advanced Research Program Agency (DARPA) contract awarded to Intermetrics, IBM, and Texas Instruments in 1983. The latest VHDL standard is IEEE 1097-2002.

Virtual Address   The logical or program address generated by the CPU in response to executing a program. Whenever the CPU generates an address, it is always in terms of virtual address space.

Virtual Machine   1. A hypothetical computer. 2. A self-contained operating environment that gives the illusion of the existence of a separate physical machine. 3. A software emulation of a real machine.

Virtual Memory   A method that uses the hard disk as an extension to RAM, thus increasing the available address space a process can use.

Viterbi Decoder   A specialized circuit employed in magnetic media that selects the most likely bit pattern. See PRML.

VLIW Architecture (Very Long Instruction Word)   An architectural characteristic in which each instruction can specify multiple scalar operations.

VLSI (Very-Large-Scale Integration)   Integrated circuits with more than 10,000 components per chip. The technology used in the fourth generation of computers.

Volatile Memory   Memory that is lost when power is switched off.

von Neumann Architecture   A stored-program machine architecture consisting of a CPU, an ALU, registers, and main memory.

von Neumann Bottleneck   The name given to the single path between main memory and the control unit of the CPU. The single path forces alternation of instruction and execution cycles and often results in a bottleneck, or slowing of the system.

Wall Clock Time   Also called elapsed time, this is the only true measure of computer performance, especially when the wall clock time is measured as the system is running *your* program.

WAN   Acronym for wide area network. WANs can cover multiple cities or the entire world.

Watchdog Timer   A specialized circuit used in embedded systems that guards against system hangs and infinite loops. Watchdog timers typically contain a register that is periodically decremented. The program running in the embedded system periodically resets the timer to indicate system liveness.

Wear Leveling   A technique used to evenly distribute erase-write operations across an entire solid-state drive in order to prevent excessive localized memory cell wear.

Weighted Arithmetic Mean   An arithmetic mean that is found by taking the products of the frequency of a set of results (expressed as a percentage) with the values of the results. The weighted arithmetic mean gives a mathematical expectation of the behavior of a system and may also be called weighted average.

Weighted Numbering System   A numeration system in which a value is represented through increasing powers of a radix (or base). The binary and decimal number systems are examples of weighted numbering systems. Roman numerals do not fall into this class.

Whetstone   A benchmarking program that is floating-point intensive with many calls to library routines for computation of trigonometric and exponential functions. Results are reported in Kilo-Whetstone Instructions per Second (KWIPS) or Mega-Whetstone Instructions per Second (MWIPS).

Wide Area Network   See WAN.

Winchester Disk   Any hard disk that is housed in a sealed unit. The name derives from the code name IBM used during the development of this technology. Today, all hard disks are enclosed in sealed units, but the name "Winchester" has persisted.

Word   An addressable group of contiguous bits. Words commonly consist of 16 bits, 32 bits, or 64 bits; however, some early architectures employed word sizes that were not multiples of 8.

Word Field (also Offset Field)   That part of an address that specifies the unique word in a given block or page.

Word-Addressable   Each word (not necessarily each byte) has its own address.

Write-Back   A cache update policy that updates main memory only when a cache block is selected to be removed from cache. Allows inconsistencies between a stored cache value and its corresponding memory value.

Write-Through   A cache update policy that updates both the cache and the main memory simultaneously on every write.

Zoned-Bit Recording   The practice of increasing disk capacity by making all disk sectors approximately the same size, placing more sectors on the outer tracks than on the inner tracks. Other types of recording methods have the same number of sectors on all tracks of the disk.

Answers and Hints for Selected Exercises

Chapter 1

1. Between hardware and software, one provides more speed, the other provides more flexibility. (Which one is which?) Hardware and software are related through the Principle of Equivalence of Hardware and Software. Can one solve a problem where the other cannot?

3. One million, or 10^6

10. 0.75 micron

Chapter 2

1. a) 121222_3

   b) 10202_5

   c) 4266_7

   d) 6030_9

7. a) 11010.11001

   b) 11000010.00001

   c) 100101010.110011

   d) 10000.000111

16. a) Signed-magnitude: 01001101

     One's complement: 01001101

     Two's complement: 01001101 Excess-127: 11001100

b) Signed-magnitude: 10101010

One's complement: 11010101

Two's complement: 11010110 Excess-127: 1010101

28. a) Smallest negative: 100000 (-31)   Largest positive: 011111 (31)

32. a) 10110000

b) 00110000

c) 10000000

34. a) 00111010

b) 00101010

c) 01011110

36. a) 111100

38. a) 1001

40. 104

42. Hint: Begin the trace as follows:

j	(Binary)	k	(Binary)
0	0000	-3	1100
1	0001	-4	1011 (1100 + 1110) (where last carry is added
			to sum doing one's complement addition)
2	0010	-5	1010 (1011 + 1110)
3	0011	-6	1001 (1010 + 1110)
4	0100	-7	1000 (1001 + 1110)
5	0101	7	0111 (1000 + 1110) (This is overflow—but you can ignore.)

46.

0	1	1	1	1	0	1	0

Error = 2.4%

57. a) Binary value   00000000   00000001   00100111

b) ASCII   10110010   00111001   00110101

c) Packed BCD   00000000   00101001   01011100

68. The error is in bit 5.

73. a) 1101 remainder 110

b) 111 remainder 1100

c) 100111 remainder 110

d) 11001 remainder 1000

77. Code word: 1011001011

Chapter 3

1. a)

x	y	z	yz	(xy)'	z(xy)'	yz + z(xy)'
0	0	0	0	1	0	0
0	0	1	0	1	1	1
0	1	0	0	1	0	0
0	1	1	1	1	1	1
1	0	0	0	1	0	0
1	0	1	0	1	1	1
1	1	0	0	0	0	0
1	1	1	1	0	0	1

b)

x	y	z	(y' + z)	x(y' + z)	xyz	x(y'+z) + xyz
0	0	0	1	0	0	0
0	0	1	1	0	0	0
0	1	0	0	0	0	0
0	1	1	1	0	0	0
1	0	0	1	1	0	1
1	0	1	1	1	0	1
1	1	0	0	0	0	0
1	1	1	1	1	1	1

3. $F(x, y, z) = xy'(x + z)$

$$F'(x, y, z) = (xy'(x + z))'$$
$$= (xy')' + (x + z)'$$
$$= (x' + y) + (x'z')$$

5. $F(w, x, y, z) = xz' (x'yz + x) + y(w'z + x')$

$$F'(w, x, y, z) = (xz'(x'yz + x) + y(w'z + x'))'$$
$$= (xz'(x'yz + x))' (y(w'z + x'))'$$
$$= ((xz')' + (x'yz + x)') (y'+ (w'z + x')')$$
$$= ((x' + z'') + (x''+ y' + z')(x')) (y' + ((w''+ z')(x'')))$$
$$= ((x' + z) + (x + y'+ z')(x')) (y' + (w + z')(x'))$$

8. Invalid. One method of proof uses a truth table. A more challenging approach using identities employs the relation a XOR $b = ab' + a'b$.

15. a)

$$
\begin{aligned}
x(yz + y'z) + xy + x'y + xz &= x(yz + y'z) + y(x + x') + xz && \text{Distributive} \\
&= x(yz + y'z) + y(1) + xz && \text{Inverse} \\
&= x(yz + y'z) + y + xz && \text{Identity} \\
&= xz(y + y') + y + xz && \text{Distributive and Commutative} \\
&= xz(1) + y + xz && \text{Inverse} \\
&= xz + xz + y && \text{Identity and Commutative} \\
&= xz + y && \text{Idempotent}
\end{aligned}
$$

b)

$$
\begin{aligned}
xyz'' + (y + z)' + x'yz &= xyz + (y + z)' + x'yz && \text{Double Complement} \\
&= xyz + y'z' + x'yz && \text{DeMorgan} \\
&= xyz + x'yz + y'z' && \text{Commutative} \\
&= xz(y' + y) + y'z' && \text{Distributive} \\
&= xz(1) + y'z' && \text{Inverse} \\
&= xz + y'z' && \text{Identity}
\end{aligned}
$$

c)

$$
\begin{aligned}
z(xy' + z)(x + y') &= z(xxy' + xy'y' + xz + y'z) && \text{Distributive/Commutative} \\
&= z(xy' + xy' + xz + y'z) && \text{Idempotent} \\
&= xy'z + xy'z + xzz + y'zz && \text{Distributive/Commutative} \\
&= xy'z + xz + y'z && \text{Idempotent} \\
&= xy'z + y'z + xz && \text{Commutative} \\
&= y'z(x + 1) + xz && \text{Distributive} \\
&= y'z(1) + xz && \text{Null} \\
&= y'z + xz && \text{Identity}
\end{aligned}
$$

17. a)

$$
\begin{aligned}
x(y + z)(x' + z') &= x(x'y + yz' + x'z + zz') && \text{Distributive/Commutative} \\
&= xx'y + xyz' + xx'z + xzz' && \text{Distributive} \\
&= 0 + xyz' + 0 + 0 && \text{Inverse/Null} \\
&= xyz' && \text{Identity}
\end{aligned}
$$

19.

$$
\begin{aligned}
x(x' + y) &= xx' + xy && \text{Distributive} \\
&= 0 + xy && \text{Inverse} \\
&= xy && \text{Identity}
\end{aligned}
$$

22. $F(x, y, z) = x'y'z' + x'yz' + xy'z + xyz' + xyz$

25.

x	y	z	xy'	x'y	xz	y'z	xy' + x'y + xz + y'z
0	0	0	0	0	0	0	0
0	0	1	0	0	0	1	1
0	1	0	0	1	0	0	1
0	1	1	0	1	0	0	1
1	0	0	1	0	0	0	0
1	0	1	1	0	1	1	1
1	1	0	0	0	0	0	0
1	1	1	0	0	1	0	1

The complemented sum of two products forms is $(x'y'z' + x'y'z)'$.

33.

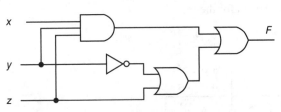

36.

x	y	z	F
0	0	0	1
0	0	1	1
0	1	0	1
0	1	1	1
1	0	0	0
1	0	1	1
1	1	0	0
1	1	1	1

49. The values assigned for the inputs (the card encoding), determine the exact design of each reader. One encoding is shown in the table below.

Encoding	Employee Class	Has authorization to enter:				
		Supply Closet	Server Room	Employee Lounge	Executive Lounge	Executive Washroom
00	IT workers		X	X		
01	Secretary	X		X	X	
10	Big Boss				X	X
11	Janitor	X	X	X	X	X

Based on this coding, the card reader for the server room can be implemented as shown below:

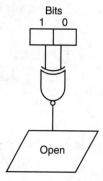

What is the design for the rest?

50.

X	Y	A	Next State	
			A	B
0	0	0	0	1
0	0	1	1	0
0	1	0	0	1
0	1	1	0	1
1	0	0	1	1
1	0	1	1	0
1	1	0	1	0
1	1	1	0	1

54.

X	Y	Z(Q)	Next State	
			S	Q
0	0	0	0	0
0	0	1	1	0
0	1	0	1	0
0	1	1	0	1
1	0	0	1	0
1	0	1	0	1
1	1	0	0	1
1	1	1	1	1

57. Start by numbering the lines between the flip-flops as shown:

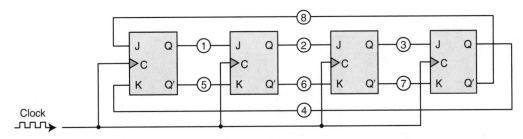

Complete the following chart for $t = 0$ through 8:

t	Lines that are "off"	Lines that are "on"
0	1,2,3,4	5,6,7,8
1	????	????
...	...	...
8	????	????

Chapter 3 Focus on Kamaugh Maps

3A.1. a) $x'z + xz'$

   b) $x'z + x'y + xy'z'$

3A.4. a) $w'z' + w'y'z' + wyz$

   b) $w'x' + wx + w'y + yz' + x'z'$ or $w'x' + wx + xy + x'z'$

3A.6. a) $x'z' + w'xz + w'xy$

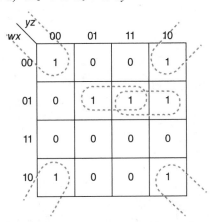

3A.6. b) $x'y' + wx'z'$

3A.8. $x'y'z + x'yz + xy'z + xyz = x'z(y' + y) + xz(y' + y)$
$$= x'z + xz$$
$$= z(x' + x)$$
$$= z$$

3A.9. a) $x + y'z$ (We don't want to include the "don't care" as it doesn't help us.)
   b) $x'z' + w'z$

Chapter 4

4. a) There are 2M $\times$ 4 bytes, which equals $2 \times 2^{20} \times 2^2 = 2^{23}$ total bytes, so 23 bits are needed for an address.

   b) There are 2M words, which equals $2 \times 2^{20} = 2^{21}$, so 21 bits are required for an address.

10. a) 16 (8 rows of 2 columns)

   b) 2

   c) 256K $= 2^{18}$, so 18 bits

   d) 8

   e) 2M $= 2^{21}$, so 21 bits

   f) Bank 0 (000)

   g) Bank 6 (110)

15. a) There are 2^{20} bytes, which can all be addressed using addresses 0 through $2^{20} - 1$ with 20-bit addresses.

   b) There are only 2^{19} words, and addressing each requires using addresses 0 through $2^{19} - 1$.

23.

A	108
One	109
S1	106
S2	103

26. a) `Store 007`

Chapter 5

1.

Address →	00	01	10	11
a) Big endian	00	00	12	34
b) Little endian	34	12	00	00

6. a) $0xFE01 = 1111\ 1110\ 0000\ 0001_2 = -511_{10}$

  b) $0x01FE = 0000\ 0001\ 1111\ 1110_2 = 510_{10}$

10. 6×2^{12}

12. a) $X\ Y \times W\ Z \times V\ U \times +\ +$

21.

Mode	Value
Immediate	0x1000
Direct	0x1400
Indirect	0x1300
Indexed	0x1000

27. a) 8

  b) 16

  c) 2^{16}

  d) $2^{24} - 1$

Chapter 6

1. a) $2^{20}/2^4 = 2^{16}$

  b) 20-bit addresses with 11 bits in the tag field, 5 in the block field, and 4 in the offset field

  c) Block 22 (or block 0x16)

4. a) $2^{16}/2^5 = 2^{11}$

  b) 16 bit addresses with 11 bits in the tag field and 5 bits in the offset field

  c) Because it's associative cache, it can map anywhere.

7. Each address has 27 bits, and there are 7 in the tag field, 14 in the set field, and 6 in the offset field.

19. Program Address
Space

Main Memory
Address Space

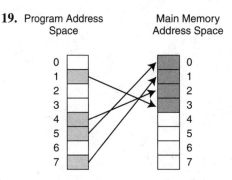

Chapter 7

1. 1.28 or 28% ($S = 1.2766; f = 0.65; k = 1.5$)

9. a) Choose the disk upgrade. This will cost $216.20 per 1% improvement versus $268.24 for the CPU.

b) The disk upgrade gives the greater improvement: 36.99% versus 18.64% for the processor.

c) The break-even point would be a disk upgrade costing $9922 or a CPU upgrade costing $4031.

12. a) A CPU should disable all interrupts before it enters an interrupt service routine, so the interrupt shouldn't happen in the first place.

b) It is not a problem.

c) If interrupts are disabled, the second interrupt would never happen, so it is not a problem.

22. Some people think that retrieving specific data from a particular disk is not a "random" act.

24. Rotational delay (average latency) = 7200 RPM = 120 rev/sec = 0.008333 sec/rev = 8.333 ms per revolution. (Alternatively, 60,000 ms per minute/7200 revolutions per minute = 8.333 ms per revolution.) The average is half of this, or 4.17 ms.

28. a) 256 MB (1 MB = 2^{20} B)

b) 11 ms

32. 28.93 MB/track

39.

Specifications	
Hours/year	8760
Cost per kWh	0.1
Active percentage	0.25
Active watts	14.4
Idle percentage	0.75
Idle watts	9.77

Hours active/yr	$0.25 \times 8760 = 2190$	
kWatts consumed active $2190 \times 14.4 \div 1000$		$= 31.536$
Hours idle/yr	$0.75 \times 8760 = 6570$	
kWatts consumed idle $6570 \times 9.77 \div 1000$		$= 64.1889$
	Total kW	95.7249
	Energy cost/yr	\$9.57
	$\times$ 5 disks	\$47.85
	$\times$ 5 years	\$239.25
	+ disk costs \$300 $\times$ 10	\$3,239.25

Facilities	
Fixed cost per GB per month	0.01
Number of GB	$\times$ 8000
Total cost per month	= 80
Number of months	$\times$ 60
Total facilities cost	\$4,800.00

Grand total:	\$8,039.25

Chapter 8

5. If processes share a specific set of resources, it might be reasonable to group them as a subsystem. If a given set of processes is used for testing the system, it would be wise to group them as a subsystemv because if they crash or do something "weird," only the subsystem in which they are running is affected. If you are giving access to a specific group of people for a limited time or to limited resources, you may want these user processes to be grouped as a subsystem as well.

7. Nonrelocatable code is often used when code needs to be more compact. Therefore, it is common in embedded systems that have space constraints (such as your microwave or your car computer). Nonrelocatable code is also faster, so it is used in systems that are sensitive to small timing delays, such as real-time systems. Relocatable code requires hardware support, so nonrelocatable code would be used in those situations that might not have that support (such as in Nintendo).

9. Dynamic linking saves disk space (why?), results in fewer system errors (why?), and allows for code sharing. However, dynamic linking can cause load-time delays, and if dynamic link library routines are changed, others using modified libraries could end up with difficult bugs to trace.

19. Java is first compiled into byte code. This intermediate byte code is then interpreted by the JVM.

21. a) A race condition occurs when different computational results (e.g., output, values of data variables) occur depending on the particular timing and resulting order of execution of statements across separate threads, processes, or transactions.

Suppose we have the following two transactions accessing an account with an initial balance of 500:

```
Transaction A                Transaction B
Get Balance of Account       Get Balance of Account
Add 100 to Balance           Subtract 100 from Balance
Store new Balance            Store new Balance
```

The value of the new balance depends on the order in which the transactions are run. What are the possible values for the new balance?

b) Race conditions can be prevented by running transactions in isolation and providing atomicity. Atomic transactions in databases are ensured via locking.

c) Using locks can result in deadlocks. Suppose Transaction T1 gets an exclusive lock on data item X (which means no other transaction can share the lock), and then Transaction T2 gets an exclusive lock on data item Y. Now suppose T1 needs to hold on to X but now needs Y, and T2 must hold on to Y but now needs X. We have a deadlock because each is waiting on the other and will not release the lock that it has.

Chapter 9

1. RISC machines limit the instructions that can access memory to load and store instructions only. This means that all other instructions use registers. This requires fewer cycles and speeds up the execution of the code and, thus, the performance of the hardware. The goal for RISC architectures is to achieve single-cycle instructions, which would not be possible if instructions had to access memory instead of registers.

3. "Reduced" originally meant providing a set of minimal instructions that could carry out all essential operations: data movement, ALU operations, and branching. However, the main objective in RISC machines today is to simplify instructions so they can execute more quickly. Each instruction performs only one operation, they are all the same size, they have only a few different layouts, and all arithmetic operations must be performed between registers (data in memory cannot be used as an operand).

5. 128

9. During a context switch, all information about the currently executing process must be saved, including the values in the register windows. When the process is restored, the values in the register windows must be restored as well. Depending on the size of the windows, this could be a very time-consuming process.

11. a) SIMD: single instruction, multiple data. One specific instruction executes on multiple pieces of data. For example, a vector processor adding arrays uses one instruction ($C[i] = A[i] + B[i]$), but can perform this instruction on several pieces of data ($C[1] = A[1] + B[1]$, $C[2] = A[2] + B[2]$, $C[3] = A[3] + B[3]$, etc.), depending on how many ALUs the processor contains.

13. *Loosely coupled* and *tightly coupled* are terms that describe how multiprocessors deal with memory. If there is one large, centralized, shared memory, we say the system is tightly coupled. If there are multiple, physically distributed memories, we say the system is loosely coupled.

17. SIMD: data parallelism; MIMD: control or task parallelism. Why?

19. Whereas superscalar processors rely on both the hardware (to arbitrate dependencies) and the compiler (to generate approximate schedules), VLIW processors rely *entirely* on the compiler. Therefore, VLIW moves the complexity completely to the compiler.

20. Both architectures feature a small number of parallel pipelines for processing instructions. However, the VLIW architecture relies on the compiler for prepackaging and scheduling the instructions in a correct and efficient way. In the superscalar architecture, instruction scheduling is done by hardware.

21. Distributed systems allow for sharing as well as redundancy.

23. When adding processors to a crossbar interconnection network, the number of crossbar switches grows to an unmanageable size very quickly. Bus networks suffer from potential bottlenecks and contention issues.

25. With write-through, the new value is immediately flushed through to the server. This keeps the server constantly up-to-date, but writing takes longer (losing the speed increase that caching typically provides). With write-back, the new value is flushed to the server after a given delay. This maintains the speed increase, but means that if the server crashes before the new data is flushed, some data may be lost. This is a good example to illustrate that performance improvements often come at a price.

27. Yes, individual neurons take input, process it, and provide output. This output is then used by another neuron "down the line." However, the neurons themselves work in parallel.

29. While the network is learning, indications of incorrect output are used to make adjustments to the weights in the network. These adjustments are based on various optimization algorithms. The learning is complete when the weighted average converges to a given value.

Chapter 10

2. Small embedded systems have no need to perform the complicated power-on self-test (POST) sequence that is carried out by personal systems. For one thing, embedded systems memories are much smaller and thus take less time for power-on checks. Secondly, peripheral devices on most embedded systems—if they exist at all—are fewer and simpler than those connected to most personal computers. This means less hardware to check and fewer drivers—if any—to load.

8. Interrupt latency is the elapsed (wall clock) time between the occurrence of an interrupt and the execution of the first instruction of the interrupt service routine (ISR). In order to execute the first instruction of the ISR, the thread currently executing in the CPU must be suspended: A context switch takes place. The interrupt latency must therefore be greater than the context switch time.

Chapter 11

1. The weighted average execution time of System C is 2170 / 5 = 434. Thus, we have (563.5 / 434 = 1.298387 − 1) × 100 = 30%. System A's performance has degraded by (9563.5 / 79 − 1) × 100 = 641.4%.

3. System A: Arithmetic mean = 400; Geometric means: 1, 0.7712, and 1.1364

   System B: Arithmetic mean = 525; Geometric means: 1.1596, 1, and 1.3663

   System C: Arithmetic mean = 405; Geometric means: 0.7946, 0.6330, and 1

7. This is the fallacy of incomplete information. Why?

9. There is no value in doing this. Each release consists of a different set of programs, so the results cannot be compared.

11. The best benchmark in this situation would be the SPEC CPU series. Why?

13. First, be diplomatic. Suggest that the group investigate whether TPC-C benchmarks are available for this system. Whether or not TPC-C figures are available, you may want to educate this individual as to the meaning of Amdahl's Law and why a fast CPU will not necessarily determine whether the entire system will handle your workload.

24. **a)** 5.8 cycles/instruction (Be sure you can show your work to arrive at this answer.)

   b) 5.8 MHz (Why?)

   c) 13.25

Chapter 12

5. The payload (data) of the TCP segment should be made as large as possible so that the network overhead required to send the segment is minimized. If the payload consisted of only 1 or 2 bytes, the network overhead would be at least an order of magnitude greater than the data transmitted.

9. **a)** Class B

   b) Class C

   c) Class A

11. **a)** We will assume that no options are set in the TCP or IP headers and ignore any session shutdown messages. There are 20 bytes in the TCP header and 20 bytes in the IP header. For a file size of 1024 bytes, using a payload of 128 bytes, 8 payloads will have to be sent. Thus, 8 TCP and IP headers. With 40 bytes of overhead per transmission unit, we have 8 × 40 bytes of overhead added to the 1024 payload bytes, giving a total transmission of 1344 bytes. The overhead percentage is 320 ÷ 1344 × 100% = 23.8%.

   b) The minimal IPv6 header is 40 bytes long. Added to the 20 bytes in the TCP header, each transmission contains 60 overhead bytes, for a total of 480 bytes to send the 8 payloads. The overhead percentage is this: 480 ÷ 1504 × 100% or 31.9%.

13. **a)** Bytes 1500 through 1599

   b) Byte 1799

19. **a)** Signal-to-noise ratio (dB) = $10 \ \log_{10} \dfrac{2898 \text{ dB}}{40 \text{ dB}} = 18.6 \text{ dB}$

   b) $0.32 \text{ dB} = 10 \ \log_{10} \dfrac{\text{Signal dB}}{35 \text{ dB}} \Rightarrow \text{Signal dB} = 37.68 \text{ dB}$

Chapter 13

5. The host adapter always has the highest device number so that it will always win arbitration for the bus. "Fast and wide" SCSI-3 interfaces can support as many as 32 devices; therefore, the host adapter will always be device number 31.

Appendix A

3. A more efficient linked list implementation will put three pointers on each node of the list. What does the extra pointer point to?

5.

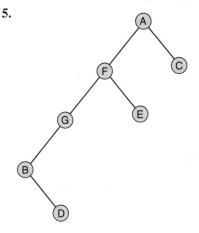

Index